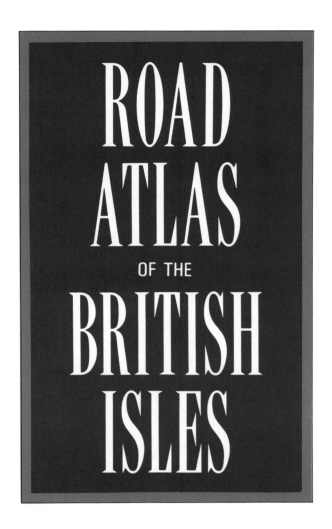

1 : 200,000
Approximately 3 miles to 1 inch

THE TOURIST'S BRITISH ISLES

1st edition September 1990

© The Automobile Association 1990

Published by The Automobile Association, Fanum House, Basingstoke, Hampshire RG21 2EA

ISBN 074 95 00794

Printed by L.E.G.O. SpA, Italy

The contents of this book are believed correct at the time of printing. Nevertheless, the publisher can accept no responsibility for errors or omissions, or for changes in the details given.

Mapping produced by the Cartographic Department of The Automobile Association. This atlas has been compiled and produced from the Automaps database utilising electronic and computer technology.

Every effort has been made to ensure that the contents of our new database are correct. However, if there are any errors or omissions, please write to the Cartographic Editor, Publishing Division, The Automobile Association, Fanum House, Basingstoke, Hampshire RG21 2EA

A CIP catalogue record for this book is available from the British Library.

•Contents

THE ATLAS

THE TOURIST'S BRITISH ISLES
·SYMBOLS·

Rochester Castle, in Kent, is a fine example of Norman military architecture.

Whether you are looking to spend an afternoon with the family or want to plan a holiday, knowing exactly where to go and what you can see when you get there can often be a problem. The following pages have been designed to give you an idea of what is on offer wherever you happen to be visiting.

Your needs could be as simple as locating a suitable place to enjoy a picnic, where to launch your boat for a day's sailing or where you can find further information about the area.

Whatever your requirement, some 50 symbols, highlighting over 8,000 features of interest, give you a chance to choose what interests you.

Pages 6 to 48 give a taste of what can be seen and where to find it.

Each place located on the atlas by the use of red symbols, has been chosen because it is open and has reasonable access for the public. Although some places may not be open to the public, they have been

included simply because they are an interesting feature or land mark, waterfall, windmill etc.

The AA is constantly checking and updating these entries in its atlases and other publications to ensure accurate, up-to-date information is given. All the attractions featured in 2000 Days Out, published annually by the AA, are highlighted in this atlas by the red symbols. The atlas, however, includes even more places and the information on locations such as country parks, nature reserves, nature trails, RSPB sites and Forest Parks, is supplied by the numerous authorities and national bodies such as the Countryside Commission, the Forestry Commission and many others.

There is a wide range of interests to choose from.

For cultural tastes, museums, art galleries, historic houses, castles, abbeys and cathedrals are featured. A stately home like Stourhead, in Somerset, may be more famous for its garden than its house and will therefore be depicted by the red garden symbol. Others, like

Chatsworth, in Derbyshire, which are better known for the architectural splendour of the house, even though they are also renowned for their garden features, will be indicated by the red house symbol. Larger, specific garden features, classified as arboreta, are depicted accordingly. Major sporting venues such as athletics stadia, county cricket grounds and horse racing courses are located by appropriate symbols. It is not possible to indicate league football grounds because of their large numbers and the limitations of the map scale. However, some are shown on the town plans at the back of the atlas where appropriate.

For those who like to participate rather than spectate, outdoor and leisure-type facilities, such as ski slopes, golf courses and coastal launching sites for boats are located.

If you have a particular interest in Ancient Britain, you can choose from the various hill-forts, Roman antiquities and prehistoric monuments which are found throughout the country. Even battle sites, where the course of history

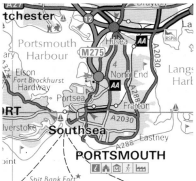

The places behind Portsmouth's tourist symbols. **Left** *Tourist Information at The Hard.* **Below left** *Industrial Interest with restored steam pumping engines at Eastney.* **Below right** *The Cathedral.* **Right** HMS Warrior, *just one of the city's many Museums.*

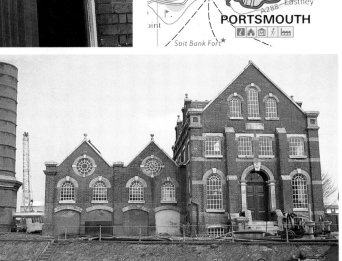

has often been changed, are shown. Some of these have interpretative centres which help you to relive and understand the events that occurred there.

Animal lovers can visit the major wildlife collections (both mammals and birds), zoos, and aquaria, or see nature in the wild at one of the numerous nature reserves, Forest Parks and RSPB sites. Another option is to follow one of the nature trails through the countryside. The more adventurous can attempt part or all of one of the national trails which traverse some of Britain's most spectacular scenic areas.

Industrial interest covers a wide spectrum from heritage centres and museums to mills, mines and slate caverns. Preserved railways, many of which served these industries in the past, now delight the public with a taste of the golden days of steam.

Family days out are catered for by the theme parks. The AA has selected eight of these for inclusion on that basis that they provide multi-purpose entertainment and leisure facilities and have numerous

fairground attractions that are unnervingly described as 'white knuckle' rides. Along with the country parks, they make ideal places to spend the whole day rather than just a quick visit.

Picnic sites are selected and inspected by the AA on a regular basis and are easily accessible, being sited on or by A and B roads. AA Viewpoints are shown if they offer vistas of at least 180 degrees, and many have panoramic 360 degree views.

Other places of interest which are worth visiting but do not fall easily into the categories symbolised are indicated by a small red star alongside their name. There is a great variety of these – waterfalls, water mills, visitor centres and market crosses, among others.

New additions for the 1990s include the National Parks of England and Wales and the National Scenic Areas of Scotland, along with Heritage Coasts and pollution-free beaches.

When the red symbols are boxed, this indicates the attractions are in urban areas. Some of these places

may seem bare compared to the surrounding countryside, however, it may be that one symbol for a museum covers several museums in the town, but it is not practical to include them all because of space limitations.

Ireland is included in this special tourist section, and places of interest are located in the atlas, but the scale of mapping does not allow a large selection. The symbols used are slightly different in some cases to those for England, Scotland and Wales. See page 156.

Wherever possible, the red pictorial symbols used in the atlas are based on the Department of Transport's brown tourist signposts, so that the maps relate with the road signs. In addition to all this information in the special tourist spreads, a month by month calendar on pages 46 and 47 tells you which customs and events occur throughout the year. This can assist you in deciding when to go. Page 48 describes the services offered by Britain's Tourist Information Centres to help you get the most out of your visits.

Abbey, cathedral or priory

Ruined abbey, cathedral or priory

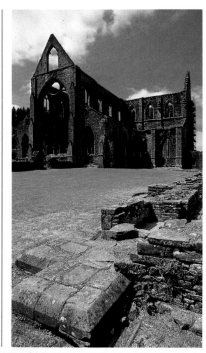

Top *Tintern Abbey: majestic roofless ruin beside the River Wye in Gwent. Above St David's Cathedral, Dyfed, where the bones of St David lie.*

Abbeys
Cathedrals
Priories

Augustinian, Benedictine, Cistercian and Dominican – the monastic orders which preserved ideals and scholarship after the fall of Rome have left a rich heritage in stone across Britain. Each imposing ruin or active place of worship tells its own story. All evoke a sense of wonder at the faith and industry of the medieval builders and monks. Which of any of them is the loveliest, however, will for ever be a matter of personal preference.

Burnt down in 1174, four years after Becket's murder, the choir of **Canterbury Cathedral** was rebuilt in a manner worthy of the martyr and appears today much as it was in the early 16th century. The 'Altar of the Sword's Point' and a modern cruciform sculpture, dedicated in 1986, mark the site of Becket's martyrdom. The long vistas back to the nave, at a lower level than the choir aisles show the evolution of Gothic style over three centuries.

The west front of **York**, the largest Gothic church north of the Alps, presents an almost 13th-century 'French' outline, with its glorious façades. The Minster contains the largest single collection of medieval stained glass in England – the west window painted in 1339 by Master Robert and the east window, the work of John Thornton of Coventry between 1405 and 1408. The Pilgrim Window dates from about 1312 and the Bellfounders Window was given by Richard Tunnoc, buried in the Minster in 1330.

A fire, started by lightning on 9 July, 1984, destroyed much of the south transept. Craftsmen, incorporating 20th-century improvements for future safety, restored the medieval beauty of the transept, reopened by the Queen in October, 1988.

Embodiment of the spirit of the nation, **Westminster**, the Norman abbey of Edward the Confessor took on its Gothic appearance after its rebuilding by Henry III. Fortunately, when the 600-year-old Benedictine community was disbanded, the buildings were spared. The Lady Chapel houses the Confessor's shrine, ringed by the tombs of five kings and three queens. In the centre is the Coronation Chair and below the oaken seat the Stone of Scone.

In the Sanctuary beyond the choir every monarch since the Conqueror has been crowned, with the exception of Edward V and Edward VIII. Early Parliaments met in the Chapter House, and the Henry VII Chapel has a superb fan-vaulted roof – the most glorious, some would say, in the country. Near the West Door lies the 'Unknown Warrior', brought back from France after World War I to sleep among the nation's great.

On its rocky promontory dominating the city and a loop in the River Wear the Norman architecture of **Durham Cathedral** gives an impression, inside as well as out, of overwhelming power. Huge deeply-grooved columns alternating with massive piers support gallery, clerestory and beautiful vault. The Early English Chapel of the Nine Altars is a 13th-century addition, its tall lancet windows paralleled only in the now ruined Fountains Abbey. In the Treasury are evocative relics of the 7th-century St Cuthbert, including his tiny portable altar, his delicate gold pectoral cross and the remains of his original carved oak coffin.

One of the most delicate of England's cathedrals must be **Salisbury**, built in the forty years following 1220, of local silver-grey limestone, with pointed arches and soaring windows. The spire, at 404 feet, is the tallest in the country. It is such inspired work that it blends perfectly with the rest, though crossing piers of clustered black marble had to be reinforced in the 15th century to support the added 6,500 tons.

Wells is the first cathedral church in the Early English style. Its west front is still, despite Puritan vandalism, one of England's richest displays of 13th-century sculpture. Inside, the most striking feature are the inverted arches, built from 1338 to 1348 to combat subsidence of the tower.

The Norman crypt and transepts of **Winchester Cathedral** survive, the rest being 13th- and 14th-century. At 556 feet it is the longest Gothic church in Europe. Saved from demolition in 1652 by a petition of the citizens, it was again saved at the beginning of this century by a diver, William Walker. Working alone, from 1906 to 1912, in pitch dark waters of the marshy foundations, he replaced the rotting 13th-century beech tree raft on which the cathedral had originally been built with cement.

Near York are three jewels – Beverley, Selby and Ripon. **Beverley Minster** houses the Percy Tomb, the most splendid of British Decorated funerary monuments. It shares, with St Mary's Church nearby, wonderful misericords and the largest collection of carvings of medieval musical instruments anywhere in the world.

Benedictine **Selby Abbey**, founded 1069, pre-dates Durham. The west front ranges in style from strength and simplicity to later elegance. The easternmost arches of the nave have distorted spectacularly, due to a high water table. High up above the south side of the choir is a 14th-century window with the arms of the Washington family – the 'Stars and Stripes' motif of the American flag.

Ripon Cathedral is built over the tiny 11 by 8 ft Saxon crypt of St Wilfrid's Church, one of the few Saxon structures left in England. The cathedral has a beautiful Early English west front. One woodcarver, working from 1939 to 1945, replaced all the 'idolatrous images' on the choir screen, destroyed by Puritans in 1643.

There are modern cathedrals too. The new **Coventry Cathedral** appears to grow out of the old St Michael's and the overwhelming

impression is of height, light and colour. South-facing angled windows enable sunlight to flood the nave with colour. Dominating the whole cathedral is the huge tapestry designed by Graham Sutherland, *Christ in Glory*.

Liverpool's **Anglican Cathedral** is, in the words of Sir John Betjeman, 'vastness, strength and height no words can describe'. Sir Giles Gilbert Scott designed Britain's largest cathedral in medieval style but on a scale which no medieval builders would have attempted. His memorial is set in the floor of the central space under the tower. He, a Catholic, is buried just outside the West Door.

The **Metropolitan Cathedral of Christ the King** in Liverpool, often irreverently called 'Paddy's Wigwam', stands above the huge crypt of the cathedral which Sir Edwin Lutyens started before the war. Inside the 194ft circular nave, every member of the 2,300 congregation has an uninterrupted view of the white marble High Altar.

A cathedral conveys 'city status' on a town, however small. Pass through the gatehouse at **St David's**, Dyfed, and the lichen-encrusted purple stone of Wales's greatest church is dramatically revealed. It was restored in Decorated Gothic style after an earthquake in 1248 and the whole building slopes upwards some 14 feet from west to east – an unnerving first glimpse for the visitor entering at the western end

of the nave. The relics of St David rest in an oak and iron reliquary, hidden at the Reformation and discovered during restoration work in 1866.

St Asaph Cathedral, in Clwyd, is on the site of a monastic community founded in AD570. It houses the tomb of Bishop William Morgan, translator of the Bible into Welsh, and the 16th-century Bible itself, which was used at the Investiture of the Prince of Wales in 1969.

Henry VIII's Dissolution left a legacy of ruined religious centres across the country, many of which still survive today in all their shattered glory.

Perhaps one of the most magnificent monastic ruins is **Rievaulx Abbey**, 2 miles north-west of Helmsley. It was founded in 1131 and is the first Cistercian house in the north of England. The name, pronounced 'Reevo', comes from Rye Vallis or valley of the River Rye, above which it stands, surrounded by wooded hills. Its chief glory is its choir built *c* 1225. The scale of the buildings give an idea of the activities and work of the 600 and more monks and lay brothers who lived here in the 13th century.

The Cistercian community of **Fountains Abbey**, near Ripon, became the centre of an enormous enterprise, with fish-farms, forestry,

Right The ancient kings of Northumbria lie buried near Tynemouth Priory. Below Cistercian Fountains Abbey, now part of the Studley Royal estate.

iron-workings, and, above all, sheep, which funded its building. It was one of the first foundations to be sold by Henry VIII in 1540. In 1768 the Aislabie family bought it as a picturesque addition to their Studley Royal estate.

The condition of the Benedictine **Whitby Abbey** cannot wholly be blamed on King Henry. The gaunt ruins of the clifftop site, chosen by St Hilda in AD657, became the setting for Bram Stoker's *Dracula* and suffered further indignity when they were bombarded by German warships during World War I.

The 7th-century buildings at **Much Wenlock** were destroyed by the Danes and later refounded by Leofric, husband of Lady Godiva. Today's ruins are the remains of the church built in the 1220s by Prior Humbert, whose lodging is one of the finest examples of English domestic architecture from around the 1500s.

Abbey, cathedral or priory

Ruined abbey, cathedral or priory

Castle

Castles

Maiden Castle to Balmoral, Mousa Broch to Dover – Britain is rich in castles dating from Bronze to Victorian ages. The very name 'castle', conjuring up visions of power, of menace and later of opulence, has often been affected by builders of lesser dwellings.

Castles begin with the hill-forts of the Bronze Age and stone brochs of pre-Christian Scotland, primarily refuges for men and cattle in time of local warfare. The ruins of Norman timber-built motte and bailey castles – a stone keep on a mound, surrounded by a defensive wall – later converted by the Plantagenets to stone fortresses, still dominate many towns, river crossings and strategic points across the country.

These were not solely refuges, but administrative headquarters, stores and living quarters. Even in times of peace they would have been bustling centres of activity; in time of war, life must have been pretty chaotic, with garrisons, stores, cattle and weaponry increased and as many of the local population as

Below *Orford Castle, in Suffolk, has a remarkable 18-sided polygonal keep.* Inset *The Welsh border castle of Goodrich, in the Wye Valley.*

could be squeezed in taking refuge in the bailey. Castles were not designed for passive defence but for vigorous action. They were not safe refuges in which to avoid conflict, but ingeniously contrived to make the enemy fight at a disadvantage – they were meant to be costly to capture – both in time and in lives.

Henry II (1154–1189), after the mayhem of Stephen's reign 'took every castle of England into his hands', destroyed about 500 unlicensed castles and founded a line of castle-building kings – Richard, John, Henry III, Edward I and III.

Visiting some of these castles, it needs only a little imagination to bring to life the history of their times. The castles of Edward I (1272–1307) around the coast of North Wales are symbols of the organising ability and engineering skills as well as reminders of the vast expense of castle building in the Middle Ages.

Norman and Plantagenet castles vary to suit the site on which they are built but the first criterion was always that of aggressive defence. Where possible a ditch or moat – dry or flooded – was dug, to prevent besiegers tunnelling under the walls. Towers without sharp

corners were less likely to be undermined, and so became the fashion.

From about 1268, the date of **Caerphilly Castle** in Mid Glamorgan, the defenders of the outer curtain wall and its towers would be supported by covering fire from higher inner walls. A formidable array of outworks defends gateways and sluices, further protected by drawbridge and portcullis. Barbicans and towers ensured that attackers were subjected to murderous flanking cross-fire before they got anywhere near anything so flammable as a wooden gate.

Caerphilly, at 30 acres the largest castle in Wales, surpassed only by **Dover** and **Windsor**, is sufficiently well preserved to give a vivid idea of the way these defensive ideas worked together. It has wide water defences, in imitation of those which Henry III had built at **Kenilworth** and which Simon de Montfort held so successfully against him. Edward I, on his return from the Crusade, liked what he saw at Caerphilly and began to turn the **Tower of London** into a concentric castle. He also introduced at **Caernarfon** and **Conwy** an idea from his campaigns in Gascony –

the 'bastide' – an extension of the bailey to enclose a small town in which traders, labourers and craftsmen could live under the protection of the castle.

Edward I's castle building in North Wales is well documented and throws fascinating light on the feudal power and organisation at the King's command. Ditch diggers were recruited from the Fens and marched across by mounted serjeants – to discourage deserters – to dig the canal around **Rhuddlan Castle**.

At **Conwy**, Edward's young Spanish queen, Eleanor, homesick for the courts and fountains of her native Castile, had a small garden and fishpond built in the castle's east barbican. In the hot summer of 1283 a labourer hauled water from the well, to 'water the Queen's new grass'. Here at Conwy it is believed that Eleanor introduced one of our favourite summer flowers – the sweet pea.

At **Caernarfon Castle** where his son, later Edward II, was born on 25 April, 1284, Edward sought to bring Arthurian and Welsh legends to life and make the seat of his government in Wales a new imperial Constantinople. Octagonal towers are set in a single curtain wall, banded with red sandstone in imitation of those of the 5th-century Turkish capital. Defended passages within the thickness of the masonry and ingenious triple arrow slits allowed three bowmen a wide angle of fire through only one external opening.

The more settled times of the Tudor dynasty after the Wars of the Roses reduced the military significance of the castle. Gunpowder played no little part in this. Castles continued to be built, but design changed. Henry VIII began a series of symmetrically planned coastal 'artillery forts' from the Thames to Dorset, in 1538. **Deal**, **Walmer** and **Sandgate** are three, but these were garrisoned rather than lived in – the garrisons complaining that 'they stank of gunpowder and dogs'. Comfort and elegance dictated the style of Elizabethan and Jacobean buildings, though many were still castellated and defensible.

The Civil War saw many castles used again as strongpoints. They stood up so well, even to improved 17th-century firepower, that the victorious Parliamentarians decreed that those which had been so vigorously defended should be 'slighted' – demolished so as to make them useless for military purposes. Some of these 'ruins Cromwell knocked about a bit', if not too badly damaged, became the

Castle

Above *Caernarfon Castle, Gwynedd, built by Edward I to subdue the Welsh.* Right *St Andrew's 13th-century castle overlooks the North Sea.*

local prison and the Norman word for the keep – *donjon* – became the English dungeon.

In Scotland, Northumberland, Cumbria and the troubled lands of the Borders, there are over 1,100 'castles' of one sort or another, excluding the baronial houses of the last 200 years. Most are tower houses or 'peles', built in stone, for timber was always short in the region, and usually several storeys high. **Craigievar**, west of Aberdeen, is the masterpiece of this uniquely Scottish style. Seven storeys high with, even today, few windows in its pink granite walls, it must have been a formidable sight for any would-be attacker.

Many peles have been absorbed into later houses. **Traquair House** west of Galashiels, now more 'château' than castle, claims to be the oldest continuously inhabited house in Scotland. Buried within the north-east corner is a pele tower dating back to the reign of Alexander I (1107– 24).

Stirling Castle which looked down on Edward II's ignominious defeat at Bannockburn in 1314, was still an earthen and timber construction. The 'Gateway to the Highlands' was transformed under the Stuarts, first into a stone fortress, then into a splendid Renaissance royal palace.

Castles lived on in the romantic imaginations of later centuries. Sir Charles Cavendish, son of Bess of Hardwick, built his mansion at **Bolsover**, Derbyshire, in the 1620s with the turrets, crenellations and medieval fancies so popular with the Elizabethans. As tastes began to rebel against Classical symmetry and long for 'the good old days', mock medieval 'castles' were built

and some genuine 14th-century castles, such as **Croft**, in Shropshire, were 'gothicized'.

William Burges built two for the Marquess of Bute, at **Cardiff** and **Castell Coch**, reconstructing the motte and bailey castle the Normans had built at Cardiff within a Roman fort into an extravaganza rivalling the creations of Ludwig of Bavaria – with a medieval tower suite complete with smoking room, Gothic chapel and banqueting hall. At Castell Coch, to the north of Cardiff, Burges transformed the ruins of a keep destroyed in the 15th century into a mock 13th-century retreat. Its conical roofs recall the illustrations in the Duc de Berri's 'Book of Hours' but the thick walls have arrow slits and 'murder holes' and a portcullis and drawbridge which function.

The last such conceit built in Britain was designed by Edwin Lutyens – who in 1901 had made a comfortable home for the publisher of *Country Life* magazine within the ramparts of **Lindisfarne**, off the Northumbrian coast. For 20 years, from 1910, **Castle Drogo**, Lutyens' composite Norman and Tudor 'castle' arose overlooking the River Teigne in Devon, home to the founder of the Home & Colonial Stores and is – to date, at any rate – Britain's 'last castle'.

Historic house

Historic Houses

The Greek historian, Thucydides said 'Men, not walls, make a city' – the same holds true for a house and the human stories of the builders, owners or residents add interest to it, however humble, however grand. Membership of the National Trust and English Heritage – an outlay quickly recouped if you are going to visit even half a dozen properties in a season – will give you a wonderful selection from which to choose, rich in architecture and in treasures, but above all in personalities.

The name 'Mote' at **Ightham Mote** in Kent, recalls the 'moot', the council which met here, in the Great Hall, dating from 1340. Three centuries of continuous ownership by the Selby family have left their mark, from Jacobean fireplaces through 17th-century wallpaper to Victorian bedrooms – all told there are 600 years of England's history to be discerned at Ightham.

Ightham Mote, Kent, is one of the best examples of a medieval manor house.

Built in 1340 by a Lord Mayor of London, the Great Hall at **Penshurst Place** in Kent is the finest to have survived. Birthplace of the Elizabethan courtier, soldier and poet Sir Philip Sidney, the house remains in the same family today. Later ranges of building have left it light and airy. The Long Gallery marries house to garden and medieval to Renaissance, a fitting memorial to the man who personified all that was best in the Elizabethan age.

The Elizabethan house Bess of Hardwick built with Sir William Cavendish at **Chatsworth** in Derbyshire has been absorbed into the present house. Chatsworth is the home of the Cavendish family, the Dukes of Devonshire, the first of whom, in the early 1700s, transformed the house into a baroque palace, a second Versailles. Treasures are everywhere – in the Painted Hall, the State Rooms, Sculpture Gallery – works by famous artists, painters and sculptors abound. The Library has over 17,000 volumes, among them those of Henry Cavendish, the 18th-century discoverer of hydrogen. Capability Brown laid out much of the garden, but retained Grillet's 1696 Cascade, the sound of the water varying as it falls over steps of different height. Joseph Paxton, too, worked here, and his Great Conservatory was the forerunner of the Crystal Palace.

Montacute in Somerset is one of the least altered of late Elizabethan houses. Begun in the year of the Armada, it expresses the rise to power of an astute lawyer, Edward Phelips. He led the prosecution of Guy Fawkes and became Speaker of the House of Commons. The house, with its mullioned front and statues standing in their lofty niches, is the masterpiece of a local genius, William Arnold. No one, though, who has seen the charming Elizabethan pavilions can ever doubt the delicacy and humour of this Elizabethan mason who has so completely captured his master's wish to display his continuing good fortune.

After a spell in the Tower and a stiff fine, Sir John Thynne retired to his Wiltshire estate at **Longleat**, following his support of the disgraced Lord Protector to Edward VI. He began Longleat in about 1546, and today it is still home to the Thynne family, now the Marquesses of Bath. The Great Hall, with its 16th-century fireplace and hunting scenes, is the least altered part of the house. Sir John broke from the tradition of the Elizabethan 'E-shaped' house and built around two inner courts. The top floor of

the house was the library and home of Thomas Ken, Bishop of Bath and Wells, who was given refuge here when he fell foul of both James II and William and Mary. Lord Bath, an innovator like his ancestor, opened his house to the public in 1949 and since 1966 has run a 600-acre safari park, a 'drive-through' reserve of giraffe, rhinoceros, elephants, tigers – and the well-known 'Lions of Longleat'.

Bess of Hardwick married four times, each time increasing her fortune. She married Sir William Cavendish when she was 27 and their second son inherited Chatsworth. She left her fourth husband, the Earl of Shrewsbury, for his alleged infatuation with his prisoner, Mary, Queen of Scots. Then, aged 70, she began to build **Hardwick Hall**. The accounts of the building reflect the imperiousness of the owner who, living a hundred yards away in her old hall, strode across to inspect and criticise every day. Her descendants preferred Chatsworth and Hardwick remained, frozen in time, one of the purest examples of 16th-century design and decor in the country, a memorial to the indomitable woman, whose portrait stares down from the tapestried wall of the Long Gallery.

Robert Cecil, first Earl of Salisbury, builder of **Hatfield House**, Hertfordshire, was adviser to both Elizabeth I and James I. James suggested that Robert Cecil exchange the house his father, Lord Burghley, had built at Theobalds, for the palace at Hatfield – a 'suggestion' he could scarcely refuse. Between 1607 and 1611, Cecil built himself a vast new house nearby.

Great Halls and Long Galleries were by then going out of fashion, but Hatfield would have lost much had Cecil not been traditionalist enough to include them. His own quarters and the guest wing, however, have smaller rooms. Here conversation and gracious living could flourish. The style of the great house was changing. It was a later Cecil, Marquess of Salisbury, three times Prime Minister to Queen Victoria, and amateur scientist, who installed electricity in 1881 and it is reported that *'the naked wires on the Gallery ceiling tended to burst into flame, being extinguished by members of the family who threw cushions at them before returning to their conversation'*.

The magnificent Restoration house, **Weston Park**, on the Shropshire–Staffordshire border, was designed single-handed by Lady Elizabeth Wilbraham. In the library is her copy of Palladio's *First Book of Architecture*, with her notes

Historic house

headed 'for building Weston House, 1671'.

By the time **Petworth** was built, 70 years or so after Hatfield, Long Galleries and Great Halls had gone completely from the English building scene. The house passed by marriage from the Percys to the 'Proud Duke' of Somerset, who began building – using his wife's fortune – in 1688. The name and skill of Grinling Gibbons will always be associated with Petworth. His mastery of limewood carving is complete. The house also boasts excellent tracery work by Jonathan Ritson, and the Marble Hall has wonderful carving by John Selden, the Duke's estate carpenter.

Just to the south of Wrexham lies **Erddig**. It was completed by a local mason in 1689 and owned by the Yorke family since 1733, who collected much and threw little away! Subsidence from coal mining almost destroyed the house and restoration began in 1973. The interest of the house is not in its architecture or its treasures, but in the relationship that a local family maintained with their servants. Portraits of master and servant hang in drawing room and servants' hall, many with little poems and descriptions. There are frequent group photographs of the whole staff, enabling us to follow some servants right through their careers. Erddig is one of the few houses to show the public the maids' bedrooms as well as the public rooms. Here, 200 years of the

Above Vanbrugh's spectacular Castle Howard, in North Yorkshire.
Right The beautiful Georgian mansion of Mellerstain, in the Borders.

running of a self contained estate come vividly to life.

Soldier, turned dramatist on his return to England in 1692, John Vanbrugh came to the notice of Charles Howard, 3rd Earl of Carlisle, perhaps through his popular and bawdy plays. Howard chose this enthusiastic amateur to build him a home fitted to the position of an Earl, and so **Castle Howard** came about. Vanbrugh was widely helped by one of Sir Christopher Wren's assistants, Nicholas Hawksmoor, who turned Vanbrugh's ideas into working drawings. Castle Howard impresses but does not overawe, as does their later work at Blenheim. At the heart of the house is the Great Hall, rising 70 feet through two storeys into the painted dome. It is the most light-hearted but impressive concept of English architecture. Treasures and portraits abound, including one of a stricken Henry VIII, painted by Holbein just after the execution of Catherine Howard, and a portrait of her uncle, Thomas Howard, who escaped the block only because the King died on the day appointed for his execution.

The story of **Blenheim Palace** is full of powerful men and women. It was built for John Churchill, Duke of Marlborough. Queen Anne instigated the idea of the palace as a

reward for Churchill's victory over the French and Bavarians at the battle of Blenheim. She later quarrelled with Sarah, Duchess of Marlborough, as did Vanbrugh, the architect. Sarah wanted a comfortable country house and Vanbrugh wanted something even greater than Castle Howard. Sir Winston Churchill, born here, became Prime Minister at a time when a man of Marlborough's character was again needed.

William Adam began to build **Mellerstain** in the Scottish borders for George Baillie in 1725, and his son, Robert, finished it in 1770. It is the interiors, by Robert, that are the main attraction, for William was never able to finish the exterior as planned and it lacks a noble central block. The colours Adam used to perfection in his decorations of the 18th-century rooms make them among the most beautiful in Europe.

*Concorde 01 is on show at the Imperial
War Museum, Duxford, Cambridgeshire.*

Museums
Art Galleries

Among the prized possessions of
the British Museum in its early days
were a landscape painted on a
spider's web, a two-headed chicken,
Chinese shoes, figures of King
William III and Queen Mary carved
out of walnut shells and various
unpleasant-looking things preserved
in spirits and hidden in the
basement in case they might
frighten pregnant women. A far cry
from the British Museum of today
with its Elgin Marbles, Assyrian
winged bulls, and the Sutton Hoo
treasure included in its fabulous
array of objects from every corner of
the globe.

The ancestors of today's museums
and art galleries were the collections
of classical sculptures and
antiquities formed during the
Renaissance period by rulers,
wealthy churchmen and merchant
princes like the Medicis of Florence.
They were inspired by the
devouring interest which had
sprung up in ancient Greece and
Rome. With interest also rapidly
developing in science, others
assembled natural history collections
and 'cabinets of curiosities', which
contained animal bones, weapons,
coins, shells, oddly shaped plants or
stones – anything that took the
collector's fancy.

In England the two John
Tradescants, father and son, who
were keen naturalists, plant-hunters
and gardeners to Charles I in the
17th century, formed a substantial
collection, or 'museum' as it was
called: one of its star pieces was a
stuffed dodo. The collection passed
to Elias Ashmole, the antiquary,
herald and pioneer Freemason, who
added to it and passed it on in turn
to Oxford University. Twelve wagon
loads of objects were conveyed to
Oxford, to form the nucleus of the
Ashmolean Museum, opened to the
public in 1683 and the oldest
museum in Britain.

The Ashmolean today glories in
its Egyptian mummy cases and
medieval jewellery, its Old Master
paintings and British art, but it still
honours Ashmole's memory and
items from the original Tradescant
collection can be seen, with other
curiosities such as Guy Fawkes's
lantern.

The **British Museum** opened its
doors in London to 'studious and
curious persons' in 1759, the word
'museum' now meaning the
building in which a collection was
kept rather than the collection itself.
It was established by Parliament and
funded by a state lottery to house
the collections of Robert Harley, Earl
of Oxford, and the books and
manuscripts assembled by Sir
Robert Cotton – which included the
Lindisfarne Gospels and two copies
of Magna Carta. Also included was
the astonishing collection of no less
than 79,575 objects put together by
Sir Hans Sloane. A successful
London doctor, Sloane's fanatical
zeal as a collector extended to
classical antiquities, coins, jewels,
fossils, plants, butterflies, zoological
specimens and oddities of every
kind. Those who came to feast their
eyes on these items consisted, as
the Trustees reported in 1784,
'chiefly of Mechanics and persons of
the lower Classes'.

Zeal to improve and educate
'persons of the lower classes' gained
strength in the 19th century,
especially in the heavily populated
towns created by the industrial
revolution, and prompted the
establishment of numerous
museums and art galleries. The
splendid **City Art Gallery** in
Manchester, for example, was
opened in 1834 and is today noted
for its superb Victorian and Pre-
Raphaelite paintings. The
**Birmingham Museum and Art
Gallery** was founded in 1867 and
the building it now occupies was
opened in 1885. Approximately a
hundred museums opened in
Britain in the 1870s and '80s.

The Victorian boom in museums
and art galleries was also stimulated
by an ambition to promote scientific
and technological advance and to
improve standards of design. This
was why the **Victoria & Albert
Museum** in London was founded by
the Prince Consort in 1852,
originally as a 'museum of
manufactures', in the wake of the
Great Exhibition of the previous
year.

National and civic pride were also
a factor. The **National Gallery** in

London is now the country's premier collection of Western painting down to 1900 (developments since then are the preserve of the **Tate Gallery**). It was founded in 1824 to emulate the national art galleries already established in Vienna, Paris, Berlin and other European capitals. The government bought 38 paintings to start it off, from the collection of a banker, Sir John Julius Angerstein: they included the Rubens *Rape of the Sabine Women*, two Rembrandts and Raphael's *Portrait of Julius II*.

Major museums and galleries generally have two functions, and there is often a tension between them. The obvious function is to instruct and entertain the public. The other, carried on out of the public eye, is the advancement of scholarship. An example of this dual role is the **National Museum of Wales** in Cardiff, opened in 1927 (in a building which has leaked ever since). It was founded to inform both the Welsh and the rest of the world about Wales, which it does. But its own staff and visiting academics work behind the scenes on collections far too voluminous for public display – 230,000 pressed plant specimens, more than 300,000 fossils, serried multitudes of dead beetles.

The museum is also a good example of the fact that the functions of an institution of this kind today go far beyond the display of objects in showcases. Activities include lectures, the loan of items to schools, and guided family walks with experts from the staff discoursing learnedly along the way.

Museums like this take a wide range of subjects for their province. Others concentrate on specialised areas. There is a museum of Scottish tartans at **Comrie**, for example, of stained glass at **Ely**, of horse racing at **Newmarket**. Military museums concentrate on regiments: the **Durham Light Infantry** in Durham, the **Staffordshire Regiment** in Lichfield, the **Rifle Brigade** at Winchester. Some museums concentrate on World War II, such as the **German Occupation Museum** in Guernsey. Portsmouth has an unrivalled battery of naval attractions, with the excellent **Royal Naval Museum**, Nelson's flagship **HMS** *Victory*, the Tudor warship *Mary Rose* and the **Submarine Museum** in Gosport among others.

There are museums which concentrate on a single famous person: **John Bunyan** in Bedford, **Jane Austen** at Chawton, **Captain Cook** in Middlesbrough, **Barbara Hepworth** at St Ives and galleries which preserve a collection formed by a single person or family – the enchanting **Lady Lever Art Gallery** at Port Sunlight, for instance, or the gorgeous **Bowes Museum** at Barnard Castle. Some of the most rewarding preserve a collection accumulated by a business firm: **Colman's Mustard** in Norwich, the **Harvey's Wine Museum** in Bristol, the **Pilkington Glass Museum** in St Helen's, the **Bass Museum of Brewing** at Burton on Trent, treasures of **Minton** at Stoke-on-Trent, **Wedgwood** at Barlaston, **Royal Crown Derby** in Derby.

There are agricultural museums, costume museums, museums which collect whole buildings, like the **Weald and Downland Museum** in Sussex. So does the sparkling **Welsh Folk Museum** in St Fagans, founded in 1947, and an example of the growing post-war interest in the lives of ordinary people in the past. The **North of England Open Air Museum** at Beamish in County Durham, which is showered with awards like confetti, re-creates the way of life of working-class people in the North around the turn of the century.

Since the 1950s there has been a second museum boom, on a far greater scale than the first. There were perhaps 700 museums all told in Britain when World War II ended. There are now more than 2000. A substantial number of these, about a third, are independent institutions, not set up by the government or the local authorities, but by private operators. To survive, they depend on their ability to attract and please paying customers, and among them are some of the best museums in the country. The **National Motor Museum** at Beaulieu in Hampshire has more than 250 historic vehicles on show and visitors are carried in moving 'pods' past displays which show how motoring developed in Britain from the late 19th century on, and how it may develop in the future. In Shropshire there is the marvellous **Ironbridge Gorge** complex of museums, bringing one of the key sites of the industrial revolution to life. In the old canal docks at Gloucester is the immensely enjoyable and nostalgic **Robert Opie Collection** of packets, wrappers, tins and advertising material, a museum of all our domestic yesterdays.

The best independents have contributed to the general enlivening of museums over the last 20 years. The old, musty institution of yore, full of mournful stuffed birds, prehistoric flint implements and dauntingly uninformative captions, is now a collector's item, if you can find one.

Some of the newest museums and galleries have been encouraged or funded by local authorities bent on developing tourist attractions to bring visitors and money into an area. In Bradford, for example, the **National Museum of Photography, Film and Television** opened in 1983, with the biggest cinema screen in Britain. It has galleries with 'interactive displays', where you can see yourself reading the news on TV!

There are teapots to admire in **Norwich**, trams to ride at **Crich** in Derbyshire, pork pies in **Melton Mowbray** and buns in **Abingdon**, voices in Lincolnshire dialect to listen to on the telephone in **Lincoln**, while the **Town Docks Museum** in Hull echoes to the voices of whales moaning in the deep. Certainly no one could sensibly complain of a lack of variety and interest in Britain's museums and galleries today.

Museum or art gallery

Below *The ship's wheel of HMS* Warrior *on show at Portsmouth.* Bottom *One of the locomotives at the National Railway Museum, in York.*

Industrial interest

Preserved railway or steam centre

Industrial Interest Preserved Railways and Steam Centres

Agriculture, industry and transport are the three principal activities through which successive generations have altered the appearance and character of Britain's landscape. Far back in the Stone Age there were axe factories in the Lake District and men wielding deer antlers as picks were digging shafts 40ft deep to mine for flint in Norfolk and Sussex. Since then the face of the land has been scarred wherever opportunity offered, by quarrying for building stone and mining for coal, iron ore, copper, lead and tin.

The great majority of Britain's sites of industrial interest today are legacies from the industrial revolution. They date roughly from the 1750s on, when water power and subsequently steam power were harnessed to the mass production of goods in mills and factories. The products were efficiently transported to customers along

Below Handsome 18th-century Quarry Bank Mill, at Styal in Cheshire. Bottom The splendid iron bridge in Ironbridge in Shropshire.

improved roads, later by canals and in the 19th century by railways.

Interest in preserving what was left of the old industrial heritage gathered strength after World War II. The term 'industrial archaeology' was coined in about 1950 and since then some exceptionally impressive sites have been rescued from dereliction or threatened destruction.

Perhaps the single most important one is the **Ironbridge Gorge** in Shropshire, where the River Severn cuts its way through steep, wooded hills. Here in the mining village of Coalbrookdale, the Darby dynasty of ironmasters succeeded in 1709 in smelting iron with coke – a fundamental advance in technology which led to the mass production of iron. It was in Coalbrookdale that the great Iron Bridge across the Severn was cast, the first important iron bridge in the world. The bridge is still there and the complex of museums and sites in the area today includes blast furnaces and engines, and a charmingly restored 1890s industrial community at **Blists Hill**, with a working foundry, a candle mill, other installations and railway exhibits.

The Darby family and other ironmasters pressed on to exploit the use of steam. One of the pioneers was John Wilkinson, known as 'Iron-Mad Wilkinson' because of his passionate advocacy of iron for every conceivable use. He wore an iron hat, was buried in an iron coffin when he died in 1808, and an iron obelisk was raised to his memory. It was Wilkinson who patented the method of boring cylinders which made James Watt's steam engine a practical proposition. His ironworks at **Bersham**, near Wrexham in North Wales, is today the centrepiece of an industrial heritage centre. This itself is on an eight-mile trail which traces the industrial history of this area from Roman times to the present day.

Another pioneer was Richard Arkwright, the Lancashire barber turned textile magnate, who built a water-powered cotton mill in the 1770s at **Cromford** in Derbyshire, with model housing for his factory hands. The site is being restored by the Arkwright Society. In Cheshire the National Trust owns **Quarry Bank Mill** at Styal, where another factory town was created round the cotton mill by the Greg family from the 1780s on. The machinery is running again, cotton goods woven in the mill are on sale and visitors can see the huge 85ft waterwheel, the village and the house where the pauper children lived.

The vast, dinosaur-like wheels and engines of the early industrial

age always attract and awe visitors. Lead mining was long an important industry on the northern moors and an enormous wheel is the most striking feature of the **Killhope Lead Mine** in Weardale, County Durham. In Cornwall giant engines were needed to pump water out of the shafts of tin mines driven 2,000ft deep and sometimes far out under the sea. The ruined engine houses and chimney stacks of abandoned tin mines are a dramatic and melancholy feature of the Cornish landscape. The National Trust preserves two of the engines at **East Pool Mine**, near Camborne. North of St Austell, in the strange white moonscape of china clay heaps, the 19th-century **Wheal Martyn** pit is a museum of the industry.

The titanic 1876 steam engine which pumped Brighton's water up from 160ft below ground has been restored, with many other engines, at the **British Engineerium** in Hove. Machinery clatters and rattles energetically away at the **Stott Park Bobbin Mill** in Cumbria, now in the care of English Heritage. This bobbin factory built in the 1830s is virtually unchanged. Wheels turn and fan-belts flap alarmingly at **Camden Works** in Bath, in the former brass foundry of J B Bowler. Here the most elementary safety precautions were ignored. The firm also made dubious aerated soft drinks. Nothing was ever thrown away at Bowler's and the whole ramshackle place is a delight.

Scotland is not as rich in industrial sites as it might be, but drinks of quite a different kind can be sampled in a clutch of whisky distilleries in the Dufftown area. There is a 70-mile, eight-distillery Whisky Trail for enthusiasts, who are urged to let someone else do the driving.

Coal mining and ironworking were carried on for centuries on a small scale in the Forest of Dean. One of the eerier experiences in Britain is to make your way down into the echoing tunnels and caverns of the **Clearwell Caves Iron Mine**, which had its heyday between 1850 and 1900.

In Wales, among the mountains of Snowdonia, there are dramatic sites where the hillsides are torn and broken by quarrying for slate, the principal industry of the area for 200 years until quite recently. At the **Llechwedd Slate Caverns** near Blaenau Ffestiniog, visitors are taken deep underground into the tunnels and caverns, and there are demonstrations of the skilled art of slate-splitting. Close by is the **Gloddfa Ganol Slate Mine**, once the biggest in the world. At Llanberis there is a museum of the

industry in the workshops of the now-closed **Dinorwic Quarry**.

The country's most dramatic and convincing coal mining museum is in South Wales. This is **Big Pit**, near Blaenafon in Gwent, in a colliery which closed in 1980. You go down almost 300ft in the cage, wearing your miner's helmet with lamp – which you need – and an ex-miner guides the party through the tunnels.

The application of steam power to transport created the great age of railways in Britain in the 19th and 20th centuries. The landscape was changed for ever by the Herculean works involved, the construction of embankments, cuttings and tunnels, the throwing of noble bridges and soaring viaducts across rivers and valleys. The sight of a powerful steam locomotive hammering along the rails at full tilt under a plume of smoke, the screaming of its whistle echoing across country, became part of the right order of things. When steam gave way to diesel and electric power, and much-loved branch lines were closed down in the 1950s and '60s, preservation societies formed to keep steam lines running or restore them to operation.

Many of the preserved lines go through particularly attractive stretches of country. The **Severn Valley Railway** runs more trains than any other, for 16 miles close to the River Severn between Bridgnorth, Bewdley and Kidderminster. Among its steam warhorses are some fine old Great Western locomotives.

The **Bluebell Railway** in Sussex has five miles of track between Sheffield Park and Horsted Keynes, through woods shining with bluebells in the spring. The **North Yorkshire Moors Railway** steams the 18 miles from Pickering to Grosmont through superlative scenery in the North York Moors National Park, and runs a Pullman service regularly. There are gaslit stations on the **Keighley and Worth Valley Railway**, whose headquarters are at Haworth in the Brontë Country. The **Lakeside & Haverthwaite Railway** puffs amicably through the Cumbrian woods to connect with the steamers on Lake Windermere.

In 19th-century England and Scotland the standard gauge of 4ft 8½in held sway, but elsewhere, especially in mountainous areas, a narrow gauge might be better suited to the terrain – the **Isle of Man Railway**'s 15-mile line from Douglas to Port Erin, has a 3ft gauge. Wales has a special reputation for its 'great little trains', on which the traveller can enjoy the steam, the shining paintwork and polished brass, and extremely spectacular scenery.

The **Vale of Rheidol Railway**, for instance, which opened in 1902, clanks its way along the mountainsides and round sharp bends from Aberystwyth to the famous beauty spot of the Devil's Bridge. The **Ffestiniog Railway**, originally built to haul slate, clambers up into Snowdonia from the harbour of Porthmadog past lakes and waterfalls and into the mountains. Some of its genial, round-faced engines have been making the trip for a hundred years. The **Talyllyn Railway**, which has been running since 1865, travels seven miles inland from Tywyn on Cardigan Bay, with splendid mountain prospects. This was the first railway in Britain to be saved from destruction by volunteers. It set an example many were glad to follow.

A vintage steam engine on the Brecon Mountain Railway near Merthyr Tydfil.

Industrial interest

Preserved railway or steam centre

Garden

Arboretum

Gardens
Arboreta

'An Englishman's home is his castle' and round his castle he creates a garden. Despite – or perhaps because of – the vagaries of our climate, the closeness of the Gulf Stream and the collections brought back from all over the world particularly in the 18th and 19th centuries, Britain has a wonderful heritage of gardens and arboreta.

The **Royal Horticultural Society**, inaugurated in 1804, has gardens at **Wisley**, near Woking, **Rosemoor**, in Devon, as well as close affiliations with the College of Horticulture, at **Pershore** and Liverpool University Botanic Garden, at **Ness**, on the Wirral. The RHS has, since 1889, published '*The Garden*', describing what can be seen, when and where. At all these places, keen gardeners can readily obtain advice and information.

The **Royal Botanic Garden** at Kew was established in 1759, in the reign of George II. Joining the traditional Victorian Palm and Temperate Houses, is Kew's latest feature, the Princess of Wales Conservatory, a

The gardens at Bodnant, Gwynedd, are among the most beautiful in Britain.

complex of 10 independently controlled climatic environments, growing a range of plants from desert to tropical forest species.

Since 1965 the National Trust property at **Wakehurst Place**, near Ardingly, has been 'Kew in the Country' and it is here that a national seed bank is maintained.

As we become increasingly aware of the fragile nature of our planet's eco-system, plant collections and gene banks are more and more a vital part of horticulture. The National Council for the Conservation of Plants and Gardens has, since 1982, co-ordinated collections such as the magnolias at **Savill Garden**, near Windsor, violas at **Leicester University**, clematis at **Tenbury**, peonies at **Hidcote** and rhododendrons at **Leonardslee**, **Nymans** and at **Exbury**. **Abbotsbury**, in Devon, looks after eucalyptus and in scores of smaller gardens, amateurs as well as professionals nurture border plants, primroses, celandines, buddleias and asters. For bigger specimens, arboreta play their part. Seventeen miles of pathways lead through the 500 acres of the Forestry Commission's **Westonbirt Arboretum** in Gloucestershire, where plantings have been

continuous for 150 years. Oak, chestnut, pine and beech shelter more exotic specimens, such as acers and willows, azaleas and rhododendrons.

The **Granada Arboretum**, in Manchester and the National Trust's **Winkworth Arboretum**, in Surrey, maintain sorbus and malus. Winter-flowering plants such as daphnes, honeysuckle, camellias and viburnum can be seen at the **Hillier Arboretum**, near Romsey and plants which flourish on chalky soils are the speciality of **Hidcote Manor Garden**, north of Chipping Campden.

Many of the gardens lovingly tended in the past have now been restored. At **New Place**, in Surrey, the Edwardian garden of Gertrude Jekyll was recovered from beneath couch grass and poppies. At East Grinstead, the mullioned windows of 16th-century **Gravetye Manor** now reflect the glory of a Victorian garden created by William Robinson. At **Erddig**, near Wrexham, another 18th-century design has been re-created in the grounds of the National Trust house and **Culpeper Flower Garden** now flourishes at **Leeds Castle**, in Kent, 17th-century home of the Culpeper family. The 18th-century garden at

Painshill Park in Surrey was laid out in the 1740s by Charles Hamilton. Sadly decayed, the combination of classical architecture, lake and landscaping is being restored and it may once again rival the garden of Hamilton's friend, Henry Hoare at Stourhead.

Gardens stretch the length and breadth of the British Isles. **Inverewe**, in Wester Ross, despite its northern latitude, enjoys frost-free conditions, due to the warm North Atlantic Drift, and **Tresco Abbey Gardens** in the Scilly Isles, created and maintained since 1834 by successive generations of the same family relishes mild, moist weather. In the 1790s garden of 13th-century **Drum Castle**, near Aberdeen, a collection illustrating the development of roses from the 17th-century has recently been created by the National Trust for Scotland.

The **University Botanic Gardens** at St Andrews, training ground for future professionals, also provide a well laid out and informative garden for the visitor. Its high point is the peat, water and rock complex simulating the natural progression from mountain crag to scree to meadow and bog. The **Royal Botanic Garden**, in Edinburgh, second oldest in the country after Oxford, also has a superb rock garden and, like the new conservatory at Kew, grows the astonishing *Victoria Amazonica* water lily, its huge leaves capable of supporting a small child, but which grow from seed annually.

Across on the west coast are the gardens of **Brodick Castle**, on the Isle of Arran. Sir John Ramsden, then owner of **Muncaster Castle**, in Cumbria, after a visit to Brodick sent his hostess some rhododendrons for her garden – in all 80 tons! In 1953 an expedition to Burma brought back hundreds more plants and yet more varieties, most of which flourish in the mild climate.

At **Belsay**, north of Newcastle, English Heritage has restored the gardens, partly in the quarry used by Charles Monck, a keen member of the Horticultural Society. At **Thorp Perrow**, near Ripon, there is a Cherry Avenue which is a riot of blossom in May. Several 'autumn bays' provide colour from September to November and there is a Rowan Avenue, with spring blossom and autumn berries.

John Aislabie, Chancellor of the Exchequer at the time of the South Sea Bubble, retired to his estate at **Studley Royal**, in Yorkshire, albeit under something of a cloud. The garden he designed is a work of true inspiration, anticipating Stourhead by 40 years. It now incorporates the ready-made 'folly', so essential to Romantic landscaping, acquired when his son purchased the nearby Fountains Abbey.

Harlow Car Botanical Garden, near Harrogate, has been since 1948 the headquarters of the Northern Horticultural Society, working closely with the RHS and offering a similar range of walks, workshops and demonstrations as Wisley. **Newby Hall**, near Ripon, has something to delight the eye all year round, but is best known for its display of roses in early summer and its herbaceous border plants.

At **Eaton Hall**, Eccleston, near Chester, there is an unheated glasshouse 120yds long, with camellias which are usually at their best in April. **Bodnant**, near Llandudno, always associated with the Aberconway family, has rhododendrons, azaleas, magnolias and camellias. Here, too, there is a wonderful laburnum walk where, on a sunny day in May, you can walk through a tunnel of glorious yellow blossom. Near Welshpool is **Powis Castle**, once the home of Clive of India. Its terraces are one of the few remaining medieval-style gardens in the country.

Doddington Hall, south-west of Lincoln, was built by the Elizabethan architect, Smythson, who designed Longleat and Hardwick Hall. The garden, even as late as 1919, had cattle grazing on the lawns, but now the walled west garden is full of the old-fashioned roses for which Doddington is famous, as well as a profusion of irises.

Near Colchester, **Beth Chatto's Garden** covering 12 acres, has developed into a centre where gardeners can pick up hints on what grows best in hard-baked sandy soil, sour silt or waterlogged clay. At **Sissinghurst**, in Kent, the garden of this Tudor house is a monument to Victoria Sackville-West who, in the 1930s, created walks where each of the gardens opening off had its own colour scheme.

In **Sheffield Park**, near East Grinstead, famous for its autumn colours, you can wander away from the lakeside rhododendrons and discover the wonderful collection of conifers. One group of Maritime pines is reputed to have been planted by Sir Joseph Banks, a founder of the RHS. David Douglas, after whom the Douglas Fir is named, brought Monterey pines here from California and there is a dwarf Siberian pine planted in the 1920s, which has just about reached five feet and can thus be highly recommended for the small garden!

The National Trust property at **Kingston Lacy** in Dorset, has a delightful fernery planted with snowdrops for an early effect and the Cedar Walk has carefully recorded plantings by the Duke of Wellington, King Edward VII, the Kaiser and King George V, who planted an oak here to commemorate his Coronation. At **Stourhead**, north of Shaftesbury, lake, bridge, temples and grottoes combine to achieve one of the finest 'landscaped' gardens in the world, the creation of Henry Hoare in the 1740s, a generation before Capability Brown began diverting rivers and moving mountains around many of the great houses of his day.

Penjerrick, in Cornwall, was begun in the 1830s and many exotic plants here were grown from seed brought into nearby Falmouth by clipper captains, but rhododendrons remain one of its glories.

Wherever you go, at no matter what season of the year, there are gardens to be enjoyed all over Britain. Provided you do not pick a Bank Holiday weekend, in most cases you will find someone ready to pass on the secret of their success to you.

Garden

Arboretum

Hillier Arboretum in Hampshire.

Country park

The forested slopes at Afan Argoed resemble those in Switzerland.

Country Parks

In the 1960s and '70s, increasing affluence, more leisure time, more cars and faster roads combined to bring the open countryside within the reach of far more people. The number of townspeople and suburbanites driving out for a day in the country was growing rapidly and there was a need to accommodate the demand without spoiling the countryside which everyone was eager to enjoy.

In 1966 a government white paper on 'Leisure in the Countryside' suggested the establishment of country parks and the idea was taken up in the Countryside Acts which followed. The two Countryside Commissions, one for England and Wales, the other for Scotland, were given the responsibility for stimulating the creation of country parks, providing advice and grants of taxpayers' money to projects they approved.

Most of the country parks have been set up by local authorities. One of their fundamental functions is to make available country places where visitors know they have a right to be. Opinion polls and studies have shown time and time again that people are held back from enjoying the countryside by an uneasy feeling that they may be trespassing or at least not wanted. A country park is a place where you are welcome. It is also a place where there will be toilets and somewhere to park the car.

There are now more than 200 country parks in Britain, varying considerably in size and character. The larger ones have visitor centres where you will find information about the landscape, the wildlife and often the area's history; wardens or rangers who keep an eye on things and provide help and information when needed; way-marked paths; amusements for children, and refreshments.

Country parks are usually open every day during daylight hours, and in the great majority of them admission is free, though boating, bowls or other special facilities may have to be paid for. Activities vary from one park to another – from riding, fishing, hang-gliding and grass-skiing to orienteering, golfing, boating and sailing.

Some of the earliest country parks were areas which were already heavily visited and where better facilities were needed. An example is **Box Hill**, near Dorking in Surrey, named after the rare wild box trees on the chalk hill. For centuries past people have loved to walk there and admire the views over the Weald. Much of the area is owned by the National Trust and there is a car park, information room and shop.

Another case in point is **Butser Hill**, a much-visited beauty spot on the A3 south of Petersfield where

Hampshire County Council created the **Queen Elizabeth Country Park**, opened by the Queen in 1976. The park covers 1,400 acres of downs, Forestry Commission beechwoods and stands of yew at the western edge of the South Downs Way footpath. There are splendid views from the top of Butser Hill, a nature reserve and waymarked trails, with downland plants and flowers to see, woodpeckers, butterflies and deer. The Ancient Farm Research Project here farms the way Iron Age man did 2000 years ago, and the park has an information centre with an audio-visual programme, a café and a picnic area.

Another heavily visited area is the **Brimham Rocks Country Park** on the moors near Pateley Bridge in North Yorkshire. The rocks, weathered into strange shapes over the centuries, drew sightseers in such numbers that the area was in danger of being badly damaged. It is owned by the National Trust and the threat to the Rocks has been brought under control.

Since country parks were intended primarily for town dwellers, they tend to be more numerous close to heavily populated urban areas. They are not thick on the ground in Norfolk and Suffolk, for example, but there is quite a concentration of them in Essex, nearer London. One of these is the attractive **Hatfield Forest Country Park**, near Bishop's Stortford, an area of ancient hunting forest which was only just rescued from the developer's grasp in the 1920s and which is famous for its hornbeams and its nightingales.

Similarly, there are fewer country parks in North and Central Wales than in the former mining and industrial areas of South Wales. One of the biggest and best is **Margam Country Park**, near Port Talbot. Its 850 acres include what were once the stately grounds of the Mansel family's fine house. There are landscaped gardens, a deer park, a handsome orangery which is used for concerts, a theatre, a large maze and boating on the lake, which is also occupied by swans, coots and moorhens. A herd of Glamorgan cattle and an Iron Age hill-fort with commanding views over the Bristol Channel adds to its enormous appeal. There is an adventure playground, and a heronry in the nature reserve, and there are skylarks and buzzards. Just outside the park is the ruined church of 12th-century Margam Abbey.

Many other parks have solved the problem of what to do with fine country estates the owners can no longer keep up. **Mount Edgcumbe Country Park**, which looks out over Plymouth Sound, preserves the formal gardens with their statues and fountains laid out for the Edgcumbe family in the 18th century. Stretching for miles along the coast, it boasts follies, woods, a deer park and a fabulous collection of camellias.

Many country parks, by contrast, have contributed to the reclamation of derelict industrial wasteland. East of Sheffield, on the border of Yorkshire and Derbyshire, the **Rother Valley Country Park** has arisen phoenix-like from an area of opencast coal mining, with 350,000 freshly planted trees and no less than three lakes for fishing and watersports. There are footpaths and visitors can hire cycles to ride along the network of bicycle tracks.

The **Strathclyde Country Park** in the south-eastern outskirts of Glasgow was formally opened in 1978. Millions of pounds were spent to take a derelict, stagnant wasteland of exhausted colliery workings and desolate spoil heaps and turn it back into pleasant countryside. The River Clyde was diverted to create a 200-acre loch, trees and shrubs and long stretches of grass were planted, paths were laid out by the loch and picnic areas and car parks provided.

Now the trees have matured. The loch, almost two miles long, is a watersports centre for sailing, canoeing and waterskiing. There is a golf course and sports pitches, an interpretation centre and a nature reserve which attracts wintering whooper swans and other waterfowl. Also inside the park are the remains of a Roman fort and a peculiar 19th-century mausoleum, which was constructed for the Dukes of Hamilton but turned out to have such a noisy echo in the chapel inside that it was impossible to use it.

Country park landscapes vary from the heath and scrub of **Cannock Chase** in Staffordshire to the giant trees in **Sherwood Forest**, the ducal landscape by Capability Brown not far away in **Clumber Park** in Nottinghamshire, and on to the deer and rugged rocks of **Bradgate Park** in Leicestershire, with the ruins of the house in which the tragic Lady Jane Grey grew up. On top of **Ham Hill** in Somerset, the grassed-over stone quarries make a wonderful arena for hide-and-seek. On **Berry Head**, south of Torbay in South Devon, towering cliffs command bracing views of the English Channel and the nests of kittiwakes and guillemots. The need to protect the wild orchids and other rare plants here was one reason why the local council bought the land in 1968. Further on along the Channel coast, at the **Lepe Country Park** in Hampshire, you can look across the Solent to the Isle of Wight and idly watch the ships and the black-headed gulls go by.

One question which remains is: are the visitors at country parks enjoying real countryside or a mock-up? Nowadays the Countryside Commission believes that the parks should be treated less as ends in themselves and more as gateways to the true countryside beyond.

Brimham Rocks, in North Yorkshire, where the rocks form weird shapes.

Theme park

The 'Thunder River' rapid-water ride, for all the family, at Thorpe Park.

Theme Parks

The British theme park has its spiritual ancestor across the Atlantic. Disneyland, which opened in Anaheim in the southern suburbs of Los Angeles in 1955, combined four basic characteristics. First there was a central theme – the world of Disney cartoons and films. Second, there were illusions, using the latest technology, and visitors experienced a simulated river trip in the African jungle, or thought they were going deep underwater in a submarine, when in fact they were only a few inches beneath the surface. Next, there were 'white knuckle' rides – an exciting roller-coaster, a terrifying helter-skelter and other thrilling fairground rides, again using the latest technology. And last, Disneyland catered for the motor car, the family with children and modern mass tourism, with a parking lot of gargantuan proportions and an ample supply of toilets and places to eat.

The lessons of Disneyland were absorbed and put to use at **Alton Towers**, the 500-acre 'leisure park' in Staffordshire which is now attracting two and a half million visitors a year. Alton Towers employs a staff of 1400 people during the summer and has six different restaurants, of varying types and price levels, with innumerable kiosks scattered about the grounds selling ice-creams and soft drinks. There is no single central theme, but six 'themed areas', which include Fantasy World, Aqualand and Kiddies Kingdom. Among the 'white knuckle' rides are the gravity-defying Corkscrew Roller-coaster, which lives up to its name, as well as the New Black Hole, the Alton Beast, and the water-based Log Flume

and Grand Canyon Rapids Ride.

There are gentler rides for those of nervous disposition or with small children, with a beautiful carousel, and a mass of indoor attractions and Disney-style parades with bands, floats and performers in life-size animal costumes.

In addition to all this is a wonderful Victorian Gothic ruin and some of the most spectacular gardens in the country, inherited from the Earls of Shrewsbury, whose country seat Alton Towers used to be. The 15th and 16th Earls constructed an enormous pseudo-medieval fantasy palace here, replete with towers and spires, turrets and battlements. A W Pugin himself, the high priest of Victorian Gothic, was called in to preside over the interior decor. Outside, meanwhile, a fortune was spent to lay out a magnificent park and gardens. Lakes and pools were dug out, fed by water brought from a spring two miles off. Terraces, miles of walks, giant stairways and grand glasshouses were built at colossal expense by an army of workmen.

The future Queen Victoria visited Alton in 1832, at the age of 13, and was entertained to luncheon on gold plates. The Chinese-style Pagoda Fountain was built, and shoots a jet of water 70ft high. A Swiss cottage was erected on the hillside to provide a fine prospect over the grounds while a blind Welsh harper was stationed there to play soothing music. Today it is a restaurant.

In later years it proved impossible to keep the house up and the mansion fell into the condition of picturesque ruin in which visitors see it now. The gardens were properly maintained, however, and are a delight to walk in today.

More 'white knuckle' rides can be found by the adventurous at the **Chessington World of Adventures**, in Surrey. 'This Ride Is Not For The

Faint-Hearted' one sign warns. There is a 'blood chilling' roller-coaster called the Vampire, which zooms along at tree-top height and dives underground. It is set in a 'Transylvania' village which also has a bubble works fantasy ride for children through a simulated fizzy pop factory, and a restaurant wittily named the Black Forest Chateau.

The theme areas at Chessington feature encounters with horrible science fiction monsters, and Calamity Canyon, where there's a Wild West trading post, a shooting gallery and a roller-coaster called the Runaway Mine Train. In the Mystic East area visitors see the Palace of the Nine Dragons, the Giant Buddha and the Cambodian temple of Angkor Wat, and go on a 'dragon river' water ride through a bamboo jungle, where the boat is attacked by a crocodile. In addition, Chessington has a zoo, a circus, a miniature railway, plenty of eating places, and live entertainment with bands, dancers, clowns, street performers and 'madcap' characters in costume.

Halfway between Derby and Nottingham may seem an odd place to meet cowboys and shoot-outs, but the Wild West is one of the main themes at the **American Adventure**, near Ilkeston in Derbyshire. Pistol-packing posses career through town, bullets fly and saloon girls squeal as badmen get their come-uppances. There is live entertainment in Lazy Lil's Saloon and jazz on a Mississippi riverboat.

The numerous rides include a double-drop log flume in Thunder Canyon and a charge through the raging torrents of the Great Niagara Rapids. Or you can take a triple-looping roller-coaster called the Missile and blast off to the stars from Space Port USA. There are special attractions to keep small children happy in Pioneer Playland, including a cartoon cinema.

At the **Pleasurewood Hills American Theme Park**, near Lowestoft in Suffolk, southern fried chicken is on the menu, and attractions range from the evil Rattlesnake roller-coaster and the New Tempest, which hangs you upside down 100ft in the air, to a water-borne voyage to Aladdin's Cave, a land of dinosaurs, fairground big wheels, a spooky haunted castle and shows by performing sea lions and parrots.

In Yorkshire, near Ripon, the **Lightwater Valley Theme Park**, in the 1970s a peaceful pig farm, prides itself on the sheer appalling terror of its 'white knuckle' rides. It opened the longest roller-coaster ride in the world in 1990, at a cost of over £5 million, running 2,400 metres (close

to 1½ miles) with a drop of 158ft and a top speed of about 60mph. This joined a nightmare ride called The Rat, which runs entirely underground in pitch darkness, 'through smelly sewers alive with the shrieks and shrills of rats' – rated tops for sheer horror by the *Daily Mirror*.

There are calmer pleasures at Lightwater Valley, too – a nine-hole golf course, three boating lakes, an old-fashioned fairground, a miniature railway, and a shopping centre. There is skate boarding, a go-kart track, an adventure playground for smaller children, and a theatre with live entertainment.

At Charnock Richard in Lancashire, there awaits 'an enchanted day out for the whole family' in 'the magical kingdom' of **Camelot**. The theme here is the world of King Arthur and his heroic knights of the Round Table. Knights in full armour thunder into combat on their chargers in the jousting arena. Jesters and grotesque animal figures wander about. A chilling roller-coaster hurtles into the Tower of Terror, where something unspeakable called the Beast lurks in its dark lair. Guinevere's swan ride negotiates Merlin's magic mountain, the Grail trail crosses a swinging rope bridge and Sir Bedevere's Bridge leads to the enchantments of the Wild Wood.

You can eat at the Round Table Burger Bar, naturally, but altogether Camelot has 28 outlets selling food and drink. It reckons to cook 2½ miles of sausages every season, as well as 250,000 pounds of dragon burgers and 315,000 pounds of chips.

The 'family leisure park' at **Thorpe Park**, near Chertsey in Surrey, is close to both the M3 and the M25. It opened in 1979 on the site of old gravel workings, which gave it plenty of lakes and pools. Water skiing, wind surfing and other watersports rank high among its pleasures, water barges carry visitors from one area of the park to another and there are river-boat restaurants.

The original theme was Britain's maritime history, but now, with the need to attract repeat visitors, the emphasis has changed. 'White knuckle' rides are not particularly important here and the park concentrates more on entertainments and amusements which families with children aged about four to 14 can all enjoy together. There is live entertainment at two theatres, lots of street entertainers, musicians, clowns and giant sub-Disney animal grotesques, and a large amusement centre with

video games and one-arm bandits. The log flume ride in the Canadian Rockies theme area has a drop of 50ft and there is a fast Space Station Zero ride, but more typical is the complete working farm, which operates as it did in the 1930s. A simulated medieval town square has a double-decker carousel and other attractions include a nature trail, miniature railway, roller skating rink, crazy golf and a cartoon cinema.

All theme parks are geared to a safe, enjoyable family day out, and you pay once, on entry, and get the rides and other attractions thrown in. Alton Towers is the kingpin in terms of visitor figures, but the numbers rung up at the other parks – over a million and a quarter at Thorpe Park, and a similar figure at Chessington – suggest that this type of transatlantic family attraction is in Britain to stay.

The 'Runaway Mine Train' at Chessington World of Adventures.

Theme Park

Zoo

*Wildlife
collection
– mammals*

*Wildlife
collection
– birds*

Aquarium

Zoos
Wildlife Collections
Aquaria

The oldest picture of an elephant in England is in Exeter Cathedral, a 13th-century wood carving under one of the choir seats. It is quite likely to be a portrait of a real African elephant, the one which was presented to Henry III by the King of France in 1253. Its arrival in England created a sensation and people flocked to see the great beast as it tramped from the port of Sandwich to London.

Zoos

The century before, Henry I had established a menagerie at Woodstock in Oxfordshire. It was later moved to the Tower of London and survived there until well into the 19th century. The public was let in to see the animals, which in 1609, consisted of 11 lions, two leopards, a jackal, two mountain cats, three eagles and two owls.

Kings and noblemen continued to keep private menageries, but the 19th century saw the creation of public zoological gardens – zoos for short – as part of the same educational and improving impulse responsible for the establishment of so many museums. The first in the field was the **Regent's Park Zoo** in London, laid out by Decimus Burton and opened in 1828 by the recently founded Zoological Society of London. The animals from the Tower were moved here.

Municipal zoos now opened, combining serious study of animals with public instruction and entertainment. In Dublin, for example, the Royal Zoological Society of Ireland opened a zoo in **Phoenix Park** in 1830. It gained a substantial reputation for breeding lions, as **Glasgow Zoo** breeds porcupines and Edinburgh Zoo is famous for its penguins.

Wildlife Collections

After World War II, a tide of disapproval set in against the old-fashioned 19th-century zoo, which seemed little better than a prison with its cramped cages and unnatural conditions, and against the whole attitude to animals which this type of zoo was felt to represent. The consequence was the modernisation of many zoos and the coming of the safari park and a new style of wildlife collection.

The development of the open-range zoo, where animals roam in large enclosures instead of being penned in cages, had begun in 1931, when the Zoological Society of London opened a country branch at **Whipsnade Park** in Bedfordshire, near Dunstable. Whipsnade covers

The famous lions of Longleat.

more than 500 acres, most of the animals live in herds in sizeable paddocks and well over 90 per cent of them were born in the zoo. In the last 30 years many other zoos have moved closer to the open-range system.

Britain's first safari park opened in 1966 at **Longleat** in Wiltshire, the palatial Elizabethan seat of the Marquess of Bath. The prime movers in the enterprise were the Marquess himself and Jimmy Chipperfield, of the well-known circus family, an experienced supplier of wild animals to zoos. The idea was for visitors to drive through the spacious enclosures where the animals roamed: in other words, for a change, the animals would be free and the public confined. The project proved extremely popular.

Lions were the first, and have always been the foremost attraction at Longleat, but many other animals can be seen there today – including the country's only white Bengal tiger, as well as white rhinos, camels, giraffes and gorillas. The monkeys enjoy riding on visitors' cars and there are boat trips to see hippos and sea lions. In some areas visitors can leave their cars and stroll about or even have a picnic among the animals. Like other safari parks, Longleat depends on and provides for the motor car, and there is plenty of parking with no problem about finding a restaurant or a toilet.

The Duke of Bedford was not far behind in opening a safari park of his own at his stately Bedfordshire mansion of **Woburn**. Jimmy Chipperfield was again involved. But Woburn already had a distinguished history of keeping and breeding wild animals. Père David's deer are named after a French missionary, who saw the only remaining herd of them in the imperial park outside Peking where they were kept in the 19th century. A few animals were grudgingly shipped out to European zoos, and

Flamingos at Slimbridge Wildfowl Trust

when the Chinese herd was wiped out, the 16 Père David's deer in Europe were the only ones left. The 11th Duke of Bedford rounded all 16 up in 1894 and settled them in his park at Woburn, where they prospered and multiplied. All the Père David's deer in the world are descended from them, and in 1985 some were sent back to China, to the same park outside Peking.

Woburn also played a part in saving the European bison from extinction. The Père David's deer are still there, and so are the bison, but the **Woburn Wild Animal Kingdom** today is Britain's largest drive-through collection of wild creatures. A ride in aerial cars gives a bird's eye view of the park, and there are performing sea lions, and even performing macaws.

A wildlife collection of an entirely different flavour can be enjoyed at **Chillingham**, in Northumberland, where visitors can cautiously inspect the 50-strong herd of wild white cattle. With their wicked, curving horns, they are the nearest thing to prehistoric cattle still in existence. They have been kept in the park at Chillingham for centuries and have never been crossbred.

John Aspinall has set up two Kent

Zoo

Wildlife collection – mammals

Wildlife collection – birds

Aquarium

zoo parks: **Howletts**, near Canterbury, famous for breeding gorillas and African elephants, and its sister at **Port Lympne**, near Hythe. Here magnificent Siberian tigers, black rhino and the country's only breeding colony of majestic Barbary lions loll about in aristocratic splendour.

Breeding animals, and especially breeding species which in the wild are threatened with extinction, has become an important function of zoos, safari parks and wildlife collections, and a key justification of their existence. **Chester Zoo**, for example, which ranks second only to London in its tally of visitors and has a wide range of animals in attractive grounds, has successfully bred orang-utans, Madagascan tree boas and rare fruit bats, among other species. **Bristol Zoo**, where the creatures on view range from tigers to tarantulas and penguins to piranhas, counts gorillas and orang-utans, Persian leopards, colobus monkeys and long-tailed macaques among its breeding successes. **Twycross Zoo**, near Atherstone in Warwickshire, a small zoo with a remarkable collection of apes and monkeys, has a notable breeding record and **Marwell**, near Winchester, breeds rare Sumatran tigers and the endangered oryx.

In 1947 there were only 50 breeding pairs of the Hawaiian geese called ne ne left in the world, all of them in Hawaii. The species was saved by successful breeding at the Wildfowl Trust reserve at **Slimbridge** in Gloucestershire, founded by the late Sir Peter Scott. Some of the birds from here were later sent back to Hawaii in the hope of re-establishing them in their native land.

The splendid Slimbridge reserve is on the bank of the River Severn. Other Wildfowl Trust reserves include those at **Arundel** in Sussex, **Washington** in Tyne and Wear, and **Caerlaverock** in Scotland. At **Stagsden** in Bedfordshire is one of the first specialist bird collections in Britain. The Bird Gardens concentrate on cranes, but there are 150 species or more on view in all. **Birdworld**, near Farnham in Surrey, has a collection ranging from tiny hummingbirds to outsize ostriches, and is successfully breeding Humboldt penguins.

Aquaria
The first public aquarium in Britain opened in London in 1853. It was not until a hundred years later that the first massive sea aquariums, or oceanariums, opened in the United States, with huge tanks containing

The 'Penguin' Parade – the star attraction at Edinburgh Zoo.

hundreds of fish of different species swimming together. The example has been followed in Britain, for example at the **Sea Life Centre** in Weymouth, which opened in 1983 with the biggest display tank in Europe. Visitors can see dolphins and porpoises, British sharks, octopus and squid and evil-looking conger eels, and fish in drifting droves. There is a special flatfish tank and a tank with a simulated sunken wreck and the marine life that would gather around it. There are also 'touch pools' and plenty of fun for children.

Of the same genre, but on a much more modest scale, is **Anglesey Sea Zoo**, near Brynsiencyn, close to the shore of the Menai Strait, with its tanks of fish, lobsters and crabs from the local waters and 'touch tank' for the children.

There is still plenty of enjoyment, and discoveries to be made, at the more old-fashioned aquaria in seaside towns, like those at **Plymouth** and **Eastbourne**, and at **Brighton**, where there are dolphin and sea lion shows. While wildlife is increasingly threatened in the wild, it flourishes in British zoos, safari parks and aquaria.

Nature reserve

Nature trail

RSPB site

Nature Reserves
Nature Trails
RSPB Sites

Brownsea Island is a much-treasured Dorset beauty spot, a 500-acre island in Poole Harbour, accessible only by boat. It has an honoured place in the history of the Boy Scouts, as it was here in 1907 that General Baden-Powell held his first scout camp. A succession of wealthy and sometimes eccentric owners preserved the island from contamination by development until, with the death of the last of them in 1961, it passed to the National Trust. It was then a wildly overgrown paradise for red squirrels, the late owner's peacocks, Sika deer, herons and seabirds. The National Trust has protected it ever since and thousands of visitors go there every year to enjoy the beaches, walk the heathland and woodland glades and admire stunning views of the Dorset coast.

A substantial area of the island is sealed off against casual visitors dropping in, though parties are guided round at regular intervals. This is a nature reserve, managed by the Dorset Trust for Nature Conservation, with a heronry, two lakes and a marsh fringed with reeds, where wildfowl congregate in

A view from a hide overlooking Welney Wildfowl Refuge, in Norfolk.

safety – terns and oystercatchers, godwits and sandpipers, dunlins and redshanks.

Nature Reserves

Unlike a National Park or a country park, a nature reserve is not protected for the sake of human visitors, but for the sake of the wild creatures, birds, insects and rare plants, and the habitats and conditions they need to survive and flourish. Many nature reserves are open to the general public, at others a permit may be needed or access may be limited, but some are closed altogether.

As long ago as 1912 the need to set aside areas in which threatened species could survive was recognised with the founding of the Society for the Promotion of Nature Reserves by the prescient naturalist Charles Rothschild. When he died the movement lost impetus. After World War II, however, the pressure of expanding population and expanding leisure time bore so heavily on the country's wildlife that something plainly needed to be done. In 1949 the government set up the Nature Conservancy Council (NCC) as its wildlife protection arm, and one of the new body's responsibilities was 'to establish, manage and maintain nature reserves'.

At the same time vigorous county and local wildlife protection trusts were forming and establishing nature reserves of their own. Charles Rothschild's society re-emerged into the limelight as the national organisation and mouthpiece of these groups, as the Royal Society for Nature Conservation.

Today Britain has more than 2,000 nature reserves, occupying more than half a million acres of land between them. Some are managed by the NCC, but a far larger number are run by the county or local trusts for nature conservation, naturalists' trusts or wildlife trusts. Others are owned and managed by the Forestry Commission, others again by local authorities and conservation bodies.

From a visitor's point of view, nature reserves supply a way of seeing and coming close to the full range of Britain's wildlife and plant life without any danger of trespassing or going where one is not wanted. They can be found on the coast and inland, on high ground and on low, in a great variety of countryside.

At **Caerlaverock**, for instance, on the Solway Firth coast of Scotland, the NCC established a reserve in 1957 on the low-lying saltmarshes among muddy flats and creeks. Multitudes of birds feed and roost there: golden plovers in legions,

greylag geese, pintail and all manner of ducks and waders. Thousands of barnacle geese fly in from the Arctic every winter, and there are birds of prey, as well as saltmarsh plants in abundance. This is also one of the breeding grounds of the rare and noisy natterjack toad. Visitor access is limited, partly because the flats and creeks are dangerous when the tide sweeps suddenly in. There is also a Wildfowl Trust refuge close by and the romantic pink ruin of Caerlaverock Castle to visit.

By contrast, not so many miles away inland, east of Newton Stewart, the NCC runs the **Cairnsmore of Fleet** nature reserve, largely a trackless waste of peat and heather moorland, bog and mountainside. It is important as the home of red deer, wild goats and ravens. Access is again restricted.

Similarly, there is a cluster of contrasting nature reserves in the Gower Peninsula of South Wales, which is famed for packing a remarkable variety of scenery into a small area, and for the accompanying wealth of wildlife. At **Cwmllwyd Wood**, west of Swansea, for instance, West Glamorgan County Council has a reserve of oak woods, grassland and marsh, with hides from which to watch snipe and woodcock. At **Oxwich** on the south coast there is an NCC reserve of quite different character in an area of sand dunes, wooded headlands and marshes, explored by nature trails. Keep an eye out for adders on the slopes.

RSPB Sites
Some of the most rewarding nature reserves in the country belong to the Royal Society for the Protection of Birds (RSPB). Founded in 1889, the RSPB is devoted to the conservation of wild birds. It has built up a portfolio of well over a hundred reserves in which the habitats of breeding and wintering birds and birds of passage are preserved.

Some of the RSPB reserves are as far flung as the **Orkneys** and **Shetlands**, but most of them are more accessible. There is one at **Dungeness** on the Kent coast, where the nuclear power station broods over a desolate landscape of shingle beach, ponds and abandoned gravel workings, and tangled gorse and brambles. But there is plenty of life here – marsh frogs, plants like viper's bugloss, and waterfowl in huge numbers, with many migrating birds making a landfall at this point.

Up in Lancashire, at **Leighton Moss** near Silverdale, the RSPB preserves an area of swamp,

The 300ft high cliffs of Marwick Head's RSPB reserve, Orkney.

shallow meres and scrubland. Here bitterns boom and breed among the reeds and marsh harriers pass by in spring, while below are otters, deer, bats and beautiful wild orchids.

Though the primary purpose of a reserve is protection, the RSPB welcomes visitors – the general public as well as its own members – so as to encourage public sympathy and support for conservation. Trails and hides are provided to help visitors see as much as possible, while interfering as little as possible with the birds.

Nature Trails
Other institutions generally take the same attitude. One device for helping visitors make the most of a reserve is a nature trail, a path equipped perhaps with a self-guiding leaflet explaining what can be seen along it, or informative notices at points along the way, or a combination of both.

Nature trails are not confined to nature reserves. They can be found on farms which are open to the public – there are many on Forestry Commission land which are often combined with other attractions. At the **Landmark Visitor Centre** at Carrbridge, in Strathspey in the Highland Region of Scotland, there is a nature trail through the pinewoods as well as an adventurous treetop trail and a sculpture park. At the **Dean Heritage Centre** in the Forest of Dean, south of Cinderford, a nature trail is an outdoors alternative to craftsmen's workshops and a museum.

There is a particularly enticing nature trail at the **Broadlands Conservation Centre**, deep in the heart of the Norfolk Broads at Ranworth. Organised by the

Norfolk Naturalists' Trust, it runs through woods and marshes to a building on piles at the edge of Ranworth Broad. Inside is a gallery with an excellent view of the birds on the water (Ranworth Church, incidentally, is famous for the view from the top of its tower).

A spectacular trail on **Skomer Island**, off the south-west tip of Wales, is run by the West Wales Naturalists' Trust, with viewing points for watching seabirds and seals. Puffins and stormy petrels breed here, and you can also see choughs, ravens and peregrine falcons.

On the other side of the country, in complete contrast, is the low-lying island of **Lindisfarne**, embalmed in mudflats at low tide. Sea aster, thrift and eelgrass flourish here, and delectable orchids grow, with myriads of birds whirling and calling in winter. Brent geese fly in from the Arctic. Also here are the ruins of a medieval priory and Lindisfarne Castle.

It is not always necessary, however, to go far from big centres of population to find rewarding nature trails. There are several on **Witley Common**, south-west of Guildford along the A3, where the National Trust owns much of the heath. The oddity here is to find chalk country plants growing, because chalk was brought in to make a parade ground for a former army camp on the common. There are oaks, silver birches and chestnuts, many birds, rabbits, foxes and deer. Like other reserves, it is a place where the visitor can be close to nature without necessarily being far from home.

Nature reserve

Nature trail

RSPB site

National trail

National Trails

Enthusiasm for long distance walking has grown apace in Britain since World War II, as part of a general quickening of appetite for exploring and enjoying the countryside at first hand, away from main roads and crowded tourist spots. The first national long distance walking route, the Pennine Way, was declared open in 1965. Since then many more paths have been established. Ten of them are now classified by the Countryside Commission as 'national trails'. These are continuous routes over substantial distances, which can take a week or more to traverse: though, of course, many people enjoy walking for only a few hours or a day or two on part of one of the routes.

The ten national trails in England and Wales are: the Cleveland Way; the North Downs Way; the Offa's Dyke Path; the Peddars Way and Norfolk Coast Path; the Pembrokeshire Coast Path; the Pennine Way; the Ridgeway Path; the South Downs Way; the South

Below Offa's Dyke Path traces the 8th-century English—Welsh boundary. *Bottom* The 50 miles of the Peddar's Way, in Norfolk, follow a Roman road.

West Coast path, and the Wolds Way. Placed end to end, these 10 routes together cover approximately 1,750 miles. Three of them are in the South of England, one is in East Anglia, two are in Wales and the Marches, and three in the North. There are also three more long distance walking routes in Scotland.

The founding father of this whole network was the late Tom Stephenson, of the Ramblers' Association, who in 1935 put forward the idea of a continuous public footpath running the whole length of the Pennine Chain to the Cheviots and the Scots Border. It took 30 years during which much opposition had to be overcome, but he lived to see his brainchild brought safely to birth as the Pennine Way.

The **Pennine Way** runs 250 miles up the backbone of England from the High Peak in Derbyshire to the Border. It starts in the Peak District National Park and crosses two other National Parks – the Yorkshire Dales and Northumberland – as well as an Area of Outstanding Natural Beauty in the North Pennines.

You can walk it either way, naturally, but travelling from south to north keeps the weather at the walker's back and the route is usually described in this direction. It starts at Edale in the delectable valley of the River Noe, close to Castleton and its deep, eerie limestone caverns. The Way goes up across the Kinder Scout plateau (there are alternative routes here, and elsewhere along the trail) to the aptly named wasteland of Bleaklow. Then by Blackstone Edge, with its exceptionally well preserved stretch of Roman road, and across the Calder Valley close to Hebden Bridge, where the rows of millhands' houses cling to the steep hillsides, to the beauty spot of Hardcastle Crags. North from here are the wild moors of the Brontë Country, near Haworth, and the bleak scenery and atmosphere of *Wuthering Heights* at the ruined farmhouse at Withins.

The Way crosses the Craven district to reach the tremendous limestone scenery of the Yorkshire Dales National Park: 'a strange landscape,' as the great fell-walker Wainwright has written, 'almost lunar, in places awesome, in places beautiful, and everywhere fascinating.' From Malham, the beetling gorge of Gordale Scar is a mile or so off the path, which scrambles up the sheer curving cliff of Malham Cove, close to 250ft (76m) high, to the cracked and fissured limestone 'pavement' on top. Malham Tarn is the lake where Charles Kingsley was inspired by

the idea for *The Water Babies*. Further on is the isolated hump of Pen-y-ghent, 2,273ft (693m).

On to Ribblesdale and to Wensleydale, at Hawes, and close to Hardraw Force, where the water tumbles over a 100ft rock. Further on is Middleton in Teesdale and the Way follows the swirling, rock-strewn Tees to three spectacular waterfalls in succession: Low Force, High Force and Cauldron Snout, where the river boils and rages down the rock ledges for 200ft. At the stupendous horseshoe of High Cup Nick an immense abyss opens, whose sides are sheer for almost 1000ft.

Northwards again, up the valley of the South Tyne to Hadrian's Wall, getting on for 1,900 years old now, but still swooping athletically over the crags. The Way follows it for nine miles, passing Housesteads, where there are the remains of a substantial Roman fort, with legionary latrines and a museum. Then the route lies on north over heathery moors to Bellingham, across Redesdale and through the forest to the high Cheviots, the lonely open spaces of the Northumberland National Park, and the Border at last, coming to a final grateful halt at Kirk Yetholm.

The **Wolds Way** in the old East Riding of Yorkshire is about as unlike the Pennine Way as two walking routes in the same country could conceivably be. In length, by comparison, the Wolds Way is a mere pygmy of 79 miles all told. It is easy going where the Pennine Way is hard. And instead of daring the wild and lonely places, and scenes of spectacular grandeur, the Wolds Way walker is in placid, pretty country and never far from a small town or a village, a bed, a meal, a drink.

Open since 1982, the Wolds Way begins at Hessle on the north bank of the Humber and runs under the northern end of the mighty Humber Suspension Bridge. Then the route heads north to the Yorkshire Wolds, rounded chalk hills with attractive valleys. The path lies through farming country and woods, over gentle slopes, along farm tracks and roads. A point of special interest is the deserted village of Wharram Percy, north of Thixendale. It was abandoned in Tudor times and only the ruined church is still standing.

From the northern scarp of the Wolds there are fine views across the Vale of Pickering to the North York Moors, and later to the North Sea as the footpath comes to the Victorian seaside resort of Filey. It passes close to Filey Brigg, a mile-long finger of rock protruding into the sea, going on along the cliffs to

join the Cleveland Way.

The **Cleveland Way** was the second long distance footpath to be opened, in 1969. It steers its course northwards along the Yorkshire coast by Scarborough and Whitby to Saltburn. There it turns inland and changes course to the south-west, to spend the rest of its energies in the Cleveland Hills and the North York Moors National Park before coming to an end at Helmsley, not far from the haunting ruins of Rievaulx Abbey.

The **Pembrokeshire Coast Path**, 180 miles round Wales's south-western corner, and the **South West Coast Path** both take the walker through heroic coastal scenery of massive sea-beaten cliffs, coves and sandy beaches, lighthouses, vast seaward panoramas and superlative sunsets. The South West Coast Path follows the entire coastline from Minehead on the Bristol Channel in Somerset, along the North Devon shore, all round Cornwall by Land's End and the Lizard, back along the South Devon coast and the Dorset shoreline to finish on the edge of Poole Harbour.

The longest of the Scottish long distance paths is the **Southern Upland Way**, 212 miles clear across the country between Cockburnspath, east of Dunbar on the North Sea shore, and Portpatrick, looking out over the Irish Sea from the Rhinns of Galloway. This is a demanding route over a great variety of Border landscape, and positively dripping in history – passing through the Lammermuirs and the Scott Country, by the austere Jacobite mansion of Traquair, past St Mary's Loch and across the wild country of the Galloway Forest Park.

The 95 miles of the **West Highland Way**, opened in 1980, also make a romantic pilgrimage. The route is by Loch Lomond, across bleak Rannoch Moor and past the grim mountain gates of Glen Coe to Kinlochleven and Fort William, in the shadow of Ben Nevis.

The English and Welsh paths, too, have historic roots. **Offa's Dyke Path**, which is quite heavily trampled in some sections but satisfactorily lonely in others, runs the whole length of the Welsh Marches for 168 miles. From Chepstow on the River Severn it goes up the entrancing Wye Valley and along the edge of the Brecon Beacons National Park, then makes its way through the solitary, eerie Shropshire Hills and over the Clwydian Range to reach the coast of North Wales at Prestatyn. For about one-third of the distance it follows the line of the formidable bank and ditch constructed by Offa, 8th-century King of Mercia, to mark and defend his frontier with the Welsh.

The **North Downs Way**, similarly, 140 miles from Farnham to Dover and Folkestone, in part runs along the traditional medieval pilgrims' route to Canterbury, to the shrine of St Thomas Becket. The **South Downs** runs 106 miles on prehistoric tracks from towering Beachy Head across Sussex and Hampshire to Winchester, commanding on the way wonderful views over the English Channel and across the Sussex Weald. The **Peddars Way**, again, follows an ancient track from the Suffolk border across Norfolk to the coast, and the **Ridgeway Path** across Wiltshire is an immensely ancient route, passing close to the important prehistoric monuments of Avebury, Wayland's Smithy and the White Horse of Uffington. On these timeworn, well-trodden ways, today's walkers tread in the footsteps of travellers of long ago.

National trail

A view from Benbrack Hill, along the Southern Upland Way in Galloway.

Cave

Prehistoric monument

Hill-fort

Roman antiquity

Stonehenge is one of the most famous prehistoric monuments in Europe.

Caves
Prehistoric Monuments
Hill-forts
Roman Antiquities
As the last great Ice Age held Britain in its grip, early man and the animals he hunted with increasingly sophisticated stone weapons, followed shifts of climate. Small family groups took refuge from the sleet-lashed tundra in many natural limestone caverns.

Caves
Creswell Crags, in Derbyshire, one of the most important Palaeolithic sites in Britain, has a Visitor Centre which illustrates the life they must have led, both in the main cave and in nearby **Pin Hole** and **Robin Hood's Cave**. At **Cheddar Gorge**, Gough's Cave and Cox's Cave have displays in a nearby museum. Other caves worth visiting are the remains of mine workings for lead and later for semi-precious fluorspar near Castleton, Derbyshire – the Treak Cliff and **Speedwell Caverns**, near Buxton, as well as the **Blue John Cavern** itself.

Prehistoric Monuments
Long after the retreating glaciers and rising sea levels had submerged the mud flats to the east of Britain, agriculturalists arrived from Europe.

By about 5,000BC, they had given the British upland landscape a basic appearance which was to remain largely unchanged until the introduction of intensive farming methods in the 20th century. But in that landscape began to appear burial mounds and much larger monuments.

Most famous must be **Stonehenge**, but from **Callanish**, on the Isle of Lewis, through **Arbor Low** and the **Nine Ladies**, near Matlock, to the **Rollright Stones**, north of Oxford, similar circles have filled later generations with awe. Possibly built, like **Castlerigg** in Cumbria and the **Ring of Brodgar** on Orkney, in connection with solar or lunar observation and associated rituals, the 'alignments' so often attributed to these circles, and to groups such as the **Devil's Arrows**, near Boroughbridge, should be treated with caution. Stonehenge pre-dates the Druid cult by 3,000 years and yet, in the Romantic age and the 19th century was thought to have been a Druid temple. In today's 'computer climate' it has become, for some, an astronomical calculator.

Orientation to the rising and setting sun does appear to have influenced the builders of most of the megalithic burial mounds in Britain. One of these, at **Newgrange**, north of Dublin, a splendid example of Neolithic

carving in its own right, is so aligned that the midwinter sunrise casts a beam directly into the tomb chamber. Newgrange pre-dates Stonehenge by a thousand years and the positions of earth and sun, of sunrise – midwinter or midsummer – have changed, but the east-west alignments remain an intriguing facet of the study of all these monuments.

The village of **Avebury** is set within another huge stone circle and earthwork rampart. An interesting museum here displays finds and explains the way in which rampart and circle were constructed.

Stonehenge has seen many phases in its construction, from its origins in 3,000BC to its present form, which dates from around 1,800BC. The sheer manpower involved is amazing. Four million cubic feet of chalk were dug out at Avebury, using antler picks. This and the hauling on raft and sledge of the Stonehenge bluestones from the Preseli Mountains in Wales and the transport of the 80 huge sarsens from the Marlborough Downs, tell us something of the beliefs and about the organisational ability of the builders of both monuments. Illiterate agriculturalists they may have been – certainly they were ignorant of the use of iron – and yet their kings and priests were able to organise and plan huge civil engineering projects.

Associated with Stonehenge is the huge circular timber building – **Woodhenge**. It is not difficult to imagine a conical thatched roof supported by timber uprights, their positions now marked by concrete posts. When was it built? Around 2750 BC – that at least is known. Why was it built? Who used it? There is no scatter of the usual debris associated with hut circles and their domestic middens, so Woodhenge and the nearby **Durrington Walls** site would seem to have had a public and ceremonial function. Perhaps the forest of tree trunk pillars recalled forest groves which had long had religious significance. At Woodhenge a three-year-old child, its skull split, was buried, perhaps as a dedication, at the centre of the complex. When the timbers at last decayed, a memorial stone was placed at the centre of the circle.

Silbury Hill, near Avebury, has so far yielded up few of its secrets. Why this 130ft mound, covering over five acres at its base, was raised is still a mystery. Trenches have been dug, seeking a burial somewhere within, but all these excavations have found is that it was very carefully built. Inside the turf mound is a stepped cone of compacted chalk rubble, each layer being finished with smooth chalk blocks. The steps were later filled with earth except for the topmost one, still visible as a terrace. The fact that the whole of the Stonehenge circle would fit comfortably within this topmost terrace gives an idea of the scale of the mound.

Carbon-14 dating has placed its construction at around 2,600 BC – and the trenches have told us that it was started in July or August, for right at the core have been found winged ants – but maybe there is a more important burial still to be discovered. Nearby is **West Kennet Long Barrow** and its sarsen façade – burial chamber perhaps, of the chieftains who commanded the building of Avebury.

Hill-forts

The 'Beaker Folk', so called from the distinctive pottery vessels found in their graves, arrived in Britain around 2,700 BC. They brought with them the Aryan roots of our language and their knowledge of metal working was gradually learnt by the established communities into which they merged. By 1,800 BC the British climate was deteriorating and tribes vied for workable land. Local chiefs gained power and protected their arable land and pasture from the safety of upland hill-forts, which gradually became tribal 'capitals'

rather than merely bolt holes in case of war.

Thousands of these hill-forts dot the landscape, and many were inhabited well into the Roman age. **Ingleborough**, just north of the National Park Centre at Clapham, North Yorkshire, is the highest in Britain. Life must have been very hard on this high windswept plateau. Earlier settlers in the area possibly made themselves a warmer home in the cave systems nearby, at **Ingleborough Show Cave** and **Gaping Gill**. One of the largest and most important hill-forts in Britain is **Maiden Castle**. Built initially around 300BC, it finally fell to Vespasian's troops in AD43. Boards around the two-mile perimeter provide much information and the museum in nearby Dorchester displays finds from the site.

Often associated with these hill-forts are the figures carved into the chalk hillsides – horses and giant figures – but only a handful can be said with certainty to be 'pre-historic'. **Uffington White Horse**, between Swindon and Wantage, certainly is. Overlooking the Ridgeway Path, an ancient trade route across the north Berkshire Downs, its disintegrated simplicity resembles the horses – tribal totems, perhaps – which feature on Celtic coinage. The **Cerne Abbas Giant**, north of Dorchester, is probably not more than 1,500 years old, but its club-wielding phallic figure possibly represents Hercules, part of a god-cult which flourished around AD100. The Iron Age enclosure above him was used for May Day and fertility ceremonies long after the foundation of the nearby Benedictine priory in the 10th century. **Wilmington Long Man**, near Alfriston, inland from Beachy Head, could well be Romano-British, too.

From 700BC onwards, Celtic settlers brought their language, their chariots and a love of finery, gold and ornaments. Iron swords gave them an ascendancy in battle over the native Britons, who were pushed westwards. Celtic immigrant groups shared a common dialect but their lack of any concept of 'nationhood' left their society an easy prey to the civilising might of Rome.

Roman Antiquities

The lure of corn, gold, iron, slaves and hunting dogs was enough to make the Romans decide that an invasion of Britannia in the summer of AD43 was worthwhile. By AD70 50 or more towns were linked by a network of roads. 'Lex Romana' tamed the unruly land and Latin became yet another rootstock from

which English would eventually spring. Evidence of Roman military occupation is everywhere – from **Hadrian's Wall** and the lighthouse in **Dover Castle**, to the legionary fortress at **Caerleon** in Gwent.

Many of the civilising influences of Rome can still be seen today – an aqueduct which supplied fresh water 12 miles along the Frome Valley to Dorchester, sewers in Lincoln, Colchester and York and bath houses. The finest of these, at **Bath**, is rivalled by the complex of baths and exercise halls at Viroconium, near **Wroxeter**. Theatres such as those of Verulamium and Caerleon, and the busy shopping centres which developed around the forum or the town gates, attracted people to the towns. Mosaic floors like those at **Aldborough**, in Yorkshire, reflect a very comfortable style of life. This wealth is mirrored, too, by the remains of many Roman villas such as those at Lullingstone, near **Eynsford** in Kent, **Fishbourne** in Sussex and **Chedworth** in Gloucestershire.

Below *Westbury White Horse, on Bratton Down, Wiltshire.* Bottom *Housesteads Fort along Hadrian's Wall, in Northumbria.*

Cave

Prehistoric monument

Hill-fort

Roman antiquity

Battle site with year

THE BATTLE OF FLODDEN FIELD
9th September 1513

Above *The site of the Battle of Flodden.* Inset *A display board at Flodden chronicles the battle which was fought here.* Top right *According to tradition, men watched London's Great Fire from Outwood Mill, Surrey.* Bottom *Porthcurno's Minack open-air theatre.*

Windmill

Other place of interest

| Battlefields
| Windmills
| Other Places of Interest

Normans and Plantagenets, wars in Scotland and Wales, the Wars of the Roses, the Civil War and the Jacobite risings, have all left the map of Britain dotted with 'crossed swords' symbols. In the 250 years that separate us from Culloden, in 1746, the last battle on British soil, farming, roads and railways, canals and houses have changed the fields on which the history of the nation was written.

Battlefields

We do not commemorate our battles as lavishly as the Visitor Centres at places such as Waterloo or Gettysburg, but there are still fields where there is something to be seen today. Facilities are available, mainly in the tourist season, for organised groups to be taken round and it is worth telephoning to see whether you can join one.

The Battle of **Hastings**, on 14 October 1066, certainly changed things in England. Stories of the battle are well enough known – Harold's forced march of 250 miles from battle against the Norwegian king at Stamford Bridge, near York, to meet the Norman invaders; the Norman minstrel Taillefer charging

the shield-wall; the hail of arrows harassing the axemen; the final stand of the house-carles around the royal standard of Wessex. All are vividly recalled in an audio-visual presentation in the Tourist Office on the green just opposite the gateway of the Abbey which William founded, its altar traditionally on the spot where Harold fell. Now an English Heritage property, the pathways around and overlooking main sectors of the battlefield are well signposted, with information boards at regular intervals.

In the **Bannockburn** Heritage Centre the full story of the battle of 24 June, 1314, is graphically told in an audio-visual entitled *The Forging of a Nation.* On the field itself is preserved the Borestone, where Robert the Bruce raised his banner before this decisive culmination of the Wars of Independence.

From the top of the Durham Cathedral tower the battlefield of **Neville's Cross** can be seen as it was by the monks who gave 'moral support' by singing hymns there in 1346. A leaflet explaining the battle is available from the Tourist Office and a half mile walk from the city brings the visitor to the battlefield itself.

An exhibition is mounted on **Bosworth** battlefield, near Sutton

Cheney, with an audio-visual presentation including scenes from Laurence Olivier's *Richard III*. There is a battlefield trail, with another information centre halfway round at Shenton Station. Here, Richard of Gloucester, uncle of the Princes in the Tower, met his end, having found no one to answer his cry 'My Kingdom for a horse!'

At a call from France for help from the 'Auld Alliance', James IV of Scotland marched into England. On Pipers Hill, at **Flodden Edge**, is a monument 'To the Brave of both Nations', with the battlefield spread out below. A booklet and map from nearby Coldstream enable you to follow the course of the battle. King Henry VIII had left the old Earl of Surrey, a veteran of Bosworth, to defend the north. Surrey had borrowed the banner of St Cuthbert, obviously a powerful morale raiser, from Durham Cathedral. But it was artillery fire that stung the Scots into premature offensive action, allowing English archers to reach the crest of Pipers' Hill and pour a murderous arrow storm into the massed pikemen below. Flodden was the last major battle won largely by the longbow.

The Castle Inn, in **Edgehill**, was built on the spot where King Charles raised his Standard. There

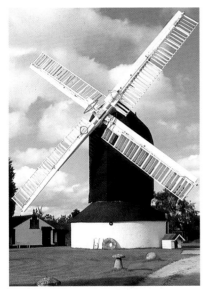

Battle site with year

Windmill

Other place of interest

is a memorial on the field below and a map and guidebook will enable you to follow the course of the fighting. Neither side seemed willing to strike the first blow until a Parliamentary gunner spotted the King on the hill, fired – and missed. Prince Rupert charged – found an ally in the inaptly named Sir Faithful Fortescue, one of the Parliamentary cavalry commanders – and they all dashed the two miles or so to Kineton, where they rested their horses and indulged in a little light looting. Roundhead foot soldiers were about to finish off the exhausted Royalists when they were attacked owing to the opportune return of Prince Rupert and the cavalry. Captain John Smith, of the King's Lifeguard, met a party of Roundheads escorting a Royalist prisoner and the Royal Standard which they had just captured. The prisoner recognised Smith and called to him. Smith charged, killed one Roundhead, wounded another and the other four fled. He was knighted on the spot by the King for recovering the Standard, which had not been in Parliamentary hands above fifteen minutes.

In the village of **Naseby** is a museum with dioramas and a ten minute commentary of different stages of the battle of 14 July, 1645.

Should the museum be closed, then try the village shop or the church for the descriptive leaflet and map, which will make the whole encounter more easy to follow.

A drive up the Naseby – Sibbertoft road takes you to a monument marking the position from which Cromwell led his cavalry to win the day and from where there is a good view over the whole battlefield.

Information about the battle of **Worcester**, 3 September, 1651, is available from both the Tourist Office and the Civil War Centre at the Commandery. Worcester was the scene of the first and last battles of the war. During the summer, frequent 're-enactments' are staged by several groups, particularly in September.

Sedgemoor, the last battle fought on English soil, on 6 July, 1685, followed the landing by the Duke of Monmouth, illegitimate son of Charles II, to claim the throne of James II. A stone monument marks the site of the battle, and information can be obtained from the Admiral Blake Museum in Bridgwater.

The Battle of Culloden, on the moors outside Inverness, ended the Jacobite Rising in 1746. Bonnie Prince Charlie, with the help of Flora Macdonald, escaped 'over the sea to Skye' and the Stuart cause was swept away. The whole story is graphically told in the Visitor Centre on the battlefield, which has been restored to its 18th-century appearance, but now dotted with emotive memorial cairns and the Graves of the Clans, on which no heather ever grows.

Since Culloden, we may be thankful that no armies have fought on British soil – only *above* it, in 1940. Aerial bombardment brought the realities of war much closer to the public than did any of the very localized combats of the previous 700 years.

Windmills

Few things add as much atmosphere to the countryside as a windmill. They have drained marshlands and ground corn since medieval times. One tradition suggests that they were introduced by crusaders returning home from the wars. Whether or not this is true, we know for a fact that they were first built here some eight centuries ago. None of the original structures remain, but some have survived a few hundred years. Still in working order is **Berney Arms Mill**, in Norfolk, from the top of which there is a splendid view and the working wind pump at **Wicken Fen**, a remnant of the wetlands drowned by Dutch engineers, which

became England's first nature reserve, in 1899. **Bourn Mill**, near Cambridge, is a 17th-century 'post mill', the oldest surviving mill in the country. Unlike the conical tower windmills with a rotating cap, here the sails and machinery all turn together, revolving round a central post. A tide mill has stood on the river bank at **Woodbridge** in Suffolk since the 12th century and the present one was working until 1956, when the shaft of the waterwheel broke. Careful restoration has successfully restored it to working condition.

Other Places of Interest

There is a wide range of other places of interest which are well worth visiting. From waterfalls, wells, bridges and towers to dovecotes, follies, monuments and parks, Britain has something to offer every visitor.

Not far from Land's End, on the cliffs near Porthcurno, is the **Minack Theatre**, carved out of the living rock in the 1930s, with the sea as a backdrop for the stage. North of Tavistock is **Lydford Gorge**, a deep wooded gorge with the lovely White Lady Waterfall at the end of a mile or so walk.

Further along the coast, north-west of Weymouth, the extraordinary Chesil Beach, a 12-mile long pebble bank, shelters the **Abbotsbury Swannery**, where swans were bred for the table by the monks as long ago as the 14th century. Today it is a breeding haven for hundreds of wild mute swans. At St Fagans, to the west of Cardiff, is the **Welsh Folk Museum**, a collection of rural buildings from the 17th century onwards from all over Wales, carefully re-erected in the grounds of St Fagans Castle, an elegant Elizabethan mansion.

Waterfalls abound, but one not to be missed is **Hardraw Force**, north of Hawes, North Yorkshire, a spectacular 90ft drop into a glen which has been used for brass band contests – a great local tradition – on account of its splendid acoustics. Further north, near Moffat on the A708, is one of Scotland's highest falls, the **Grey Mare's Tail**, where Loch Skeen plunges 200ft to meet Moffat Water.

Shire horses, Clydesdales and Suffolk Punches have ploughed England's fields – and delivered England's beer – for centuries. In the **National Shire Horse Centre**, at Plymouth, there is stabling dating back to 1772 and three parades a day are staged in summer. Courage Breweries have a **Shire Horse Centre** near Maidenhead, as do Whitbread at their **Hop Farm**, on the B2015, east of Tonbridge.

AA viewpoint

Picnic site

Agricultural showground

AA Viewpoints
Picnic Sites
Agricultural Showgrounds
The **Clee Hills** of Shropshire, in the Welsh Marches, are in a remote and exceptionally attractive area of the country – an official Area of Outstanding Natural Beauty, in fact. They are 'young' hills, geologically, jagged and more impressive than their official height statistics would suggest, and in the past were heavily quarried for coal, building stone, iron and copper. A wealth of folklore still attaches to them, with sinister tales of witches and evil forces. They are also the site of the first AA viewpoint in the country, established in 1951.

AA Viewpoints
The viewpoint is on the A4117, 6 miles east of Ludlow. In the immediate foreground to the north is the bulk of Titterstone Clee, 1750ft (533m) with its aerials and radar dishes, and one of the biggest Iron Age hill-forts in Britain on its summit. Beyond the hill is the long,

Below The picnic site at David Marshall Lodge, Aberfoyle.
Bottom View of South Stack lighthouse from the AA viewpoint on Anglesey.

wooded ridge of Wenlock Edge and to the west beyond Ludlow rise the mountains of Wales.

Since 1951 more than 40 AA viewpoints have been opened. They are all easily accessible by car and have a plaque to identify landmarks and places of interest in the area. Each viewpoint has a prospect of at least 180 degrees, and some command wider vistas still. The **Cockleroy** viewpoint, 2 miles south of Linlithgow in the Lothian region of Scotland, has marvellous views over the full 360 degrees. To the east the eye ranges over Edinburgh to the Firth of Forth, to the south-east lie the Pentland Hills, in the west is Glasgow and in the north the outlying bastions of the Highlands.

The viewpoint is in the Beecraigs Country Park, among the Bathgate Hills, with trails through the woodland, a reservoir with hides for watching the numerous waterfowl and a deer farm with a viewing platform. At Linlithgow are the romantic ruins of the palace of the Stuart kings, where Mary, Queen of Scots was born, and the church where she was christened. Not far away is Torphichen Preceptory, once the Scottish base of the crusading order of the Knights of St John of Jerusalem. A little to the south there are superlative views again, from Cairnpapple Hill, where prehistoric men buried their dead over a period of 2,500 years and more.

On the other side of Glasgow, the **Lyle Hill** viewpoint is just outside the former shipbuilding town of Greenock, the birthplace of James Watt and during World War II the principal Free French naval base. The viewpoint is near the war memorial to those sailors, an anchor surmounted by a Cross of Lorraine. Down below is the Firth of Clyde and its swarming ferries. To the north and north-west lie Holy Loch and the woods and mountains of the Argyll Forest Park on the Cowal Peninsula, with the serrated crests of The Cobbler in the distance. West and south-west are the Isle of Bute, separated from the mainland by the narrow Kyles of Bute, the Isle of Arran rising to Goat Fell, and beyond Arran, the Kintyre Peninsula.

Far away at the other end of the country, in Cornwall, the majestic harbour of Carrick Roads was an important United States Navy base during the war. The AA viewpoint is on **Pendennis Point**, outside Falmouth, commanding a sweeping prospect of the harbour and out to the English Channel and the Lizard Peninsula. Close at hand is the round keep of Pendennis Castle,

one of the artillery strongpoints built along the coast in Henry VIII's time against attack by the French. Across the water is its other half, St Mawes Castle. These twin fortresses have done their job, and no enemy force has ever attempted to penetrate Carrick Roads.

Another AA viewpoint with naval connections lies eastward along the coast, on **Portsdown Hill** in Hampshire, a mile north of Cosham. Immediately to the south sprawls Portsmouth, with its historic harbour and the Royal Navy dockyard where Nelson's HMS *Victory* rests in honourable retirement. Birds wheel above the Farlington Marshes at the northern end of Langstone Harbour and the eagle eye pierces 10 miles across the the Solent to the Isle of Wight. For visitors who would like something to eat as well as watch, there is a picnic site here.

So there is at the AA viewpoint at **David Marshall Lodge**, the Forestry Commission visitor centre in the scenic Trossachs area, in the Central region of Scotland, a mile north of Aberfoyle on A821. There are spectacular views here of Ben Lomond, the Highland mountains and the valleys of the Forth.

The haunting beauty of the Trossachs – 'So wondrous wild, the whole might seem the scenery of a fairy dream' – with its lochs, peaks and 'wildering forest' – was hymned by Sir Walter Scott in 1810 in his immensely popular poem *The Lady of the Lake*. To add to its romantic attractions, much of the area was Rob Roy country.

Strictly speaking, the Trossachs ('the cross places' in Gaelic) means the narrow belt of land between Loch Katrine and Loch Achray, but the name is more often used broadly for the whole area between Loch Lomond and Callander. Much of it is now in the Forestry Commission's enormous Queen Elizabeth Forest Park. After Scott, tourists began to flock to the area in such numbers that the local landowner, the Duke of Montrose, built the road north from Aberfoyle which is now the A821, or Duke's Road. There are parking places and a picnic site along it, and more along the Forestry Commission's one-way Achray Forest Drive, which leaves the Duke's Road to make its way seven miles through the woods, by Loch Drunkie and Loch Achray. There are more scenic viewpoints here and a waymarked forest walk.

Picnic Sites
One of the Countryside Commission's achievements has been to stimulate local authorities to

AA viewpoint

Picnic site

Agricultural showground

provide places where motorists could pull off the road to enjoy a picnic. Opinion surveys and studies repeatedly made it clear that many people were deterred from enjoying the countryside by an uneasy fear of trespassing or going where they were not wanted, and an official picnic spot is somewhere where you know you are entitled to be. Although most sites have been organised by county councils, many have been provided by the Forestry Commission, others by the National Trust and by private landowners.

Many sites provide a view of attractive scenery or are close to an outstanding attraction. There is one near the ruins of **Mount Grace Priory**, for instance, the medieval Carthusian monastery near Osmotherley in North Yorkshire (where each of the tiny hermit-like cells had running water, incidentally) and there is one close to the **Hardraw Force** waterfall, off the Pennine Way. In Wales there are several with views of **Llyn Clywedog**, near Llanidloes in Powys, a 3-mile long reservoir. An old iron mine can also be visited here, and not far away is another picnic site beside the infant River Severn, as it starts its long journey to the sea from the high moors of Plynlimon. There are more looking over **Lake Vyrnwy** in Powys, a beautiful 1880s reservoir with wooded shores and a striking Victorian Gothic tower. In England too, reservoirs make pleasing picnic spots, as at **Rutland Water** in Leicestershire, or **Grafham Water** in Cambridgeshire.

Agricultural Showgrounds
The 'traditional' English landscape of green fields, hedgerows and narrow lanes was created by the agricultural revolution of the 18th century, which introduced improved farming methods. County agricultural societies were formed, to spread knowledge of the new ways and raise standards. They organised annual county shows at which farmers and breeders showed off their achievements and competed against each other. For 200 years and more these agricultural shows have been part of the accustomed round of country life, with their marquees and bands, their displays of the latest farm machinery and equipment, and their classes for heavy horses, cattle and sheep. One of the oldest is the **Royal Bath and West Show**, which can trace its history back to 1777 and draws 100,000 people every year to its permanent showground near Shepton Mallet in Somerset.

Before the War, the county shows normally moved around from one

country estate or farmer's fields to another, year by year. After 1945 cost of staging a show escalated alarmingly. Some shows folded up, some amalgamated and others established permanent showgrounds. The leader in the field was the Yorkshire Agricultural Society, which planted its **Great Yorkshire Show** on a permanent site at Harrogate. The **Royal Highland Show** chose a location at Ingliston, near Forfar, for its shows.

Other leading shows which have equipped themselves with fixed locations include the **Three Counties** at Great Malvern (the three counties being Herefordshire, Worcestershire and Gloucestershire), the **South of England** at Ardingly in Sussex, the **Royal Cornwall** at Wadebridge, the

A plaque marking the AA viewpoint on Sugar Loaf Mountain in Wales.

East of England near Peterborough and the **Royal Welsh** at Builth Wells. The Royal Agricultural Society of England, founded in 1838, held its first show at Oxford the following year. The 'Royal' moved about the country every year until 1963, when it settled at Stoneleigh in Warwickshire, in a permanent home where the **National Agriculture Centre** evolved in the 1970s. The agricultural shows have had heavy weather to come through in recent years, but they have survived, and altogether are estimated to attract about three million visitors a year to share country triumphs and pleasures.

Horse racing

Show jumping and equestrian circuit

Horse Racing
Show Jumping and
Equestrian Circuits
Athletics Stadia
Motor Racing Circuits

Becher's Brook . . . Valentine's . . . the Canal Turn . . . the Chair. The familiar litany of names conjures up **Aintree** on Grand National Day – the jostle at the start, the crash and crackle of horse meeting thorn-and-fir fence, horses and jockeys falling, the clamour of the crowd. The early history of the great race is obscure, but it is usually traced back to the Grand Liverpool Steeplechase of 1839. That race was won by a horse appropriately named Lottery and that was the year the gallant Captain Becher, a well-known gentleman rider of the day, fell into the brook that bears his name. His horse, named Conrad, fell in as well.

Horse Racing

A steeplechase, as the name implies, did not originally take place on a course at all. A by-product of hunting, it was a wild pell-mell gallop across country over hedges and ditches, towards a distant steeple or other agreed marker. Not

World famous Derby Day, at Epsom Race Course in Surrey.

until the 19th century did organised racing over artificial jumps on a set course begin. Racing started at Aintree in 1829, on the course owned by the Earls of Sefton for another 120 years. The course, in a dreary northern suburb of Liverpool, has the most formidable fences in the sport, and in 1928 a horse named Tipperary Tim won the Grand National simply by being the only finisher, of 42 starters. Far and away the most famous horse associated with Aintree and the National, however, is Red Rum, the only three-time winner (in 1973, 1974 and 1977).

The most prestigious steeplechase course in England is at **Cheltenham**, in a delightful country situation outside the town, at Prestbury Park, under the looming Cotswold bulwark of Cleeve Hill. It is a testing track on heavy clay. The major event of the year is the Cheltenham Gold Cup in March, first held in 1924. The great horse Golden Miller won it five years in succession from 1932 to 1936 (and in 1934 won the Grand National as well). The Champion Hurdle at Cheltenham is the premier hurdle event in the country.

The capital of the flat racing industry is across the other side of the country at **Newmarket**. The

town developed as a racing and breeding centre for 'the sport of kings' under royal patronage. Charles II rode his own horses in races there: hence the name Rowley Mile for one of Newmarket's two courses, from the king's nickname, Old Rowley. In the mid-18th century the aristocratic Jockey Club was founded at Newmarket. It owns the two courses and Newmarket Heath, the open country around the town on which strings of staggeringly valuable racehorses can be seen exercising. It occupies a suitably august red brick building in the centre of the town, and nearby is the highly enjoyable National Horseracing Museum, which opened in 1983.

Two of the five 'classic' races are held at Newmarket: the Two Thousand Guineas, and the One Thousand Guineas for fillies only, inaugurated in 1809 and 1814 respectively. Both are run on the Rowley Mile course, which has a long flat straight, followed by a dip and rise to the finish. Long races cannot easily be seen from the grandstands because the course was laid out long before the days of packed modern race crowds.

The most famous race in the world is run early in June every year at **Epsom**. It is named after the

12th Earl of Derby, though it might easily have been called the Bunbury. Lord Derby and Sir Charles Bunbury tossed a coin in 1780 to decide the name of a new race for three-year-old colts and fillies. As if in compensation, Bunbury's horse Diomed won the first Derby, and Lord Derby had to wait until 1787 to win with Sir Peter Teazle.

The other classic race at Epsom, the Oaks, restricted to fillies, was first run in 1779 and was named after a house which Lord Derby had taken nearby.

W P Frith's well-known painting *Derby Day* gives a vivid impression of the occasion in Victorian times, when it was virtually a public holiday. Huge numbers of people swarmed to enjoy a day out and all the fun of the fair on Epsom Downs. The Derby course is more or less level for the first three-quarters of a mile and then drops to a sharp turn at Tattenham Corner before the run-in.

The last of the classics, in September, is the oldest: the St Leger, which goes all the way back to 1776 and is named after a prominent Yorkshire sportsman of the time. It is run at **Doncaster**, on the Town Moor, the common land outside the town which, as at Epsom, was the natural place for the races.

One of the oldest courses in the country, and one of the oddest, is the Roodee at **Chester**, where there was apparently organised racing in Henry VIII's time. The course has the River Dee on one side with the old city wall on the other and is circular, with almost no straight. At **York**, there was racing on the Knavesmire, common land outside the city, early in the 18th century. Here in August is contested the Gimcrack Stakes, named in honour of a famous grey. The sport's most attractive setting is claimed by **Goodwood**, near Chichester in Sussex, where the course was laid out by the 3rd Duke of Richmond with the first meeting staged in 1801.

The smartest social occasion of the racing year is the **Royal Ascot** meeting in June, attended by the Queen, with a royal procession up the straight in carriages and much media fuss about fashionable hats. Races were first held at Ascot, in Berkshire, in 1711. The King George VI and Queen Elizabeth Diamond Stakes, run in July with the richest prize money in the sport, was inaugurated in 1951 to mark the Festival of Britain.

Showjumping and Equestrian Circuits

The first show jumping contest on record was held in London in 1869. From 1912 the sport was regularly included in the Olympic Games, but it is only since 1945 that it has attracted strong public and media interest. The popular Horse of the Year Show, at **Wembley Arena** in London, dates from 1949. The same year saw the first horse trials at **Badminton**, in Avon, on a testing course laid out in the grounds of his palatial mansion by the Duke of Beaufort. Himself a redoubtable huntsman, the duke was determined to do something about the indifferent showing of the British equestrian team in the 1948 Olympics. The Three Day Event at Badminton in the spring now draws spectators in thousands. In 1984 Lucinda Green won Badminton for a record sixth time, on six different horses. Another stately home course is the one at **Burghley House**, near Stamford, in the grounds of the palace of the Cecils, right-hand men to Elizabeth I and James I. The Marquess of Exeter, a former Olympic athlete, offered a home for a three day event here, first held in 1961. The Burghley Horse Trials in September are now firmly established as a prestigious occasion in the show jumping calendar.

The sport's equivalent of Aintree and Epsom combined is the course at **Hickstead** in Sussex, opened in 1960 at his home by a leading rider, Douglas Bunn, to provide a permanent arena with formidable obstacles. The first British Show Jumping Derby was held there in 1961.

Athletics Stadia

Athletics is less well equipped with tracks and grounds than other major sports. The principal arena for international athletics is at the **Crystal Palace** in South London, where a 12,000-seater stadium was opened in 1964. Ten years later, an all-weather track was installed in the town stadium at **Gateshead**, and home-town athlete Brendan Foster set a new 3,000m world record to celebrate. The cross-country course at Gateshead is also well-known.

Motor Racing Circuits

The magic name from the early history of motor racing in England is **Brooklands**, the track near Weybridge in Surrey which, sadly, closed in 1939. Every great figure of the early days raced there, and John Cobb set a lap record of 143mph in a Napier-Railton in 1935. Another leading venue was **Donington Park**, near Derby, where Grand Prix events were held in the 1930s. During the War the site was taken over by the Army. Years later the circuit was reopened for racing, in the 1970s. The Motor Museum there has a notable collection of Grand Prix racing cars.

Since 1945 the two major British circuits have been Silverstone and Brands Hatch. **Silverstone**, in Northamptonshire near Towcester, opened in 1948 on a former airfield, hence the name Hangar Straight for part of the course. The British Grand Prix is often staged there, or alternatively at **Brands Hatch**, near Farningham in Kent. It opened for Formula Three racing in 1949 and in 1960 opened the Grand Prix course.

Athletics stadium

Motor racing circuit

A rider in the TT races, held every June on the Isle of Man.

Golf course

County cricket ground

National rugby ground

A scene at Lord's, the home of Middlesex Country Cricket Club.

Golf Courses
County Cricket Grounds
National Rugby Grounds
Ski Slopes
Coastal Launching Sites
Of all the world's great golf courses, the most august is the venerable and venerated Old Course at **St Andrews** in Scotland, where the Victorian clubhouse of the Royal and Ancient Golf Club is the temple and citadel of the game. A links, or seaside course – as all the country's top courses are – the Old Course is 4 miles in length and so many golfers are keen to play it that it normally opens at 6 o'clock in the morning. The notorious par 4 17th, or Roadhole, is said to have driven

more great golfers to rage and bitter despair than any other golf hole in the world.

Golf Courses
Golf was played at St Andrews on the springy turf beside the North Sea as long ago as the 15th century, it seems, and when 22 noblemen and gentlemen founded the Society of St Andrews Golfers in 1754, they described the game as an 'ancient and healthful exercise'. The club was dubbed 'royal' in 1834 by King William IV and became the governing body of the game.

Another illustrious club is the Honourable Company of Edinburgh Golfers, which was founded in 1744 (as the Gentlemen Golfers of Leith), ten years before the Royal and Ancient. It drew up the first set of

rules, which the R and A adopted. The club now has its headquarters at **Muirfield**, a famous championship course on the outskirts of the village of Gullane, east of Edinburgh. It is close to the shore of the Firth of Forth, whose invigorating breezes are claimed to account for the great age which the Edinburgh Golfers commonly attain. The course is known for its meticulously constructed bunkers. Jack Nicklaus won his first British Open at Muirfield in 1966 and Nick Faldo won there in 1987.

There is a clutch of notable courses across on the Ayrshire shore, on hillocky ground on the sandy turf and coarse grass beside the sea. The **Prestwick** club organised the first British Open championship in 1860 and it was played there many times, but after 1925 the course was no longer big enough for the crowds which the event was beginning to attract. Few of them are these days.

Royal Troon, just to the north, has holes with names – they start with Seal and go on to Postage Stamp and Rabbit. In the 1973 Open two holes-in-one were scored at Postage Stamp. One was by the veteran American Gene Sarazen and the other by the amateur David Russell, who happened to be respectively the oldest and the youngest players in the field.

There is another group of redoubtable courses in England along the Lancashire coast. **Royal Lytham and St Anne's**, near Blackpool, was in open countryside when the club was founded in 1886, but is now an oasis in a desert of housing estates. Here, the first Ladies Open was played in 1893 and Tony Jacklin had his Open triumph in 1969. Near Southport is another crack course, **Royal Birkdale**, and further south on the tip of the Wirral Peninsula, is **Hoylake**, where the first British Amateur championship was contested in 1885. The demanding course is no longer considered adequate to cope with Open crowds. The Open is still played over the **Royal St George's** course at Sandwich on the Kent coast, one of the toughest in Britain, and the scene of a famous fictitious match in Ian Fleming's *Goldfinger*.

Other courses are celebrated not for the championships fought out over them, but for their associations with heroic figures of the past. The legendary James Braid, five times Open champion, was professional at **Walton Heath** in Surrey for 45 years until he died in 1950 at the age of 80. On his birthday he invariably went out and played the course in as many strokes as his age or less.

His contemporary, the incomparable John Henry Taylor, learned his golf at the **Royal North Devon's** links at Westward Ho!, on the bumpy sandy ground of the Burrows, grazed by horses, cows and sheep as well as golfers.

Speaking of animals on a course, in 1934 the professional at the **St Margaret's at Cliffe** club in Kent killed a cow with his tee shot to the 18th. And in 1975 at **Scunthorpe**, Humberside, a drive at the 14th hole, named the Mallard, hit and killed a mallard duck in flight.

Cricket Grounds

Cricket, like golf, emerged from the mists of obscurity into the light of history in the 18th century. The most famous ground in the country, and the world, is **Lord's** in the St John's Wood district of London. It takes its name from its original proprietor, a Yorkshireman named Thomas Lord, who came to London in 1787, was connected with the founding of the MCC (Marylebone Cricket Club) and opened the St John's Wood ground in 1812.

Lord's is also the home of the Middlesex County Cricket Club. The original pavilion, a one-room hut, and the tavern provided by Thomas Lord have been replaced over the years by a Victorian pavilion and modern stands. The grand entrance gates to the ground were specially designed in 1923 as a memorial to W G Grace, the greatest cricketer of his age, and Lord's now has a good museum of cricket.

The other famous London ground is the **Oval**, in Kennington, south of the river. Originally a market garden, and long famed for a fine view of the local gasometers, the ground has been the headquarters of the Surrey county club since its formation in a nearby pub in 1845. Like Lord's, the Oval is a regular Test match arena. The highest innings ever recorded in Test cricket was notched up there in 1938, when England scored 903 for 7 declared, with Len Hutton making 364.

One of cricket's most attractive settings is the county ground at **Worcester**, where the cathedral rises nobly in the background across the Severn. The drawback is that when the river floods, as in 1990, the pitch is covered with tons of thick black mud. Another attractive county cricket arena is the St Lawrence ground at **Canterbury** in Kent. The Canterbury Week cricket festival has been held there since 1847.

The ground at **Old Trafford** in the southern suburbs of Manchester has seen many a Test match and many a tussle between the red rose of Lancashire and the white rose of Yorkshire. The principal Yorkshire

ground is at **Headingley**, a couple of miles from the centre of Leeds. Two other grounds regularly used for Test cricket are **Trent Bridge** in Nottingham, where cricket has been played since 1838, and **Edgbaston**, the Warwickshire county ground in Birmingham.

Rugby Grounds

Rugby's equivalent of Lord's is the 'cabbage patch' at **Twickenham**, a market garden bought by the Rugby Union in 1907. The choice was fiercely criticised for being too far from Piccadilly Circus, but the motor car has changed all that and the ground has been developed into a spanking modern arena. For Welsh rugby men, however, the holy of holies of their national game is **Cardiff Arms Park**, beside the River Taff close to the heart of the city, where the stands echo on great occasions to the impassioned sound of Welsh singing. The Cardiff Football Club began to practise on a piece of meadow here beside the river in 1876. Today it is a thoroughly up-to-date arena with

base for the nearby Cairngorms Ski Area, with its chairlifts and ski tows.

There are cross-country ski trails of varying degrees of difficulty in this area, too. The other main Scottish ski areas are **Glenshee**, south of Braemar on the A93, Britain's highest main road; the **Lecht** area on the A939 near Tomintoul; and the **Glencoe** area above the A82, where the road crosses Rannoch Moor.

Coastal Launching Sites

Sailing has also become more popular. Most of its enthusiasts are weekend sailors, who do not go far from shore, and there are boat launching sites at harbours and marinas all round the coast, from **St Ives** harbour in Cornwall to **Thurso Bay** on the north coast of Scotland. They vary from the broad, sheltered expanses of **Carrick Roads** or **Plymouth Sound** to the flat shingle shore at **Deal** in Kent, close to the historic anchorage of The Downs, or the exposed Suffolk coastline at **Walberswick** or **Southwold**.

Natural ski slope

Artificial ski slope

Coastal launching site

Above *The clubhouse at St Andrew's.* Right *Skiing in the Cairngorms, one of Scotland's busiest resorts.*

two stadiums. The two other home international grounds are **Murrayfield** in Edinburgh and **Lansdowne Road** in Dublin.

Ski Slopes

Increasing affluence since 1945 has brought skiing within the reach of far more people than before, and although all the major ski slopes are abroad, a skiing industry has developed in Scotland. The Highland village of **Aviemore**, a quiet haven for anglers and mountaineers, was transformed into a thriving winter sports resort in the 1960s. There are ski schools and dry-ski slopes, and Aviemore is the

Above *Looking across Embleton Bay, a
view from Dunstanburgh Castle.*
Left *Spectacular rock formation at
Elegug stacks, Pembrokeshire.*

Heritage Coasts
Pollution-free Beaches

For centuries the white cliffs of
Dover have stood as symbols of
English nationhood, independence
and pride, confronting foes across
the Channel with unyielding
defiance. It was the sight of the
white cliffs which told generations
of weary English travellers that they
were nearing home. Today, to keep
the white cliffs unspoiled, they have
to be protected as two four-mile
stretches of Heritage Coast, either
side of Dover.

Heritage Coasts

Before World War II, concern was
growing about the substantial areas
of coastline which had been ruined
by commercial development and the
threat that what was left would go
the same way, disappearing under
an ever-rising tide of cliff-top
bungalows and caravan sites. The
Coastal Preservation Committee
mounted a campaign in the 1930s.
During the War, the distinguished
geographer J A Steers surveyed the
coast for the government, and his
work would later be the basis on
which Heritage Coasts were chosen.

In 1965 the National Trust,
thoroughly alarmed, launched
Enterprise Neptune, a campaign to
raise money to buy threatened
coastline. This campaign continues
and the Trust now owns and
protects more than one mile in
every six along the shoreline of
England, Wales and Northern
Ireland: including the **Giant's
Causeway** on the scenic North
Antrim seacoast of Northern Ireland
and more than a quarter of the
entire coast of **Cornwall**.

In 1970 the Countryside
Commission recommended to the
government that scenically
outstanding stretches of
undeveloped coast should be
designated as Heritage Coasts and
protected against undesirable
development. This was duly set in
train and by the end of the 1980s
there were some 850 miles of
Heritage Coast in total, amounting
to a little over 30 per cent of the
coastline of England and Wales. In
Scotland more than 20 stretches of
coastline of scenic, ecological or
environmental importance have
been designated by the Scottish
Development Department as
Preferred Conservation Zones.

The Heritage Coasts reflect much
of the wide variety of scenery and
wildlife of the shores of England
and Wales. Atop the sheer chalk
cliffs of **Dover**, **Beachy Head** and
the **Seven Sisters** orchids grow, and
they make good places to watch
jackdaws and swallows as well as
seabirds. Right across on the other
side of the country, the granite **Isles
of Scilly** lie 28 miles out to sea off
Land's End. In legend the islands
are all that is left above the surface
of the lost land of Lyonesse, which
sank beneath the waves when King
Arthur's reign came to an end.

The local environmental trust
manages 40 miles of Heritage Coast
in the Scillies, where the long
Atlantic rollers cream on sandy
beaches and rocky coves. The mild
climate fosters a wealth of wildlife –
snails and worms, sea urchins and
anemones in the sand or in rock
pools, seaweed trailing and
undulating in the waves. Manx
shearwaters, stormy petrels and
puffins breed here and there are
multitudes of terns and gulls.
Marram and sand sedge grow in the
dunes, with the dwarf pansy –
found only here and in the Channel
Islands.

The **Suffolk** Heritage Coast is
altogether different. This is a
reticent, understated shore of low
cliffs under enormous skies, and
shingle beaches where the sea's
melancholy retreating roar rattles
the pebbles. The sea has swallowed
up stretches of this coast, but

contrariwise has constructed the shingle bulk of Orford Ness and the long shingle spit that runs six miles down to North Weir Point. Martello towers stud the shoreline. The country's principal breeding colony of avocets has been established by the RSPB in the reserve at Havergate Island. Further north is the Sizewell nuclear power station, and beyond is the RSPB reserve at Minsmere. Here among the marshes and shallow 'scrapes', or lagoons, are more avocets, as well as bitterns, marsh harriers, nightingales and nightjars, all told the largest number of breeding bird species on any British reserve.

Bird sanctuaries are again a feature of the **North Norfolk** Heritage Coast between Holme-next-the-Sea and Weybourne. This is a hauntingly desolate coast and another shifting shoreline, which has left places 'next the sea' – like Holme, Cley and Wells – marooned some distance inland. Along the shore an almost unbroken succession of nature reserves protects the saltmarshes, sand dunes and shingle spits, where mats of sea lavender edge the muddy inlets. Hundreds of species of moths gladden the hearts of entomologists here, and there are birds in millions. Rarities sometimes seen include hoopoes and ospreys. The nature reserve on Scolt Head Island is famous for its nesting terns, and there are more at Blakeney Point.

Though it faces the same North Sea, the **North Yorkshire and Cleveland** Heritage Coast is a different matter altogether. Lying north of Scarborough and on either side of Whitby, this is the seaward edge of the North York Moors National Park, a line of high cliffs and bays, dramatic headlands and narrow, wooded ravines. Fishing villages huddle in deep clefts, and this is where the great explorer Captain Cook first learned his seamanship. Geologically it is an area of unusual interest and pieces of jet picked up along the shore are the foundation of the trade in Whitby jet ornaments. At Robin Hood's Bay the village houses crowd above each other on a 1-in-3 gradient.

Further up the same coast is the **North Northumberland** area, where there is a different landscape again, with miles of delectable sandy beaches, many of them owned by the National Trust. There are no titanic cliffs here, but low, rocky headlands thrust into the sea. On one of them sprawls ruined Dunstanburgh Castle, lazily menacing like a lion lying in the sun. Bamburgh Castle looks out seawards to the Farne Islands bird

sanctuaries, and there are memories here of gallant Grace Darling, the lighthouse keeper's daughter who in 1838, rowed out in a storm to rescue shipwrecked sailors. The tides race in across the gleaming mudflats to cut Lindisfarne off from the mainland.

The only Heritage Coast in Cumbria and Lancashire is the short section round **St Bees Head**. The sheer red sandstone cliffs here command views of the Isle of Man on a clear day and the seabirds wheel and cry – fulmars, herring gulls, black-headed gulls and kittiwakes. Thrift, harebell and wild thyme grow by the cliff path.

The Great Orme is another dramatic headland with stark cliffs, looming above Llandudno on the North Wales coast slopes. Further south, miles more of formidable cliff scenery have been designated as Heritage Coasts: around the **Lleyn Peninsula**, along the **Pembrokeshire** shore and in **Devon**, **Cornwall** and **Dorset**.

Heritage Coasts have a great variety of owners, not all of whom are equally conscientious in their stewardship: from the National Trust, the RSPB and other conservation bodies to county councils, local authorities, farmers, private estates and individuals. The Countryside Commission itself gives advice and financial help, but does not own any of the land.

Where a piece of Heritage Coast is owned by an organisation like the National Trust or the RSPB, the public can feel cast-iron certain there will be proper protection. Matters are not as straightforward along the other Heritage Coasts. Here, each area has a Heritage Coast plan,

drawn up by the local authority on Countryside Commission guidelines. The aim is to involve all local interests in a common approach to the management of the area, to conserve it and to encourage locals and visitors to take tender care of it.

Pollution Free Beaches
Quite apart from the physical constitution of the coastline, there is concern about polluted beaches. In 1988 one-third of the bathing beaches in England, Wales and Northern Ireland failed to meet EEC standards of cleanliness: sewage levels in the water were too high. This was at least an improvement on 1986, when half the beaches had failed the test. The great majority of bathing beaches in Cornwall, Devon, Dorset, East Anglia, Wales and Northern Ireland were passed as clean. Along the Kent, Sussex and Hampshire shore, in southern Northumberland, and especially in the North-West, the situation was not so good.

Large amounts of money are being spent on the problem. The Marine Conservation society publishes *The Good Beach Guide*, which gives lists and details of the country's cleanest beaches. These include most of those which have won a Blue Flag award from the Tidy Britain Group. The Blue Flag winners are mostly town beaches; those which are cleaned every day during the season and where water cleanliness is high. More beaches in Britain are clean than are not, but there is still work to be done.

Alum Bay, Isle of Wight, whose colourful sands are sold as souvenirs.

Heritage Coast

Pollution free beach

National Park

National Parks

Wordsworth, in his *Guide to the Lakes* wrote: 'the Lakes are a sort of national property, in which every man has a right and interest who has an eye to perceive and a heart to enjoy'. In the 19th century 'being outdoors' was seen as being good for body and soul.

Earlier this century, on many wild moors shooting took precedence over amenities for walkers. In the Peak District, an area much appreciated by those wishing to escape for a while from nearby large industrial communities, a mass trespass took place on Kinder Scout in 1932 and five men were arrested and imprisoned.

The Standing Committee on National Parks – (SCNP) – met for the first time on 26 May, 1936, the start of an organised effort to protect and to make available to all the wild landscapes of Britain. The Council for National Parks now oversees the 11 National Parks in Britain, which have been set up since the National Parks and Access to the Countryside Act became law in 1949.

Reservoirs, power lines, roads, quarrying, forestry, TV transmitter

A spectacular view towards Derwent Dale, in the Peak District.

masts, power boats, caravan sites, even the tourists themselves, by eroding footpaths – all are potential threats to the preservation of the National Parks. But, provided informed and responsible public opinion and a spirit of co-operation prevail, all these amenities will be available to future generations.

It is fitting that, after the Kinder Scout protest, the **Peak District** should have been established as the first National Park. The Pennine Way was opened on the anniversary of the protest in 1965 and follows the backbone of England from Edale in Derbyshire, across Hadrian's Wall, to Kirk Yetholm, in the Cheviots. Seventeen million people live within a couple of hours' drive of the park and many come to enjoy walking the deep dales of the White Peak or the dramatic moors and peat bogs of the Dark Peak. Fishing, cycling and rock climbing on the gritstone edges have been joined as leisure activities by gliding and hang-gliding. An Iron Age fort on Mam Tor overlooks Roman lead workings and the mine near Castleton, where deposits of decorative fluorspar – Blue John – have been worked since Roman times. Heather covers one third of the Park and provides food for the red grouse.

Largest of the National Parks, the **Lake District** combines mountain and lake, woodland and farmland. Moving ice shaped these troughs and corries and glacial rubble dammed the valleys, but the underlying rock dictated whether the hills were softly rounded, like Skiddaw, or wildly rugged, like Scafell and Helvellyn. Broad-leaved woodland like the Borrowdale and Witherslack woods, of great interest to conservationists, cover about five per cent of the Park.

The Snowdon massif is the heartland of the **Snowdonia National Park** and Cader Idris is one of the most popular areas. Half a million people reach Snowdon Summit each year and only a quarter of them admit to using the railway! Many fewer visit the Aran Mountains in the south, or the rugged Rhynogydd. Harlech Castle lies on part of the Park's 20 or so miles of sweeping sandy coastline, backed by beautiful mountain scenery. For the 'railway buff' there are six narrow-gauge railways to enjoy and to the 5,000 acres of ancient broad-leaved woodland have been added another 5,000, which with commercial forestry, now cover over 10 per cent of the Park.

Two plateaux make up **Dartmoor**, largest and wildest stretch of open country in southern Britain, rising to over 2,000ft (610m). Covered with blanket bog and heather moorland, they are divided by the River Dart. Granite tors protrude near the edges, where other rivers have eroded deep valleys. Over a third of the Park is farmland and the high northern moors have been a military training area since the 1870s. The Dartmoor pony – descendant of ponies turned out to graze in the Middle Ages – grazes much of the lower lying heather moorland. There are hundreds of ancient sites – chambered tombs, hill-forts and stone circles – in the Park and medieval crosses and waymarks can still be useful to today's traveller.

The **Pembrokeshire Coast National Park**, the smallest of the Parks, hugs the coast and is only three miles wide along most of its length. Steep cliffs display spectacularly folded and twisted rock formations, while sheltered bays invite bathing and scuba-diving. Offshore, islands such as Skomer and Skokholm support huge colonies of seabirds, among them the world's largest concentration of Manx shearwaters and puffins. Inland from the Milford Haven oil terminal, with its facilities for 300,000-ton tankers, is the Daugleddau, a drowned river valley with dense woodlands and in the north, the windswept moorlands of the Preseli Hills, source of the 'bluestones' of Stonehenge.

Though Middlesbrough and York are not far away, the **North Yorks Moors** is a relatively quiet Park. The moors rise sharply from Pickering in the south, Teesside in the north and the Vale of York in the west. The eastern boundary is the sea, with Staithes, home of Captain Cook, and Whitby (outside the Park boundaries), famous for its clifftop Abbey and its jet – a fossilised black amber – so popular with the Victorians. Rievaulx and Rosedale Abbeys are within the Park, as is Mount Grace Priory, the best preserved Carthusian priory in Britain. Evidence of man's occupation of the high moors ranges from the burial mounds of the neolithic farmers who first cleared the land to the giant golf ball-like radar domes of the Fylingdales early warning system.

Nearly half of the **Yorkshire Dales** is farmland, but there is little woodland. Over four centuries the monasteries' sheep walks developed into the start of a road system across the fells, the best known today being the green lane between Kilnsey and Malham. Miles of dry stone walling are a man-made feature of the landscape, as is the Settle-Carlisle railway with its spectacular Ribblehead Viaduct. Public transport facilities being poor,

the Dalesrail scheme makes recreational use of this line for walkers, who form the second largest group of visitors, after the touring motorist. As well as a part of the Pennine Way, there are popular areas for walkers and day trippers around Malham Cove and Tarn, with its unique limestone pavement 'grikes', sheltered habitats for lime- and shade-loving plants. Aysgarth Falls, in Wensleydale, attracts over half a million visitors a year. There is a 'Bunk House Barns' project, offering basic shelter for walkers in field barns which used to over-winter the dairy cattle.

R D Blackmore's *Lorna Doone* has made **Exmoor** known to many, as has Williamson's *Tarka the Otter*. The heartland, rising to 1,500ft (460m), from Chapman Barrows to Dunkery Beacon is still the windswept haunt of falcon and hawk. The 'hog's back' cliffs along the coast are broken by deep valleys with waterfalls which make protected breeding sites for seabirds. Exmoor is known for its Bronze and Iron Age sites, and a recent aerial survey has added over 2000 fresh areas to be investigated. The medieval Tarr Steps bridge in the Barle Valley is a popular tourist attraction. With the Quantocks, Exmoor is the last secure habitat in the south of

England for the red deer. The numbers of Exmoor ponies, adapted to rough grazing and wild winters, are declining, but a small herd has been established to maintain the breed.

Cheviot sheep graze the open moorland which makes up most of the **Northumberland National Park**. Remote from all settlements and mostly above 1,000ft (300m), it is often a harsh environment and must have seemed the end of the world to Roman legionaries from sunny Spain and Italy who manned Hadrian's Wall, part of which runs along the southern edge of the Park. Housesteads Fort and Vindolanda have interesting Visitor Centres and museums. Otterburn and other battles over the 300 years up to the Union of Crowns in 1603 have given rise to many a Border Ballad.

The **Brecon Beacons**, four high red sandstone mountain blocks, divide the ancient rocks of mid-Wales from the coalfields and industrialisation further south. From the Black Mountains, near Hay-on-Wye, through the Brecon Beacons and Fforest Fawr, the Park stretches to Black Mountain in the west. Along its southern edge a limestone belt provides a dramatic change in scenery with hundreds of sink-holes and cave systems. The most

spectacular are the Dan-yr-Ogof Caves, on the A4067, at the head of the Tawe valley. The ruins of Carreg Cennen castle, a 13th-century stronghold on sheer limestone cliffs, lie just off the A40, near Llandeilo.

The **Broads Authority**, the latest member, was rejected together with the Sussex Downs, from the twelve candidates in 1949, but was established as a National Park on 1 April, 1989. We owe Britain's most famous stretch of inland waterways to the peat-digging activities of our ancestors in the 9th century, which caused flooding in the 14th, and its survival as a recreational area to the strenuous efforts of the Broads Authority, in the 1980s, to halt the environmental degradation. Algae flourished on increased nutrients from effluents and fertilisers, the water 'died', reed cover was lost and the banks became eroded. Much has been done, but care is still needed, particularly from those holidaymakers who agree with Ratty, in *The Wind in the Willows* that 'There is nothing – absolutely nothing – half so much worth doing as simply messing about in boats'.

National Park

Hound Tor, an example of Dartmoor's striking landscape.
Inset *The deep waters of Llyn Cau, from Cader Idris, Gwynedd.*

National Scenic Area (Scotland)

National Scenic Areas (Scotland)
Where England and Wales have National Parks, Scotland has National Scenic Areas. There are 40 of them, designated in 1978 by the Countryside Commission for Scotland, established to conserve Scotland's natural beauty and improve public access to and enjoyment of it. Though the Commission's stated policy is not 'to see land in Scotland managed as though it were a museum', the National Scenic Areas are protected from development which would harm their scenic qualities. Between them they cover close to one eighth of the total area of Scotland.

Inevitably, the great majority of these National Scenic Areas lie in the Highlands and Islands, along or north of the Highland Line, the geological fault which separates Highland from Lowland Scotland. It runs diagonally from south-west to north-east clear across the country from the Isle of Arran to Stonehaven on the east coast. North and west of this line Scotland's wilder, more solitary, most spectacular and least spoiled landscapes are to be found. The land to the south and east is far more given to farming and industry, and some of it is heavily populated.

A few of the areas lie south of the Highland Line, however. In the Borders, for instance, the **Eildon and Leaderfoot** area includes the uncannily beautiful Eildon Hills. The Leader Water runs south to join the River Tweed below the three volcanic Eildon peaks, the highest rising to 1385ft (422m). These

Looking out to Scarista Bay, from Borve on the west coast of Harris.

shapely hills are steeped in legend and romance. King Arthur and his gallant knights of the Round Table are said to lie sleeping beneath them, under an enchantment, awaiting the time of their recall to life. It was here that Thomas the Rhymer, the 13th-century poet and prophet, encountered the Queen of Fairyland. Dressed all in green, and very fair, she took him away to her magic realm for seven years and gave him the power to see into the future. Here, below the hills, lies ruined Melrose Abbey, where the heart of Robert the Bruce was buried, and close by is Abbotsford, the house Sir Walter Scott built for himself in the countryside he loved.

Scott's immensely popular poems and novels whetted the appetite of prospective tourists for his native land. The process was helped along by Queen Victoria and Prince Albert, who made themselves a Highland retreat at Balmoral in the 1840s. They loved to go stalking deer in the mountains, picnicking at the remote shielings, or shepherds' huts, and fishing for trout in a lumbering rowing boat on Loch Muick.

The region today is the **Deeside and Lochnagar** National Scenic Area, which is the only one in the Grampian Region. The high granite ridge of Lochnagar, a favourite with climbers, rises to 3786ft (1154m) to the south of Braemar, in an area of mountain and forest where the River Dee flows past Balmoral Castle on its way to the North Sea at Aberdeen. Lord Byron wrote rhapsodically of 'the crags that are wild and majestic, the steep frowning slopes of dark Lochnagar'. Ever since Queen Victoria's time,

the Highland Gathering at Braemar has been regularly attended by the royal family and marks the annual apogee of the Highland Games season.

From Deeside westwards, the pass called the Lairg Ghru runs through another National Scenic Area, negotiating the heart of the **Cairngorm Mountains** on its way to Speyside. This is the largest tract of land above 3,000ft (915m) in Britain. Rearing up between Braemar and the valley of the Spey, the lofty granite summits of Ben Macdhui, Braeriach, Cairn Toul and Cairn Gorm itself all clear 4,000ft (1220m) and are outstripped in height only by Ben Nevis.

The lures of hill walking, rock climbing and wintersports draw visitors here. The Forestry Commission manages an extensive Forest Park, and near Loch an Eilein are Scots pines at least 250 years old. A hundred square miles of nature reserve lies to the south of Glen More and includes both Braeriach and Cairn Toul. Arctic and Alpine plant rarities grow here, with all sorts of mosses and ferns. Reindeer were reintroduced a few years ago and red deer and wildcat roam the mountainsides. Golden eagles soar above the corries and capercaillies make popping noises like corks in the woods.

Scottish scenery is renowned not only for its breathtaking grandeur, its harmony of sky and mountain and water, but for the romantic and often violent history which seems to cling still to every peak and corrie, every pass and glen. The **Ben Nevis** and **Glen Coe** area contains both the highest mountain in Britain at 4408ft (1344m) and one of the most notorious localities in all Scotland's bloody and tragic past. Ben Nevis, which is more of a hump than a peak, can be climbed fairly easily in good weather, though it will take a good many hours up and down, and there are colossal views from the top on a clear day. In Fort William, down below the mountain, the West Highland Museum illuminates the natural and the human history of the district.

To the south are the peaks which tower above Glen Coe, on an overcast day one of the bleakest and most melancholy places in the British Isles. The celebrated and treacherous massacre of the local Macdonalds by a party of Campbell soldiery occurred on a bitter February night in 1692. The site of the Macdonald settlement and much of the surrounding country is now owned by the National Trust for Scotland, which has a visitor centre in the glen. There is also a folk museum in Glencoe village. Further

south still, and part of the National Scenic Area, is the brooding wasteland of Rannoch Moor, with its peaty bogs and lochans, vividly described in an episode of Robert Louis Stevenson's *Kidnapped*.

Famed again in song and story are the **Cuillin Hills** of the Isle of Skye, which reach up in savage splendour above dramatic Loch Coruisk. These are black, jagged, precipitous, sinister mountains, the highest peak being Sgurr Alasdair at 3309ft (1009m). The Cuillins are an irresistible magnet to rock climbers, but they have an old reputation for treachery – compasses go oddly astray, mists descend suddenly, climbers are lost and cut off. Among marginally safer attractions on Skye are Talisker malt whisky and the MacLeods' ancestral castle at Dunvegan with its singularly daunting dungeon.

There is wonderful mountain and loch scenery again to the north, where six massive ranges rear their peaks to the sky in the National Scenic Area of **Wester Ross**. The sun glitters on Loch Maree and its islands, and the warmth of the North Atlantic Drift fosters a subtropical paradise in the luxuriant gardens at Inverewe, at the head of Loch Ewe. The gardens were created from the 1860s on by Osgood Mackenzie on what was initially barren peat wasteland.

The island of Foula is included in the **Shetlands** National Scenic Area, and so is Fair Isle, familiar from weather forecasts. In the Orkneys

the island of **Hoy** is protected, with its dramatic isolated 450ft (137m) stack, the Old Man of Hoy. Man-made Orkney attractions include the Stone Age village of Skara Brae and the enormous Stone Age tomb of Maes Howe, as well as the cathedral of St Magnus in Kirkwall.

Though most of the National Scenic Areas protect mountain scenery, one of them is centred on the old town of **Dunkeld** in the Tayside Region, where the River Tay sweeps past the ruined cathedral among its lawns and sheltering trees. There are memorials in the church to a renowned Scottish regiment, the Black Watch, and to the Scottish Horse, a regiment raised by the Duke of Atholl to fight in the Boer War. An attractive walk through the woods by the River Braan leads to a waterfall and an 18th-century folly. Not far away in the opposite direction is the Loch of Lowes nature reserve, run by the Scottish Wildlife Trust, where visitors who are lucky may see ospreys. Macbeth's Birnam Wood is not far away either.

Lying across the Highland Line are the 'bonnie banks' of **Loch Lomond**, 24 miles long and the largest stretch of inland water in Britain. This is another National Scenic Area. The narrow northern end of the loch protrudes into the Highlands between Ben Vorlich and Ben Lomond, both over 3,000ft (915m). The southern end, with its numerous islands, lies in more

Top *The rocks and tumbling waters of the River Dee, in Royal Deeside.* Above *Beinn Alligin's peak, with Upper Loch Torridon in the foreground.*

placid country. The burial place of the outlawed Clan MacGregor is on the island of Inchaillach, which is part of the nature reserve at the lower end of the loch.

To the south-west there is a return to mountain landscape in the National Scenic Area of **North Arran**, among the jagged heights of this island in the Firth of Clyde. The highest is Goat Fell at 2866ft (874m), which can be climbed from the town of Brodick and offers wonderful views, stretching on a clear day to England, Ireland and the Isle of Man. It is to be hoped that the National Scenic Areas will continue to reward Scots and their visitors for many generations to come.

Forest Park

Forest Drive

Forest Parks
Forest Drives

Long ago, before man began to make his mark, most of the land surface of Britain was thickly covered with trees. Far back in the New Stone Age, 6,000 years ago or more, farmers began to fell and burn the woodlands to make clearings for crops and pasture stock. By the Middle Ages more than 80 per cent of the original woodland cover had been cleared. Little is left today of the tangled Wealden forest through which the defeated English were chased by William the Conqueror's Normans after Hastings, or of the oaks and glades of Sherwood Forest where Robin Hood and his outlaws hunted.

In this century huge new man-made forests have been created by the Forestry Commission, set up in 1919 to repair the ravages of World War I, when no timber was imported. The Commission's principal purpose has always been a commercial one, to grow saleable timber. It planted pine, larch and spruce – fast-growing softwood trees that thrive in poor soil and are ready for harvesting in 25 or 30 years – and it has been fiercely criticised for its regimented ranks of

This vast, wooded region of Argyll became Scotland's first Forest Park.

conifers marching monotonously over hill and dale. Increasingly, however, the Commission has recognised the importance of its role as a provider of recreation and its responsibility to the environment.

Forest Parks

In Scotland, where it is the largest landowner, the Commission began to create Forest Parks in scenically attractive areas. The first of them, set under way as far back as 1935, was the **Argyll Forest Park**, extending over 100 square miles of the Cowal Peninsula in the Strathclyde region. Lying between Loch Fyne and Loch Long, it is mountain country, long dominated by the Campbell clan, who feuded with the local Lamonts. The ruined Campbell hold of Carrick Castle glowers out over Loch Goil, and the churchyard of Kilmun on Holy Loch was the traditional burying place of the Campbell chiefs.

Visitors can enjoy driving the forest roads, walking on miles of tracks, pony trekking, fishing, sailing and waterskiing. Deer, wildcats, otters, golden eagles and ravens live here. Near the head of Loch Long are fine peaks, including The Cobbler at 2891ft (881m) and the pass called 'Rest and be Thankful' on the A83, named from the inscription on a stone seat that used to be there. Close to the

southern end of Loch Eck, Benmore House, weirdly and wonderfully Scots Baronial, was given to the Forestry Commission in 1928. The Younger Botanic Garden here is open to the public and is celebrated for its marvellous azaleas and rhododendrons. A brook runs through Puck's Glen, a narrow cleft among the rocks with rare mosses and ferns.

Further south and more than twice as big in area is the **Galloway Forest Park**, designated in 1943, a wild area of wooded mountains, moorland, lochs and streams lying to the north of Newton Stewart. There are ten peaks above 2000ft (610m), the highest being Merrick, 2766ft (843m) near the centre of the park. There is climbing, walking, fishing and swimming to enjoy, and a tremendous richness of wildlife – deer, wild goats, pine martens, wildcats, red squirrels, golden eagles and hen harriers.

There are miles of trails for walkers, but motor roads are few and far between in this part of the world. North of Newton Stewart, Loch Trool, bowered among wooded slopes, has a good forest trail. The main road in the park is the Queen's Drive, or more prosaically the A712, from New Galloway to Newton Stewart. Bruce's Stone marks the place where Robert the Bruce scored an early

victory over the English and the man-made Clatteringshaws Loch is part of a hydro-electric scheme. The Galloway Deer Museum is informative not only about the deer but the park and its wildlife in general. The Raiders' Road Forest Drive turns off to the south and follows an old cattle thieves' route through the woods for 10 miles beside the Black Water of Dee, with bathing places and picnic spots.

The **Glen More Forest Park** is in the National Scenic Area of the Cairngorms. The **Queen Elizabeth Forest Park**, designated in 1953, links two National Scenic Areas, Loch Lomond and the Trossachs. In the Tayside Region there is pony trekking, mountain biking and fishing in the **Tummel Forest Park**, with numerous walks of varying length and degrees of difficulty. Forestry Commission walks are graded as 'Easy', 'Strenuous' and 'Difficult'. There are camp sites, picnic sites and plenty of car parks, with deer, red squirrels and capercaillies to watch. The forest here has mostly been planted since World War II, but a specially enticing attraction is a guided walk through the magically named Black Wood of Rannoch. On the south shore of Loch Rannoch, this is one of the rare remaining fragments of the great Caledonian pine forest, which once stretched for hundreds of miles. The visitor centre for the Forest Park is above Loch Tummel at the Queen's View, where you can stand in the footsteps of Queen Victoria, who admired the prospect in 1866. She also admired the Pass of Killiecrankie, not far away, a wooded gorge and battlefield where the National Trust for Scotland has a visitor centre.

The Forest Park idea spread from Scotland south into England. The **Border Forest Park**, designated in 1955, straddles the high sparse moors on both sides of the Anglo-Scots border, where so many raiding and rustling parties rode about their nefarious business in past centuries. Ruins of pele towers and castles testify to a violent history of feuding and marauding. At the heart of the park lies Kielder Water, a spectacular man-made reservoir seven miles long in the valley of the North Tyne, holding 40 million gallons of water. Ferry boats ply across it in the summer, and it is reached by the 12-mile Kielder Forest Drive from the A68. The drive runs past viewpoints and picnic spots to the Forestry Commission's visitor centre at Kielder Castle. In the remoter areas, you may catch sight of red deer, wild goats, blue hares and red squirrels.

On a much smaller scale is the **Grizedale Forest Park**, occupying a slice of Lake District scenery between Coniston Water and Esthwaite Water, south-west of Hawkshead. There are walks and guided tours, orienteering courses, cycle trails, a disabled trail, and a theatre. A trail bears witness to past industries: bloomeries where iron ore was smelted, charcoal pits, potash pits for soap-making, kilns, a tannery, and a blast furnace.

The **North Riding Forest Park** lies north-east of Pickering in the rolling landscape of the North York Moors. Centred on the Dalby Valley, in the Middle Ages it was part of the much larger royal hunting forest of Pickering. A nine-mile forest drive takes the motorist gently through the woodland today, with an ample supply of parking pull-offs and places for a picnic. Self-guiding walks lead off for those who want to stretch their legs. Part of the drive follows the Staindale Beck, which was dammed to create an attractive lake, and there is a walk from here to the strange rock formations called the Bridestones, in a nature reserve run by the National Trust and the Yorkshire Wildlife Trust.

Forest Drives

Where there is no Forest Park, there is still occasionally a forest drive: as in the **Hamsterley Forest**, the largest area of woodland in County Durham. It covers 5,000 acres west of Bishop Auckland, off the A68. The Forestry Commission bought the estate from the last Surtees owner, a descendant of the famous Victorian sporting novelist R S Surtees. The drive runs for four miles along the Bedburn Beck and the Spurlswood Beck, through

Right Helpful information at the Visitor Centre in the Borders Forest Park. *Below* Kielder Forest Drive, between Kielder Castle and Redesdale.

woodland which sports much pine and fir, spruce and larch. There are no less than 60 varieties of tree here all told, with oak and ash, beech and thorn among them. Red squirrels and roe deer, bats and lizards frequent these woods and there are large numbers of woodpeckers and fungi. There are waymarked walks, though more adventurous visitors can explore wherever they like.

In South Wales, meanwhile, it takes a tough cyclist to manage the splendid **Cwmcarn Forest Drive**. The seven-mile drive starts at an excellent new visitor centre south of Abercarn, near Newport. Higher up are picnic places and barbecue spots with commanding views across country and to the Bristol Channel. Walks lead off at intervals, including one which climbs to the summit. The trees are mostly spruce, larch and pine, but oaks, beeches and rowans temper the conifers.

The drive runs through part of the Forestry Commission's Ebbw Forest, a distant man-made descendant of the ancient forest of Machen, which was eaten away over the centuries by sheep and charcoal burners and finally fell victim to the devouring demand for timber in the South Wales coal mines. So here man has put back something of what he has destroyed.

Forest Park

Forest Drive

THE TOURIST'S BRITISH ISLES
·CALENDAR·

SPRING

MARCH

Whuppity Scoorie
Lanark, Strathclyde
(March 1)

Ideal Home Exhibition
Earls Court, London
(early March to early April)

Belfast Musical Festival
Belfast
(March – 3rd week)

Oxford v Cambridge Boat Race
Putney to Mortlake, London
(late March or early April)

Midgley Pace Egg Play
Calder Valley, West Yorkshire
(Good Friday)

Nutters Dance
Bacup, Lancashire
(Easter Saturday)

Easter Parade
Battersea Park, London
(Easter Monday)

Harness Horse Parade
Regent's Park, London
(Easter Monday)

Hare Pie Scramble and Bottle Kicking
Hallaton, Leicestershire
(Easter Monday)

Hocktide Festival
Hungerford, Berkshire
(Easter Tuesday)

Northumbria Gathering
Morpeth, Northumbria
(week after Easter)

APRIL

The Grand National
Aintree, Merseyside
(April – 2nd Saturday)

Shakespeare's Birthday Celebrations
Stratford-upon-Avon, Warwickshire
(April 21)

Spring Flower Show
Harrogate, North Yorkshire
(late April)

Badminton Three Day Event
Badminton, Avon
(late April or early May)

MAY

May Morning Ceremony
Oxford
(May 1)

Royal May Day Celebrations
Knutsford, Cheshire
(May – 1st Saturday)

Flower Parade
Spalding, Lincolnshire
(early May)

Furry Dance
Helston, Cornwall
(May 8)

Garland Day
Abbotsbury, Dorset
(May 13)

Goat Fell Race
Isle of Arran, Strathclyde
(May – 2nd or 3rd Saturday)

Bath International Festival of the Arts
Bath, Avon
(late May to early June)

Chelsea Flower Show
Royal Hospital, Chelsea, London
(late May to early June)

TT Motorcycle Races
Isle of Man
(late May to early June)

Arbor Tree Day
Aston on Clun, Shropshire
(late May)

Garland Day
Castleton, Derbyshire
(May 29)

Dickens Festival
Rochester, Kent
(late May or early June)

Royal Bath and West Show
Shepton Mallet, Somerset
(late May or early June)

Woolsack Races
Tetbury, Gloucestershire
(Spring Bank Holiday)

SUMMER

JUNE

The Derby
Epsom, Surrey
(June – 1st Wednesday)

Scuttlebrook Wake
Chipping Campden, Gloucestershire
(Saturday following Spring Bank Holiday)

Appleby Horse Fair
Appleby, Cumbria
(June – 2nd Tuesday and Wednesday)

Trooping the Colour
Horse Guards Parade, London
(June – 2nd Saturday)

Royal Cornwall Show
Wadebridge, Cornwall
(June – 2nd week)

Aldeburgh Festival of Music and the Arts
Aldeburgh, Suffolk
(June – 2nd to 4th weeks)

Selkirk Common Riding
Selkirk, Borders
(mid-June)

Three Counties Agricultural Show
Great Malvern, Hereford & Worcester
(mid-June)

Stour Music Festival
Boughton Aluph, Kent
(June – 2nd half)

Royal Highland Show
Ingliston, Lothian
(June – 3rd week)

Royal Ascot Race Meeting
Ascot, Berkshire
(late June)

Wimbledon Lawn Tennis Championships
Wimbledon, London
(late June to early July)

JULY

Tynwald Day
Isle of Man
(July 5)

Henley Royal Regatta
Henley on Thames, Oxfordshire
(July – 1st week)

Cheltenham International Festival of Music
Cheltenham, Gloucestershire
(July – 1st and 3rd weeks)

British Rose Festival
Gardens of the Rose, Chiswell Green, Hertfordshire
(July – 1st or 2nd week)

Royal International Agricultural Show
Stoneleigh, Warwickshire
(early July)

Great Yorkshire Agricultural Show
Harrogate, North Yorkshire
(July – 2nd week)

International Musical Eisteddfod
Llangollen, Clwyd
(early July)

Sham Fight
Scarva, Co Down
(July 13)

Royal Welsh Show
Builth Wells, Powys
(July – 3rd week)

Black Cherry Fair
Chertsey, Surrey
(July – 3rd Saturday)

Royal Tournament
Earls Court, London
(mid-July)

Buxton International Arts Festival
Buxton, Derbyshire
(mid-July to early August)

Tweedmouth Salmon Feast
Tweedmouth, Northumberland
(Sunday after July 18)

Tolpuddle Martyrs Procession
Tolpuddle, Dorset
(July – 3rd Sunday)

Durham Miners Gala
Durham
(July – Saturday of 2nd
week)

Croagh Patrick Pilgrimage
Near Wexford, Co Mayo
(July – last Sunday)

AUGUST

Royal National Eisteddfod
Varying locations in Wales
(August – 1st week)

The Burry Man Festival
Queensferry, Lothian
(August – 2nd Friday)

Cowes Week
Cowes, Isle of Wight
(August – 2nd week)

Puck Fair
Killorglin, Co Kerry
(August 10–12)

Marymass Festival
Irvine, Strathclyde
(August – 2nd or 3rd
weeks)

**Edinburgh International
Festival**
Edinburgh
(August – last three weeks)

Priddy Sheep Fair
Priddy, Somerset
(mid-August)

Grasmere Sports
Grasmere, Cumbria
(Thursday nearest
August 20)

Burning of Bartle
West Witton, North
Yorkshire
(Saturday nearest
August 24)

Oul' Lammas Fair
Ballycastle, Co Antrim
(August – last Tuesday)

Plague Sunday Service
Eyam, Derbyshire
(August – last Sunday)

Navy Days
Plymouth and Portsmouth
(August Bank Holiday)

AUTUMN

SEPTEMBER

Ben Nevis Hill Race
Fort William, Highland
(September – 1st Saturday)

Braemar Gathering
Braemar, Grampian
(September – 1st Saturday)

Hop Hoodening
Canterbury, Kent
(early September)

St Giles's Fair
Oxford
(September – 1st full week)

Horn Dance
Abbots Bromley,
Staffordshire
(Monday after 1st Sunday
following September 4)

Burghley Horse Trials
Burghley House, Stamford
(early September)

Blackpool Illuminations
Blackpool, Lancashire
(early September to early
November)

International Air Show
Farnborough, Hampshire
(September – 1st week)

**Clarinbridge Oyster
Festival**
Clarinbridge, Co Galway
(early or mid-September)

**World Carriage Driving
Championships**
Windsor, Berkshire
(September – 3rd week)

Victorian Festival
Llandrindod Wells, Powys
(September – 3rd week)

**Great Autumn Flower
Show**
Harrogate, North Yorkshire
(mid-September)

Dr Johnson's Birthday
Lichfield, Staffordshire
(on or near September 18)

Egremont Crab Fair
Egremont, Cumbria
(Saturday nearest
September 18)

Barnstaple Old Fair
Barnstaple, Devon
(September – 3rd week)

**Painswick Church
Clipping**
Painswick, Gloucestershire
(September – 3rd week)

Dublin Theatre Festival
Dublin
(late September to early
October)

OCTOBER

Nottingham Goose Fair
Nottingham
(early October)

Tavistock Goose Fair
Tavistock, Devon
(October 10)

Pack Monday Fair
Sherborne, Dorset
(1st Monday after
October 10)

Border Shepherds Show
Alwinton, Northumberland
(October – 2nd week)

Horse of the Year Show
Wembley Arena, London
(mid-October)

Stratford Mop Fair
Stratford-upon-Avon,
Warwickshire
(mid-October)

Wexford Opera Festival
Wexford, Co Mayo
(late October to
mid-November)

NOVEMBER

**London to Brighton
Veteran Car Run**
Hyde Park Corner, London
(November – 1st Sunday)

Guy Fawkes Night
Lewes, East Sussex, and
elsewhere
(November 5)

Tar-Barrel Rolling
Ottery St Mary, Devon
(November 5)

Lord Mayor's Show
Guildhall to the Strand,
London
(November – 2nd Saturday)

Belfast Festival at Queen's
Belfast
(mid to late November)

**Contemporary Music
Festival**
Huddersfield, West
Yorkshire
(late November)

WINTER

DECEMBER

Royal Smithfield Show
London
(early December)

**Festival of Carols and
Lessons**
King's College Chapel,
Cambridge
(December 24)

Ba' Games
Kirkwall, Orkney Islands
(December 25 and
January 1)

Greatham Sword Dance
Greatham, Cleveland
(December 26)

**Allendale Tar-Barrel
Ceremony**
Allendale, Northumberland
(December 31)

Fireball Ceremony
Stonehaven, Grampian
(December 31)

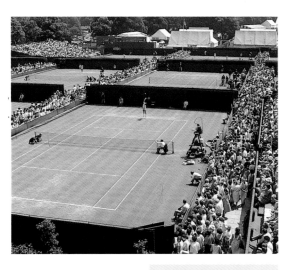

Flambeaux Procession
Comrie, Tayside
(December 31)

JANUARY

Haxey Hood Game
Haxey, Humberside
(January 5 or 6)

Straw Bear Festival
Whittlesey, Cambridgeshire
(Friday and Saturday
before Plough Monday)

Plough Stots Service
Goathland, North
Yorkshire
(Monday after January 6)

Burning the Clavie
Burghead, Grampian
(January 11)

Wassailing the Apple Tree
Carhampton, Somerset
(January 17)

Up Helly Aa
Lerwick, Shetland Islands
(January – last Tuesday)

FEBRUARY

Jorvik Viking Festival
York, North Yorkshire
(February – whole month)

Pancake Day Race
Olney, Buckinghamshire
(Shrove Tuesday)

Shrovetide Football
Ashbourne, Derbyshire
(Shrove Tuesday)

Shrovetide Skipping
Scarborough, North
Yorkshire
(Shrove Tuesday)

Left *Traditional maypole
dancing at Chipping Campden
in Gloucestershire.*
Inset *A familiar sight in The
Mall, the Household Cavalry.*
Above *Wimbledon draws the
crowds each summer.*
Below *May Day celebrations
in Oxford, which were started
in the mid-17th century.*

Tourist Information Centre

Tourist Information Centre (Summer only)

Tourist Information Centres

With over 800 offices nationwide, Britain's Tourist Information Centres offer a free service, welcoming calls both in person and by phone.

Whatever your query – whether you are looking for something new to do on a Sunday, somewhere to take the family for the day or simply a good place to eat, your local Tourist Information Centre is only too willing to help.

The staff at each centre have details on just about everything within a 50-mile radius and this is backed up by a comprehensive range of brochures, pamphlets and guides both free and for sale.

They can help with excursions and outings, giving you details and route directions to a variety of places, from castles and craft centres to model villages and museums; tell you which bus to catch, the best place for a picnic, or a walk or a scenic drive. They can even advise on which restaurant is likely to provide a high-chair for the baby or which stately home involves a lot of walking about. They also have details of local events: concerts, carnivals, festivals and fêtes and

Inside the London Tourist Board Information Centre at Victoria.

what is on in town in the evenings.

Another invaluable service is to offer on-the-spot help with finding places to stay. Most centres have up-to-date lists of all kinds of holiday accommodation in the area such as hotels, holiday homes and campsites. They can make local reservations for you, if available, or reservations at any other town which has a centre offering this facility, for the same or the following day. A fee or deposit may be payable for these services.

Most of the centres keep regular office hours from 9 to 5, Monday to Friday, but many are also open at weekends or for longer periods, especially in the summer. Some, however, are open from Easter to September only, but you can always refer your enquiries to the nearest all-year-round centre.

Britain's Tourist Information Centres are at your service and are always happy to help, no matter what the query.

The following signs indicate where you will find a Tourist Information Centre in a town.

– directional sign for road traffic

– sign for pedestrians

– this sign means a Tourist Information Centre is just a few yards away

ROAD ATLAS

OF THE

BRITISH ISLES

•Using this atlas

ROUTE PLANNING
Specially designed route planning maps, showing a basic road network of motorways, primary routes and most A roads, help you plan long distance journeys quickly and easily.

ATLAS
Clear, easy-to-read mapping helps you to plan more detailed journeys, and provides a wealth of information for the motorist. All motorways, primary, A and B roads and unclassified roads are shown. The atlas also identifies those roads outside urban areas which are under construction. Additional features include rivers, lakes and reservoirs, railway lines, interesting places to visit, picnic sites and Tourist Information Centres, and to assist you in estimating journey length, distances are shown in miles between blue marker symbols.

A road   Motorway

Primary routes

Unclassified road   Motorways and junctions   Railway   B road   Road under construction

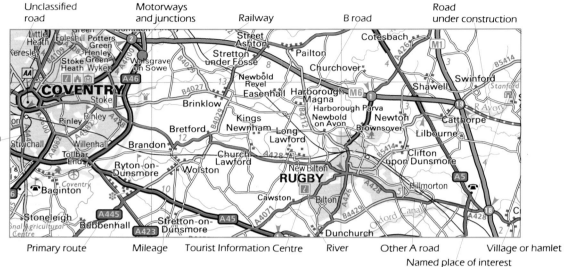

Urban area

Primary route   Mileage   Tourist Information Centre   River   Other A road   Village or hamlet

Named place of interest

FERRY AND RAIL ROUTES
Coastal stretches of mapping provide basic off-shore information including ferry routes within Great Britain and to the Continent, to assist you in planning journeys overseas. Throughout the atlas, railway lines with stations and level crossings are shown, to assist with general navigation or rail travel requirements.

Level crossing

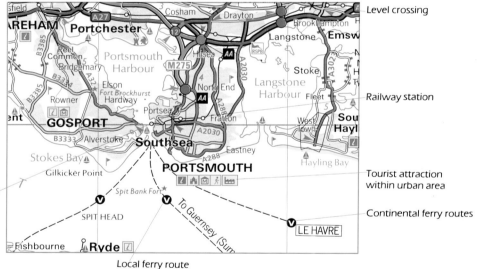

Railway station

Tourist attraction within urban area

Continental ferry routes

AA Port Shop

Local ferry route

TOURISM AND LEISURE
Red pictorial symbols and red type, highlight numerous places of interest, catering for every taste. Red symbols within yellow boxes show tourist attractions in towns. Use them to plan days out or places to visit on holiday. Remember to check opening times before you visit to avoid disappointment.

Heritage coast

Place of interest located and named

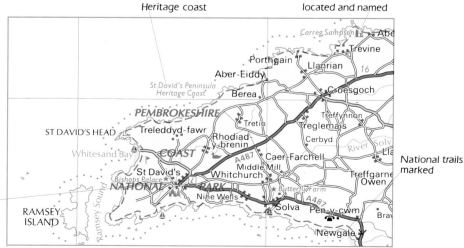

National trails marked

Tourist Information Centre

•Using this atlas

PORTS AND AIRPORTS
Maps show the major Channel and east coast ports, plus detailed maps of the main airports in Britain, giving approach roads as well as car parking facilities, and information about garages, hotels and public transport services. The map on page 119 locates *all* British ports and airports.

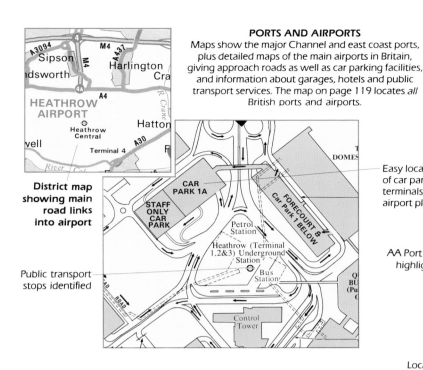

District map showing main road links into airport

Public transport stops identified

Easy location of car parks and terminals on airport plan

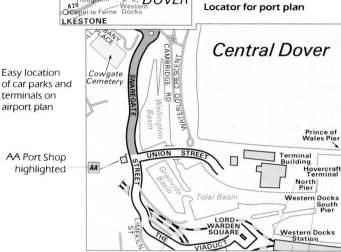

District map showing main road links

Road number for major approach roads

Locator for port plan

AA Port Shop highlighted

Local approach road named

Ship piers, ferry and hovercraft terminals and railway station clearly shown

TOWN PLANS
Up-to-date, fully-indexed town plans show AA recommended roads and other practical information such as one way streets, car parks and restricted roads, making navigation much easier. Area plans show major road networks into and out of the region.

Area map showing main road links and neighbouring towns

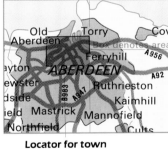

Locator for town plan

AA recommended throughroutes clearly identified

Town parking facilities

Major buildings and places of interest highlighted and named

Street index with every plan
Aberdeen
Abbotsford Lane	C2-D2
Academy Street	C4-D4
Advocates Road	E8
Affleck Street	D3
Albert Quay	E3-F3
Albert Place	A5-A6
Albert Street	A4-A5
Albert Terrace	A4-A5
Albury Place	B2-C2
Albury Road	B2-C2-C3
Albyn Grove	A4

Churches located

Pedestrian areas located

One way streets shown

LONDON
Easy-to-read, fully-indexed street maps of Inner London, provide a simple guide to finding your way around the city.

One way systems clearly shown

Underground railway stations located and named

Major places of tourist interest shown

Open spaces and parks highlighted

Garage parking identified

AA recommended routes for easier navigation

Alphabetical street index

III

•Signs and symbols

To assist you in journey planning and making the most of the comprehensive information contained in this atlas, it helps if you understand the signs on the roads and the symbols used on the maps. The principal benefit of the Department of Transport road signs is that the primary road signs (green) indicate the most *straightforward* route between one town and another. They do not necessarily indicate the most *direct* route, but it should be remembered that direct routes may not be the quickest, or the easiest to follow.

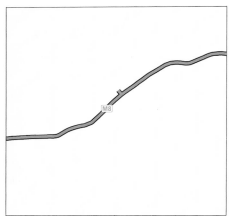

MOTORWAYS
On the map – all motorways are blue. Motorway signposts have white lettering on a blue background. Advance direction signs approaching an interchange generally include the junction number in a black box. On the map, the junction number appears in white on a solid *blue* circle.

A white number on a solid *red* circle indicates restricted access on or off the motorway at that point.

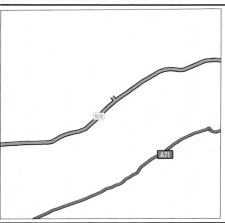
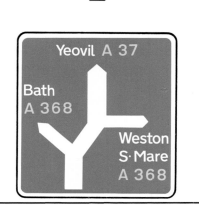

PRIMARY ROUTES
On the map – all the primary routes are green. The signposts on primary roads are also green, with white lettering and yellow numbers. Apart from the motorways, primary routes are the most important traffic routes in both urban and rural areas. They form a network of throughroutes connecting 'primary towns', which are generally places of traffic importance. Primary routes are usually along A roads.

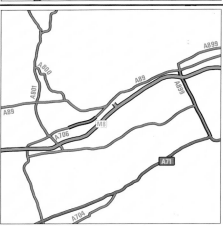
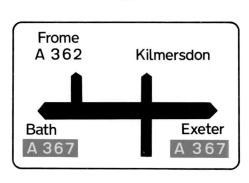

A ROADS
On the map – all A roads are shown in red, unless part of the primary network when they are green. The signposts along these roads have black lettering on a white background. At a junction with a primary route, the primary road number appears yellow in a green box.

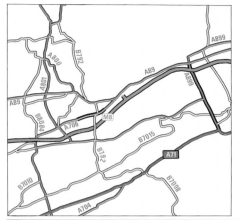

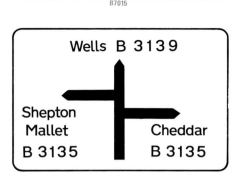

B ROADS
On the map – all B roads not in the primary network are represented in yellow. The signs on B roads are black lettering on a white background, the same as for A roads.

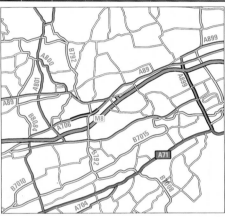

UNCLASSIFIED ROADS
On the map – all unclassified (unnumbered) roads are white. New signposts along unclassified roads are usually of the 'local direction' type. These have black lettering on a white background with a blue border. Many minor roads still have pre-World War II 'finger' post signs.

PLACE NAMES
Throughout the atlas, the size of lettering and its style is an indication of the size and importance of a place or location. This is generally related to population. All places with over 3,000 inhabitants are shown, plus there is a selection of smaller locations which are useful navigation points or possible destinations in some of the more isolated rural areas.

The section of map below highlights the various population categories and explains the difference in the size and style of lettering. The name London is a special category as it has a population in excess of 8 million.

Stourbridge
Places with this style and size of lettering include major towns and cities with populations between 50,000 and 200,000.

Birmingham
Places using this style and size of lettering indicate cities and very large towns with populations between 200,000 and 500,000.

King's Norton
This style and size of lettering is used to show suburban locations within large urban areas. Their population size is included within the 200,000 and 500,000 category.

Chaddesley Corbett
This style and size of lettering is used to show villages and hamlets with less than 3,000 inhabitants. In isolated rural areas in the north a selection of crossroads and farms are shown in slightly smaller lettering–Auchnotteroch

Bromsgrove
Metropolitan Districts, larger market and developing towns with populations between 10,000 and 50,000 are indicated by this size and style of lettering.

Alvechurch
Locations shown in this style and size of lettering are generally small market towns or developing communities situated on the fringes of large urban areas. Their populations vary between 3,000 and 10,000 inhabitants.

v

•Journey planning

Whether you are planning a journey for business or for pleasure, this atlas will make it much easier. A little preparation can save valuable time.

Alertness
If you are planning a long journey, or just going out for the day, it is essential you set out feeling alert and confident. Tired, frustrated drivers are a potential danger to themselves, to their passengers and to other road users. You will feel more capable of dealing with unexpected situations, and have a more comfortable journey if you plan ahead.

CHECK LIST
On long journeys, in particular, it pays to make a check list of things to do, even down to cancelling the milk and papers, taking the dog to the kennels, making sandwiches and a thermos, checking the roof rack and locking the door. We all forget something at some time or other! Have you never set off without having to stop just a few miles from home to wonder if you had remembered to turn the gas off?

PREPARATION
How to get there
The special route planning maps will help you to plan a basic route, and the atlas will enable you to make a more detailed one. (Taking a note of road numbers, towns and directions is useful, as this reduces the need to consult the atlas on the way.)

Distance and time
One of the fundamental considerations to be taken into account when planning any journey is how far it is. The mileage chart on the inside back cover will help you estimate the distance and this in turn can help you calculate your journey time. On the atlas, distances between places are indicated as blue numbers between blue arrowheads eg. ◀ 14 ▶ Do not forget to allow extra time for peak hours and holiday weekends.

Motorways
Despite ever-increasing traffic, motorways are still the quickest and most efficient means of travelling across the country. The map on pages xx–xxi gives an overall picture of the system.

A Roads
London is the hub for the spokes of roads numbered A1 to A6, and Edinburgh is the hub for the A7, A8 and A9.

Starting with the A1 running north from London, the roads radiate clockwise: the A2 runs generally east, the A3 south-west etc. This system has made the numbering of other roads very simple. Generally, the lower the subsequent number, the closer the road's starting point to London — similarly to Edinburgh.

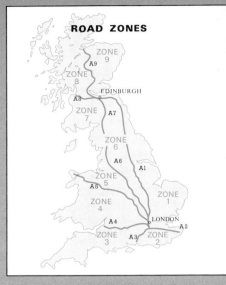

ROAD ZONES

DELAYS AND HOLD-UPS
Radio
Frequent radio bulletins are issued by the BBC and Independent Local radio stations on road conditions, possible hold-ups etc, and these can be of great assistance. By tuning in to the local stations as you pass through the area, you can avoid delays, and prepare yourself to make changes to your route. However, local radio does not yet cover the entire country. For radio

frequencies consult the regional route planning pages.

AA Roadwatch

However, if you require this information *before* setting out, you can call AA Roadwatch. This service provides information (updated every 15 minutes) on major roadworks and weather conditions for the whole country, and can be used as part of your basic journey planning. (See the regional route planning pages)

Getting the most out of the maps

The mapping contains a wide range of practical information for the motorist. Not only does it show the existing road network, but it also shows new roads which are due to be opened shortly or within approximately the next 12 months. It even indicates where A and B roads are very narrow in the Scottish Highlands. Passing bays are usually provided on these roads at regular intervals.

In addition you can use the atlas to plan trips and days out. Look for the special red tourist symbols and red names. The attractions highlighted in this way range from the cultural and historic — abbeys, museums, stately homes, to the sporting — cricket, golf, gliding, horseracing, and include Tourist Information Centres and AA viewpoints.

You can find any place listed in the index by using the National Grid, which is explained in simple terms below.

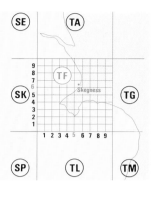

FINDING YOUR PLACE

One of the unique features of AA mapping is the use of the National Grid system.

It covers Britain with an imaginary network of squares, using blue horizontal lines called northings and vertical lines called eastings.

On the atlas pages these lines are numbered along the bottom and up the left hand side.

Each entry in the index is followed by a page number, two letters denoting an area on the map and a 4-figure grid reference. You will not need to use the two letters for simple navigation, but they come in useful if you want to use your map in relation to the rest of the country and other map series.

For quick reference, the 4 figures of the grid reference in the index are arranged so that the 1st and 3rd are in bolder type than the 2nd and 4th.

The 1st figure shows which number

along the bottom to locate, and the 3rd figure, which number up the left hand side. These will indicate the square in which you will find the place name. However, to pinpoint a place more accurately, you use the 2nd and 4th numbers also. The 2nd will tell you how many imaginary tenths along the bottom line to go from the 1st number, and the 4th will tell you how many tenths up the line to go from the 3rd number.

Where these two lines intersect, you will locate your place. Eg Skegness 77 TF **5**6**6**3. Skegness is located on page 77, within grid square 56, in National Grid square TF. Its exact location is **5**6**6**3.

If you find you get the numbers confused, it might help if you can imagine entering a house, walking in the door and along a corridor first, and then going up the stairs, then you will remember how to get them in the correct order.

•The South West and South Wales

The maps and charts at the beginning of this atlas are designed to help you plan your journey with ease and economy.

The following Route Planning Maps indicate the page grids and page numbers for easy reference to the atlas. In addition, you will find regional radio frequencies on the relevant pages and AA Roadwatch numbers on the South, East Anglia and East Midlands pages.

Finding it

Look for the place name you want in the index section at the back of the atlas. The name is followed by a page number and a National Grid reference. Turn to the atlas page indicated and use the National Grid reference to pinpoint the place.

The National Grid and how to use are explained on page VII.

Getting there

Having found your destination in the main atlas, find the nearest large town. This will be shown on the following Route Planning Maps, pages VIII-XVII. These maps show the principal routes throughout Britain and a basic route can be planned from them. A special feature of these maps is that a key to the atlas pages is super-imposed—making place location much easier. A more detailed route can then be worked out from the main atlas. Taking a note of road numbers and directions reduces the need to stop and consult the atlas on the way.

How far?

The length of the journey is a fundamental consideration when a journey is being planned. The mileage chart on the inside back cover gives the distance between main towns and can be used to make a rough calculation of the total journey length. You should then be able to estimate the time needed for the journey.

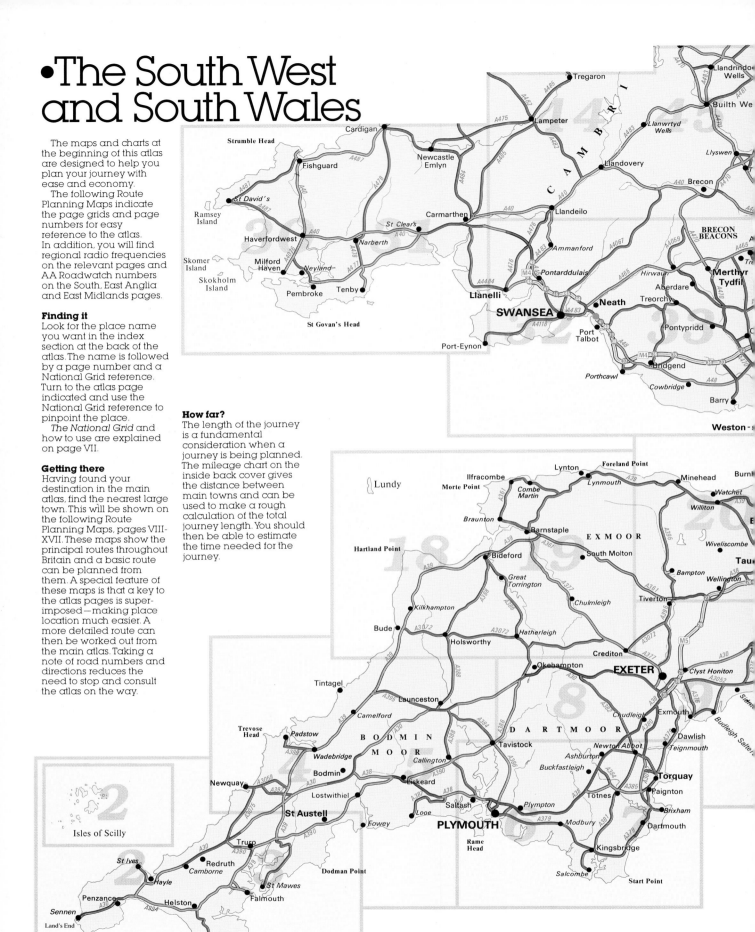

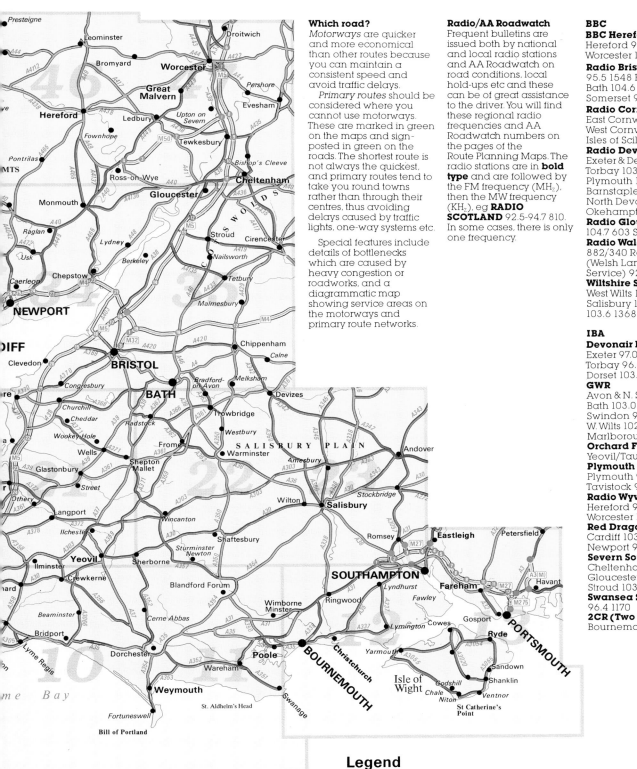

Which road?

Motorways are quicker and more economical than other routes because you can maintain a consistent speed and avoid traffic delays.

Primary routes should be considered where you cannot use motorways. These are marked in green on the maps and sign-posted in green on the roads. The shortest route is not always the quickest, and primary routes tend to take you round towns rather than through their centres, thus avoiding delays caused by traffic lights, one-way systems etc.

Special features include details of bottlenecks which are caused by heavy congestion or roadworks, and a diagrammatic map showing service areas on the motorways and primary route networks.

Radio/AA Roadwatch

Frequent bulletins are issued both by national and local radio stations and AA Roadwatch on road conditions, local hold-ups etc and these can be of great assistance to the driver. You will find these regional radio frequencies and AA Roadwatch numbers on the pages of the Route Planning Maps. The radio stations are in **bold type** and are followed by the FM frequency (MH_2), then the MW frequency (KH_2), eg **RADIO SCOTLAND** 92.5-94.7 810. In some cases, there is only one frequency.

BBC
BBC Hereford & Worcester
Hereford 94.7 819
Worcester 104.0 738
Radio Bristol
95.5 1548 Bristol 94.9 1548
Bath 104.6 1548 Central
Somerset 95.5 1323
Radio Cornwall
East Cornwall 95.2 657
West Cornwall 103.9 630
Isles of Scilly 96.0 630
Radio Devon
Exeter & Devon 95.8 990
Torbay 103.4 1458
Plymouth 103.4 855
Barnstaple 94.8 801
North Devon 103.4 801
Okehampton 96.0 801
Radio Gloucestershire
104.7 603 Stroud 95.0
Radio Wales
882/340 Radio Cymru
(Welsh Language
Service) 92.5-94.5
Wiltshire Sound
West Wilts 104.3 1332
Salisbury 103.5 North Wilts
103.6 1368

IBA
Devonair Radio
Exeter 97.0 666
Torbay 96.4 954 E. Devon/
Dorset 103.0 666
GWR
Avon & N. Som. 96.3 1260
Bath 103.0 1260
Swindon 97.2 1161
W. Wilts 102.2 936
Marlborough 96.5
Orchard FM
Yeovil/Taunton 102.6
Plymouth Sound
Plymouth 97.0 1152.
Tavistock 96.6 1152
Radio Wyvern
Hereford 97.6 954
Worcester 102.8 1530
Red Dragon Radio
Cardiff 103.2 1359
Newport 97.4 1305
Severn Sound
Cheltenham and
Gloucester 102.4 774.
Stroud 103.0 774
Swansea Sound
96.4 1170
2CR (Two Counties Radio)
Bournemouth 97.2 828.

Legend

Motorway	
Motorway under construction	
Primary route single carriageway	
Primary route dual carriageway	
Other A roads	
Motorway junction	⑦
Motorway junction with limited entries or exits.	⑦

Scale 16 miles to 1 inch

0 ... 10 ... 20 mls

0 ... 10 ... 20 ... 30 kms

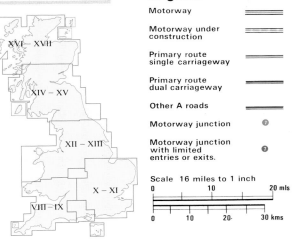

ENGLAND

ENGLISH CHANNEL

FRANCE

152

•The South, East Anglia and East Midlands

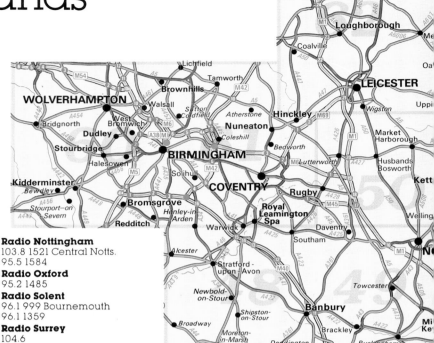

BBC

BBC CWR (Coventry & Warwick)
Coventry 94.8
Warwickshire 103.7

BBC Essex
103.5 765 N.E. Essex 103.5
729 S.E. Essex 95.3 1530

Greater London Radio
94.9 1458

Radio Berkshire
104.1 Henley 94.6 Reading
104.4 Windsor 95.4

Radio Cambridgeshire
96.0 1026 Peterborough
& W. Cambs. 95.7 1449

Radio Derby
104.5 1116 Derby 94.2 1116
Bakewell & Matlock 95.3
Buxton 96

Radio Bedfordshire
95.5 630 Bedford 95.5 1161
Luton & Dunstable 103.8
630 Bletchley 104.5 630

Radio Kent
96.7 1035 Tunbridge Wells
96.7 1602 East Kent 104.2
774

Radio Leicester
95.1 837 N.W. Leicester
104.9

Radio Norfolk
East Norfolk 95.1 855
West Norfolk 104.4 873

Radio Northampton
104.2 1107 Corby 103.6 1107

Radio Nottingham
103.8 1521 Central Notts.
95.5 1584

Radio Oxford
95.2 1485

Radio Solent
96.1 999 Bournemouth
96.1 1359

Radio Surrey
104.6

Radio Sussex
Brighton & Worthing 95.3
1485 East Sussex & part of
West Sussex 104.5 1161
Crawley & Horsham 95.1
1368 Newhaven 95.0
1485

Radio W.M. (West Midlands)
95.6 1458 Wolverhampton
95.6 828

IBA

BRMB Radio
Birmingham 96.4 1152

Capital Radio
95.8 1548

Chiltern Radio
Bedford 96.9 792
Luton 97.6 828
Northampton 96.6 1557

CN FM
Cambridge & Newmarket
103.0

County Sound
Guildford 96.4 1476
Haslemere 97.1 1476

Essex Radio
Chelmsford 102.6 1359
Southend 96.3 1431

Fox FM
Oxford 102.6 Banbury 97.4

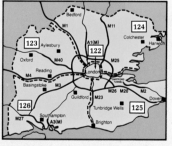
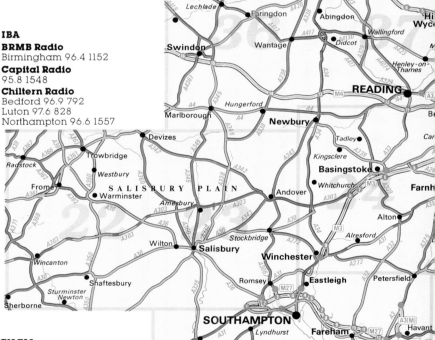

Hereward Radio
Peterborough 102.7 133.2
Horizon Radio
Milton Keynes 103.3
Invicta Radio
Kent 103.1 1242
Canterbury 102.8 603
Thanet 95.9 603
Dover/Folkestone 97.0
603 Ashford 96.1 603
Leicester Sound
Leicester 103.2 1260
LBC
97.3 1152
Mercia Sound
Coventry 97.0 1359
Leamington Spa 102.9
1359
Northants 96
96.0 1557
Ocean Sound
Southampton, S.W. Hants &
I.O.W. 103.2 1557
Winchester 96.7
Portsmouth, S.E. Hants &
Chichester 97.5 1170
Radio 210
Thames Valley 97.0 1431
Basingstoke, Andover
102.9 1431
Radio Broadland
Gt. Yarmouth & Norwich
102.4 1152
Radio Mercury
Crawley/Reigate 102.7
1521 Horsham 97.5 1521
Radio Orwell
Ipswich 97.1 1170
Saxon Radio
Bury St. Edmunds 96.4
1251
Southern Sound
Brighton 103.5 1323
Eastbourne 102.4 1323
Hastings 97.5 1323
Newhaven 96.9 1323

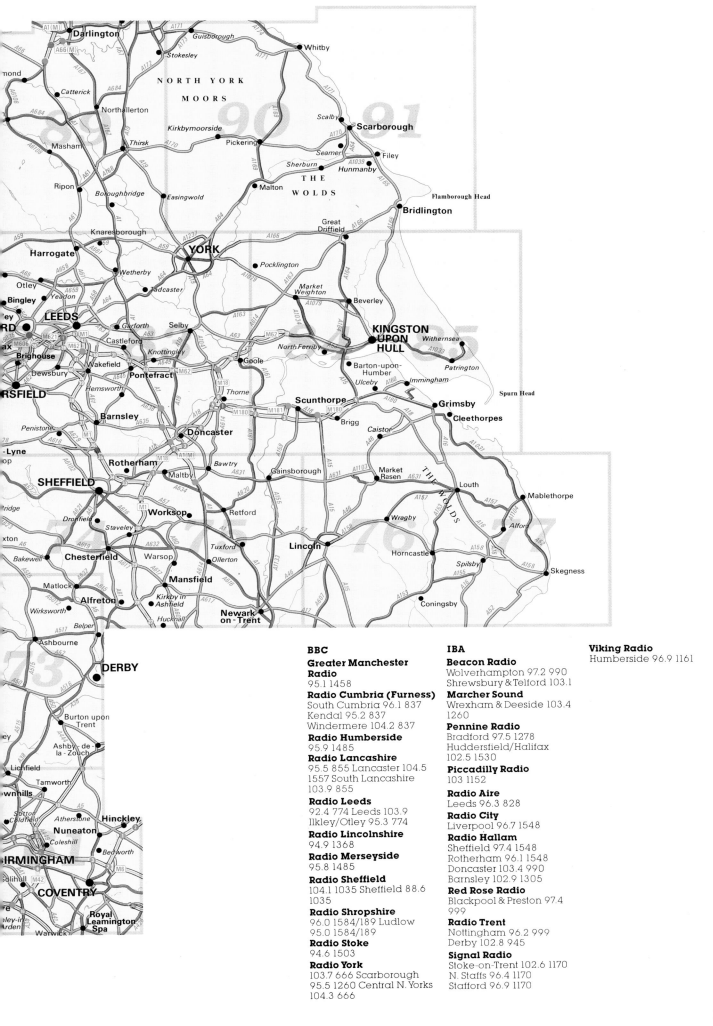

BBC

Greater Manchester Radio
95.1 1458

Radio Cumbria (Furness)
South Cumbria 96.1 837
Kendal 95.2 837
Windermere 104.2 837

Radio Humberside
95.9 1485

Radio Lancashire
95.5 855 Lancaster 104.5
1557 South Lancashire
103.9 855

Radio Leeds
92.4 774 Leeds 103.9
Ilkley/Otley 95.3 774

Radio Lincolnshire
94.9 1368

Radio Merseyside
95.8 1485

Radio Sheffield
104.1 1035 Sheffield 88.6
1035

Radio Shropshire
96.0 1584/189 Ludlow
95.0 1584/189

Radio Stoke
94.6 1503

Radio York
103.7 666 Scarborough
95.5 1260 Central N. Yorks
104.3 666

IBA

Beacon Radio
Wolverhampton 97.2 990
Shrewsbury & Telford 103.1

Marcher Sound
Wrexham & Deeside 103.4
1260

Pennine Radio
Bradford 97.5 1278
Huddersfield/Halifax
102.5 1530

Piccadilly Radio
103 1152

Radio Aire
Leeds 96.3 828

Radio City
Liverpool 96.7 1548

Radio Hallam
Sheffield 97.4 1548
Rotherham 96.1 1548
Doncaster 103.4 990
Barnsley 102.9 1305

Red Rose Radio
Blackpool & Preston 97.4
999

Radio Trent
Nottingham 96.2 999
Derby 102.8 945

Signal Radio
Stoke-on-Trent 102.6 1170
N. Staffs 96.4 1170
Stafford 96.9 1170

Viking Radio
Humberside 96.9 1161

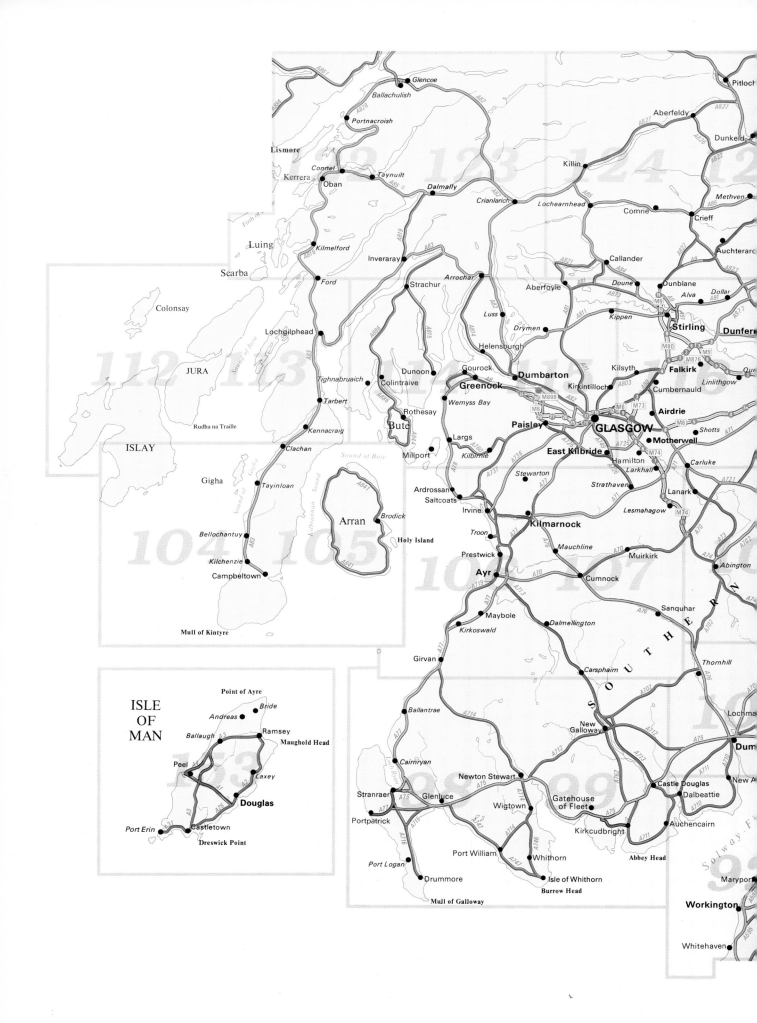

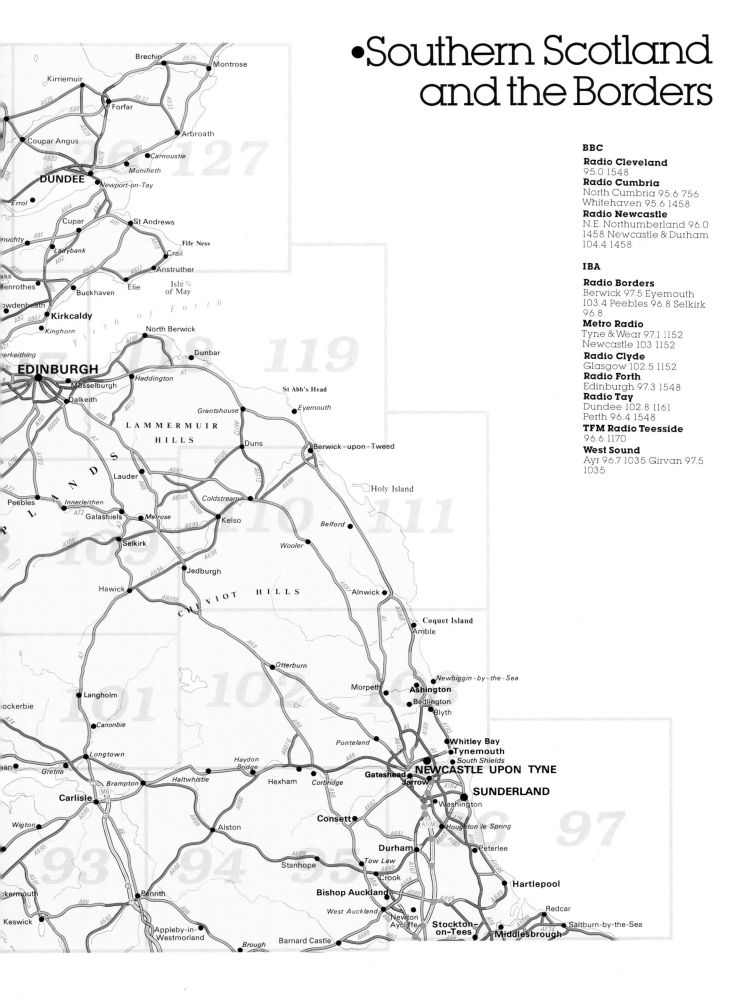

•Southern Scotland and the Borders

BBC

Radio Cleveland
95.0 1548
Radio Cumbria
North Cumbria 95.6 756
Whitehaven 95.6 1458
Radio Newcastle
N.E. Northumberland 96.0
1458 Newcastle & Durham
104.4 1458

IBA

Radio Borders
Berwick 97.5 Eyemouth
103.4 Peebles 96.8 Selkirk
96.8
Metro Radio
Tyne & Wear 97.1 1152
Newcastle 103 1152
Radio Clyde
Glasgow 102.5 1152
Radio Forth
Edinburgh 97.3 1548
Radio Tay
Dundee 102.8 1161
Perth 96.4 1548
TFM Radio Teesside
96.6 1170
West Sound
Ayr 96.7 1035 Girvan 97.5
1035

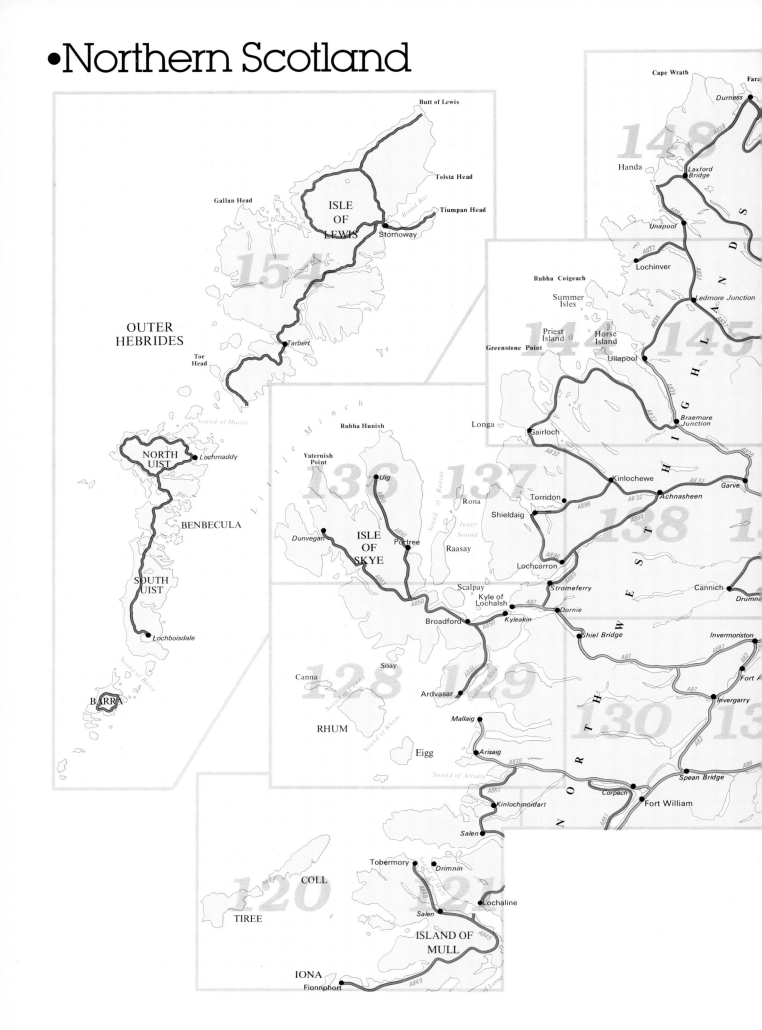

•Northern Scotland

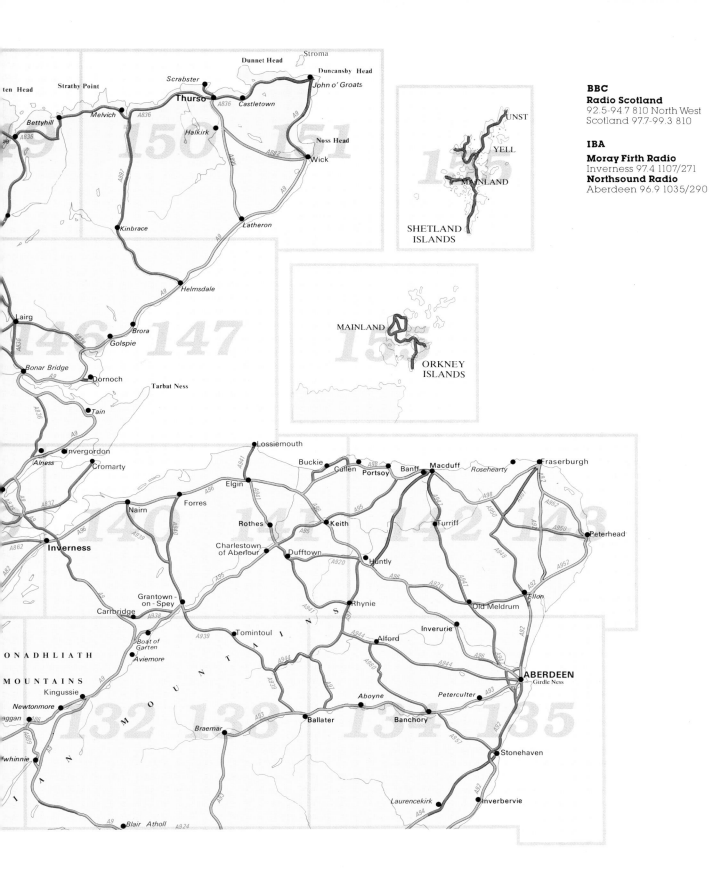

SHETLAND
ISLANDS

MAINLAND

ORKNEY
ISLANDS

•The Channel Tunnel

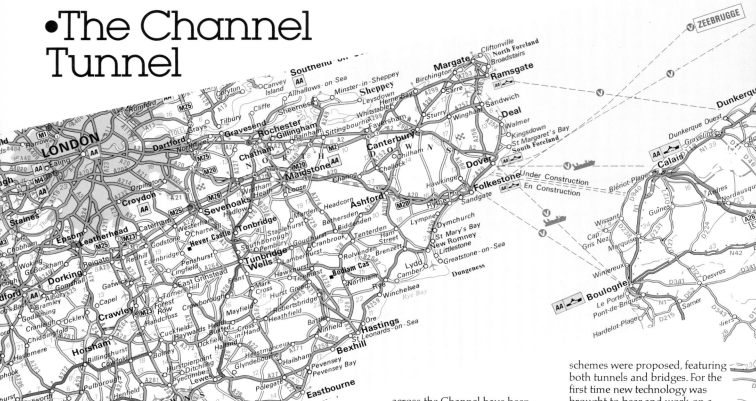

THE Channel Tunnel, the largest construction project Europe has seen in the 20th century, will play a vital role in creating an integrated Europe and in building a free market economy within the Continent. The impact of the tunnel on road transport will be immense, bringing about major changes in patterns of business

A model of the Channel Tunnel terminus at Folkestone, Kent

and commercial travel, as well as tourism. Unaffected by weather, and with careful consideration given to security and the threats posed by breakdowns, fire and acts of terrorism, the tunnel will provide a dependable and quick cross-Channel connection. It will also be a vital link in the expanding European motorway network.

A double dream
The opening of the tunnel will fulfil an engineering and economic dream that has lasted for nearly 200 years. Since 1802 at least 70 schemes for building a fixed link

across the Channel have been proposed, some of the earliest of which were included in Napoleon's plans for the invasion of England. Since then, the fear of invasion and other military and political concerns have brought many subsequent schemes to an end. In the 1880s a tunnel was driven for over a mile under the Channel from a site near Shakespeare Cliff before military and political pressure brought the project to a standstill, and another tunnelling attempt in the 1920s met the same fate. In the late 1960s the idea came to life again, helped by the breaking down of traditional trade and political barriers within Europe and many new fixed link

schemes were proposed, featuring both tunnels and bridges. For the first time new technology was brought to bear and work on a tunnel started briefly in 1974 before political concerns again brought things to an end.

Signing the treaties
By the 1980s some form of fixed link between Britain and Europe had become an economic necessity, and on 12 February 1986 Prime Minister Margaret Thatcher and President Francois Mitterand signed a treaty agreeing the terms for the building and operating of the Channel Tunnel. This treaty was ratified on 29 July 1987 and a 55 year concession to construct and operate the tunnel was granted to Eurotunnel. Work was soon under way on the largest privately funded construction scheme ever. Teething troubles caused delays at first, but soon the giant boring machines were carving their way under the Channel from sites near Folkestone in Kent and Sangatte, south of Calais, with a target to link up in stages from late 1990 onwards.

The building of the tunnel has aroused great public interest, and special exhibition centres opened at both English and French terminal sites have become popular tourist attractions, with hundreds of thousands of visitors coming to find out about the tunnel.

Trains take the strain
The Channel Tunnel is actually three parallel bores, comprising two running tunnels 25 feet (7.6m) in diameter and a central service tunnel 16 feet (4.8m) in diameter. Their total length is 30.7 miles (49km), of which 23.6 (38) are under the sea. For most of their length they lie between 80 and 130 feet (25 and 40m) below the

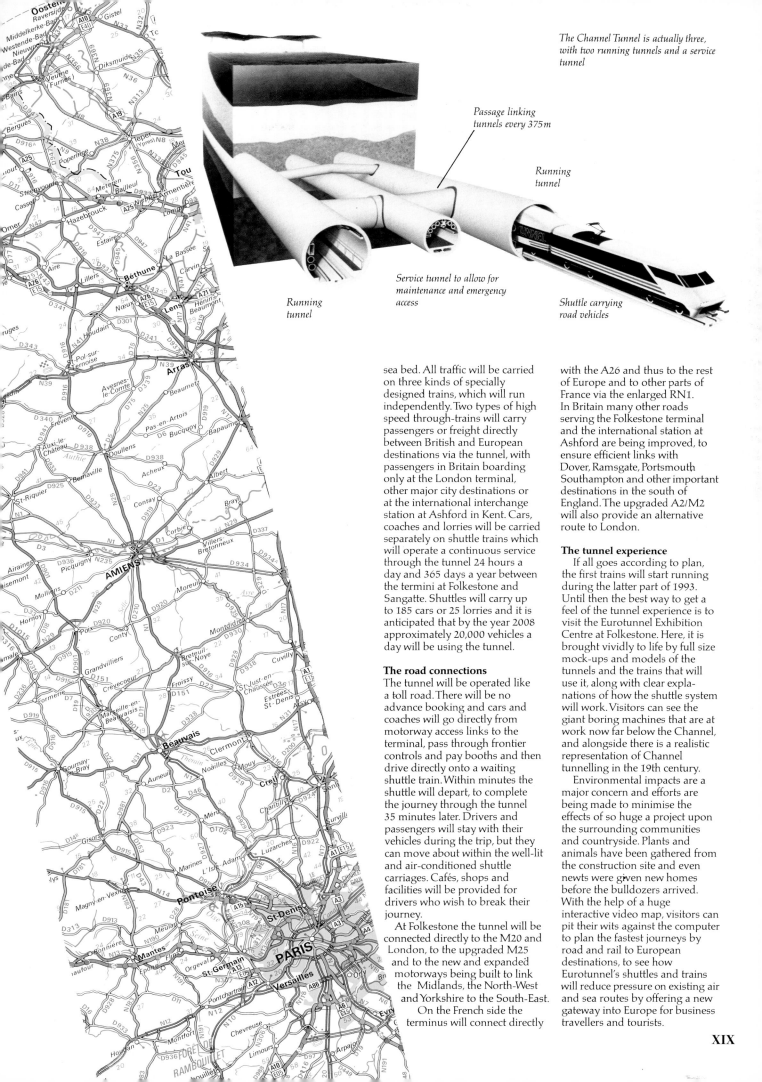

The Channel Tunnel is actually three, with two running tunnels and a service tunnel

Passage linking tunnels every 375m

Running tunnel

Running tunnel

Service tunnel to allow for maintenance and emergency access

Shuttle carrying road vehicles

sea bed. All traffic will be carried on three kinds of specially designed trains, which will run independently. Two types of high speed through-trains will carry passengers or freight directly between British and European destinations via the tunnel, with passengers in Britain boarding only at the London terminal, other major city destinations or at the international interchange station at Ashford in Kent. Cars, coaches and lorries will be carried separately on shuttle trains which will operate a continuous service through the tunnel 24 hours a day and 365 days a year between the termini at Folkestone and Sangatte. Shuttles will carry up to 185 cars or 25 lorries and it is anticipated that by the year 2008 approximately 20,000 vehicles a day will be using the tunnel.

The road connections

The tunnel will be operated like a toll road. There will be no advance booking and cars and coaches will go directly from motorway access links to the terminal, pass through frontier controls and pay booths and then drive directly onto a waiting shuttle train. Within minutes the shuttle will depart, to complete the journey through the tunnel 35 minutes later. Drivers and passengers will stay with their vehicles during the trip, but they can move about within the well-lit and air-conditioned shuttle carriages. Cafés, shops and facilities will be provided for drivers who wish to break their journey.

At Folkestone the tunnel will be connected directly to the M20 and London, to the upgraded M25 and to the new and expanded motorways being built to link the Midlands, the North-West and Yorkshire to the South-East. On the French side the terminus will connect directly

with the A26 and thus to the rest of Europe and to other parts of France via the enlarged RN1. In Britain many other roads serving the Folkestone terminal and the international station at Ashford are being improved, to ensure efficient links with Dover, Ramsgate, Portsmouth Southampton and other important destinations in the south of England. The upgraded A2/M2 will also provide an alternative route to London.

The tunnel experience

If all goes according to plan, the first trains will start running during the latter part of 1993. Until then the best way to get a feel of the tunnel experience is to visit the Eurotunnel Exhibition Centre at Folkestone. Here, it is brought vividly to life by full size mock-ups and models of the tunnels and the trains that will use it, along with clear explanations of how the shuttle system will work. Visitors can see the giant boring machines that are at work now far below the Channel, and alongside there is a realistic representation of Channel tunnelling in the 19th century.

Environmental impacts are a major concern and efforts are being made to minimise the effects of so huge a project upon the surrounding communities and countryside. Plants and animals have been gathered from the construction site and even newts were given new homes before the bulldozers arrived. With the help of a huge interactive video map, visitors can pit their wits against the computer to plan the fastest journeys by road and rail to European destinations, to see how Eurotunnel's shuttles and trains will reduce pressure on existing air and sea routes by offering a new gateway into Europe for business travellers and tourists.

•Regional roadworks and bottlenecks

BOTTLENECKS

Roadworks and the sheer volume of traffic in an area can cause major delays and disruption to your journey if you come across them unawares. Knowing where they are likely to occur means you can alter your route to avoid them or allow more time for travelling. This list, and its accompanying map, highlights the major bottlenecks on motorways and primary routes. These are caused by traffic congestion or long term roadworks as predicted by the AA for 1991. Information on problems within major towns and cities is not included.

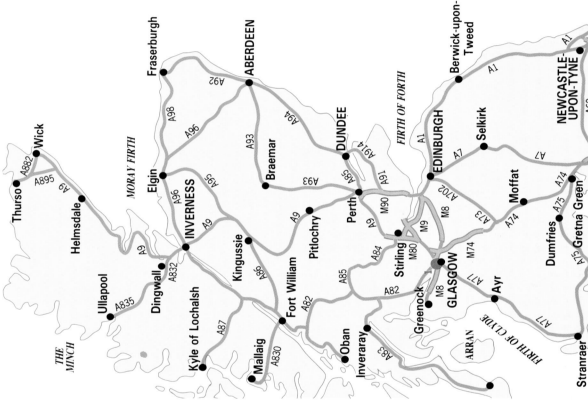

15 Newport
M4 junctions 25-26
Peak times – heavy congestion due to volume of traffic and road construction.

16 Severn Bridge
M4
Peak times – heavy congestion due to volume of traffic.

17 Bristol
M5 junctions 14-20
Summer Saturdays – southbound congestion due to volume of traffic.

18 Penmaenmawr
A55
Peak periods, especially summer weekends – congestion due to volume of traffic and road construction.

19 Conwy
A55
Peak periods, especially summer weekends – congestion due to volume of traffic.

20 Porthmadog
A487
Summer weekends – congestion at toll gate due to volume of traffic and toll collection.

21 Plymouth
A38 and A374 (Marsh Mills Roundabout)
Peak periods, especially summer weekends – heavy congestion due to volume of traffic and road construction.

22 Tamar Bridge
A38
Peak periods, especially summer weekends – heavy congestion due to volume of traffic.

23 Indian Queens and Fraddon
A30 and A39
Summer Saturdays – congestion due to volume of traffic.

24 Reigate
M25 junctions 7-8
Clockwise, peak periods – congestion due to slow moving lorries.

25 Dartford Tunnel
M25 and A282
Both directions, peak periods daily, and weekends from Easter to October, particularly Bank Holidays – congestion due to volume of traffic and toll collection.

26 Uxbridge
M25 junctions 15-16
Anti-clockwise morning rush hour; clockwise evening rush hour – congestion due to volume of traffic.

27 St Albans-Luton
M1 junctions 6-10
Southbound, Monday to Friday, morning rush hour; northbound, Friday evening rush hour – congestion due to volume of traffic.

28 Rayleigh Weir Roundabout
A127 and A129
Construction of underpass until early 1992.

29 Camberley-Chertsey
M3 junctions 2-4
Eastbound, morning rush hour – congestion due to volume of traffic.

30 West Wycombe
M40 junctions 4-5
Road widening until late 1991.

ISLE OF MAN

ISLE OF WIGHT

THE WASH

CAERNARFON BAY

CARDIGAN BAY

BRISTOL CHANNEL

1 Glasgow
M8 junctions 8-25
Monday to Friday,
morning and evening
rush hours —heavy
congestion due to
volume of traffic.

2 Ambleside
A591 and A593
Bank Holidays. July and
August —daily heavy
congestion due to
volume of traffic,
especially Saturdays.

3 Windermere
A591 and A592
Bank Holidays. July and
August —daily heavy
congestion due to
volume of traffic,
especially Saturdays.

4 Selby
A63
Delays at toll bridge
especially when swing
bridge is opened.

5 Leeds
A58(M)
Inner Ring Road, during
rush hours —congestion
due to volume of traffic.

6 Lancaster
A6 and A589
One-way system,
especially for
Morecambe/Heysham:
traffic —general
congestion due to
volume of traffic.

7 Preston
M6 between M61 and
M55, junctions 30-32
Monday to Friday,
morning and evening
rush hours, also summer
weekends —heavy
congestion due to
volume of traffic.

8 Thelwall Viaduct
M6 junctions 20a-21a
Monday to Friday,
morning and evening
rush hours —congestion
due to volume of traffic.

9 Manchester
M62 and M63
South, west and north of
city Monday to Friday,
morning and evening
rush hours —heavy
congestion due to
volume of traffic.

10 Birmingham
M6 junctions 6-12
Monday to Friday,
morning and evening
rush hours, also Friday
late evening in summer—
heavy congestion due to
volume of traffic.

11 Shrewsbury
A5
Second weekend of
August, Friday and
Saturday —congestion
due to flower show traffic.

12 Worcester
M5 junctions 6-8
Possible congestion due
to widening work,
scheduled to start 1991.

13 Silverstone
A43
Grand Prix weekend —
congestion due to
volume of traffic.

14 Swansea
A48 between M4
junctions 41 and 44
Peak times —heavy
congestion due to
volume of traffic and
motorway construction

31 Eastleigh
A33
Conversion to motorway
until summer 1991.

XXI

•Motorway and primary route service areas

This map shows, in diagrammatic form, service areas on the motorways and primary routes.

The companies running them are shown after the name of the service area. They are leased from the Department of Transport and, as such, are required to cater for the basic needs of long-distance travellers, including the disabled – up to 2 hours free parking, refreshments, toilets, telephones and fuel 24 hours a day. Many include additional facilities at the operators' discretion such as shops, breakdown and repair services, picnic areas, business and banking facilities, overnight parking for caravans and special changing areas for babies, plus accommodation.

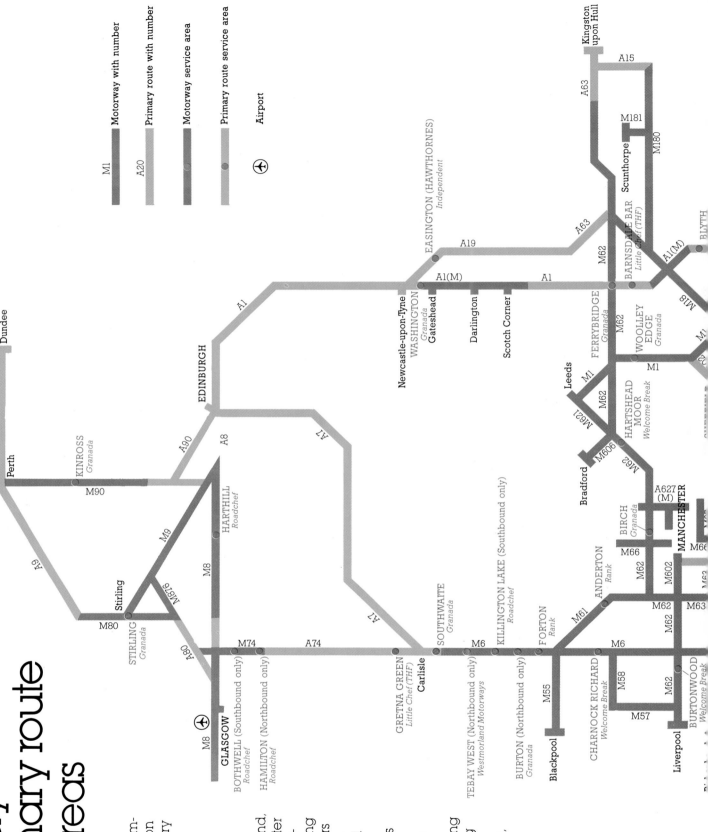

Legend:
- M1 — Motorway with number
- A20 — Primary route with number
- Motorway service area
- Primary route service area
- ✈ Airport

Dundee

A85

Perth

M90

KINROSS
Granada

A90

A9

M9

Stirling

M80

STIRLING
Granada

A80

M876

HARTHILL
Roadchef

M8

A8

EDINBURGH

A1

A7

BOTHWELL (Southbound only)
Roadchef

HAMILTON (Northbound only)
Roadchef

M74

M8

GLASGOW ✈

A74

GRETNA GREEN
Little Chef (THF)

Carlisle

SOUTHWAITE
Granada

TEBAY WEST (Northbound only)
Westmorland Motorways

KILLINGTON LAKE (Southbound only)
Roadchef

BURTON (Northbound only)
Granada

FORTON
Rank

M6

M55

Blackpool

CHARNOCK RICHARD
Welcome Break

M61

ANDERTON
Rank

M58

M57

BURTONWOOD
Welcome Break

Liverpool

M62

A627
(M)

M66

MANCHESTER

BIRCH
Granada

M66

M602

M63

M6

Bradford

M606

M62

Leeds

M1

M621

HARTSHEAD MOOR
Welcome Break

M62

WOOLLEY EDGE
Granada

M1

FERRYBRIDGE
Granada

M62

Newcastle-upon-Tyne

WASHINGTON
Granada

Gateshead

A1(M)

Darlington

A1

Scotch Corner

A19

EASINGTON (HAWTHORNES)
Independent

A63

BARNSDALE BAR
Little Chef (THF)

A1(M)

A18

M18

BLYTH

Scunthorpe

M181

M180

A15

A63

Kingston upon Hull

SHEFFIELD

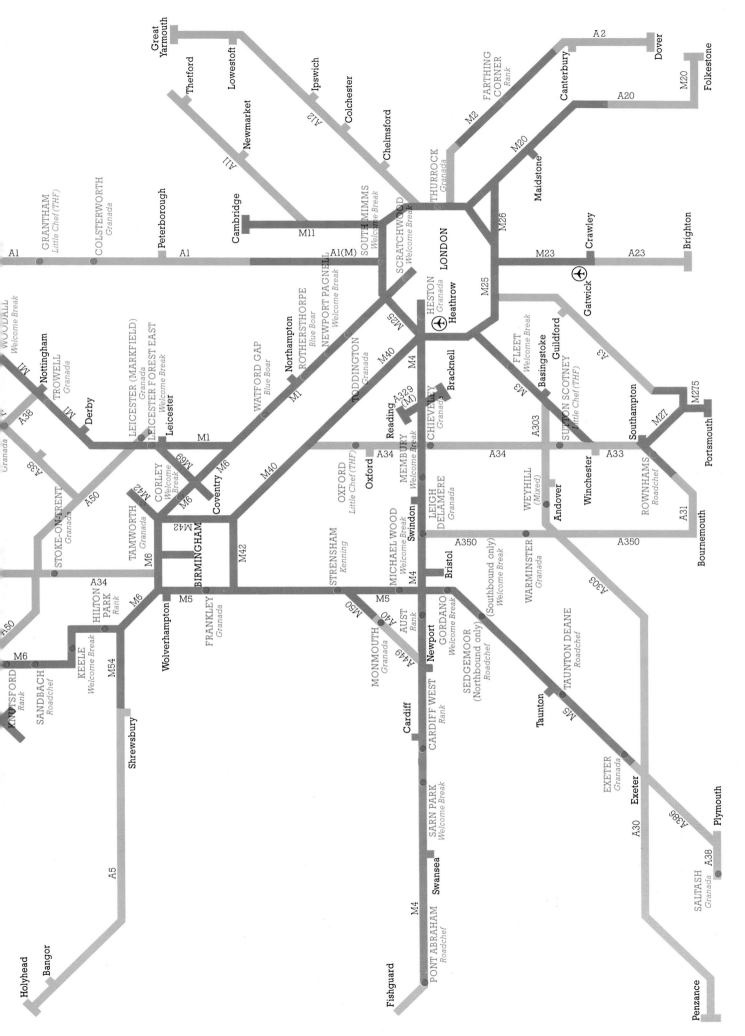

•Map pages

XXIV

•Map symbols

MOTORING INFORMATION

M4	Motorway with number
11	Motorway junction with and without number
3	Motorway junction with limited access
S	Motorway service area
	Motorway and junction under construction
A4	Primary route single/dual carriageway
S	Primary route service area
A1123	Other A road single/dual carriageway
B2070	B road single/dual carriageway
	Unclassified road single/dual carriageway
	Road under construction
	Narrow primary, other A or B road with passing places (Scotland)
	Road tunnel
	Steep gradient (arrows point downhill)
Toll	Road toll
5	Distance in miles between symbols

V	Vehicle ferry – Great Britain
CHERBOURG V	Vehicle ferry – Continental
H	Hovercraft ferry
⊕	Airport
H	Heliport
	Railway line/in tunnel
X	Railway station and level crossing
AA	AA Shop – full services
AA	AA Roadside Shop – limited services
AA	AA Port Shop – open as season demands
☎	AA telephone
☎	BT telephone in isolated places
	Urban area/village
628 ▲	Spot height in metres
	River, canal, lake
	Sandy beach
	County boundary
	National boundary
88	Page overlap and number

TOURIST INFORMATION

i	Tourist Information Centre
i	Tourist Information Centre (summer only)
	Abbey, cathedral or priory
	Ruined abbey, cathedral or priory
	Castle
	Historic house
M	Museum or art gallery
	Industrial interest
	Garden
	Arboretum
	Country park
	Agricultural showground
	Theme park
	Zoo
	Wildlife collection – mammals
	Wildlife collection – birds
	Aquarium
	Nature reserve
RSPB	RSPB site
	Nature trail
.....	Forest drive
- - -	National trail
☀	AA viewpoint
	Picnic site

	Hill fort
	Roman antiquity
	Prehistoric monument
X	Battle site with year
	Preserved railway/ steam centre
	Cave
	Windmill
	Golf course
	County cricket ground
	Rugby Union national ground
	International athletics stadium
	Horse racing
	Show jumping/equestrian circuit
	Motor racing circuit
	Coastal launching site
	Ski slope – natural
	Ski slope – artificial
★	Other places of interest
	Boxed symbols indicate attractions within urban areas
	National Park (England & Wales)
	National Scenic Area (Scotland)
	Forest Park
	Heritage Coast
	Blue flag beach

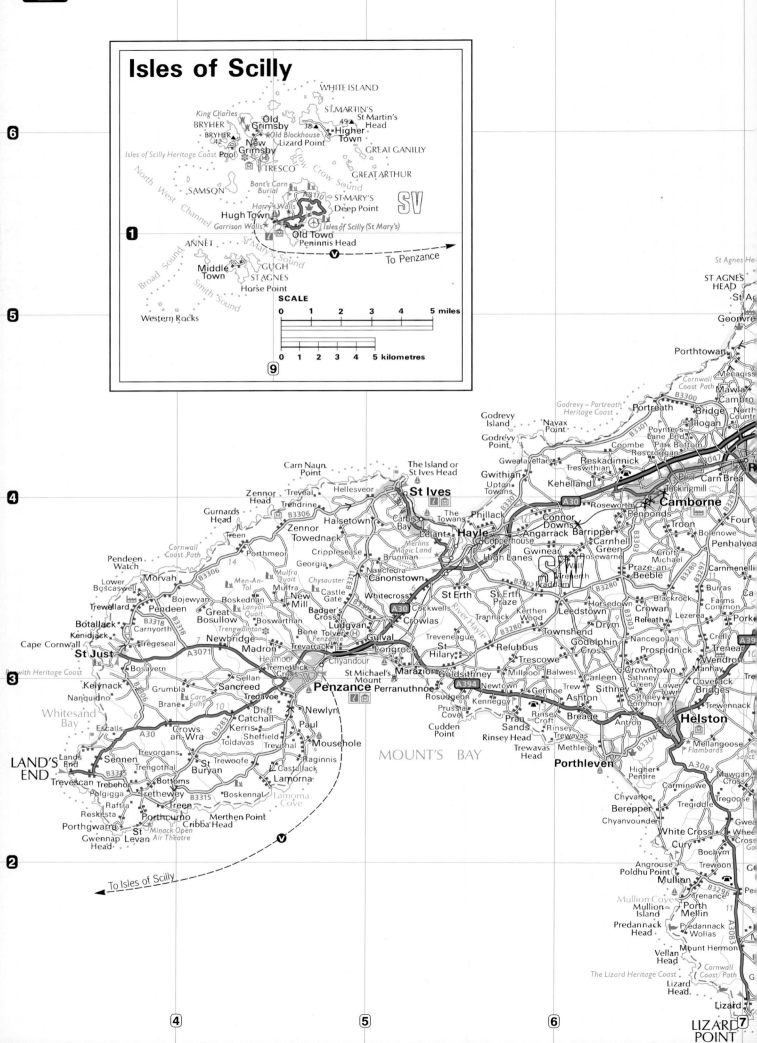

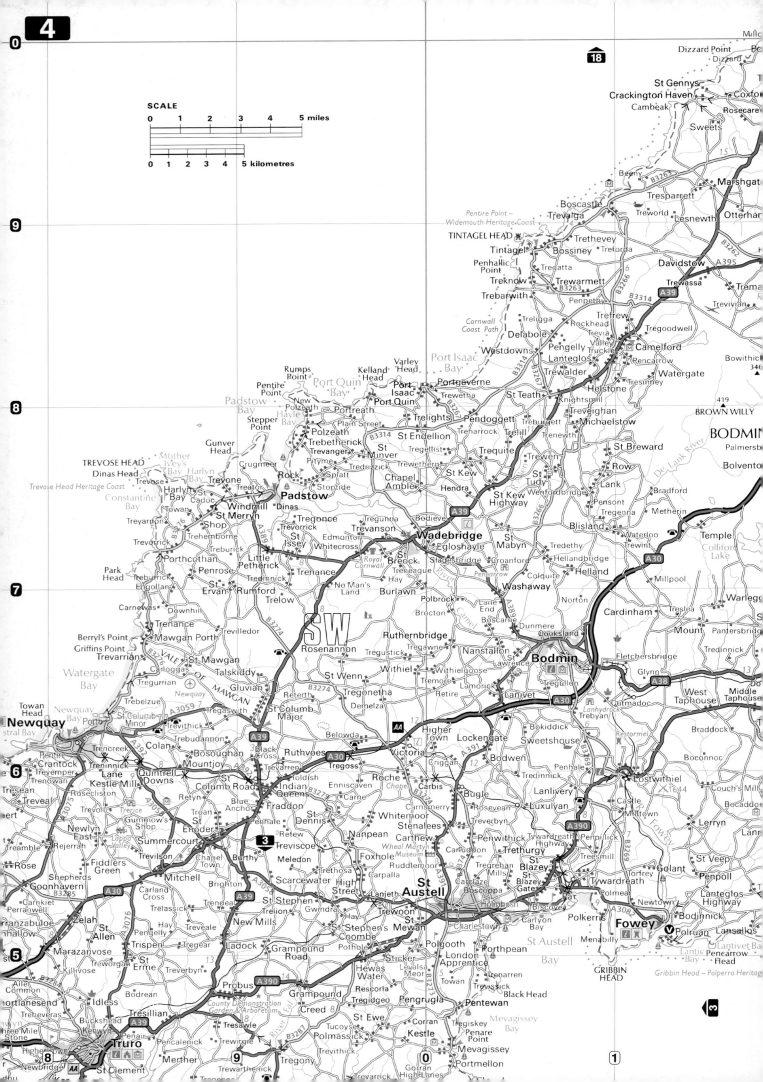

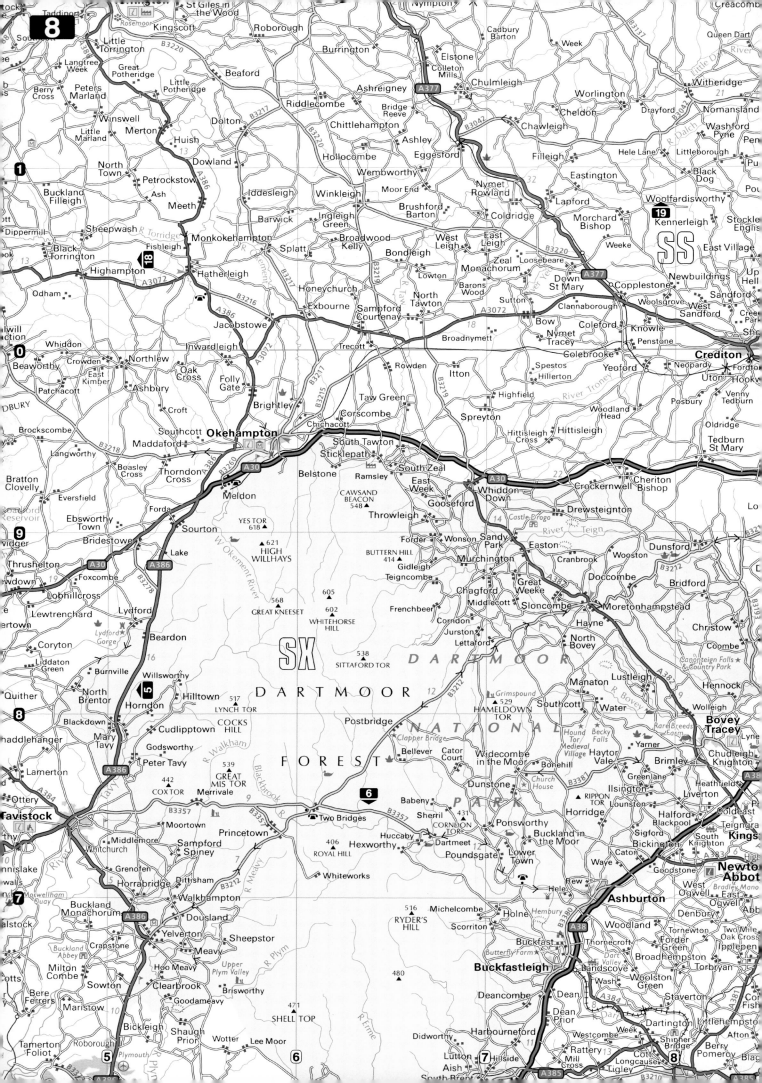

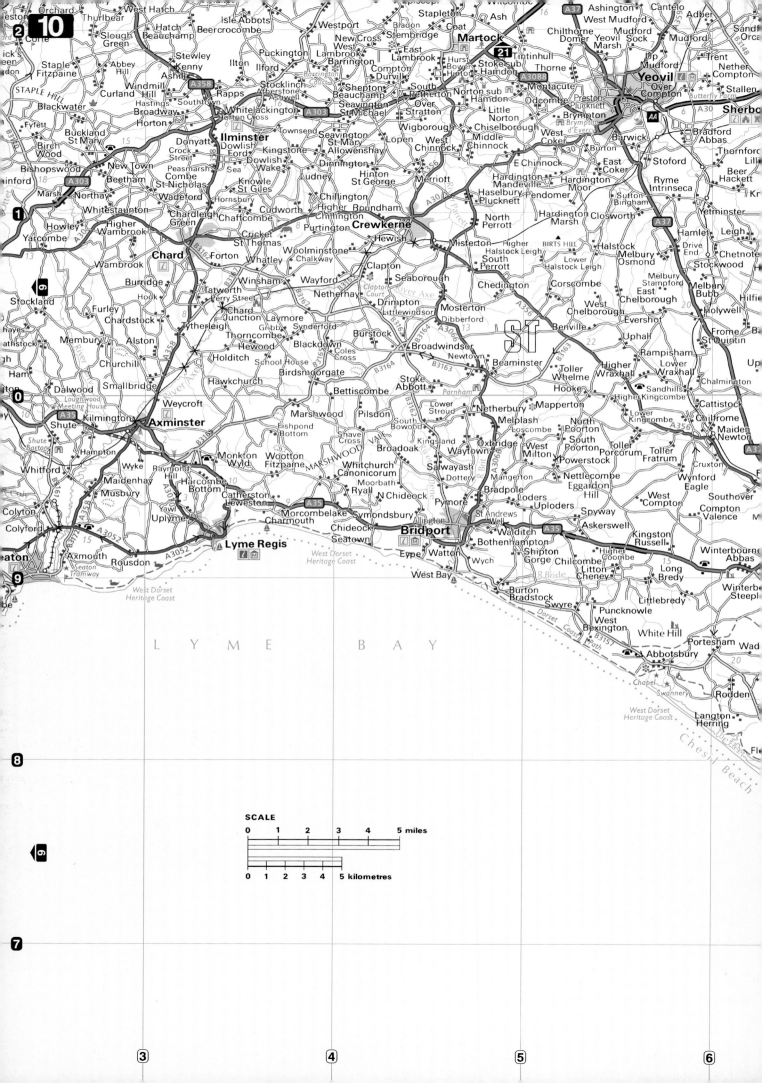

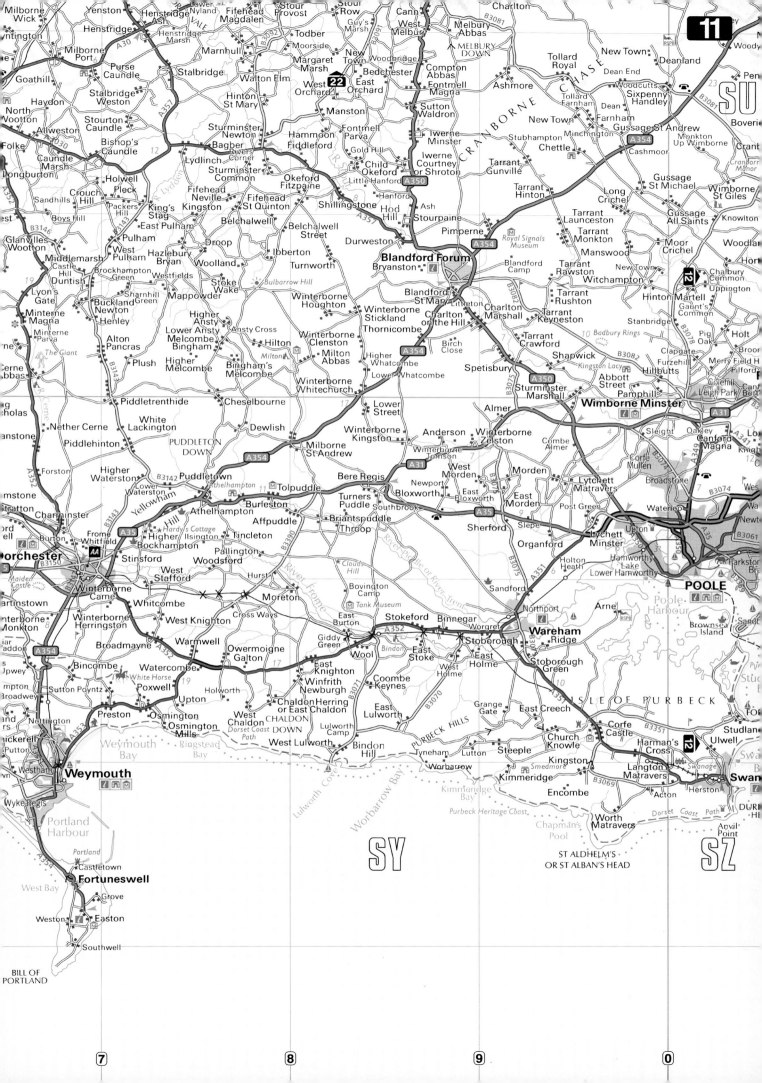

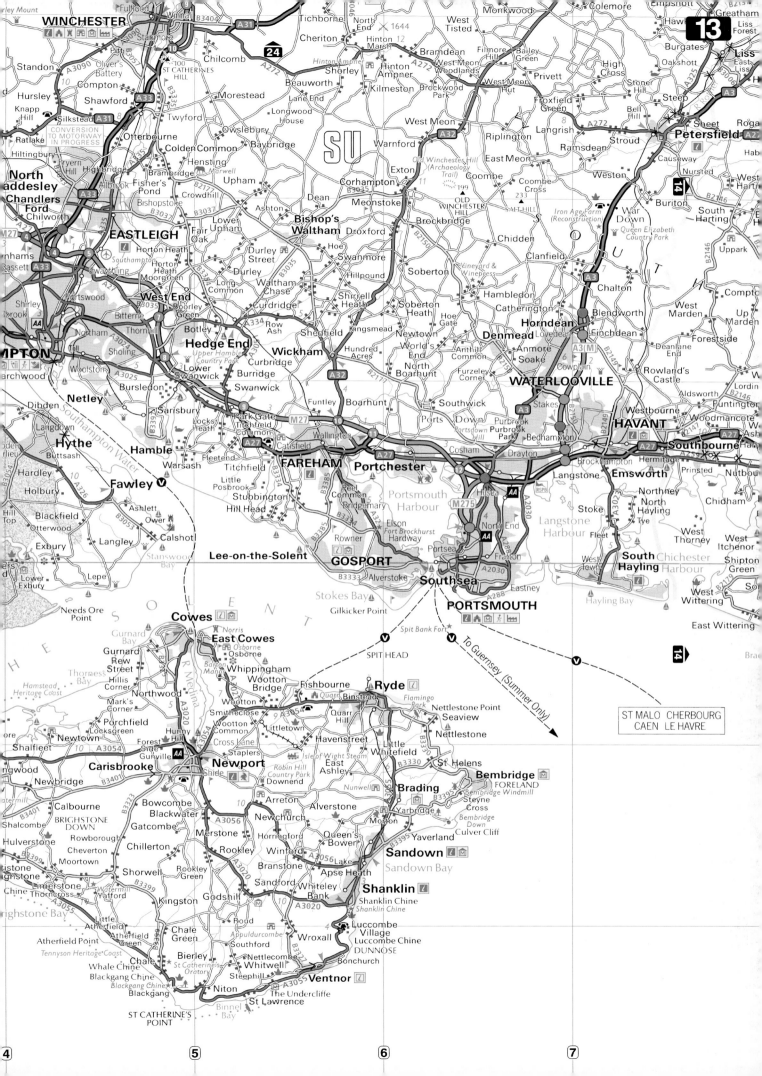

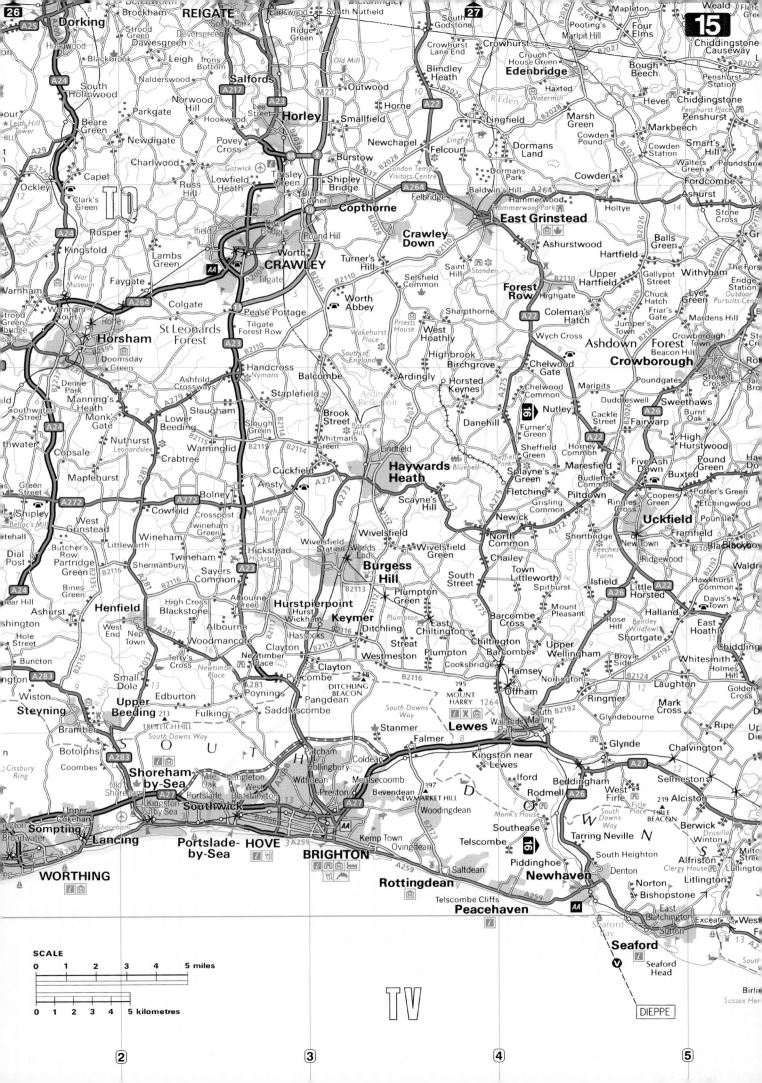

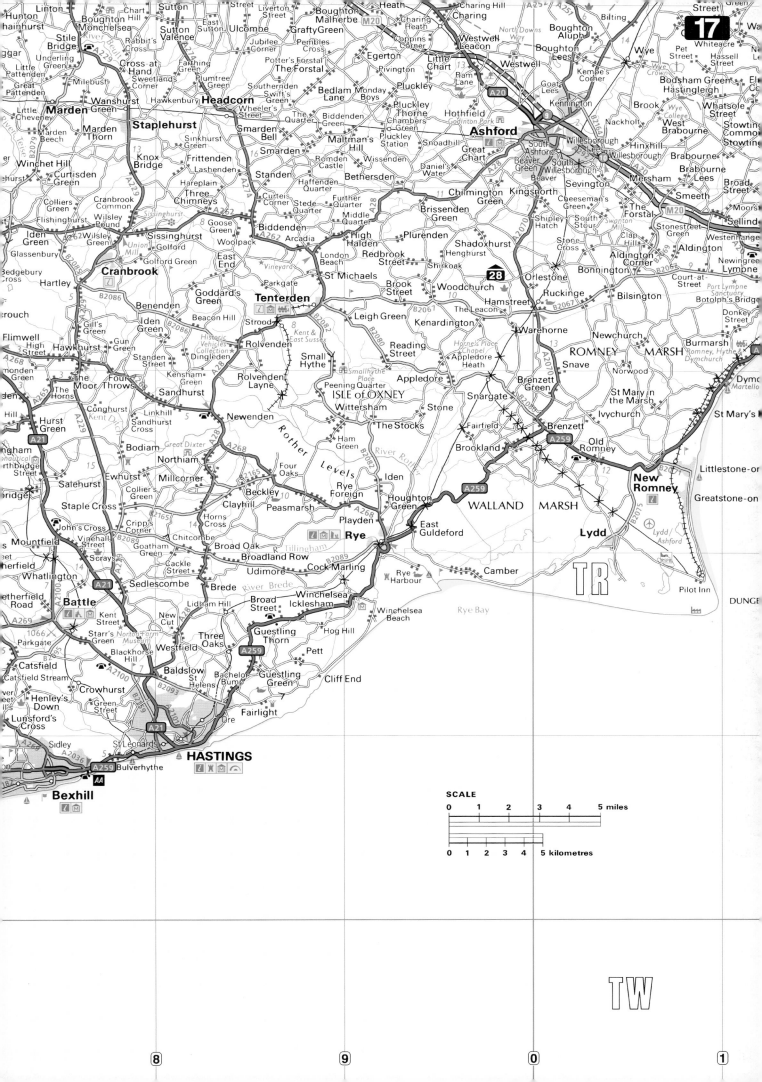

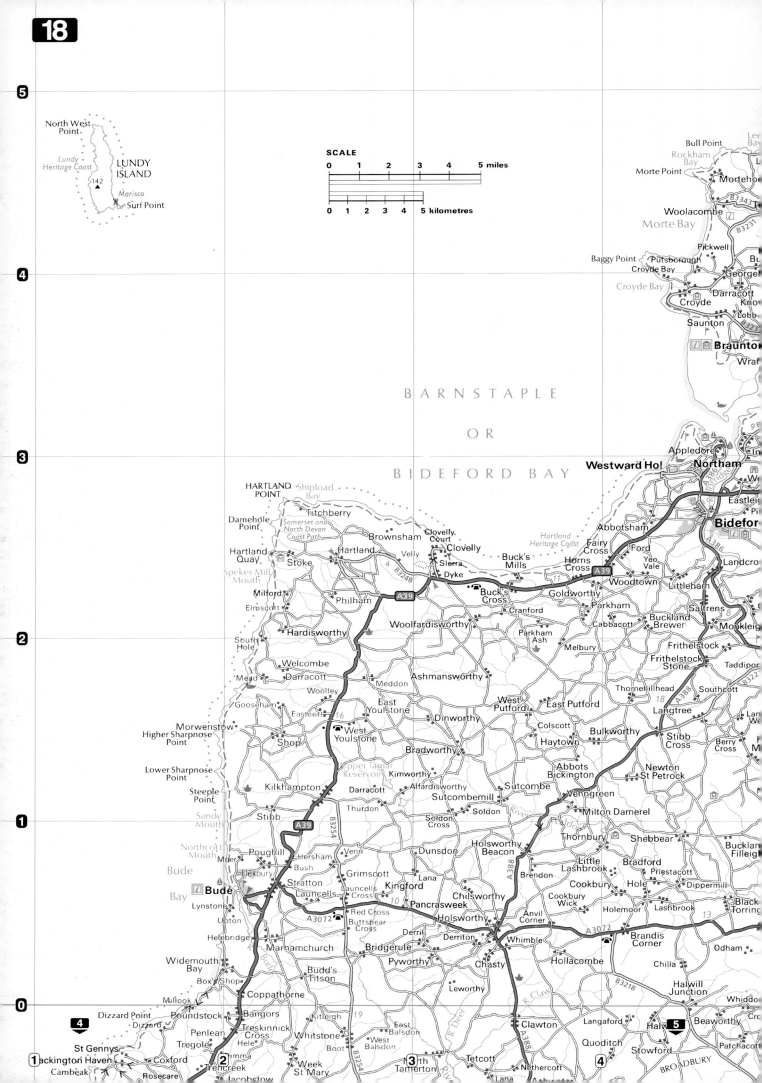

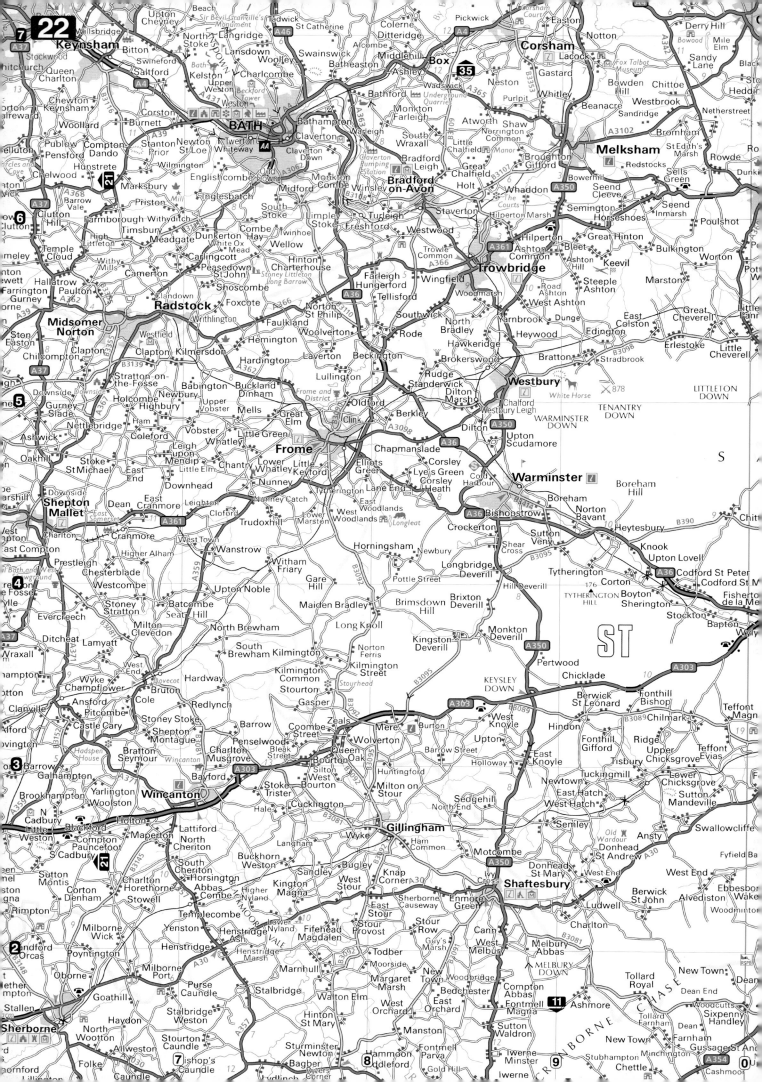

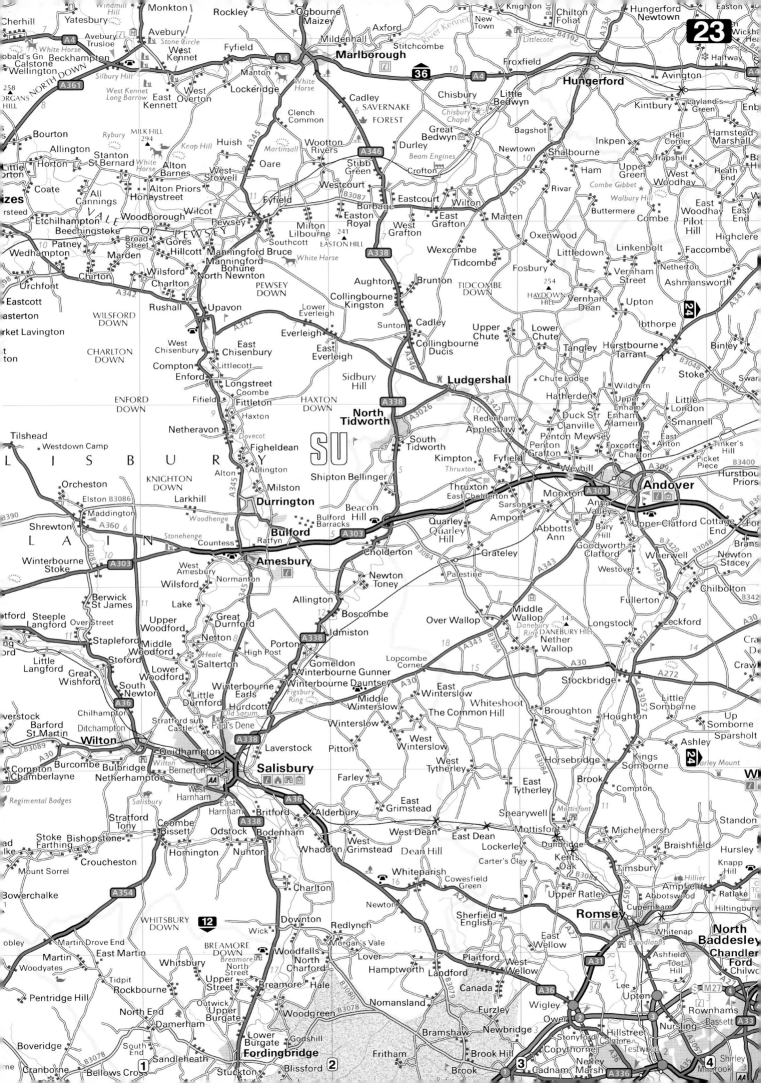

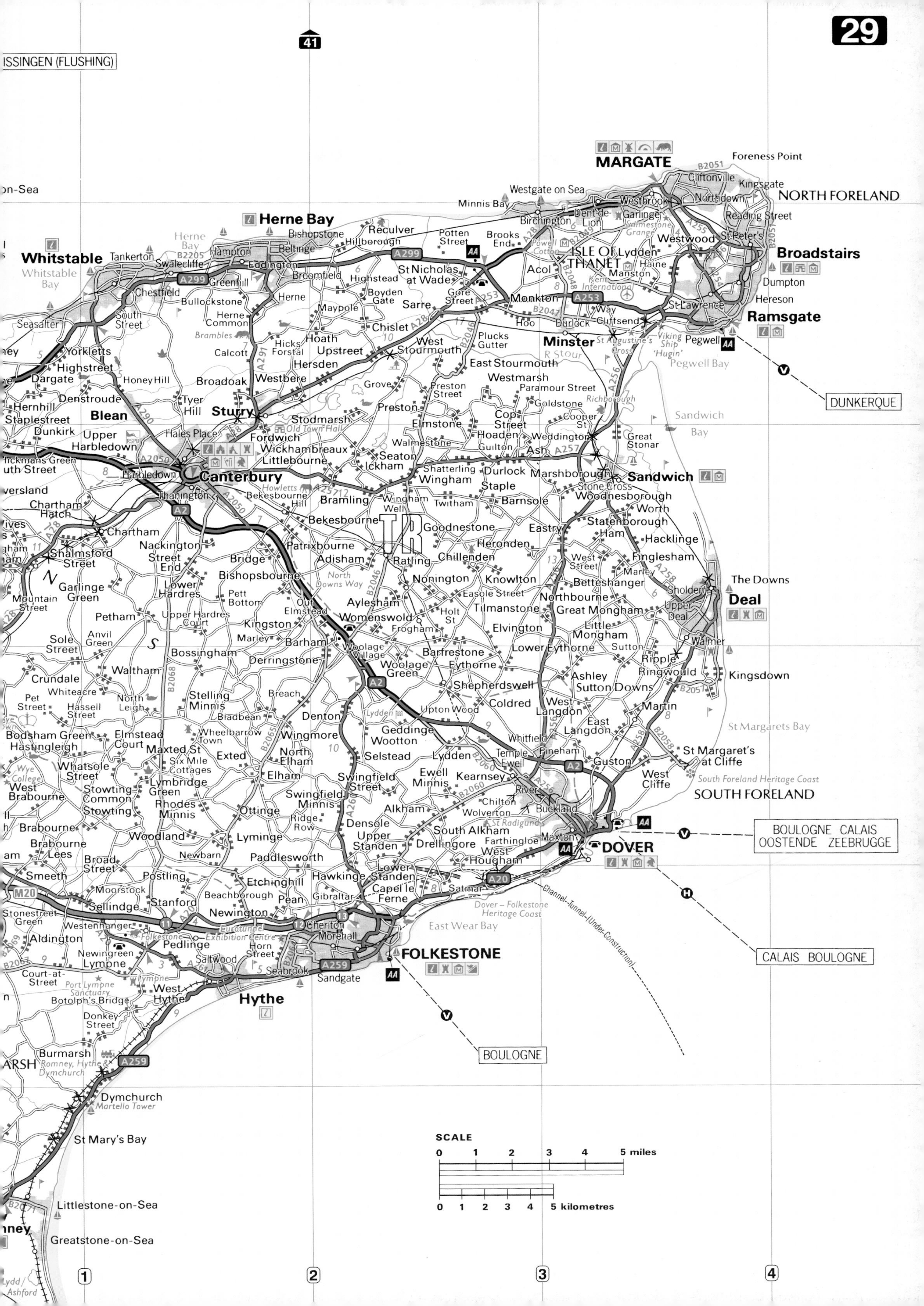

ISSINGEN (FLUSHING)

on-Sea

MARGATE
Foreness Point
Westgate on Sea
Cliftonville Kingsgate
Minnis Bay
Westbrook Northdown **NORTH FORELAND**
Birchington Dent-de- Garlinge
Herne Bay Lion Reading Street
Bishopstone Reculver Potten Brooks Powell Westwood St Peter's
Hilborough Street End Cotton
Herne Hampton Beltinge Kent
Bay Grange
Whitstable Tankerton Greenhill St Nicholas Westbrook **Broadstairs**
Whitstable Swalecliffe at Wade Highstead ISLE OF Lydden
Bay Chestfield Boyden Sarre Acol **THANET** Haine Dumpton
Seasalter South Broomfield Gate Gore Street Monkton Manston Hereson
Street Bullockstone Herne Maypole Chislet Hoo Durlock Cliffsend St Lawrence **Ramsgate**
Yorkletts Herne Hoath Upstreet West **Minster** Viking Pegwell
Highstreet Common Calcott Hersden Stourmouth Plucks R Stour Ship
Dargate Honey Hill Broadoak Westbere Gutter St Augustine's 'Hugin' Pegwell Bay
Hernhill Tyer Grove East Stourmouth Cross
Denstroude Hill **Sturry** Preston Westmarsh Richborough **DUNKERQUE**
Staplestreet **Blean** Stodmarsh Paramour Street Sandwich
Dunkirk Upper Hales Place Fordwich Preston Goldstone Bay
Harbledown Wickhambreaux Cop Cooper
versland Harbledown **Canterbury** Littlebourne Seaton Hoaden Street St Great Stonar
Chartham Thanington Ickham Guilton Weddington
Hatch Bekesbourne Walmestone Ash A257 **Sandwich**
ives Chartham Bekesbourne Hill Shatterling Durlock Marshborough
Shalmsford Bramling Wingham Staple Woodnesborough
Street Patrixbourne Twitham Barnsole Worth
N Nackington Bishopsbourne Adisham Wingham Statenborough
Garlinge Street Bridge Well Goodnestone Eastry Ham Hacklinge
Green End Ratling Heronden Finglesham
Mountain Lower Pett Chillenden Betteshanger **Deal**
Street Petham Hardres Bottom Out Knowlton West Marley The Downs
Sole Elmstead Aylesham Nonington Street Sholden
Street Kingston Womenswold Easole Street Northbourne Upper
Crundale Anvil Marley Holt Tilmanstone Great Mongham Deal
Pet Whiteacre Green Barham St Frogham Deal Walmer
Street Hassell Bossingham Derringstone Woolage Elvington Little
Waltham North Village Barfreston Lower Eythorne Mongham Ripple Ringwould
Bodsham Green Leigh Breach Woolage Eythorne Ashley Sutton Kingsdown
Hastingleigh Stelling Green Shepherdswell Sutton Downs
Elmstead Minnis Bladbean Coldred West Martin
Whatsole Court Maxted St Denton Langdon
Street Six Mile Wingmore Geddinge East St Margarets Bay
West Stowting Cottages North Wootton Whitfield Langdon
Brabourne Common Wheelbarrow Elham Selstead Lydden West South Foreland Heritage Coast
Stowting Town Upton Wood Temple Cliffe St Margaret's
Brabourne Rhodes Exted Swingfield Ewell Ewell Pineham **SOUTH FORELAND** at Cliffe
am Lees Minnis Ottinge Street Minnis Kearsney Guston
Broad Woodland Elham Swingfield River West
Street Lyminge Minnis Alkham Chilton **DOVER** Cliffe **BOULOGNE CALAIS**
Smeeth Newbarn Ridge Densole Wolverton Buckland Maxton **OOSTENDE ZEEBRUGGE**
M20 Paddlesworth Row Upper South Alkham Farthingloe West
Postling Etchinghill Standen Drellingore Hougham **CALAIS BOULOGNE**
Stonestreet Moorstock Hawkinge Lower-
Green Stanford Beachborough Pean Capel le Standen
Sellindge Newington Gibraltar Ferne Satmar
Aldington Westenhanger 11 Euratunnel East Wear Bay
Lympne Folkestone Cheriton Morehall Dover-Folkestone
Newingreen Pedlinge Exhibition Centre **FOLKESTONE** Heritage Coast
Court-at- Lympne Horn Channel-Tunnel-(Under-Construction)
Street Port Lympne Saltwood Street
Sanctuary West Seabrook Sandgate
Donkey Hythe
Street **Hythe** **BOULOGNE**

Burmarsh Romney, Hythe
RSH & Dymchurch
Dymchurch
Martello Tower

St Mary's Bay

Littlestone-on-Sea
nney
Greatstone-on-Sea

SCALE

0 1 2 3 4 5 miles

0 1 2 3 4 5 kilometres

Lydd/
Ashford

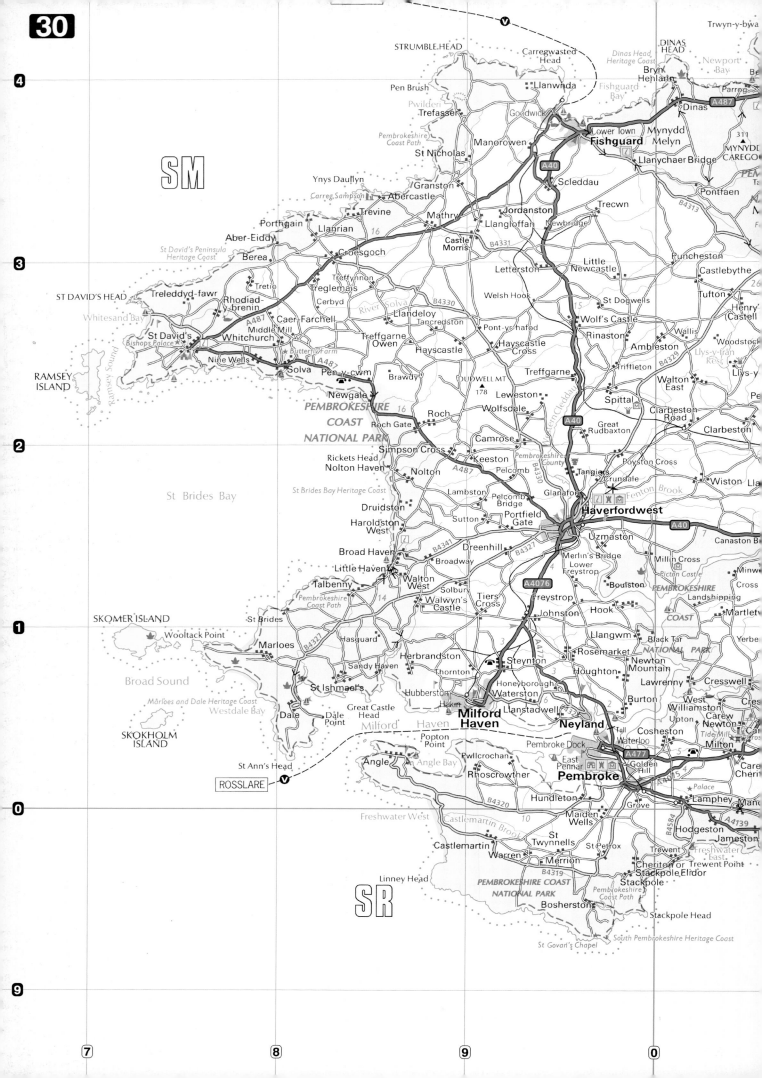

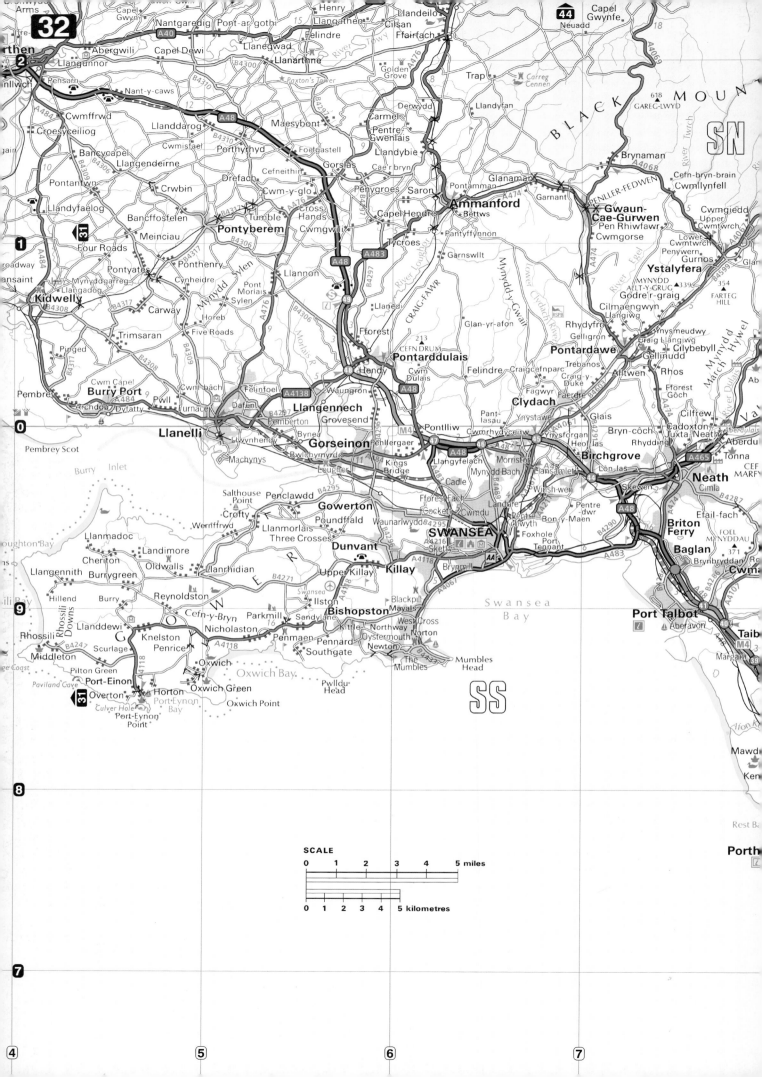

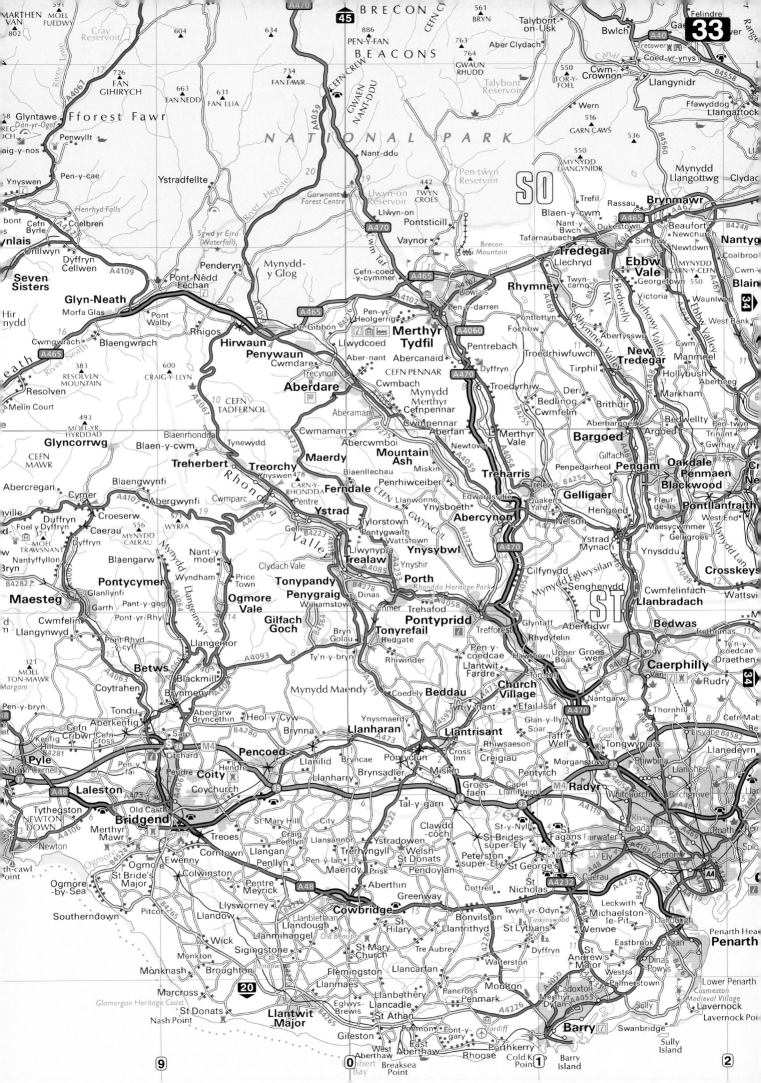

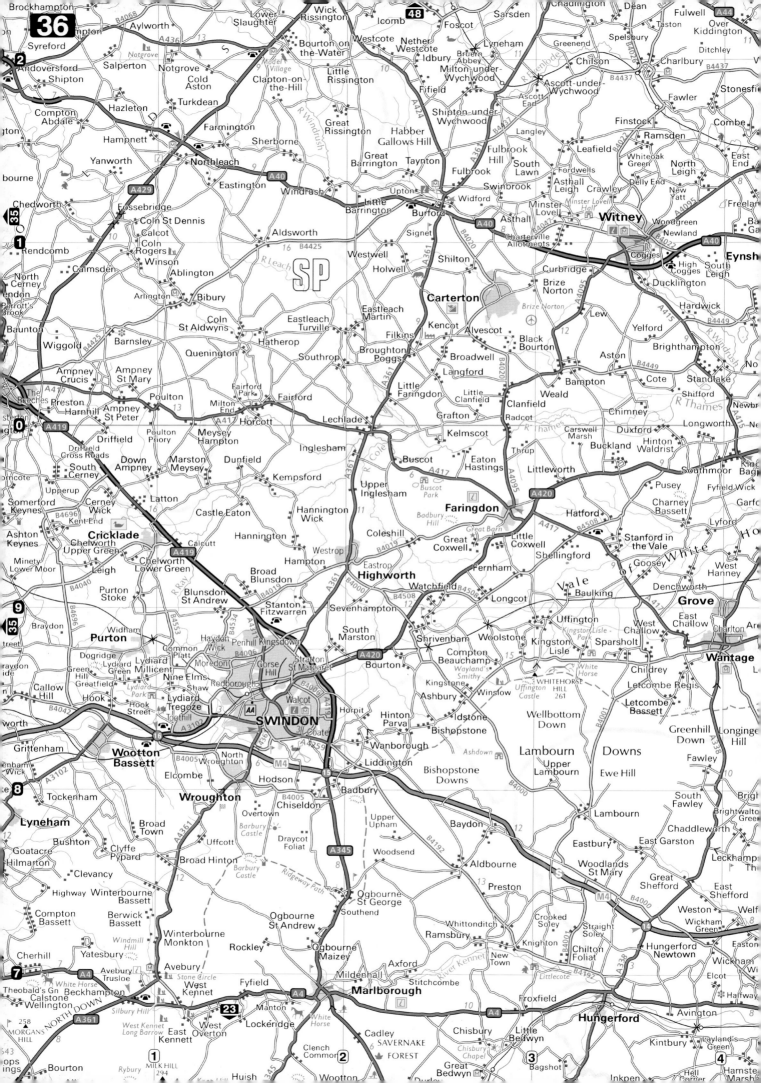

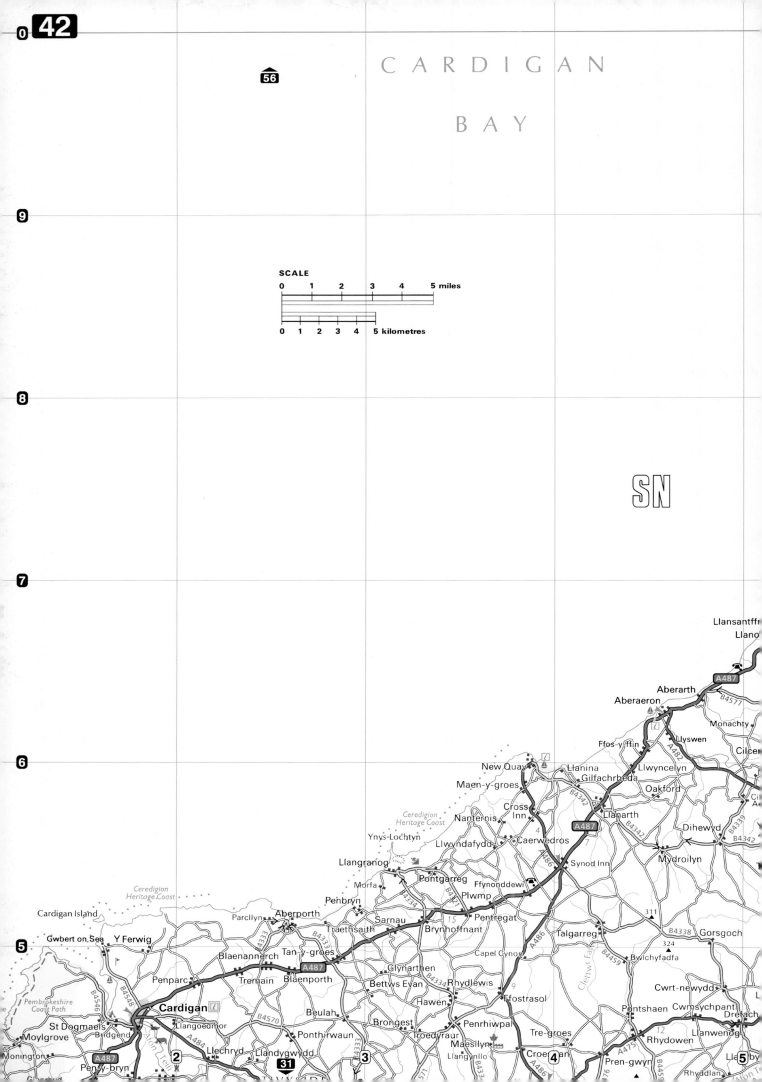

C A R D I G A N

B A Y

9

SCALE

0   1   2   3   4   5 miles

0   1   2   3   4   5 kilometres

8

SN

7

Llansantffr
Llano

A487

Aberarth
Aberaeron

Monachty

Ffos-y-ffin   Llyswen

New Quay   Llanina   Llwyncelyn   Cilce

Maen-y-groes   Gilfachrheda

Oakford   Ci
A

Cross   B4342

Nanternis   Inn   Llanarth

Ceredigion   A487   Dihewyd   B4342

Heritage Coast   Caerwedros   B4342

Ynys-Lochtyn   Llwyndafydd   Mydroilyn

Llangranog   Synod Inn

Morfa   Pontgarreg   311

Penbryn   Ffynonddewi

Ceredigion   Plwmp

Heritage Coast   15   Pentregat   B4338

Cardigan Island   Parcllyn   Aberporth   Sarnau   Talgarreg   Gorsgoch

Gwbert on Sea   Y Ferwig   Traethsaith   Brynhoffnant   324

5   Capel Cynon   Bwlchyfadfa

Pembrokeshire   Blaenannerch   Tan-y-groes

Coast Path   A487   Glynarthen   Cwrt-newydd

Penparc   Bettws Evan   Rhydlewis   Pontshaen   Cwmsychpant

Tremain   Blaenporth   Efostrasol   Drefach

St Dogmaels   Beulah   Hawen   Tre-groes   Llanwenog

Moylgrove   Cardigan   Brongest   Penrhiwpal   Rhydowen   Lla
5

Monington   Langoedmor   Ponthirwaun   Troedyraur   Maesllyn   Croe   Pren-gwyn

Pen-y-bryn   A487   Llechryd   Llandygwydd   Llangynllo   Rhyddlan

2   31   3   4   5

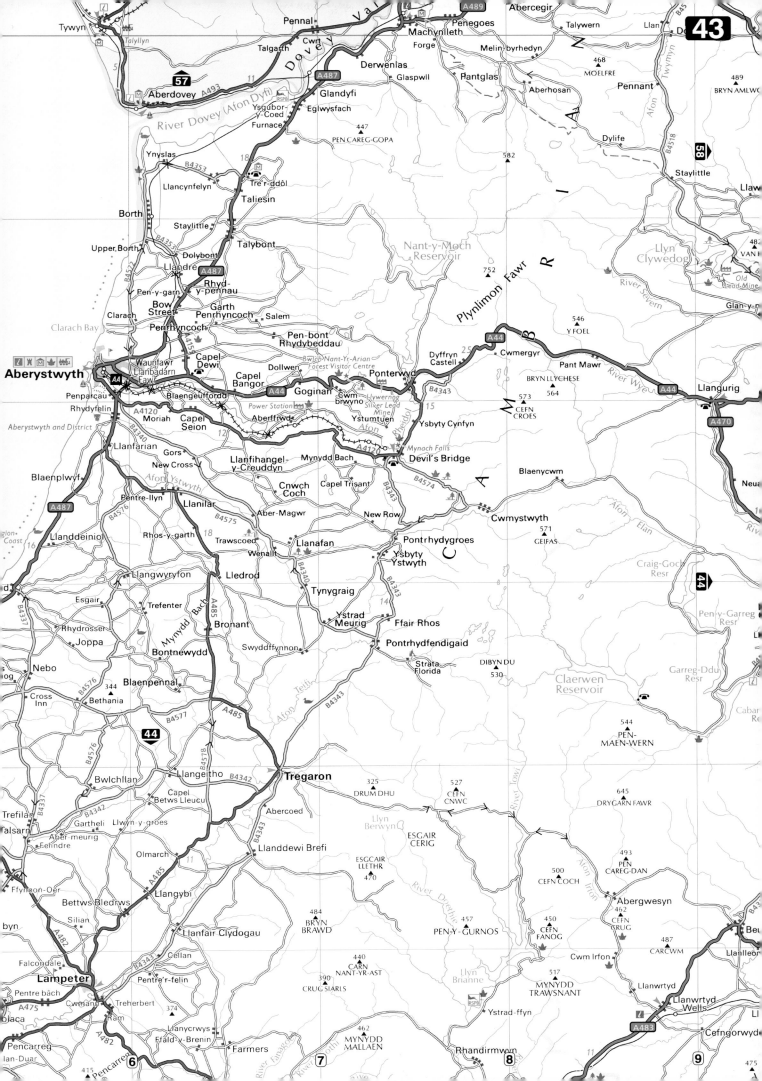

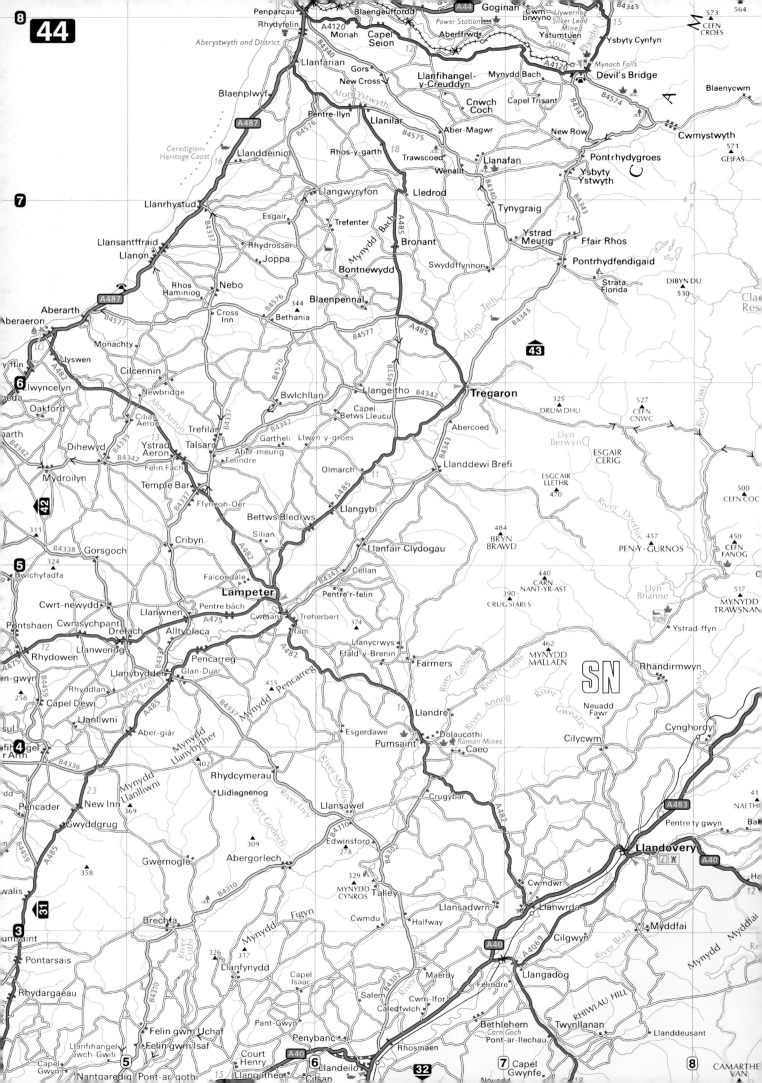

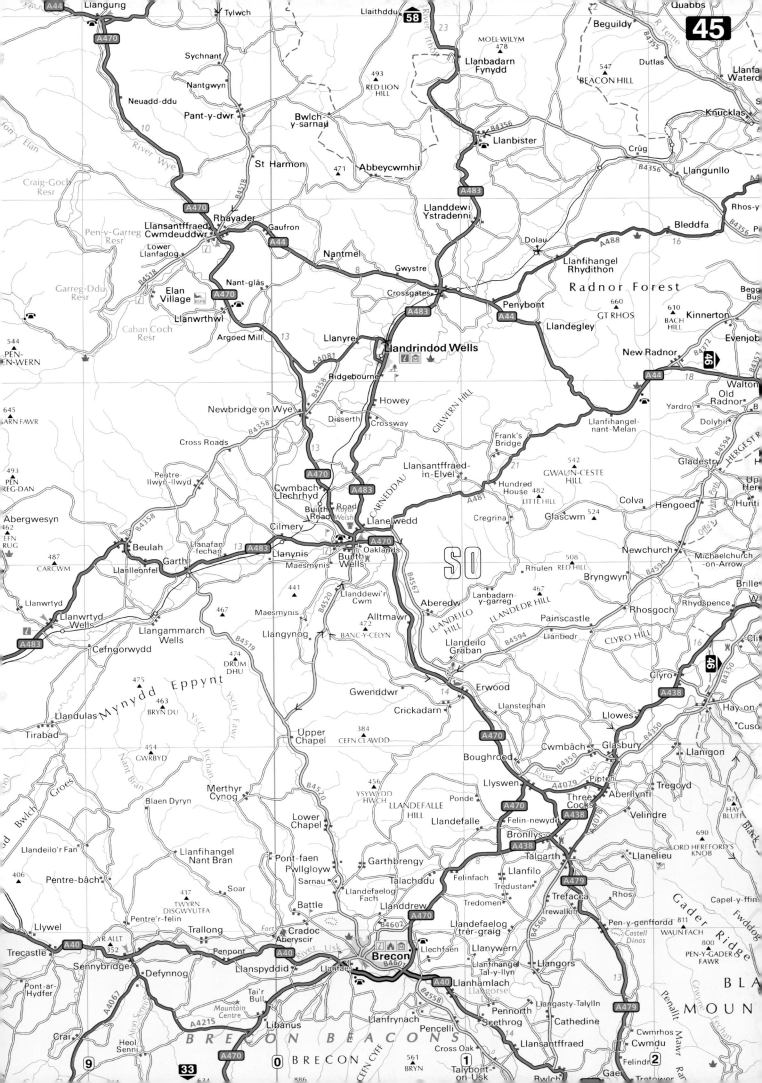

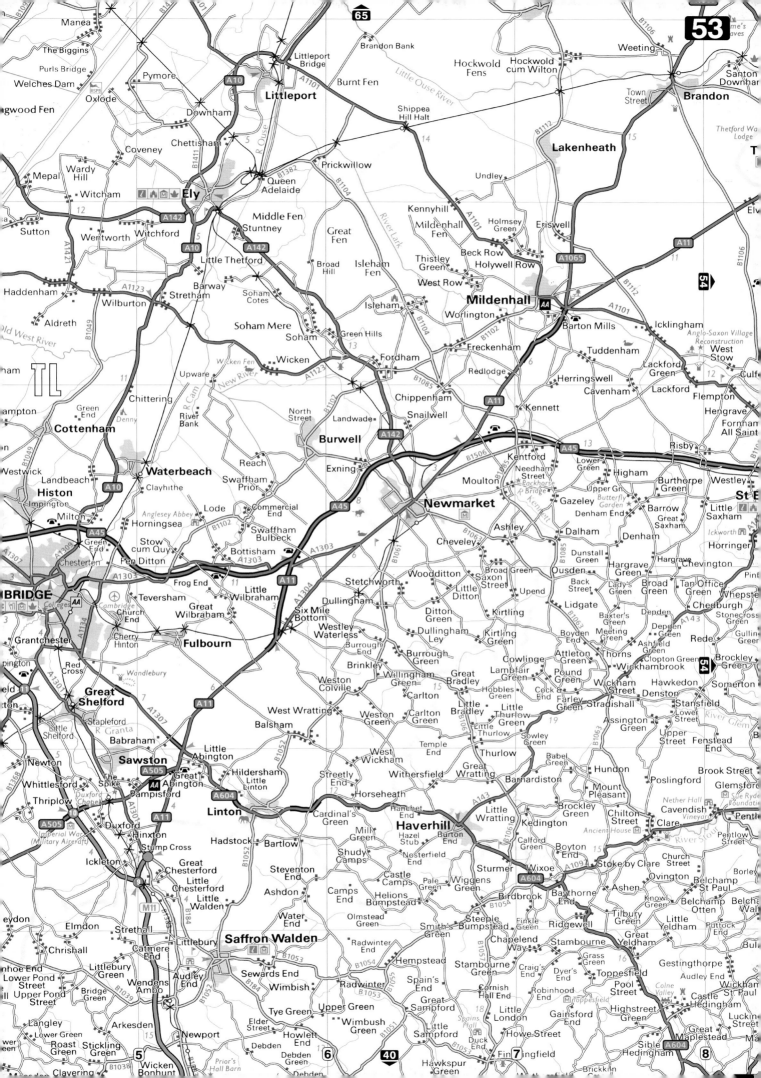

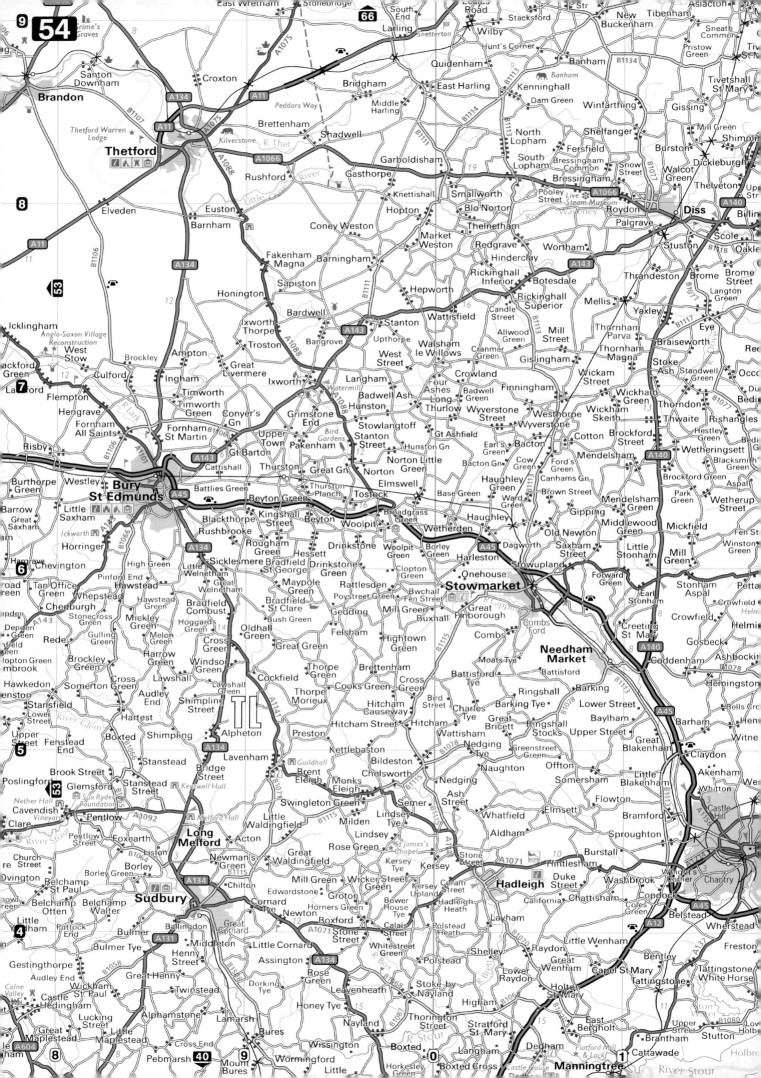

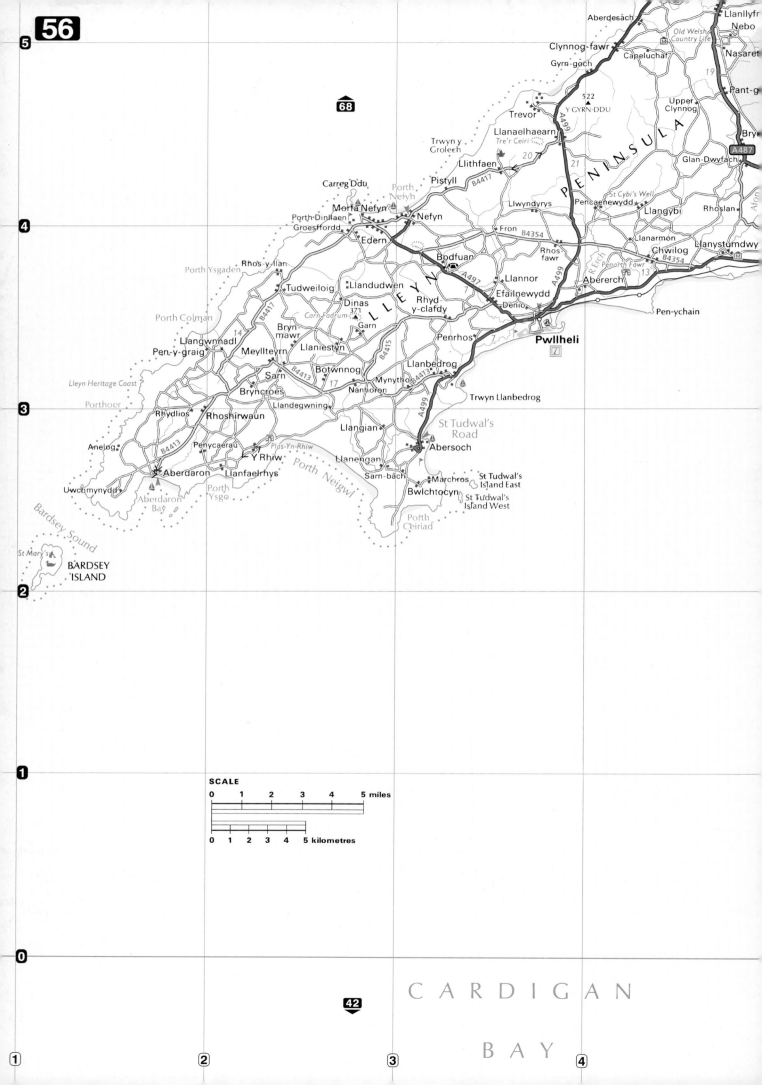

68

5

4

3

2

1

0

1   2   3   4

Aberdesách
Llanllyfr
Nebo
Clynnog-fawr
Gyrn-goch
Capeluchaf
Nasaret
Old Welsh
Country Life
522
Y GYRN-DDU
Upper
Clynnog
Pant-g
Trevor
Glan-Dwyfach
Bry
A499
Llanaelhaearn
19
PENINSULA
A487
Trwyn y
Grolech
Tre'r Ceiri
20
21
Rhoslan
Llithfaen
B4417
St Cybi's Well
Pistyll
Pencaenewydd
Llangybi
Carreg Ddu
Llwyndyrys
Porth
Nefyn
Morfa Nefyn
Nefyn
Fron
B4354
Llanarmon
Chwilog
Llanystumdwy
Porth Dinllaen
Rhos
fawr
R Erch
Penarth Fawr
B4354
Groesffordd
Edern
Bodfuan
A497
Abererch
13
Rhos-y-llan
Porth Ysgaden
A499
LLEYN
Llannor
Pen-ychain
Llandudwen
Tudweiloig
Efailnewydd
Denio
Rhyd
y-clafdy
Porth Colman
Dinas
Carn-Fadrum
371
Garn
Penrhos
Pwllheli
Bryn-
mawr
Llaniestyn
B4417
14
Llangwnnadl
7
Meyllteyrn
Llanbedrog
Pen-y-graig
Botwnnog
B4415
Lleyn Heritage Coast
Sarn
B4413
Mynytho
B4413
Trwyn Llanbedrog
Porthoer
17
Nanhoron
Bryncroes
A499
3
Rhydlios
Llandegwning
St Tudwal's
Road
Rhoshirwaun
Llangian
Anelog
B4413
Abersoch
Penycaerau
Plas-Yn-Rhiw
Y Rhiw
Llanengan
Sarn-bach
Aberdaron
Llanfaelrhys
Marchros
St Tudwal's
Island East
Uwchmynydd
Porth Neigwl
Bwlchtocyn
St Tudwal's
Island West
Aberdaron
Bay
Porth
Ysgo
Porth
Ceiriad
Bardsey Sound
St Mary's
BARDSEY
ISLAND
2

1

CARDIGAN

42

BAY

SCALE

0   1   2   3   4   5 miles

0   1   2   3   4   5 kilometres

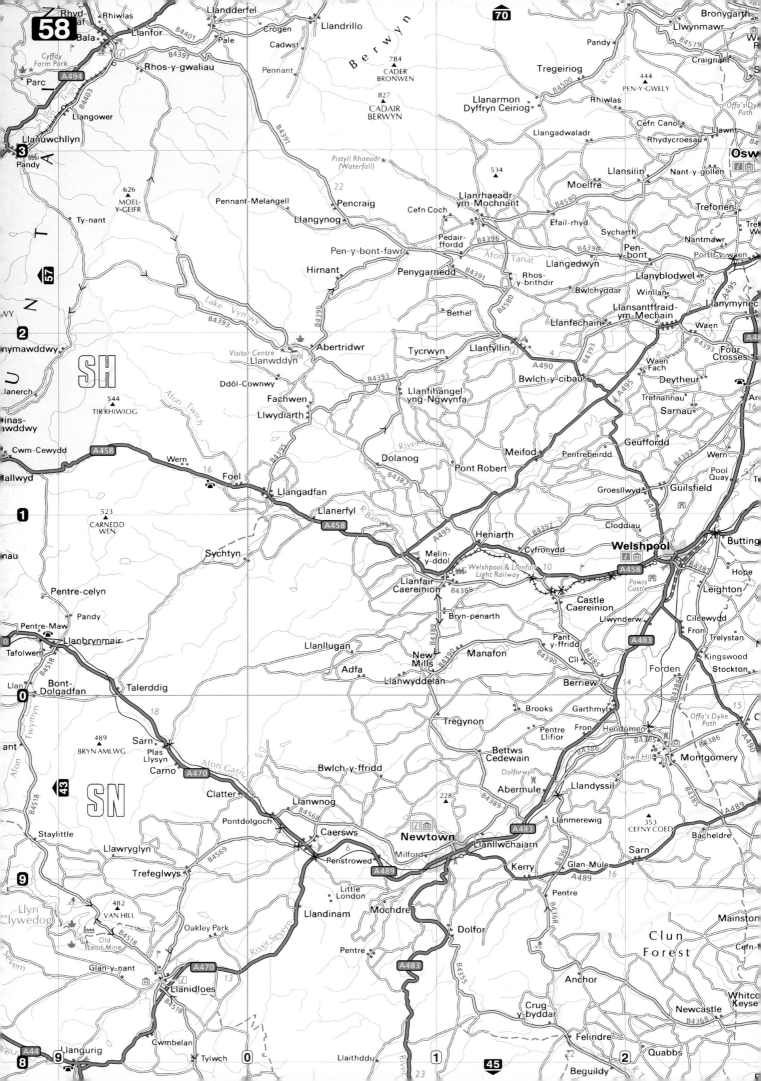

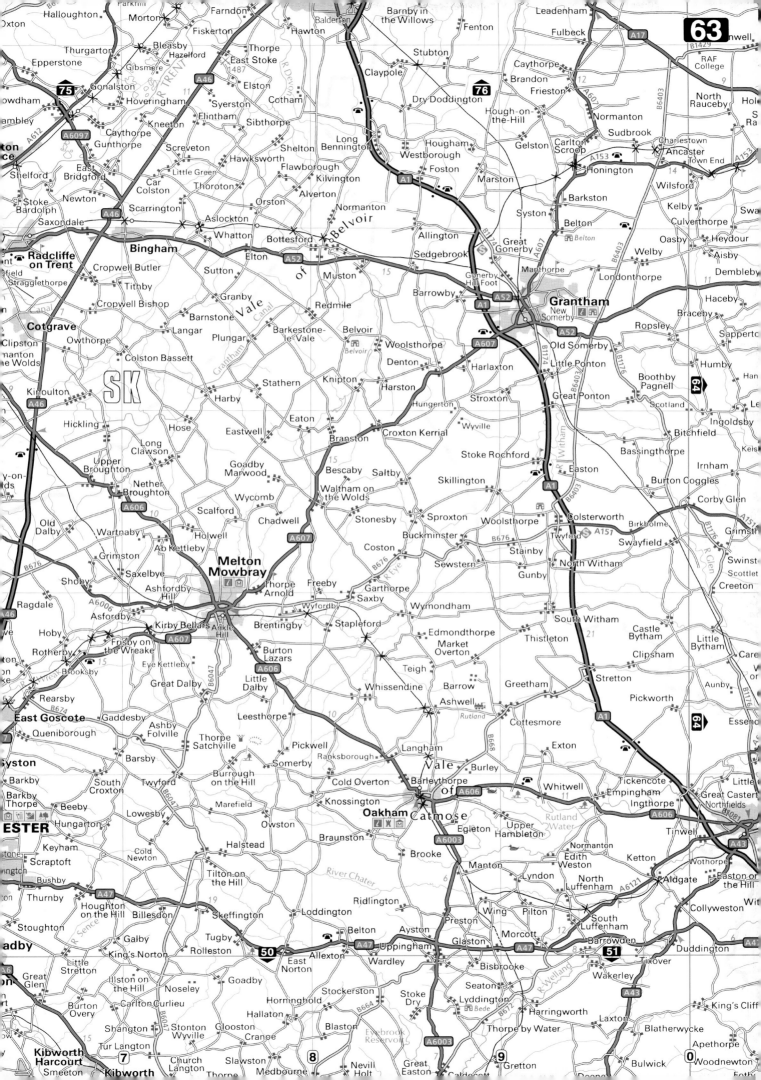

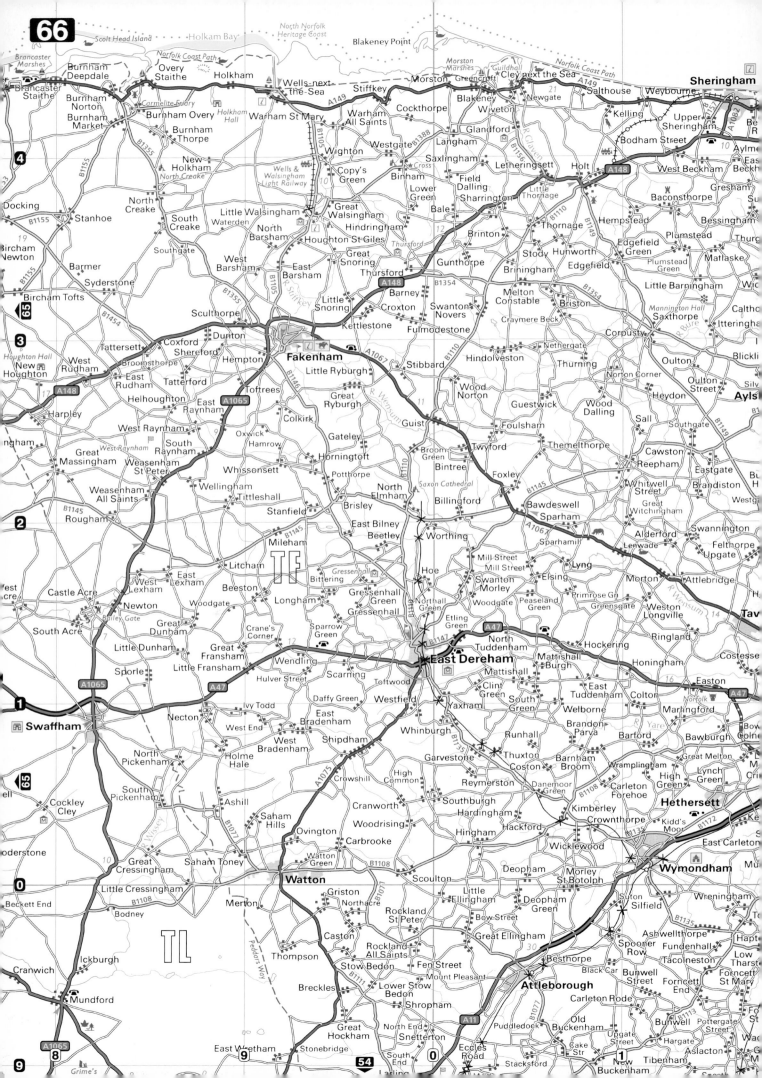

SCALE

0 1 2 3 4 5 miles

0 1 2 3 4 5 kilometres

East Runton
Cromer
Overstrand
Sidestrand
Felbrigg
Crossdale Street
Trimingham
Northrepps
Gimingham
Southrepps
Mundesley
Thorpe Market
Lower Street
Trunch
Knapton
Paston
Bacton
Bradfield
Old Hall Street
Edingthorpe
Walcott
Suffield
Antingham
Swafield
Edingthorpe Green
Witton
Ridlington
Happisburgh
Colby
Banningham
North Walsham
Spa Common
Ridlington Street
Crostwight
Whimpwell Green
Happisburgh Common
Hempstead
Tungate
Felmingham
Meeting House Hill
Honing
Lessingham
Ingham Corner
Waxham
Skeyton Corner
Bengates
Briggate
East Ruston
Ingham
Sea Palling
Burgh next Aylsham
Skeyton
Westwick
Worstead
Dilham
Stalham
Calthorpe Street
Swanton Abbot
Frankfort
Smallburgh
Stalham Green
Hickling
Oxnead
Lamas
Scottow
Sloley
Tunstead
Low Street
Pennygate
Sutton
Hickling Green
Horsey Corner
Brampton
Sco Ruston
Wood Street
Hickling Heath
Hill Common
Horsey
Buxton
Little Hautbois
Market Street
Crowgate Street
Neatishead
Barton Turf
Catfield Common
West Somerton
Stratton Strawless
St James
Catfield
Hickling Broad
Horsey Windpump
Waterloo
Horstead
Coltishall
Threehammer Common
Irstead
Sharp Green
Potter Heigham
Winterton-on-Sea
Hainford
Belaugh
Hoveton
Ludham
Martham
East Somerton
Frettenham
Wroxham
Johnson's Street
Bastwick
Cess
Newton St Faith
Crostwick
Upper Street
Horning
A1062
Repps
Hemsby
Hemsby Hole
Horsham St Faith
Spixworth
Rackheath
Salhouse
Woodbastwick
Upper Street
Thurne
Clippesby
Rollesby
Ormesby St Michael
Newport
Scratby
Broadland Conservation Centre
Burgh St Margaret
Ormesby Broad
New Rackheath
Panxworth
Town Green
Ranworth
Pilson Green
Cargate Green
California
Thorpe End
Little Plumstead
South Walsham
Upton
Billockby
Thrigby
Filby
Mautby
Ormesby St Margaret
NORWICH
Witton
Hemblington
Great Plumstead
Burlingham Green
Acle
Stokesby
West End
West Caister
Caister-on-Sea
Thorpe St Andrew
North Burlingham
Runham
Lingwood
Blofield
Beighton
Moulton St Mary
Tunstall
THE BROADS
Runham
GREAT YARMOUTH
Postwick
Damgate
Halvergate
Brundall
Strumpshaw
South Burlingham
Southtown
New Lakenham
Old Lakenham
Trowse Newton
Kirby Bedon
Surlingham
Buckenham
Southwood
Freethorpe
Wickhampton
Burgh Castle
Bramerton
Hassingham
Freethorpe Common
Berney Arms
Bradwell
Gorleston on Sea
Caister St Edmund
Framingham Pigot
Rockland St Mary
Cantley
Southwood
Witton Green
Pettitts Crafts
Belton
Elm Grove
Dunston
Armingham
Framingham Earl
Claxton
Carleton St Peter
Limpenhoe
Langley Street
Reedham
Hobland Hall
Upper Stoke
Stoke Holy Cross
Yelverton
Ashby St Mary
Hardley Street
Nogdam End
Fritton
Swainsthorpe
Howe
Alpington
Mill Common
Thurton
Norton Subcourse
Lower Thurlton
St Olaves
Lound
Hopton on Sea
Hawe's Green
Shotesham
Bergh Apton
Chedgrave
Thurlton
Thorpe
Herringfleet
Somerleyton
Blundeston
Corton
Saxlingham Thorpe
Stubbs Green
High Gn
Brooke
Mundham
Loddon
Hales
Haddiscoe
Tasburgh
Saxlingham Nethergate
Kirstead Green
Seething
Raveningham
Hales Hall
Upper Tasburgh
Saxlingham Green
Thwaite St Mary
Maypole Green
Toft Monks
Wheatacre
Hempnall
Woodton
Kirby Cane
Stockton
Aldeby
Burgh St Peter
Oulton Broad
LOWESTOFT
Stratton St Michael
Fritton
Hempnall Green
Topcroft
Hedenham
Ellingham
Bull's Green
Kirkley
Morningthorpe
Lundy Green
Topcroft Street
Upgate Street
Ditchingham
Broome
Geldeston
Gillingham
Barnby
Pleasurewood Hills
Gunton
Shelton
Shelton Green
Bungay
Wainford
Shipmeadow
Worlingham
Paketield
Hardwick
Mettingham
Carlton Colville

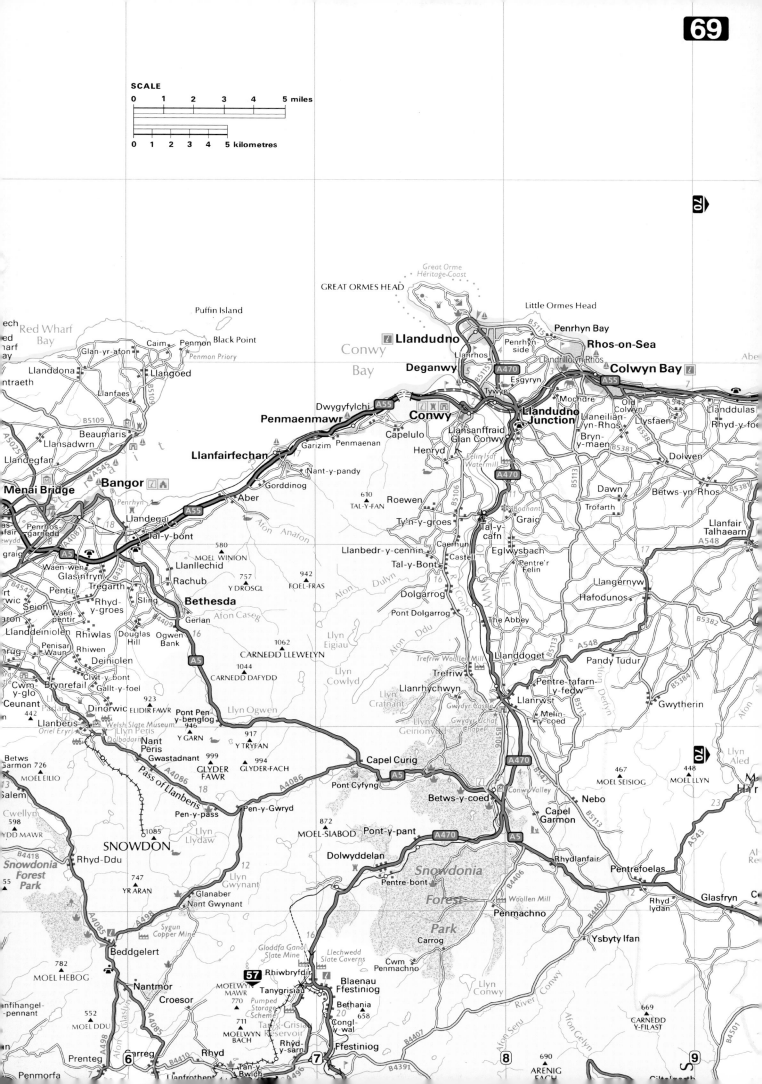

SCALE

0 1 2 3 4 5 miles

0 1 2 3 4 5 kilometres

GREAT ORMES HEAD

Great Orme
Heritage Coast

Puffin Island

Black Point

Little Ormes Head

Penrhyn Bay

Llandudno

Rhos-on-Sea

Conwy
Bay

Penrhyn-side

Llanrhos

Deganwy

Llandrillo-yn-Rhos

Colwyn Bay

Red Wharf
Bay

Caim Penmon

Glan-yr-afon

Penmon Priory

Llangoed

Esgyryn

Mochdre

Old
Colwyn

Llanddulas

Llanddona

Llanfaes

Dwygyfylchi

A55

Conwy

Llandudno
Junction

Llaneilian-
yn-Rhos

Llysfaen

Rhyd-y-foe

Penmaenmawr

Tywyn

Bryn-
y-maen

Betws-yn-Rhos

Penmaenan

Llansanffraid
Glan Conwy

Garizim

Beaumaris

Llansadwrn

Dolwen

Llanfairfechan

Henryd

Llandegfan

Nant-y-pandy

Gorddinog

Roewen

Dawn

Menai Bridge

Bangor

Aber

TAL-Y-FAN
610

Tyʼn-y-groes

Graig

Bodnant

Trofarth

Llanfair
Talhaearn

Penrhyn

Llandegai

Tal-y-
cafn

Eglwysbach

Hafodunos

Penrhos-
garnedd

Tal-y-bont

MOEL WINION

Llanbedr-y-cennin

580

Caerhun

Pentre'r
Felin

Llangernyw

Llanllechid

Castell

Waen-wen

Glasinfryn

Pentir

Rachub

Y DROSGL
757

FOEL-FRAS
942

Tal-y-Bont

The Abbey

Seion

Rhyd-
y-groes

Tregarth

Bethesda

Dolgarrog

Gwytherin

Llanddeiniolen

Gerlan

Afon Caseg

Pont Dolgarrog

Llanddoget

Pandy Tudur

Rhiwlas

Douglas
Hill

Ogwen
Bank

A5

Llyn
Eigiau

Trefriw Woollen Mill

Waen-
pentir

Penisar
Waun

Rhiwen

1062

Trefriw

Pentre-tafarn-
y-fedw

Deiniolen

CARNEDD LLEWELYN

Llyn
Cowlyd

Llanrhychwyn

Melin-
y-coed

Cwm-
y-glo

Clwt-y-bont

Gallt-y-foel

1044

CARNEDD DAFYDD

Llanrwst

Ceunant

923

Llyn Ogwen

Gwydir Castle

442

Dinorwic

ELIDIR FAWR

Pont Pen-
y-benglog

946

Gwydyr Uchaf
Chapel

Brynrefail

Welsh Slate Museum

Y GARN
917

Llyn
Geirionydd

Llanberis

Oriel Eryri

Dolbadarn

Llyn Peris

Y TRYFAN

Betws
Garmon

726

MOEL EILIO

Nant
Peris

Gwastadnant

GLYDER
FAWR
999

GLYDER-FACH
994

Capel Curig

MOEL SEISIOG
467

MOEL LLYN
448

Llyn
Aled

Pass of Llanberis

Pont Cyfyng

Conwy Valley

Nebo

Salem

Pen-y-pass

A5

Betws-y-coed

Cwellyn

598

DD MAWR

SNOWDON

1085

Pen-y-Gwryd

Llyn
Llydaw

MOEL-SIABOD
872

Pont-y-pant

Capel
Garmon

Pentrefoelas

Snowdonia
Forest Park

Rhyd-Ddu

747

YR ARAN

Llyn
Gwynant

Dolwyddelan

Rhydlanfair

Rhyd
lydan

Glasfryn

Glanaber

Nant Gwynant

Pentre-bont

Snowdonia

Forest

Woollen Mill

Beddgelert

Sygun
Copper Mine

Penmachno

Park

782

MOEL HEBOG

Nantmor

Croesor

MOELWYN
MAWR
770

Rhiwbryfdir

Gloddfa Ganol
Slate Mine

Llechwedd
Slate Caverns

Cwm
Penmachno

Carrog

Ysbyty Ifan

552

MOEL DDU

Tanygrisiau

57

Pumped
Storage
Scheme

Blaenau
Ffestiniog

Bethania

Llyn
Conwy

669

CARNEDD
Y-FILAST

Prenteg

711

MOELWYN
BACH

Rhyd-
y-sarn

Congl-
y-wal

Ffestiniog

690

ARENIG
FACH

Carreg

Rhyd

Tan-y-
Bwlch

6

7

8

9

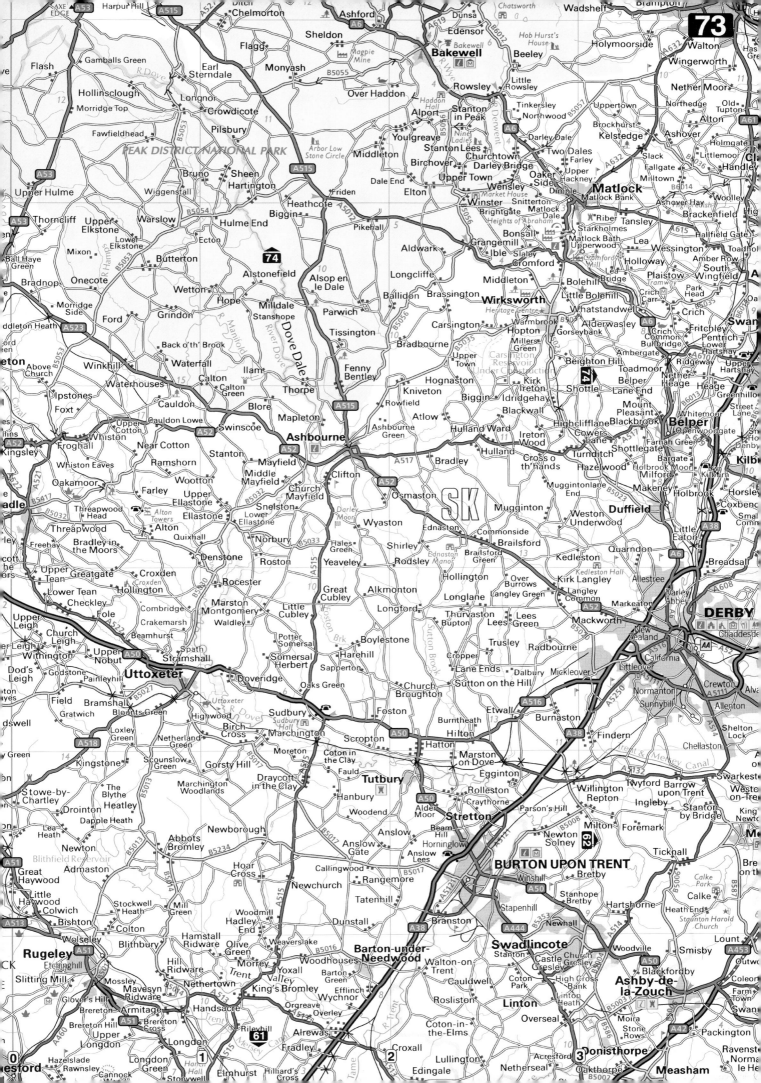

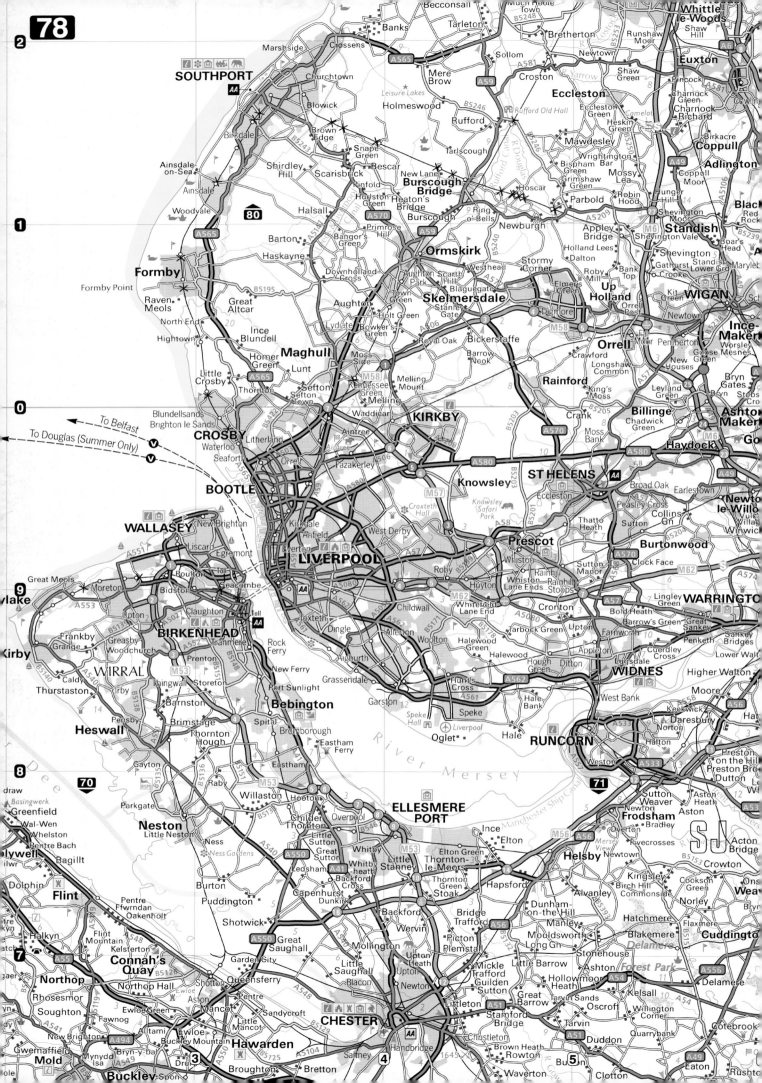

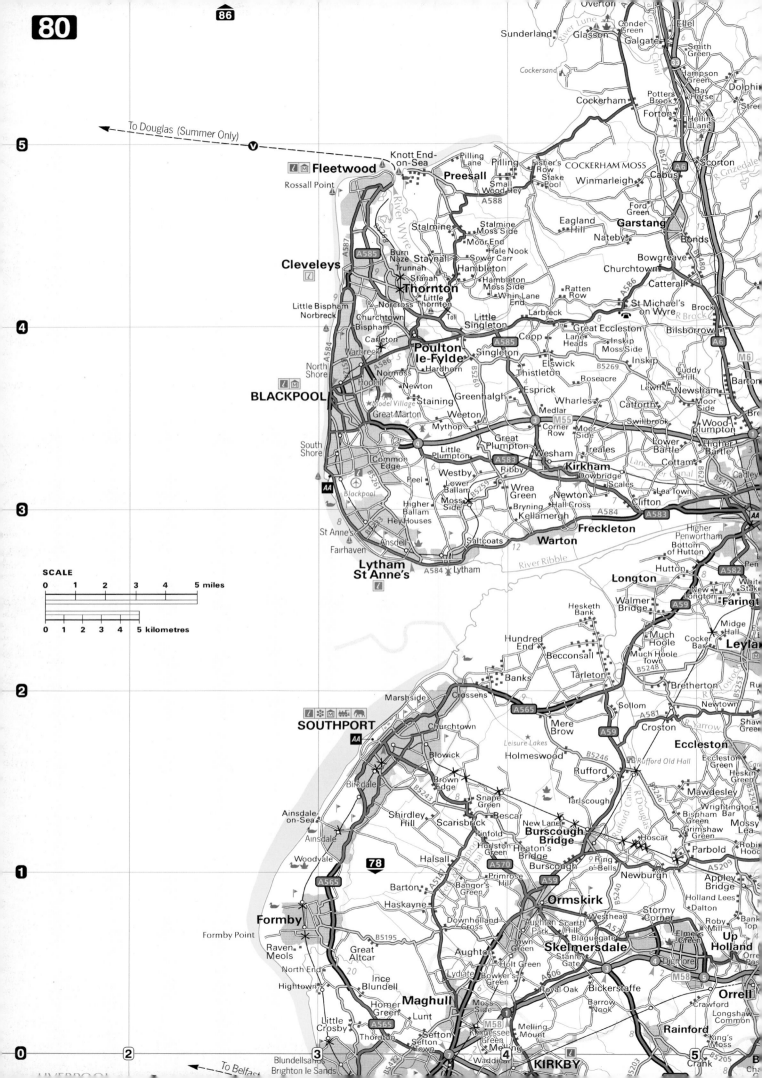

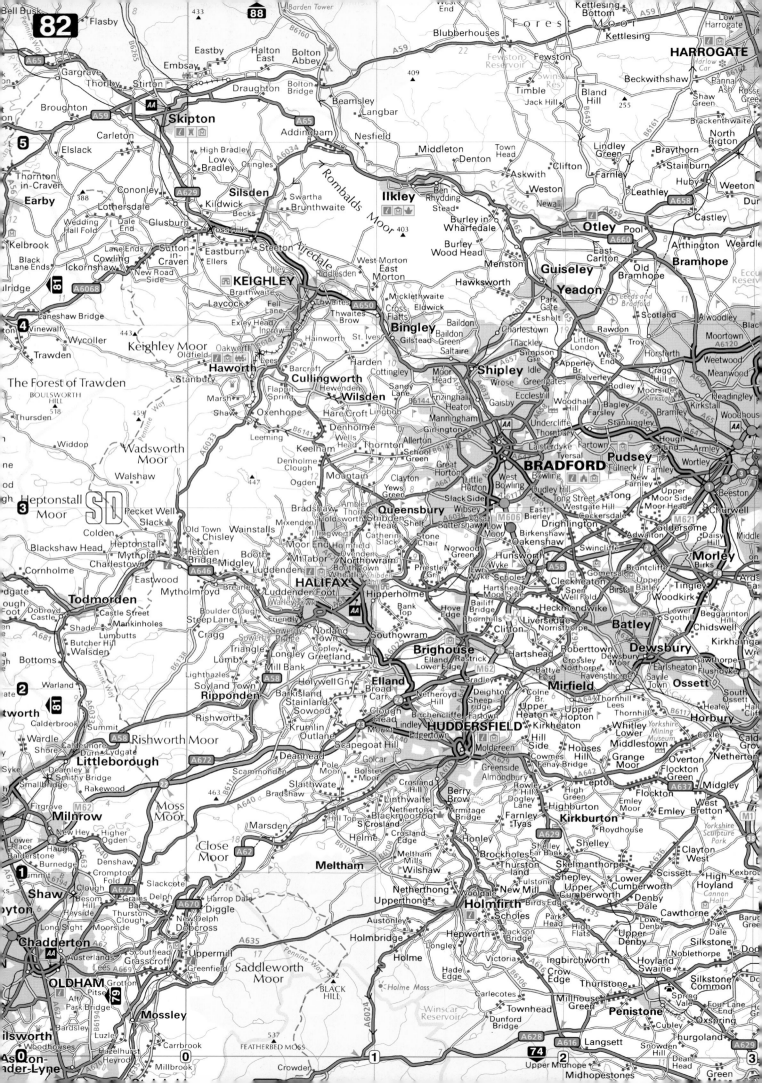

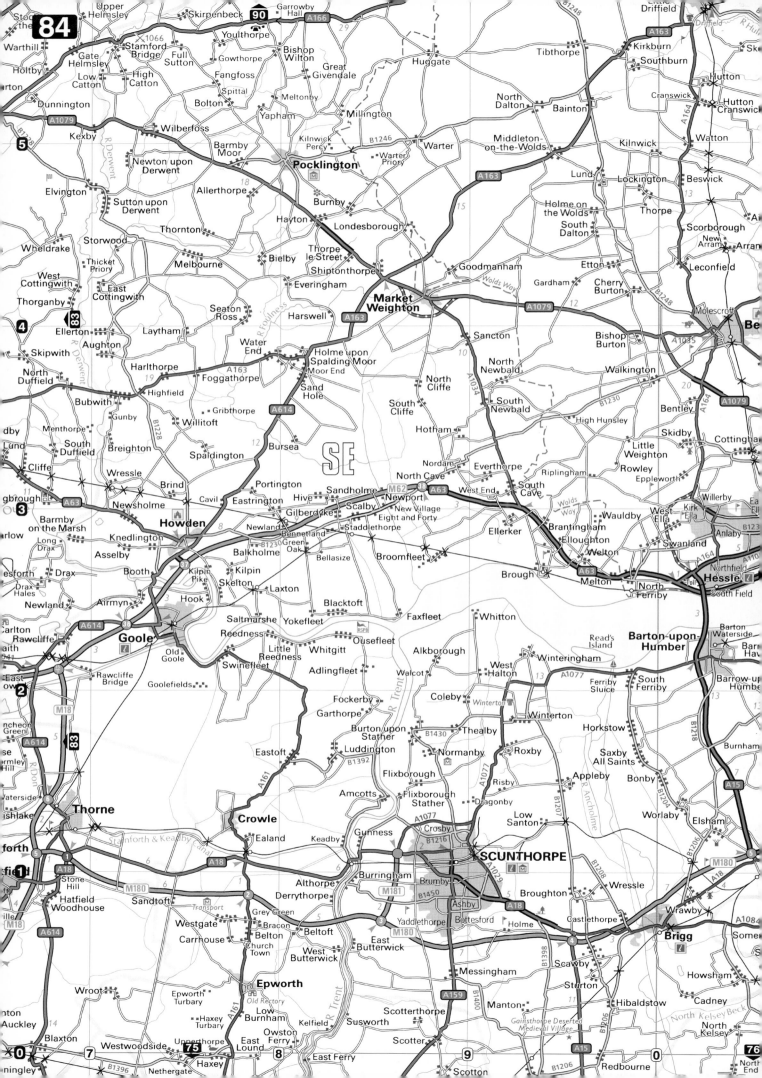

91

nsford
Gembling
Ulrome
Foston on the Wolds
Beeford
Dringhoe
Skipsea
Skipsea Brough
Upton
North Frodingham
A165
Dunnington
Atwick
Bewholme
Nunkeeling
olme
Burshill
Brandesburton
Hornsea Mere
Hornsea
RSPB
Hornsea Pottery
Leven
Catwick
Seaton
Rolston
B1244
Little Catwick
Sigglesthorne
Goxhill
Mappleton
Mappleton Sands
Little Hatfield
Routh
Long Riston
Rise
Great Hatfield
Great Cowden
B1243
North End
Arnold
B1242
Withernwick
North Skirlaugh
New Ellerby
Meaux
Marton
Aldbrough
ansey
South Skirlaugh
West Newton
East Newton
hearne
A165
Old Ellerby
Etherdwick
17
Wawne
Swine
13
Flinton
Burton Constable Hall
Garton
Grimston
Dunswell
Coniston
Thirtleby
B1238
Sproatley
Humbleton
Fitling
Hilston
B1237
Ganstead
Wyton
Lelley
Owstwick
North End
Tunstall
Sutton on Hull
Bilton
B1239
Elstronwick
Danthorpe
Stoneferry
B1220
East End
Preston
Burton Pidsea
Roos
Waxholme
A1165
AA
Marfleet
A1033
West End
Rimswell
Owthorne
A1103
KINGSTON UPON HULL
Haven Side
Hedon
Burstwick
B1362
West End
Withernsea
Paull
Thorngumbald
Halsham
East End
Hollym
Ryehill
16
Keyingham
Winestead
A1033
Holmpton
New Holland
Ottringham
A1033
North End
Goxhill
TA
Patrington
Out Newton
South End
B1445
East Halton
Welwick
Thornton Abbey
Sunk Island
Weeton
Easington
Thornton Curtis
North Killingholme
Skeffling
South End
South Killingholme
Kilnsea
Ulceby Skitter
A160
A1173
Immingham Dock
B1211
10
Ulceby
A1173
Spurn Head Heritage Coast
Habrough
Immingham
15
A180
SPURN HEAD
A180
Croxton
B1211
B1210
Stallingborough
GRIMSBY
Kirmington
Brocklesby
A18
Healing
Great Coates
ROTTERDAM (EUROPOORT)
ZEEBRUGGE
Melton Ross
Humberside
Great Limber
Keelby
Little Coates
West Marsh
Cleethorpes
12
A1173
Aylesby
Old Clee
by
Riby
A46
Nunsthorpe
Humberston
Clixby
Bradley
Scartho
A1098
Laceby
A16
sby 9
Irby upon Humber
B1203
New Waltham
Caistor
Cabourne
Swallow
7
Barnoldby le Beck
Holton le Clay
Tetney Lock
Nettleton
Cuxwold
Beelsby
Brigsley
North End
Tetney
North Cotes
A46
A1173
Hatcliffe
Ashby cum Fenby
Waithe
A1033
77
Rothwell
West Ravendale
Grainsby
A18
Marshchapel
East
B1201
Eskham

1   2   3   4

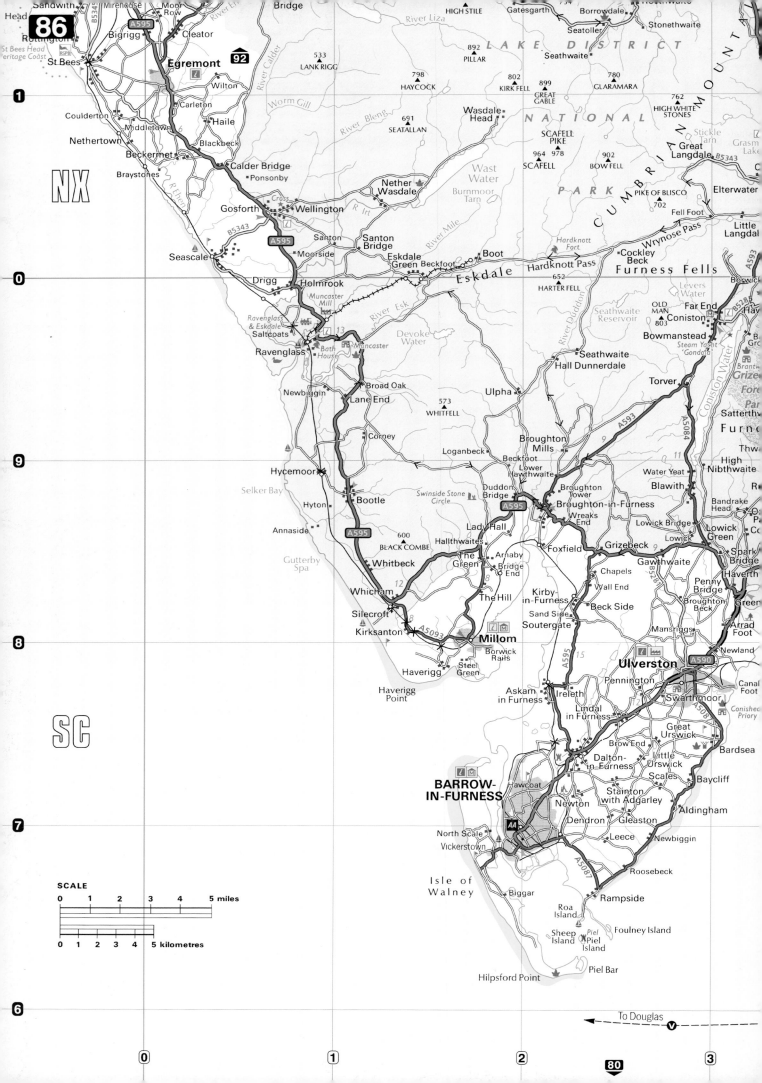

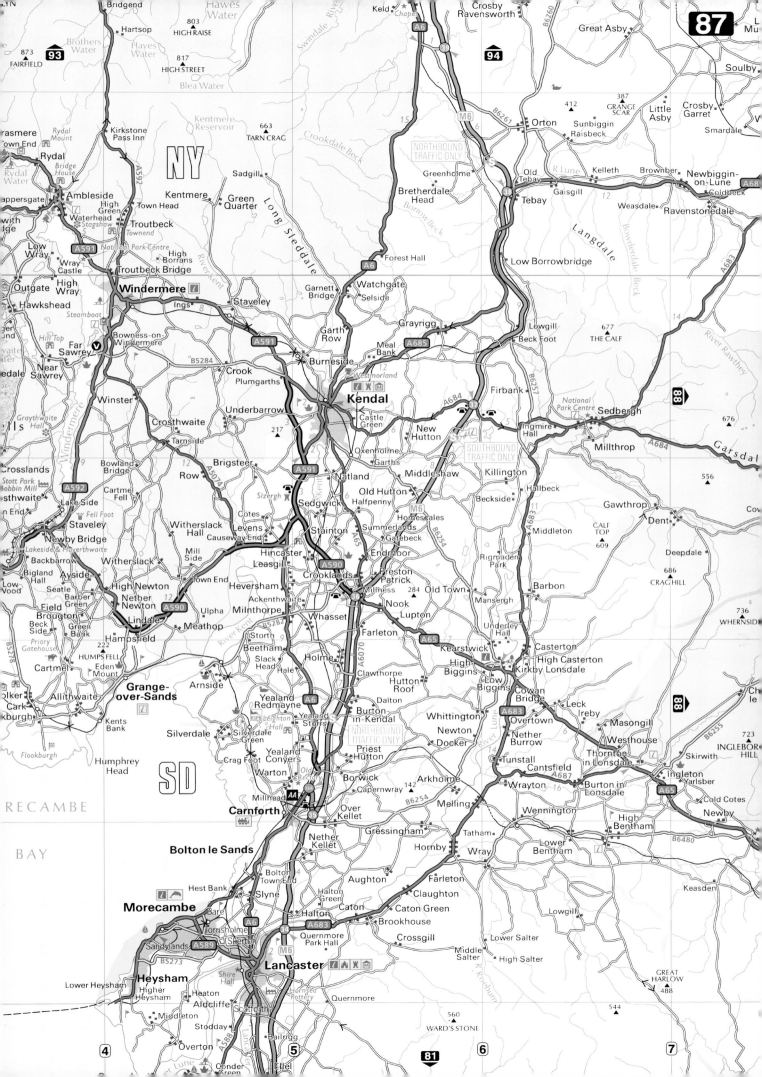

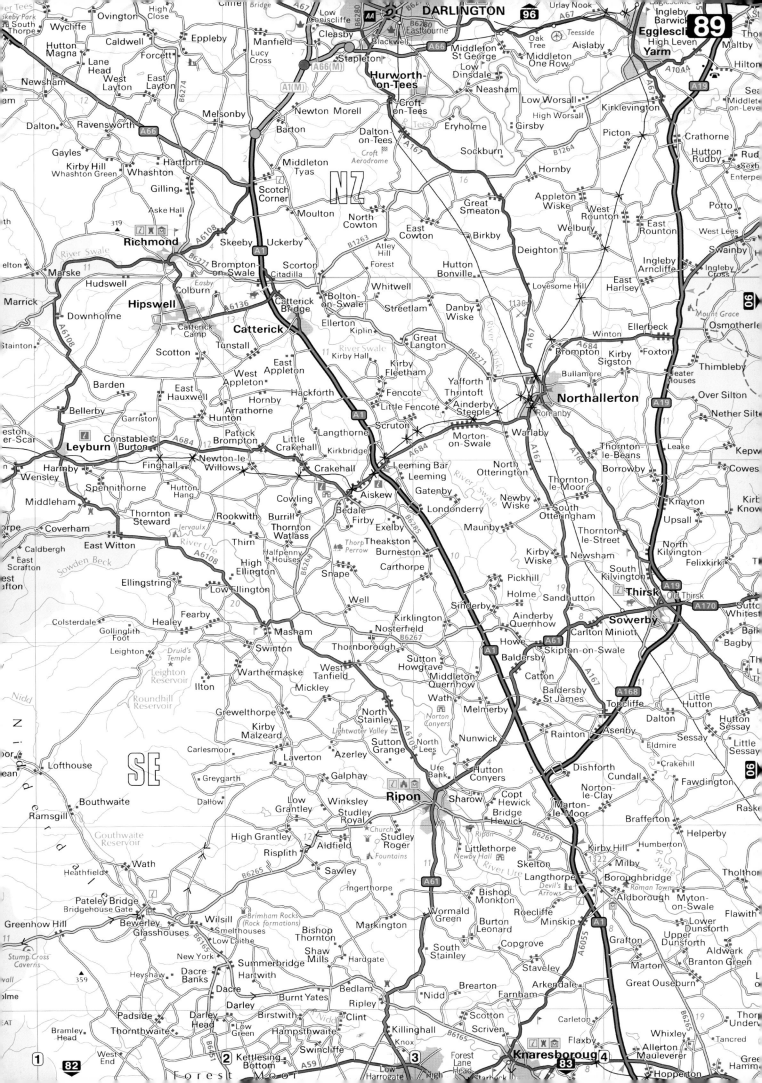

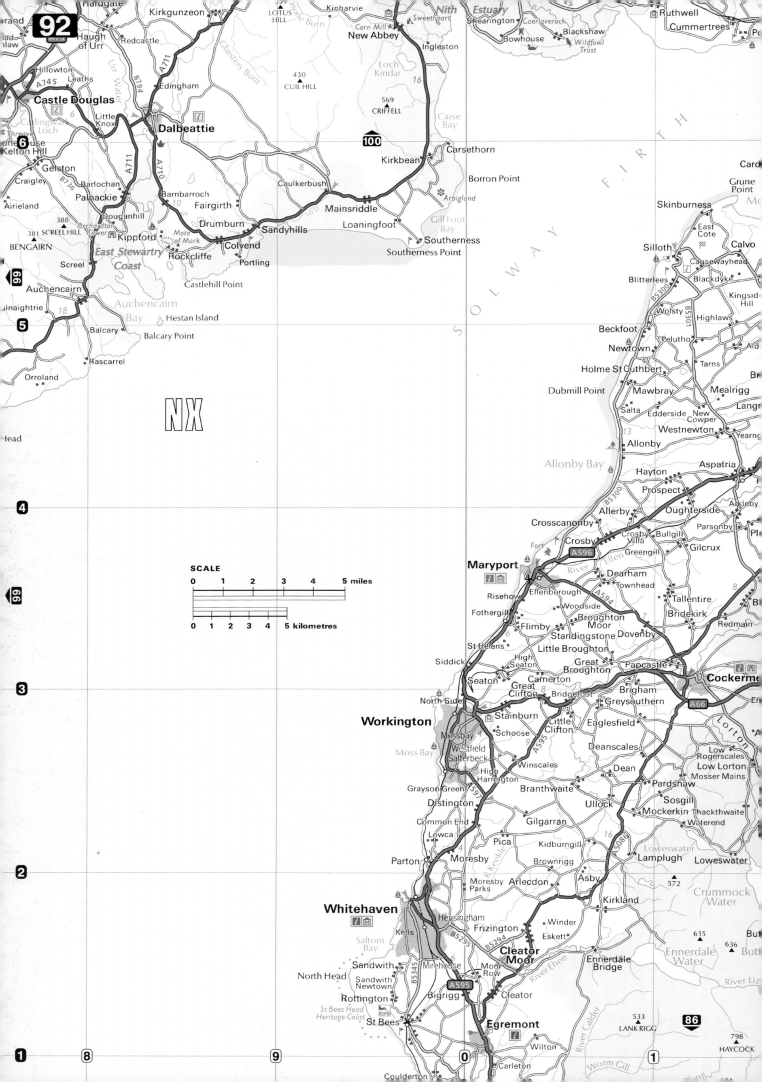

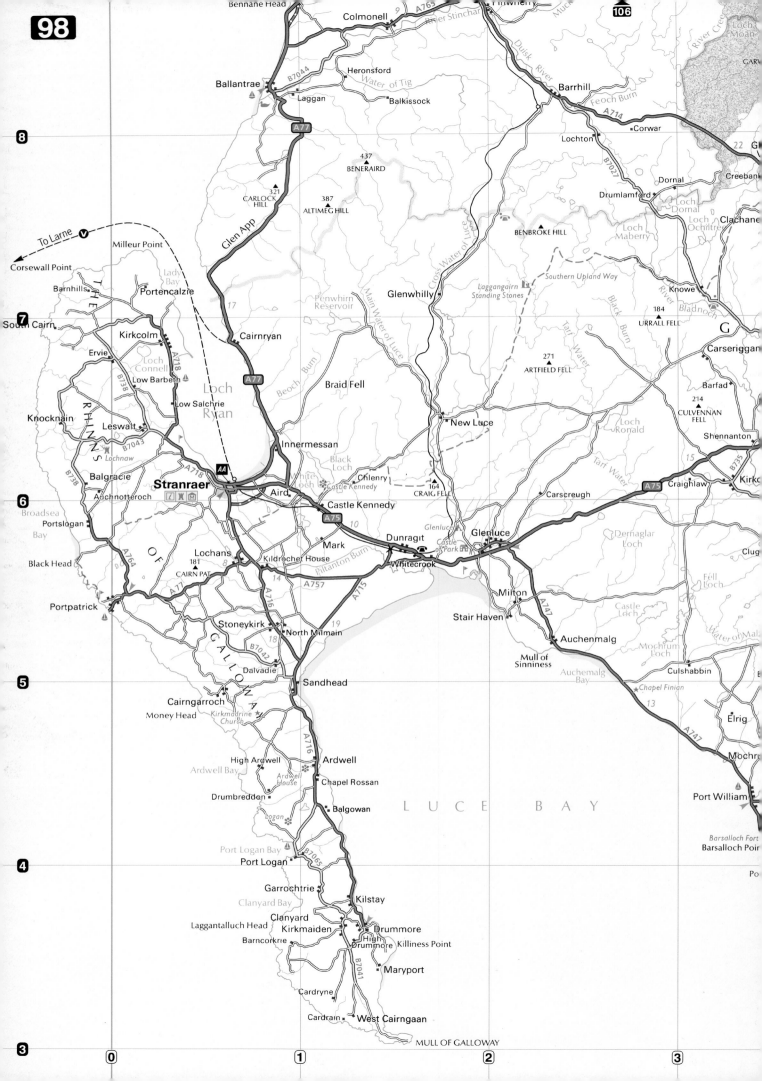

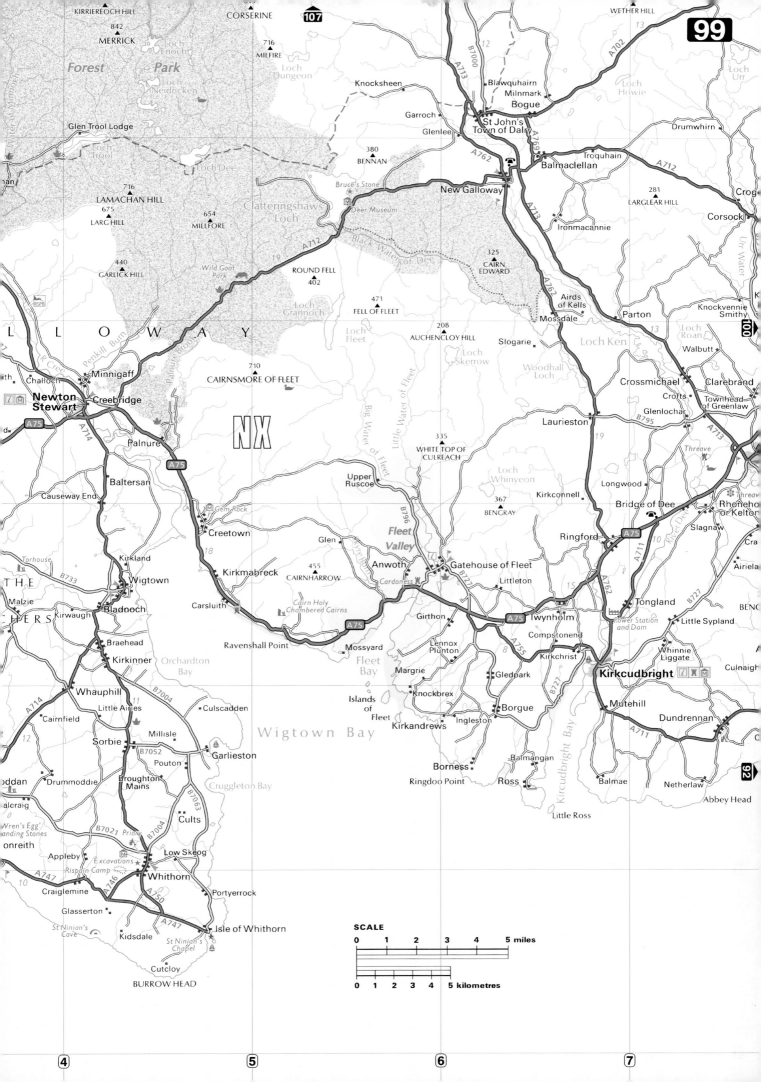

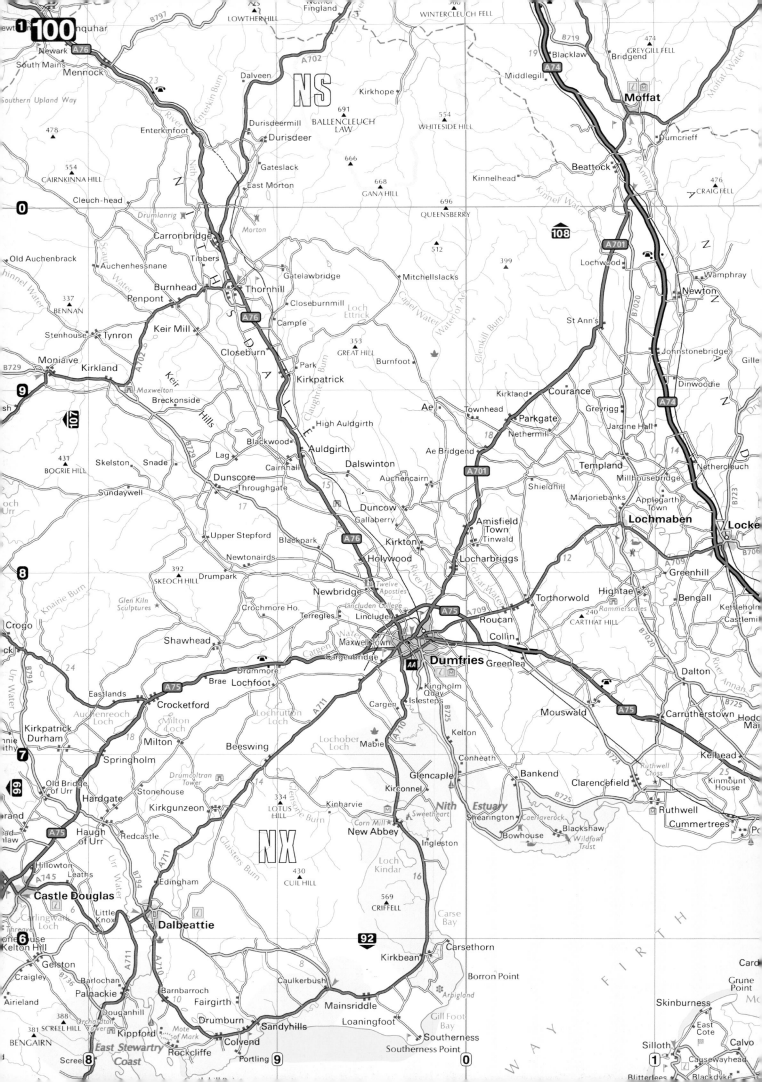

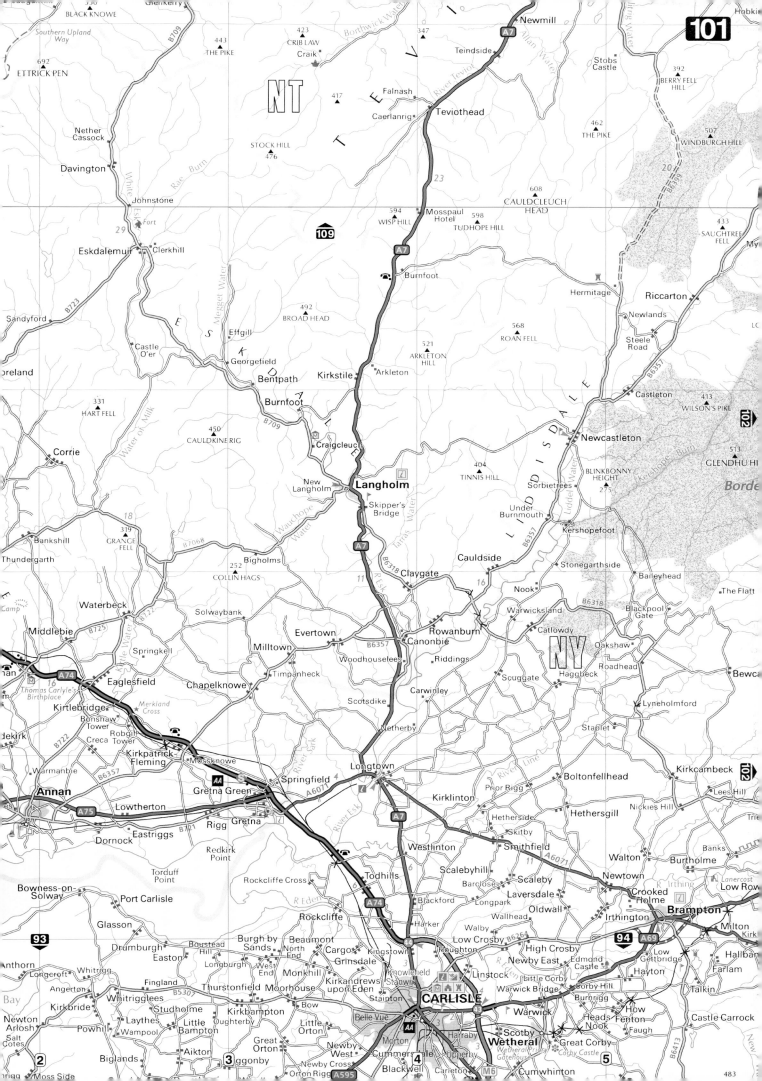

HILL
Hobkirk
Chesters
414
BROWNDEAN
Blindburn
Barrow Burn
500
SHILLHOPE LAW

16
A6088
Letham

393
WOFFEE HEAD
Carter Bar
Shillmoor
Biddlestone
Newton
Burr

Camps

THE
500
HUNGRY LAW
NT
NORTHUMBERLAND
Alwinton
Newton

Linshiels
A68
Ramshope
448
BLACK KIP
110

553
CARTER FELL
Catcleugh Reservoir
NATIONAL
Harbottle
Holystone

Byrness
13
368
CORBY PIKE

PARK

602
PEEL FELL
551
OH ME EDGE
River Rede
Rochester
301
THE BEACON

Myredykes
425
HINDHOPE LAW
Camp
Horsley
17

Elishaw
1388

403
LOCH KNOWE
213
MONKSIDE
Otterburn
Elsdon
B6341
DOL

Kielder
397
EARL'S SEAT
Troughend
Old Town
Rayless

9
Kielder Water
Highgreen Manor
Black Middens Bastle House
9

307
WHITE HILL
Gatehouse
Greenhaugh
West Woodburn
East Woodburn
Ray Fell

order
Forest
Park
Falstone
Lanehead
Charlton
Fort
Kirkwh

Stannersburn
Hott
Bellingham
Ridsdale
15

NORTHUMBERLAND
Hesleyside
Redesmouth
B6320
A68
Sweethope Loughs

395
BOLTS LAW
NATIONAL
PARK
Pennine Way
Gr Bavir

8
519
SIGHTY CRAG
492
BLACK KNOWE
Chirdon Burn
Birtley
Carrycoats Hall
Thockri

e Flatt
313
SPY RIGG
Churnsike Lodge
325
ROUND TOP
NY
Wark
Chipchase Castle
Park End
Great Swinburne
Litt Swinb

355
BARRON'S PIKE
Stonehaugh
Simonburn
Nunwick
Gunnerton
Barrasford
Colw

Bewcastle
Black Fell
Wark's Burn
12

101
265
GREEN RIGG
River Irthing
Broomlee Lough
B6318
Carrawburgh Temple of Mithras
Humshaugh
Walwick
Chollerton

7
Greenlee Lough
Housesteads
17
Grindon Hill
Settlingstones
Chollerford
Hadrian's Wall

Hill
B6318
Fort
Gilsland
Hadrian's Wall
Chesterholm (Vindolanda)
Newbrough
Chesters Fort
Wall
Fallowfield

Trermain
Birdoswald
Westend Town
Thorngrafton
Chesterwood
Fourstones
High Warden
Acomb
S

Upper Denton
Greenhead
Haltwhistle
Melkridge
Henshaw
Bardon Mill
A69
Wharmley
Warden
Oakwood
Anick
Cor

A69
Haydon Bridge
Bridge End
B6531

w Row
255
DENTON FELL
Plenmeller
Redburn
Beltingham
Ridley
A686
Elrington
Hexham
A695 Dilst

6
house A689
Coalfell
Tindale
Park
Langley Castle
Langley
B6305
Diptonmill

Midgeholme
Lambley
Coanwood
94
Fellhouse Fell
Deanraw
West Dipton Burn
Dye House
Ordley
Steel

Forest Head
Halton Lea Gate
Stonehouse
Wolf Hills
Whitfield
Catton
Whitley Chapel

621
COLD FELL
Eals
Whitfield Hall
Thornley Gate
Allendale Town
357
DUKESFIELD FELL

522
GLENDUE FELL
Knarsdale
Bearsbridge
Nineb ks

rrock

521

443

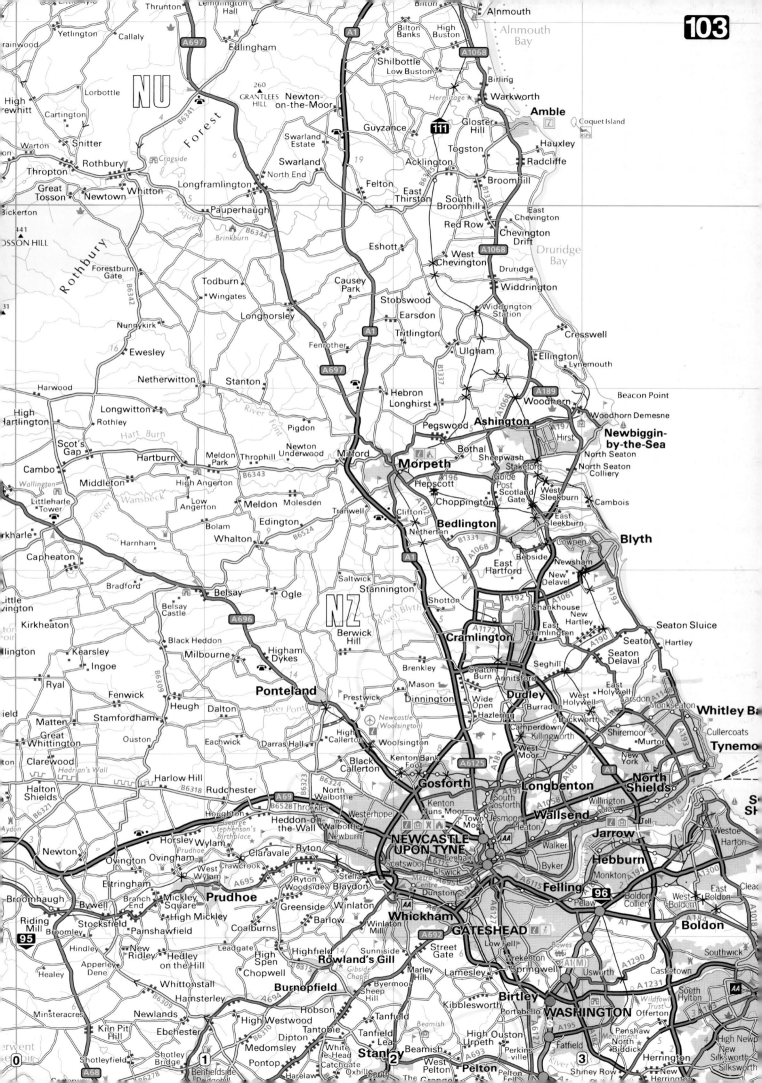

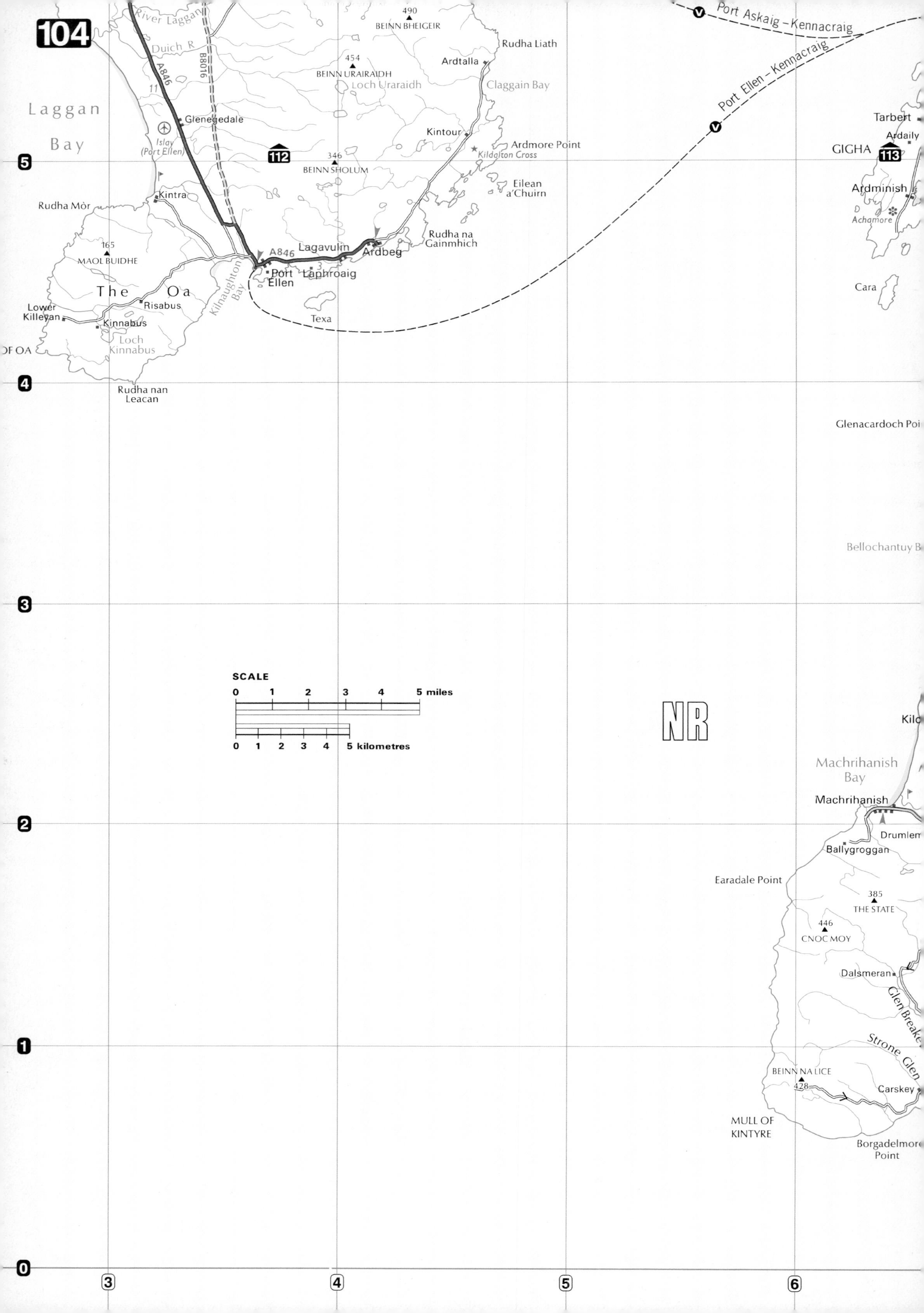

River Laggan

490
BEINN BHEIGEIR ▲

Rudha Liath

Duich R

A846

B8016

454
BEINN URAIRAIDH ▲

Ardtalla

Loch Uraraidh

Claggain Bay

Port Ellen – Kennacraig

Tarbert

Ardaily

Laggan

11

Glenegedale

✈

Islay
(Port Ellen)

Kintour

112

346
BEINN SHOLUM

GIGHA

113

Bay

5

Ardmore Point

★ Kildalton Cross

Ardminish

Achamore ❊

Rudha Mòr

Kintra

Eilean
a'Chuirn

Cara

165 ▲
MAOL BUIDHE

Lagavulin

A846

Ardbeg

Rudha na
Gainmhich

Laphroaig

Kilnaughton Bay

Port
Ellen

3

The   O a

Risabus

Glenacardoch Poi

Lower
Killeyan

Kinnabus

Texa

Loch
Kinnabus

OF OA

4

Rudha nan
Leacan

Bellochantuy B

3

SCALE

| 0 | 1 | 2 | 3 | 4 | 5 miles |

| 0 | 1 | 2 | 3 | 4 | 5 kilometres |

NR

Kilo

Machrihanish
Bay

Machrihanish

2

Drumlem

Ballygroggan

Earadale Point

385 ▲
THE STATE

446 ▲
CNOC MOY

Dalsmeran

1

Glen Breake

Strone Glen

BEINN NA LICE
428 ▲

Carskey

MULL OF
KINTYRE

Borgadelmore
Point

0

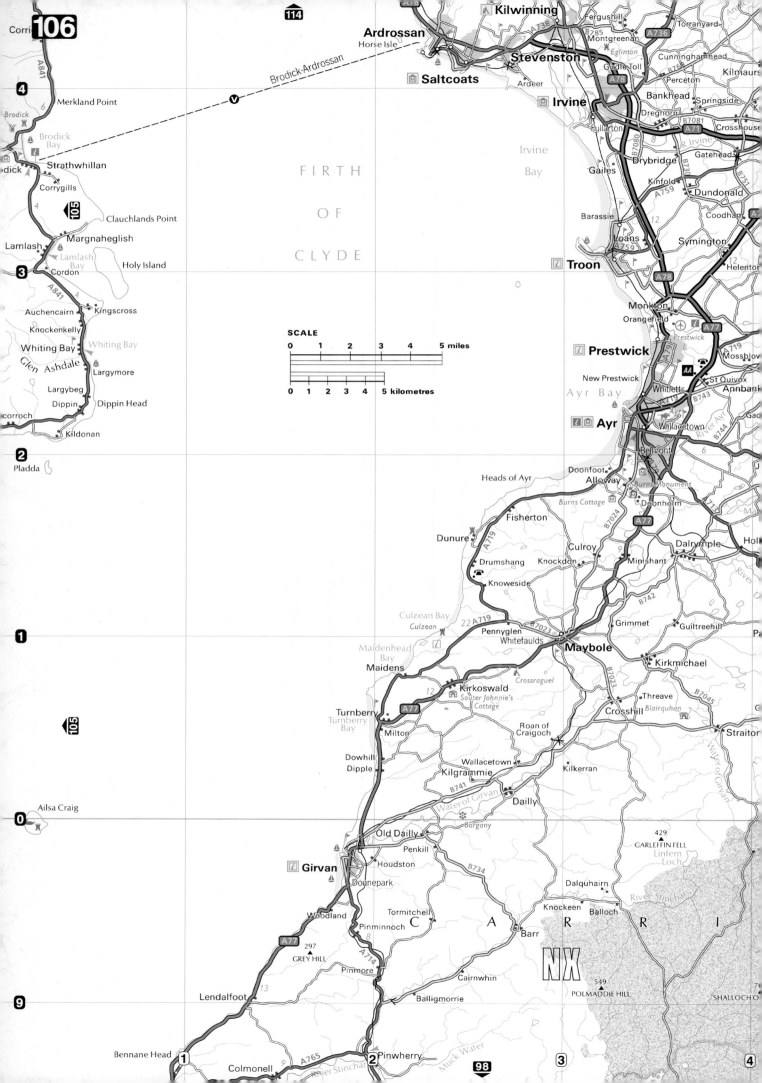

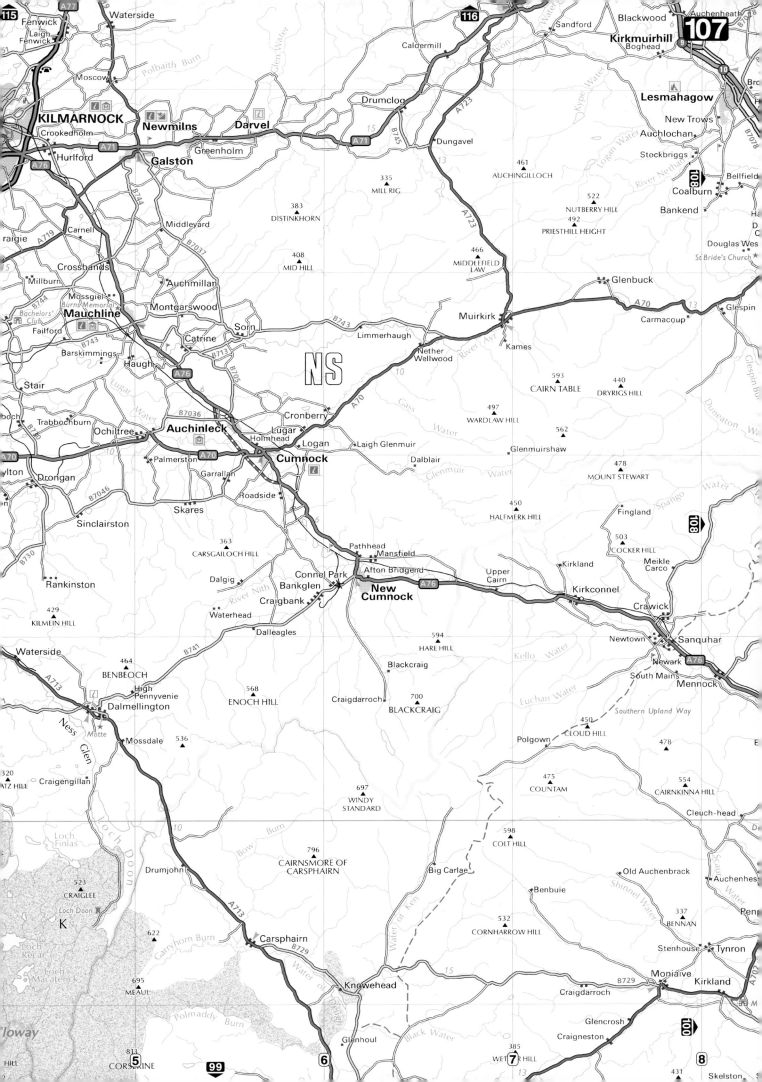

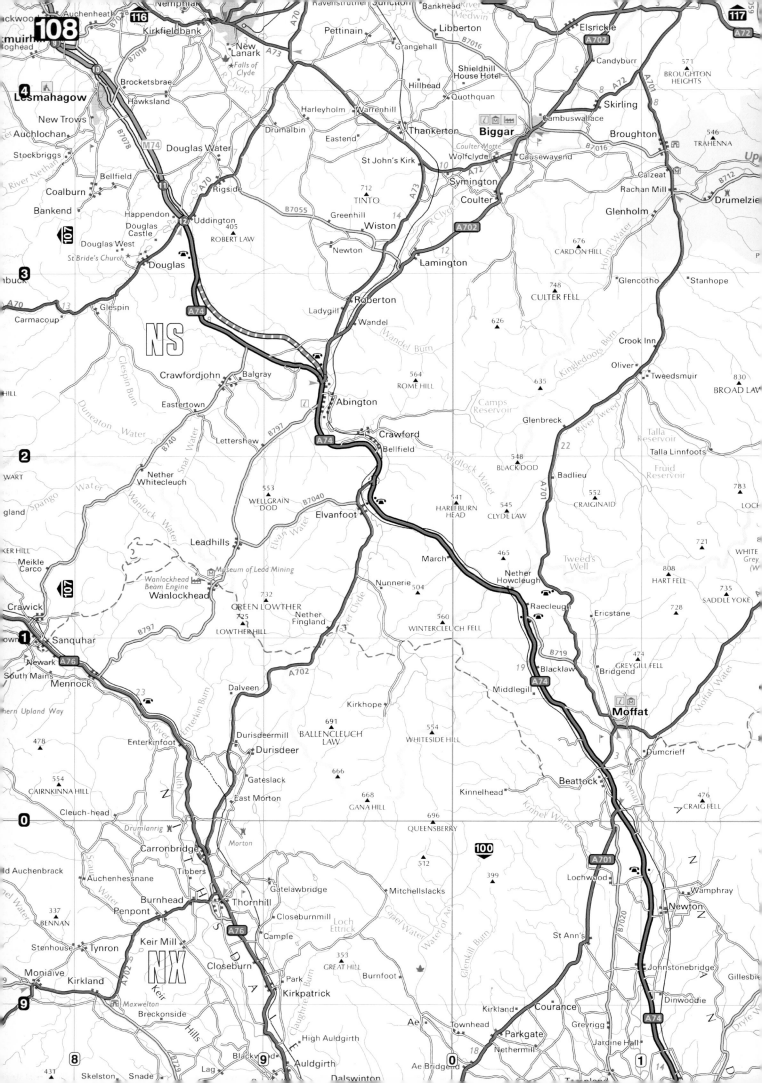

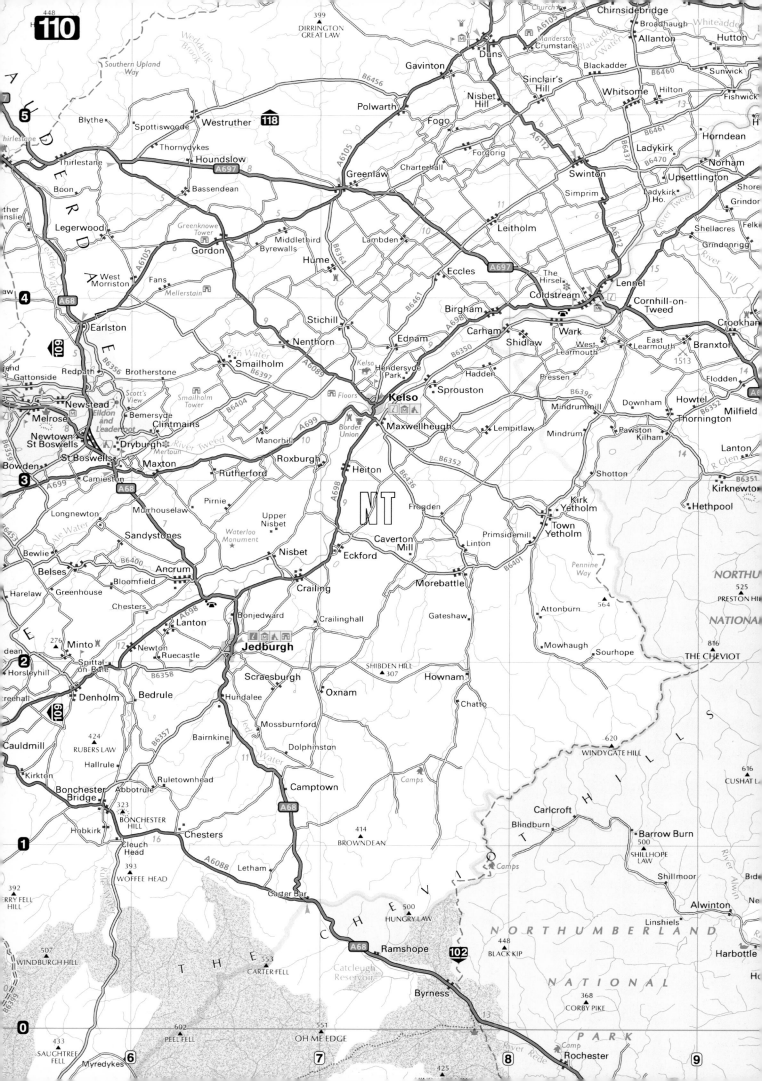

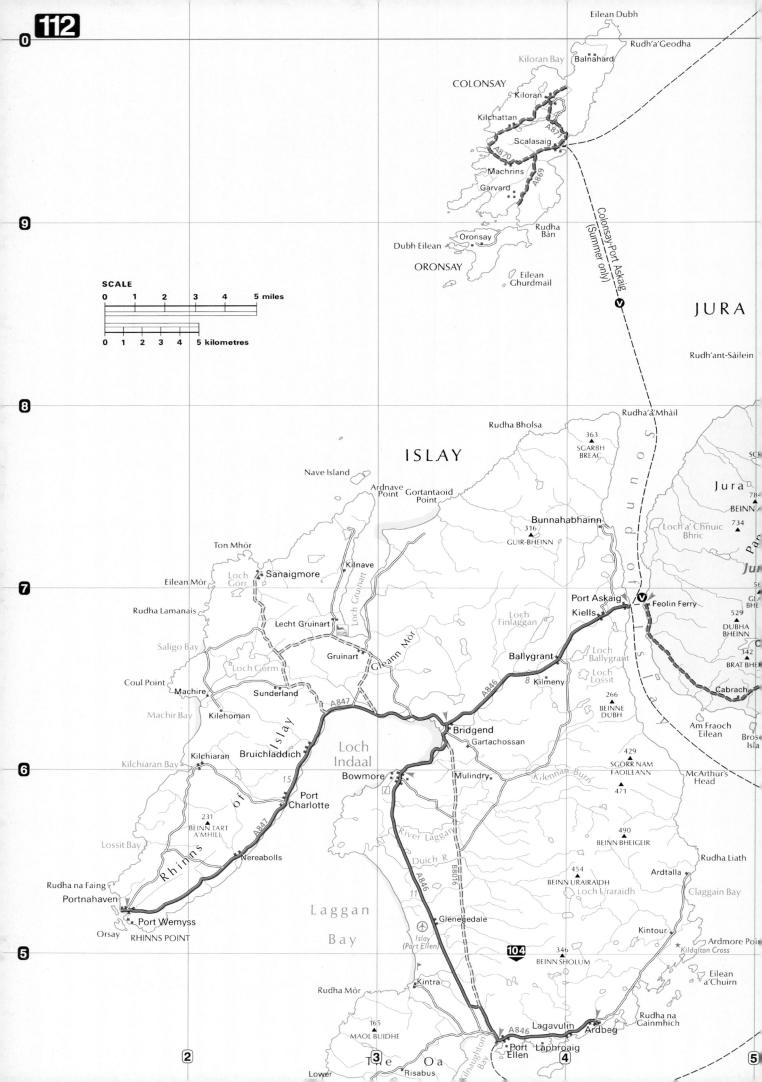

SCALE

0   1   2   3   4   5 miles

0   1   2   3   4   5 kilometres

Eilean Dubh

Rudh'a'Geodha

Kiloran Bay   Balnahard

COLONSAY

Kiloran

Kilchattan

Scalasaig

Machrins

Garvard

Oronsay

Dubh Eilean

ORONSAY

Rudha Bàn

Eilean
Ghurdmail

Colonsay-Port Askaig
(Summer only)

JURA

Rudh'ant-Sàilein

ISLAY

Rudha Bholsa

Rudha'a'Mhàil

363
SGARBH
BREAC

Jura

784
BEIN

Nave Island

Ardnave
Point

Gortantaoid
Point

Bunnahabhainn

316
GUIR-BHEINN

Loch a' Chnuic
Bhric

734

Ton Mhòr

Loch
Gorr

Sanaigmore

Kilnave

Rudha Lamanais

Lecht Gruinart

Loch Gruinart

Gleann Mòr

Loch
Finlaggan

Port Askaig
Kiells

Feolin Ferry

529

Saligo Bay

Gruinart

Ballygrant

Loch
Ballygrant

DUBHA
BHEINN

Loch Gorm

Sunderland

A847

Kilmeny

8

Loch
Lossit

342
BRAT BHE

Coul Point

Machire

266
BEINNE
DUBH

Am Fraoch
Eilean

Cabrach

Bros
Isla

Machir Bay

Kilchoman

Rhinns of Islay

A846

Bridgend

Gartachossan

Kilchiaran Bay

Kilchiaran

Bruichladdich

Loch
Indaal

Bowmore

Mulindry

Kilennan Burn

429
SGÒRR NAM
FAOILEANN

McArthur's
Head

Port
Charlotte

471

231
BEINN TART
A'MHILL

A847

15

River Laggan

490
BEINN BHEIGEIR

Lossit Bay

Nereabolls

Duich R

A846

B8016

454
BEINN URAIRAIDH

Ardtalla

Rudha Liath

Loch Uraraidh

Claggain Bay

Rudha na Faing

Portnahaven

Port Wemyss

Orsay

RHINNS POINT

Laggan

Bay

11

Islay
(Port Ellen)

Glenegedale

104

346
BEINN SHOLUM

Kintour

Ardmore Poi
Kildalton Cross

Eilean
a'Chuirn

Rudha Mòr

Kintra

Lagavulin

Ardbeg

Rudha na
Gainmhich

165
MAOL BUIDHE

A846

Port
Ellen

Laphroaig

Lower
Risabus

T h e   O a

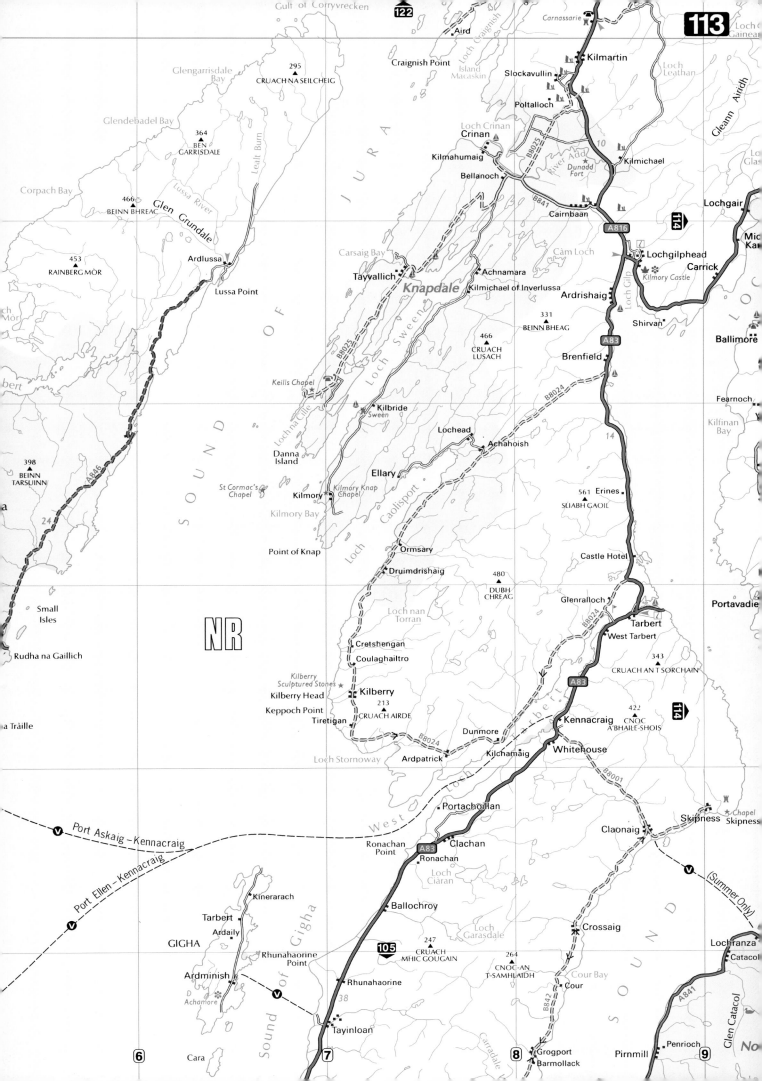

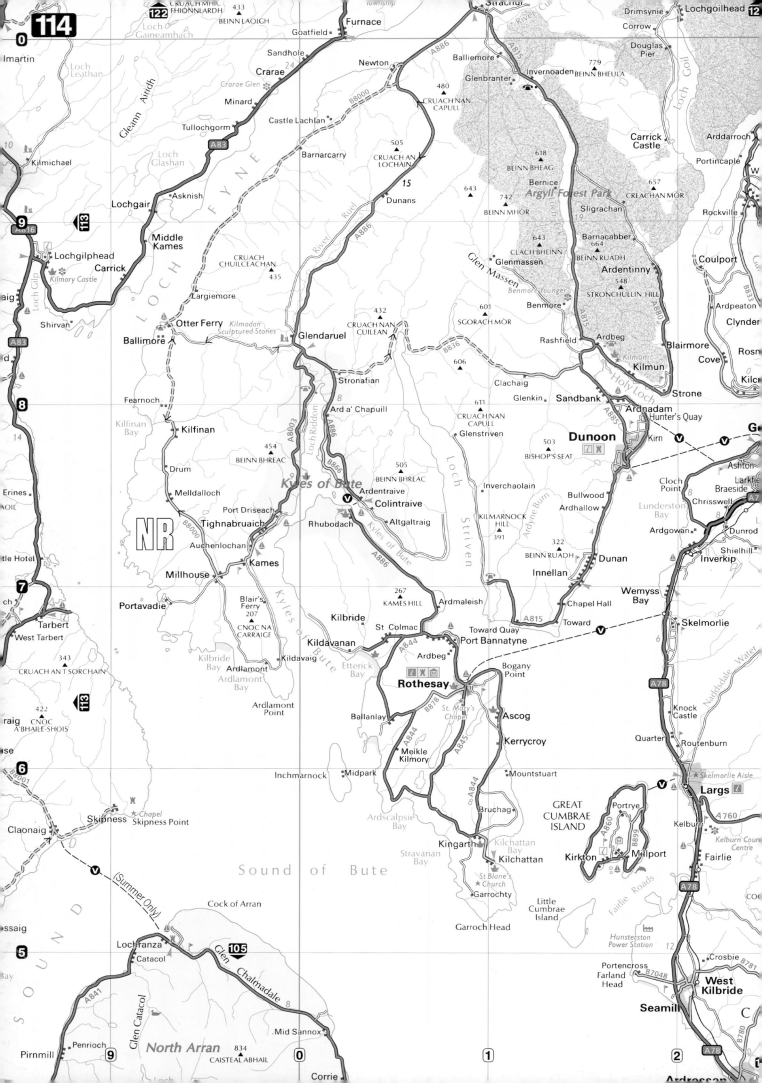

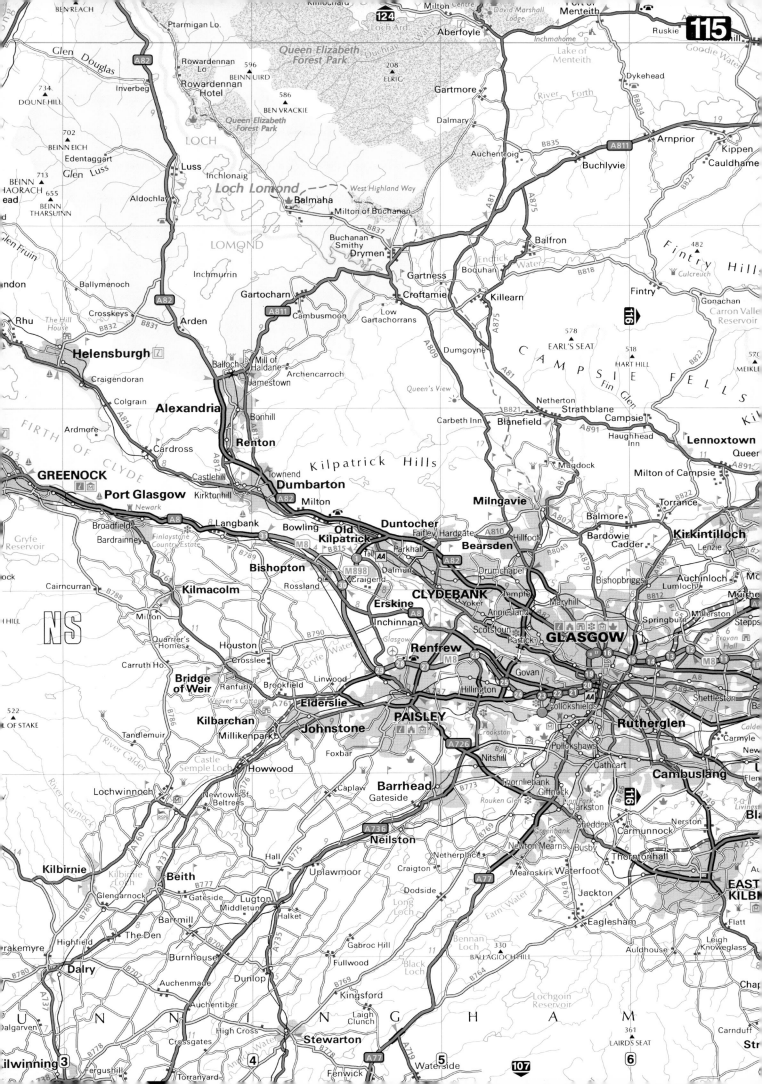

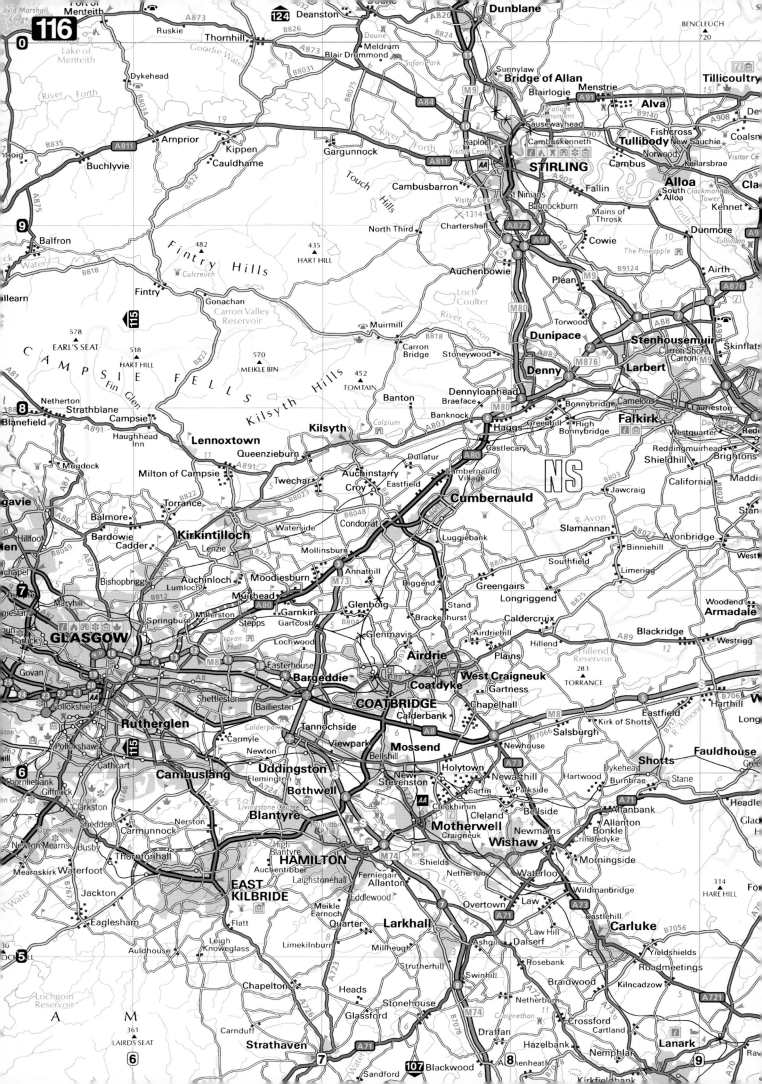

SCALE

0   1   2   3   4   5 miles

0 1 2 3 4   5 kilometres

NU

bar ℹ

oxburn
1650   Barns Ness
        East Barns
            Chapel Point
            Skateraw
        Thorntonloch
Innerwick   Crowhill

319   Dunglass   Reed Point
COCKLAW HILL   Collegiate   Pease
            Church   Bay   Siccar Point   Fast Castle Head
Oldhamstocks   Cockburnspath

            Ecclaw   196   ST ABB'S HEAD
391   Southern   BROWN RIG
HEART LAW   Upland Way   St Abbs

                                        Coldingham Bay
        Butterdean   Grantshouse   Coldingham
                21
        Quixwood   Houndwood   22
                                            ℹ 🏛
Abbey St Bathans   Heugh Head   Cairncross   Eyemouth
Ellemford   Edin's   262
        Hall Broch   HORSELEY HILL   B6438   Reston A1
        14   Auchencrow   Ayton   Burnmouth
BERMUIR   325
        COCKBURN
        LAW   Marygold   Lamberton
    B6355   Marshall Meadows Bay
99   Lintlaw   B6437
NGTON   Preston   North Northumberland
AT LAW Primrosehill   East   Chirnside   Edington Foulden   Heritage Coast
        B6365   Cumledge   Blanerne   A1
            Edrom   15   Tithe Barn
        Church   Chirnsidebridge   1333 ✕   A6105
                    Broadhaugh   Whiteadder
Gavinton   Manderston   Allanton   Hutton   Water
        Duns   Crumstane   Barracks
                                    Paxton   Town Ramparts ℹ 🏛
Polwarth   Sinclair's Blackadder   B6460   Sunwick   Berwick-upon-Tweed
        Nisbet Hill   Hilton   Fishwick   Tweedmouth
110   Hill   Whitsome   13   Loanend   East Ord   Spittal
    Fogo   A698   Huds Head
Greenlaw   B6456   B6461   Horncliffe   111   Unthank
    A6105   Charterhall   Forgorig   Horndean   Murton
        A6112   Ladykirk   Thornton   Scremerston
            Swinton   B6470   Norham   West Allerdean   Cheswick
    Simprim   Ladykirk   Upsettlington   Shoreswood
7   8   Ho.   Grindon   B6354   Ancroft A1 Goswick
    11 Leitholm   9   Shellacres   Felkington   0   Haggerston

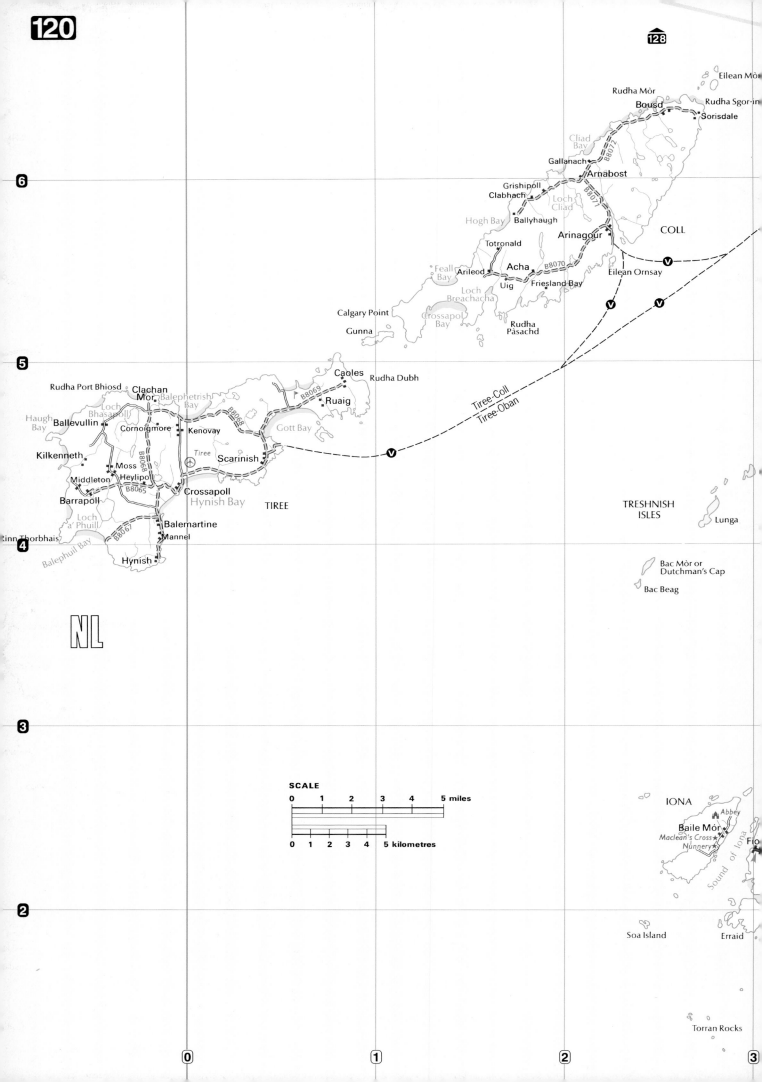

128

Eilean Mòr

Rudha Mòr

Rudha Sgor-in

Bousd

Sorisdale

Cliad
Bay

Gallanach

Arnabost

Grishipoll

Clabhach

Loch
Cliad

COLL

Hogh Bay   Ballyhaugh

Arinagour

Totronald

Feall
Bay

Arileod   **Acha**   B8070

Uig   Friesland Bay

Eilean Ornsay

Loch
Breachacha

Calgary Point

Crossapol
Bay

Rudha
Pàsachd

Gunna

5

Caoles   Rudha Dubh

Rudha Port Bhiosd   **Clachan**   Balephetrish
Mòr   Bay   B8069   Ruaig

Tiree-Coll

Tiree-Oban

Loch
Bhasapoll

Haugh
Bay   **Ballevullin**   B8068

Cornoigmore   Kenovay   Gott Bay

Kilkenneth   Tiree

B8068   Moss   **Scarinish**

Middleton   Heylipoll

Barrapoll   B8065   **Crossapoll**
Hynish Bay   **TIREE**

TRESHNISH
ISLES

Lunga

Loch
a' Phuill

Rinn Thorbhais   **Balemartine**
Mannel   B8067

Balephuil Bay

4   Hynish

Bac Mòr or
Dutchman's Cap

Bac Beag

NL

3

SCALE

0   1   2   3   4   5 miles

IONA

Abbey

0   1   2   3   4   5 kilometres

Baile Mòr
Maclean's Cross
Nunnery

Fio

Sound of Iona

2

Soa Island   Erraid

Torran Rocks

0   **1**   **2**   **3**

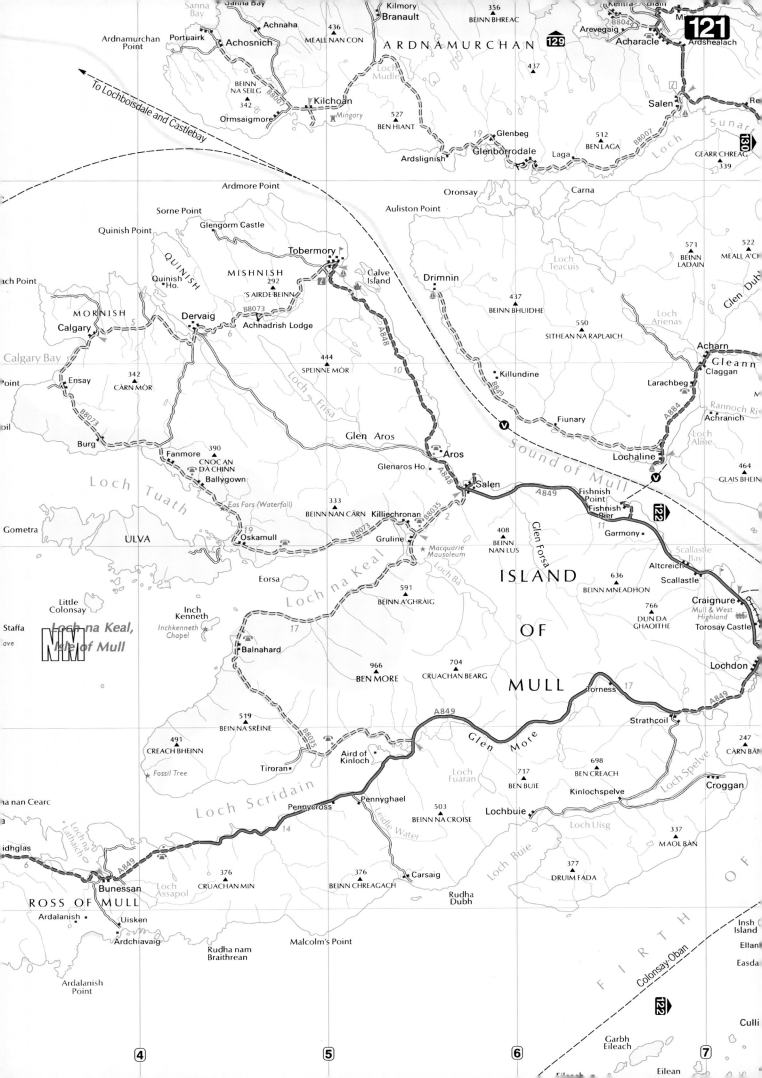

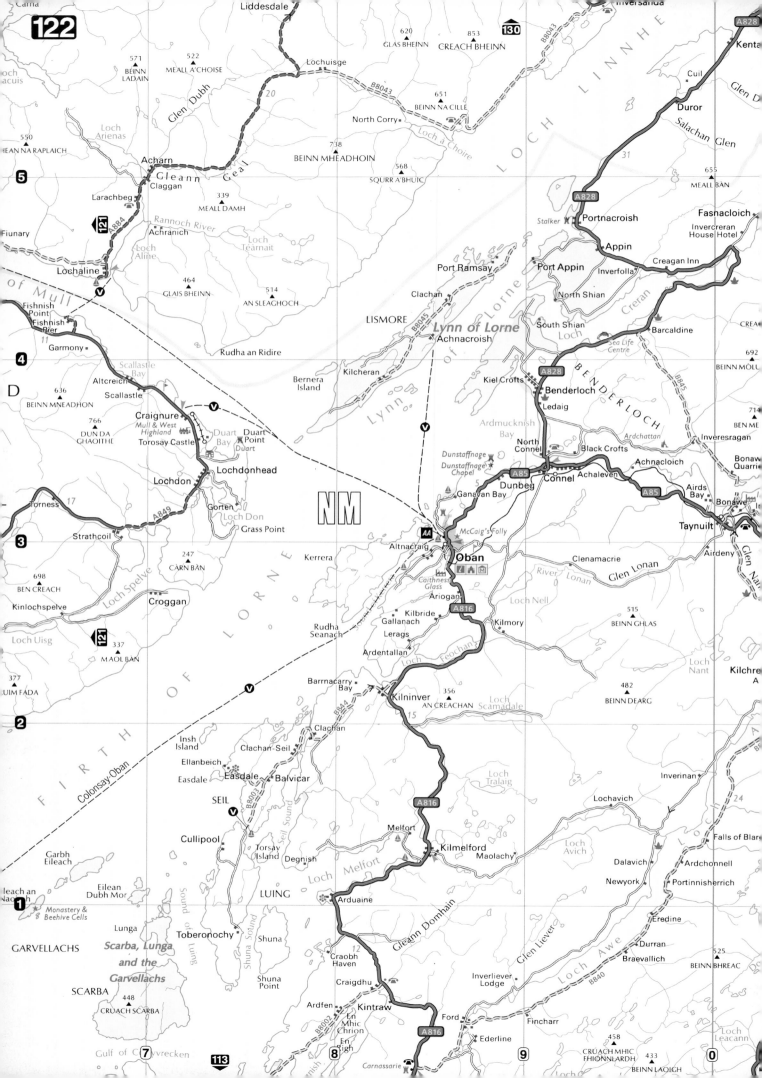

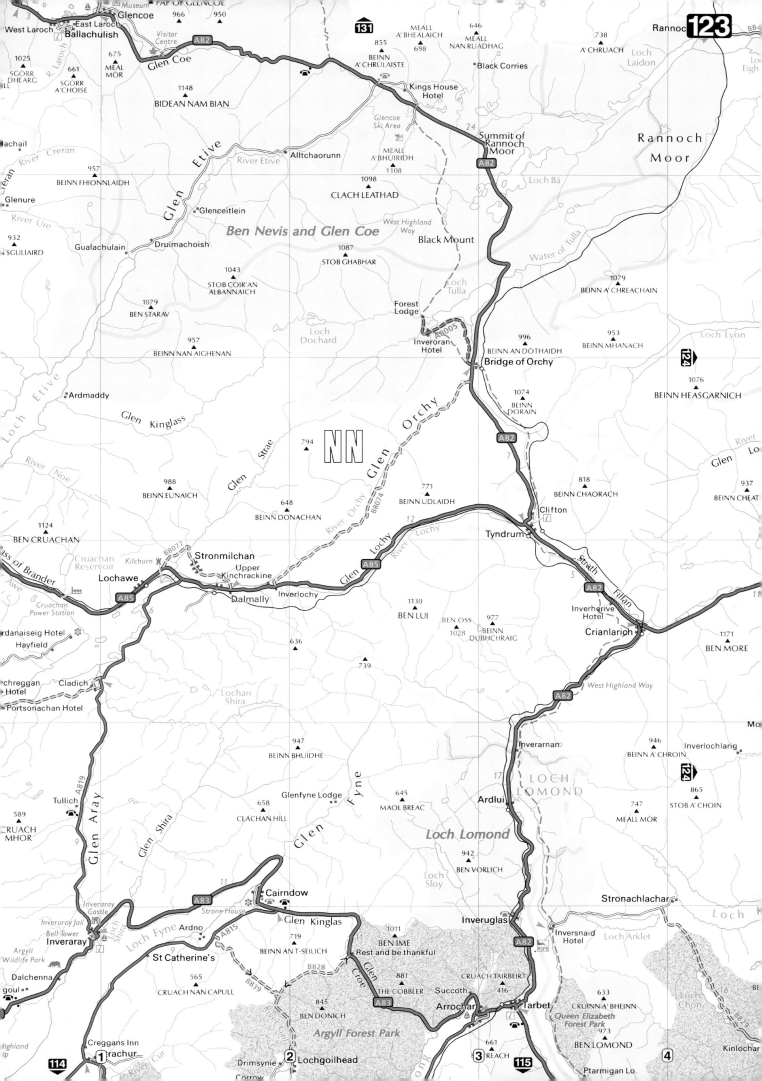

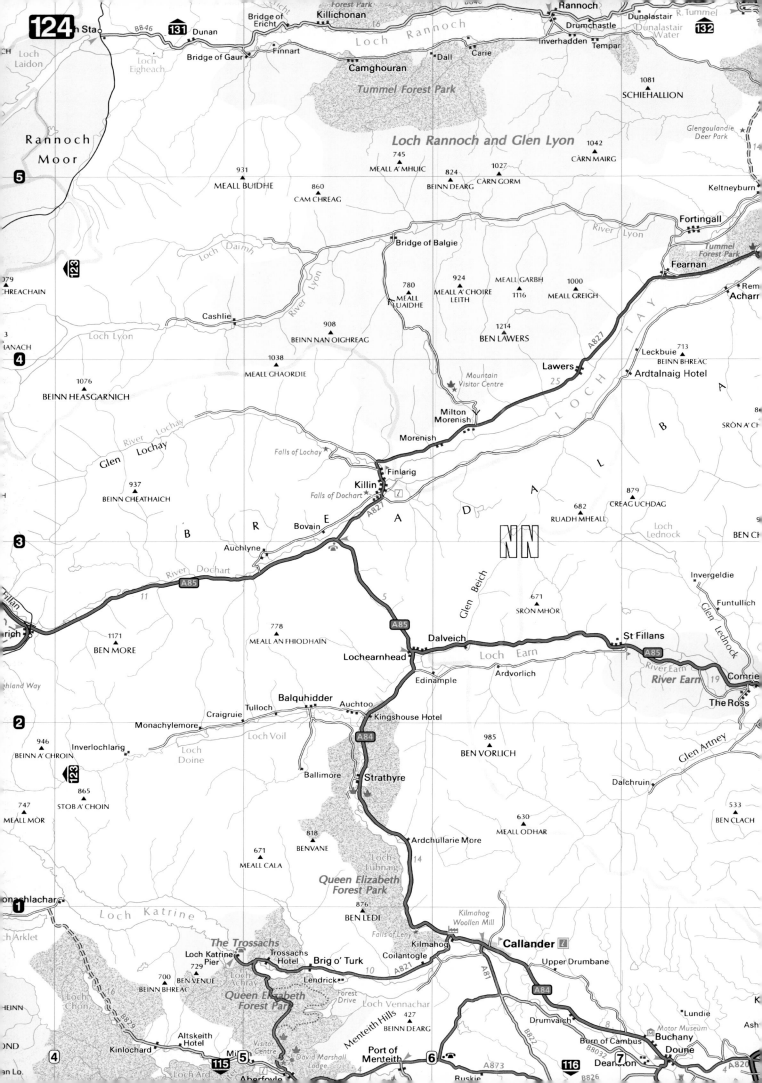

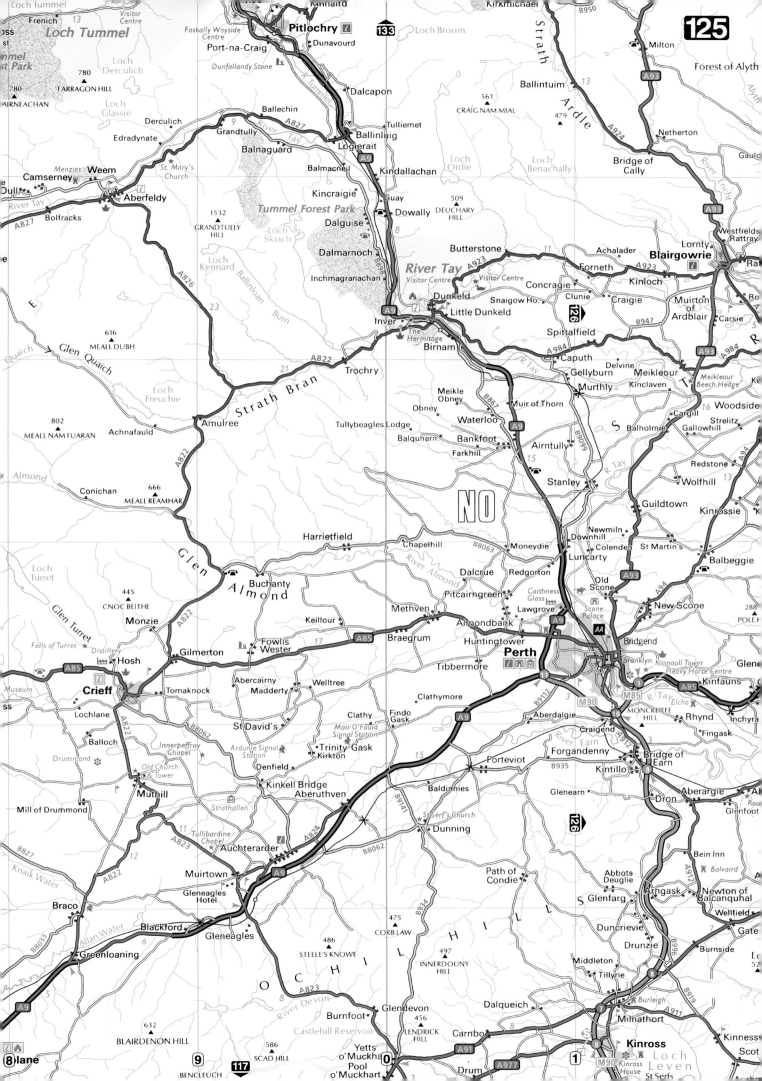

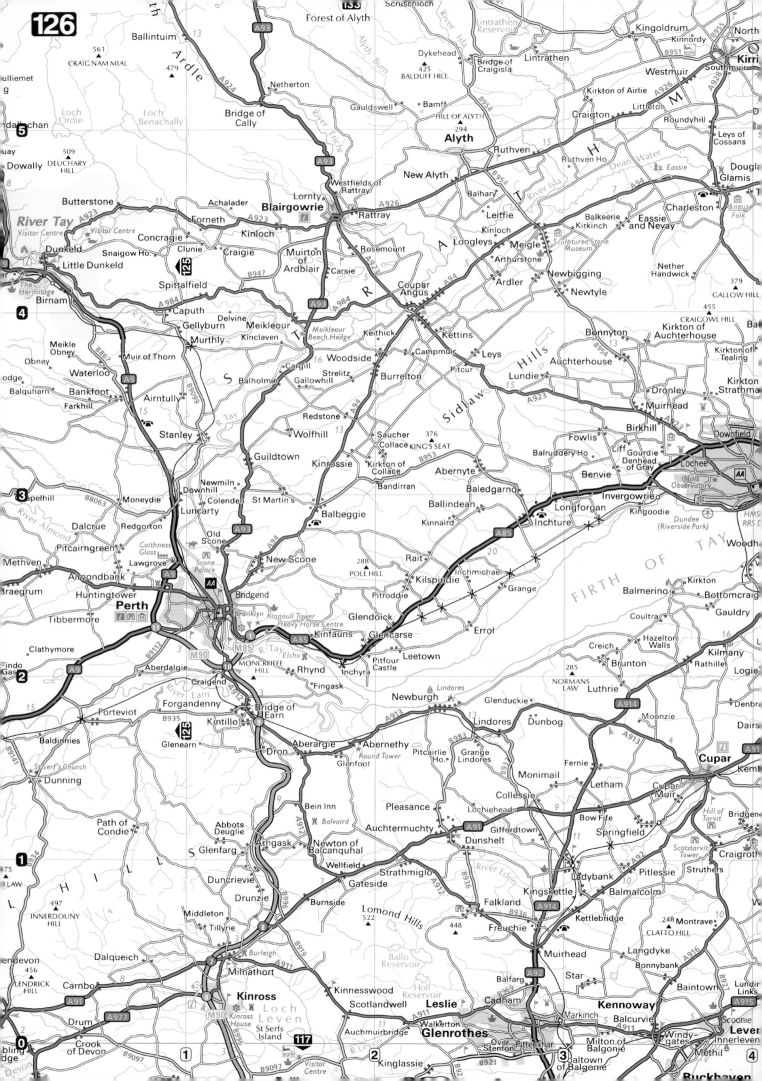

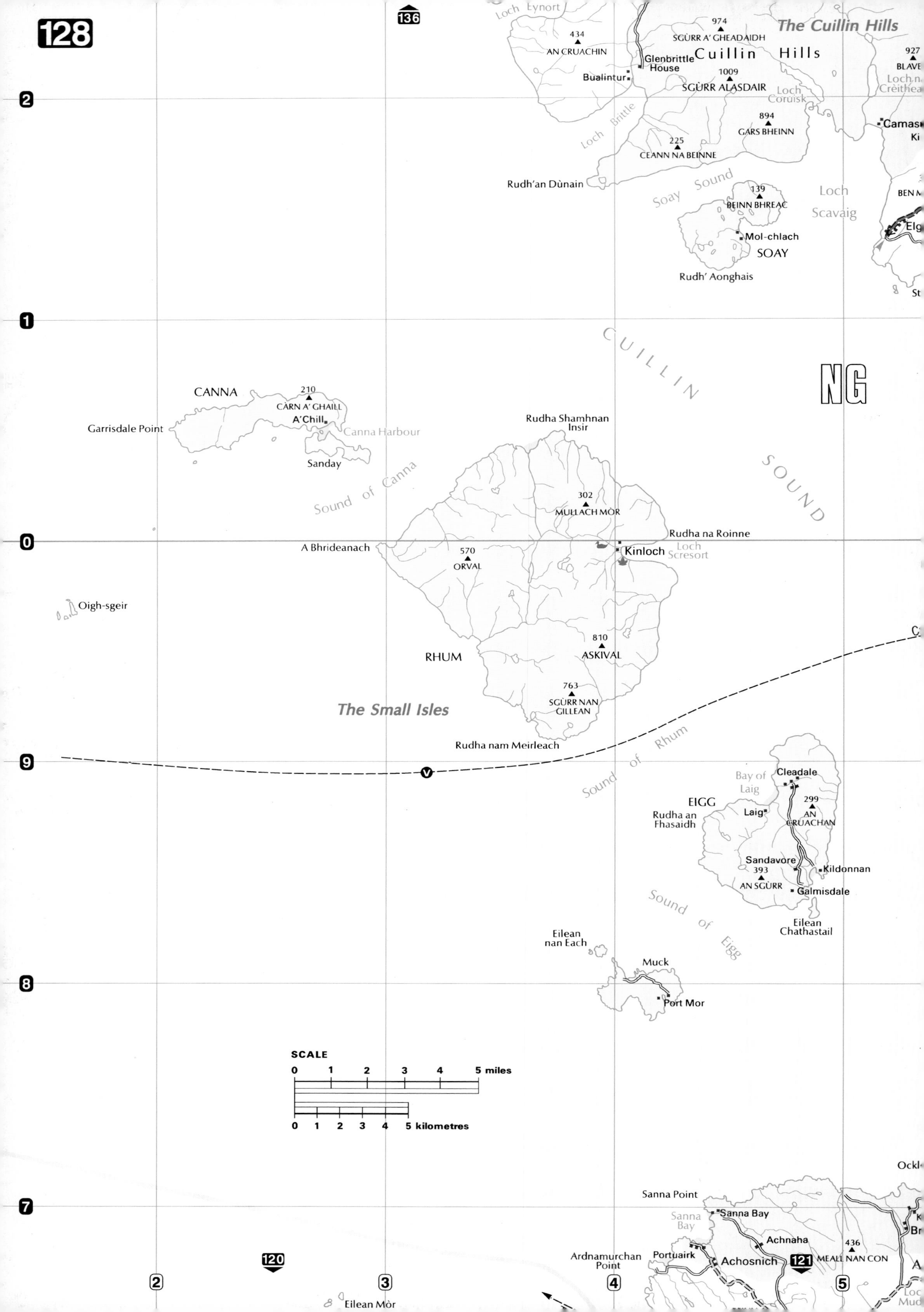

Loch Eynort

974
SGÙRR A' GHEADAIDH

The Cuillin Hills

434
AN CRUACHIN

Glenbrittle
House

Cuillin Hills

927
BLAVE

Bualintur

1009
SGÙRR ALASDAIR

Loch Coruisk

Loch n
Crèithea

2

Loch Brittle

894
GARS BHEINN

Camas
Ki

225
CEANN NA BEINNE

Soay Sound

139
BEINN BHREAC

*Loch
Scavaig*

BEN M

Rudh'an Dùnain

Mol-chlach

Elg

St

SOAY

Rudh' Aonghais

1

NG

CANNA

210
CÀRN A' GHAILL

A'Chill

Canna Harbour

Rudha Shamhnan
Insir

C
U
I
L
L
I
N

Garrisdale Point

Sanday

Sound of Canna

302
MULLACH MÒR

S
O
U
N
D

0

A Bhrideanach

570
ORVAL

*Loch
Scresort*

Kinloch

Rudha na Roinne

Oigh-sgeir

810
ASKIVAL

C

RHUM

763
SGÙRR NAN
GILLEAN

The Small Isles

Rudha nam Meirleach

Sound of Rhum

9

V

Cleadale

*Bay of
Laig*

EIGG

299
AN
CRUACHAN

Rudha an
Fhasaidh

Laig

393
AN SGÙRR

Sandavore

Kildonnan

Galmisdale

Eilean
nan Each

*Sound
of
Eigg*

Eilean
Chathastail

Muck

8

Port Mor

SCALE

0   1   2   3   4   5 miles

0 1 2 3 4   5 kilometres

Sanna Point

Ockl

7

*Sanna
Bay*

Sanna Bay

Achnaha

436
MEALL NAN CON

K
Br

Ardnamurchan
Point

Portuairk

Achosnich

121

Eilean Mòr

Loch
Mud

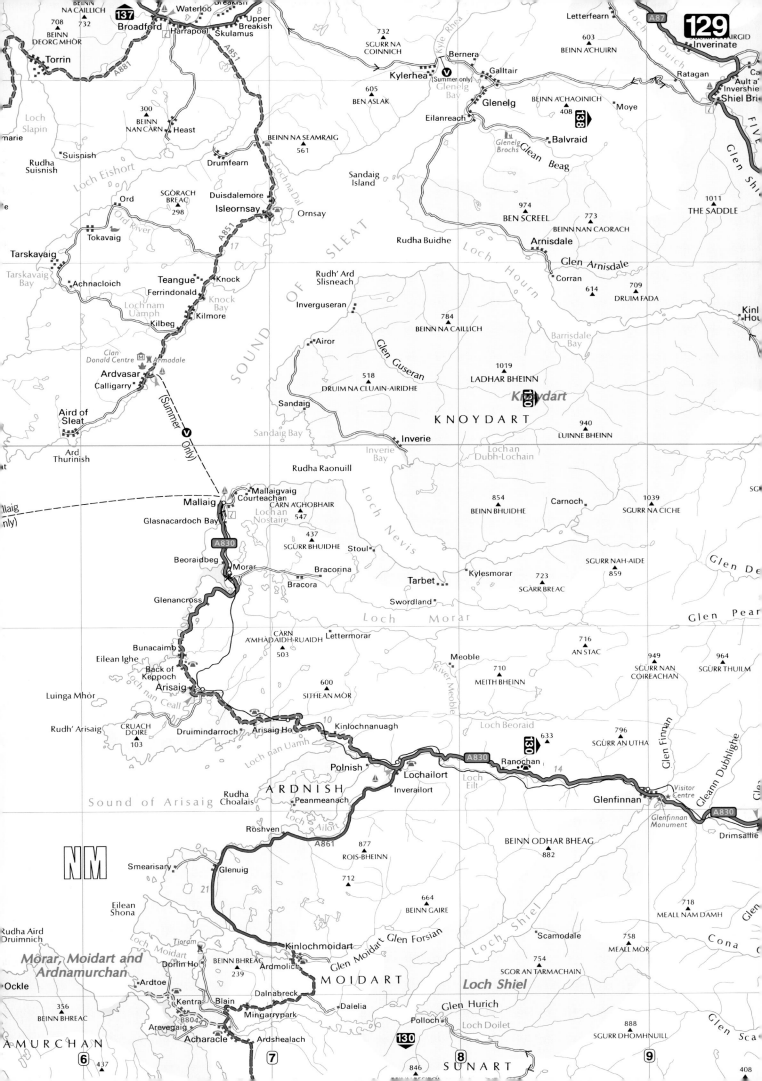

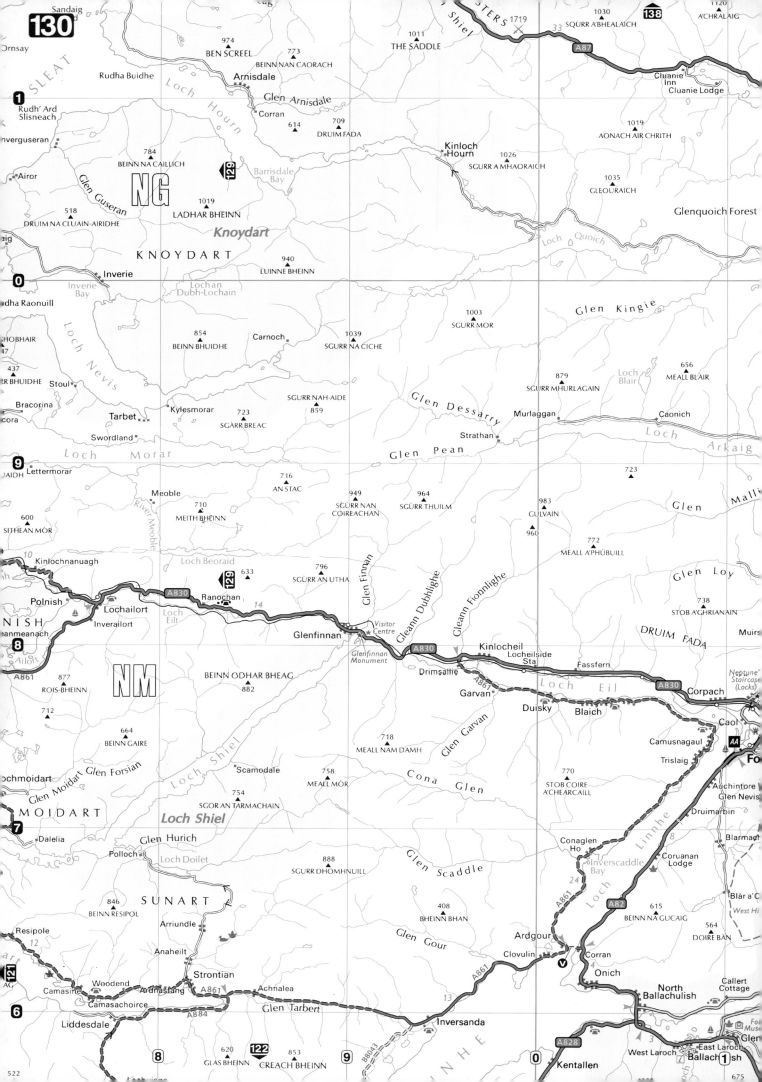

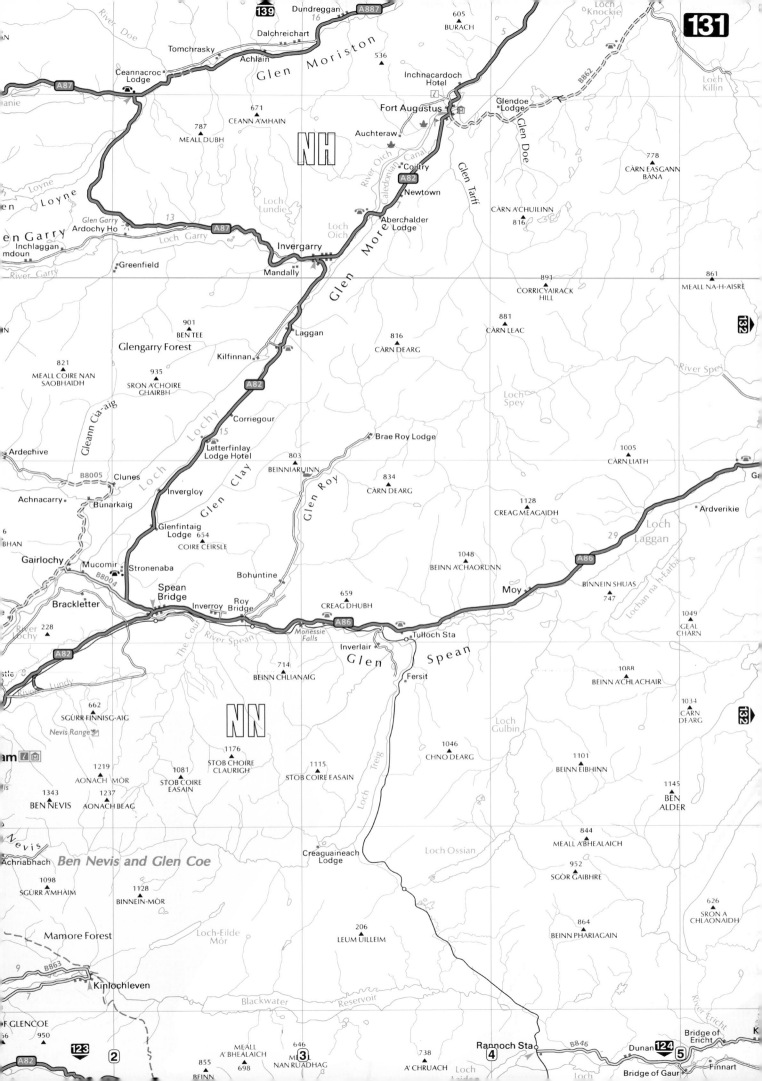

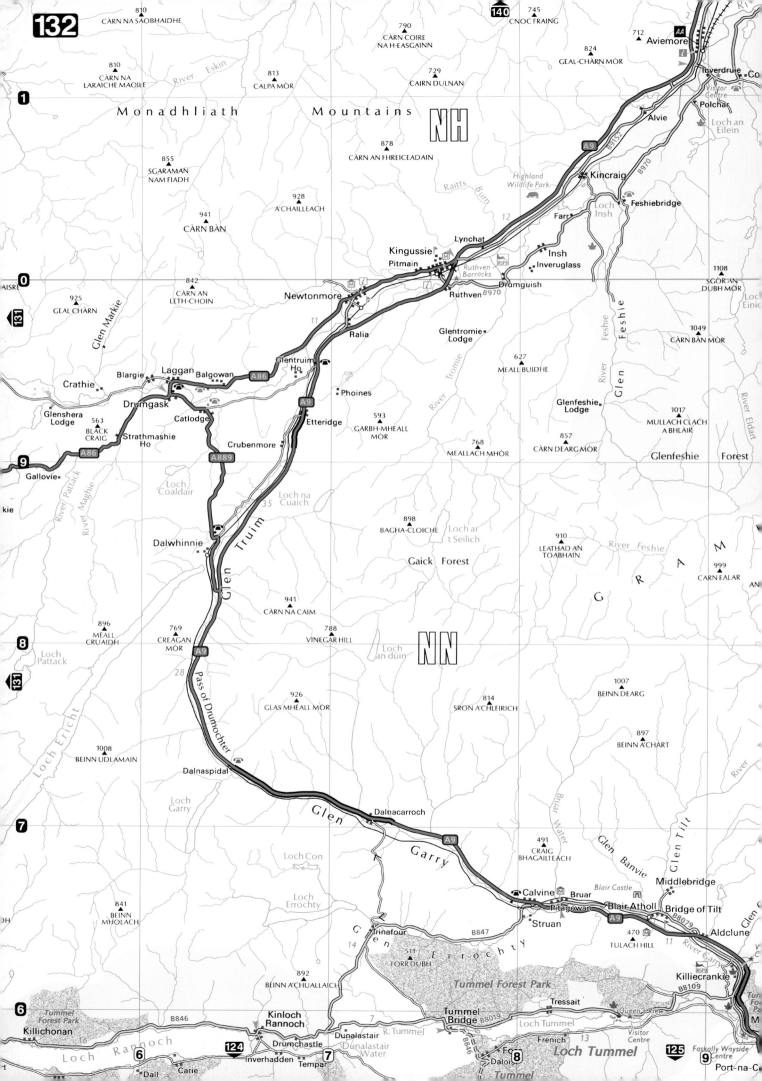

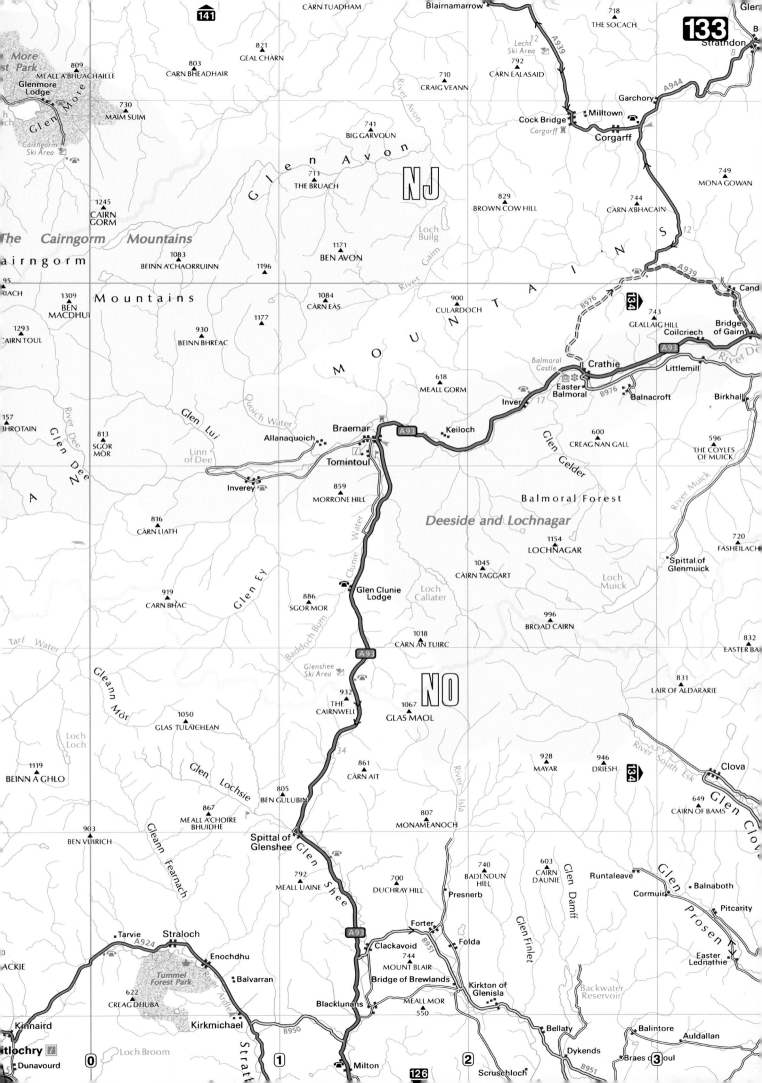

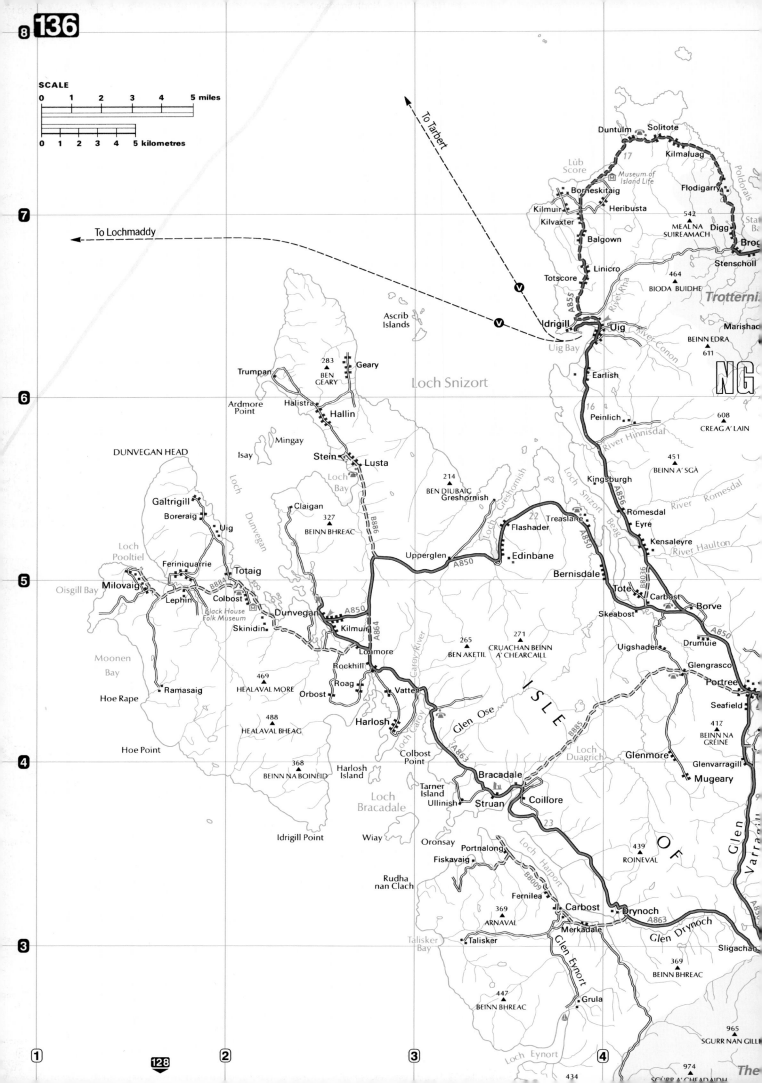

SCALE

0 1 2 3 4 5 miles

0 1 2 3 4 5 kilometres

7

To Lochmaddy →

6

5

4

3

2 1

To Tarbert

Duntulm Solitote
Kilmaluag
Borneskitaig
Museum of Island Life
Kilmuir Heribusta Flodigarry
Kilvaxter
Balgown 542 Digg
MEAL NA SUIREAMACH
Totscore Linicro 464 Stenscholl
BIODA BUIDHE Trotterni.
Idrigill Uig Marishad
Uig Bay BEINN EDRA 611
NG
Earlish
Ascrib Islands Peinlich 608 CREAG A' LAIN
Loch Snizort
451 BEINN A' SGÀ
Trumpan 283 BEN GEARY Geary
Ardmore Point Halistra Kingsburgh
Hallin Romesdal
Mingay Stein Lusta Eyre
Isay 214 BEN DIUBAIG Kensaleyre
Greshornish
Galtrigill Flashader Treaslane River Haulton
Boreraig Claigan Edinbane Bernisdale
Uig 327 BEINN BHREAC Upperglen A850 Tote Carbost
Feriniquarrie Totaig Skeabost Borve
Milovaig Colbost Dunvegan Uigshader
Lephin Black House Folk Museum Skinidin Kilmuir 265 BEN AKETIL 271 CRUACHAN BEINN A' CHEARCAILL Drumuie
Oisgill Bay Loinmore Glengrasco
Moonen Bay Rockhill Portree
Ramasaig 469 HEALAVAL MORE Roag Vatten Seafield
Hoe Rape Orbost 417 BEINN NA GRÉINE
Hoe Point 488 HEALAVAL BHEAG Harlosh ISLE Glenmore
368 BEINN NA BOINEID Harlosh Island Colbost Point Glen Ose Glenvarragill
Loch Bracadale Tarner Island Bracadale Mugeary
Idrigill Point Wiay Ullinish Struan Coillore 439 ROINEVAL O
Oronsay Portnalong F
Fiskavaig
Rudha nan Clach Fernilea
Talisker Bay 369 ARNAVAL Carbost Drynoch Glen Drynoch
Talisker Merkadale Sligachan
447 BEINN BHREAC Grula 369 BEINN BHREAC
965 SGURR NAN GILL
974
434 SGURR A' CHEAD
The

North Erradale

Londubh   MEALL NA

B8021

Poolewe

Big Sand

Longa Island

A832

Strath

Smithstown

Auchtercairn

Loch

Gairloch

Gairloch

Heritage
Museum

421

MEALL AN DOIREIN

Eilean
Horrisdale

Charlestown

144

Port
Henderson

B8056

Loch Mar

Badachro

Opinan

20

South Erradale

Tal

Red Point

619

BEINN BHREAC

Craig

River

Loch
Torridon

985

Rudha na Fearn

Lower Diabaig

138

BEINN ALLIGIN

Loch
Diabaig

Fearnbeg

Arinacrinachd

Alligin Shuas

Inveralligin

10.

Cuaig

Kenmore

Torridon Ho

LIATH

ISLAND
OF
RONA

Ardheslaig

Torri

Kalnalkill

Upper   Loch   Torridon

Loch
Shieldaig

Shieldaig
Island

Annat

Lonbain

492

AN GARBH-MHEALL

Shieldaig

Loch
Damh

Wester Ros

Eilean
Tigh

493

CROIC-BHEINN

902

BEINN DAMH

MAC

Eilean
Fladday

Glenshieldaig

Umachan

Forest

Manish Point

Loch
Arnish

Torran

Loch
Lundie

BEINN DAMH

Arnish

Brochel

River Applecross

895

BEINN BHAN

Loch
Coultrie

14

730

SGURR A GHARAIDH

ISLAND
OF
RAASAY

Applecross
Bay

Applecross

Milton

SGÙRR
A'CHAORACHAIN
774

Kirkton

12

Camusteel

Camusterrach

Lochcarron

ANAVAIG

Bealach-Na-Ba

Ardarroch

Camastianavaig

Slumbay

Tianavaig
Bay
Ollach

DÙN
CAAN
444

Rudha
na' Leac

Toscaig

Loch Kishorn

BAD A CHREAMHA
394

Oskaig

Kishorn
Island

Upper
Ollach

Clachan

310

BEINN NA LEAC

B883

Inverarish

Eyre Point

River Toscaig

Loch Carron

Strome

Ardnarf

The
raes

Suisnish
Point

Eilean
Meadhonach

Eilean
Mòr

Plockton

Stromeferry

horran

Caolas Mor

CROWLIN
ISLANDS

Port-an-Eorna

Duirinish

15

Sconser

SCALPAY

67

Longay

Drumbuie

BEINN RAIMH
447

773

AMAIG

396

MULLACH NA
CARN

Pabay

Badicaul

138

YE

Dunan

Loch Ainort

27

Kyle of Lochalsh

Balmacara

Lochalsh House
& Garden

Auchtertyre

Conchra

Nostie

Luib

Caolas Scalpay

Kyleakin

Kirkton

Ardelve

Bunda

564

GLAS BHEINN
MHÒR

A850

Corry

A854 Bay

Lower
Breakish

A850

Loch Alsh

Eilean Donan

Dornie

Carndu

Hills

129

6

BEINN
NA LLICH
708   732

Waterloo

Upper
Breakish

7

Rhea

8

Letterfearn

9

Keppo

A87

Broadford

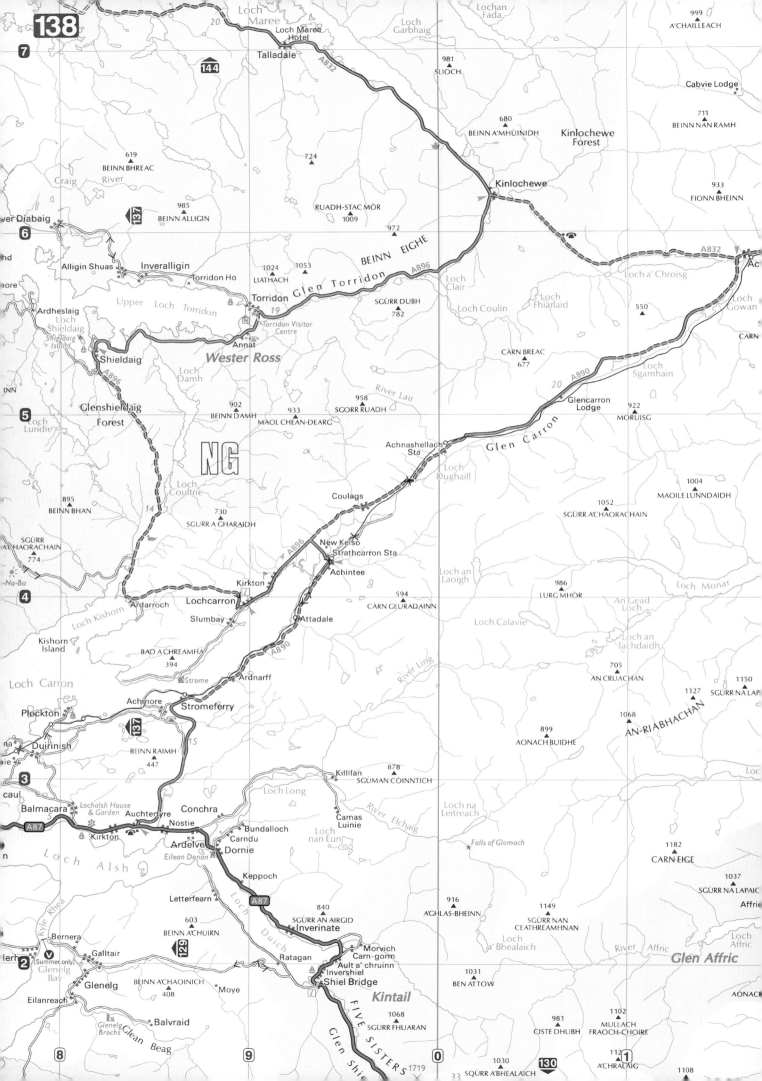

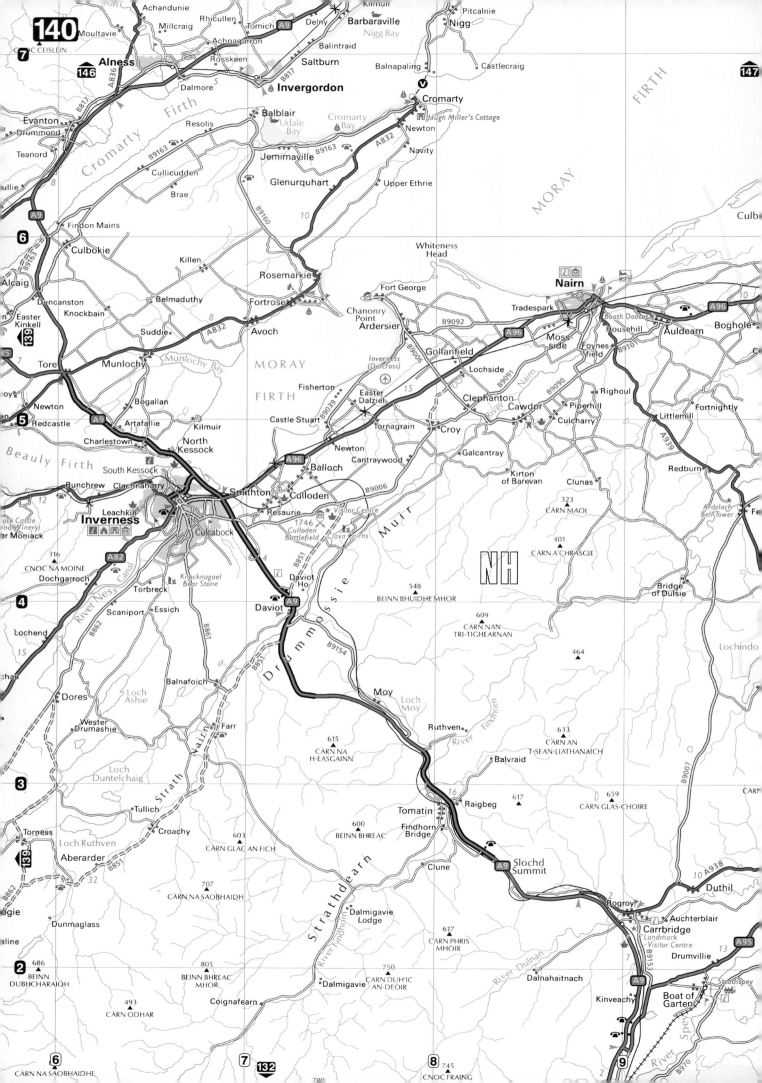

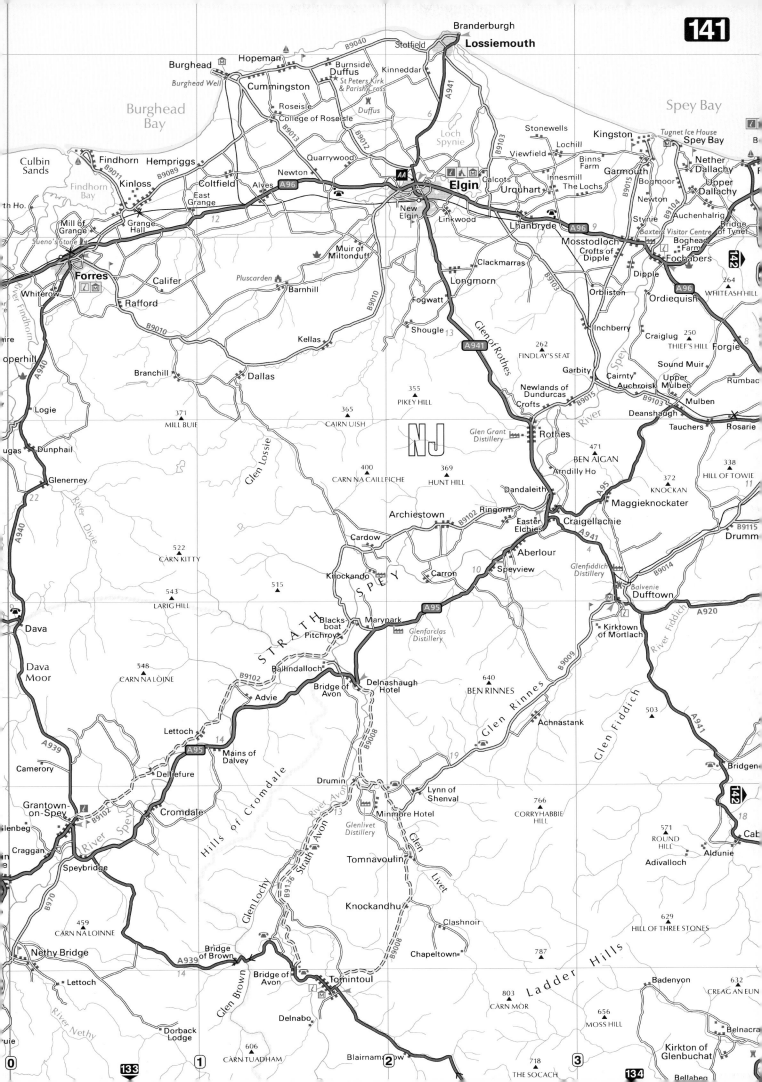

Troup Head
Cullykhan Bay
Crovie
21
Pennan
Protstonhill
Roseharty
Sandhaven
Kinnairds Head
Fraserburgh
Pittulie
Peathill
Craigiefold
Coburby
Percyhorner
Pitblae
Kirktown
Fraserburgh Bay
Cairnbulg
Inverallochy
New Aberdour
Boyndlie
Mid Ardlaw
B9031
B9032
A98
10
Memsie
A92
St Combs
Netherbrae
221
BRACKLAMORE HILL
New Pitsligo
B9030
Strichen
Newburgh
A981
234
WAUGHTON HILL
Rathen
Lonmay
Crimonmogate
Loch of Strathbeg
Old Rattray
Rattray Head
Crofts of Savoch
A952
Crimond
Blackhill
18
New Byth
Bonnykelly
Garmond
Oldwhat
Balthangie
13
inestown
New Leeds
B9093
Longhill
Leys
Denhead
Backfolds
Kirktown
St Fergus
Rora
A952
Fetterangus
Dunshillock
Deer Abbey
Mintlaw
A92
Longside
Inverugie
Buchanhaven
Peterhead
B9170
New Deer
Maud
B9106
Fedderate
6
B9029
Old Deer
Visitor Centre
Blackhill of Clackriach
Bulwark
Stuartfield
Millbreck
A950
Inverquhomery
Nether Kinmundy
Little Dens
Hillhead of Cocklaw
Peterhead Bay
Burnhaven
A948
Maryhill
Slacks of Cairnbanno
Millbrex
Drymuir
Nethermuir
Clola
Blackhill
Boddam
Buchan Ness
B9170
Kirkton
Knaven
Kinnadie
NK
Stirling
B9030
Cottown
Cairnorrie
Auchnagatt
12
Inkhorn
Coldwells
Kinknockie
Blackhill
Coldwells
Lendrum Terrace
B9005
thenty
Brownhill
Muirtack
14
Hatton
Auchiries
Bullers of Buchan
North Haven
A952
dhead
Haddo
Methlick
R Ythan
Arthrath
Birness
A92
Bogbrae
17
A975
Chapel Hill
Cruden Bay
Port Errol
Bay of Cruden
The Skares
14
B9005
Barthol Chapel
Earlsford
Haddo
Auchedly
Wedderlairs
Medieval Tomb
Ythsie
Tulloch
Jarves
A948
Kinharrachie
Artrochie
Auchmacoy
Craigdam
Tolquhon
Ellon
Esslemont
Kirkton of Logie Buchan
Collieston
Kirktown of Slains
Idrum
A920
Carnbrogie
Pitmedden
B9000
32
Kirktown of Bourtie
Udny Green
Housieside
Whiterashes
Woodland
Pettymuk
B999
Culterculle
A947
Nether Crimond
Tillygreig
urie
Straloch
B993
Reisque
Newmachar
B979
Causeyend
Delfrigs
17
Kinmuck
ll Church
Whitecairns
Belhelvie
B9000
Newburgh
Foveran
A92
Kinmundy
B977
Hatton of Fintray
Dyce Symbol Stones
Overton
Parkhill
Potterton
8
6
B977
135
9
B997
R Don
B999
Blackdog
Dyce
Aberdeen
0
1

SCALE
0 1 2 3 4 5 miles
0 1 2 3 4 5 kilometres

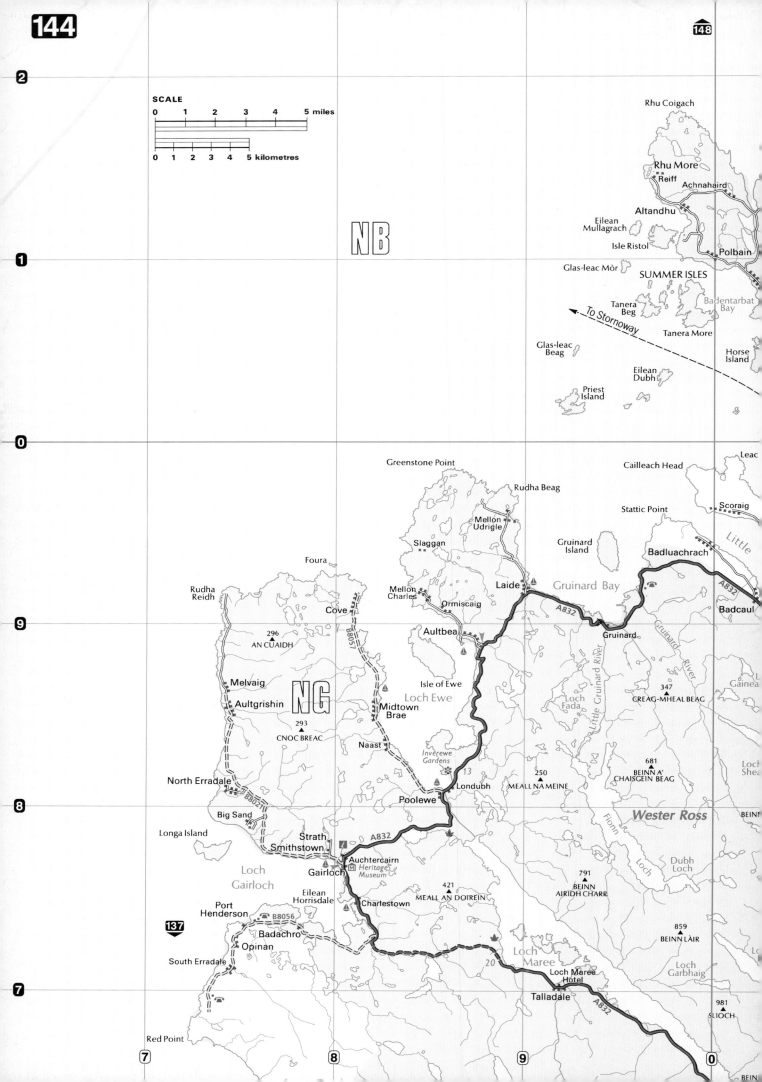

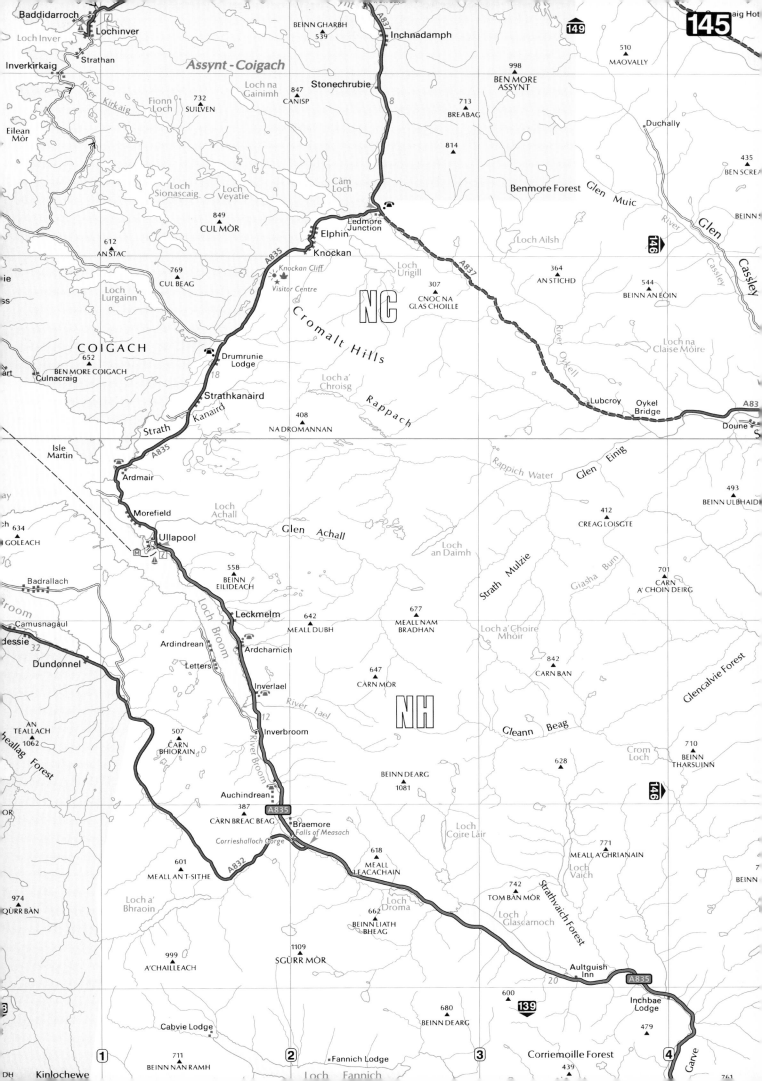

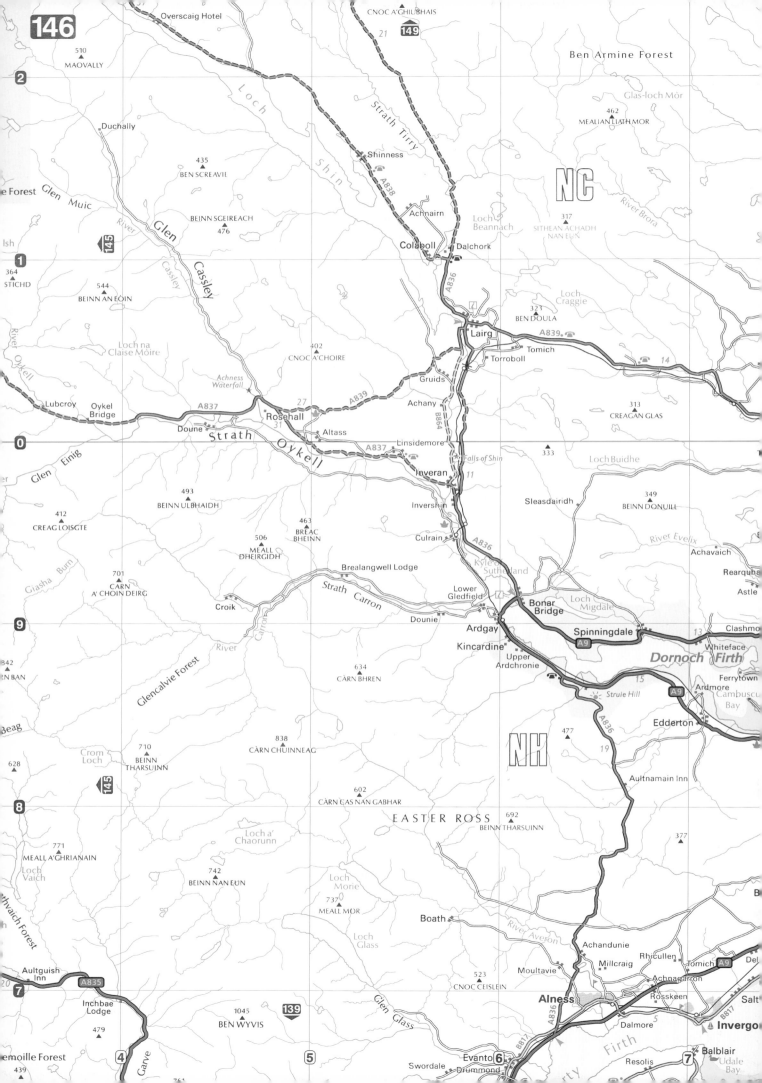

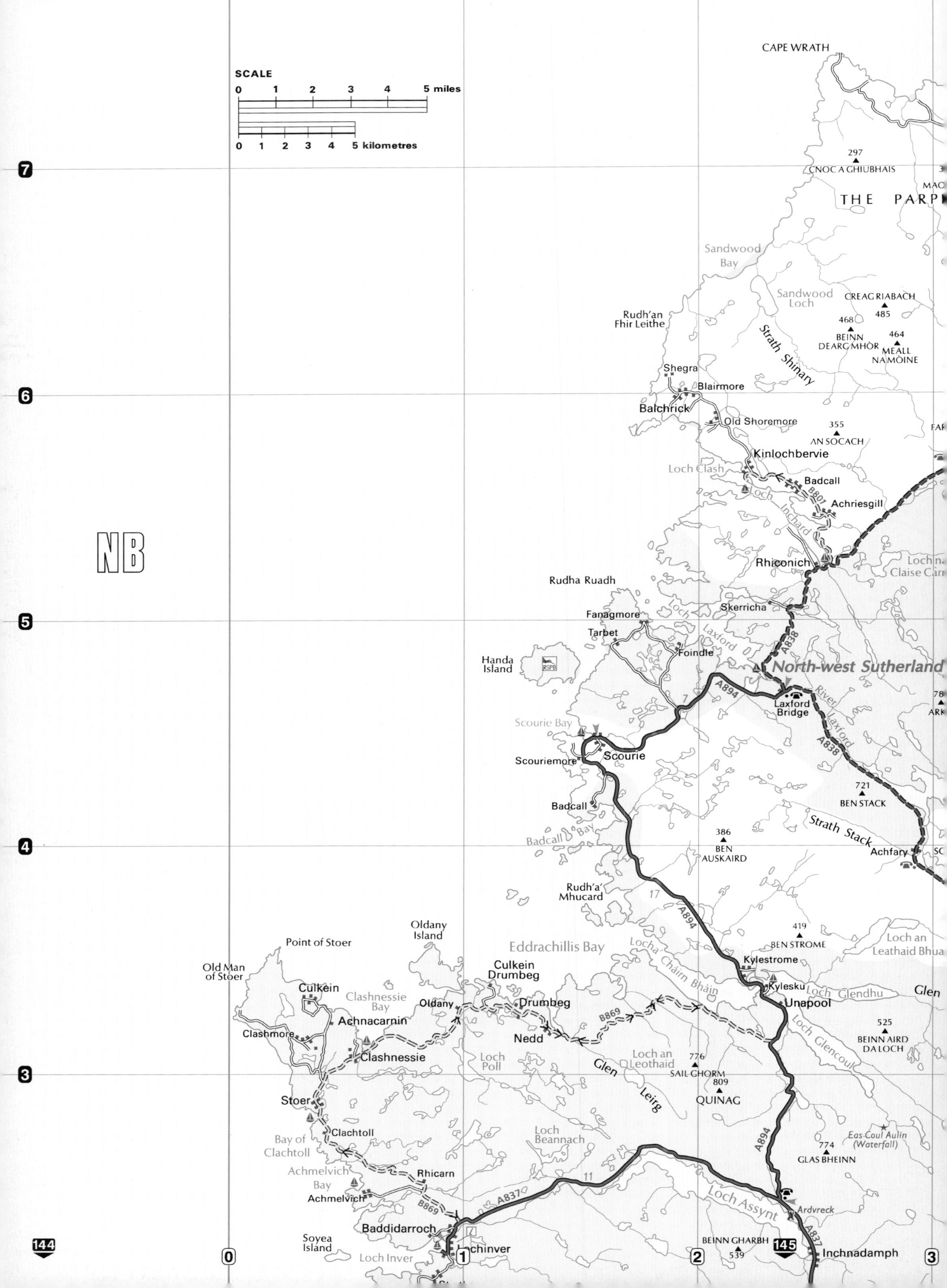

NB

SCALE

0　1　2　3　4　5 miles

0　1　2　3　4　5 kilometres

CAPE WRATH

CNOC A GHIUBHAIS
297 ▲

THE PARP

MAC

Sandwood
Bay

Sandwood
Loch

CREAG RIABACH
▲ 485
Rudh'an
Fhir Leithe
468 ▲
BEINN
DEARG MHÒR
464 ▲
MEALL
NA MÒINE

Strath Shinary

Shegra
Blairmore
Balchrick
Old Shoremore
355 ▲
AN SOCACH
Kinlochbervie
FAR

Loch Clash
Badcall
Loch Inchard
B801
Achriesgill

Rhiconich
Loch na
Claise Carr

Rudha Ruadh

Fanagmore
Tarbet
Foindle
Skerricha

A838
Loch

Handa
Island
RSPB
Laxford
▲ North-west Sutherland
River Laxford
78
ARK

Scourie Bay
A894
Laxford
Bridge

Scouriemore
Scourie
7

Strath Stack
721 ▲
BEN STACK

Badcall

Badcall Bay
386 ▲
BEN
AUSKAIRD
Achfary
SC

Rudh'a'
Mhucard
A894
17

419 ▲
BEN STROME
Loch an
Leathaid Bhua

Oldany
Island

Point of Stoer

Eddrachillis Bay
Loch a Chàirn Bhàin
Kylestrome
Kylesku
Unapool
Loch Glendhu
Glen

Old Man
of Stoer
Culkein
Culkein
Drumbeg
B869
Oldany
Drumbeg
Loch Glencoul
525 ▲
BEINN AIRD
DA LOCH

Clashnessie
Bay
Achnacarnin
Nedd
776 ▲
SAIL GHORM

Clashmore
Clashnessie
Loch
Poll
Glen
Leirg
809 ▲
QUINAG

Stoer
Loch an
Leothaid

Eas-Coul-Aulin
(Waterfall)
774 ▲
GLAS BHEINN

Clachtoll
Loch
Beannach
A894

Bay of
Clachtoll
Achmelvich
Bay
Rhicarn
11
A837
Loch Assynt
Ardvreck
A837

Achmelvich
B869

Soyea
Island
Baddidarroch
chinver

BEINN GHARBH
539 ▲
Inchnadamph

Loch Inver

7
6
5
4
3

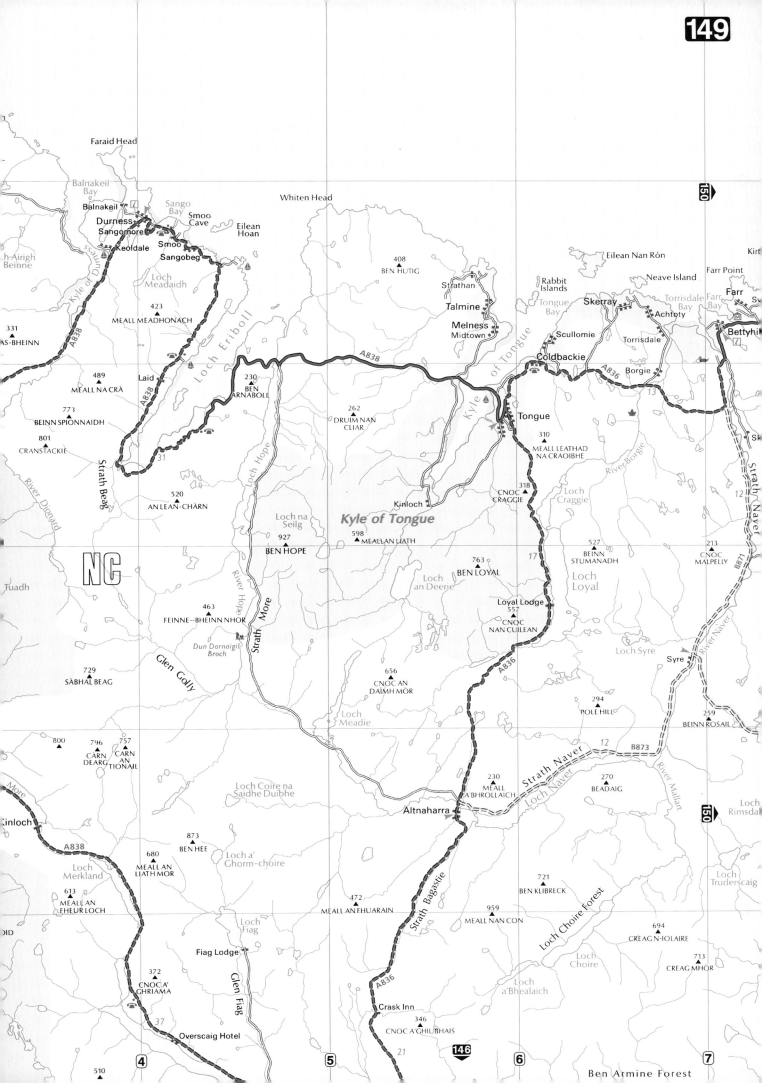

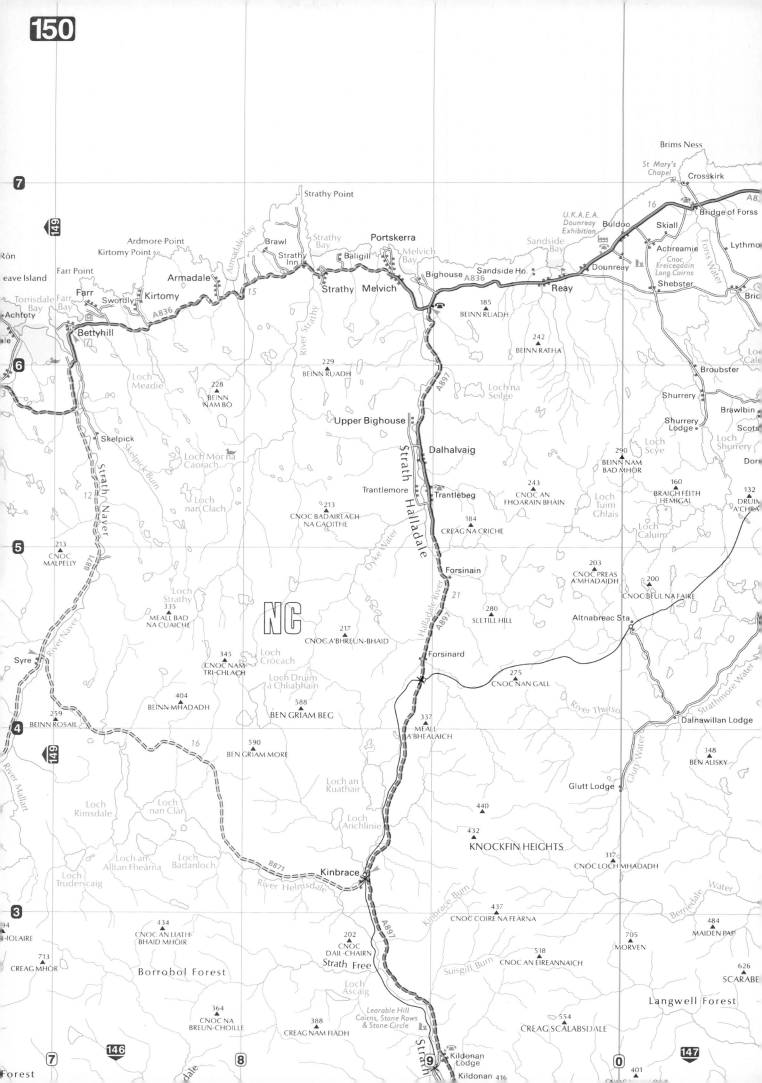

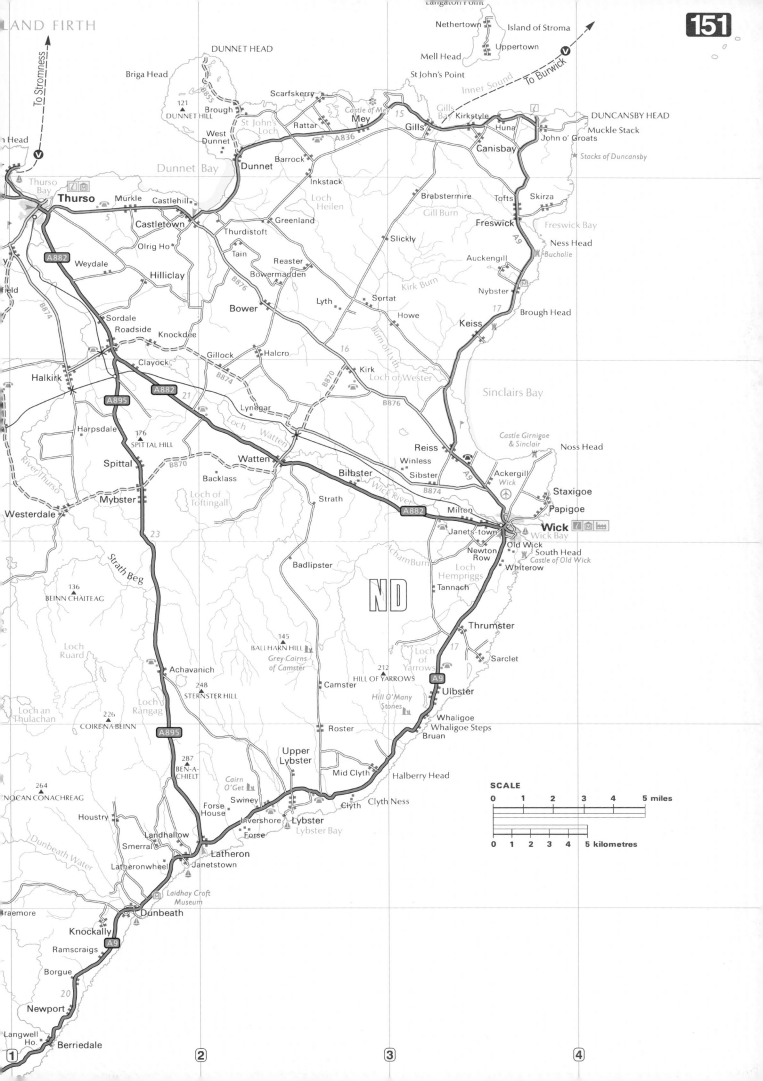

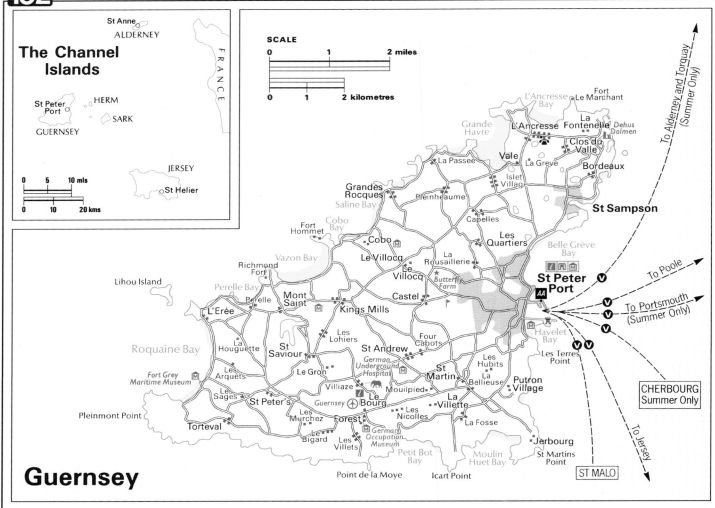

The Channel Islands

St Anne
ALDERNEY

FRANCE

St Peter Port
HERM
SARK
GUERNSEY

JERSEY
St Helier

SCALE
0   5   10 mls
0   10   20 kms

SCALE
0   1   2 miles
0   1   2 kilometres

To Alderney and Torquay (Summer Only)

L'Ancresse Bay
Le Fort Marchant
Grande Havre
L'Ancresse
La Fontenelle
La Dehus Dolmen
Clos du Valle
Vale
La Grève
Bordeaux
La Passee
St Sampson
Grandes Rocques
Pleinheaume
Capelles
Les Quartiers
Belle Grève Bay
Fort Hommet
Cobo Bay
Saline Bay
Cobo
Le Villocq
La Rousaillerie
Butterfly Farm
St Peter Port
To Poole
Richmond Fort
Vazon Bay
Le Villocq
Castel
Havelet Bay
To Portsmouth (Summer Only)
Lihou Island
Perelle Bay
Perelle
Mont Saint
Kings Mills
Les Terres Point
L'Erée
Four Cabots
Les Lohiers
St Andrew
German Underground Hospital
Les Hubits
La Bellieuse
Putron Village
CHERBOURG Summer Only
Roquaine Bay
La Houguette
St Saviour
Le Gron
St Martin
Les Murchez
Les Arquets
Villiaze
Moulpied
Fort Grey Maritime Museum
Les Sages
St Peter's
Le Bourg
Guernsey
Les Nicolles
La Villette
La Fosse
To Jersey
Pleinmont Point
Forest
Les Bigard
Les Villets
German Occupation Museum
Jerbourg
St Martins Point
ST MALO
Torteval
Petit Bot Bay
Point de la Moye
Icart Point
Moulin Huet Bay

Guernsey

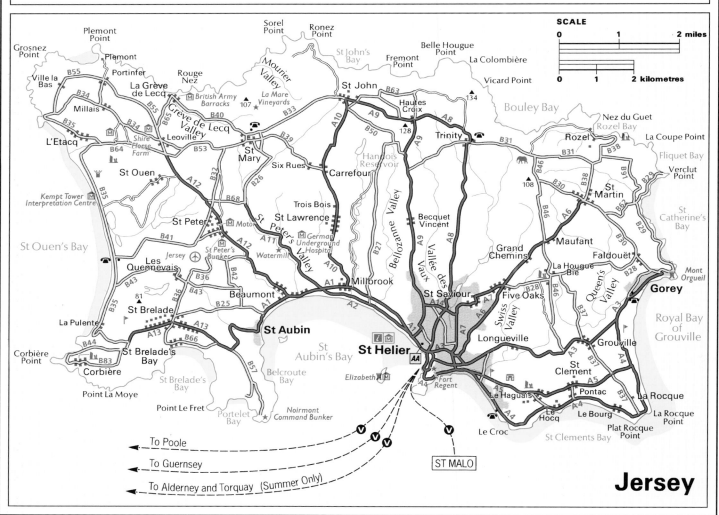

SCALE
0   1   2 miles
0   1   2 kilometres

Grosnez Point
Plemont Point
Plemont
Sorel Point
Ronez Point
Belle Hougue Point
Ville la Bas
Portinfer
B55
Rouge Nez
Mourier Valley
St John's Bay
Fremont Point
La Colombière
Vicard Point
Bouley Bay
La Grève de Lecq
British Army Barracks
La Mare Vineyards
St John
Hautes Croix
Millais
B34
B55
Grève de Lecq Valley
B40
107
B33
A10
A9
A8
Nez du Guet
Rozel Bay
L'Etacq
B35
B65
Leoville
Shire Horse Farm
St Mary
B39
128
Trinity
Rozel
La Coupe Point
B64
B53
Six Rues
Hambie Reservoir
B31
B38
Fliquet Bay
B32
B26
Carrefour
B50
B46
St Martin
Verclut Point
St Ouen
Trois Bois
108
B30
B38
B91
Kempt Tower Interpretation Centre
B68
St Lawrence
German Underground Hospital
Bellozanne Valley
Vallée des Vaux
Maufant
Faldouët
St Catherine's Bay
St Peter
Motor
Becquet Vincent
B46
La Hougue Bie
B28
Mont Orgueil
B41
St Peter's Valley
Grand Chemins
B28
Queen's Valley
B29
St Ouen's Bay
A12
Jersey
St Peter's Bunker
Watermill
St Saviour
Five Oaks
B37
B28
Gorey
Les Quennevais
B36
A11
A10
Millbrook
A14
A7
Swiss Valley
Grouville
Royal Bay of Grouville
81
B36
B43
Beaumont
B25
A1
A2
St Helier
Longueville
A3
St Brelade
La Pulente
A13
B66
St Aubin
St Clement
A5
Corbière Point
B44
B83
St Brelade's Bay
A13
B51
St Aubin's Bay
A1
AA
Le Haguais
Pontac
La Rocque
Corbière
Belcroute Bay
Elizabeth
Fort Regent
A4
Le Bourg
Point La Moye
St Brelade's Bay
A4
Le Hocq
La Rocque Point
Point Le Fret
Portelet Bay
Noirmont Command Bunker
Le Croc
Plat Rocque Point
St Clements Bay

To Poole
To Guernsey
To Alderney and Torquay (Summer Only)
ST MALO

Jersey

Isle of Man

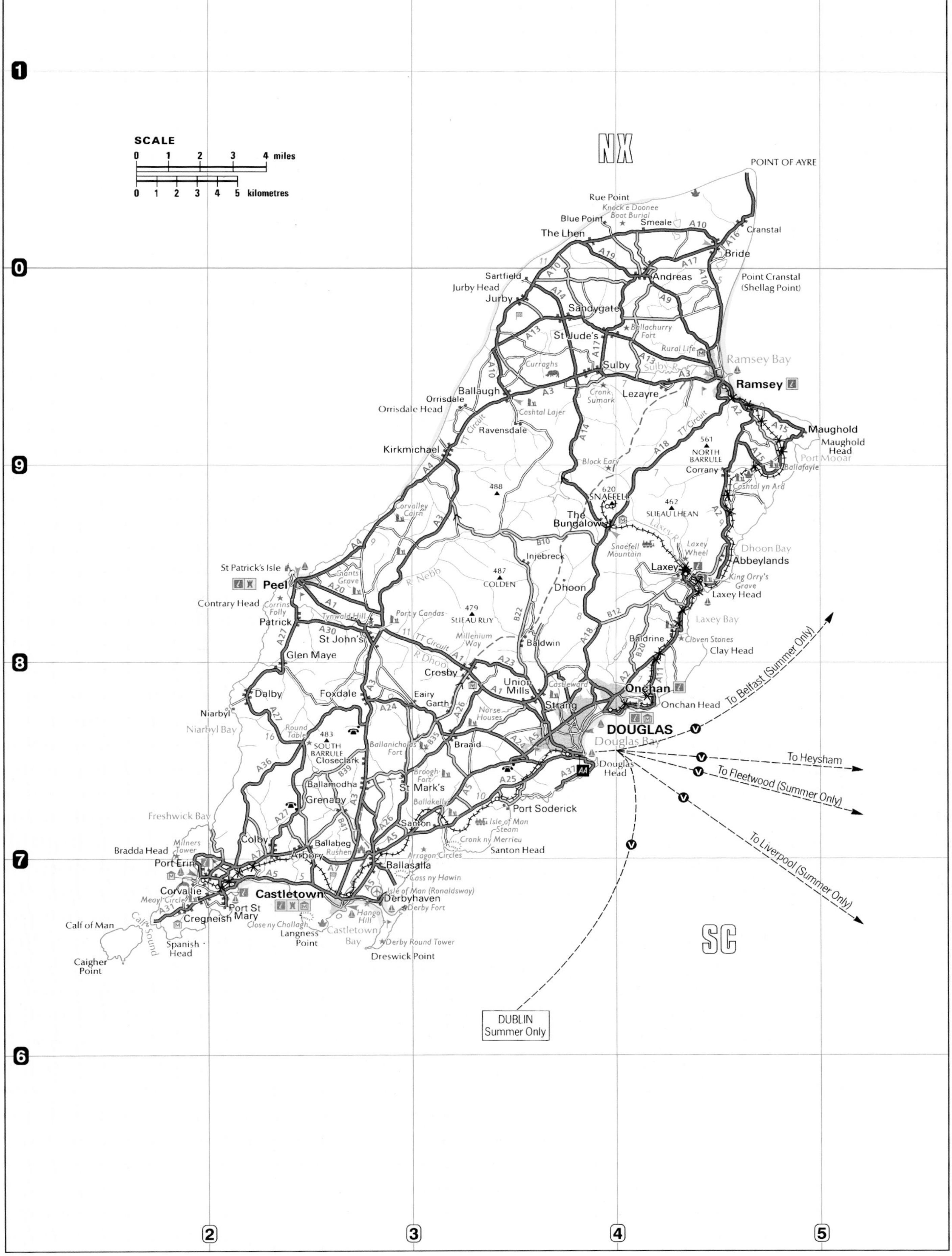

SCALE

0 1 2 3 4 miles

0 1 2 3 4 5 kilometres

NX

POINT OF AYRE

Rue Point
Knock e Doonee Boot Burial
Blue Point
Smeale
The Lhen
Cranstal
Bride
Sartfield
Andreas
Point Cranstal (Shellag Point)
Jurby Head
Jurby
Sandygate
St Jude's
Ballachurry Fort
Rural Life
Ramsey Bay
Sulby
Ramsey
Curraghs
Sulby R.
Ballaugh
Lezayre
Orrisdale
Cronk Sumark
Orrisdale Head
Coshtal Lajer
Maughold
Maughold Head
Ravensdale
561 NORTH BARRULE
Port Mooar
Kirkmichael
Block Eary
Corrany
Ballafayle
Coshtal yn Ard
620 SNAEFELL
462 SLIEAU LHEAN
488
Corvalley Cairn
The Bungalow
Dhoon Bay
Abbeylands
Injebreck
Laxey Wheel
Snaefell Mountain
Laxey
King Orry's Grave
St Patrick's Isle
Giants Grave
487 COLDEN
Laxey Head
Peel
R. Nebb
Laxey Bay
Contrary Head
Corrins Folly
Port y Candas
479 SLIEAU RUY
Dhoon
Laxey R.
Cloven Stones
Clay Head
Patrick
Tynwald Hill
TT Circuit
B22
Baldwin
Baldrine
St John's
Millenium Way
To Belfast (Summer Only)
Glen Maye
Crosby
R. Dhoo
Union Mills
Castleward
Onchan
Dalby
Foxdale
Eairy Garth
Norse Houses
Strang
Onchan Head
To Heysham
Niarbyl
A24
Braaid
DOUGLAS
To Fleetwood (Summer Only)
Niarbyl Bay
Round Table
483 SOUTH BARRULE
Ballanicholas Fort
Broogh Fort
Douglas Bay
Douglas Head
Closeclark
St Mark's
Ballakelly
To Liverpool (Summer Only)
Ballamodha
Grenaby
Ballakilley
Isle of Man Steam
Port Soderick
Freshwick Bay
Santon
Cronk ny Merriue
Milners Tower
Colby
Ballabeg
Arragon Circles
Santon Head
Bradda Head
Arbory
Ballasalla
Cass ny Hawin
Port Erin
Rushen
Isle of Man (Ronaldsway)
SC
Corvallie
Meayl Circle
Port St Mary
Castletown
Derbyhaven
Derby Fort
Calf of Man
Cregneish
Close ny Chollagh
Hango Hill
Castletown Bay
Caigher Point
Spanish Head
Langness Point
Derby Round Tower
Dreswick Point

DUBLIN Summer Only

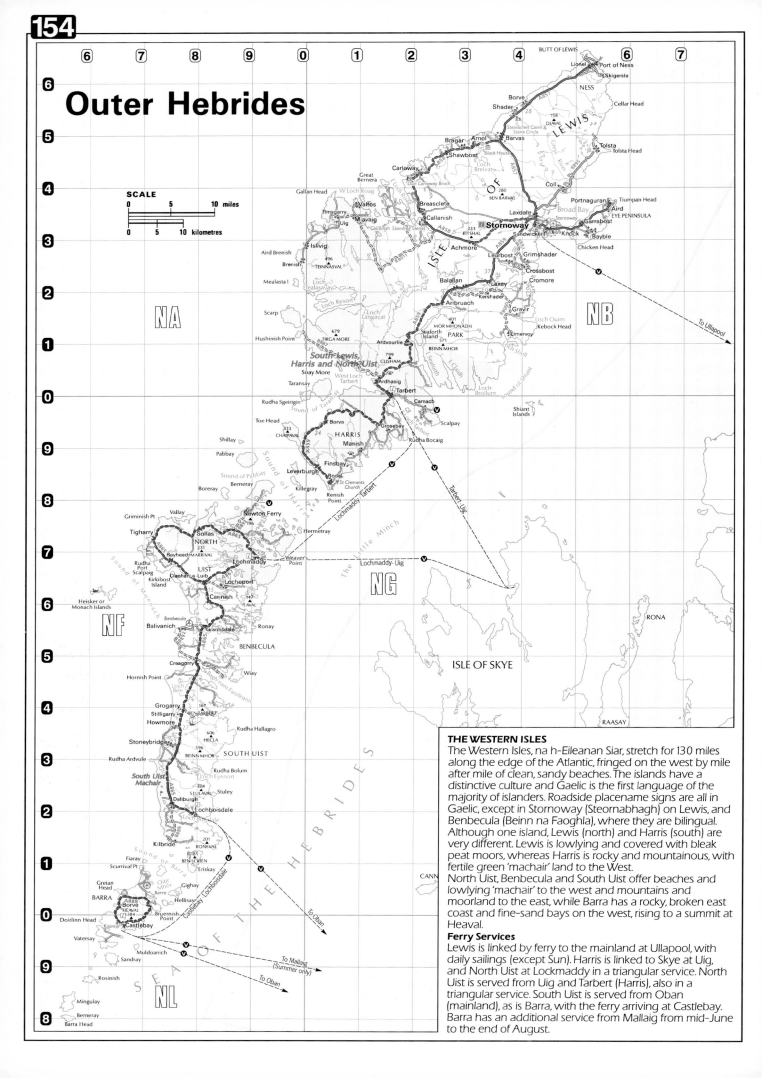

Outer Hebrides

THE WESTERN ISLES
The Western Isles, na h-Eileanan Siar, stretch for 130 miles along the edge of the Atlantic, fringed on the west by mile after mile of clean, sandy beaches. The islands have a distinctive culture and Gaelic is the first language of the majority of islanders. Roadside placename signs are all in Gaelic, except in Stornoway (Steornabhagh) on Lewis, and Benbecula (Beinn na Faoghla), where they are bilingual. Although one island, Lewis (north) and Harris (south) are very different. Lewis is lowlying and covered with bleak peat moors, whereas Harris is rocky and mountainous, with fertile green 'machair' land to the West.
North Uist, Benbecula and South Uist offer beaches and lowlying 'machair' to the west and mountains and moorland to the east, while Barra has a rocky, broken east coast and fine-sand bays on the west, rising to a summit at Heaval.

Ferry Services
Lewis is linked by ferry to the mainland at Ullapool, with daily sailings (except Sun). Harris is linked to Skye at Uig, and North Uist at Lockmaddy in a triangular service. North Uist is served from Uig and Tarbert (Harris), also in a triangular service. South Uist is served from Oban (mainland), as is Barra, with the ferry arriving at Castlebay. Barra has an additional service from Mallaig from mid-June to the end of August.

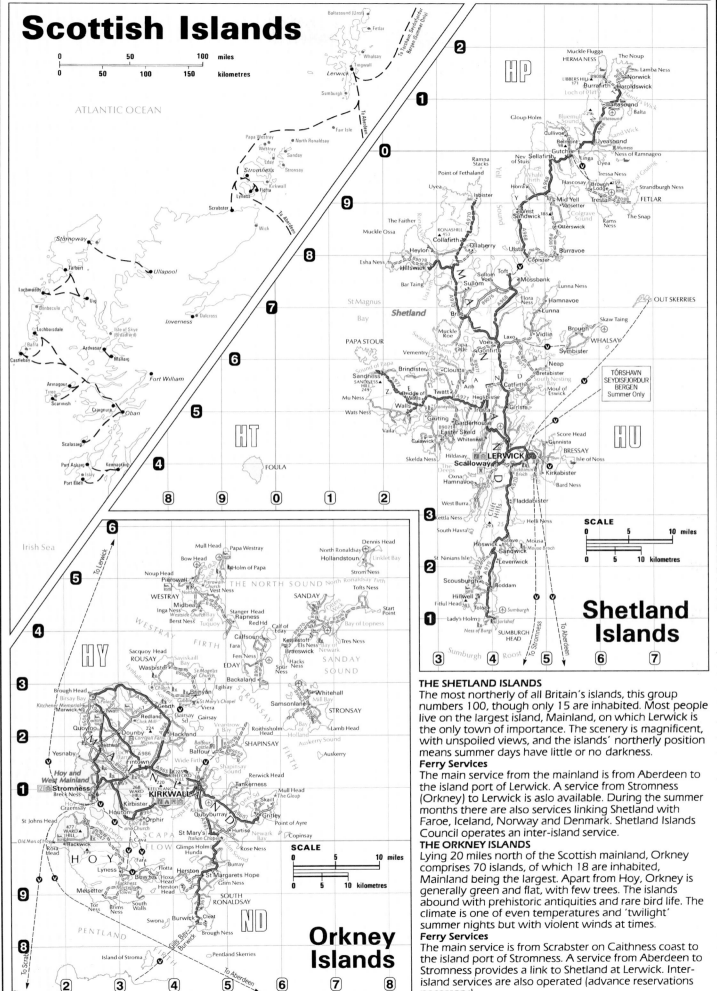

Scottish Islands

50 miles 100
50 100 150 kilometres

ATLANTIC OCEAN

Shetland Islands

THE SHETLAND ISLANDS
The most northerly of all Britain's islands, this group numbers 100, though only 15 are inhabited. Most people live on the largest island, Mainland, on which Lerwick is the only town of importance. The scenery is magnificent, with unspoiled views, and the islands' northerly position means summer days have little or no darkness.
Ferry Services
The main service from the mainland is from Aberdeen to the island port of Lerwick. A service from Stromness (Orkney) to Lerwick is aslo available. During the summer months there are also services linking Shetland with Faroe, Iceland, Norway and Denmark. Shetland Islands Council operates an inter-island service.
THE ORKNEY ISLANDS
Lying 20 miles north of the Scottish mainland, Orkney comprises 70 islands, of which 18 are inhabited, Mainland being the largest. Apart from Hoy, Orkney is generally green and flat, with few trees. The islands abound with prehistoric antiquities and rare bird life. The climate is one of even temperatures and 'twilight' summer nights but with violent winds at times.
Ferry Services
The main service is from Scrabster on Caithness coast to the island port of Stromness. A service from Aberdeen to Stromness provides a link to Shetland at Lerwick. Inter-island services are also operated (advance reservations necessary).

Orkney Islands

1   **2**

Abbeydorney G2
Abbeyfeale G2
Abbeyleix G4
Adamstown G4
Adare G2
Adrigole H2
Ahascragh F3
Ahoghill D5
Allihies H1
Anascaul H1
Annalong E5
Annestown H4
Antrim D5
Ardagh G2
Ardara D3
Ardcath F5
Ardee E4
Ardfert G2
Ardfinnan G3
Ardglass E5
Ardgroom H1
Arklow G5
Arless G4
Armagh D4
Armoy D5
Arthurstown H4
Arvagh E4
Ashbourne F4
Ashford D5
Askeaton G2
Athboy E4
Athea G2
Athenry F3
Athleague F3
Athlone F3
Athy F4
Augher D4
Aughnacloy D4
Aughrim G5
Avoca G5

Balieborough E4
Balbriggan F5
Balla G2
Ballacolla G4
Ballaghaderreen E3
Ballina G2
Ballina E2
Ballinafad E3
Ballinagh E4
Ballinakill G4
Ballinalee E3
Ballinamallard D4
Ballinamore E3
Ballinascarty H2
Ballinasloe F3
Ballindine E2
Ballineen H2
Ballingarry G3
Ballingarry G2
Ballingeary H2
(Beal Atha an Ghaorfthaidh)
Ballinhassig H3
Ballinlough E3
Ballinrobe E2
Ballinspittle H2
Ballintober E3
Ballintra D3
Ballivor F4
Ballon G4
Ballybaun F3
Ballybay G4
Ballybofey D3
Ballybunion G2
Ballycanew G5
Ballycarry D5
Ballycastle D2
Ballycastle C5
Ballyclare D5
Ballyconnelly F1
Ballycotton H3
Ballycumber F3
Ballydehob J2
Ballydesmond H2
Ballyduff H3
Ballyduff G2
Ballyfarnan E3
Ballygalley D5
Ballygar F3
Ballygawley D5
Ballygowan D5
Ballyhaise E4
Ballyhale G4
Ballyhaunis E3
Ballyhean E2
Ballyheige G1
Ballyjamesduff E4
Ballykeeran F3
Ballylanders G3
Ballylongford G2
Ballylooby G4
Ballyliffan G4
Ballymahon F3
Ballymakeery H2
Ballymaloe H3
Ballymena D5
Ballymoe E3
Ballymoney C4
Ballymore F3
Ballymore Eustace F4
Ballymote E3
Ballynahinch D5
Ballynure D5

Ballyragget G4
Ballyroan G4
Ballyronan D4
Ballysadare E3
Ballyshannon D3
Ballyvaughan F2
Ballywalter D5
Balrothery F5
Baltimore J2
Baltinglass G4
Banagher F3
Banbridge D5
Bandon H2
Bangor D5
Bangor Erris E2
Bansha G3
Banteer H2
Bantry H2
Barryporeen H3
Beaufort H2
Belcoo D3
Belfast D5
Belgooly H3
Bellaghy D4
Belleek D3
Belmullet D2
(Beal an Mhuirhead)
Belturbet E4
Benburb D4
Bennetsbridge G4
Beragh D4
Birr F3
Blacklion D3
Blackwater G5
Blarney H3
Blessington F4
Boherbue H2
Borris G4
Borris-in-Ossory G3
Borrisokane F3
Borrisoleigh G3
Boyle E3
Bracknagh F4
Bray F5
Bridgetown H4
Brittas F4
Broadford G3
Broadford G2
Broughshane D5
Bruff G3
Bruree G3
Bunclody G4
Buncrana C4
Bundoran D3
Bunnahowen D2
Bunnyconnellan E2
Bushmills C4
Butler's Bridge E4
Buttevant H2

Cadamstown F3
Caherconlish G3
Caherdaniel H1
Cahir G3
Cahirciveen H1
Caledon D4
Callan G4
Caltra F3
Camolin G4
Camp G1
Cappagh White G3
Cappamore G3
Cappoquin H3
Carlanstown E4
Carlingford E5
Carlow G4
Carndonagh C4
Carnew G4
Carnlough C5
Carracastle E3
Carrick D3
(An Charraig)
Carrickfergus D5
Carrickmacross E4
Carrickmore D4
Carrick-on-Shannon E3
Carrigahorig F3
Carrigaline H3
Carrigallen E3
Carriganimmy H2
Carrigans C4
Carrigtohill H3
Carrowkeel C4
Carryduff D5
Cashel G3
Castlebar E2
Castlebellingham E5
Castleblayney E4
Castlebridge G4
Castlecomer G4
Castle Cove H1
Castlederg D4
Castledermot G4
Castleisland G2
Castlemaine H2
Castlemartyr H3
Castleplunkett E3
Castlepollard E4
Castlerea E3
Castlerock C4
Castleshane E4
Castletown F4
Castletownbere H1

Castletownroche H3
Castletownshend J2
Castlewellan E5
Causeway G2
Cavan E4
Ceanannus Mor (Kells) E4
Celbridge F4
Charlestown E3
Clady D4
Clane F4
Clara F3
Clarecastle G2
Claremorris E2
Clarinbridge F2
Clashmore H3
Claudy C4
Cliffony D3
Clogan F3
Clogh G4
Clogheen H3
Clogher D4
Clohamon G4
Clonakilty H2
Clonard F4
Clonaslee F3
Clonbulloge F4
Clonbur (An Fhairche) E2
Clondalkin F4
Clones E4
Clonmany C4
Clonmel G3
Clonmellon E4
Clonmore G3
Clonony F3
Clonoulty G3
Clonroche G4
Clontibret E4
Cloonbannin H2
Cloondara F3
Cloonkeen H2
Cloonlara G3
Clough D5
Cloughjordan F3
Cloyne H3
Coagh D4
Coalisland D4
Cobh H3
Coleraine C4
Collinstown E4
Collon E4
Collooney E3
Comber D5
Conna H3
Cookstown D4
Coole E4
Cooraclare G2
Cootehill E4
Cork H3
Cork Airport H3
Cornamona F2
Corofin F2
Courtmacsherry H2
Courtown Harbour G5
Craigavon D5
Craughwell F3
Creggs E3
Cresslough C3
Croagh G2
Crolly (Croithli) C3
Crookedwood E4
Crookhaven J1
Crookstown H2
Croom G2
Crossakeel E4
Cross Barry H2
Crosshaven H3
Crossmaglen E4
Crossmolina E2
Crumlin D5
Crusheen F2
Culdaff C4
Culleybackey D5
Curracloe G4
Curraghboy F3
Curry E3

Daingean F4
Delvin E4
Derrygonnelly D3
Derrylin E4
Dervock C4
Dingle (An Daingean) H1
Doagh D5
Donaghadee D5
Donaghmore G3
Donegal D3
Doneraile H3
Doonbeg G2
Douglas H3
Downpatrick D5
Dowra E3
Draperstown D4
Drimoleague H2
Dripsey H2
Drogheda E5
Dromahair D3
Dromcolliher H3
Dromore D5
Dromore D4
Dromore West D2
Drum E4
Drumconrath E4

Drumkeeran E3
Drumlish E3
Drumod E3
Drumquin D4
Drumshanbo E3
Drumsna E3
Duagh G2
Dublin F5
Duleek E4
Dunboyne F4
Duncormick H4
Dundalk E5
Dunderrow H2
Dundrum B5
Dunfanaghy C4
Dungannon D4
Dungarvan H3
Dungarvan E4
Dungiven C4
Dunglow C3
Dungourney H3
Dunkineely D3
Dun Laoghaire F5
Dunlavin F4
Dunleer E4
Dunloy C5
Dunmanway H2
Dunmore East H4
Dunmurry D5
Dunshauglin F4
Durrow G4
Durrus H2

Eaky D2
Edenderry F4
Edgeworthstown E3
Eglinton C4
Elphin E3
Emyvale D4
Enfield F4
Ennis F2
Enniscorthy G4
Enniscrone D2
Enniskean H2
Enniskillen D4
Ennistymon F2
Eyrecourt F3

Farnaght E3
Farranfore H2
Feakle F3
Fenagh E3
Fermoy H3
Ferns G4
Fethard H4
Fethard G4
Finnea E4
Fintona D4
Fivemiletown D4
Fontstown F4
Foulksmills H4
Foxford E2
Foynes G2
Freemount G2
Frenchpark E3
Freshford G4
Fuerty E3

Galbally G3
Galway F2
Garrison D3
Garvagh C4
Geashill F4
Gilford D5
Glandore J2
Glanmire H3
Glanworth H3
Glaslough D4
Glassan F3
Glenamoy E3
Glenarm C5
Glenavy D5
Glenbeigh H1
Glencolumbkille D3
(Gleann Cholm Cille)
Glendalough E5
Glenealy G5
Glenfarne D3
Glengarriff H2
Glenmore G4
Glenties D3
Glenville H3
Glin G2
Glinsk F2
(Glinsce)
Golden G3
Goleen J1
Goresbridge G4
Gorey G5
Gort F2
Gortin D4
Gowran G4
Graiguenamanagh G4
Grallagh G3
Granard E4
Grange D3
Greencastle D5
Greyabbey D5
Greystones F5
Gulladuff D4

Hacketstown G4
Headford F2

Herbertstown G3
Hillsborough D5
Hilltown E5
Holycross G3
Holywood D5
Howth F5

Inch H1
Inchigeelagh H2
Inishannon H2

Johnstown G3

Kanturk H2
Keadue E3
Keady E4
Keel E1
Keenagh E3
Kells D5
Kenmare H2
Kesh D3
Kilbeggan F4
Kilberry E4
Kilbrittain H2
Kilcar D3
(Cill Charthaigh)
Kilcock F4
Kilcolgan F2
Kilconnell F3
Kilconnell F2
Kilcoole F5
Kilcormac F3
Kilcullen F4
Kilcurry E4
Kildare F4
Kildavin G4
Kildorrery H3
Kildress D4
Kilfenora F2
Kilfinnane G3
Kilgarvan H2
Kilkee G2
Kilkeel E5
Kilkelly E2
Kilkenny G4
Kilkieran F2
(Cill Ciarain)
Kilkinlea G3
Kill H4
Killadysert G2
Killala D2
Killaloe G3
Killarney H2
Killashandra E4
Killashee E3
Killeagh H3
Killeigh F4
Killenaule G3
Killimer G2
Killimor F3
Killiney F5
Killinick H4
Killorglin H1
Killough E5
Killucan F4
Killybegs D3
Killyleagh D5
Kilmacanoge F5
Kilmacrenan C3
Kilmacthomas H4
Kilmaganny G4
Kilmaine E2
Kilmallock G3
Kilmanagh G4
Kilmanahan G3
Kilmeaden H4
Kilmeage F4
Kilmeedy G2
Kilmichael H2
Kilmore Quay H4
Kilnaleck E4
Kilrea C4
Kilrush G2
Kilsheelan G3
Kiltealy G4
Kiltegan G4
Kiltimagh E2
Kiltoom F3
Kingscourt E4
Kinlough D3
Kinnegad F4
Kinnitty F3
Kinsale H3
Kinvarra F2
Kircubbin D5
Knock E2
Knockcroghery E3
Knocklofty G3
Knockmahon H4
Knocktopher G4

Lahinch F2
Lanesborough E3
Laragh E3
Laragh G4
Laugh H1
Laurencetown F3
Leap J2
Leenene H1
Leighlinbridge G4
Leitrim E3
Leixlip F4
Lemybrien H3
Letterfrack E2

Letterkenny C3
Lifford D4
Limavady C4
Limerick G3
Lisbellaw D4
Lisburn D5
Liscarroll G2
Lisdoonvarna F2
Lismore H3
Lisnaskea D4
Listowel G2
Loghill G2
Londonderry C4
Longford E3
Loughbrickland D5
Loughgall D4
Loughglinn E3
Loughrea F3
Louisburgh E2
Lucan F4
Lurgan D5
Lusk F5

Macroom H2
Maghera E5
Maghera D5
Magherafelt D4
Maguiresbridge D4
Malahide F5
Malin C4
Malin More D3
Mallow H2
Manorhamilton D3
Markethill D4
Maynooth F4
Maze D5
Middletown D4
Midleton H3
Milford C4
Millstreet H2
Milltown F4
Milltown Malbay G2
Mitchelstown H3
Moate F3
Mohill E3
Molls Cap H2
Monaghan E4
Monasterevin F4
Moneygall G3
Moneymore D4
Monivea F3
Mooncoin H4
Moorfields D5
Mount Bellew F3
Mount Charles D3
Mountmellick F4
Mountrath F4
Mountshannon F3
Mourne Abbey H3
Moville C4
Moy D4
Moylett E4
Moynalty E4
Moyvore F3
Muckross H2
Muff C4
Muine Bheag G4
Mullaboy D4
Mullagh F4
Mullinavat G4
Mullingar F4
Myshall G4

Naas F4
Nad H2
Naul F5
Navan E4
Neale E2
Nenagh G3
Newbliss E4
Newcastle D5
Newcastle West G2
Newinn G3
Newmarket H2
Newmarket-on-Fergus G2
Newport G3
Newport E2
New Ross G4
Newry G5
Newtown G4
Newtownabbey D5
Newtownards D5
Newtown Butler E4
Newtown Forbes E3
Newtownhamilton E4
Newtown Mount Kennedy F5
Newtownstewart D4
Nobber E4

Oilgate G4
Oldcastle E4
Omagh D4
Omeath E5
Oola G3
Oranmore F2
Oughterard F2
Ovens H2

Pallasgreen G3
Parknasilla H1
Partry E2
Passage East H4
Passage West H3

Patrickswell G2
Paulstown G4
Pettigo D3
Plumbridge D4
Pomeroy D4
Portadown D4
Portaferry D5
Portarlington F4
Portavogie D5
Portglenone D4
Port Laoise F4
Portmarnock F5
Portrane F5
Portroe G3
Portrush C4
Portstewart C4
Portumna F3
Poyntzpass D5

Raharney F4
Randalstown D5
Rasharkin C4
Rathangen F4
Rathcoole F4
Rathcormack H3
Rathdowney G3
Rathdrum D5
Rathfriland E5
Rathkeale G2
Rath Luric G2
(Charleville)
Rathmelton C4
Rathmolyon F4
Rathmore H2
Rathmullan C4
Rathnew G5
Rathowen E4
Rathvilty G4
Ratoath F4
Ray C4
Ring H3
(An Rinn)
Ringaskiddy H3
Riverstown E3
Rockcorry E4
Roosky E3
Rosapenna C3
Rosebercon G4
Roscommon F3
Roscrea F3
Ross Carberry J2
Rosscor D3
Rosses Point E3
Rosslare Harbour H4
Rosslea E4
Rostrevor E5
Roundstone F2
Roundwood F5
Rush F5

St Johnstown C4
Saintfield D5
Sallins F4
Scarriff G3
Scartaglen H2
Scarva D5
Schull J2
Scramoge E3
Scribbagh D3
Seskinore D4
Shanagolden G2
Shannon Airport G2
Shannonbridge F3
Shercock E4
Shillelagh G4
Shinrone F3
Shrule F2
Silvermines G3
Sion Mills D4
Sixmilebridge G2
Skerries F5
Skibbereen J2
Slane E4
Sligo E3
Smithborough E4
Sneem H1
Spiddal F2
(An Spideal)
Sporthouse Cross Roads H4
Stewartstown D4
Stonyford G4
Strabane D4

Stradbally F4
Stradone E4
Strandhill D3
Strangford D5
Stranorlar D3
Stratford E3
Strokestown E3
Summerhill F4
Swanlinbar E3
Swatragh D4
Swinford E2
Swords F5

Taghmon G4
Tagoat H4
Tahilla H1
Tallaght F5
Tallow G3
Tallowbridge H3
Tandragee D5
Tang F3
Tarbert G2
Templemore G3
Templepatrick D5
Templetouhy G3
Termonfeckin E5
Thomas Street F3
Thomastown G4
Thurles G3
Timahoe G4
Timoleague H2
Tinahely G4
Tipperary G3
Tobercurry E3
Tobermore D4
Togher F3
Toomyvara G3
Toormore J1
Tralee G2
Tramore H4
Trim F4
Tuam F3
Tuamgraney G3
Tulla G2
Tullamore F4
Tullow G4
Tulsk E3
Turlough G2
Tyholland D4
Tyrrellspass F4

Urlingford G3

Virginia E4
Waddington D4
Warrenpoint E5
Waterford H4
Watergrasshill H3
Waterville H1
Westport E2
Wexford H4
Whitegate H3
Whitehead D5
Wicklow G5
Woodenbridge G5
Woodford F3

Youghal H3

B C D E

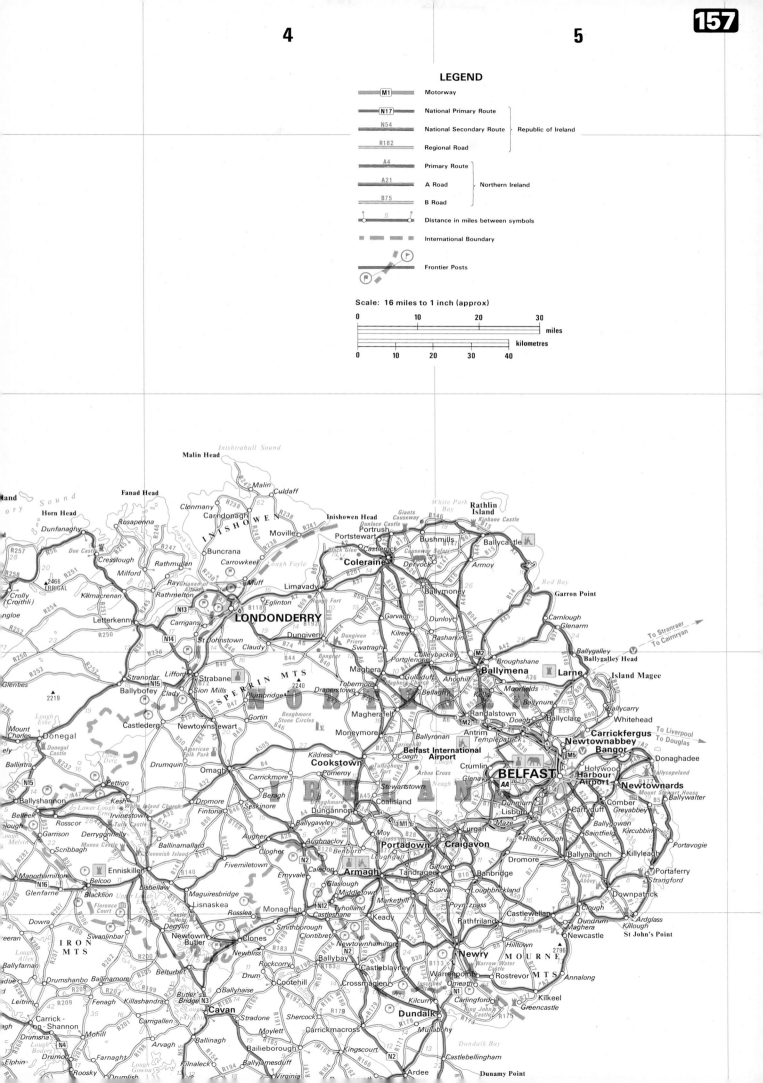

4   5

LEGEND

M1	Motorway
N17	National Primary Route
N54	National Secondary Route } Republic of Ireland
R182	Regional Road
A4	Primary Route
A21	A Road } Northern Ireland
B75	B Road
5	Distance in miles between symbols
	International Boundary
	Frontier Posts

Scale: 16 miles to 1 inch (approx)

0   10   20   30   miles

0   10   20   30   40   kilometres

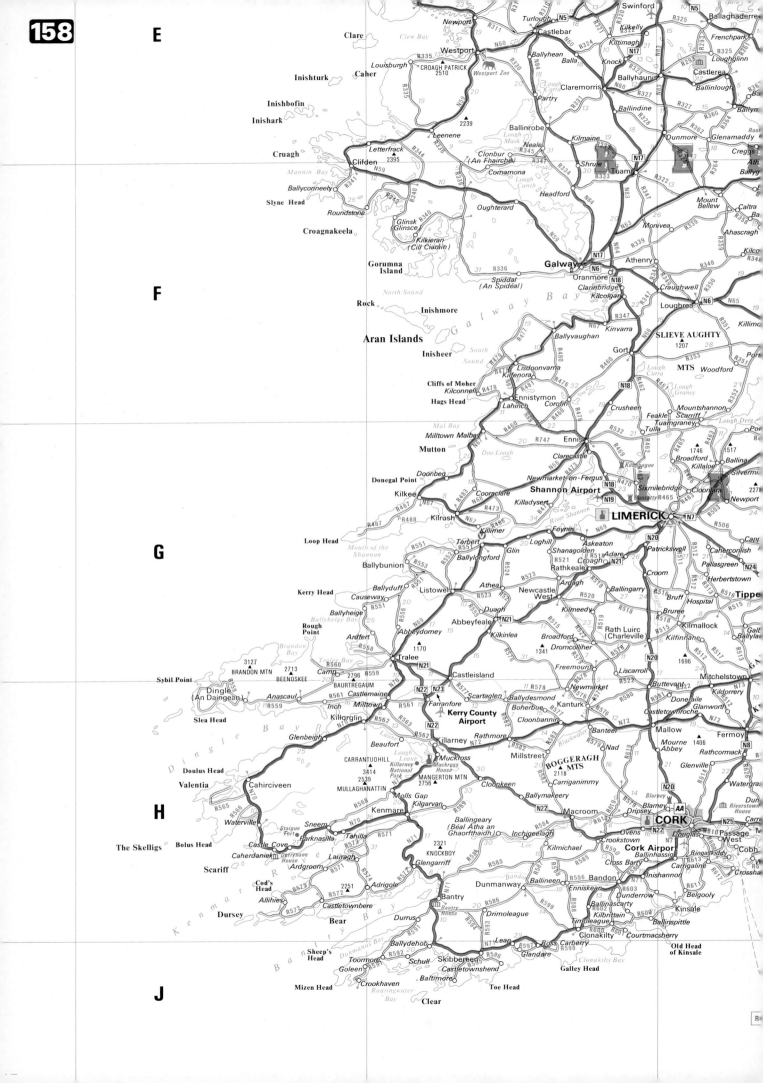

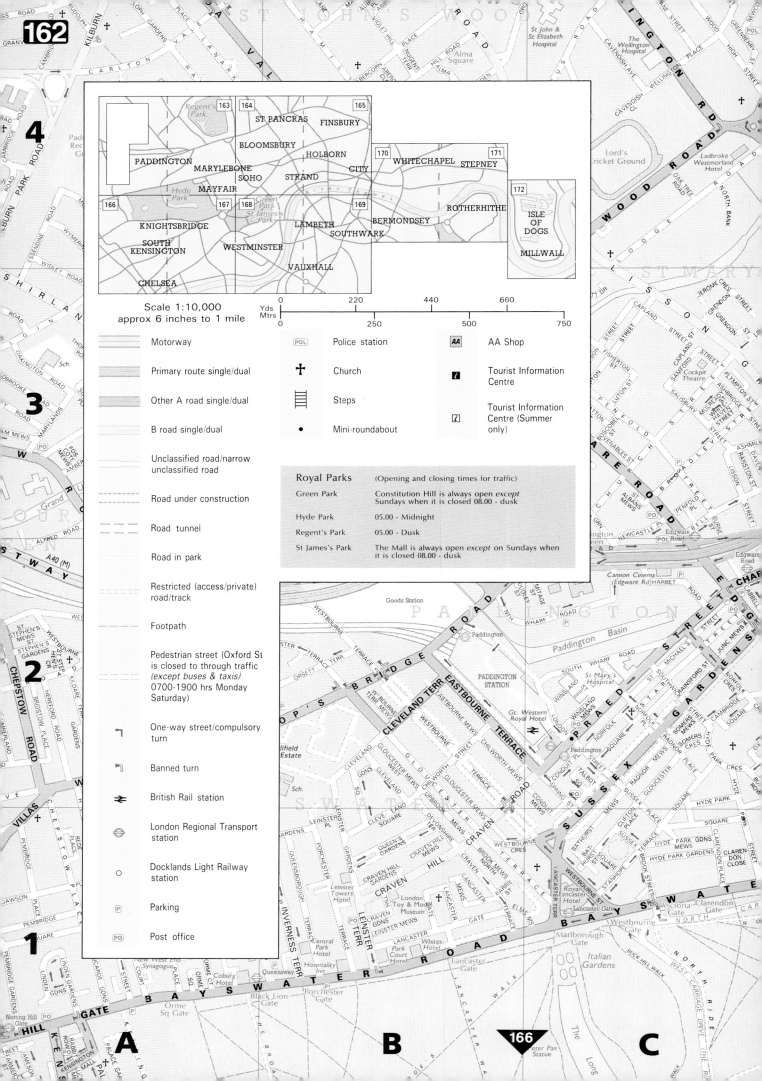

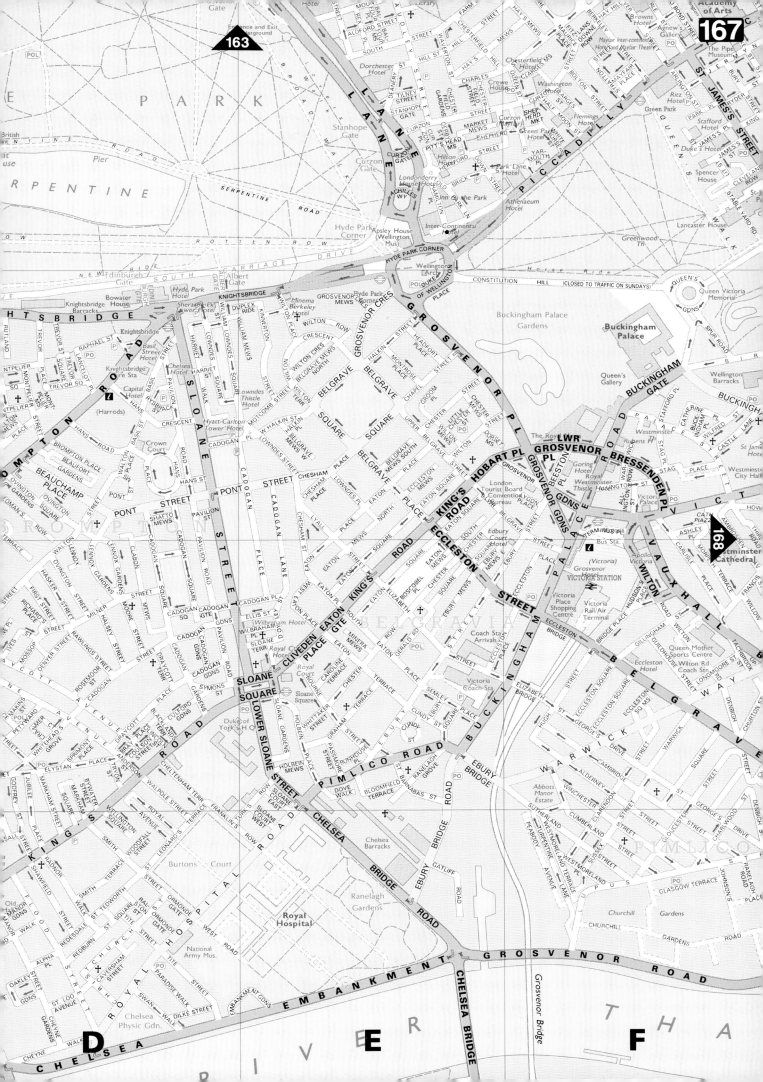

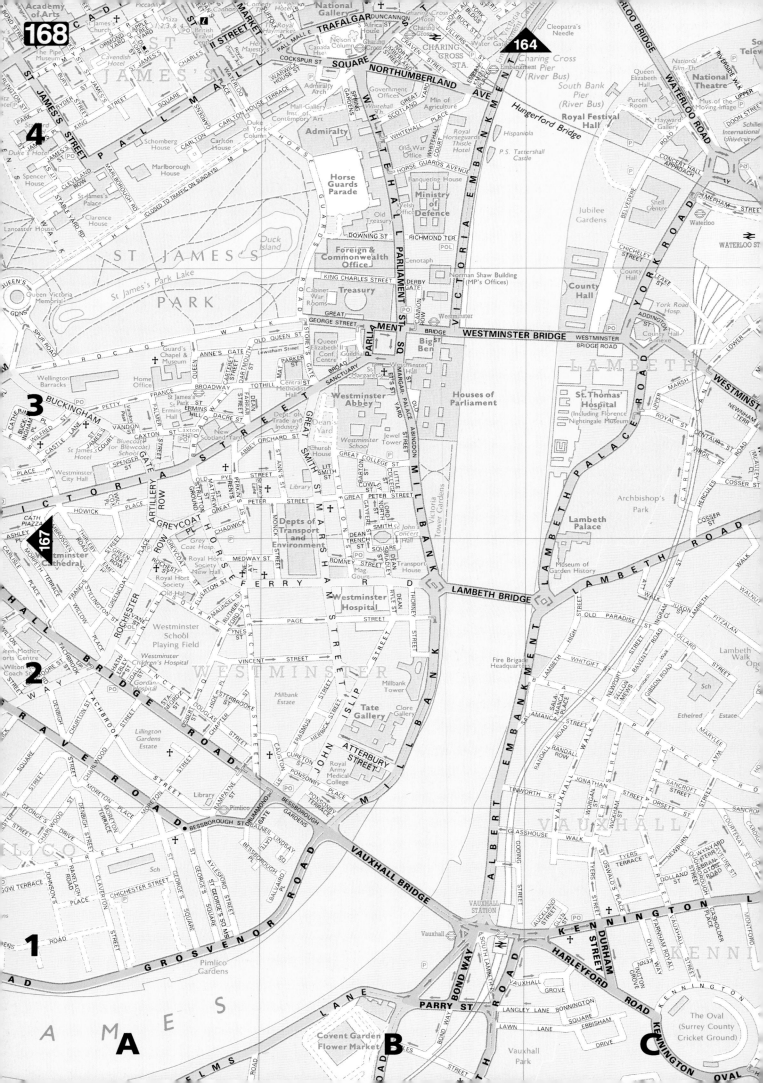

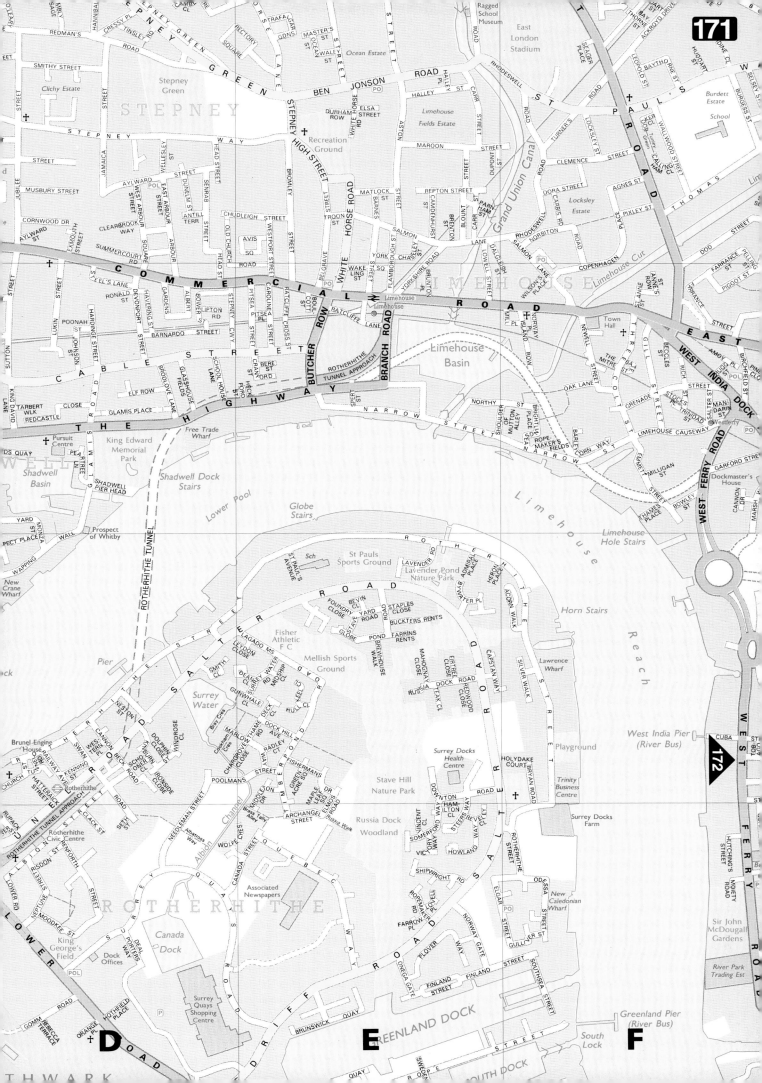

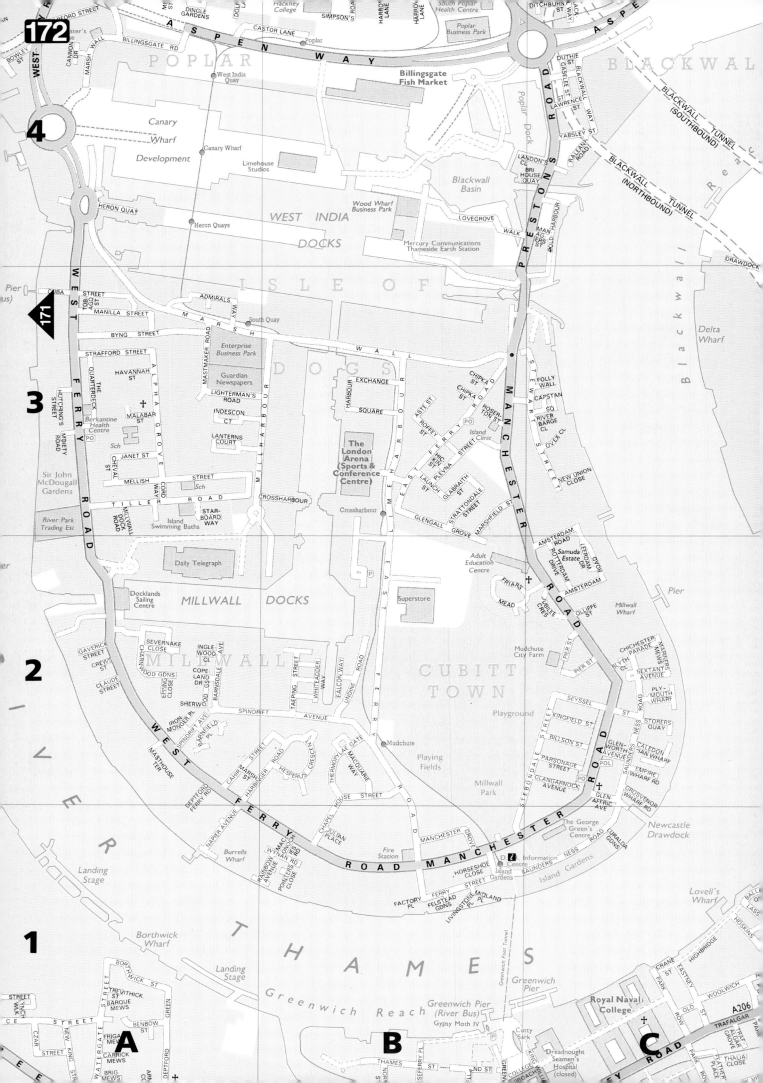

In the index, the street names are listed in alphabetical order and written in full, but may be abbreviated on the map. Postal codes are listed where information is available. Each entry is followed by its map page number in bold type and an arbitrary letter and figure grid reference eg Exhibition Road SW7 166 C3. Turn to page '166'. The letter 'C' refers to the grid square located at the bottom of the page. The figure '3' refers to the grid square located at the lefthand side of the page. Exhibition Road is found within the intersecting square. SW7 refers to the postcode.

180

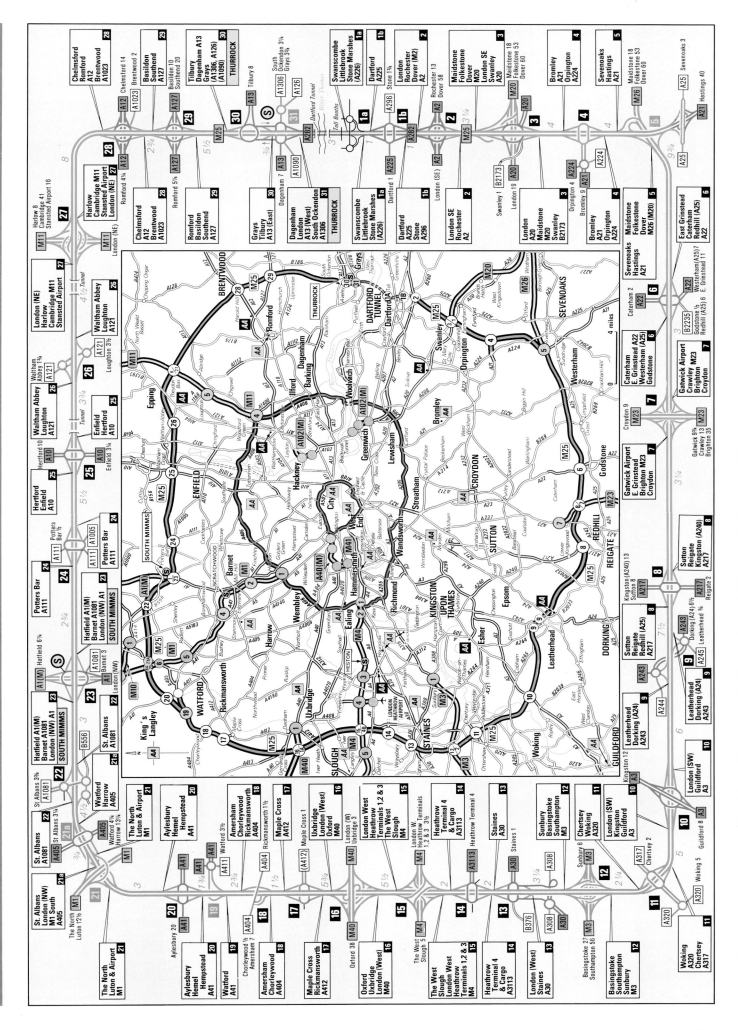

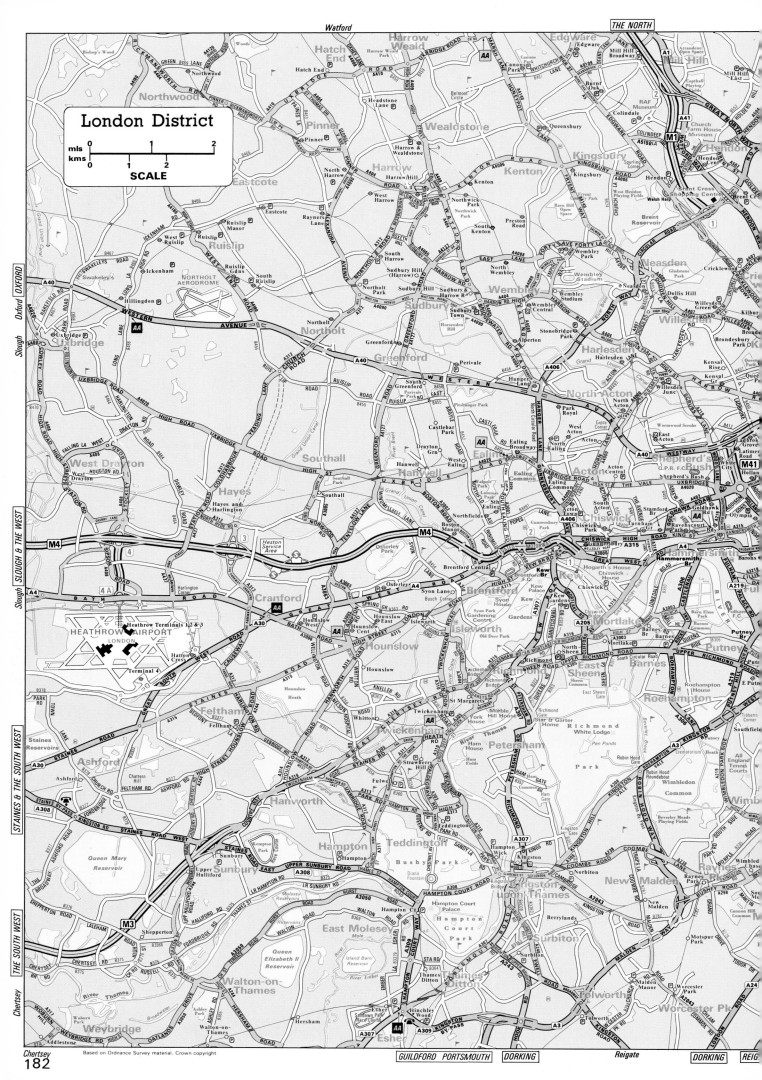

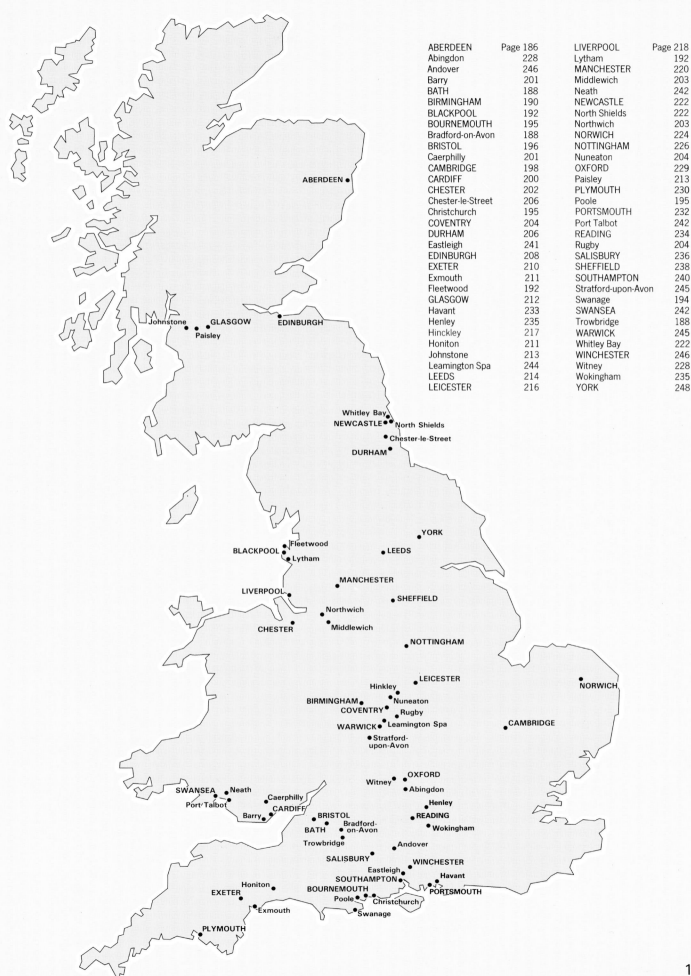

•Town plans

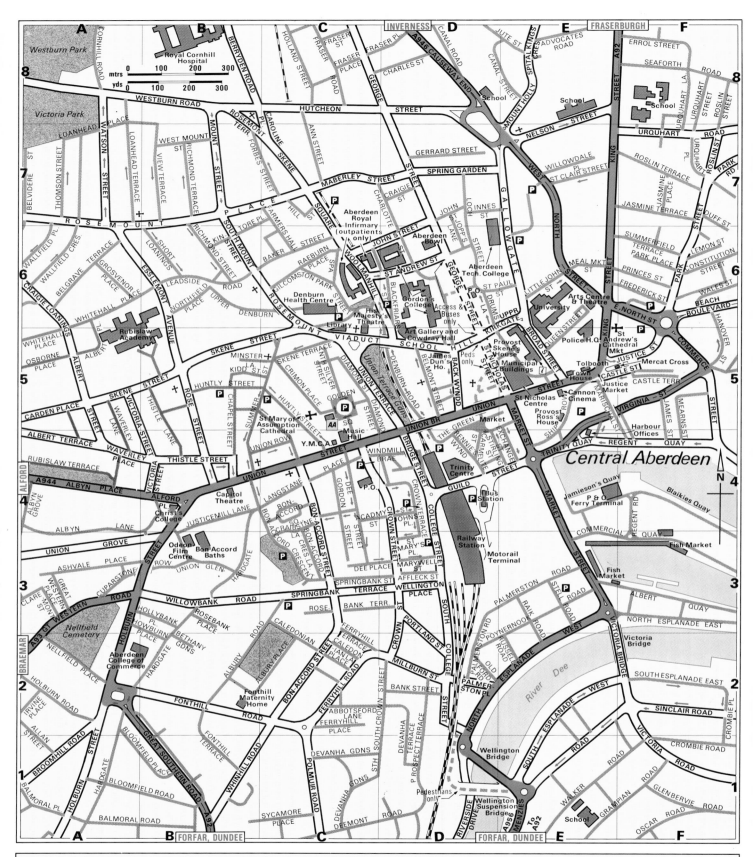

Aberdeen

Granite gives Aberdeen its especial character; but this is not to say that the city is a grim or a grey place, the granites used are of many hues – white, blue, pink and grey. Although the most imposing buildings date from the 19th century, granite has been used to dramatic effect since at least as early as the 15th century. From that time dates St Machar's Cathedral, originally founded in AD580,

but rebuilt several times, especially after a devasting fire started on the orders of Edward III of England in 1336. St Machar's is in Old Aberdeen, traditionally the ecclesiastical and educational hub of the city, while 'New' Aberdeen (actually no newer) has always been the commercial centre. Even that definition is deceptive, for although Old Aberdeen has King's College, founded in 1494, New Aberdeen has Marischal College, founded almost exactly a century later (but rebuilt in 1844)

and every bit as distinguished as a seat of learning. Both establishments functioned as independent universities until they were merged in 1860 to form Aberdeen University. The North Sea oil boom has brought many changes to the city, some of which threatened its character. But even though high-rise buildings are now common, the stately façades, towers and pillars of granite still reign supreme and Union Street remains one of the best thoroughfares in Britain.

186

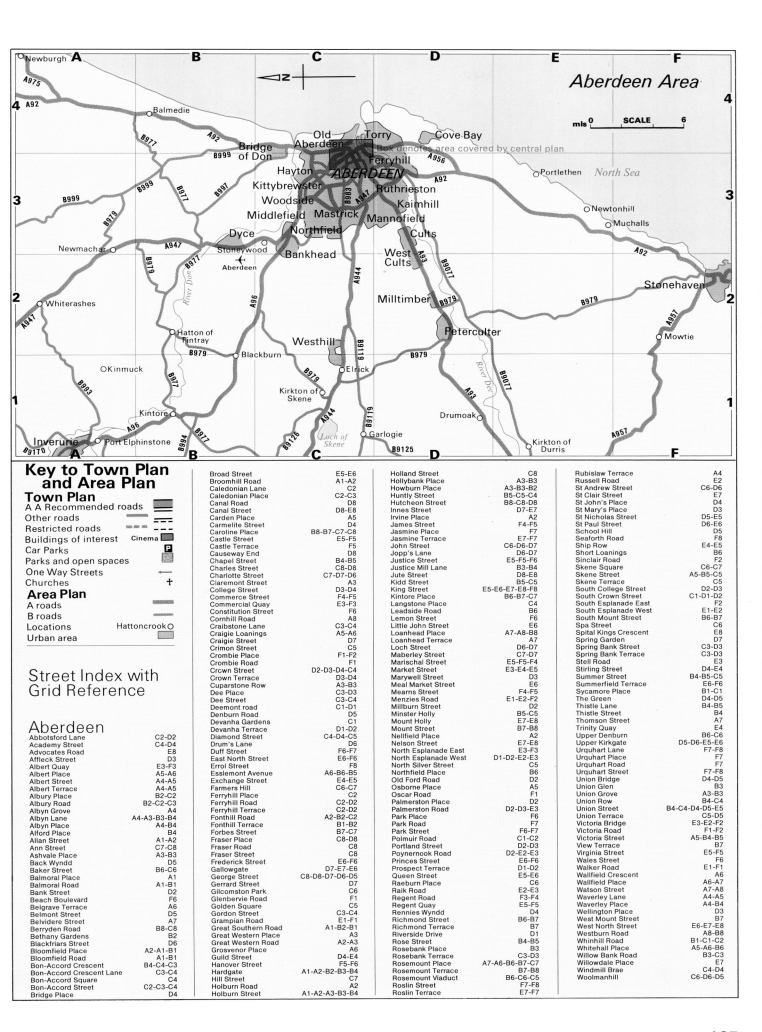

Aberdeen Area

Box denotes area covered by central plan

North Sea

SCALE mls 0 — 6

Key to Town Plan and Area Plan

Town Plan
A A Recommended roads
Other roads
Restricted roads
Buildings of interest — Cinema
Car Parks — P
Parks and open spaces
One Way Streets →
Churches — +

Area Plan
A roads
B roads
Locations — Hattoncrook ○
Urban area

Street Index with Grid Reference

Aberdeen

Street	Grid
Abbotsford Lane	C2-D2
Academy Street	C4-D4
Advocates Road	E8
Affleck Street	D3
Albert Quay	E3-F3
Albert Place	A5-A6
Albert Street	A4-A5
Albert Terrace	A4-A5
Albury Place	B2-C2
Albury Road	B2-C2-C3
Albyn Grove	A4
Albyn Lane	A4-A3-B3-B4
Albyn Place	A4-B4
Alford Place	B4
Allan Street	A1-A2
Ann Street	C7-C8
Ashvale Place	A3-B3
Back Wyndd	D5
Baker Street	B6-C6
Balmoral Place	A1
Balmoral Road	A1-B1
Bank Street	D2
Beach Boulevard	F6
Belgrave Terrace	A6
Belmont Street	D5
Belvidere Street	A7
Berryden Road	B8-C8
Bethany Gardens	B2
Blackfriars Street	D6
Bloomfield Place	A2-A1-B1
Bloomfield Road	A1-B1
Bon-Accord Crescent	B4-C4-C3
Bon-Accord Crescent Lane	C3-C4
Bon-Accord Square	C4
Bon-Accord Street	C2-C3-C4
Bridge Place	D4

Street	Grid
Broad Street	E5-E6
Broomhill Road	A1-A2
Caledonian Lane	C2
Caledonian Place	C2-C3
Canal Road	D8
Canal Street	D8-E8
Carden Place	A5
Carmelite Street	D4
Caroline Place	B8-B7-C7-C8
Castle Street	E5-F5
Castle Terrace	D8
Causeway End	D8
Chapel Street	B4-B5
Charles Street	C8-D8
Charlotte Street	C7-D7-D6
Claremont Street	A3
College Street	D3-D4
Commerce Street	F4-F5
Commercial Quay	E3-F3
Constitution Street	F6
Cornhill Road	A8
Craibstone Lane	C3-C4
Craigie Loanings	A5-A6
Craigie Street	D7
Crimon Street	C5
Crombie Place	F1-F2
Crombie Road	F1
Crown Street	D2-D3-D4-C4
Crown Terrace	D3-D4
Cuparstone Row	A3-B3
Dee Place	C3-D3
Dee Street	C3-C4
Deemont road	C1-D1
Denburn Road	D5
Devanha Gardens	C1
Devanha Terrace	D1-D2
Diamond Street	C4-D4-C5
Drum's Lane	D6
Duff Street	F6-F7
East North Street	E6-F6
Errol Street	F8
Esslemont Avenue	A6-B6-B5
Exchange Street	E4-E5
Farmers Hill	C6-C7
Ferryhill Place	C2
Ferryhill Road	C2-D2
Ferryhill Terrace	C2-D2
Fonthill Road	A2-B2-C2
Fonthill Terrace	B1-B2
Forbes Street	B7-C7
Fraser Place	C8-D8
Fraser Road	C8
Fraser Street	C8
Frederick Street	E6-F6
Gallowgate	D7-E7-E6
George Street	C8-D8-D7-D6-D5
Gerrard Street	D7
Gilcomston Park	C6
Glenbervie Road	F1
Golden Square	C5
Gordon Street	C3-C4
Grampian Road	E1-F1
Great Southern Road	A1-B2-B1
Great Western Place	A3
Great Western Road	A2-A3
Grosvenor Place	A6
Guild Street	D4-E4
Hanover Street	F5-F6
Hardgate	A1-A2-B2-B3-B4
Hill Street	C7
Holburn Road	A2
Holburn Street	A1-A2-A3-B3-B4

Street	Grid
Holland Street	C8
Hollybank Place	A3-B3
Howburn Place	A3-B3-B2
Huntly Street	B5-C5-C4
Hutcheon Street	B8-C8-D8
Innes Street	D7-E7
Irvine Place	A2
James Street	F4-F5
Jasmine Place	F7
Jasmine Terrace	E7-F7
John Street	C6-D6-D7
Jopp's Lane	D6-D7
Justice Street	E5-F5-F6
Justice Mill Lane	B3-B4
Jute Street	D8-E8
Kidd Street	B5-C5
King Street	E5-E6-E7-E8-F8
Kintore Place	B6-B7-C7
Langstone Place	C4
Leadside Road	B6
Lemon Street	F6
Little John Street	E6
Loanhead Place	A7-A8-B8
Loanhead Terrace	A7
Loch Street	D6-D7
Maberley Street	C7-D7
Marischal Street	E5-F5-F4
Market Street	E3-E4-E5
Marywell Street	D3
Meal Market Street	E6
Mearns Street	F4-F5
Menzies Road	E1-E2-F2
Millburn Street	D2
Minster Holly	B5-C5
Mount Holly	E7-E8
Mount Street	B7-B8
Nellfield Place	A2
Nelson Street	E7-E8
North Esplanade East	E3-F3
North Esplanade West	D1-D2-E2-E3
North Silver Street	C5
Northfield Place	B6
Old Ford Road	D2
Osborne Place	A5
Oscar Road	F1
Palmerston Place	D2
Palmerston Road	D2-D3-E3
Park Place	F6
Park Road	F7
Park Street	F6-F7
Polmuir Road	C1-C2
Portland Street	D2-D3
Poynernook Road	D2-E2-E3
Princes Street	E6-F6
Prospect Terrace	D1-D2
Queen Street	E5-E6
Raeburn Place	C6
Raik Road	E2-E3
Regent Road	F3-F4
Regent Quay	E5-F5
Rennies Wyndd	D4
Richmond Street	B6-B7
Richmond Terrace	B7
Riverside Drive	D1
Rose Street	B4-B5
Rosebank Place	B3
Rosebank Terrace	C3-D3
Rosemount Place	A7-A6-B6-B7-C7
Rosemount Terrace	B7-B8
Rosemount Viaduct	B6-C6-C5
Roslin Street	F7-F8
Roslin Terrace	E7-F7

Street	Grid
Rubislaw Terrace	A4
Russell Road	E2
St Andrew Street	C6-D6
St Clair Street	E7
St John's Place	D4
St Mary's Place	D3
St Nicholas Street	D5-E5
St Paul Street	D6-E6
School Hill	D5
Seaforth Road	F8
Ship Row	E4-E5
Short Loanings	B6
Sinclair Road	F2
Skene Square	C6-C7
Skene Street	A5-B5-C5
Skene Terrace	C5
South College Street	D2-D3
South Crown Street	C1-D1-D2
South Esplanade East	F2
South Esplanade West	E1-E2
South Mount Street	B6-B7
Spa Street	C6
Spital Kings Crescent	E8
Spring Garden	D7
Spring Bank Street	C3-D3
Spring Bank Terrace	C3-D3
Stell Road	E3
Stirling Street	D4-E4
Summer Street	B4-B5-C5
Summerfield Terrace	E6-F6
Sycamore Place	B1-C1
The Green	D4-D5
Thistle Lane	B4-B5
Thistle Street	B4
Thomson Street	A7
Trinity Quay	E4
Upper Denburn	B6-C6
Upper Kirkgate	D5-D6-E5-E6
Urquhart Lane	F7-F8
Urquhart Place	F7
Urquhart Road	F7
Urquhart Street	F7-F8
Union Bridge	D4-D5
Union Glen	B3
Union Grove	A3-B3
Union Row	B4-C4
Union Street	B4-C4-D4-D5-E5
Union Terrace	C5-D5
Victoria Bridge	E3-E2-F2
Victoria Road	F1-F2
Victoria Street	A5-B4-B5
View Terrace	B7
Virginia Street	E5-F5
Wales Street	F5
Walker Road	E1-F1
Wallfield Crescent	A6
Wallfield Place	A6-A7
Watson Street	A7-A8
Waverley Lane	A4-A5
Waverley Place	A4-B4
Wellington Place	D3
West Mount Street	B7
West North Street	E6-E7-E8
Westburn Road	A8-B8
Whinhill Road	B1-C1-C2
Whitehall Place	A5-A6-B6
Willow Bank Road	B3-C3
Willowdale Place	E7
Windmill Brae	C4-D4
Woolmanhill	C6-D6-D5

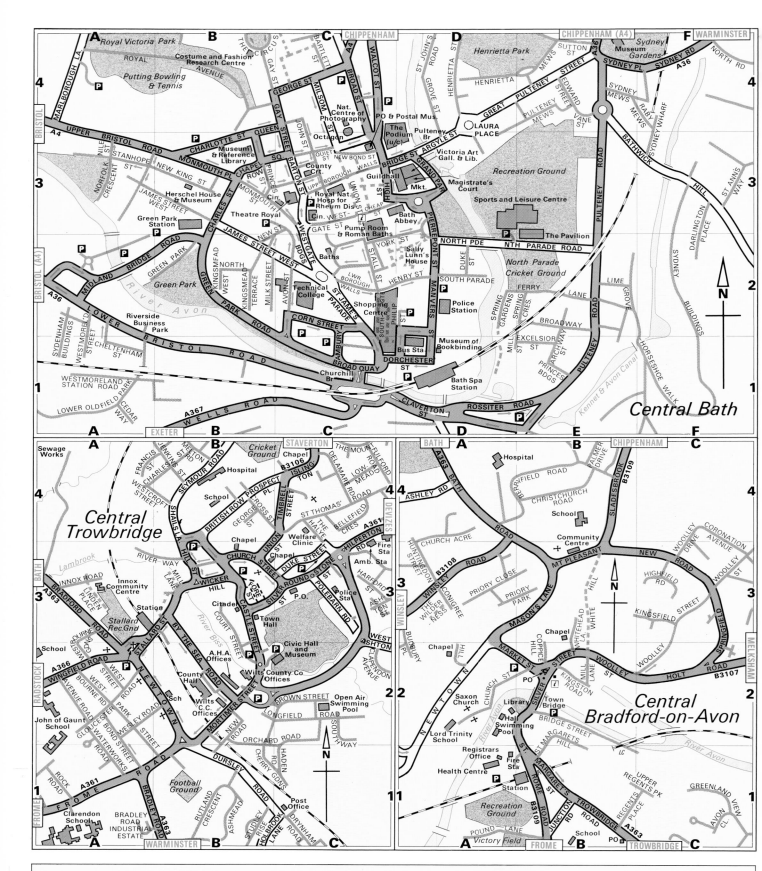

Bath

This unique city combines Britain's most impressive collection of Roman relics with the country's finest Georgian townscape. Its attraction to Romans and fashionable 18th-century society alike was its mineral springs, which are still seen by thousands of tourists who visit the Roman Baths every year. They are now the centre-piece of a Roman museum, where exhibits give a vivid impression of life 2000 years ago. The adjacent Pump Room to which the waters were piped for drinking was a focal point of social life in 18th-and 19th-century Bath.

The Georgian age of elegance also saw the building of Bath's perfectly proportioned streets, terraces and crescents. The finest examples are Queen Square, the Circus, and Royal Crescent, all built of golden local stone. Overlooking the Avon from the west is the great tower of Bath Abbey - sometimes called the "Lantern of the West"

because of its large and numerous windows.

Bath has much to delight the museum-lover. The Holburne Museum in Great Pulteney Street houses collections of silver, porcelain, paintings, furniture and glass of all periods.

The Assembly Rooms in Bennett Street, very much a part of the social scene in Georgian Bath, are now the home of the Museum of Costume with displays illustrating fashion through the ages.

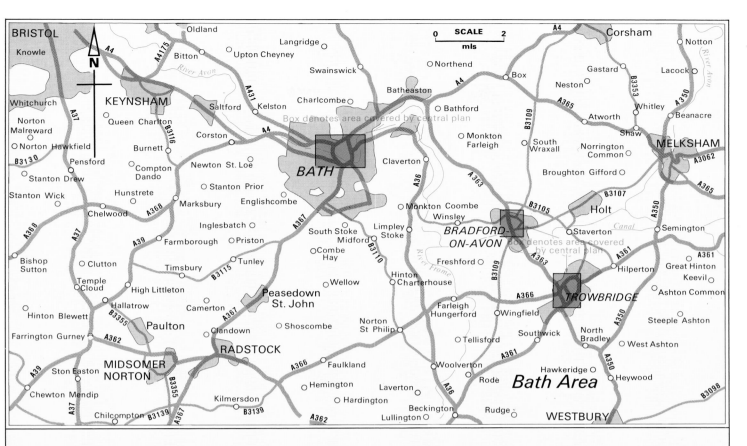

Key to Town Plan and Area Plan

Town Plan

A A Recommended roads
Other roads
Restricted roads
Buildings of interest — Library
Car Parks — P
Parks and open spaces
Churches — †

Area Plan

A roads
B roads
Locations — Box ○
Urban Area

Street Index with Grid Reference

Central Bath

Ambury	C1-C2
Archway Street	E1-E2
Argyle Street	D3-D4
Avon Street	C2
Bartlett Street	C4
Barton Street	C3
Bathwick Hill	E3-F3
Bridge Street	C3-D3
Broadway	E2
Broad Street	C3-C4
Broad Quay	C1
Chapel Row	D3
Charles Street	B2-B3
Charlotte Street	B3-B4
Cheap Street	C3
Cheltenham Street	A1
Claverton Street	C1-D1
Corn Street	C2
Darlington Place	F2-F3
Dorchester Street	C1-D1
Duke Street	D2
Edward Street	E4
Excelsior Street	E1
Ferry Lane	D2-E2
Gay Street	B4-C4-C3
George Street	B4-C4
Grand Parade	D3
Great Pulteney Street	D4-E4
Green Park	A2-B2
Green Park Road	B1-B2-C2-C1
Grove Street	D3-D4
Henrietta Mews	D4-E4
Henrietta Street	D4
Henry Street	C2-D2
High Street	C3
Horseshoe Walk	F1
James Street West	A3-B3-B2-C2
John Street	C3-C4
Kingsmead North	B2
Kingsmead Terrace	B2
Kingsmead West	B2
Laura Place	D3-D4
Lime Grove	E2-F2-F1
Lower Bristol Road	A2-A1-B1-C1
Lower Borough Walls	C2
Lower Oldfield Park	A1
Manvers Street	D1-D2
Marlborough Lane	A4
Midland Bridge Road	A2-B2-B3
Milk Street	B2
Mill Street	D1
Milsom Street	C3-C4
Monmouth Place	B3
Monmouth Street	B3-C3
New Street	B2-B3-C3
New Bond Street	C3
New King Street	A3-B3
Nile Street	A3
Norfolk Crescent	A3
North Parade	D2
North Parade Road	D2-E2
North Road	F4
Philip Street	C1-C2-D2
Pierrepont Street	E1
Princes Buildings	E1
Princes Street	B3
Pulteney Mews	E4
Pulteney Road	E1-E2-E3-E4
Queen Square	B3-B4-C4-C3
Quiet Street	C3
Raby Mews	E4-F4
Rossiter Road	D1-E1
Royal Avenue	A4-B4
St Ann's Way	F3
St Jame's Parade	C2
St John's Road	D4r
Southgate	C1-C2
South Parade	D2
Spring Crescent	E1
Spring Gardens	D2
Stall Street	C2-C3
Stanhope Street	A3
Sutton Street	E4
Sydenham Buildings	A1-A2
Sydney Buildings	F1-F2-F3
Sydney Mews	E4-F4
Sydney Place	E4-F4
Sydney Road	F4
Sydney Wharf	F3-F4
The Circus	B4
Union Street	C3
Upper Borough Walls	C3
Upper Bristol Road	A4-A3-B3
Vane Street	E4
Walcot Street	C3-C4
Wells Road	A1-B1-C1
Westgate Buildings	C2-C3
Westgate Street	C3
Westmoreland Station Road	A1
Westmoreland Street	A1
York Street	C2-D2-D3

Trowbridge

Ashmead	D1
Ashton Street	C3
Avenue Road	A2
Bellefield Crescent	C4
Bond Street	A1-A2
Bradford Road	A2-A3
Bradley Road	A1-B1
British Row	B4
Brown Street	B2-C2
Bythesea Road	B2-B3
Castle Street	B2-B3
Charles Street	A4-B4
Cherry Gardens	B1-C1
Church Street	B3-C3
Clapendon Avenue	C2
Court Street	B2-B3
Cross Street	B4-C4
Delamare Road	C4
Dynham Road	C1
Duke Street	C3-C4
Dursley Road	B1-C1
Fore Street	B3
Francis Street	A4-B4
Frome Road	A1-B1
Fulford Road	C4
George Street	B4
Gloucester Road	A2
Haden Road	C1
Harford Street	C3
Hill Street	B3
Hilperton Road	C3-C4
Holbrook Lane	B1-C1
Innox Road	A3
Islington	C4
Jenkins Street	A4-B4
Linden Place	A3
Longfield Road	B2-C2
Lowmead	C4
Melton Road	B4
Mill Lane	B3
Mortimer Street	B2
New Road	B1-B2
Newtown	A2-B2
Orchard Road	B1-B2-C2-C1
Park Street	A2-A1-B1
Polebarn Road	C3
Prospect Place	D4-C4
River Way	A3-B3
Rock Road	A1
Roundstone Street	C3
Rutland Crescent	B1
St Thomas' Road	C4
Seymour Road	B4
Shails Lane	B3-B4
Silver Street	B3-C3
Southway	C2
Stallard Street	A2-A3-B3
Studley Rise	B1
The Hayle	C4
The Mount	B4
Timbrell Street	C4
Union Street	B3-B4-C4-C3
Waterworks Road	A1-A2
Wesley Road	A2-B2
West Street	A2
West Ashton	C2-C3
Westbourne Gardens	A2-A3
Westbourne Road	A2
Westcroft Street	A4-B4
Wicker Hill	B3
Wingfield Road	A2

Bradford-upon-Avon

Ashley Road	A4
Avon Close	C1
Bath Road	A3-A4-B4-B3
Berryfield Road	A4-B4
Bridge Street	B2
Christchurch Road	B4
Christchurch Road	B4
Church Acre	A4
Church Street	A2-B2
Conigre Hill	A2-A3
Coppice Hill	B2-B3
Coronation Avenue	C3-C4
Greenland View	C1
Highfield Road	C3
Holt Road	B2-C2
Huntingdon Street	A3
Kingston Road	B2
Junction Road	B1
Market Street	A2-B2
Masons Lane	A3-B3
Mill Lane	B2
Mount Pleasant	B3
Newtown	A1-A2-A3
New Road	B3-C3
Palmer Drive	B4
Pound Lane	A1-B1
Priory Close	A3-B3
Priory Park	A3-B3
Regents Place	B1-C1
Rome Road	B1
St Margaret's Place	B1-B2
St Margaret's Street	B1-C2
Silver Street	B2
Sladesbrook	B3-B4
Springfield	C2-C3
The Wilderness	A3
Trowbridge Road	B1
Upper Regents Park	B1-C1
White Hill	B2-B3
Whitehead Lane	B2-B3
Winsley Road	A3-A4
Woolley Drive	C3-C4
Woolley Street	C2-C3

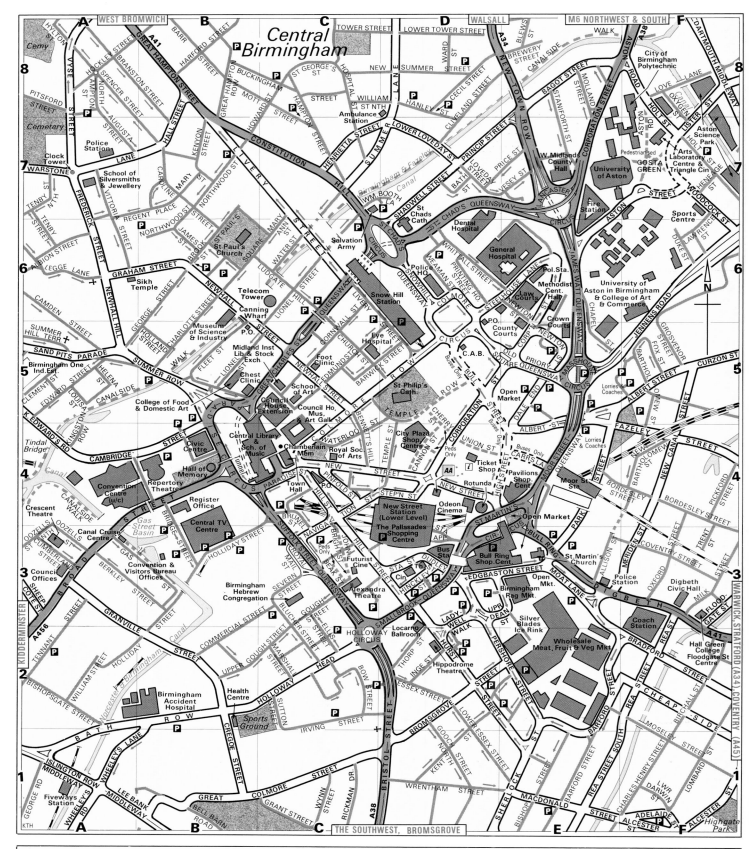

Birmingham

It is very difficult to visualise Birmingham as it was before it began the growth which eventually made it the second-largest city in England. When the Romans were in Britain it was little more than a staging post on Icknield Street. Throughout medieval times it was a sleepy agricultural centre in the middle of a heavily-forested region. Timbered houses clustered together round a green that was

eventually to be called the Bull Ring. But by the 16th century, although still a tiny and unimportant village by today's standards, it had begun to gain a reputation as a manufacturing centre. Tens of thousands of sword blades were made here during the Civil War. Throughout the 18th century more and more land was built on. In 1770 the Birmingham Canal was completed, making trade very much easier and increasing the town's development dramatically. All of that pales into near

insignificance compared with what happened in the 19th century. Birmingham was not represented in Parliament until 1832 and had no town council until 1838. Yet by 1889 it had already been made a city, and after only another 20 years it had become the second largest city in England. Many of Birmingham's most imposing public buildings date from the 19th century, when the city was growing so rapidly. Surprisingly, the city has more miles of waterway than Venice.

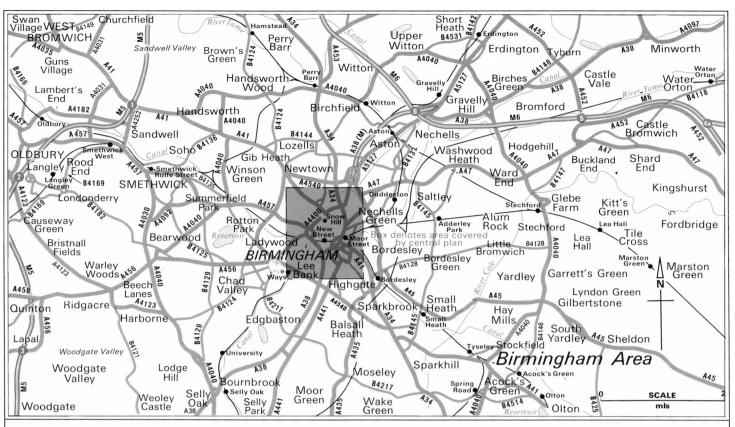

Key to Town Plan and Area Plan

Town Plan

AA Recommended roads	
Restricted roads	
Other roads	
Buildings of interest	Station
One Way Streets	←
Car Parks	P
Parks and open spaces	
Churches	†

Area Plan

A roads	
B roads	
Locations	Meer End ○
Urban area	

Street Index with Grid Reference

Birmingham

Adelaide Street	F1
Albert Street	E4-E5-F5
Albion Street	A6
Alcester Street	F1
Allison Street	E3
Aston Road	F8-E8-F8-F7
Aston Street	E6-E7-F7
Augusta Street	A7-A8
Bagot Street	E8
Barford Street	E1-E2-F2
Barr Street	B8
Bartholomew Street	F4-F5
Barwick Street	C5-D5
Bath Row	A1-A2-B2
Bath Street	D7
Beak Street	C3
Bell Barn Road	B1
Bennett's Hill	C4-C5
Berkley Street	A3-B3
Birchall Street	F1-F2
Bishop Street	E1
Bishopsgate Street	A2
Blews Street	E8
Blucher Street	C2-C3
Bordesley Street	E4-F4-F3
Bow Street	C2
Bradford Street	E3-E2-F2
Branston Street	A8-B8-B7
Brewery Street	E8
Bridge Street	B3-B4
Bristol Street	C1-D1-D2-C2
Broad Street	A2-A3-A4-B4
Bromsgrove Street	D1-D2-E2
Brook Street	B6
Brunel Street	C3-C4
Buckingham Street	B8-C8
Bull Ring	E3
Bull Street	D5-E5-E4

Cambridge Street	A4-B4-B5
Camden Street	A5-A6
Cannon Street	D4
Caroline Street	B6-B7
Carrs Lane	E4
Cecil Street	D8
Chapel Street	E5-E6
Charles Henry Street	F1
Charlotte Street	B5-B6
Cheapside	F1-F2
Cherry Street	D4-D5
Church Street	C6-C5-D5
Clement Street	A5
Cliveland Street	D7-D8-E8
Colmore Circus	D5-D6
Colmore Row	C4-C5-D5
Commercial Street	B2-B3-C3
Constitution Hill	B7-C7
Cornwall Street	C5-C6
Corporation Street	D4-D5-E5-E6-E7-E8-F8
Coventry Street	E3-F3
Cregoe Street	B1-B2
Cumberland Street	A3
Curzon Street	F5
Dale End	E4-E5
Dartmouth Middleway	F7-F8
Digbeth	E3-F3
Dudley Street	D3
Duke Street	F6
Edgbaston Street	D3-E3
Edmund Street	C5-D5
Edward Street	A5
Ellis Street	C2-C3
Essex Street	D2
Fazeley Street	E5-E4-F4
Fleet Street	B5
Floodgate Street	F3
Fox Street	F5
Frederick Street	A6-A7
Gas Street	A3-B3
George Road	A1
George Street	A5-B5-B6
Gooch Street North	D1-D2
Gosta Green	F7
Gough Street	C3
Graham Street	A6-B6
Grant Street	C1
Granville Street	A3-A2-B2
Great Charles St Queensway	B5-C5-C6
Great Colmore Street	B1-C1-D1
Great Hampton Row	B8
Great Hampton Street	A8-B8
Grosvenor Street	F5-F6
Hall Street	B7-B8
Hampton Street	C7-C8
Harford Street	B8
Hanley Street	D7-D8
Helena Street	A5
Heneage Street	F7
Henrietta Street	C7-D7
High Street	D4-E4
Hill Street	C4-C3-D3
Hinckley Street	D3
Hockley Street	A8-B8
Holland Street	B5
Holliday Street	A2-B2-B3-C3-C4
Holloway Circus	C2-C3-D3-D2
Holloway Head	B2-C2
Holt Street	F7-F8
Hospital Street	C7-C8
Howard Street	B7-C7-C8
Hurst Street	D3-D2-E2-E1

Hylton Street	A8
Inge Street	D2
Irving Street	C2-D2
Islington Row Middleway	A1
James Street	B6
James Watt Queensway	E5-E6
Jennens Road	E5-F5-F6
John Bright Street	C3-C4
Kent Street	D1-D2
Kenyon Street	B7
King Edward's Road	A4-A5
Kingston Row	A4
Ladywell Walk	D2-D3
Lancaster Circus	E6-E7
Lawrence Street	F6-F7
Lee Bank Middleway	A1-B1
Legge Lane	A6
Lionel Street	B5-C5-C6
Lister Street	F7-F8
Livery Street	B7-C7-C6-D6-D5
Lombard Street	F1-F2
Louisa Street	A5
Love Lane	F8
Loveday Street	D7
Lower Darwin Street	F1
Lower Essex Street	D2-D1-E1
Lower Loveday Street	D7
Lower Tower Street	D8
Ludgate Hill	B6-C6
Macdonald Street	E1-F1
Marshall Street	C2
Mary Street	B7
Mary Ann Street	C6-C7
Masshouse Circus	E5
Meriden Street	E3-F3
Milk Street	F3
Moat Lane	E3
Molland Street	E8
Moor Street Queensway	E4-E5
Moseley Street	E2-F2-F1
Mott Street	B8-C8-C7
Navigation Street	C3-C4
New Street	C4-D4
New Bartholomew Street	F4
New Canal Street	F4-F5
Newhall Hill	A5-A6
Newhall Street	B6-B5-C5
New Summer Street	C8-D8
Newton Street	E5
New Town Row	D8-E8-E7
Northampton Street	A8
Northwood Street	B6-B7
Old Square	D5-E5
Oozells Street	A3-A4
Oozells Street North	A3-A4
Oxford Street	F3-F4
Oxygen Street	F7-F8
Paradise Circus	B4-B5
Paradise Street	C4
Park Street	E3-E4
Pershore Street	D3-D2-E2
Pickford Street	F4
Pinfold Street	C4
Pitsford Street	A8
Price Street	D7-E7
Princip Street	D7-E7-E8
Printing House Street	D6
Priory Queensway	E5
Rea Street	E2-F2-F3
Rea Street South	E1-F1-F2
Regent Place	A7-B7
Rickman Drive	C1

Royal Mail Street	C3
St Chad's Circus	C7-C6-D6
St Chad's Queensway	D6-D7-E7
St George's Street	C8
St Martin's Circus	D3-D4-E4-E3
St Paul's Square	B7-B6-C6
Sand Pits Parade	A5
Severn Street	C3
Shadwell Street	D6-D7
Sheepcote Street	A3
Sherlock Street	D1-E1-E2
Smallbrook Queensway	C3-D3
Snow Hill Queensway	D6
Spencer Street	A8-A7-B7
Staniforth Street	E7-E8
Station Approach	D3
Station Street	D3
Steelhouse Lane	D6-E6
Stephenson Street	C4-D4
Suffolk Street Queensway	B4-C4-C3
Summer Hill Terrace	A5
Summer Row	A5-B5
Summer Lane	C7-D7-D8
Sutton Street	C2
Temple Row	C5-D5
Temple Street	D4-D5
Tenby Street	A6-A7
Tenby Street North	A7
Tennant Street	A2-A3
Thorp Street	D2-D3
Tower Street	C8-D8
Trent Street	F3-F4
Union Street	D4
Upper Dean Street	D3-E3
Upper Gough Street	B2-C2-C3
Vesey Street	D7-E7
Vittoria Street	A6-A7
Vyse Street	A7-A8
Ward Street	D8
Warstone Lane	A7-B7
Water Street	C6
Waterloo Street	C4-C5-D5
Weaman Street	D6
Wheeley's Lane	A1-B1-B2
Wheeley's Road	A1
Whittall Street	D6-E6
William Booth Lane	C7-D7
William Street	A2
William Street North	C8-D8
Woodcock Street	F6-F7
Wrentham Street	D1-E1
Wynn Street	C1

191

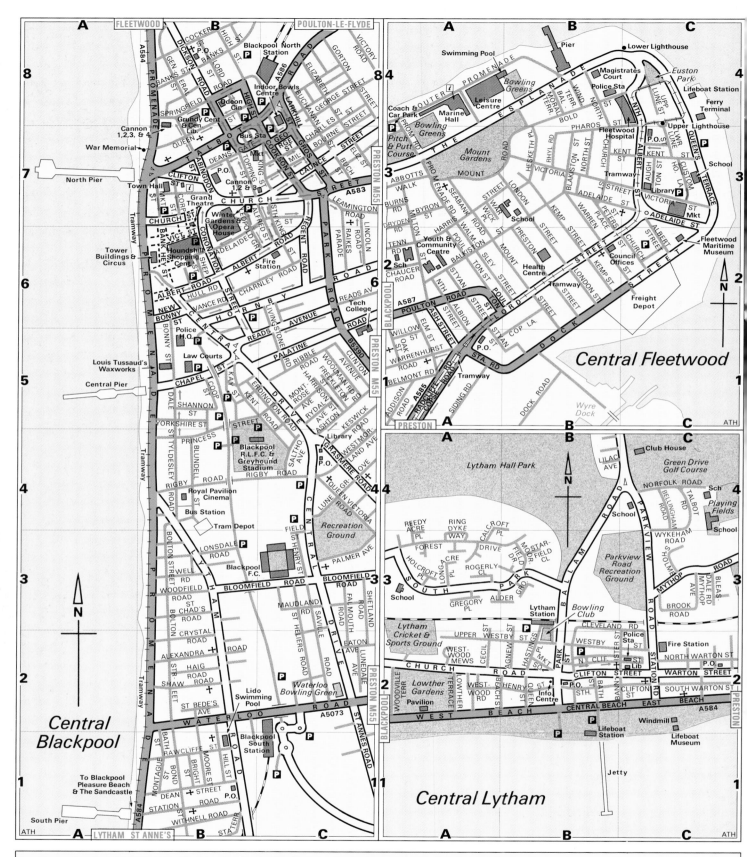

Central Fleetwood

Central Blackpool

Central Lytham

Blackpool

No seaside resort is regarded with greater affection than Blackpool. It is still the place where millions of North Country folk spend their holidays; its famous illuminations draw visitors from all over the world. It provides every conceivable kind of traditional holiday entertainment, and in greater abundance than any other seaside resort in Britain. The famous tower – built in the 1890s as a replica of the Eiffel Tower – the three piers, seven miles of promenade, five miles of illuminations, countless guesthouses, huge numbers of pubs, shops, restaurants and cafes play host to eight million visitors a year.

At the base of the tower is a huge entertainment complex that includes a ballroom, a circus and an aquarium. Other 19th-century landmarks are North Pier and Central Pier, the great Winter Gardens and Opera House and the famous trams that still run along the promenade – the only electric trams still operating in Britain. The most glittering part of modern Blackpool is the famous Golden Mile, packed with amusements, novelty shops and snack stalls. Every autumn it becomes part of the country's most extravagant light show – the illuminations – when the promenade is ablaze with neon representations of anything and everything from moon rockets to the Muppets. Autumn is also the time when Blackpool is a traditional venue for political party conferences.

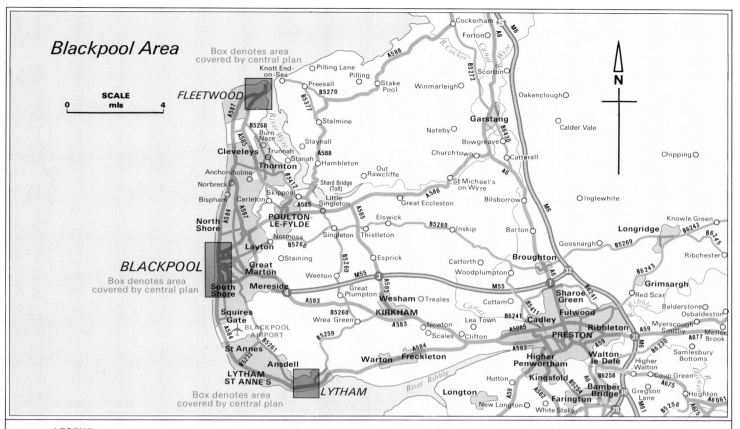

Blackpool Area

Box denotes area covered by central plan

FLEETWOOD

BLACKPOOL
Box denotes area covered by central plan

LYTHAM
ST ANNE'S
Box denotes area covered by central plan

LYTHAM

SCALE
0   mls   4

N

LEGEND

Town Plan
AA Recommended roads
Restricted roads
Other roads
Buildings of interest   Hall
Car parks   P
Parks and open spaces

Area Plan
A roads
B roads
Locations   Trunnah ○
Urban area

Street Index with Grid Reference

Blackpool

Abingdon Street	B7
Adelaide Street	B6-B7-C7
Albert Road	B6-C6
Alexandra Road	B2
Alfred Street	B7-C7-C6
Ashton Road	C4-C5
Bank Hey Street	B6-B7
Banks Street	B8
Bath Street	B1-B2
Bloomfield Road	B3-C3
Blundell Street	B4
Bolton Street	B2-B3-B4
Bond Street	B1-B2
Bonny Street	B5-B6
Bright Street	B1
Buchanan Street	C7-C8
Caunce Street	C7-C8
Central Drive	B6-B5-C5-C4-C3-C2
Chapel Street	B5
Charles Street	C7-C8
Charnley Road	B6-C6
Church Street	B7-C7
Clifton Street	B7
Clinton Avenue	C5
Cocker Street	B8
Cookson Street	B8-B7-C7
Coop Street	B5
Coronation Street	B5-B6-B7
Corporation Street	B7
Crystal Road	B2

Dale Street	B4-B5
Deansgate	B7-C7
Dean Street	B1
Dickson Road	B7-B8
Eaton Avenue	C2
Erdington Road	B5-C5-C4
Elizabeth Street	C7-C8
Falmouth Road	C2-C3
Field Street	C3
Freckleton Street	C5
General Street	B8
George Street	C7-C8
Gorton Street	C8
Grasmere Road	C4
Grosvenor Street	C7
Haig Road	B2
Harrison Street	C5
Henry Street	C3
High Street	B8
Hill Street	B1
Hornby Road	B6-C6
Hull Road	B6
Kay Street	B5
Kent Road	B5-C5-C4
Keswick Road	C4-C5-C6
King Street	C7
Larkhill Street	C8
Leamington Road	C7
Leopold Grove	B7-B6-C6
Lincoln Road	C6-C7
Livingstone Road	C5-C6
Lonsdale Road	B3
Lord Street	B8
Lune Grove	C4
Lunedale Avenue	C2
Lytham Road	B1-B2-B3-B4
Market Street	B7
Maudland Road	B3-C3
Milbourne Street	C7-C8
Montague Street	B1
Montrose Avenue	B5-C5
Moore Street	B2
New Bonny Street	B5-B6
Palatine Road	B5-C5-C6
Palmer Avenue	C3
Park Road	C5-C6-C7
Princes Street	B4-B5-C5
Promenade	B1-B2-B3-B4-B5-B6-A6-A7-B7-B8
Queen Street	B7-B8
Queen Victoria Road	C3-C4
Raikes Parade	C6-C7
Rawcliffe Street	B1
Reads Avenue	B5-C5-C6
Regent Road	C6-C7
Ribble Road	C5
Rigby Road	B4-C4
Rydal Avenue	C5
St Annes Road	C1-C2
St Bede's Avenue	B2
St Chad's Road	B3
St Heliers Road	C2-C3
Salthouse Avenue	C4
Saville Road	C2-C3
Shannon Street	B5
Shaw Road	B2
Sheppard Street	B6
Shetland Road	C2-C3
South King Street	C6-C7
Springfield Road	B8

Station Road	B1
Station Terrace	B1
Talbot Road	B7-B8-C8
Topping Street	B7
Tyldesley Road	B4
Vance Road	B6
Victoria Street	B6
Victory Road	C8
Waterloo Road	B2-C2
Wellington Road	B3
Westmorland Avenue	C4
Withnell Road	B1
Woodfield Road	B3
Woolman Road	C5
Yorkshire Street	B5

Fleetwood

Abbots Walk	A3
Adelaide Street	B3-C3-C2
Addison Road	A1
Albert Street	C2-C3
Ash Street	A1-A2
Aughton Street	C3
Balmoral Terrace	B4
Belmont Road	A1
Blakiston Street	A2-B2-B3
Bold Street	B4-C4
Burns Road	A3
Byron Street	A3
Chaucer Road	A2
Church Street	C2
Cop Lane	A1-B1-B2
Copse Road	A1
Custom House Lane	C3
Dock Road	B1
Dock Street	B1-B2-C2
Dryden Road	A2-A3
Elm Street	A1-A2
Harris Street	A2-A3-B3
Hesketh Place	B3
Kemp Street	B2-B3
Kent Street	B3-C3
London Street	B2-B3
Lord Street	A1-A2-B2-C2-C3
Lower Lune Street	C3
Milton Street	A2-A3
Mount Road	A3-B3
Mount Street	A2-B2
North Albert Street	C3-C4
North Albion Street	A1-A2
North Church Street	B3-B4
North Street	B3
Oak Street	A1
Outer Promenade	A4-B4
Pharos Street	B3-C3-C4
Poulton Road	A2
Poulton Street	A2
Preston Street	B2
Promenade Road	A3-A4
Queen's Terrace	C3-C4
Radcliffe Road	A1
Rhyl Street	B3
St Peters Place	B2-B3
Seabank Road	A2-A3

Siding Road	A1
Station Road	A1
Styan Street	A2-A1-B1
Tennyson Road	A2
The Esplanade	A3-A4-B4
Upper Lune Street	C4
Victoria Street	B3-C3
Walmsley Street	A3-A2-B2
Warrenhurst Road	A1
Warren Street	B3-B2-C2
Warwick Place	A3
Willow Street	A1
Windsor Terrace	B4

Lytham

Agnew Street	B2-B3
Alder Grove	A3-B3
Ballam Road	B2-B3-B4-C4
Bath Street	B2
Beach Street	B2
Bellingham Road	C4
Bleasdale Road	A1
Brook Road	C3
Calcroft Place	A3-B4
Cecil Street	A2-A3
Central Beach	B2-C2
Church Road	A2-B2
Cleveland Road	B3-C3
Clifton Street	B2-C2
East Beach	C2
Forest Drive	A3-B3
Gregory Place	A3
Hastings Place	B2-B3
Henry Street	B2
Holcroft Place	A3
Lilac Avenue	B4
Longacre Place	A3
Lowther Terrace	A2
Market Square	B2
Moorfield Drive	B3
Mythop Avenue	C3
Mythop Road	C3
Norfolk Road	C4
North Clifton Street	B2-C2
North Warton Street	C2
Park Street	B2
Parkview Road	C2-C3-C4
Queen Street	B2
Reedy Acre Place	A3-A4
Ring Dyke Way	A3
Rogerly Close	A3
South Clifton Street	B2-C2
South-Holme	C3
South Park	A3-B3
South Warton Street	C2
Starfield Close	B3
Station Road	C2
Talbot Road	C4
Upper Westby Street	A2-B2
Warton Street	C2
West Beach	A2-B2
Westby Street	B2-C2
Westwood Mews	A2
Westwood Road	A2

Woodville Terrace	A2
Wykeham Road	C3-C4

ATH

Street Index with Grid Reference

Bournemouth

Albert Road	C3-D3
Avenue Road	B3-C3
Bath Road	D2-E2-E3-E4-F4
Beacon Road	C1
Bodorgan Road	C4
Bourne Avenue	B3-C3
Bradbourne Road	B3
Braidley Road	B3-B4
Branksome Wood Gardens	A4
Branksome Wood Road	A4
Cambridge Road	A2-A3
Central Drive	B4
Chine Crescent	A1
Chine Crescent Road	A1-A2
Christchurch Road	F4
Commercial Road	B2
Cotlands Road	F4
Cranbourne Road	B2-C2
Crescent Road	A3-B3
Cumnor Road	E4
Dean Park Crescent	C4-D4
Dean Park Road	C4
Durley Chine Road	A1-A2
Durley Chine Road South	A1
Durley Gardens	A1-A2
Durley Road	A1-A2-B1
Durrant Road	B4
East Overcliff Drive	E2-F2-F3
Exeter Crescent	C2
Exeter Park Road	C2-D2
Exeter Road	C2-D2
Fir Vale Road	D3-D4
Gervis Place	C3-D3
Gervis Road	E3-F3
Glenfern Road	D3-E3-E4
Grove Road	E3-F3
Hahnemann Road	A1-B1-B2
Hinton Road	D2-D3-E2
Holdenhurst Road	F4
Kensington Drive	A4
Kerley Road	C1
Lansdowne Road	E4-F4
Lorne Park Road	E4
Madeira Road	D4-E4
Marlborough Road	A2
Meyrick Road	F3-F4
Norwich Avenue	A2
Norwich Avenue West	A3
Norwich Road	A2-B2
Old Christchurch Road	D3-D4-E4-F4
Orchard Street	C2-C3
Parsonage Road	D3-E3
Poole Hill	A2-B2
Poole Road	A2
Post Office Road	C3
Priory Road	C1-C2
Purbeck Road	B2
Richmond Gardens	C4
Richmond Hill	C3-C4
Richmond Hill Drive	C4
Russell Cotes Road	E2
Somerville Road	A2
St Michael's Road	B2-B1-C1
St Peter's Road	D3-E3
St Stephen's Road	B3-B4-C4-C3
St Stephen's Way	C4
Stafford Road	E4
Suffolk Road	A3-B3
Surrey Road	A3
Terrace Road	B2-C2
The Triangle	B2-B3
Tregonwell Road	B2-C2-C1
Trinity Road	E4
Undercliffe Drive	D1-D2-E1-E2-F2
Upper Hinton Road	D2-D3-E2
Upper Norwich Road	A2-B2
Upper Terrace Road	B2-C2
Wessex Way	A3-A4-B4-C4-D4-E4
West Cliff Gardens	B1
West Cliff Promenade	B1-C1-D1-C1
West Cliff Road	A1-B1
Westhill Road	A2-B2-B1
Westover Road	D2-D3
West Promenade	C1-D1
Wimborne Road	C4
Wootton Gardens	E3-E4
Wootton Mount	E4
Yelverton Road	C3-D3

Christchurch

Albion Road	A4
Arcadia Road	A4
Arthur Road	B3
Avenue Road	A3-B3-B4
Avon Road West	A3-A4-B4
Bargates	B2-B3
Barrack Road	A4-A3-B2-B3

Beaconsfield Road	B2-B3
Bridge Street	C2
Bronte Avenue	B4
Canberra Road	A4
Castle Street	B2-C2
Christchurch By-Pass	B2-C2-C3
Clarendon Road	A3-B3
Douglas Avenue	A2-B2
Endfield Road	A4
Fairfield	B3
Fairfield Drive	A2
Fairmile Road	A4-B4-B3
Flambard Avenue	B4
Gardner Road	A3-A4
Gleadows Avenue	A2-B2
Grove Road East	A3-B3
Grove Road West	A3
High Street	B2
Iford Lane	A1
Jumpers Avenue	A4
Jumpers Road	A3-A4-B4
Kings Avenue	A2-B2
Manor Road	B2
Milhams Street	B2-C2
Mill Road	B3-B4
Portfield Road	A3-B3
Queens Avenue	B1
Quay Road	B1
River Lea Road	B2
Soapers Lane	B1
Saxonbury Road	A1
St John's Road	A2
St Margarets Avenue	B1
Sopers Lane	B1-B2
South View Road	A1-B1
Stony Lane	C4-C3-C2
Stour Road	B3-B2-A1-A2
Stourbank Road	B2
The Grove	A4
Tuckton Road	A1
Twynham Avenue	B2-B3
Walcott Avenue	A4-B4
Waterloo Place	C2
Wickfield Avenue	B1-B2
Wick Lane	A1-B1-B2
Willow Drive	A1-B1
Willow Way	A1-B1
Windsor Road	A3

Poole

Ballard Road	B1-C1
Church Street	A1
Dear Hay Lane	A2-B2
Denmark Road	C3
East Quay Road	B1
East Street	B1
Elizabeth Road	B1-B2
Emerson Road	B1-B2
Esplanade	B3
Garland Road	C4
Green Road	B2-B1-C1
Heckford Road	C3-C4
High Street	A1-B1-B2
Hill Street	B2
Johns Road	C3-C4
Jolliffe Road	C4
Kingland Road	B2-C2
Kingston Road	C3-C4
Lagland Street	B1-B2
Longfleet Road	C3
Maple Road	C3-C4
Mount Pleasant Road	C2-C3
Newfoundland Drive	C1
New Orchard	A1-A2
North Street	B2
Old Orchard	B1
Parkstone Road	C1-C2
Perry Gardens	B1
Poole Bridge	A1
Sandbourne Road	C4
St Mary's Road	C3
Seldown Lane	C2-C3
Shaftesbury Road	C3
Skinner Street	B1
South Road	B2
Stanley Road	B1
Sterte Avenue	A4-B4
Sterte Road	B2-B3-B4
Stokes Avenue	B4-C4
Strand Street	A1-B1
Tatnam Road	B4-C4
The Quay	A1-B1
Towngate Bridge	B2-B3
West Quay Road	A1-A2-B2
West Street	A1-A2-B2
Wimborne Road	B3-C3-C4

Swanage

Argyle Road	A2
Atlantic Road	A1-B1
Battlemead	B4
Beach Gardens	B4
Bon Accord Road	B1
Broad Road	C1
Cauldron Avenue	B4
Cauldron Barn Road	A4-B4
Cauldron Crescent	A4
Church Hill	A2
Clifton Road	B4
Cluny Crescent	B1-C1
Court Hill	A2
Court Road	A2
Cowlease	A1-A2
Cranborne Road	B2
De Moulham Road	B3-B4
D'uberville Drive	A4-B4
Eldon Terrace	B2
Encombe Road	C1
Exeter Road	B1-C1
Gannets Park	B3
Gilbert Road	A2-B2
Gordon Road	B1
Grosvenor Road	C1
Hanbury Road	A2
High Street	A2-B3
Ilminster Road	B2-B3
Institute Road	B2-B2
Kings Road	A2-B2
Kings Road East	B2
Kings Road West	A2
Locarno Road	A2
Manor Road	B1-C1
Manwell Drive	A1
Manwell Road	A1
Mariners Drive	A1
Marshall Row	C1
Mount Pleasant Lane	B1-B2
Mountscar	A1
Newton Road	B1
Northbrook Road	A2-A3-B3-B4
Osborne Road	A1
Park Road	C1
Princess Road	A2
Prospect Crescent	A3
Peveril Heights	C1
Peveril Point Road	C1
Priests Road	C1
Queens Mead	B1
Queens Road	A1-B1-C1
Rabling Road	A3-B3
Rempstone Road	B2-B3
Richmond Road	A1
St Vast's Road	B1
Sentry Road	C1
Seymer Road	C1
Shore Road	B3-B4

Springfield Road	B2
Stafford Road	B1-B2
Station Road	B2
Sunridge Close	B1
Taunton Road	C1
The Parade	C2
Townsend Road	A1
Ulwell Road	B4
Victoria Avenue	A3-B3
Vivian Park	B4
Walrond Road	A3-B3

LEGEND

AA Recommended roads	
Other roads	
Restricted roads	
Buildings of interest	Sta
AA Centre	AA
Churches	†
Car parks	P
One Way streets	
Parks and open spaces	

STT

Bournemouth

Until the beginning of the 19th-century the landscape was open heath. Bournemouth's rise began in Victorian times when the idea of seaside holidays was very new. In the next 50 years it had become a major resort. Holidaymakers today enjoy miles of sandy beaches, a mild climate and beautiful setting, along with a tremendous variety of amenities, including some of the best shopping in the south. Entertainments range from variety shows, cinemas, opera and the world famous Bournemouth Symphony Orchestra.

Christchurch is situated at the confluence of the rivers Avon and Stour which flow into Christchurch Harbour at Mudeford. The Priory Church dominates the town with its many attractive walks and old buildings.

Poole is famous for the large natural harbour and Poole Quay with its unique historical interest.

The Maritime Museum illustrates the town's associations with the sea since prehistoric times and the famous Poole Pottery offers guided tours of its workshops with exhibits of pottery past and present.

Swanage is one of Dorset's most popular holiday resorts that has still retained much of its Victorian influence. Dramatic coastal scenery with cliff top walks and many places of interest are within easy reach.

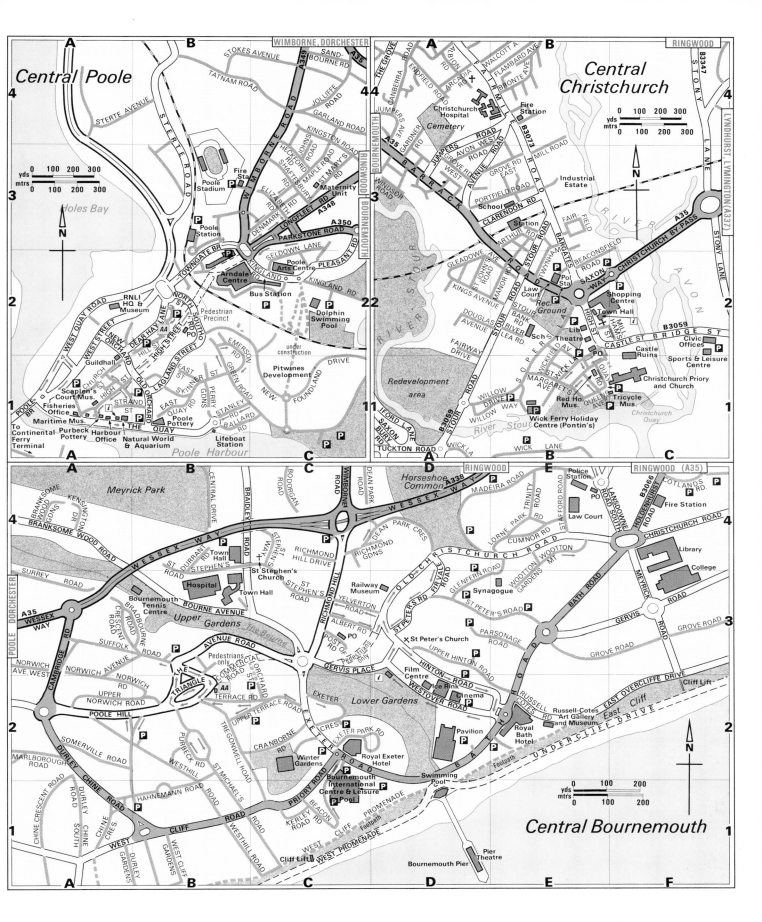

BOURNEMOUTH
The pier, safe sea-bathing, golden sands facing south and sheltered by steep cliffs, and plenty of amenities for the holiday maker make Bournemouth one of the most popular resorts on the south coast of England.

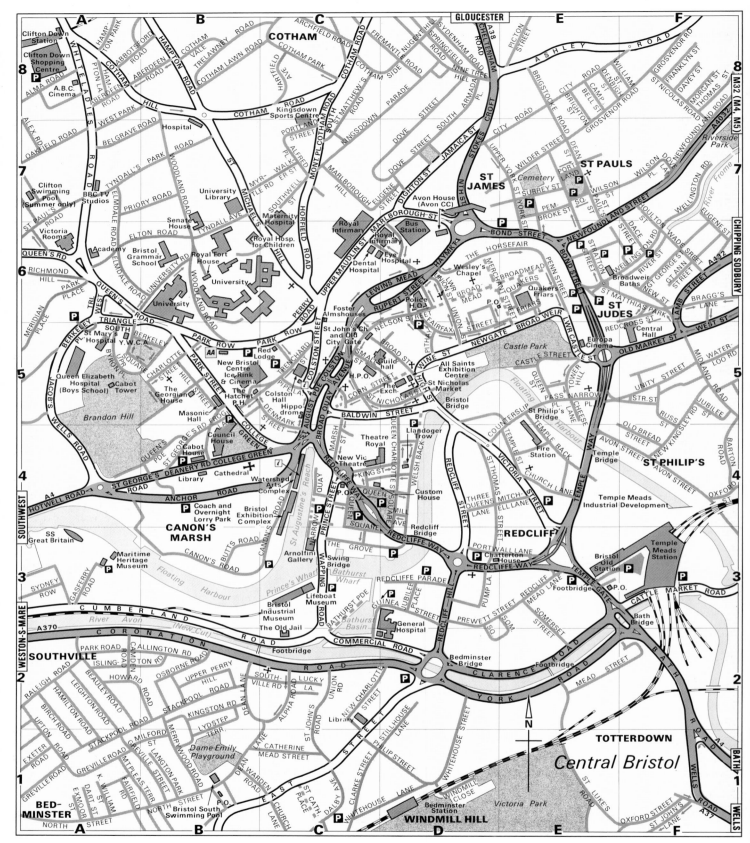

Bristol

One of Britain's most historic seaports, Bristol retains many of its visible links with the past, despite terrible damage inflicted during bombing raids in World War II. Most imposing is the cathedral, founded as an abbey church in 1140. Perhaps even more famous than the cathedral is the Church of St Mary Redcliffe. Ranking among the finest churches in the country, it owes much of its splendour to 14th- and 15th-century merchants who bestowed huge sums of money on it.

The merchant families brought wealth to the whole of Bristol, and their trading links with the world are continued in today's modern aerospace and technological industries. Much of the best of Bristol can be seen in the area of the Floating Harbour. Several of the old warehouses have been converted into museums, galleries and exhibition centres. Among them are genuinely picturesque old pubs, the best known which is the Llandoger Trow. It is a timbered 17th-century house, the finest of its kind in Bristol. Further up the same street - King Street - is the Theatre Royal, built in 1766 and the oldest theatre in the country. In Corn Street, the heart of the business area, is a magnificent 18th-century corn exchange. In front of it are the four pillars known as the 'nails', on which merchants used to make cash transactions, hence to 'pay on the nail';

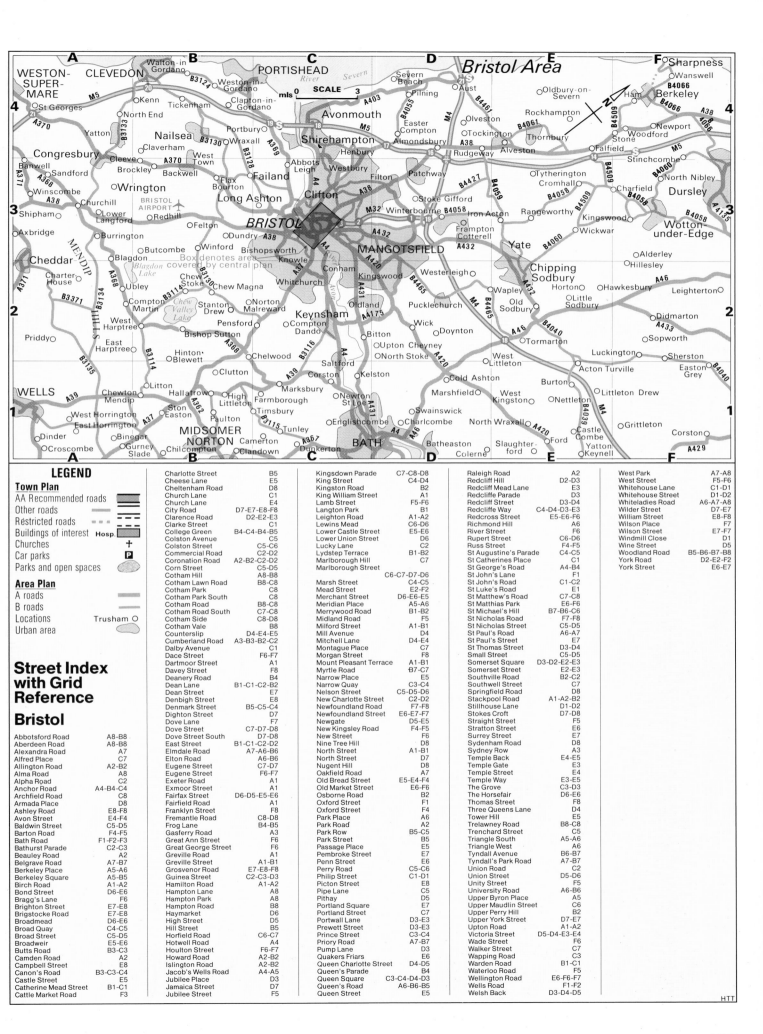

LEGEND

Town Plan

AA Recommended roads	
Other roads	
Restricted roads	
Buildings of interest	Hosp.
Churches	+
Car parks	P
Parks and open spaces	

Area Plan

A roads	
B roads	
Locations	Trusham ○
Urban area	

Street Index with Grid Reference

Bristol

Abbotsford Road	A8-B8	Charlotte Street	B5	Kingsdown Parade	C7-C8-D8	Raleigh Road	A2
Aberdeen Road	A8-B8	Cheese Lane	E5	King Street	C4-D4	Redcliff Hill	D2-D3
Alexandra Road	A7	Cheltenham Road	D8	Kingston Road	B2	Redcliff Mead Lane	E3
Alfred Place	C7	Church Lane	C1	King William Street	A1	Redcliffe Parade	D3
Allington Road	A2-B2	Church Lane	E4	Lamb Street	F5-F6	Redcliff Street	D3-D4
Alma Road	A8	City Road	D7-E7-E8-F8	Langton Park	B1	Redcliffe Way	C4-D4-D3-E3
Alpha Road	C2	Clarence Road	D2-E2-E3	Leighton Road	A1-A2	Redcross Street	E5-E6-F6
Anchor Road	A4-B4-C4	Clarke Street	C1	Lewins Mead	C6-D6	Richmond Hill	A6
Archfield Road	C8	College Green	B4-C4-B4-B5	Lower Castle Street	E5-E6	River Street	F6
Armada Place	D8	Colston Avenue	C5	Lower Union Street	D6	Rupert Street	C6-D6
Ashley Road	E8-F8	Colston Street	C5-C6	Lucky Lane	C2	Russ Street	F4-F5
Avon Street	E4-F4	Commercial Road	C2-D2	Lydstep Terrace	B1-B2	St Augustine's Parade	C4-C5
Baldwin Street	C5-D5	Coronation Road	A2-B2-C2-D2	Marlborough Hill	C7	St Catherines Place	C1
Barton Road	F4-F5	Corn Street	C5-D5	Marlborough Street		St George's Road	A4-B4
Bath Road	F1-F2-F3	Cotham Hill	A8-B8		C6-C7-D7-D6	St John's Lane	B1
Bathurst Parade	C2-C3	Cotham Lawn Road	B8-C8	Marsh Street	C4-C5	St John's Road	C1-C2
Beauley Road	A2	Cotham Park	C8	Mead Street	E2-F2	St Luke's Road	E1
Belgrave Road	A7-B7	Cotham Park South	C8	Merchant Street	D6-E6-E5	St Matthew's Road	C7-C8
Berkeley Place	A5-A6	Cotham Road	B8-C8	Meridian Place	A5-A6	St Matthias Park	E6-F6
Berkeley Square	A5-B5	Cotham Road South	C7-C8	Merrywood Road	B1-B2	St Michael's Hill	B7-B6-C6
Birch Road	A1-A2	Cotham Side	C8-D8	Midland Road	F5	St Nicholas Road	F7-F8
Bond Street	D6-E6	Cotham Vale	B8	Milford Street	A1-B1	St Nicholas Street	C5-D5
Bragg's Lane	F6	Countership	D4-E4-E5	Mill Avenue	D4	St Paul's Road	A6-A7
Brighton Street	E7-E8	Cumberland Road	A3-B3-B2-C2	Mitchell Lane	D4-E4	St Paul's Street	E7
Brigstocke Road	E7-E8	Dalby Avenue	C1	Montague Place	C7	St Thomas Street	D3-D4
Broadmead	D6-E6	Dace Street	F6-F7	Morgan Street	F8	Small Street	C5-D5
Broad Quay	C4-C5	Dartmoor Street	A1	Mount Pleasant Terrace	A1-B1	Somerset Square	D3-D2-E2-E3
Broad Street	C5-D5	Davey Street	F8	Myrtle Road	B7-C7	Somerset Street	E2-E3
Broadweir	E5-E6	Deanery Road	B4	Narrow Place	E5	Southville Road	B2-C2
Butts Road	B3-C3	Dean Lane	B1-C1-C2-B2	Narrow Quay	C3-C4	Southwell Street	C7
Camden Road	A2	Dean Street	E7	Nelson Street	C5-D5-D6	Springfield Road	D8
Campbell Street	E8	Denbigh Street	E8	New Charlotte Street	C2-D2	Stackpool Road	A1-A2-B2
Canon's Road	B3-C3-C4	Denmark Street	B5-C5-C4	Newfoundland Road	F7-F8	Stillhouse Lane	D1-D2
Castle Street	E5	Dighton Street	D7	Newfoundland Street	E6-E7-E7-F7	Stokes Croft	D7-D8
Catherine Mead Street	B1-C1	Dove Lane	F7	Newgate	D5-E5	Straight Street	F5
Cattle Market Road	F3	Dove Street	C7-D7-D8	New Kingsley Road	F4-F5	Stratton Street	E6
		Dove Street South	D7-D8	New Street	F6	Surrey Street	E7
		East Street	B1-C1-C2-D2	Nine Tree Hill	D8	Sydenham Road	D8
		Elmdale Road	A7-A6-B6	North Street	A1-B1	Sydney Row	A3
		Elton Road	A6-B6	North Street	D7	Temple Back	E4-E5
		Eugene Street	C7-D7	Nugent Hill	D8	Temple Gate	E3
		Eugene Street	F6-F7	Oakfield Road	A7	Temple Street	E4
		Exeter Road	A1	Old Bread Street	E5-E4-F4	Temple Way	E3-E5
		Exmoor Street	A1	Old Market Street	E6-F6	The Grove	C3-D3
		Fairfax Street	D6-D5-E5-E6	Osborne Road	B2	The Horsefair	D6-E6
		Fairfield Road	A1	Oxford Street	F1	Thomas Street	F8
		Franklyn Street	F8	Oxford Street	F4	Three Queens Lane	D4
		Fremantle Road	C8-D8	Park Place	A6	Tower Hill	E5
		Frog Lane	B4-B5	Park Road	A2	Trelawney Road	B8-C8
		Gasferry Road	A3	Park Row	B5-C5	Trenchard Street	C5
		Great Ann Street	F6	Park Street	B5	Triangle South	A5-A6
		Great George Street	F6	Passage Place	E5	Triangle West	A6
		Greville Road	A1	Pembroke Street	E7	Tyndall Avenue	B6-B7
		Greville Street	A1-B1	Penn Street	E6	Tyndall's Park Road	A7-B7
		Grosvenor Road	E7-E8-F8	Perry Road	C5-C6	Union Road	C2
		Guinea Street	C2-C3-D3	Philip Street	C1-D1	Union Street	D5-D6
		Hamilton Road	A1-A2	Picton Street	E8	Unity Street	F5
		Hampton Lane	A8	Pipe Lane	C5	University Road	A6-B6
		Hampton Park	A8	Pithay	D5	Upper Byron Place	A5
		Hampton Road	B8	Portland Square	E7	Upper Maudlin Street	C6
		Haymarket	D6	Portland Street	C7	Upper Perry Hill	B2
		High Street	D5	Portwall Lane	D3-E3	Upper York Street	D7-E7
		Hill Street	D3-E3	Prewett Street	E3	Upton Road	A1-A2
		Horfield Road	C6-C7	Prince Street	C3-C4	Victoria Street	D5-D4-E3-E4
		Hotwell Road	A4	Priory Road	A7-B7	Wade Street	F6
		Houlton Street	F6-F7	Pump Lane	D3	Walker Street	C7
		Howard Road	A2-B2	Quakers Friars	E6	Wapping Road	C3
		Islington Road	A2-B2	Queen Charlotte Street	D4-D5	Warden Road	B1-C1
		Jacob's Wells Road	A4-A5	Queen's Parade	B4	Waterloo Road	F5
		Jubilee Place	D3	Queen Square	C3-C4-D4-D3	Wellington Road	E6-F6-F7
		Jamaica Street	D7	Queen's Road	A6-B6-B5	Wells Road	F1-F2
		Jubilee Street	F5	Queen Street	E5	Welsh Back	D3-D4-D5

West Park	A7-A8
West Street	F5-F6
Whitehouse Lane	C1-D1
Whitehouse Street	D1-D2
Whiteladies Road	A6-A7-A8
Wilder Street	D7-E7
William Street	E8-F8
Wilson Place	F7
Wilson Street	E7-F7
Windmill Close	D1
Wine Street	D5
Woodland Road	B5-B6-B7-B8
York Road	D2-E2-F2
York Street	E6-E7

197

HTT

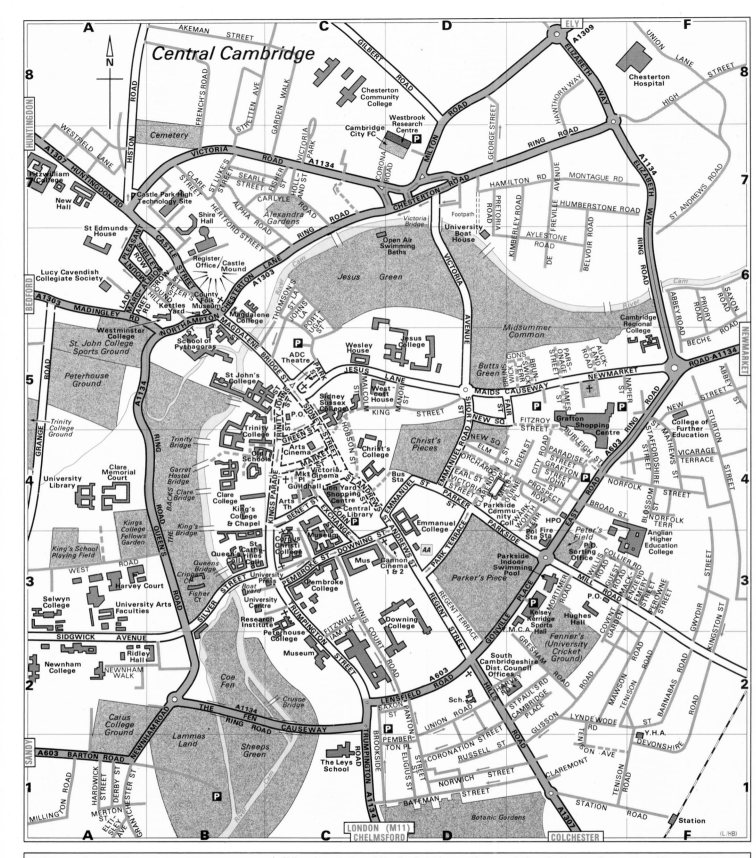

Cambridge

Few views in England, perhaps even in Europe, are as memorable as that from Cambridge's Backs towards the colleges. Dominating the scene, in every sense, is King's College Chapel. One of the finest Gothic buildings anywhere, it was built in three stages from 1446 to 1515.

No one would dispute that the chapel is Cambridge's masterpiece, but there are dozens of buildings here that would be the finest in any other town or city. Most are colleges, or are attached to colleges, and it is the university which permeates every aspect of Cambridge's landscape and life. In all there are 33 university colleges in the city, and nearly all have buildings and features of great interest. Guided tours of the colleges are available.

Cambridge can provide a complete history of English architecture. The oldest surviving building is the tower of St Benet's Church dating back to before the Norman Conquest, and its most famous church is the Church of the Holy Sepulchre, one of only four round churches of its kind.

Of the many notable museums in Cambridge, the Fitzwilliam Museum contains some of the best collections of ceramics, paintings, coins, medals and Egyptian, Greek and Roman antiquities outside London.

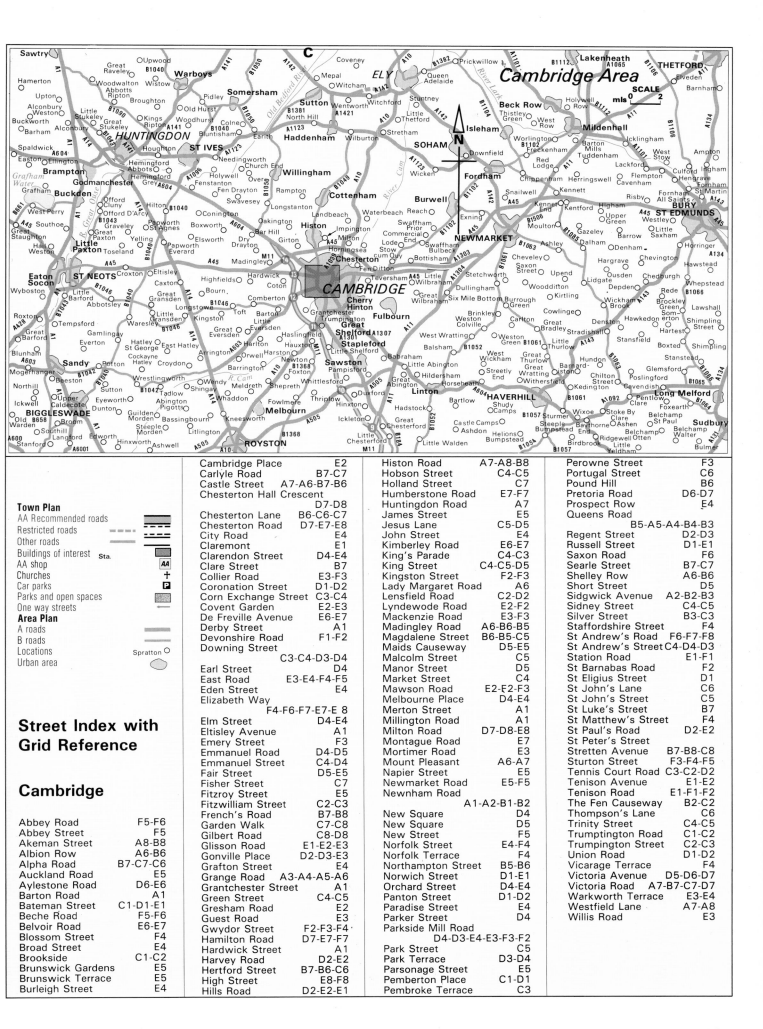

Cambridge Area

SCALE

mls 0 ___ 2

Town Plan

AA Recommended roads	
Restricted roads	
Other roads	
Buildings of interest	Sta.
AA shop	AA
Churches	+
Car parks	P
Parks and open spaces	
One way streets	←

Area Plan

A roads	
B roads	
Locations	Spratton ○
Urban area	

Street Index with Grid Reference

Cambridge

Abbey Road	F5-F6
Abbey Street	F5
Akeman Street	A8-B8
Albion Row	A6-B6
Alpha Road	B7-C7-C6
Auckland Road	E5
Aylestone Road	D6-E6
Barton Road	A1
Bateman Street	C1-D1-E1
Beche Road	F5-F6
Belvoir Road	E6-E7
Blossom Street	F4
Broad Street	E4
Brookside	C1-C2
Brunswick Gardens	E5
Brunswick Terrace	E5
Burleigh Street	E4

Cambridge Place	E2
Carlyle Road	B7-C7
Castle Street	A7-A6-B7-B6
Chesterton Hall Crescent	D7-D8
Chesterton Lane	B6-C6-C7
Chesterton Road	D7-E7-E8
City Road	E4
Claremont	E1
Clarendon Street	D4-E4
Clare Street	B7
Collier Road	E3-F3
Coronation Street	D1-D2
Corn Exchange Street	C3-C4
Covent Garden	E2-E3
De Freville Avenue	E6-E7
Derby Street	A1
Devonshire Road	F1-F2
Downing Street	C3-C4-D3-D4
Earl Street	D4
East Road	E3-E4-F4-F5
Eden Street	E4
Elizabeth Way	F4-F6-F7-E7-E 8
Elm Street	D4-E4
Eltisley Avenue	A1
Emery Street	F3
Emmanuel Road	D4-D5
Emmanuel Street	C4-D4
Fair Street	D5-E5
Fisher Street	C7
Fitzroy Street	E5
Fitzwilliam Street	C2-C3
French's Road	B7-B8
Garden Walk	C7-C8
Gilbert Road	C8-D8
Glisson Road	E1-E2-E3
Gonville Place	D2-D3-E3
Grafton Street	E4
Grange Road	A3-A4-A5-A6
Grantchester Street	A1
Green Street	C4-C5
Gresham Road	E2
Guest Road	E3
Gwydor Street	F2-F3-F4
Hamilton Road	D7-E7-F7
Hardwick Street	A1
Harvey Road	D2-E2
Hertford Street	B7-B6-C6
High Street	E8-F8
Hills Road	D2-E2-E1

Histon Road	A7-A8-B8
Hobson Street	C4-C5
Holland Street	C7
Humberstone Road	E7-F7
Huntingdon Road	A7
James Street	E5
Jesus Lane	C5-D5
John Street	E4
Kimberley Road	E6-E7
King's Parade	C4-C3
King Street	C4-C5-D5
Kingston Street	F2-F3
Lady Margaret Road	A6
Lensfield Road	C2-D2
Lyndewode Road	E2-F2
Mackenzie Road	E3-F3
Madingley Road	A6-B6-B5
Magdalene Street	B6-B5-C5
Maids Causeway	D5-E5
Malcolm Street	C5
Manor Street	D5
Market Street	C4
Mawson Road	E2-F2-F3
Melbourne Place	D4-E4
Merton Street	A1
Millington Road	A1
Milton Road	D7-D8-E8
Montague Road	E7
Mortimer Road	E3
Mount Pleasant	A6-A7
Napier Street	E5
Newmarket Road	E5-F5
Newnham Road	A1-A2-B1-B2
New Square	D4
New Square	D5
New Street	F5
Norfolk Street	E4-F4
Norfolk Terrace	F4
Northampton Street	B5-B6
Norwich Street	D1-E1
Orchard Street	D4-E4
Panton Street	D1-D2
Paradise Street	E5
Parker Street	D4
Parkside Mill Road	D4-D3-E4-E3-F3-F2
Park Street	C5
Park Terrace	D3-D4
Parsonage Street	E5
Pemberton Place	C1-D1
Pembroke Terrace	C3

Perowne Street	F3
Portugal Street	C6
Pound Hill	B6
Pretoria Road	D6-D7
Prospect Row	E4
Queens Road	B5-A5-A4-B4-B3
Regent Street	D2-D3
Russell Street	D1-E1
Saxon Road	F6
Searle Street	B7-C7
Shelley Row	A6-B6
Short Street	D5
Sidgwick Avenue	A2-B2-B3
Sidney Street	C4-C5
Silver Street	B3-C3
Staffordshire Street	F4
St Andrew's Road	F6-F7-F8
St Andrew's Street	C4-D4-D3
Station Road	E1-E2
St Barnabas Road	F2
St Eligius Street	D1
St John's Lane	C6
St John's Street	C5
St Luke's Street	B7
St Matthew's Street	F4
St Paul's Road	D2-E2
St Peter's Street	
Stretten Avenue	B7-B8-C8
Sturton Street	F3-F4-F5
Tennis Court Road	C3-C2-D2
Tenison Avenue	E1-E2
Tenison Road	E1-F1-F2
The Fen Causeway	B2-C2
Thompson's Lane	C6
Trinity Street	C4-C5
Trumpington Road	C1-C2
Trumpington Street	C2-C3
Union Road	D1-D2
Vicarage Terrace	F4
Victoria Avenue	D5-D6-D7
Victoria Road	A7-B7-C7-D7
Warkworth Terrace	E3-E4
Westfield Lane	A7-A8
Willis Road	E3

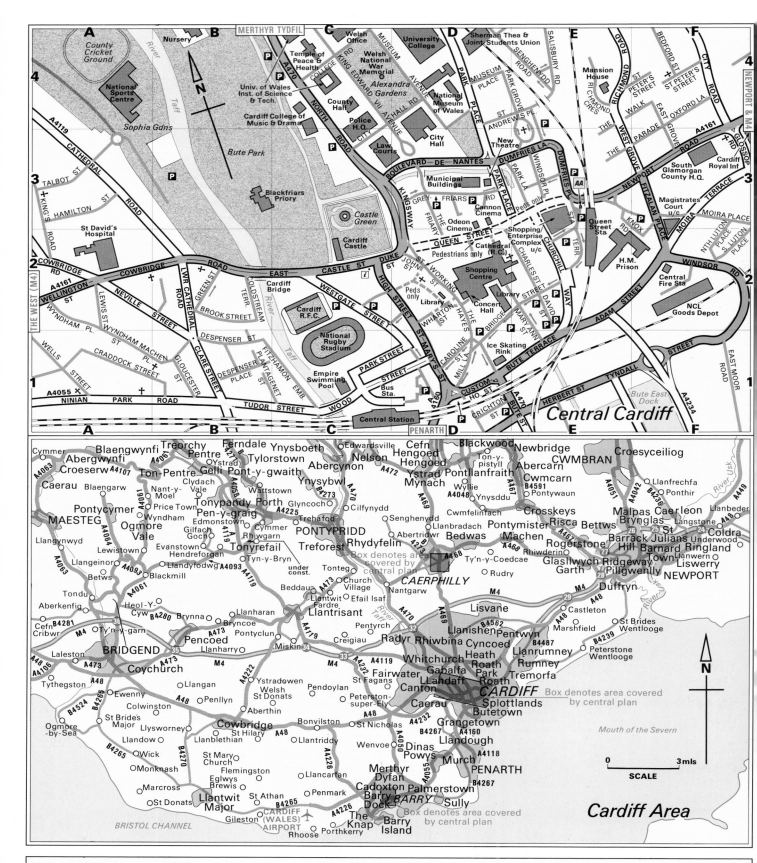

Cardiff

Strategically important to both the Romans and the Normans, Cardiff slipped from prominence in medieval times and remained a quiet market town in a remote area until it was transformed – almost overnight – by the effects of the Industrial Revolution. The valleys of South Wales were a principal source of iron and coal – raw materials which helped to change the shape and course of

the 19th-century world. Cardiff became a teeming export centre; by the end of the 19th century it was the largest coal-exporting city in the world.

Close to the castle – an exciting place with features from Roman times to the 19th century – is the city's civic centre – a fine concourse of buildings dating largely from the early part of the 20th century. Among them is the National Museum of Wales – a superb collection of art and antiquities from Wales and around the world.

Barry has sandy beaches, landscaped gardens and parks, entertainment arcades and funfairs. Like Cardiff it grew as a result of the demand for coal and steel, but now its dock complex is involved in the petrochemical and oil industries.

Caerphilly is famous for two things – a castle and cheese. The cheese is no longer made here, but the 13th-century castle, slighted by Cromwell, still looms above its moat. No castle in Britain – except Windsor – is larger.

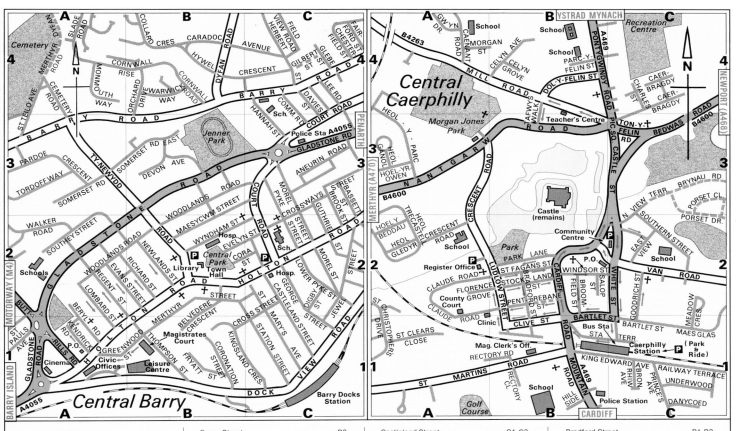

LEGEND

Town Plan

AA recommended route	
Restricted roads	
Other roads	
Buildings of interest	Cinema ■
Car parks	P
Parks and open spaces	▲
One way streets	⌐

Area Plan

A roads	
B roads	
Locations	Glyncoch ○
Urban area	

Street Index with Grid Reference

Cardiff

Adam Street	E1-E2-F2
Bedford Street	F4
Boulevard de Nantes	C3-D3
Bridge Street	D1-D2-E2
Brook Street	B2
Bute Street	D1-E1
Bute Terrace	D1-E1
Caroline Street	D1
Castle Street	C2
Cathedral Street	A4-A3-B3-B2-A2
Charles Street	D2-E2
Churchill Way	E2-E3
City Hall Road	C3-C4-D4
City Road	F4
Clare Street	B1
Coldstream Terrace	B2
College Road	C4
Cowbridge Road	A2
Cowbridge Road East	A2-B2-C2
Craddock Street	A1-B1
Crichton Street	D1
Customhouse Street	D1
David Street	E2
Despenser Place	B1
Despenser Street	B1
Duke Street	C2-D2
Dumfries Lane	D3-E3
Dumfries Place	E3
East Grove	F4-F3
East Moor Road	F1
Fitzalan Place	F3-F2
Fitzhamon Embankment	B1-C1
Glossop Road	F3
Gloucester Street	B1

Green Street	B2
Greyfriars Road	D3
Hamilton Street	A3
Herbert Street	E1
High Street	C2-D2
King Edward VII Avenue	C4-D4-D3-C3
King's Road	A2-A3
Kingsway	C3-D3-D2
Knox Road	E3-F3-F2
Lewis Street	A2
Lower Cathedral Road	B1-B2
Machen Place	A1-B1
Mary Ann Street	E1-E2
Mill Lane	D1
Moira Place	F3
Moira Terrace	F2-F3
Museum Avenue	C4-D4
Museum Place	D4
Neville Street	A2-B2-B1
Newport Road	E3-F3-F4
Ninian Park Road	A1-B1
North Luton Place	F2-F3
North Road	B4-C4-C3
Oxford Lane	F4
Park Grove	D4-E4
Park Lane	D3-E3
Park Place	D4-D3-E3
Park Street	C1-D1
Plantagenet Street	B1-C1
Queen Street	D2-D3
Richmond Crescent	E4
Richmond Road	E4
St Andrew's Place	D4-E4
St John Street	D2
St Mary's Street	D1-D2
St Peter's Street	E4-F4
Salisbury Road	E4
Senghenydd Road	D4-E4
South Luton Place	F2-F3
Station Terrace	E2-E3
The Friary	D2-D3
The Hayes	D1-D2
The Parade	E3-F3-F4
The Walk	E3-E4-F4
Talbot Street	A3
Tudor Street	B1-C1
Tyndall Street	E1-F1
Wellington Street	A2
Wells Street	A1
Westgate Street	C2-D2-D1
West Grove	E4-E3-F3
Wharton Street	D2
Windsor Place	E3
Windsor Road	F2
Wood Street	C1-D1
Working Street	D2
Wyndham Place	A2
Wyndham Street	A1-A2

Barry

Aneurin Road	C3
Barry Road	A3-A4-B3-B4-C4
Bassett Street	C2-C3
Belvedere Crescent	B1-B2
Beryl Road	A1-A2
Brook Street	C2-C3
Buttrills Road	A1-A2
Caradoc Avenue	B4-C4

Castleland Street	C1-C2
Cemetery Road	A3-A4
Chesterfield Street	C4
Collard Crescent	B4
Commercial Road	C3-C4
Cora Street	B2-C2
Cornwall Rise	A3-A4
Cornwall Road	B4
Coronation Street	B1
Cross Street	B1-C1-C2
Crossways Street	C2-C3
Court Road	C2-C3-C4
Davies Street	C3-C4
Devon Avenue	B3
Digby Street	C2
Dock View Road	B1-C1-C2
Dyfan Road	B4
Evans Street	A2-B2
Evelyn Street	B2-C2
Fairford Street	C4
Field View Road	C4
Fryatt Street	B1
George Street	C1-C2
Gilbert Street	C4
Gladstone Road	A1-A2-B2-B3-C3
Glebe Street	C2
Greenwood Street	A1-B1
Guthrie Street	C3-C2
Hannah Street	C4-C3
Herbert Street	C4
Holton Road	A1-B1-B2-C2
Hywell Crescent	B4-C4
Jewel Street	C1-C2
Kendrick Road	A1
Kingsland Crescent	B1-C1
Lee Road	C4
Lombard Street	A1-A2
Lower Pyke Street	C2
Maesycwm Street	B2-B3-C3
Merthyr Dyfan Road	A4
Merthyr Street	B1-B2-C2
Monmouth Way	A4
Morel Street	C2-C3
Newlands Street	B2
Orchard Drive	B3-B4
Pardoe Crescent	A3
Pyke Street	C3-C2
Regent Street	A2-B2
Richard Street	A2-B2
St Mary's Avenue	C1-C2
St Pauls Avenue	A1
St Teilo Avenue	A3-A4
Slade Road	A4
Somerset Road	A3
Somerset Road East	A3-B3
Southey Street	A2-A3
Station Street	C1
Thompson Street	B1
Tordoff Way	A3
Ty-Newydd Road	A3-B3-B2
Walker Road	A2
Warwick Way	B4
Woodlands Road	A2-B2-B3-C3
Wyndham Street	B2-C2

Bradford Street	B1-B2
Broomfield Street	B2
Bronrhiw Avenue	C1
Brynau Road	C3
Caenant Road	A4
Caer Bragdy	C4
Cardiff Road	B1-B2
Castle Street	C3
Celyn Avenue	B4
Celyn Grove	B4
Charles Street	C4
Claude Road	A1-A2-B2
Clive Street	B1-B2
Crescent Rod	A2-A3-B3
Danycoed	C1
Dol-y-Felen Street	B4
East View	C2
Florence Grove	A2-B2
Goodrich Street	C1-C2
Gwyn Drive	A4
Heol Ganol	A3
Heol Gledyr	A2
Heol Trecastell	A2-A3
Hillside	B1
Heol y Beddau	A2
Heol-yr-Owen	A3
King Edward Avenue	B1-C1
Ludlow Street	A2-B2-B1
Maes Glas	C1
Meadow Crescent	C1-C2
Mill Road	A4-B4-B3
Morgan Street	A4-B4
Mountain Road	B1
Nantgarw Road	A3-B3
North View Terrace	C2-C3
Parc-y-Felin Street	B4
Park Lane	B2
Pentrebone Street	B2
Piccadilly Square	C3
Pontygwindy Road	B4-C4
Porset Close	C3
Porset Drive	C2-C3
Prince's Avenue	C1
Railway Terrace	C1
Rectory Road	A1-B1
Rectory Close	B1
St Christopher's Drive	A1-A2
St Clears Close	A1
St Fagans Street	B2
St Martins Road	A1-B1
Salop Street	B2
Southern Street	C2-C3
Station Terrace	B1-C1
Stockland Street	B2
Tafwy Walk	B3-B4
Ton-y-Felin Road	C3
Underwood	C1
Van Road	C2
White Street	C2
Windsor Street	B2

Caerphilly

Bartlet Street	B2-B1-C1
Bedwas Road	C3-C4

LTH

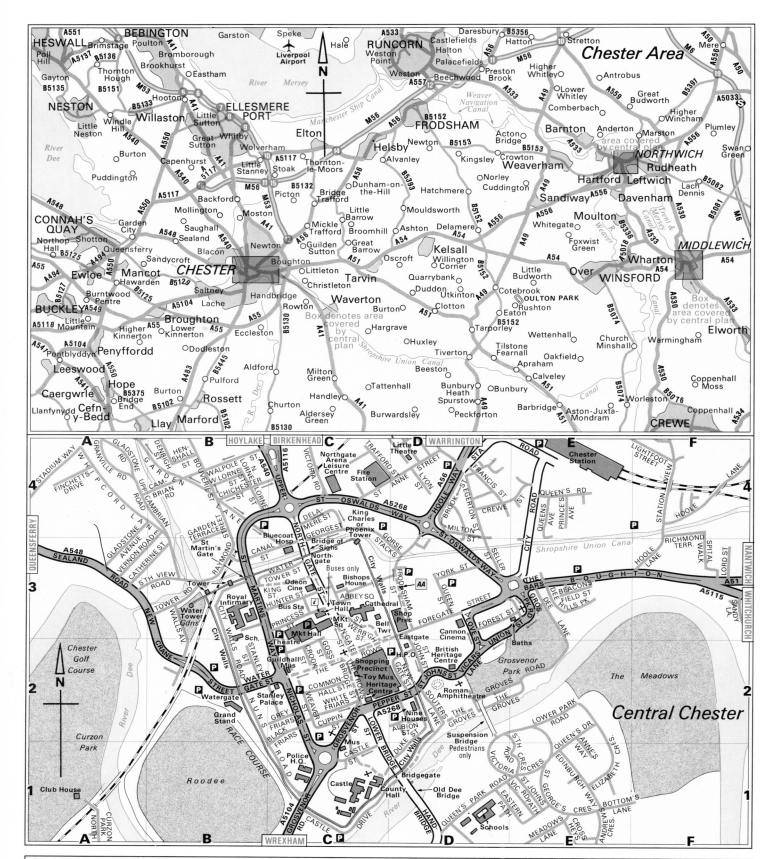

Chester

Chester is the only English city to have preserved the complete circuit of its Roman and medieval walls. On the west side, the top of the walls is now at pavement level, but on the other three sides the walk along the ramparts is remarkable. Two of the old watchtowers contain small museums: the Water Tower, built to protect the old river port, displays relics of medieval Chester; King Charles's Tower, from which Charles I watched the defeat of the Royalist army at the Battle of Rowton Moor in 1645, portrays Chester's role in the Civil War.

Looking down from the top of the Eastgate, crowned with the ornate and gaily-coloured Jubilee Clock erected in 1897, the view down the main street, the old Roman *Via Principalis*, reveals a dazzling display of the black-and-white timbered buildings for which Chester is famous. One of these, Providence House, bears the inscription 'God's Providence is Mine Inheritance', carved in thanks for sparing the survivors of the plague of 1647 that ravaged the city.

On either side of Eastgate, Watergate and Bridge Street are the Rows, a feature unique to Chester, and dating back at least to the 13th century. These covered galleries of shops, raised up at first-floor level, protected pedestrians from weather and traffic. Chester's magnificent cathedral has beautifully carved choir stalls.

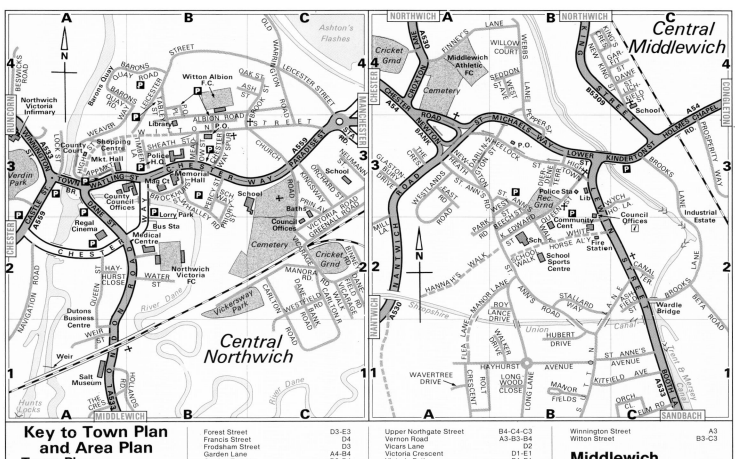

Key to Town Plan and Area Plan

Town Plan

AA Recommended roads	
Other roads	
Restricted roads	
Buildings of interest	College
AA Service Centre	AA
Car Parks	P
Parks and open spaces	
Churches	+

Area Plan

A roads	
B roads	
Locations	DuddonO
Urban area	
Locks	

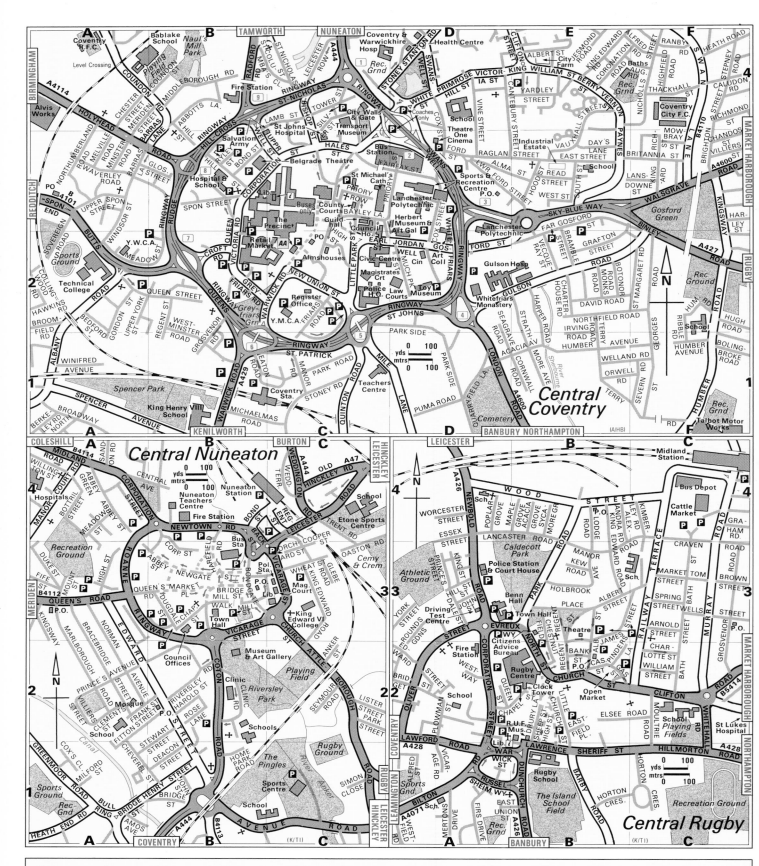

Coventry

Few British towns were as battered by the Blitz as Coventry. A raid in November 1940 flattened most of the city and left the lovely cathedral church a gaunt shell with only the tower and spire still standing. Rebuilding started almost immediately. Symbolising the creation of the new from the ashes of the old is Sir Basil Spence's cathedral, completed in 1962 beside the bombed ruins.

A few medieval buildings have survived intact in the city. St Mary's Guildhall is a finely restored 14th-century building with an attractive minstrels' gallery. Whitefriars Monastery now serves as a local museum. The Herbert Art Gallery and Museum has several collections. Coventry is an important manufacturing centre – most notably for cars – and it is also a university city with the fine campus of the University of Warwick some four miles from the centre.

Nuneaton is an industrial town to the north of Coventry with two distinguished old churches – St Nicholas' and St Mary's. Like Coventry it was badly damaged in the war and its centre has been rebuilt.

Rugby was no more than a sleepy market town until the arrival of the railway. Of course it did have the famous Rugby School, founded in 1567 and one of the country's foremost educational establishments. The railway brought industry – still the town's mainstay.

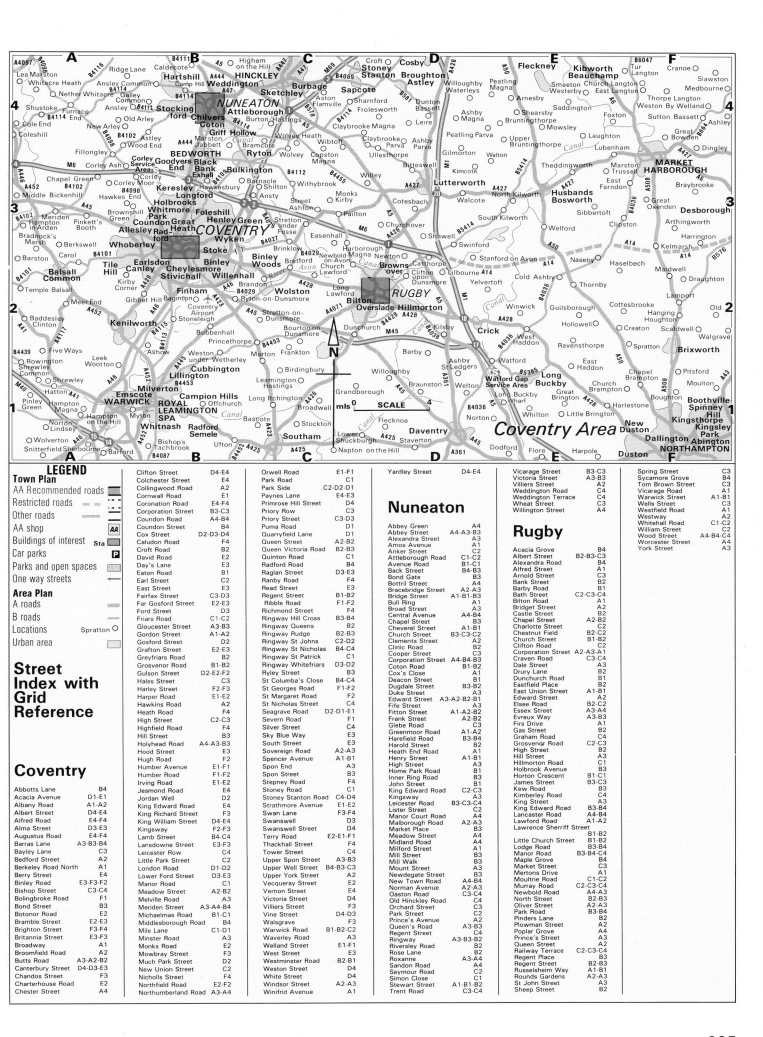

Coventry Area map

LEGEND

Town Plan

- AA Recommended roads
- Restricted roads
- Other roads
- AA shop — AA
- Buildings of interest — Sta
- Car parks — P
- Parks and open spaces
- One way streets →

Area Plan

- A roads
- B roads
- Locations — Spratton ○
- Urban area

Street Index with Grid Reference

Coventry

Abbotts Lane	B4
Acacia Avenue	D1-E1
Albany Road	A1-A2
Albert Street	D4-E4
Alfred Road	E4-F4
Alma Street	D3-E3
Augustus Road	E4-F4
Barras Lane	A3-B3-B4
Bayley Lane	C3
Bedford Street	A2
Berkeley Road North	A1
Berry Street	E4
Binley Road	E3-F3-F2
Bishop Street	C3-C4
Bolingbroke Road	F1
Bond Street	B3
Botoner Road	E2
Bramble Street	E2-E3
Brighton Street	F3-F4
Britannia Street	E3-F3
Broadway	A1
Broomfield Road	A2
Butts Road	A3-A2-B2
Canterbury Street	D4-D3-E3
Chandos Street	F3
Charterhouse Road	E2
Chester Street	A4

Clifton Street	D4-E4
Colchester Street	E4
Collingwood Road	A2
Cornwall Road	E1
Coronation Road	E4-F4
Corporation Street	B3-C3
Coundon Road	A4-B4
Coundon Street	B4
Cox Street	D2-D3-D4
Caludon Road	F4
Croft Road	B2
David Road	E2
Day's Lane	E3
Eaton Road	B1
Earl Street	C2
East Street	E3
Fairfax Street	C3-D3
Far Gosford Street	E2-E3
Ford Street	D3
Friars Road	C1-C2
Gloucester Street	A3-B3
Gordon Street	A1-A2
Gosford Street	D2
Grafton Street	E2-E3
Greyfriars Road	B2
Grosvenor Road	B1-B2
Gulson Street	D2-E2-F2
Hales Street	C3
Harley Street	F2-F3
Harper Road	E1-E2
Hawkins Road	A2
Heath Road	F4
High Street	C2-C3
Highfield Road	F4
Hill Street	B3
Holyhead Road	A4-A3-B3
Hood Street	E3
Hugh Road	F2
Humber Avenue	E1-F1
Humber Road	F1-F2
Irving Road	E1-E2
Jesmond Road	F2
Jordan Well	D2
King Edward Road	E4
King Richard Street	F3
King William Street	D4-E4
Kingsway	F2-F3
Lamb Street	B4-C4
Lansdowne Street	E3-F3
Leicester Row	C4
Little Park Street	C2
London Road	D1-D2
Lower Ford Street	D3-E3
Manor Road	C1
Meadow Street	A2-B2
Melville Road	A3
Meriden Street	A3-A4-B4
Michaelmas Road	B1-C1
Middlesborough Road	B4
Mile Lane	C1-D1
Minster Road	A3
Monks Road	F2
Mowbray Street	F3
Much Park Street	D2
New Union Street	C2
Nicholls Street	F4
Northfield Road	E2-F2
Northumberland Road	A3-A4

Orwell Road	E1-F1
Park Road	C1
Park Side	C2-D2-D1
Paynes Lane	E4-E3
Primrose Hill Street	D4
Priory Row	C3
Priory Street	C3-D3
Puma Road	D1
Quarryfield Lane	D1
Queen Street	A2-B2
Queen Victoria Road	B2-B3
Quinton Road	C1
Radford Road	B4
Raglan Street	D3-E3
Ranby Road	F4
Read Street	E3
Regent Street	B1-B2
Ribble Road	F1-F2
Richmond Street	F4
Ringway Hill Cross	B3-B4
Ringway Queens	B2
Ringway Rudge	B2-B3
Ringway St Johns	C2-D2
Ringway St Nicholas	B4-C4
Ringway St Patrick	C1
Ringway Whitefriars	D3-D2
Ryley Street	B3
St Columba's Close	B4-C4
St Georges Road	F1-F2
St Margaret Road	F2
St Nicholas Street	C4
Seagrave Road	D2-D1-E1
Severn Road	F1
Silver Street	C4
Sky Blue Way	E3
South Street	E3
Sovereign Road	A2-A3
Spencer Avenue	A1-B1
Spon End	A3
Spon Street	B3
Stepney Road	F4
Stoney Road	C1
Stoney Stanton Road	C4-D4
Strathmore Avenue	E1-E2
Swan Lane	F3-F4
Swanswell	D3
Swanswell Street	D4
Terry Road	E2-E1-F1
Thackhall Street	F4
Tower Street	C4
Upper Spon Street	A3-B3
Upper Well Street	B4-B3-C3
Upper York Street	A2
Vecquaray Street	E2
Vernon Street	E4
Victoria Street	D4
Villiers Street	F3
Vine Street	D4-D3
Walsgrave	F3
Warwick Road	B1-B2-C2
Waverley Road	A3
Welland Street	E1-F1
West Street	E3
Westminster Road	B2-B1
Weston Street	D4
White Street	D4
Windsor Street	A2-A3
Winifrid Avenue	A1

Yardley Street	D4-E4

Nuneaton

Abbey Green	A4
Abbey Street	A4-A3-B3
Alexandra Street	A1
Amos Avenue	A1
Anker Street	C2
Attleborough Road	C1-C2
Avenue Road	B1-C1
Back Street	B4-B3
Bond Gate	B3
Bottril Street	A4
Bracebridge Street	A2-A3
Bridge Street	A1-B1-B3
Bull Ring	A1
Broad Street	A2
Central Avenue	A4-B4
Chapel Street	B3
Cheverel Street	A1-B1
Church Street	B3-C3-C2
Clements Street	A2
Clinic Road	B2
Cooper Street	C2
Corporation Street	A4-B4-B3
Coton Road	B1-B2
Cox's Close	A1
Deacon Street	A2
Dugdale Street	B3-B2
Duke Street	B3
Edward Street	A3-A2-B2-B1
Fife Street	A3
Fitton Street	A1-A2-B2
Frank Street	A2-B2
Glebe Road	B2
Greenmoor Road	A1-A2
Harefield Road	B3-B4
Harold Street	B2
Heath End Road	A1
Henry Street	A1-B1
High Street	A3
Home Park Road	B1
Inner Ring Road	B2
John Street	B1
King Edward Road	C2-C3
Kingsway	A3
Leicester Road	B3-C3-C4
Lister Street	C2
Manor Court Road	A4
Malborough Road	A2-A3
Market Place	B3
Meadow Street	A4
Midland Road	A4
Milford Street	A1
Mill Street	B3
Mill Walk	B3
Mount Street	A3
Newdegate Street	B3
New Town Road	A4-B4
Norman Avenue	A2-A3
Oaston Road	C3-C4
Old Hinckley Road	A4
Orchard Street	C3
Park Street	C2
Prince's Avenue	A3
Queen's Road	A3-B3
Regent Street	B3
Ringway	A3-B3-B2
Riversley Road	B2
Rose Lane	A3-A4
Roxanne	A4
Sandon Road	A4
Seymour Road	B2
Simon Close	C1
Stewart Street	A1-B1-B2
Trent Road	C3-C4

Vicarage Street	B3-C3
Victoria Street	A3-B3
Villiers Street	A2
Weddington Road	C4
Weddington Terrace	C4
Wheat Street	C3
Willington Street	A4

Rugby

Acacia Grove	B4
Albert Street	B2-B3-C3
Alexandra Road	B4
Alfred Street	A1
Arnold Street	C3
Bank Street	B2
Barby Road	B1
Bath Street	C2-C3-C4
Bilton Road	A1
Bridget Street	A2
Castle Street	C2
Chapel Street	A2-B2
Charlotte Street	C2
Chestnut Field	B2-C2
Church Street	B1-B2
Clifton Road	C2
Corporation Street	A2-A3-A1
Craven Road	C3-C4
Dale Street	A3
Drury Lane	B1
Dunchurch Road	B1
Eastfield Place	B2
East Union Street	A1-B1
Edward Street	A2
Elsee Road	B2-C2
Essex Street	A3-A4
Evreux Way	A3-B3
Firs Drive	A1
Gas Street	B2
Graham Road	A3
Grosvenor Road	C2-C3
High Street	B2
Hill Street	A3
Hillmorton Road	C1
Holbrook Avenue	B3
Horton Crescent	B1-C1
James Street	B3-C3
Kew Road	B3
Kimberley Road	C4
King Street	A3
King Edward Road	B3-B4
Lancaster Road	A4-B4
Lawford Road	A1-A2
Lawrence Sherriff Street	B1-B2
Little Church Street	B1-B2
Lodge Road	B3-B4
Manor Road	B3-B4-C4
Maple Grove	B4
Market Street	C3
Mertons Drive	A1
Moultrie Road	C1-C2
Murray Road	C2-C3-C4
Newbold Road	A4-A3
North Street	B2-B3
Oliver Street	A3
Park Road	B3-B4
Pinders Lane	B2
Plowman Street	A2
Poplar Grove	A4
Prince's Street	A3
Queen Street	A3
Railway Terrace	C2-C3-C4
Regent Place	B3
Regent Street	B2-B3
Russelsheim Way	A1-B1
Rounds Gardens	A2-A3
St John Street	A3
Sheep Street	B2

Spring Street	C3
Sycamore Grove	B4
Tom Brown Street	C3
Vicarage Road	A1
Warwick Street	A1-B1
Wells Street	A2
Westfield Road	A1
Westway	A2
Whitehall Road	C1-C2
William Street	C2
Wood Street	A4-B4-C4
Worcester Street	A4
York Street	A3

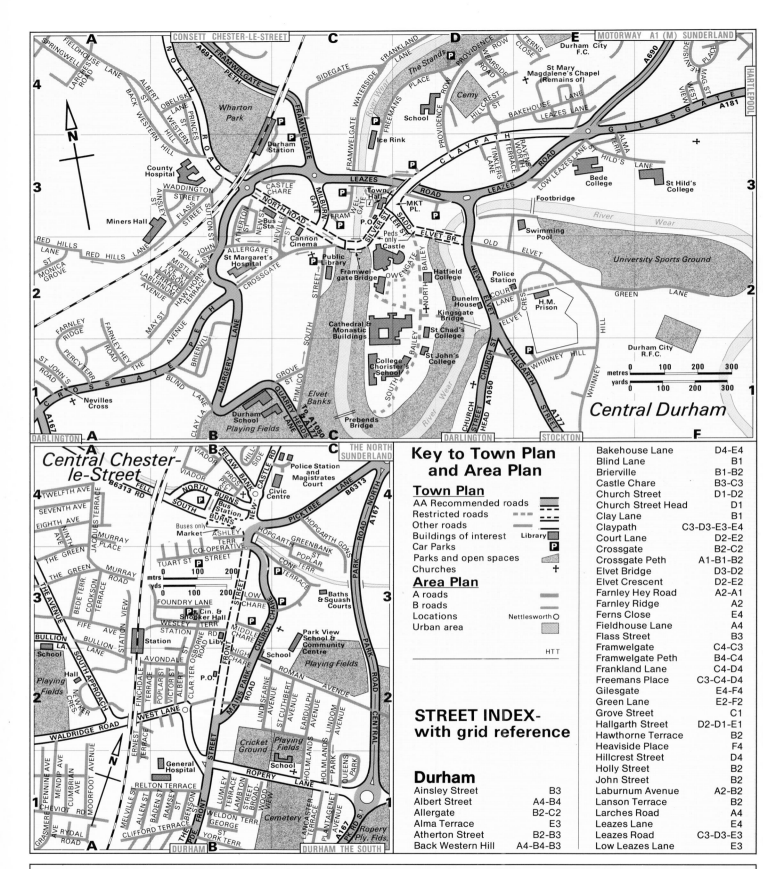

Key to Town Plan and Area Plan

Town Plan

- AA Recommended roads
- Restricted roads
- Other roads
- Buildings of interest — Library
- Car Parks — P
- Parks and open spaces
- Churches — +

Area Plan

- A roads
- B roads
- Locations — Nettlesworth ○
- Urban area

HTT

STREET INDEX- with grid reference

Durham

Ainsley Street	B3
Albert Street	A4-B4
Allergate	B2-C2
Alma Terrace	E3
Atherton Street	B2-B3
Back Western Hill	A4-B4-B3
Bakehouse Lane	D4-E4
Blind Lane	B1
Brierville	B1-B2
Castle Chare	B3-C3
Church Street	D1-D2
Church Street Head	D1
Clay Lane	B1
Claypath	C3-D3-E3-E4
Court Lane	D2-E2
Crossgate	B2-C2
Crossgate Peth	A1-B1-B2
Elvet Bridge	D3-D2
Elvet Crescent	D2-E2
Farnley Hey Road	A2-A1
Farnley Ridge	A2
Ferns Close	E4
Fieldhouse Lane	A4
Flass Street	B3
Framwelgate	C4-C3
Framwelgate Peth	B4-C4
Frankland Lane	C4-D4
Freemans Place	C3-C4-D4
Gilesgate	E4-F4
Green Lane	E2-F2
Grove Street	C1
Hallgarth Street	D2-D1-E1
Hawthorne Terrace	B2
Heaviside Place	F4
Hillcrest Street	D4
Holly Street	B2
John Street	B2
Laburnum Avenue	A2-B2
Lanson Terrace	B2
Larches Road	A4
Leazes Lane	E4
Leazes Road	C3-D3-E3
Low Leazes Lane	E3

Durham

The castle and the cathedral stand side by side high above the city like sentinels, dramatically symbolising the military and religious power Durham wielded in the past. Its origins date from about 995 when the remains of St Cuthbert arrived from Lindisfarne and his shrine was a popular centre of pilgrimage. Soon after that early fortifications were built, later replaced by a stone castle which became the residence of the Prince-Bishops of Durham – powerful feudal rulers appointed by the King. Today the city's university, the oldest in England after Oxford and Cambridge, occupies the castle and most of the buildings around peaceful, secluded Palace Green. The splendid Norman cathedral, sited on the other side of the Green, is considered to be one of the finest in Europe. Its combination of strength and size, tempered with grace and beauty, is awe-inspiring.

Under the shadow of these giants the old city streets, known as vennels, ramble down the bluff past the 17th-century Bishop Cosin's House and the old grammar school, to the thickly-wooded banks of the Wear. Here three historic bridges link the city's heart with the pleasant Georgian suburbs on the other side of the river.

Although Durham is not an industrial city, it has become the venue for the North-East miners' annual Gala Day in July.

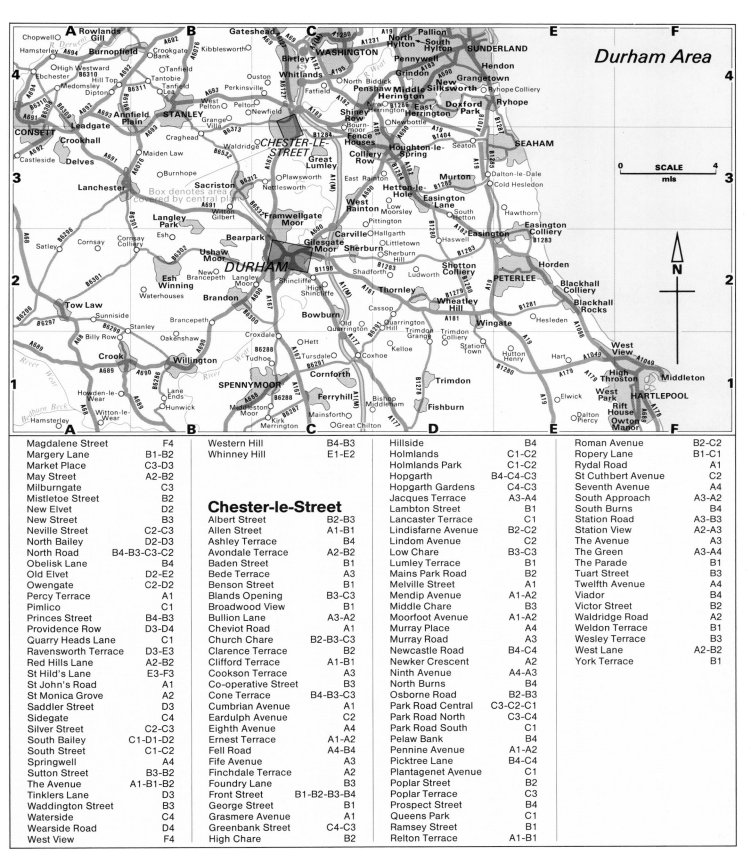

Durham Area

SCALE 0 — 4 mls

N

Magdalene Street	F4	Western Hill	B4-B3	
Margery Lane	B1-B2	Whinney Hill	E1-E2	
Market Place	C3-D3			
May Street	A2-B2			
Milburngate	C3			
Mistletoe Street	B2	**Chester-le-Street**		
New Elvet	D2	Albert Street	B2-B3	
New Street	B3	Allen Street	A1-B1	
Neville Street	C2-C3	Ashley Terrace	B4	
North Bailey	D2-D3	Avondale Terrace	A2-B2	
North Road	B4-B3-C3-C2	Baden Street	B1	
Obelisk Lane	B4	Bede Terrace	A3	
Old Elvet	D2-E2	Benson Street	B1	
Owengate	C2-D2	Blands Opening	B3-C3	
Percy Terrace	A1	Broadwood View	B1	
Pimlico	C1	Bullion Lane	A3-A2	
Princes Street	B4-B3	Cheviot Road	A1	
Providence Row	D3-D4	Church Chare	B2-B3-C3	
Quarry Heads Lane	C1	Clarence Terrace	B2	
Ravensworth Terrace	D3-E3	Clifford Terrace	A1-B1	
Red Hills Lane	A2-B2	Cookson Terrace	A3	
St Hild's Lane	E3-F3	Co-operative Street	B3	
St John's Road	A1	Cone Terrace	B4-B3-C3	
St Monica Grove	A2	Cumbrian Avenue	A1	
Saddler Street	D3	Eardulph Avenue	C2	
Sidegate	C4	Eighth Avenue	A4	
Silver Street	C2-C3	Ernest Terrace	A1-A2	
South Bailey	C1-D1-D2	Fell Road	A4-B4	
South Street	C1-C2	Fife Avenue	A3	
Springwell	A4	Finchdale Terrace	A2	
Sutton Street	B3-B2	Foundry Lane	B3	
The Avenue	A1-B1-B2	Front Street	B1-B2-B3-B4	
Tinklers Lane	D3	George Street	B1	
Waddington Street	B3	Grasmere Avenue	A1	
Waterside	C4	Greenbank Street	C4-C3	
Wearside Road	D4	High Chare	B2	
West View	F4			

Hillside	B4	Roman Avenue	B2-C2
Holmlands	C1-C2	Ropery Lane	B1-C1
Holmlands Park	C1-C2	Rydal Road	A1
Hopgarth	B4-C4-C3	St Cuthbert Avenue	C2
Hopgarth Gardens	C4-C3	Seventh Avenue	A4
Jacques Terrace	A3-A4	South Approach	A3-A2
Lambton Street	B1	South Burns	B4
Lancaster Terrace	C1	Station Road	A3-B3
Lindisfarne Avenue	B2-C2	Station View	A2-A3
Lindom Avenue	C2	The Avenue	A3
Low Chare	B3-C3	The Green	A3-A4
Lumley Terrace	B1	The Parade	B1
Mains Park Road	B2	Tuart Street	B3
Melville Street	A1	Twelfth Avenue	A4
Mendip Avenue	A1-A2	Viador	B4
Middle Chare	B3	Victor Street	B2
Moorfoot Avenue	A1-A2	Waldridge Road	A2
Murray Place	A4	Weldon Terrace	B1
Murray Road	A3	Wesley Terrace	B3
Newcastle Road	B4-C4	West Lane	A2-B2
Newker Crescent	A2	York Terrace	B1
Ninth Avenue	A4-A3		
North Burns	B4		
Osborne Road	B2-B3		
Park Road Central	C3-C2-C1		
Park Road North	C3-C4		
Park Road South	C1		
Pelaw Bank	B4		
Pennine Avenue	A1-A2		
Picktree Lane	B4-C4		
Plantagenet Avenue	C1		
Poplar Street	B2		
Poplar Terrace	C3		
Prospect Street	B4		
Queens Park	C1		
Ramsey Street	B1		
Relton Terrace	A1-B1		

DURHAM
High above the wooded banks of the River Wear, Durham's castle and cathedral crown the steep hill on which the city is built. They share the site with several of the university's attractive old buildings.

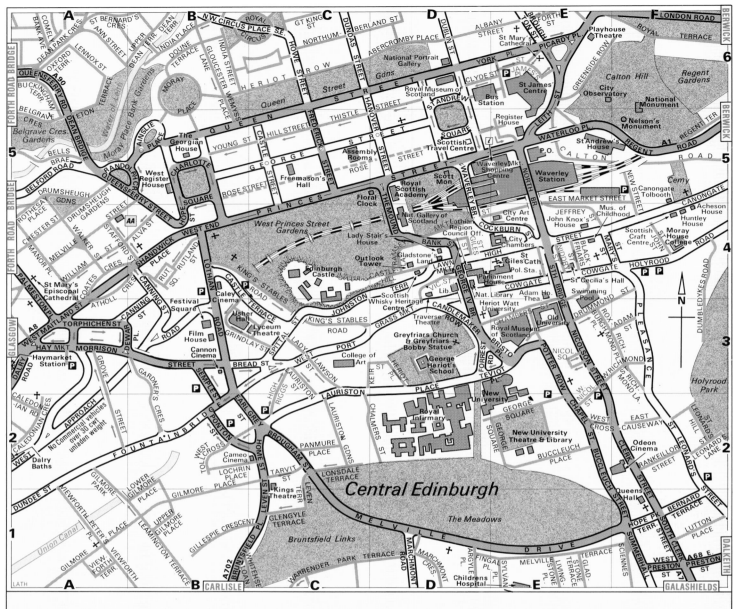

Key to Town Plan and Area Plan

Town Plan
A A Recommended roads
Other roads
Restricted roads
Buildings of intrest — Gallery
Car Parks — P
Parks and open spaces
A A Service Centre — AA
Churches — +

Area Plan
A roads
B roads
Locations — Newcraighall O
Urban area

Edinburgh

Scotland's ancient capital, dubbed the "Athens of the North", is one of the most splendid cities in the whole of Europe. Its buildings, its history and its cultural life give it an international importance which is celebrated every year in its world-famous festival. The whole city is overshadowed by the craggy castle which seems to grow out of the rock itself. There has been a fortress here since the 7th century and most of the great figures of Scottish history have been associated with it. The old town grew up around the base of Castle Rock within the boundaries of the defensive King's Wall and, unable to spread outwards, grew upwards in a maze of tenements. However, during the 18th century new prosperity from the shipping trade resulted in the building of the New Town and the regular, spacious layout of the Georgian development makes a striking contrast with the old hotch-potch of streets. Princes Street is the main east-west thoroughfare with excellent shops on one side and Princes Street Gardens with their famous floral clock on the south side.

As befits such a splendid capital city there are numerous museums and art galleries packed with priceless treasures. Among these are the famous picture gallery in 16th-century Holyroodhouse, the present Royal Palace, and the fascinating and unusual Museum of Childhood.

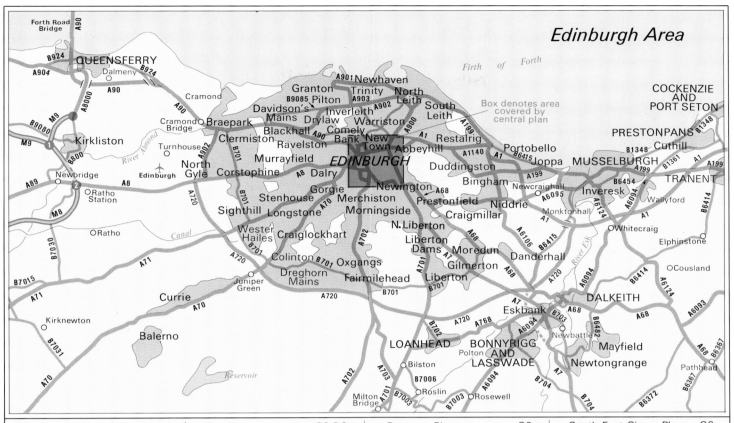

Edinburgh Area

East Market Street E5-E4-F4-F5	Kier Street C3-D3	Panmure Place C2	South East Circus Place C6
East Preston Street F1	King's Stables Road B4-C4-C3	Picardy Place E6	Spittal Street C3
Eton Terrace A5-A6	Lady Lawson Street C3	Pleasance F3-F4	Stafford Street A4-B4
Fingal Place D1-E1	Lauriston Gardens C2	Ponton Street B2-C2	Summerhall F1
Forrest Road D3	Lauriston Place C2-C3-D3	Potter Row E2-E3	Sylvan Place E1
Fountain Bridge A2-B2-B3-C3	Lauriston Street C2-C3	Princes Street B4-C4-C5-D5-E5	The Mound D4-D5
Frederick Street C5	Lawn Market D4	Queen Street B5-C5-C6-D6	Tarvit Street C2
Forth Street E6	Leamington Terrace A1-B1	Queensferry Road A5-A6	Teviot Place D3-E3
Gardeners Crescent B2-B3	Leith Street E4-E6	Queensferry Street A5-B5-B4	Thistle Street C5-D5-D6
George IV Bridge D3-D4	Lennox Street A6	Ramsy Lane D4	Torphichen Street A3
George Square E2	Leven Street C1-C2	Randoplph Crescent A5-B5	Upper Dean Terrace B6
George Street B5-C5-D5	Leven Terrace C1-C2	Rankeillor Street F2	Upper Gilmore Place B1
Gillespie Crescent B1-C1	Livingtone Place E1	Regent Road E5-F5	Victoria Street D4
Gilmore Park A1-A2	Lochrin Place B2-C2	Regent Terrace F5	Viewforth A1-B1
Gilmore Place A1-B1-B2-C2	London Road F6	Richmond Lane F2-F3	viewforth Terrace A1
Gladstone Terrace E1	Lonsdale Terrace C2	Richmond Place E3-F3	Walker Street A4-A5
Glengyle Terrace C1	Lothian Road B3-B4	Rose Street B5-C5-D5	Warrender Park Terr D1
Gloucester Lane B6	Lower Gilmore Place B1-B2	Rothesay Place A4-A5	Waterloo Place E5
Grass Market D3	Lutton Place F1	Roxbury Place E3	Waverley Bridge D4-D5
Great King Street C6	Manor Place A4	Royal Circus B6-C6	Wemyss Place B5-B6
Greenside Row E6-F6	Marchmont Crescent D1	Royal Terrace E6-F6	West Approach Road A2-A3-B3
Grindley Street B3-C3	Marchmont Road D1	Rutland Square B4	West Cross-Causeway E2
Grove Street A2-A3	Market Street D4-D4	Rutland Street B4	West End B4
Hanover Street C6-D6-D5	Melville Drive C2-C1-D1-E1-F1	St Andrew Square D5-D6	West Nicolson Street E2-E3
Hay Market A3	Melville Street A4-B4-B5	St Bernard's Crescent A6-B6	West Maitland Street A3-A4
Heriot Place D3	Melville Terrace E1-F1	St Giles Street D4	West Port C3
High Riggs C2-C3	Moray Place B5-B6	St James's Place E6	West Preston Street F1
High Street D4-E4	Morriston Street A3-B3	St John Street F4	West Richmond Street E3-F3
Hill Street C5	New Street F4-F5	St Leonards Hill F2	West Tollcross B2
Holyrood Road F4	Nicolson Square E3	St Leonards Lane F2	Whitehouse Loan B1-C1
Home Street C2	Nicolson Street E3-E2-F2	St Leonards Street F1-F2	William Street A4
Hope Park Terrace F1	Niddry Street E4	St Mary's Street E4-F4	York Place D6-E6
Hope Street B4	North Bridge E4-E5	St Peter Place A1	Young Street B5-C5
Howe Street C6	North West Circus Place B6	Sciennes F1	
India Place B6	Northumberland Street C6-D6	Semples Street B2-B3	
India Street B6	Oxford Terrace A6	Shandwick Place B4	
Jeffrey Street E4	Palmerston Place A3-A4	South Bridge E3-E4	
Johnston Terrace C3-C4-D4		South Clerk Street F1	

EDINBURGH
Holyrood Palace orginated as a guest house for the Abbey of Holyrood in the 16th century, but most of the present building was built for Charles II. Mary Queen of Scots was one of its most famous inhabitants.

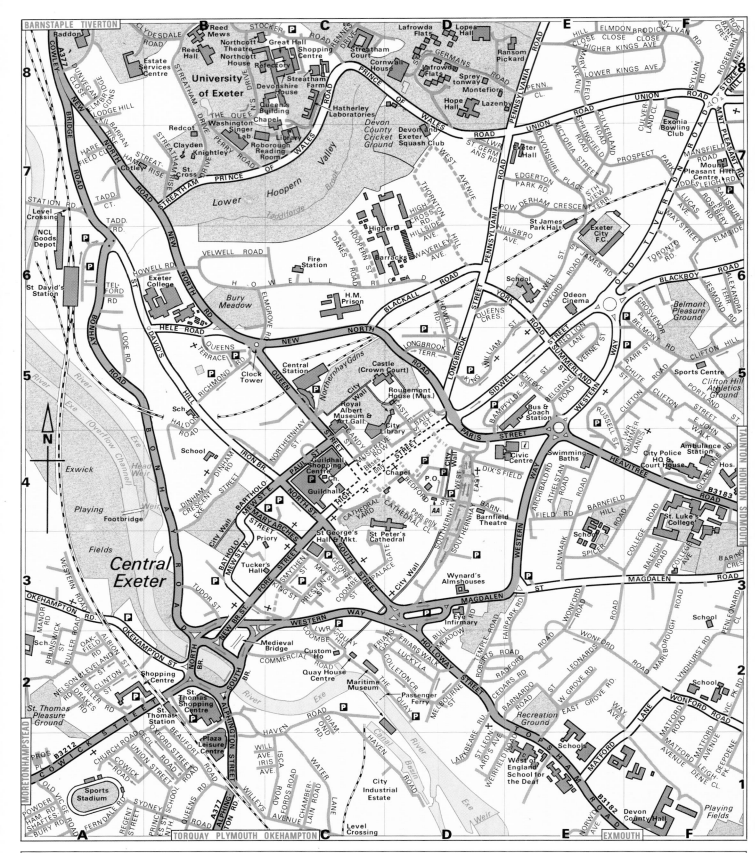

Exeter

The cathedral is Exeter's greatest treasure. Founded in 1050, but rebuilt by the Normans during the 12th-century and again at the end of the 13th-century, it has many beautiful and outstanding features - especially the exquisite rib-vaulting of the nave. Most remarkable, perhaps, is the fact that it still stood after much around it was flattened during the bombing raids in World War II.

There are still plenty of reminders of Old Exeter; Roman and medieval walls circle parts of the city;

14th-century underground passages can be explored; the Guildhall is 15th-century; and Sir Francis Drake is said to have met his explorer companions at Mol's Coffee House. Of the city's ancient churches the most interesting are St Mary Steps, St Mary Arches and St Martin's. The extensive Maritime Museum has over 100 boats from all over the world. Other museums include the Rougemont House, the Devonshire Regiment and the Royal Albert Memorial Museum and Art Gallery.

Exmouth has a near-perfect position at the

mouth of the Exe estuary. On each side it has expanses of sandy beach, on another a wide estuary alive with wildfowl and small boats, while inland is beautiful Devon countryside.

Honiton is famous for traditional hand-made lace and pottery which can still be bought in the busy town.

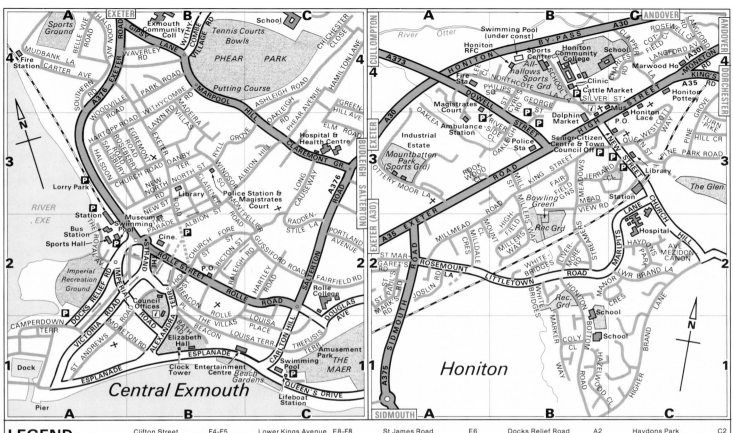

Central Exmouth

Honiton

LEGEND

- AA Recommended roads
- Other roads
- Restricted roads
- Buildings of interest
- Churches
- Car parks
- Parks, open spaces
- One way streets

Street Index with Grid Reference

Exeter

Albion Street	A2	Clifton Street	F4-F5
Alexandra Terrace	F6	Clinton Street	A2
Alphington Road	B1	Clydesdale Road	A8-B8
Alphington Street	B1-B2	College Avenue	F3
Archibald Road	E4	College Road	F3-F4
Athelstan Road	E4	Colleton Crescent	C2-D2
Bailey Street	D5	Commercial Road	B2-C2
Bampfylde Street	D4-D5-E5	Coombe Street	C3
Baring Crescent	F3	Cowick Road	A1
Barnado Road	E2	Cowick Street	A1-A2-B2
Barnfield Hill	E4-F4	Cowley Bridge Road	A6-A7-A8
Barnfield Road	D4-E4	Culverland Close	F7-F8
Bartholomew Street East	B4-C4	Culverland Road	E7-E8
Bartholomew Street West	B3	Danes Road	C6
Bedford Street	D4	Deepdene Park	F1
Belgrave Road	E5	Denmark Road	F3-F4
Belmont Road	F6-F5	Devonshire Place	E7
Blackall Road	C6-D6	Diamond Road	C2-C1
Blackboy Road	F6	Dineham Crescent	B4
Bonhay Road	A5-B4-B3	Dinham Road	B4
Brodick Close	F8	Dix's Field	D4
Brunswick Street	A2	Drakes Road	A2
Buller Road	A2-A3	Dunvegan Close	A8
Bull Meadow Road	D2	East John Walk	F4-F5
Castle Street	D5	East Grove Road	E2
Cathedral Close	D4	Edgerton Park Road	E7
Cathedral Yard	C4	Elmbridge Gardens	A8
Cecil Road	A1-B1	Elmdon Close	E8-F8
Cedars Road	E2	Elmgrove Road	B6-C6-B5
Chamberlain Road	C1	Elmside	F6
Cheeke Street	E5	Exe Street	B4
Church Road	A1-A2-B2	Fairpark Road	E2-E3
Chute Street	E5-F5	Ferndale Road	A1
Clevedon Street	A2	Fords Road	C1
Clifton Hill	F5	Fore Street	B3-C3
Clifton Road	E5-F5	Friars Gate	C2-D2
		Friars Walk	D2
		Gandy Street	C4
		George Street	C3
		Gladstone Road	F4
		Grosvenor Place	F3
		Haldon Road	B4-B5
		Harefield Close	A7
		Haven Road	C1-C2-D1
		Heavitree Road	E4-F4
		Hele Road	B6-B5
		Highcross Road	A1
		Higher Kings Avenue	E8-F8
		High Street	C4-D4-D5
		Hill Close	E8
		Hillsborough Avenue	D6-E6
		Hillside Avenue	D6
		Holloway Street	D2
		Hoopern Street	C6-C7
		Howell Road	A6-D6
		Iddesleigh Road	F7
		Iris Avenue	B1-C1
		Iron Bridge	B4-C4
		Isca Road	C1
		Jesmond Road	F6-F5-F6
		Kilbarran Rise	A7-A8
		King Street	C3
		King William Street	D5-E5-E6
		Larkbeare Road	D1-D2
		Leighdene Close	F1
		Lodge Hill	A8
		Longbrook Street	D5-D6
		Longbrook Terrace	D5
		Looe Road	A5-A6
		Lower Coombe Street	C2

Lower Kings Avenue	E8-F8	St James Road	E6
Lower St Germans Road	D7	St Leonards Avenue	D1-E1
Lower Summerlands	F4	St Leonards Road	E2-E3
Lucas Avenue	F7	Salisbury Road	F7-F6
Lucky Lane	D2	School Road	B1
Lyndhurst Road	F2	Shaftesbury Road	A1
Magdalen Road	E3-F3	Sidwell Street	D5-E5-E6
Magdalen Street	D3-E3	Smythen Street	C3
Manor Road	A3	South Bridge	B2
Mansfield Road	F7	Southernhay East	D3-D4
Market Street	C3	Southernhay West	D3-D4
Marlborough Road	F2-F3	South Street	D3
Mary Arches Street	B4-C3	South View Terrace	E7
Maryfield Avenue	A3	Spicer Road	E3-E4-F4
Matford Avenue	F2-F1-F2	Springfield Road	E8-E7
Matford Lane	E1-F1-F2	Station Road	E2
Matford Road	F1-F2	Stocker Road	B8-C8
May Street	F7-F6	Stoke Hill	F8
Melbourne Street	D2	Streatham Drive	B7-B8
Mount Pleasant Road	F8-F7	Streatham Rise	A7-B7
Musgrave Row	C4-C5	Summerland Street	E5
Nelson Road	A2	Sydney Road	A1-B1
New Bridge Street	B2-B3	Sylvan Road	F8
New North Road	A7-B6-C6-D5	Taddiforde Court	A7
North Bridge	B2	Taddiforde Road	A6-A7
Northernhay Street	C4-C5	Telford Road	A6
North Street	C4	Temple Road	D2-D3
Norwood Avenue	E1	The Quay	C2-D2
Oakfield Road	A2	The Queen's Drive	B8
Oakhampton Street	A2-B2	Thornton Hill	D7-D6
Okehampton Road	A3-A2-B2	Topsham Road	E2-E1-F1
Old Tiverton Road	E6-F7	Toronto Road	F6
Old Vicarage Road	A1	Tudor Street	B4
Oxford Road	E6	Union Road	E7-E8-F8
Oxford Street	B1-B2	Union Street	A1-B1
Palace Gate	C3-D3	Velwell Road	B6-C6
Paris Street	D5-D4-E4	Verney Street	E5
Parr Street	F5	Victoria Park Road	F2
Paul Street	C4	Victoria Street	E7
Penleonard Close	F3	Water Lane	C1
Pennsylvania Close	E8	Waverley Avenue	C6
Pennsylvania Road	D6-E8	Way Avenue	C2
Perry Road	B7	Weirfield Road	D1-E1
Portland Street	F5	Well Street	E6
Powderham Crescent	D7-E7	West Avenue	D7
Powderham Road	A1	Western Road	A3
Preston Street	C3	Western Way	E3-E5, C3
Prince of Wales Road	B7-C8-D7	West Grove Road	E2
Princes Street North	B2	Willeys Avenue	B1-C1
Prospect Park	E7-F7	Williams Avenue	B1-C1
Prospect Place	A1	Wonford Road	E3-E2-F2
Quay Hill	C2	York Road	D6-E6-E5
Queens Crescent	D6		
Queens Road	B1		
Queen Street	B5-C5-C4		
Queens Terrace	C4		
Radford Road	D2-E2		
Raleigh Road	F3		
Red Lion Lane	E5		
Regent Street	A1		
Rennes Drive	C8		
Richmond Road	B5		
Roberts Road	D2-E2		
Rosebank Crescent	F8		
Rosebarn Lane	F8		
Rosebery Road	F6-F7		
Russell Street	E5		
St David's Hill	A6-B5		
St Germans Road	D8-E8		

Exmouth

Albion Hill	B3-C3	Docks Relief Road	A2
Albion Street	B2-B3	Douglas Avenue	C1-C2
Alexandra Terrace	B1-B2	Egremont Road	B3
Ashleigh Road	C4	Elm Road	C3
Bath Road	B1-B2	Esplanade	A1-B1-C1
Beacon Place	B2	Exeter Road	B3-A4
Belle View Road	A4	Fairfield Road	B3
Bicton Street	B2-B2	Fore Street	B2-C2
Camperdown Terrace	A1	Gipsy Lane	A4-B4
Carter Avenue	A2	Green Hill Avenue	C3-C4
Carlton Hill	C1-C2	Gussiford Road	C2
Chichester Close	C3	Halsdon Avenue	C4
Church Road	A3-B3	Hamilton Lane	C4
Church Street	B2	Hartley Road	C2
Claremont Grove	C3	Hartopp Road	A3-B3
Clarence Road	B3	Halsdon Road	A3
Danby Terrace	B3	High Street	B2
		Imperial Road	A2-B1
		Lawn Road	B3
		Long Causeway	C3
		Louisa Place	B1-C1
		Louisa Terrace	B1-C1
		Lyndhurst Road	A4-B4
		Madeira Villas	B3-B4
		Marpool Hill	B3-B4
		Montpellier Road	B3-B2-C2
		Moreton Road	A1-B1
		Mudbank Lane	A4
		New North Road	B3
		New Street	B3
		North Street	B3
		Oakleigh Road	C3-C4
		Park Road	B4
		Phear Avenue	C3-C4
		Portland Avenue	C2
		Queens Drive	C1
		Raddenstile Lane	C2
		Raleigh Road	B2-C2
		Rolle Road	B2-C2
		Rolle Street	B2
		Rolle Villas	B1-B2
		Roseberry Road	A3-B3
		Ryll Grove	B3-C3
		St Andrews Road	A1-B1-B2
		Salisbury Road	A3-B3
		Salterton Road	C2-C3
		Southern Road	A4
		The Beacon	B1-B2
		The Parade	B2
		The Strand	B2
		The Royal Avenue	A2
		Trefusis Terrace	C1
		Victoria Road	A1-A2-B2
		Waverley Road	B4
		Windsor Square	B3
		Withycombe Road	B3-B4
		Withycombe Village Road	B4
		Woodville Road	A3-A4-B4

Haydons Park	C2	
Hazelwood Close	B1	
Higher Brand Lane	C1-C2	
Highfield	B2	
High Street	B3-C4	
Hill Crescent	C3	
Honiton Bottom Road	B1-B2	
Honiton By-Pass	A4-B4	
Jerrard Close	B3-C3	
Jerrard Crescent	C3	
Joslin Road	A2	
King's Road	C4	
Kings Street	B3	
Langford Avenue	C4	
Langford Road	C4	
Lee Close	A4	
Littledown Road	A2	
Livermore Road	B2	
Lower Brand Lane	C2	
Manor Crescent	B2-C2	
Marker Way	B1	
Marlpits Lane	C2	
Mead View Road	B3	
Milldale Crescent	A2	
Millers Way	B2-B3	
Millmead Road	A2-B3	
Mill Street	B3	
Monkton Road	C3	
Mount Close	A2	
New Street	C3	
Northcote Lane	B4	
Oaklea	A3	
Oakleigh	B3	
Ottery Moor Lane	A3	
Philips Square	B3	
Pine Grove	C3-C4	
Pine Park Road	C3	
Queen Street	B3	
Riverside Close	B3	
Rookwood Close	A3	
Rosemount Lane	A2	
Rosewell Close	C4	
St Cyre's Road	B4	
St Margaret's Road	A2	
St Mark's Road	A2	
St Paul's Road	A2	
School Lane	B4	
Sidmouth Road	A1-A2	
Silver Street	B4-C4	
Streamers Meadows	B2-B3	
Turnpike	C3	
Westcott Way	C3	
Whitebridges	B2	

Honiton

Avenue Mezidon-Canon	C2
Charles Road	C4
Church Hill	C2-C3
Clapper Lane	C4
Coly Close	B1
Cotfield Close	C4
Dowell Street	A4-B3
Exeter Road	A2-B3
Fairfield Gardens	B3
George Street	B4

211

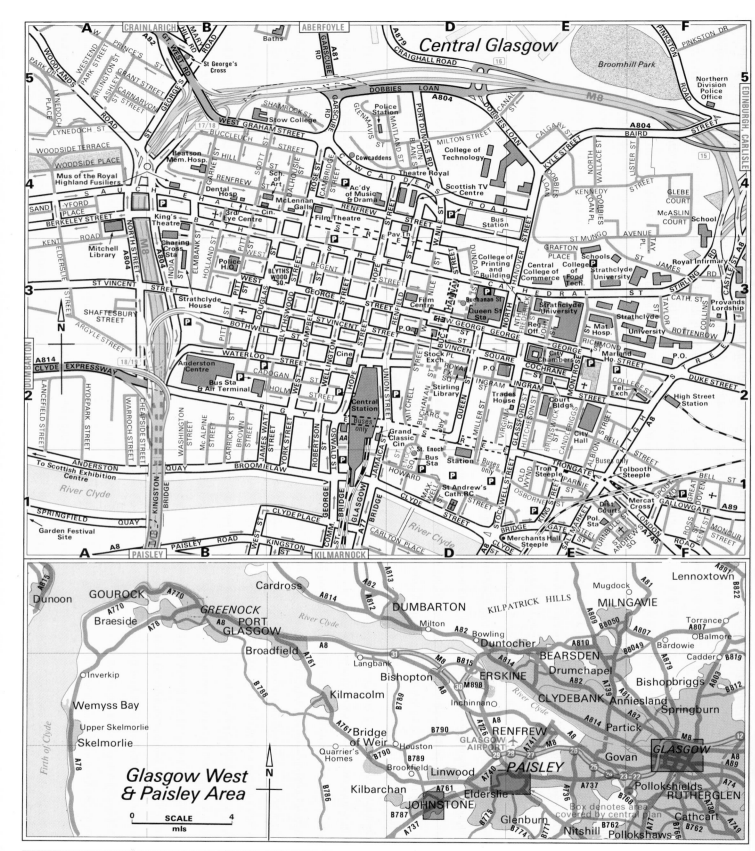

Glasgow

Although much of Glasgow is distinctly Victorian in character, its roots go back very many centuries. It's best link with the past is the Cathedral, in High Street. Founded in the 6th-century, it has features from many succeeding centuries, including an exceptional 13th-century crypt. Nearby is Provand's Lordship, the city's oldest house. It dates from 1471 and is now a museum. Two much larger museums are to be found a little out of the centre the Art Gallery and Museum contains one of the

finest collections of paintings in Britain, while the Hunterian Museum, attached to the University, covers geology, archaeology, ethnography and more general subjects. On Glasgow Green is People's Palace - a museum of city life. Most imposing of the Victorian buildings are the City Chambers and City Hall which was built in 1841 as a concert hall. A new International Concert Hall has now been built.

Paisley is famous for the lovely fabric pattern to which it gives its name. It was taken from

fabrics brought from the Near East in the early 19th-century, and its manufacture, along with the production of thread, is still important. Coats Observatory is one of the best equipped in the country.

Johnstone grew rapidly as a planned industrial town in the 19th-century, but suffered from the effects of the Industrial Revolution. Today, engineering is the main industry.

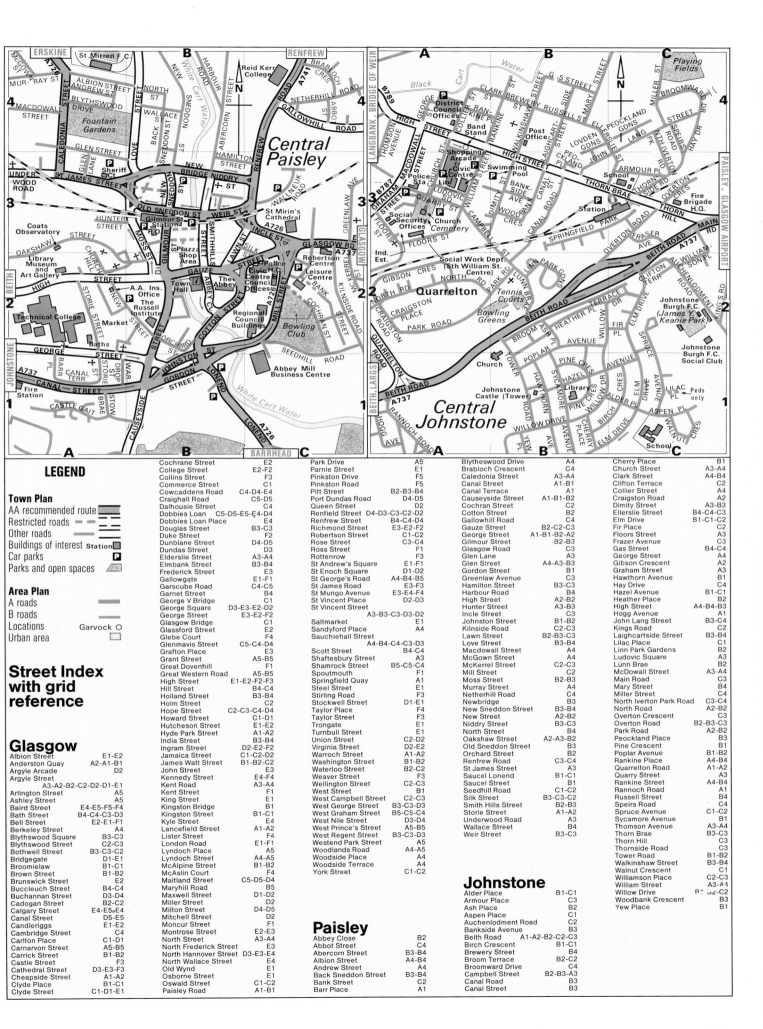

LEGEND

Town Plan

AA recommended route
Restricted roads
Other roads
Buildings of interest — Station
Car parks — P
Parks and open spaces

Area Plan

A roads
B roads
Locations — Garvock O
Urban area

Street Index with grid reference

Glasgow

Albion Street	E1-E2
Anderston Quay	A2-A1-B1
Argyle Arcade	D2
Argyle Street	A3-A2-B2-C2-D2-D1-E1
Arlington Street	A5
Ashley Street	A5
Baird Street	E4-E5-F5-F4
Bath Street	B4-C4-C3-D3
Bell Street	E2-E1-F1
Berkeley Street	A5
Blythswood Square	B3-C3
Blythswood Street	C2-C3
Bothwell Street	B3-C3-C2
Bridgegate	D1-E1
Broomielaw	B1-C1
Brown Street	B1-B2
Brunswick Street	E2
Buccleuch Street	B4-C4
Buchanan Street	D3-D4
Cadogan Street	B2-C2
Calgary Street	E4-E5-E4
Canal Street	D5-E5
Candleriggs	E1-E2
Cambridge Street	C4
Carlton Place	C1-D1
Carnarvon Street	A5-B5
Carrick Street	B1-B2
Castle Street	F3
Cathedral Street	D3-E3-F3
Cheapside Street	A1-A2
Clyde Place	B1-C1
Clyde Street	C1-D1-E1
Cochrane Street	E2
College Street	E2-F2
Collins Street	F3
Commerce Street	C1
Cowcaddens Road	C4-D4-E4
Craighall Road	C5-D5
Dalhousie Street	C4
Dobbies Loan	C5-D5-E5-E4-D4
Dobbies Loan Place	E5
Douglas Street	B3-C3
Duke Street	F2
Dunblane Street	D4-D5
Dundas Street	D3
Elderslie Street	A3-A4
Elmbank Street	B3-B4
Frederick Street	E3
Gallowgate	E1-F1
Garnet Street	B4
Garscube Road	C4-C5
George V Bridge	C1
George Square	D3-E3-E2-D2
George Street	E3-E2-F2
Glasgow Bridge	C1
Glassford Street	E2
Glebe Court	F4
Glenmavis Street	C5-C4-D4
Grafton Place	E3
Grant Street	A5-B5
Great Dovenhill	F1
Great Western Road	A5-B5
High Street	E1-E2-F2-F3
Hill Street	B4-C4
Holland Street	B3-B4
Holm Street	C2
Hope Street	C2-C3-C4-D4
Howard Street	D1-D1
Hutcheson Street	E1-E2
Hyde Park Street	A1-A2
India Street	B3-B4
Ingram Street	D2-E2-F2
Jamaica Street	C1-C2-D2
James Watt Street	B1-B2-C2
John Street	E3
Kennedy Street	E4-F4
Kent Road	A3-A4
Kent Street	F1
King Street	E1
Kingston Bridge	B1
Kingston Street	B1-C1
Kyle Street	E4
Lancefield Street	A1-A2
Lister Street	F4
London Road	E1-F1
Lyndoch Place	A5
Lyndoch Street	A4-A5
McAlpine Street	B1-B2
McAslin Court	F4
Maitland Street	C5-D5-D4
Maryhill Road	B5
Maxwell Street	D1-D2
Miller Street	D2
Milton Street	D4-D5
Mitchell Street	D2
Moncur Street	F1
Montrose Street	E2-E3
North Street	A3-A4
North Frederick Street	E3
North Hannover Street	D3-E3-E4
North Wallace Street	E4
Old Wynd	E1
Osborne Street	E1
Oswald Street	C1-C2
Paisley Road	A1-B1
Park Drive	A5
Parnie Street	E1
Pinkston Drive	F5
Pinkston Road	F5
Pitt Street	B2-B3-B4
Port Dundas Road	D4-D5
Queen Street	D2
Renfield Street	D4-D3-C3-C2-D2
Renfrew Street	C4
Richmond Street	E3-E2-F2
Robertson Street	C1-C2
Rose Street	C3-C4
Ross Street	F1
Rottenrow	F3
St Andrew's Square	E1-F1
St Enoch Square	D1-D2
St George's Road	A4-B4-B5
St James Road	E3-F3
St Mungo Avenue	E3-E4-F4
St Vincent Place	D2-D3
St Vincent Street	A3-B3-C3-D3-D2
Saltmarket	E1
Sandyford Place	A4
Sauchiehall Street	A4-B4-C4-C3-D3
Scott Street	B4-C4
Shaftesbury Street	A3
Shamrock Street	B5-C5-C4
Spoutmouth	F1
Springfield Quay	A1
Steel Street	E1
Stirling Road	F3
Stockwell Street	D1-E1
Taylor Place	F4
Taylor Street	F3
Trongate	E1
Turnbull Street	E1
Union Street	C2-D2
Virginia Street	D2-E2
Warroch Street	A1-A2
Washington Street	B1-B2
Waterloo Street	B2-C2
Weaver Street	F3
Wellington Street	C2-C3
West Street	B1
West Campbell Street	C2-C3
West George Street	B3-C3-D3
West Graham Street	B5-C5-C4
West Nile Street	D3-D4
West Prince's Street	A5-B5
West Regent Street	B3-C3-D3
Westend Park Street	A5
Woodlands Road	A4-A5
Woodside Place	A4
Woodside Terrace	A4
York Street	C1-C2

Paisley

Abbey Close	B2
Abbot Street	C4
Abercorn Street	B3-B4
Albion Street	A4-B4
Andrew Street	A4
Back Sneddon Street	B3-B4
Bank Street	C2
Barr Place	A1
Blytheswood Drive	A4
Brabloch Crescent	C4
Caledonia Street	A3-A4
Canal Street	A1-B1
Canal Terrace	A1
Causeyside Street	A1-B1-B2
Cochran Street	C2
Cotton Street	B2
Gallowhill Road	C4
Gauze Street	B2-C2-C3
George Street	A1-B1-B2-A2
Gilmour Street	B2-B3
Glasgow Road	A3
Glen Lane	A3
Glen Street	A4-A3-B3
Gordon Street	B1
Greenlaw Avenue	C3
Hamilton Street	B3-C3
Harbour Road	B4
High Street	A2-B2
Hunter Street	A3-B3
Incle Street	C3
Johnston Street	B1-B2
Kilnside Road	C2-C3
Lawn Street	B2-B3-C3
Love Street	B3-B4
Macdowall Street	A4
McGown Street	A4
McKerrel Street	C2-C3
Mill Street	C2
Moss Street	B2-B3
Murray Street	A4
Netherhill Road	C4
Newbridge	B3
New Sneddon Street	B3-B4
New Street	A2-B2
Niddry Street	B3-C3
North Street	B4
Oakshaw Street	A2-A3-B2
Old Sneddon Street	B3
Orchard Street	B2
Renfrew Road	C3-C4
St James Street	A3
Saucel Lonend	B1-C1
Saucel Street	B1
Seedhill Road	C1-C2
Silk Street	B3-C3-C2
Smith Hills Street	B2-B3
Storie Street	A1-A2
Underwood Road	A3
Wallace Street	B4
Weir Street	B3-C3

Johnstone

Alder Place	B1-C1
Armour Place	C3
Ash Place	B2
Aspen Place	C1
Auchenlodment Road	C2
Bankside Avenue	B3
Beith Road	A1-A2-B2-C2-C3
Birch Crescent	B1-C1
Brewery Street	B4
Broom Terrace	B2-C2
Broomward Drive	C4
Campbell Street	B2-B3-A3
Canal Road	B3
Canal Street	B3
Cherry Place	B1
Church Street	A3-A4
Clark Street	A4-B4
Clifton Terrace	C2
Collier Street	A4
Craigston Road	A2
Dimity Street	A3-B3
Ellerslie Street	B4-C4-C3
Elm Drive	B1-C1-C2
Fir Place	C2
Floors Street	A3
Frazer Avenue	C3
Gas Street	B4-C4
George Street	A4
Gibson Crescent	A2
Graham Street	A3
Hawthorn Avenue	B1
Hay Drive	C4
Hazel Avenue	B1-C1
Heather Place	B2
High Street	A4-B4-B3
Hogg Avenue	A1
John Lang Street	B3-C3
Kings Road	C2
Laighcartside Street	B3-B4
Lilac Place	C1
Linn Park Gardens	B2
Ludovic Square	A3
Lunn Brae	B2
McDowall Street	A3-A4
Main Road	C3
Mary Street	B4
Miller Street	C4
North Iverton Park Road	C3-C4
North Road	A2-B2
Overton Crescent	C3
Overton Road	B2-B3-C3
Park Road	A2-B2
Peockland Place	B3
Pine Crescent	B1
Poplar Avenue	B1-B2
Rankine Place	A4-B4
Quarrelton Road	A1-A2
Quarry Street	A3
Rankine Street	A4-B4
Rannoch Road	A1
Russell Street	B4
Speirs Road	C4
Spruce Avenue	C1-C2
Sycamore Avenue	B1
Thomson Avenue	A3-A4
Thorn Brae	B3-C3
Thorn Hill	C3
Thornside Road	C3
Tower Road	B1-B2
Walkinshaw Street	B3-B4
Walnut Crescent	C1
Williamson Place	C2-C3
William Street	A3-A4
Willow Drive	B1-B2-C2
Woodbank Crescent	B3
Yew Place	B1

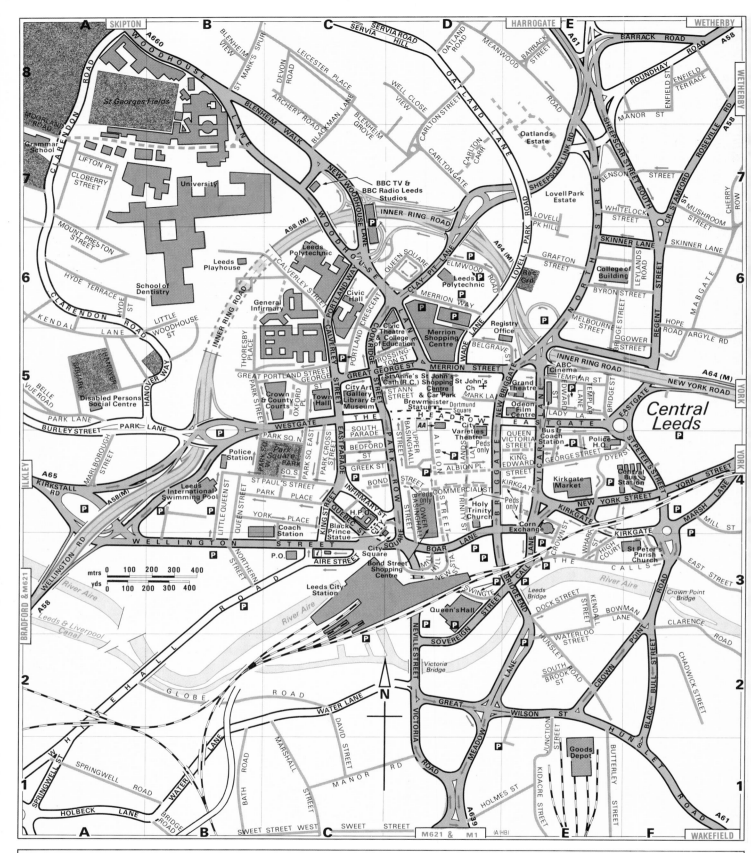

Leeds

In the centre of Leeds is its town hall – a monumental piece of architecture with a 225ft clock-tower. It was opened by Queen Victoria in 1858, and has been a kind of mascot for the city ever since. It exudes civic pride; such buildings could only have been created in the heyday of Victorian prosperity and confidence. Leeds' staple industry has always been the wool trade, but it

only became a boom town towards the end of the 18th century, when textile mills were introduced. Today, the wool trade and ready-made clothing (Mr Hepworth and Mr Burton began their work here) are still important, though industries like paper, leather, furniture and electrical equipment are prominent.

Across Calverley Street from the town hall is the City Art Gallery, Library and Museum. Its collections include sculpture by Henry Moore, who

was a student at Leeds School of Art. Nearby is the Headrow, Leeds' foremost shopping thoroughfare. On it is the City Varieties Theatre, venue for many years of the famous television programme 'The Good Old Days'. Off the Headrow are several shopping arcades, of which Leeds has many handsome examples. Leeds has a good number of interesting churches; perhaps the finest is St John's, unusual in that it dates from 1634, a time when few churches were built.

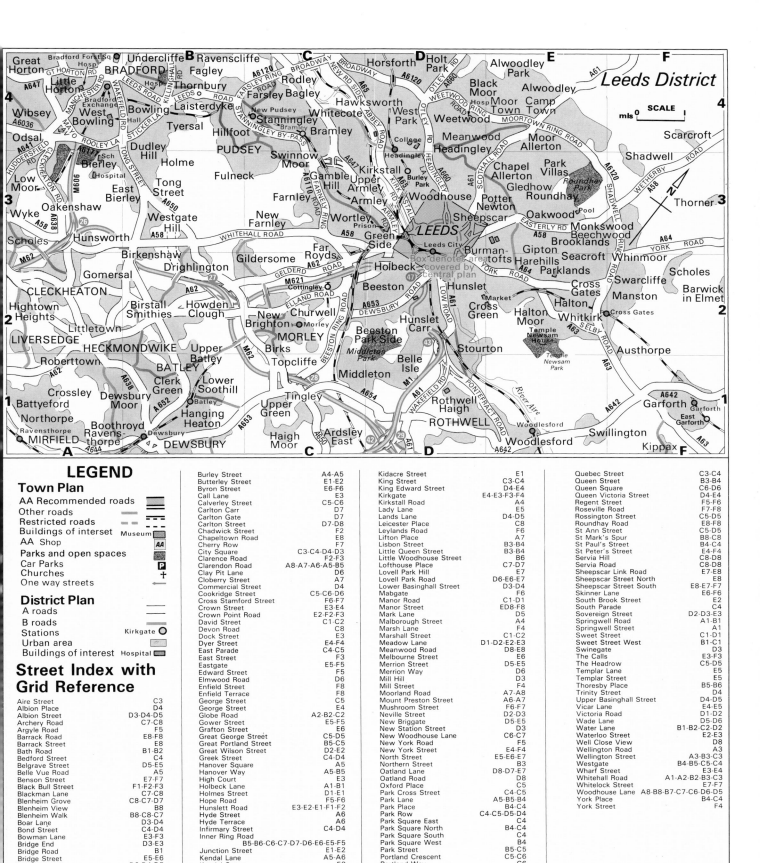

Leeds District

SCALE — mls 0

LEGEND

Town Plan

AA Recommended roads	
Other roads	
Restricted roads	
Buildings of interset	Museum
AA Shop	AA
Parks and open spaces	
Car Parks	P
Churches	+
One way streets	←

District Plan

A roads	
B roads	
Stations	Kirkgate O
Urban area	
Buildings of interest	Hospital

Street Index with Grid Reference

Street	Grid
Aire Street	C3
Albion Place	D4
Albion Street	D3-D4-D5
Archery Road	C7-C8
Argyle Road	F5
Barrack Road	E8-F8
Barrack Street	E8
Bath Road	B1-B2
Bedford Street	C4
Belgrave Street	D5-E5
Belle Vue Road	A5
Benson Street	E7-F7
Black Bull Street	F1-F2-F3
Blackman Lane	C7-C8
Blenheim Grove	C8-C7-D7
Blenheim View	B8
Blenheim Walk	B8-C8-C7
Boar Lane	D3-D4
Bond Street	C4-D4
Bowman Lane	E3-F3
Bridge End	D3-E3
Bridge Road	B1
Bridge Street	E5-E6
Briggate	D3-D4-D5
Burley Street	A4-A5
Butterley Street	E1-E2
Byron Street	E6-F6
Call Lane	E3
Calverley Street	C5-C6
Carlton Carr	D7
Carlton Gate	D7
Carlton Street	D7-D8
Chadwick Street	F2
Chapeltown Road	E8
Cherry Row	F7
City Square	C3-C4-D4-D3
Clarence Road	F2-F3
Clarendon Road	A8-A7-A6-A5-B5
Clay Pit Lane	D6
Cloberry Street	A7
Commercial Street	D4
Cookridge Street	C5-C6-D6
Cross Stamford Street	F6-F7
Crown Street	E3-E4
Crown Point Road	E2-F2-F3
David Street	C1-C2
Devon Road	C8
Dock Street	E3
Dyer Street	E4-F4
East Parade	C4-C5
East Street	F3
Eastgate	E5-F5
Edward Street	F5
Elmwood Road	D6
Enfield Street	F8
Enfield Terrace	F8
George Street	C5
George Street	E4
Globe Road	A2-B2-C2
Gower Street	E5-F5
Grafton Street	E6
Great George Street	C5-D5
Great Portland Street	B5-C5
Great Wilson Street	D2-E2
Greek Street	C4-D4
Hanover Square	A5
Hanover Way	A5-B5
High Court	E3
Holbeck Lane	A1-B1
Holmes Street	D1-E1
Hope Road	F5-F6
Hunslett Road	E3-E2-E1-F1-F2
Hyde Street	A6
Hyde Terrace	A6
Infirmary Street	C4-D4
Inner Ring Road	B5-B6-C6-C7-D7-D6-E6-E5-F5
Junction Street	E1-E2
Kendal Lane	A5-A6
Kendal Street	E3
Kidacre Street	E1
King Street	C3-C4
King Edward Street	D4-E4
Kirkgate	E4-E3-F3-F4
Kirkstall Road	A4
Lady Lane	E5
Lands Lane	D4-D5
Leicester Place	C8
Leylands Road	F6
Lifton Place	A7
Lisbon Street	B3-B4
Little Queen Street	B3-B4
Little Woodhouse Street	B6
Lofthouse Place	C7-D7
Lovell Park Hill	E7
Lovell Park Road	D6-E6-E7
Lower Basinghall Street	D3-D4
Mabgate	F6
Manor Road	C1-D1
Manor Street	ED8-F8
Mark Lane	D5
Malborough Street	A4
Marsh Lane	F4
Marshall Street	C1-C2
Meadow Lane	D1-D2-E2-E3
Meanwood Road	D8-E8
Melbourne Street	E6
Merrion Street	D5-E5
Merrion Way	D6
Mill Hill	D3
Mill Street	F4
Moorland Road	A7-A8
Mount Preston Street	A6-A7
Mushroom Street	F6-F7
Neville Street	D2-D3
New Briggate	D5-E5
New Station Street	D3
New Woodhouse Lane	C6-C7
New York Road	F5
New York Street	E4-F4
North Street	E5-E6-E7
Northern Street	B3
Oatland Lane	D8-D7-E7
Oatland Road	D8
Oxford Place	C5
Park Cross Street	C4-C5
Park Lane	A5-B5-B4
Park Place	B4-C4
Park Row	C4-C5-D5-D4
Park Square East	C4
Park Square North	B4-C4
Park Square South	C4
Park Square West	B4
Park Street	B5-C5
Portland Crescent	C5-C6
Portland Way	C6
Quebec Street	C3-C4
Queen Street	B3-B4
Queen Square	C6-D6
Queen Victoria Street	D4-E4
Regent Street	F5-F6
Roseville Road	F7-F8
Rossington Street	C5-D5
Roundhay Road	E8-F8
St Ann Street	C5-D5
St Mark's Spur	B8-C8
St Paul's Street	B4-C4
St Peter's Street	E4-F4
Servia Hill	C8-D8
Servia Road	C8-D8
Sheepscar Link Road	E7-E8
Sheepscar Street North	E8
Sheepscar Street South	E8-E7-F7
Skinner Lane	E6-F6
South Brook Street	E2
South Parade	C4
Sovereign Street	D2-D3-E3
Springwell Road	A1-B1
Springwell Street	A1
Sweet Street	C1-D1
Sweet Street West	B1-C1
Swinegate	D3
The Calls	E3-F3
The Headrow	C5-D5
Templar Lane	E5
Templar Street	E5
Thoresby Place	B5-B6
Trinity Street	D4
Upper Basinghall Street	D4-D5
Vicar Lane	E4-E5
Victoria Road	D1-D2
Wade Lane	D5-D6
Water Lane	B1-B2-C2-D2
Waterloo Street	E2-E3
Well Close View	D8
Wellington Road	A3
Wellington Street	A3-B3-C3
Westgate	B4-B5-C5-C4
Wharf Street	E3-E4
Whitehall Road	A1-A2-B2-B3-C3
Whitelock Street	E7-F7
Woodhouse Lane	A8-B8-B7-C7-C6-D6-D5
York Place	B4-C4
York Street	F4

LEEDS
Offices now occupy the handsome twin-towered Civic Hall which stands in Calverley Street in front of the new buildings of Leeds Polytechnic. This area of the city – the commercial centre – has been extensively redeveloped

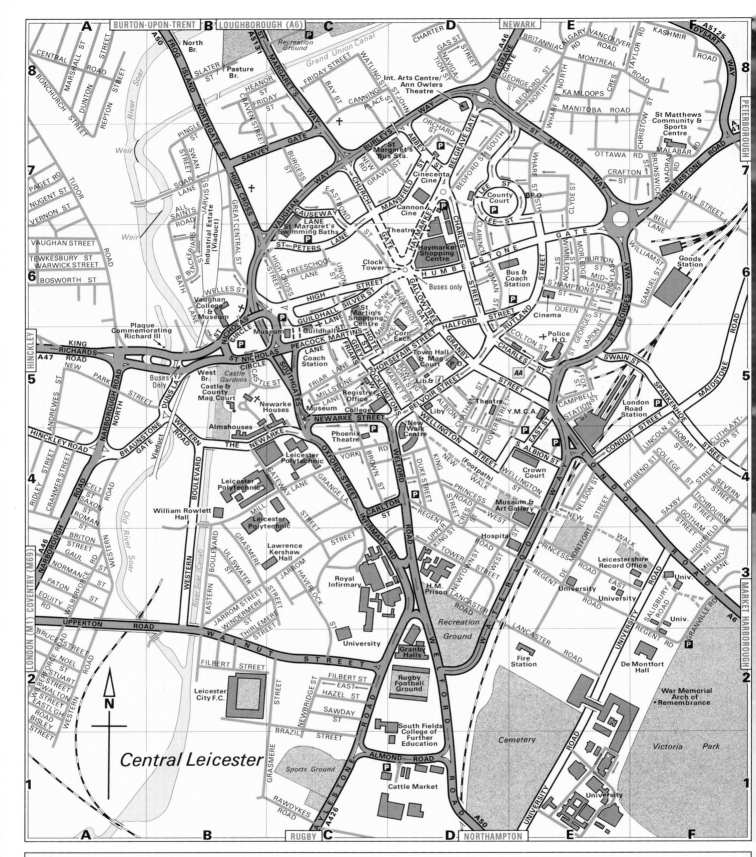

Leicester

A regional capital in Roman times, Leicester has retained many buildings from its eventful and distinguished past. Today the city is a thriving modern place, a centre for industry and commerce, serving much of the Midlands. Among the most outstanding monuments from the past is the Jewry Wall, a great bastion of Roman masonry. Close by are remains of the Roman baths and several other contemporary buildings. Attached is a museum covering all periods from prehistoric times to 1500. Numerous other museums include the Wygston's House Museum of Costume, with displays covering the period 1769 to 1924; Newarke House, with collections showing changing social conditions in Leicester through four hundred years; and Leicestershire Museum and Art Gallery, with collections of drawings, paintings, ceramics, geology and natural history.

The medieval Guildhall has many features of interest, including a great hall, library and police cells. Leicester's castle, although remodelled in the 17th century, retains a 12th-century great hall. The Church of St Mary de Castro, across the road from the castle, has features going back at least as far as Norman times; while St Nicholas's Church is even older, with Roman and Saxon foundations. St Martin's Cathedral dates mainly from the 13th to 15th centuries and has a notable Bishop's throne.

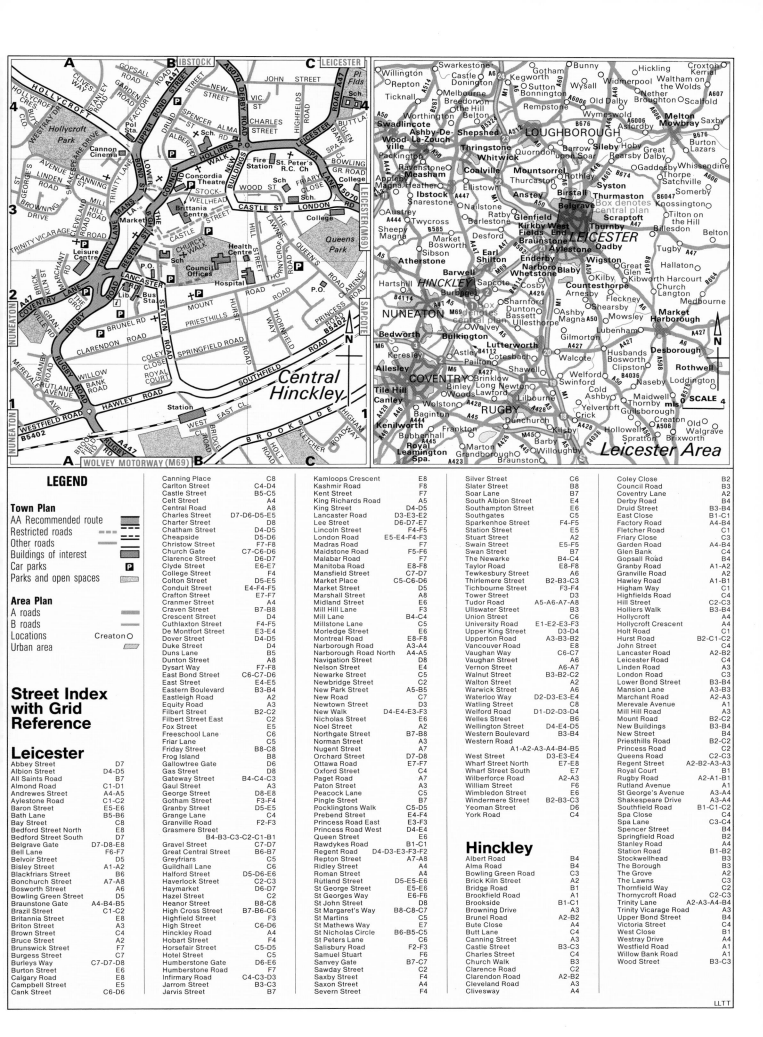

LEGEND

Town Plan

- AA Recommended route
- Restricted roads
- Other roads
- Buildings of interest
- Car parks **P**
- Parks and open spaces

Area Plan

- A roads
- B roads
- Locations Creaton ○
- Urban area

Street Index with Grid Reference

Leicester

Abbey Street	D7
Albion Street	D4-D5
All Saints Road	B7
Almond Road	C1-D1
Andrewes Street	A4-A5
Aylestone Road	C1-C2
Baron Street	E5-E6
Bath Lane	B5-B6
Bay Street	C8
Bedford Street North	E8
Bedford Street South	D7
Belgrave Gate	D7-D8-E8
Bell Lane	F6-F7
Belvoir Street	D5
Bisley Street	A1-A2
Blackfriars Street	B6
Bonchurch Street	A7-A8
Bosworth Street	A6
Bowling Green Street	D5
Braunstone Gate	A4-B4-B5
Brazil Street	C1-C2
Britannia Street	E8
Briton Street	A3
Brown Street	C4
Bruce Street	A2
Brunswick Street	F7
Burgess Street	C7
Burleys Way	C7-D7-D8
Burton Street	E6
Calgary Road	E8
Campbell Street	E5
Cank Street	C6-D6
Canning Place	C8
Carlton Street	C4-D4
Castle Street	B5-C5
Celt Street	A4
Central Road	A8
Charles Street	D7-D6-D5-E5
Charter Street	D8
Chatham Street	D4-D5
Cheapside	D5-D6
Christow Street	F7-F8
Church Gate	C7-C6-D6
Clarence Street	D6-D7
Clyde Street	E6-E7
College Street	F4
Colton Street	D5-E5
Conduit Street	E4-F4-F5
Crafton Street	E7-F7
Cranmer Street	A4
Craven Street	B7-B8
Crescent Street	D4
Cuthlaxton Street	F4-F5
De Montfort Street	E3-E4
Dover Street	D4-D5
Duke Street	D4
Duns Lane	B5
Dunton Street	A8
Dysart Way	F7-F8
East Bond Street	C6-C7-D6
East Street	E4-E5
Eastern Boulevard	B3-B4
Eastleigh Road	A2
Equity Road	A3
Filbert Street	B2-C2
Filbert Street East	C2
Fox Street	E5
Freeschool Lane	C6
Friar Lane	C5
Friday Street	B8-C8
Frog Island	B8
Gallowtree Gate	D6
Gas Street	D8
Gateway Street	B4-C4-C3
Gaul Street	A3
George Street	D8-E8
Gotham Street	F3-F4
Granby Street	D5-E5
Grange Lane	C4
Granville Road	F2-F3
Grasmere Street	B4-B3-C3-C2-C1-B1
Gravel Street	C7-D7
Great Central Street	B6-B7
Greyfriars	C5
Guildhall Lane	C6
Halford Street	D5-E6-E6
Haverlock Street	C2-C3
Haymarket	D6-D7
Hazel Street	C2
Heanor Street	B8-C8
High Cross Street	B7-B6-C6
Highfield Street	F3
High Street	C6-D6
Hinckley Road	A4
Hobart Street	F4
Horsefair Street	C5-D5
Hotel Street	C5
Humberstone Gate	D6-E6
Humberstone Road	F7
Infirmary Road	C4-C3-D3
Jarrom Street	B3-C3
Jarvis Street	B7
Kamloops Crescent	E8
Kashmir Road	F8
Kent Street	F7
King Richards Road	A5
King Street	D4-D5
Lancaster Road	D3-E3-E2
Lee Street	D6-D7-E7
Lincoln Street	F4-F5
London Road	E5-E4-F4-F3
Madras Road	F7
Maidstone Road	F5-F6
Malabar Road	F7
Manitoba Road	E8-F8
Mansfield Street	C7-D7
Market Place	C5-C6-D6
Market Street	D5
Marshall Street	A8
Midland Street	E6
Mill Hill Lane	F3
Mill Lane	B4-C4
Millstone Lane	C5
Morledge Street	E6
Montreal Road	E8-F8
Narborough Road	A3-A4
Narborough Road North	A4-A5
Navigation Street	D8
Nelson Street	E4
Newarke Street	C5
Newbridge Street	C2
New Park Street	A5-B5
New Road	C7
Newtown Street	D3
New Walk	D4-E4-E3-F3
Nicholas Street	E6
Noel Street	A2
Northgate Street	B7-B8
Norman Street	A3
Nugent Street	A7
Orchard Street	D7-D8
Ottawa Road	E7-F7
Oxford Street	C4
Paget Road	A7
Paton Street	A3
Peacock Lane	C5
Pingle Street	B7
Pocklingtons Walk	C5-D5
Prebend Street	E4-F4
Princess Road East	E3-F3
Princess Road West	D4-E4
Queen Street	E6
Rawdykes Road	B1-C1
Regent Road	D4-D3-E3-F3-F2
Repton Street	A7-A8
Ridley Street	A4
Roman Street	A4
Rutland Street	D5-E5-E6
St George Street	E5-E6
St Georges Way	E6-F6
St John Street	D8
St Margaret's Way	B8-C8-C7
St Martins	C5
St Mathews Way	E7
St Nicholas Circle	B6-B5-C5
St Peters Lane	C6
Salisbury Road	F2-F3
Samuel Stuart	F4
Sanvey Gate	B7-C7
Sawday Street	C2
Saxby Street	F4
Saxon Street	A4
Severn Street	F4
Silver Street	C6
Slater Street	B8
Soar Lane	B7
South Albion Street	E4
Southampton Street	E6
Southgates	C5
Sparkenhoe Street	F4-F5
Station Street	E5
Stuart Street	A2
Swain Street	E5-F5
Swan Street	B7
The Newarke	B4-C4
Taylor Road	E8-F8
Tewkesbury Street	A6
Thirlemere Street	B2-B3-C3
Tichbourne Street	F3-F4
Tower Street	D3
Tudor Road	A5-A6-A7-A8
Ullswater Street	B3
Union Street	C6
University Road	E1-E2-E3-F3
Upper King Street	D3-D4
Upperton Road	A3-B3-B2
Vancouver Road	E8
Vaughan Way	C6-C7
Vaughan Street	A6
Vernon Street	A6-A7
Walnut Street	B3-B2-C2
Walton Street	A2
Warwick Street	A4
Waterloo Way	D2-D3-E3-E4
Watling Street	C8
Welford Road	D1-D2-D3-D4
Welles Street	B6
Wellington Street	D4-E4-D5
Western Boulevard	B3-B4
Western Road	A1-A2-A3-A4-B4-B5
West Street	D3-E3-E4
Wharf Street North	E7-E8
Wharf Street South	E7
Wilberforce Road	A2-A3
William Street	F6
Wimbledon Street	E6
Windermere Street	B2-B3-C3
Yeoman Street	D6
York Road	C4

Hinckley

Albert Road	B4
Alma Road	B4
Bowling Green Road	C3
Brick Kiln Street	A2
Bridge Road	B1
Brookfield Road	A1
Brookside	B1-C1
Browning Drive	A3
Brunel Road	A2-B2
Bute Close	A4
Butt Lane	C4
Canning Street	C4
Castle Street	B3-C3
Charles Street	C4
Church Walk	B3
Clarence Road	C2
Clarendon Road	A2-B2
Cleveland Road	A3
Clivesway	A4
Coley Close	B2
Council Road	B3
Coventry Lane	A2
Derby Road	B4
Druid Street	B3-B4
East Close	B1-C1
Factory Road	A4-B4
Fletcher Road	C1
Friary Close	C3
Garden Road	A4-B4
Glen Bank	C4
Gopsall Road	B4
Granby Road	A1-A2
Granville Road	A2
Hawley Road	A1-B1
Higham Way	C4
Highfields Road	C2-C3
Hill Street	C2-C3
Holliers Walk	B3-B4
Hollycroft	A4
Hollycroft Crescent	A4
Holt Road	C1
Hurst Road	B2-C1-C2
John Street	C4
Lancaster Road	A2-B2
Leicester Road	C4
Linden Road	A3
London Road	C3
Lower Bond Street	B3-B4
Mansion Lane	A3-B3
Marchant Road	A2-A3
Merevale Avenue	A1
Mill Hill Road	A1
Mount Road	B2-C2
New Buildings	B3-B4
New Street	B4
Priesthills Road	B2-C2
Princess Road	C2
Queens Road	C2-C3
Regent Street	A2-B2-A3-A3
Royal Court	B1
Rugby Road	A2-A1-B1
Rutland Avenue	A1
St George's Avenue	A3-A4
Shakespeare Drive	A4
Southfield Road	B1-C1-C2
Spa Close	C4
Spa Lane	C3-C4
Spencer Street	B4
Springfield Road	B2
Stanley Road	B4
Station Road	B1-B2
Stockwellhead	B3
The Borough	B3
The Grove	A2
The Lawns	C3
Thornfield Way	C3
Thornycroft Road	C2-C3
Trinity Lane	A2-A3-A4-B4
Trinity Vicarage Road	A3
Upper Bond Street	B4
Victoria Street	C4
West Close	B1
Westray Drive	A4
Westfield Road	A1
Willow Bank Road	A1
Wood Street	B3-C3

LLTT

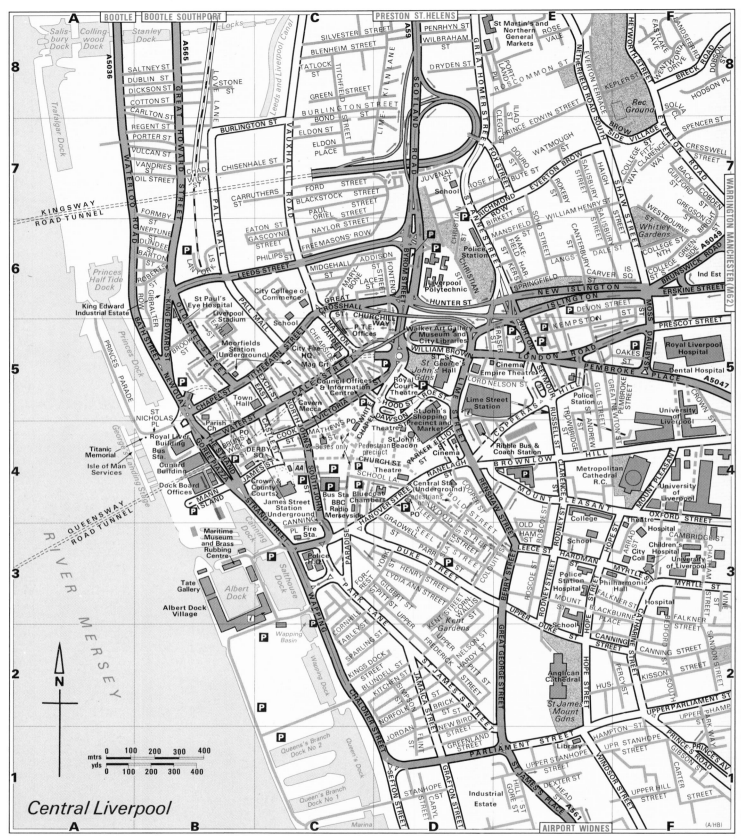

Central Liverpool

Liverpool

Although its dock area has been much reduced, Liverpool was at one time second only to London in pre-eminence as a port. Formerly the centrepiece of the docks area are three monumental buildings - the Dock Board Offices, built in 1907 with a huge copper-covered dome; the Cunard Building, dating from 1912 and decorated with an abundance of ornamental carving; and best-known of all, the world-famous Royal Liver Building, with the two 'liver birds' crowning its twin cupolas.

Some of the city's best industrial buildings have fallen into disuse in recent years, but some have been preserved as monuments of the idustrial age. One has become a maritime museum housing full-sized craft and a workshop where maritime crafts are demonstrated. Other museums and galleries include the Walker Art Gallery, with excellent collections of European painting and sculpture; Liverpool City Libraries, one of the oldest and largest public libraries in Britain, with a vast collection of books and manuscripts; and Bluecoat

Chambers, a Queen Anne building now used as a gallery and concert hall. Liverpool has two outstanding cathedrals: the Roman Catholic, completed in 1967 in an uncompromising controversial style; and the Protestant, constructed in the great tradition of Gothic architecture, but begun in 1904 and only recently completed.

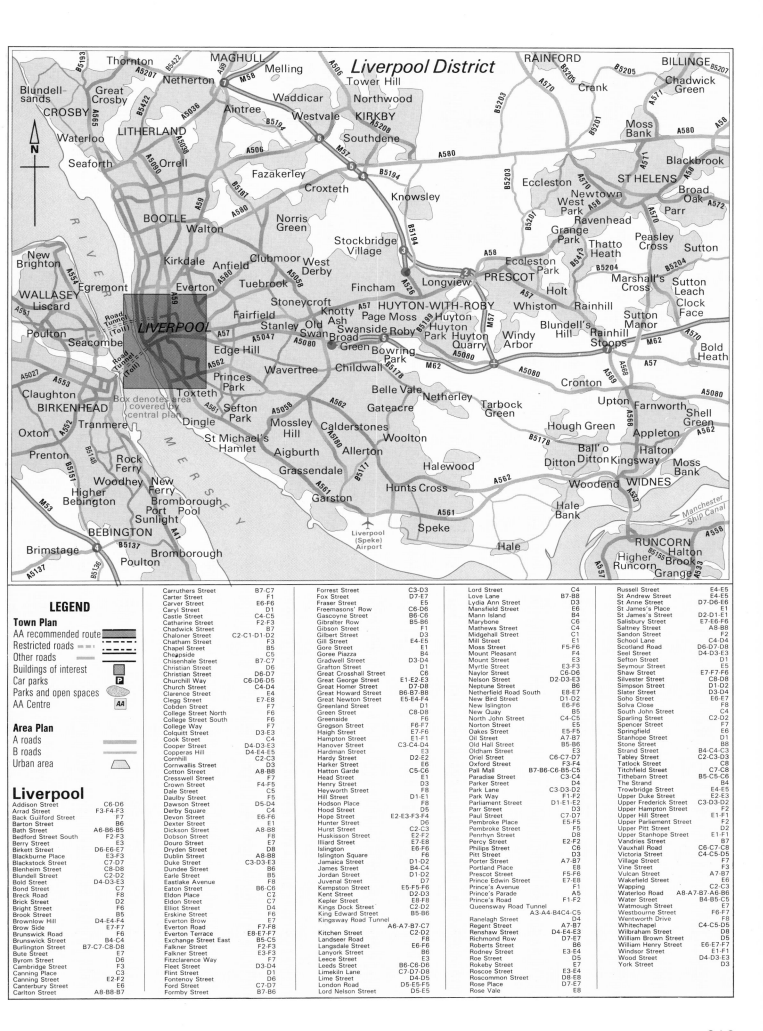

Liverpool District

LEGEND

Town Plan

- AA recommended route
- Restricted roads
- Other roads
- Buildings of interest
- Car parks [P]
- Parks and open spaces
- AA Centre [AA]

Area Plan

- A roads
- B roads
- Urban area

Liverpool

Addison Street	C6-D6
Arrad Street	F3-F4-F3
Back Guilford Street	F7
Barton Street	B6
Bath Street	A6-B6-B5
Bedford Street South	F2-F3
Berry Street	E3
Birkett Street	D6-E6-E7
Blackburne Place	E3-F3
Blackstock Street	C7-D7
Blenheim Street	C8-D8
Blundell Street	C2-D2
Bold Street	D4-D3-E3
Bond Street	C7
Breck Road	F8
Brick Street	D2
Bright Street	F6
Brook Street	B5
Brownlow Hill	D4-E4-F4
Brow Side	E7-F7-F7
Brunswick Road	F6
Brunswick Street	B4-C4
Burlington Street	B7-C7-C8-D8
Bute Street	E7
Byrom Street	D6
Cambridge Street	F3
Canning Place	C3
Canning Street	E2-F2
Canterbury Street	E6
Carlton Street	A8-B8-B7
Carruthers Street	B7-C7
Carter Street	F1
Carver Street	E6-F6
Caryl Street	D1
Castle Street	C4-C5
Catharine Street	F2-F3
Chadwick Street	B7
Chaloner Street	C2-C1-D1-D2
Chatham Street	F3
Chapel Street	B5
Cheapside	C5
Chisenhale Street	B7-C7
Christian Street	D6
Christian Street	D6-D7
Churchill Way	C6-D6-D5
Church Street	C4-D4
Clarence Street	E4
Clegg Street	E7-E8
Cobden Street	F7
College Street North	F6
College Street South	F6
College Way	F7
Colquitt Street	D3-E3
Cook Street	C4
Cooper Street	D4-D3-E3
Copperas Hill	D4-E4-E5
Cornhill	C2-C3
Cornwallis Street	A8-B8
Cotton Street	A8-B8
Cresswell Street	F7
Crown Street	F4-F5
Dale Street	C5
Daulby Street	F5
Dawson Street	D5-D4
Derby Square	C4
Devon Street	E6-F6
Dexter Street	E1
Dickson Street	A8-B8
Dobson Street	F8
Douro Street	E7
Dryden Street	D8
Dublin Street	A8-B8
Duke Street	C3-D3-E3
Dundee Street	B6
Earle Street	B5
Eastlake Avenue	F8
Eaton Street	B6-C6
Eldon Place	C7
Eldon Street	C7
Elliot Street	D4
Erskine Street	F6
Everton Brow	E7
Everton Road	F7-F8
Everton Terrace	E8-E7-F7
Exchange Street East	B5-C5
Falkner Street	F2-F3
Falkner Street	E3-F3
Fitzclarence Way	F7
Fleet Street	D3-D4
Flint Street	D1
Fontenoy Street	D6
Ford Street	C7-D7
Formby Street	B7-B6
Forrest Street	C3-D3
Fox Street	D7-E7
Fraser Street	E5
Freemasons' Row	C6-D6
Gascoyne Street	B6-C6
Gibraltar Row	B5-B6
Gibson Street	F1
Gilbert Street	D3
Gill Street	E4-E5
Gore Street	E1
Goree Piazza	B4
Gradwell Street	D3-D4
Grafton Street	D1
Great Crosshall Street	C6
Great George Street	E1-E2-E3
Great Homer Street	D7-D8
Great Howard Street	B6-B7-B8
Great Newton Street	E5-E4-F4
Greenland Street	D1
Green Street	C8-D8
Greenside	F6
Gregson Street	F6-F7
Haigh Street	E7-F6
Hampton Street	E1-F1
Hanover Street	C3-C4-D4
Hardman Street	E3
Hardy Street	D2-E2
Harker Street	E6
Hatton Garde	C5-C6
Head Street	E1
Henry Street	D3
Heyworth Street	F8
Hill Street	D1-E1
Hodson Place	F8
Hood Street	D5
Hope Street	E2-E3-F3-F4
Hunter Street	D6
Hurst Street	C2-C3
Huskisson Street	E2-F2
Illiard Street	E7-E8
Islington	E6-F6
Islington Square	F6
Jamaica Street	D1-D2
James Street	B4-C4
Jordan Street	D1-D2
Juvenal Street	D7
Kempston Street	E5-F5-F6
Kent Street	D2-D3
Kepler Street	E8-F8
Kings Dock Street	C2-D2
King Edward Street	B5-B6
Kingsway Road Tunnel	A6-A7-B7-C7
Kitchen Street	C2-D2
Landseer Road	F8
Langsdale Street	E6-F6
Lanyork Street	B6
Leece Street	E3
Leeds Street	B6-C6-D6
Limekiln Lane	C7-D7-D8
Lime Street	D4-D5
London Road	D5-E5-F5
Lord Nelson Street	D5-E5
Lord Street	C4
Love Lane	B7-B8
Lydia Ann Street	D3
Mansfield Street	E6
Mann Island	B4
Marybone	C6
Mathews Street	C4
Midgehall Street	C1
Mill Street	E1
Moss Street	F5-F6
Mount Pleasant	F4
Mount Street	E3
Myrtle Street	E3-F3
Naylor Street	C6-D6
Nelson Street	D2-D3-E3
Neptune Street	B6
Netherfield Road South	E8-E7
New Bird Street	D1-D2
New Islington	E6-F6
New Quay	B5
North John Street	C4-C5
Norton Street	E5
Oakes Street	A7-B7
Oil Street	B5-B6
Old Hall Street	B5-B6
Oldham Street	E3
Oriel Street	C6-C7-D7
Oxford Street	F3-F4
Pall Mall	B7-B6-C6-B5-C5
Paradise Street	C3-C4
Parker Street	D4
Park Lane	C3-D3-D2
Park Way	F1-F2
Parliament Street	D1-E1-E2
Parr Street	D3
Paul Street	C7-D7
Pembroke Place	E5-F5
Pembroke Street	F5
Penrhyn Street	D8
Percy Street	E2-F2
Philips Street	C6
Pitt Street	D3
Porter Street	A7-B7
Portland Place	E8
Prescot Street	F5-F6
Prince Edwin Street	E7-E8
Prince's Avenue	F1
Prince's Parade	A5
Prince's Road	F1-F2
Queensway Road Tunnel	A3-A4-B4C4-C5
Ranelagh Street	D4
Regent Street	A7-B7
Renshaw Street	D4-E4-E3
Richmond Row	D7-E7
Roberts Street	B6
Rodney Street	E3-E4
Roe Street	D5
Rokeby Street	E7
Roscoe Street	E3
Roscommon Street	D8-E8
Rose Place	D7-E7
Rose Vale	E8
Russell Street	E4-E5
St Andrew Street	E4-E5
St Anne Street	D7-D6-E6
St James's Place	E1
St James's Street	D2-D1-E1
Salisbury Street	E7-E6-F6
Saltney Street	A8-B8
Sandon Street	F2
School Lane	C4-D4
Scotland Road	D6-D7-D8
Seel Street	D4-D3-E3
Sefton Street	D1
Seymour Street	E5
Shaw Street	E7-F7-F6
Silvester Street	C8-D8
Simpson Street	D1-D2
Slater Street	D3-D4
Soho Street	E6-E7
Solva Close	F8
South John Street	C4
Sparling Street	C2-D2
Spencer Street	F7
Springfield	E6
Stanhope Street	E1
Stone Street	B8
Strand Street	B4-C4-C3
Tabley Street	C2-C3-D3
Tatlock Street	C8
Titchfield Street	C7-C8
Tithebarn Street	B5-C5-C6
The Strand	B4
Trowbridge Street	E4-E5
Upper Duke Street	E2-E3
Upper Frederick Street	C3-D3-D2
Upper Hampton Street	F2
Upper Hill Street	E1-F1
Upper Parliament Street	F1
Upper Pitt Street	D2
Upper Stanhope Street	E1-F1
Vandries Street	B7
Vauxhall Road	C6-C7-C8
Victoria Street	C4-C5-D5-C6
Village Street	F3
Vine Street	F3
Vulcan Street	A7-B7
Wakefield Street	E6
Wapping	C2-C3
Waterloo Road	A8-A7-B7-A6-B6
Water Street	B4-B5-C5
Wentmouth Street	E7
Westbourne Street	F6-F7
Wentworth Drive	F8
Whitechapel	C4-C5-D4
Wilbraham Street	D5
William Brown Street	D5
William Henry Street	E6-E7-F7
Windsor Street	E1-F1
Wood Street	D4-D3-E3
York Street	D3

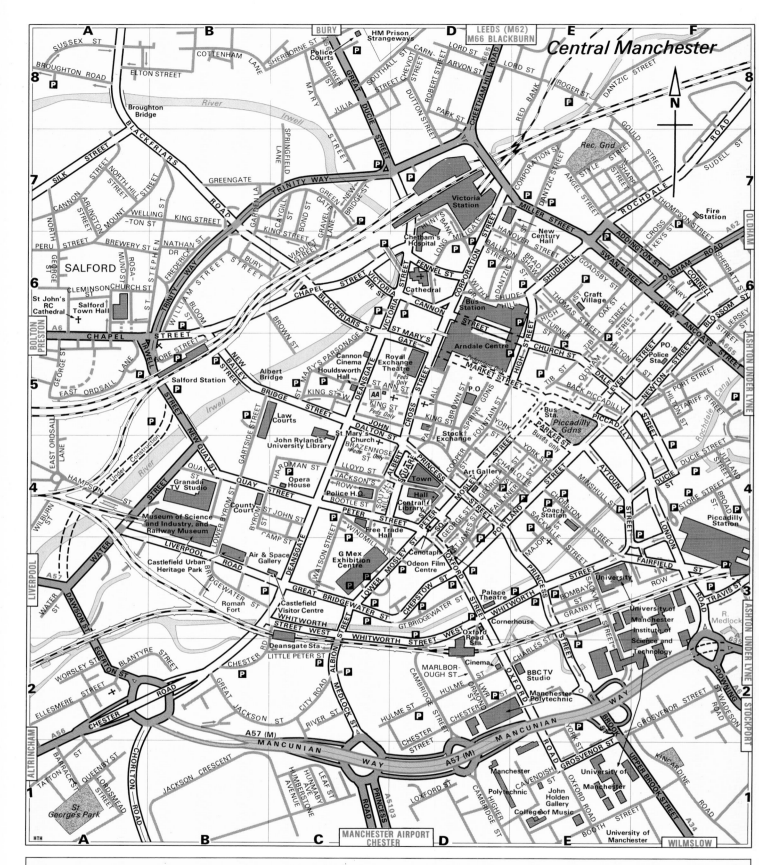

Manchester

The gigantic conurbation called Greater Manchester covers a staggering 60 square miles, reinforcing Manchester's claim to be Britain's second city. Commerce and industry are vital aspects of the city's character, but it is also an important cultural centre - the Halle Orchestra has its home at the Free Trade Hall (a venue for many concerts besides classical music), there are several theatres, a library

(the John Rylands) which houses one of the most important collections of books in the world, and a number of museums and galleries, including the Whitworth Gallery with its lovely watercolours.

Like many great cities it suffered badly during the bombing raids of World War II, but some older buildings remain, including the town hall, a huge building designed in Gothic style by Alfred Waterhouse and opened in 1877. Manchester Cathedral dates mainly from the 15th century and is noted for its fine tower and outstanding carved

woodwork. Nearby is Chetham's Hospital, also 15th-century and now housing a music school. Much new development has taken place, and more is planned. Shopping precincts cater for the vast population, and huge hotels have provided services up to international standards. The Museum of Science and Industry opened in 1980, inside the worlds first passenger railway station, with exhibits from the Industrial Revolution to the Space Age.

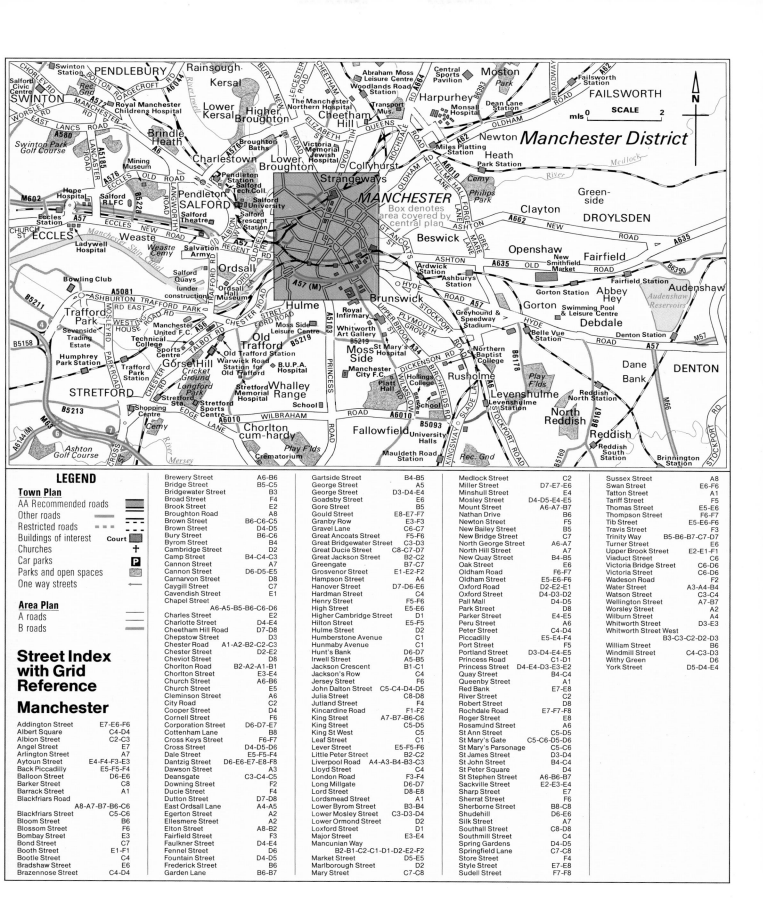

SCALE

LEGEND

Town Plan

AA Recommended roads	
Other roads	
Restricted roads	
Buildings of interest	Court
Churches	+
Car parks	P
Parks and open spaces	
One way streets	←

Area Plan

A roads	
B roads	

Street Index with Grid Reference

Manchester

Addington Street	E7-E6-F6
Albert Square	C4-D4
Albion Street	C2-C3
Angel Street	E7
Arlington Street	A7
Aytoun Street	E4-F4-F3-E3
Back Piccadilly	E5-F5-F4
Balloon Street	D6-E6
Barker Street	C8
Barrack Street	A1
Blackfriars Road	A8-A7-B7-B6-C6
Blackfriars Street	C5-C5-C6
Bloom Street	B6
Blossom Street	F6
Bombay Street	E3
Bond Street	C7
Booth Street	E1-F1
Bootle Street	C4
Bradshaw Street	E6
Brazennose Street	C4-D4

Brewery Street	A6-B6
Bridge Street	B5-C5
Bridgewater Street	B3
Broad Street	F4
Brook Street	E2
Broughton Road	A8
Brown Street	B6-C6-C5
Brown Street	D4-D5
Bury Street	B6-C6
Byrom Street	B4
Cambridge Street	D2
Camp Street	B4-C4-C3
Cannon Street	A7
Cannon Street	D6-D5-E5
Carnarvon Street	D8
Caygill Street	C7
Cavendish Street	E1
Chapel Street	A6-A5-B5-B6-C6-D6
Charles Street	E2
Charlotte Street	D4-E4
Cheetham Hill Road	D7-D8
Chepstow Street	D3
Chester Road	A1-A2-B2-C2-C3
Chester Street	D2-E2
Cheviot Street	D8
Chorlton Road	B2-A2-A1-B1
Chorlton Street	E3-E4
Church Street	A6-B6
Church Street	E5
Cleminson Street	A6
City Road	C2
Cooper Street	D4
Cornell Street	F6
Corporation Street	D6-D7-E7
Cottenham Lane	B8
Cross Keys Street	F6-F7
Cross Street	D4-D5-D6
Dale Street	E5-F5-F4
Dantzig Street	D6-E6-E7-E8-F8
Dawson Street	A3
Deansgate	C3-C4-C5
Downing Street	F2
Ducie Street	F4
Dutton Street	D7-D8
East Ordsall Lane	A4-A5
Egerton Street	A2
Ellesmere Street	A2
Elton Street	A8-B2
Fairfield Street	F3
Faulkner Street	D4-E4
Fennel Street	D6
Fountain Street	D4-D5
Frederick Street	B6
Garden Lane	B6-B7

Gartside Street	B4-B5
George Street	A5
George Street	D3-D4-E4
Goadsby Street	E6
Gore Street	B5
Gould Street	E8-E7-F7
Granby Row	E3-F3
Gravel Lane	C6-C7
Great Ancoats Street	F5-F6
Great Bridgewater Street	C3-D3
Great Ducie Street	C8-C7-D7
Great Jackson Street	B2-C2
Greengate	B7-C7
Grosvenor Street	E1-E2-F2
Hampson Street	A4
Hanover Street	D7-D6-E6
Hardman Street	C4
Henry Street	F5-F6
High Street	E5-E6
Higher Cambridge Street	D1
Hilton Street	E5-F5
Hulme Street	D2
Humberstone Avenue	C1
Hunmaby Avenue	C1
Hunt's Bank	D6-D7
Irwell Street	A5-B5
Jackson Crescent	B1-C1
Jackson's Row	C4
Jersey Street	F6
John Dalton Street	C5-C4-D4-D5
Julia Street	C8-D8
Jutland Street	F4
Kincardine Road	F1-F2
King Street	A7-B7-B6-C6
King Street	C5-D5
King St West	C5
Leaf Street	C1
Lever Street	E5-F5-F6
Little Peter Street	B2-C2
Liverpool Road	A4-A3-B4-B3-C3
Lloyd Street	C4
London Road	F3-F4
Long Millgate	D6-D7
Lord Street	D8-E8
Lordsmead Street	A1
Lower Byrom Street	B3-B4
Lower Mosley Street	C3-D3-D4
Lower Ormond Street	D2
Loxford Street	D1
Major Street	E3-E4
Mancunian Way	B2-B1-C2-C1-D1-D2-E2-F2
Market Street	D5-E5
Marlborough Street	D2
Mary Street	C7-C8

Medlock Street	C2
Miller Street	D7-E7-E6
Minshull Street	E4
Mosley Street	D4-D5-E4-E5
Mount Street	A6-A7-B7
Nathan Drive	B6
Newton Street	F5
New Bailey Street	B5
New Bridge Street	C7
North George Street	A6-A7
North Hill Street	A7
New Quay Street	B4-B5
Oak Street	E6
Oldham Road	F6-F7
Oldham Street	E5-E6-F6
Oxford Road	D2-E2-E1
Oxford Street	D4-D3-D2
Pall Mall	D4-D5
Park Street	D8
Parker Street	E4-E5
Peru Street	A6
Peter Street	C4-D4
Piccadilly	E5-E4-F4
Port Street	F5
Portland Street	D3-D4-E4-E5
Princess Road	C1-D1
Princess Street	D4-E4-D3-E3-E2
Quay Street	B4-C4
Queenby Street	A1
Red Bank	E7-E8
River Street	C2
Robert Street	D8
Rochdale Road	E7-F7-F8
Roger Street	E8
Rosamund Street	A6
St Ann Street	C5-D5
St Mary's Gate	C5-C6-D5-D6
St Mary's Parsonage	C5-C6
St James Street	D3-D4
St John Street	B4-C4
St Peter Square	D4
St Stephen Street	A6-B6-B7
Sackville Street	E2-E3-E4
Sharp Street	E7
Sherrat Street	F6
Sherborne Street	B8-C8
Shudehill	D6-E6
Silk Street	A7
Southall Street	C8-D8
Southmill Street	C4
Spring Gardens	D4-D5
Springfield Lane	C7-C8
Store Street	F4
Style Street	E7-E8
Sudell Street	F7-F8

Sussex Street	A8
Swan Street	E6-F6
Tatton Street	A1
Tariff Street	F5
Thomas Street	E5-E6
Thompson Street	F6-F7
Tib Street	E5-E6-F6
Travis Street	F3
Trinity Way	B5-B6-B7-C7-D7
Turner Street	E6
Upper Brook Street	E2-E1-F1
Viaduct Street	C6
Victoria Bridge Street	C6-D6
Victoria Street	C6-D6
Wadeson Road	F2
Water Street	A3-A4-B4
Watson Street	C3-C4
Wellington Street	A7-B7
Whitworth Street	D3-E3
Whitworth Street West	B3-C3-C2-D2-D3
William Street	B6
Windmill Street	C4-C3-D3
Withy Green	D6
York Street	D5-D4-E4

MANCHESTER

The Barton Swing Bridge carries the Bridgewater Canal over the Manchester Ship Canal, which links Manchester with the sea nearly 40 miles away. Completed in 1894, the canal is navigable by vessels up to 15,000 tons.

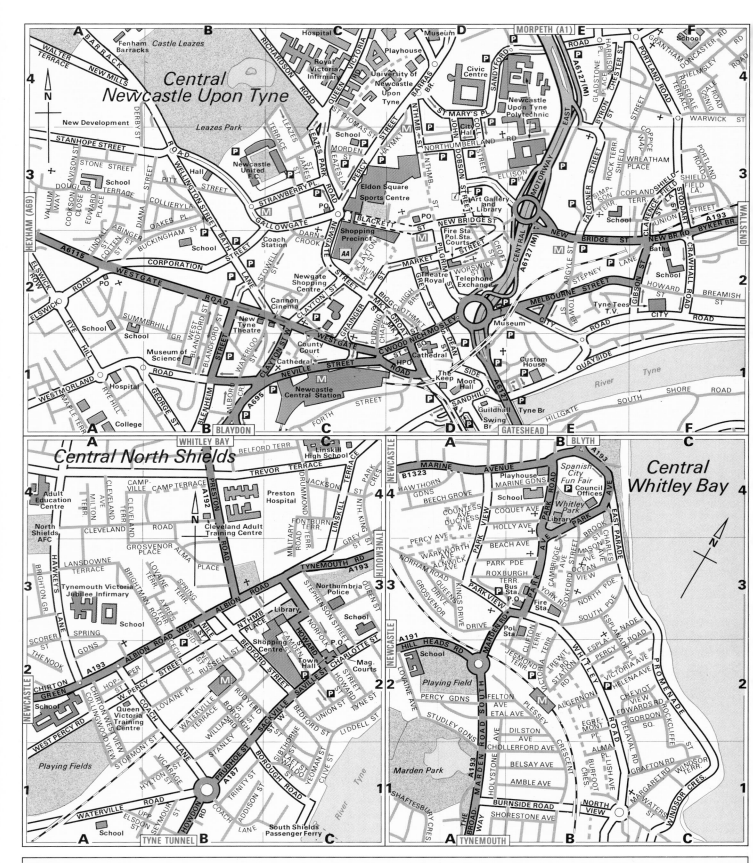

Newcastle

Six bridges span the Tyne at Newcastle; they all help to create a striking scene, but the most impressive is the High Level Bridge, built by Robert Stephenson in 1845-49 and consisting of two levels, one for the railway and one for the road. It is from the river that some of the best views of the city can be obtained. Grey Street is Newcastle's most handsome thoroughfare. It dates from the time, between 1835 and 1840, when much of this part of the city was replanned and rebuilt. Elegant façades curve up to Grey's Monument. Close to the Monument is the Eldon Centre, combining sports facilities and shopping centre to form an integrated complex which is one of the largest of its kind in Europe. Newcastle has many museums. The industrial background of the city is traced in the Museum of Science and Engineering, while the Laing Art Gallery and Museum covers painting, costumes and local domestic history. The Hancock Museum has an exceptional natural history collection and the John George Joicey Museum has period displays in a 17th-century almshouse. In Black Gate is one of Britain's most unusual museums – a collection of over 100 sets of bagpipes. Within the University precincts are three further museums. Of the city's open spaces, Town Moor is the largest. At nearly 1,000 acres it is big enough to feel genuinely wild.

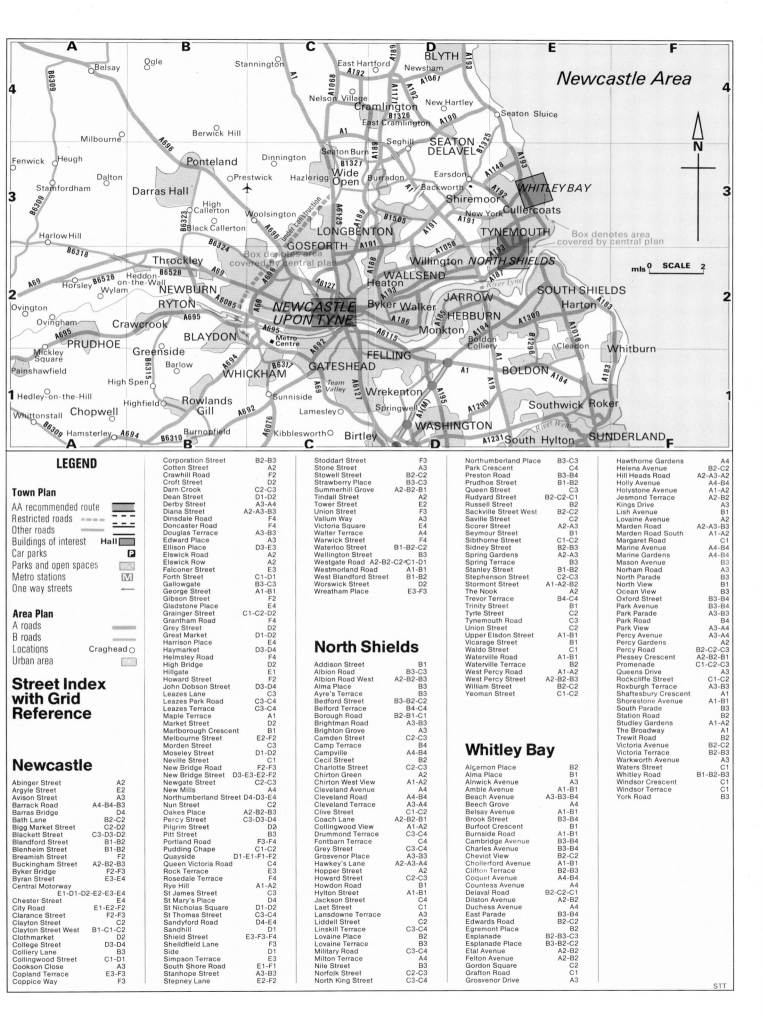

LEGEND

Town Plan

AA recommended route
Restricted roads
Other roads
Buildings of interest **Hall**
Car parks **P**
Parks and open spaces
Metro stations **M**
One way streets ←

Area Plan

A roads
B roads
Locations Craghead ○
Urban area

Street Index with Grid Reference

Newcastle

Abinger Street	A2
Argyle Street	E2
Avison Street	A3
Barrack Road	A4-B4-B3
Barras Bridge	D4
Bath Lane	B2-C2
Bigg Market Street	C2-D2
Blackett Street	C3-D3-D2
Blandford Street	B1-B2
Blenheim Street	B1-B2
Breamish Street	F2
Buckingham Street	A2-B2-B3
Byker Bridge	F2-F3
Byran Street	E3-E4
Central Motorway	E1-D1-D2-E2-E3-E4
Chester Street	E4
City Road	E1-E2-F2
Clarance Street	F2-F3
Clayton Street	C2
Clayton Street West	B1-C1-C2
Clothmarket	D2
College Street	D3-D4
Colliery Lane	B3
Collingwood Street	C1-D1
Cookson Close	A3
Copland Terrace	E3-F3
Coppice Way	F3

Corporation Street	B2-B3
Cotten Street	A2
Crawhill Road	F2
Croft Street	D2
Darn Crook	C2-C3
Dean Street	D1-D2
Derby Street	A3-A4
Diana Street	A2-A3-B3
Dinsdale Road	F4
Doncaster Road	F4
Douglas Terrace	A3-B3
Edward Place	A3
Ellison Place	D3-E3
Elswick Road	A2
Elswick Row	A2
Falconer Street	E3
Forth Street	C1-D1
Gallowgate	B3-C3
George Street	A1-B1
Gibson Street	F2
Gladstone Place	E4
Grainger Street	C1-C2-D2
Grantham Road	F4
Grey Street	D2
Great Market	D1-D2
Harrison Place	E4
Haymarket	D3-D4
Helmsley Road	F4
High Bridge	D2
Hillgate	E1
Howard Street	F2
John Dobson Street	D3-D4
Leazes Lane	C3
Leazes Park Road	C3-C4
Leazes Terrace	C3-C4
Maple Terrace	A1
Market Street	D2
Marlborough Crescent	B1
Melbourne Street	E2-F2
Morden Street	C3
Moseley Street	D1-D2
Neville Street	C1
New Bridge Road	F2-F3
New Bridge Street	D3-E3-E2-F2
Newgate Street	C2-C3
New Mills	A4
Northumberland Street	D4-D3-D4
Nun Street	C2
Oakes Place	A2-B2-B3
Percy Street	C3-D3-D4
Pilgrim Street	D2
Pitt Street	B3
Portland Road	F3-F4
Pudding Chape	C1-C2
Quayside	D1-E1-F1-F2
Queen Victoria Road	C4
Rock Terrace	E3
Rosedale Terrace	F4
Rye Hill	A1-A2
St James Street	C3
St Mary's Place	D4
St Nicholas Square	D1-D2
St Thomas Street	C3-C4
Sandyford Road	D4-E4
Sandhill	D1
Shield Street	E3-F3-F4
Sheildfield Lane	F3
Side	D1
Simpson Terrace	E3
South Shore Road	E1-F1
Stanhope Street	A3-B3
Stepney Lane	E2-F2

Stoddart Street	F3
Stone Street	A3
Stowell Street	B2-C2
Strawberry Place	B3-C3
Summerhill Grove	A2-B2-B1
Tindall Street	A2
Tower Street	E2
Union Street	F3
Vallum Way	A3
Victoria Square	E4
Walter Terrace	A4
Warwick Street	F4
Waterloo Street	B1-B2-C2
Wellington Street	B3
Westgate Road	A2-B2-C2-C1-D1
Westmorland Road	A1-B1
West Blandford Street	B1-B2
Worswick Street	D2
Wreatham Place	E3-F3

North Shields

Addison Street	B1
Albion Road	B3-C3
Albion Road West	A2-B2-B3
Alma Place	B3
Ayre's Terrace	B3
Bedford Street	B3-B2-C2
Belford Terrace	B4-C4
Borough Road	B2-B1-C1
Brightman Road	A3-B3
Brighton Grove	A3
Camden Street	C2-C3
Camp Terrace	B4
Campville	A4-B4
Cecil Street	B2
Charlotte Street	C2-C3
Chirton Green	A2
Chirton West View	A1-A2
Cleveland Avenue	A4
Cleveland Road	A4-B4
Cleveland Terrace	A3-A4
Clive Street	C1-C2
Coach Lane	A2-B2-B1
Collingwood View	A1-A2
Drummond Terrace	C3-C4
Fontbarn Terrace	C4
Grey Street	C3-C4
Grosvenor Place	A3-B3
Hawkey's Lane	A2-A3-A4
Hopper Street	A2
Howard Street	C2-C3
Howdon Road	B1
Hylton Street	A1-B1
Jackson Street	C4
Laet Street	C1
Lansdowne Terrace	A3
Liddell Street	C2
Linskill Terrace	C3-C4
Lovaine Place	B2
Lovaine Terrace	B3
Military Road	C3-C4
Milton Terrace	A4
Nile Street	B3
Norfolk Street	C2-C3
North King Street	C3-C4

Northumberland Place	B3-C3
Park Crescent	C4
Preston Road	B3-B4
Prudhoe Street	B1-B2
Queen Street	C3
Rudyard Street	B2-C2-C1
Russell Street	B2
Sackville Street West	B2-C2
Saville Street	C2
Scorer Street	A2-A3
Seymour Street	B1
Sibthorne Street	C1-C2
Sidney Street	B2-B3
Spring Gardens	A2-A3
Spring Terrace	B3
Stanley Street	B1-B2
Stephenson Street	C2-C3
Stormont Street	A1-A2-B2
The Nook	A2
Trevor Terrace	B4-C4
Trinity Street	B1
Tyrfe Street	C2
Tynemouth Road	C3
Union Street	C2
Upper Elsdon Street	A1-B1
Vicarage Street	B1
Waldo Street	C1
Waterville Road	A1-B1
Waterville Terrace	B2
West Percy Road	A1-A2
West Percy Street	A2-B2-B3
William Street	B2-C2
Yeoman Street	C1-C2

Whitley Bay

Algernon Place	B2
Alma Place	B1
Alnwick Avenue	A3
Amble Avenue	A1-B1
Beach Avenue	A3-B3-B4
Beech Grove	A4
Belsay Avenue	A1-B1
Brook Street	B3-B4
Burfoot Crescent	B1
Burnside Road	A1-B1
Cambridge Avenue	B3-B4
Charles Avenue	B3-B4
Cheviot View	B2-C2
Chollerford Avenue	A1-B1
Clifton Terrace	B2-B3
Coquet Avenue	A4-B4
Countess Avenue	A4
Delaval Road	B2-C2-C1
Dilston Avenue	A2-B2
Duchess Avenue	A4
East Parade	B3-B4
Edwards Road	B2-C2
Egremont Place	B2
Esplanade	B2-B3-B4
Esplanade Place	B3-B2-C2
Etal Avenue	A2-B2
Felton Avenue	A2-B2
Gordon Square	C2
Grafton Road	C1
Grosvenor Drive	A3

Hawthorne Gardens	A4
Helena Avenue	B2-C2
Hill Heads Road	A2-A3-A2
Holly Avenue	A4-B4
Holystone Avenue	A1-A2
Jesmond Terrace	A2-B2
Kings Drive	A3
Lish Avenue	B1
Lovaine Avenue	A2
Marden Road	A2-A3-B3
Marden Road South	A1-A2
Margaret Road	C1
Marine Avenue	A4-B4
Marine Gardens	A4-B4
Mason Avenue	B3
Norham Road	A3
North Parade	B3
North View	B1
Ocean View	B3
Oxford Street	B3-B4
Park Avenue	B3-B4
Park Parade	A3-B3
Park Road	A3-B3
Park View	A3-A4
Percy Avenue	A3-A4
Percy Gardens	A2
Percy Road	B2-C2-C3
Plessey Crescent	A2-B2-B1
Promenade	C1-C2-C3
Queens Drive	A3
Rockcliffe Street	C1-C2
Roxburgh Terrace	A3-B3
Shaftesbury Crescent	A1
Shorestone Avenue	A1-B1
South Parade	B3
Station Road	B2
Studley Gardens	A1-A2
The Broadway	A1
Trewit Road	B2
Victoria Avenue	B2-C2
Victoria Terrace	B2-B3
Warkworth Avenue	A3
Waters Street	C1
Whitley Road	B1-B2-B3
Windsor Crescent	C1
Windsor Terrace	C1
York Road	B3

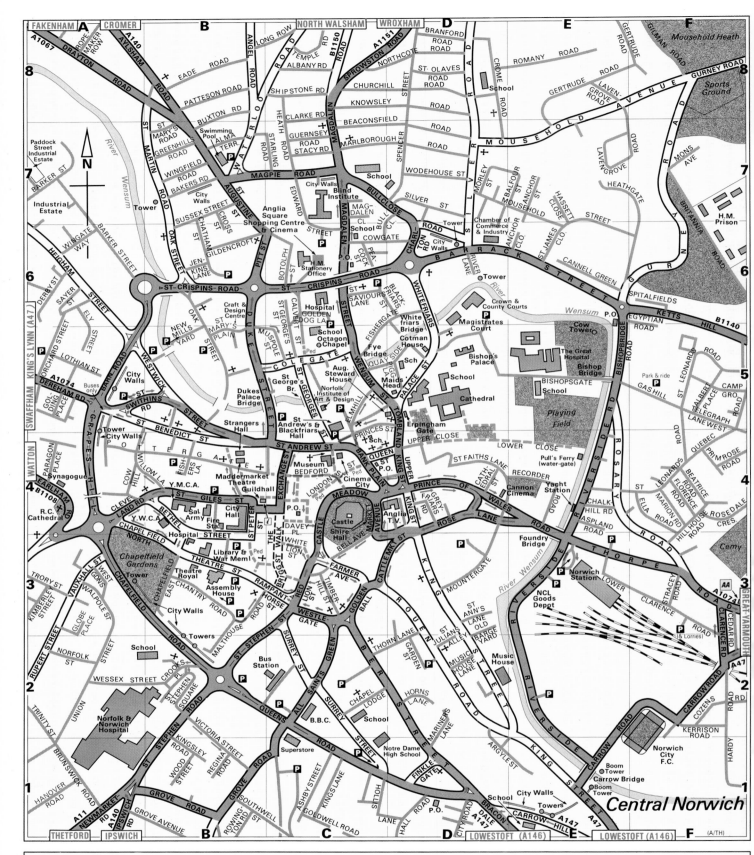

Norwich

Fortunately the heart has not been ripped out of Norwich to make way for some bland precinct, so its ancient character has been preserved. Narrow alleys run between the streets – sometimes opening out into quiet courtyards, sometimes into thoroughfares packed with people, sometimes into lanes which seem quite deserted. It is a unique place, with something of interest on every corner.

The cathedral was founded in 1096 by the city's first bishop, Herbert de Losinga. Among its most notable features are the nave, with its huge pillars, the bishop's throne (a Saxon survival unique in Europe) and the cloisters with their matchless collection of roof bosses. Across the city is the great stone keep of the castle, set on a mound and dominating all around it. It dates from Norman times, but was refaced in 1834. The keep now forms part of Norwich Castle Museum – an extensive and

fascinating collection. Other museums are Bridewell Museum – collections relating to local crafts and industries within a 14th-century building – and Strangers' Hall, a genuinely 'old world' house, rambling and full of surprises, both in its tumble of rooms and in the things which they contain. Especially picturesque parts of the city are Elm Hill – a street of ancient houses; Tombland – with two gateways into the Cathedral Close; and Pull's Ferry – a watergate by the river.

224

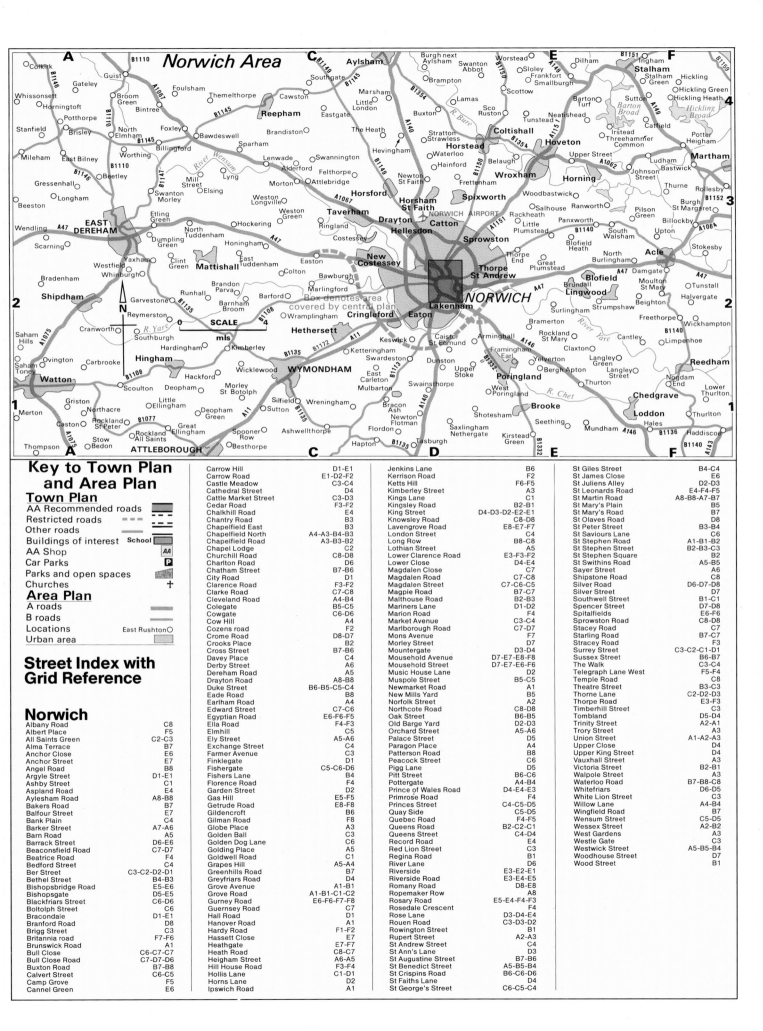

Norwich Area

Key to Town Plan and Area Plan

Town Plan

AA Recommended roads	
Restricted roads	
Other roads	
Buildings of interest	School
AA Shop	AA
Car Parks	P
Parks and open spaces	
Churches	+

Area Plan

A roads	
B roads	
Locations	East Rushton ○
Urban area	

Street Index with Grid Reference

Norwich

Albany Road	C8
Albert Place	F5
All Saints Green	C2-C3
Alma Terrace	B7
Anchor Close	E6
Anchor Street	E7
Angel Road	B8
Argyle Street	D1-E1
Ashby Street	C1
Aspland Road	E4
Aylesham Road	A8-B8
Bakers Road	B7
Balfour Street	E7
Bank Plain	C4
Barker Street	A7-A6
Barn Road	A5
Barrack Street	D6-E6
Beaconsfield Road	C7-D7
Beatrice Road	F4
Bedford Street	C4
Ber Street	C3-C2-D2-D1
Bethel Street	B4-B3
Bishopsbridge Road	E5-E6
Bishopsgate	D5-E5
Blackfriars Street	C6-D6
Boltolph Street	C6
Bracondale	D1-E1
Branford Road	D8
Brigg Street	C3
Britannia road	F7-F6
Brunswick Road	A1
Bull Close	C6-C7-C7
Bull Close Road	C7-D7-D6
Buxton Road	B7-B8
Calvert Street	C6-C5
Camp Grove	F5
Cannel Green	E6

Carrow Hill	D1-E1
Carrow Road	E1-D2-F2
Castle Meadow	C3-C4
Cathedral Street	D4
Cattle Market Street	C3-D3
Cedar Road	F3-F2
Chalkhill Road	E4
Chantry Road	B3
Chapelfield East	E4
Chapelfield Road	B3
Chapelfield North	A4-A3-B4-B3
Chapelfield Road	A3-B3-B2
Chapel Lodge	C2
Churchill Road	C8-D8
Charlton Road	D6
Chatham Street	B7-B6
City Road	D1
Clarence Road	F3-F2
Clarke Road	C7-C8
Cleveland Road	A4-B4
Colegate	C6-D6
Cowgate	C6-D6
Cow Hill	A4
Cozens road	F2
Crome Road	D8-D7
Crooks Place	B2
Cross Street	B7-B6
Davey Place	C4
Derby Street	A6
Dereham Road	A5
Drayton Road	A8-B8
Duke Street	B6-B5-C5-C4
Eade Road	B8
Earlham Road	A4
Edward Street	C7-C6
Egyptian Road	E6-F6-F5
Ella Road	F4-F3
Elmhill	C5
Ely Street	A5-A6
Exchange Street	C4
Farmer Avenue	C3
Finklegate	C5-C6-D6
Fishergate	C5
Fishers Lane	B4
Florence Road	F4
Garden Street	D2
Gas Hill	E5-F5
Getrude Road	E8-F8
Gildencroft	B6
Gilman Road	F8
Globe Place	A3
Golden Ball	C3
Golden Dog Lane	C6
Golding Place	A5
Goldwell Road	C1
Grapes Hill	A5-A4
Greenhills Road	B7
Greyfriars Road	D4
Grove Avenue	A1-B1
Grove Road	A1-B1-C1-C2
Gurney Road	E6-F6-F7-F8
Guernsey Road	C7
Hall Road	D1
Hanover Road	A1
Hardy Road	F1-F2
Hassett Close	E7
Heathgate	E7-F7
Heath Road	C8-C7
Heigham Street	A6-A5
Hill House Road	F3-F4
Hollis Lane	C1-D1
Horns Lane	D2
Ipswich Road	A1

Jenkins Lane	B6
Kerrison Road	F2
Ketts Hill	F6-F5
Kimberley Street	A3
Kings Lane	C1
Kingsley Road	B2-B1
King Street	D4-D3-D2-E2-E1
Knowsley Road	C8-D8
Lavengrove Road	E8-E7-F7
London Street	C4
Long Row	B8-C8
Lothian Street	A5
Lower Clarence Road	E3-F3-F2
Lower Close	D4-E4
Magdalen Close	C7
Magdalen Road	C7-C8
Magdalen Street	C7-C6-C5
Magpie Road	B7-C7
Malthouse Road	B2-B3
Mariners Lane	D1-D2
Marion Road	F4
Market Avenue	C3-C4
Marlborough Road	C7-D7
Mons Avenue	F7
Morley Street	D7
Mountergate	D3-D4
Mousehold Avenue	D7-E7-E8-F8
Mousehold Street	D7-E7-E6-F6
Music House Lane	D2
Muspole Street	B5-C5
Newmarket Road	A1
New Mills Yard	B5
Norfolk Street	A2
Northcote Road	C8-D8
Oak Street	B6-B5
Old Barge Yard	D2-D3
Orchard Street	A5-A6
Palace Street	D5
Paragon Place	A4
Patterson Road	B8
Peacock Street	C6
Pigg Lane	D5
Pitt Street	B6-C6
Pottergate	A4-B4
Prince of Wales Road	D4-E4-E3
Primrose Road	F4
Princes Street	C4-C5-D5
Quay Side	C5-D5
Quebec Road	F4-F5
Queens Road	B2-C2-C1
Queens Street	C4-D4
Record Road	E4
Red Lion Street	C3
Regina Road	B1
River Lane	D6
Riverside	E3-E2-E1
Riverside Road	E3-E4-E5
Romany Road	D8-E8
Ropemaker Row	A8
Rosary Road	E5-E4-F4-F3
Rosedale Crescent	F4
Rose Lane	D3-D4-E4
Rouen Road	C3-D3-D2
Rowington Street	B1
Rupert Street	A2-A3
St Andrew Street	C4
St Ann's Lane	D3
St Augustine Street	B7-B6
St Benedict Street	A5-B5-B4
St Crispins Road	B6-C6-D6
St Faiths Lane	D4
St George's Street	C6-C5-C4

St Giles Street	B4-C4
St James Close	E6
St Juliens Alley	D2-D3
St Leonards Road	E4-F4-F5
St Martin Road	A8-B8-A7-B7
St Mary's Plain	B5
St Mary's Road	B7
St Olaves Road	D8
St Peter Street	B3-B4
St Saviours Lane	C6
St Stephen Road	A1-B1-B2
St Stephen Street	B2-B3-C3
St Stephen Square	B2
St Swithins Road	A5-B5
Sayer Street	A6
Shipstone Road	C8
Silver Road	D6-D7-D8
Silver Street	D7
Southwell Street	B1-C1
Spencer Street	D7-D8
Spitalfields	E6-F6
Sprowston Road	C8-D8
Stacey Road	C7
Starling Road	B7-C7
Stracey Road	F3
Surrey Street	C3-C2-C1-D1
Sussex Street	B6-B7
The Walk	C3-C4
Telegraph Lane West	F5-F4
Temple Road	C8
Theatre Street	B3-C3
Thorne Lane	C2-D2-D3
Thorpe Road	E3-F3
Timberhill Street	C3
Tombland	D5-D4
Trinity Street	A2-A1
Trory Street	A3
Union Street	A1-A2-A3
Upper Close	D4
Upper King Street	D4
Vauxhall Street	A3
Victoria Street	B2-B1
Walpole Street	A3
Waterloo Road	B7-B8-C8
Whitefriars	D6-D5
White Lion Street	C3
Willow Lane	A4-B4
Wingfield Road	B7
Wensum Street	C5-D5
Wessex Street	A2-B2
West Gardens	A3
Westle Gate	C3
Westwick Street	A5-B5-B4
Woodhouse Street	D7
Wood Street	B1

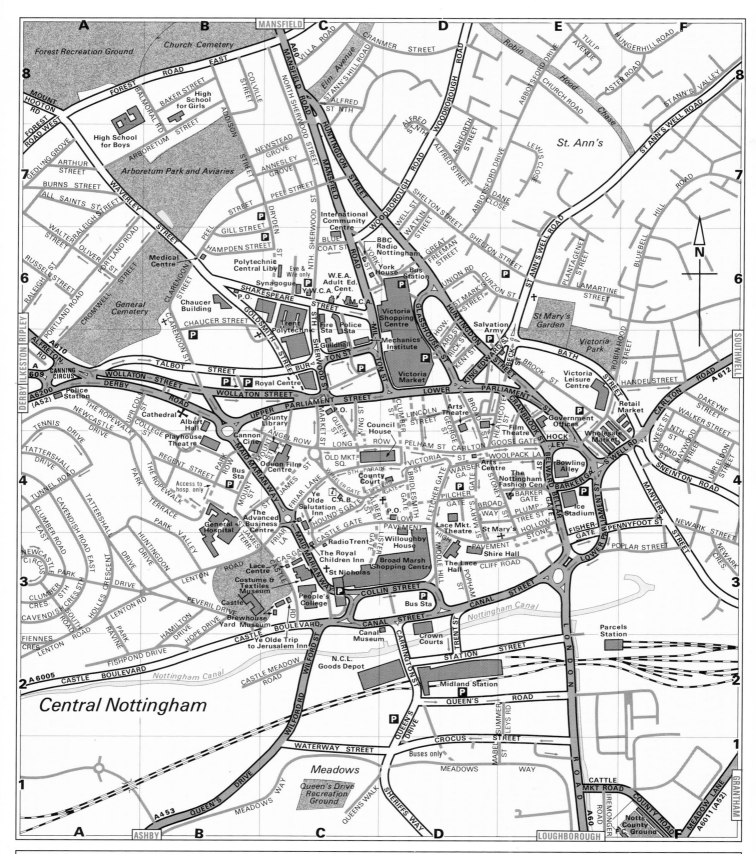

Central Nottingham

Nottingham

Hosiery and lace were the foundations upon which Nottingham's prosperity was built. The stockings came first – a knitting machine for these had been invented by a Nottinghamshire man as early as 1589 – but a machine called a 'tickler', which enabled simple patterns to be created in the stocking fabric, prompted the development of machine-made lace. The earliest fabric was produced in 1768, and an example from not much later than that is kept in the city's Castlegate Costume and Textile Museum. In fact, the entire history of lacemaking is beautifully explained in this converted row of Georgian terraces. The Industrial Museum at Wollaton Park has many other machines and exhibits tracing the development of the knitting industry, as well as displays on the other industries which have brought wealth to the city – tobacco, pharmaceuticals, engineering and printing. At Wollaton Hall is a natural history museum, while nearer the centre are the Canal Museum and the Brewhouse Yard Museum, a marvellous collection which shows items from daily life in the city up to the present day. Nottingham is not complete without mention of Robin Hood, the partly mythical figure whose statue is in the castle grounds. Although the castle itself has Norman foundations, the present structure is largely Victorian. It is now a museum.

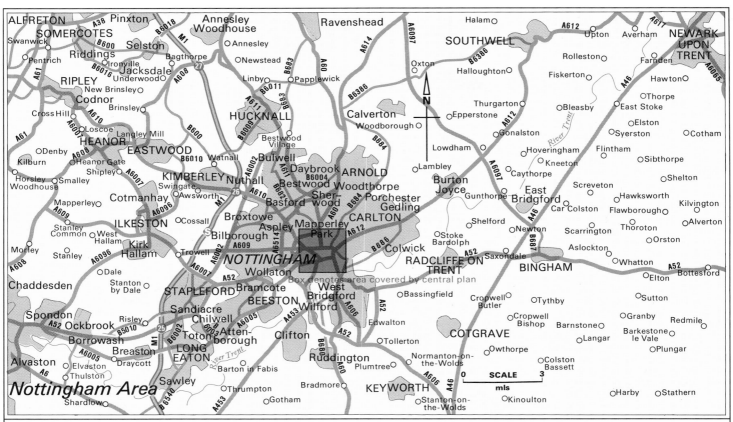

Nottingham Area

Key to Town Plan and Area Plan

Town Plan

AA Recommended roads	
Restricted roads	
Other roads	
Buildings of interest	Theatre
Car Parks	P
Parks and open spaces	
Churches	+
One Way Streets	→

Area Plan

A roads	
B roads	
Locations	Bagthorpe○
Urban area	

Street Index with Grid Reference

Nottingham

Abbotsford Drive	D6-D7-D7-E7-E8
Addison Street	B8-B7
Albert Street	C4
Alfred Street	D7
Alfred Street North	C8, D7-D8
Alfreton Road	A5-A6
All Saints Street	A7
Angel Row	B5-B4-C4
Annesley Grove	B7-C7
Ashforth Street	D7-D8
Aster Road	E8-F8
Arboretum Street	A7-B7-B8
Arthur Street	A7
Baker Street	B8
Balmoral Road	A8-B8-B7
Barker Gate	E4
Bath Street	E5-F5
Beck Street	E5
Bellar Gate	E4
Belward Street	E4
Bluebell Hill Road	F6-F7
Bluecoat Street	C6
Bond Street	F4
Bridlesmith Gate	D4
Broad Street	D4-D5
Broadway	D4-E4
Brook Street	E5
Burns Street	A7

Burton Street	C5
Canal Street	C3-D3-E3
Canning Circus	A5
Carlton Road	F5
Carlton Street	D4
Carrington Street	D2-D3
Castle Boulevard	A2-B2-B3-C3
Castle Gate	C3-C4
Castle Meadow Road	B2-C2
Castle Road	C3
Cattle Market Road	E1-F1
Cavendish Crescent South	A3
Cavendish Road East	A3-A4
Chaucer Street	B5-B6
Church Road	E8
Clarendon Street	B5-B6
Cliff Road	D3-E3
Clumber Crescent South	A3
Clumber Road East	A3-A4
Clumber Street	D4-D5
College Street	A5-B5-B4
Collin Street	C3-D3
Colville Street	B8
County Road	F1
Cranbrook Street	E4-E5
Cranmer Street	C8-D8
Crocus Street	D1-E1
Cromwell Street	A5-A6-B6
Curzon Street	D6-E6
Dane Close	D7-E7
Dakeyne Street	F5
Derby Road	A5-B5
Dryden Street	C6-C7
Fiennes Crescent	A2
Fishergate	E3-E4
Fishpond Drive	A2-B2
Fletcher Gate	D4
Forest Road East	A8-B8-C8
Forest Road West	A7-A8
Friar Lane	C3-C4
Gedling Grove	A7
George Street	D4-D5
Glasshouse Street	D5-D6
Gill Street	B6-C6
Goldsmith Street	B6-C6-C5
Goose Gate	D4-E4
Great Freeman Street	D6
Hamilton Drive	B2-B3
Hampden Street	B6-C6
Handel Street	E5-F5
Haywood Street	F4-F5
Heathcote Street	D4-D5-E5
High Pavement	D4-D3-E3
Hockley	E4
Holles Crescent	A3
Hollowstone	E3-E4

Hope Drive	B2-B3
Hound's Gate	C4
Howard Street	D5-D6
Hungerhill Road	E8-F8
Huntingdon Drive	A4-A3-B3
Huntingdon Street	C8-D7-D6-E5
Iremonger Road	E1
Kent Street	D5
King Edward Street	D5-E5
King Street	C4-C5
Lamartine Street	E6-F6
Lenton Road	A2-A3-B3
Lewis Close	E7
Lincoln Street	D5
Lister Gate	C3-C4
London Road	E1-E2-E3
Long Row	C4-D4
Lower Parliament Street	D5-E4-E3
Low Pavement	C4-D4
Mabel Street	E1
Maid Marian Way	B4-C4-C3
Mansfield Road	C6-C7-C8
Manvers Street	F3-F4
Market Street	C4-C5
Meadow Lane	F1
Meadows Way	B1-C1-D1-E1
Middle Hill	D3-D4
Milton Street	C6-C5-D5
Mount Hooton Road	A8
Mount Street	B4-C4
Newark Crescent	F3
Newark Street	F3-F4
Newcastle Circus	A3
Newcastle Drive	A4-A5
Newstead Grove	B7-C7
North Street	F4-F5
North Sherwood Street	C6-C7-C8
Old Market Square	C4
Oliver Street	A6
Park Drive	A3-B3
Park Ravine	A2-A3
Park Row	B4
Park Terrace	A4-B4
Park Valley	A4-B4-B3
Peel Street	B6-B7-C7
Pelham Street	D4
Pennyfoot Street	E4-F4
Peveril Drive	B3
Pilcher Gate	D4
Plantagenet Street	E6
Plumptree Street	E4
Popham Street	D3
Poplar Street	E3-F3
Portland Road	A5-A6-A7
Queen's Drive	B1-C1, D1-D2
Queen's Road	D2-E2

Queen Street	C4-C5
Queen's Walk	C1
Raleigh Street	A6-A7
Regent Street	B4
Rick Street	D5
Robin Hood Street	E5-F5-F6
Russell Street	A6
St Ann's Hill Road	C8
St Ann's Valley	F7-F8
St Ann's Well Road	E5-E6-E7-F7-F8
St James Street	C4
St James Terrace	B4-B3-C3
St Mark's Street	D6
St Mary's Gate	D3-D4
St Peters Gate	C4-D4
Shakespeare Street	B6-C6
Shelton Street	D7-D6-E6
Sheriff's Way	D1
Sneinton Road	F4
South Parade	C4-D4
South Road	A3
South Sherwood Street	C5-C6
Southwell Road	E4-F4
Station Street	D2-E2
Stony Street	D4-E4
Summer Leys Road	E1
Talbot Street	A5-B5-C5
Tattershall Drive	A4-A3-B3
Tennis Drive	A4-A5-A4
The Ropewalk	A5-A4-B4
Trent Street	D2-D3
Tulip Avenue	E8
Tunnel Road	A4
Union Road	D6
Upper College Street	A5-B5
Upper Eldon Street	F4
Upper Parliament Street	B5-C5-D5
Victoria Street	D4
Villa Road	C8
Walker Street	F4-F5
Walter Street	A6-A7
Warser Gate	D4
Waterway Street	C1-D1
Watkin Street	D6-D7
Waverely Street	A8-A7-B7-B6
Wellington Street	D6-D7
West Street	F4-F5
Wheeler Gate	C4
Wilford Road	C1-C2
Wilford Street	C2-C3
Wollaton Street	A5-B5-C5
Woodborough Road	C6-C7-D7-D8
Woolpack Lane	D4-E4
York Street	C6-D6

LBTT

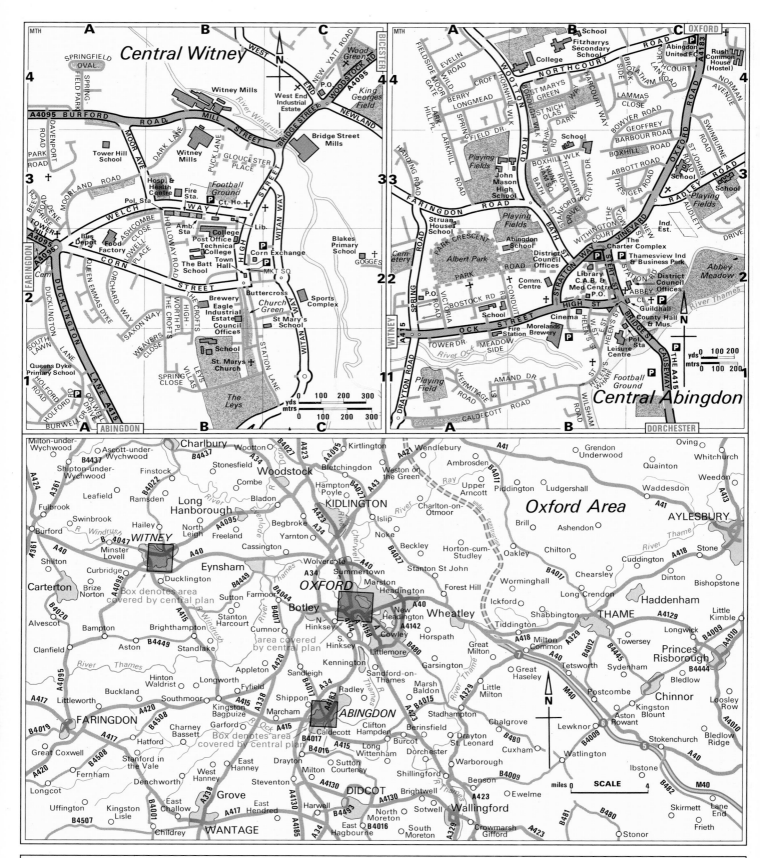

Oxford

From Carfax (at the centre of the city) round to Magdalen Bridge stretches High Street, one of England's best and most interesting thoroughfares. Shops rub shoulders with churches and colleges, alleyways lead to ancient inns and to a large covered market, and little streets lead to views of some of the finest architecture to be seen anywhere. Catte Street, beside St Mary's Church (whose lovely tower gives a panoramic view of Oxford), opens out into Radcliffe Square, dominated by the Radcliffe Camera, a great round structure built in 1749. Close by is the Bodleian Library, one of the finest collections of books and manuscripts in the world. All around are ancient college buildings. Close to Magdalen Bridge is Magdalen College, founded in 1448 and certainly not to be missed. Across the High Street are the Botanical Gardens, founded in 1621 and the oldest such foundation in England. Footpaths lead through Christ Church Meadow to Christ Church College and the cathedral. Tom Tower is the college's most notable feature; the cathedral is actually its chapel and is the smallest cathedral in England. Among much else not to be missed in Oxford is the Ashmolean Museum, whose vast collections of precious and beautiful objects from all over the world repay many hours of study; perhaps the loveliest treasure is the 9th-century Alfred Jewel.

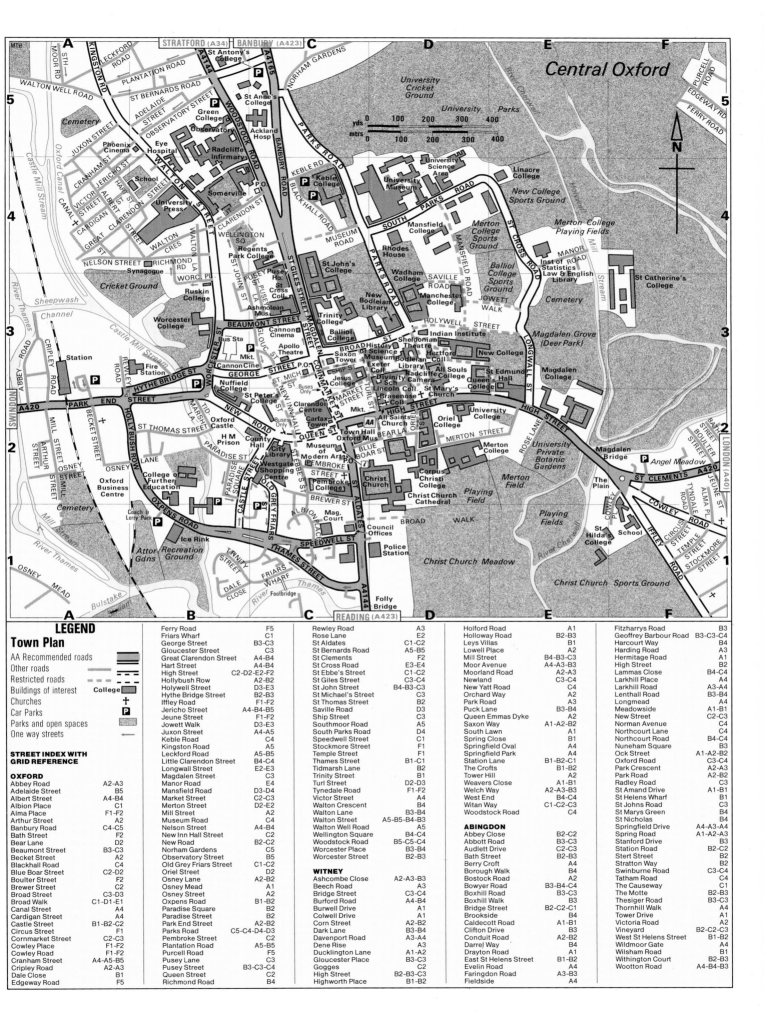

Central Oxford

LEGEND

Town Plan

- AA Recommended roads
- Other roads
- Restricted roads
- Buildings of interest — College
- Churches — †
- Car Parks — P
- Parks and open spaces
- One way streets — ←

STREET INDEX WITH GRID REFERENCE

OXFORD

Abbey Road	A2-A3
Adelaide Street	B5
Albert Street	A4-B4
Albion Place	C1
Alma Place	F1-F2
Arthur Street	A2
Banbury Road	C4-C5
Bath Street	F2
Bear Lane	D2
Beaumont Street	B3-C3
Becket Street	A2
Blackhall Road	C4
Blue Boar Street	C2-D2
Boulter Street	F2
Brewer Street	C2
Broad Street	C3-D3
Broad Walk	C1-D1-E1
Canal Street	A4
Cardigan Street	A4
Castle Street	B1-B2-C2
Circus Street	F1
Cornmarket Street	C2-C3
Cowley Place	F1-F2
Cowley Road	F1-F2
Cranham Street	A4-A5-B5
Cripley Road	A2-A3
Dale Close	B1
Edgeway Road	F5
Ferry Road	F5
Friars Wharf	C1
George Street	B3-C3
Gloucester Street	C3
Great Clarendon Street	A4-B4
Hart Street	A4
High Street	C2-D2-E2-F2
Hollybush Row	A2-B2
Holywell Street	D3-E3
Hythe Bridge Street	B2-B3
Iffley Road	F1-F2
Jericho Street	A4-B4-B5
Jeune Street	F1-F2
Jowett Walk	D3-E3
Juxon Street	A4-A5
Keble Road	C4
Kingston Road	A5
Leckford Road	A5-B5
Little Clarendon Street	B4-C4
Longwall Street	E2-E3
Magdalen Street	C3
Manor Road	E4
Mansfield Road	D3-D4
Market Street	C2-C3
Merton Street	D2-E2
Mill Street	A2
Museum Road	C4
Nelson Street	A4-B4
New Inn Hall Street	C2
New Road	B2-C2
Norham Gardens	C5
Observatory Street	B5
Old Grey Friars Street	C1-C2
Oriel Street	D2
Osney Lane	A2-B2
Osney Mead	A1
Osney Street	A2
Oxpens Road	B1-B2
Paradise Square	B2
Paradise Street	B2
Park End Street	A2-B2
Parks Road	C5-C4-D4-D3
Pembroke Street	C2
Plantation Road	A5-B5
Purcell Road	F5
Pusey Lane	C4
Pusey Street	B3-C3-C4
Queen Street	C2
Richmond Road	B4
Rewley Road	A3
Rose Lane	E2
St Aldates	C1-C2
St Bernards Road	A5-B5
St Clements	F2
St Cross Road	E3-E4
St Ebbe's Street	C1-C2
St Giles Street	C3-C4
St John Street	B4-B3-C3
St Michael's Street	C3
St Thomas Street	B2
Saville Road	D3
Ship Street	C3
Southmoor Road	A5
South Parks Road	D4
Speedwell Street	C1
Stockmore Street	F1
Temple Street	F1
Thames Street	B1-C1
Tidmarsh Lane	B2
Trinity Street	B1
Turl Street	D2-D3
Tynedale Road	F1-F2
Victor Street	A4
Walton Crescent	A4
Walton Lane	B3-B4
Walton Street	A5-B5-B4-B3
Walton Well Road	A5
Wellington Square	B4-C4
Woodstock Road	B5-C5-C4
Worcester Place	B3-B4
Worcester Street	B2-B3

WITNEY

Ashcombe Close	A2-A3-B3
Beech Road	A3
Bridge Street	C3-C4
Burford Road	A4-B4
Burwell Drive	A1
Colwell Drive	A1
Corn Street	A2-B2
Dark Lane	B3-B4
Davenport Road	A3-A4
Dene Rise	A3
Ducklington Lane	A1-A2
Gloucester Place	B3-C3
Gogges	C2
High Street	B2-B3-C3
Highworth Place	B1-B2
Holford Road	A1
Holloway Road	B2-B3
Leys Villas	B1
Lowell Place	A2
Mill Street	B4-B3-C3
Moor Avenue	A4-A3-B3
Moorland Road	A2-A3
Newland	C3-C4
New Yatt Road	C4
Orchard Way	A2
Park Road	A3
Puck Lane	B3-B4
Queen Emmas Dyke	A2
Saxon Way	A1-A2-B2
South Lawn	A1
Spring Close	B1
Springfield Oval	A4
Springfield Park	A4
Station Lane	B1-B2-C1
The Crofts	B1-B2
Tower Hill	A2
Weavers Close	A1-B1
Welch Way	A2-A3-B3
West End	B4-C4
Witan Way	C1-C2-C3
Woodstock Road	C4

ABINGDON

Abbey Close	B2-C2
Abbott Road	B3-C3
Audlett Drive	C2-C3
Bath Street	B2-B3
Berry Croft	A4
Borough Walk	B4
Bostock Road	A4
Bowyer Road	B3-B4-C4
Boxhill Road	B3-C3
Boxhill Walk	B3
Bridge Street	B2-C2-C1
Brookside	B4
Caldecott Road	A1-B1
Clifton Drive	B3
Conduit Road	A2-B2
Darrel Way	B4
Drayton Road	A1
East St Helens Street	B1-B2
Evelin Road	A4
Faringdon Road	A3-B3
Fieldside	A4
Fitzharrys Road	B3
Geoffrey Barbour Road	B3-C3-C4
Harcourt Way	B4
Harding Road	A3
Hermitage Road	A1
High Street	C4
Lammas Close	B4-C4
Larkhill Place	A4
Larkhill Road	A3-A4
Lenthall Road	B3-B4
Longmead	A4
Meadowside	A1-B1
New Street	C2-C3
Norman Avenue	C4
Northcourt Lane	C4
Northcourt Road	B4-C4
Nuneham Square	B3
Ock Street	A1-A2-B2
Oxford Road	C3-C4
Park Crescent	A2-A3
Park Road	A2-B2
Radley Road	C3
St Amand Drive	A1-B1
St Helens Wharf	B1
St Johns Road	C3
St Marys Green	B4
St Nicholas	B4
Springfield Drive	A4-A3-B3
Spring Road	A1-A2-B3
Stanford Drive	B3
Station Road	B2-C2
Stert Street	B2
Stratton Way	B2
Swinburne Road	C3-C4
Tatham Road	B2
The Causeway	C1
The Motte	B2-B3
Thesiger Road	B3-C3
Thornhill Walk	A4
Tower Drive	A1
Victoria Road	A2
Vineyard	B2-C2-C3
West St Helens Street	B1-B2
Wildmoor Gate	A4
Wilsham Road	B1
Withington Court	B2-B3
Wootton Road	A4-B4-B3

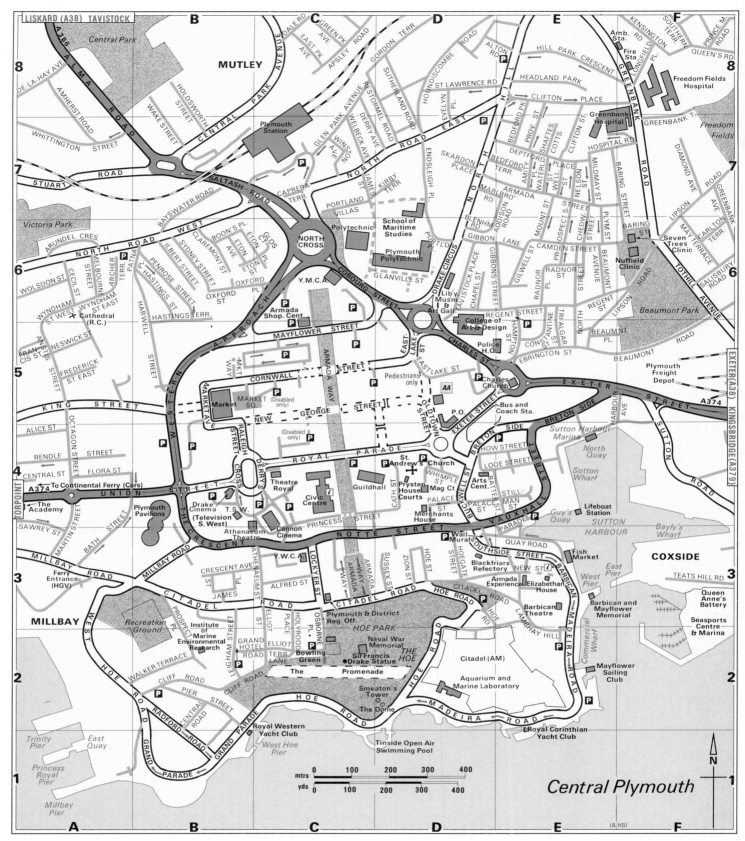

Plymouth

Ships, sailors and the sea permeate every aspect of Plymouth's life and history. Its superb natural harbour - Plymouth Sound - has ensured its importance as a port, yachting centre and naval base (latterly at Devonport) over many centuries. Sir Francis Drake is undoubtedly the city's most famous sailor. His statue stands on the Hoe - where he really did play bowls before tackling the Spanish Armada. Also on the Hoe are Smeaton's

Tower, which once formed the upper part of the third Eddystone Lighthouse, and the impressive Royal Naval War Memorial. Just east of the Hoe is the Royal Citadel, an imposing fortress built in 1666 by order of Charles II. North is Sutton Harbour, perhaps the most atmospheric part of Plymouth. Here fishing boats bob up and down in a harbour whose quays are lined with attractive old houses, inns and warehouses. One of the memorials on Mayflower Quay just outside the harbour commemorates the sailing of the Mayflower from

here in 1620. Plymouth's shopping centre was built after the old centre was badly damaged in World War II. Nearby is the 200ft-high tower of the impressive modern Civic Centre. Some buildings escaped destruction, including the Elizabethan House and the 500-year-old Prysten House. Next door is St Andrew's Church, with stained glass by John Piper.

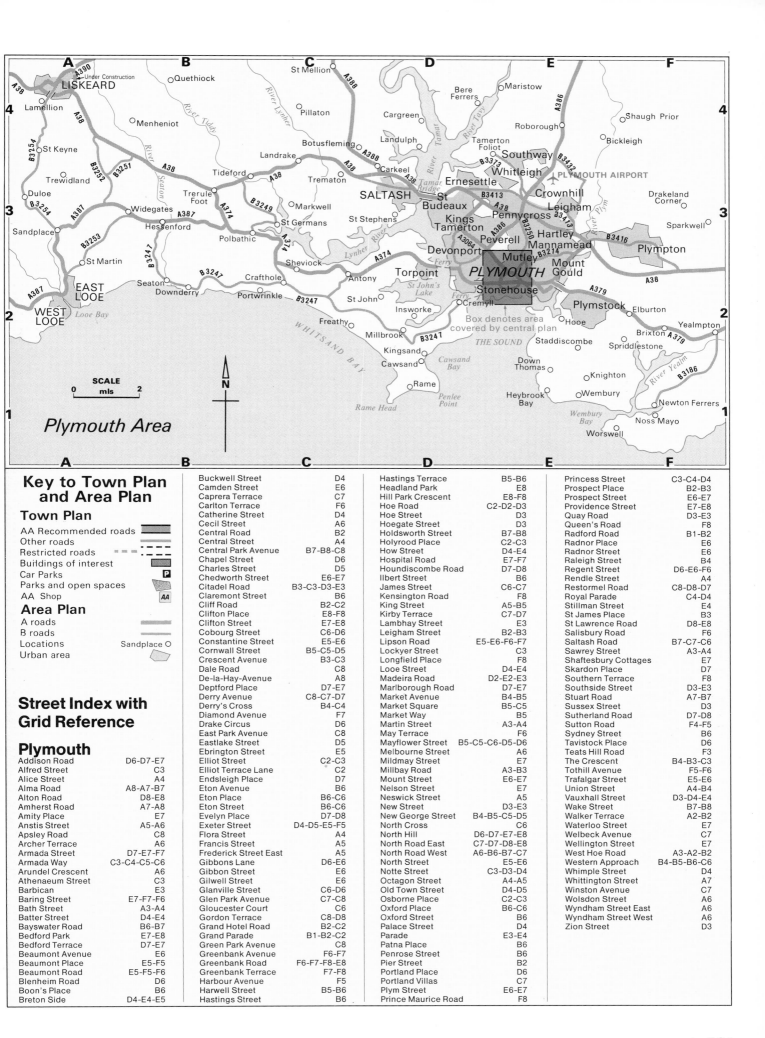

Key to Town Plan and Area Plan

Town Plan

AA Recommended roads
Other roads
Restricted roads
Buildings of interest
Car Parks — P
Parks and open spaces
AA Shop — AA

Area Plan

A roads
B roads
Locations — Sandplace ○
Urban area

Street Index with Grid Reference

Plymouth

Street	Grid
Addison Road	D6-D7-E7
Alfred Street	C3
Alice Street	A4
Alma Road	A8-A7-B7
Alton Road	D8-E8
Amherst Road	A7-A8
Amity Place	E7
Anstis Street	A5-A6
Apsley Road	C8
Archer Terrace	A6
Armada Street	D7-E7-F7
Armada Way	C3-C4-C5-C6
Arundel Crescent	A6
Athenaeum Street	C3
Barbican	E3
Baring Street	E7-F7-F6
Bath Street	A3-A4
Batter Street	D4-E4
Bayswater Road	B6-B7
Beaumont Avenue	E6
Beaumont Place	E5-F5
Beaumont Road	E5-F5-F6
Blenheim Road	D6
Boon's Place	B6
Breton Side	D4-E4-E5
Buckwell Street	D4
Camden Street	E6
Caprera Terrace	C7
Carlton Terrace	F6
Catherine Street	D4
Cecil Street	A6
Central Road	B2
Central Street	A4
Central Park Avenue	B7-B8-C8
Chapel Street	D6
Charles Street	D5
Chedworth Street	E6-E7
Citadel Road	B3-C3-D3-E3
Claremont Street	B6
Cliff Road	B2-C2
Clifton Place	E8-F8
Clifton Street	E7-E8
Cobourg Street	C6-D6
Constantine Street	E5-E6
Cornwall Street	B5-C5-D5
Crescent Avenue	B3-C3
Dale Road	C8
De-la-Hay-Avenue	A8
Deptford Place	D7-E7
Derry Avenue	C8-C7-D7
Derry's Cross	B4-C4
Diamond Avenue	F7
Drake Circus	D6
East Park Avenue	C8
Eastlake Street	D5
Ebrington Street	E5
Elliot Street	C2-C3
Elliot Terrace Lane	C2
Endsleigh Place	D7
Eton Avenue	B6
Eton Place	B6-C6
Eton Street	B6-C6
Evelyn Place	D7-D8
Exeter Street	D4-D5-E5-F5
Flora Street	A4
Francis Street	A5
Frederick Street East	A5
Gibbons Lane	D6-E6
Gibbon Street	E6
Gilwell Street	E6
Glanville Street	C6-D6
Glen Park Avenue	C7-C8
Gloucester Court	C6
Gordon Terrace	C8-D8
Grand Hotel Road	B2-C2
Grand Parade	B1-B2-C2
Green Park Avenue	C8
Greenbank Avenue	F6-F7
Greenbank Road	F6-F7-F8-E8
Greenbank Terrace	F7-F8
Harbour Avenue	F5
Harwell Street	B5-B6
Hastings Street	B6
Hastings Terrace	B5-B6
Headland Park	E8
Hill Park Crescent	E8-F8
Hoe Road	C2-D2-D3
Hoe Street	D3
Hoegate Street	D3
Holdsworth Street	B7-B8
Holyrood Place	C2-C3
How Street	D4-E4
Hospital Road	E7-F7
Houndiscombe Road	D7-D8
Ilbert Street	B6
James Street	C6-C7
Kensington Road	F8
King Street	A5-B5
Kirby Terrace	C7-D7
Lambhay Street	E3
Leigham Street	B2-B3
Lipson Road	E5-E6-F6-F7
Lockyer Street	C3
Longfield Place	F8
Looe Street	D4-E4
Madeira Road	D2-E2-E3
Marlborough Road	D7-E7
Market Avenue	B4-B5
Market Square	B5-C5
Market Way	B5
Martin Street	A3-A4
May Terrace	F6
Mayflower Street	B5-C5-C6-D5-D6
Melbourne Street	A6
Mildmay Street	E6
Millbay Road	A3-B3
Mount Street	E6-E7
Nelson Street	E7
Neswick Street	A5
New Street	D3-E3
New George Street	B4-B5-C5-D5
North Cross	C6
North Hill	D6-D7-E7-E8
North Road East	C7-D7-D8-E8
North Road West	A6-B6-B7-C7
North Street	E5-E6
Notte Street	C3-D3-D4
Octagon Street	A4-A5
Old Town Street	D4-D5
Osborne Place	C2-C3
Oxford Place	B6-C6
Oxford Street	B6
Palace Street	D4
Parade	E3-E4
Patna Place	B6
Penrose Street	B6
Pier Street	B2
Portland Place	D6
Portland Villas	C7
Plym Street	E6-E7
Prince Maurice Road	F8
Princess Street	C3-C4-D4
Prospect Place	B2-B3
Prospect Street	E6-E7
Providence Street	E7-E8
Quay Road	D3-E3
Queen's Road	F8
Radford Road	B1-B2
Radnor Place	E6
Radnor Street	E6
Raleigh Street	B4
Regent Street	D6-E6-F6
Rendle Street	A4
Restormel Road	C8-D8-D7
Royal Parade	C4-D4
Stillman Street	E4
St James Place	B3
St Lawrence Road	D8-E8
Salisbury Road	F6
Saltash Road	B7-C7-C6
Sawrey Street	A3-A4
Shaftesbury Cottages	E7
Skardon Place	D7
Southern Terrace	F8
Southside Street	D3-E3
Stuart Road	A7-B7
Sussex Street	D3
Sutherland Road	D7-D8
Sutton Road	F4-F5
Sydney Street	B6
Tavistock Place	D6
Teats Hill Road	F3
The Crescent	B4-B3-C3
Tothill Avenue	F5-F6
Trafalgar Street	E5-E6
Union Street	A4-B4
Vauxhall Street	D3-D4-E4
Wake Street	B7-B8
Walker Terrace	A2-B2
Waterloo Street	E7
Welbeck Avenue	C7
Wellington Street	E7
West Hoe Road	A3-A2-B2
Western Approach	B4-B5-B6-C6
Whimple Street	D4
Whittington Street	A7
Winston Avenue	C7
Wolsdon Street	A6
Wyndham Street East	A6
Wyndham Street West	A6
Zion Street	D3

231

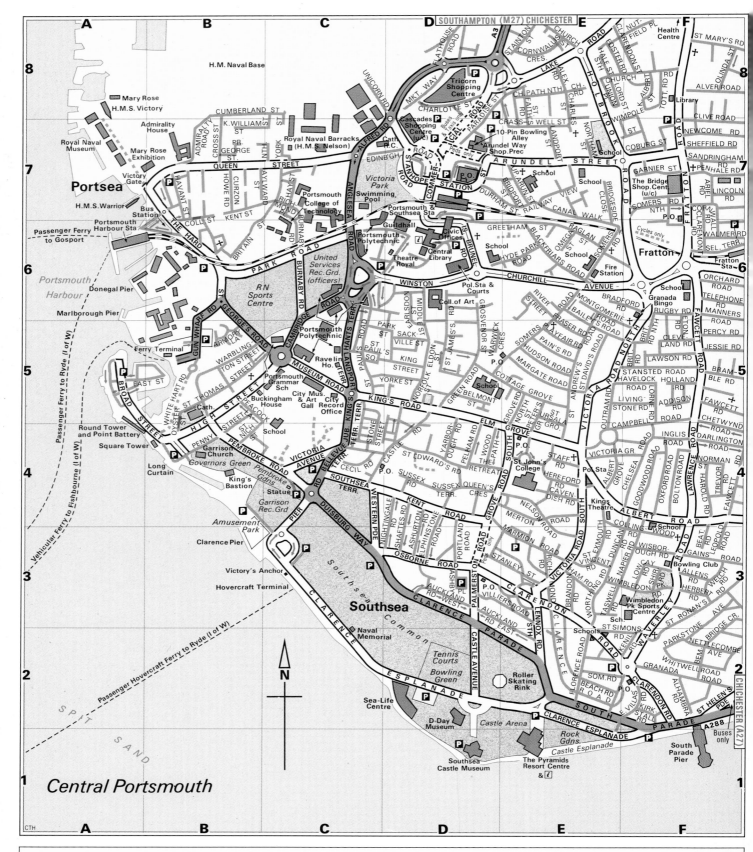

Portsmouth

Richard the Lionheart first recognised the strategic importance of Portsea Island and ordered the first docks, and later the town to be built. Succeeding monarchs improved the defences and extended the docks which now cover some 300 acres - as befits Britain's premier naval base. Of the defensive fortifications, Fort Widley and the Round Tower are the best preserved remains. Three famous ships

rest in Portsmouth; HMS Victory, the Mary Rose and HMS Warrior. The former, Lord Nelson's flagship, has been fully restored and the adjacent Royal Naval museum houses numerous relics of Trafalgar. The Mary Rose, built by Henry VIII, lay on the sea bed off Southsea until she was spectacularly raised in 1982. She has now been put on display and there is an exhibition of artefacts that have been recovered from her. HMS Warrior is the worlds first iron hulled warship.

Portsmouth suffered greatly from bombing in World War II and the centre has been almost completely rebuilt. However, the old town clustered around the harbour mouth escaped severe damage and, now restored, forms an attractive and fashionable area of the city.

Southsea, Portsmouth's near neighbour, developed in the 19th century as an elegant seaside resort with fine houses and terraces, an esplanade and an extensive seafront common.

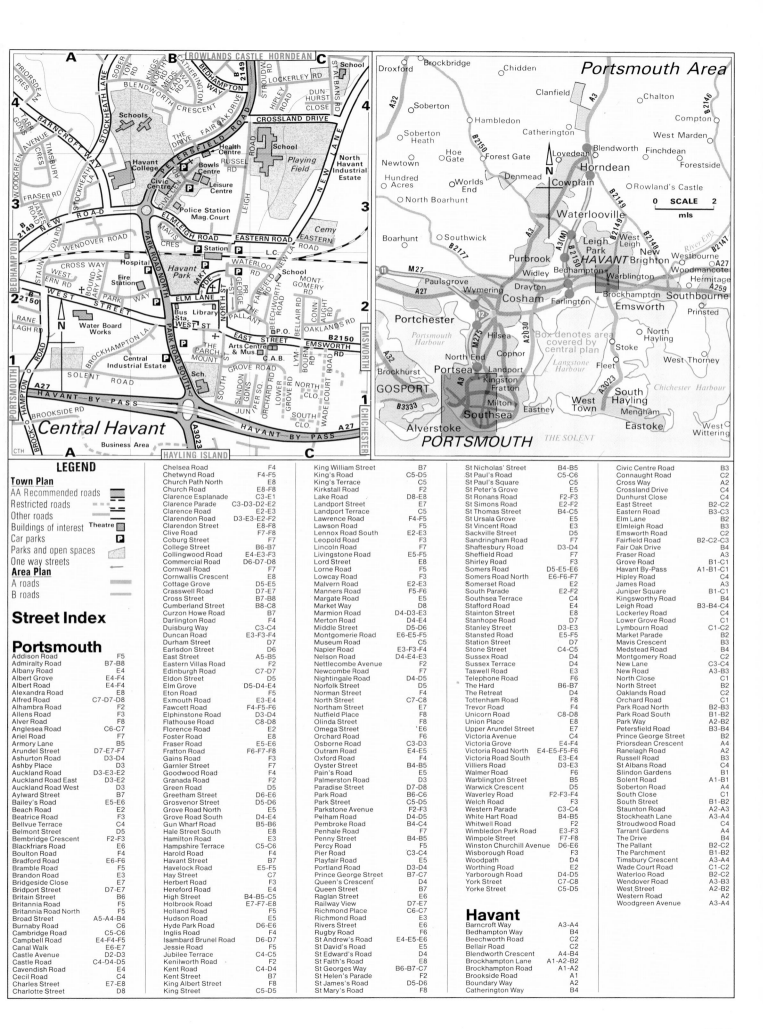

Central Havant

Business Area

Portsmouth Area

LEGEND

Town Plan

AA Recommended roads
Restricted roads
Other roads
Buildings of interest — Theatre
Car parks
Parks and open spaces
One way streets

Area Plan

A roads
B roads

Street Index

Portsmouth

Addison Road	F5
Admiralty Road	B7-B8
Albany Road	E4
Albert Grove	E4-F4
Albert Road	E4-F4
Alexandra Road	E8
Alfred Road	C7-D7-D8
Alhambra Road	F2
Allens Road	F3
Alver Road	C6-C7
Anglesea Road	F7
Ariel Road	F7
Armory Lane	B5
Arundel Street	D7-E7-F7
Ashurton Road	D3-D4
Ashby Place	D3
Auckland Road	D3-E3-E2
Auckland Road East	D3-E2
Auckland Road West	D3
Aylward Street	B7
Bailey's Road	E5-E6
Beach Road	E2
Beatrice Road	F3
Bellvue Terrace	C4
Belmont Street	D5
Bembridge Crescent	F2-F3
Blackfriars Road	E6
Boulton Road	F4
Bradford Road	E6-F6
Bramble Road	F5
Brandon Road	E3
Bridgeside Close	E7
Bridport Street	D7-E7
Britain Street	B6
Britannia Road	F5
Britannia Road North	F5
Broad Street	A5-A4-B4
Burnaby Road	C6
Cambridge Road	C5-C6
Campbell Road	E4-F4-F5
Canal Walk	E6-E7
Castle Avenue	D2-D3
Castle Road	C4-D4-D5
Cavendish Road	C4
Cecil Road	C4
Charles Street	E7-E8
Charlotte Street	D8

Chelsea Road	F4
Chetwynd Road	F4-F5
Church Path North	E8
Church Road	E8-F8
Clarence Esplanade	C3-E1
Clarence Parade	C3-D3-D2-E2
Clarence Road	E2-E3
Clarendon Road	D3-E3-E2-F2
Clarendon Street	E8-F8
Clive Road	F7-F8
Coburg Street	F7
College Street	B6-B7
Collingwood Road	E4-E3-F3
Commercial Road	D6-D7-D8
Cornwall Road	F7
Cornwallis Crescent	E8
Cottage Grove	D5-E5
Crasswell Road	D7-E7
Cross Street	B7-B8
Cumberland Street	B8-C8
Curzon Howe Road	B7
Darlington Road	F4
Duisburg Way	C3-C4
Duncan Road	E3-F3-F4
Durham Street	D7
Earlsdon Street	D6
East Street	A5-B5
Eastern Villas Road	F2
Edinburgh Road	C7-D7
Eldon Street	D5
Elm Grove	D5-D4-E4
Eton Road	F5
Exmouth Road	E3-E4
Fawcett Road	F4-F5-F6
Elphinstone Road	D3-D4
Flathouse Road	C8-D8
Florence Road	E2
Foster Road	E8
Fraser Road	E5-E6
Fratton Road	F6-F7-F8
Gains Road	F3
Garnier Street	F7
Goodwood Road	F4
Granada Road	F2
Green Road	D5
Greetham Street	D6-E6
Grosvenor Street	D5-D6
Grove Road North	E5
Grove Road South	D4-E4
Gun Wharf Road	B5-B6
Hale Street South	E8
Hamilton Road	E3
Hampshire Terrace	C5-C6
Harold Road	F4
Havant Street	B7
Havelock Road	E5-F5
Hay Street	C7
Herbert Road	F3
Hereford Road	E4
High Street	B4-B5-C5
Holbrook Road	E7-F7-E8
Holland Road	F5
Hudson Road	E5
Hyde Park Road	D6-E6
Inglis Road	F4
Isambard Brunel Road	D6-D7
Jessie Road	F5
Jubilee Terrace	C4-C5
Kenilworth Road	F2
Kent Road	C4-D4
Kent Street	B7
King Albert Street	F8
King Street	C5-D5

King William Street	B7
King's Road	C5-D5
King's Terrace	C5
Kirkstall Road	F2
Lake Road	D8-E8
Landport Street	E7
Landport Terrace	C5
Lawrence Road	F4-F5
Lawson Road	F5
Lennox Road South	E2-E3
Leopold Road	F3
Lincoln Road	E7
Livingstone Road	E5-F5
Lord Street	E8
Lorne Road	F5
Lowcay Road	F3
Malvern Road	E2-E3
Manners Road	F5-F6
Margate Road	E5
Market Way	D8
Marmion Road	D4-D3-E3
Merton Road	D4-E4
Middle Street	D5-D6
Montgomerie Road	E6-E5-F5
Museum Road	C5
Napier Road	E3-F3-F4
Nelson Road	D4-E4-E3
Nettlecombe Avenue	F2
Newcombe Road	F7
Nightingale Road	D4-D5
Norfolk Street	D5
Norman Street	F4
North Street	C7-C8
Northam Street	E7
Nutfield Place	F8
Olinda Street	F8
Omega Street	E6
Orchard Road	F6
Osborne Road	C3-D3
Outram Road	E4-E5
Oxford Road	F4
Oyster Street	B4-B5
Pain's Road	E5
Palmerston Road	D3
Paradise Street	D7-D8
Park Road	B6-C6
Park Street	C5-D5
Parkstone Avenue	F2-F3
Pelham Road	D5
Pembroke Road	B4-C4
Penhale Road	F7
Penny Street	B4-B5
Percy Road	F5
Pier Road	C3-C4
Playfair Road	E5
Portland Road	D3-D4
Prince George Street	B7-C7
Queen's Crescent	D4
Queen Street	B7
Raglan Street	E6
Railway View	D7-E7
Richmond Place	C6-C7
Richmond Road	E3
Rivers Street	E6
Rugby Road	F6
St Andrew's Road	E4-E5-E6
St David's Road	E5
St Edward's Road	D4
St Faith's Road	E8
St Georges Way	B6-B7-C7
St Helen's Parade	F2
St James's Road	D5-D6
St Mary's Road	F8

St Nicholas' Street	B4-B5
St Paul's Road	C5-C6
St Paul's Square	C5
St Peter's Grove	E5
St Ronans Road	F2-F3
St Simons Road	E2-F2
St Thomas Street	B4-C5
St Ursula Grove	E5
St Vincent Road	E3
Sackville Street	D5
Sandringham Road	F7
Shaftesbury Road	D3-D4
Sheffield Road	F7
Shirley Road	F3
Somers Road	D5-E5-E6
Somers Road North	E6-F6-F7
Somerset Road	E2
South Parade	E2-F2
Southsea Terrace	C4
Stafford Road	E4
Stainton Street	E8
Stanhope Road	D7
Stanley Street	D3-E3
Stansted Road	E5-F5
Station Street	D7
Stone Street	C4-C5
Sussex Road	D4
Sussex Terrace	D4
Taswell Road	E3
Telephone Road	F5
The Hard	B6-B7
The Retreat	D4
Tottenham Road	F8
Trevor Road	F4
Unicorn Road	C8-D8
Union Place	E8
Upper Arundel Street	E7
Victoria Avenue	C4
Victoria Grove	E4-F4
Victoria Road North	E4-E5-F5-F6
Victoria Road South	E3-E4
Villiers Road	D3-E3
Walmer Road	F6
Warblington Street	B5
Warwick Crescent	D5
Waverley Road	F2-F3-F4
Welch Road	F3
Western Parade	C3-C4
White Hart Road	B4-B5
Whitwell Road	F2
Wimbledon Park Road	E3-F3
Wimpole Street	F7-F8
Winston Churchill Avenue	D6-E6
Wisborough Road	F3
Woodpath	D4
Worthing Road	E2
Yarborough Road	D4-D5
York Street	C7-C8
Yorke Street	C5-D5

Havant

Barncroft Way	A3-A4
Bedhampton Way	B4
Beechworth Road	C2
Bellair Road	C2
Blendworth Crescent	A4-B4
Brockhampton Lane	A1-A2-B2
Brockhampton Road	A1-A2
Brookside Road	A1
Boundary Way	A2
Catherington Way	B4
Civic Centre Road	B3
Connaught Road	C2
Cross Way	A2
Crossland Drive	C4
Dunhurst Close	C4
East Street	B2-C2
Eastern Road	B3-C3
Elm Lane	B2
Elmleigh Road	B3
Emsworth Road	C2
Fairfield Road	B2-C2-C3
Fair Oak Drive	B4
Fraser Road	A3
Grove Road	B1-C1
Havant By-Pass	A1-B1-C1
Hipley Road	C4
James Road	A3
Juniper Square	B1-C1
Kingsworthy Road	C2
Leigh Road	B3-B4-C4
Lockerley Road	C4
Lower Grove Road	C1
Lymbourn Road	C1-C2
Market Parade	B2
Mavis Crescent	B3
Medstead Road	B4
Montgomery Road	C2
New Lane	C3-C4
New Road	A3-B3
North Close	C1
North Street	C2
Oaklands Road	C2
Orchard Road	C1
Park Road North	B2-B3
Park Road South	B1-B2
Park Way	A2-B2
Petersfield Road	B3-B4
Prince George Street	B2
Priorsdean Crescent	A4
Ranelagh Road	A2
Russell Road	B3
St Albans Road	C4
Slindon Gardens	B1
Solent Road	A1-B1
Soberton Road	A4
South Close	C1
South Street	B1-B2
Staunton Road	A2-A3
Stockheath Lane	A3-A4
Stroudwood Road	A4
Tarrant Gardens	A4
The Drive	B4
The Pallant	B2-C2
The Parchment	B1-B2
Timsbury Crescent	A3-A4
Wade Court Road	C1-C2
Waterloo Road	B2-C2
Wendover Road	A3-B3
West Street	A2-B2
Western Road	A2
Woodgreen Avenue	A3-A4

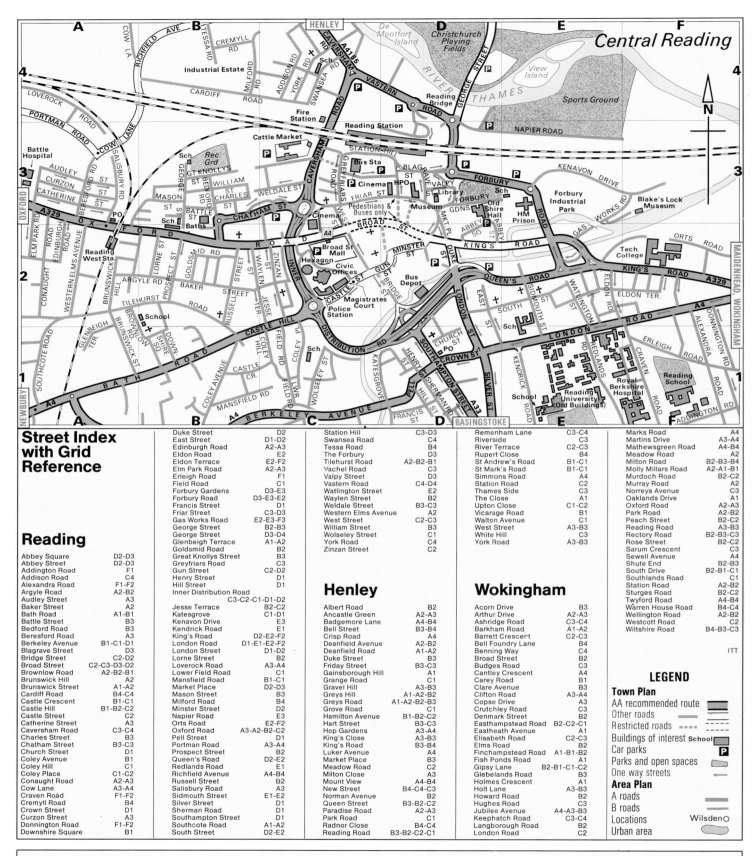

Central Reading

Street Index with Grid Reference

Reading

Abbey Square	D2-D3
Abbey Street	D2-D3
Addington Road	F1
Addison Road	C4
Alexandra Road	F1-F2
Argyle Road	A2-B2
Audley Street	A3
Baker Street	A2
Bath Road	A1-B1
Battle Street	B3
Bedford Road	B3
Beresford Road	A3
Berkeley Avenue	B1-C1-D1
Blagrave Street	D3
Bridge Street	C2-D2
Broad Street	C2-C3-D3-D2
Brownlow Road	A2-B2-B1
Brunswick Hill	A2
Brunswick Street	A1-A2
Cardiff Road	B4-C4
Castle Crescent	B1-C1
Castle Hill	B1-B2-C2
Castle Street	C2
Catherine Street	A3
Caversham Road	C3-C4
Charles Street	B3
Chatham Street	B3-C3
Church Street	D1
Coley Avenue	B1
Coley Hill	C1
Coley Place	C1-C2
Conaught Road	A2-A3
Cow Lane	A3-A4
Craven Road	F1-F2
Cremyll Road	B4
Crown Street	D1
Curzon Street	A3
Donnington Road	F1-F2
Downshire Square	B1
Duke Street	D2
East Street	D1-D2
Edinburgh Road	A2-A3
Eldon Road	E2
Eldon Terrace	E2-F2
Elm Park Road	A2-A3
Erleigh Road	F1
Field Road	C1
Forbury Gardens	D3-E3
Forbury Road	D3-E3-E2
Francis Street	D1
Friar Street	C3-D3
Gas Works Road	E2-E3-F3
George Street	B2-B3
George Street	D3-D4
Glenbeigh Terrace	A1-A2
Goldsmid Road	B2
Great Knollys Street	B3
Greyfriars Road	C3
Gun Street	C2-D2
Henry Street	D1
Hill Street	D1
Inner Distribution Road	C3-C2-C1-D1-D2
Jesse Terrace	B2-C2
Katesgrove	C1-D1
Kenavon Drive	E3
Kendrick Road	E1
King's Road	D2-E2-F2
London Road	D1-E1-E2-F2
London Street	D1-D2
Lorne Street	B2
Loverock Road	A3-A4
Lower Field Road	C1
Mansfield Road	B1-C1
Market Place	D2-D3
Mason Street	B3
Milford Road	B4
Minster Street	D2
Napier Road	E3
Orts Road	E2-F2
Oxford Road	A3-A2-B2-C2
Pell Street	D1
Portman Road	A3-A4
Prospect Street	B2
Queen's Road	D2-E2
Redlands Road	E1
Richfield Avenue	A4-B4
Russell Street	B2
Salisbury Road	A3
Sidmouth Street	E1-E2
Silver Street	D1
Sherman Road	D1
Southampton Street	D1
Southcote Road	A1-A2
South Street	D2-E2
Station Hill	C3-D3
Swansea Road	C4
Tessa Road	B4
The Forbury	D3
Tilehurst Road	A2-B2-B1
Vachel Road	C3
Valpy Street	D3
Vastern Road	C4-D4
Watlington Street	E2
Waylen Street	B2
Weldale Street	B3-C3
Western Elms Avenue	A2
West Street	C2-C3
William Street	B3
Wolseley Street	C1
York Road	C4
Zinzan Street	C2

Henley

Albert Road	B2
Ancastle Green	A2-A3
Badgemore Lane	A4-B4
Bell Street	B3-B4
Crisp Road	A4
Deanfield Avenue	A2-B2
Deanfield Road	A1-A2
Duke Street	B3
Friday Street	B3-C3
Gainsborough Hill	A1
Grange Road	C1
Gravel Hill	A3-B3
Greys Hill	A1-A2-B2
Greys Road	A1-A2-B2-B3
Grove Road	C1
Hamilton Avenue	B1-B2-C2
Hart Street	B3-C3
Hop Gardens	A3-A4
King's Close	A3-B3
King's Road	B3-B4
Luker Avenue	A4
Market Place	B3
Meadow Road	C2
Milton Close	A3
Mount View	A4-B4
New Street	B4-C4-C3
Norman Avenue	B2
Queen Street	B3-B2-C2
Paradise Road	A2-A3
Park Road	C1
Radnor Close	B4-C4
Reading Road	B3-B2-C2-C1

Wokingham

Acorn Drive	B3
Arthur Drive	A2-A3
Ashridge Road	C3-C4
Barkham Road	A1-A2
Barrett Crescent	C2-C3
Bell Foundry Lane	B4
Benning Way	C4
Broad Street	B2
Budges Road	C3
Cantley Crescent	A4
Carey Road	B1
Clare Avenue	B3
Clifton Road	A3-A4
Copse Drive	A3
Crutchley Road	C3
Denmark Street	B2
Easthampstead Road	B2-C2-C1
Eastheath Avenue	A1
Elisabeth Road	C2-C3
Elms Road	B2
Finchampstead Road	A1-B1-B2
Fish Ponds Road	A1
Gipsy Lane	B2-B1-C1-C2
Glebelands Road	B3
Holmes Crescent	A1
Holt Lane	A3-B3
Howard Road	B2
Hughes Road	C3
Jubilee Avenue	A4-A3-B3
Keephatch Road	C3-C4
Langborough Road	B2
London Road	C2

Marks Road	A4
Martins Drive	A3-A4
Mathewsgreen Road	A4-B4
Meadow Road	A2
Milton Road	B2-B3-B4
Molly Millars Road	A2-A1-B1
Murdoch Road	B2-C2
Murray Road	A2
Norreys Avenue	C3
Oaklands Drive	A1
Oxford Road	A2-A3
Park Road	A2-B2
Peach Street	B2-C2
Reading Road	A3-B3
Rectory Road	B2-B3-C3
Rose Street	B2-C2
Sarum Crescent	C3
Sewell Avenue	A4
Shute End	B2-B3
South Drive	B2-B1-C1
Southlands Road	C1
Station Road	A2-B2
Sturges Road	B2-C2
Twyford Road	A4-B4
Warren House Road	B4-C4
Wellington Road	A3-B3
Westcott Road	C2
Wiltshire Road	B4-B3-C3

ITT

LEGEND

Town Plan

- AA recommended route
- Other roads
- Restricted roads
- Buildings of interest — School
- Car parks — P
- Parks and open spaces
- One way streets

Area Plan

- A roads
- B roads
- Locations — Wilsden○
- Urban area

Reading

Shopping and light industry first spring to mind when thinking of Reading, but the town actually has a long and important history. Its rise to significance began in 1121 when Henry I founded an abbey here which became the third most important in England. However, after the Dissolution of the Monasteries, only a few ruins were left. Reading also used to be one of the major centres of the medieval cloth trade, but, already declining in the early 17th century, this source of income was reduced still further as a result of Civil War disturbances.

A fascinating collection of all types of farm implements and domestic equipment can be found in the extremely comprehensive Museum of English Rural Life, situated in the University Campus at Whiteknights Park. The town's own museum has major displays about nearby Silchester – the powerful Roman town of *Calleva*.

Henley-on-Thames, famous for its annual rowing regatta, is a lovely old town, well-provided with old coaching inns, Georgian façades and numerous listed buildings.

Wokingham has been a market town for centuries and over the years has been known for its silk industry and its bell-foundry. Half-timbered gabled houses can be seen in the town centre, although modern development surrounds it.

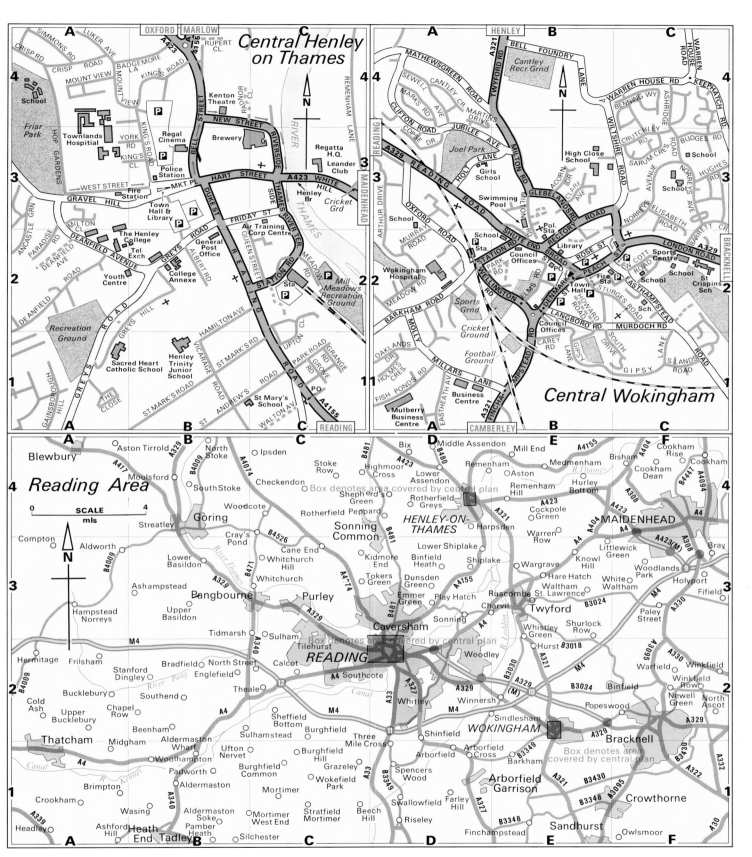

READING

Whiteknights, which consists of 300 acres of landscaped parkland, provides Reading's modern university with an incomparable campus setting and includes a conservation area and a biological reserve for research purposes.

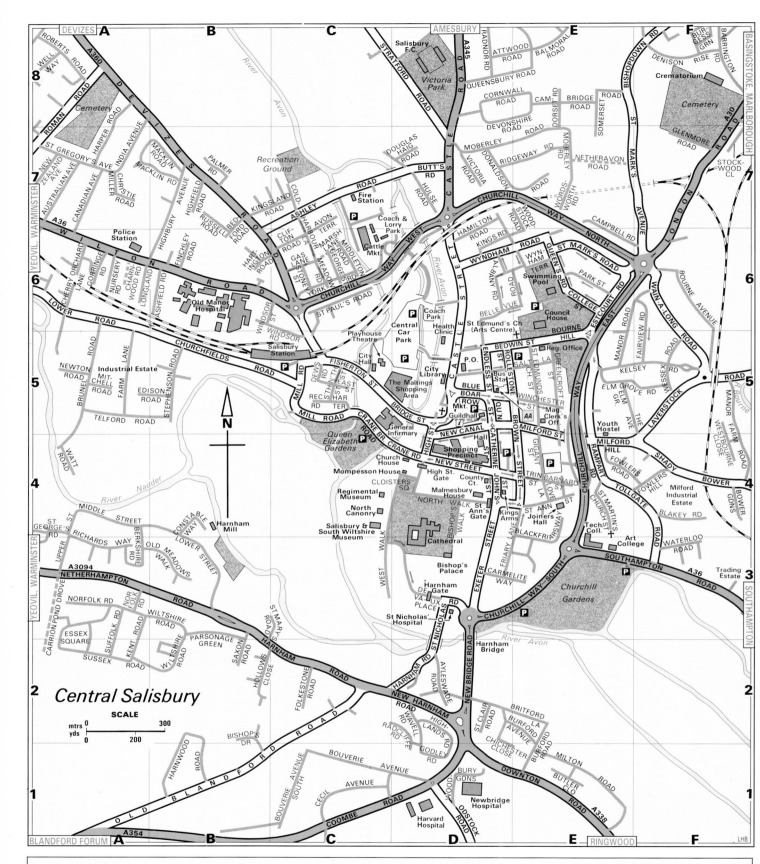

Salisbury

Its attractive site where the waters of the Avon and Nadder meet, its beautiful cathedral and its unspoilt centre put Salisbury among England's finest cities. In 1220 the people of the original settlement at Old Sarum, two miles to the north, moved down to the plain and laid the first stone of the cathedral.

Within 38 years it was completed and the result

is a superb example of Early English architecture. The cloisters are the largest in England and the spire the tallest in Britain. All the houses within the Cathedral Close were built for cathedral functionaries, and although many have Georgian facades, most date back to the 13th century. Mompesson House is one of the handsome mansions here and as it belongs to the National Trust, its equally fine interior can be seen. Another building houses the Museum of the Duke of Edinburgh's Royal Regiment, At one time, relations

between the clergy and the citizens of Salisbury were not always harmonious, so the former built a protective wall around the Close.

The streets of the modern city follow the medieval grid pattern of squares, or 'chequers', and the tightly-packed houses provide a very pleasing townscape. Salisbury was granted its first charter in 1227 and flourished as a market and wool centre; there is still a twice-weekly market in the spacious square.

236

Salisbury Area

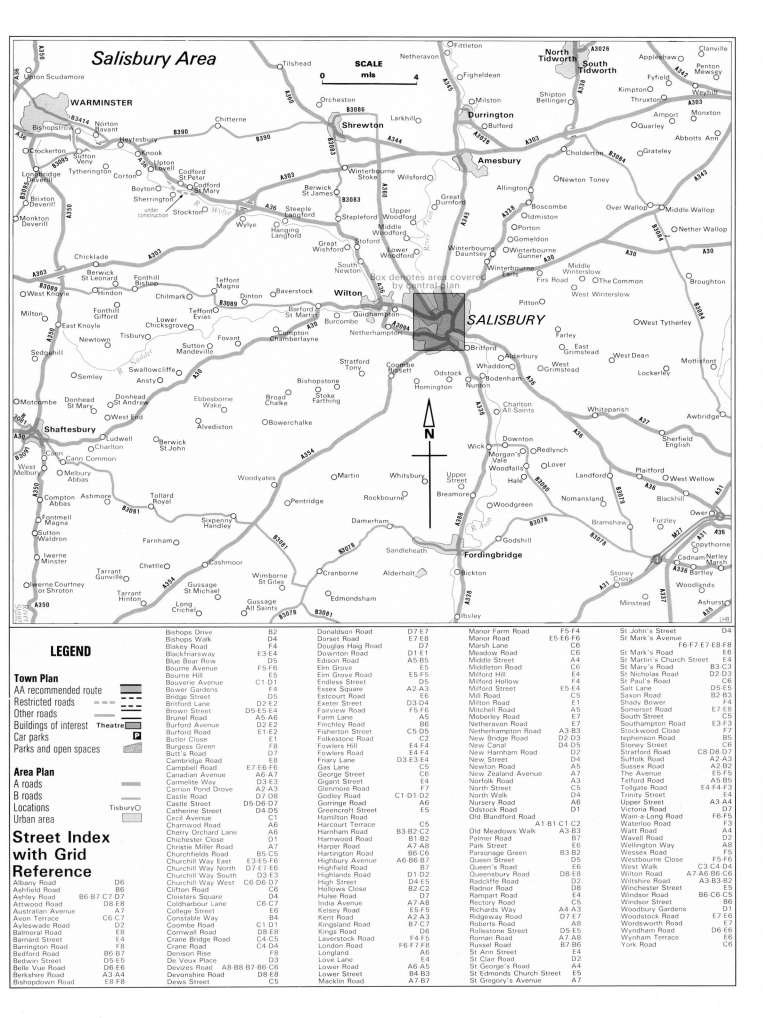

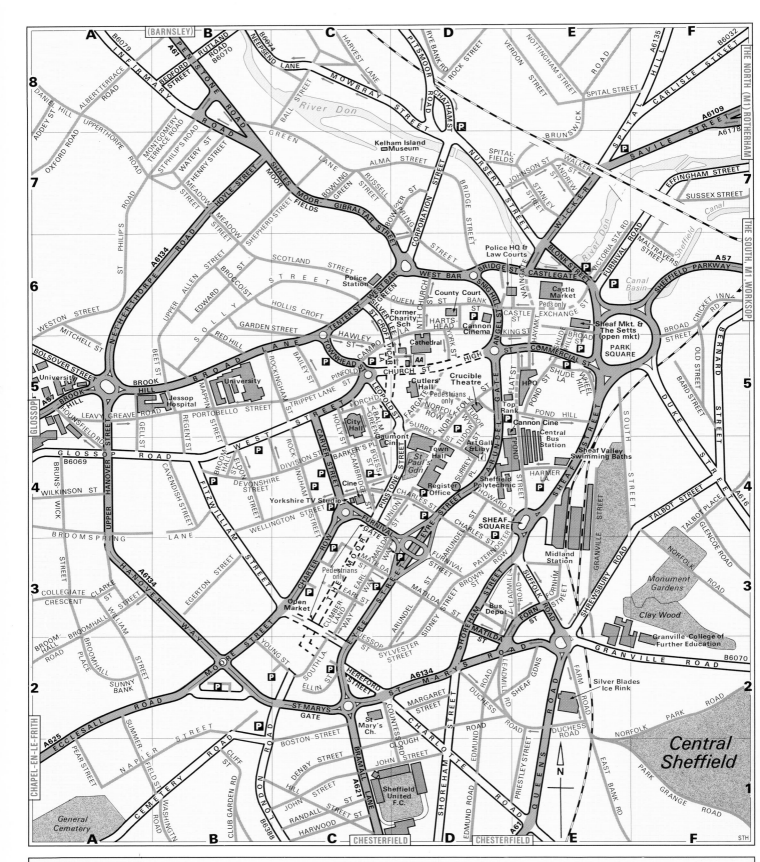

Sheffield

Cutlery – which has made the name of Sheffield famous throughout the world – has been manufactured here since at least as early as the time of Chaucer. The god of blacksmiths, Vulcan, is the symbol of the city's industry, and he crowns the town hall, which was opened in 1897 by Queen Victoria. At the centre of the industry, however, is Cutlers' Hall, the headquarters of the Company of Cutlers. This society was founded in 1624 and has the right to grant trade marks to articles of a sufficiently high standard. In the hall is the company's collection of silver, with examples of craftsmanship dating back every year to 1773. A really large collection of cutlery is kept in the city museum. Steel production, a vital component of the industry, was greatly improved when the crucible process was invented here in 1740. At Abbeydale Industrial Hamlet, 3½ miles south-west of the city centre, is a complete restored site open as a museum and showing 18th-century methods of steel production. Sheffield's centre, transformed since World War II, is one of the finest and most modern in Europe. There are no soot-grimed industrial eyesores here, for the city has stringent pollution controls and its buildings are carefully planned and set within excellent landscaping projects. Many parks are set in and around the city, and the Pennines are within easy reach.

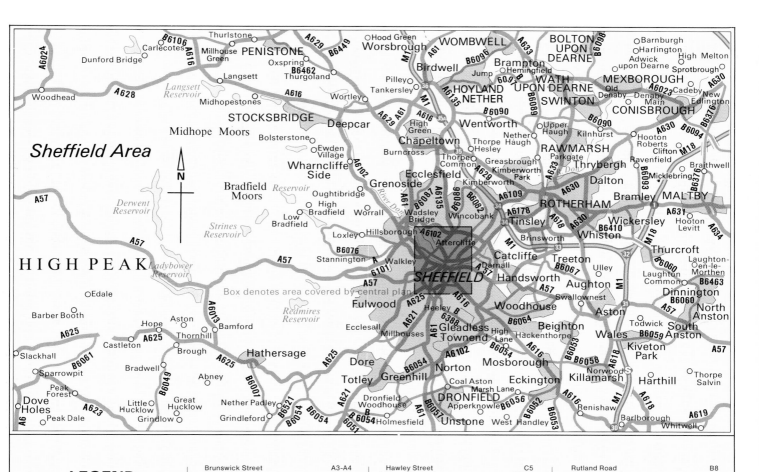

Sheffield Area

LEGEND

Town Plan
- AA Recommended roads
- Other roads
- Restricted roads
- Buildings of interest
- One Way streets
- Car Parks
- Parks and open spaces

Area Plan
- A roads
- B roads
- Locations — Hartshead ○
- Urban area

Street Index with grid reference

Sheffield

Addey Street	A7-A8
Albert Terrace Road	A8
Alma Street	C7 D7
Andrew Street	E7
Angel Street	D5-D6
Arundel Gate	D4-D5
Arundel Street	C2-D2-D3-D4
Bailey Street	C5
Ball Street	C8
Balm Green	C4-C5
Bank Street	D6
Bard Street	F5
Barker's Pool	C4-C5-D5
Bedford Street	B8
Beet Street	B5
Bernard Street	F4-F5-F6
Blonk Street	E6
Bolsover Street	A5
Boston Street	C1-C2
Bower Street	C7-D7
Bowling Green	C7
Bramall Lane	C1-C2
Bridge Street	D7-D6-E6
Broad Lane	B5-C5-C6
Broad Street	E6-F5-F6
Brocco Street	B6
Brook Hill	A5-B5
Broomhall Place	A2
Broomhall Road	A2
Broomhall Street	A2-A3-B4
Broomspring Lane	A4-B4
Brown Street	D3

Brunswick Street	A3-A4
Brunswick Road	E7-E8
Burgess Street	C4
Cambridge Street	C4
Campo Lane	C5-D5-D6
Carlisle Street	F8
Carver Street	C4-C5
Castle Street	D6-E6
Castlegate	E6
Cavendish Street	B4
Cemetery Road	A1-B1-B2
Charles Street	D3-D4
Charlotte Road	C2-D2-D1-E1
Charter Row	C3-C4
Chatham Street	D7-D8
Church Street	C5-D5
Clarke Street	A3
Cliff Street	B1
Clough Road	C1-D1-D2
Club Garden Road	B1
Collegiate Crescent	A3
Commercial Street	E5
Corporation Street	D6-D7
Countess Road	C2-D2-D1
Cricket Inn Road	F6
Cumberland Way	C3
Daniel Hill	A8
Denby Street	C1
Devonshire Street	B4-C4
Division Street	C4
Duchess Road	D2-E2
Duke Street	F4-F5
Earl Street	C3
Earl Way	C3
East Bank Road	E1-E2
Ecclesall Road	A1-A2-B2
Edmund Road	D1-D2
Edward Street	B6
Effingham Street	F7
Egerton Street	B3
Eldon Street	B4
Ellin Street	C2
Eyre Street	C2-C3-D3-D4
Exchange Street	E6
Fargate	D5
Farm Road	E2
Fitzwilliam Street	B4-B3-C3
Flat Street	E5
Fornham Street	E3
Furnival Gate	C3-C4-D3-D4
Furnival Road	E6-F6-F7
Furnival Street	D3
Garden Street	B6-C6-C5
Gell Street	A4-A5
Gibraltar Street	C7-C6-D6
Glencoe Road	F3-F4
Glossop Road	A4-B4
Granville Road	E2-F2
Granville Street	E3-E4
Green Lane	B8-C8-C7
Hanover Way	A3-B3-B2
Harmer Lane	E4
Hartshead	D6
Harwood Street	C1
Harvest Lane	C8

Hawley Street	C5
Haymarket	E5-E6
Henry Street	B7
Hereford Street	C2
High Street	D5-E5
Hill Street	B1-C1
Hollis Croft	B6-C6
Holly Street	C4-C5
Hounsfield Road	A4-A5
Howard Street	D4-E4
Hoyle Street	B7
Infirmary Road	A8-B8 B7
Jessop Street	C2
John Street	C1-D1
Johnson Street	D7-E7
King Street	D5-E5-E6
Leadmill Road	D2-D3-E3
Leavy Greave Road	A5-B5
Lee Croft	C5-C6
Leopold Street	C5-D5
London Road	C1-B1-B2-C2
Maltravers Street	F6
Mappin Street	B4-B5
Margaret Street	D2
Matilda Street	C3-D3-D2
Matilda Way	C3
Meadow Street	B6-B7
Mitchell Street	A5-A6
Montgomery Terrace Road	A7-B7-B8
Moorfields	C7
Moore Street	B2-B3-C3
Mowbray Street	C8-D8-D7
Napier Street	A1-B1-B2
Neepsend Lane	B8-C8
Netherthorpe Road	A5-A6-B6-B7
Norfolk Park Road	E1-E2-F2
Norfolk Road	F3-F4
Norfolk Row	D5
Norfolk Street	D4-D5
North Church Street	D6
Nottingham Street	E8
Nursery Street	D7-E7-E6
Old Street	F5-F6
Orchard Lane	C5
Oxford Road	A7-A8
Park Grange Road	E1-F1
Park Square	E5-E6-F6-F5
Paternoster Row	D3-D4-E4
Pear Street	A1
Penistone Road	B7-B8
Pinfold Street	C5
Pinstone Street	C4-D4-D5
Pitsmoor Road	D8
Pond Hill	E5
Pond Street	E4-E5
Portobello Street	B5-C5
Priestley Street	D1-E1-E2
Queen Street	C6-D6
Queen's Road	E1-E2
Randall Street	C1
Red Hill	B5-B6
Regent Street	B4-B5
Rock Street	D8
Rockingham Street	B5-C5-C4
Russell Street	C7

Rutland Road	B8
Rye Bank Road	D8
St Mary's Gate	C2
St Mary's Road	C2-D2-E2
St Philip's Road	A6-A7-B7-B8
Savile Street	E7-F7-F8
Scotland Street	B6-C6
Shales Moor	B7-C7
Sheaf Gardens	D2-E2
Sheaf Street	E4-E5
Sheffield Parkway	F6
Shepherd Street	B6-B7-C7
Shoreham Street	D1-D2-D3-E3
Shrewsbury Road	E3-E4-F3-F4
Shude Lane	E5
Shude Hill	E5-E6
Sidney Street	D3
Silver Street	C6
Snig Hill	D6
Solly Street	B5-B6-C6
South Lane	C2
South Street	E4-E5
Spital Hill	E7-E8-F8
Spital Street	E8-F8
Spitalfields	D7-E7
Spring Street	D6-D7
Stanley Street	E7
Suffolk Road	E3
Summerfield Street	A2-A1-B1
Sunny Bank	A2
Surrey Place	D4
Surrey Street	D4-D5
Sussex Street	F7
Sylvester Street	C2-D2
Talbot Place	F4
Talbot Street	F4
Tenter Street	C6
The Moor	C3-C4
Townhead Street	C5
Trippet Lane	C5
Tudor Street	D4-D5
Tudor Way	D5
Union Street	C4-D4
Upper Allen Street	B6
Upper Hanover Street	A3-A4-A5
Upperthorpe Road	A7-A8
Verdon Street	D8-E8
Vicar Lane	C5-D5
Victoria Station Road	E6-E7-F7
Waingate	E6
Walker Street	E7
Washington Road	B1
Watery Street	B7-B8
Wellington Street	B4-C4
West Bar	D6
West Bar Green	C6-D6
West Street	B4-B5-C5
Weston Street	A5-A6
Wheel Hill	E5
Wicker	E6-E7
Wilkinson Street	A4
William Street	A2-A3
York Street	D5-D6
Young Street	B2-C2

239

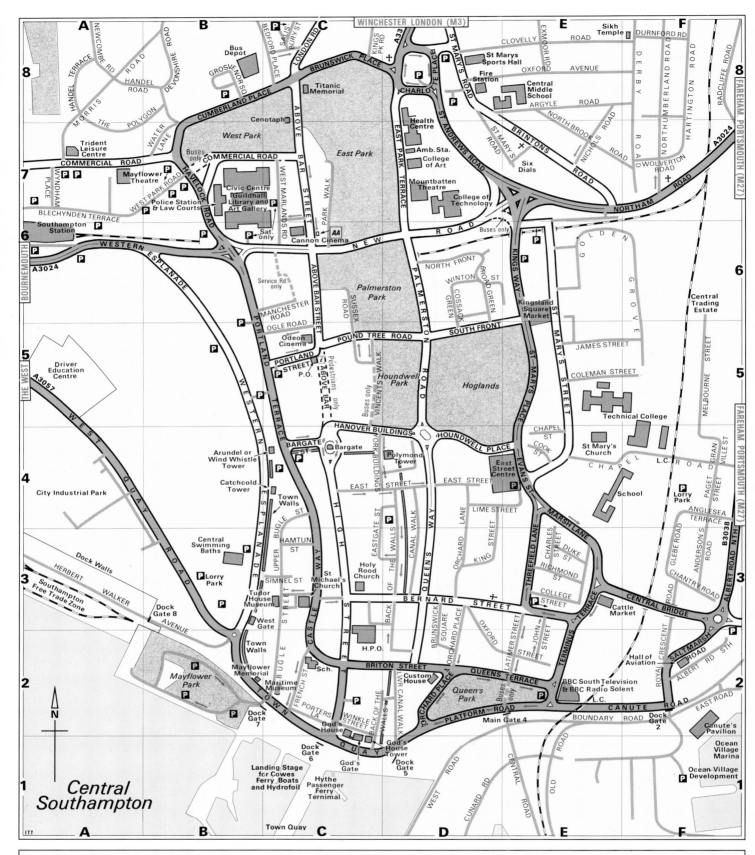

Southampton

In the days of the great ocean-going liners, Southampton was Britain's premier passenger port. Today container traffic is more important, but cruise liners still berth there. A unique double tide caused by the Solent waters, and protection from the open sea by the Isle of Wight, has meant that Southampton has always been a superb and important port. Like many great cities it was devastated by bombing raids during World War II. However, enough survives to make the city a fascinating place to explore. Outstanding are the town walls, which stand to their original height in some places, especially along Western Esplanade. The main landward entrance to the walled town was the Bargate – a superb medieval gateway with a Guildhall (now a museum) on its upper floor. The best place to appreciate old Southampton is in and around St Michael's Square. Here is St Michael's Church, oldest in the city and founded in 1070. Opposite is Tudor House Museum, a lovely gabled building housing much of interest. Down Bugle Street are old houses, with the town walls, pierced by the 13th-century West Gate, away to the right. At the corner of Bugle Street is the Wool House Maritime Museum, contained in a 14th-century warehouse. On the quayside is God's House Tower, part of the town's defences and now an archaeological museum.

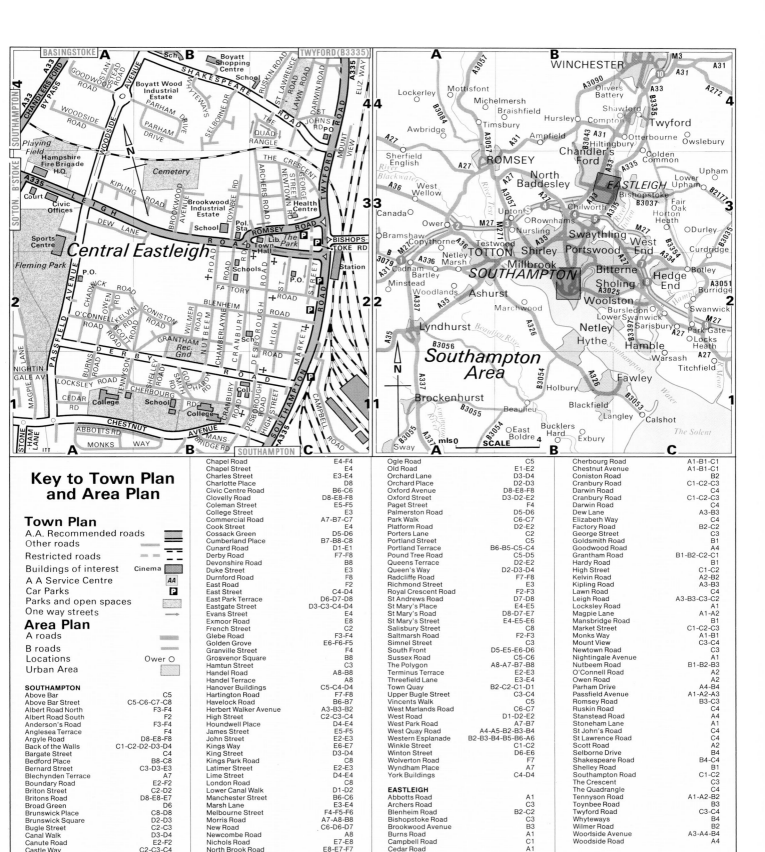

SOUTHAMPTON

Although liners still use Southampton's docks which handled all the great ocean-going passenger ships before the age of air travel replaced sea travel, the port is chiefly used by commercial traffic today.

241

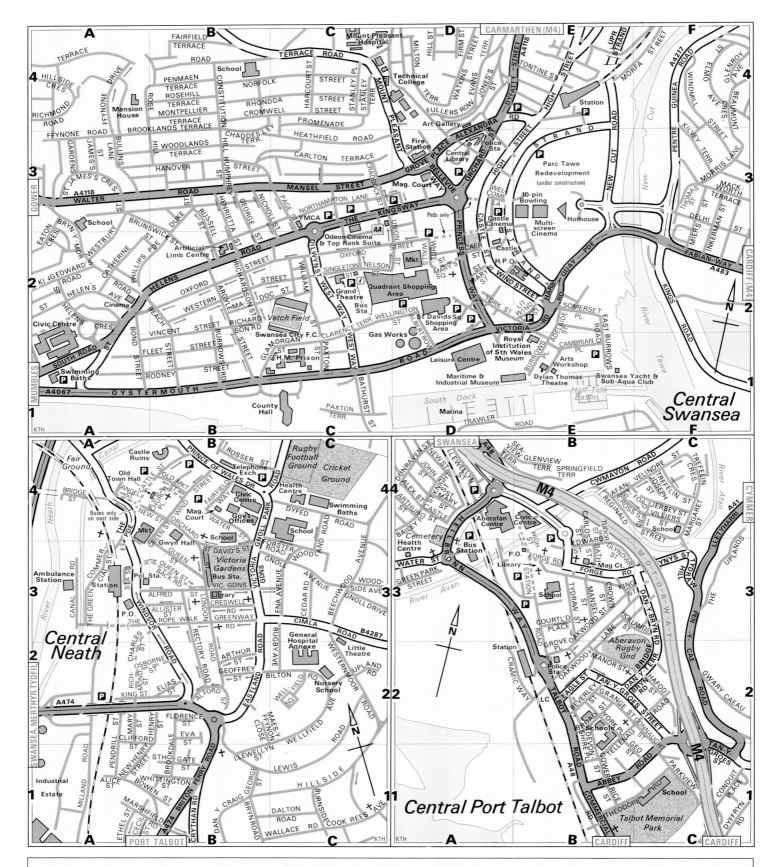

Swansea

Like nearly all towns in the valleys and along the coast of Glamorgan, Swansea grew at an amazing speed during the Industrial Revolution. Ironworks, non-ferrous metal smelting works and mills and factories of every kind were built to produce the goods which were exported from the city's docks. There had been a settlement here from very early times - the city's name is derived from Sweyn's Ea

- Ea means island, and Sweyn was a Viking pirate who had a base here. Heavy industry is still pre-eminent in the area, but commerce is of increasing importance and the university exerts a strong influence. Hundreds of acres of parkland and open space lie in and around the city, and just to the west is the Gower, one of the most beautiful areas of Wales. The history of Swansea is traced in the Maritime and Industrial Museum and Royal Institution of South Wales Museum, while the Glynn Vivian Art Gallery contains notable paintings and

porcelain.

Neath and *Port Talbot* are, like Swansea, dominated by heavy industry. Neath was once a Roman station, and later had a castle and an abbey, ruins of which can still be seen. Port Talbot has been an industrial centre since 1770, when a copper-smelting works was built. Steelworks and petrochemical works stretch for miles around Swansea Bay.

242

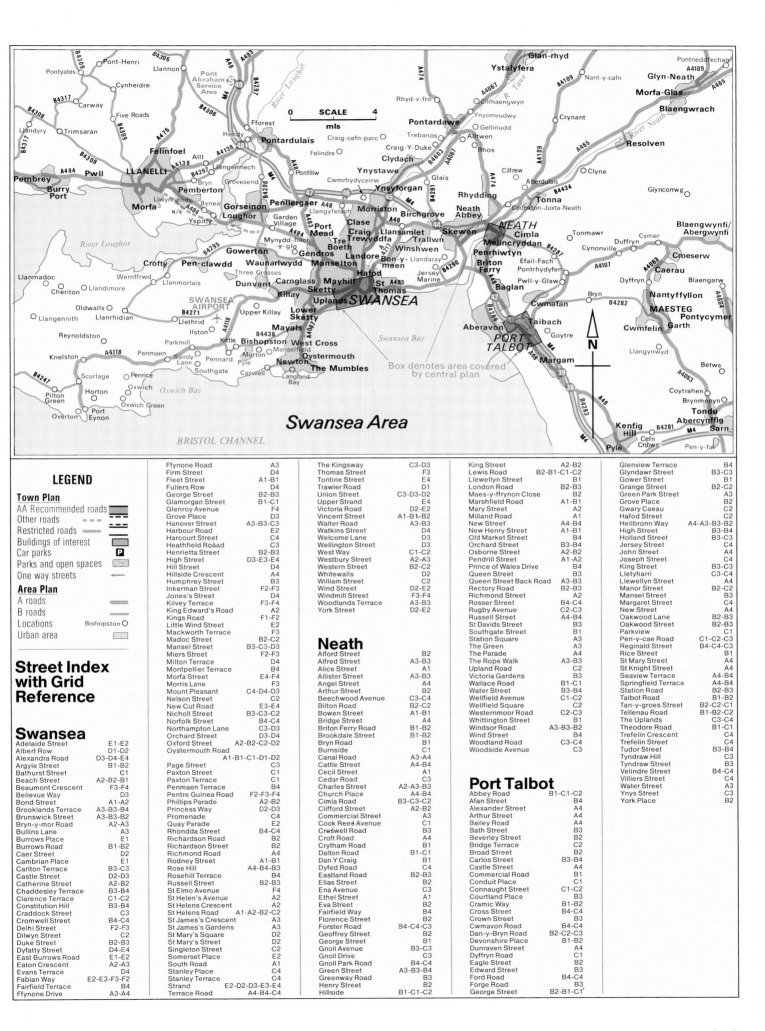

Swansea Area

SCALE 0 — 4 mls

BRISTOL CHANNEL

Box denotes area covered by central plan

LEGEND

Town Plan
- AA Recommended roads
- Other roads
- Restricted roads
- Buildings of interest
- Car parks [P]
- Parks and open spaces
- One way streets

Area Plan
- A roads
- B roads
- Locations   Bishopston ○
- Urban area

Street Index with Grid Reference

Swansea

Adelaide Street	E1-E2
Albert Row	D1-D2
Alexandra Road	D3-D4-E4
Argyle Street	B1-B2
Bathurst Street	C1
Beach Street	A2-B2-B1
Beaumont Crescent	F3-F4
Bellevue Way	D3
Bond Street	A1-A2
Brooklands Terrace	A3-B3-B4
Brunswick Street	A3-B3-B2
Bryn-y-mor Road	A2-A3
Bullins Lane	A3
Burrows Place	E1
Burrows Road	B1-B2
Caer Street	D2
Cambrian Place	E1
Carlton Terrace	B3-C3
Castle Street	D2-D3
Catherine Street	A2-B2
Chaddesley Terrace	B3-B4
Clarence Terrace	C1-C2
Constitution Hill	B3-B4
Craddock Street	C3
Cromwell Street	B4-C4
Delhi Street	F2-F3
Dilwyn Street	C2
Duke Street	B2-B3
Dyfatty Street	D4-E4
East Burrows Road	E1-E2
Eaton Crescent	A2-A3
Evans Terrace	D4
Fabian Way	E2-E3-F3-F2
Fairfield Terrace	B4
Ffynone Drive	A3-A4

Ffynone Road	A3
Firm Street	D4
Fleet Street	A1-B1
Fullers Row	D4
George Street	B2-B3
Glamorgan Street	B1-C1
Glenroy Avenue	F4
Grove Place	D3
Hanover Street	A3-B3-C3
Harbour Road	E2
Harcourt Street	C4
Heathfield Road	C3
Henrietta Street	B2-B3
High Street	D3-E3-E4
Hill Street	D4
Hillside Crescent	A4
Humphrey Street	B3
Inkerman Street	F2-F3
Jones's Street	D4
Kilvey Terrace	F3-F4
King Edward's Road	A2
Kings Road	F1-F2
Little Wind Street	E2
Mackworth Terrace	F3
Madoc Street	B2-C2
Mansel Street	B3-C3-D3
Miers Street	F2-F3
Milton Terrace	D4
Montpellier Terrace	B4
Morfa Street	E4-F4
Morris Lane	F3
Mount Pleasant	C4-D4-D3
Nelson Street	C2
New Cut Road	E3-E4
Nicholl Street	B3-C3-C2
Norfolk Street	B4-C4
Northampton Lane	C3-D3
Orchard Street	D3-D4
Oxford Street	A2-B2-C2-D2
Oystermouth Road	A1-B1-C1-D1-D2
Page Street	C3
Paxton Street	C1
Paxton Terrace	C1
Penmaen Terrace	B4
Pentre Guinea Road	F2-F3-F4
Phillips Parade	A2-B2
Princess Way	D2-D3
Promenade	C4
Quay Parade	E2
Rhondda Street	B4-C4
Richardson Road	B2
Richardson Street	B2
Richmond Road	A4
Rodney Street	A1-B1
Rose Hill	A4-B4-B3
Rosehill Terrace	B4
Russell Street	B2-B3
St Elmo Avenue	F4
St Helen's Avenue	A2
St Helens Crescent	A2
St Helens Road	A1-A2-B2-C2
St James's Crescent	A3
St James's Gardens	A3
St Mary's Square	D2
St Mary's Street	D2
Singleton Street	C2
Somerset Place	E2
South Road	A1
Stanley Place	C4
Stanley Terrace	C4
Strand	E2-D2-D3-E3-E4
Terrace Road	A4-B4-C4

The Kingsway	C3-D3
Thomas Street	F3
Tontine Street	E4
Trawler Road	D1
Union Street	C3-D3-D2
Upper Strand	E4
Victoria Road	D2-E2
Vincent Street	A1-B1-B2
Walter Road	A3-B3
Watkins Street	D4
Welcome Lane	D3
Wellington Street	D3
West Way	C1-C2
Westbury Street	A2-A3
Western Street	B2-C2
Whitewalls	D2
William Street	C2
Wind Street	D2-E2
Windmill Street	F3-F4
Woodlands Terrace	A3-B3
York Street	D2-E2

Neath

Alford Street	B2
Alfred Street	A3-B3
Alice Street	A1
Allister Street	A3-B3
Angel Street	A4
Arthur Street	B2
Beechwood Avenue	C3-C4
Bilton Road	B2-C2
Bowen Street	A1-B1
Bridge Street	A4
Briton Ferry Road	B1-B2
Brookdale Street	B1-B2
Bryn Road	B1
Burnside	C1
Canal Road	A3-A4
Cattle Street	A4-B4
Cecil Street	A1
Cedar Road	C3
Charles Street	A2-A3-B3
Church Place	A4-B4
Cimla Road	B3-C3-C2
Clifford Street	A2-B2
Commercial Street	A3
Cook Rees Avenue	C1
Creswell Road	B3
Croft Road	A4
Crytham Road	B1
Dalton Road	B1-C1
Dan Y Craig	B1
Dyfed Street	C4
Eastland Road	B2-B3
Elias Street	B2
Ena Avenue	C3
Ethel Street	A1
Eva Street	B2
Fairfield Way	B4
Florence Street	B2
Forster Road	B4-C4-C3
Geoffrey Street	B2
George Street	B1
Gnoll Avenue	B3-C3
Gnoll Drive	C3
Gnoll Park Road	B4-C4
Green Street	A3-B3-B4
Greenway Road	B3
Henry Street	B2
Hillside	B1-C1-C2

King Street	A2-B2
Lewis Road	B2-B1-C1-C2
Llewellyn Street	B1
London Road	B2-B3
Maes-y-ffrynon Close	B2
Marshfield Road	A1-B1
Mary Street	A2
Milland Road	A1
New Street	A4-B4
New Henry Street	A1-B1
Old Market Street	B4
Orchard Street	B3-B4
Osborne Street	A2-B2
Pendrill Street	A1-A2
Prince of Wales Drive	B4
Queen Street	B3
Queen Street Back Road	A3-B3
Rectory Road	B2-B3
Richmond Street	A2
Rosser Street	B4-C4
Rugby Avenue	C2-C3
Russell Street	A4-B4
St Davids Street	B3
Southgate Street	B1
Station Square	A3
The Green	A3
The Parade	A4
The Rope Walk	A3-B3
Upland Road	C2
Victoria Gardens	B3
Wallace Road	B1-C1
Water Street	B3-B4
Wellfield Avenue	C1-C2
Wellfield Square	C2
Westernmoor Road	C2-C3
Whittington Street	B1
Windsor Road	A3-B3-B2
Wind Street	B4
Woodland Road	C3-C4
Woodside Avenue	C3

Port Talbot

Abbey Road	B1-C1-C2
Afan Street	B4
Alexander Street	A4
Arthur Street	A4
Bailey Road	A4
Bath Street	B3
Beverley Street	B2
Bridge Terrace	C2
Broad Street	B2
Carlos Street	B3-B4
Castle Street	A4
Commercial Road	B1
Conduit Place	C1
Connaught Street	C1-C2
Courtland Place	B3
Cramic Way	B1-B2
Cross Street	B4-C4
Crown Street	B3
Cwmavon Road	B4-C4
Dan-y-Bryn Road	B2-C2-C3
Devonshire Place	B1-B2
Dunraven Street	A4
Dyffryn Road	C1
Eagle Street	B2
Edward Street	B3
Ford Road	B4-C4
Forge Road	B3
George Street	B2-B1-C1

Glenview Terrace	B4
Glyndawr Street	B3-C3
Gower Street	B1
Grange Street	B2-C2
Green Park Street	A3
Grove Place	B2
Gwary Caeau	C2
Hafod Street	C2
Heilbronn Way	A4-A3-B3-B2
High Street	B3-B4
Holland Street	B3-C3
Jersey Street	C4
John Street	A4
Joseph Street	C4
King Street	B3-C3
Lletyharri	C3-C4
Llewellyn Street	A4
Manor Street	B2-C2
Mansel Street	B3
Margaret Street	C4
New Street	A4
Oakwood Lane	B2-B3
Oakwood Street	B2-B3
Parkview	C1
Pen-y-cae Road	C1-C2-C3
Reginald Street	B4-C4-C3
Rice Street	B1
St Mary Street	A4
St Knight Street	A4
Seaview Terrace	A4-B4
Springfield Terrace	A4-B4
Station Road	B2-B3
Talbot Road	B1-B2
Tan-y-groes Street	B2-C2-C1
Tellenau Road	B1-B2-C2
The Uplands	C3-C4
Theodore Road	B1-C1
Trefelin Crescent	C4
Trefelin Street	C4
Tudor Street	B3-B4
Tyndraw Hill	C3
Tyndraw Street	B3
Velindre Street	B4-C4
Villiers Street	C4
Water Street	A3
Ynys Street	C3
York Place	B2

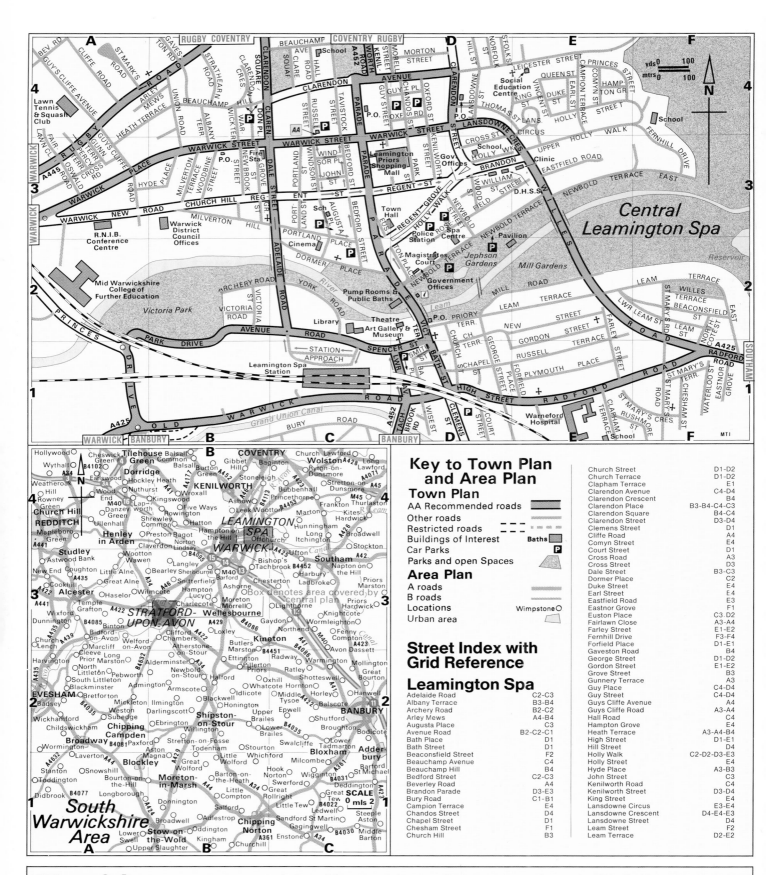

Key to Town Plan and Area Plan

Town Plan
AA Recommended roads
Other roads
Restricted roads
Buildings of Interest — Baths
Car Parks — P
Parks and open Spaces

Area Plan
A roads
B roads
Locations — Wimpstone ○
Urban area

Street Index with Grid Reference

Leamington Spa

Adelaide Road	C2-C3
Albany Terrace	B3-B4
Archery Road	B2-C2
Arley Mews	A4-B4
Augusta Place	C3
Avenue Road	B2-C2-C1
Bath Place	D1
Bath Street	D1
Beaconsfield Street	F2
Beauchamp Avenue	C4
Beauchamp Hill	B4
Bedford Street	C2-C3
Beverley Road	A4
Brandon Parade	D3-E3
Bury Road	C1-B1
Campion Terrace	E4
Chandos Street	D4
Chapel Street	D1
Chesham Street	F1
Church Hill	B3
Church Street	D1-D2
Church Terrace	D1-D2
Clapham Terrace	E1
Clarendon Avenue	C4-D4
Clarendon Crescent	B4
Clarendon Place	B3-B4-C4-C3
Clarendon Square	B4-C4
Clarendon Street	D3-D4
Clemens Street	D1
Cliffe Road	A4
Comyn Street	E4
Court Street	D1
Cross Road	A3
Cross Street	D3
Dale Street	B3-C3
Dormer Place	C2
Duke Street	E4
Earl Street	E4
Eastfield Road	E3
Eastnor Grove	F1
Euston Place	C3-D2
Fairlawn Close	A3-A4
Farley Street	E1-E2
Fernhill Drive	F3-F4
Forfield Place	D1-E1
Gaveston Road	B4
George Street	D1-D2
Gordon Street	E1-E2
Grove Street	B3
Gunnery Terrace	A3
Guy Place	C4-D4
Guy Street	C4-D4
Guys Cliffe Avenue	A4
Guys Cliffe Road	A3-A4
Hall Road	C4
Hampton Grove	E4
Heath Terrace	A3-A4-B4
High Street	D1-E1
Hill Street	D4
Holly Walk	C2-D2-D3-E3
Holly Street	E4
Hyde Place	A3-B3
John Street	C3
Kenilworth Road	C4
Kenilworth Street	D3-D4
King Street	E4
Lansdowne Circus	E3-E4
Lansdowne Crescent	D4-E4-E3
Lansdowne Street	D4
Leam Street	F2
Leam Terrace	D2-E2

Warwick

The old county town of the shire, Warwick lies in the shadow of its massive, historic castle which occupies the rocky ridge above the River Avon. Thomas Beauchamp and his son built the huge towers and curtain walls in the 14th century, but it was the Jacobean holders of the earldom, the Grevilles, who transformed the medieval stronghold into a nobleman's residence. In 1694,

the heart of the town was almost completely destroyed by fire and the few medieval buildings that survived lie on the outskirts of the present 18th-century centre. Of these Oken House, now a doll museum, and Lord Leycester's Hospital, almshouses dating back to the 14th century, are particularly striking.

Stratford-upon-Avon, as the birthplace of William Shakespeare, England's most famous poet and playwright, is second only to London as a

tourist attraction. This charming old market town is a living memorial to him; his plays are performed in the Royal Shakespeare Theatre which dominates the river bank, a waxwork museum specialises in scenes from his works, and his childhood home in Henley Street is a museum.

Leamington Spa, an inland spa on the River Leam, gained the prefix 'Royal' after Queen Victoria had visited it in 1838, and the town has been a fashionable health resort ever since.

244

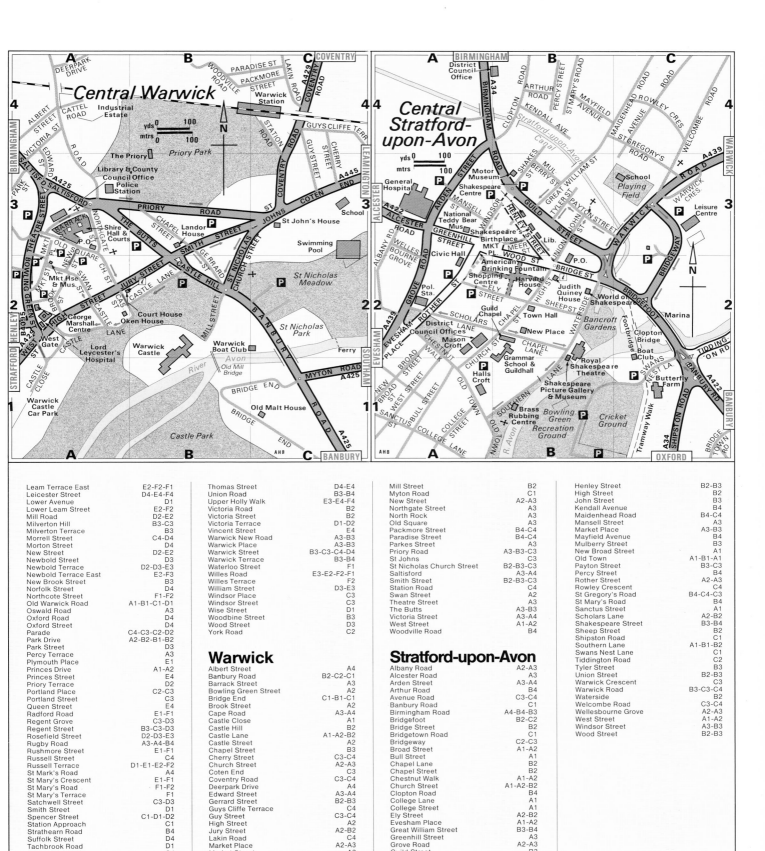

Central Warwick

Central Stratford-upon-Avon

Leam Terrace East	E2-F2-F1	Thomas Street	D4-E4	Mill Street	B2	Henley Street	B2-B3
Leicester Street	D4-E4-F4	Union Road	B3-B4	Myton Road	C1	High Street	B2
Lower Avenue	D1	Upper Holly Walk	E3-E4-F4	New Street	A2-A3	John Street	B3
Lower Leam Street	E2-F2	Victoria Road	B2	Northgate Street	A3	Kendall Avenue	B4
Mill Road	D2-E2	Victoria Street	B2	North Rock	A3	Maidenhead Road	B4-C4
Milverton Hill	B3-C3	Victoria Terrace	D1-D2	Old Square	A3	Mansell Street	A3
Milverton Terrace	B3	Vincent Street	E4	Packmore Street	B4-C4	Market Place	A3-B3
Morrell Street	C4-D4	Warwick New Road	A3-B3	Paradise Street	B4-C4	Mayfield Avenue	B4
Morton Street	D4	Warwick Place	A3-B3	Parkes Street	A3	Mulberry Street	B3
New Street	D2-E2	Warwick Street	B3-C3-C4-D4	Priory Road	A3-B3-C3	New Broad Street	A1
Newbold Street	D3	Warwick Terrace	B3-B4	St Johns	C3	Old Town	A1-B1-A1
Newbold Terrace	D2-D3-E3	Waterloo Street	F1	St Nicholas Church Street	B2-B3-C3	Payton Street	B3-C3
Newbold Terrace East	E3-F3	Willes Road	E3-E2-F2-F1	Saltisford	A3-A4	Percy Street	B4
New Brook Street	B3	Willes Terrace	F2	Smith Street	B2-B3-C3	Rother Street	A2-A3
Norfolk Street	D4	William Street	D3-E3	Station Road	C4	Rowley Crescent	C4
Northcote Street	F1-F2	Windsor Place	C3	Swan Street	A2	St Gregory's Road	B4-C4-C3
Old Warwick Road	A1-B1-C1-D1	Windsor Street	C3	Theatre Street	A3	St Mary's Road	B4
Oswald Road	A3	Wise Street	D1	The Butts	A3-B3	Sanctus Street	A1
Oxford Road	D4	Woodbine Street	B3	Victoria Street	A3-A4	Scholars Lane	A2-B2
Oxford Street	D4	Wood Street	D3	West Street	A1-A2	Shakespeare Street	B3-B4
Parade	C4-C3-C2-D2	York Road	C2	Woodville Road	B4	Sheep Street	B2
Park Drive	A2-B2-B1-B2					Shipston Road	C1
Park Street	D3					Southern Lane	A1-B1-B2
Percy Terrace	A3	**Warwick**		**Stratford-upon-Avon**		Swans Nest Lane	C1
Plymouth Place	E1	Albert Street	A4	Albany Road	A2-A3	Tiddington Road	C2
Princes Drive	A1-A2	Banbury Road	B2-C2-C1	Alcester Road	A3	Tyler Street	B3
Princes Street	E4	Barrack Street	A3	Arden Street	A3-A4	Union Street	B2-B3
Priory Terrace	D2	Bowling Green Street	A2	Arthur Road	B4	Warwick Crescent	C3
Portland Place	C2-C3	Bridge End	C1-B1-C1	Avenue Road	C3-C4	Warwick Road	B3-C3-C4
Portland Street	C3	Brook Street	A2	Banbury Road	C1	Waterside	B2
Queen Street	E4	Cape Road	A3-A4	Birmingham Road	A4-B4-B3	Welcombe Road	C3-C4
Radford Road	E1-F1	Castle Close	A1	Bridgefoot	B2-C2	Wellesbourne Grove	A2-A3
Regent Grove	C3-D3	Castle Hill	B2	Bridge Street	B2	West Street	A1-A2
Regent Street	B3-C3-D3	Castle Lane	A1-A2-B2	Bridgetown Road	C1	Windsor Street	A3-B3
Rosefield Street	D2-D3-E3	Castle Street	B2	Bridgeway	C2-C3	Wood Street	B2-B3
Rugby Road	A3-A4-B4	Chapel Street	B3	Broad Street	A1-A2		
Rushmore Street	E1-F1	Cherry Street	C3-C4	Bull Street	A1		
Russell Street	C4	Church Street	A2-A3	Chapel Lane	B2		
Russell Terrace	D1-E1-E2-F2	Coten End	C3	Chapel Street	B2		
St Mark's Road	A4	Coventry Road	C3-C4	Chestnut Walk	A1-A2		
St Mary's Crescent	E1-F1	Deerpark Drive	A4	Church Street	A1-A2-B2		
St Mary's Road	F1-F2	Edward Street	A3-A4	Clopton Road	B4		
St Mary's Terrace	F1	Gerrard Street	B2-B3	College Lane	A1		
Satchwell Street	C3-D3	Guys Cliffe Terrace	C4	College Street	A1		
Smith Street	D1	Guy Street	C3-C4	Ely Street	A2-B2		
Spencer Street	C1-D1-D2	High Street	A2	Evesham Place	A1-A2		
Station Approach	C1	Jury Street	A2-B2	Great William Street	B3-B4		
Strathearn Road	B4	Lakin Road	C4	Greenhill Street	A3		
Suffolk Street	D4	Market Place	A2-A3	Grove Road	A2-A3		
Tachbrook Road	D1	Market Street	A2	Guild Street	B3		
Tavistock Street	C4						

WARWICK
These pretty brick and timbered cottages standing in the shadow of the great medieval towers of Warwick Castle are among the few buildings in the town that survived a devastating fire in the late 17th century.

245

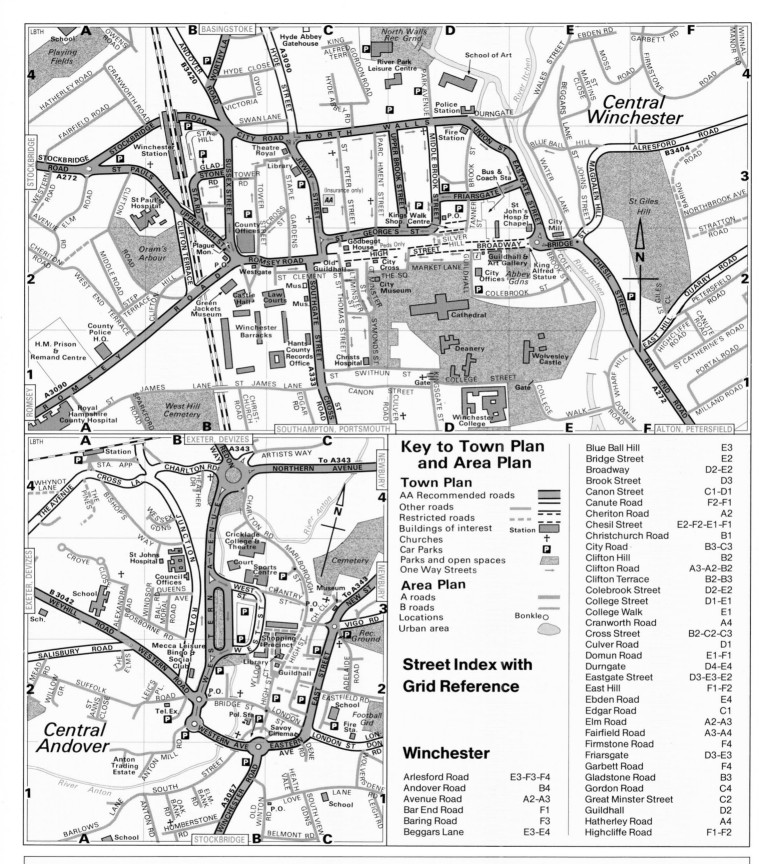

Key to Town Plan and Area Plan

Town Plan

AA Recommended roads	
Other roads	
Restricted roads	
Buildings of interest	Station
Churches	†
Car Parks	P
Parks and open spaces	
One Way Streets	→

Area Plan

A roads	
B roads	
Locations	Bonkle○
Urban area	

Street Index with Grid Reference

Winchester

Winchester

King Alfred designated Winchester capital of England, a status it retained until after the Norman Conquest. Although gradually eclipsed by London, the city maintained close links with the Crown until the reign of Charles II.

Tucked away unobtrusively in the heart of Winchester is the impressive cathedral which encompasses Norman, and all the later Gothic styles of architecture. William of Wykeham was a bishop here in the 14th century and it was he who founded Winchester College, one of the oldest and most famous public schools in England. The buildings lie just outside the peaceful, shady Close where Pilgrims' Hall can be visited. Nearby are the Bishop's Palace and remains of Wolvesley Castle, one of Winchester's two Norman castles. Of the other, only the Great Hall, just outside the Westgate survives. Here hangs the 14th-century Round Table associated with the legend of King Arthur.

The streets of the city, which cover a remarkably small area, are lined with many charming old buildings of different periods. A walk along the pedestrianised High Street takes you past the former Guildhall - now a bank - and the old Butter Cross, into the Broadway where a statue of King Alfred stands near the River Itchen. A delightful path follows the river alongside the remnants of the old city walls.

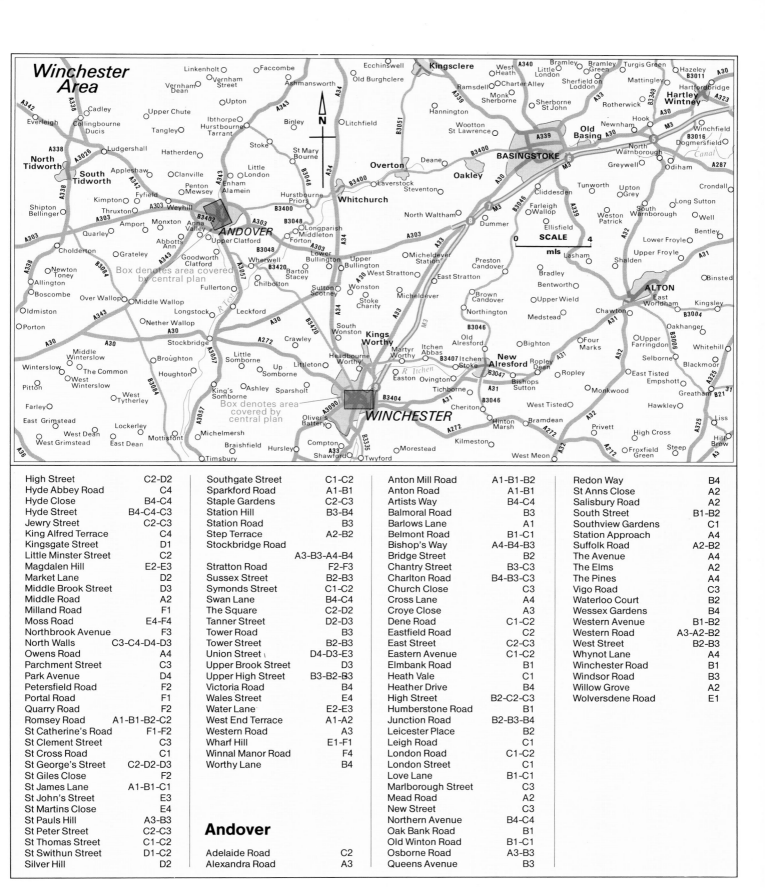

Winchester Area

Box denotes area covered by central plan

Box denotes area covered by central plan

High Street	C2-D2	Southgate Street	C1-C2	Anton Mill Road	A1-B1-B2	Redon Way	B4
Hyde Abbey Road	C4	Sparkford Road	A1-B1	Anton Road	A1-B1	St Anns Close	A2
Hyde Close	B4-C4	Staple Gardens	C2-C3	Artists Way	B4-C4	Salisbury Road	A2
Hyde Street	B4-C4-C3	Station Hill	B3-B4	Balmoral Road	B3	South Street	B1-B2
Jewry Street	C2-C3	Station Road	B3	Barlows Lane	A1	Southview Gardens	C1
King Alfred Terrace	C4	Step Terrace	A2-B2	Belmont Road	B1-C1	Station Approach	A4
Kingsgate Street	D1	Stockbridge Road		Bishop's Way	A4-B4-B3	Suffolk Road	A2-B2
Little Minster Street	C2		A3-B3-A4-B4	Bridge Street	B2	The Avenue	A4
Magdalen Hill	E2-E3	Stratton Road	F2-F3	Chantry Street	B3-C3	The Elms	A2
Market Lane	D2	Sussex Street	B2-B3	Charlton Road	B4-B3-C3	The Pines	A4
Middle Brook Street	D3	Symonds Street	C1-C2	Church Close	C3	Vigo Road	C3
Middle Road	A2	Swan Lane	B4-C4	Cross Lane	A4	Waterloo Court	B2
Milland Road	F1	The Square	C2-D2	Croye Close	A3	Wessex Gardens	B4
Moss Road	E4-F4	Tanner Street	D2-D3	Dene Road	C1-C2	Western Avenue	B1-B2
Northbrook Avenue	F3	Tower Road	B3	Eastfield Road	C2	Western Road	A3-A2-B2
North Walls	C3-C4-D4-D3	Tower Street	B2-B3	East Street	C2-C3	West Street	B2-B3
Owens Road	A4	Union Street	D4-D3-E3	Eastern Avenue	C1-C2	Whynot Lane	A4
Parchment Street	C3	Upper Brook Street	D3	Elmbank Road	B1	Winchester Road	B1
Park Avenue	D4	Upper High Street	B3-B2-B3	Heath Vale	C1	Windsor Road	B3
Petersfield Road	F2	Victoria Road	B4	Heather Drive	B4	Willow Grove	A2
Portal Road	F1	Wales Street	E4	High Street	B2-C2-C3	Wolversdene Road	E1
Quarry Road	F2	Water Lane	E2-E3	Humberstone Road	B1		
Romsey Road	A1-B1-B2-C2	West End Terrace	A1-A2	Junction Road	B2-B3-B4		
St Catherine's Road	F1-F2	Western Road	A3	Leicester Place	B2		
St Clement Street	C3	Wharf Hill	E1-F1	Leigh Road	C1		
St Cross Road	C1	Winnal Manor Road	F4	London Road	C1-C2		
St George's Street	C2-D2-D3	Worthy Lane	B4	London Street	C1		
St James Lane	A1-B1-C1			Love Lane	B1-C1		
St John's Street	E3			Marlborough Street	C3		
St Martins Close	E4			Mead Road	A2		
St Pauls Hill	A3-B3	**Andover**		New Street	C3		
St Peter Street	C2-C3			Northern Avenue	B4-C4		
St Thomas Street	C1-C2	Adelaide Road	C2	Oak Bank Road	B1		
St Swithun Street	D1-C2	Alexandra Road	A3	Old Winton Road	B1-C1		
Silver Hill	D2			Osborne Road	A3-B3		
				Queens Avenue	B3		

WINCHESTER
Standing on the site of the old Hall of Court in the Broadway is the city's Guildhall. Built in 1873, its style was influenced by Northampton Town Hall. It is now a centre for culture and the arts.

247

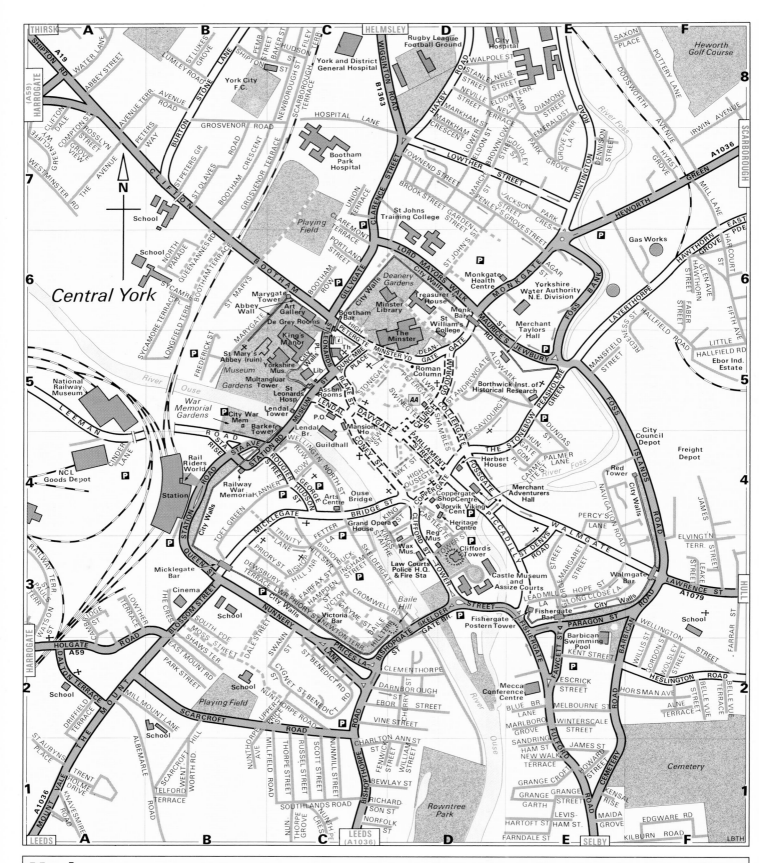

York

York Minster, unquestionably the city's outstanding glory, is considered to be one of the greatest cathedral churches in Europe. It is especially famous for its lovely windows which contain more than half the medieval stained glass in England.

Great medieval walls enclose the historic city centre and their three-mile circuit offers magnificent views of the Minster, York's numerous fine buildings, churches and the River Ouse. The ancient streets consist of a maze of alleys and lanes, some of them so narrow that the overhanging upper storeys of the houses almost touch. The most famous of these picturesque streets is The Shambles, formerly the butchers' quarter of the city, but now colonised by antique and tourist shops. York flourished throughout Tudor, Georgian and Victorian times and handsome buildings from these periods also feature throughout the city.

The Castle Museum gives a fascinating picture of York as it used to be and the Heritage Centre interprets the social and architectural history of the city. Other places of exceptional note in this city of riches include the Merchant Adventurer's Hall; the Treasurer's House, now owned by the National Trust and filled with fine paintings and furniture; the Jorvik Viking Centre, where there is an exciting restoration of the original Viking settlement at York, and the National Railway Museum.

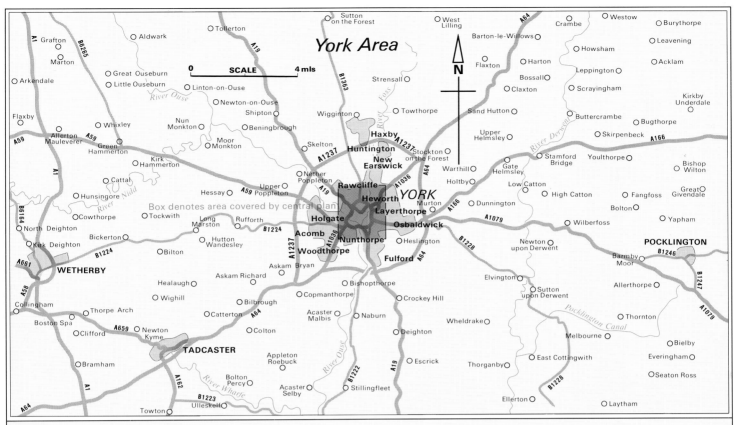

York Area

SCALE
0 — 4 mls

Box denotes area covered by central plan

Key to Town Plan and Area Plan

Town Plan

AA Recommended roads
Other roads
Restricted roads
Buildings of interest   Station
Churches
Car Parks
Parks and open spaces
AA Service Centre
One Way Streets

Area Plan

A roads
B roads
Locations   Fangfoss ○
Urban area

Street Index with Grid Reference

York

Abbey Street	A8
Agar Street	E6
Albemarle Road	A2-A1-B1
Aldwark	D5-E5
Alne Terrace	F2
Amber Street	E8
Ann Street	D1
Avenue Road	B8
Avenue Terrace	A7-A8-B8
Baile Hill Terrace	C2-C3-D3
Baker Street	C8
Barbican Road	E2-F2-F3-E3
Belle Vue Street	F2
Belle Vue Terrace	F2
Bewlay Street	C1-D1
Bishopgate Street	C2-D2-D3
Bishophill Junior	C3
Bishophill Senior	C3
Bishopthorpe Road	C1-C2
Blake Street	C5
Blossom Street	B2-B3
Blue Bridge Lane	E2
Bootham	B6-C6
Bootham Crescent	B7-C7-C8
Bootham Row	C6
Bootham Terrace	B6
Bridge Street	C4-D4
Brook Street	D7
Brownlow Street	D7-E7-E8
Buckingham Street	C3
Burton Stone Lane	B7-B8
Cambridge Street	A2-A3
Carmelite Street	D4-E4
Castlegate	D3-D4
Cemetery Road	E1-E2
Charlton Street	C1-D1
Cherry Street	D2
Church Street	D5
Cinder Lane	A4
Claremont Terrace	C6-C7
Clarence Street	C6-C7-D7
Clementhorpe	C2-D2
Clifford Street	D3-D4
Clifton	A8-A7-B7
Clifton Dale	A7-A8
Colliergate	D4-D5
Compton Street	A7-A8
Coppergate	D4
Cromwell Road	C3-D3
Cygnet Street	C2
Dale Street	B2-B3
Dalton Terrace	A2
Darnborough Street	C2-D2
Davygate	C5-C4-D4-D5
Deangate	D5
Dennison Street	E7
Dewsbury Terrace	B3-C3
Diamond Street	E8
Dodsworth Avenue	E8-F8-F7
Driffield Terrace	A2
Dudley Street	D7-E7
Duncombe Place	C5
Dundas Street	E4-E5
East Parade	F6-F7
East Mount Road	B2
Ebor Street	C2-D2
Edgware Road	F1
Eldon Terrace	D8-E8
Elvington Terrace	F3
Emerald Street	E7-E8
Escrick Street	E2
Faber Street	F6
Fairfax Street	C3
Farndale Street	E1
Farrar Street	F2-F3
Fawcett Street	E2-E3
Fenwick Street	C1-D1
Fetter Lane	C3-C4
Fifth Avenue	F5-F6
Filey Terrace	C8
Fishergate	E2-E3
Foss Bank	D7
Fossgate	D4
Foss Islands Road	E4-E5-F5-F4
Frederick Street	B5
Fulford Road	E1-E2
Garden Street	D7
George Hudson Street	C4
George Street	E3-E4
Gillygate	C5
Glen Avenue	F6
Goodramgate	D5-D6
Gordon Street	F2
Grange Croft	E1
Grange Garth	E1

Grange Street	E1
Greencliffe Way	A7-A8
Grosvenor Road	B8-C8
Grosvenor Terrace	B6-B7-C7-C8
Grove Terrace Lane	E7-E8
Grove View	A7
Hallfield Road	F5-F6
Hampden Street	C3
Harcourt Street	F6
Harloft Street	E1
Hawthorn Grove	F6
Hawthorne Street	F6
Haxby Road	D7-D8
Heslington Road	E2-F2
Heworth Green	E6-E7-F7
High Ousegate	D4
High Petergate	C5-C6
Holgate Road	A2-A3-B3
Hope Street	E3
Horsman Avenue	E2-F2
Hospital Lane	C8
Howard Street	E1
Hudson Street	C8
Hungate	E4
Huntington Road	E6-E7-E8
Hyrst Grove	F7
Irwin Avenue	F7-F8
Jackson Street	D7-E7
James Street	E1
James Street	F3-F4
Jewbury	E5
Kensal Rise	E1
Kent Street	E2
Kilburn Road	E1-F1
Kings Staithe	C4-D4-D3
King Street	C4-D4
Knavesmire Road	A1
Kyme Street	C3
Lawrence Street	F3
Layerthorpe	E5-E6-F6
Lead Mill Lane	E3
Leake Street	F3
Leeman Road	A5-A4-B5-B4
Lendal Coney Street	C5-C4-D4
Levisham Street	D1
Little Hallfield Road	F5
Long Close Lane	E3-F3
Longfield Terrace	B5-B6
Lord Mayors Walk	C6-D6
Lumley Road	B8
Love Lane	A1-A2
Lower Eldon Street	D7
Lower Petergate	D5
Lower Priory Street	C3
Lowther Street	D7-E7
Lowther Terrace	A3
Maida Grove	E1
Mansfield Street	E5
March Street	D7
Margaret Street	E3
Market Street	D4
Markham Crescent	D7-D8
Markham Street	D7-D8
Marlborough Grove	E2
Marygate	B5-B6-C6
Melbourne Street	E2
Micklegate	B3-B4-C4
Millfield Road	C1-C2
Mill Lane	F7
Mill Mount Lane	A2-B2

Minster Yard	C5-D5
Monkgate	D6-E6
Moss Street	B2-B3
Mount Vale	A1
Museum Street	C5
Navigation Road	E4-E3-F3
Nelson Street	D8
Neville Street	D8
Neville Terrace	D8-E8
Newborough Street	C8
New Street	C4-C5
Newton Terrace	C2-C3
New Walk Terrace	E1
Norfolk Street	C1-D1
North Parade	B6
North Street	C4
Nunmill Street	C1-C2
Nunnery Lane	B3-C3-C2
Nunthorpe Avenue	B1-B2
Nunthorpe Grove	C1
Nunthorpe Road	B2-C2
Palmer Lane	E4
Paragon Street	E3-F3
Park Crescent	E7
Park Grove	E7-E8
Park Street	B2
Parliament Street	D4-D5
Peasholme Green	E5
Pembroke Street	B8
Penley's Grove Street	D7-E7-E8
Percy's Lane	E4
Peters Way	A7-B7-B8
Piccadilly	D4-D3-E3-E4
Portland Street	C6
Pottery Lane	F8
Prices Lane	C2
Priory Street	B3-C3
Queen Annes Road	B6
Queen Street	B3
Railway Terrace	A3
Redness Street	F5-F6
Richardson Street	C1-D1
Rosslyn Street	A7
Rougier Street	C4
Russel Street	C1-C2
St Andrewgate	D5
St Aubyns Place	A1
St Benedict Road	C2
St Denys Road	E3-E4
St Johns Street	D6-D7
St Leonards Place	D5-D6
St Lukes Grove	B8
St Marys	B6
St Maurices	D6-D5-E5
St Olaves Road	B7-B8
St Pauls Terrace	A3
St Peters Grove	B7
St Saviourgate	D4-D5-E5
Sandringham Street	E1
Saxon Place	E8-F8
Scarborough Terrace	C8
Scarcroft Hill	B1-B2
Scarcroft Road	A2-B2-C2-C1
Scott Street	C1-C2
Shambles	D4-D5
Shaws Terrace	B2-B3
Shipton Road	A8
Shipton Street	B8-C8
Skeldergate	C4-C3-D3
Skeldergate Bridge	D3

South Esplanade	D3
Southlands Road	C1
South Parade	B2-B3
Stanley Street	D8
Station Avenue	B4
Station Rise	B4
Station Road	B3-B4-C4-C5
Stonegate	C5-D5
Swann Street	C9
Swinegate	D5
Sycamore Place	B6
Sycamore Terrace	A5-B5-B6
Tanner Row	B4-C4
Telford Terrace	B1
The Avenue	A7
The Crescent	B3
The Mount	A1-A2-B2
The Stonebow	D4-E4-E5
Thorpe Street	C1-C2
Toft Green	B3-B4
Tower Street	D4-D3-D3
Townend Street	D7
Trent Holme Drive	A1
Trinity Lane	C3-C4
Union Terrace	C7
Upper Price Street	B2-C2
Victor Street	C3
Vine Street	C2-D2
Walmgate	D4-E4-E3-F3
Walpole Street	D8-E8
Water Lane	A8
Watson Street	A2-A3
Wellington Row	C4
Wellington Street	F2-F3
Wentworth Road	B1
Westminster Road	A7
William Street	D1
Willis Street	F2-F3
Winterscale Street	E2
Wolsley Street	F2

249

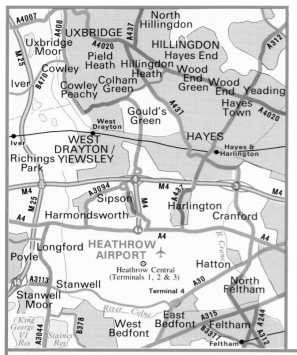

Airports and Seaports

Most people who leave Britain by air or sea use the airports and seaports detailed in these pages. The maps indicate the approach roads into each complex with information on parking and telephone numbers through which details on costs and other travel information can be obtained. The hotels listed are AA-appointed, and the garages have been selected because they provide adequate long term parking facilities. HEATHROW AIRPORT Tel 081-759 4321 (Airport Information)

Heathrow one of the world's busiest international airports, lies sixteen miles west of London. The airport is situated on the Piccadilly Underground line at Heathrow Central station. It is also served by local bus and long distance coach services. For short term parking multi-storey car parks are sited at each of the passenger terminals Tel: 081-745 7160 (terminals 1,2,3) 081-759 4931 (terminal 4). Charges for the long term car parks on the northern perimeter road are designed to encourage their use for a stay in excess of four hours. A free coach takes passengers to and from the terminals. Commercial garages offering long-term parking facilities within easy reach of the airport include: Quo-Vadis Airport Parking Tel: 081-759 2778; Airways Cranford Parking Tel: 081-759

9661; Flyaway Car Storage Tel: 081-759 1567 or 2020; and National Car Parks Tel: 081-759 9878. Car Hire: Avis Rent-A-Car Tel: 081-897 2621; Budget Rent-A-Car Tel: 081-759 2216; Godfrey Davis Europcar Tel: 081-897 0811/5; Guy Salmon Tel: 081-897 0541; Hertz Rent-A-Car Tel: 081-897 3347; Kenning Car Hire Tel: 081-759 9701 and EuroDollar Rent-A-Car Tel: 081-897-3232. The 4-star hotels in the area are The Excelsior Tel: 081-759 6611; the Heathrow Penta Tel: 081-897 6363; the Holiday Inn Tel: (0895) 445555. The 3-star hotels are the Berkeley Arms Tel: 081-897 2121; the Ariel Tel: 081-759 2552; the Post House Tel: 081-759 2323; and the Skyway Tel: 081-759 6311.

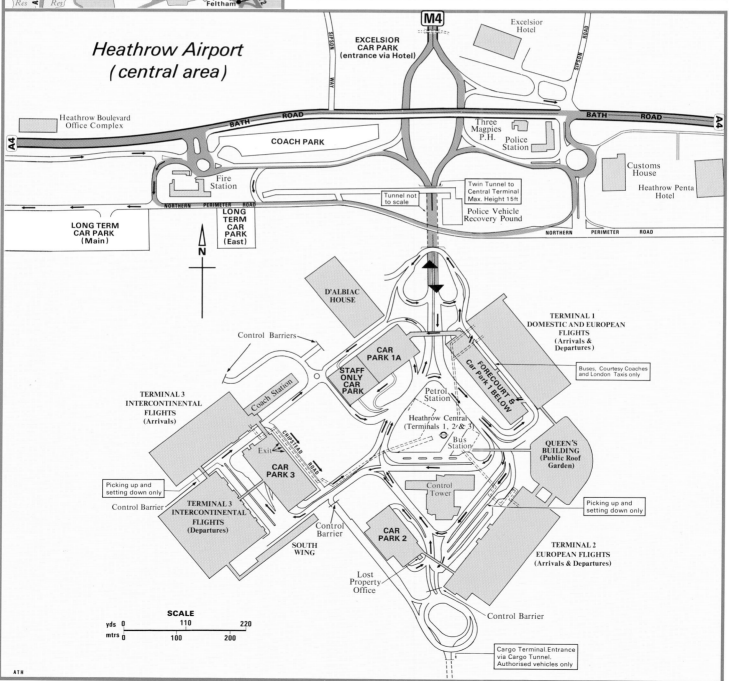

Heathrow Airport (central area)

SCALE

| yds | 0 | | 110 | | 220 |
| mtrs | 0 | 100 | | 200 | |

ATH

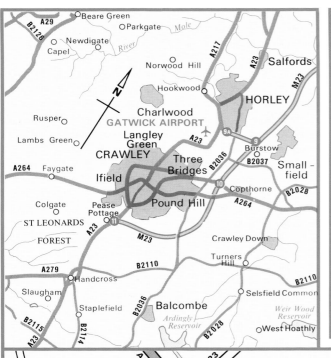

GATWICK AIRPORT Tel: (0293) 28822 or 081-668 4211.
London's second airport is served by regular bus and coach services.
There is a fast 15-minute rail service linking London (Victoria) with
Gatwick 24 hours a day. Parking: ample multi-storey and open-air
car parking is available. For latest prices tel: Gatwick (0293) 789812
South Terminal, and Gatwick (0293) 502747 for North Terminal.

MANCHESTER AIRPORT Tel: 061-489 3000. Situated nine miles
south of the city. Manchester Airport provides regular scheduled
services for many of the leading airlines. A spacious concourse,
restaurants and parking facilities are available for passengers. For
parking enquiries Tel: 061-489 3723 or 061-489 3000 ext 4635 or
2021.

LUTON AIRPORT Tel:(0582)405100. Used mainly for package
holiday tour operators, the airport has ample open-air car parking.
Covered garage space is available from Central Car Storage Tel:
(0582) 26189 or (0582)20957 for a booking form. Allow five
weeks.

BIRMINGHAM AIRPORT Tel: 021-767 5511. A three-storey
terminal building gives access from the first floor to the Maglev
transit system which offers a 90 second shuttle service to
Birmingham International Railway Station. Multi-storey parking for
800 cars and surface parking is available for 4,400 cars. Tel:
021-767 7861.

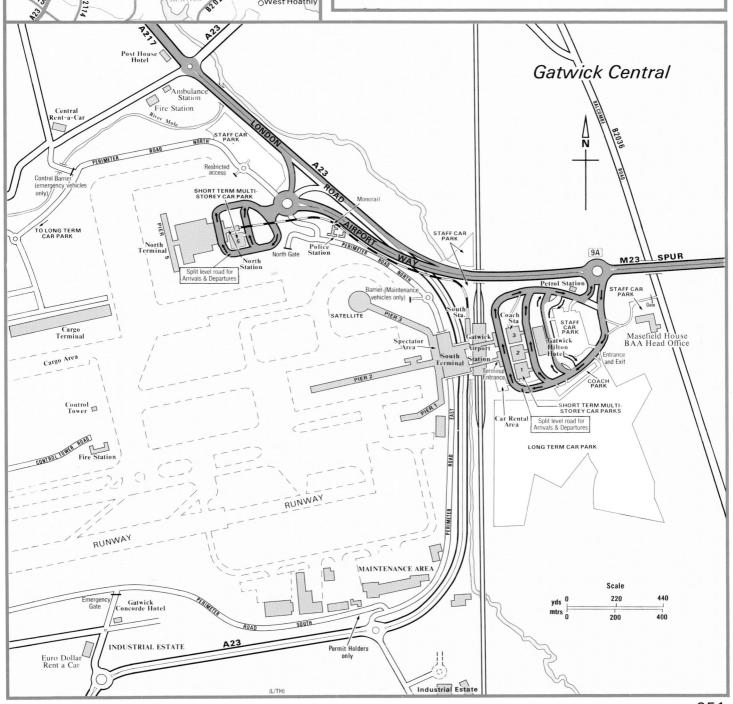

Gatwick Central

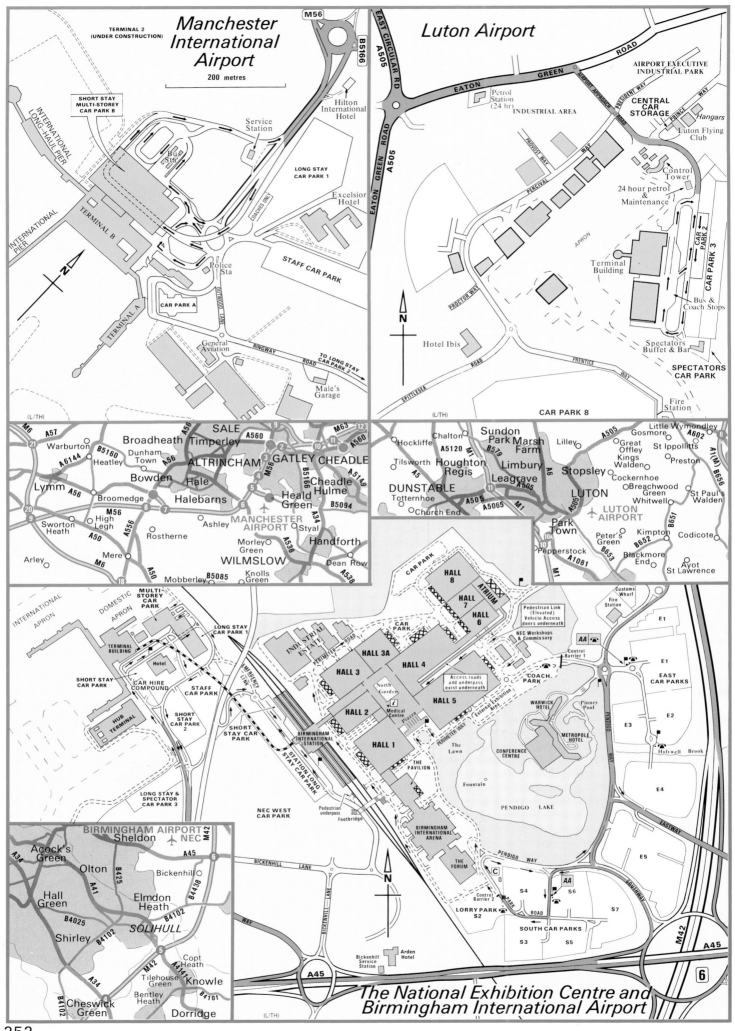

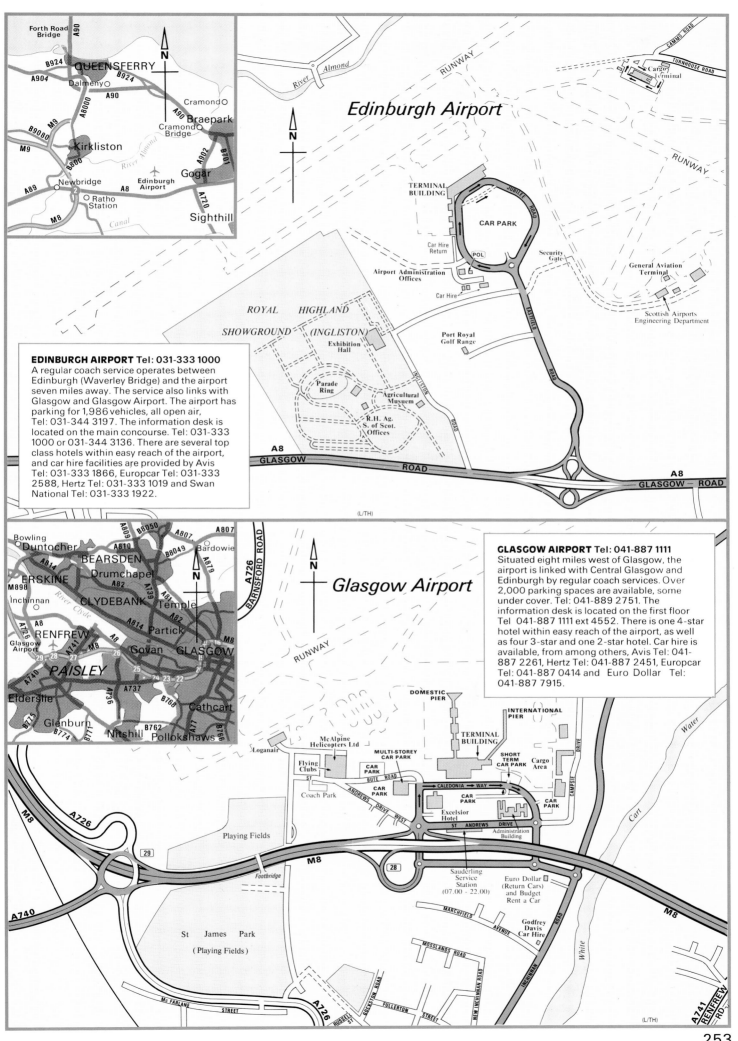

Edinburgh Airport

EDINBURGH AIRPORT Tel: 031-333 1000

A regular coach service operates between Edinburgh (Waverley Bridge) and the airport seven miles away. The service also links with Glasgow and Glasgow Airport. The airport has parking for 1,986 vehicles, all open air, Tel: 031-344 3197. The information desk is located on the main concourse. Tel: 031-333 1000 or 031-344 3136. There are several top class hotels within easy reach of the airport, and car hire facilities are provided by Avis Tel: 031-333 1866, Europcar Tel: 031-333 2588, Hertz Tel: 031-333 1019 and Swan National Tel: 031-333 1922.

Glasgow Airport

GLASGOW AIRPORT Tel: 041-887 1111

Situated eight miles west of Glasgow, the airport is linked with Central Glasgow and Edinburgh by regular coach services. Over 2,000 parking spaces are available, some under cover. Tel: 041-889 2751. The information desk is located on the first floor Tel 041-887 1111 ext 4552. There is one 4-star hotel within easy reach of the airport, as well as four 3-star and one 2-star hotel. Car hire is available, from among others, Avis Tel: 041-887 2261, Hertz Tel: 041-887 2451, Europcar Tel: 041-887 0414 and Euro Dollar Tel: 041-887 7915.

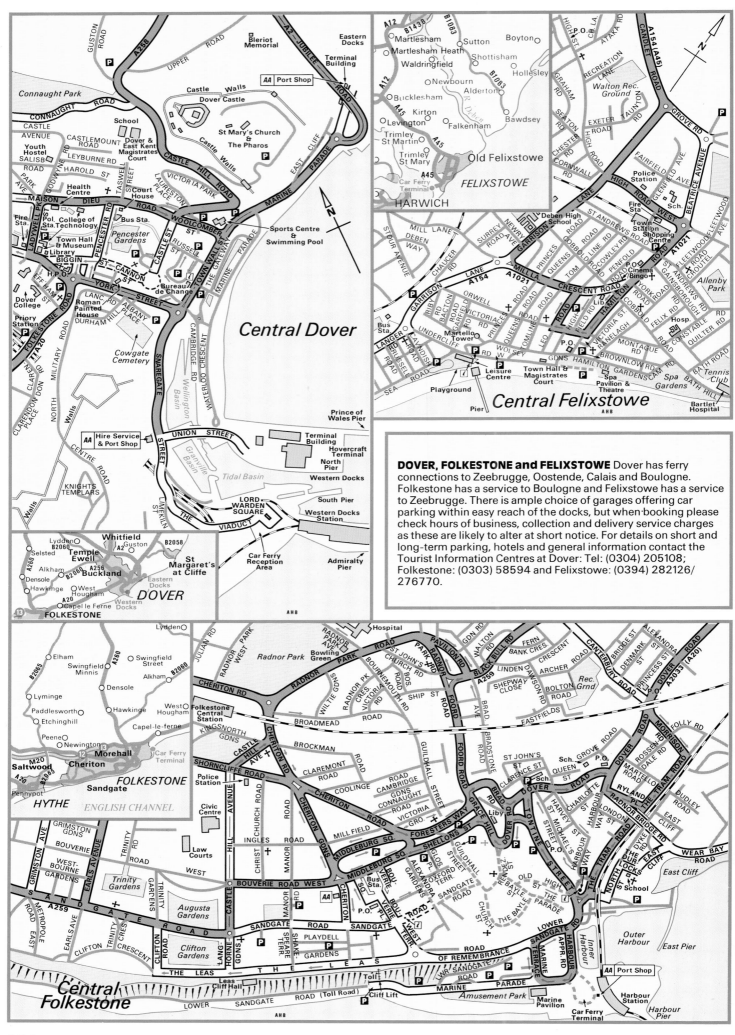

DOVER, FOLKESTONE and FELIXSTOWE Dover has ferry connections to Zeebrugge, Oostende, Calais and Boulogne. Folkestone has a service to Boulogne and Felixstowe has a service to Zeebrugge. There is ample choice of garages offering car parking within easy reach of the docks, but when booking please check hours of business, collection and delivery service charges as these are likely to alter at short notice. For details on short and long-term parking, hotels and general information contact the Tourist Information Centres at Dover: Tel: (0304) 205108; Folkestone: (0303) 58594 and Felixstowe: (0394) 282126/ 276770.

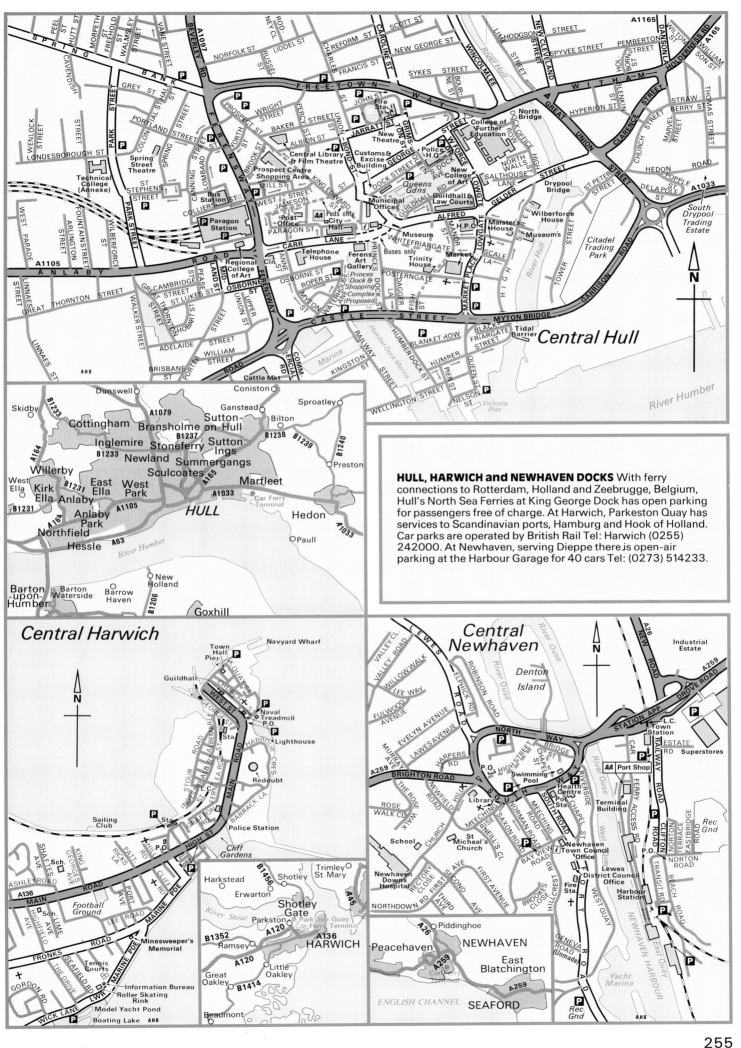

HULL, HARWICH and NEWHAVEN DOCKS With ferry connections to Rotterdam, Holland and Zeebrugge, Belgium, Hull's North Sea Ferries at King George Dock has open parking for passengers free of charge. At Harwich, Parkeston Quay has services to Scandinavian ports, Hamburg and Hook of Holland. Car parks are operated by British Rail Tel: Harwich (0255) 242000. At Newhaven, serving Dieppe there is open-air parking at the Harbour Garage for 40 cars Tel: (0273) 514233.

•Index

Each placename entry in this index is identified by its county or region name. These are shown in italics. A list of the abbreviated forms used is given below.

To locate a placename in the atlas turn to the map page number indicated in bold type in the index and use the 4 figure grid reference.

e g   Hythe Kent **29** TR1634 is found on page '**29**'. The two letters 'TR' refer to the National Grid. To pin point our example the first bold figure '**1**' is found along the bottom edge of the page. The following figure '**6**' indicates how many imaginary tenths to move east of line '**1**'. The next bold figure '**3**' is found along the left hand side of the page. The last figure '**4**' shows how many imaginary tenths to move north of line '**3**'. You will locate Hythe where these two lines intersect.

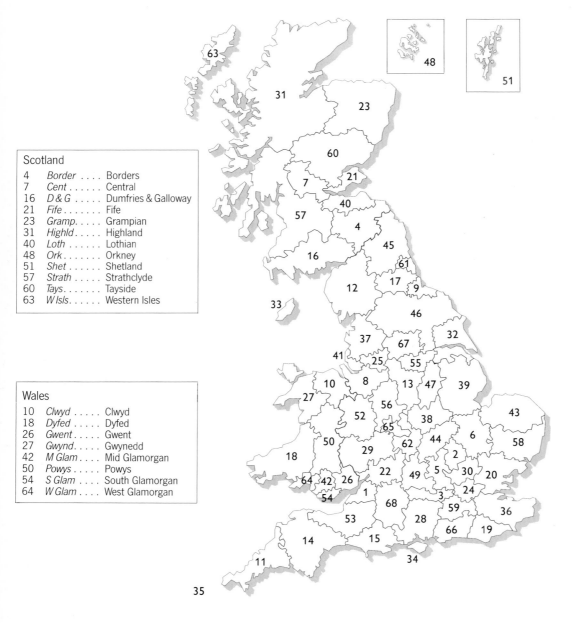

Scotland

4	*Border*	Borders
7	*Cent*	Central
16	*D & G*	Dumfries & Galloway
21	*Fife*	Fife
23	*Gramp.*	Grampian
31	*Highld*	Highland
40	*Loth*	Lothian
48	*Ork*	Orkney
51	*Shet*	Shetland
57	*Strath*	Strathclyde
60	*Tays.*	Tayside
63	*W Isls.*	Western Isles

Wales

10	*Clwyd*	Clwyd
18	*Dyfed*	Dyfed
26	*Gwent*	Gwent
27	*Gwynd.*	Gwynedd
42	*M Glam*	Mid Glamorgan
50	*Powys*	Powys
54	*S Glam*	South Glamorgan
64	*W Glam*	West Glamorgan

England

1	*Avon*	Avon
2	*Beds*	Bedfordshire
3	*Berks*	Berkshire
5	*Bucks*	Buckinghamshire
6	*Cambs*	Cambridgeshire
8	*Ches*	Cheshire
9	*Cleve.*	Cleveland
11	*Cnwll.*	Cornwall
12	*Cumb*	Cumbria
13	*Derbys*	Derbyshire
14	*Devon*	Devon
15	*Dorset.*	Dorset
17	*Dur.*	Durham
19	*E.Susx.*	East Sussex
20	*Essex*	Essex
22	*Gloucs.*	Gloucestershire
24	*Gt Lon.*	Greater London
25	*Gt Man*	Greater Manchester
28	*Hants*	Hampshire
29	*H & W*	Hereford & Worcester
30	*Herts.*	Hertfordshire
32	*Humb*	Humberside
33	*IOM*	Isle of Man
34	*IOW.*	Isle of Wight
35	*IOS*	Isles of Scilly
36	*Kent*	Kent
37	*Lancs*	Lancashire
38	*Leics*	Leicestershire
39	*Lincs.*	Lincolnshire
41	*Mersyd*	Merseyside
43	*Norfk*	Norfolk
44	*Nhants*	Northamptonshire
45	*Nthumb.*	Northumberland
46	*N York*	North Yorkshire
47	*Notts.*	Nottinghamshire
49	*Oxon*	Oxfordshire
52	*Shrops*	Shropshire
53	*Somset*	Somerset
55	*S York*	South Yorkshire
56	*Staffs*	Staffordshire
58	*Suffk.*	Suffolk
59	*Surrey*	Surrey
61	*T & W.*	Tyne & Wear
62	*Warwks*	Warwickshire
65	*W Mids*	West Midland
66	*W Susx*	West Sussex
67	*W York*	West Yorkshire
68	*Wilts*	Wiltshire

A'Chill Amblecote

A'Chill Highld 128 NG2705
Ab Kettleby Leics 63 SK7223
Ab Lench H & W 47 SP0151
Abbas Combe Somset 22 ST7022
Abberley H & W 47 SO7567
Abberley Common H & W 47 SO7467
Abberton H & W 47 SO9953
Abberton Essex 41 TM0019
Abberwick Nthumb 111 NU1313
Abbess Roding Essex 40 TL5711
Abbey Devon 9 ST1410
Abbey Dore H & W 46 SO3830
Abbey Green Staffs 72 SJ9757
Abbey Hill Somset 10 ST2718
Abbey St. Bathans Border 119 NT7661
Abbey Town Cumb 93 NY1750
Abbey Village Lancs 81 SD6422
Abbey Wood Gt Lon 27 TQ4779
Abbeycwmhir Powys 45 SO0571
Abbeydale S York 74 SK3281
Abbeylands IOM 153 SC4585
Abbeystead Lancs 81 SD5654
Abbot's Chair Derbys 74 SK0290
Abbot's Salford Warwks 48 SP0650
Abbotrule Border 110 NT6113
Abbots Bickington Devon 18 SS3813
Abbots Bromley Staffs 73 SK0724
Abbots Deuglie Tays 126 NO1111
Abbots Langley Herts 26 TL0901
Abbots Leigh Avon 34 ST5474
Abbots Morton H & W 48 SP0255
Abbots Ripton Cambs 52 TL2377
Abbots Worthy Hants 24 SU4932
Abbotsbury Dorset 10 SY5785
Abbotsford Border 109 NT5034
Abbotsham Devon 18 SS4226
Abbotskerswell Devon 7 SX8568
Abbotsleigh Devon 7 SX8048
Abbotsley Cambs 52 TL2256
Abbotstone Hants 24 SU5634
Abbotswood Hants 23 SU3623
Abbott Street Dorset 11 ST9800
Abbotts Ann Hants 23 SU3243
Abcott Shrops 46 SO3978
Abdon Shrops 59 SO5786
Abenhall Gloucs 35 SO6717
Aber Gwynd 69 SH6572
Aber Clydach Powys 33 SO1021
Aber-Magwr Dyfed 43 SN6673
Aber-arad Dyfed 31 SN3140
Aber-banc Dyfed 31 SN3541
Aber-giar Dyfed 44 SN5040
Aber-meurig Dyfed 44 SN5656
Aber-nant M Glam 33 SO0103
Aberaeron Dyfed 42 SN4562
Aberaman M Glam 33 SO0100
Aberangell Powys 57 SH8410
Aberarder Highld 140 NH6225
Aberargie Tays 126 NO1615
Aberarth Dyfed 42 SN4763
Aberavon W Glam 32 SS7489
Aberbargoed M Glam 33 SO1500
Aberbeeg Gwent 33 SO2002
Abercanaid M Glam 33 SO0503
Abercairny Tays 125 NN9222
Abercarn Gwent 33 ST2194
Abercastle Dyfed 30 SM8533
Abercegir Powys 57 SH8001
Aberchalder Lodge Highld 131 NH3403
Aberchirder Gramp 142 NJ6252
Abercraf Powys 33 SN8212
Abercregan W Glam 33 SS8496
Abercrombie Fife 127 NO5102
Abercwmboi M Glam 33 ST0299
Abercych Dyfed 31 SN2441
Abercynon M Glam 33 ST0794
Aberdalgie Tays 125 NO0720
Aberdare Powys 33 SO0002
Aberdaron Gwynd 56 SH1726
Aberdeen Gramp 135 NJ9306
Aberdesach Gwynd 68 SH4251
Aberdour Fife 117 NT1985
Aberdovey Gwynd 43 SN6196
Aberdulais W Glam 32 SS7799
Aberedw Powys 45 SO0847
Abereiddy Dyfed 30 SM7931
Abererch Gwynd 56 SH3936
Aberfan M Glam 33 SO0700
Aberfeldy Tays 125 NN8549
Aberffraw Gwynd 68 SH3569
Aberffrwd Dyfed 43 SN6878
Aberford W York 83 SE4337
Aberfoyle Cent 115 NN5200
Abergarw M Glam 33 SS9184
Abergarwed W Glam 33 SN8102
Abergavenny Gwent 34 SO2914
Abergele Clwyd 70 SH9477
Abergorlech Dyfed 44 SN5833
Abergwesyn Powys 45 SN8552
Abergwili Dyfed 31 SN4320
Abergwydol Powys 57 SH7903
Abergwynfi W Glam 33 SS8995
Abergynolwyn Gwynd 57 SH6806
Aberhosan Powys 43 SN8197
Aberkenfig M Glam 33 SS8984
Aberlady Loth 118 NT4679
Aberlemno Tays 127 NO5255
Aberllefenni Gwynd 57 SH7609
Aberllynfi Powys 45 SO1737
Aberlour Gramp 141 NJ2642
Abermorddu Clwyd 71 SJ3056
Abermule Powys 58 SO1594
Abernant Dyfed 31 SN3323
Abernethy Tays 126 NO1816
Abernyte Tays 126 NO2531
Aberporth Dyfed 42 SN2651
Abersoch Gwynd 56 SH3127
Abersychan Gwent 34 SO2603
Aberthin S Glam 33 ST0074
Abertillery Gwent 33 SO2104
Abertridwr Powys 58 SJ0319
Abertridwr M Glam 33 ST1289
Abertysswg M Glam 33 SO1305
Aberuthven Tays 125 NN9815
Aberyscir Powys 45 SN9929
Aberystwyth Dyfed 43 SN5881
Abingdon Oxon 37 SU4997
Abinger Surrey 14 TQ1145
Abinger Hammer Surrey 14 TQ0947
Abington Strath 108 NS9323
Abington Nhants 50 SP7861
Abington Pigotts Cambs 39 TL3044
Ablington Gloucs 36 SP1007
Ablington Wilts 23 SU1546
Abney Derbys 74 SK1980
Above Church Staffs 73 SK0150
Aboyne Gramp 134 NO5298
Abram Gt Man 78 SD6001
Abriachan Highld 139 NH5535
Abridge Essex 27 TQ4696
Abson Avon 35 ST7074
Abthorpe Nhants 49 SP6446
Aby Lincs 77 TF4078
Acaster Malbis N York 83 SE5845
Acaster Selby N York 83 SE5741
Accott Devon 19 SS6432
Accrington Lancs 81 SD7628
Acha Strath 120 NM1854
Achahoish Strath 113 NR7877
Achalader Tays 126 NO1245
Achaleven Strath 122 NM9233
Achanalt Highld 139 NH2661
Achandunie Highld 146 NH6472
Achany Highld 146 NC5602
Acharacle Highld 121 NM6767
Acharn Tays 124 NN7543
Achavanich Highld 151 ND1842
Achduart Highld 145 NC0403
Achfary Highld 148 NC2939
Achiltibuie Highld 144 NC0208
Achinhoan Strath 105 NR7516
Achintee Highld 138 NG9441
Achlain Highld 131 NH2812
Achmelvich Highld 148 NC0524
Achmore W Isls 154 NB3029
Achmore Highld 138 NG8533
Achnacarnin Highld 148 NC0432
Achnacarry Highld 131 NN1787
Achnacloich Highld 129 NG5908
Achnacloich Strath 122 NM9534
Achnaconeran Highld 139 NH4118
Achnacroish Strath 122 NM8541
Achnadrish Lodge Strath 121 NM4652
Achnafauld Tays 125 NN8736
Achnagarron Highld 146 NH6870
Achnaha Highld 128 NM4668
Achnahaird Highld 144 NC0013
Achnairn Highld 146 NC5512
Achnalea Highld 130 NM8561
Achnamara Strath 113 NR7887
Achnasheen Highld 138 NH1658
Achnashellach Station Highld 138 NH0048
Achnastank Gramp 141 NJ2733
Achosnich Highld 121 NM4467
Achranich Highld 122 NM7047
Achreamie Highld 150 ND0166
Achriabhach Highld 131 NN1468
Achriesgill Highld 148 NC2554
Achtoty Highld 149 NC6762
Achurch Nhants 51 TL0283
Achvaich Highld 146 NH7194
Ackenthwaite Cumb 87 SD5081
Ackergill Highld 151 ND3553
Acklam Cleve 97 NZ4817
Acklam N York 90 SE7861
Ackleton Shrops 60 SO7698
Acklington Nthumb 103 NU2301
Ackton W York 83 SE4121
Ackworth Moor Top W York 83 SE4316
Acle Norfk 67 TG4010
Acock's Green W Mids 61 SP1283
Acol Kent 29 TR3067
Acomb Nthumb 102 NY9366
Acomb N York 83 SE5651
Acombe Somset 9 ST1914
Aconbury H & W 46 SO5133
Acre Lancs 81 SD7924
Acrefair Clwyd 70 SJ2743
Acresford Derbys 61 SK2913
Acton Ches 71 SJ6352
Acton Staffs 72 SJ8241
Acton Shrops 59 SO3185
Acton H & W 47 SO8467
Acton Dorset 11 SY9978
Acton Suffk 54 TL8945
Acton Gt Lon 26 TQ2080
Acton Beauchamp H & W 47 SO6850
Acton Bridge Ches 71 SJ6075
Acton Burnell Shrops 59 SJ5302
Acton Green H & W 47 SO6950
Acton Park Clwyd 71 SJ3451
Acton Pigott Shrops 59 SJ5402
Acton Round Shrops 59 SO6395
Acton Scott Shrops 59 SO4589
Acton Trussell Staffs 72 SJ9318
Acton Turville Avon 35 ST8080
Adbaston Staffs 72 SJ7627
Adber Dorset 21 ST5920
Adbolton Notts 62 SK5938
Adderbury Oxon 49 SP4735
Adderley Shrops 72 SJ6640
Adderstone Nthumb 111 NU1330
Addiewell Loth 117 NS9962
Addingham W York 82 SE0749
Addington Bucks 49 SP7428
Addington Gt Lon 27 TQ3664
Addington Kent 28 TQ6559
Addiscombe Gt Lon 27 TQ3366
Addlestone Surrey 26 TQ0564
Addlestonemore Surrey 26 TQ0565
Addlethorpe Lincs 77 TF5468
Adeney Shrops 72 SJ6918
Adeyfield Herts 38 TL0708
Adfa Powys 58 SJ0601
Adforton H & W 46 SO4071
Adisham Kent 29 TR2253
Adlestrop Gloucs 48 SP2426
Adlingfleet Humb 84 SE8421
Adlington Lancs 81 SD6013
Adlington Ches 79 SJ9180
Admaston Shrops 59 SJ6313
Admaston Staffs 73 SK0423
Admington Warwks 48 SP2045
Adsborough Somset 20 ST2729
Adscombe Somset 20 ST1837
Adstock Bucks 49 SP7329
Adstone Nhants 49 SP5951
Adswood Gt Man 79 SJ8888
Adversane W Susx 14 TQ0723
Advie Highld 141 NJ1234
Adwalton W York 82 SE2328
Adwell Oxon 37 SU6999
Adwick Le Street S York 83 SE5308
Adwick upon Dearne S York 83 SE4701
Ae D & G 100 NX9889
Ae Bridgend D & G 100 NY0186
Affetside Gt Man 81 SD7513
Affleck Gramp 142 NJ5540
Affpuddle Dorset 11 SY8093
Affric Lodge Highld 138 NH1822
Afon-wen Clwyd 70 SJ1371
Afton Devon 7 SX8462
Afton IOW 12 SZ3486
Afton Bridgend Strath 107 NS6213
Agglethorpe N York 89 SE0885
Aigburth Mersyd 78 SJ3886
Aike Humb 84 TA0446
Aiketgate Cumb 94 NY4846
Aikhead Cumb 93 NY2349
Aikton Cumb 93 NY2753
Ailby Lincs 77 TF4376
Ailey H & W 46 SO3348
Ailsworth Cambs 64 TL1198
Ainderby Quernhow N York 89 SE3480
Ainderby Steeple N York 89 SE3392
Aingers Green Essex 41 TM1120
Ainsdale Mersyd 80 SD3112
Ainsdale-on-Sea Mersyd 80 SD2912
Ainstable Cumb 94 NY5246
Ainsworth Gt Man 79 SD7610
Ainthorpe N York 90 NZ7007
Aintree Mersyd 78 SJ3898
Aird W Isls 154 NB5635
Aird Strath 113 NM7600
Aird D & G 98 NX0960
Aird of Kinloch Strath 121 NM5228
Aird of Sleat Highld 129 NG5900
Airdeny Strath 122 NM9929
Airdrie Strath 116 NS7565
Airdriehill Strath 116 NS7867
Airds Bay Strath 122 NM9932
Airds of Kells D & G 99 NX6770
Airieland D & G 99 NX7556
Airmyn Humb 84 SE7224
Airntully Tays 125 NO0935
Airor Highld 129 NG7205
Airth Cent 116 NS9087
Airton N York 88 SD9059
Aisby Lincs 76 SK8692
Aisby Lincs 64 TF0138
Aisgill Cumb 88 SD7797
Aish Devon 7 SX6960
Aish Devon 7 SX8458
Aiskew N York 89 SE2788
Aislaby Cleve 89 NZ4012
Aislaby N York 90 NZ8608
Aislaby N York 90 SE7785
Aisthorpe Lincs 76 SK9480
Aith Shet 155 HU3455
Akeld Nthumb 111 NT9529
Akeley Bucks 49 SP7037
Akenham Suffk 54 TM1449
Albaston Devon 6 SX4270
Alberbury Shrops 59 SJ3614
Albert Street Clwyd 70 SJ2660
Albourne W Susx 15 TQ2516
Albourne Green W Susx 15 TQ2616
Albrighton Shrops 59 SJ4918
Albrighton Shrops 60 SJ8004
Alburgh Norfk 55 TM2687
Albury Oxon 37 SP6505
Albury Herts 39 TL4324
Albury Surrey 14 TQ0447
Albury End Herts 39 TL4223
Albury Heath Surrey 14 TQ0646
Alby Hill Norfk 67 TG1934
Alcaig Highld 139 NH5657
Alcaston Shrops 59 SO4587
Alcester Warwks 48 SP0857
Alcester Lane End W Mids 61 SP0780
Alciston E Susx 16 TQ5005
Alcombe Wilts 35 ST8169
Alconbury Cambs 52 TL1875
Alconbury Weston Cambs 52 TL1777
Aldborough N York 89 SE4066
Aldborough Norfk 66 TG1834
Aldbourne Wilts 36 SU2676
Aldbrough Humb 85 TA2438
Aldbury Herts 38 SP9612
Aldcliffe Cumb 87 SD4660
Aldclune Tays 132 NN8964
Aldeburgh Suffk 55 TM4656
Aldeby Norfk 67 TM4493
Aldenham Herts 26 TQ1498
Alder Moor Staffs 73 SK2226
Alderbury Wilts 23 SU1827
Aldercar Derbys 62 SK4447
Alderford Norfk 66 TG1218
Alderholt Dorset 12 SU1212
Alderley Gloucs 35 ST7690
Alderley Edge Ches 79 SJ8478
Aldermans Green W Mids 61 SP3683
Aldermaston Berks 24 SU5965
Alderminster Warwks 48 SP2348
Aldershot Hants 25 SU8650
Alderton Shrops 59 SJ4924
Alderton Gloucs 47 SP0033
Alderton Nhants 49 SP7446
Alderton Wilts 35 ST8482
Alderton Suffk 55 TM3441
Alderwasley Derbys 73 SK3053
Aldfield N York 89 SE2669
Aldford Ches 71 SJ4159
Aldgate Leics 63 SK9804
Aldham Essex 40 TL9126
Aldham Suffk 54 TM0545
Aldingbourne W Susx 14 SU9205
Aldingham Cumb 86 SD2870
Aldington H & W 48 SP0644
Aldington Kent 29 TR0736
Aldington Corner Kent 29 TR0636
Aldivalloch Gramp 141 NJ3526
Aldochlay Strath 115 NS3591
Aldon Shrops 46 SO4379
Aldoth Cumb 92 NY1448
Aldreth Cambs 53 TL4473
Aldridge W Mids 61 SK0500
Aldringham Suffk 55 TM4461
Aldro N York 90 SE8162
Aldsworth Gloucs 36 SP1509
Aldsworth W Susx 14 SU7608
Aldunie Gramp 141 NJ3626
Aldwark N York 89 SE4663
Aldwark Derbys 74 SK2257
Aldwick W Susx 14 SZ9198
Aldwincle Nhants 51 TL0081
Aldworth Berks 37 SU5579
Alexandria Strath 115 NS3979
Aley Somset 20 ST1838
Alfardisworthy Devon 18 SS2911
Alfington Devon 9 SY1197
Alfold Surrey 14 TQ0333
Alfold Bars W Susx 14 TQ0333
Alfold Crossways Surrey 14 TQ0335
Alford Gramp 142 NJ5715
Alford Somset 21 ST6032
Alford Lincs 77 TF4575
Alfreton Derbys 74 SK4155
Alfrick H & W 47 SO7453
Alfrick Pound H & W 47 SO7452
Alfriston E Susx 16 TQ5103
Algarkirk Lincs 64 TF2935
Alhampton Somset 21 ST6234
Alkborough Humb 84 SE8821
Alkerton Gloucs 35 SO7705
Alkerton Oxon 48 SP3743
Alkham Kent 29 TR2542
Alkington Shrops 71 SJ5339
Alkmonton Derbys 73 SK1838
All Cannings Wilts 23 SU0661
All Saints South Elmham Suffk 55 TM3482
All Stretton Shrops 59 SO4595
Allaleigh Devon 7 SX8053
Allanaquoich Gramp 133 NO1291
Allanbank Strath 116 NS8458
Allanton Strath 116 NS7454
Allanton Strath 116 NS8457
Allanton Border 119 NT8654
Allardice Gramp 135 NO8173
Allaston Gloucs 35 SO6304
Allbrook Hants 13 SU4521
Allen End Warwks 61 SP1696
Allen's Green Herts 39 TL4516
Allendale Town Nthumb 95 NY8355
Allenheads Nthumb 95 NY8645
Allensford Dur 95 NZ0750
Allensmore H & W 46 SO4635
Allenton Derbys 62 SK3732
Aller Devon 19 SS7625
Aller Somset 21 ST4029
Allerby Cumb 92 NY0839
Allercombe Devon 9 SY0494
Allerford Somset 20 SS9046
Allerston N York 90 SE8782
Allerthorpe Humb 84 SE7847
Allerton W York 82 SE1234
Allerton Mersyd 78 SJ3987
Allerton Bywater W York 83 SE4227
Allerton Mauleverer N York 89 SE4157
Allesley W Mids 61 SP3080
Allestree Derbys 62 SK3439
Allet Common Cnwll 3 SW7948
Allexton Leics 51 SK8100
Allgreave Ches 72 SJ9767
Allhallows Kent 28 TQ8377
Allhallows-on-Sea Kent 40 TQ8478
Alligin Shuas Highld 137 NG8357
Allimore Green Staffs 72 SJ8519
Allington Lincs 63 SK8540
Allington Wilts 35 ST8975
Allington Wilts 23 SU0663
Allington Wilts 23 SU2039
Allington Dorset 10 SY4693
Allington Kent 28 TQ7557
Allithwaite Cumb 87 SD3876
Alloa Cent 116 NS8892
Allonby Cumb 92 NY0842
Alloway Strath 106 NS3318
Allowenshay Somset 10 ST3913
Allscott Shrops 59 SJ6113
Allscott Shrops 60 SO7396
Alltami Clwyd 70 SJ2665
Alltchaorunn Highld 123 NN1951
Alltmawr Powys 45 SO0746
Alltwalis Dyfed 31 SN4431
Alltwen W Glam 32 SN7303
Alltyblaca Dyfed 44 SN5245
Allweston Dorset 11 ST6614
Allwood Green Suffk 54 TM0472
Almeley H & W 46 SO3351
Almeley Wooton H & W 46 SO3352
Almer Dorset 11 SY9199
Almholme S York 83 SE5808
Almington Staffs 72 SJ7034
Almodington W Susx 14 SZ8297
Almondbank Tays 125 NO0625
Almondbury W York 82 SE1614
Almondsbury Avon 34 ST6084
Alne N York 90 SE4965
Alnesbourn Priory Suffk 55 TM1940
Alness Highld 146 NH6569
Alnham Nthumb 111 NT9810
Alnmouth Nthumb 111 NU2410
Alnwick Nthumb 111 NU1813
Alperton Gt Lon 26 TQ1883
Alphamstone Essex 54 TL8735
Alpheton Suffk 54 TL8750
Alphington Devon 9 SX9190
Alpington Norfk 67 TG2901
Alport Derbys 74 SK2264
Alpraham Ches 71 SJ5859
Alresford Essex 41 TM0621
Alrewas Staffs 61 SK1614
Alsager Ches 72 SJ7955
Alsagers Bank Staffs 72 SJ7948
Alshot Somset 20 ST1935
Alsop en le Dale Derbys 73 SK1554
Alston Cumb 94 NY7146
Alston Devon 10 ST3002
Alston Sutton Somset 21 ST4151
Alstone Gloucs 47 SO9832
Alstone Somset 21 ST3146
Alstone Green Staffs 72 SJ8518
Alstonefield Staffs 73 SK1355
Alswear Devon 19 SS7222
Alt Gt Man 79 SD9403
Altandhu Highld 144 NB9812
Altarnun Cnwll 5 SX2281
Altass Highld 146 NC5000
Altcreich Strath 122 NM6938
Altgaltraig Strath 114 NS0473
Altham Lancs 81 SD7732
Althorne Essex 40 TQ9198
Althorpe Humb 84 SE8309
Altnabreac Station Highld 150 ND0045
Altnacraig Strath 122 NM8429
Altnaharra Highld 149 NC5635
Altofts W York 83 SE3823
Alton Staffs 73 SK0741
Alton Derbys 74 SK3664
Alton Wilts 23 SU1546
Alton Hants 24 SU7139
Alton Barnes Wilts 23 SU1062
Alton Pancras Dorset 11 ST7002
Alton Priors Wilts 23 SU1162
Altrincham Gt Man 79 SJ7687
Alva Cent 116 NS8897
Alvanley Ches 71 SJ4974
Alvaston Derbys 62 SK3833
Alvechurch H & W 60 SP0272
Alvecote Warwks 61 SK2404
Alvediston Wilts 22 ST9723
Alveley Shrops 60 SO7584
Alverdiscott Devon 19 SS5225
Alverstoke Hants 13 SZ6098
Alverstone IOW 13 SZ5785
Alverthorpe W York 82 SE3121
Alverton Notts 63 SK7942
Alves Gramp 141 NJ1362
Alvescot Oxon 36 SP2704
Alveston Warwks 48 SP2356
Alveston Avon 35 ST6388
Alvie Highld 132 NH8609
Alvingham Lincs 77 TF3691
Alvington Gloucs 34 SO6000
Alwalton Cambs 64 TL1396
Alwinton Nthumb 110 NT9106
Alwoodley W York 82 SE2840
Alwoodley Gates W York 82 SE3140
Alyth Tays 126 NO2448
Amber Hill Lincs 76 TF2346
Amber Row Derbys 74 SK3856
Ambergate Derbys 74 SK3451
Amberley Gloucs 35 SO8501
Amberley W Susx 14 TQ0213
Ambirstone E Susx 16 TQ5911
Amble Nthumb 103 NU2604
Amblecote W Mids 60 SO8985

Ambler Thorn

Atherstone on Stour

Ambler Thorn *W York*	**82**	SE0929
Ambleside *Cumb*	**87**	NY3704
Ambleston *Dyfed*	**30**	SN0025
Ambrosden *Oxon*	**37**	SP6019
Amcotts *Humb*	**84**	SE8514
America *Cambs*	**53**	TL4378
Amersham *Bucks*	**26**	SU9597
Amersham on the Hill *Bucks*	**26**	SU9798
Amerton *Staffs*	**73**	SJ9927
Amesbury *Wilts*	**23**	SU1541
Amington *Staffs*	**61**	SK2304
Amisfield Town *D & G*	**100**	NY0082
Amlwch *Gwynd*	**68**	SH4492
Ammanford *Dyfed*	**32**	SN6212
Amotherby *N York*	**90**	SE7473
Ampfield *Hants*	**13**	SU4023
Ampleforth *N York*	**90**	SE5878
Ampney Crucis *Gloucs*	**36**	SP0601
Ampney St. Mary *Gloucs*	**36**	SP0802
Ampney St. Peter *Gloucs*	**36**	SP0801
Amport *Hants*	**23**	SU3044
Ampthill *Beds*	**38**	TL0337
Ampton *Suffk*	**54**	TL8671
Amroth *Dyfed*	**31**	SN1608
Amwell *Herts*	**39**	TL1613
Anaheilt *Highld*	**130**	NM8162
Ancaster *Lincs*	**63**	SK9843
Anchor *Shrops*	**58**	SO1785
Ancroft *Nthumb*	**111**	NT9945
Ancrum *Border*	**110**	NT6224
Ancton *W Susx*	**14**	SU9800
Anderby *Lincs*	**77**	TF5275
Andersea *Somset*	**21**	ST3333
Andersfield *Somset*	**20**	ST2434
Anderson *Dorset*	**11**	SY8897
Anderton *Ches*	**79**	SJ6475
Anderton *Cnwll*	**6**	SX4351
Andover *Hants*	**23**	SU3645
Andoversford *Gloucs*	**35**	SP0219
Andreas *IOM*	**153**	SC4199
Anelog *Gwynd*	**56**	SH1527
Anerley *Gt Lon*	**27**	TQ3369
Anfield *Mersyd*	**78**	SJ3692
Angarrack *Cnwll*	**2**	SW5838
Angarrick *Cnwll*	**3**	SW7937
Angelbank *Shrops*	**46**	SO5776
Angersleigh *Somset*	**20**	ST1918
Angerton *Cumb*	**93**	NY2257
Angle *Dyfed*	**30**	SM8603
Angmering *W Susx*	**14**	TQ0604
Angram *N York*	**88**	SD8899
Angram *N York*	**83**	SE5248
Angrouse *Cnwll*	**2**	SW6619
Anick *Nthumb*	**102**	NY9465
Ankerville *Highld*	**147**	NH8174
Ankle Hill *Leics*	**63**	SK7518
Anlaby *Humb*	**84**	TA0328
Anmer *Norfk*	**65**	TF7429
Anmore *Hants*	**13**	SU6611
Anna Valley *Hants*	**23**	SU3543
Annan *D & G*	**101**	NY1966
Annaside *Cumb*	**86**	SD0986
Annat *Highld*	**138**	NG8954
Annat *Strath*	**122**	NN0322
Annathill *Strath*	**116**	NS7270
Annbank *Strath*	**106**	NS4023
Annesley *Notts*	**75**	SK5053
Annesley Woodhouse *Notts*	**75**	SK4953
Annfield Plain *Dur*	**96**	NZ1651
Anniesland *Strath*	**115**	NS5368
Annitsford *T & W*	**103**	NZ2674
Annscroft *Shrops*	**59**	SJ4507
Ansdell *Lancs*	**80**	SD3428
Ansford *Somset*	**21**	ST6433
Ansley *Warwks*	**61**	SP3091
Anslow *Staffs*	**73**	SK2125
Anslow Gate *Staffs*	**73**	SK1924
Anslow Lees *Staffs*	**73**	SK2024
Ansteadbrook *Surrey*	**14**	SU9332
Anstey *Leics*	**62**	SK5508
Anstey *Hants*	**24**	SU7240
Anstey *Herts*	**39**	TL4033
Anstruther *Fife*	**127**	NO5703
Anstruther Easter *Fife*	**127**	NO5704
Ansty *Warwks*	**61**	SP4083
Ansty *Wilts*	**22**	ST9526
Ansty *W Susx*	**15**	TQ2923
Ansty Cross *Dorset*	**11**	ST7603
Anthill Common *Hants*	**13**	SU6312
Anthony's *Surrey*	**26**	TQ0161
Anthorn *Cumb*	**93**	NY1958
Antingham *Norfk*	**67**	TG2533
Antony *Cnwll*	**5**	SX4054
Antrobus *Ches*	**79**	SJ6480
Antron *Cnwll*	**2**	SW6327
Anvil Corner *Devon*	**18**	SS3704
Anvil Green *Kent*	**29**	TR1049
Anwick *Lincs*	**76**	TF1150
Anwoth *D & G*	**99**	NX5856
Aperfield *Gt Lon*	**27**	TQ4158
Apes Dale *H & W*	**60**	SO9972
Apethorpe *Nhants*	**51**	TL0295
Apeton *Staffs*	**72**	SJ8518
Apley *Lincs*	**76**	TF1075
Apperknowle *Derbys*	**74**	SK3878
Apperley *Gloucs*	**47**	SO8628
Apperley Bridge *W York*	**82**	SE1937
Apperley Dene *Nthumb*	**95**	NZ0558
Appersett *N York*	**88**	SD8690
Appin *Strath*	**122**	NM9346
Appleby *D & G*	**99**	NX4140
Appleby *Humb*	**84**	SE9514
Appleby Magna *Leics*	**61**	SK3109
Appleby Parva *Leics*	**61**	SK3008
Appleby Street *Herts*	**27**	TL3304
Appleby-in-Westmorland *Cumb*	**94**	NY6820
Applecross *Highld*	**137**	NG7144
Appledore *Devon*	**18**	SS4630
Appledore *Devon*	**9**	ST0614
Appledore *Kent*	**17**	TQ9529
Appledore Heath *Kent*	**17**	TQ9530
Appleford *Oxon*	**37**	SU5293
Applegarth Town *D & G*	**100**	NY1084
Applehaigh *S York*	**83**	SE3512
Appleshaw *Hants*	**23**	SU3048
Applethwaite *Cumb*	**93**	NY2625
Appleton *Ches*	**78**	SJ5186
Appleton *Oxon*	**37**	SP4401
Appleton Roebuck *N York*	**83**	SE5542
Appleton Wiske *N York*	**89**	NZ3804
Appleton-le-Moors *N York*	**90**	SE7387
Appleton-le-Street *N York*	**90**	SE7373
Appletreehall *Border*	**109**	NT5117
Appletreewick *N York*	**88**	SE0560
Appley *Somset*	**20**	ST0721
Appley Bridge *Lancs*	**78**	SD5209
Apse Heath *IOW*	**13**	SZ5683
Apsley End *Beds*	**38**	TL1232
Apsley Heath *Warwks*	**61**	SP0970
Apuldram *W Susx*	**14**	SU8403
Arbirlot *Tays*	**127**	NO6040
Arboll *Highld*	**147**	NH8781
Arborfield *Berks*	**24**	SU7567
Arborfield Cross *Berks*	**24**	SU7666
Arbory *IOM*	**153**	SC2470
Arbourthorne *S York*	**74**	SK3785
Arbroath *Tays*	**127**	NO6441
Arbuthnott *Gramp*	**135**	NO8074
Arcadia *Kent*	**28**	TQ8836
Archddu *Dyfed*	**32**	SN4401
Archdeacon Newton *Dur*	**96**	NZ2517
Archencarroch *Strath*	**115**	NS4182
Archiestown *Gramp*	**141**	NJ2244
Arclid Green *Ches*	**72**	SJ7861
Ard a'Chapuill *Strath*	**114**	NS0179
Ardaily *Strath*	**104**	NR6450
Ardalanish *Strath*	**121**	NM3619
Ardanaiseig Hotel *Strath*	**123**	NN0824
Ardarroch *Highld*	**137**	NG8339
Ardarroch *Strath*	**114**	NS2494
Ardbeg *Strath*	**104**	NR4146
Ardbeg *Strath*	**114**	NS0766
Ardbeg *Strath*	**114**	NS1583
Ardcharnich *Highld*	**145**	NH1788
Ardchiavaig *Strath*	**121**	NM3818
Ardchonnel *Strath*	**122**	NM9812
Ardchullarie More *Cent*	**124**	NN5813
Arddleen *Powys*	**58**	SJ2616
Ardechive *Highld*	**131**	NN1490
Ardeer *Strath*	**106**	NS2740
Ardeley *Herts*	**39**	TL3027
Ardelve *Highld*	**138**	NG8627
Arden *Strath*	**115**	NS3684
Ardens Grafton *Warwks*	**48**	SP1154
Ardentinny *Strath*	**114**	NS1887
Ardersier *Highld*	**140**	NH7855
Ardessie *Highld*	**145**	NH0689
Ardfen *Strath*	**122**	NM8004
Ardgay *Highld*	**146**	NH5990
Ardgour *Highld*	**130**	NN0163
Ardgowan *Strath*	**114**	NS2073
Ardhallow *Strath*	**114**	NS1674
Ardhasig *W Isls*	**154**	NB1202
Ardheslaig *Highld*	**137**	NG7855
Ardindrean *Highld*	**145**	NH1588
Ardingly *W Susx*	**15**	TQ3429
Ardington *Oxon*	**36**	SU4388
Ardington Wick *Oxon*	**36**	SU4389
Ardlamont *Strath*	**114**	NR9865
Ardleigh *Essex*	**41**	TM0529
Ardleigh Heath *Essex*	**41**	TM0430
Ardler *Tays*	**126**	NO2642
Ardley *Oxon*	**49**	SP5427
Ardley End *Essex*	**39**	TL5214
Ardlui *Strath*	**123**	NN3115
Ardlussa *Strath*	**113**	NR6487
Ardmaddy *Strath*	**123**	NN0837
Ardmair *Highld*	**145**	NH1198
Ardmaleish *Strath*	**114**	NS0768
Ardminish *Strath*	**104**	NR6448
Ardmolich *Highld*	**129**	NM7172
Ardmore *Highld*	**146**	NH7086
Ardmore *Strath*	**115**	NS3178
Ardnadam *Strath*	**114**	NS1780
Ardnagrask *Highld*	**139**	NH5249
Ardnarff *Highld*	**138**	NG8935
Ardnastang *Highld*	**130**	NM8061
Ardno *Strath*	**123**	NN1508
Ardochy House *Highld*	**131**	NH2002
Ardpatrick *Strath*	**113**	NR7660
Ardpeaton *Strath*	**114**	NS2185
Ardrishaig *Strath*	**113**	NR8585
Ardrossan *Strath*	**106**	NS2342
Ardshealach *Highld*	**121**	NM6867
Ardsley *S York*	**83**	SE3805
Ardsley East *W York*	**82**	SE3025
Ardslignish *Highld*	**121**	NM5661
Ardtalla *Strath*	**112**	NR4654
Ardtalnaig Hotel *Tays*	**124**	NN7039
Ardtoe *Highld*	**129**	NM6270
Arduaine *Strath*	**122**	NM7910
Ardvasar *Highld*	**129**	NG6303
Ardverikie *Highld*	**131**	NN5087
Ardvorlich *Tays*	**124**	NN6322
Ardvourlie *W Isls*	**154**	NB1810
Ardwell *D & G*	**98**	NX1045
Ardwick *Gt Man*	**79**	SJ8597
Areley Kings *H & W*	**60**	SO7970
Arevegaig *Highld*	**129**	NM6568
Arford *Hants*	**14**	SU8236
Argoed *Shrops*	**59**	SJ3220
Argoed *Gwent*	**33**	ST1799
Argoed Mill *Powys*	**45**	SN9963
Argos Hill *E Susx*	**16**	TQ5728
Aribrauch *W Isls*	**154**	NB2417
Aridhglas *Strath*	**120**	NM3123
Arileod *Strath*	**120**	NM1655
Arinacrinachd *Highld*	**137**	NG7458
Arinagour *Strath*	**120**	NM2257
Ariogan *Strath*	**122**	NM8627
Arisaig *Highld*	**129**	NM6586
Arisaig House *Highld*	**129**	NM6984
Arkendale *N York*	**89**	SE3861
Arkesden *Essex*	**39**	TL4834
Arkholme *Lancs*	**87**	SD5871
Arkleby *Cumb*	**92**	NY1439
Arkleton *D & G*	**101**	NY3791
Arkley *Gt Lon*	**26**	TQ2295
Arksey *S York*	**83**	SE5807
Arkwright Town *Derbys*	**74**	SK4270
Arle *Gloucs*	**47**	SO9223
Arlecdon *Cumb*	**92**	NY0419
Arlescote *Warwks*	**48**	SP3848
Arlesey *Beds*	**39**	TL1936
Arleston *Shrops*	**60**	SJ6609
Arley *Ches*	**79**	SJ6680
Arley *Warwks*	**61**	SP2890
Arlingham *Gloucs*	**35**	SO7010
Arlington *Gloucs*	**36**	SP1006
Arlington *Devon*	**19**	SS6140
Arlington *E Susx*	**16**	TQ5407
Arlington Beccott *Devon*	**19**	SS6241
Armadale *Highld*	**150**	NC7864
Armadale *Loth*	**116**	NS9368
Armaside *Cumb*	**92**	NY1527
Armathwaite *Cumb*	**94**	NY5046
Arminghall *Norfk*	**67**	TG2504
Armitage *Staffs*	**73**	SK0715
Armitage Bridge *W York*	**82**	SE1313
Armley *W York*	**82**	SE2833
Armshead *Staffs*	**72**	SJ9348
Armston *Nhants*	**51**	TL0685
Armthorpe *S York*	**83**	SE6204
Arnabost *Strath*	**120**	NM2159
Arnaby *Cumb*	**86**	SD1884
Arncliffe *N York*	**88**	SD9371
Arncliffe Cote *N York*	**88**	SD9470
Arncroach *Fife*	**127**	NO5105
Arndilly House *Gramp*	**141**	NJ2847
Arne *Dorset*	**11**	SY9788
Arnesby *Leics*	**50**	SP6192
Arnfield *Derbys*	**79**	SK0197
Arngask *Tays*	**126**	NO1410
Arnicle *Strath*	**105**	NR7138
Arnisdale *Highld*	**130**	NG8410
Arnish *Highld*	**137**	NG5948
Arniston *Loth*	**118**	NT3362
Arnol *W Isls*	**154**	NB3148
Arnold *Notts*	**62**	SK5845
Arnold *Humb*	**85**	TA1241
Arnprior *Cent*	**116**	NS6194
Arnside *Cumb*	**87**	SD4578
Aros *Strath*	**121**	NM5645
Arowry *Clwyd*	**71**	SJ4639
Arrad Foot *Cumb*	**86**	SD3080
Arram *Humb*	**84**	TA0344
Arrathorne *N York*	**89**	SE2093
Arreton *IOW*	**13**	SZ5386
Arrington *Cambs*	**52**	TL3250
Arriundle *Highld*	**130**	NM8264
Arrochar *Strath*	**123**	NN2904
Arrow *Warwks*	**48**	SP0856
Arrowfield Top *H & W*	**61**	SP0374
Arscott *Shrops*	**59**	SJ4307
Artafallie *Highld*	**140**	NH6349
Arthington *W York*	**82**	SE2644
Arthingworth *Nhants*	**50**	SP7581
Arthog *Gwynd*	**57**	SH6414
Arthrath *Gramp*	**143**	NJ9636
Arthursdale *W York*	**83**	SE3737
Artrochie *Gramp*	**143**	NK0031
Arundel *W Susx*	**14**	TQ0106
Asby *Cumb*	**92**	NY0620
Ascog *Strath*	**114**	NS1062
Ascot *Berks*	**25**	SU9268
Ascott *Warwks*	**48**	SP3234
Ascott Earl *Oxon*	**36**	SP3018
Ascott-under-Wychwood *Oxon*	**36**	SP3018
Asenby *N York*	**89**	SE3975
Asfordby *Leics*	**63**	SK7019
Asfordby Hill *Leics*	**63**	SK7219
Asgarby *Lincs*	**64**	TF1145
Asgarby *Lincs*	**77**	TF3366
Ash *Devon*	**19**	SS5208
Ash *Somset*	**20**	ST2822
Ash *Somset*	**21**	ST4720
Ash *Dorset*	**11**	ST8610
Ash *Surrey*	**25**	SU9051
Ash *Devon*	**7**	SX8349
Ash *Kent*	**27**	TQ6064
Ash *Kent*	**29**	TR2858
Ash Green *Warwks*	**61**	SP3384
Ash Green *Surrey*	**25**	SU9049
Ash Magna *Shrops*	**71**	SJ5739
Ash Mill *Devon*	**19**	SS7823
Ash Parva *Shrops*	**71**	SJ5739
Ash Priors *Somset*	**20**	ST1529
Ash Street *Suffk*	**54**	TM0146
Ash Thomas *Devon*	**9**	ST0010
Ash Vale *Surrey*	**25**	SU8951
Ashampstead *Berks*	**37**	SU5676
Ashampstead Green *Berks*	**37**	SU5677
Ashbocking *Suffk*	**54**	TM1754
Ashbocking Green *Suffk*	**54**	TM1854
Ashbourne *Derbys*	**73**	SK1746
Ashbourne Green *Derbys*	**73**	SK1948
Ashbrittle *Somset*	**20**	ST0521
Ashburnham Place *E Susx*	**16**	TQ6814
Ashburton *Devon*	**7**	SX7570
Ashbury *Oxon*	**36**	SU2685
Ashbury *Devon*	**5**	SX5098
Ashby *Humb*	**84**	SE8908
Ashby Folville *Leics*	**63**	SK7012
Ashby Magna *Leics*	**50**	SP5690
Ashby Parva *Leics*	**50**	SP5288
Ashby Puerorum *Lincs*	**77**	TF3271
Ashby St. Ledgers *Nhants*	**50**	SP5768
Ashby St. Mary *Norfk*	**67**	TG3202
Ashby by Partney *Lincs*	**77**	TF4266
Ashby cum Fenby *Humb*	**77**	TA2500
Ashby de la Launde *Lincs*	**76**	TF0555
Ashby-de-la-Zouch *Leics*	**62**	SK3516
Ashchurch *Gloucs*	**47**	SO9233
Ashcombe *Avon*	**21**	ST3361
Ashcombe *Devon*	**9**	SX9179
Ashcott *Somset*	**21**	ST4336
Ashdon *Essex*	**53**	TL5842
Ashe *Hants*	**24**	SU5350
Asheldham *Essex*	**41**	TL9701
Ashen *Essex*	**53**	TL7442
Ashendon *Bucks*	**37**	SP7014
Asheridge *Bucks*	**38**	SP9304
Ashfield *Cent*	**124**	NN7803
Ashfield *Hants*	**12**	SU3619
Ashfield *Suffk*	**55**	TM2062
Ashfield Green *Suffk*	**53**	TL7655
Ashfield Green *Suffk*	**55**	TM2573
Ashfields *Shrops*	**72**	SJ7026
Ashfold Crossways *W Susx*	**15**	TQ2328
Ashford *Derbys*	**74**	SK1969
Ashford *Devon*	**19**	SS5335
Ashford *Devon*	**7**	SX6948
Ashford *Surrey*	**26**	TQ0771
Ashford *Kent*	**28**	TR0142
Ashford Bowdler *Shrops*	**46**	SO5170
Ashford Carbonel *Shrops*	**46**	SO5270
Ashford Hill *Hants*	**24**	SU5562
Ashgill *Strath*	**116**	NS7850
Ashill *Devon*	**9**	ST0811
Ashill *Somset*	**10**	ST3217
Ashill *Norfk*	**66**	TF8804
Ashingdon *Essex*	**40**	TQ8693
Ashington *Nthumb*	**103**	NZ2687
Ashington *Somset*	**21**	ST5621
Ashington *W Susx*	**15**	TQ1315
Ashkirk *Border*	**109**	NT4722
Ashlett *Hants*	**13**	SU4603
Ashleworth *Gloucs*	**47**	SO8125
Ashleworth Quay *Gloucs*	**47**	SO8125
Ashley *Staffs*	**72**	SJ7636
Ashley *Ches*	**79**	SJ7784
Ashley *Nhants*	**50**	SP7990
Ashley *Devon*	**19**	SS6511
Ashley *Wilts*	**22**	ST8268
Ashley *Gloucs*	**35**	ST9394
Ashley *Hants*	**23**	SU3831
Ashley *Hants*	**12**	SZ2595
Ashley *Cambs*	**53**	TL6961
Ashley *Kent*	**29**	TR3048
Ashley Green *Bucks*	**38**	SP9705
Ashley Moor *H & W*	**46**	SO4767
Ashmansworth *Hants*	**24**	SU4157
Ashmansworthy *Devon*	**18**	SS3418
Ashmead Green *Gloucs*	**35**	ST7699
Ashmill *Devon*	**5**	SX3995
Ashmore *Dorset*	**11**	ST9117
Ashmore Green *Berks*	**24**	SU5069
Ashorne *Warwks*	**48**	SP3057
Ashover *Derbys*	**74**	SK3463
Ashover Hay *Derbys*	**74**	SK3460
Ashow *Warwks*	**61**	SP3170
Ashperton *H & W*	**47**	SO6441
Ashprington *Devon*	**7**	SX8157
Ashreigney *Devon*	**19**	SS6313
Ashridge Park *Herts*	**38**	SP9912
Ashtead *Surrey*	**26**	TQ1857
Ashton *Ches*	**71**	SJ5069
Ashton *H & W*	**46**	SO5164
Ashton *Nhants*	**49**	SP7649
Ashton *Somset*	**21**	ST4149
Ashton *Hants*	**13**	SU5419
Ashton *Cnwll*	**2**	SW6028
Ashton *Cnwll*	**5**	SX3868
Ashton *Devon*	**8**	SX8584
Ashton *Cambs*	**64**	TF1005
Ashton *Nhants*	**51**	TL0588
Ashton Common *Wilts*	**22**	ST8958
Ashton Hill *Wilts*	**22**	ST9057
Ashton Keynes *Wilts*	**36**	SU0494
Ashton Watering *Avon*	**21**	ST5369
Ashton under Hill *H & W*	**47**	SO9937
Ashton upon Mersey *Gt Man*	**79**	SJ7892
Ashton-under-Lyne *Gt Man*	**79**	SJ9399
Ashurst *Hants*	**12**	SU3310
Ashurst *W Susx*	**15**	TQ1715
Ashurst *Kent*	**16**	TQ5138
Ashurstwood *W Susx*	**15**	TQ4136
Ashwater *Devon*	**5**	SX3895
Ashwell *Leics*	**63**	SK8613
Ashwell *Herts*	**39**	TL2639
Ashwell End *Herts*	**39**	TL2540
Ashwellthorpe *Norfk*	**66**	TM1497
Ashwick *Somset*	**21**	ST6348
Ashwicken *Norfk*	**65**	TF7018
Ashwood *Staffs*	**60**	SO8688
Askam in Furness *Cumb*	**86**	SD2177
Aske Hall *N York*	**89**	NZ1703
Askern *S York*	**83**	SE5613
Askerswell *Dorset*	**10**	SY5292
Askett *Bucks*	**38**	SP8105
Askham *Cumb*	**94**	NY5123
Askham *Notts*	**75**	SK7374
Askham Bryan *N York*	**83**	SE5548
Askham Richard *N York*	**83**	SE5347
Asknish *Strath*	**114**	NR9391
Askrigg *N York*	**88**	SD9491
Askwith *N York*	**82**	SE1648
Aslackby *Lincs*	**64**	TF0830
Aslacton *Norfk*	**54**	TM1590
Aslockton *Notts*	**63**	SK7440
Asney *Somset*	**21**	ST4636
Aspall *Suffk*	**54**	TM1664
Aspatria *Cumb*	**92**	NY1441
Aspenden *Herts*	**39**	TL3528
Asperton *Lincs*	**64**	TF2637
Aspley *Staffs*	**72**	SJ8133
Aspley Guise *Beds*	**38**	SP9335
Aspley Heath *Beds*	**38**	SP9334
Aspull *Gt Man*	**78**	SD6108
Aspull Common *Gt Man*	**79**	SJ6498
Asselby *Humb*	**84**	SE7127
Asserby *Lincs*	**77**	TF4977
Asserby Turn *Lincs*	**77**	TF4777
Assington *Suffk*	**54**	TL9338
Assington Green *Suffk*	**53**	TL7751
Astbury *Ches*	**72**	SJ8461
Astcote *Nhants*	**49**	SP6753
Asterby *Lincs*	**77**	TF2679
Asterley *Shrops*	**59**	SJ3707
Asterton *Shrops*	**59**	SO3991
Asthall *Oxon*	**36**	SP2811
Asthall Leigh *Oxon*	**36**	SP3013
Astle *Highld*	**146**	NH7391
Astley *Gt Man*	**79**	SD7000
Astley *W York*	**83**	SE3828
Astley *Shrops*	**59**	SJ5218
Astley *H & W*	**47**	SO7867
Astley *Warwks*	**61**	SP3189
Astley Abbots *Shrops*	**60**	SO7096
Astley Bridge *Gt Man*	**81**	SD7111
Astley Cross *H & W*	**47**	SO8069
Astley Green *Gt Man*	**79**	SJ7099
Astley Town *H & W*	**47**	SO7968
Aston *Clwyd*	**71**	SJ3067
Aston *Shrops*	**59**	SJ5328
Aston *Ches*	**71**	SJ5578
Aston *Shrops*	**59**	SJ6109
Aston *Ches*	**71**	SJ6146
Aston *Staffs*	**72**	SJ7541
Aston *Staffs*	**72**	SJ8923
Aston *Staffs*	**72**	SJ9130
Aston *Derbys*	**74**	SK1783
Aston *S York*	**75**	SK4685
Aston *H & W*	**46**	SO4662
Aston *H & W*	**46**	SO4671
Aston *Shrops*	**60**	SO8093
Aston *W Mids*	**61**	SP0888
Aston *Oxon*	**36**	SP3403
Aston *Berks*	**37**	SU7884
Aston *Herts*	**39**	TL2722
Aston Abbotts *Bucks*	**38**	SP8420
Aston Botterell *Shrops*	**59**	SO6384
Aston Cantlow *Warwks*	**48**	SP1460
Aston Clinton *Bucks*	**38**	SP8812
Aston Crews *H & W*	**47**	SO6723
Aston Cross *Gloucs*	**47**	SO9433
Aston End *Herts*	**39**	TL2724
Aston Eyre *Shrops*	**59**	SO6594
Aston Fields *H & W*	**47**	SO9669
Aston Flamville *Leics*	**50**	SP4692
Aston Heath *Ches*	**71**	SJ5678
Aston Ingham *H & W*	**47**	SO6823
Aston Magna *Gloucs*	**48**	SP1935
Aston Pigott *Shrops*	**59**	SJ3305
Aston Rogers *Shrops*	**59**	SJ3406
Aston Rowant *Oxon*	**37**	SU7299
Aston Sandford *Bucks*	**37**	SP7507
Aston Somerville *H & W*	**48**	SP0438
Aston Subedge *Gloucs*	**48**	SP1441
Aston Tirrold *Oxon*	**37**	SU5586
Aston Upthorpe *Oxon*	**37**	SU5586
Aston juxta Mondrum *Ches*	**72**	SJ6456
Aston le Walls *Nhants*	**49**	SP4950
Aston on Clun *Shrops*	**59**	SO3981
Aston-in-Makerfield *Gt Man*	**78**	SJ5798
Aston-on-Trent *Derbys*	**62**	SK4129
Astonlane *Shrops*	**59**	SO6494
Astrop *Nhants*	**49**	SP5036
Astrope *Herts*	**38**	SP8914
Astwick *Beds*	**39**	TL2138
Astwith *Derbys*	**75**	SK4464
Astwood *H & W*	**47**	SO9365
Astwood *Bucks*	**38**	SP9547
Astwood Bank *H & W*	**48**	SP0462
Aswarby *Lincs*	**64**	TF0639
Aswardby *Lincs*	**77**	TF3770
Atch Lench *H & W*	**48**	SP0350
Atcham *Shrops*	**59**	SJ5409
Athelhampton *Dorset*	**11**	SY7694
Athelington *Suffk*	**55**	TM2171
Athelney *Somset*	**21**	ST3428
Athelstaneford *Loth*	**118**	NT5377
Atherfield Green *IOW*	**13**	SZ4679
Atherington *Devon*	**19**	SS5922
Atherington *W Susx*	**14**	TQ0000
Atherstone *Warwks*	**61**	SP3097
Atherstone *Somset*	**10**	ST3816
Atherstone on Stour *Warwks*	**48**	SP2051

Atherton Barlow

Atherton *Gt Man* 79 SD6703
Atley Hill *N York* 89 NZ2802
Atlow *Derbys* 73 SK2248
Attadale *Highld* 138 NG9238
Attenborough *Notts* 62 SK5034
Atterby *Lincs* 76 SK9792
Attercliffe *S York* 74 SK3788
Atterley *Shrops* 59 SO6397
Atterton *Leics* 61 SP3598
Attleborough *Warwks* 61 SP3790
Attleborough *Norfk* 66 TM0495
Attlebridge *Norfk* 66 TG1216
Attleton Green *Suffk* 53 TL7454
Attonburn *Border* 110 NT8122
Atwick *Humb* 85 TA1850
Atworth *Wilts* 22 ST8565
Auberrow *H & W* 46 SO4947
Aubourn *Lincs* 76 SK9262
Auchagallon *Strath* 105 NR8934
Auchedly *Gramp* 143 NJ8933
Auchenblae *Gramp* 135 NO7279
Auchenbowie *Cent* 116 NS7987
Auchencairn *D & G* 92 NX7951
Auchencairn *D & G* 100 NX9884
Auchencrow *Border* 119 NT8560
Auchendinny *Loth* 117 NT2561
Auchengray *Strath* 117 NS9954
Auchenhalrig *Gramp* 141 NJ3761
Auchenheath *Strath* 108 NS8043
Auchenhessnane *D & G* 100 NX8096
Auchenlochan *Strath* 114 NR9772
Auchenmade *Strath* 115 NS3548
Auchenmalg *D & G* 98 NX2352
Auchentibber *Strath* 116 NS6755
Auchentiber *Strath* 115 NS3647
Auchentroig *Cent* 115 NS5493
Auchindrean *Highld* 145 NH1980
Auchininna *Gramp* 142 NJ6546
Auchinleck *Strath* 107 NS5521
Auchinloch *Strath* 116 NS6570
Auchinstarry *Strath* 116 NS7176
Auchintore *Highld* 130 NN0972
Auchiries *Gramp* 143 NK0737
Auchlee *Gramp* 135 NO8996
Auchleven *Gramp* 142 NJ6224
Auchlochan *Strath* 107 NS7937
Auchlossan *Gramp* 134 NJ5601
Auchlyne *Cent* 124 NN5129
Auchmacoy *Gramp* 143 NJ9931
Auchmillan *Strath* 107 NS5129
Auchmithie *Tays* 127 NO6743
Auchmuirbridge *Fife* 126 NO2101
Auchnacree *Tays* 134 NO4663
Auchnagatt *Gramp* 143 NJ9241
Auchnangoul *Strath* 123 NN0605
Auchnotteroch *D & G* 98 NW9960
Auchroisk *Gramp* 141 NJ3351
Auchronie *Tays* 134 NO4480
Auchterarder *Tays* 125 NN9412
Auchteraw *Highld* 131 NH3507
Auchterblair *Highld* 140 NH9222
Auchtercairn *Highld* 144 NG8077
Auchterhouse *Tays* 126 NO3337
Auchterless *Gramp* 142 NJ7141
Auchtermuchty *Fife* 126 NO2311
Auchterneed *Highld* 139 NH4959
Auchtertool *Fife* 117 NT2190
Auchtertyre *Highld* 138 NG8427
Auchtoo *Cent* 124 NN5520
Auckengill *Highld* 151 ND3663
Auckley *S York* 75 SE6400
Audenshaw *Gt Man* 79 SJ9197
Audlem *Ches* 72 SJ6543
Audley *Staffs* 72 SJ7950
Audley End *Essex* 39 TL5337
Audley End *Essex* 54 TL8137
Audley End *Suffk* 54 TL8553
Audmore *Staffs* 72 SJ8321
Audnam *W Mids* 60 SO8986
Aughertree *Cumb* 93 NY2538
Aughton *Lancs* 78 SD3905
Aughton *Lancs* 87 SD5567
Aughton *Humb* 84 SE7038
Aughton *S York* 75 SK4586
Aughton *Wilts* 23 SU2356
Aughton Park *Lancs* 78 SD4006
Auldallan *Tays* 134 NO3158
Auldearn *Highld* 140 NH9255
Aulden *H & W* 46 SO4654
Auldgirth *D & G* 100 NX9186
Auldhame *Loth* 118 NT5984
Auldhouse *Strath* 116 NS6250
Ault Hucknall *Derbys* 75 SK4665
Ault a' chruinn *Highld* 138 NG9420
Aultbea *Highld* 144 NG8789
Aultgrishin *Highld* 144 NG7485
Aultguish Inn *Highld* 145 NH3570
Aultmore *Gramp* 142 NJ4053
Aultnagoire *Highld* 139 NH5423
Aultnamain Inn *Highld* 146 NH6681
Aunby *Lincs* 64 TF0214
Aunk *Devon* 9 ST0400
Aunsby *Lincs* 64 TF0438
Aust *Avon* 34 ST5788
Austendike *Lincs* 64 TF2821
Austerfield *Notts* 75 SK6694
Austerlands *Gt Man* 79 SD9505
Austhorpe *W York* 83 SE3733
Austonley *W York* 82 SE1107
Austrey *Warwks* 61 SK2906
Austwick *N York* 88 SD7668
Authorpe *Lincs* 77 TF3980
Authorpe Row *Lincs* 77 TF5373
Avebury *Wilts* 36 SU1069
Avebury Trusloe *Wilts* 36 SU0969
Aveley *Essex* 27 TQ5680
Avening *Gloucs* 35 ST8898
Averham *Notts* 75 SK7654
Aveton Gifford *Devon* 7 SX6947
Aviemore *Highld* 132 NH8913
Avington *Berks* 23 SU3767
Avoch *Highld* 140 NH7055
Avon *Dorset* 12 SZ1498
Avon Dassett *Warwks* 49 SP4150
Avonbridge *Cent* 116 NS9172
Avonmouth *Avon* 34 ST5178
Avonwick *Devon* 7 SX7158
Awkley *Avon* 34 ST5985
Awliscombe *Devon* 9 ST1301
Awre *Gloucs* 35 SO7008
Awsworth *Notts* 62 SK4844
Axborough *H & W* 60 SO8579
Axbridge *Somset* 21 ST4354
Axford *Wilts* 36 SU2370
Axford *Hants* 24 SU6043
Axminster *Devon* 10 SY2998
Axmouth *Devon* 10 SY2591
Axton *Clwyd* 70 SJ1080
Aycliffe *Dur* 96 NZ2822
Aylburton *Gloucs* 34 SO6101
Ayle *Cumb* 94 NY7149
Aylesbeare *Devon* 9 SY0392
Aylesbury *Bucks* 38 SP8213
Aylesby *Humb* 85 TA2007
Aylesford *Kent* 28 TQ7359
Aylesham *Kent* 29 TR2452
Aylestone *Leics* 50 SK5700
Aylestone Park *Leics* 50 SK5800
Aylmerton *Norfk* 66 TG1839
Aylsham *Norfk* 67 TG1926
Aylton *H & W* 47 SO6537
Aylworth *Gloucs* 36 SP1021
Aymestrey *H & W* 46 SO4265
Aynho *Nhants* 49 SP5133
Ayot Green *Herts* 39 TL2214
Ayot St. Lawrence *Herts* 39 TL1916
Ayot St. Peter *Herts* 39 TL2115
Ayr *Strath* 106 NS3321
Aysgarth *N York* 88 SE0088
Ayshford *Devon* 9 ST0415
Ayside *Cumb* 87 SD3983
Ayston *Leics* 51 SK8600
Aythorpe Roding *Essex* 40 TL5815
Ayton *Border* 119 NT9260
Azerley *N York* 89 SE2574

B

Babbacombe *Devon* 7 SX9265
Babbington *Notts* 62 SK4943
Babbinswood *Shrops* 59 SJ3329
Babbs Green *Herts* 39 TL3916
Babcary *Somset* 21 ST5628
Babel *Dyfed* 44 SN8235
Babel Green *Suffk* 53 TL7348
Babell *Clwyd* 70 SJ1573
Babeny *Devon* 7 SX6775
Babington *Somset* 22 ST7051
Bablock Hythe *Oxon* 36 SP4304
Babraham *Cambs* 53 TL5150
Babworth *Notts* 75 SK6880
Bachau *Gwynd* 68 SH4383
Bache *Shrops* 59 SO4681
Bacheldre *Powys* 58 SO2492
Bachelor Bump *E Susx* 17 TQ8412
Back Street *Suffk* 53 TL7458
Back o' th' Brook *Staffs* 73 SK0751
Back of Keppoch *Highld* 129 NM6587
Backaland *Ork* 155 HY5630
Backbarrow *Cumb* 87 SD3584
Backe *Dyfed* 31 SN2615
Backfolds *Gramp* 143 NK0252
Backford *Ches* 71 SJ3971
Backford Cross *Ches* 71 SJ3873
Backies *Highld* 147 NC8302
Backlass *Highld* 151 ND2053
Backwell *Avon* 21 ST4968
Backworth *T & W* 103 NZ3072
Bacon's End *W Mids* 61 SP1888
Baconsthorpe *Norfk* 66 TG1236
Bacton *H & W* 46 SO3732
Bacton *Norfk* 67 TG3433
Bacton *Suffk* 54 TM0567
Bacton Green *Suffk* 54 TM0365
Bacup *Lancs* 81 SD8622
Badachro *Highld* 137 NG7873
Badbury *Wilts* 36 SU1980
Badby *Nhants* 49 SP5658
Badcall *Highld* 148 NC1541
Badcall *Highld* 148 NC2455
Badcaul *Highld* 144 NH0291
Baddeley Edge *Staffs* 72 SJ9150
Baddeley Green *Staffs* 72 SJ9151
Baddesley Clinton *Warwks* 61 SP2070
Baddesley Ensor *Warwks* 61 SP2798
Baddidarroch *Highld* 145 NC0822
Badenscoth *Gramp* 142 NJ6938
Badenyon *Gramp* 141 NJ3319
Badgall *Cnwll* 5 SX2486
Badgeney *Cambs* 65 TL4397
Badger *Shrops* 60 SO7699
Badger's Cross *Cnwll* 2 SW4833
Badgers Mount *Kent* 27 TQ4962
Badgeworth *Gloucs* 35 SO9019
Badgworth *Somset* 21 ST3952
Badharlick *Cnwll* 5 SX2686
Badicaul *Highld* 137 NG7529
Badingham *Suffk* 55 TM3068
Badlesmere *Kent* 28 TR0153
Badlieu *Border* 108 NT0518
Badlipster *Highld* 151 ND2448
Badluachrach *Highld* 144 NG9994
Badninish *Highld* 147 NH7594
Badrallach *Highld* 145 NH0691
Badsey *H & W* 48 SP0743
Badshot Lea *Surrey* 25 SU8648
Badsworth *W York* 83 SE4614
Badwell Ash *Suffk* 54 TL9868
Badwell Green *Suffk* 54 TM0169
Bag Enderby *Lincs* 77 TF3571
Bagber *Dorset* 11 ST7513
Bagby *N York* 89 SE4680
Bagendon *Gloucs* 35 SP0106
Bagginswood *Shrops* 60 SO6881
Baggrow *Cumb* 93 NY1741
Bagham *Kent* 29 TR0753
Bagillt *Clwyd* 70 SJ2175
Baginton *Warwks* 61 SP3474
Baglan *W Glam* 32 SS7492
Bagley *W York* 82 SE2235
Bagley *Shrops* 59 SJ4027
Bagley *Somset* 21 ST4645
Bagmore *Hants* 24 SU6544
Bagnall *Staffs* 72 SJ9250
Bagnor *Berks* 24 SU4569
Bagot *Shrops* 46 SO5873
Bagshot *Wilts* 23 SU3165
Bagshot *Surrey* 25 SU9063
Bagstone *Avon* 35 ST6987
Bagthorpe *Notts* 75 SK4651
Bagworth *Leics* 62 SK4408
Bagwy Llydiart *H & W* 46 SO4426
Baildon *W York* 82 SE1539
Baildon Green *W York* 82 SE1439
Baile Mor *Strath* 120 NM2824
Bailey Green *Hants* 13 SU6627
Baileyhead *Cumb* 101 NY5179
Bailiff Bridge *W York* 82 SE1425
Baillieston *Strath* 116 NS6764
Bailrigg *Lancs* 87 SD4858
Bainbridge *N York* 88 SD9390
Bainshole *Gramp* 142 NJ6035
Bainton *Humb* 84 SE9652
Bainton *Oxon* 49 SP5827
Bainton *Cambs* 64 TF0906
Baintown *Fife* 126 NO3503
Bairnkine *Border* 110 NT6515
Baker Street *Essex* 40 TQ6381
Baker's End *Herts* 39 TL3917
Bakewell *Derbys* 74 SK2168
Bala *Gwynd* 58 SH9235
Balallan *W Isls* 154 NB2920
Balbeg *Highld* 139 NH4431
Balbeggie *Tays* 126 NO1629
Balblair *Highld* 139 NH5145
Balblair *Highld* 140 NH7066
Balby *S York* 75 SE5600
Balcary *D & G* 92 NX8149
Balchraggan *Highld* 139 NH5343
Balchrick *Highld* 148 NC1960
Balcombe *W Susx* 15 TQ3130
Balcombe Lane *W Susx* 15 TQ3132
Balcomie Links *Fife* 127 NO6209
Balcurvie *Fife* 118 NO3400
Baldersby *N York* 89 SE3578
Baldersby St. James *N York* 89 SE3676
Balderstone *Lancs* 81 SD6332
Balderstone *Gt Man* 79 SD9010
Balderton *Notts* 75 SK8151
Baldhu *Cnwll* 3 SW7743
Baldinnie *Fife* 127 NO4211
Baldinnies *Tays* 125 NO0216
Baldock *Herts* 39 TL2434
Baldovie *Tays* 127 NO4533
Baldrine *IOM* 153 SC4281
Baldslow *E Susx* 17 TQ8013
Baldwin *IOM* 153 SC3581
Baldwin's Gate *Staffs* 72 SJ7939
Baldwin's Hill *Surrey* 15 TQ3839
Baldwinholme *Cumb* 93 NY3351
Bale *Norfk* 66 TG0136
Baledgarno *Tays* 126 NO2730
Balemartine *Strath* 120 NL9841
Balerno *Loth* 117 NT1666
Balfarg *Fife* 126 NO2803
Balfield *Tays* 134 NO5468
Balfour *Ork* 155 HY4716
Balfron *Cent* 115 NS5489
Balgaveny *Gramp* 142 NJ6540
Balgavies *Tays* 127 NO5451
Balgonar *Fife* 117 NT0293
Balgowan *Highld* 132 NN6494
Balgowan *D & G* 98 NX1142
Balgown *Highld* 136 NG3868
Balgracie *D & G* 98 NW9860
Balgray *Tays* 126 NO4038
Balhalgardy *Gramp* 142 NJ7523
Balham *Gt Lon* 27 TQ2873
Balhary *Tays* 126 NO2646
Balholmie *Tays* 126 NO1436
Baligill *Highld* 150 NC8565
Balintore *Highld* 147 NH8675
Balintore *Tays* 133 NO2859
Balintraid *Highld* 146 NH7370
Balivanich *W Isls* 154 NF7755
Balk *N York* 89 SE4780
Balkeerie *Tays* 126 NO3244
Balkholme *Humb* 84 SE7828
Balkissock *Strath* 98 NX1482
Ball *Shrops* 59 SJ3026
Ball Green *Staffs* 72 SJ8952
Ball Haye Green *Staffs* 72 SJ9856
Ball Hill *Hants* 24 SU4163
Ball's Green *Gloucs* 35 ST8699
Ballabeg *IOM* 153 SC2570
Ballachgair *Strath* 105 NR7727
Ballachulish *Highld* 130 NN0858
Ballamodha *IOM* 153 SC2773
Ballantrae *Strath* 98 NX0882
Ballards Gore *Essex* 40 TQ9092
Ballards Green *Warwks* 61 SP2791
Ballasalla *IOM* 153 SC2870
Ballater *Gramp* 134 NO3695
Ballaugh *IOM* 153 SC3493
Ballchraggan *Highld* 147 NH7675
Ballechin *Tays* 125 NN9353
Ballencrieff *Loth* 118 NT4878
Ballevullin *Strath* 120 NL9546
Ballidon *Derbys* 73 SK2054
Balliekine *Strath* 105 NR8739
Balliemore *Strath* 114 NS1099
Balligmorrie *Strath* 106 NX2290
Ballimore *Cent* 124 NN5317
Ballimore *Strath* 114 NR9283
Ballindalloch *Gramp* 141 NJ1636
Ballindean *Tays* 126 NO2529
Ballingdon *Essex* 54 TL8640
Ballinger Common *Bucks* 38 SP9103
Ballingham *H & W* 46 SO5731
Ballingry *Fife* 117 NT1797
Ballinluig *Tays* 125 NN9752
Ballinshoe *Tays* 126 NO4153
Ballintuim *Tays* 126 NO1055
Balloch *Highld* 140 NH7247
Balloch *Tays* 125 NN8419
Balloch *Strath* 106 NX3295
Ballochroy *Strath* 106 NR7352
Ballogie *Gramp* 134 NO5795
Balls Cross *W Susx* 14 SU9826
Balls Green *E Susx* 16 TQ4936
Ballygown *Strath* 121 NM4343
Ballygrant *Strath* 112 NR3966
Ballygroggan *Strath* 104 NR6219
Ballyhaugh *Strath* 120 NM1758
Ballymenoch *Strath* 115 NS3086
Ballymichael *Strath* 105 NR9231
Balmacara *Highld* 137 NG8028
Balmaclellan *D & G* 99 NX6579
Balmacneil *Tays* 125 NN9750
Balmae *D & G* 99 NX6844
Balmaha *Cent* 115 NS4290
Balmalcolm *Fife* 126 NO3208
Balmangan *D & G* 99 NX6445
Balmedie *Gramp* 143 NJ9618
Balmer Heath *Shrops* 59 SJ4434
Balmerino *Fife* 126 NO3524
Balmerlawn *Hants* 12 SU3003
Balmore *Strath* 115 NS5973
Balmuchy *Highld* 147 NH8678
Balmuir *Tays* 127 NO5648
Balmule *Fife* 117 NT2088
Balmullo *Fife* 127 NO4220
Balnaboth *Tays* 134 NO3166
Balnacoil Lodge *Highld* 147 NC8011
Balnacroft *Gramp* 133 NO2894
Balnafoich *Highld* 140 NH6835
Balnaguard *Tays* 125 NN9451
Balnahard *Strath* 121 NM4534
Balnahard *Strath* 112 NR4199
Balnain *Highld* 139 NH4430
Balnakeil *Highld* 149 NC3968
Balnapaling *Highld* 147 NH7969
Balquharn *Tays* 125 NO0235
Balquhidder *Cent* 124 NN5320
Balruddery House *Tays* 126 NO3132
Balsall *W Mids* 61 SP2376
Balsall Common *W Mids* 61 SP2377
Balsall Heath *W Mids* 61 SP0784
Balsall Street *W Mids* 61 SP2276
Balscote *Oxon* 48 SP3942
Balsham *Cambs* 53 TL5850
Baltasound *Shet* 155 HP6208
Balterley *Staffs* 72 SJ7650
Balterley Green *Staffs* 72 SJ7650
Baltersan *D & G* 99 NX4261
Balthangie *Gramp* 143 NJ8351
Baltonsborough *Somset* 21 ST5434
Balvicar *Strath* 122 NM7616
Balvraid *Highld* 129 NG8416
Balvraid *Highld* 140 NH8231
Balwest *Cnwll* 2 SW5930
Bamber Bridge *Lancs* 81 SD5625
Bamber's Green *Essex* 40 TL5722
Bamburgh *Nthumb* 111 NU1734
Bamff *Tays* 126 NO2251
Bamford *Gt Man* 81 SD8612
Bamford *Derbys* 74 SK2083
Bampton *Cumb* 94 NY5118
Bampton *Oxon* 36 SP3103
Bampton *Devon* 20 SS9522
Bampton Grange *Cumb* 94 NY5218
Banavie *Highld* 130 NN1177
Banbury *Oxon* 49 SP4540
Banc-y-ffordd *Dyfed* 31 SN4037
Bancffosfelem *Dyfed* 32 SN4811
Banchory *Gramp* 135 NO6995
Banchory-Devenick *Gramp* 135 NJ9002
Bancycapel *Dyfed* 31 SN4214
Bancyfelin *Dyfed* 31 SN3218
Bandirran *Tays* 126 NO2030
Bandrake Head *Cumb* 86 SD3187
Banff *Gramp* 142 NJ6863
Bangor *Gwynd* 69 SH5772
Bangor's Green *Lancs* 78 SD3709
Bangor-is-y-coed *Clwyd* 71 SJ3845
Bangors *Cnwll* 18 SX2099
Banham *Norfk* 54 TM0687
Bank *Hants* 12 SU2807
Bank Ground *Cumb* 86 SD3196
Bank Newton *N York* 81 SD9053
Bank Street *H & W* 47 SO6362
Bank Top *Lancs* 78 SD5207
Bank Top *W York* 82 SE1024
Bankend *Strath* 108 NS8033
Bankend *D & G* 100 NY0268
Bankfoot *Tays* 125 NO0635
Bankglen *Strath* 107 NS5912
Bankhead *Gramp* 135 NJ9009
Bankhead *Strath* 106 NS3739
Banknock *Cent* 116 NS7779
Banks *Cumb* 101 NY5664
Banks *Lancs* 80 SD3920
Banks Green *H & W* 47 SO9967
Bankshill *D & G* 101 NY1982
Banningham *Norfk* 67 TG2129
Bannister Green *Essex* 40 TL6920
Bannockburn *Cent* 116 NS8190
Banstead *Surrey* 27 TQ2559
Bantham *Devon* 7 SX6643
Banton *Strath* 116 NS7480
Banwell *Avon* 21 ST3959
Bapchild *Kent* 28 TQ9263
Bapton *Wilts* 22 ST9938
Bar Hill *Cambs* 52 TL3863
Barassie *Strath* 106 NS3232
Barbaraville *Highld* 146 NH7472
Barber Booth *Derbys* 74 SK1184
Barber Green *Cumb* 87 SD3982
Barbieston *Strath* 107 NS4317
Barbon *Cumb* 87 SD6282
Barbridge *Ches* 71 SJ6156
Barbrook *Devon* 19 SS7147
Barby *Nhants* 50 SP5470
Barcaldine *Strath* 122 NM9641
Barcheston *Warwks* 48 SP2639
Barclose *Cumb* 101 NY4462
Barcombe *E Susx* 15 TQ4114
Barcombe Cross *E Susx* 15 TQ4115
Barcroft *W York* 82 SE0437
Barden *N York* 89 SE1493
Barden Park *Kent* 16 TQ5746
Bardfield End Green *Essex* 40 TL6231
Bardfield Saling *Essex* 40 TL6826
Bardney *Lincs* 76 TF1269
Bardon *Leics* 62 SK4412
Bardon Mill *Nthumb* 102 NY7764
Bardowie *Strath* 115 NS5873
Bardown *E Susx* 16 TQ6629
Bardrainney *Strath* 115 NS3373
Bardsea *Cumb* 86 SD3074
Bardsey *W York* 83 SE3643
Bardsley *Gt Man* 79 SD9201
Bardwell *Suffk* 54 TL9473
Bare *Lancs* 87 SD4564
Bareppa *Cnwll* 3 SW7729
Barewood *H & W* 46 SO3856
Barfad *D & G* 98 NX3266
Barford *Warwks* 48 SP2760
Barford *Norfk* 66 TG1107
Barford St. John *Oxon* 49 SP4433
Barford St. Martin *Wilts* 23 SU0531
Barford St. Michael *Oxon* 49 SP4332
Barfrestone *Kent* 29 TR2650
Bargate *Derbys* 62 SK3546
Bargeddie *Strath* 116 NS6964
Bargoed *M Glam* 33 ST1599
Bargrennan *D & G* 98 NX3577
Barham *Cambs* 52 TL1375
Barham *Suffk* 54 TM1451
Barham *Kent* 29 TR2050
Barholm *Lincs* 64 TF0810
Barkby *Leics* 63 SK6309
Barkby Thorpe *Leics* 63 SK6309
Barkers Green *Shrops* 59 SJ5228
Barkestone-le-Vale *Leics* 63 SK7734
Barkham *Berks* 25 SU7766
Barking *Suffk* 54 TM0753
Barking *Gt Lon* 27 TQ4484
Barking Tye *Suffk* 54 TM0652
Barkingside *Gt Lon* 27 TQ4489
Barkisland *W York* 82 SE0519
Barkla Shop *Cnwll* 3 SW7350
Barkston *N York* 83 SE4936
Barkston *Lincs* 63 SK9341
Barkway *Herts* 39 TL3835
Barlaston *Staffs* 72 SJ8938
Barlavington *W Susx* 14 SU9716
Barlborough *Derbys* 75 SK4777
Barlby *N York* 83 SE6333
Barlestone *Leics* 62 SK4205
Barley *Lancs* 81 SD8240
Barley *Herts* 39 TL4038
Barley Hole *S York* 74 SK3697
Barleycroft End *Herts* 39 TL4327
Barleythorpe *Leics* 63 SK8409
Barling *Essex* 40 TQ9389
Barlings *Lincs* 76 TF0774
Barlochan *D & G* 92 NX8157
Barlow *T & W* 96 NZ1561
Barlow *N York* 83 SE6428

Barlow Berrier

Barlow *Derbys* 74 SK3474
Barmby Moor *Humb* 84 SE7748
Barmby on the Marsh *Humb* 83 SE6928
Barmer *Norfk* 66 TF8133
Barming Heath *Kent* 28 TQ7255
Barmollack *Strath* 105 NR8043
Barmouth *Gwynd* 57 SH6116
Barmpton *Dur* 96 NZ3118
Barmston *Humb* 91 TA1659
Barnaby Green *Suffk* 55 TM4780
Barnacabber *Strath* 114 NS1789
Barnacarry *Strath* 114 NS0094
Barnack *Cambs* 64 TF0705
Barnacle *Warwks* 61 SP3884
Barnard Castle *Dur* 95 NZ0516
Barnard Gate *Oxon* 36 SP4010
Barnardiston *Suffk* 53 TL7148
Barnbarroch *D & G* 92 NX8456
Barnburgh *S York* 83 SE4803
Barnby *Suffk* 55 TM4789
Barnby Dun *S York* 83 SE6109
Barnby Moor *Notts* 75 SK6684
Barnby in the Willows *Notts* 76 SK8552
Barncorkrie *D & G* 98 NX0935
Barnes *Gt Lon* 26 TQ2276
Barnes Street *Kent* 16 TQ6447
Barnet *Gt Lon* 26 TQ2496
Barnet Gate *Gt Lon* 26 TQ2195
Barnetby le Wold *Humb* 84 TA0509
Barney *Norfk* 66 TF9932
Barnham *W Susx* 14 SU9503
Barnham *Suffk* 54 TL8779
Barnham Broom *Norfk* 66 TG0807
Barnhead *Tays* 135 NO6657
Barnhill *Gramp* 141 NJ1457
Barnhill *Tays* 127 NO4731
Barnhill *Ches* 71 SJ4854
Barnhills *D & G* 98 NW9871
Barningham *Dur* 89 NZ0810
Barningham *Suffk* 54 TL9676
Barnoldby le Beck *Humb* 85 TA2303
Barnoldswick *Lancs* 81 SD8746
Barns Green *W Susx* 14 TQ1226
Barnsley *S York* 83 SE3406
Barnsley *Shrops* 60 SO7592
Barnsley *Gloucs* 36 SP0704
Barnsole *Kent* 29 TR2756
Barnstaple *Devon* 19 SS5633
Barnston *Mersyd* 78 SJ2783
Barnston *Essex* 40 TL6419
Barnstone *Notts* 63 SK7335
Barnt Green *H & W* 60 SP0173
Barnton *Loth* 117 NT1874
Barnton *Ches* 71 SJ6375
Barnwell All Saints *Nhants* 51 TL0484
Barnwell St. Andrew *Nhants* 51 TL0584
Barnwood *Gloucs* 35 SO8518
Baron's Cross *H & W* 46 SO4758
Barons Wood *Devon* 8 SS7003
Baronwood *Cumb* 94 NY5143
Barr *Strath* 106 NX2794
Barrachan *D & G* 99 NX3649
Barrapoll *Strath* 120 NL9442
Barras *Cumb* 88 NY8511
Barrasford *Nthumb* 102 NY9173
Barrets Green *Ches* 71 SJ5859
Barrhead *Strath* 115 NS4958
Barrhill *Strath* 98 NX2382
Barrington *Somset* 10 ST3818
Barrington *Cambs* 52 TL3849
Barripper *Cnwll* 2 SW6338
Barrmill *Strath* 115 NS3651
Barrnacarry Bay *Strath* 122 NM8122
Barrock *Highld* 151 ND2570
Barrow *Lancs* 81 SD7338
Barrow *Shrops* 59 SJ6500
Barrow *Leics* 63 SK8815
Barrow *Gloucs* 47 SO8824
Barrow *Somset* 22 ST7231
Barrow *Suffk* 53 TL7663
Barrow Bridge *Gt Man* 81 SD6811
Barrow Burn *Nthumb* 110 NT8610
Barrow Gurney *Avon* 21 ST5268
Barrow Haven *Humb* 84 TA0622
Barrow Hill *Derbys* 74 SK4275
Barrow Nook *Lancs* 78 SD4402
Barrow Street *Wilts* 22 ST8330
Barrow Vale *Avon* 21 ST6460
Barrow upon Soar *Leics* 62 SK5717
Barrow upon Trent *Derbys* 62 SK3528
Barrow's Green *Ches* 78 SJ5287
Barrow's Green *Ches* 72 SJ6857
Barrow-in-Furness *Cumb* 86 SD2068
Barrow-upon-Humber *Humb* 84 TA0620
Barroway Drove *Norfk* 65 TF5703
Barrowby *Lincs* 63 SK8736
Barrowden *Leics* 51 SK9400
Barrowford *Lancs* 81 SD8539
Barry *Tays* 127 NO5334
Barry *S Glam* 20 ST1268
Barry Island *S Glam* 20 ST1166
Barsby *Leics* 63 SK6911
Barsham *Suffk* 55 TM3989
Barskimmings *Strath* 107 NS4825
Barston *W Mids* 61 SP2078
Bartestree *H & W* 46 SO5640
Barthol Chapel *Gramp* 143 NJ8133
Bartholomew Green *Essex* 40 TL7221
Barthomley *Ches* 72 SJ7652
Bartley *Hants* 12 SU3012
Bartley Green *W Mids* 60 SP0081
Bartlow *Cambs* 53 TL5845
Barton *Cumb* 94 NY4826
Barton *N York* 89 NZ2208
Barton *Lancs* 78 SD3509
Barton *Lancs* 80 SD5137
Barton *Ches* 71 SJ4454
Barton *H & W* 46 SO2957
Barton *Gloucs* 48 SP0925
Barton *Warwks* 48 SP1051
Barton *Oxon* 37 SP5507
Barton *Devon* 7 SX9167
Barton *Cambs* 52 TL4055
Barton Bendish *Norfk* 65 TF7105
Barton End *Gloucs* 35 ST8498
Barton Green *Staffs* 73 SK1717
Barton Hartshorn *Bucks* 49 SP6430
Barton Mills *Suffk* 53 TL7173
Barton Seagrave *Nhants* 51 SP8877
Barton St. David *Somset* 21 ST5432
Barton Stacey *Hants* 24 SU4341
Barton Town *Devon* 19 SS6840
Barton Turf *Norfk* 67 TG3522
Barton Waterside *Humb* 84 TA0222
Barton in Fabis *Notts* 62 SK5132
Barton in the Beans *Leics* 62 SK3906
Barton in the Clay *Beds* 38 TL0830
Barton on Sea *Hants* 12 SZ2393
Barton upon Irwell *Gt Man* 79 SJ7697
Barton-Upon-Humber *Humb* 84 TA0221
Barton-le-Street *N York* 90 SE7274
Barton-le-Willows *N York* 90 SE7163
Barton-on-the-Heath *Warwks* 48 SP2532
Barton-under-Needwood *Staffs* 73 SK1818
Barugh *S York* 82 SE3108
Barugh Green *S York* 82 SE3107
Barvas *W Isls* 154 NB3649
Barway *Cambs* 53 TL5575
Barwell *Leics* 50 SP4496
Barwick *Devon* 8 SS5907
Barwick *Somset* 10 ST5513
Barwick *Herts* 39 TL3819
Barwick in Elmet *W York* 83 SE4037
Baschurch *Shrops* 59 SJ4221
Bascote *Warwks* 48 SP4063
Bascote Heath *Warwks* 48 SP3962
Base Green *Suffk* 54 TM0163
Basford Green *Staffs* 72 SJ9851
Bashall Eaves *Lancs* 81 SD6943
Bashall Town *Lancs* 81 SD7142
Bashley *Hants* 12 SZ2496
Basildon *Berks* 37 SU6078
Basildon *Essex* 40 TQ7189
Basingstoke *Hants* 24 SU6352
Baslow *Derbys* 74 SK2572
Bason Bridge *Somset* 21 ST3446
Bassaleg *Gwent* 34 ST2786
Bassendean *Border* 110 NT6245
Bassenthwaite *Cumb* 93 NY2332
Bassett *Hants* 13 SU4216
Bassingbourn *Cambs* 39 TL3343
Bassingfield *Notts* 62 SK6137
Bassingham *Lincs* 76 SK9060
Bassingthorpe *Leics* 63 SK9628
Bassus Green *Herts* 39 TL3025
Bastad *Kent* 27 TQ6055
Baston *Lincs* 64 TF1113
Bastwick *Norfk* 67 TG4217
Batch *Somset* 21 ST3255
Batchworth *Herts* 26 TQ0694
Batchworth Heath *Herts* 26 TQ0792
Batcombe *Somset* 22 ST6938
Bate Heath *Ches* 79 SJ6879
Batecombe *Dorset* 10 ST6103
Batford *Herts* 38 TL1415
Bath *Avon* 22 ST7464
Bath Side *Essex* 41 TM2532
Bathampton *Avon* 22 ST7766
Bathealton *Somset* 20 ST0823
Batheaston *Avon* 22 ST7767
Bathford *Avon* 22 ST7866
Bathgate *Loth* 117 NS9768
Bathley *Notts* 75 SK7759
Bathpool *Somset* 20 ST2526
Bathpool *Cnwll* 5 SX2874
Bathville *Loth* 116 NS9367
Bathway *Somset* 21 ST5952
Batley *W York* 82 SE2224
Batsford *Gloucs* 48 SP1833
Batson *Devon* 7 SX7339
Batt's Corner *Surrey* 25 SU8240
Battersby *N York* 90 NZ5907
Battersea *Gt Lon* 27 TQ2776
Battisborough Cross *Devon* 6 SX5948
Battisford *Suffk* 54 TM0554
Battisford Tye *Suffk* 54 TM0354
Battle *Powys* 45 SO0130
Battle *E Susx* 17 TQ7515
Battleborough *Somset* 21 ST3450
Battledown *Gloucs* 35 SO9621
Battledykes *Tays* 127 NO4555
Battlefield *Shrops* 59 SJ5117
Battlesbridge *Essex* 40 TQ7894
Battlesden *Beds* 38 SP9628
Battleton *Somset* 20 SS9127
Battlies Green *Suffk* 54 TL9064
Battramsley Cross *Hants* 12 SZ3198
Battye Ford *W York* 82 SE1920
Baughton *H & W* 47 SO8841
Baughurst *Hants* 24 SU5860
Baulds *Gramp* 134 NO6093
Baulking *Oxon* 36 SU3191
Baumber *Lincs* 76 TF2274
Baunton *H & W* 35 SP0104
Baveney Wood *Shrops* 60 SO6979
Baverstock *Wilts* 23 SU0332
Bawburgh *Norfk* 66 TG1508
Bawdeswell *Norfk* 66 TG0420
Bawdrip *Somset* 21 ST3439
Bawdsey *Suffk* 55 TM3440
Bawtry *Notts* 75 SK6493
Baxenden *Lancs* 81 SD7726
Baxter's Green *Suffk* 53 TL7557
Baxterley *Warwks* 61 SP2896
Baxton *Kent* 28 TQ8959
Bay Horse *Lancs* 80 SD4952
Bayble *W Isls* 154 NB5231
Baybridge *Nthumb* 95 NY9550
Baybridge *Hants* 13 SU5223
Baycliff *Cumb* 86 SD2872
Baydon *Wilts* 36 SU2878
Bayford *Somset* 22 ST7229
Bayford *Herts* 39 TL3108
Bayhead *W Isls* 154 NF7468
Bayley's Hill *Kent* 27 TQ5151
Baylham *Suffk* 54 TM1051
Baynard's Green *Oxon* 49 SP5429
Baysdale Abbey *N York* 90 NZ6206
Baysham *H & W* 46 SO5727
Bayston Hill *Shrops* 59 SJ4808
Baythorne End *Essex* 53 TL7242
Bayton *H & W* 60 SO6973
Bayton Common *H & W* 60 SO7173
Bayworth *Oxon* 37 SP4901
Beach *Avon* 35 ST7071
Beachampton *Bucks* 49 SP7736
Beachamwell *Norfk* 65 TF7505
Beachborough *Kent* 29 TR1638
Beachley *Gloucs* 34 ST5591
Beacon *Devon* 9 ST1805
Beacon End *Essex* 41 TL9524
Beacon Hill *Notts* 75 SK8153
Beacon Hill *Surrey* 14 SU8736
Beacon Hill *E Susx* 16 TQ5030
Beacon Hill *Kent* 17 TQ8232
Beacon's Bottom *Bucks* 37 SU7895
Beaconsfield *Bucks* 26 SU9490
Beacontree *Gt Lon* 27 TQ4786
Beadlam *N York* 90 SE6584
Beadlow *Beds* 38 TL1038
Beadnell *Nthumb* 111 NU2229
Beaford *Devon* 19 SS5515
Beal *Nthumb* 111 NU0642
Beal *N York* 83 SE5325
Bealbury *Cnwll* 5 SX3766
Bealsmill *Cnwll* 5 SX3576
Beam Hill *Staffs* 73 SK2325
Beamhurst *Staffs* 73 SK0536
Beaminster *Dorset* 10 ST4701
Beamish *Dur* 96 NZ2253
Beamsley *N York* 82 SE0752
Bean *Kent* 27 TQ5872
Beanacre *Wilts* 22 ST9066
Beanley *Nthumb* 111 NU0818
Beardon *Devon* 5 SX5184
Beardwood *Lancs* 81 SD6629
Beare *Devon* 9 SS9901
Beare Green *Surrey* 15 TQ1742
Bearley *Warwks* 48 SP1860
Bearley Cross *Warwks* 48 SP1761
Bearpark *Dur* 96 NZ2343
Bearsbridge *Nthumb* 94 NY7857
Bearsden *Strath* 115 NS5372
Bearstead *Kent* 28 TQ8055
Bearstone *Shrops* 72 SJ7239
Bearwood *W Mids* 60 SP0286
Beatley Heath *Herts* 27 TQ2599
Beattock *D & G* 108 NT0802
Beauchamp Roding *Essex* 40 TL5809
Beauchief *S York* 74 SK3381
Beaudesert *Warwks* 48 SP1565
Beaufort *Gwent* 33 SO1611
Beaulieu *Hants* 12 SU3802
Beauly *Highld* 139 NH5246
Beaumaris *Gwynd* 69 SH6076
Beaumont *Jersey* 152 JS0000
Beaumont *Cumb* 93 NY3459
Beaumont *Essex* 41 TM1624
Beaumont Hill *Dur* 96 NZ2918
Beausale *Warwks* 61 SP2470
Beauworth *Hants* 13 SU5726
Beaver *Kent* 28 TR0040
Beaver Green *Kent* 28 TR0041
Beaworthy *Devon* 18 SX4699
Beazley End *Essex* 40 TL7429
Bebington *Mersyd* 78 SJ3383
Bebside *Nthumb* 103 NZ2781
Beccles *Suffk* 55 TM4289
Becconsall *Lancs* 80 SD4523
Beck Foot *Cumb* 87 SD6196
Beck Hole *N York* 90 NZ8202
Beck Row *Suffk* 53 TL6977
Beck Side *Cumb* 86 SD2382
Beck Side *Cumb* 87 SD3780
Beckbury *Shrops* 60 SJ7601
Beckenham *Gt Lon* 27 TQ3769
Beckering *Lincs* 76 TF1280
Beckermet *Cumb* 86 NY0106
Beckett End *Norfk* 65 TL7798
Beckfoot *Cumb* 92 NY0949
Beckfoot *Cumb* 86 NY1600
Beckfoot *Cumb* 86 SD1989
Beckford *H & W* 47 SO9736
Beckhampton *Wilts* 23 SU0868
Beckingham *Notts* 75 SK7789
Beckingham *Lincs* 76 SK8753
Beckington *Somset* 22 ST8051
Beckjay *Shrops* 46 SO3977
Beckley *Oxon* 37 SP5611
Beckley *Hants* 12 SZ2296
Beckley *E Susx* 17 TQ8523
Becks *W York* 82 SE0345
Beckside *Cumb* 87 SD6187
Beckton *Gt Lon* 27 TQ4381
Beckwithshaw *N York* 82 SE2653
Becquet Vincent *Jersey* 152 JS0000
Bedale *N York* 89 SE2688
Bedburn *Dur* 95 NZ0931
Bedchester *Dorset* 11 ST8517
Beddau *M Glam* 33 ST0585
Beddgelert *Gwynd* 69 SH5948
Beddingham *E Susx* 16 TQ4407
Beddington *Gt Lon* 27 TQ3065
Beddington Corner *Gt Lon* 27 TQ2866
Bedfield *Suffk* 55 TM2166
Bedfield Little Green *Suffk* 55 TM2365
Bedford *Beds* 38 TL0449
Bedgebury Cross *Kent* 17 TQ7134
Bedham *W Susx* 14 TQ0122
Bedhampton *Hants* 13 SU7006
Bedingfield *Suffk* 54 TM1768
Bedingfield Green *Suffk* 54 TM1866
Bedingfield Street *Suffk* 54 TM1768
Bedlam *N York* 89 SE2661
Bedlam Lane *Kent* 28 TQ8845
Bedlington *T & W* 103 NZ2681
Bedlinog *M Glam* 33 SO0901
Bedminster *Avon* 34 ST5871
Bedminster Down *Avon* 34 ST5770
Bedmond *Herts* 38 TL0903
Bednall *Staffs* 72 SJ9517
Bedrule *Border* 110 NT6017
Bedstone *Shrops* 46 SO3676
Bedwas *M Glam* 33 ST1789
Bedwellty *Gwent* 33 SO1600
Bedworth *Warwks* 61 SP3687
Bedworth Woodlands *Warwks* 61 SP3487
Beeby *Leics* 63 SK6608
Beech *Staffs* 72 SJ8538
Beech *Hants* 24 SU6938
Beech Hill *Berks* 24 SU6964
Beechingstoke *Wilts* 23 SU0859
Beedon *Berks* 37 SU4878
Beedon Hill *Berks* 37 SU4877
Beeford *Humb* 85 TA1253
Beeley *Derbys* 74 SK2667
Beelsby *Humb* 85 TA2001
Beenham *Berks* 24 SU5868
Beer *Somset* 21 ST4031
Beer *Devon* 9 SY2289
Beer Hackett *Dorset* 10 ST6011
Beercrocombe *Somset* 21 ST3220
Beesands *Devon* 7 SX8140
Beesby *Lincs* 77 TF4680
Beeson *Devon* 7 SX8140
Beeston *W York* 82 SE2830
Beeston *Ches* 71 SJ5358
Beeston *Notts* 62 SK5236
Beeston *Norfk* 66 TF9015
Beeston *Beds* 52 TL1648
Beeston Regis *Norfk* 66 TG1642
Beeswing *D & G* 100 NX8969
Beetham *Cumb* 87 SD4979
Beetham *Somset* 10 ST2712
Beetley *Norfk* 66 TF9718
Began *S Glam* 34 ST2283
Begbroke *Oxon* 37 SP4614
Begdale *Cambs* 65 TF4506
Begelly *Dyfed* 31 SN1107
Beggar's Bush *Powys* 46 SO2664
Beggarinton Hill *W York* 82 SE2724
Beguildy *Powys* 45 SO1979
Beighton *S York* 75 SK4483
Beighton *Norfk* 67 TG3808
Beighton Hill *Derbys* 73 SK2951
Bein Inn *Tays* 126 NO1513
Beith *Strath* 115 NS3553
Bekesbourne *Kent* 29 TR1955
Bekesbourne Hill *Kent* 29 TR1856
Belaugh *Norfk* 67 TG2818
Belbroughton *H & W* 60 SO9277
Belchalwell *Dorset* 11 ST7909
Belchalwell Street *Dorset* 11 ST7909
Belchamp Otten *Essex* 54 TL8041
Belchamp St. Paul *Essex* 53 TL7942
Belchamp Walter *Essex* 54 TL8240
Belchford *Lincs* 77 TF2975
Belford *Nthumb* 111 NU1034
Belgrave *Leics* 62 SK5906
Belhelvie *Gramp* 143 NJ9417
Belhinnie *Gramp* 142 NJ4627
Bell Bar *Herts* 39 TL2505
Bell Busk *N York* 81 SD9056
Bell End *H & W* 60 SO9477
Bell Heath *H & W* 60 SO9477
Bell Hill *Hants* 13 SU7324
Bell o' th'Hill *Ches* 71 SJ5245
Bellabeg *Gramp* 134 NJ3513
Belladrum *Highld* 139 NH5142
Bellanoch *Strath* 113 NR7992
Bellasize *Humb* 84 SE8227
Bellaty *Tays* 133 NO2359
Belle Vue *Cumb* 92 NY1131
Belle Vue *Cumb* 93 NY3756
Belle Vue *W York* 83 SE3419
Belleau *Lincs* 77 TF4078
Bellerby *N York* 89 SE1192
Bellever *Devon* 8 SX6577
Bellfield *Strath* 108 NS8234
Bellfield *Strath* 108 NS9620
Bellimoor *H & W* 46 SO3840
Bellingdon *Bucks* 38 SP9405
Bellingham *Nthumb* 102 NY8383
Belloch *Strath* 105 NR6737
Bellochantuy *Strath* 104 NR6632
Bellows Cross *Dorset* 12 SU0613
Bells Cross *Suffk* 54 TM1552
Bells Yew Green *E Susx* 16 TQ6135
Bellshill *Nthumb* 111 NU1230
Bellside *Strath* 116 NS8058
Bellsquarry *Loth* 117 NT0465
Belluton *Avon* 21 ST6164
Belmaduthy *Highld* 140 NH6456
Belmont *Shet* 155 HP5600
Belmont *Strath* 106 NS3419
Belmont *Lancs* 81 SD6715
Belmont *Gt Lon* 27 TQ2562
Belnacraig *Gramp* 141 NJ3716
Belowda *Cnwll* 4 SW9661
Belper *Derbys* 62 SK3447
Belper Lane End *Derbys* 74 SK3349
Belsay *Nthumb* 103 NZ0978
Belsay Castle *Nthumb* 103 NZ0878
Belses *Border* 110 NT5725
Belsford *Devon* 7 SX7659
Belsize *Herts* 26 TL0300
Belstead *Suffk* 54 TM1241
Belstone *Devon* 8 SX6293
Belthorn *Lancs* 81 SD7124
Beltinge *Kent* 29 TR1967
Beltingham *Nthumb* 102 NY7863
Beltoft *Humb* 84 SE8006
Belton *Humb* 84 SE7806
Belton *Leics* 62 SK4420
Belton *Leics* 63 SK8101
Belton *Lincs* 63 SK9339
Belton *Norfk* 67 TG4802
Beltring *Kent* 28 TQ6747
Belvedere *Gt Lon* 27 TQ4978
Belvoir *Leics* 63 SK8133
Bembridge *IOW* 13 SZ6488
Bemersley Green *Staffs* 72 SJ8854
Bemersyde *Border* 110 NT5933
Bemerton *Wilts* 23 SU1230
Bempton *Humb* 91 TA1972
Ben Rhydding *W York* 82 SE1347
Benacre *Suffk* 55 TM5184
Benbuie *D & G* 107 NX7196
Benderloch *Strath* 122 NM9038
Benenden *Kent* 17 TQ8033
Benfield *D & G* 99 NX3763
Benfieldside *Dur* 95 NZ0952
Bengall *D & G* 100 NY1178
Bengates *Norfk* 67 TG3027
Bengeworth *H & W* 48 SP0443
Benhall Green *Suffk* 55 TM3961
Benhall Street *Suffk* 55 TM3561
Benholm *Gramp* 135 NO8069
Beningbrough *N York* 90 SE5257
Benington *Lincs* 77 TF3946
Benington *Herts* 39 TL2923
Benllech *Gwynd* 68 SH5182
Benmore *Strath* 114 NS1385
Bennacott *Cnwll* 5 SX2992
Bennan *Strath* 105 NR9921
Bennet Head *Cumb* 93 NY4423
Bennetland *Humb* 84 SE8228
Bennett End *Bucks* 37 SU7897
Bennington Sea End *Lincs* 65 TF4145
Benniworth *Lincs* 76 TF2081
Benny *Cnwll* 4 SX1192
Benover *Kent* 28 TQ7048
Benson *Oxon* 37 SU6291
Bentfield Green *Essex* 39 TL5025
Benthall *Shrops* 60 SJ6602
Bentham *Gloucs* 35 SO9116
Benthoul *Gramp* 135 NJ8003
Bentlawn *Shrops* 59 SJ3301
Bentley *S York* 83 SE5605
Bentley *Warwks* 61 SP2895
Bentley *Hants* 25 SU7844
Bentley *Humb* 84 TA0136
Bentley *Suffk* 54 TM1138
Bentley Heath *W Mids* 61 SP1675
Bentley Rise *S York* 83 SE5604
Benton *Devon* 19 SS6536
Bentpath *D & G* 101 NY3190
Bentwichen *Devon* 19 SS7333
Bentworth *Hants* 24 SU6640
Benvie *Tays* 126 NO3231
Benville *Dorset* 10 ST5303
Benwick *Cambs* 52 TL3490
Beoley *H & W* 48 SP0669
Beoraidbeg *Highld* 129 NM6793
Bepton *W Susx* 14 SU8618
Berden *Essex* 39 TL4629
Bere Alston *Devon* 6 SX4466
Bere Ferrers *Devon* 6 SX4563
Bere Regis *Dorset* 11 SY8494
Berea *Dyfed* 30 SM7930
Berepper *Cnwll* 2 SW6523
Bergh Apton *Norfk* 67 TG3001
Berhill *Somset* 21 ST4436
Berinsfield *Oxon* 37 SU5696
Berkeley *Gloucs* 35 ST6899
Berkeley Heath *Gloucs* 35 ST6999
Berkeley Road *Gloucs* 35 SO7200
Berkhamsted *Herts* 38 SP9907
Berkley *Somset* 22 ST8049
Berkswell *W Mids* 61 SP2479
Bermondsey *Gt Lon* 27 TQ3479
Bernera *Highld* 129 NG8020
Bernice *Strath* 114 NS1391
Bernisdale *Highld* 136 NG4050
Berrick Prior *Oxon* 37 SU6294
Berrick Salome *Oxon* 37 SU6293
Berriedale *Highld* 147 ND1222
Berrier *Cumb* 93 NY3929

Berriew Bleasby

Berriew *Powys* 58 SJ1801
Berrington *Nthumb* 111 NU0043
Berrington *Shrops* 59 SJ5206
Berrington *H & W* 46 SO5767
Berrington Green *H & W* 46 SO5766
Berrow *Somset* 20 ST2951
Berry Brow *W York* 82 SE1314
Berry Cross *Devon* 18 SS4714
Berry Down Cross *Devon* 19 SS5743
Berry Hill *Dyfed* 30 SN0640
Berry Hill *Gloucs* 34 SO5712
Berry Pomeroy *Devon* 7 SX8261
Berry's Green *Gt Lon* 27 TQ4359
Berryhillock *Gramp* 142 NJ5054
Berryhillock *Gramp* 142 NJ5060
Berrynarbor *Devon* 19 SS5646
Bersham *Clwyd* 71 SJ3049
Berthengam *Clwyd* 70 SJ1179
Berwick *E Susx* 16 TQ5105
Berwick Bassett *Wilts* 36 SU0973
Berwick Hill *Nthumb* 103 NZ1775
Berwick St. James *Wilts* 23 SU0739
Berwick St. John *Wilts* 22 ST9422
Berwick St. Leonard *Wilts* 22 ST9233
Berwick-upon-Tweed *Nthumb* 119 NT9953
Bescaby *Leics* 63 SK8126
Bescar *Cumb* 80 SD3913
Besford *Shrops* 59 SJ5525
Besford *H & W* 47 SO9144
Besom Hill *Gt Man* 79 SD9508
Bessacarr *S York* 75 SE6100
Bessels Leigh *Oxon* 37 SP4501
Besses o' th' Barn *Gt Man* 79 SD8005
Bessingby *Humb* 91 TA1566
Bessingham *Norfk* 66 TG1636
Bestbeech Hill *E Susx* 16 TQ6231
Besthorpe *Notts* 75 SK8264
Besthorpe *Norfk* 66 TM0595
Beswick *Humb* 84 TA0147
Betchworth *Surrey* 26 TQ2150
Bethania *Gwynd* 57 SH7044
Bethania *Dyfed* 43 SN5763
Bethel *Gwynd* 68 SH3970
Bethel *Gwynd* 68 SH5265
Bethel *Gwynd* 70 SH9839
Bethel *Powys* 58 SJ1021
Bethersden *Kent* 28 TQ9240
Bethesda *Gwynd* 69 SH6266
Bethesda *Dyfed* 31 SN0918
Bethlehem *Dyfed* 44 SN6825
Bethnal Green *Gt Lon* 27 TQ3482
Betley *Staffs* 72 SJ7548
Betsham *Kent* 27 TQ6071
Betteshanger *Kent* 29 TR3152
Bettisfield *Clwyd* 59 SJ4635
Betton *Shrops* 72 SJ6936
Betton Strange *Shrops* 59 SJ5009
Bettws *Gwent* 34 ST2890
Bettws Bledrws *Dyfed* 44 SN5952
Bettws Cedewain *Powys* 58 SO1296
Bettws Evan *Dyfed* 42 SN3047
Betws Gerfil Goch *Clwyd* 70 SJ0346
Bettws-Newydd *Gwent* 34 SO3606
Bettyhill *Highld* 150 NC7061
Betws *Dyfed* 32 SN6311
Betws *M Glam* 33 SS9086
Betws Garmon *Gwynd* 69 SH5357
Betws-y-coed *Gwynd* 69 SH7956
Betws-yn-Rhos *Clwyd* 69 SH9073
Beulah *Dyfed* 42 SN2846
Beulah *Powys* 45 SN9251
Bevendean *E Susx* 15 TQ3306
Bevercotes *Notts* 75 SK6972
Beverley *Humb* 84 TA0339
Beverstone *Gloucs* 35 ST8694
Bevington *Gloucs* 35 ST6596
Bewaldeth *Cumb* 93 NY2034
Bewcastle *Cumb* 101 NY5674
Bewdley *H & W* 60 SO7875
Bewerley *N York* 89 SE1565
Bewholme *Humb* 85 TA1649
Bewlbridge *Kent* 16 TQ6834
Bewlie *Border* 109 NT5525
Bexhill *E Susx* 17 TQ7407
Bexley *Gt Lon* 27 TQ4973
Bexley Heath *Gt Lon* 27 TQ4875
Bexleyhill *W Susx* 14 SU9125
Bexwell *Norfk* 65 TF6303
Beyton *Suffk* 54 TL9363
Beyton Green *Suffk* 54 TL9363
Bibstone *Avon* 35 ST6991
Bibury *Gloucs* 36 SP1106
Bicester *Oxon* 49 SP5823
Bickenhill *W Mids* 61 SP1882
Bicker *Lincs* 64 TF2237
Bicker Bar *Lincs* 64 TF2438
Bicker Gauntlet *Lincs* 64 TF2139
Bickershaw *Gt Man* 79 SD6201
Bickerstaffe *Lancs* 78 SD4404
Bickerton *Nthumb* 103 NT9900
Bickerton *N York* 83 SE4550
Bickerton *Ches* 71 SJ5052
Bickerton *Devon* 7 SX8139
Bickford *Staffs* 60 SJ8814
Bickington *Devon* 19 SS5332
Bickington *Devon* 7 SX8072
Bickleigh *Devon* 9 SS9407
Bickleigh *Devon* 6 SX5262
Bickleton *Devon* 19 SS5030
Bickley *N York* 91 SE9191
Bickley *Ches* 71 SJ5348
Bickley *H & W* 47 SO6371
Bickley *Gt Lon* 27 TQ4268
Bickley Moss *Ches* 71 SJ5448
Bicknacre *Essex* 40 TL7802
Bicknoller *Somset* 20 ST1139
Bicknor *Kent* 28 TQ8658
Bickton *Hants* 12 SU1412
Bicton *Shrops* 59 SJ4415
Bicton *Shrops* 59 SO2983
Bicton *H & W* 46 SO4764
Bidborough *Kent* 16 TQ5643
Bidden *Hants* 24 SU7049
Biddenden *Kent* 28 TQ8538
Biddenden Green *Kent* 28 TQ8842
Biddenham *Beds* 38 TL0250
Biddestone *Wilts* 35 ST8673
Biddisham *Somset* 21 ST3853
Biddlesden *Bucks* 49 SP6340
Biddlestone *Nthumb* 111 NT9508
Biddulph *Staffs* 72 SJ8858
Biddulph Moor *Staffs* 72 SJ9058
Bideford *Devon* 18 SS4526
Bidford-on-Avon *Warwks* 48 SP1052
Bidston *Mersyd* 78 SJ2890
Bielby *Humb* 84 SE7843
Bieldside *Gramp* 135 NJ8702
Bierley *IOW* 13 SZ5078
Bierton *Bucks* 38 SP8415
Big Balcraig *D & G* 99 NX3843
Big Carlae *D & G* 107 NX6597
Big Sand *Highld* 144 NG7578
Bigbury *Devon* 7 SX6646
Bigbury-on-Sea *Devon* 7 SX6544
Bigby *Lincs* 84 TA0507
Biggar *Strath* 108 NT0437
Biggar *Cumb* 86 SD1966
Biggin *N York* 83 SE5434
Biggin *Derbys* 74 SK1559
Biggin *Derbys* 73 SK2549
Biggin Hill *Gt Lon* 27 TQ4159
Biggleswade *Beds* 39 TL1944
Bigholms *D & G* 101 NY3180
Bighouse *Highld* 150 NC8964
Bighton *Hants* 24 SU6134
Bigland Hall *Cumb* 87 SD3583
Biglands *Cumb* 93 NY2553
Bignor *W Susx* 14 SU9814
Bigrigg *Cumb* 92 NY0013
Bilborough *Notts* 62 SK5241
Bilbrook *Staffs* 60 SJ8703
Bilbrook *Somset* 20 ST0341
Bilbrough *N York* 83 SE5346
Bilbster *Highld* 151 ND2853
Bildershaw *Dur* 96 NZ2024
Bildeston *Suffk* 54 TL9949
Bill Street *Kent* 28 TQ7370
Billacott *Cnwll* 5 SX2690
Billericay *Essex* 40 TQ6794
Billesdon *Leics* 63 SK7202
Billesley *Warwks* 48 SP1456
Billingborough *Lincs* 64 TF1133
Billinge *Mersyd* 78 SD5200
Billingford *Norfk* 66 TG0120
Billingford *Norfk* 54 TM1678
Billingham *Cleve* 97 NZ4624
Billinghay *Lincs* 76 TF1554
Billingley *S York* 83 SE4304
Billingshurst *W Susx* 14 TQ0825
Billingsley *Shrops* 60 SO7085
Billington *Lancs* 81 SD7235
Billington *Staffs* 72 SJ8820
Billington *Beds* 38 SP9422
Billockby *Norfk* 67 TG4313
Billy Row *Dur* 96 NZ1637
Bilsborrow *Lancs* 80 SD5139
Bilsby *Lincs* 77 TF4776
Bilsham *W Susx* 14 SU9702
Bilsington *Kent* 17 TR0434
Bilsthorpe *Notts* 75 SK6460
Bilsthorpe Moor *Notts* 75 SK6560
Bilston *Loth* 117 NT2664
Bilston *W Mids* 60 SO9596
Bilstone *Leics* 62 SK3605
Bilting *Kent* 28 TR0549
Bilton *Nthumb* 111 NU2210
Bilton *N York* 83 SE4749
Bilton *Warwks* 50 SP4873
Bilton *Humb* 85 TA1632
Bilton Banks *Nthumb* 111 NU2010
Binbrook *Lincs* 76 TF2093
Binchester Blocks *Dur* 96 NZ2232
Bincombe *Dorset* 11 SY6884
Binegar *Somset* 21 ST6149
Bines Green *W Susx* 15 TQ1817
Binfield *Berks* 25 SU8471
Binfield Heath *Oxon* 37 SU7477
Bingfield *Nthumb* 102 NY9772
Bingham *Notts* 63 SK7039
Bingham's Melcombe *Dorset* 11 ST7702
Bingley *W York* 82 SE1039
Bings *Shrops* 59 SJ5318
Binham *Norfk* 66 TF9839
Binley *W Mids* 61 SP3778
Binley *Hants* 24 SU4253
Binnegar *Dorset* 11 SY8887
Binniehill *Cent* 116 NS8572
Binns Farm *Gramp* 141 NJ3164
Binscombe *Surrey* 25 SU9645
Binsey *Oxon* 37 SP4907
Binstead *Hants* 25 SU7740
Binstead *IOW* 13 SZ5892
Binsted *W Susx* 14 SU9806
Binton *Warwks* 48 SP1454
Bintree *Norfk* 66 TG0123
Binweston *Shrops* 59 SJ3004
Birch *Gt Man* 79 SD8507
Birch *Essex* 40 TL9419
Birch Close *Dorset* 11 ST8803
Birch Cross *Staffs* 73 SK1230
Birch Green *Herts* 39 TL2911
Birch Green *Essex* 40 TL9418
Birch Heath *Ches* 71 SJ5461
Birch Hill *Ches* 71 SJ5173
Birch Vale *Derbys* 74 SK0286
Birch Wood *Somset* 9 ST2414
Bircham Newton *Norfk* 65 TF7733
Bircham Tofts *Norfk* 65 TF7732
Birchanger *Essex* 39 TL5122
Birchencliffe *W York* 82 SE1218
Bircher *H & W* 46 SO4765
Birchfield *W Mids* 61 SP0790
Birchgrove *W Glam* 32 SS7098
Birchgrove *S Glam* 33 ST1679
Birchgrove *E Susx* 15 TQ4029
Birchington *Kent* 29 TR3069
Birchley Heath *Warwks* 61 SP2894
Birchmoor Green *Beds* 38 SP9534
Birchover *Derbys* 74 SK2362
Birchyfield *H & W* 47 SO6453
Bircotes *Notts* 75 SK6391
Bird End *W Mids* 60 SP0194
Bird Street *Suffk* 54 TM0052
Birdbrook *Essex* 53 TL7041
Birdforth *N York* 90 SE4875
Birdham *W Susx* 14 SU8200
Birdingbury *Warwks* 50 SP4368
Birdlip *Gloucs* 35 SO9214
Birdoswald *Cumb* 102 NY6166
Birds Edge *W York* 82 SE2007
Birds Green *Essex* 40 TL5808
Birdsall *N York* 90 SE8165
Birdsgreen *Shrops* 60 SO7785
Birdsmoorgate *Dorset* 10 ST3900
Birdwell *S York* 83 SE3401
Birdwood *Gloucs* 35 SO7418
Birgham *Border* 110 NT7939
Birichin *Highld* 147 NH7592
Birkacre *Lancs* 81 SD5714
Birkby *N York* 89 NZ3202
Birkdale *Mersyd* 80 SD3214
Birkenbog *Gramp* 142 NJ5365
Birkenhead *Mersyd* 78 SJ3288
Birkenhills *Gramp* 142 NJ7445
Birkenshaw *W York* 82 SE2028
Birkhall *Gramp* 134 NO3493
Birkhill *Tays* 126 NO3534
Birkhill *D & G* 109 NT2015
Birkholme *Lincs* 63 SK9623
Birkin *N York* 83 SE5326
Birks *W York* 82 SE2626
Birkshaw *Nthumb* 102 NY7765
Birley *H & W* 46 SO4553
Birley Carr *S York* 74 SK3392
Birling *Nthumb* 111 NU2406
Birling *Kent* 28 TQ6860
Birling Gap *E Susx* 16 TV5596
Birlingham *H & W* 47 SO9343
Birmingham *W Mids* 61 SP0786
Birnam *Tays* 125 NO0341
Birness *Gramp* 143 NJ9933
Birse *Gramp* 134 NO5697
Birsemore *Gramp* 134 NO5297
Birstall *W York* 82 SE2225
Birstall *Leics* 62 SK5909
Birstwith *N York* 89 SE2359
Birthorpe *Lincs* 64 TF1033
Birtley *Nthumb* 102 NY8778
Birtley *T & W* 96 NZ2756
Birtley *H & W* 46 SO3669
Birts Street *H & W* 47 SO7836
Bisbrooke *Leics* 51 SP8899
Biscathorpe *Lincs* 76 TF2284
Biscovey *Cnwll* 3 SX0552
Bish Mill *Devon* 19 SS7425
Bisham *Berks* 26 SU8485
Bishampton *H & W* 47 SO9951
Bishop Auckland *Dur* 96 NZ2028
Bishop Burton *Humb* 84 SE9839
Bishop Middleham *Dur* 96 NZ3231
Bishop Monkton *N York* 89 SE3266
Bishop Norton *Lincs* 76 SK9892
Bishop Sutton *Avon* 21 ST5859
Bishop Thornton *N York* 89 SE2563
Bishop Wilton *Humb* 84 SE7955
Bishop's Castle *Shrops* 59 SO3288
Bishop's Cleeve *Gloucs* 47 SO9627
Bishop's Frome *H & W* 47 SO6648
Bishop's Green *Hants* 24 SU5063
Bishop's Green *Essex* 40 TL6217
Bishop's Itchington *Warwks* 48 SP3857
Bishop's Norton *Gloucs* 47 SO8424
Bishop's Nympton *Devon* 19 SS7523
Bishop's Offley *Staffs* 72 SJ7729
Bishop's Stortford *Herts* 39 TL4821
Bishop's Sutton *Hants* 24 SU6032
Bishop's Tachbrook *Warwks* 48 SP3161
Bishop's Tawton *Devon* 19 SS5729
Bishop's Waltham *Hants* 13 SU5517
Bishop's Wood *Staffs* 60 SJ8309
Bishop's Caundle *Dorset* 11 ST6913
Bishopbridge *Lincs* 76 TF0391
Bishopbriggs *Strath* 116 NS6070
Bishops Cannings *Wilts* 23 SU0364
Bishops Gate *Surrey* 25 SU9871
Bishops Hull *Somset* 20 ST2024
Bishops Lydeard *Somset* 20 ST1729
Bishopsbourne *Kent* 29 TR1852
Bishopsteignton *Devon* 7 SX9073
Bishopstoke *Hants* 13 SU4619
Bishopston *Warwks* 48 SP1956
Bishopston *W Glam* 32 SS5789
Bishopstone *H & W* 46 SO4143
Bishopstone *Bucks* 38 SP8010
Bishopstone *Wilts* 23 SU0625
Bishopstone *Wilts* 36 SU2483
Bishopstone *E Susx* 16 TQ4701
Bishopstone *Kent* 26 TQ2068
Bishopstrow *Wilts* 22 ST8943
Bishopswood *Somset* 10 ST2612
Bishopsworth *Avon* 21 ST5768
Bishopthorpe *N York* 83 SE5947
Bishopton *Strath* 115 NS4371
Bishopton *Dur* 96 NZ3621
Bishton *Staffs* 73 SK0220
Bishton *Gwent* 34 ST3887
Bisley *Gloucs* 35 SO9005
Bisley *Surrey* 25 SU9559
Bisley Camp *Surrey* 25 SU9357
Bispham *Lancs* 80 SD3140
Bispham Green *Lancs* 80 SD4813
Bissoe *Cnwll* 3 SW7741
Bisterne *Hants* 12 SU1401
Bitchet Green *Kent* 27 TQ5654
Bitchfield *Lincs* 63 SK9828
Bittadon *Devon* 19 SS5441
Bittaford *Devon* 7 SX6656
Bittering *Norfk* 66 TF9417
Bitterley *Shrops* 46 SO5677
Bitterne *Hants* 13 SU4513
Bitteswell *Leics* 50 SP5385
Bitton *Avon* 35 ST6869
Bix *Oxon* 37 SU7284
Blaby *Leics* 50 SP5697
Black Bourton *Oxon* 36 SP2804
Black Callerton *T & W* 103 NZ1769
Black Car *Norfk* 66 TM0995
Black Corner *W Susx* 15 TQ2939
Black Corries *Highld* 123 NN2956
Black Crofts *Strath* 122 NM9234
Black Cross *Cnwll* 4 SW9060
Black Dog *Devon* 19 SS8009
Black Heddon *Nthumb* 103 NZ0775
Black Lane *Gt Man* 79 SD7708
Black Lane Ends *Lancs* 81 SD9243
Black Moor *W York* 82 SE2939
Black Notley *Essex* 40 TL7620
Black Street *Suffk* 55 TM5186
Black Tar *Dyfed* 30 SM9909
Black Torrington *Devon* 18 SS4605
Blackadder *Border* 119 NT8452
Blackawton *Devon* 7 SX8051
Blackbank *Warwks* 61 SP3586
Blackbeck *Cumb* 86 NY0207
Blackborough *Devon* 9 ST0909
Blackborough End *Norfk* 65 TF6615
Blackboys *E Susx* 16 TQ5220
Blackbrook *Staffs* 72 SJ7638
Blackbrook *Derbys* 62 SK3347
Blackbrook *Surrey* 15 TQ1846
Blackburn *Gramp* 135 NJ8212
Blackburn *Loth* 117 NS9865
Blackburn *Lancs* 81 SD6827
Blackcraig *Strath* 107 NS6308
Blackden Heath *Ches* 79 SJ7871
Blackdog *Gramp* 135 NJ9513
Blackdown *Dorset* 10 ST3903
Blackdown *Devon* 5 SX5079
Blackdyke *Cumb* 92 NY1452
Blackenall Heath *W Mids* 60 SK0002
Blacker *S York* 83 SE3309
Blacker Hill *S York* 83 SE3602
Blackfield *Hants* 13 SU4402
Blackford *Tays* 125 NN8908
Blackford *Cumb* 101 NY3961
Blackford *Somset* 21 ST4147
Blackford *Somset* 21 ST6526
Blackford Bridge *Gt Man* 79 SD8007
Blackfordby *Leics* 62 SK3217
Blackgang *IOW* 13 SZ4876
Blackhall Colliery *Dur* 97 NZ4539
Blackhaugh *Border* 109 NT4238
Blackheath *W Mids* 60 SO9786
Blackheath *Suffk* 55 TM4274
Blackheath *Surrey* 14 TQ0346
Blackheath *Gt Lon* 27 TQ3876
Blackhill *Gramp* 143 NK0039
Blackhill *Gramp* 143 NK0755
Blackhill *Dur* 95 NZ0851
Blackhorse *Devon* 9 SX9893
Blackhorse Hill *E Susx* 17 TQ7714
Blackjack *Lincs* 64 TF2639
Blackland *Somset* 19 SS8336
Blackland *Wilts* 22 SU0168
Blacklaw *D & G* 108 NT0408
Blackley *Gt Man* 79 SD8502
Blacklunans *Tays* 133 NO1460
Blackmarstone *H & W* 46 SO5038
Blackmill *M Glam* 33 SS9386
Blackmoor *Avon* 21 ST4661
Blackmoor *Hants* 14 SU7733
Blackmoorfoot *W York* 82 SE0913
Blackmore *Essex* 40 TL6001
Blackmore End *Herts* 39 TL1716
Blackmore End *Essex* 40 TL7430
Blackness *Loth* 117 NT0579
Blacknest *Hants* 25 SU7941
Blacknest *Berks* 25 SU9568
Blacko *Lancs* 81 SD8541
Blackpark *D & G* 100 NX9281
Blackpill *W Glam* 32 SS6190
Blackpool *Lancs* 80 SD3036
Blackpool *Devon* 7 SX8547
Blackpool *Devon* 7 SX8174
Blackpool Gate *Cumb* 101 NY5377
Blackridge *Loth* 116 NS8967
Blackrock *Gwent* 33 SO2112
Blackrock *Gwent* 34 ST5188
Blackrock *Cnwll* 2 SW6534
Blackrod *Gt Man* 78 SD6110
Blacksboat *Gramp* 141 NJ1838
Blackshaw *D & G* 100 NY0465
Blackshaw Head *W York* 82 SD9527
Blacksmith's Green *Suffk* 54 TM1465
Blacksnape *Lancs* 81 SD7121
Blackstone *W Susx* 15 TQ2316
Blackthorn *Oxon* 37 SP6219
Blackthorpe *Suffk* 54 TL9063
Blacktoft *Humb* 84 SE8324
Blacktop *Gramp* 135 NJ8604
Blackwall *Derbys* 73 SK2548
Blackwater *Somset* 10 ST2615
Blackwater *Hants* 25 SU8459
Blackwater *Cnwll* 3 SW7346
Blackwater *IOW* 13 SZ5086
Blackwaterfoot *Strath* 105 NR9028
Blackwell *Cumb* 93 NY4053
Blackwell *Dur* 89 NZ2713
Blackwell *Derbys* 74 SK1272
Blackwell *Derbys* 75 SK4458
Blackwell *H & W* 60 SO9972
Blackwell *Warwks* 48 SP2443
Blackwellsend Green *Gloucs* 47 SO7825
Blackwood *Strath* 116 NS7844
Blackwood *D & G* 100 NX9087
Blackwood *Gwent* 33 ST1797
Blackwood Hill *Staffs* 72 SJ9255
Blacon *Ches* 71 SJ3868
Bladbean *Kent* 29 TR1847
Bladnoch *D & G* 99 NX4254
Bladon *Oxon* 37 SP4514
Bladon *Somset* 21 ST4220
Blaen Dyryn *Powys* 45 SN9336
Blaen-y-Coed *Dyfed* 31 SN3427
Blaen-y-cwm *Gwent* 33 SO1311
Blaen-y-cwm *M Glam* 33 SS9298
Blaenannerch *Dyfed* 42 SN2448
Blaenau Ffestiniog *Gwynd* 57 SH7045
Blaenavon *Gwent* 34 SO2508
Blaenawey *Gwent* 34 SO2919
Blaenffos *Dyfed* 31 SN1937
Blaengarw *M Glam* 33 SS9092
Blaengeuffardd *Dyfed* 43 SN6480
Blaengwrach *W Glam* 33 SN8605
Blaengwynfi *W Glam* 33 SS8996
Blaenllechau *M Glam* 33 ST0097
Blaenpennal *Dyfed* 43 SN6264
Blaenplwyf *Dyfed* 43 SN5775
Blaenporth *Dyfed* 42 SN2648
Blaenrhondda *M Glam* 33 SS9299
Blaenwaun *Dyfed* 31 SN2327
Blaenycwm *Dyfed* 43 SN8275
Blagdon *Somset* 20 ST2118
Blagdon *Avon* 21 ST5059
Blagdon *Devon* 7 SX8561
Blagdon Hill *Somset* 9 ST2117
Blagill *Cumb* 94 NY7347
Blaguegate *Lancs* 78 SD4506
Blaich *Highld* 130 NN0376
Blain *Highld* 129 NM6769
Blaina *Gwent* 33 SO2008
Blair Atholl *Tays* 132 NN8665
Blair Drummond *Cent* 116 NS7399
Blairgowrie *Tays* 126 NO1745
Blairingone *Fife* 117 NS9896
Blairlogie *Cent* 116 NS8396
Blairmore *Highld* 148 NC1959
Blairmore *Strath* 114 NS1983
Blairnamarrow *Gramp* 141 NJ2015
Blairs Ferry *Strath* 114 NR9869
Blaisdon *Gloucs* 35 SO7017
Blake End *Essex* 40 TL7023
Blakebrook *H & W* 60 SO8276
Blakedown *H & W* 60 SO8878
Blakeley Lane *Staffs* 72 SJ9746
Blakemere *Ches* 71 SJ5571
Blakemere *H & W* 46 SO3641
Blakemore *Devon* 7 SX7660
Blakeney *Gloucs* 35 SO6707
Blakeney *Norfk* 66 TG0243
Blakenhall *Ches* 72 SJ7247
Blakenhall *W Mids* 60 SO9197
Blakeshall *H & W* 60 SO8381
Blakesley *Nhants* 49 SP6250
Blanchland *Nthumb* 95 NY9650
Bland Hill *N York* 82 SE2053
Blandford Camp *Dorset* 11 ST9107
Blandford Forum *Dorset* 11 ST8806
Blandford St. Mary *Dorset* 11 ST8805
Blankney *Lincs* 76 TF0660
Blantyre *Strath* 116 NS6957
Blar a' Chaorainn *Highld* 130 NN1066
Blargie *Highld* 132 NN6094
Blarmachfoldach *Highld* 130 NN0969
Blashford *Hants* 12 SU1506
Blaston *Leics* 51 SP8095
Blatherwycke *Nhants* 51 SP9795
Blawith *Cumb* 86 SD2888
Blawquhairn *D & G* 99 NX6282
Blaxhall *Suffk* 55 TM3656
Blaxton *S York* 75 SE6700
Blaydon *T & W* 103 NZ1863
Bleadney *Somset* 21 ST4845
Bleadon *Somset* 21 ST3456
Bleak Street *Somset* 22 ST7631
Blean *Kent* 29 TR1260
Bleasby *Lincs* 75 SK7149
Bleasby *Lincs* 76 TF1384

Bradworthy

Bromsberrow

Bradworthy *Devon*	18	SS3214
Brae *Shet*	155	HU3568
Brae *Highld*	140	NH6662
Brae *D & G*	100	NX8674
Brae Roy Lodge *Highld*	131	NN3391
Braeface *Cent*	116	NS7880
Braegrum *Tays*	125	NO0025
Braehead *Tays*	127	NO6952
Braehead *Strath*	117	NS9550
Braehead *D & G*	99	NX4152
Braelangwell Lodge *Highld*	146	NH5192
Braemar *Gramp*	133	NO1591
Braemore *Highld*	150	ND0829
Braemore *Highld*	145	NH2079
Braes of Coul *Tays*	133	NO2857
Braes of Enzie *Gramp*	142	NJ3957
Braeside *Strath*	114	NS2374
Braeswick *Ork*	155	HY6137
Braevallich *Strath*	122	NM9507
Brafferton *Dur*	96	NZ2921
Brafferton *N York*	89	SE4370
Brafield-on-the-Green *Nhants*	51	SP8258
Bragar *W Isls*	154	NB2947
Bragbury End *Herts*	39	TL2621
Braidwood *Strath*	116	NS8448
Brailsford *Derbys*	73	SK2541
Brailsford Green *Derbys*	73	SK2541
Brain's Green *Gloucs*	35	SO6609
Braintree *Essex*	40	TL7523
Braiseworth *Suffk*	54	TM1371
Braishfield *Hants*	23	SU3725
Braithwaite *Cumb*	93	NY2323
Braithwaite *W York*	82	SE0341
Braithwell *S York*	75	SK5394
Braken Hill *W York*	83	SE4216
Bramber *W Susx*	15	TQ1810
Brambridge *Hants*	13	SU4721
Bramcote *Notts*	62	SK5037
Bramcote *Warwks*	61	SP4088
Bramdean *Hants*	24	SU6128
Bramerton *Norfk*	67	TG2904
Bramfield *Herts*	39	TL2915
Bramfield *Suffk*	55	TM3973
Bramford *Suffk*	54	TM1246
Bramhall *Gt Man*	79	SJ8984
Bramham *W York*	83	SE4242
Bramhope *W York*	82	SE2543
Bramley *W York*	82	SE2435
Bramley *Derbys*	74	SK3978
Bramley *S York*	75	SK4892
Bramley *Hants*	24	SU6458
Bramley *Surrey*	25	TQ0044
Bramley Corner *Hants*	24	SU6359
Bramley Green *Hants*	24	SU6658
Bramley Head *N York*	89	SE1258
Bramling *Kent*	29	TR2256
Brampford Speke *Devon*	9	SX9298
Brampton *Cumb*	101	NY5361
Brampton *Cumb*	94	NY6723
Brampton *S York*	83	SE4101
Brampton *Lincs*	76	SK8479
Brampton *Norfk*	67	TG2223
Brampton *Cambs*	52	TL2170
Brampton *Suffk*	55	TM4381
Brampton Abbotts *H & W*	46	SO6026
Brampton Ash *Nhants*	50	SP7987
Brampton Bryan *H & W*	46	SO3772
Brampton-en-le-Morthen *S York*	75	SK4887
Bramshall *Staffs*	73	SK0532
Bramshaw *Hants*	12	SU2615
Bramshill *Hants*	24	SU7461
Bramshott *Hants*	14	SU8432
Bramwell *Somset*	21	ST4329
Bramwell *Somset*	21	ST4329
Bran End *Essex*	40	TL6525
Branault *Highld*	128	NM5269
Brancaster *Norfk*	65	TF7743
Brancaster Staithe *Norfk*	66	TF7944
Brancepeth *Dur*	96	NZ2237
Branch End *Nthumb*	103	NZ0661
Branchill *Gramp*	141	NJ0852
Brand End *Lincs*	64	TF3745
Brand Green *Gloucs*	47	SO7328
Branderburgh *Gramp*	141	NJ2371
Brandesburton *Humb*	85	TA1147
Brandeston *Suffk*	55	TM2460
Brandis Corner *Devon*	18	SS4104
Brandiston *Norfk*	66	TG1421
Brandon *Nthumb*	111	NU0417
Brandon *Dur*	96	NZ2340
Brandon *Lincs*	76	SK9048
Brandon *Warwks*	50	SP4176
Brandon *Suffk*	53	TL7886
Brandon Bank *Cambs*	53	TL6288
Brandon Creek *Norfk*	65	TL6091
Brandon Parva *Norfk*	66	TG0708
Brandsby *N York*	90	SE5872
Brandy Wharf *Lincs*	76	TF0196
Brane *Cnwll*	2	SW4028
Branksome *Dorset*	12	SZ0492
Branksome Park *Dorset*	12	SZ0590
Bransbury *Hants*	24	SU4242
Bransby *Lincs*	76	SK8978
Branscombe *Devon*	9	SY1988
Bransford *H & W*	47	SO7952
Bransgore *Hants*	12	SZ1897
Bransley *Shrops*	47	SO6575
Branson's Cross *H & W*	61	SP0970
Branston *Staffs*	73	SK2221
Branston *Leics*	63	SK8129
Branston *Lincs*	76	TF0166
Branston Booths *Lincs*	76	TF0668
Branstone *IOW*	13	SZ5583
Brant Broughton *Lincs*	76	SK9154
Brantham *Suffk*	54	TM1034
Branthwaite *Cumb*	92	NY0525
Branthwaite *Cumb*	93	NY2937
Brantingham *Humb*	84	SE9429
Branton *Nthumb*	111	NU0416
Branton *S York*	83	SE6401
Branton Green *N York*	89	SE4362
Branxton *Nthumb*	110	NT8937
Brassey Green *Ches*	71	SJ5260
Brassington *Derbys*	73	SK2254
Brasted *Kent*	27	TQ4755
Brasted Chart *Gt Lon*	27	TQ4653
Brathens *Gramp*	135	NO6798
Bratoft *Lincs*	77	TF4764
Brattleby *Lincs*	76	SK9481
Bratton *Shrops*	59	SJ6413
Bratton *Somset*	20	SS9446
Bratton *Wilts*	22	ST9152
Bratton Clovelly *Devon*	5	SX4691
Bratton Fleming *Devon*	19	SS6437
Bratton Seymour *Somset*	22	ST6729
Braughing *Herts*	39	TL3925
Braughing Friars *Herts*	39	TL4124
Braunston *Leics*	63	SK8306
Braunston *Nhants*	50	SP5466
Braunstone *Leics*	62	SK5502
Braunton *Devon*	18	SS4836
Brawby *N York*	90	SE7378
Brawdy *Dyfed*	30	SM8524
Brawl *Highld*	150	NC8166
Brawlbin *Highld*	150	ND0757
Braworth *N York*	90	NZ5007
Bray *Berks*	26	SU9079
Bray Shop *Cnwll*	5	SX3374
Bray's Hill *E Susx*	16	TQ6714
Braybrooke *Nhants*	50	SP7684
Braydon *Wilts*	36	SU0488
Braydon Brook *Wilts*	35	ST9891
Braydon Side *Wilts*	35	SU0185
Brayford *Devon*	19	SS6834
Braystones *Cumb*	86	NY0106
Braythorn *N York*	82	SE2449
Brayton *N York*	83	SE6030
Braywick *Berks*	26	SU8979
Braywoodside *Berks*	26	SU8775
Brazacott *Cnwll*	5	SX2691
Breach *Kent*	28	TQ8465
Breach *Kent*	29	TR1947
Breachwood Green *Herts*	39	TL1522
Breaden Heath *Shrops*	59	SJ4436
Breadsall *Derbys*	62	SK3639
Breadstone *Gloucs*	35	SO7000
Breadward *H & W*	46	SO2854
Breage *Cnwll*	2	SW6128
Breakachy *Highld*	139	NH4644
Bream *Gloucs*	34	SO6005
Breamore *Hants*	12	SU1517
Brean *Somset*	20	ST2956
Brearley *W York*	82	SE0225
Brearton *N York*	89	SE3261
Breasclete *W Isls*	154	NB2135
Breaston *Derbys*	62	SK4533
Brechfa *Dyfed*	44	SN5230
Brechin *Tays*	134	NO6060
Breckles *Norfk*	66	TL9594
Breckonside *D & G*	100	NX8489
Brecon *Powys*	45	SO0428
Bredbury *Gt Man*	79	SJ9291
Brede *E Susx*	17	TQ8218
Bredenbury *H & W*	46	SO6056
Bredfield *Suffk*	55	TM2653
Bredgar *Kent*	28	TQ8860
Bredhurst *Kent*	28	TQ7962
Bredon *H & W*	47	SO9236
Bredon's Hardwick *H & W*	47	SO9135
Bredon's Norton *H & W*	47	SO9339
Bredwardine *H & W*	46	SO3344
Breedon on the Hill *Leics*	62	SK4022
Breich *Loth*	117	NS9560
Breightmet *Gt Man*	79	SD7409
Breighton *Humb*	84	SE7033
Breinton *H & W*	46	SO4739
Bremhill *Wilts*	35	ST9773
Bremridge *Devon*	19	SS6929
Brenchley *Kent*	28	TQ6741
Brendon *Devon*	18	SS3607
Brendon *Devon*	19	SS7748
Brenfield *Strath*	113	NR8482
Brenish *W Isls*	154	NA9925
Brenkley *T & W*	103	NZ2175
Brent Eleigh *Suffk*	54	TL9448
Brent Knoll *Somset*	21	ST3350
Brent Mill *Devon*	7	SX6959
Brent Pelham *Herts*	39	TL4330
Brentford *Gt Lon*	26	TQ1777
Brentingby *Leics*	63	SK7818
Brentwood *Essex*	27	TQ5993
Brenzett *Kent*	17	TR0027
Brenzett Green *Kent*	17	TR0128
Brereton *Staffs*	73	SK0516
Brereton Cross *Staffs*	73	SK0615
Brereton Green *Ches*	72	SJ7764
Brereton Heath *Ches*	72	SJ8065
Brereton Hill *Staffs*	73	SK0515
Bressingham *Norfk*	54	TM0780
Bressingham Common *Norfk*	54	TM0981
Bretabister *Shet*	155	HU4857
Bretby *Derbys*	73	SK2922
Bretford *Warwks*	50	SP4377
Bretforton *H & W*	48	SP0944
Bretherdale Head *Cumb*	87	NY5705
Bretherton *Lancs*	80	SD4720
Brettenham *Norfk*	54	TL9383
Brettenham *Suffk*	54	TL9654
Bretton *Clwyd*	71	SJ3563
Bretton *Derbys*	74	SK2078
Brewer Street *Surrey*	27	TQ3251
Brewers End *Essex*	39	TL5521
Brewood *Staffs*	60	SJ8808
Briantspuddle *Dorset*	11	SY8193
Brick End *Essex*	40	TL5725
Brick Houses *S York*	74	SK3081
Bricket Wood *Herts*	26	TL1202
Brickkiln Green *Essex*	40	TL7331
Bricklehampton *H & W*	47	SO9742
Bride *IOM*	153	NX4401
Bridekirk *Cumb*	92	NY1133
Bridell *Dyfed*	31	SN1742
Bridestowe *Devon*	5	SX5189
Brideswell *Gramp*	142	NJ5738
Bridford *Devon*	8	SX8186
Bridge *Cnwll*	2	SW6744
Bridge *Kent*	29	TR1854
Bridge End *Cumb*	93	NY3748
Bridge End *Nthumb*	102	NY8965
Bridge End *Dur*	95	NZ0236
Bridge End *Cumb*	86	SD1884
Bridge End *Devon*	7	SX6946
Bridge End *Lincs*	64	TF1436
Bridge End *Beds*	38	TL0050
Bridge End *Essex*	40	TL6731
Bridge End *Surrey*	26	TQ0756
Bridge Fields *Leics*	62	SK4827
Bridge Green *Essex*	39	TL4636
Bridge Hewick *N York*	89	SE3370
Bridge Reeve *Devon*	19	SS6613
Bridge Sollers *H & W*	46	SO4142
Bridge Street *Suffk*	54	TL8749
Bridge Trafford *Ches*	71	SJ4571
Bridge of Alford *Gramp*	142	NJ5617
Bridge of Avon *Gramp*	141	NJ1835
Bridge of Balgie *Tays*	124	NN5746
Bridge of Brewlands *Tays*	133	NO1961
Bridge of Brown *Highld*	141	NJ1120
Bridge of Cally *Tays*	126	NO1351
Bridge of Canny *Gramp*	135	NO6597
Bridge of Craigisla *Tays*	126	NO2553
Bridge of Dee *D & G*	99	NX7359
Bridge of Don *Gramp*	135	NJ9409
Bridge of Dulsie *Highld*	140	NH9341
Bridge of Dye *Gramp*	135	NO6586
Bridge of Earn *Tays*	126	NO1318
Bridge of Ericht *Tays*	131	NN5258
Bridge of Feugh *Gramp*	135	NO7094
Bridge of Forss *Highld*	150	ND0368
Bridge of Gairn *Gramp*	134	NO3597
Bridge of Gaur *Tays*	124	NN5056
Bridge of Orchy *Strath*	123	NN2939
Bridge of Tilt *Tays*	132	NN8765
Bridge of Tynet *Gramp*	141	NJ3861
Bridge of Walls *Shet*	155	HU2752
Bridge of Weir *Strath*	115	NS3965
Bridge of Westfield *Highld*	150	ND0664
Bridgefoot *Cumb*	92	NY0529
Bridgehampton *Somset*	21	ST5624
Bridgehill *Dur*	95	NZ0951
Bridgehouse Gate *N York*	89	SE1565
Bridgemary *Hants*	13	SU5803
Bridgend *Gramp*	141	NJ3731
Bridgend *Gramp*	142	NJ5135
Bridgend *Gramp*	142	NJ7249
Bridgend *Tays*	126	NO1224
Bridgend *Fife*	126	NO3911
Bridgend *Tays*	134	NO5368
Bridgend *Strath*	112	NR3362
Bridgend *Loth*	117	NT0475
Bridgend *D & G*	108	NT0708
Bridgend *Border*	109	NT5235
Bridgend *Cumb*	93	NY4014
Bridgend *Dyfed*	42	SN1745
Bridgend *M Glam*	33	SS9079
Bridgend *Devon*	6	SX5548
Bridgerule *Devon*	18	SS2702
Bridges *Shrops*	59	SO3996
Bridgetown *Somset*	20	SS9233
Bridgetown *Devon*	5	SX3389
Bridgeyate *Avon*	35	ST6872
Bridgham *Norfk*	54	TL9685
Bridgnorth *Shrops*	60	SO7193
Bridgtown *Staffs*	60	SJ9808
Bridgwater *Somset*	20	ST2937
Bridlington *Humb*	91	TA1866
Bridport *Dorset*	10	SY4692
Bridstow *H & W*	46	SO5824
Brierfield *Lancs*	81	SD8436
Brierley *W York*	83	SE4010
Brierley *H & W*	46	SO4955
Brierley *Gloucs*	35	SO6215
Brierley Hill *W Mids*	47	SO9169
Brierton *Cleve*	97	NZ4730
Briery *Cumb*	93	NY2824
Brig o'Turk *Cent*	124	NN5306
Brigg *Humb*	84	TA0007
Briggate *Norfk*	67	TG3127
Briggswath *N York*	90	NZ8608
Brigham *Cumb*	92	NY0830
Brigham *Cumb*	93	NY2823
Brigham *Humb*	85	TA0753
Brighouse *W York*	82	SE1422
Brighstone *IOW*	13	SZ4282
Brightgate *Derbys*	74	SK2659
Brighthampton *Oxon*	36	SP3803
Brightholmlee *Derbys*	74	SK2895
Brightley *Devon*	8	SX6097
Brightling *E Susx*	16	TQ6820
Brightlingsea *Essex*	41	TM0817
Brighton *Cnwll*	3	SW9054
Brighton *E Susx*	15	TQ3104
Brighton le Sands *Mersyd*	78	SJ3098
Brightons *Cent*	116	NS9277
Brightor *Cnwll*	5	SX3561
Brightwalton *Berks*	36	SU4279
Brightwalton Green *Berks*	36	SU4278
Brightwalton Holt *Berks*	36	SU4377
Brightwell *Oxon*	37	SU5790
Brightwell *Suffk*	55	TM2543
Brightwell Baldwin *Oxon*	37	SU6595
Brightwell Upperton *Oxon*	37	SU6594
Brignall *Dur*	95	NZ0712
Brigsley *Humb*	85	TA2501
Brigsteer *Cumb*	87	SD4889
Brigstock *Nhants*	51	SP9485
Brill *Bucks*	37	SP6513
Brill *Cnwll*	3	SW7229
Brilley *H & W*	46	SO2648
Brimfield *H & W*	46	SO5267
Brimfield Cross *H & W*	46	SO5368
Brimington *Derbys*	74	SK4073
Brimley *Devon*	8	SX8077
Brimpsfield *Gloucs*	35	SO9312
Brimpton *Berks*	24	SU5564
Brimscombe *Gloucs*	35	SO8702
Brimstage *Mersyd*	78	SJ3082
Brincliffe *S York*	74	SK3284
Brind *Humb*	84	SE7430
Brindham *Somset*	21	ST5139
Brindister *Shet*	155	HU2857
Brindle *Lancs*	81	SD5924
Brineton *Staffs*	60	SJ8013
Bringhurst *Leics*	51	SP8492
Brington *Cambs*	51	TL0875
Briningham *Norfk*	66	TG0434
Brinkely *Notts*	75	SK7153
Brinkhill *Lincs*	77	TF3773
Brinkley *Cambs*	53	TL6354
Brinklow *Warwks*	50	SP4379
Brinkworth *Wilts*	35	SU0184
Brinscall *Lancs*	81	SD6221
Brinscombe *Somset*	21	ST4251
Brinsea *Avon*	21	ST4461
Brinsley *Notts*	75	SK4548
Brinsop *H & W*	46	SO4444
Brinsworth *S York*	74	SK4289
Brinton *Norfk*	66	TG0335
Brinyan *Ork*	155	HY4327
Brisco *Cumb*	93	NY4252
Brisley *Norfk*	66	TF9421
Brislington *Avon*	35	ST6270
Brissenden Green *Kent*	28	TQ9439
Bristol *Avon*	34	ST5972
Briston *Norfk*	66	TG0632
Brisworthy *Devon*	6	SX5665
Britannia *Lancs*	81	SD8821
Britford *Wilts*	23	SU1627
Brithdir *Gwynd*	57	SH7618
Brithdir *M Glam*	33	SO1401
British *Gwent*	34	SO2503
British Legion Village *Kent*	28	TQ7257
Briton Ferry *W Glam*	32	SS7394
Britwell Salome *Oxon*	37	SU6792
Brixham *Devon*	7	SX9255
Brixton *Devon*	6	SX5552
Brixton *Gt Lon*	27	TQ3175
Brixton Deverill *Wilts*	22	ST8638
Brixworth *Nhants*	50	SP7470
Brize Norton *Oxon*	36	SP2907
Broad Alley *H & W*	47	SO8867
Broad Blunsdon *Wilts*	36	SU1491
Broad Campden *Gloucs*	48	SP1537
Broad Carr *W York*	82	SE0919
Broad Chalke *Wilts*	23	SU0325
Broad Clough *Lancs*	81	SD8623
Broad Ford *Kent*	28	TQ7139
Broad Green *H & W*	47	SO7756
Broad Green *H & W*	60	SO9970
Broad Green *Cambs*	53	TL6859
Broad Green *Suffk*	53	TL7859
Broad Green *Essex*	40	TL8823
Broad Haven *Dyfed*	30	SM8613
Broad Hill *Cambs*	53	TL5976
Broad Hinton *Wilts*	36	SU1075
Broad Laying *Hants*	24	SU4362
Broad Marston *H & W*	48	SP1446
Broad Meadow *Staffs*	72	SJ8348
Broad Oak *Cumb*	86	SD1194
Broad Oak *Mersyd*	78	SJ5395
Broad Oak *H & W*	34	SO4821
Broad Oak *Hants*	24	SU7551
Broad Oak *E Susx*	17	TQ8219
Broad Road *Suffk*	55	TM2676
Broad Street *Wilts*	23	SU1059
Broad Street *Essex*	39	TL5516
Broad Street *Kent*	28	TQ7672
Broad Street *Kent*	28	TQ8356
Broad Street *E Susx*	17	TQ8616
Broad Street *Kent*	29	TR1139
Broad Street Green *Essex*	40	TL8509
Broad Town *Wilts*	36	SU0977
Broad's Green *Essex*	40	TL6912
Broadbottom *Gt Man*	79	SJ9993
Broadbridge *W Susx*	14	SU8105
Broadbridge Heath *W Susx*	15	TQ1431
Broadclyst *Devon*	9	SX9897
Broadfield *Strath*	115	NS3373
Broadfield *Dyfed*	31	SN1303
Broadford *Highld*	129	NG6423
Broadford Bridge *W Susx*	14	TQ0921
Broadgairhill *Border*	109	NT2010
Broadgate *Lincs*	64	TF3610
Broadgrass Green *Suffk*	54	TL9663
Broadhaugh *Border*	119	NT8655
Broadheath *Gt Man*	79	SJ7689
Broadheath *H & W*	47	SO6665
Broadhembury *Devon*	9	ST1004
Broadhempston *Devon*	7	SX8066
Broadholme *Notts*	76	SK8874
Broadland Row *E Susx*	17	TQ8319
Broadlay *Dyfed*	31	SN3709
Broadley *Gramp*	142	NJ3961
Broadley *Gt Man*	81	SD8816
Broadley Common *Essex*	39	TL4206
Broadmayne *Dorset*	11	SY7286
Broadmere *Hants*	24	SU6247
Broadmoor *Dyfed*	31	SN0906
Broadmoor *Gloucs*	35	SO6415
Broadnymett *Devon*	8	SS7001
Broadoak *Clwyd*	71	SJ3658
Broadoak *Gloucs*	35	SO6912
Broadoak *Dorset*	10	SY4396
Broadoak *E Susx*	16	TQ6022
Broadoak *Kent*	29	TR1761
Broadstairs *Kent*	29	TR3967
Broadstone *Gwent*	34	SO5102
Broadstone *Shrops*	59	SO5489
Broadstone *Dorset*	11	SZ0095
Broadwater *Herts*	39	TL2422
Broadwater *W Susx*	15	TQ1404
Broadwaters *H & W*	60	SO8477
Broadway *Dyfed*	31	SN2910
Broadway *Dyfed*	31	SN3808
Broadway *H & W*	48	SP0937
Broadway *Somset*	10	ST3215
Broadway *Suffk*	55	TM3979
Broadwell *Gloucs*	34	SO5811
Broadwell *Gloucs*	48	SP2027
Broadwell *Oxon*	36	SP2504
Broadwell *Warwks*	50	SP4565
Broadwey *Dorset*	11	SY6683
Broadwindsor *Dorset*	10	ST4302
Broadwood Kelly *Devon*	8	SS6106
Broadwoodwidger *Devon*	5	SX4189
Brobury *H & W*	46	SO3444
Brochel *Highld*	137	NG5846
Brock *Lancs*	80	SD5140
Brock's Green *Hants*	24	SU5061
Brockamin *H & W*	47	SO7753
Brockbridge *Hants*	13	SU6118
Brockdish *Norfk*	55	TM2179
Brockencote *H & W*	60	SO8873
Brockenhurst *Hants*	12	SU3002
Brocketsbrae *Strath*	108	NS8239
Brockford Green *Suffk*	54	TM1265
Brockford Street *Suffk*	54	TM1167
Brockhall *Nhants*	49	SP6362
Brockham *Surrey*	15	TQ1949
Brockhampton *H & W*	46	SO5931
Brockhampton *Gloucs*	47	SO9326
Brockhampton *Gloucs*	36	SP0322
Brockhampton Green *Dorset*	11	ST7106
Brockholes *W York*	82	SE1510
Brockhurst *Derbys*	74	SK3364
Brockhurst *Warwks*	50	SP4683
Brocklebank *Cumb*	93	NY3042
Brocklesby *Lincs*	85	TA1311
Brockley *Avon*	21	ST4666
Brockley *Suffk*	54	TL8371
Brockley Green *Suffk*	53	TL7247
Brockley Green *Suffk*	54	TL8254
Brockleymoor *Cumb*	94	NY4937
Brockmoor *W Mids*	60	SO9088
Brockscombe *Devon*	5	SX4695
Brockton *Shrops*	59	SJ3104
Brockton *Shrops*	60	SJ7103
Brockton *Staffs*	72	SJ8131
Brockton *Shrops*	59	SO3285
Brockton *Shrops*	59	SO5794
Brockwell *Gwent*	34	SO5401
Brockwood Park *Hants*	13	SU6226
Brockworth *Gloucs*	35	SO8916
Brocton *Staffs*	72	SJ9619
Brocton *Cnwll*	4	SX0168
Brodick *Strath*	105	NS0135
Brodie *Gramp*	140	NH9757
Brodsworth *S York*	83	SE5007
Brogaig *Highld*	136	NG4767
Brogborough *Beds*	38	SP9638
Broken Cross *Ches*	79	SJ6873
Broken Cross *Ches*	79	SJ8973
Brokenborough *Wilts*	35	ST9189
Brokerswood *Wilts*	22	ST8352
Bromborough *Mersyd*	78	SJ3582
Brome *Suffk*	54	TM1376
Brome Street *Suffk*	54	TM1576
Bromeswell *Suffk*	55	TM3050
Bromfield *Cumb*	93	NY1746
Bromfield *Shrops*	46	SO4876
Bromham *Wilts*	22	ST9665
Bromham *Beds*	38	TL0051
Bromley *S York*	74	SK3298
Bromley *Shrops*	60	SO7395
Bromley *W Mids*	60	SO9088
Bromley *Gt Lon*	27	TQ4069
Bromley Common *Gt Lon*	27	TQ4266
Bromley Cross *Essex*	41	TM0627
Bromlow *Shrops*	59	SJ3201
Brompton *N York*	89	SE3796
Brompton *N York*	91	SE9482
Brompton *Shrops*	59	SJ5408
Brompton *Kent*	28	TQ7668
Brompton Ralph *Somset*	20	ST0832
Brompton Regis *Somset*	20	SS9531
Brompton-on-Swale *N York*	89	SE2199
Bromsash *H & W*	47	SO6524
Bromsberrow *Gloucs*	47	SO7433

Carnwath Cherry Burton

Carnwath Strath 117 NS9846
Carnyorth Cnwll 2 SW3733
Carol Green W Mids 61 SP2577
Carpalla Cnwll 3 SW9654
Carperby N York 88 SE0089
Carr Gt Man 81 SD7816
Carr S York 75 SK5090
Carr Gate W York 82 SE3123
Carr Shield Nthumb 95 NY8047
Carr Vale Derbys 75 SK4669
Carradale Strath 105 NR8138
Carrbridge Highld 140 NH9022
Carrbrook Gt Man 79 SD9800
Carrefour Jersey 152 JS0000
Carreglefn Gwynd 68 SH3889
Carrhouse Humb 84 SE7706
Carrick Fife 127 NO4422
Carrick Strath 114 NR9086
Carrick Castle Strath 114 NS1994
Carriden Cent 117 NT0181
Carrington Loth 117 NT3160
Carrington Gt Man 79 SJ7492
Carrington Lincs 77 TF3155
Carrismerry Cnwll 4 SX0158
Carrog Gwynd 69 SH7647
Carrog Clwyd 70 SJ1043
Carron Gramp 141 NJ2241
Carron Cent 116 NS8882
Carron Bridge Cent 116 NS7483
Carronbridge D & G 100 NX8698
Carronshore Cent 116 NS8983
Carrow Hill Gwent 34 ST4390
Carruth House Strath 115 NS3566
Carrutherstown D & G 100 NY1071
Carrville Dur 96 NZ3043
Carrycoats Hall Nthumb 102 NY9279
Carsaig Strath 121 NM5421
Carscreugh D & G 98 NX2260
Carse Gray Tays 127 NO4553
Carseriggan D & G 98 NX3167
Carsethorn D & G 92 NX9959
Carshalton Gt Lon 27 TQ2764
Carsie Tays 126 NO1742
Carsington Derbys 73 SK2553
Carskey Strath 104 NR6508
Carsluith D & G 99 NX4854
Carsphairn D & G 107 NX5693
Carstairs Strath 116 NS9345
Carstairs Junction Strath 117 NS9545
Carswell Marsh Oxon 36 SU3299
Carter Bar Border 110 NT6907
Carter's Clay Hants 23 SU3024
Carters Green Essex 39 TL5110
Carterton Oxon 36 SP2806
Carterway Heads Nthumb 95 NZ0451
Carthew Cnwll 3 SX0056
Carthorpe N York 89 SE3083
Cartington Nthumb 103 NU0204
Cartland Strath 116 NS8646
Cartledge Derbys 74 SK3276
Cartmel Cumb 87 SD3878
Cartmel Fell Cumb 87 SD4188
Carway Dyfed 32 SN4606
Carwinley Cumb 101 NY4072
Cashe's Green Gloucs 35 SO8205
Cashmoor Dorset 11 ST9713
Cassington Oxon 37 SP4511
Cassop Colliery Dur 96 NZ3438
Castel Guern 152 GN0000
Castell Gwynd 69 SH7669
Castell-y-bwch Gwent 34 ST2792
Casterton Lancs 87 SD6279
Castle Cnwll 4 SX0958
Castle Acre Norfk 66 TF8115
Castle Ashby Nhants 51 SP8659
Castle Bolton N York 88 SE0391
Castle Bromwich W Mids 61 SP1489
Castle Bytham Lincs 63 SK9818
Castle Caereinion Powys 58 SJ1605
Castle Camps Cambs 53 TL6242
Castle Carrock Cumb 94 NY5455
Castle Cary Somset 21 ST6432
Castle Combe Wilts 35 ST8477
Castle Donington Leics 62 SK4427
Castle Douglas D & G 99 NX7662
Castle Eaton Wilts 36 SU1496
Castle Eden Dur 96 NZ4238
Castle End Cambs 64 TF1208
Castle Frome H & W 47 SO6645
Castle Gate Cnwll 2 SW4934
Castle Green Cumb 87 SD5392
Castle Green Surrey 25 SU9761
Castle Gresley Derbys 73 SK2717
Castle Hedingham Essex 53 TL7835
Castle Hill Suffk 54 TM1446
Castle Hill Kent 28 TQ6942
Castle Kennedy D & G 98 NX1159
Castle Lachlan Strath 114 NS0195
Castle Morris Dyfed 30 SM9031
Castle O'er D & G 101 NY2492
Castle Pulverbatch Shrops 59 SJ4202
Castle Rising Norfk 65 TF6624
Castle Street W York 82 SD9524
Castle Stuart Highld 140 NH7449
Castlebay W Isls 154 NL6698
Castlebythe Dyfed 30 SN0229
Castlecary Strath 116 NS7878
Castlecraig Highld 147 NH8269
Castlecroft W Mids 60 SO8797
Castleford W York 83 SE4225
Castlehill Highld 151 ND1968
Castlehill Strath 116 NS8451
Castlehill Border 109 NT2135
Castlemartin Dyfed 30 SR9198
Castlemilk D & G 100 NY1577
Castlemorton H & W 47 SO7937
Castleside Dur 95 NZ0748
Castlethorpe Humb 84 SE9807
Castlethorpe Bucks 38 SP8044
Castleton Border 101 NY5189
Castleton N York 90 NZ6807
Castleton Gt Man 79 SD8810
Castleton Derbys 74 SK1582
Castleton Gwent 34 ST2583
Castletown Highld 151 ND1967
Castletown T & W 96 NZ3658
Castletown IOM 153 SC2667
Castletown Dorset 11 SY6874
Castley N York 82 SE2646
Caston Norfk 66 TL9597
Castor Cambs 64 TL1298
Cat's Ash Gwent 34 ST3790
Catacol Strath 105 NR9149
Catbrook Gwent 35 SO5102
Catch Clwyd 70 SJ2070
Catchall Cnwll 2 SW4228
Catchem's Corner W Mids 61 SP2576
Catchgate Dur 96 NZ1652
Catcliffe S York 74 SK4288
Catcomb Wilts 35 SU0076
Catcott Somset 21 ST3939
Catcott Burtle Somset 21 ST4043
Caterham Surrey 27 TQ3455
Catfield Norfk 67 TG3821
Catfield Common Norfk 67 TG4021
Catfirth Shet 155 HU4354
Catford Gt Lon 27 TQ3773
Catforth Lancs 80 SD4735
Cathcart Strath 115 NS5860
Cathedine Powys 45 SO1425
Catherine Slack W York 82 SE0928
Catherine de-Barnes Heath W Mids 61 SP1780
Catherington Hants 13 SU6914
Catherston Leweston Dorset 10 SY3694
Catherton Shrops 47 SO6578
Cathpair Border 118 NT4646
Catisfield Hants 13 SU5506
Catley Lane Head Gt Man 81 SD8715
Catley Southfield H & W 47 SO6844
Catlodge Highld 132 NN6392
Catlow Lancs 81 SD8836
Catlowdy Cumb 101 NY4576
Catmere End Essex 39 TL4939
Catmore Berks 37 SU4580
Caton Lancs 87 SD5364
Caton Devon 7 SX7872
Caton Green Lancs 87 SD5565
Cator Court Devon 8 SX6877
Catrine Strath 107 NS5225
Catsfield E Susx 17 TQ7213
Catsfield Stream E Susx 17 TQ7113
Catsham Somset 21 ST5533
Catshill H & W 60 SO9573
Catstree Shrops 60 SO7496
Catsyke W York 83 SE4224
Cattadale Strath 105 NR6710
Cattal N York 83 SE4454
Cattawade Suffk 41 TM1033
Catterall Lancs 80 SD4942
Catteralslane Shrops 71 SJ5640
Catterick N York 89 SE2397
Catterick Bridge N York 89 SE2299
Catterick Camp N York 89 SE1897
Catterlen Cumb 94 NY4833
Catterton N York 83 SE5145
Catteshall Surrey 25 SU9844
Catthorpe Leics 50 SP5578
Cattishall Suffk 54 TL8865
Cattistock Dorset 10 SY5999
Catton Cumb 95 NY8257
Catton N York 89 SE3678
Catton Norfk 67 TG2312
Catwick Humb 85 TA1345
Catworth Cambs 51 TL0873
Caudle Green Gloucs 35 SO9410
Caulcott Oxon 49 SP5024
Caulcott Beds 38 TL0042
Cauldcots Tays 127 NO6547
Cauldhame Cent 116 NS6493
Cauldmill Border 109 NT5315
Cauldon Staffs 73 SK0749
Cauldon Lowe Staffs 73 SK0747
Cauldside D & G 101 NY4480
Cauldwell Derbys 73 SK2517
Caulkerbush D & G 92 NX9257
Caundle Marsh Dorset 11 ST6713
Caunsall H & W 60 SO8581
Caunton Notts 75 SK7460
Causeway Hants 13 SU7422
Causeway End D & G 99 NX4260
Causeway End Cumb 87 SD4885
Causeway End Essex 40 TL6819
Causewayend Strath 108 NT0336
Causewayhead Cent 116 NS8095
Causewayhead Cumb 92 NY1253
Causey Park Nthumb 103 NZ1794
Causeyend Gramp 143 NJ9419
Cavendish Suffk 54 TL8046
Cavenham Suffk 53 TL7670
Caversfield Oxon 49 SP5825
Caversham Berks 24 SU7274
Caverswall Staffs 72 SJ9542
Caverton Mill Border 110 NT7425
Cavil Humb 84 SE7730
Cawdor Highld 140 NH8450
Cawkwell Lincs 77 TF2879
Cawood N York 83 SE5737
Cawsand Cnwll 6 SX4350
Cawston Warwks 50 SP4773
Cawston Norfk 66 TG1323
Cawthorn N York 90 SE7788
Cawthorne S York 82 SE2808
Caxton Cambs 52 TL3058
Caxton End Cambs 52 TL2759
Caxton End Cambs 52 TL3157
Caxton Gibbet Cambs 52 TL2960
Caynham Shrops 46 SO5573
Caythorpe Notts 63 SK6845
Caythorpe Lincs 76 SK9348
Cayton N York 91 TA0583
Ceannacroc Lodge Highld 131 NH2211
Ceciliford Gwent 34 SO5003
Cefn Gwent 34 ST2788
Cefn Berain Clwyd 70 SH9969
Cefn Byrle Powys 33 SN8311
Cefn Canel Clwyd 58 SJ2331
Cefn Coch Powys 58 SJ1026
Cefn Cribwr M Glam 33 SS8582
Cefn Cross M Glam 33 SS8682
Cefn Mably M Glam 34 ST2283
Cefn-Einion Shrops 58 SO2886
Cefn-brith Clwyd 70 SH9350
Cefn-bryn-brain Dyfed 32 SN7413
Cefn-coed-y-cymmer M Glam 33 SO0308
Cefn-ddwysarn Gwynd 70 SH9638
Cefn-mawr Clwyd 70 SJ2842
Cefn-y-bedd Clwyd 71 SJ3156
Cefn-y-pant Dyfed 31 SN1925
Cefneithin Dyfed 32 SN5513
Cefngorwydd Powys 45 SN9045
Cefnpennar M Glam 33 SO0300
Ceint Gwynd 68 SH4875
Cellan Dyfed 44 SN6149
Cellarhead Staffs 72 SJ9547
Cellerton Cumb 94 NY4925
Celynen Gwent 33 ST2195
Cemaes Gwynd 68 SH3793
Cemmaes Powys 57 SH8406
Cemmaes Road Powys 57 SH8104
Cenarth Dyfed 31 SN2641
Cerbyd Dyfed 30 SM8227
Ceres Fife 126 NO4011
Cerne Abbas Dorset 11 ST6601
Cerney Wick Gloucs 36 SU0796
Cerrigceinwen Gwynd 68 SH4274
Cerrigydrudion Clwyd 70 SH9548
Cess Norfk 67 TG4417
Ceunant Gwynd 69 SH5361
Chaceley Gloucs 47 SO8530
Chacewater Cnwll 3 SW7544
Chackmore Bucks 49 SP6835
Chacombe Nhants 49 SP4944
Chadbury H & W 47 SP0146
Chadderton Gt Man 79 SD9005
Chadderton Fold Gt Man 79 SD9006
Chaddesden Derbys 62 SK3836
Chaddesley Corbett H & W 60 SO8973
Chaddlehanger Devon 5 SX4678
Chaddleworth Berks 36 SU4178
Chadlington Oxon 36 SP3321
Chadshunt Warwks 48 SP3453
Chadwell Shrops 60 SJ7814
Chadwell Leics 63 SK7824
Chadwell End Beds 51 TL0865
Chadwell Heath Gt Lon 27 TQ4888
Chadwell St. Mary Essex 40 TQ6478
Chadwick H & W 47 SO8369
Chadwick End W Mids 61 SP2073
Chadwick Green Mersyd 78 SJ5299
Chaffcombe Somset 10 ST3510
Chagford Devon 8 SX7087
Chailey E Susx 15 TQ3919
Chainbridge Cambs 27 TL4200
Chainhurst Kent 28 TQ7248
Chalbury Common Dorset 12 SU0206
Chaldon Surrey 27 TQ3155
Chaldon Herring or East Chaldon Dorset 11 SY7983
Chale IOW 13 SZ4877
Chale Green IOW 13 SZ4879
Chalfont Common Bucks 26 TQ0092
Chalfont St. Giles Bucks 26 SU9893
Chalfont St. Peter Bucks 26 TQ0090
Chalford Gloucs 35 SO8802
Chalford Oxon 37 SP7200
Chalford Wilts 22 ST8650
Chalgrove Oxon 37 SU6396
Chalgrove Beds 38 TL0127
Chalk Kent 28 TQ6773
Chalk End Essex 40 TL6310
Chalkhouse Green Berks 37 SU7178
Chalkway Somset 10 ST3707
Chalkwell Kent 28 TQ8963
Challaborough Devon 7 SX6544
Challacombe Devon 19 SS6940
Challoch D & G 99 NX3866
Challock Lees Kent 28 TR0050
Chalmington Dorset 10 ST5900
Chalton Hants 13 SU7315
Chalton Beds 38 TL0326
Chalton Beds 52 TL1450
Chalvey Berks 26 SU9679
Chalvington E Susx 16 TQ5109
Chambers Green Kent 28 TQ9243
Chandler's Cross Herts 26 TQ0698
Chandler's Ford Hants 13 SU4319
Chandlers Cross H & W 47 SO7738
Channel's End Beds 51 TL1056
Chantry Somset 22 ST7146
Chantry Suffk 54 TM1443
Chapel Cumb 93 NY2231
Chapel Fife 117 NT2593
Chapel Allerton W York 82 SE3037
Chapel Allerton Somset 21 ST4050
Chapel Amble Cnwll 4 SW9975
Chapel Brampton Nhants 50 SP7266
Chapel Chorlton Staffs 72 SJ8137
Chapel Cross E Susx 16 TQ6120
Chapel End Warwks 61 SP3393
Chapel End Beds 38 TL0542
Chapel End Beds 51 TL1058
Chapel End Cambs 52 TL1282
Chapel Field Gt Man 79 SD7906
Chapel Green Warwks 61 SP2785
Chapel Green Warwks 49 SP4660
Chapel Haddlesey N York 83 SE5826
Chapel Hall Strath 114 NS1369
Chapel Hill Gramp 143 NK0635
Chapel Hill N York 83 SE3446
Chapel Hill Gwent 59 SO5399
Chapel Hill Lincs 76 TF2054
Chapel Lawn Shrops 46 SO3176
Chapel Leigh Somset 20 ST1229
Chapel Milton Derbys 74 SK0581
Chapel Rossan D & G 98 NX1044
Chapel Row Berks 24 SU5769
Chapel Row Essex 40 TL7900
Chapel Row E Susx 16 TQ6312
Chapel St. Leonards Lincs 77 TF5672
Chapel Stile Cumb 86 NY3205
Chapel Town Cnwll 3 SW8855
Chapel le Dale N York 88 SD7377
Chapel of Garioch Gramp 142 NJ7124
Chapel-en-le-Frith Derbys 74 SK0580
Chapelbridge Cambs 64 TL2993
Chapelend Way Essex 53 TL7039
Chapelgate Lincs 65 TF4124
Chapelhall Strath 116 NS7862
Chapelhill Tays 125 NO0030
Chapelknowe D & G 101 NY3173
Chapels Cumb 86 SD2383
Chapelton Tays 127 NO6247
Chapelton Strath 116 NS6848
Chapelton Devon 19 SS5726
Chapeltown Gramp 141 NJ2320
Chapeltown Lancs 81 SD7315
Chapeltown S York 74 SK3596
Chapmans Well Devon 5 SX3593
Chapmanslade Wilts 22 ST8247
Chapmore End Herts 39 TL3216
Chappel Essex 40 TL8928
Charaton Cnwll 5 SX3069
Chard Somset 10 ST3208
Chard Junction Somset 10 ST3404
Chardleigh Green Somset 10 ST3110
Chardstock Devon 10 ST3004
Charfield Avon 35 ST7292
Chargrove Gloucs 35 SO9219
Charing Kent 28 TQ9549
Charing Heath Kent 28 TQ9249
Charing Hill Kent 28 TQ9550
Charingworth Gloucs 48 SP1939
Charlbury Oxon 36 SP3519
Charlcombe Avon 22 ST7467
Charlcutt Wilts 35 ST9875
Charlecote Warwks 48 SP2656
Charles Devon 19 SS6832
Charles Tye Suffk 54 TM0252
Charleshill Surrey 25 SU8944
Charleston Tays 126 NO3845
Charlestown Highld 144 NG8174
Charlestown Highld 140 NH6448
Charlestown Gramp 135 NJ9300
Charlestown Fife 117 NT0683
Charlestown Gt Man 79 SD8100
Charlestown W York 82 SD9726
Charlestown W York 82 SE1638
Charlestown Derbys 74 SK0392
Charlestown Lincs 63 SK9844
Charlestown Cnwll 3 SX0351
Charlestown Dorset 11 SY6579
Charlesworth Derbys 79 SK0092
Charlinch Somset 20 ST2338
Charlton Nthumb 102 NY8184
Charlton Shrops 59 SJ5911
Charlton H & W 60 SO8371
Charlton H & W 47 SP0045
Charlton Nhants 49 SP5335
Charlton Somset 20 ST2926
Charlton Somset 21 ST6343
Charlton Wilts 22 ST9022
Charlton Wilts 35 ST9588
Charlton Wilts 23 SU1156
Charlton Wilts 23 SU1723
Charlton Hants 23 SU3547
Charlton Oxon 36 SU4088
Charlton W Susx 14 SU8812
Charlton Herts 39 TL1728
Charlton Gt Lon 27 TQ4178
Charlton Abbots Gloucs 48 SP0324
Charlton Adam Somset 21 ST5328
Charlton Hill Shrops 59 SJ5807
Charlton Horethorne Somset 22 ST6623
Charlton Kings Gloucs 35 SO9621
Charlton Mackrell Somset 21 ST5328
Charlton Marshall Dorset 11 ST9004
Charlton Musgrove Somset 22 ST7229
Charlton on the Hill Dorset 11 ST8903
Charlton-on-Otmoor Oxon 37 SP5616
Charlwood Hants 24 SU6731
Charlwood Surrey 15 TQ2441
Charminster Dorset 11 SY6792
Charmouth Dorset 10 SY3693
Charndon Bucks 49 SP6724
Charney Bassett Oxon 36 SU3894
Charnock Green Lancs 81 SD5516
Charnock Richard Lancs 81 SD5515
Charsfield Suffk 55 TM2556
Chart Corner Kent 28 TQ7950
Chart Hill Kent 28 TQ7949
Chart Sutton Kent 28 TQ8049
Charter Alley Hants 24 SU5958
Charterhall Border 110 NT7647
Charterhouse Somset 21 ST4955
Chartershall Cent 116 NS7990
Charterville Allotments Oxon 36 SP3110
Chartham Kent 29 TR1054
Chartham Hatch Kent 29 TR1056
Charton Surrey 26 TQ0869
Chartridge Bucks 38 SP9303
Chartway Street Kent 28 TQ8350
Charwelton Nhants 49 SP5356
Chase Terrace Staffs 61 SK0309
Chasetown Staffs 61 SK0408
Chastleton Oxon 48 SP2429
Chasty Devon 18 SS3402
Chatburn Lancs 81 SD7644
Chatcull Staffs 72 SJ7934
Chatham Gwent 33 ST2188
Chatham Kent 28 TQ7567
Chatham Green Essex 40 TL7115
Chathill Nthumb 111 NU1827
Chatley H & W 47 SO8561
Chattenden Kent 28 TQ7572
Chatter End Essex 39 TL4725
Chatteris Cambs 52 TL3985
Chatterton Lancs 81 SD7918
Chattisham Suffk 54 TM0942
Chatto Border 110 NT7717
Chatton Nthumb 111 NU0528
Chawleigh Devon 19 SS7112
Chawley Oxon 37 SP4604
Chawston Beds 52 TL1556
Chawton Hants 24 SU7037
Chaxhill Gloucs 35 SO7414
Chazey Heath Oxon 37 SU6977
Cheadle Gt Man 79 SJ8688
Cheadle Staffs 73 SK0043
Cheadle Heath Gt Man 79 SJ8789
Cheadle Hulme Gt Man 79 SJ8786
Cheam Gt Lon 26 TQ2463
Cheapside Berks 25 SU9469
Chearsley Bucks 37 SP7110
Chebsey Staffs 72 SJ8528
Checkendon Oxon 37 SU6683
Checkley Ches 72 SJ7346
Checkley Staffs 73 SK0237
Checkley Green Ches 72 SJ7245
Chedburgh Suffk 53 TL7957
Cheddar Somset 21 ST4553
Cheddington Bucks 38 SP9217
Cheddleton Staffs 72 SJ9752
Cheddleton Heath Staffs 72 SJ9853
Cheddon Fitzpaine Somset 20 ST2427
Chedglow Wilts 35 ST9493
Chedgrave Norfk 67 TM3699
Chedington Dorset 10 ST4805
Chediston Suffk 55 TM3577
Chediston Green Suffk 55 TM3578
Chedworth Gloucs 36 SP0512
Chedzoy Somset 21 ST3437
Cheesden Gt Man 81 SD8216
Cheeseman's Green Kent 28 TR0338
Cheetham Hill Gt Man 79 SD8401
Cheetwood Gt Man 79 SJ8399
Cheldon Devon 19 SS7313
Chelford Ches 79 SJ8174
Chellaston Derbys 62 SK3730
Chellington Beds 51 SP9555
Chelmarsh Shrops 60 SO7288
Chelmick Shrops 59 SO4791
Chelmondiston Suffk 55 TM2037
Chelmorton Derbys 74 SK1169
Chelmsford Essex 40 TL7007
Chelmsley Wood W Mids 61 SP1887
Chelsea Gt Lon 27 TQ2778
Chelsfield Gt Lon 27 TQ4864
Chelsham Surrey 27 TQ3758
Chelston Somset 20 ST1521
Chelsworth Suffk 54 TL9748
Cheltenham Gloucs 35 SO9422
Chelveston Nhants 51 SP9969
Chelvey Avon 21 ST4668
Chelwood Avon 21 ST6361
Chelwood Common E Susx 15 TQ4128
Chelwood Gate E Susx 15 TQ4130
Chelworth Wilts 35 ST9694
Chelworth Lower Green Wilts 36 SU0892
Chelworth Upper Green Wilts 36 SU0893
Cheney Longville Shrops 59 SO4284
Chenies Bucks 26 TQ0198
Chepstow Gwent 34 ST5393
Chequerbent Gt Man 79 SD6706
Chequers Corner Norfk 65 TF4908
Cherhill Wilts 36 SU0370
Cherington Warwks 48 SP2936
Cherington Gloucs 35 ST9098
Cheriton W Glam 32 SS4593
Cheriton Devon 19 SS7346
Cheriton Hants 24 SU5828
Cheriton Kent 29 TR2037
Cheriton Bishop Devon 8 SX7793
Cheriton Fitzpaine Devon 9 SS8606
Cheriton or Stackpole Elidor Dyfed 30 SR9897
Cherrington Shrops 72 SJ6619
Cherry Burton Humb 84 SE9841

Corran Cross Lanes

Corran *Highld* 130 NG8409
Corran *Highld* 130 NN0263
Corran *Cnwll* 3 SW9946
Corrany *IOM* 153 SC4589
Corrie *Strath* 105 NS0242
Corrie *D & G* 101 NY2086
Corriecravie *Strath* 105 NR9223
Corriegour *Highld* 131 NN2692
Corriemoille *Highld* 139 NH3663
Corrimony *Highld* 139 NH3730
Corringham *Lincs* 76 SK8691
Corringham *Essex* 40 TQ7083
Corris *Gwynd* 57 SH7508
Corris Uchaf *Gwynd* 57 SH7408
Corrow *Strath* 114 NN1800
Corry *Highld* 137 NG6424
Corrygills *Strath* 105 NS0335
Cors-y-Gedol *Gwynd* 57 SH6022
Corscombe *Dorset* 10 ST5105
Corscombe *Devon* 8 SX6296
Corse *Gramp* 142 NJ6040
Corse *Gloucs* 47 SO7826
Corse Lawn *Gloucs* 47 SO8330
Corsham *Wilts* 35 ST8770
Corsindae *Gramp* 135 NJ6808
Corsley *Wilts* 22 ST8246
Corsley Heath *Wilts* 22 ST8245
Corsock *D & G* 99 NX7675
Corston *Avon* 22 ST6965
Corston *Wilts* 35 ST9283
Corstorphine *Loth* 117 NT1972
Cortachy *Tays* 134 NO3959
Corton *Wilts* 22 ST9340
Corton *Suffk* 67 TM5497
Corton Denham *Somset* 21 ST6322
Coruanan Lodge *Highld* 130 NN0668
Corvallie *IOM* 153 SC1968
Corwar *Strath* 98 NX2780
Corwen *Clwyd* 70 SJ0743
Coryates *Dorset* 10 SY6285
Coryton *Devon* 5 SX4583
Coryton *Essex* 40 TQ7382
Cosby *Leics* 50 SP5495
Coseley *W Mids* 60 SO9494
Cosford *Shrops* 60 SJ8005
Cosgrove *Nhants* 38 SP7942
Cosham *Hants* 13 SU6505
Cosheston *Dyfed* 30 SN0003
Coshieville *Tays* 124 NN7749
Cossall *Notts* 62 SK4842
Cossall Marsh *Notts* 62 SK4842
Cossington *Leics* 62 SK6013
Cossington *Somset* 21 ST3540
Costallack *Cnwll* 2 SW4525
Costessey *Norfk* 66 TG1711
Costock *Notts* 62 SK5726
Coston *Leics* 63 SK8422
Coston *Norfk* 66 TG0506
Cote *Oxon* 36 SP3502
Cote *Somset* 21 ST3444
Cotebrook *Ches* 71 SJ5765
Cotehill *Cumb* 93 NY4650
Cotes *Cumb* 87 SD4886
Cotes *Staffs* 72 SJ8434
Cotes *Leics* 62 SK5520
Cotes Heath *Staffs* 72 SJ8334
Cotesbach *Leics* 50 SP5382
Cotgrave *Notts* 63 SK6435
Cotham *Notts* 63 SK7947
Cothelstone *Somset* 20 ST1831
Cotherstone *Dur* 95 NZ0119
Cothill *Oxon* 37 SU4699
Cotleigh *Devon* 9 ST2002
Cotmanhay *Derbys* 62 SK4543
Coton *Shrops* 59 SJ5334
Coton *Staffs* 72 SJ8120
Coton *Staffs* 72 SJ9731
Coton *Staffs* 61 SK1804
Coton *Nhants* 50 SP6771
Coton *Cambs* 52 TL4058
Coton Clanford *Staffs* 72 SJ8723
Coton Hayes *Staffs* 72 SJ9832
Coton Hill *Shrops* 59 SJ4813
Coton Park *Derbys* 73 SK2617
Coton in the Clay *Staffs* 73 SK1628
Coton in the Elms *Derbys* 73 SK2415
Cott *Devon* 7 SX7861
Cottage End Hants 24 SU4143
Cottam *Lancs* 80 SD5032
Cottam *Humb* 91 SE9964
Cottam *Notts* 75 SK8179
Cottenham *Cambs* 53 TL4467
Cotterdale *N York* 88 SD8393
Cottered *Herts* 39 TL3129
Cotteridge *W Mids* 61 SP0480
Cotterstock *Nhants* 51 TL0490
Cottesbrooke *Nhants* 50 SP7173
Cottesmore *Leics* 63 SK9013
Cottingham *Nhants* 51 SP8490
Cottingham *Humb* 84 TA0432
Cottingley *W York* 82 SE1137
Cottisford *Oxon* 49 SP5831
Cottivett *Cnwll* 5 SX3662
Cotton *Suffk* 54 TM0666
Cotton End *Beds* 38 TL0845
Cotton Tree *Lancs* 81 SD9039
Cottown *Gramp* 142 NJ5026
Cottown *Gramp* 142 NJ7615
Cottown *Gramp* 143 NJ8140
Cottrell *S Glam* 33 ST0774
Cotts *Devon* 6 SX4365
Cotwall *Shrops* 59 SJ6017
Cotwalton *Staffs* 72 SJ9234
Couch's Mill *Cnwll* 4 SX1459
Coughton *H & W* 34 SO5921
Coughton *Warwks* 48 SP0860
Coulaghailtro *Strath* 113 NR7165
Coulags *Highld* 138 NG9645
Coulderton *Cumb* 86 NX9808
Coull *Gramp* 134 NJ5102
Coulport *Strath* 114 NS2187
Coulsdon *Gt Lon* 27 TQ2959
Coulter *Strath* 108 NT0234
Coultershaw Bridge *W Susx* 14 SU9719
Coultings *Somset* 20 ST2241
Coulton *N York* 90 SE6373
Coultra *Fife* 126 NO3523
Cound *Shrops* 59 SJ5505
Coundlane *Shrops* 59 SJ5705
Coundon *Dur* 96 NZ2329
Coundon Grange *Dur* 96 NZ2228
Countersett *N York* 88 SD9187
Countess *Wilts* 23 SU1542
Countess Cross *Essex* 40 TL8631
Countess Wear *Devon* 9 SX9489
Countesthorpe *Leics* 50 SP5895
Countisbury *Devon* 19 SS7449
Coup Green *Lancs* 81 SD5927
Coupar Angus *Tays* 126 NO2239
Coupland *Nthumb* 110 NT9330
Coupland *Cumb* 94 NY7118
Cour *Strath* 105 NR8248
Courance *D & G* 100 NY0590
Court Henry *Dyfed* 32 SN5522
Court-at-Street *Kent* 17 TR0935
Courteachan *Highld* 129 NM6897
Courteenhall *Nhants* 49 SP7653
Courtsend *Essex* 41 TR0293
Courtway *Somset* 20 ST2033
Cousland *Loth* 118 NT3768
Cousley Wood *E Susx* 16 TQ6533
Cove *Highld* 144 NG8191
Cove *Gramp* 135 NJ9501
Cove *Strath* 114 NS2282
Cove *Devon* 20 SS9619
Cove *Hants* 25 SU8555
Cove Bottom *Suffk* 55 TM4979
Covehithe *Suffk* 55 TM5282
Coven *Staffs* 60 SJ9106
Coven Lawn *Staffs* 60 SJ9005
Coveney *Cambs* 53 TL4882
Covenham St. Bartholomew *Lincs* 77 TF3394
Covenham St. Mary *Lincs* 77 TF3394
Coventry *W Mids* 61 SP3378
Coverack *Cnwll* 3 SW7818
Coverack Bridges *Cnwll* 2 SW6630
Coverham *N York* 89 SE1086
Covington *Cambs* 51 TL0570
Cow Green *Suffk* 54 TM0565
Cow Honeybourne *H & W* 48 SP1143
Cowan Bridge *Lancs* 87 SD6376
Cowbeech *E Susx* 16 TQ6114
Cowbit *Lincs* 64 TF2518
Cowbridge *S Glam* 33 SS9974
Cowdale *Derbys* 74 SK0771
Cowden *Kent* 16 TQ4640
Cowden Pound *Kent* 16 TQ4642
Cowden Station *Kent* 16 TQ4741
Cowdenbeath *Fife* 117 NT1691
Cowdenburn *Border* 117 NT2052
Cowers Lane *Derbys* 73 SK3046
Cowes *IOW* 13 SZ4996
Cowesby *N York* 89 SE4689
Cowesfield Green *Wilts* 23 SU2523
Cowfold *W Susx* 15 TQ2122
Cowgill *Cumb* 88 SD7586
Cowhill *Avon* 34 ST6091
Cowie *Cent* 116 NS8389
Cowley *Derbys* 74 SK3376
Cowley *Gloucs* 35 SO9614
Cowley *Oxon* 37 SP5304
Cowley *Oxon* 49 SP6628
Cowley *Devon* 9 SX9095
Cowley *Gt Lon* 26 TQ0582
Cowling *Lancs* 81 SD5917
Cowling *N York* 82 SD9643
Cowling *N York* 89 SE2387
Cowlinge *Suffk* 53 TL7154
Cowmes *W York* 82 SE1815
Cowpe *Lancs* 81 SD8320
Cowpen *Nthumb* 103 NZ2981
Cowpen Bewley *Cleve* 97 NZ4824
Cowplain *Hants* 13 SU6810
Cowshill *Dur* 95 NY8540
Cowslip Green *Avon* 21 ST4861
Cowthorpe *N York* 83 SE4252
Cox Common *Suffk* 55 TM4082
Coxall *Shrops* 46 SO3774
Coxbank *Ches* 72 SJ6541
Coxbench *Derbys* 62 SK3743
Coxbridge *Somset* 21 ST5436
Coxford *Cnwll* 4 SX1696
Coxford *Norfk* 66 TF8529
Coxgreen *Staffs* 60 SO8086
Coxheath *Kent* 28 TQ7451
Coxhoe *Dur* 96 NZ3136
Coxley *W York* 82 SE2717
Coxley *Somset* 21 ST5343
Coxley Wick *Somset* 21 ST5243
Coxpark *Cnwll* 5 SX4072
Coxtie Green *Essex* 27 TQ5696
Coxwold *N York* 90 SE5377
Coychurch *M Glam* 33 SS9379
Coylton *Strath* 107 NS4219
Coylumbridge *Highld* 132 NH9111
Coytrahen *M Glam* 33 SS8885
Crab Orchard *Dorset* 12 SU0806
Crabbs Cross *H & W* 48 SP0465
Crabtree *W Susx* 15 TQ2125
Crabtree Green *Clwyd* 71 SJ3344
Crackenthorpe *Cumb* 94 NY6622
Crackington Haven *Cnwll* 4 SX1496
Crackley *Staffs* 72 SJ8350
Crackley *Warwks* 61 SP2973
Crackleybank *Shrops* 60 SJ7611
Crackpot *N York* 88 SD9796
Cracoe *N York* 88 SD9760
Craddock *Devon* 9 ST0812
Cradle End *Herts* 39 TL4521
Cradley *H & W* 47 SO7347
Cradoc *Powys* 45 SO0130
Crafthole *Cnwll* 5 SX3654
Crafton *Bucks* 38 SP8819
Crag Foot *Lancs* 87 SD4873
Cragg *W York* 82 SE0023
Cragg Hill *W York* 82 SE2437
Caggan *Highld* 141 NJ0226
Craghead *Dur* 96 NZ2150
Crai *Powys* 45 SN8924
Craibstone *Gramp* 142 NJ4959
Craibstone *Gramp* 135 NJ8710
Craichie *Tays* 127 NO5047
Craig Llangiwg *W Glam* 32 SN7204
Craig Penllyn *S Glam* 33 SS9777
Craig's End *Essex* 53 TL7137
Craig-y-Duke *W Glam* 32 SN7002
Craig-y-nos *Powys* 33 SN8415
Craigburn *Border* 117 NT2354
Craigcefnparc *W Glam* 32 SN6702
Craigdam *Gramp* 143 NJ8430
Craigdarroch *Strath* 107 NS6306
Craigdarroch *D & G* 107 NX7391
Craigdhu *Strath* 122 NM8205
Craigearn *Gramp* 142 NJ7214
Craigellachie *Gramp* 141 NJ2844
Craigend *Tays* 126 NO1120
Craigend *Strath* 115 NS4670
Craigendoran *Strath* 115 NS3181
Craigengillan *Strath* 107 NS4702
Craighlaw *D & G* 98 NX3061
Craigie *Tays* 126 NO1143
Craigie *Strath* 107 NS4232
Craigiefold *Gramp* 143 NJ9165
Craiglemine *D & G* 99 NX4039
Craiglcleuch *D & G* 101 NY3486
Craigley *D & G* 99 NX7658
Craiglockhart *Fife* 117 NT2271
Craiglug *Gramp* 141 NJ3355
Craigmillar *Loth* 117 NT3071
Craignant *Shrops* 58 SJ2535
Craigneston *D & G* 107 NX7587
Craigneuk *Strath* 116 NS7756
Craignure *Strath* 122 NM7236
Craigo *Tays* 135 NO6864
Craigrothie *Fife* 126 NO3810
Craigruie *Cent* 124 NN4920
Craigton *Gramp* 135 NJ8301
Craigton *Tays* 126 NO3250
Craigton *Tays* 127 NO5138
Craigton *Strath* 115 NS4954
Craik *Border* 109 NT3408
Crail *Fife* 127 NO6107
Crailing *Border* 110 NT6824
Crailinghall *Border* 110 NT6922
Crakehall *N York* 89 SE2489
Crakehill *N York* 89 SE4273
Crakemarsh *Staffs* 73 SK0936
Crambe *N York* 90 SE7364
Cramlington *Nthumb* 103 NZ2676
Cramond *Loth* 117 NT1976
Cramond Bridge *Loth* 117 NT1775
Cranage *Ches* 79 SJ7568
Cranberry *Staffs* 72 SJ8235
Cranborne *Dorset* 12 SU0513
Cranbrook *Devon* 8 SX7489
Cranbrook *Kent* 28 TQ7736
Cranbrook Common *Kent* 28 TQ7838
Crane Moor *S York* 82 SE3001
Crane's Corner *Norfk* 66 TF9113
Cranfield *Beds* 38 SP9542
Cranford *Devon* 18 SS3421
Cranford *Gt Lon* 26 TQ1076
Cranford St. Andrew *Nhants* 51 SP9277
Cranford St. John *Nhants* 51 SP9276
Cranham *Gloucs* 35 SO8913
Cranham *Gt Lon* 27 TQ5786
Cranhill *Warwks* 48 SP1253
Crank *Mersyd* 78 SJ5099
Cranleigh *Surrey* 14 TQ0539
Cranmer Green *Suffk* 54 TM0171
Cranmore *Somset* 22 ST6643
Cranmore *IOW* 13 SZ3990
Cranoe *Leics* 50 SP7695
Cransford *Suffk* 55 TM3164
Cranshaws *Border* 118 NT6861
Cranstal *IOM* 153 NX4602
Cranswick *Humb* 84 TA0252
Crantock *Cnwll* 4 SW7960
Cranwell *Lincs* 76 TF0349
Cranwich *Norfk* 65 TL7794
Cranworth *Norfk* 66 TF9804
Craobh Haven *Strath* 122 NM7907
Crapstone *Devon* 6 SX5067
Crarae *Strath* 114 NR9897
Crask Inn *Highld* 149 NC5224
Crask of Aigas *Highld* 139 NH4642
Craster *Nthumb* 111 NU2519
Craswall *H & W* 46 SO2735
Crateford *Staffs* 60 SJ9009
Cratfield *Suffk* 55 TM3175
Crathes *Gramp* 135 NO7596
Crathie *Highld* 132 NN5793
Crathie *Gramp* 133 NO2695
Crathorne *N York* 89 NZ4407
Craven Arms *Shrops* 59 SO4382
Crawcrook *T & W* 103 NZ1363
Crawford *Strath* 108 NS9520
Crawford *Lancs* 78 SD4902
Crawfordjohn *Strath* 108 NS8823
Crawick *D & G* 107 NS7811
Crawley *Oxon* 36 SP3412
Crawley *Hants* 24 SU4235
Crawley *W Susx* 15 TQ2636
Crawley Down *W Susx* 15 TQ3437
Crawley Side *Dur* 95 NY9940
Crawshawbooth *Lancs* 81 SD8125
Crawton *Gramp* 135 NO8779
Cray *N York* 88 SD9479
Cray's Pond *Oxon* 37 SU6380
Crayford *Gt Lon* 27 TQ5175
Crayke *N York* 90 SE5670
Craymere Beck *Norfk* 66 TG0631
Crays Hill *Essex* 40 TQ7192
Craythorne *Staffs* 73 SK2426
Craze Lowman *Devon* 9 SS9814
Crazies Hill *Oxon* 37 SU7980
Creacombe *Devon* 18 SS3219
Creagan Inn *Strath* 122 NM9744
Creagorry *W Isls* 154 NF7948
Creaguaineach Lodge *Highld* 131 NN3068
Creamore Bank *Shrops* 59 SJ5130
Creaton *Nhants* 50 SP7071
Creca *D & G* 101 NY2270
Credenhill *H & W* 46 SO4543
Crediton *Devon* 8 SS8300
Creebank *D & G* 98 NX3477
Creebridge *D & G* 99 NX4165
Creech Heathfield *Somset* 20 ST2727
Creech St. Michael *Somset* 20 ST2725
Creed *Cnwll* 3 SW9347
Creedy Park *Devon* 8 SS8301
Creekmouth *Gt Lon* 27 TQ4581
Creeting St. Mary *Suffk* 54 TM0956
Creeton *Lincs* 64 TF0120
Creetown *D & G* 99 NX4759
Creggans Inn *Strath* 123 NN0902
Cregneish *IOM* 153 SC1867
Cregrina *Powys* 45 SO1252
Creich *Fife* 126 NO3221
Creigiau *M Glam* 33 ST0781
Crelly *Cnwll* 2 SW6732
Cremyll *Cnwll* 6 SX4553
Cressage *Shrops* 59 SJ5904
Cressbrook *Derbys* 74 SK1673
Cresselly *Dyfed* 30 SN0606
Cressex *Bucks* 26 SU8492
Cressing *Essex* 40 TL7920
Cresswell *Nthumb* 103 NZ2993
Cresswell *Staffs* 72 SJ9739
Cresswell *Dyfed* 30 SN0506
Creswell *Derbys* 75 SK5274
Creswell Green *Staffs* 61 SK0710
Cretingham *Suffk* 55 TM2260
Cretshengan *Strath* 113 NR7166
Crew Green *Powys* 59 SJ3215
Crewe *Ches* 71 SJ4253
Crewe *Ches* 72 SJ7056
Crewe Green *Ches* 72 SJ7255
Crewkerne *Somset* 10 ST4409
Crews Hill *H & W* 35 SO6722
Crews Hill Station *Herts* 27 TL3000
Crewton *Derbys* 62 SK3733
Crianlarich *Strath* 123 NN3825
Cribbs Causeway *Avon* 34 ST5780
Cribyn *Dyfed* 44 SN5250
Criccieth *Gwynd* 56 SH4938
Crich *Derbys* 74 SK3454
Crich Carr *Derbys* 74 SK3354
Crich Common *Derbys* 74 SK3553
Crichton *Loth* 118 NT3862
Crick *Nhants* 50 SP5872
Crick *Gwent* 34 ST4890
Crickadarn *Powys* 45 SO0942
Cricket St. Thomas *Somset* 10 ST3708
Crickheath *Shrops* 59 SJ2922
Crickhowell *Powys* 33 SO2118
Cricklade *Wilts* 36 SU0993
Cricklewood *Gt Lon* 26 TQ2385
Cridling Stubbs *N York* 83 SE5221
Crieff *Tays* 125 NN8621
Criggan *Cnwll* 4 SX0160
Criggion *Powys* 59 SJ2915
Crigglestone *W York* 82 SE3116
Crimble *Gt Man* 81 SD8611
Crimond *Gramp* 143 NK0556
Crimonmogate *Gramp* 143 NK0358
Crimplesham *Norfk* 65 TF6503
Crimscote *Warwks* 48 SP2347
Crinan *Strath* 113 NR7894
Crindledyke *Strath* 116 NS8356
Cringleford *Norfk* 67 TG1905
Cringles *N York* 82 SE0448
Crinow *Dyfed* 31 SN1214
Cripp's Corner *E Susx* 17 TQ7721
Cripplesease *Cnwll* 2 SW5036
Cripplestyle *Dorset* 12 SU0812
Crizeley *H & W* 46 SO4532
Croachy *Highld* 140 NH6527
Croanford *Cnwll* 4 SX0371
Crochmare House *D & G* 100 NX8977
Crock Street *Somset* 10 ST3213
Crockenhill *Kent* 27 TQ5067
Crocker End *Oxon* 37 SU7086
Crocker's Ash *H & W* 34 SO5316
Crockerhill *W Susx* 14 SU9206
Crockernwell *Devon* 8 SX7592
Crockerton *Wilts* 22 ST8642
Crocketford *D & G* 100 NX8372
Crockey Hill *N York* 83 SE6246
Crockham Hill *Kent* 27 TQ4450
Crockhurst Street *Kent* 16 TQ6245
Crockleford Heath *Essex* 41 TM0426
Croes-lan *Dyfed* 42 SN3844
Croes-y-mwyalch *Gwent* 34 ST3092
Croes-y-pant *Gwent* 34 SO3104
Croeserw *W Glam* 33 SS8795
Croesgoch *Dyfed* 30 SM8330
Croesor *Gwynd* 57 SH6344
Croesyceiliog *Dyfed* 31 SN4016
Croesyceiliog *Gwent* 34 ST3096
Croft *Ches* 79 SJ6393
Croft *Leics* 50 SP5195
Croft *Devon* 5 SX5296
Croft *Lincs* 77 TF5061
Croft Michael *Cnwll* 2 SW6637
Croft-on-Tees *N York* 89 NZ2809
Croftamie *Cent* 115 NS4785
Crofton *Cumb* 93 NY3050
Crofton *W York* 83 SE3817
Crofton *Wilts* 23 SU2562
Crofton *Devon* 9 SX9680
Crofts *Gramp* 141 NJ2850
Crofts *D & G* 99 NX7365
Crofts of Dipple *Gramp* 141 NJ3259
Crofts of Savoch *Gramp* 143 NK0460
Crofty *W Glam* 32 SS5294
Crogen *Gwynd* 58 SJ0036
Croggan *Strath* 122 NM7027
Croglin *Cumb* 94 NY5747
Crogo *D & G* 99 NX7576
Croik *Highld* 146 NH4591
Cromarty *Highld* 140 NH7867
Crombie *Fife* 117 NT0584
Cromdale *Highld* 141 NJ0728
Cromer *Norfk* 67 TG2242
Cromer *Herts* 39 TL2928
Cromford *Derbys* 73 SK2956
Cromhall *Avon* 35 ST6990
Cromhall Common *Avon* 35 ST6989
Cromore *W Isls* 154 NB4021
Crompton Fold *Gt Man* 79 SD9409
Cromwell *Notts* 75 SK7961
Cronberry *Strath* 107 NS6022
Crondall *Hants* 25 SU7948
Cronton *Mersyd* 78 SJ4988
Crook *Dur* 96 NZ1635
Crook *Cumb* 87 SD4695
Crook of Devon *Tays* 117 NO0400
Crook Inn *Border* 108 NT1026
Crookdake *Cumb* 93 NY1943
Crooke *Gt Man* 78 SD5507
Crooked End *Gloucs* 35 SO6217
Crooked Holme *Cumb* 101 NY5161
Crooked Soley *Wilts* 36 SU3172
Crookedholm *Strath* 107 NS4537
Crookes *S York* 74 SK3287
Crookhall *Dur* 95 NZ1150
Crookham *Nthumb* 110 NT9138
Crookham *Berks* 24 SU5464
Crookham Village *Hants* 25 SU7952
Crooklands *Cumb* 87 SD5383
Cropper *Derbys* 73 SK2335
Cropredy *Oxon* 49 SP4646
Cropston *Leics* 62 SK5510
Cropthorne *H & W* 47 SO9945
Cropton *N York* 90 SE7589
Cropwell Bishop *Notts* 63 SK6835
Cropwell Butler *Notts* 63 SK6837
Crosbie *Strath* 114 NS2149
Crosby *Cumb* 92 NY0738
Crosby *IOM* 153 SC3279
Crosby *Humb* 84 SE8912
Crosby *Mersyd* 78 SJ3198
Crosby Garret *Cumb* 88 NY7209
Crosby Ravensworth *Cumb* 94 NY6214
Crosby Villa *Cumb* 92 NY0939
Croscombe *Somset* 21 ST5944
Crosemere *Shrops* 59 SJ4329
Cross *Somset* 21 ST4154
Cross Ash *Gwent* 34 SO4019
Cross Bush *W Susx* 14 TQ0306
Cross Coombe *Cnwll* 3 SW7251
Cross End *Beds* 51 TL0658
Cross End *Essex* 54 TL8534
Cross Flatts *W York* 82 SE1040
Cross Gates *W York* 83 SE3534
Cross Green *Staffs* 60 SJ9105
Cross Green *Devon* 5 SX3888
Cross Green *Suffk* 54 TL8353
Cross Green *Suffk* 54 TL8955
Cross Green *Suffk* 54 TL9852
Cross Hands *Dyfed* 31 SN0712
Cross Hands *Dyfed* 32 SN5612
Cross Hill *Derbys* 74 SK4148
Cross Hills *N York* 82 SE0145
Cross Houses *Shrops* 59 SJ5307
Cross Houses *Shrops* 60 SO6991
Cross Inn *Dyfed* 42 SN3957
Cross Inn *Dyfed* 43 SN5464
Cross Inn *M Glam* 33 ST0582
Cross Keys *Wilts* 35 ST8771
Cross Lane *IOW* 13 SZ5089
Cross Lane Head *Shrops* 60 SO7195
Cross Lanes *N York* 90 SE5364
Cross Lanes *Clwyd* 71 SJ3746
Cross Lanes *Cnwll* 2 SW6921
Cross Lanes *Cnwll* 3 SW7642

D

Dean Head Drummond

Dean Head *S York* 74 SE2600
Dean Prior *Devon* 7 SX7363
Dean Row *Ches* 79 SJ8781
Dean Street *Kent* 28 TQ7453
Deanburnhaugh *Border* 109 NT3911
Deancombe *Devon* 7 SX7264
Deane *Gt Man* 79 SD6907
Deane *Hants* 24 SU5450
Deanhead *W York* 82 SE0415
Deanland *Dorset* 22 ST9918
Deanlane End *W Susx* 13 SU7412
Deanraw *Nthumb* 102 NY8162
Deanscales *Cumb* 92 NY0926
Deanshanger *Nhants* 49 SP7639
Deanshaugh *Gramp* 141 NJ3550
Deanston *Cent* 116 NN7101
Dearham *Cumb* 92 NY0736
Dearnley *Gt Man* 81 SD9215
Debach *Suffk* 55 TM2454
Debden *Essex* 39 TL5533
Debden Cross *Essex* 40 TL5831
Debden Green *Essex* 40 TL5732
Debden Green *Essex* 27 TQ4398
Debenham *Suffk* 54 TM1763
Deblin's Green *H & W* 47 SO8148
Dechmont *Loth* 117 NT0370
Dechmont Road *Loth* 117 NT0269
Deddington *Oxon* 49 SP4631
Dedham *Essex* 41 TM0533
Dedham Heath *Essex* 41 TM0531
Dedworth *Berks* 26 SU9476
Deene *Nhants* 51 SP9492
Deenethorpe *Nhants* 51 SP9591
Deepcar *S York* 74 SK2897
Deepcut *Surrey* 25 SU9057
Deepdale *Cumb* 88 SD7184
Deepdale *N York* 88 SD8979
Deeping Gate *Lincs* 64 TF1509
Deeping St. James *Lincs* 64 TF1609
Deeping St. Nicholas *Lincs* 64 TF2115
Deerhurst *Gloucs* 47 SO8730
Deerhurst Walton *Gloucs* 47 SO8828
Deerton Street *Kent* 28 TQ9762
Defford *H & W* 47 SO9143
Defynnog *Powys* 45 SN9227
Deganwy *Gwynd* 69 SH7779
Degnish *Strath* 122 NM7812
Deighton *N York* 89 NZ3801
Deighton *W York* 82 SE1519
Deighton *N York* 83 SE6244
Deiniolen *Gwynd* 69 SH5763
Delabole *Cnwll* 4 SX0683
Delamere *Ches* 71 SJ5668
Delfrigs *Gramp* 143 NJ9620
Dell Quay *W Susx* 14 SU8302
Delley *Devon* 19 SS5424
Delliefure *Highld* 141 NJ0730
Delly End *Oxon* 36 SP3513
Delmonden Green *Kent* 17 TQ7330
Delnabo *Gramp* 141 NJ1517
Delnashaugh Hotel *Gramp* 141 NJ1835
Delny *Highld* 146 NH7372
Delph *Gt Man* 82 SD9807
Delves *Dur* 95 NZ1149
Delvine *Tays* 126 NO1240
Dembleby *Lincs* 64 TF0437
Demelza *Cnwll* 4 SW9763
Denaby *S York* 75 SK4899
Denaby Main *S York* 75 SK4999
Denbies *Surrey* 26 TQ1450
Denbigh *Clwyd* 70 SJ0566
Denbrae *Fife* 126 NO3818
Denbury *Devon* 7 SX8268
Denby *Derbys* 62 SK3946
Denby Bottles *Derbys* 62 SK3846
Denby Dale *W York* 82 SE2208
Denchworth *Oxon* 36 SU3891
Dendron *Cumb* 86 SD2470
Denel End *Beds* 38 TL0335
Denfield *Tays* 125 NN9517
Denford *Nhants* 51 SP9976
Dengie *Essex* 41 TL9802
Denham *Suffk* 53 TL7561
Denham *Suffk* 55 TM1974
Denham *Bucks* 26 TQ0487
Denham End *Suffk* 53 TL7663
Denham Green *Suffk* 55 TM1974
Denham Green *Bucks* 26 TQ0488
Denhead *Gramp* 143 NJ9952
Denhead *Fife* 127 NO4613
Denhead of Gray *Tays* 126 NO3531
Denholm *Border* 110 NT5718
Denholme *W York* 82 SE0734
Denholme Clough *W York* 82 SE0732
Denio *Gwynd* 56 SH3635
Denmead *Hants* 13 SU6512
Denmore *Gramp* 135 NJ9411
Denne Park *W Susx* 15 TQ1628
Dennington *Suffk* 55 TM2867
Denny *Cent* 116 NS8082
Dennyloanhead *Cent* 116 NS8080
Denshaw *Gt Man* 82 SD9710
Denside *Gramp* 135 NO8095
Densole *Kent* 29 TR2141
Denston *Suffk* 53 TL7652
Denstone *Staffs* 73 SK0940
Denstroude *Kent* 29 TR1061
Dent *Cumb* 87 SD7086
Dent-de-Lion *Kent* 29 TR3269
Denton *Dur* 96 NZ2118
Denton *N York* 82 SE1448
Denton *Gt Man* 79 SJ9295
Denton *Lincs* 63 SK8632
Denton *Oxon* 37 SP5902
Denton *Nhants* 51 SP8358
Denton *Cambs* 52 TL1587
Denton *Norfk* 55 TM2788
Denton *E Susx* 16 TQ4502
Denton *Kent* 28 TQ6673
Denton *Kent* 29 TR2147
Denver *Norfk* 65 TF6001
Denwick *Nthumb* 111 NU2014
Deopham *Norfk* 66 TG0400
Deopham Green *Norfk* 66 TM0499
Depden *Suffk* 53 TL7857
Depden Green *Suffk* 53 TL7756
Deptford *Wilts* 22 SU0138
Deptford *Gt Lon* 27 TQ3777
Derby *Derbys* 62 SK3536
Derbyhaven *IOM* 153 SC2867
Derculich *Tays* 125 NN8852
Deri *M Glam* 33 SO1201
Derril *Devon* 18 SS3003
Derringstone *Kent* 29 TR2049
Derrington *Staffs* 72 SJ8922
Derriton *Devon* 18 SS3303
Derry Hill *Wilts* 35 ST9670
Derrythorpe *Humb* 84 SE8208
Dersingham *Norfk* 65 TF6830
Dervaig *Strath* 121 NM4352
Derwen *Clwyd* 70 SJ0750
Derwenlas *Powys* 57 SN7298
Desborough *Nhants* 51 SP8083
Desford *Leics* 62 SK4703
Deskford *Gramp* 142 NJ5061
Detchant *Nthumb* 111 NU0836
Detling *Kent* 28 TQ7958
Deuxhill *Shrops* 60 SO6987
Devauden *Gwent* 34 ST4898
Devil's Bridge *Dyfed* 43 SN7376
Deviock *Cnwll* 5 SX3155
Devitts Green *Warwks* 61 SP2790
Devizes *Wilts* 22 SU0061
Devonport *Devon* 6 SX4554
Devonside *Cent* 116 NS9196
Devoran *Cnwll* 3 SW7939
Dewarton *Loth* 118 NT3763
Dewlish *Dorset* 11 SY7798
Dewsbury *W York* 82 SE2421
Dewsbury Moor *W York* 82 SE2321
Deytheur *Powys* 58 SJ2317
Dhoon *IOM* 153 SC3784
Dial *Avon* 21 ST5366
Dial Green *W Susx* 14 SU9227
Dial Post *W Susx* 15 TQ1519
Dibberford *Dorset* 10 ST4504
Dibden *Hants* 13 SU4008
Dibden Purlieu *Hants* 13 SU4106
Dickens Heath *W Mids* 61 SP1176
Dickleburgh *Norfk* 54 TM1682
Didbrook *Gloucs* 48 SP0531
Didcot *Oxon* 37 SU5290
Diddington *Cambs* 52 TL1965
Diddlebury *Shrops* 59 SO5085
Didley *H & W* 46 SO4532
Didling *W Susx* 14 SU8318
Didmarton *Gloucs* 35 ST8287
Didsbury *Gt Man* 79 SJ8491
Didworthy *Devon* 7 SX6862
Digby *Lincs* 76 TF0854
Digg *Highld* 136 NG4668
Diggle *Gt Man* 82 SE0007
Digmore *Lancs* 78 SD4905
Digswell *Herts* 39 TL2415
Digswell Water *Herts* 39 TL2514
Dihewyd *Dyfed* 44 SN4855
Dilham *Norfk* 67 TG3325
Dilhorne *Staffs* 72 SJ9743
Dillington *Cambs* 52 TL1365
Dilston *Nthumb* 102 NY9763
Dilton *Wilts* 22 ST8548
Dilton Marsh *Wilts* 22 ST8449
Dilwyn *H & W* 46 SO4154
Dimma *Cnwll* 5 SX1997
Dimple *Gt Man* 81 SD7015
Dinas *Gwynd* 56 SH2735
Dinas *Dyfed* 30 SN0138
Dinas *Dyfed* 31 SN2730
Dinas *M Glam* 33 ST0091
Dinas *Cnwll* 4 SW9274
Dinas Dinlle *Gwynd* 68 SH4455
Dinas Powys *S Glam* 33 ST1571
Dinas-Mawddwy *Gwynd* 57 SH8515
Dinder *Somset* 21 ST5744
Dinedor *H & W* 46 SO5336
Dingestow *Gwent* 34 SO4510
Dingle *Mersyd* 78 SJ3687
Dingleden *Kent* 17 TQ8131
Dingley *Nhants* 50 SP7787
Dingwall *Highld* 139 NH5458
Dinham *Gwent* 34 ST4792
Dinmael *Clwyd* 70 SJ0044
Dinnet *Gramp* 134 NO4598
Dinnington *T & W* 103 NZ2073
Dinnington *S York* 75 SK5285
Dinnington *Somset* 10 ST4012
Dinorwic *Gwynd* 69 SH5961
Dinton *Bucks* 37 SP7610
Dinton *Wilts* 22 SU0131
Dinwoodie *D & G* 100 NY1190
Dinworthy *Devon* 18 SS3015
Dipford *Somset* 20 ST2021
Dipley *Hants* 24 SU7457
Dippen *Strath* 105 NR7937
Dippenhall *Surrey* 25 SU8146
Dippermill *Devon* 18 SS4406
Dippertown *Devon* 5 SX4284
Dippin *Strath* 105 NS0422
Dipple *Gramp* 141 NJ3258
Dipple *Strath* 106 NS2002
Diptford *Devon* 7 SX7256
Dipton *Dur* 96 NZ1554
Diptonmill *Nthumb* 102 NY9361
Dirleton *Loth* 118 NT5184
Dirt Pot *Nthumb* 95 NY8545
Discoed *Powys* 46 SO2764
Diseworth *Leics* 62 SK4524
Dishforth *N York* 89 SE3873
Disley *Ches* 79 SJ9784
Diss *Norfk* 54 TM1180
Disserth *Powys* 45 SO0358
Distington *Cumb* 92 NY0023
Ditchampton *Wilts* 23 SU0831
Ditchburn *Nthumb* 111 NU1320
Ditcheat *Somset* 21 ST6236
Ditchingham *Norfk* 67 TM3391
Ditchley *Oxon* 36 SP3820
Ditchling *E Susx* 15 TQ3215
Ditherington *Shrops* 59 SJ5014
Ditteridge *Wilts* 35 ST8169
Dittisham *Devon* 6 SX5370
Dittisham *Devon* 7 SX8655
Ditton *Ches* 78 SJ4986
Ditton *Kent* 28 TQ7158
Ditton Green *Cambs* 53 TL6558
Ditton Priors *Shrops* 59 SO6089
Dixton *Gwent* 34 SO5113
Dixton *Gloucs* 47 SO9830
Dizzard *Cnwll* 4 SX1698
Dobcross *Gt Man* 82 SD9906
Dobroyd Castle *W York* 81 SD9323
Dobwalls *Cnwll* 5 SX2165
Doccombe *Devon* 8 SX7786
Dochgarroch *Highld* 140 NH6140
Docker *Lancs* 87 SD5774
Docking *Norfk* 65 TF7636
Docklow *H & W* 46 SO5657
Dockray *Cumb* 93 NY2649
Dockray *Cumb* 93 NY3921
Dod's Leigh *Staffs* 73 SK0134
Dodbrooke *Devon* 7 SX7444
Dodd's Green *Ches* 71 SJ6043
Doddinghurst *Essex* 27 TQ5999
Doddington *Nthumb* 111 NT9932
Doddington *Lincs* 76 SK8970
Doddington *Shrops* 46 SO6176
Doddington *Cambs* 52 TL4090
Doddington *Kent* 28 TQ9357
Doddiscombsleigh *Devon* 8 SX8586
Doddshill *Norfk* 65 TF6930
Doddy Cross *Cnwll* 5 SX3062
Dodford *H & W* 60 SO9373
Dodford *Nhants* 49 SP6160
Dodington *Somset* 20 ST1740
Dodington *Avon* 35 ST7580
Dodleston *Ches* 71 SJ3661
Dodscott *Devon* 19 SS5419
Dodside *Strath* 115 NS5053
Dodworth *S York* 83 SE3105
Dodworth Bottom *S York* 83 SE3204
Dodworth Green *S York* 83 SE3004
Doe Bank *W Mids* 61 SP1197
Doe Lea *Derbys* 75 SK4666
Dog Village *Devon* 9 SX9896
Dogdyke *Lincs* 76 TF2055
Dogley Lane *W York* 82 SE1813
Dogmersfield *Hants* 25 SU7852
Dogridge *Wilts* 36 SU0887
Dogsthorpe *Cambs* 64 TF1901
Dol-for *Powys* 57 SH8106
Dol-gran *Dyfed* 31 SN4334
Dolanog *Powys* 58 SJ0612
Dolau *Powys* 45 SO1467
Dolbenmaen *Gwynd* 56 SH5043
Doley *Shrops* 72 SJ7429
Dolfor *Powys* 58 SO1087
Dolgarrog *Gwynd* 69 SH7767
Dolgellau *Gwynd* 57 SH7217
Dolgoch *Gwynd* 57 SH6504
Doll *Highld* 147 NC8803
Dollar *Cent* 117 NS9698
Dollarbeg *Cent* 117 NS9796
Dollarfield *Cent* 117 NS9697
Dolley Green *Powys* 46 SO2865
Dollwen *Dyfed* 43 SN6881
Dolphin *Clwyd* 70 SJ1973
Dolphinholme *Lancs* 80 SD5253
Dolphinstom *Border* 110 NT6815
Dolphinton *Strath* 117 NT1046
Dolton *Devon* 19 SS5712
Dolwen *Clwyd* 69 SH8874
Dolwyddelan *Gwynd* 69 SH7352
Dolybont *Dyfed* 33 SN6288
Dolyhir *Powys* 46 SO2457
Domgay *Powys* 58 SJ2818
Doncaster *S York* 83 SE5703
Doncaster Carr *S York* 83 SE5801
Donehill *Devon* 8 SX7277
Donhead St. Andrew *Wilts* 22 ST9124
Donhead St. Mary *Wilts* 22 ST9024
Donibristle *Fife* 117 NT1688
Doniford *Somset* 20 ST0842
Donington *Lincs* 64 TF2035
Donington Southing *Lincs* 64 TF2034
Donington on Bain *Lincs* 76 TF2382
Donisthorpe *Leics* 61 SK3113
Donkey Street *Kent* 17 TR1032
Donkey Town *Surrey* 25 SU9360
Donnington *Shrops* 59 SJ5708
Donnington *Shrops* 60 SJ7114
Donnington *H & W* 47 SO7034
Donnington *Gloucs* 48 SP1928
Donnington *Berks* 24 SU4668
Donnington *W Susx* 14 SU8501
Donnington Wood *Shrops* 60 SJ7012
Donyatt *Somset* 10 ST3314
Doomsday Green *W Susx* 15 TQ1929
Doonfoot *Strath* 106 NS3219
Doonholm *Strath* 106 NS3317
Dorback Lodge *Highld* 141 NJ0716
Dorchester *Oxon* 37 SU5794
Dorchester *Dorset* 11 SY6990
Dordon *Warwks* 61 SK2500
Dore *S York* 74 SK3181
Dores *Highld* 140 NH5934
Dorking *Surrey* 15 TQ1649
Dorlin House *Highld* 129 NM6671
Dormans Land *Surrey* 16 TQ4041
Dormans Park *Surrey* 15 TQ3940
Dormington *H & W* 46 SO5840
Dormston *H & W* 47 SO9857
Dorn *Gloucs* 48 SP2034
Dornal *Strath* 98 NX2976
Dorney *Berks* 26 SU9378
Dornie *Highld* 138 NG8826
Dornoch *Highld* 147 NH7989
Dornock *D & G* 101 NY2366
Dorrery *Highld* 150 ND0754
Dorridge *W Mids* 61 SP1775
Dorrington *Shrops* 59 SJ4702
Dorrington *Shrops* 72 SJ7340
Dorrington *Lincs* 76 TF0852
Dorsington *Warwks* 48 SP1349
Dorstone *H & W* 46 SO3141
Dorton *Bucks* 37 SP6814
Dosthill *Staffs* 61 SP2199
Dottery *Dorset* 10 SY4595
Doublebois *Cnwll* 5 SX1964
Douganhill *D & G* 92 NX8155
Doughton *Gloucs* 35 ST8791
Douglas *Strath* 108 NS8330
Douglas *IOM* 153 SC3775
Douglas Castle *Strath* 108 NS8431
Douglas Hill *Gwynd* 69 SH6065
Douglas Pier *Strath* 114 NS1999
Douglas Water *Strath* 108 NS8736
Douglas West *Strath* 108 NS8231
Douglas and Angus *Tays* 127 NO4233
Douglastown *Tays* 126 NO4147
Dougarie *Strath* 105 NR8837
Dounby *Ork* 155 HY2920
Doune *Highld* 146 NC4400
Doune *Cent* 116 NN7201
Dounepark *Strath* 106 NX1897
Dounie *Highld* 146 NH5690
Dounreay *Highld* 150 ND0065
Dousland *Devon* 6 SX5369
Dovaston *Shrops* 59 SJ3521
Dove Green *Notts* 75 SK4652
Dove Holes *Derbys* 74 SK0777
Dovenby *Cumb* 92 NY0933
Dover *Gt Man* 78 SD6000
Dover *Kent* 29 TR3141
Dovercourt *Essex* 41 TM2431
Doverdale *H & W* 47 SO8666
Doveridge *Derbys* 73 SK1133
Doversgreen *Surrey* 15 TQ2548
Dowally *Tays* 125 NO0048
Dowbridge *Lancs* 80 SD4331
Dowdeswell *Gloucs* 35 SP0019
Dowhill *Strath* 106 NS2003
Dowlais *M Glam* 33 SO0607
Dowland *Devon* 19 SS5610
Dowlish Ford *Somset* 10 ST3513
Dowlish Wake *Somset* 10 ST3712
Down Ampney *Gloucs* 36 SU0996
Down Hatherley *Gloucs* 35 SO8622
Down St. Mary *Devon* 8 SS7404
Down Thomas *Devon* 6 SX5050
Downacarey *Devon* 5 SX3790
Downderry *Cnwll* 5 SX3154
Downe *Gt Lon* 27 TQ4361
Downend *Avon* 35 ST6577
Downend *Gloucs* 35 ST8398
Downend *Berks* 37 SU4775
Downend *IOW* 13 SZ5387
Downfield *Tays* 126 NO3932
Downgate *Cnwll* 5 SX2871
Downgate *Cnwll* 5 SX3672
Downham *Nthumb* 110 NT8633
Downham *Lancs* 81 SD7844
Downham *Cambs* 53 TL5284
Downham *Gt Lon* 27 TQ3871
Downham *Essex* 40 TQ7296
Downham Market *Norfk* 65 TF6103
Downhead *Somset* 21 ST5625
Downhead *Somset* 22 ST6945
Downhill *Tays* 125 NO0930
Downhill *Cnwll* 4 SW8669
Downholland Cross *Lancs* 78 SD3606
Downholme *N York* 89 SE1197
Downies *Gramp* 135 NO9294
Downing *Clwyd* 70 SJ1578
Downley *Bucks* 26 SU8495
Downside *Somset* 21 ST6244
Downside *Somset* 21 ST6450
Downside *Surrey* 26 TQ1057
Downton *Wilts* 12 SU1821
Downton *Hants* 12 SZ2693
Downton on the Rock *H & W* 46 SO4273
Dowsby *Lincs* 64 TF1129
Dowsdale *Lincs* 64 TF2810
Dowsland Green *Essex* 40 TL8724
Doxey *Staffs* 72 SJ8923
Doxford *Nthumb* 111 NU1823
Doynton *Avon* 35 ST7274
Draethen *M Glam* 34 ST2287
Draffan *Strath* 116 NS7945
Dragonby *Humb* 84 SE9014
Dragons Green *W Susx* 15 TQ1423
Drakeholes *Notts* 75 SK7090
Drakelow *H & W* 60 SO8180
Drakemyre *Strath* 115 NS2950
Drakes Broughton *H & W* 47 SO9248
Drakes Cross *H & W* 61 SP0876
Drakewalls *Cnwll* 6 SX4270
Draughton *N York* 82 SE0352
Draughton *Nhants* 50 SP7676
Drax *N York* 83 SE6726
Drax Hales *N York* 83 SE6725
Draycot Foliat *Wilts* 36 SU1777
Draycote *Warwks* 50 SP4470
Draycott *Derbys* 62 SK4433
Draycott *H & W* 47 SO8548
Draycott *Shrops* 60 SO8093
Draycott *Gloucs* 48 SP1835
Draycott *Somset* 21 ST4751
Draycott *Somset* 21 ST5521
Draycott in the Clay *Staffs* 73 SK1528
Draycott in the Moors *Staffs* 72 SJ9840
Drayford *Devon* 19 SS7813
Draynes *Cnwll* 5 SX2169
Drayton *H & W* 60 SO8975
Drayton *Oxon* 49 SP4241
Drayton *Leics* 51 SP8392
Drayton *Somset* 21 ST4024
Drayton *Oxon* 37 SU4894
Drayton *Hants* 13 SU6705
Drayton *Lincs* 64 TF2439
Drayton *Norfk* 66 TG1813
Drayton Bassett *Staffs* 61 SK1900
Drayton Beauchamp *Bucks* 38 SP9011
Drayton Parslow *Bucks* 38 SP8328
Drayton St Leonard *Oxon* 37 SU5996
Drebley *N York* 88 SE0559
Dreenhill *Dyfed* 30 SM9214
Drefach *Dyfed* 31 SN3538
Drefach *Dyfed* 44 SN4945
Drefach *Dyfed* 32 SN5213
Drefelin *Dyfed* 31 SN3637
Dreghorn *Strath* 106 NS3538
Drellingore *Kent* 29 TR2441
Drem *Loth* 118 NT5079
Dresden *Staffs* 72 SJ9142
Drewsteignton *Devon* 8 SX7391
Driffield *Gloucs* 36 SU0799
Driffield *Humb* 91 TA0257
Driffield Cross Roads *Gloucs* 36 SU0698
Drift *Cnwll* 2 SW4328
Drigg *Cumb* 86 SD0699
Drighlington *W York* 82 SE2228
Drimnin *Highld* 121 NM5554
Drimpton *Dorset* 10 ST4104
Drimsallie *Highld* 130 NM9578
Drimsynie *Strath* 114 NN1901
Dringhoe *Humb* 85 TA1454
Dringhouses *N York* 83 SE5849
Drinkstone *Suffk* 54 TL9561
Drinkstone Green *Suffk* 54 TL9660
Drinsey Nook *Notts* 76 SK8773
Drive End *Dorset* 10 ST5808
Driver's End *Herts* 39 TL2220
Drointon *Staffs* 73 SK0226
Droitwich Spa *H & W* 47 SO8963
Dron *Tays* 126 NO1416
Dronfield *Derbys* 74 SK3578
Dronfield Woodhouse *Derbys* 74 SK3378
Drongan *Strath* 107 NS4418
Dronley *Tays* 126 NO3435
Droop *Dorset* 11 ST7508
Dropping Well *S York* 74 SK3994
Droxford *Hants* 13 SU6018
Droylsden *Gt Man* 79 SJ9097
Druid *Clwyd* 70 SJ0443
Druids Heath *W Mids* 61 SK0502
Druidston *Dyfed* 30 SM8616
Druimachoish *Highld* 123 NN1246
Druimarbin *Highld* 130 NN0770
Druimdrishaig *Strath* 113 NR7370
Druimindarroch *Highld* 129 NM6884
Drum *Tays* 117 NO0400
Drum *Strath* 114 NR9276
Drumalbin *Strath* 108 NS9038
Drumbeg *Highld* 148 NC1232
Drumblade *Gramp* 142 NJ5840
Drumblair House *Gramp* 142 NJ6343
Drumbreddon *D & G* 98 NX0843
Drumbuie *Highld* 137 NG7730
Drumburgh *Cumb* 93 NY2659
Drumburn *D & G* 92 NX8854
Drumchapel *Strath* 115 NS5270
Drumchastle *Tays* 132 NN6858
Drumclog *Strath* 107 NS6438
Drumeldrie *Fife* 127 NO4403
Drumelzier *Border* 108 NT1334
Drumfearn *Highld* 129 NG6716
Drumfrennie *Gramp* 135 NO7298
Drumgask *Highld* 132 NN6193
Drumhead *Gramp* 134 NO6092
Drumin *Gramp* 141 NJ1830
Drumjohn *D & G* 107 NX5297
Drumlamford *Strath* 98 NX2876
Drumlasie *Gramp* 135 NJ6405
Drumleaning *Cumb* 93 NY2751
Drumlemble *Strath* 104 NR6619
Drumlithie *Gramp* 135 NO7880
Drummoddie *D & G* 99 NX3845
Drummond *Highld* 140 NH6065

Drummore East Pennard

Drummore D & G 98 NX1336
Drummore D & G 100 NX9074
Drummuir Gramp 141 NJ3843
Drumnadrochit Highld 139 NH5030
Drumnagorrach Gramp 142 NJ5252
Drumore Strath 105 NR7022
Drumpark D & G 100 NX8779
Drumrunie Lodge Highld 145 NC1604
Drumshang Strath 106 NS2514
Drumtroddan D & G 99 NX3645
Drumuie Highld 136 NG4546
Drumvaich Cent 124 NN6704
Drumvillie Highld 140 NH9420
Drumwalt D & G 98 NX3053
Drumwhirn D & G 99 NX7480
Drunzie Tays 126 NO1308
Druridge Nthumb 103 NZ2796
Drury Clwyd 71 SJ2964
Dry Doddington Lincs 63 SK8546
Dry Drayton Cambs 52 TL3861
Dry Sandford Oxon 37 SP4600
Dry Street Essex 40 TQ6986
Drybeck Cumb 94 NY6615
Drybridge Gramp 142 NJ4362
Drybridge Strath 106 NS3536
Drybrook Gloucs 35 SO6417
Dryburgh Border 110 NT5932
Dryhope Border 109 NT2624
Drym Cnwll 2 SW6133
Drymen Cent 115 NS4788
Drymuir Gramp 143 NJ9046
Drynoch Highld 136 NG4031
Dryton Shrops 59 SJ5905
Dubford Gramp 143 NJ7963
Dublin Suffk 54 TM1669
Duchally Highld 145 NC3817
Duck End Beds 38 TL0544
Duck End Cambs 52 TL2464
Duck End Essex 40 TL6526
Duck Street Hants 23 SU3249
Duck's Cross Beds 52 TL1156
Duckend Green Essex 40 TL7223
Duckington Ches 71 SJ4851
Ducklington Oxon 36 SP3507
Duddingston Loth 117 NT2872
Duddington Nhants 51 SK9800
Duddlestone Somset 20 ST2321
Duddleswell E Susx 16 TQ4628
Duddlewick Shrops 59 SO6583
Duddo Nthumb 110 NT9342
Duddon Ches 71 SJ5164
Duddon Bridge Cumb 86 SD1988
Dudleston Shrops 71 SJ3438
Dudleston Heath Shrops 59 SJ3736
Dudley T & W 103 NZ2573
Dudley W Mids 60 SO9490
Dudley Hill W York 82 SE1830
Dudley Port W Mids 60 SO9691
Dudnill Shrops 47 SO6474
Dudsbury Dorset 12 SZ0798
Dudswell Herts 38 SP9609
Duffield Derbys 62 SK3443
Duffryn M Glam 33 SS8495
Dufftown Gramp 141 NJ3240
Duffus Gramp 141 NJ1668
Dufton Cumb 94 NY6825
Duggleby N York 90 SE8767
Duirinish Highld 137 NG7831
Duisdalemore Highld 129 NG7013
Duisky Highld 130 NN0076
Duke Street Suffk 54 TM0742
Dukestown Gwent 33 SO1410
Dukinfield Gt Man 79 SJ9397
Dulas Gwynd 68 SH4789
Dulcote Somset 21 ST5644
Dulford Devon 9 ST0706
Dull Tays 125 NN8049
Dullatur Strath 116 NS7476
Dullingham Cambs 53 TL6357
Dullingham Ley Cambs 53 TL6456
Dulnain Bridge Highld 141 NH9925
Duloe Cnwll 5 SX2358
Duloe Beds 52 TL1560
Dulverton Somset 20 SS9127
Dulwich Gt Lon 27 TQ3373
Dumbarton Strath 115 NS3975
Dumbleton Gloucs 47 SP0135
Dumcrieff D & G 108 NT1003
Dumfries D & G 100 NX9776
Dumgoyne Cent 115 NS5283
Dummer Hants 24 SU5846
Dumpton Kent 29 TR3966
Dun Tays 135 NO6659
Dunalastair Tays 132 NN7158
Dunan Highld 137 NG5828
Dunan Tays 124 NN4757
Dunan Strath 114 NS1571
Dunans Strath 114 NS0491
Dunavourd Tays 125 NN9657
Dunaverty Strath 105 NR6807
Dunball Somset 21 ST3141
Dunbar Loth 118 NT6778
Dunbeath Highld 151 ND1629
Dunbeg Strath 122 NM8833
Dunblane Cent 116 NN7801
Dunbog Fife 126 NO2817
Dunbridge Hants 23 SU3226
Duncanston Highld 139 NH5856
Duncanstone Gramp 142 NJ5726
Dunchideock Devon 9 SX8787
Dunchurch Warwks 50 SP4871
Duncote Nhants 49 SP6750
Duncow D & G 100 NX9683
Duncrievie Tays 126 NO1309
Duncton W Susx 14 SU9617
Dundee Tays 126 NO4030
Dundon Somset 21 ST4832
Dundonald Strath 106 NS3634
Dundonnell Highld 145 NH0987
Dundraw Cumb 93 NY2149
Dundreggan Highld 131 NH3214
Dundrennan D & G 99 NX7447
Dundry Avon 21 ST5666
Dunecht Gramp 135 NJ7509
Dunfermline Fife 117 NT0987
Dunfield Gloucs 36 SU1497
Dunford Bridge S York 82 SE1502
Dungate Kent 28 TQ9159
Dungavel Strath 107 NS6537
Dunge Wilts 22 ST8954
Dunglass Loth 119 NT7671
Dungworth S York 74 SK2789
Dunham Notts 75 SK8074
Dunham Town Gt Man 79 SJ7387
Dunham Woodhouses Gt Man 79 SJ7287
Dunham-on-the-Hill Ches 71 SJ4772
Dunhampstead H & W 47 SO9160
Dunhampton H & W 47 SO8466
Dunholme Lincs 76 TF0279
Dunino Fife 127 NO5311
Dunipace Cent 116 NS8083
Dunk's Green Kent 27 TQ6152
Dunkeld Tays 125 NO0242
Dunkerton Avon 22 ST7159
Dunkeswell Devon 9 ST1407
Dunkeswick W York 82 SE3047
Dunkirk Ches 71 SJ3872
Dunkirk Staffs 72 SJ8152
Dunkirk Avon 35 ST7885
Dunkirk Wilts 22 ST9962
Dunkirk Kent 29 TR0759
Dunlappie Tays 134 NO5867
Dunley H & W 47 SO7869
Dunley Hants 24 SU4553
Dunlop Strath 115 NS4049
Dunmaglass Highld 140 NH5922
Dunmere Cnwll 4 SX0467
Dunmore Strath 113 NR7961
Dunmore Cent 116 NS8989
Dunn Street Kent 28 TQ7961
Dunnet Highld 151 ND2171
Dunnichen Tays 127 NO5048
Dunning Tays 125 NO0114
Dunnington N York 83 SE6652
Dunnington Warwks 48 SP0654
Dunnington Humb 85 TA1551
Dunnockshaw Lancs 81 SD8127
Dunoon Strath 114 NS1776
Dunphail Gramp 141 NJ0048
Dunragit D & G 98 NX1557
Dunrod Strath 114 NS2273
Duns Border 119 NT7853
Duns Tew Oxon 49 SP4528
Dunsa Derbys 74 SK2470
Dunsby Lincs 64 TF1026
Dunscar Gt Man 81 SD7113
Dunscore D & G 100 NX8684
Dunscroft S York 83 SE6409
Dunsdale Cleve 97 NZ6019
Dunsden Green Oxon 37 SU7377
Dunsdon Devon 18 SS3008
Dunsfold Surrey 14 TQ0035
Dunsford Devon 8 SX8189
Dunshelt Fife 126 NO2410
Dunshillock Gramp 143 NJ9848
Dunsill Notts 75 SK4661
Dunsley N York 90 NZ8511
Dunsley Staffs 60 SO8583
Dunsmore Bucks 38 SP8605
Dunsop Bridge Lancs 81 SD6649
Dunstable Beds 38 TL0122
Dunstall Staffs 73 SK1820
Dunstall Common H & W 47 SO8843
Dunstall Green Suffk 53 TL7460
Dunstan Nthumb 111 NU2419
Dunstan Steads Nthumb 111 NU2422
Dunster Somset 20 SS9943
Duntson T & W 96 NZ2362
Dunston Staffs 72 SJ9217
Dunston Lincs 76 TF0662
Dunston Norfk 67 TG2202
Dunston Heath Staffs 72 SJ9017
Dunstone Devon 6 SX5951
Dunstone Devon 7 SX7175
Dunsville S York 83 SE6407
Dunswell Humb 85 TA0735
Dunsyre Strath 117 NT0748
Dunterton Devon 5 SX3779
Dunthrop Oxon 48 SP3528
Duntisbourne Abbots Gloucs 35 SO9607
Duntisbourne Rouse Gloucs 35 SO9805
Duntish Dorset 11 ST6906
Duntocher Strath 115 NS4973
Dunton Bucks 38 SP8224
Dunton Norfk 66 TF8830
Dunton Beds 39 TL2344
Dunton Bassett Leics 50 SP5490
Dunton Green Kent 27 TQ5157
Dunton Wayletts Essex 40 TQ6590
Duntulm Highld 136 NG4174
Dunure Strath 106 NS2515
Dunvant W Glam 32 SS5993
Dunvegan Highld 136 NG2547
Dunwich Suffk 55 TM4770
Dunwood Staffs 72 SJ9455
Durdar Cumb 93 NY4051
Durgan Cnwll 3 SW7727
Durham Dur 96 NZ2742
Durisdeer D & G 108 NS8903
Durisdeermill D & G 108 NS8804
Durkar W York 82 SE3116
Durleigh Somset 20 ST2736
Durley Wilts 23 SU2364
Durley Hants 13 SU5116
Durley Street Hants 13 SU5217
Durlock Kent 29 TR2757
Durlock Kent 29 TR3164
Durlow Common H & W 47 SO6339
Durmgley Tays 127 NO4250
Durn Gt Man 82 SD9416
Durness Highld 149 NC4068
Duror Highld 122 NM9754
Durran Highld 151 ND1963
Durrington Wilts 23 SU1544
Durrington W Susx 14 TQ1105
Dursley Gloucs 35 ST7598
Dursley Cross Gloucs 35 SO6920
Durston Somset 20 ST2928
Durweston Dorset 11 ST8508
Duston Nhants 49 SP7261
Duthil Highld 140 NH9324
Dutlas Powys 45 SO2177
Dutson Cnwll 5 SX3485
Dutton Ches 71 SJ5779
Duxford Oxon 36 SP3600
Duxford Cambs 53 TL4846
Dwygyfylchi Gwynd 69 SH7376
Dwyran Gwynd 68 SH4465
Dyce Gramp 135 NJ8812
Dye House Nthumb 95 NY9358
Dyer's End Essex 53 TL7238
Dyfatty Dyfed 32 SN4401
Dyffryn M Glam 33 SO0603
Dyffryn S Glam 33 ST0971
Dyffryn Ardudwy Gwynd 57 SH5823
Dyffryn Castell Dyfed 43 SN7782
Dyffryn Cellwen W Glam 33 SN8510
Dyke Gramp 140 NH9858
Dyke Devon 18 SS3123
Dyke Lincs 64 TF1022
Dykehead Tays 126 NO2453
Dykehead Tays 134 NO3859
Dykehead Cent 115 NS5997
Dykehead Strath 116 NS8759
Dykelands Gramp 135 NO7068
Dykends Tays 133 NO2557
Dykeside Gramp 142 NJ7243
Dylife Powys 43 SN8694
Dymchurch Kent 17 TR1029
Dymock Gloucs 47 SO7031
Dyrham Avon 35 ST7475
Dysart Fife 117 NT3093
Dyserth Clwyd 70 SJ0578

E

Eachway H & W 60 SO9876
Eachwick Nthumb 103 NZ1171
Eagland Hill Lancs 80 SD4345
Eagle Lincs 76 SK8766
Eagle Barnsdale Lincs 76 SK8865
Eagle Manor Lincs 76 SK8868
Eaglescliffe Cleve 96 NZ4215
Eaglesfield Cumb 92 NY0928
Eaglesfield D & G 101 NY2374
Eaglesham Strath 115 NS5751
Eagley Gt Man 81 SD7112
Eairy IOM 153 SC2977
Eakring Notts 75 SK6762
Ealand Humb 84 SE7811
Ealing Gt Lon 26 TQ1780
Eals Nthumb 94 NY6756
Eamont Bridge Cumb 94 NY5228
Earby Lancs 81 SD9046
Earcroft Lancs 81 SD6823
Eardington Shrops 60 SO7290
Eardisland H & W 46 SO4158
Eardisley H & W 46 SO3149
Eardiston Shrops 59 SJ3725
Eardiston H & W 47 SO6968
Earith Cambs 52 TL3875
Earl Shilton Leics 50 SP4697
Earl Soham Suffk 55 TM2363
Earl Sterndale Derbys 74 SK0966
Earl Stonham Suffk 54 TM1059
Earl's Croome H & W 47 SO8642
Earl's Down E Susx 16 TQ6419
Earl's Green Suffk 54 TM0366
Earle Nthumb 111 NT9826
Earlestown Mersyd 78 SJ5795
Earley Berks 24 SU7472
Earlham Norfk 67 TG1908
Earlish Highld 136 NG3861
Earls Barton Nhants 51 SP8563
Earls Colne Essex 40 TL8528
Earls Common H & W 47 SO9559
Earlsditton Shrops 47 SO6275
Earlsdon W Mids 61 SP3278
Earlsferry Fife 118 NO4800
Earlsfield Gt Lon 27 TQ2573
Earlsford Gramp 143 NJ8334
Earlsheaton W York 82 SE2621
Earlston Strath 106 NS4035
Earlston Border 110 NT5738
Earlswood Warwks 61 SP1174
Earlswood Surrey 15 TQ2749
Earlswood Common Gwent 34 ST4594
Earnley W Susx 14 SZ8196
Earnshaw Bridge Lancs 80 SD5222
Earsdon Nthumb 103 NZ1993
Earsdon T & W 103 NZ3272
Earsham Norfk 55 TM3288
Earswick N York 90 SE6157
Eartham W Susx 14 SU9309
Easby N York 90 NZ5708
Easebourne W Susx 14 SU9023
Easenhall Warwks 50 SP4679
Eashing Surrey 25 SU9443
Easington Nthumb 111 NU1234
Easington Dur 96 NZ4143
Easington Cleve 97 NZ7417
Easington Bucks 37 SP6810
Easington Oxon 37 SU6697
Easington Humb 85 TA3919
Easington Colliery Dur 96 NZ4344
Easington Lane T & W 96 NZ3646
Easingwold N York 90 SE5269
Easole Street Kent 29 TR2652
Eassie and Nevay Tays 126 NO3344
East Aberthaw S Glam 20 ST0366
East Allington Devon 7 SX7748
East Anstey Devon 19 SS8626
East Anton Hants 23 SU3747
East Appleton N York 89 SE2395
East Ashey IOW 13 SZ5888
East Ashling W Susx 14 SU8107
East Aston Hants 24 SU4445
East Ayton N York 91 SE9985
East Balsdon Cnwll 5 SX2898
East Bank Gwent 33 SO2105
East Barkwith Lincs 76 TF1681
East Barming Kent 28 TQ7254
East Barnby N York 90 NZ8212
East Barnet Gt Lon 27 TQ2795
East Barns Loth 119 NT7176
East Barsham Norfk 66 TF9133
East Beckham Norfk 66 TG1639
East Bedfont Gt Lon 26 TQ0873
East Bergholt Suffk 54 TM0734
East Bierley W York 82 SE1929
East Bilney Norfk 66 TF9519
East Blanerne Border 119 NT8457
East Blatchington E Susx 16 TQ4800
East Bloxworth Dorset 11 SY8894
East Boldon T & W 96 NZ3661
East Boldre Hants 12 SU3700
East Bolton Nthumb 111 NU1216
East Bower Somset 21 ST3237
East Bradenham Norfk 66 TF9308
East Brent Somset 21 ST3451
East Bridgford Notts 63 SK6943
East Briscoe Dur 95 NY9719
East Buckland Devon 19 SS6831
East Budleigh Devon 9 SY0684
East Burnham Bucks 26 SU9584
East Burton Dorset 11 SY8287
East Butsfield Dur 95 NZ1145
East Butterwick Humb 84 SE8306
East Calder Loth 117 NT0867
East Carleton Norfk 66 TG1701
East Carlton W York 82 SE2143
East Carlton Nhants 51 SP8389
East Challow Oxon 36 SU3888
East Charleton Devon 7 SX7642
East Chelborough Dorset 10 ST5505
East Chevington Nthumb 103 NZ2699
East Chiltington E Susx 15 TQ3715
East Chinnock Somset 10 ST4913
East Chisenbury Wilts 23 SU1452
East Cholderton Hants 23 SU2945
East Clandon Surrey 26 TQ0651
East Claydon Bucks 49 SP7325
East Clevedon Avon 34 ST4171
East Coker Somset 10 ST5412
East Combe Somset 20 ST1631
East Compton Somset 21 ST6141
East Cornworthy Devon 7 SX8455
East Cote Cumb 92 NY1255
East Cottingwith Humb 84 SE7042
East Coulston Wilts 22 ST9554
East Cowes IOW 13 SZ5095
East Cowick Humb 83 SE6620
East Cowton N York 89 NZ3003
East Cramlington Nthumb 103 NZ2776
East Cranmore Somset 22 ST6743
East Creech Dorset 11 SY9382
East Curthwaite Cumb 93 NY3348
East Dean H & W 35 SO6520
East Dean Hants 23 SU2726
East Dean W Susx 14 SU9012
East Dean E Susx 16 TV5598
East Dereham Norfk 66 TF9913
East Down Devon 19 SS6041
East Drayton Notts 75 SK7775
East Dulwich Gt Lon 27 TQ3375
East Dundry Avon 21 ST5766
East Ella Humb 84 TA0529
East End Oxon 36 SP3915
East End Bucks 38 SP9344
East End Beds 38 SP9642
East End Avon 34 ST4770
East End Somset 22 ST6746
East End Hants 24 SU4161
East End Hants 12 SZ3696
East End Humb 85 TA1931
East End Humb 85 TA2927
East End Beds 51 TL1055
East End Essex 39 TL4210
East End Herts 39 TL4527
East End Kent 17 TQ8335
East End Kent 28 TQ9673
East Everleigh Wilts 23 SU2053
East Farleigh Kent 28 TQ7353
East Farndon Nhants 50 SP7184
East Ferry Lincs 75 SK8199
East Firsby Lincs 76 TF0085
East Fortune Loth 118 NT5479
East Garforth W York 83 SE4133
East Garston Berks 36 SU3576
East Ginge Oxon 37 SU4486
East Goscote Leics 63 SK6413
East Grafton Wilts 23 SU2560
East Grange Gramp 141 NJ0961
East Green Suffk 55 TM4065
East Grimstead Wilts 23 SU2227
East Grinstead W Susx 15 TQ3938
East Guldeford E Susx 17 TQ9321
East Haddon Nhants 50 SP6668
East Hagbourne Oxon 37 SU5288
East Halton Humb 85 TA1319
East Ham Gt Lon 27 TQ4283
East Hanney Oxon 36 SU4193
East Hanningfield Essex 40 TL7701
East Hardwick W York 83 SE4618
East Harling Norfk 54 TL9986
East Harlsey N York 89 SE4299
East Harnham Wilts 23 SU1428
East Harptree Avon 21 ST5655
East Hartburn Cleve 96 NZ4217
East Hartford Nthumb 103 NZ2679
East Harting W Susx 14 SU7919
East Hatch Wilts 22 ST9228
East Hatley Cambs 52 TL2850
East Hauxwell N York 89 SE1693
East Haven Tays 127 NO5836
East Heath Berks 25 SU7967
East Heckington Lincs 64 TF1944
East Hedleyhope Dur 96 NZ1540
East Helmsdale Highld 147 ND0315
East Hendred Oxon 37 SU4588
East Heslerton N York 91 SE9276
East Hewish Avon 21 ST4064
East Hoathly E Susx 16 TQ5216
East Holme Dorset 11 SY8986
East Holywell T & W 103 NZ3073
East Horndon Essex 40 TQ6389
East Horrington Somset 21 ST5846
East Horsley Surrey 26 TQ0952
East Horton Nthumb 111 NU0330
East Howe Dorset 12 SZ0795
East Huntington N York 83 SE6155
East Huntspill Somset 21 ST3445
East Hyde Beds 38 TL1217
East Ilkerton Devon 19 SS7147
East Ilsley Berks 37 SU4980
East Keal Lincs 77 TF3863
East Kennett Wilts 23 SU1167
East Keswick W York 83 SE3644
East Kilbride Strath 116 NS6354
East Kimber Devon 5 SX4998
East Kirkby Lincs 77 TF3362
East Knighton Dorset 11 SY8185
East Knowstone Devon 19 SS8423
East Knoyle Wilts 22 ST8830
East Kyloe Nthumb 111 NU0639
East Lambrook Somset 10 ST4318
East Langdon Kent 29 TR3346
East Langton Leics 50 SP7292
East Laroch Highld 130 NN0858
East Lavant W Susx 14 SU8608
East Lavington W Susx 14 SU9416
East Layton N York 89 NZ1609
East Leake Notts 62 SK5526
East Learmouth Nthumb 110 NT8637
East Leigh Devon 8 SS6905
East Leigh Devon 7 SX6852
East Leigh Devon 7 SX7657
East Lexham Norfk 66 TF8517
East Linton Loth 118 NT5877
East Liss Hants 14 SU7827
East Lockinge Oxon 36 SU4287
East Lound Humb 75 SK7899
East Lulworth Dorset 11 SY8682
East Lutton N York 91 SE9469
East Lydford Somset 21 ST5731
East Malling Kent 28 TQ7056
East Malling Heath Kent 28 TQ6955
East Marden W Susx 14 SU8014
East Markham Notts 75 SK7373
East Martin Hants 12 SU0719
East Marton N York 81 SD9050
East Meon Hants 13 SU6822
East Mere Devon 9 SS9916
East Mersea Essex 41 TM0414
East Molesey Surrey 26 TQ1467
East Morden Dorset 11 SY9194
East Morton D & G 108 NS8800
East Morton W York 82 SE0942
East Ness N York 90 SE6978
East Newton Humb 85 TA2638
East Norton Leics 50 SK7800
East Oakley Hants 24 SU5749
East Ogwell Devon 7 SX8370
East Orchard Dorset 11 ST8317
East Ord Nthumb 119 NT9751
East Panson Devon 5 SX3692
East Parley Dorset 12 SZ1097
East Peckham Kent 28 TQ6648
East Pennar Dyfed 30 SM9602
East Pennard Somset 21 ST5937

East Perry

Ervie

East Perry *Cambs* 52 TL1566
East Poringland *Norfk* 67 TG2701
East Portlemouth *Devon* 7 SX7538
East Prawle *Devon* 7 SX7836
East Preston *W Susx* 14 TQ0602
East Pulham *Dorset* 11 ST7209
East Putford *Devon* 18 SS3616
East Quantoxhead *Somset* 20 ST1343
East Rainham *Kent* 28 TQ8267
East Rainton *T & W* 96 NZ3347
East Ravendale *Lincs* 76 TF2399
East Raynham *Norfk* 66 TF8825
East Rigton *W York* 83 SE3743
East Rolstone *Avon* 21 ST3962
East Rounton *N York* 89 NZ4203
East Rudham *Norfk* 66 TF8228
East Runton *Norfk* 67 TG1942
East Ruston *Norfk* 67 TG3427
East Saltoun *Loth* 118 NT4767
East Scrafton *N York* 89 SE0884
East Sheen *Gt Lon* 26 TQ2075
East Shefford *Berks* 36 SU3874
East Sleekburn *Nthumb* 103 NZ2883
East Somerton *Norfk* 67 TG4719
East Stoke *Notts* 75 SK7549
East Stoke *Dorset* 11 SY8686
East Stour *Dorset* 22 ST8022
East Stourmouth *Kent* 29 TR2662
East Stowford *Devon* 19 SS6326
East Stratton *Hants* 24 SU5440
East Sutton *Kent* 28 TQ8349
East Taphouse *Cnwll* 4 SX1863
East Thirston *Nthumb* 89 NZ1900
East Tilbury *Essex* 28 TQ6877
East Tisted *Hants* 24 SU7032
East Torrington *Lincs* 76 TF1483
East Tuddenham *Norfk* 66 TG0711
East Tytherley *Hants* 23 SU2929
East Tytherton *Wilts* 35 ST9674
East Village *Devon* 8 SS8405
East Wall *Shrops* 59 SO5293
East Walton *Norfk* 65 TF7416
East Water *Somset* 21 ST5350
East Week *Devon* 8 SX6692
East Wellow *Hants* 12 SU3020
East Wemyss *Fife* 118 NT3497
East Whitburn *Loth* 117 NS9665
East Wickham *Gt Lon* 27 TQ4677
East Williamston *Dyfed* 31 SN0904
East Winch *Norfk* 65 TF6916
East Winterslow *Wilts* 23 SU2434
East Wittering *W Susx* 14 SZ7997
East Witton *N York* 89 SE1486
East Woodburn *Nthumb* 102 NY9086
East Woodhay *Hants* 24 SU4061
East Woodlands *Somset* 22 ST7944
East Worldham *Hants* 24 SU7538
East Wretham *Norfk* 54 TL9190
East Youlstone *Devon* 18 SS2715
Eastbourne *Dur* 89 NZ3013
Eastbourne *E Susx* 16 TV6199
Eastbridge *Suffk* 55 TM4566
Eastbrook *S Glam* 33 ST1671
Eastburn *W York* 82 SE0144
Eastbury *Berks* 36 SU3477
Eastbury *Herts* 26 TQ1092
Eastby *N York* 82 SE0154
Eastchurch *Kent* 28 TQ9871
Eastcombe *Gloucs* 35 SO8904
Eastcote *W Mids* 61 SP1979
Eastcote *Nhants* 49 SP6853
Eastcote *Gt Lon* 26 TQ1088
Eastcott *Cnwll* 18 SS2515
Eastcott *Wilts* 23 SU0255
Eastcourt *Wilts* 35 ST9792
Eastcourt *Wilts* 23 SU2361
Eastdown *Devon* 7 SX8249
Eastend *Strath* 108 NS9537
Eastend *Essex* 40 TQ9492
Easter Balmoral *Gramp* 133 NO2694
Easter Compton *Avon* 34 ST5782
Easter Dalziel *Highld* 140 NH7550
Easter Elchies *Gramp* 141 NJ2744
Easter Howgate *Tays* 117 NT2463
Easter Kinkell *Highld* 139 NH5755
Easter Lednathie *Tays* 134 NO3463
Easter Moniack *Highld* 139 NH5543
Easter Ord *Gramp* 135 NJ8304
Easter Pitkierie *Fife* 127 NO5606
Easter Skeld *Shet* 155 HU3144
Eastergate *W Susx* 14 SU9405
Easterhouse *Strath* 116 NS6865
Eastern Green *W Mids* 61 SP2879
Easterton *Wilts* 23 SU0254
Eastertown *Strath* 108 NS8622
Eastertown *Somset* 21 ST3454
Eastfield *Strath* 116 NS7475
Eastfield *Cent* 116 NS8964
Eastfield *N York* 91 TA0484
Eastgate *Dur* 95 NY9538
Eastgate *Lincs* 64 TF1019
Eastgate *Norfk* 66 TG1423
Eastham *Mersyd* 78 SJ3680
Eastham Ferry *Mersyd* 78 SJ3681
Easthampstead *Berks* 25 SU8667
Easthampton *H & W* 46 SO4063
Easthope *Shrops* 59 SO5695
Easthorpe *Notts* 75 SK7053
Easthorpe *Essex* 40 TL9121
Eastington *Gloucs* 36 SP1213
Eastington *Devon* 19 SS7408
Eastlands *D & G* 100 NX8172
Eastleach Martin *Gloucs* 36 SP2004
Eastleach Turville *Gloucs* 36 SP1905
Eastleigh *Devon* 18 SS4827
Eastleigh *Hants* 13 SU4519
Eastling *Kent* 28 TQ9656
Eastly End *Surrey* 26 TQ0368
Eastmoor *Norfk* 65 TF7303
Eastney *Hants* 13 SZ6698
Eastnor *H & W* 47 SO7237
Eastoft *Humb* 84 SE8016
Easton *Cumb* 93 NY2759
Easton *Lincs* 63 SK9326
Easton *Somset* 21 ST5147
Easton *Wilts* 35 ST8970
Easton *Berks* 24 SU4172
Easton *Hants* 24 SU5132
Easton *Devon* 8 SX7289
Easton *Dorset* 11 SY6971
Easton *IOW* 12 SZ3486
Easton *Norfk* 66 TG1310
Easton *Cambs* 52 TL1371
Easton *Suffk* 55 TM2858
Easton Grey *Wilts* 35 ST8887
Easton Maudit *Nhants* 51 SP8858
Easton Royal *Wilts* 23 SU2060
Easton on the Hill *Nhants* 64 TF0104
Easton-in-Gordano *Avon* 34 ST5175
Eastpeek *Devon* 5 SX3494
Eastrea *Cambs* 64 TL2997
Eastriggs *D & G* 101 NY2466
Eastrington *Humb* 84 SE7929
Eastrop *Wilts* 36 SU2092
Eastry *Kent* 29 TR3054
Eastshaw *W Susx* 14 SU8724
Eastville *Lincs* 77 TF4056
Eastwell *Leics* 63 SK7728
Eastwick *Herts* 39 TL4311
Eastwood *W York* 82 SD9726
Eastwood *Notts* 62 SK4646
Eastwood *Essex* 40 TQ8688
Eastwood End *Cambs* 65 TL4292
Eathorpe *Warwks* 48 SP3969
Eaton *Ches* 71 SJ5763
Eaton *Ches* 72 SJ8765
Eaton *Notts* 75 SK7077
Eaton *Leics* 63 SK7928
Eaton *Shrops* 59 SO3789
Eaton *Shrops* 59 SO5089
Eaton *Oxon* 37 SP4403
Eaton *Norfk* 67 TG2006
Eaton Bishop *H & W* 46 SO4439
Eaton Bray *Beds* 38 SP9720
Eaton Constantine *Shrops* 59 SJ5906
Eaton Ford *Beds* 52 TL1759
Eaton Green *Beds* 38 SP9621
Eaton Hastings *Oxon* 36 SU2598
Eaton Mascott *Shrops* 59 SJ5305
Eaton Socon *Beds* 52 TL1759
Eaton upon Tern *Shrops* 72 SJ6523
Eaves Brow *Ches* 79 SJ6393
Eaves Green *W Mids* 61 SP2682
Ebberston *N York* 91 SE8982
Ebbesborne Wake *Wilts* 22 ST9924
Ebbw Vale *Gwent* 33 SO1609
Ebchester *Dur* 95 NZ1055
Ebdon *Avon* 21 ST3664
Ebford *Devon* 9 SX9887
Ebley *Gloucs* 35 SO8205
Ebnal *Ches* 71 SJ4948
Ebnall *H & W* 46 SO4758
Ebrington *Gloucs* 48 SP1840
Ebsworthy Town *Devon* 5 SX5090
Ecchinswell *Hants* 24 SU4959
Ecclaw *Loth* 119 NT7568
Ecclefechan *D & G* 101 NY1974
Eccles *Border* 110 NT7641
Eccles *Gt Man* 79 SJ7798
Eccles *Kent* 28 TQ7360
Eccles Green *H & W* 46 SO3748
Eccles Road *Norfk* 54 TM0189
Ecclesall *S York* 74 SK3284
Ecclesfield *S York* 74 SK3593
Ecclesgreig *Gramp* 135 NO7465
Eccleshall *Staffs* 72 SJ8329
Eccleshill *W York* 82 SE1736
Ecclesmachan *Loth* 117 NT0573
Eccleston *Lancs* 80 SD5217
Eccleston *Ches* 71 SJ4162
Eccleston *Mersyd* 78 SJ4895
Eccleston Green *Lancs* 80 SD5216
Echt *Gramp* 135 NJ7405
Eckford *Border* 110 NT7026
Eckington *Derbys* 75 SK4379
Eckington *H & W* 47 SO9241
Ecton *Staffs* 74 SK0958
Ecton *Nhants* 51 SP8263
Edale *Derbys* 74 SK1285
Edburton *W Susx* 15 TQ2311
Edderside *Cumb* 92 NY1045
Edderton *Highld* 146 NH7084
Eddington *Kent* 29 TR1867
Eddleston *Border* 117 NT2447
Eddlewood *Strath* 116 NS7153
Eden Mount *Cumb* 87 SD4077
Edenbridge *Kent* 16 TQ4446
Edenfield *Lancs* 81 SD8019
Edenhall *Cumb* 94 NY5632
Edenham *Lincs* 64 TF0621
Edensor *Derbys* 74 SK2469
Edentaggart *Strath* 115 NS3293
Edenthorpe *S York* 83 SE6206
Ederline *Strath* 122 NM8702
Edern *Gwynd* 56 SH2739
Edgarley *Somset* 21 ST5238
Edgbaston *W Mids* 61 SP0684
Edgcombe *Cnwll* 2 SW7133
Edgcott *Bucks* 37 SP6722
Edgcott *Devon* 19 SS8438
Edge *Shrops* 59 SJ3908
Edge *Gloucs* 35 SO8409
Edge End *Gloucs* 34 SO5913
Edge Green *Ches* 71 SJ4851
Edgebolton *Shrops* 59 SJ5721
Edgefield *Norfk* 66 TG0934
Edgefield Green *Norfk* 66 TG0934
Edgefold *Gt Man* 79 SD7005
Edgerley *Shrops* 59 SJ3518
Edgertown *W York* 82 SE1317
Edgeside *Lancs* 81 SD8322
Edgeworth *Gloucs* 35 SO9406
Edgeworthy *Devon* 19 SS8413
Edgiock *H & W* 48 SP0461
Edgmond *Shrops* 72 SJ7119
Edgmond Marsh *Shrops* 72 SJ7120
Edgton *Shrops* 59 SO3885
Edgware *Gt Lon* 26 TQ1991
Edgworth *Lancs* 81 SD7416
Edial *Staffs* 61 SK0808
Edinample *Cent* 124 NN6022
Edinbane *Highld* 136 NG3451
Edinburgh *Loth* 117 NT2573
Edingale *Staffs* 61 SK2111
Edingham *D & G* 100 NX8363
Edingley *Notts* 75 SK6655
Edingthorpe *Norfk* 67 TG3132
Edingthorpe Green *Norfk* 67 TG3031
Edington *Border* 119 NT8956
Edington *Nthumb* 103 NZ1582
Edington *Somset* 21 ST3839
Edington *Wilts* 22 ST9253
Edington Burtle *Somset* 21 ST3943
Edingworth *Somset* 21 ST3653
Edith Weston *Leics* 63 SK9205
Edithmead *Somset* 21 ST3249
Edlesborough *Bucks* 38 SP9719
Edlingham *Nthumb* 111 NU1109
Edlington *Lincs* 76 TF2371
Edmond Castle *Cumb* 94 NY4958
Edmondsham *Dorset* 12 SU0611
Edmondsley *Dur* 96 NZ2349
Edmondthorpe *Leics* 63 SK8517
Edmonton *Cnwll* 4 SW9672
Edmonton *Gt Lon* 27 TQ3492
Edmundbyers *Dur* 95 NZ0150
Ednam *Border* 110 NT7337
Ednaston *Derbys* 73 SK2341
Edradynate *Tays* 125 NN8751
Edrom *Border* 119 NT8255
Edstaston *Shrops* 59 SJ5132
Edstone *Warwks* 48 SP1962
Edvin Loach *H & W* 47 SO6658
Edwalton *Notts* 62 SK5935
Edwardstone *Suffk* 54 TL9442
Edwardsville *M Glam* 33 ST0896
Edwinsford *Dyfed* 44 SN6334
Edwinstowe *Notts* 75 SK6266
Edworth *Beds* 39 TL2241
Edwyn Ralph *H & W* 47 SO6457
Edzell *Tays* 134 NO6068
Efail Isaf *M Glam* 33 ST0884
Efail-fach *W Glam* 32 SS7895
Efail-rhyd *Clwyd* 58 SJ1626
Efailnewydd *Gwynd* 56 SH3535
Efailwen *Dyfed* 31 SN1325
Efenechtyd *Clwyd* 70 SJ1155
Effgill *D & G* 101 NY3092
Effingham *Surrey* 26 TQ1153
Efflinch *Staffs* 73 SK1816
Efford *Devon* 9 SS8901
Egbury *Hants* 24 SU4352
Egerton *Gt Man* 81 SD7014
Egerton *Kent* 28 TQ9147
Eggesford *Devon* 19 SS6811
Eggington *Beds* 38 SP9525
Egginton *Derbys* 73 SK2628
Egglescliffe *Cleve* 89 NZ4113
Eggleston *Dur* 95 NY9923
Egham *Surrey* 25 TQ0071
Egham Wick *Surrey* 25 SU9870
Eginswell *Devon* 7 SX8866
Egleton *Leics* 63 SK8707
Eglingham *Nthumb* 111 NU1019
Egloshayle *Cnwll* 4 SX0072
Egloskerry *Cnwll* 5 SX2786
Eglwys Cross *Clwyd* 71 SJ4740
Eglwys-Brewis *S Glam* 20 ST0068
Eglwysbach *Gwynd* 69 SH8070
Eglwysfach *Dyfed* 43 SN6996
Eglwyswrw *Dyfed* 31 SN1438
Egmanton *Notts* 75 SK7368
Egremont *Cumb* 86 NY0110
Egremont *Mersyd* 78 SJ3192
Egton *N York* 90 NZ8006
Egton Bridge *N York* 90 NZ8004
Eight Ash Green *Essex* 40 TL9425
Eight and Forty *Humb* 84 SE8529
Eilanreach *Highld* 129 NG8018
Elan Village *Powys* 45 SN9364
Elberton *Avon* 34 ST6088
Elbridge *W Susx* 14 SU9101
Elburton *Devon* 6 SX5353
Elcombe *Wilts* 36 SU1280
Elcot *Berks* 36 SU3969
Elder Street *Essex* 53 TL5734
Eldernell *Cambs* 64 TL3298
Eldersfield *H & W* 47 SO7931
Elderslie *Strath* 115 NS4463
Eldmire *N York* 89 SE4274
Eldon *Dur* 96 NZ2328
Eldwick *W York* 82 SE1240
Elfhill *Gramp* 135 NO8085
Elford *Nthumb* 111 NU1831
Elford *Staffs* 61 SK1810
Elgin *Gramp* 141 NJ2162
Elgol *Highld* 128 NG5213
Elham *Kent* 29 TR1744
Elie *Fife* 118 NO4900
Elilaw *Nthumb* 111 NT9708
Elim *Gwynd* 68 SH3584
Eling *Hants* 12 SU3612
Elishaw *Nthumb* 102 NY8595
Elkesley *Notts* 75 SK6975
Elkstone *Gloucs* 35 SO9612
Ella *Gramp* 142 NJ6459
Ellanbeich *Strath* 122 NM7417
Elland *W York* 82 SE1120
Elland Lower Edge *W York* 82 SE1221
Ellary *Strath* 113 NR7376
Ellastone *Staffs* 73 SK1143
Ellel *Lancs* 80 SD4856
Ellemford *Border* 119 NT7260
Ellen's Green *Surrey* 14 TQ0935
Ellenborough *Cumb* 92 NY0435
Ellenbrook *Gt Man* 79 SD7201
Ellenhall *Staffs* 72 SJ8426
Ellerbeck *N York* 89 SE4396
Ellerby *N York* 90 NZ7914
Ellerdine Heath *Shrops* 59 SJ6122
Ellerhayes *Devon* 9 SS9702
Elleric *Strath* 123 NN0448
Ellerker *Humb* 84 SE9229
Ellers *N York* 82 SE0043
Ellerton *N York* 89 SE2598
Ellerton *Humb* 84 SE7039
Ellerton *Shrops* 72 SJ7125
Ellesborough *Bucks* 38 SP8306
Ellesmere *Shrops* 59 SJ3934
Ellesmere Port *Ches* 71 SJ4076
Ellicombe *Somset* 20 SS9844
Ellingham *Nthumb* 111 NU1725
Ellingham *Hants* 12 SU1408
Ellingham *Norfk* 67 TM3592
Ellingstring *N York* 89 SE1783
Ellington *Nthumb* 103 NZ2791
Ellington *Cambs* 52 TL1671
Ellington Thorpe *Cambs* 52 TL1670
Elliots Green *Somset* 22 ST7945
Ellisfield *Hants* 24 SU6446
Ellishader *Highld* 137 NG5065
Ellistown *Leics* 62 SK4309
Ellon *Gramp* 143 NJ9530
Ellonby *Cumb* 93 NY4235
Ellough *Suffk* 55 TM4486
Elloughton *Humb* 84 SE9428
Ellwood *Gloucs* 34 SO5908
Elm *Cambs* 65 TF4707
Elm Green *Essex* 40 TL7705
Elm Grove *Norfk* 67 TG4803
Elm Park *Gt Lon* 27 TQ5385
Elmbridge *H & W* 47 SO9068
Elmdon *W Mids* 61 SP1783
Elmdon *Essex* 39 TL4639
Elmdon Heath *W Mids* 61 SP1680
Elmer *W Susx* 14 SU9800
Elmer's Green *Lancs* 78 SD5006
Elmers End *Gt Lon* 27 TQ3668
Elmesthorpe *Leics* 50 SP4696
Elmhurst *Staffs* 61 SK1112
Elmley Castle *H & W* 47 SO9841
Elmley Lovett *H & W* 47 SO8769
Elmore *Gloucs* 35 SO7815
Elmore Back *Gloucs* 35 SO7616
Elms Green *H & W* 47 SO7266
Elmscott *Devon* 18 SS2321
Elmsett *Suffk* 54 TM0546
Elmstead Heath *Essex* 41 TM0622
Elmstead Market *Essex* 41 TM0624
Elmstead Row *Essex* 41 TM0621
Elmsted Court *Kent* 29 TR1144
Elmstone *Kent* 29 TR2660
Elmstone Hardwicke *Gloucs* 47 SO9125
Elmswell *Humb* 91 SE9958
Elmswell *Suffk* 54 TL9964
Elmton *Derbys* 75 SK5073
Elphin *Highld* 145 NC2111
Elphinstone *Loth* 118 NT3970
Elrick *Gramp* 135 NJ8106
Elrig *D & G* 98 NX3248
Elrington *Nthumb* 102 NY8563
Elsdon *Nthumb* 102 NY9393
Elsecar *S York* 74 SK3899
Elsenham *Essex* 39 TL5326
Elsfield *Oxon* 37 SP5410
Elsham *Humb* 84 TA0312
Elsick House *Gramp* 135 NO8894
Elsing *Norfk* 66 TG0516
Elslack *N York* 81 SD9349
Elson *Shrops* 59 SJ3735
Elson *Hants* 13 SU6002
Elsrickle *Strath* 108 NT0643
Elstead *Surrey* 25 SU9043
Elsted *W Susx* 14 SU8119
Elstob *Dur* 96 NZ3323
Elston *Lancs* 81 SD5932
Elston *Notts* 63 SK7647
Elston *Wilts* 23 SU0644
Elstone *Devon* 19 SS6716
Elstow *Beds* 38 TL0546
Elstree *Herts* 26 TQ1795
Elstronwick *Humb* 85 TA2232
Elswick *T & W* 103 NZ2263
Elswick *Lancs* 80 SD4238
Elsworth *Cambs* 52 TL3163
Elterwater *Cumb* 86 NY3204
Eltham *Gt Lon* 27 TQ4274
Eltisley *Cambs* 52 TL2759
Elton *Cleve* 96 NZ4017
Elton *Gt Man* 81 SD7911
Elton *Ches* 71 SJ4575
Elton *Derbys* 74 SK2260
Elton *Notts* 63 SK7638
Elton *H & W* 46 SO4570
Elton *Gloucs* 35 SO7014
Elton *Cambs* 51 TL0893
Elton Green *Ches* 71 SJ4574
Eltringham *Nthumb* 103 NZ0762
Elvaston *Derbys* 62 SK4032
Elveden *Suffk* 54 TL8280
Elvetham Hall *Hants* 25 SU7856
Elvingston *Loth* 118 NT4674
Elvington *N York* 84 SE7047
Elvington *Kent* 29 TR2750
Elwell *Devon* 19 SS6631
Elwick *Nthumb* 111 NU1136
Elwick *Cleve* 97 NZ4532
Elworth *Ches* 72 SJ7361
Elworthy *Somset* 20 ST0834
Ely *S Glam* 33 ST1476
Ely *Cambs* 53 TL5480
Emberton *Bucks* 38 SP8849
Embleton *Nthumb* 111 NU2322
Embleton *Cumb* 92 NY1629
Embleton *Dur* 96 NZ4129
Embo *Highld* 147 NH8192
Embo Street *Highld* 147 NH8091
Emborough *Somset* 21 ST6151
Embsay *N York* 82 SE0053
Emery Down *Hants* 12 SU2808
Emley *W York* 82 SE2413
Emley Moor *W York* 82 SE2313
Emmbrook *Berks* 25 SU8069
Emmer Green *Berks* 37 SU7276
Emmett Carr *Derbys* 75 SK4577
Emmington *Oxon* 37 SP7402
Emneth *Cambs* 65 TF4807
Emneth Hungate *Norfk* 65 TF5107
Empingham *Leics* 63 SK9508
Empshott *Hants* 24 SU7531
Empshott Green *Hants* 24 SU7431
Emsworth *Hants* 13 SU7406
Enborne *Berks* 24 SU4365
Enborne Row *Hants* 24 SU4463
Enchmarsh *Shrops* 59 SO5096
Encombe *Dorset* 11 SY9478
Enderby *Leics* 50 SP5399
Endmoor *Cumb* 87 SD5384
Endon *Staffs* 72 SJ9253
Endon Bank *Staffs* 72 SJ9253
Enfield *Gt Lon* 27 TQ3597
Enfield Lock *Gt Lon* 27 TQ3698
Enfield Wash *Gt Lon* 27 TQ3598
Enford *Wilts* 23 SU1351
Engine Common *Avon* 35 ST6984
England's Gate *H & W* 46 SO5451
Englefield *Berks* 24 SU6272
Englefield Green *Surrey* 25 SU9971
Englesea-brook *Ches* 72 SJ7551
English Bicknor *Gloucs* 34 SO5815
English Frankton *Shrops* 59 SJ4529
Englishcombe *Avon* 22 ST7162
Engollan *Cnwll* 4 SW8670
Enham-Alamein *Hants* 23 SU3649
Enmore *Somset* 20 ST2435
Enmore Green *Dorset* 22 ST8523
Ennerdale Bridge *Cumb* 92 NY0615
Enniscaven *Cnwll* 4 SW9659
Enochdhu *Tays* 133 NO0662
Ensay *Strath* 121 NM3648
Ensbury *Dorset* 12 SZ0896
Ensdon *Shrops* 59 SJ4017
Ensis *Devon* 19 SS5626
Enson *Staffs* 72 SJ9328
Enstone *Oxon* 48 SP3724
Enterkinfoot *D & G* 108 NS8504
Enterpen *N York* 89 NZ4605
Enville *Staffs* 60 SO8286
Enys *Cnwll* 3 SW7836
Epney *Gloucs* 35 SO7611
Epperstone *Notts* 75 SK6548
Epping *Essex* 27 TL4502
Epping Green *Herts* 39 TL2906
Epping Green *Essex* 39 TL4305
Epping Upland *Essex* 39 TL4404
Eppleby *N York* 89 NZ1713
Eppleworth *Humb* 84 TA0131
Epsom *Surrey* 26 TQ2160
Epwell *Oxon* 48 SP3540
Epworth *Humb* 84 SE7803
Epworth Turbary *Humb* 84 SE7603
Erbistock *Clwyd* 71 SJ3541
Erdington *W Mids* 61 SP1191
Ericstane *D & G* 108 NT0711
Eridge Green *E Susx* 16 TQ5535
Eridge Station *E Susx* 16 TQ5434
Erines *Strath* 113 NR8575
Erisey *Cnwll* 2 SW7117
Eriswell *Suffk* 53 TL7278
Erith *Gt Lon* 27 TQ5177
Erlestoke *Wilts* 22 ST9653
Ermington *Devon* 6 SX6353
Erpingham *Norfk* 67 TG1931
Erriottwood *Kent* 28 TQ9459
Errogie *Highld* 139 NH5622
Errol *Tays* 126 NO2422
Erskine *Strath* 115 NS4770
Ervie *D & G* 98 NX0067

Erwarton Fisherford

Erwarton *Suffk* 55 TM2234
Eryholme *N York* 89 NZ3208
Eryrys *Clwyd* 70 SJ2057
Escalls *Cnwll* 2 SW3627
Escomb *Dur* 96 NZ1830
Escott *Somset* 20 ST0937
Escrick *N York* 83 SE6242
Esgair *Dyfed* 31 SN3728
Esgair *Dyfed* 43 SN5868
Esgairgeiliog *Powys* 57 SH7606
Esgyryn *Gwynd* 69 SH8078
Esh *Dur* 96 NZ1944
Esh Winning *Dur* 96 NZ1942
Esher *Surrey* 26 TQ1364
Esholt *W York* 82 SE1840
Eshott *Nthumb* 103 NZ2097
Eshton *N York* 81 SD9356
Eskadale *Highld* 139 NH4540
Eskbank *Loth* 118 NT3266
Eskdale Green *Cumb* 86 NY1400
Eskdalemuir *D & G* 101 NY2597
Eskett *Cumb* 92 NY0516
Eskham *Lincs* 77 TF3698
Eskholme *S York* 83 SE6317
Esperley Lane Ends *Dur* 96 NZ1324
Esprick *Lancs* 80 SD4036
Essendine *Leics* 64 TF0412
Essendon *Herts* 39 TL2708
Essich *Highld* 140 NH6439
Essington *Staffs* 60 SJ9603
Esslemont *Gramp* 143 NJ9229
Esthorpe *Lincs* 64 TF0623
Eston *Cleve* 97 NZ5418
Etal *Nthumb* 110 NT9339
Etchilhampton *Wilts* 23 SU0460
Etchingham *E Susx* 17 TQ7126
Etchinghill *Staffs* 73 SK0218
Etchinghill *Kent* 29 TR1639
Etchingwood *E Susx* 16 TQ5022
Etherdwick *Humb* 85 TA2337
Etling Green *Norfk* 66 TG0113
Etloe *Gloucs* 35 SO6806
Eton *Berks* 26 SU9677
Eton Wick *Berks* 26 SU9478
Etruria *Staffs* 72 SJ8647
Etteridge *Highld* 132 NN6892
Ettersgill *Dur* 95 NY8829
Ettiley Heath *Ches* 72 SJ7360
Ettingshall *W Mids* 60 SO9396
Ettington *Warwks* 48 SP2749
Etton *Humb* 84 SE9743
Etton *Cambs* 64 TF1406
Ettrick *Border* 109 NT2714
Ettrick Hill *Border* 109 NT2514
Ettrickbridge *Border* 109 NT3824
Etwall *Derbys* 73 SK2631
Eudon George *Shrops* 60 SO6888
Euston *Suffk* 54 TL8979
Euximoor Drove *Cambs* 65 TL4898
Euxton *Lancs* 81 SD5519
Evancoyd *Powys* 46 SO2663
Evanton *Highld* 140 NH6066
Evedon *Lincs* 76 TF0947
Evelith *Shrops* 60 SJ7405
Evelix *Highld* 147 NH7790
Evenjobb *Powys* 46 SO2662
Evenley *Oxon* 49 SP5834
Evenlode *Gloucs* 48 SP2129
Evenwood *Dur* 96 NZ1524
Evenwood Gate *Dur* 96 NZ1624
Evercreech *Somset* 21 ST6438
Everingham *Humb* 84 SE8042
Everleigh *Wilts* 23 SU2053
Everley *N York* 91 SE9788
Eversfield *Devon* 5 SX4792
Evershot *Beds* 38 SP9833
Evershot *Dorset* 10 ST5704
Eversley *Hants* 25 SU7762
Eversley Cross *Hants* 25 SU7961
Everthorpe *Humb* 84 SE9031
Everton *Mersyd* 78 SJ3491
Everton *Notts* 75 SK6990
Everton *Hants* 12 SZ2894
Everton *Beds* 52 TL2051
Evertown *D & G* 101 NY3576
Evesbatch *H & W* 47 SO6948
Evesham *H & W* 48 SP0344
Evington *Leics* 62 SK6203
Ewden Village *S York* 74 SK2796
Ewdness *Shrops* 60 SO7396
Ewell *Surrey* 26 TQ2262
Ewell Minnis *Kent* 29 TR2643
Ewelme *Oxon* 37 SU6491
Ewen *Gloucs* 35 SU0097
Ewenny *M Glam* 33 SS9077
Ewerby *Lincs* 76 TF1247
Ewerby Thorpe *Lincs* 76 TF1347
Ewesley *Nthumb* 103 NZ0591
Ewhurst *Surrey* 14 TQ0940
Ewhurst *E Susx* 17 TQ7924
Ewhurst Green *Surrey* 14 TQ0939
Ewloe *Clwyd* 71 SJ3066
Ewloe Green *Clwyd* 71 SJ2966
Ewood *Lancs* 81 SD6725
Ewood Bridge *Lancs* 81 SD7920
Eworthy *Devon* 5 SX4495
Ewshot *Hants* 25 SU8149
Ewyas Harold *H & W* 46 SO3828
Exbourne *Devon* 8 SS6002
Exbury *Hants* 13 SU4200
Exceat *E Susx* 16 TV5199
Exebridge *Somset* 20 SS9324
Exelby *N York* 89 SE2987
Exeter *Devon* 9 SX9292
Exford *Somset* 19 SS8538
Exfordsgreen *Shrops* 59 SJ4505
Exhall *Warwks* 48 SP1055
Exhall *Warwks* 61 SP3485
Exlade Street *Oxon* 37 SU6581
Exley Head *W York* 82 SE0440
Exminster *Devon* 9 SX9487
Exmouth *Devon* 9 SY0081
Exning *Cambs* 53 TL6265
Exted *Kent* 29 TR1744
Exton *Leics* 63 SK9211
Exton *Somset* 20 SS9233
Exton *Hants* 13 SU6120
Exton *Devon* 9 SX9886
Exwick *Devon* 9 SX9093
Eyam *Derbys* 74 SK2176
Eydon *Nhants* 49 SP5449
Eye *H & W* 46 SO4964
Eye *Cambs* 64 TF2202
Eye *Suffk* 54 TM1473
Eye Green *Cambs* 64 TF2303
Eye Kettleby *Leics* 63 SK7316
Eyemouth *Border* 119 NT9464
Eyeworth *Beds* 52 TL2545
Eyhorne Street *Kent* 28 TQ8354
Eyke *Suffk* 55 TM3151
Eynesbury *Beds* 52 TL1859
Eynsford *Kent* 27 TQ5465
Eynsham *Oxon* 36 SP4309
Eype *Dorset* 10 SY4491
Eyre *Highld* 136 NG4153
Eythorne *Kent* 29 TR2849
Eyton *Clwyd* 71 SJ3544
Eyton *Shrops* 59 SJ3714
Eyton *Shrops* 59 SJ4422
Eyton *Shrops* 59 SO3787
Eyton *H & W* 46 SO4761
Eyton on Severn *Shrops* 59 SJ5806
Eyton upon the Weald Moor *Shrops* 72 SJ6515

F

Faccombe *Hants* 23 SU3857
Faceby *N York* 90 NZ4903
Fachwen *Powys* 58 SJ0316
Facit *Lancs* 81 SD8819
Fackley *Notts* 75 SK4761
Faddiley *Ches* 71 SJ5852
Fadmoor *N York* 90 SE6789
Faerdre *W Glam* 32 SN6901
Failand *Avon* 34 ST5171
Failford *Strath* 107 NS4626
Failsworth *Gt Man* 79 SD8901
Fair Oak *Hants* 13 SU4918
Fair Oak Green *Hants* 24 SU6660
Fairbourne *Gwynd* 57 SH6113
Fairburn *N York* 83 SE4727
Fairfield *Derbys* 74 SK0673
Fairfield *H & W* 60 SO9475
Fairfield *Kent* 17 TQ9626
Fairford *Gloucs* 36 SP1501
Fairford Park *Gloucs* 36 SP1501
Fairgirth *D & G* 92 NX8756
Fairhaven *Lancs* 80 SD3227
Fairlie *Strath* 114 NS2054
Fairlight *E Susx* 17 TQ8511
Fairmile *Devon* 9 SY0897
Fairmile *Surrey* 26 TQ1161
Fairnilee *Border* 109 NT4532
Fairoak *Staffs* 72 SJ7632
Fairseat *Kent* 27 TQ6261
Fairstead *Essex* 40 TL7616
Fairwarp *E Susx* 16 TQ4626
Fairwater *S Glam* 33 ST1477
Fairy Cross *Devon* 18 SS4024
Fakenham *Norfk* 66 TF9229
Fakenham Magna *Suffk* 54 TL9176
Fala *Loth* 118 NT4460
Fala Dam *Loth* 118 NT4361
Falcondale *Dyfed* 44 SN5649
Falcut *Nhants* 49 SP5942
Faldingworth *Lincs* 76 TF0684
Faldouet *Jersey* 152 JS0000
Falfield *Gloucs* 35 ST6893
Falkenham *Suffk* 55 TM2939
Falkirk *Cent* 116 NS8880
Falkland *Fife* 126 NO2507
Fallgate *Derbys* 74 SK3561
Fallin *Cent* 116 NS8391
Falloden *Nthumb* 111 NU1922
Fallowfield *Nthumb* 102 NY9268
Fallowfield *Gt Man* 79 SJ8593
Falls of Blarghour *Strath* 122 NM9913
Falmer *E Susx* 15 TQ3509
Falmouth *Cnwll* 3 SW8032
Falnash *Border* 109 NT3905
Falstone *Nthumb* 102 NY7287
Fanagmore *Highld* 148 NC1749
Fancott *Beds* 38 TL0127
Fanellan *Highld* 139 NH4942
Fangdale Beck *N York* 90 SE5694
Fangfoss *Humb* 84 SE7653
Fanmore *Strath* 121 NM4144
Fannich Lodge *Highld* 139 NH2266
Fans *Border* 110 NT6140
Far Bletchley *Bucks* 38 SP8533
Far Cotton *Nhants* 49 SP7559
Far End *Cumb* 86 SD3098
Far Forest *H & W* 60 SO7275
Far Green *Gloucs* 35 SO7700
Far Moor *Gt Man* 78 SD5204
Far Oakridge *Gloucs* 35 SO9203
Far Sawrey *Cumb* 87 SD3795
Far Thorpe *Lincs* 77 TF2674
Farcet *Cambs* 64 TL2094
Farden *Shrops* 46 SO5775
Fareham *Hants* 13 SU5606
Farewell *Staffs* 61 SK0811
Farforth *Lincs* 77 TF3178
Faringdon *Oxon* 36 SU2895
Farington *Lancs* 80 SD5325
Farkhill *Tays* 125 NO0435
Farlam *Cumb* 94 NY5558
Farleigh *Avon* 21 ST5069
Farleigh *Devon* 7 SX7553
Farleigh *Surrey* 27 TQ3760
Farleigh Hungerford *Somset* 22 ST8057
Farleigh Wallop *Hants* 24 SU6247
Farlesthorpe *Lincs* 77 TF4774
Farleton *Cumb* 87 SD5380
Farleton *Lancs* 87 SD5767
Farley *Staffs* 73 SK0644
Farley *Derbys* 74 SK2962
Farley *Wilts* 23 SU2229
Farley Green *Suffk* 53 TL7353
Farley Green *Surrey* 14 TQ0545
Farley Hill *Berks* 24 SU7464
Farleys End *Gloucs* 35 SO7614
Farlington *N York* 90 SE6167
Farlow *Shrops* 59 SO6380
Farm Town *Leics* 62 SK3916
Farmborough *Avon* 22 ST6660
Farmbridge End *Essex* 40 TL6211
Farmcote *Shrops* 60 SO7791
Farmcote *Gloucs* 48 SP0628
Farmers *Dyfed* 44 SN6444
Farmington *Gloucs* 36 SP1315
Farmoor *Oxon* 37 SP4506
Farms Common *Cnwll* 2 SW6734
Farmtown *Gramp* 142 NJ5051
Farnachty *Gramp* 142 NJ4261
Farnah Green *Derbys* 62 SK3347
Farnborough *Warwks* 49 SP4349
Farnborough *Berks* 36 SU4381
Farnborough *Hants* 25 SU8753
Farnborough *Gt Lon* 27 TQ4464
Farnborough Park *Hants* 25 SU8755
Farnborough Street *Hants* 25 SU8756
Farncombe *Surrey* 25 SU9744
Farndish *Beds* 51 SP9263
Farndon *Ches* 71 SJ4154
Farndon *Notts* 75 SK7651
Farnell *Tays* 127 NO6255
Farnham *N York* 89 SE3460
Farnham *Dorset* 11 ST9515
Farnham *Surrey* 25 SU8346
Farnham *Essex* 39 TL4724
Farnham *Suffk* 55 TM3660
Farnham Common *Bucks* 26 SU9585
Farnham Green *Essex* 39 TL4625
Farnham Royal *Bucks* 26 SU9583
Farningham *Kent* 27 TQ5467
Farnley *N York* 82 SE2148
Farnley *W York* 82 SE2532
Farnley Tyas *W York* 82 SE1612
Farnsfield *Notts* 75 SK6456
Farnworth *Gt Man* 79 SD7306
Farnworth *Ches* 78 SJ5187
Farr *Highld* 150 NC7163
Farr *Highld* 140 NH6833
Farr *Highld* 132 NH8203
Farraline *Highld* 139 NH5621
Farringdon *Devon* 9 SY0191
Farrington Gurney *Avon* 21 ST6355
Farsley *W York* 82 SE2135
Farther Howegreen *Essex* 40 TL8401
Farthing Green *Kent* 28 TQ8146
Farthing Street *Gt Lon* 27 TQ4262
Farthinghoe *Nhants* 49 SP5339
Farthingloe *Kent* 29 TR2940
Farthingstone *Nhants* 49 SP6154
Fartown *W York* 82 SE1518
Fartown *W York* 82 SE2233
Farway Street *Devon* 9 SY1895
Fasnacloich *Strath* 122 NN0247
Fasnakyle *Highld* 139 NH3128
Fassfern *Highld* 130 NN0278
Fatfield *T & W* 96 NZ2954
Faugh *Cumb* 94 NY5154
Fauld *Staffs* 73 SK1728
Faulkbourne *Essex* 40 TL7917
Faulkland *Somset* 22 ST7354
Fauls *Shrops* 59 SJ5832
Faversham *Kent* 28 TR0161
Fawdington *N York* 89 SE4372
Fawdon *Nthumb* 111 NU0315
Fawfieldhead *Staffs* 74 SK0763
Fawkham Green *Kent* 27 TQ5865
Fawler *Oxon* 36 SP3717
Fawley *Berks* 36 SU3981
Fawley *Hants* 13 SU4503
Fawley *Bucks* 37 SU7586
Fawley Chapel *H & W* 46 SO5929
Fawnog *Clwyd* 70 SJ2466
Fawsley *Nhants* 49 SP5656
Faxfleet *Humb* 84 SE8624
Faygate *W Susx* 15 TQ2134
Fazakerley *Mersyd* 78 SJ3796
Fazeley *Staffs* 61 SK2001
Fearby *N York* 89 SE1981
Fearn *Highld* 147 NH8378
Fearnan *Tays* 124 NN7244
Fearnbeg *Highld* 137 NG7359
Fearnhead *Ches* 79 SJ6390
Fearnoch *Strath* 114 NR9279
Featherstone *W York* 83 SE4221
Featherstone *Staffs* 60 SJ9305
Feckenham *H & W* 47 SP0162
Fedderate *Gramp* 143 NJ8949
Feering *Essex* 40 TL8720
Feetham *N York* 88 SD9898
Feizor *N York* 88 SD7867
Felbridge *Surrey* 15 TQ3739
Felbrigg *Norfk* 67 TG2039
Felcourt *Surrey* 15 TQ3841
Felday *Surrey* 14 TQ1144
Felden *Herts* 38 TL0404
Felin Fach *Dyfed* 44 SN5355
Felin gwm Isaf *Dyfed* 44 SN5023
Felin gwm Uchaf *Dyfed* 44 SN5024
Felin-newydd *Powys* 45 SO1135
Felindre *Dyfed* 32 SN5521
Felindre *Dyfed* 44 SN5555
Felindre *Dyfed* 44 SN7027
Felindre *Powys* 58 SO1681
Felindre Farchog *Dyfed* 31 SN1039
Felinfach *Powys* 45 SO0933
Felinfoel *Dyfed* 32 SN5102
Felixkirk *N York* 89 SE4684
Felixstowe *Suffk* 55 TM3034
Felixstoweferry *Suffk* 55 TM3237
Felkington *Nthumb* 110 NT9444
Felkirk *W York* 83 SE3812
Fell Foot *Cumb* 86 NY2903
Fell Lane *W York* 82 SE0440
Fell Side *Cumb* 93 NY3037
Felling *T & W* 96 NZ2762
Felmersham *Beds* 51 SP9957
Felmingham *Norfk* 67 TG2529
Felpham *W Susx* 14 SZ9499
Felsham *Suffk* 54 TL9457
Felsted *Essex* 40 TL6720
Feltham *Gt Lon* 26 TQ1073
Felthamhill *Gt Lon* 26 TQ0971
Felthorpe *Norfk* 66 TG1618
Felton *Nthumb* 103 NU1800
Felton *H & W* 46 SO5748
Felton *Avon* 21 ST5265
Felton Butler *Shrops* 59 SJ3917
Feltwell *Norfk* 53 TL7190
Fen Ditton *Cambs* 53 TL4860
Fen Drayton *Cambs* 52 TL3368
Fen End *W Mids* 61 SP2274
Fen End *Lincs* 64 TF2420
Fen Street *Norfk* 66 TL9895
Fen Street *Suffk* 54 TM1862
Fenay Bridge *W York* 82 SE1815
Fence *Lancs* 81 SD8237
Fence *S York* 75 SK4485
Fencehouses *T & W* 96 NZ3250
Fencote *N York* 89 SE2893
Fencott *Oxon* 37 SP5716
Fendike Corner *Lincs* 77 TF4560
Fenham *Nthumb* 111 NU0840
Fenham *T & W* 103 NZ2265
Feniscliffe *Lancs* 81 SD6526
Feniscowles *Lancs* 81 SD6425
Feniton *Devon* 9 SY1099
Fenn Green *Shrops* 60 SO7783
Fenn Street *Kent* 28 TQ7975
Fenny Bentley *Derbys* 73 SK1749
Fenny Bridges *Devon* 9 SY1198
Fenny Compton *Warwks* 49 SP4152
Fenny Drayton *Leics* 61 SP3596
Fenny Stratford *Bucks* 38 SP8734
Fenrother *Nthumb* 103 NZ1792
Fenstanton *Cambs* 52 TL3168
Fenstead End *Suffk* 54 TL8050
Fenton *Cumb* 94 NY5056
Fenton *Staffs* 72 SJ8944
Fenton *Notts* 75 SK7983
Fenton *Lincs* 76 SK8476
Fenton *Lincs* 76 SK8751
Fenton *Cambs* 52 TL3279
Fenton Town *Nthumb* 111 NT9733
Fenwick *Strath* 107 NS4643
Fenwick *Nthumb* 111 NU0640
Fenwick *Nthumb* 103 NZ0572
Fenwick *S York* 83 SE5916
Feock *Cnwll* 3 SW8238
Feolin Ferry *Strath* 112 NR4469
Feriniquarrie *Highld* 136 NG1750
Fern *Tays* 134 NO4861
Ferndale *M Glam* 33 SS9996
Ferndown *Dorset* 12 SU0700
Ferness *Highld* 140 NH9645
Fernham *Oxon* 36 SU2991
Fernhill Heath *H & W* 47 SO8759
Fernhurst *W Susx* 14 SU8928
Fernie *Fife* 126 NO3115
Ferniegair *Strath* 116 NS7354
Fernilea *Highld* 136 NG3732
Fernilee *Derbys* 79 SK0178
Ferny Common *H & W* 46 SO3651
Ferriby Sluice *Humb* 84 SE9720
Ferrindonald *Highld* 129 NG6608
Ferring *W Susx* 14 TQ0902
Ferry Point *Highld* 146 NH7385
Ferrybridge *W York* 83 SE4824
Ferryden *Tays* 127 NO7156
Ferryhill *Dur* 96 NZ2832
Ferryside *Dyfed* 31 SN3610
Ferrytown *Highld* 146 NH7387
Fersfield *Norfk* 54 TM0683
Fersit *Highld* 131 NN3577
Feshiebridge *Highld* 132 NH8504
Fetcham *Surrey* 26 TQ1455
Fetterangus *Gramp* 143 NJ9850
Fettercairn *Gramp* 135 NO6573
Fewcott *Oxon* 49 SP5428
Fewston *N York* 82 SE1954
Ffair Rhos *Dyfed* 43 SN7368
Ffairfach *Dyfed* 32 SN6321
Ffawyddog *Powys* 33 SO2018
Ffestiniog *Gwynd* 57 SH7042
Ffordd-Las *Clwyd* 70 SJ1264
Fforest *Dyfed* 32 SN5704
Fforest *Gwent* 34 SO2820
Fforest Fach *W Glam* 32 SS6295
Fforest Goch *W Glam* 32 SN7401
Ffostrasol *Dyfed* 42 SN3747
Ffrith *Clwyd* 70 SJ2855
Ffynnon-Oer *Dyfed* 44 SN5353
Ffynnongroew *Clwyd* 70 SJ1382
Ffynonddewi *Dyfed* 42 SN3852
Fiag Lodge *Highld* 149 NC4528
Fickleshole *Surrey* 27 TQ3860
Fiddes *Gramp* 135 NO8080
Fiddington *Gloucs* 47 SO9231
Fiddington *Somset* 20 ST2140
Fiddleford *Dorset* 11 ST8013
Fiddlers Green *Cnwll* 3 SW8155
Fiddlers Hamlet *Essex* 27 TL4701
Field *Staffs* 73 SK0233
Field Broughton *Cumb* 87 SD3881
Field Dalling *Norfk* 66 TG0038
Field Head *Leics* 62 SK4909
Fieldhead *Cumb* 93 NY4539
Fife Keith *Gramp* 142 NJ4250
Fifehead Magdalen *Dorset* 22 ST7821
Fifehead Neville *Dorset* 11 ST7610
Fifehead St. Quinton *Dorset* 11 ST7710
Fifield *Oxon* 36 SP2418
Fifield *Wilts* 23 SU1450
Fifield *Berks* 26 SU9076
Figheldean *Wilts* 23 SU1547
Filands *Wilts* 35 ST9388
Filby *Norfk* 67 TG4613
Filey *N York* 91 TA1180
Filgrave *Bucks* 38 SP8648
Filkins *Oxon* 36 SP2304
Filleigh *Devon* 19 SS6627
Filleigh *Devon* 19 SS7410
Fillingham *Lincs* 76 SK9485
Fillongley *Warwks* 61 SP2887
Filmore Hill *Hants* 13 SU6627
Filton *Avon* 34 ST6079
Fimber *Humb* 91 SE8960
Finavon *Tays* 127 NO4956
Fincham *Norfk* 65 TF6806
Finchampstead *Berks* 25 SU7963
Fincharr *Strath* 122 NM9003
Finchdean *Hants* 13 SU7312
Finchingfield *Essex* 40 TL6832
Finchley *Gt Lon* 27 TQ2690
Findern *Derbys* 73 SK3030
Findhorn *Gramp* 141 NJ0364
Findhorn Bridge *Highld* 140 NH8027
Findo Gask *Tays* 125 NO0019
Findochty *Gramp* 142 NJ4667
Findon *Gramp* 135 NO9397
Findon *W Susx* 14 TQ1208
Findon Mains *Highld* 140 NH6060
Findrack House *Gramp* 134 NJ6004
Finedon *Nhants* 51 SP9172
Fingal Street *Suffk* 55 TM2169
Fingask *Gramp* 142 NJ7827
Fingask *Tays* 126 NO1619
Fingest *Bucks* 37 SU7791
Finghall *N York* 89 SE1889
Fingland *D & G* 107 NS7517
Fingland *Cumb* 93 NY2557
Finglesham *Kent* 29 TR3353
Fingringhoe *Essex* 41 TM0220
Finkle Green *Essex* 53 TL7040
Finkle Street *S York* 74 SK3099
Finlarig *Cent* 124 NN5733
Finmere *Oxon* 49 SP6332
Finnart *Tays* 124 NN5157
Finningham *Suffk* 54 TM0669
Finningley *Notts* 75 SK6799
Finsbay *W Isls* 154 NG0786
Finstall *H & W* 60 SO9770
Finsthwaite *Cumb* 87 SD3687
Finstock *Oxon* 36 SP3616
Fintown *Ork* 155 HY3513
Fintry *Gramp* 142 NJ7554
Fintry *Cent* 116 NS6186
Finzean *Gramp* 134 NO5993
Fionnphort *Strath* 120 NM3023
Fir Tree *Dur* 96 NZ1434
Firbank *Cumb* 87 SD6293
Firbeck *S York* 75 SK5688
Firby *N York* 89 SE2686
Firby *N York* 90 SE7466
Firgrove *Gt Man* 81 SD9113
Firsby *Lincs* 77 TF4562
Fishbourne *W Susx* 14 SU8304
Fishbourne *IOW* 13 SZ5592
Fishburn *Dur* 96 NZ3632
Fishcross *Cent* 116 NS8995
Fisher *W Susx* 14 SU8700
Fisher's Pond *Hants* 13 SU4820
Fisher's Row *Lancs* 80 SD4148
Fisherford *Gramp* 142 NJ6735

275

Gabroc Hill Gollanfield

G

Gabroc Hill *Strath* 115 NS4550
Gaddesby *Leics* 63 SK6813
Gaddesden Row *Herts* 38 TL0512
Gadfa *Gwynd* 68 SH4689
Gadgirth *Strath* 106 NS4022
Gadlas *Shrops* 59 SJ3737
Gaer *Powys* 33 SO1721
Gaer-llwyd *Gwent* 34 ST4496
Gaerwen *Gwynd* 68 SH4871
Gagingwell *Oxon* 48 SP4025
Gailes *Strath* 106 NS3235
Gailey *Staffs* 60 SJ9110
Gainford *Dur* 96 NZ1716
Gainsborough *Lincs* 75 SK8189
Gainsford End *Essex* 53 TL7235
Gairloch *Highld* 144 NG8076
Gairlochy *Highld* 131 NN1784
Gairneybridge *Tays* 117 NT1397
Gaisby *W York* 82 SE1536
Gaisgill *Cumb* 87 NY6305
Gaitsgill *Cumb* 93 NY3846
Galashiels *Border* 109 NT4936
Galby *Leics* 50 SK6900
Galcantray *Highld* 140 NH8148
Galgate *Lancs* 80 SD4855
Galhampton *Somset* 21 ST6329
Gallaberry *D & G* 100 NX9682
Gallanach *Strath* 120 NM2161
Gallanach *Strath* 122 NM8326
Gallantry Bank *Ches* 71 SJ5153
Gallatown *Fife* 117 NT2994
Galley Common *Warwks* 61 SP3091
Galleywood *Essex* 40 TL7003
Gallovie *Highld* 132 NN5589
Gallowfauld *Tays* 127 NO4342
Gallowhill *Tays* 126 NO1635
Gallows Green *H & W* 47 SO9362
Gallowstree Common *Oxon* 37 SU6980
Gallt-y-foel *Gwynd* 69 SH5862
Galltair *Highld* 129 NG8120
Gally Hill *Hants* 25 SU8051
Gallypot Street *E Susx* 16 TQ4735
Galmisdale *Highld* 128 NM4784
Galmpton *Devon* 7 SX6940
Galmpton *Devon* 7 SX8856
Galphay *N York* 89 SE2572
Galston *Strath* 107 NS5036
Giltbrook *Notts* 62 SK4845
Galton *Dorset* 11 SY7785
Galtrigill *Highld* 136 NG1854
Gamballs Green *Staffs* 74 SK0367
Gambles Green *Essex* 40 TL7614
Gamblesby *Cumb* 94 NY6039
Gamelsby *Cumb* 93 NY2552
Gamesley *Gt Man* 79 SK0194
Gamlingay *Cambs* 52 TL2452
Gamlingay Cinques *Cambs* 52 TL2352
Gamlingay Great Heath *Beds* 52 TL2151
Gammersgill *N York* 88 SE0582
Gamrie *Gramp* 143 NJ7962
Gamston *Notts* 75 SK7176
Ganarew *H & W* 34 SO5216
Ganavan Bay *Strath* 122 NM8632
Gang *Cnwll* 5 SX3068
Ganllwyd *Gwynd* 57 SH7324
Gannachy *Tays* 134 NO5970
Ganstead *Humb* 85 TA1434
Ganthorpe *N York* 90 SE6870
Ganton *N York* 91 SE9977
Ganwick Corner *Herts* 27 TQ2599
Gappah *Devon* 9 SX8677
Garbity *Gramp* 141 NJ3152
Garboldisham *Norfk* 54 TM0081
Garchory *Gramp* 134 NJ3010
Garden City *Clwyd* 71 SJ3269
Garden Village *Derbys* 74 SK2698
Gardeners Green *Berks* 25 SU8266
Gardenstown *Gramp* 143 NJ8064
Garderhouse *Shet* 155 HU3347
Gardham *Humb* 84 SE9542
Gare Hill *Somset* 22 ST7840
Garelochhead *Strath* 114 NS2491
Garford *Oxon* 36 SU4296
Garforth *W York* 83 SE4033
Garforth Bridge *W York* 83 SE3932
Gargrave *N York* 81 SD9354
Gargunnock *Cent* 116 NS7094
Garizim *Gwynd* 69 SH6975
Garlic Street *Norfk* 55 TM2183
Garlieston *D & G* 99 NX4746
Garlinge *Kent* 29 TR3369
Garlinge Green *Kent* 29 TR1152
Garlogie *Gramp* 135 NJ7805
Garmond *Gramp* 143 NJ8052
Garmondsway *Dur* 96 NZ3434
Garmony *Strath* 121 NM6640
Garmouth *Gramp* 141 NJ3364
Garmston *Shrops* 59 SJ6006
Garn *Gwynd* 56 SH2834
Garn-Dolbenmaen *Gwynd* 56 SH4943
Garnant *Dyfed* 32 SN6713
Garnett Bridge *Cumb* 87 SD5299
Garnkirk *Strath* 116 NS6768
Garnswllt *W Glam* 32 SN6209
Garrabost *W Isls* 154 NB5133
Garrallan *Strath* 107 NS5418
Garras *Cnwll* 2 SW7023
Garreg *Gwynd* 57 SH6141
Garrigill *Cumb* 94 NY7441
Garriston *N York* 89 SE1592
Garroch *D & G* 99 NX5981
Garrochtrie *D & G* 98 NX1138
Garrochty *Strath* 114 NS0953
Garros *Highld* 136 NG4962
Garrowby Hall *Humb* 90 SE7957
Garsdale *Cumb* 88 SD7489
Garsdale Head *Cumb* 88 SD7891
Garsdon *Wilts* 35 ST9687
Garshall Green *Staffs* 72 SJ9633
Garsington *Oxon* 37 SP5802
Garstang *Lancs* 80 SD4945
Garston *Mersyd* 78 SJ4084
Garston *Herts* 26 TL1100
Gartachossan *Strath* 112 NR3461
Gartcosh *Strath* 116 NS6967
Garth *IOM* 153 SC3177
Garth *Clwyd* 70 SJ2542
Garth *Powys* 45 SN9549
Garth *Powys* 46 SO2772
Garth *M Glam* 33 SS8690
Garth *Gwent* 34 ST3492
Garth Penrhyncoch *Dyfed* 43 SN6484
Garth Row *Cumb* 87 SD5297
Garthbrengy *Powys* 45 SO0433
Gartheli *Dyfed* 44 SN5856
Garthmyl *Powys* 58 SO1999
Garthorpe *Humb* 84 SE8418
Garthorpe *Leics* 63 SK8320
Garths *Cumb* 87 SD5489
Gartley *Gramp* 142 NJ5232
Gartmore *Cent* 115 NS5297
Gartness *Cent* 115 NS5086
Gartness *Strath* 116 NS7864
Gartocharn *Strath* 115 NS4286
Garton *Humb* 85 TA2635
Garton End *Cambs* 64 TF1900
Garton-on-the-Wolds *Humb* 91 SE9759
Gartsherrie *Strath* 116 NS7265
Gartymore *Highld* 147 ND0114
Garvald *Loth* 118 NT5870
Garvan *Highld* 130 NM9777
Garvard *Strath* 112 NR3791
Garve *Highld* 139 NH3961
Garvestone *Norfk* 66 TG0207
Garvock *Strath* 114 NS2570
Garway *H & W* 34 SO4522
Garway Common *H & W* 34 SO4622
Garway Hill *H & W* 46 SO4425
Gasper *Wilts* 22 ST7633
Gass *Strath* 106 NS4105
Gastard *Wilts* 22 ST8868
Gasthorpe *Norfk* 54 TL9781
Gaston Green *Essex* 39 TL4917
Gatcombe *IOW* 13 SZ4985
Gate Burton *Lincs* 76 SK8382
Gate Helmsley *N York* 83 SE6955
Gatebeck *Cumb* 87 SD5485
Gateford *Notts* 75 SK5781
Gateforth *N York* 83 SE5628
Gatehead *Strath* 106 NS3936
Gatehouse *Nthumb* 102 NY7889
Gatehouse of Fleet *D & G* 99 NX5956
Gateley *Norfk* 66 TF9624
Gatenby *N York* 89 SE3287
Gates Heath *Ches* 71 SJ4760
Gatesgarth *Cumb* 93 NY1915
Gateshaw *Border* 110 NT7722
Gateshead *T & W* 96 NZ2562
Gateside *Fife* 126 NO1809
Gateside *Tays* 127 NO4344
Gateside *Strath* 115 NS3653
Gateside *Strath* 115 NS4858
Gateslack *D & G* 108 NS8902
Gathurst *Gt Man* 78 SD5407
Gatley *Gt Man* 79 SJ8488
Gatton *Surrey* 27 TQ2752
Gattonside *Border* 109 NT5435
Gaufron *Powys* 45 SN9968
Gauldry *Fife* 126 NO3723
Gauldswell *Tays* 126 NO2151
Gaulkthorn *Lancs* 81 SD7526
Gaultree *Norfk* 65 TF4907
Gaunt's Common *Dorset* 12 SU0205
Gaunt's End *Essex* 39 TL5525
Gaunton's Bank *Ches* 71 SJ5647
Gautby *Lincs* 76 TF1772
Gavinton *Border* 119 NT7652
Gawber *S York* 83 SE3207
Gawcott *Bucks* 49 SP6831
Gawsworth *Ches* 79 SJ8969
Gawthorpe *W York* 82 SE2721
Gawthrop *Cumb* 87 SD6987
Gawthwaite *Cumb* 86 SD2784
Gay Bowers *Essex* 40 TL7904
Gay Street *W Susx* 14 TQ0820
Gaydon *Warwks* 48 SP3653
Gayhurst *Bucks* 38 SP8446
Gayle *N York* 88 SD8688
Gayles *N York* 89 NZ1207
Gayton *Mersyd* 78 SJ2780
Gayton *Staffs* 72 SJ9828
Gayton *Nhants* 49 SP7054
Gayton *Norfk* 65 TF7219
Gayton Thorpe *Norfk* 65 TF7418
Gayton le Marsh *Lincs* 77 TF4284
Gaywood *Norfk* 65 TF6320
Gazeley *Suffk* 53 TL7264
Gear *Cnwll* 3 SW7224
Geary *Highld* 136 NG2661
Gedding *Suffk* 54 TL9457
Geddinge *Kent* 29 TR2346
Geddington *Nhants* 51 SP8983
Gedling *Notts* 62 SK6142
Gedney *Lincs* 65 TF4024
Gedney Broadgate *Lincs* 65 TF4022
Gedney Drove End *Lincs* 65 TF4629
Gedney Dyke *Lincs* 65 TF4126
Gedney Hill *Lincs* 64 TF3311
Gee Cross *Gt Man* 79 SJ9593
Geldeston *Norfk* 67 TM3991
Gelli *M Glam* 33 SS9794
Gelli *Gwent* 34 ST2792
Gelli Gynan *Clwyd* 70 SJ1854
Gellifor *Clwyd* 70 SJ1262
Gelligaer *M Glam* 33 ST1396
Gelligron *W Glam* 32 SN7104
Gellilydan *Gwynd* 57 SH6839
Gellinudd *W Glam* 32 SN7303
Gelly *Dyfed* 31 SN0819
Gellyburn *Tays* 125 NO0939
Gellywen *Dyfed* 31 SN2723
Gelston *D & G* 92 NX7758
Gelston *Lincs* 63 SK9145
Gembling *Humb* 91 TA1057
Gentleshaw *Staffs* 61 SK0511
George Green *Bucks* 26 SU9981
George Nympton *Devon* 19 SS7023
Georgefield *D & G* 101 NY2991
Georgeham *Devon* 18 SS4639
Georgia *Cnwll* 2 SW4836
Georth *Ork* 155 HY3625
Gerlan *Gwynd* 69 SH6366
Germansweek *Devon* 5 SX4394
Germoe *Cnwll* 2 SW5829
Gerrans *Cnwll* 3 SW8735
Gerrards Cross *Bucks* 26 TQ0088
Gerrick *Cleve* 90 NZ7012
Gestingthorpe *Essex* 54 TL8138
Geuffordd *Powys* 58 SJ2114
Gib Hill *Ches* 79 SJ6478
Gibraltar *Kent* 29 TR2038
Gibsmere *Notts* 75 SK7148
Giddeahall *Wilts* 35 ST8674
Giddy Green *Dorset* 11 SY8386
Gidea Park *Gt Lon* 27 TQ5290
Gidleigh *Devon* 8 SX6788
Giffnock *Strath* 115 NS5658
Gifford *Loth* 118 NT5368
Giffordtown *Fife* 126 NO2811
Giggleswick *N York* 88 SD8063
Gilberdyke *Humb* 84 SE8329
Gilbert Street *Hants* 24 SU6432
Gilbert's Cross *Staffs* 60 SO8187
Gilbert's End *H & W* 47 SO8342
Gilchriston *Loth* 118 NT4865
Gilcrux *Cumb* 92 NY1138
Gildersome *W York* 82 SE2429
Gildingwells *S York* 75 SK5585
Gilesgate Moor *Dur* 96 NZ2942
Gileston *S Glam* 20 ST0166
Gilfach *M Glam* 33 ST1598
Gilfach Goch *M Glam* 33 SS9790
Gilfachrheda *Dyfed* 42 SN4158
Gilgarran *Cumb* 92 NY0323
Gill *Cumb* 93 NY4429
Gill's Green *Kent* 17 TQ7532
Gillamoor *N York* 90 SE6889
Gillesbie *D & G* 100 NY1691
Gilling *N York* 89 NZ1805
Gilling East *N York* 90 SE6176
Gillingham *Dorset* 22 ST8026
Gillingham *Norfk* 67 TM4191
Gillingham *Kent* 28 TQ7768
Gillock *Highld* 151 ND2159
Gillow Heath *Staffs* 72 SJ8858
Gills *Highld* 151 ND3272
Gilmanscleuch *Border* 109 NT3321
Gilmerton *Tays* 125 NN8823
Gilmerton *Loth* 117 NT2868
Gilmonby *Dur* 95 NY9912
Gilmorton *Leics* 50 SP5787
Gilsland *Nthumb* 102 NY6366
Gilson *Warwks* 61 SP1989
Gilstead *W York* 82 SE1239
Gilston *Herts* 39 TL4413
Gilwern *Gwent* 34 SO2414
Gimingham *Norfk* 67 TG2836
Ginclough *Ches* 79 SJ9576
Ginger Green *E Susx* 16 TQ6212
Gipping *Suffk* 54 TM0763
Gipsey Bridge *Lincs* 77 TF2849
Girdle Toll *Strath* 106 NS3440
Girlington *W York* 82 SE1334
Girlsta *Shet* 155 HU4250
Girsby *Cleve* 89 NZ3508
Girtford *Beds* 52 TL1649
Girthon *D & G* 99 NX6053
Girton *Notts* 75 SK8265
Girton *Cambs* 53 TL4262
Girvan *Strath* 106 NX1897
Gisburn *Lancs* 81 SD8248
Gisleham *Suffk* 55 TM5188
Gislingham *Suffk* 54 TM0771
Gissing *Norfk* 54 TM1485
Gittisham *Devon* 9 SY1398
Gladestry *Powys* 45 SO2355
Gladsmuir *Loth* 118 NT4573
Glais *W Glam* 32 SN7000
Glaisdale *N York* 90 NZ7705
Glamis *Tays* 126 NO3846
Glan-Duar *Dyfed* 44 SN5243
Glan-Mule *Powys* 58 SO1690
Glan-rhyd *W Glam* 32 SN7809
Glan-y-don *Clwyd* 70 SJ1679
Glan-y-llyn *M Glam* 33 ST1183
Glan-y-nant *Powys* 58 SN9384
Glan-yr-afon *Gwynd* 69 SH6080
Glan-yr-afon *Gwynd* 70 SH9140
Glan-yr-afon *Gwynd* 70 SJ0142
Glanaber *Gwynd* 69 SH6351
Glanafon *Dyfed* 30 SM9617
Glanaman *Dyfed* 32 SN6713
Glandford *Norfk* 66 TG0441
Glandwr *Dyfed* 31 SN1928
Glandyfi *Dyfed* 43 SN6996
Glangrwyne *Powys* 34 SO2416
Glanrhyd *Dyfed* 31 SN1442
Glanton *Nthumb* 111 NU0714
Glanton Pike *Nthumb* 111 NU0514
Glanvilles Wootton *Dorset* 11 ST6708
Glapthorn *Nhants* 51 TL0290
Glapwell *Derbys* 75 SK4766
Glasbury *Powys* 45 SO1739
Glascoed *Clwyd* 70 SH9973
Glascoed *Gwent* 34 SO3301
Glascote *Staffs* 61 SK2203
Glascwm *Powys* 45 SO1552
Glasfryn *Clwyd* 70 SH9250
Glasgow *Strath* 115 NS5865
Glasinfryn *Gwynd* 69 SH5868
Glasnacardoch Bay *Highld* 129 NM6795
Glasnakille *Highld* 128 NG5313
Glaspwll *Powys* 43 SN7397
Glass Houghton *W York* 83 SE4324
Glassel *Gramp* 135 NO6599
Glassenbury *Kent* 28 TQ7536
Glasserton *D & G* 99 NX4237
Glassford *Strath* 116 NS7247
Glasshouse *Gloucs* 35 SO7021
Glasshouse Hill *Gloucs* 35 SO7020
Glasshouses *N York* 89 SE1764
Glasson *Cumb* 101 NY2560
Glasson *Lancs* 80 SD4456
Glassonby *Cumb* 94 NY5738
Glasterlaw *Tays* 127 NO5951
Glaston *Leics* 51 SK8900
Glastonbury *Somset* 21 ST5038
Glatton *Cambs* 52 TL1586
Glazebrook *Ches* 79 SJ6992
Glazebury *Ches* 79 SJ6797
Glazeley *Shrops* 60 SO7088
Gleadsmoss *Ches* 79 SJ8168
Gleaston *Cumb* 86 SD2570
Gledhow *W York* 82 SE3137
Gledpark *D & G* 99 NX6250
Gledrid *Shrops* 59 SJ3036
Glemsford *Suffk* 54 TL8348
Glen *D & G* 99 NX5457
Glen Clunie Lodge *Gramp* 133 NO1383
Glen Maye *IOM* 153 SC2379
Glen Nevis House *Highld* 130 NN1272
Glen Parva *Leics* 50 SP5798
Glen Trool Lodge *D & G* 99 NX4080
Glenancross *Highld* 129 NM6691
Glenaros House *Strath* 121 NM5544
Glenbarr *Strath* 105 NR6736
Glenbeg *Highld* 121 NM5862
Glenbervie *Gramp* 135 NO7680
Glenboig *Strath* 116 NS7268
Glenborrodale *Highld* 121 NM6061
Glenbranter *Strath* 114 NS1197
Glenbreck *Border* 108 NT0521
Glenbrittle House *Highld* 128 NG4121
Glenbuck *Strath* 107 NS7429
Glencally *Tays* 134 NO3562
Glencaple *D & G* 100 NX9968
Glencarron Lodge *Highld* 138 NH0650
Glencarse *Tays* 126 NO1921
Glenceitlein *Highld* 123 NN1548
Glencoe *Highld* 130 NN1058
Glencothe *Border* 108 NT0829
Glencraig *Fife* 117 NT1894
Glencrosh *D & G* 107 NX7689
Glendaruel *Strath* 114 NR9983
Glendevon *Tays* 125 NN9904
Glendoe Lodge *Highld* 131 NH4009
Glendoick *Tays* 126 NO2022
Glenduckie *Fife* 126 NO2818
Gleneagles *Tays* 125 NN9208
Glenearn *Tays* 126 NO1016
Glenegedale *Strath* 112 NR3351
Glenelg *Highld* 129 NG8119
Glenerney *Gramp* 141 NJ0146
Glenfarg *Tays* 126 NO1310
Glenfeshie Lodge *Highld* 132 NN8493
Glenfield *Leics* 62 SK5406
Glenfinnan *Highld* 130 NM9080
Glenfinntaig Lodge *Highld* 131 NN2286
Glenfoot *Tays* 126 NO1815
Glenfyne Lodge *Strath* 123 NN2215
Glengarnock *Strath* 115 NS3252
Glengolly *Highld* 151 ND1065
Glengorm Castle *Strath* 121 NM4457
Glengrasco *Highld* 136 NG4444
Glenholm *Border* 108 NT1033
Glenhoul *D & G* 107 NX6187
Glenkerry *Border* 109 NT2710
Glenkin *Strath* 114 NS1280
Glenkindie *Gramp* 142 NJ4314
Glenlee *D & G* 99 NX6080
Glenlochar *D & G* 99 NX7364
Glenloig *Strath* 105 NR9435
Glenluce *D & G* 98 NX1957
Glenmark *Tays* 134 NO4183
Glenmassen *Strath* 114 NS1088
Glenmavis *Strath* 116 NS7467
Glenmore *Highld* 136 NG4340
Glenmore Lodge *Highld* 133 NH9709
Glenmuirshaw *Strath* 107 NS6920
Glenquiech *Tays* 134 NO4261
Glenralloch *Strath* 113 NR8569
Glenridding *Cumb* 93 NY3817
Glenrothes *Fife* 117 NO2700
Glenshero Lodge *Highld* 132 NN5592
Glenstriven *Strath* 114 NS0878
Glentham *Lincs* 76 TF0090
Glentromie Lodge *Highld* 132 NN7897
Glentrool Village *D & G* 98 NX3578
Glentruim House *Highld* 132 NN6894
Glentworth *Lincs* 76 SK9488
Glenuig *Highld* 129 NM6677
Glenure *Strath* 123 NN0448
Glenurquhart *Highld* 140 NH7462
Glenvarragill *Highld* 136 NG4739
Glenwhilly *D & G* 98 NX1771
Glespin *Strath* 108 NS8127
Glewstone *H & W* 34 SO5521
Glinton *Cambs* 64 TF1505
Glooston *Leics* 50 SP7595
Glororum *Nthumb* 111 NU1633
Glossop *Derbys* 74 SK0393
Gloster Hill *Nthumb* 103 NU2504
Gloucester *Gloucs* 35 SO8318
Glover's Hill *Staffs* 73 SK0516
Glusburn *N York* 82 SE0045
Glutt Lodge *Highld* 150 ND0036
Gluvian *Cnwll* 4 SW9164
Glympton *Oxon* 36 SP4221
Glyn Ceiriog *Clwyd* 70 SJ2038
Glyn-Neath *W Glam* 33 SN8806
Glynarthen *Dyfed* 42 SN3148
Glyncorrwg *W Glam* 33 SS8798
Glynde *E Susx* 16 TQ4509
Glyndebourne *E Susx* 16 TQ4510
Glyndyfrdwy *Clwyd* 70 SJ1442
Glynn *Cnwll* 4 SX1165
Glyntaff *M Glam* 33 ST0889
Glyntawe *Powys* 33 SN8416
Glynteg *Dyfed* 31 SN3538
Gnosall *Staffs* 72 SJ8220
Gnosall Heath *Staffs* 72 SJ8220
Goadby *Leics* 50 SP7598
Goadby Marwood *Leics* 63 SK7726
Goat Lees *Kent* 28 TR0145
Goatacre *Wilts* 35 SU0276
Goatfield *Strath* 114 NN0100
Goatham Green *E Susx* 17 TQ8120
Goathill *Dorset* 11 ST6717
Goathland *N York* 90 NZ8301
Goathurst *Somset* 20 ST2534
Goathurst Common *Kent* 27 TQ4952
Gobowen *Shrops* 59 SJ3033
Godalming *Surrey* 25 SU9643
Godameavy *Devon* 6 SX5364
Goddard's Corner *Suffk* 55 TM2868
Goddard's Green *Kent* 17 TQ8134
Godford Cross *Devon* 9 ST1302
Godington *Bucks* 49 SP6427
Godley *Gt Man* 79 SJ9595
Godmanchester *Cambs* 52 TL2470
Godmanstone *Dorset* 11 SY6697
Godmersham *Kent* 28 TR0550
Godney *Somset* 21 ST4842
Godolphin Cross *Cnwll* 2 SW6031
Godre'r-graig *W Glam* 32 SN7506
Godshill *Hants* 12 SU1715
Godshill *IOW* 13 SZ5281
Godstone *Staffs* 73 SK0134
Godstone *Surrey* 27 TQ3551
Godsworthy *Devon* 5 SX5277
Godwinscroft *Hants* 12 SZ1996
Goetre *Gwent* 34 SO3206
Goff's Oak *Herts* 27 TL3202
Gogar *Loth* 117 NT1672
Goginan *Dyfed* 43 SN6881
Golan *Gwynd* 57 SH5242
Golant *Cnwll* 3 SX1254
Golberdon *Cnwll* 5 SX3271
Golborne *Gt Man* 78 SJ6097
Golcar *W York* 82 SE0915
Gold Hill *Dorset* 11 ST8213
Gold Hill *Cambs* 65 TL5392
Goldcliff *Gwent* 34 ST3683
Golden Cross *E Susx* 16 TQ5312
Golden Green *Kent* 16 TQ6348
Golden Grove *Dyfed* 32 SN5919
Golden Hill *Dyfed* 30 SM9802
Golden Pot *Hants* 24 SU7143
Golden Valley *Derbys* 74 SK4251
Goldenhill *Staffs* 72 SJ8553
Golders Green *Gt Lon* 26 TQ2487
Goldfinch Bottom *Berks* 24 SU5063
Goldhanger *Essex* 40 TL9008
Golding *Shrops* 59 SJ5403
Goldington *Beds* 38 TL0750
Golds Green *W Mids* 60 SO9893
Goldsborough *N York* 90 NZ8314
Goldsborough *N York* 83 SE3856
Goldsithney *Cnwll* 2 SW5430
Goldstone *Kent* 27 TQ2961
Goldstone *Shrops* 72 SJ7028
Goldsworth *Surrey* 25 SU9958
Goldthorpe *S York* 83 SE4604
Goldworthy *Devon* 18 SS3922
Golford *Kent* 28 TQ7936
Golford Green *Kent* 28 TQ7936
Gollanfield *Highld* 140 NH8053

Griff Hardwick

Griff *Warwks* 61 SP3689
Griffithstown *Gwent* 34 ST2998
Griffydam *Leics* 62 SK4118
Griggs Green *Hants* 14 SU8231
Grimeford Village *Lancs* 81 SD6112
Grimesthorpe *S York* 74 SK3689
Grimethorpe *S York* 83 SE4109
Grimley *H & W* 47 SO8360
Grimmet *Strath* 106 NS3210
Grimoldby *Lincs* 77 TF3988
Grimpo *Shrops* 59 SJ3526
Grimsargh *Lancs* 81 SD5834
Grimsby *Humb* 85 TA2710
Grimscote *Nhants* 49 SP6553
Grimscott *Cnwll* 18 SS2606
Grimshader *W Isls* 154 NB4025
Grimshaw *Lancs* 81 SD7024
Grimshaw Green *Lancs* 80 SD4912
Grimsthorpe *Lincs* 64 TF0422
Grimston *Leics* 63 SK6821
Grimston *Humb* 85 TA2735
Grimston *Norfk* 65 TF7222
Grimston Hill *Notts* 75 SK6865
Grimstone *Dorset* 10 SY6394
Grimstone End *Suffk* 54 TL9368
Grinacombe Moor *Devon* 5 SX4191
Grindale *Humb* 91 TA1271
Grindle *Shrops* 60 SJ7503
Grindleford *Derbys* 74 SK2477
Grindleton *Lancs* 81 SD7545
Grindley Brook *Shrops* 71 SJ5242
Grindlow *Derbys* 74 SK1877
Grindon *Nthumb* 110 NT9144
Grindon *Cleve* 96 NZ3925
Grindon *Staffs* 73 SK0854
Grindon Hill *Nthumb* 102 NY8268
Grindonrigg *Nthumb* 110 NT9243
Gringley on the Hill *Notts* 75 SK7390
Grinsdale *Cumb* 93 NY3758
Grinshill *Shrops* 59 SJ5223
Grinton *N York* 88 SE0498
Grishipoll *Strath* 120 NM1859
Grisling Common *E Susx* 16 TQ4322
Gristhorpe *N York* 91 TA0981
Griston *Norfk* 66 TL9499
Gritley *Ork* 155 HY5504
Grittenham *Wilts* 36 SU0382
Grittleton *Wilts* 35 ST8580
Grizebeck *Cumb* 86 SD2384
Grizedale *Cumb* 86 SD3394
Groby *Leics* 62 SK5207
Groes *Clwyd* 70 SJ0064
Groes-Wen *M Glam* 33 ST1286
Groes-faen *M Glam* 33 ST0680
Groesffordd *Gwynd* 56 SH2739
Groesffordd Marli *Clwyd* 70 SJ0073
Groesllwyd *Powys* 58 SJ2111
Groeslon *Gwynd* 68 SH4755
Groeslon *Gwynd* 68 SH5260
Grogport *Strath* 105 NR8144
Gromford *Suffk* 55 TM3858
Gronant *Clwyd* 70 SJ0983
Groom's Hill *H & W* 47 SP0154
Groombridge *E Susx* 16 TQ5337
Grosebay *W Isls* 154 NG1593
Grosmont *N York* 90 NZ8305
Grosmont *Gwent* 46 SO4024
Grossington *Gloucs* 35 SO7302
Groton *Suffk* 54 TL9641
Grotton *Gt Man* 79 SD9604
Grouville *Jersey* 152 JS0000
Grove *Notts* 75 SK7479
Grove *Dyfed* 30 SM9900
Grove *Bucks* 38 SP9122
Grove *Oxon* 36 SU4090
Grove *Dorset* 11 SY6972
Grove *Kent* 29 TR2362
Grove Green *Kent* 28 TQ7856
Grove Park *Gt Lon* 27 TQ4072
Grove Vale *W Mids* 61 SP0394
Grovenhurst *Kent* 28 TQ7140
Grovesend *W Glam* 32 SN5900
Grovesend *Avon* 35 ST6589
Grubb Street *Kent* 27 TQ5869
Gruids *Highld* 146 NC5603
Gruinard *Highld* 144 NG9489
Gruinart *Strath* 112 NR2966
Grula *Highld* 136 NG3826
Gruline *Strath* 121 NM5440
Grumbla *Cnwll* 2 SW4029
Grundisburgh *Suffk* 55 TM2251
Gruting *Shet* 155 HU2749
Gualachulain *Highld* 123 NN1145
Guanockgate *Lincs* 64 TF3710
Guardbridge *Fife* 127 NO4518
Guarlford *H & W* 47 SO8145
Guay *Tays* 125 NN9948
Guestling Green *E Susx* 17 TQ8513
Guestling Thorn *E Susx* 17 TQ8516
Guestwick *Norfk* 66 TG0626
Guide *Lancs* 81 SD7025
Guide Bridge *Gt Man* 79 SJ9297
Guilden Down *Shrops* 59 SO3082
Guilden Morden *Cambs* 39 TL2744
Guilden Sutton *Ches* 71 SJ4468
Guildford *Surrey* 25 SU9949
Guildstead *Kent* 28 TQ8262
Guildtown *Tays* 126 NO1331
Guilsborough *Nhants* 50 SP6772
Guilsfield *Powys* 58 SJ2211
Guilton *Kent* 29 TR2858
Guiltreehill *Strath* 106 NS3610
Guineaford *Devon* 19 SS5537
Guisborough *Cleve* 97 NZ6015
Guiseley *W York* 82 SE1942
Guist *Norfk* 66 TG0025
Guiting Power *Gloucs* 48 SP0924
Gullane *Loth* 118 NT4882
Gulling Green *Suffk* 54 TL8256
Gulval *Cnwll* 2 SW4831
Gulworthy *Devon* 6 SX4572
Gumfreston *Dyfed* 31 SN1001
Gumley *Leics* 50 SP6889
Gummow's Shop *Cnwll* 4 SW8657
Gun Green *Kent* 17 TQ7731
Gun Hill *Warwks* 61 SP2889
Gun Hill *E Susx* 16 TQ5614
Gunby *Humb* 84 SE7035
Gunby *Lincs* 63 SK9121
Gunby *Lincs* 77 TF4666
Gundleton *Hants* 24 SU6133
Gunn *Devon* 19 SS6333
Gunnerside *N York* 88 SD9598
Gunnerton *Nthumb* 102 NY9074
Gunness *Humb* 84 SE8411
Gunnislake *Devon* 6 SX4371
Gunnista *Shet* 155 HU5043
Gunthorpe *Notts* 63 SK6844
Gunthorpe *Cambs* 64 TF1802
Gunthorpe *Norfk* 66 TG0134
Gunton *Suffk* 67 TM5395
Gunville *IOW* 13 SZ4788
Gupworthy *Somset* 20 SS9734
Gurnard *IOW* 13 SZ4795
Gurnett *Ches* 79 SJ9271
Gurney Slade *Somset* 21 ST6249
Gurnos *W Glam* 32 SN7709
Gushmere *Kent* 28 TR0457
Gussage All Saints *Dorset* 11 SU0010
Gussage St. Michael *Dorset* 11 ST9811
Guston *Kent* 29 TR3244
Gutcher *Shet* 155 HU5499
Guthrie *Tays* 127 NO5650
Guy's Marsh *Dorset* 22 ST8420
Guyhirn *Cambs* 65 TF4003
Guyhirn Gull *Cambs* 65 TF3904
Guyzance *Nthumb* 103 NU2103
Gwaenysgor *Clwyd* 70 SJ0781
Gwalchmai *Gwynd* 68 SH3876
Gwastadnant *Gwynd* 69 SH6157
Gwaun-Cae-Gurwen *W Glam* 32 SN6911
Gwbert on Sea *Dyfed* 42 SN1650
Gwealavellan *Cnwll* 2 SW6041
Gwealeath *Cnwll* 2 SW6922
Gweek *Cnwll* 2 SW7026
Gwehelog *Gwent* 34 SO3804
Gwenddwr *Powys* 45 SO0643
Gwendreath *Cnwll* 3 SW7217
Gwennap *Cnwll* 3 SW7340
Gwenter *Cnwll* 3 SW7417
Gwernaffield *Clwyd* 70 SJ2065
Gwernesney *Gwent* 34 SO4101
Gwernogle *Dyfed* 44 SN5333
Gwernymynydd *Clwyd* 70 SJ2162
Gwersyllt *Clwyd* 71 SJ3153
Gwespyr *Clwyd* 70 SJ1183
Gwindra *Cnwll* 3 SW9552
Gwinear *Cnwll* 2 SW5937
Gwithian *Cnwll* 2 SW5841
Gwredog *Gwynd* 68 SH4085
Gwrhay *Gwent* 33 ST1899
Gwyddelwern *Clwyd* 70 SJ0746
Gwyddgrug *Dyfed* 44 SN4635
Gwynfryn *Clwyd* 70 SJ2552
Gwystre *Powys* 45 SO0665
Gwytherin *Clwyd* 69 SH8761
Gyfelia *Clwyd* 71 SJ3245
Gyrn-goch *Gwynd* 68 SH4048

H

Habberley *Shrops* 59 SJ3903
Habberley *H & W* 60 SO8177
Habergham *Lancs* 81 SD8033
Habertoft *Lincs* 77 TF5069
Habin *W Susx* 14 SU8022
Habrough *Humb* 85 TA1413
Hacconby *Lincs* 64 TF1025
Haceby *Lincs* 64 TF0236
Hacheston *Suffk* 55 TM3059
Hack Green *Ches* 72 SJ6448
Hackenthorpe *S York* 74 SK4183
Hackford *Norfk* 66 TG0502
Hackforth *N York* 89 SE2492
Hackland *Ork* 155 HY3920
Hackleton *Nhants* 51 SP8055
Hacklinge *Kent* 29 TR3454
Hackman's Gate *H & W* 60 SO8978
Hackness *N York* 91 SE9790
Hackness *Somset* 21 ST3345
Hackney *Gt Lon* 27 TQ3484
Hackthorn *Lincs* 76 SK9982
Hackthorpe *Cumb* 94 NY5423
Hacton *Gt Lon* 27 TQ5585
Hadden *Border* 110 NT7836
Haddenham *Bucks* 37 SP7308
Haddenham *Cambs* 53 TL4675
Haddington *Loth* 118 NT5173
Haddington *Lincs* 76 SK9162
Haddiscoe *Norfk* 67 TM4497
Haddo *Gramp* 143 NJ8337
Haddon *Cambs* 64 TL1392
Hade Edge *W York* 82 SE1404
Hademore *Staffs* 61 SK1708
Hadfield *Derbys* 74 SK0296
Hadham Cross *Herts* 39 TL4218
Hadham Ford *Herts* 39 TL4321
Hadleigh *Suffk* 54 TM0242
Hadleigh *Essex* 40 TQ8187
Hadleigh Heath *Suffk* 54 TL9941
Hadley *Shrops* 60 SJ6711
Hadley *H & W* 47 SO8564
Hadley End *Staffs* 73 SK1320
Hadley Wood *Gt Lon* 27 TQ2698
Hadlow *Kent* 27 TQ6350
Hadlow Down *E Susx* 16 TQ5324
Hadnall *Shrops* 59 SJ5220
Hadstock *Essex* 53 TL5644
Hadzor *H & W* 47 SO9162
Haffenden Quarter *Kent* 28 TQ8840
Hafod-y-bwch *Clwyd* 71 SJ3147
Hafod-y-coed *Gwent* 34 SO2200
Hafodunos *Clwyd* 69 SH8666
Hafodyrynys *Gwent* 34 ST2298
Haggate *Lancs* 81 SD8735
Haggbeck *Cumb* 101 NY4773
Haggerston *Nthumb* 111 NU0443
Haggington Hill *Devon* 19 SS5547
Haggs *Cent* 116 NS7879
Hagley *H & W* 46 SO5641
Hagley *H & W* 60 SO9180
Hagnaby *Lincs* 77 TF3462
Hagworthingham *Lincs* 77 TF3469
Haigh *Gt Man* 78 SD6009
Haighton Green *Lancs* 81 SD5634
Hail Weston *Cambs* 52 TL1662
Haile *Cumb* 86 NY0308
Hailes *Gloucs* 48 SP0430
Hailey *Oxon* 37 SU6485
Hailey *Herts* 39 TL3710
Hailsham *E Susx* 16 TQ5909
Hainault *Gt Lon* 27 TQ4591
Haine *Kent* 29 TR3566
Hainford *Norfk* 67 TG2218
Hainton *Lincs* 76 TF1884
Hainworth *W York* 82 SE0638
Haisthorpe *Humb* 91 TA1264
Hakin *Dyfed* 30 SM8905
Halam *Notts* 75 SK6754
Halbeath *Fife* 117 NT1288
Halberton *Devon* 9 ST0112
Halcro *Highld* 151 ND2360
Hale *Cumb* 87 SD5078
Hale *Ches* 78 SJ4782
Hale *Gt Man* 79 SJ7786
Hale *Somset* 22 ST7427
Hale *Hants* 12 SU1818
Hale *Surrey* 25 SU8448
Hale Bank *Ches* 78 SJ4784
Hale Green *E Susx* 16 TQ5514
Hale Nook *Lancs* 80 SD3944
Hale Street *Kent* 28 TQ6749
Halebarns *Gt Man* 79 SJ7985
Hales *Staffs* 72 SJ7134
Hales *Norfk* 67 TM3797
Hales Green *Derbys* 73 SK1841
Hales Place *Kent* 29 TR1459
Halesgate *Lincs* 64 TF3226
Halesowen *W Mids* 60 SO9683
Halesworth *Suffk* 55 TM3877
Halewood *Mersyd* 78 SJ4585
Halewood Green *Mersyd* 78 SJ4486
Halford *Shrops* 59 SO4383
Halford *Warwks* 48 SP2645
Halford *Devon* 7 SX8174
Halfpenny *Cumb* 87 SD5387
Halfpenny Green *Staffs* 60 SO8291
Halfpenny Houses *N York* 89 SE2284
Halfway *S York* 75 SK4381
Halfway *Dyfed* 44 SN6430
Halfway *Powys* 44 SN8232
Halfway *Berks* 24 SU4068
Halfway Bridge *W Susx* 14 SU9321
Halfway House *Shrops* 59 SJ3411
Halfway Houses *Kent* 28 TQ9372
Halifax *W York* 82 SE0925
Halistra *Highld* 136 NG2459
Halket *Strath* 115 NS4252
Halkirk *Highld* 151 ND1359
Halkyn *Clwyd* 70 SJ2171
Hall *Strath* 115 NS4154
Hall Cliffe *W York* 82 SE2918
Hall Cross *Lancs* 80 SD4230
Hall Dunnerdale *Cumb* 86 SD2195
Hall End *W Mids* 60 SP0092
Hall End *Beds* 38 TL0045
Hall End *Beds* 38 TL0737
Hall Green *Ches* 72 SJ8356
Hall Green *W Mids* 61 SP1181
Hall's Green *Herts* 39 TL2728
Hall's Green *Essex* 39 TL4108
Hallam Fields *Derbys* 62 SK4739
Halland *E Susx* 16 TQ4916
Hallaton *Leics* 50 SP7896
Hallatrow *Avon* 21 ST6357
Hallbankgate *Cumb* 94 NY5859
Hallbeck *Cumb* 87 SD6288
Hallen *Avon* 34 ST5580
Hallfield Gate *Derbys* 74 SK3958
Hallgarth *Dur* 96 NZ3243
Hallin *Highld* 136 NG2558
Halling *Kent* 28 TQ7063
Hallington *Nthumb* 102 NY9875
Hallington *Lincs* 77 TF3085
Halliwell *Gt Man* 79 SD6910
Halloughton *Notts* 75 SK6951
Hallow *H & W* 47 SO8258
Hallow Heath *H & W* 47 SO8259
Hallrule *Border* 110 NT5914
Hallsands *Devon* 7 SX8138
Hallthwaites *Cumb* 86 SD1885
Halltoft End *Lincs* 64 TF3645
Hallworthy *Cnwll* 4 SX1787
Hallyne *Border* 109 NT1940
Halmer End *Staffs* 72 SJ7948
Halmond's Frome *H & W* 47 SO6747
Halnaker *W Susx* 14 SU9007
Halsall *Lancs* 78 SD3710
Halse *Nhants* 49 SP5640
Halse *Somset* 20 ST1428
Halsetown *Cnwll* 2 SW5038
Halsham *Humb* 85 TA2727
Halsinger *Devon* 19 SS5138
Halstead *Leics* 63 SK7505
Halstead *Essex* 40 TL8130
Halstead *Kent* 27 TQ4861
Halstock *Dorset* 10 ST5308
Halsway *Somset* 20 ST1337
Haltcliff Bridge *Cumb* 93 NY3636
Haltham *Lincs* 77 TF2463
Halton *Nthumb* 103 NY9967
Halton *Lancs* 87 SD5064
Halton *W York* 83 SE3533
Halton *Clwyd* 71 SJ3039
Halton *Ches* 78 SJ5481
Halton *Bucks* 38 SP8710
Halton East *N York* 82 SE0454
Halton Fenside *Lincs* 77 TF4263
Halton Gill *N York* 88 SD8776
Halton Green *Lancs* 87 SD5165
Halton Holegate *Lincs* 77 TF4165
Halton Lea Gate *Nthumb* 94 NY6458
Halton Quay *Cnwll* 5 SX4165
Halton Shields *Nthumb* 103 NZ0168
Halton West *N York* 81 SD8454
Haltwhistle *Nthumb* 102 NY7064
Halvergate *Norfk* 67 TG4106
Halwell *Devon* 7 SX7753
Halwill *Devon* 18 SX4299
Halwill Junction *Devon* 18 SS4400
Ham *Gloucs* 35 SO9721
Ham *Devon* 9 ST2301
Ham *Somset* 20 ST2825
Ham *Somset* 22 ST6748
Ham *Gloucs* 35 ST6898
Ham *Wilts* 23 SU3262
Ham *Gt Lon* 26 TQ1772
Ham *Kent* 29 TR3254
Ham Common *Dorset* 22 ST8125
Ham Green *H & W* 47 SO7544
Ham Green *H & W* 47 SP0163
Ham Green *Avon* 34 ST5375
Ham Green *Kent* 28 TQ8468
Ham Green *Kent* 17 TQ8926
Ham Hill *Kent* 28 TQ6960
Ham Street *Somset* 21 ST5534
Hamble *Hants* 13 SU4806
Hambleden *Bucks* 37 SU7886
Hambledon *Hants* 13 SU6414
Hambledon *Surrey* 25 SU9638
Hambleton *Lancs* 80 SD3742
Hambleton *N York* 83 SE5530
Hambleton Moss Side *Lancs* 80 SD3842
Hambridge *Somset* 21 ST3921
Hambridge *Somset* 21 ST5936
Hambrook *Avon* 35 ST6478
Hambrook *W Susx* 14 SU7806
Hamels *Herts* 39 TL3724
Hameringham *Lincs* 77 TF3167
Hamerton *Cambs* 52 TL1379
Hamilton *Strath* 116 NS7255
Hamlet *Dorset* 10 ST5908
Hamlins *E Susx* 16 TQ5908
Hammerpot *W Susx* 14 TQ0605
Hammersmith *Gt Lon* 26 TQ2378
Hammerwich *Staffs* 61 SK0707
Hammerwood *E Susx* 16 TQ4339
Hammond Street *Herts* 39 TL3304
Hammoon *Dorset* 11 ST8114
Hamnavoe *Shet* 155 HU3735
Hamnavoe *Shet* 155 HU4971
Hampden Park *E Susx* 16 TQ6002
Hampden Row *Bucks* 26 SP8501
Hamperden End *Essex* 40 TL5730
Hampnett *Gloucs* 36 SP0915
Hampole *S York* 83 SE5010
Hampreston *Dorset* 12 SZ0598
Hampsfield *Cumb* 87 SD4080
Hampson Green *Lancs* 80 SD4954
Hampstead *Gt Lon* 27 TQ2685
Hampstead Norrey's *Berks* 37 SU5276
Hampsthwaite *N York* 89 SE2559
Hampt *Cnwll* 5 SX3874
Hampton *Shrops* 60 SO7486
Hampton *H & W* 48 SP0243
Hampton *Wilts* 36 SU1892
Hampton *Gt Lon* 26 TQ1369
Hampton *Kent* 29 TR1568
Hampton Bishop *H & W* 46 SO5637
Hampton Green *Ches* 71 SJ5149
Hampton Heath *Ches* 71 SJ5049
Hampton Loade *Shrops* 60 SO7486
Hampton Lovett *H & W* 47 SO8865
Hampton Lucy *Warwks* 48 SP2557
Hampton Poyle *Oxon* 37 SP5015
Hampton Wick *Gt Lon* 26 TQ1769
Hampton in Arden *W Mids* 61 SP2080
Hampton on the Hill *Warwks* 48 SP2564
Hamptworth *Wilts* 12 SU2419
Hamrow *Norfk* 66 TF9124
Hamsey *E Susx* 15 TQ4012
Hamsey Green *Gt Lon* 27 TQ3559
Hamstall Ridware *Staffs* 73 SK1019
Hamstead *W Mids* 61 SP0592
Hamstead *IOW* 13 SZ4091
Hamstead Marshall *Berks* 24 SU4165
Hamsterley *Dur* 95 NZ1156
Hamsterley *Dur* 96 NZ1231
Hamstreet *Kent* 17 TR0033
Hamwood *Avon* 21 ST3756
Hamworthy *Dorset* 11 SY9991
Hanbury *Staffs* 73 SK1727
Hanbury *H & W* 47 SO9664
Hanby *Lincs* 64 TF0231
Hanchet End *Suffk* 53 TL6446
Hanchurch *Staffs* 72 SJ8441
Hand Green *Ches* 71 SJ5460
Hand and Pen *Devon* 9 SY0495
Handale *Cleve* 97 NZ7215
Handbridge *Ches* 71 SJ4065
Handcross *W Susx* 15 TQ2629
Handforth *Ches* 79 SJ8583
Handley *Ches* 71 SJ4657
Handley *Derbys* 74 SK3761
Handley Green *Essex* 40 TL6501
Handsacre *Staffs* 73 SK0915
Handsworth *S York* 74 SK4186
Handsworth *W Mids* 61 SP0489
Handy Cross *Bucks* 26 SU8590
Hanford *Staffs* 72 SJ8741
Hanford *Dorset* 11 ST8411
Hanging Langford *Wilts* 23 SU0337
Hangleton *W Susx* 14 TQ0803
Hangleton *E Susx* 15 TQ2607
Hanham *Avon* 35 ST6472
Hankelow *Ches* 72 SJ6645
Hankerton *Wilts* 35 ST9790
Hankham *E Susx* 16 TQ6105
Hanley *Staffs* 72 SJ8847
Hanley Castle *H & W* 47 SO8442
Hanley Child *H & W* 47 SO6565
Hanley Swan *H & W* 47 SO8142
Hanley William *H & W* 47 SO6766
Hanlith *N York* 88 SD8961
Hanmer *Clwyd* 71 SJ4539
Hannaford *Devon* 19 SS6029
Hannah *Lincs* 77 TF4979
Hannington *Nhants* 51 SP8170
Hannington *Wilts* 36 SU1793
Hannington *Hants* 24 SU5355
Hannington Wick *Wilts* 36 SU1795
Hanscombe End *Beds* 38 TL1133
Hanslope *Bucks* 38 SP8046
Hanthorpe *Lincs* 64 TF0823
Hanwell *Oxon* 49 SP4343
Hanwell *Gt Lon* 26 TQ1579
Hanworth *Norfk* 67 TG1935
Hanworth *Gt Lon* 26 TQ1271
Happendon *Strath* 108 NS8533
Happisburgh *Norfk* 67 TG3831
Happisburgh Common *Norfk* 67 TG3728
Hapsford *Ches* 71 SJ4774
Hapton *Lancs* 81 SD7931
Hapton *Norfk* 66 TM1796
Harberton *Devon* 7 SX7758
Harbertonford *Devon* 7 SX7856
Harbledown *Kent* 29 TR1357
Harborne *W Mids* 60 SP0284
Harborough Magna *Warwks* 50 SP4778
Harborough Parva *Warwks* 50 SP4878
Harbottle *Nthumb* 102 NT9304
Harbourneford *Devon* 7 SX7162
Harbours Hill *H & W* 47 SO9565
Harbridge *Hants* 12 SU1410
Harbridge Green *Hants* 12 SU1410
Harbury *Warwks* 48 SP3759
Harby *Leics* 63 SK7431
Harby *Notts* 76 SK8770
Harcombe *Devon* 9 SX8881
Harcombe *Devon* 9 SY1590
Harcombe Bottom *Devon* 10 SY3395
Harden *W York* 82 SE0838
Harden *W Mids* 60 SK0100
Hardenhuish *Wilts* 35 ST9174
Hardgate *Gramp* 135 NJ7901
Hardgate *Strath* 115 NS5072
Hardgate *D & G* 100 NX8167
Hardgate *N York* 89 SE2662
Hardham *W Susx* 14 TQ0317
Hardhorn *Lancs* 80 SD3537
Hardingham *Norfk* 66 TG0403
Hardings Wood *Staffs* 72 SJ8254
Hardingstone *Nhants* 49 SP7657
Hardington *Somset* 22 ST7452
Hardington Mandeville *Somset* 10 ST5111
Hardington Marsh *Somset* 10 ST5009
Hardington Moor *Somset* 10 ST5112
Hardisworthy *Devon* 18 SS2320
Hardley *Hants* 13 SU4205
Hardley Street *Norfk* 67 TG3701
Hardmead *Bucks* 38 SP9347
Hardraw *N York* 88 SD8691
Hardsough *Lancs* 81 SD7920
Hardstoft *Derbys* 75 SK4363
Hardway *Somset* 22 ST7234
Hardway *Hants* 13 SU6001
Hardwick *S York* 75 SK4885
Hardwick *Lincs* 76 SK8675
Hardwick *W Mids* 61 SP0798
Hardwick *Oxon* 36 SP3806

Hardwick Hempton

Hardwick *Oxon* 49 SP5729
Hardwick *Bucks* 38 SP8019
Hardwick *Nhants* 51 SP8469
Hardwick *Cambs* 52 TL3758
Hardwick *Norfk* 55 TM2289
Hardwick Green *H & W* 47 SO8133
Hardwicke *Gloucs* 35 SO7912
Hardwicke *Gloucs* 47 SO9027
Hardy's Green *Essex* 40 TL9320
Hare Croft *W York* 82 SE0835
Hare Green *Essex* 41 TM1025
Hare Hatch *Berks* 37 SU8077
Hare Street *Herts* 39 TL3929
Hare Street *Essex* 39 TL4209
Hare Street *Essex* 27 TL5300
Harebeating *E Susx* 16 TQ5910
Hareby *Lincs* 77 TF3365
Harefield *Gt Lon* 26 TQ0590
Harehill *Derbys* 73 SK1735
Harehills *W York* 82 SE3135
Harehope *Nthumb* 111 NU0920
Harelaw *Border* 109 NT5323
Harelaw *Dur* 96 NZ1652
Hareplain *Kent* 28 TQ8339
Haresceugh *Cumb* 94 NY6042
Harescombe *Gloucs* 35 SO8310
Haresfield *Gloucs* 35 SO8010
Harestock *Hants* 24 SU4631
Harewood *W York* 83 SE3245
Harewood End *H & W* 46 SO5227
Harford *Devon* 6 SX6359
Hargate *Norfk* 66 TM1191
Hargrave *Ches* 71 SJ4862
Hargrave *Nhants* 51 TL0370
Hargrave *Suffk* 53 TL7760
Hargrave Green *Suffk* 53 TL7759
Harker *Cumb* 101 NY3960
Harkstead *Suffk* 54 TM1834
Harlaston *Staffs* 61 SK2110
Harlaxton *Lincs* 63 SK8832
Harle Syke *Lancs* 81 SD8635
Harlech *Gwynd* 57 SH5831
Harlescott *Shrops* 59 SJ4916
Harlesden *Gt Lon* 26 TQ2183
Harlesthorpe *Derbys* 75 SK4976
Harleston *Devon* 7 SX7945
Harleston *Suffk* 54 TM0160
Harleston *Norfk* 55 TM2483
Harlestone *Nhants* 49 SP7064
Harley *Shrops* 59 SJ5901
Harley *S York* 74 SK3698
Harleyholm *Strath* 108 NS9238
Harlington *S York* 83 SE4802
Harlington *Beds* 38 TL0330
Harlington *Gt Lon* 26 TQ0877
Harlosh *Highld* 136 NG2841
Harlow *Essex* 39 TL4611
Harlow Hill *Nthumb* 103 NZ0768
Harlthorpe *Humb* 84 SE7337
Harlton *Cambs* 52 TL3852
Harlyn Bay *Cnwll* 4 SW8775
Harman's Cross *Dorset* 11 SY9880
Harmby *N York* 89 SE1289
Harmer Green *Herts* 39 TL2515
Harmer Hill *Shrops* 59 SJ4822
Harmondsworth *Gt Lon* 26 TQ0577
Harmston *Lincs* 76 SK9662
Harnage *Shrops* 59 SJ5604
Harnham *Nthumb* 103 NZ0781
Harnhill *Gloucs* 36 SP0600
Harold Hill *Gt Lon* 27 TQ5392
Harold Wood *Gt Lon* 27 TQ5590
Haroldston West *Dyfed* 30 SM8615
Haroldswick *Shet* 155 HP6312
Harome *N York* 90 SE6481
Harpenden *Herts* 38 TL1314
Harpford *Devon* 9 SY0990
Harpham *Humb* 91 TA0861
Harpley *H & W* 47 SO6861
Harpley *Norfk* 65 TF7825
Harpole *Nhants* 49 SP6961
Harpsdale *Highld* 151 ND1355
Harpsden *Oxon* 37 SU7680
Harpswell *Lincs* 76 SK9389
Harpur Hill *Derbys* 74 SK0671
Harpurhey *Gt Man* 79 SD8501
Harraby *Cumb* 93 NY4154
Harracott *Devon* 19 SS5527
Harrapool *Highld* 129 NG6523
Harrietfield *Tays* 125 NN9829
Harrietsham *Kent* 28 TQ8652
Harringay *Gt Lon* 27 TQ3188
Harrington *Nhants* 50 SP7780
Harrington *Lincs* 77 TF3671
Harringworth *Nhants* 51 SP9197
Harriseahead *Staffs* 72 SJ8655
Harriston *Cumb* 92 NY1541
Harrogate *N York* 82 SE3054
Harrold *Beds* 51 SP9457
Harrop Dale *Gt Man* 82 SE0008
Harrow *Gt Lon* 26 TQ1588
Harrow Green *Suffk* 54 TL8654
Harrow Weald *Gt Lon* 26 TQ1591
Harrow on the Hill *Gt Lon* 26 TQ1587
Harrowbarrow *Cnwll* 5 SX4070
Harrowden *Beds* 38 TL0647
Harrowgate Village *Dur* 96 NZ2917
Harston *Leics* 63 SK8331
Harston *Cambs* 53 TL4250
Harswell *Humb* 84 SE8240
Hart *Cleve* 97 NZ4734
Hart Station *Cleve* 97 NZ4836
Hartburn *Nthumb* 103 NZ0885
Hartest *Suffk* 54 TL8352
Hartfield *E Susx* 16 TQ4735
Hartford *Ches* 71 SJ6372
Hartford *Somset* 20 SS9529
Hartford *Cambs* 52 TL2572
Hartford End *Essex* 40 TL6817
Hartfordbridge *Hants* 25 SU7757
Hartforth *N York* 89 NZ1606
Harthill *Loth* 116 NS9064
Harthill *Ches* 71 SJ4955
Harthill *S York* 75 SK4980
Hartington *Derbys* 74 SK1260
Hartland *Devon* 18 SS2524
Hartland Quay *Devon* 18 SS2224
Hartlebury *H & W* 60 SO8471
Hartlepool *Cleve* 97 NZ5032
Hartley *Cumb* 88 NY7808
Hartley *Nthumb* 103 NZ3475
Hartley *Kent* 27 TQ6066
Hartley *Kent* 17 TQ7634
Hartley Green *Staffs* 72 SJ9829
Hartley Green *Kent* 27 TQ6067
Hartley Wespall *Hants* 24 SU6958
Hartley Wintney *Hants* 24 SU7656
Hartlip *Kent* 28 TQ8464
Hartoft End *N York* 90 SE7493
Harton *T & W* 103 NZ3765
Harton *N York* 90 SE7061
Harton *Shrops* 59 SO4888
Hartpury *Gloucs* 47 SO7924
Hartshead *W York* 82 SE1822
Hartshead Moor Side *W York* 82 SE1625
Hartshill *Staffs* 72 SJ8546
Hartshill *Warwks* 61 SP3194
Hartshorne *Derbys* 62 SK3221
Hartside *Nthumb* 111 NT9716
Hartsop *Cumb* 93 NY4013
Hartswell *Somset* 20 ST0827
Hartwell *Nhants* 38 SP7850
Hartwith *N York* 89 SE2161
Hartwood *Strath* 116 NS8459
Hartwoodmyres *Border* 109 NT4324
Harvel *Kent* 28 TQ6563
Harvington *H & W* 60 SO8775
Harvington *H & W* 48 SP0549
Harwell *Notts* 75 SK6891
Harwell *Oxon* 37 SU4989
Harwich *Essex* 41 TM2531
Harwood *Nthumb* 95 NY8233
Harwood *Nthumb* 103 NZ0189
Harwood *Gt Man* 79 SD7410
Harwood Dale *N York* 91 SE9695
Harwood Lee *Gt Man* 81 SD7411
Harworth *Notts* 75 SK6191
Hasbury *W Mids* 60 SO9582
Hascombe *Surrey* 25 TQ0039
Haselbeach *Nhants* 50 SP7177
Haselbury Plucknett *Somset* 10 ST4710
Haseley *Warwks* 48 SP2367
Haseley Green *Warwks* 48 SP2369
Haseley Knob *Warwks* 61 SP2371
Haselor *Warwks* 48 SP1257
Hasfield *Gloucs* 47 SO8227
Hasguard *Dyfed* 30 SM8509
Haskayne *Lancs* 78 SD3508
Hasketon *Suffk* 55 TM2450
Hasland *Derbys* 74 SK3969
Hasland Green *Derbys* 74 SK3968
Haslemere *Surrey* 14 SU9032
Haslingden *Lancs* 81 SD7823
Haslingfield *Cambs* 52 TL4052
Haslington *Ches* 72 SJ7355
Haslington Grane *Lancs* 81 SD7522
Hassall *Ches* 72 SJ7657
Hassall Green *Ches* 72 SJ7858
Hassell Street *Kent* 29 TR0946
Hassendean *Border* 109 NT5420
Hassingham *Norfk* 67 TG3605
Hassness *Cumb* 93 NY1816
Hassocks *W Susx* 15 TQ3015
Hassop *Derbys* 74 SK2272
Haste Hill *Surrey* 14 SU9032
Hasthorpe *Lincs* 77 TF4869
Hastingleigh *Kent* 29 TR0945
Hastings *Somset* 10 ST3116
Hastings *E Susx* 17 TQ8209
Hastingwood *Essex* 39 TL4807
Hastoe *Herts* 38 SP9209
Haswell *Dur* 96 NZ3743
Haswell Plough *Dur* 96 NZ3742
Hatch *Beds* 52 TL1547
Hatch Beauchamp *Somset* 20 ST3020
Hatch End *Beds* 51 TL0760
Hatch End *Herts* 26 TQ1390
Hatchet Gate *Hants* 12 SU3701
Hatching Green *Herts* 38 TL1312
Hatchmere *Ches* 71 SJ5571
Hatcliffe *Humb* 76 TA2100
Hatfield *S York* 83 SE6609
Hatfield *H & W* 46 SO5959
Hatfield *Herts* 39 TL2308
Hatfield Broad Oak *Essex* 39 TL5416
Hatfield Heath *Essex* 39 TL5215
Hatfield Peverel *Essex* 40 TL7911
Hatfield Woodhouse *S York* 83 SE6708
Hatford *Oxon* 36 SU3395
Hatherden *Hants* 23 SU3450
Hatherleigh *Devon* 8 SS5404
Hathern *Leics* 62 SK5022
Hatherop *Gloucs* 36 SP1505
Hathersage *Derbys* 74 SK2381
Hathersage Booths *Derbys* 74 SK2480
Hatherton *Ches* 72 SJ6847
Hatherton *Staffs* 60 SJ9510
Hatley St. George *Cambs* 52 TL2751
Hatt *Cnwll* 5 SX4062
Hattingley *Hants* 24 SU6437
Hatton *Gramp* 143 NK0537
Hatton *Tays* 127 NO4642
Hatton *Ches* 78 SJ5982
Hatton *Derbys* 73 SK2130
Hatton *Shrops* 59 SO4790
Hatton *Warwks* 48 SP2367
Hatton *Lincs* 76 TF1776
Hatton *Gt Lon* 26 TQ0975
Hatton Heath *Ches* 71 SJ4561
Hatton of Fintray *Gramp* 143 NJ8316
Haugh *Strath* 107 NS4925
Haugh *W York* 81 SD9311
Haugh *Lincs* 77 TF4175
Haugh Head *Nthumb* 111 NU0026
Haugh of Glass *Gramp* 142 NJ4238
Haugh of Urr *D & G* 100 NX8066
Haugham *Lincs* 77 TF3381
Haughhead Inn *Strath* 116 NS6079
Haughley *Suffk* 54 TM0262
Haughley Green *Suffk* 54 TM0264
Haughton *Powys* 59 SJ3018
Haughton *Shrops* 59 SJ3726
Haughton *Shrops* 59 SJ5516
Haughton *Shrops* 60 SJ7408
Haughton *Staffs* 72 SJ8620
Haughton *Notts* 75 SK6872
Haughton *Shrops* 60 SO6896
Haughton Green *Gt Man* 79 SJ9393
Haughton Moss *Ches* 71 SJ5756
Haughton le Skerne *Dur* 96 NZ3116
Haultwick *Herts* 39 TL3323
Haunton *Staffs* 61 SK2310
Hautes Croix *Jersey* 152 JS0000
Hauxley *Nthumb* 103 NU2703
Hauxton *Cambs* 53 TL4452
Havannah *Ches* 72 SJ8664
Havant *Hants* 13 SU7106
Haven *H & W* 46 SO4054
Haven Bank *Lincs* 76 TF2352
Haven Side *Humb* 85 TA1827
Havenstreet *IOW* 13 SZ5690
Havercroft *W York* 83 SE3913
Haverfordwest *Dyfed* 30 SM9515
Haverhill *Suffk* 53 TL6745
Haverigg *Cumb* 86 SD1578
Havering-atte-Bower *Essex* 27 TQ5193
Haversham *Bucks* 38 SP8242
Haverthwaite *Cumb* 87 SD3483
Haverton Hill *Cleve* 97 NZ4822
Havyat *Avon* 21 ST4761
Havyatt *Somset* 21 ST5338
Hawarden *Clwyd* 71 SJ3165
Hawbridge *H & W* 47 SO9049
Hawbush Green *Essex* 40 TL7820
Hawcoat *Cumb* 86 SD2071
Hawe's Green *Norfk* 67 TM2399
Hawen *Dyfed* 42 SN3446
Hawes *N York* 88 SD8789
Hawford *H & W* 47 SO8460
Hawick *Border* 109 NT5014
Hawk Green *Gt Man* 79 SJ9687
Hawkchurch *Devon* 10 ST3400
Hawkedon *Suffk* 53 TL7953
Hawkenbury *Kent* 28 TQ8045
Hawkeridge *Wilts* 22 ST8653
Hawkerland *Devon* 9 SY0588
Hawkes End *W Mids* 61 SP2982
Hawkesbury *Warwks* 61 SP3784
Hawkesbury *Avon* 35 ST7686
Hawkesbury Upton *Avon* 35 ST7786
Hawkhill *Nthumb* 111 NU2212
Hawkhurst *Kent* 17 TQ7530
Hawkhurst Common *E Susx* 16 TQ5217
Hawkinge *Kent* 29 TR2139
Hawkley *Hants* 24 SU7429
Hawkridge *Devon* 19 SS8630
Hawksdale *Cumb* 93 NY3648
Hawkshaw *Gt Man* 81 SD7615
Hawkshead *Cumb* 87 SD3598
Hawkshead Hill *Cumb* 86 SD3398
Hawksland *Strath* 108 NS8439
Hawkspur Green *Essex* 40 TL6532
Hawkstone *Shrops* 59 SJ5830
Hawkswick *N York* 88 SD9570
Hawksworth *W York* 82 SE1641
Hawksworth *Notts* 63 SK7543
Hawkwell *Essex* 40 TQ8591
Hawley *Hants* 25 SU8657
Hawley *Kent* 27 TQ5471
Hawling *Gloucs* 36 SP0622
Hawnby *N York* 90 SE5489
Haworth *W York* 82 SE0337
Hawstead *Suffk* 54 TL8559
Hawstead Green *Suffk* 54 TL8658
Hawthorn *Dur* 96 NZ4145
Hawthorn *M Glam* 33 ST0987
Hawthorn *Hants* 24 SU6733
Hawthorn Hill *Berks* 25 SU8773
Hawthorn Hill *Lincs* 76 TF2155
Hawthorpe *Lincs* 64 TF0427
Hawton *Notts* 75 SK7851
Haxby *N York* 90 SE6058
Haxby Gates *N York* 83 SE6056
Haxey *Humb* 75 SK7799
Haxey Turbary *Humb* 84 SE7501
Haxted *Surrey* 16 TQ4245
Haxton *Wilts* 23 SU1449
Hay *Cnwll* 3 SW8651
Hay *Cnwll* 3 SW9243
Hay *Cnwll* 3 SW9552
Hay *Cnwll* 4 SW9770
Hay Green *Norfk* 65 TF5418
Hay Street *Herts* 39 TL3926
Hay-on-Wye *Powys* 45 SO2342
Haydock *Mersyd* 78 SJ5697
Haydon *Somset* 20 ST2523
Haydon *Dorset* 11 ST6715
Haydon Bridge *Nthumb* 102 NY8464
Haydon Wick *Wilts* 36 SU1387
Haye *Cnwll* 5 SX3570
Hayes *Gt Lon* 26 TQ0980
Hayes *Gt Lon* 27 TQ4066
Hayes End *Gt Lon* 26 TQ0882
Hayfield *Strath* 123 NN0723
Hayfield *Derbys* 74 SK0386
Haygate *Shrops* 59 SJ6410
Hayhillock *Tays* 127 NO5242
Hayle *Cnwll* 2 SW5537
Hayley Green *W Mids* 60 SO9582
Haymoor Green *Ches* 72 SJ6850
Hayne *Devon* 9 SS9515
Hayne *Devon* 8 SX7685
Haynes *Beds* 38 TL0740
Haynes West End *Beds* 38 TL0640
Hayscastle *Dyfed* 30 SM8925
Hayscastle Cross *Dyfed* 30 SM9125
Haysden *Kent* 16 TQ5745
Hayton *Cumb* 92 NY1041
Hayton *Cumb* 94 NY5157
Hayton *Humb* 84 SE8245
Hayton *Notts* 75 SK7284
Hayton's Bent *Shrops* 59 SO5280
Haytor Vale *Devon* 8 SX7777
Haytown *Devon* 18 SS3814
Haywards Heath *W Susx* 15 TQ3324
Haywood *S York* 83 SE5812
Haywood *H & W* 46 SO4834
Haywood Oaks *Notts* 75 SK6055
Hazards Green *E Susx* 16 TQ6812
Hazel Grove *Gt Man* 79 SJ9287
Hazel Street *Kent* 28 TQ6939
Hazel Stub *Suffk* 53 TL6544
Hazelbank *Strath* 116 NS8345
Hazelbury Bryan *Dorset* 11 ST7408
Hazeleigh *Essex* 40 TL8203
Hazeley *Hants* 24 SU7458
Hazelhurst *Gt Man* 79 SD9600
Hazelslade *Staffs* 60 SK0212
Hazelton Walls *Fife* 126 NO3322
Hazelwood *Derbys* 62 SK3245
Hazlemere *Bucks* 26 SU8895
Hazlerigg *T & W* 103 NZ2472
Hazles *Staffs* 73 SK0047
Hazleton *Gloucs* 36 SP0718
Heacham *Norfk* 65 TF6737
Headbourne Worthy *Hants* 24 SU4832
Headbrook *H & W* 46 SO2854
Headcorn *Kent* 28 TQ8344
Headingley *W York* 82 SE2836
Headington *Oxon* 37 SP5207
Headlam *Dur* 96 NZ1818
Headless Cross *H & W* 48 SP0365
Headlesscross *Strath* 116 NS9158
Headley *Hants* 24 SU5162
Headley *Hants* 14 SU8236
Headley *Surrey* 26 TQ2054
Headley Down *Hants* 14 SU8336
Headley Heath *H & W* 61 SP0676
Headon *Notts* 75 SK7476
Heads *Strath* 116 NS7247
Heads Nook *Cumb* 94 NY5054
Heage *Derbys* 74 SK3750
Healaugh *N York* 88 SE0199
Healaugh *N York* 83 SE5047
Heald Green *Gt Man* 79 SJ8485
Heale *Devon* 19 SS6446
Heale *Somset* 20 ST2420
Heale *Somset* 21 ST3825
Healey *Nthumb* 95 NZ0158
Healey *Lancs* 81 SD8816
Healey *N York* 89 SE1780
Healey *W York* 82 SE2719
Healeyfield *Dur* 95 NZ0648
Healing *Humb* 85 TA2110
Heamoor *Cnwll* 2 SW4631
Heanor *Derbys* 62 SK4346
Heanton Punchardon *Devon* 19 SS5035
Heapey *Lancs* 81 SD5920
Heapham *Lincs* 76 SK8788
Hearn *Hants* 14 SU8337
Hearts Delight *Kent* 28 TQ8862
Heasley Mill *Devon* 19 SS7332
Heast *Highld* 129 NG6417
Heath *W York* 83 SE3520
Heath *Derbys* 75 SK4567
Heath Common *W Susx* 14 TQ0915
Heath End *Leics* 62 SK3621
Heath End *Warwks* 48 SP2360
Heath End *Hants* 24 SU4161
Heath End *Hants* 24 SU5862
Heath End *Surrey* 25 SU8549
Heath End *Bucks* 26 SU8898
Heath Green *H & W* 61 SP0771
Heath Hayes *Staffs* 60 SK0110
Heath Hill *Shrops* 60 SJ7613
Heath House *Somset* 21 ST4146
Heath Town *W Mids* 60 SO9399
Heath and Reach *Beds* 38 SP9228
Heathbrook *Shrops* 59 SJ6228
Heathcote *Shrops* 72 SJ6528
Heathcote *Derbys* 74 SK1460
Heathencote *Nhants* 49 SP7147
Heather *Leics* 62 SK3910
Heathfield *N York* 89 SE1367
Heathfield *Somset* 20 ST1626
Heathfield *Devon* 8 SX8376
Heathfield *E Susx* 16 TQ5821
Heathstock *Devon* 9 ST2402
Heathton *Shrops* 60 SO8192
Heatley *Gt Man* 79 SJ7088
Heatley *Staffs* 73 SK0626
Heaton *T & W* 103 NZ2666
Heaton *Lancs* 87 SD4460
Heaton *Gt Man* 79 SD6909
Heaton *W York* 82 SE1335
Heaton *Staffs* 72 SJ9562
Heaton Chapel *Gt Man* 79 SJ8891
Heaton Mersey *Gt Man* 79 SJ8690
Heaton Norris *Gt Man* 79 SJ8890
Heaton's Bridge *Lancs* 80 SD4011
Heaverham *Kent* 27 TQ5758
Heaviley *Gt Man* 79 SJ9088
Heavitree *Devon* 9 SX9492
Hebburn *T & W* 103 NZ3164
Hebden *N York* 88 SE0263
Hebden Bridge *W York* 82 SD9927
Hebden Green *Ches* 71 SJ6365
Hebing End *Herts* 39 TL3122
Hebron *Nthumb* 103 NZ1989
Hebron *Dyfed* 31 SN1827
Heckfield *Hants* 24 SU7160
Heckfield Green *Suffk* 54 TM1875
Heckfordbridge *Essex* 40 TL9421
Heckington *Lincs* 64 TF1444
Heckmondwike *W York* 82 SE1824
Heddington *Wilts* 22 ST9966
Heddon-on-the-Wall *Nthumb* 103 NZ1366
Hedenham *Norfk* 67 TM3193
Hedge End *Hants* 13 SU4912
Hedgerley *Bucks* 26 SU9687
Hedgerley Green *Bucks* 26 SU9787
Hedging *Somset* 20 ST3029
Hedley on the Hill *Nthumb* 95 NZ0759
Hednesford *Staffs* 60 SJ9912
Hedon *Humb* 85 TA1928
Hedsor *Bucks* 26 SU9086
Hegdon Hill *H & W* 46 SO5853
Heglibister *Shet* 155 HU3851
Heighington *Dur* 96 NZ2422
Heighington *Lincs* 76 TF0269
Heightington *H & W* 60 SO7671
Heiton *Border* 110 NT7130
Hele *Devon* 19 SS5347
Hele *Devon* 9 SS9902
Hele *Somset* 20 ST1824
Hele *Cnwll* 5 SX2198
Hele *Devon* 7 SX7470
Hele Lane *Devon* 19 SS7910
Helebridge *Cnwll* 18 SS2103
Helensburgh *Strath* 115 NS2982
Helenton *Strath* 106 NS3830
Helford *Cnwll* 3 SW7526
Helford Passage *Cnwll* 3 SW7626
Helhoughton *Norfk* 66 TF8626
Helions Bumpstead *Essex* 53 TL6541
Hell Corner *Berks* 23 SU3864
Helland *Cnwll* 4 SX0771
Hellandbridge *Cnwll* 4 SX0671
Hellescott *Cnwll* 5 SX2888
Hellesdon *Norfk* 67 TG2010
Hellesvear *Cnwll* 2 SW5040
Hellidon *Nhants* 49 SP5158
Hellifield *N York* 81 SD8556
Hellingly *E Susx* 16 TQ5812
Hellington *Norfk* 67 TG3103
Helmdon *Nhants* 49 SP5943
Helme *W York* 82 SE0912
Helmingham *Suffk* 54 TM1857
Helmington Row *Dur* 96 NZ1835
Helmsdale *Highld* 147 ND0315
Helmshore *Lancs* 81 SD7821
Helmsley *N York* 90 SE6183
Helperby *N York* 89 SE4469
Helperthorpe *N York* 91 SE9570
Helpringham *Lincs* 64 TF1440
Helpston *Cambs* 64 TF1205
Helsby *Ches* 71 SJ4975
Helsey *Lincs* 77 TF5172
Helston *Cnwll* 2 SW6527
Helstone *Cnwll* 4 SX0881
Helton *Cumb* 94 NY5021
Helwith *N York* 88 NZ0702
Helwith Bridge *N York* 88 SD8069
Hemblington *Norfk* 67 TG3411
Hemel Hempstead *Herts* 38 TL0507
Hemerdon *Devon* 6 SX5657
Hemingbrough *N York* 83 SE6730
Hemingby *Lincs* 76 TF2374
Hemingfield *S York* 83 SE3801
Hemingford Abbots *Cambs* 52 TL2871
Hemingford Grey *Cambs* 52 TL2970
Hemingstone *Suffk* 54 TM1454
Hemington *Somset* 22 ST7253
Hemington *Nhants* 51 TL0985
Hemley *Suffk* 55 TM2842
Hemlington *Cleve* 90 NZ5014
Hemp Green *Suffk* 55 TM3769
Hempholme *Humb* 85 TA0850
Hempnall *Norfk* 67 TM2494
Hempnall Green *Norfk* 67 TM2493
Hempriggs *Gramp* 141 NJ1063
Hempstead *Gloucs* 35 SO8116
Hempstead *Norfk* 66 TG1037
Hempstead *Norfk* 67 TG4028
Hempstead *Essex* 53 TL6338
Hempstead *Kent* 28 TQ7964
Hempton *Oxon* 49 SP4431
Hempton *Norfk* 66 TF9129

Hemsby Hittisleigh Cross

Hemsby *Norfk* 67 TG4917
Hemswell *Lincs* 76 SK9290
Hemsworth *W York* 83 SE4213
Hemyock *Devon* 9 ST1313
Henbury *Ches* 79 SJ8773
Henbury *Avon* 34 ST5678
Hendersyde Park *Border* 110 NT7435
Hendham *Devon* 7 SX7450
Hendomen *Powys* 58 SO2197
Hendon *Gt Lon* 26 TQ2389
Hendra *Cnwll* 3 SW7237
Hendra *Cnwll* 4 SX0275
Hendre *M Glam* 33 SS9381
Hendy *Dyfed* 32 SN5803
Heneglwys *Gwynd* 68 SH4276
Henfield *W Susx* 15 TQ2115
Henford *Devon* 5 SX3794
Henghurst *Kent* 28 TQ9536
Hengoed *Shrops* 58 SJ2833
Hengoed *Powys* 45 SO2253
Hengoed *M Glam* 33 ST1494
Hengrave *Suffk* 54 TL8268
Henham *Essex* 39 TL5428
Henhurst *Kent* 28 TQ6669
Heniarth *Powys* 58 SJ1208
Henlade *Somset* 20 ST2623
Henley *Shrops* 59 SO4588
Henley *Shrops* 46 SO5476
Henley *Gloucs* 35 SO9016
Henley *Somset* 21 ST4232
Henley *Dorset* 11 ST6904
Henley *W Susx* 14 SU8925
Henley *Suffk* 54 TM1551
Henley Green *W Mids* 61 SP3681
Henley Park *Surrey* 25 SU9352
Henley Street *Kent* 28 TQ6667
Henley's Down *E Susx* 17 TQ7312
Henley-in-Arden *Warwks* 48 SP1566
Henley-on-Thames *Oxon* 37 SU7682
Henllan *Clwyd* 70 SJ0268
Henllan *Dyfed* 31 SN3540
Henllan Amgoed *Dyfed* 31 SN1819
Henllys *Gwent* 34 ST2691
Henlow *Beds* 39 TL1738
Hennock *Devon* 8 SX8381
Henny Street *Essex* 54 TL8738
Henry's Moat (Castell Hendre) *Dyfed* 30 SN0427
Henryd *Gwynd* 69 SH7774
Hensall *N York* 83 SE5923
Henshaw *Nthumb* 102 NY7664
Hensingham *Cumb* 92 NX9816
Henstead *Suffk* 55 TM4885
Hensting *Hants* 13 SU4922
Henstridge *Somset* 22 ST7219
Henstridge Ash *Somset* 22 ST7220
Henstridge Marsh *Somset* 22 ST7320
Henton *Oxon* 37 SP7602
Henton *Somset* 21 ST4945
Henwick *H & W* 47 SO8355
Henwood *Cnwll* 5 SX2673
Heol Senni *Powys* 45 SN9223
Heol-las *W Glam* 32 SS6998
Heol-y-Cyw *M Glam* 33 SS9484
Hepburn *Nthumb* 111 NU0624
Hepscott *Nthumb* 103 NZ2284
Heptonstall *W York* 82 SD9828
Hepworth *W York* 82 SE1606
Hepworth *Suffk* 54 TL9874
Herbrandston *Dyfed* 30 SM8707
Hereford *H & W* 46 SO5139
Hereson *Kent* 29 TR3865
Heribusta *Highld* 136 NG3970
Heriot *Loth* 118 NT3953
Hermiston *Loth* 117 NT1870
Hermit Hill *S York* 74 SE3200
Hermitage *Border* 101 NY5095
Hermitage *Dorset* 11 ST6506
Hermitage *Berks* 24 SU5072
Hermitage *Hants* 13 SU7505
Hermon *Gwynd* 68 SH3968
Hermon *Dyfed* 31 SN2031
Herne *Kent* 29 TR1865
Herne Bay *Kent* 29 TR1768
Herne Common *Kent* 29 TR1765
Herne Pound *Kent* 28 TQ6654
Herner *Devon* 19 SS5826
Hernhill *Kent* 29 TR0660
Herodsfoot *Cnwll* 5 SX2160
Heronden *Kent* 29 TR2954
Herongate *Essex* 40 TQ6291
Heronsford *Strath* 98 NX1283
Heronsgate *Herts* 26 TQ0294
Herriard *Hants* 24 SU6646
Herring's Green *Beds* 38 TL0844
Herringfleet *Suffk* 67 TM4797
Herringswell *Suffk* 53 TL7270
Herringthorpe *S York* 75 SK4492
Herrington *T & W* 96 NZ3453
Hersden *Kent* 29 TR2062
Hersham *Cnwll* 18 SS2507
Hersham *Surrey* 26 TQ1164
Herstmonceux *E Susx* 16 TQ6410
Herston *Ork* 155 ND4191
Herston *Dorset* 11 SZ0178
Hertford *Herts* 39 TL3212
Hertford Heath *Herts* 39 TL3510
Hertingfordbury *Herts* 39 TL3012
Hesketh Bank *Lancs* 80 SD4423
Hesketh Lane *Lancs* 81 SD6141
Heskin Green *Lancs* 80 SD5315
Hesleden *Dur* 96 NZ4438
Hesleden *N York* 88 SD8874
Hesleyside *Nthumb* 102 NY8183
Heslington *N York* 83 SE6250
Hessay *N York* 83 SE5253
Hessenford *Cnwll* 5 SX3057
Hessett *Suffk* 54 TL9361
Hessle *W York* 84 TA0326
Hessle *Humb* 84 TA0326
Hest Bank *Lancs* 87 SD4666
Hestley Green *Suffk* 54 TM1567
Heston *Gt Lon* 26 TQ1277
Hestwall *Ork* 155 HY2618
Heswall *Mersyd* 78 SJ2681
Hethe *Oxon* 49 SP5929
Hethersett *Norfk* 66 TG1404
Hethersgill *Cumb* 101 NY4767
Hetherside *Cumb* 101 NY4366
Hetherson Green *Ches* 71 SJ5250
Hethpool *Nthumb* 110 NT8928
Hett *Dur* 96 NZ2836
Hetton *N York* 88 SD9658
Hetton Steads *Nthumb* 111 NU0335
Hetton-le-Hole *T & W* 96 NZ3547
Heugh *Nthumb* 103 NZ0873
Heugh Head *Border* 119 NT8762
Heugh-Head *Gramp* 134 NJ3811
Heveningham *Suffk* 55 TM3372
Hever *Kent* 16 TQ4745
Heversham *Cumb* 87 SD4983
Hevingham *Norfk* 67 TG1921
Hewas Water *Cnwll* 3 SW9649
Hewelsfield *Gloucs* 34 SO5602
Hewenden *W York* 82 SE0736
Hewish *Avon* 21 ST4064
Hewish *Somset* 10 ST4208
Hewood *Dorset* 10 ST3502
Hexham *Nthumb* 102 NY9364
Hextable *Kent* 27 TQ5170
Hexthorpe *S York* 83 SE5602
Hexton *Herts* 38 TL1030
Hexworthy *Cnwll* 5 SX3581
Hexworthy *Devon* 7 SX6572
Hey *Lancs* 81 SD8843
Hey Houses *Lancs* 80 SD3429
Heybridge *Essex* 40 TL8508
Heybridge *Essex* 40 TQ6398
Heybridge Basin *Essex* 40 TL8707
Heybrook Bay *Devon* 6 SX4949
Heydon *Norfk* 66 TG1127
Heydon *Cambs* 39 TL4339
Heydour *Lincs* 63 TF0039
Heyhead *Gt Man* 79 SJ8285
Heylipoll *Strath* 120 NL9743
Heylor *Shet* 155 HU2980
Heyrod *Gt Man* 79 SJ9799
Heysham *Lancs* 87 SD4160
Heyshaw *N York* 89 SE1761
Heyshott *W Susx* 14 SU8917
Heyside *Gt Man* 79 SD9307
Heytesbury *Wilts* 22 ST9242
Heythrop *Oxon* 48 SP3527
Heywood *Gt Man* 79 SD8510
Heywood *Wilts* 22 ST8753
Hibaldstow *Humb* 84 SE9702
Hickleton *S York* 83 SE4805
Hickling *Notts* 63 SK6928
Hickling *Norfk* 67 TG4124
Hickling Green *Norfk* 67 TG4123
Hickling Heath *Norfk* 67 TG4022
Hickmans Green *Kent* 29 TR0658
Hicks Forstal *Kent* 29 TR1863
Hickstead *W Susx* 15 TQ2620
Hidcote Bartrim *Gloucs* 48 SP1742
Hidcote Boyce *Gloucs* 48 SP1742
High Ackworth *W York* 83 SE4417
High Angerton *Nthumb* 103 NZ0985
High Ardwell *D & G* 98 NX0745
High Auldgirth *D & G* 100 NX9187
High Bankhill *Cumb* 94 NY5542
High Beach *Essex* 27 TQ4198
High Bentham *N York* 87 SD6669
High Bewaldeth *Cumb* 93 NY2234
High Bickington *Devon* 19 SS6020
High Bickwith *N York* 88 SD8076
High Biggins *Cumb* 87 SD6078
High Blantyre *Strath* 116 NS6756
High Bonnybridge *Cent* 116 NS8379
High Borrans *Cumb* 87 NY4300
High Bradley *N York* 82 SE0049
High Bray *Devon* 19 SS6934
High Brooms *Kent* 16 TQ5941
High Bullen *Devon* 19 SS5320
High Buston *Nthumb* 111 NU2308
High Callerton *Nthumb* 103 NZ1670
High Catton *Humb* 84 SE7153
High Close *N York* 96 NZ1715
High Cogges *Oxon* 36 SP3709
High Common *Norfk* 66 TF9905
High Coniscliffe *Dur* 96 NZ2215
High Crosby *Cumb* 93 NY4559
High Cross *Strath* 115 NS4046
High Cross *Warwks* 48 SP2067
High Cross *Hants* 13 SU7126
High Cross *Cnwll* 3 SW7429
High Cross *Herts* 39 TL3618
High Cross *W Susx* 15 TQ2417
High Cross Bank *Derbys* 73 SK2817
High Disley *Ches* 79 SJ9784
High Drummore *D & G* 98 NX1235
High Dubmire *T & W* 96 NZ3250
High Easter *Essex* 40 TL6214
High Eggborough *N York* 83 SE5721
High Ellington *N York* 89 SE2083
High Ercall *Shrops* 59 SJ5917
High Etherley *Dur* 96 NZ1728
High Ferry *Lincs* 77 TF3549
High Flats *W York* 82 SE2107
High Garrett *Essex* 40 TL7727
High Grange *Dur* 96 NZ1731
High Grantley *N York* 89 SE2369
High Green *Cumb* 87 NY4103
High Green *W York* 82 SE2014
High Green *S York* 74 SK3397
High Green *Shrops* 60 SO7083
High Green *H & W* 47 SO8745
High Green *Norfk* 66 TG1305
High Green *Suffk* 54 TL8560
High Green *Norfk* 54 TM1689
High Green *Norfk* 67 TM2898
High Halden *Kent* 28 TQ8937
High Halstow *Kent* 28 TQ7875
High Ham *Somset* 21 ST4231
High Harrington *Cumb* 92 NY0025
High Harrogate *N York* 82 SE3155
High Hartlington *Nthumb* 103 NZ0288
High Haswell *Dur* 96 NZ3643
High Hatton *Shrops* 59 SJ6124
High Hawsker *N York* 91 NZ9207
High Hesket *Cumb* 93 NY4744
High Hoyland *S York* 82 SE2710
High Hunsley *Humb* 84 SE9535
High Hurstwood *E Susx* 16 TQ4926
High Hutton *N York* 90 SE7568
High Ireby *Cumb* 93 NY2237
High Kilburn *N York* 90 SE5179
High Killerby *N York* 91 TA0683
High Knipe *Cumb* 94 NY5219
High Lands *Dur* 96 NZ1226
High Lane *Ches* 79 SJ8868
High Lane *Gt Man* 79 SJ9585
High Lane *H & W* 47 SO6760
High Lanes *Cnwll* 2 SW5637
High Laver *Essex* 39 TL5208
High Legh *Ches* 79 SJ7084
High Leven *Cleve* 89 NZ4512
High Littleton *Avon* 21 ST6458
High Lorton *Cumb* 92 NY1625
High Marnham *Notts* 75 SK8070
High Melton *S York* 83 SE5001
High Mickley *Nthumb* 103 NZ0761
High Moorsley *T & W* 96 NZ3345
High Newport *T & W* 96 NZ3754
High Newton *Cumb* 87 SD4082
High Newton by-the-Sea *Nthumb* 111 NU2325
High Nibthwaite *Cumb* 86 SD2989
High Offley *Staffs* 72 SJ7826
High Ongar *Essex* 40 TL5603
High Onn *Staffs* 72 SJ8216
High Park Corner *Essex* 41 TM0320
High Pennyvenie *Strath* 107 NS4907
High Post *Wilts* 23 SU1536
High Roding *Essex* 40 TL6017
High Row *Cumb* 93 NY3535
High Row *Cumb* 93 NY3821
High Salter *Lancs* 87 SD6062
High Salvington *W Susx* 14 TQ1206
High Scales *Cumb* 93 NY1845
High Seaton *Cumb* 92 NY0231
High Shaw *N York* 88 SD8691
High Side *Cumb* 93 NY2330
High Spen *T & W* 96 NZ1359
High Stoop *Dur* 95 NZ1040
High Street *Cnwll* 3 SW9653
High Street *Cambs* 52 TL3762
High Street *Suffk* 55 TM4171
High Street *Suffk* 55 TM4355
High Street *Kent* 17 TQ7430
High Street *Kent* 29 TR0862
High Throston *Cleve* 97 NZ4833
High Town *Staffs* 60 SJ9911
High Toynton *Lincs* 77 TF2869
High Trewhitt *Nthumb* 111 NU0105
High Urpeth *Dur* 96 NZ2354
High Valleyfield *Fife* 117 NT0086
High Warden *Nthumb* 102 NY9067
High Westwood *Dur* 95 NZ1155
High Woolaston *Gloucs* 34 ST5899
High Worsall *Cleve* 89 NZ3809
High Wray *Cumb* 87 SD3799
High Wych *Herts* 39 TL4614
High Wycombe *Bucks* 26 SU8693
Higham *Lancs* 81 SD8136
Higham *S York* 82 SE3107
Higham *Derbys* 74 SK3859
Higham *Suffk* 53 TL7465
Higham *Suffk* 54 TM0335
Higham *Kent* 16 TQ6048
Higham *Kent* 28 TQ7171
Higham Dykes *Nthumb* 103 NZ1375
Higham Ferrers *Nhants* 51 SP9668
Higham Gobion *Beds* 38 TL1032
Higham Hill *Gt Lon* 27 TQ3590
Higham on the Hill *Leics* 61 SP3895
Highampton *Devon* 18 SS4804
Highams Park *Gt Lon* 27 TQ3891
Highbridge *Somset* 21 ST3247
Highbridge *Hants* 13 SU4621
Highbrook *W Susx* 15 TQ3630
Highburton *W York* 82 SE1813
Highbury *Somset* 22 ST6949
Highbury *Gt Lon* 27 TQ3185
Highclere *Hants* 24 SU4359
Highcliffe *Dorset* 12 SZ2193
Highcliffane *Derbys* 73 SK2947
Higher Alham *Somset* 22 ST6741
Higher Ansty *Dorset* 11 ST7604
Higher Ballam *Lancs* 80 SD3630
Higher Bartle *Lancs* 80 SD5033
Higher Berry End *Beds* 38 SP9834
Higher Bockhampton *Dorset* 11 SY7292
Higher Brixham *Devon* 7 SX9155
Higher Burrowton *Devon* 9 SY0097
Higher Burwardsley *Ches* 71 SJ5156
Higher Chillington *Somset* 10 ST3810
Higher Combe *Somset* 20 SS9030
Higher Coombe *Dorset* 10 SY5391
Higher Gabwell *Devon* 7 SX9169
Higher Green *Gt Man* 79 SD7000
Higher Halstock Leigh *Dorset* 10 ST5107
Higher Harpers *Lancs* 81 SD8237
Higher Heysham *Lancs* 87 SD4160
Higher Hurdsfield *Ches* 79 SJ9374
Higher Irlam *Gt Man* 79 SJ7295
Higher Kinnerton *Clwyd* 71 SJ3261
Higher Melcombe *Dorset* 11 ST7402
Higher Muddiford *Devon* 19 SS5638
Higher Nyland *Dorset* 22 ST7322
Higher Ogden *Gt Man* 82 SD9512
Higher Pentire *Cnwll* 2 SW6525
Higher Penwortham *Lancs* 80 SD5128
Higher Studfold *N York* 88 SD8170
Higher Town *IOS* 2 SV9215
Higher Town *Cnwll* 3 SW8044
Higher Town *Cnwll* 4 SX0061
Higher Tregantle *Cnwll* 5 SX4052
Higher Walton *Lancs* 81 SD5727
Higher Walton *Ches* 78 SJ5985
Higher Wambrook *Somset* 10 ST2908
Higher Waterston *Dorset* 11 SY7295
Higher Whatcombe *Dorset* 11 ST8301
Higher Wheelton *Lancs* 81 SD6022
Higher Whiteleigh *Cnwll* 5 SX2494
Higher Whitley *Ches* 78 SJ6180
Higher Wraxhall *Dorset* 10 ST5601
Higher Wych *Ches* 71 SJ4943
Higherford *Lancs* 81 SD8640
Highfield *Strath* 115 NS3150
Highfield *T & W* 96 NZ1458
Highfield *Humb* 84 SE7236
Highfield *Devon* 8 SX7097
Highfields *S York* 83 SE5406
Highgate *N York* 83 SE5918
Highgate *Gt Lon* 27 TQ2887
Highgate *E Susx* 16 TQ4234
Highgate Head *Derbys* 74 SK0486
Highgreen Manor *Nthumb* 102 NY8091
Highlane *S York* 74 SK4081
Highlaws *Cumb* 92 NY1449
Highleadon *Gloucs* 47 SO7623
Highleigh *W Susx* 14 SZ8498
Highley *Shrops* 60 SO7483
Highmoor *Cumb* 93 NY2647
Highmoor *Oxon* 37 SU7084
Highmoor Cross *Oxon* 37 SU7084
Highmoor Hill *Gwent* 34 ST4689
Highnam *Gloucs* 35 SO7817
Highnam Green *Gloucs* 35 SO7920
Highridge *Avon* 21 ST5567
Highstead *Kent* 29 TR2166
Highsted *Kent* 28 TQ9061
Highstreet Green *Surrey* 14 SU9835
Highstreet Green *Essex* 53 TL7634
Hightae *D & G* 100 NY0978
Highter's Heath *W Mids* 61 SP0879
Hightown *Mersyd* 78 SD3003
Hightown *Ches* 72 SJ8762
Hightown *Hants* 12 SU1704
Hightown Green *Suffk* 54 TL9756
Highway *H & W* 46 SO4549
Highway *Wilts* 36 SU0474
Highweek *Devon* 7 SX8472
Highwood *Staffs* 73 SK0931
Highwood Hill *Gt Lon* 26 TQ2193
Highworth *Wilts* 36 SU2092
Hilden Park *Kent* 16 TQ5747
Hildenborough *Kent* 16 TQ5648
Hildersham *Cambs* 53 TL5448
Hilderstone *Staffs* 72 SJ9534
Hilderthorpe *Humb* 91 TA1766
Hilfield *Dorset* 11 ST6305
Hilgay *Norfk* 65 TL6298
Hill *Warwks* 50 SP4566
Hill *Avon* 35 ST6495
Hill Brow *Hants* 14 SU7926
Hill Chorlton *Staffs* 72 SJ7939
Hill Cliff *Ches* 78 SJ6185
Hill Common *Somset* 20 ST1426
Hill Common *Norfk* 67 TG4122
Hill Deverill *Wilts* 22 ST8640
Hill Dyke *Lincs* 77 TF3447
Hill End *Fife* 117 NT0395
Hill End *Dur* 95 NZ0136
Hill End *Gloucs* 47 SO9037
Hill Green *Kent* 28 TQ8362
Hill Head *Hants* 13 SU5402
Hill Ridware *Staffs* 73 SK0817
Hill Side *W York* 82 SE1717
Hill Side *H & W* 47 SO7561
Hill Top *Dur* 95 NY9924
Hill Top *W York* 82 SE0712
Hill Top *W York* 83 SE3315
Hill Top *S York* 74 SK3992
Hill Top *W Mids* 60 SO9993
Hill Top *Hants* 13 SU4003
Hill of Beath *Fife* 117 NT1590
Hill of Fearn *Highld* 147 NH8377
Hillam *N York* 83 SE5028
Hillbeck *Cumb* 95 NY7915
Hillborough *Kent* 29 TR2168
Hillbutts *Dorset* 11 ST9901
Hillcott *Wilts* 23 SU1158
Hillend *Strath* 116 NS8267
Hillend *Fife* 117 NT1483
Hillend *Loth* 117 NT2566
Hillend *W Glam* 31 SS4190
Hillersland *Gloucs* 34 SO5614
Hillerton *Devon* 8 SX7298
Hillesden *Bucks* 49 SP6828
Hillesley *Avon* 35 ST7689
Hillfarrance *Somset* 20 ST1624
Hillfoot *Strath* 115 NS5472
Hillgrove *W Susx* 14 SU9428
Hillhampton *H & W* 46 SO5847
Hillhead *Strath* 108 NS9840
Hillhead *Devon* 7 SX9054
Hillhead of Cocklaw *Gramp* 143 NK0844
Hillhead of Durno *Gramp* 142 NJ7128
Hilliard's Cross *Staffs* 61 SK1511
Hilliclay *Highld* 151 ND1764
Hillingdon *Gt Lon* 26 TQ0782
Hillington *Strath* 115 NS5164
Hillington *Norfk* 65 TF7225
Hillis Corner *IOW* 13 SZ4793
Hillmorton *Warwks* 50 SP5373
Hillock Vale *Lancs* 81 SD7629
Hillowtan *D & G* 100 NX7763
Hillpool *H & W* 60 SO8976
Hillpound *Hants* 13 SU5715
Hills Town *Derbys* 75 SK4869
Hillside *T & W* 135 NO6960
Hillside *Gramp* 135 NO9197
Hillside *Devon* 7 SX7060
Hillstreet *Hants* 12 SU3416
Hillswick *Shet* 155 HU2877
Hilltown *Devon* 8 SX5380
Hillwell *Shet* 155 HU3714
Hilmarton *Wilts* 35 SU0175
Hilperton *Wilts* 22 ST8759
Hilperton Marsh *Wilts* 22 ST8659
Hilsea *Hants* 13 SU6503
Hilston *Humb* 85 TA2833
Hilston Park *Gwent* 34 SO4418
Hiltingbury *Hants* 13 SU4221
Hilton *Border* 119 NT8750
Hilton *Cumb* 94 NY7320
Hilton *Dur* 96 NZ1622
Hilton *Cleve* 89 NZ4611
Hilton *Derbys* 73 SK2430
Hilton *Shrops* 60 SO7795
Hilton *Dorset* 11 ST7802
Hilton *Cambs* 52 TL2966
Hilton of Cadboll *Highld* 147 NH8776
Himbleton *H & W* 47 SO9458
Himley *Staffs* 60 SO8891
Hincaster *Cumb* 87 SD5084
Hinckley *Leics* 50 SP4294
Hinderclay *Suffk* 54 TM0276
Hinderwell *N York* 97 NZ7916
Hindford *Shrops* 59 SJ3333
Hindhead *Surrey* 14 SU8835
Hindle Fold *Lancs* 81 SD7332
Hindley *Nthumb* 95 NZ0459
Hindley *Gt Man* 78 SD6104
Hindley Green *Gt Man* 79 SD6403
Hindlip *H & W* 47 SO8858
Hindolveston *Norfk* 66 TG0329
Hindon *Wilts* 22 ST9132
Hindringham *Norfk* 66 TF9836
Hingham *Norfk* 66 TG0202
Hinksford *Staffs* 60 SO8689
Hinnington *Shrops* 60 SJ7404
Hinstock *Shrops* 72 SJ6925
Hintlesham *Suffk* 54 TM0843
Hinton *Shrops* 59 SJ4008
Hinton *H & W* 46 SO3338
Hinton *Shrops* 59 SO6582
Hinton *Gloucs* 35 SO6803
Hinton *Avon* 35 ST7376
Hinton *Hants* 12 SZ2195
Hinton Admiral *Hants* 12 SZ2096
Hinton Ampner *Hants* 13 SU6027
Hinton Blewett *Somset* 21 ST5956
Hinton Charterhouse *Avon* 22 ST7758
Hinton Green *H & W* 48 SP0240
Hinton Marsh *Hants* 24 SU5828
Hinton Martell *Dorset* 11 SU0106
Hinton Parva *Wilts* 36 SU2383
Hinton St. George *Somset* 10 ST4212
Hinton St. Mary *Dorset* 11 ST7816
Hinton Waldrist *Oxon* 36 SU3799
Hinton on the Green *H & W* 48 SP0240
Hinton-in-the-Hedges *Nhants* 49 SP5636
Hints *Staffs* 61 SK1502
Hints *Shrops* 46 SO6174
Hinwick *Beds* 51 SP9361
Hinxhill *Kent* 28 TR0442
Hinxton *Cambs* 53 TL4945
Hinxworth *Herts* 39 TL2340
Hipperholme *W York* 82 SE1225
Hipswell *N York* 89 SE1898
Hirn *Gramp* 135 NJ7200
Hirnant *Powys* 58 SJ0422
Hirst *Nthumb* 103 NZ2787
Hirst Courtney *N York* 83 SE6124
Hirwaen *Clwyd* 70 SJ1361
Hirwaun *M Glam* 33 SN9505
Hiscott *Devon* 19 SS5426
Histon *Cambs* 53 TL4463
Hitcham *Suffk* 54 TL9851
Hitcham Causeway *Suffk* 54 TL9852
Hitcham Street *Suffk* 54 TL9851
Hitchin *Herts* 39 TL1829
Hither Green *Gt Lon* 27 TQ3874
Hittisleigh *Devon* 8 SX7395
Hittisleigh Cross *Devon* 8 SX7395

Hive Humberstone

Hive *Humb* 84 SE8230
Hixon *Staffs* 73 SK0025
Hoaden *Kent* 29 TR2759
Hoar Cross *Staffs* 73 SK1323
Hoarwithy *H & W* 46 SO5429
Hoath *Kent* 29 TR2064
Hoathly *Kent* 28 TQ6536
Hobarris *Shrops* 46 SO3178
Hobbles Green *Suffk* 53 TL7053
Hobbs Cross *Essex* 27 TQ4799
Hobkirk *Border* 110 NT5811
Hobland Hall *Norfk* 67 TG5001
Hobsick *Notts* 75 SK4549
Hobson *Dur* 96 NZ1756
Hoby *Leics* 63 SK6617
Hockering *Norfk* 66 TG0713
Hockerton *Notts* 75 SK7156
Hockley *Ches* 79 SJ9383
Hockley *Staffs* 61 SK2200
Hockley *W Mids* 61 SP2779
Hockley *Essex* 40 TQ8392
Hockley Heath *W Mids* 61 SP1572
Hockliffe *Beds* 38 SP9726
Hockwold cum Wilton *Norfk* 53 TL7388
Hockworthy *Devon* 20 ST0319
Hoddesdon *Herts* 39 TL3708
Hoddleston *Lancs* 81 SD7122
Hoddom Cross *D & G* 101 NY1873
Hoddom Mains *D & G* 100 NY1572
Hodgehill *Ches* 79 SJ8269
Hodgeston *Dyfed* 30 SS0399
Hodnet *Shrops* 59 SJ6128
Hodsall Street *Kent* 27 TQ6263
Hodsock *Notts* 75 SK6185
Hodson *Wilts* 36 SU1780
Hodthorpe *Derbys* 75 SK5376
Hoe *Hants* 13 SU5617
Hoe *Norfk* 66 TF9916
Hoe Gate *Hants* 13 SU6213
Hoff *Cumb* 94 NY6717
Hog Hill *E Susx* 17 TQ8815
Hogben's Hill *Kent* 28 TR0356
Hoggards Green *Suffk* 54 TL8856
Hoggeston *Bucks* 38 SP8024
Hoghton *Lancs* 81 SD6125
Hoghton Bottoms *Lancs* 81 SD6227
Hognaston *Derbys* 73 SK2350
Hogrill's End *Warwks* 61 SP2292
Hogsthorpe *Lincs* 77 TF5372
Holbeach *Lincs* 64 TF3624
Holbeach Bank *Lincs* 64 TF3527
Holbeach Clough *Lincs* 64 TF3526
Holbeach Drove *Lincs* 64 TF3212
Holbeach Hurn *Lincs* 65 TF3926
Holbeach St. Johns *Lincs* 64 TF3518
Holbeach St. Mark's *Lincs* 64 TF3731
Holbeach St. Matthew *Lincs* 65 TF4132
Holbeck *Notts* 75 SK5473
Holbeck Woodhouse *Notts* 75 SK5472
Holberrow Green *H & W* 48 SP0259
Holbeton *Devon* 6 SX6150
Holborn *Gt Lon* 27 TQ3181
Holborough *Kent* 28 TQ7062
Holbrook *Derbys* 62 SK3644
Holbrook *S York* 75 SK4481
Holbrook *Suffk* 54 TM1636
Holbrook Moor *Derbys* 62 SK3645
Holburn *Nthumb* 111 NU0436
Holbury *Hants* 13 SU4303
Holcombe *Gt Man* 81 SD7816
Holcombe *Somset* 20 ST1129
Holcombe *Somset* 22 ST6749
Holcombe *Devon* 7 SX9574
Holcombe Brook *Gt Man* 81 SD7815
Holcombe Rogus *Devon* 20 ST0518
Holcot *Nhants* 50 SP7969
Holden *Lancs* 81 SD7749
Holden *Lancs* 81 SD8833
Holden Gate *W York* 81 SD8923
Holdenby *Nhants* 50 SP6967
Holder's Green *Essex* 40 TL6328
Holdgate *Shrops* 59 SO5689
Holdingham *Lincs* 76 TF0547
Holditch *Dorset* 10 ST3402
Holdsworth *W York* 82 SE0829
Hole *Devon* 18 SS4206
Hole Street *W Susx* 15 TQ1314
Hole-in-the-Wall *H & W* 46 SO6128
Holehouse *Derbys* 79 SK0092
Holemoor *Devon* 18 SS4205
Holford *Somset* 20 ST1541
Holgate *N York* 83 SE5851
Holker *Cumb* 87 SD3676
Holkham *Norfk* 66 TF8943
Hollacombe *Devon* 18 SS3702
Hollam *Somset* 20 SS9232
Holland Fen *Lincs* 76 TF2349
Holland Lees *Lancs* 78 SD5208
Holland-on-Sea *Essex* 41 TM1916
Hollandstoun *Ork* 155 HY7553
Hollesley *Suffk* 55 TM3544
Hollicombe *Devon* 7 SX8962
Hollies Hill *H & W* 60 SO9377
Hollin Green *Ches* 71 SJ5952
Hollingbourne *Kent* 28 TQ8455
Hollingdon *Bucks* 38 SP8727
Hollingthorpe *W York* 83 SE3831
Hollington *Staffs* 73 SK0538
Hollington *Derbys* 73 SK2239
Hollingworth *Gt Man* 79 SK0096
Hollinlane *Ches* 79 SJ8384
Hollins *Gt Man* 79 SD8107
Hollins *Staffs* 73 SJ9947
Hollins *Derbys* 74 SK3271
Hollins End *S York* 74 SK3883
Hollins Green *Ches* 79 SJ6990
Hollins Lane *Lancs* 80 SD4951
Hollinsclough *Staffs* 74 SK0666
Hollinswood *Shrops* 60 SJ7008
Hollinwood *Shrops* 59 SJ5136
Holllingrove *E Susx* 16 TQ6821
Hollocombe *Devon* 19 SS6311
Holloway *Derbys* 74 SK3256
Holloway *Wilts* 22 ST8730
Holloway *Gt Lon* 27 TQ3086
Hollowell *Nhants* 50 SP6971
Hollowmoor Heath *Ches* 71 SJ4868
Holly End *Norfk* 65 TF4906
Holly Green *H & W* 47 SO8641
Hollybush *Strath* 106 NS3915
Hollybush *Gwent* 33 SO1603
Hollybush *H & W* 47 SO7536
Hollyhurst *Ches* 71 SJ5744
Hollym *Humb* 85 TA3425
Hollywood *H & W* 61 SP0877
Holmbridge *W York* 82 SE1206
Holmbury St. Mary *Surrey* 14 TQ1143
Holmbush *Cnwll* 3 SX0352
Holmcroft *Staffs* 72 SJ9024
Holme *Cumb* 87 SD5278
Holme *W York* 82 SE1105
Holme *N York* 89 SE3582
Holme *Humb* 84 SE9206
Holme *Notts* 75 SK8059
Holme *Cambs* 52 TL1987
Holme Chapel *Lancs* 81 SD8728
Holme Green *N York* 83 SE5541
Holme Hale *Norfk* 66 TF8807
Holme Lacy *H & W* 46 SO5535
Holme Marsh *H & W* 46 SO3454
Holme Pierrepont *Notts* 62 SK6238
Holme St. Cuthbert *Cumb* 92 NY1047
Holme next the Sea *Norfk* 65 TF7043
Holme on the Wolds *Humb* 84 SE9646
Holme upon Spalding Moor *Humb* 84 SE8038
Holmer *H & W* 46 SO5042
Holmer Green *Bucks* 26 SU9097
Holmes Chapel *Ches* 72 SJ7667
Holmes Hill *E Susx* 16 TQ5312
Holmesfield *Derbys* 74 SK3277
Holmeswood *Lancs* 80 SD4316
Holmethorpe *Surrey* 27 TQ2851
Holmewood *Derbys* 75 SK4365
Holmfield *W York* 82 SE0828
Holmfirth *W York* 82 SE1408
Holmgate *Derbys* 74 SK3763
Holmhead *Strath* 107 NS5620
Holmpton *Humb* 85 TA3623
Holmrook *Cumb* 86 SD0799
Holmsey Green *Suffk* 53 TL6978
Holmshurst *E Susx* 16 TQ6425
Holmside *Dur* 96 NZ2149
Holmwood *Surrey* 15 TQ1647
Holmwrangle *Cumb* 94 NY5148
Holne *Devon* 7 SX7069
Holnest *Dorset* 11 ST6510
Holnicote *Somset* 20 SS9146
Holsworthy *Devon* 18 SS3403
Holsworthy Beacon *Devon* 18 SS3608
Holt *Clwyd* 71 SJ4053
Holt *H & W* 47 SO8362
Holt *Wilts* 22 ST8661
Holt *Dorset* 12 SU0303
Holt *Norfk* 66 TG0838
Holt End *H & W* 48 SP0769
Holt Fleet *H & W* 47 SO8263
Holt Green *Lancs* 78 SD3905
Holt Heath *H & W* 47 SO8163
Holt Heath *Dorset* 12 SU0504
Holt Street *Kent* 29 TR2551
Holtby *N York* 83 SE6754
Holton *Oxon* 37 SP6006
Holton *Somset* 22 ST6826
Holton *Suffk* 55 TM4077
Holton Heath *Dorset* 11 SY9490
Holton Hill *E Susx* 16 TQ6625
Holton St. Mary *Suffk* 54 TM0536
Holton cum Beckering *Lincs* 76 TF1181
Holton le Clay *Lincs* 85 TA2802
Holton le Moor *Lincs* 76 TF0897
Holtye *E Susx* 16 TQ4539
Holway *Clwyd* 70 SJ1876
Holwell *Leics* 63 SK7323
Holwell *Oxon* 36 SP2309
Holwell *Dorset* 11 ST6911
Holwell *Herts* 39 TL1633
Holwick *Dur* 95 NY9126
Holworth *Dorset* 11 SY7683
Holy Cross *H & W* 60 SO9278
Holy Island *Nthumb* 111 NU1241
Holybourne *Hants* 24 SU7340
Holyfield *Essex* 39 TL3803
Holyhead *Gwynd* 68 SH2482
Holylee *Border* 109 NT3937
Holymoorside *Derbys* 74 SK3369
Holyport *Berks* 26 SU8977
Holystone *Nthumb* 102 NT9502
Holytown *Strath* 116 NS7660
Holywell *Clwyd* 70 SJ1875
Holywell *Dorset* 10 ST5904
Holywell *Cnwll* 4 SW7659
Holywell *Cambs* 52 TL3370
Holywell Green *W York* 82 SE0819
Holywell Lake *Somset* 20 ST1020
Holywell Row *Suffk* 53 TL7177
Holywood *D & G* 100 NX9480
Hom Green *H & W* 34 SO5822
Homer *Shrops* 59 SJ6101
Homer Green *Mersyd* 78 SD3402
Homersfield *Suffk* 55 TM2885
Homescales *Cumb* 87 SD5587
Homington *Wilts* 23 SU1226
Honey Hill *Kent* 29 TR1161
Honey Tye *Suffk* 54 TL9535
Honeyborough *Dyfed* 30 SM9406
Honeybourne *H & W* 48 SP1144
Honeychurch *Devon* 8 SS6303
Honeystreet *Wilts* 23 SU1061
Honiley *Warwks* 61 SP2372
Honing *Norfk* 67 TG3227
Honingham *Norfk* 66 TG1011
Honington *Lincs* 63 SK9443
Honington *Warwks* 48 SP2642
Honington *Suffk* 54 TL9174
Honiton *Devon* 9 ST1600
Honley *W York* 82 SE1311
Honnington *Shrops* 72 SJ7215
Hoo *Kent* 27 TQ2964
Hoo *Kent* 28 TQ7872
Hoo End *Herts* 39 TL1820
Hoo Green *Ches* 79 SJ7182
Hoo Meavy *Devon* 6 SX5265
Hoobrook *H & W* 60 SO8374
Hood Green *S York* 82 SE3102
Hood Hill *S York* 74 SK3697
Hooe *Devon* 6 SX5052
Hooe *E Susx* 16 TQ6809
Hooe Common *E Susx* 16 TQ6910
Hoohill *Lancs* 80 SD3237
Hook *Humb* 84 SE7625
Hook *Dyfed* 30 SM9711
Hook *Devon* 10 ST3005
Hook *Wilts* 36 SU0784
Hook *Hants* 24 SU7254
Hook *Cambs* 65 TL4293
Hook *Surrey* 26 TQ1864
Hook *Kent* 27 TQ6170
Hook Bank *H & W* 47 SO8140
Hook Green *Kent* 16 TQ6535
Hook Norton *Oxon* 48 SP3533
Hook Street *Gloucs* 35 ST6799
Hook Street *Wilts* 36 SU0884
Hookagate *Shrops* 59 SJ4609
Hooke *Dorset* 10 ST5300
Hookgate *Staffs* 72 SJ7435
Hookway *Devon* 8 SX8598
Hookwood *Surrey* 15 TQ2643
Hooley *Surrey* 27 TQ2856
Hooley Bridge *Gt Man* 81 SD8511
Hooton *Ches* 71 SJ3678
Hooton Levitt *S York* 75 SK5291
Hooton Pagnell *S York* 83 SE4807
Hooton Roberts *S York* 75 SK4897
Hop Pole *Lincs* 64 TF1813
Hopcrofts Holt *Oxon* 49 SP4625
Hope *Powys* 58 SJ2507
Hope *Clwyd* 71 SJ3058
Hope *Shrops* 59 SJ3401
Hope *Staffs* 73 SK1254
Hope *Derbys* 74 SK1783
Hope *Shrops* 46 SO5974
Hope *Devon* 7 SX6740
Hope Bowdler *Shrops* 59 SO4792
Hope End Green *Essex* 40 TL5720
Hope Mansell *H & W* 35 SO6219
Hope under Dinmore *H & W* 46 SO5052
Hopehouse *Border* 109 NT2916
Hopeman *Gramp* 147 NJ1469
Hopesay *Shrops* 59 SO3983
Hopetown *W York* 83 SE3923
Hopperton *N York* 83 SE4256
Hopsford *Warwks* 50 SP4284
Hopstone *Shrops* 60 SO7894
Hopton *Shrops* 59 SJ3820
Hopton *Staffs* 72 SJ9426
Hopton *Derbys* 73 SK2653
Hopton *Suffk* 54 TL9979
Hopton Cangeford *Shrops* 59 SO5480
Hopton Castle *Shrops* 46 SO3678
Hopton Wafers *Shrops* 47 SO6376
Hopton on Sea *Norfk* 67 TM5299
Hoptonheath *Shrops* 46 SO3877
Hopwas *Staffs* 61 SK1804
Hopwood *Gt Man* 79 SD8609
Hopwood *H & W* 61 SP0375
Horam *E Susx* 16 TQ5717
Horbling *Lincs* 64 TF1135
Horbury *W York* 82 SE2918
Horcott *Gloucs* 36 SP1500
Horden *Dur* 96 NZ4440
Horderley *Shrops* 59 SO4086
Hordle *Hants* 12 SZ2795
Hordley *Shrops* 59 SJ3831
Horeb *Dyfed* 31 SN3942
Horeb *Dyfed* 32 SN4905
Horfield *Avon* 34 ST5976
Horham *Suffk* 55 TM2072
Horkesley Green *Essex* 41 TL9831
Horkesley Heath *Essex* 41 TL9829
Horkstow *Humb* 84 SE9817
Horley *Oxon* 49 SP4144
Horley *Surrey* 15 TQ2842
Horn Hill *Bucks* 26 TQ0192
Horn Street *Kent* 29 TR1836
Hornblotton Green *Somset* 21 ST5833
Hornby *N York* 89 NZ3605
Hornby *Lancs* 87 SD5868
Hornby *N York* 89 SE2293
Horncastle *Lincs* 77 TF2669
Hornchurch *Gt Lon* 27 TQ5387
Horncliffe *Nthumb* 110 NT9249
Horndean *Border* 110 NT9049
Horndean *Hants* 13 SU7013
Horndon *Devon* 5 SX5280
Horndon on the Hill *Essex* 40 TQ6683
Horne *Surrey* 15 TQ3344
Horne Row *Essex* 40 TL7704
Horner *Somset* 20 SS9045
Horners Green *Suffk* 54 TL9641
Horney Common *E Susx* 16 TQ4525
Horning *Norfk* 67 TG3417
Horninghold *Leics* 51 SP8097
Horninglow *Staffs* 73 SK2425
Horningsea *Cambs* 53 TL4962
Horningsham *Wilts* 22 ST8141
Horningtoft *Norfk* 66 TF9323
Horningtops *Cnwll* 5 SX2760
Horns Cross *Devon* 18 SS3823
Horns Cross *E Susx* 17 TQ8222
Hornsby *Cumb* 94 NY5150
Hornsby *Somset* 10 ST3310
Hornsbygate *Cumb* 94 NY5250
Hornsea *Humb* 85 TA1947
Hornsey *Gt Lon* 27 TQ3089
Hornton *Oxon* 48 SP3945
Horpit *Wilts* 36 SU2183
Horra *Shet* 155 HU4693
Horrabridge *Devon* 6 SX5169
Horridge *Devon* 7 SX7674
Horringer *Suffk* 54 TL8261
Horringford *IOW* 13 SZ5485
Horrocks Fold *Gt Man* 81 SD7012
Horrocksford *Lancs* 81 SD7543
Horsacott *Devon* 19 SS5231
Horsebridge *Shrops* 59 SJ3606
Horsebridge *Staffs* 72 SJ9553
Horsebridge *Hants* 23 SU3430
Horsebridge *Devon* 5 SX4075
Horsebridge *E Susx* 16 TQ5811
Horsebrook *Staffs* 60 SJ8810
Horsecastle *Avon* 21 ST4265
Horsedown *Cnwll* 2 SW6134
Horsegate *Lincs* 64 TF1510
Horsehay *Shrops* 60 SJ6707
Horseheath *Cambs* 53 TL6147
Horsehouse *N York* 88 SE0480
Horsell *Surrey* 25 SU9959
Horseman's Green *Clwyd* 71 SJ4441
Horsenden *Bucks* 37 SP7902
Horseshoes *Wilts* 22 ST9159
Horsey *Somset* 21 ST3239
Horsey *Norfk* 67 TG4622
Horsey Corner *Norfk* 67 TG4523
Horsford *Norfk* 67 TG1916
Horsforth *W York* 82 SE2338
Horsham *H & W* 47 SO7358
Horsham *W Susx* 15 TQ1731
Horsham St. Faith *Norfk* 67 TG2115
Horsington *Somset* 22 ST7023
Horsington *Lincs* 76 TF1968
Horsley *Nthumb* 102 NY8496
Horsley *Nthumb* 103 NZ0965
Horsley *Derbys* 62 SK3744
Horsley *Gloucs* 35 ST8497
Horsley Cross *Essex* 41 TM1227
Horsley Woodhouse *Derbys* 62 SK3944
Horsley's Green *Bucks* 37 SU7894
Horsley-Gate *Derbys* 74 SK3076
Horsleycross Street *Essex* 41 TM1228
Horsleyhill *Border* 109 NT5319
Horsmonden *Kent* 28 TQ7040
Horspath *Oxon* 37 SP5705
Horstead *Norfk* 67 TG2619
Horsted Keynes *W Susx* 15 TQ3828
Horton *Lancs* 81 SD8550
Horton *Shrops* 59 SJ4929
Horton *Shrops* 60 SJ6814
Horton *Staffs* 72 SJ9457
Horton *Nhants* 51 SP8154
Horton *Bucks* 38 SP9219
Horton *W Glam* 32 SS4785
Horton *Somset* 10 ST3214
Horton *Avon* 35 ST7584
Horton *Dorset* 12 SU0307
Horton *Wilts* 23 SU0463
Horton *Berks* 26 TQ0175
Horton Cross *Somset* 10 ST3315
Horton Green *Ches* 71 SJ4549
Horton Heath *Hants* 13 SU4916
Horton Kirby *Kent* 27 TQ5668
Horton in Ribblesdale *N York* 88 SD8071
Horton-cum-Studley *Oxon* 37 SP5912
Horwich *Gt Man* 81 SD6311
Horwich End *Derbys* 79 SK0080
Horwood *Devon* 19 SS5027
Hoscar *Lancs* 80 SD4611
Hoscote *Border* 109 NT3911
Hose *Leics* 63 SK7329
Hosey Hill *Kent* 27 TQ4553
Hosh *Tays* 125 NN8523
Hoswick *Shet* 155 HU4123
Hotham *Humb* 84 SE8934
Hothfield *Kent* 28 TQ9644
Hoton *Leics* 62 SK5722
Hott *Nthumb* 102 NY7785
Houdston *Strath* 106 NX2097
Hough *Ches* 72 SJ7151
Hough *Ches* 79 SJ8578
Hough End *W York* 82 SE2433
Hough Green *Ches* 78 SJ4886
Hough-on-the-Hill *Lincs* 63 SK9246
Hougham *Lincs* 63 SK8844
Houghton *Cumb* 93 NY4159
Houghton *Nthumb* 103 NZ1266
Houghton *Dyfed* 30 SM9807
Houghton *Hants* 23 SU3432
Houghton *Cambs* 52 TL2872
Houghton *W Susx* 14 TQ0111
Houghton Conquest *Beds* 38 TL0441
Houghton Green *Ches* 79 SJ6291
Houghton Green *E Susx* 17 TQ9222
Houghton Regis *Beds* 38 TL0123
Houghton St. Giles *Norfk* 66 TF9235
Houghton le Side *Dur* 96 NZ2221
Houghton le Spring *T & W* 96 NZ3449
Houghton on the Hill *Leics* 63 SK6703
Hound Green *Hants* 24 SU7359
Houndslow *Border* 110 NT6347
Houndsmoor *Somset* 20 ST1225
Houndwood *Border* 119 NT8463
Hounslow *Gt Lon* 26 TQ1375
Hounslow Green *Essex* 40 TL6518
Househill *Highld* 140 NH8855
Houses Hill *W York* 82 SE1916
Housieside *Gramp* 143 NJ8926
Houston *Strath* 115 NS4066
Houstry *Highld* 151 ND1534
Houton *Ork* 155 HY3104
Hove *E Susx* 15 TQ2804
Hove Edge *W York* 82 SE1324
Hoveringham *Notts* 63 SK6946
Hoveton *Norfk* 67 TG3018
Hovingham *N York* 90 SE6675
How *Cumb* 94 NY5056
How Caple *H & W* 46 SO6030
How End *Beds* 38 TL0340
Howbrook *S York* 74 SK3298
Howden *Humb* 84 SE7428
Howden-le-Wear *Dur* 96 NZ1633
Howe *Highld* 151 ND3061
Howe *N York* 89 SE3580
Howe *Norfk* 67 TM2799
Howe Bridge *Gt Man* 79 SD6602
Howe Green *Essex* 40 TL7403
Howe Street *Essex* 40 TL6914
Howe Street *Essex* 53 TL6934
Howe of Teuchar *Gramp* 143 NJ7946
Howegreen *Essex* 40 TL8301
Howell *Lincs* 76 TF1346
Howes *D & G* 101 NY1866
Howey *Powys* 45 SO0558
Howgate *Loth* 117 NT2457
Howgill *Lancs* 81 SD8246
Howick *Nthumb* 111 NU2417
Howle *Dur* 95 NZ0926
Howle *Shrops* 72 SJ6923
Howle Hill *H & W* 34 SO6020
Howlett End *Essex* 53 TL5834
Howley *Somset* 10 ST2609
Howmore *W Isls* 154 NF7536
Hownam *Border* 110 NT7719
Howrigg *Cumb* 93 NY3347
Howsham *N York* 90 SE7362
Howsham *Humb* 84 TA0404
Howt Green *Kent* 28 TQ8965
Howtel *Nthumb* 110 NT8934
Howton *H & W* 46 SO4129
Howtown *Cumb* 93 NY4419
Howwood *Strath* 115 NS3960
Hoxne *Suffk* 54 TM1777
Hoylake *Mersyd* 78 SJ2189
Hoyland Common *S York* 74 SE3600
Hoyland Nether *S York* 74 SE3700
Hoyland Swaine *S York* 82 SE2604
Hoyle *W Susx* 14 SU9018
Hoyle Mill *S York* 83 SE3506
Hubberholme *N York* 88 SD9278
Hubberston *Dyfed* 30 SM8906
Hubbert's Bridge *Lincs* 64 TF2643
Huby *N York* 82 SE2747
Huby *N York* 90 SE5665
Hucclecote *Gloucs* 35 SO8717
Hucking *Kent* 28 TQ8458
Hucknall *Notts* 75 SK5349
Huddersfield *W York* 82 SE1416
Huddington *H & W* 47 SO9457
Huddlesford *Staffs* 61 SK1509
Hudswell *N York* 89 NZ1400
Huggate *Humb* 84 SE8855
Hugglescote *Leics* 62 SK4212
Hugh Town *IOS* 2 SV9010
Hughenden Valley *Bucks* 26 SU8697
Hughley *Shrops* 59 SO5698
Huish *Devon* 19 SS5311
Huish *Wilts* 23 SU1463
Huish Champflower *Somset* 20 ST0529
Huish Episcopi *Somset* 21 ST4326
Hulberry *Kent* 27 TQ5265
Hulcote *Beds* 38 SP9438
Hulcott *Bucks* 38 SP8516
Hullaby *Devon* 7 SX6673
Hulland *Derbys* 73 SK2446
Hulland Ward *Derbys* 73 SK2546
Hullavington *Wilts* 35 ST8981
Hullbridge *Essex* 40 TQ8095
Hulme *Ches* 78 SJ6091
Hulme *Gt Man* 79 SJ8396
Hulme *Staffs* 72 SJ9345
Hulme End *Staffs* 74 SK1059
Hulme Walfield *Ches* 72 SJ8465
Hulse Heath *Ches* 79 SJ7283
Hulton Lane Ends *Gt Man* 79 SD6905
Hulver Street *Norfk* 66 TF9311
Hulver Street *Suffk* 55 TM4686
Hulverstone *IOW* 13 SZ3984
Humberston *Humb* 85 TA3105
Humberstone *Leics* 63 SK6305

282

Keillour Kinton

Keillour *Tays* **125** NN9725
Keils *Strath* **113** NR5268
Keinton Mandeville *Somset* **21** ST5430
Keir Mill *D & G* **100** NX8593
Keirsleywell Row *Nthumb* **94** NY7751
Keisby *Lincs* **64** TF0328
Keisley *Cumb* **94** NY7124
Keiss *Highld* **151** ND3461
Keith *Gramp* **142** NJ4250
Keithick *Tays* **126** NO2038
Keithock *Tays* **134** NO6063
Keithtown *Gramp* **139** NH5256
Kelbrook *Lancs* **81** SD9044
Kelburn *Strath* **114** NS2156
Kelby *Lincs* **63** TF0041
Keld *Cumb* **94** NY5514
Keld *N York* **88** NY8900
Keld Head *N York* **90** SE7884
Keldholme *N York* **90** SE7086
Kelfield *N York* **83** SE5938
Kelfield *Humb* **84** SE8201
Kelham *Notts* **75** SK7755
Kelhead *D & G* **100** NY1469
Kellacott *Devon* **5** SX4088
Kellamergh *Lancs* **80** SD4029
Kellas *Gramp* **141** NJ1654
Kellas *Tays* **127** NO4535
Kellaton *Devon* **7** SX8039
Kelleth *Cumb* **87** NY6605
Kelling *Norfk* **66** TG0942
Kellington *N York* **83** SE5524
Kelloe *Dur* **96** NZ3436
Kells *Cumb* **92** NX9616
Kelly *Devon* **5** SX3981
Kelly Bray *Cnwll* **5** SX3671
Kelmarsh *Nhants* **50** SP7379
Kelmscot *Oxon* **36** SU2499
Kelsale *Suffk* **55** TM3865
Kelsall *Ches* **71** SJ5268
Kelshall *Herts* **39** TL3336
Kelsick *Cumb* **93** NY1950
Kelso *Border* **110** NT7234
Kelstedge *Derbys* **74** SK3363
Kelstern *Lincs* **77** TF2489
Kelsterton *Clwyd* **70** SJ2770
Kelston *Avon* **22** ST7067
Keltneyburn *Tays* **124** NN7749
Kelton *D & G* **100** NX9970
Kelty *Fife* **117** NT1494
Kelvedon *Essex* **40** TL8619
Kelvedon Hatch *Essex* **27** TQ5698
Kelynack *Cnwll* **2** SW3729
Kemacott *Devon* **19** SS6647
Kemback *Fife* **126** NO4115
Kemberton *Shrops* **60** SJ7204
Kemble *Wilts* **35** ST9897
Kemble Wick *Gloucs* **35** ST9895
Kemerton *H & W* **47** SO9536
Kemeys Commander *Gwent* **34** SO3404
Kemnay *Gramp* **142** NJ7316
Kemp Town *E Susx* **15** TQ3303
Kempe's Corner *Kent* **28** TR0346
Kempley *Gloucs* **47** SO6629
Kempley Green *Gloucs* **47** SO6728
Kemps Green *Warwks* **61** SP1470
Kempsey *H & W* **47** SO8549
Kempsford *Gloucs* **36** SU1696
Kempshott *Hants* **24** SU6050
Kempston *Beds* **38** TL0347
Kempston Hardwick *Beds* **38** TL0344
Kempton *Shrops* **59** SO3682
Kemsing *Kent* **27** TQ5558
Kemsley *Kent* **28** TQ9166
Kemsley Street *Kent* **28** TQ8062
Kenardington *Kent* **17** TQ9732
Kenchester *H & W* **46** SO4342
Kencot *Oxon* **36** SP2504
Kendal *Cumb* **87** SD5192
Kenderchurch *H & W* **46** SO4028
Kendleshire *Avon* **35** ST6679
Kenfig Hill *M Glam* **33** SS8382
Kenilworth *Warwks* **61** SP2871
Kenley *Shrops* **59** SJ5500
Kenley *Gt Lon* **27** TQ3260
Kenmore *Highld* **137** NG7557
Kenmore *Tays* **124** NN7745
Kenn *Avon* **21** ST4268
Kenn *Devon* **9** SX9285
Kennacraig *Strath* **113** NR8262
Kennards House *Cnwll* **5** SX2883
Kenneggy *Cnwll* **2** SW5628
Kennerleigh *Devon* **8** SS8107
Kennessee Green *Mersyd* **78** SD3801
Kennet *Cent* **116** NS9291
Kennethmont *Gramp* **142** NJ5428
Kennett *Cambs* **53** TL7068
Kennford *Devon* **9** SX9186
Kenninghall *Norfk* **54** TM0386
Kennington *Oxon* **37** SP5201
Kennington *Kent* **28** TR0245
Kennoway *Fife* **126** NO3502
Kenny *Somset* **10** ST3117
Kennyhill *Suffk* **53** TL6679
Kennythorpe *N York* **90** SE7865
Kenovay *Strath* **120** NL9946
Kensaleyre *Highld* **136** NG4151
Kensham Green *Kent* **17** TQ8229
Kensington *Gt Lon* **27** TQ2579
Kensworth *Beds* **38** TL0319
Kensworth Common *Beds* **38** TL0317
Kent End *Wilts* **36** SU0594
Kent Green *Ches* **72** SJ8458
Kent Street *Kent* **28** TQ6654
Kent Street *E Susx* **17** TQ7816
Kent's Green *Gloucs* **47** SO7423
Kent's Oak *Hants* **23** SU3224
Kentallen *Highld* **122** NN0057
Kentchurch *H & W* **46** SO4125
Kentford *Suffk* **53** TL7066
Kentisbeare *Devon* **9** ST0608
Kentisbury *Devon* **19** SS6243
Kentisbury Ford *Devon* **19** SS6242
Kentish Town *Gt Lon* **27** TQ2884
Kentmere *Cumb* **87** NY4504
Kenton *T & W* **103** NZ2267
Kenton *Devon* **9** SX9583
Kenton *Suffk* **55** TM1965
Kenton *Gt Lon* **26** TQ1788
Kenton Bank Foot *Nthumb* **103** NZ2069
Kentra *Highld* **129** NM6569
Kents Bank *Cumb* **87** SD3975
Kenwick *Shrops* **59** SJ4230
Kenwyn *Cnwll* **3** SW8145
Kenyon *Gt Man* **79** SJ6395
Keoldale *Highld* **149** NC3866
Keppoch *Highld* **138** NG8924
Kepwick *N York* **89** SE4690
Keresley *W Mids* **61** SP3282
Keresley Green *Warwks* **61** SP3283
Kergilliak *Cnwll* **3** SW7833
Kernborough *Devon* **7** SX7941
Kerne Bridge *H & W* **34** SO5818
Kerridge *Ches* **79** SJ9376
Kerridge-end *Ches* **79** SJ9475
Kerris *Cnwll* **2** SW4427
Kerry *Powys* **58** SO1490
Kerrycroy *Strath* **114** NS1061
Kersall *Notts* **75** SK7162
Kersbrook *Devon* **9** SY0683
Kerscott *Devon* **19** SS6329
Kersey *Suffk* **54** TM0044
Kersey Tye *Suffk* **54** TL9843
Kersey Upland *Suffk* **54** TL9942
Kershader *W Isls* **154** NB3320
Kershopefoot *D & G* **101** NY4782
Kersoe *H & W* **47** SO9940
Kerswell *Devon* **9** ST0806
Kerswell Green *H & W* **47** SO8646
Kerthen Wood *Cnwll* **2** SW5833
Kesgrave *Suffk* **55** TM2245
Kessingland *Suffk* **55** TM5286
Kessingland Beach *Suffk* **55** TM5385
Kestle *Cnwll* **3** SW9845
Kestle Mill *Cnwll* **4** SW8459
Keston *Gt Lon* **27** TQ4164
Keswick *Cumb* **93** NY2623
Keswick *Norfk* **67** TG2004
Ketsby *Lincs* **77** TF3676
Kettering *Nhants* **51** SP8678
Ketteringham *Norfk* **66** TG1603
Kettins *Tays* **126** NO2338
Kettle Green *Herts* **39** TL4118
Kettlebaston *Suffk* **54** TL9650
Kettlebridge *Fife* **126** NO3007
Kettlebrook *Staffs* **61** SK2103
Kettleburgh *Suffk* **55** TM2660
Kettleholm *D & G* **100** NY1577
Kettleshulme *Ches* **79** SJ9879
Kettlesing *N York* **82** SE2256
Kettlesing Bottom *N York* **89** SE2357
Kettlestoft *Ork* **155** HY6538
Kettlestone *Norfk* **66** TF9631
Kettlethorpe *Lincs* **76** SK8475
Kettlewell *N York* **88** SD9672
Ketton *Leics* **63** SK9704
Kew *Gt Lon* **26** TQ1876
Kexbrough *S York* **82** SE3009
Kexby *N York* **84** SE7050
Kexby *Lincs* **76** SK8785
Key Green *N York* **90** NZ8004
Key Green *Ches* **72** SJ8963
Key Street *Kent* **28** TQ8764
Key's Toft *Lincs* **77** TF4858
Keyham *Leics* **63** SK6706
Keyhaven *Hants* **12** SZ3091
Keyingham *Humb* **85** TA2425
Keymer *W Susx* **15** TQ3115
Keynsham *Avon* **21** ST6568
Keysoe *Beds* **51** TL0762
Keysoe Row *Beds* **51** TL0861
Keyston *Cambs* **51** TL0475
Keyworth *Notts* **62** SK6130
Kibbear *Somset* **20** ST2222
Kibblesworth *T & W* **96** NZ2456
Kibworth Beauchamp *Leics* **50** SP6893
Kibworth Harcourt *Leics* **50** SP6894
Kidbrooke *Gt Lon* **27** TQ4176
Kidburngill *Cumb* **92** NY0621
Kidd's Moor *Norfk* **66** TG1103
Kiddemore Green *Staffs* **60** SJ8509
Kidderminster *H & W* **60** SO8376
Kiddington *Oxon* **49** SP4123
Kidlington *Oxon* **37** SP4913
Kidmore End *Oxon* **37** SU6979
Kidsdale *D & G* **99** NX4336
Kidsgrove *Staffs* **72** SJ8454
Kidstones *N York* **88** SD9581
Kidwelly *Dyfed* **31** SN4006
Kiel Crofts *Strath* **122** NM9039
Kielder *Nthumb* **102** NY6293
Kiells *Strath* **112** NR4168
Kilbeg *Highld* **129** NG6506
Kilberry *Strath* **113** NR7164
Kilbirnie *Strath* **115** NS3154
Kilbride *W Isls* **154** NF7514
Kilbride *Strath* **122** NM8525
Kilbride *Strath* **113** NR7279
Kilbride *Strath* **114** NS0367
Kilburn *N York* **90** SE5179
Kilburn *Derbys* **62** SK3845
Kilburn *Gt Lon* **26** TQ2483
Kilby *Leics* **50** SP6295
Kilchamaig *Strath* **113** NR8060
Kilchattan *Strath* **112** NR3795
Kilchattan *Strath* **114** NS1054
Kilchenzie *Strath* **105** NR6724
Kilcheran *Strath* **122** NM8239
Kilchiaran *Strath* **112** NR2060
Kilchoan *Highld* **121** NM4863
Kilchrenan *Strath* **122** NN0322
Kilconquhar *Fife* **127** NO4802
Kilcot *Gloucs* **47** SO6925
Kilcoy *Highld* **139** NH5751
Kilcreggan *Strath* **114** NS2480
Kildale *N York* **90** NZ6009
Kildalloig *Strath* **105** NR7518
Kildary *Highld* **147** NH7674
Kildavanan *Strath* **114** NS0266
Kildonan *Highld* **147** NC9120
Kildonan *Strath* **105** NS0321
Kildonan Lodge *Highld* **147** NC9022
Kildonnan *Highld* **128** NM4885
Kildrochet House *D & G* **98** NX0856
Kildrummy *Gramp* **142** NJ4617
Kildwick *N York* **82** SE0046
Kilehoman *Strath* **112** NR2163
Kilfinan *Strath* **114** NR9378
Kilfinnan *Highld* **131** NN2795
Kilgetty *Dyfed* **31** SN1207
Kilgrammie *Strath* **106** NS2502
Kilgwrrwg Common *Gwent* **34** ST4797
Kilham *Nthumb* **110** NT8832
Kilham *Humb* **91** TA0664
Kilkenneth *Strath* **120** NL9444
Kilkerran *Strath* **106** NS3003
Kilkhampton *Cnwll* **18** SS2511
Killamarsh *Derbys* **75** SK4581
Killay *W Glam* **32** SS6092
Killearn *Cent* **115** NS5286
Killen *Highld* **140** NH6758
Killerby *Dur* **96** NZ1919
Killerton *Devon* **9** SS9700
Killichonan *Tays* **132** NN5458
Killiechronan *Strath* **121** NM5441
Killiecrankie *Tays* **132** NN9162
Killilan *Highld* **138** NG9430
Killin *Cent* **124** NN5733
Killinghall *N York* **89** SE2858
Killington *Cumb* **87** SD6188
Killington *Devon* **19** SS6646
Killingworth *T & W* **103** NZ2770
Killiow *Cnwll* **3** SW8042
Killivose *Cnwll* **3** SW8049
Killochyett *Border* **118** NT4545
Killundine *Highld* **121** NM5949
Kilmacolm *Strath* **115** NS3567
Kilmahog *Cent* **124** NN6108
Kilmahumaig *Strath* **113** NR7893
Kilmaluag *Highld* **136** NG4374
Kilmany *Fife* **126** NO3821
Kilmarie *Highld* **129** NG5517
Kilmarnock *Strath* **107** NS4237
Kilmartin *Strath* **113** NR8398
Kilmaurs *Strath* **106** NS4141
Kilmelford *Strath* **122** NM8512
Kilmeny *Strath* **112** NR3965
Kilmersdon *Somset* **22** ST6952
Kilmeston *Hants* **13** SU5825
Kilmichael *Strath* **113** NR8593
Kilmichael of Inverlussa *Strath* **113** NR7786
Kilmington *Wilts* **22** ST7736
Kilmington *Devon* **10** SY2797
Kilmington Common *Wilts* **22** ST7735
Kilmington Street *Wilts* **22** ST7835
Kilmory *Strath* **122** NM8825
Kilmorack *Highld* **139** NH4944
Kilmore *Highld* **129** NG6507
Kilmory *Highld* **128** NM5270
Kilmory *Strath* **113** NR7074
Kilmuir *Highld* **136** NG2547
Kilmuir *Highld* **136** NG3770
Kilmuir *Highld* **140** NH6749
Kilmuir *Highld* **147** NH7573
Kilmun *Strath* **114** NS1781
Kiln Green *Berks* **37** SU8178
Kiln Pit Hill *Nthumb* **95** NZ0355
Kilnave *Strath* **112** NR2871
Kilncadzow *Strath* **116** NS8848
Kilndown *Kent* **16** TQ7035
Kilnhill *Cumb* **93** NY2132
Kilnhouses *Ches* **71** SJ6366
Kilnhurst *S York* **75** SK4597
Kilninver *Strath* **122** NM8221
Kilnsea *Humb* **85** TA4115
Kilnsey *N York* **88** SD9767
Kilnwick *Humb* **84** SE9949
Kilnwick Percy *Humb* **84** SE8249
Kiloran *Strath* **112** NR3996
Kilpeck *H & W* **46** SO4430
Kilpin *Humb* **84** SE7726
Kilpin Pike *Humb* **84** SE7626
Kilrie *Ches* **79** SJ7478
Kilsby *Nhants* **50** SP5671
Kilspindie *Tays* **126** NO2125
Kilstay *D & G* **98** NX1238
Kilsyth *Strath* **116** NS7178
Kiltarlity *Highld* **139** NH5041
Kilton *Cleve* **97** NZ7018
Kilton Thorpe *Cleve* **97** NZ6917
Kilvaxter *Highld* **136** NG3869
Kilve *Somset* **20** ST1442
Kilvington *Notts* **63** SK8042
Kilwinning *Strath* **106** NS3043
Kimberley *Notts* **62** SK4944
Kimberley *Norfk* **66** TG0603
Kimberworth *S York* **74** SK4093
Kimble Wick *Bucks* **38** SP8007
Kimblesworth *Dur* **96** NZ2547
Kimbolton *H & W* **46** SO5261
Kimbolton *Cambs* **51** TL1067
Kimcote *Leics* **50** SP5886
Kimmeridge *Dorset* **11** SY9179
Kimmerston *Nthumb* **111** NT9535
Kimpton *Hants* **23** SU2746
Kimpton *Herts* **39** TL1718
Kimworthy *Devon* **18** SS3112
Kinbrace *Highld* **150** NC8631
Kinbuck *Cent* **125** NN7905
Kincaple *Fife* **127** NO4618
Kincardine *Highld* **146** NH6089
Kincardine *Fife* **116** NS9387
Kincardine O'Neil *Tays* **134** NO5999
Kinclaven *Tays* **126** NO1538
Kincorth *Gramp* **135** NJ9403
Kincorth House *Gramp* **141** NJ0161
Kincraig *Highld* **132** NH8305
Kincraigie *Tays* **125** NN9849
Kindallachan *Tays* **125** NN9949
Kinerarach *Strath* **113** NR6553
Kineton *Gloucs* **48** SP0926
Kineton *Warwks* **48** SP3350
Kinfauns *Tays* **126** NO1622
Kinfig *M Glam* **32** SS8081
King Sterndale *Derbys* **74** SK0972
King's Acre *H & W* **46** SO4841
King's Bromley *Staffs* **73** SK1216
King's Cliffe *Nhants* **51** TL0097
King's Coughton *Warwks* **48** SP0859
King's Heath *W Mids* **61** SP0781
King's Hill *Warwks* **61** SP3274
King's Lynn *Norfk* **65** TF6120
King's Mills *Guern* **152** GN0000
King's Moss *Lancs* **78** SD5000
King's Newton *Derbys* **62** SK3825
King's Norton *Leics* **50** SK6800
King's Norton *W Mids* **61** SP0579
King's Nympton *Devon* **19** SS6819
King's Pyon *H & W* **46** SO4450
King's Somborne *Hants* **23** SU3531
King's Stag *Dorset* **11** ST7210
King's Stanley *Gloucs* **35** SO8103
King's Sutton *Oxon* **49** SP4936
King's Walden *Herts* **39** TL1623
Kingarth *Strath* **114** NS0956
Kingcausie *Gramp* **135** NO8699
Kingcoed *Gwent* **34** SO4305
Kingerby *Lincs* **76** TF0592
Kingford *Devon* **18** SS2806
Kingham *Oxon* **48** SP2624
Kingholm Quay *D & G* **100** NX9773
Kinglassie *Loth* **117** NT2298
Kingoldrum *Tays* **126** NO3355
Kingoodie *Tays* **126** NO3329
Kings Bridge *W Glam* **32** SS5997
Kings Caple *H & W* **46** SO5528
Kings Green *Gloucs* **47** SO7734
Kings Hill *W Mids* **60** SO9896
Kings House Hotel *Highld* **123** NN2654
Kings Langley *Herts* **26** TL0702
Kings Meaburn *Cumb* **94** NY6221
Kings Muir *Border* **109** NT2539
Kings Newnham *Warwks* **50** SP4577
Kings Ripton *Cambs* **52** TL2676
Kings Weston *Avon* **34** ST5477
Kings Worthy *Hants* **24** SU4932
Kingsand *Cnwll* **6** SX4350
Kingsash *Bucks* **38** SP8805
Kingsbarns *Fife* **127** NO5912
Kingsbridge *Somset* **20** SS9837
Kingsbridge *Devon* **7** SX7344
Kingsburgh *Highld* **136** NG3955
Kingsbury *Warwks* **61** SP2196
Kingsbury *Gt Lon* **26** TQ1988
Kingsbury Episcopi *Somset* **21** ST4321
Kingsclere *Hants* **24** SU5258
Kingscote *Gloucs* **35** ST8196
Kingscott *Devon* **19** SS5318
Kingscross *Strath* **105** NS0428
Kingsdon *Somset* **21** ST5126
Kingsdown *Wilts* **36** SU1688
Kingsdown *Kent* **29** TR3748
Kingseat *Fife* **117** NT1290
Kingsey *Bucks* **37** SP7406
Kingsfold *W Susx* **15** TQ1636
Kingsford *Strath* **115** NS4447
Kingsford *H & W* **60** SO8181
Kingsgate *Kent* **29** TR3970
Kingshall Street *Suffk* **54** TL9161
Kingsheanton *Devon* **19** SS5537
Kingshouse Hotel *Cent* **124** NN5620
Kingshurst *W Mids* **61** SP1688
Kingside Hill *Cumb* **92** NY1551
Kingskerswell *Devon* **7** SX8767
Kingskettle *Fife* **126** NO3008
Kingsland *H & W* **46** SO4461
Kingsland *Dorset* **10** SY4597
Kingsley *Ches* **71** SJ5574
Kingsley *Staffs* **73** SK0146
Kingsley *Hants* **25** SU7838
Kingsley Green *W Susx* **14** SU8930
Kingsley Park *Nhants* **49** SP7762
Kingslow *Shrops* **60** SO7998
Kingsmead *Hants* **13** SU5813
Kingsmuir *Tays* **127** NO4849
Kingsmuir *Fife* **127** NO5308
Kingsnorth *Kent* **28** TR0039
Kingstanding *W Mids* **61** SP0794
Kingsteignton *Devon* **7** SX8773
Kingsthorne *H & W* **46** SO4931
Kingsthorpe *Nhants* **49** SP7563
Kingston *Gramp* **141** NJ3365
Kingston *Loth* **118** NT5482
Kingston *Dorset* **11** ST7509
Kingston *Hants* **12** SU1401
Kingston *Cnwll* **5** SX3675
Kingston *Devon* **6** SX6347
Kingston *Dorset* **11** SY9579
Kingston *IOW* **13** SZ4781
Kingston *Cambs* **52** TL3455
Kingston *W Susx* **14** TQ0802
Kingston *Kent* **29** TR1950
Kingston Bagpuize *Oxon* **36** SU4098
Kingston Blount *Oxon* **37** SU7399
Kingston Deverill *Wilts* **22** ST8437
Kingston Lisle *Oxon* **36** SU3287
Kingston Russell *Dorset* **10** SY5791
Kingston Seymour *Avon* **21** ST4066
Kingston St. Mary *Somset* **20** ST2229
Kingston Stert *Oxon* **37** SP7200
Kingston by Sea *W Susx* **15** TQ2305
Kingston near Lewes *E Susx* **15** TQ3908
Kingston on Soar *Notts* **62** SK5027
Kingston upon Hull *Humb* **85** TA0829
Kingston upon Thames *Gt Lon* **26** TQ1869
Kingstone *Staffs* **73** SK0629
Kingstone *H & W* **46** SO4235
Kingstone *Somset* **10** ST3713
Kingstone *Oxon* **36** SU2685
Kingstown *Cumb* **93** NY3959
Kingswear *Devon* **7** SX8851
Kingswells *Gramp* **135** NJ8606
Kingswinford *W Mids* **60** SO8888
Kingswood *Powys* **58** SJ2302
Kingswood *Warwks* **61** SP1871
Kingswood *Bucks* **37** SP6919
Kingswood *Somset* **20** ST1037
Kingswood *Avon* **35** ST6473
Kingswood *Gloucs* **35** ST7491
Kingswood *Surrey* **26** TQ2455
Kingswood *Kent* **28** TQ8350
Kingswood Brook *Warwks* **61** SP1970
Kingswood Common *Staffs* **60** SJ8302
Kingswood Common *H & W* **46** SO2954
Kingthorpe *Lincs* **76** TF1275
Kington *H & W* **46** SO2956
Kington *H & W* **47** SO9956
Kington *Avon* **35** ST6290
Kington Langley *Wilts* **35** ST9276
Kington Magna *Dorset* **22** ST7622
Kington St. Michael *Wilts* **35** ST9077
Kingussie *Highld* **132** NH7500
Kingweston *Somset* **21** ST5230
Kinharrachie *Gramp* **143** NJ9231
Kinharvie *D & G* **100** NX9266
Kinkell Bridge *Tays* **125** NN9316
Kinknockie *Gramp* **143** NK0041
Kinleith *Loth* **117** NT1866
Kinlet *Shrops* **60** SO7180
Kinloch *Highld* **149** NC3434
Kinloch *Highld* **149** NC5552
Kinloch *Highld* **128** NM4099
Kinloch *Tays* **126** NO1444
Kinloch *Tays* **126** NO2644
Kinloch Hourn *Highld* **130** NG9506
Kinloch Rannoch *Tays* **132** NN6658
Kinlochard *Cent* **124** NN4502
Kinlochbervie *Highld* **148** NC2256
Kinlocheil *Highld* **130** NM9779
Kinlochewe *Highld* **138** NH0261
Kinlochleven *Highld* **131** NN1861
Kinlochmoidart *Highld* **129** NM7172
Kinlochnanuagh *Highld* **129** NM7384
Kinlochspelve *Strath* **121** NM6526
Kinloss *Gramp* **141** NJ0661
Kinmel Bay *Clwyd* **70** SH9880
Kinmount House *D & G* **100** NY1368
Kinmuck *Gramp* **143** NJ8119
Kinmundy *Gramp* **143** NJ8817
Kinnadie *Gramp* **143** NJ9743
Kinnahaird *Highld* **139** NH4755
Kinnaird *Tays* **133** NN9559
Kinnaird *Tays* **126** NO2428
Kinnaird Castle *Tays* **134** NO6357
Kinneddar *Gramp* **141** NJ2269
Kinneff *Gramp* **135** NO8574
Kinnelhead *D & G* **108** NT0201
Kinnell *Tays* **127** NO6150
Kinnerley *Shrops* **59** SJ3320
Kinnersley *H & W* **46** SO3449
Kinnersley *H & W* **47** SO8743
Kinnerton *Powys* **46** SO2463
Kinnerton *Shrops* **59** SO3796
Kinnerton Green *Clwyd* **71** SJ3361
Kinnesswood *Tays* **126** NO1702
Kinninvie *Dur* **95** NZ0521
Kinnordy *Tays* **126** NO3655
Kinoulton *Notts* **63** SK6730
Kinross *Tays* **126** NO1102
Kinrossie *Tays* **126** NO1832
Kinsbourne Green *Herts* **38** TL1016
Kinsey Heath *Ches* **72** SJ6642
Kinsham *H & W* **46** SO3665
Kinsham *H & W* **47** SO9335
Kinsley *W York* **83** SE4114
Kinson *Dorset* **12** SZ0796
Kintbury *Berks* **23** SU3866
Kintillo *Tays* **126** NO1317
Kinton *Shrops* **59** SJ3719

Kintore Langtoft

Kintore *Gramp* 143 NJ7916
Kintour *Strath* 112 NR4551
Kintra *Strath* 120 NM3125
Kintraw *Strath* 122 NM8204
Kinveachy *Highld* 140 NH9018
Kinver *Staffs* 60 SO8483
Kiplin *N York* 89 SE2897
Kippax *W York* 83 SE4130
Kippen *Cent* 116 NS6494
Kippford or Scaur *D & G* 92 NX8354
Kipping's Cross *Kent* 16 TQ6440
Kirbister *Ork* 155 HY3607
Kirby Bedon *Norfk* 67 TG2705
Kirby Bellars *Leics* 63 SK7117
Kirby Cane *Norfk* 67 TM3794
Kirby Corner *W Mids* 61 SP2976
Kirby Cross *Essex* 41 TM2120
Kirby Fields *Leics* 62 SK5203
Kirby Grindalythe *N York* 91 SE9067
Kirby Hill *N York* 89 NZ1406
Kirby Hill *N York* 89 SE3968
Kirby Knowle *N York* 89 SE4687
Kirby Misperton *N York* 90 SE7779
Kirby Muxloe *Leics* 62 SK5104
Kirby Row *Norfk* 67 TM3792
Kirby Sigston *N York* 89 SE4194
Kirby Underdale *Humb* 90 SE8058
Kirby Wiske *N York* 89 SE3784
Kirby le Soken *Essex* 41 TM2121
Kirby-in-Furness *Cumb* 86 SD2282
Kirconnel *D & G* 100 NX9868
Kirdford *W Susx* 14 TQ0126
Kirk *Highld* 151 ND2859
Kirk Bramwith *S York* 83 SE6211
Kirk Deighton *N York* 83 SE3950
Kirk Ella *Humb* 84 TA0129
Kirk Hallam *Derbys* 62 SK4540
Kirk Hammerton *N York* 83 SE4655
Kirk Ireton *Derbys* 73 SK2650
Kirk Langley *Derbys* 73 SK2838
Kirk Merrington *Dur* 96 NZ2631
Kirk Sandall *S York* 83 SE6108
Kirk Smeaton *N York* 83 SE5216
Kirk Yetholm *Border* 110 NT8228
Kirk of Shotts *Strath* 116 NS8462
Kirkabister *Shet* 155 HU4938
Kirkandrews *D & G* 99 NX6048
Kirkandrews upon Eden *Cumb* 93 NY3558
Kirkbampton *Cumb* 93 NY3056
Kirkbean *D & G* 92 NX9759
Kirkbride *Cumb* 93 NY2256
Kirkbridge *N York* 89 SE2590
Kirkbuddo *Tays* 127 NO5043
Kirkburn *Border* 109 NT2938
Kirkburn *Humb* 84 SE9855
Kirkburton *W York* 82 SE1912
Kirkby *N York* 90 NZ5305
Kirkby *Mersyd* 78 SJ4099
Kirkby *Lincs* 76 TF0592
Kirkby Fleetham *N York* 89 SE2894
Kirkby Green *Lincs* 76 TF0857
Kirkby Hall *N York* 89 SE2795
Kirkby Lonsdale *Cumb* 87 SD6178
Kirkby Malham *N York* 88 SD8960
Kirkby Mallory *Leics* 50 SK4500
Kirkby Malzeard *N York* 89 SE2374
Kirkby Mills *N York* 90 SE7085
Kirkby Overblow *N York* 83 SE3249
Kirkby Stephen *Cumb* 88 NY7708
Kirkby Thore *Cumb* 94 NY6325
Kirkby Underwood *Lincs* 64 TF0727
Kirkby Wharf *N York* 83 SE5041
Kirkby Woodhouse *Notts* 75 SK4954
Kirkby in Ashfield *Notts* 75 SK4856
Kirkby la Thorpe *Lincs* 76 TF0946
Kirkby on Bain *Lincs* 77 TF2462
Kirkbymoorside *N York* 90 SE6986
Kirkcaldy *Fife* 117 NT2892
Kirkcambeck *Cumb* 101 NY5368
Kirkchrist *D & G* 99 NX6751
Kirkcolm *D & G* 98 NX0268
Kirkconnel *D & G* 107 NS7311
Kirkconnell *D & G* 99 NX6760
Kirkcowan *D & G* 98 NX3260
Kirkcudbright *D & G* 99 NX6850
Kirkdale *Mersyd* 78 SJ3493
Kirkfieldbank *Strath* 108 NS8643
Kirkgunzeon *D & G* 100 NX8666
Kirkham *Lancs* 80 SD4232
Kirkham *N York* 90 SE7365
Kirkhamgate *W York* 82 SE2922
Kirkharle *Nthumb* 103 NZ0182
Kirkhaugh *Nthumb* 94 NY6949
Kirkheaton *Nthumb* 103 NZ0177
Kirkheaton *W York* 82 SE1818
Kirkhill *Highld* 139 NH5545
Kirkhope *Strath* 108 NS9606
Kirkhope *Border* 109 NT3723
Kirkhouse *Cumb* 94 NY5759
Kirkhouse Green *S York* 83 SE6213
Kirkibost *Highld* 129 NG5518
Kirkinch *Tays* 126 NO3044
Kirkinner *D & G* 99 NX4251
Kirkintilloch *Strath* 116 NS6573
Kirkland *D & G* 107 NS7213
Kirkland *D & G* 99 NX4356
Kirkland *D & G* 100 NX8190
Kirkland *D & G* 100 NY0389
Kirkland *Cumb* 92 NY0718
Kirkland *Cumb* 93 NY2648
Kirkland *Cumb* 94 NY6432
Kirkland Guards *Cumb* 93 NY1840
Kirkleatham *Cleve* 97 NZ5921
Kirklevington *Cleve* 89 NZ4309
Kirkley *Suffk* 67 TM5391
Kirkleyditch *Ches* 79 SJ8778
Kirklington *N York* 89 SE3181
Kirklington *Notts* 75 SK6757
Kirklinton *Cumb* 101 NY4367
Kirkliston *Loth* 117 NT1274
Kirkmabreck *D & G* 99 NX4856
Kirkmaiden *D & G* 98 NX1236
Kirkmichael *Tays* 133 NO0759
Kirkmichael *Strath* 106 NS3408
Kirkmichael *IOM* 153 SC3190
Kirkmuirhill *Strath* 107 NS7842
Kirknewton *Fife* 117 NT1166
Kirknewton *Nthumb* 110 NT9130
Kirkney *Gramp* 142 NJ5132
Kirkoswald *Strath* 106 NS2407
Kirkoswald *Cumb* 94 NY5541
Kirkpatrick *D & G* 100 NX9090
Kirkpatrick Durham *D & G* 100 NX7870
Kirkpatrick-Fleming *D & G* 101 NY2770
Kirksanton *Cumb* 86 SD1380
Kirkstall *W York* 82 SE2635
Kirkstead *Lincs* 76 TF1762
Kirkstile *Gramp* 142 NJ5235
Kirkstile *D & G* 101 NY3690
Kirkstone Pass Inn *Cumb* 87 NY4007
Kirkstyle *Highld* 151 ND3472
Kirkthorpe *W York* 83 SE3621
Kirkton *Highld* 137 NG8227
Kirkton *Highld* 138 NG9141
Kirkton *Gramp* 142 NJ6425
Kirkton *Gramp* 143 NJ8243
Kirkton *Tays* 125 NN9618
Kirkton *Fife* 126 NO3625
Kirkton *Border* 109 NT5413
Kirkton *D & G* 100 NX9781
Kirkton Manor *Border* 109 NT2238
Kirkton of Airlie *Tays* 126 NO3151
Kirkton of Auchterhouse *Tays* 126 NO3438
Kirkton of Collace *Tays* 126 NO1931
Kirkton of Craig *Tays* 127 NO6956
Kirkton of Logie Buchan *Gramp* 143 NJ9829
Kirkton of Monikie *Tays* 127 NO5138
Kirkton of Skene *Gramp* 135 NJ8007
Kirkton of Tealing *Tays* 126 NO4038
Kirkton of Strathmartine *Tays* 126 NO3735
Kirktown *Gramp* 143 NJ9965
Kirktown *Gramp* 143 NK0852
Kirktown of Alvah *Gramp* 142 NJ6760
Kirktown of Bourtie *Gramp* 143 NJ8025
Kirktown of Fetteresso *Gramp* 135 NO8486
Kirktown of Mortlach *Gramp* 141 NJ3138
Kirktown of Slains *Gramp* 143 NK0329
Kirkwall *Ork* 155 HY4411
Kirkwhelpington *Nthumb* 103 NY9984
Kirmington *Humb* 85 TA1011
Kirmond le Mire *Lincs* 76 TF1892
Kirn *Strath* 114 NS1878
Kirstead Green *Norfk* 67 TM2997
Kirtlebridge *D & G* 101 NY2372
Kirtling *Cambs* 53 TL6857
Kirtling Green *Suffk* 53 TL6855
Kirtlington *Oxon* 37 SP4919
Kirtomy *Highld* 150 NC7463
Kirton *Gramp* 134 NJ6113
Kirton *Strath* 114 NS1655
Kirton *Notts* 75 SK6969
Kirton *Lincs* 64 TF3038
Kirton *Suffk* 55 TM2740
Kirton End *Lincs* 64 TF2940
Kirton Holme *Lincs* 64 TF2642
Kirton in Lindsey *Lincs* 76 SK9398
Kirkton of Barevan *Highld* 140 NH8347
Kirkton of Durris *Gramp* 135 NO7796
Kirkton of Glenbuchat *Gramp* 141 NJ3715
Kirkton of Glenisla *Tays* 133 NO2160
Kirkton of Menmuir *Tays* 134 NO5364
Kirkton of Rayne *Gramp* 142 NJ6930
Kirkton of Strathmartine *Tays* 126 NO3735
Kirtonhill *Strath* 115 NS3875
Kirwaugh *D & G* 99 NX4054
Kislingbury *Nhants* 49 SP6959
Kit Green *Gt Man* 78 SD5405
Kite Green *Warwks* 48 SP1666
Kites Hardwick *Warwks* 50 SP4768
Kitleigh *Cnwll* 18 SX2499
Kittisford *Somset* 20 ST0822
Kittle *W Glam* 32 SS5789
Kitts Green *W Mids* 61 SP1587
Kittybrewster *Gramp* 135 NJ9207
Kitwood *Hants* 24 SU6633
Kivernoll *H & W* 46 SO4632
Kiveton Park *S York* 75 SK4982
Knaith *Lincs* 75 SK8284
Knaith Park *Lincs* 76 SK8485
Knap Corner *Dorset* 22 ST8023
Knaphill *Surrey* 25 SU9658
Knaplock *Somset* 19 SS8633
Knapp *Somset* 20 ST3025
Knapp Hill *Hants* 13 SU4023
Knapthorpe *Notts* 75 SK7458
Knapton *N York* 83 SE5652
Knapton *N York* 90 SE8876
Knapton *Norfk* 67 TG3034
Knapton Green *H & W* 46 SO4452
Knapwell *Cambs* 52 TL3362
Knaresborough *N York* 89 SE3557
Knarsdale *Nthumb* 94 NY6754
Knaven *Gramp* 143 NJ8943
Knayton *N York* 89 SE4387
Knebworth *Herts* 39 TL2520
Knedlington *Humb* 84 SE7327
Kneesall *Notts* 75 SK7064
Kneesworth *Cambs* 39 TL3444
Kneeton *Notts* 63 SK7146
Knelston *W Glam* 32 SS4688
Knenhall *Staffs* 72 SJ9237
Knettishall *Suffk* 54 TL9780
Knightacott *Devon* 19 SS6539
Knightcote *Warwks* 48 SP4054
Knightley *Staffs* 72 SJ8125
Knightley Dale *Staffs* 72 SJ8123
Knighton *Staffs* 72 SJ7240
Knighton *Staffs* 72 SJ7527
Knighton *Leics* 62 SK6001
Knighton *Powys* 46 SO2872
Knighton *Somset* 20 ST1944
Knighton *Dorset* 10 ST6111
Knighton *Wilts* 36 SU2971
Knighton *Devon* 6 SX5349
Knighton *Dorset* 12 SZ0497
Knighton on Teme *H & W* 47 SO6369
Knightsmill *Cnwll* 4 SX0780
Knightwick *H & W* 47 SO7356
Knill *H & W* 46 SO2960
Knipton *Leics* 63 SK8231
Knitsley *Dur* 95 NZ1048
Kniveton *Derbys* 73 SK2050
Knock *W Isls* 154 NB4931
Knock *Highld* 129 NG6709
Knock *Gramp* 142 NJ5452
Knock *Cumb* 94 NY6727
Knock Castle *Strath* 114 NS1963
Knockally *Highld* 151 ND1429
Knockan *Highld* 145 NC2110
Knockandhu *Gramp* 141 NJ2023
Knockando *Gramp* 141 NJ1941
Knockbain *Highld* 139 NH5543
Knockbain *Highld* 140 NH6256
Knockbrex *D & G* 99 NX5849
Knockdee *Highld* 151 ND1760
Knockdown *Wilts* 35 ST8388
Knockeen *Strath* 106 NX3195
Knockenkelly *Strath* 105 NS0427
Knockentiber *Strath* 106 NS4039
Knockespock House *Gramp* 142 NJ5423
Knockholt *Kent* 27 TQ5974
Knockholt *Kent* 27 TQ4658
Knockholt Pound *Kent* 27 TQ4859
Knockin *Shrops* 59 SJ3322
Knockinlaw *Strath* 107 NS4239
Knockmill *Kent* 27 TQ5761
Knocknain *D & G* 98 NW9764
Knocksheen *D & G* 99 NX5882
Knockvennie Smithy *D & G* 99 NX7571
Knodishall *Suffk* 55 TM4262
Knole *Somset* 21 ST4825
Knole Park *Avon* 34 ST5983
Knolls Green *Ches* 79 SJ8079
Knolton *Clwyd* 71 SJ3739
Knook *Wilts* 22 ST9341
Knossington *Leics* 63 SK8008
Knott End-on-Sea *Lancs* 80 SD3548
Knotting *Beds* 51 TL0063
Knotting Green *Beds* 51 TL0062
Knottingley *W York* 83 SE5023
Knotty Green *Bucks* 26 SU9392
Knowbury *Shrops* 46 SO5775
Knowe *D & G* 98 NX3171
Knowehead *D & G* 107 NX6090
Knoweside *Strath* 106 NS2512
Knowl Green *Essex* 53 TL7841
Knowl Hill *Berks* 37 SU8279
Knowle *Shrops* 46 SO5973
Knowle *W Mids* 61 SP1876
Knowle *Devon* 18 SS4938
Knowle *Devon* 8 SS7801
Knowle *Somset* 20 SS9643
Knowle *Devon* 9 ST0007
Knowle *Avon* 34 ST6070
Knowle *Devon* 9 SY0582
Knowle Cross *Devon* 9 SY0397
Knowle Green *Lancs* 81 SD6338
Knowle Hill *Surrey* 25 SU9966
Knowle St. Giles *Somset* 10 ST3411
Knowlton *Dorset* 12 SU0209
Knowlton *Kent* 29 TR2853
Knowsley *Mersyd* 78 SJ4395
Knowstone *Devon* 19 SS8323
Knox *N York* 89 SE2957
Knox Bridge *Kent* 28 TQ7840
Knucklas *Powys* 46 SO2574
Knuston *Nhants* 51 SP9266
Knutsford *Ches* 79 SJ7578
Knutton *Staffs* 72 SJ8347
Knypersley *Staffs* 72 SJ8856
Krumlin *W York* 82 SE0518
Kuggar *Cnwll* 3 SW7216
Kyle of Lochalsh *Highld* 137 NG7627
Kyleakin *Highld* 137 NG7526
Kylerhea *Highld* 129 NG7820
Kylesku *Highld* 148 NC2233
Kylesmorar *Highld* 129 NM8093
Kylestrome *Highld* 148 NC2234
Kyloe *Nthumb* 111 NU0540
Kynaston *Shrops* 59 SJ3520
Kynaston *H & W* 47 SO6435
Kynnersley *Shrops* 72 SJ6716
Kyre Green *H & W* 46 SO6162
Kyre Park *H & W* 47 SO6263
Kyrewood *H & W* 46 SO5967
Kyrle *Somset* 20 ST0522

L

L'Ancresse *Guern* 152 GN0000
L'Eree *Guern* 152 GN0000
L'Etacq *Jersey* 152 JS0000
La Beilleuse *Guern* 152 GN0000
La Fontenelle *Guern* 152 GN0000
La Fosse *Guern* 152 GN0000
La Greve *Guern* 152 GN0000
La Greve de Lecq *Jersey* 152 JS0000
La Hougue Bie *Jersey* 152 JS0000
La Houguette *Guern* 152 GN0000
La Passee *Guern* 152 GN0000
La Pulente *Jersey* 152 JS0000
La Rocque *Jersey* 152 JS0000
La Rousaillerie *Guern* 152 GN0000
La Villette *Guern* 152 GN0000
Labbacott *Devon* 18 SS4021
Laceby *Humb* 85 TA2106
Lacey Green *Bucks* 37 SP8200
Lach Dennis *Ches* 79 SJ7071
Lackenby *Cleve* 97 NZ5619
Lackford *Suffk* 53 TL7970
Lackford Green *Suffk* 53 TL7970
Lacock *Wilts* 22 ST9168
Ladbroke *Warwks* 49 SP4158
Ladderedge *Staffs* 72 SJ9654
Laddingford *Kent* 28 TQ6948
Lade Bank *Lincs* 77 TF3954
Ladock *Cnwll* 3 SW8950
Lady Hall *Cumb* 86 SD1986
Lady's Green *Suffk* 53 TL7559
Ladybank *Fife* 126 NO3009
Ladycross *Cnwll* 5 SX3188
Ladygill *Strath* 108 NS9428
Ladykirk *Border* 110 NT8847
Ladykirk Ho *Border* 110 NT8845
Ladywood *H & W* 47 SO8661
Ladywood *W Mids* 61 SP0586
Lag *D & G* 100 NX8786
Lagavulin *Strath* 104 NR4045
Lagg *Strath* 105 NR9521
Laggan *Highld* 131 NN2997
Laggan *Highld* 132 NN6194
Laggan *Strath* 98 NX0982
Laid *Highld* 149 NC4159
Laide *Highld* 144 NG9091
Laig *Highld* 128 NM4687
Laigh Church *Strath* 115 NS4647
Laigh Fenwick *Strath* 107 NS4542
Laigh Glenmuir *Strath* 107 NS6120
Laighstonehall *Strath* 116 NS7054
Laindon *Essex* 40 TQ6889
Lairg *Highld* 146 NC5806
Laisterdyke *W York* 82 SE1932
Laithes *Cumb* 93 NY4633
Lake *Devon* 19 SS5531
Lake *Wilts* 23 SU1339
Lake *Devon* 5 SX5289
Lake *Dorset* 11 SY9990
Lake *IOW* 13 SZ5883
Lake Side *Cumb* 87 SD3787
Lakenheath *Suffk* 53 TL7182
Laker's Green *Surrey* 14 TQ0335
Lakesend *Norfk* 65 TL5196
Lakley Lanes *Bucks* 38 SP8250
Laleham *Surrey* 26 TQ0568
Laleston *M Glam* 33 SS8779
Lamanva *Cnwll* 3 SW7631
Lamarsh *Essex* 54 TL8835
Lamas *Norfk* 67 TG2423
Lamb Roe *Lancs* 81 SD7337
Lambden *Border* 110 NT7443
Lamberhurst *Kent* 28 TQ6736
Lamberhurst Down *Kent* 16 TQ6735
Lamberton *Border* 119 NT9658
Lambfair Green *Suffk* 53 TL7153
Lambley *Nthumb* 94 NY6759
Lambley *Notts* 63 SK6345
Lambourn *Berks* 36 SU3278
Lambourne End *Essex* 27 TQ4794
Lambs Green *W Susx* 15 TQ2136
Lambston *Dyfed* 30 SM9016
Lamerton *Devon* 5 SX4577
Lamesley *T & W* 96 NZ2557
Lamington *Strath* 108 NS9731
Lamlash *Strath* 105 NS0231
Lamonby *Cumb* 93 NY4036
Lamorick *Cnwll* 4 SX0364
Lamorna *Cnwll* 2 SW4424
Lamorran *Cnwll* 3 SW8741
Lampen *Cnwll* 4 SX1867
Lampeter *Dyfed* 44 SN5747
Lampeter Velfrey *Dyfed* 31 SN1514
Lamphey *Dyfed* 30 SN0100
Lamplugh *Cumb* 92 NY0820
Lamport *Nhants* 50 SP7574
Lamyatt *Somset* 21 ST6536
Lana *Devon* 18 SS3007
Lana *Devon* 5 SX3496
Lanark *Strath* 108 NS8843
Lanarth *Cnwll* 3 SW7621
Lancaster *Lancs* 87 SD4761
Lancaut *Gloucs* 34 ST5396
Lanchester *Dur* 96 NZ1647
Lancing *W Susx* 15 TQ1804
Land-hallow *Highld* 151 ND1833
Landbeach *Cambs* 53 TL4765
Landcross *Devon* 18 SS4523
Landerberry *Gramp* 135 NJ7404
Landewednack *Cnwll* 2 SW7012
Landford *Wilts* 12 SU2519
Landimore *W Glam* 32 SS4692
Landkey *Devon* 19 SS6031
Landkey Town *Devon* 19 SS5931
Landore *W Glam* 32 SS6695
Landrake *Cnwll* 5 SX3760
Lands End *Cnwll* 2 SW3425
Landscove *Devon* 7 SX7766
Landshipping *Dyfed* 30 SN0211
Landue *Cnwll* 5 SX3579
Landulph *Cnwll* 6 SX4361
Landwade *Cambs* 53 TL6268
Landywood *Staffs* 60 SJ9805
Lane *Cnwll* 4 SW8260
Lane Bottom *Lancs* 81 SD8735
Lane End *Cumb* 86 SD1093
Lane End *Lancs* 81 SD8747
Lane End *Ches* 79 SJ6890
Lane End *Wilts* 22 ST8145
Lane End *Hants* 13 SU5525
Lane End *Bucks* 37 SU8091
Lane End *Cnwll* 4 SX0369
Lane End *Kent* 27 TQ5671
Lane Ends *Dur* 96 NZ1833
Lane Ends *Lancs* 81 SD7930
Lane Ends *N York* 82 SD9743
Lane Ends *Derbys* 73 SK2334
Lane Green *Staffs* 60 SJ8703
Lane Head *Dur* 89 NZ1211
Lane Head *Gt Man* 79 SJ6296
Lane Head *W Mids* 35 SO9700
Lane Heads *Lancs* 80 SD4339
Lane Side *Lancs* 81 SD7922
Laneast *Cnwll* 5 SX2283
Laneham *Notts* 75 SK8076
Lanehead *Dur* 95 NY8441
Laneshaw Bridge *Lancs* 81 SD9240
Langaford *Devon* 18 SX4199
Langaller *Somset* 20 ST2626
Langar *Notts* 63 SK7234
Langbank *Strath* 115 NS3873
Langbar *N York* 82 SE0951
Langbaurgh *N York* 90 NZ5511
Langcliffe *N York* 88 SD8264
Langdale End *N York* 91 SE9391
Langdon *Cnwll* 5 SX3089
Langdon Beck *Dur* 95 NY8531
Langdown *Hants* 13 SU4206
Langdyke *Fife* 126 NO3304
Langenhoe *Essex* 41 TM0018
Langford *Notts* 75 SK8258
Langford *Oxon* 36 SP2402
Langford *Devon* 9 ST0203
Langford *Avon* 21 ST4560
Langford *Beds* 39 TL1841
Langford *Essex* 40 TL8309
Langford Budville *Somset* 20 ST1122
Langford End *Beds* 52 TL1753
Langham *Leics* 63 SK8411
Langham *Dorset* 22 ST7725
Langham *Norfk* 66 TG0141
Langham *Suffk* 54 TL9769
Langham *Essex* 41 TM0333
Langham Moor *Essex* 41 TM0131
Langham Wick *Essex* 41 TM0231
Langho *Lancs* 81 SD7034
Langholm *D & G* 101 NY3684
Langley *Nthumb* 102 NY8261
Langley *Gt Man* 79 SD8506
Langley *Ches* 79 SJ9471
Langley *Derbys* 62 SK4445
Langley *Gloucs* 47 SP0028
Langley *Warwks* 48 SP1965
Langley *Oxon* 36 SP2915
Langley *Somset* 20 ST0828
Langley *Hants* 13 SU4401
Langley *W Susx* 14 SU8029
Langley *Herts* 39 TL2122
Langley *Essex* 39 TL4334
Langley *Berks* 26 TQ0178
Langley *Kent* 28 TQ8052
Langley Burrell *Wilts* 35 ST9375
Langley Castle *Nthumb* 102 NY8362
Langley Common *Derbys* 73 SK2937
Langley Green *Derbys* 73 SK2738
Langley Green *Warwks* 48 SP2062
Langley Green *Essex* 40 TL8722
Langley Marsh *Somset* 20 ST0729
Langley Mill *Derbys* 62 SK4446
Langley Moor *Dur* 96 NZ2540
Langley Park *Dur* 96 NZ2145
Langley Street *Norfk* 67 TG3601
Langleybury *Herts* 26 TL0700
Langney *E Susx* 16 TQ6302
Langold *Notts* 75 SK5886
Langore *Cnwll* 5 SX2986
Langport *Somset* 21 ST4226
Langrick *Lincs* 77 TF2648
Langridge *Avon* 35 ST7469
Langridge Ford *Devon* 19 SS5722
Langrigg *Cumb* 92 NY1645
Langrish *Hants* 13 SU7023
Langsett *S York* 74 SE2100
Langshaw *Border* 109 NT5139
Langside *Tays* 125 NN7913
Langstone *Gwent* 34 ST3789
Langstone *Hants* 13 SU7204
Langthorne *N York* 89 SE2491
Langthorpe *N York* 89 SE3867
Langthwaite *N York* 88 NZ0001
Langtoft *Humb* 91 TA0066
Langtoft *Lincs* 64 TF1212

Langton Little Barugh

Langton *Dur* 96 NZ1619
Langton *N York* 90 SE7966
Langton *Lincs* 76 TF2368
Langton *Lincs* 77 TF3970
Langton Green *Suffk* 54 TM1474
Langton Green *Kent* 16 TQ5439
Langton Herring *Dorset* 10 SY6182
Langton by Wragby *Lincs* 76 TF1476
Langtree *Devon* 18 SS4515
Langwathby *Cumb* 94 NY5733
Langwell House *Highld* 147 ND1122
Langwith *Derbys* 75 SK5370
Langworth *Lincs* 76 TF0676
Langworthy *Devon* 5 SX4894
Lanieth *Cnwll* 3 SW9752
Lanivet *Cnwll* 4 SX0464
Lank *Cnwll* 4 SX0875
Lanlivery *Cnwll* 4 SX0759
Lanner *Cnwll* 2 SW7139
Lanoy *Cnwll* 5 SX2977
Lanreath *Cnwll* 4 SX1857
Lansallos *Cnwll* 4 SX1751
Lansdown *Avon* 22 ST7268
Lanteglos *Cnwll* 4 SX0882
Lanteglos Highway *Cnwll* 3 SX1453
Lantilio-Crossenny *Gwent* 34 SO3914
Lanton *Border* 110 NT6221
Lanton *Nthumb* 110 NT9231
Lapford *Devon* 19 SS7308
Laphroaig *Strath* 104 NR3845
Lapley *Staffs* 60 SJ8712
Lapworth *Warwks* 61 SP1671
Larachbeg *Highld* 122 NM6948
Larbert *Cent* 116 NS8582
Larbreck *Lancs* 80 SD4040
Largie *Gramp* 142 NJ6131
Largiemore *Strath* 114 NR9486
Largoward *Fife* 127 NO4607
Largs *Strath* 114 NS2059
Largybeg *Strath* 105 NS0423
Largymore *Strath* 105 NS0424
Larkfield *Strath* 114 NS2475
Larkfield *Kent* 28 TQ7058
Larkhall *Strath* 116 NS7651
Larkhill *Wilts* 23 SU1244
Larling *Norfk* 54 TL9889
Lartington *Dur* 95 NZ0117
Lasborough *Gloucs* 35 ST8294
Lasham *Hants* 24 SU6742
Lashbrook *Devon* 18 SS4305
Lashenden *Kent* 28 TQ8440
Lask Edge *Staffs* 72 SJ9156
Lassodie *Fife* 117 NT1292
Lasswade *Loth* 117 NT3065
Lastingham *N York* 90 SE7290
Latcham *Somset* 21 ST4447
Latchford *Oxon* 37 SP6501
Latchford *Herts* 39 TL3920
Latchingdon and Snoreham *Essex* 40 TL8800
Latchley *Cnwll* 5 SX4173
Latebrook *Staffs* 72 SJ8453
Lately Common *Gt Man* 79 SJ6797
Lathbury *Bucks* 38 SP8744
Latheron *Highld* 151 ND2033
Latheronwheel *Highld* 151 ND1832
Lathones *Fife* 127 NO4708
Latimer *Bucks* 26 TQ0199
Latteridge *Avon* 35 ST6684
Lattiford *Somset* 22 ST6926
Latton *Wilts* 36 SU0995
Lauder *Border* 118 NT5347
Laugharne *Dyfed* 31 SN3010
Laughterton *Lincs* 76 SK8375
Laughton *Lincs* 76 SK8497
Laughton *Leics* 50 SP6688
Laughton *Lincs* 64 TF0731
Laughton *E Susx* 16 TQ4913
Laughton-en-le-Morthen *S York* 75 SK5187
Launcells *Cnwll* 18 SS2405
Launcells Cross *Cnwll* 18 SS2605
Launceston *Cnwll* 5 SX3384
Launton *Oxon* 37 SP6022
Laurencekirk *Gramp* 135 NO7171
Laurieston *Cent* 116 NS9179
Laurieston *D & G* 99 NX6864
Lavendon *Bucks* 51 SP9153
Lavenham *Suffk* 54 TL9149
Lavernock *S Glam* 20 ST1868
Laversdale *Cumb* 101 NY4762
Laverstock *Wilts* 23 SU1630
Laverstoke *Hants* 24 SU4948
Laverton *N York* 89 SE2273
Laverton *Gloucs* 48 SP0735
Laverton *Somset* 22 ST7753
Lavister *Clwyd* 71 SJ3758
Law *Strath* 116 NS8252
Law Hill *Strath* 116 NS8251
Lawers *Tays* 124 NN6739
Lawford *Somset* 20 ST1336
Lawford *Essex* 41 TM0831
Lawgrove *Tays* 125 NO0926
Lawhitton *Cnwll* 5 SX3582
Lawkland *N York* 88 SD7766
Lawkland Green *N York* 88 SD7765
Lawley *Shrops* 60 SJ6608
Lawnhead *Staffs* 72 SJ8325
Lawrence End *Herts* 38 TL1419
Lawrenny *Dyfed* 30 SN0106
Lawshall *Suffk* 54 TL8654
Lawshall Green *Suffk* 54 TL8853
Lawton *H & W* 46 SO4459
Laxay *W Isls* 154 NB3321
Laxdale *W Isls* 154 NB4234
Laxey *IOM* 153 SC4384
Laxfield *Suffk* 55 TM2972
Laxford Bridge *Highld* 148 NC2346
Laxo *Shet* 155 HU4463
Laxton *Humb* 84 SE7925
Laxton *Notts* 75 SK7267
Laxton *Nhants* 51 SP9596
Laycock *W York* 82 SE0341
Layer Breton *Essex* 40 TL9417
Layer Marney *Essex* 40 TL9217
Layer-de-la-Haye *Essex* 41 TL9620
Layham *Suffk* 54 TM0240
Layland's Green *Berks* 23 SU3866
Laymore *Dorset* 10 ST3804
Laysters Pole *H & W* 46 SO5563
Layter's Green *Bucks* 26 SU9890
Laytham *Humb* 84 SE7439
Laythes *Cumb* 93 NY2455
Lazenby *Cleve* 97 NZ5719
Lazonby *Cumb* 94 NY5439
Le Bigard *Guern* 152 GN0000
Le Bourg *Guern* 152 GN0000
Le Bourg *Jersey* 152 JS0000
Le Gron *Guern* 152 GN0000
Le Haquais *Jersey* 152 JS0000
Le Hocq *Jersey* 152 JS0000
Le Villocq *Guern* 152 GN0000
Lea *Shrops* 59 SJ4108
Lea *Derbys* 74 SK3257
Lea *Lincs* 75 SK8286
Lea *Shrops* 59 SO3589
Lea *H & W* 35 SO6521
Lea *Wilts* 35 ST9586
Lea Bridge *Derbys* 74 SK3156
Lea Heath *Staffs* 73 SK0225
Lea Marston *Warwks* 61 SP2093
Lea Town *Lancs* 80 SD4730
Lea Yeat *Cumb* 88 SD7686
Leachkin *Highld* 140 NH6344
Leadburn *Loth* 117 NT2355
Leaden Roding *Essex* 40 TL5913
Leadenham *Lincs* 76 SK9452
Leadgate *Nthumb* 95 NZ1159
Leadgate *Dur* 96 NZ1251
Leadhills *Strath* 108 NS8815
Leadingcross Green *Kent* 28 TQ8951
Leadmill *Derbys* 74 SK2380
Leafield *Oxon* 36 SP3115
Leagrave *Beds* 38 TL0523
Leahead *Ches* 72 SJ6864
Lealholm Side *N York* 90 NZ7607
Leake *N York* 89 SE4390
Leake Common Side *Lincs* 77 TF3952
Lealholm *N York* 90 NZ7607
Lealt *Highld* 137 NG5060
Leam *Derbys* 74 SK2379
Leamington Hastings *Warwks* 50 SP4467
Leamonsley *Staffs* 61 SK1009
Leap Cross *E Susx* 16 TQ5810
Leasgill *Cumb* 87 SD4983
Leasingham *Lincs* 76 TF0548
Leasingthorne *Dur* 96 NZ2530
Leatherhead *Surrey* 26 TQ1656
Leathley *N York* 82 SE2347
Leaths *D & G* 100 NX7862
Leaton *Shrops* 59 SJ4618
Leaton *Shrops* 59 SJ6111
Leaveland *Kent* 28 TR0053
Leavenheath *Suffk* 54 TL9537
Leavening *N York* 90 SE7863
Leaves Green *Gt Lon* 27 TQ4161
Lebberston *N York* 91 TA0782
Lechampstead Thicket *Berks* 36 SU4276
Lechlade *Wilts* 36 SU2199
Leck *Lancs* 87 SD6476
Leckbuie *Tays* 124 NN7040
Leckford *Hants* 23 SU3737
Leck Gruinart *Strath* 112 NR2768
Leckhampstead *Bucks* 49 SP7237
Leckhampstead *Berks* 36 SU4375
Leckhampton *Gloucs* 35 SO9419
Leckmelm *Highld* 145 NH1689
Leckwith *S Glam* 33 ST1574
Leconfield *Humb* 84 TA0143
Ledaig *Strath* 122 NM9037
Ledburn *Bucks* 38 SP9021
Ledbury *H & W* 47 SO7137
Leddington *Gloucs* 47 SO6834
Ledgemoor *H & W* 46 SO4150
Ledicot *H & W* 46 SO4162
Ledmore Junction *Highld* 145 NC2412
Ledsham *W York* 83 SE4529
Ledsham *Ches* 71 SJ3574
Ledston *W York* 83 SE4328
Ledstone *Devon* 7 SX7446
Ledwell *Oxon* 49 SP4128
Lee *Shrops* 59 SJ4032
Lee *Devon* 18 SS4846
Lee *Hants* 12 SU3617
Lee *Gt Lon* 27 TQ3875
Lee Brockhurst *Shrops* 59 SJ5427
Lee Chapel *Essex* 40 TQ6987
Lee Clump *Bucks* 38 SP9004
Lee Common *Bucks* 38 SP9103
Leeds *W York* 82 SE2932
Lee Green *Ches* 72 SJ6661
Lee Mill *Devon* 6 SX5955
Lee Moor *Devon* 6 SX5762
Lee Street *Surrey* 15 TQ2743
Lee-on-the-Solent *Hants* 13 SU5600
Leebotwood *Shrops* 59 SO4798
Leece *Cumb* 86 SD2469
Leedon *Beds* 38 SP9325
Leeds *Kent* 28 TQ8253
Leeds Beck *Lincs* 76 TF2065
Leedstown *Cnwll* 2 SW6034
Leek *Staffs* 72 SJ9856
Leek Wootton *Warwks* 48 SP2868
Leeming *W York* 82 SE0434
Leeming *N York* 89 SE2989
Leeming Bar *N York* 89 SE2889
Lees *Gt Man* 79 SD9504
Lees *W York* 82 SE0437
Lees *Derbys* 73 SK2637
Lees Green *Derbys* 73 SK2637
Lees Hill *Cumb* 101 NY5568
Leesthorpe *Leics* 63 SK7813
Leetown *Tays* 126 NO2121
Leftwich *Ches* 79 SJ6672
Legbourne *Lincs* 77 TF3784
Legburthwaite *Cumb* 93 NY3219
Legerwood *Border* 110 NT5843
Legsby *Lincs* 76 TF1385
Leicester *Leics* 62 SK5804
Leicester Forest East *Leics* 62 SK5202
Leigh *Shrops* 59 SJ3303
Leigh *Mersyd* 79 SJ6599
Leigh *H & W* 47 SO7853
Leigh *Gloucs* 47 SO8626
Leigh *Dorset* 10 ST6108
Leigh *Wilts* 36 SU0692
Leigh *Surrey* 15 TQ2246
Leigh *Kent* 16 TQ5446
Leigh Beck *Essex* 40 TQ8183
Leigh Delamere *Wilts* 35 ST8879
Leigh Green *Kent* 17 TQ9033
Leigh Knoweglass *Strath* 116 NS6350
Leigh Sinton *H & W* 47 SO7750
Leigh Woods *Avon* 34 ST5672
Leigh upon Mendip *Somset* 22 ST6947
Leigh-on-Sea *Essex* 40 TQ8286
Leighland Chapel *Somset* 20 ST0336
Leighterton *Gloucs* 35 ST8290
Leighton *N York* 89 SE1679
Leighton *Powys* 58 SJ2306
Leighton *Shrops* 59 SJ6105
Leighton *Somset* 22 ST7043
Leighton Bromswold *Cambs* 52 TL1175
Leighton Buzzard *Beds* 38 SP9225
Leinthall Earls *H & W* 46 SO4467
Leinthall Starkes *H & W* 46 SO4369
Leintwardine *H & W* 46 SO4074
Leire *Leics* 50 SP5290
Leiston *Suffk* 55 TM4462
Leitfie *Tays* 126 NO2545
Leith *Loth* 117 NT2776
Leitholm *Border* 110 NT7944
Lelant *Cnwll* 2 SW5437
Lelley *Humb* 85 TA2032
Lem Hill *H & W* 60 SO7275
Lemmington Hall *Nthumb* 111 NU1211
Lempitlaw *Border* 110 NT7832
Lemreway *W Isls* 154 NB3711
Lemsford *Herts* 39 TL2212
Lenchwick *H & W* 48 SP0347
Lendalfoot *Strath* 106 NX1390
Lendrick *Cent* 124 NN5506
Lendrum Terrace *Gramp* 143 NK1141
Lenham *Kent* 28 TQ8952
Lenham Heath *Kent* 28 TQ9149
Lenie *Highld* 139 NH5126
Lennel *Border* 110 NT8540
Lennox Plunton *D & G* 99 NX6051
Lennoxlove *Loth* 118 NT5172
Lennoxtown *Strath* 116 NS6277
Lent *Bucks* 26 SU9381
Lenton *Notts* 62 SK5539
Lenton *Lincs* 64 TF0230
Lenwade *Norfk* 66 TG0918
Lenzie *Strath* 116 NS6572
Leochel-Cushnie *Gramp* 134 NJ5210
Leominster *H & W* 46 SO4959
Leonard Stanley *Gloucs* 35 SO8003
Leoville *Jersey* 152 JS0000
Lepe *Hants* 13 SZ4498
Lephin *Highld* 136 NG1749
Leppington *N York* 90 SE7661
Lepton *W York* 82 SE2015
Lerags *Strath* 122 NM8324
Lerryn *Cnwll* 4 SX1457
Lerwick *Shet* 155 HU4741
Les Arquets *Guern* 152 GN0000
Les Hubits *Guern* 152 GN0000
Les Lohiers *Guern* 152 GN0000
Les Murchez *Guern* 152 GN0000
Les Nicolles *Guern* 152 GN0000
Les Quartiers *Guern* 152 GN0000
Les Quennevais *Jersey* 152 JS0000
Les Sages *Guern* 152 GN0000
Les Villets *Guern* 152 GN0000
Lesbury *Nthumb* 111 NU2311
Leslie *Gramp* 142 NJ5924
Leslie *Fife* 126 NO2501
Lesmahagow *Strath* 108 NS8139
Lesnewth *Cnwll* 4 SX1390
Lessingham *Norfk* 67 TG3928
Lessonhall *Cumb* 93 NY2250
Lestowder *Cnwll* 3 SW7924
Leswalt *D & G* 98 NX0163
Letchmore Heath *Herts* 26 TQ1597
Letchworth *Herts* 39 TL2232
Letcombe Bassett *Oxon* 36 SU3784
Letcombe Regis *Oxon* 36 SU3886
Letham *Fife* 126 NO3014
Letham *Tays* 127 NO5348
Letham *Border* 110 NT6709
Letham Grange *Tays* 127 NO6345
Lethenty *Gramp* 142 NJ5820
Lethenty *Gramp* 143 NJ8140
Letheringham *Suffk* 55 TM2757
Letheringsett *Norfk* 66 TG0638
Lett's Green *Kent* 27 TQ4559
Lettaford *Devon* 8 SX7084
Letterfinlay Lodge Hotel *Highld* 131 NN2491
Letterfearn *Highld* 138 NG8823
Lettermorar *Highld* 129 NM7389
Letters *Highld* 145 NH1687
Lettershaw *Strath* 108 NS8920
Letterston *Dyfed* 30 SM9429
Lettoch *Highld* 141 NJ0219
Lettoch *Highld* 141 NJ1032
Letton *H & W* 46 SO3346
Letton *H & W* 46 SO3770
Letty Green *Herts* 39 TL2810
Letwell *S York* 75 SK5686
Leuchars *Fife* 127 NO4521
Leurbost *W Isls* 154 NB3725
Levalsa Moor *Cnwll* 3 SX0049
Levedale *Staffs* 72 SJ8916
Level's Green *Essex* 39 TL4724
Leven *Fife* 118 NO3800
Leven *Humb* 85 TA1045
Levencorroch *Strath* 105 NS0021
Levens *Cumb* 87 SD4886
Levens Green *Herts* 39 TL3522
Levenshulme *Gt Man* 79 SJ8794
Levenwick *Shet* 155 HU4021
Leverburgh *W Isls* 154 NG0186
Leverington *Cambs* 65 TF4411
Leverstock Green *Herts* 38 TL0806
Leverton *Lincs* 77 TF4047
Levington *Suffk* 55 TM2339
Levisham *N York* 90 SE8390
Lew *Oxon* 36 SP3206
Lewannick *Cnwll* 5 SX2780
Lewdown *Devon* 5 SX4586
Lewes *E Susx* 15 TQ4110
Leweston *Dyfed* 30 SM9322
Leweston *Dorset* 10 ST6312
Lewis Wych *H & W* 46 SO3357
Lewisham *Gt Lon* 27 TQ3774
Lewiston *Highld* 139 NH5129
Lewknor *Oxon* 37 SU7197
Leworthy *Devon* 18 SS3201
Leworthy *Devon* 19 SS6738
Lewson Street *Kent* 28 TQ9661
Lewth *Lancs* 80 SD4836
Lewtrenchard *Devon* 5 SX4586
Lexden *Essex* 41 TL9625
Lexworthy *Somset* 20 ST2535
Ley *Cnwll* 4 SX1766
Leybourne *Kent* 28 TQ6858
Leyburn *N York* 89 SE1190
Leycett *Staffs* 72 SJ7946
Leygreen *Herts* 39 TL1624
Leyland *Lancs* 80 SD5422
Leyland Green *Mersyd* 78 SD5500
Leylodge *Gramp* 135 NJ7613
Leys *Gramp* 143 NK0052
Leys *Tays* 126 NO2537
Leys of Cossans *Tays* 126 NO3849
Leysdown-on-Sea *Kent* 28 TR0370
Leysmill *Tays* 127 NO6047
Leyton *Gt Lon* 27 TQ3786
Leytonstone *Gt Lon* 27 TQ3987
Lezant *Cnwll* 5 SX3479
Lezayre *IOM* 153 SC4294
Lezerea *Cnwll* 2 SW6833
Lhanbryde *Gramp* 141 NJ2761
Libanus *Powys* 45 SN9925
Libberton *Strath* 108 NS9943
Liberton *Loth* 117 NT2769
Lichfield *Staffs* 61 SK1109
Lickey *H & W* 60 SO9975
Lickey End *H & W* 60 SO9772
Lickey Rock *H & W* 60 SO9774
Lickfold *W Susx* 14 SU9226
Liddaton Green *Devon* 5 SX4582
Liddesdale *Highld* 130 NM7759
Liddington *Wilts* 36 SU2081
Lidgate *Derbys* 74 SK3077
Lidgate *Suffk* 53 TL7258
Lidget *S York* 75 SE6500
Lidgett *Notts* 75 SK6365
Lidham Hill *E Susx* 17 TQ8316
Lidlington *Beds* 38 SP9939
Lidsing *Kent* 28 TQ7862
Liff *Tays* 126 NO3332
Lifford *W Mids* 61 SP0580
Lifton *Devon* 5 SX3885
Liftondown *Devon* 5 SX3685
Lighthazles *W York* 82 SE0220
Lighthorne *Warwks* 48 SP3355
Lightwater *Surrey* 25 SU9362
Lightwood *Staffs* 72 SJ9241
Lightwood Green *Clwyd* 71 SJ3840
Lightwood Green *Ches* 71 SJ6342
Lilbourne *Nhants* 50 SP5676
Lilburn Tower *Nthumb* 111 NU0224
Lilleshall *Shrops* 72 SJ7315
Lilley *Berks* 37 SU4479
Lilley *Herts* 38 TL1126
Lilliesleaf *Border* 109 NT5325
Lillingstone Dayrell *Bucks* 49 SP7039
Lillingstone Lovell *Bucks* 49 SP7140
Lillington *Dorset* 10 ST6212
Lilstock *Somset* 20 ST1645
Lilyhurst *Shrops* 60 SJ7413
Limbrick *Lancs* 81 SD6016
Limbury *Beds* 38 TL0724
Lime Street *H & W* 47 SO8130
Limebrook *H & W* 46 SO3766
Limefield *Gt Man* 81 SD8012
Limekilnburn *Strath* 116 NS7050
Limekilns *Fife* 117 NT0883
Limerigg *Cent* 116 NS8571
Limerstone *IOW* 13 SZ4482
Limestone Brae *Nthumb* 95 NY7949
Limington *Somset* 21 ST5422
Limmerhaugh *Strath* 107 NS6127
Limpenhoe *Norfk* 67 TG3903
Limpley Stoke *Wilts* 22 ST7860
Limpsfield *Surrey* 27 TQ4053
Limpsfield Chart *Surrey* 27 TQ4251
Linby *Notts* 75 SK5351
Linchmere *W Susx* 14 SU8630
Lincluden *D & G* 100 NX9677
Lincoln *Lincs* 76 SK9771
Lincomb *H & W* 47 SO8268
Lincombe *Devon* 7 SX7440
Lindal in Furness *Cumb* 86 SD2475
Lindale *Cumb* 87 SD4180
Lindean *Border* 109 NT4931
Lindfield *W Susx* 15 TQ3425
Lindford *Hants* 14 SU8036
Lindley *W York* 82 SE1217
Lindley Green *N York* 82 SE2248
Lindores *Fife* 126 NO2616
Lindow End *Ches* 79 SJ8178
Lindridge *H & W* 47 SO6769
Lindsell *Essex* 40 TL6427
Lindsey *Suffk* 54 TL9745
Lindsey Tye *Suffk* 54 TL9845
Liney *Somset* 21 ST3535
Linford *Hants* 12 SU1806
Linford *Essex* 40 TQ6779
Lingbob *W York* 82 SE0935
Lingdale *Cleve* 97 NZ6716
Lingen *H & W* 46 SO3667
Lingley Green *Ches* 78 SJ5588
Lingwood *Norfk* 67 TG3508
Linicro *Highld* 136 NG3966
Linkend *H & W* 47 SO8231
Linkenholt *Hants* 23 SU3657
Linkhill *Kent* 17 TQ8127
Linkinhorne *Cnwll* 5 SX3173
Linktown *Fife* 117 NT2790
Linkwood *Gramp* 141 NJ2361
Linley *Shrops* 59 SO3592
Linley Green *H & W* 47 SO6953
Linleygreen *Shrops* 60 SO6898
Linlithgow *Loth* 117 NS9977
Linshiels *Nthumb* 110 NT8906
Linsidemore *Highld* 146 NH5499
Linslade *Beds* 38 SP9125
Linstead Parva *Suffk* 55 TM3377
Linstock *Cumb* 93 NY4258
Linthurst *H & W* 60 SO9972
Linthwaite *W York* 82 SE1014
Lintlaw *Border* 119 NT8258
Lintmill *Gramp* 142 NJ5165
Linton *Border* 110 NT7726
Linton *N York* 88 SD9962
Linton *W York* 83 SE3946
Linton *Derbys* 73 SK2716
Linton *H & W* 47 SO6625
Linton *Cambs* 53 TL5646
Linton *Kent* 28 TQ7550
Linton Heath *Derbys* 73 SK2816
Linton Hill *Gloucs* 47 SO6624
Linton-on-Ouse *N York* 90 SE4860
Lintrathen *Tays* 126 NO2854
Linwood *Strath* 115 NS4464
Linwood *Hants* 12 SU1809
Linwood *Lincs* 76 TF1186
Lionel *W Isls* 154 NB5263
Lions Green *E Susx* 16 TQ5518
Liphook *Hants* 14 SU8431
Lipley *Shrops* 72 SJ7330
Liscard *Mersyd* 78 SJ2991
Liscombe *Devon* 19 SS8732
Liskeard *Cnwll* 5 SX2564
Liss *Hants* 14 SU7727
Liss Forest *Hants* 14 SU7828
Lissett *Humb* 91 TA1458
Lissington *Lincs* 76 TF1083
Liston *Essex* 54 TL8544
Lisvane *S Glam* 33 ST1883
Litcham *Norfk* 66 TF8817
Litchard *M Glam* 33 SS9081
Litchborough *Nhants* 49 SP6354
Litchfield *Hants* 24 SU4653
Litherland *Mersyd* 78 SJ3397
Litlington *Cambs* 39 TL3142
Litlington *E Susx* 16 TQ5201
Little Abington *Cambs* 53 TL5349
Little Addington *Nhants* 51 SP9673
Little Airies *D & G* 99 NX4248
Little Almshoe *Herts* 39 TL2026
Little Alne *Warwks* 48 SP1461
Little Amwell *Herts* 39 TL3511
Little Asby *Cumb* 87 NY6909
Little Aston *Staffs* 61 SK0900
Little Atherfield *IOW* 13 SZ4679
Little Ayton *N York* 90 NZ5610
Little Baddow *Essex* 40 TL7707
Little Badminton *Avon* 35 ST8084
Little Bampton *Cumb* 93 NY2755
Little Bardfield *Essex* 40 TL6531
Little Barford *Beds* 52 TL1756
Little Barningham *Norfk* 66 TG1333
Little Barrington *Gloucs* 36 SP2012
Little Barrow *Ches* 71 SJ4769
Little Barugh *N York* 90 SE7679

Little Bayton LLangoedmor

Little Bayton *Warwks* 61 SP3585
Little Bealings *Suffk* 55 TM2247
Little Bedwyn *Wilts* 23 SU2866
Little Bentley *Essex* 41 TM1125
Little Berkhamsted *Herts* 39 TL2907
Little Billing *Nhants* 51 SP8061
Little Billington *Beds* 38 SP9322
Little Birch *H & W* 46 SO5130
Little Bispham *Lancs* 80 SD3141
Little Blakenham *Suffk* 54 TM1048
Little Blencow *Cumb* 93 NY4532
Little Bloxwich *W Mids* 60 SK0003
Little Bognor *W Susx* 14 TQ0020
Little Bolehill *Derbys* 73 SK2954
Little Bookham *Surrey* 26 TQ1254
Little Bourton *Oxon* 49 SP4544
Little Bowden *Leics* 50 SP7487
Little Bradley *Suffk* 53 TL6852
Little Brampton *H & W* 46 SO3061
Little Braxted *Essex* 40 TL8314
Little Brechin *Tays* 134 NO5862
Little Brickhill *Bucks* 38 SP9132
Little Bridgeford *Staffs* 72 SJ8727
Little Brington *Nhants* 49 SP6663
Little Bromley *Essex* 41 TM0928
Little Broughton *Cumb* 92 NY0731
Little Budworth *Ches* 71 SJ5965
Little Burstead *Essex* 40 TQ6692
Little Bytham *Lincs* 64 TF0118
Little Carlton *Notts* 75 SK7757
Little Carlton *Lincs* 77 TF3985
Little Casterton *Leics* 64 TF0109
Little Catwick *Humb* 85 TA1244
Little Catworth *Cambs* 51 TL1072
Little Cawthorpe *Lincs* 77 TF3583
Little Chalfont *Bucks* 26 SU9997
Little Charlinch *Somset* 20 ST2437
Little Chart *Kent* 28 TQ9446
Little Chatfield *Wilts* 22 ST8563
Little Chesterford *Essex* 39 TL5141
Little Cheveney *Kent* 28 TQ7243
Little Cheverell *Wilts* 22 ST9953
Little Chishill *Cambs* 39 TL4137
Little Clacton *Essex* 41 TM1618
Little Clanfield *Oxon* 36 SP2701
Little Clifton *Cumb* 92 NY0528
Little Coates *Humb* 85 TA2408
Little Comberton *H & W* 47 SO9643
Little Common *E Susx* 17 TQ7107
Little Comp *Kent* 27 TQ6356
Little Compton *Warwks* 48 SP2630
Little Corby *Cumb* 93 NY4757
Little Cornard *Suffk* 54 TL9039
Little Cowarne *H & W* 46 SO6051
Little Coxwell *Oxon* 36 SU2893
Little Crakehall *N York* 89 SE2390
Little Cransley *Nhants* 51 SP8376
Little Creaton *Nhants* 50 SP7171
Little Cressingham *Norfk* 66 TF8700
Little Crosby *Mersyd* 78 SD3201
Little Crosthwaite *Cumb* 93 NY2327
Little Cubley *Derbys* 73 SK1537
Little Dalby *Leics* 63 SK7714
Little Dens *Gramp* 143 NK0643
Little Dewchurch *H & W* 46 SO5231
Little Ditton *Cambs* 53 TL6658
Little Doward *H & W* 34 SO5416
Little Driffield *Humb* 91 TA0058
Little Dunham *Norfk* 66 TF8612
Little Dunkeld *Tays* 125 NO0342
Little Dunmow *Essex* 40 TL6521
Little Durnford *Wilts* 23 SU1234
Little Eaton *Derbys* 62 SK3641
Little Ellingham *Norfk* 66 TM0099
Little Elm *Somset* 22 ST7146
Little Everdon *Nhants* 49 SP5957
Little Eversden *Cambs* 52 TL3753
Little Faringdon *S York* 36 SP2201
Little Fencote *N York* 89 SE2893
Little Fenton *N York* 83 SE5235
Little Fransham *Norfk* 66 TF9011
Little Gaddesden *Herts* 38 SP9913
Little Garway *H & W* 46 SO4424
Little Gidding *Cambs* 52 TL1282
Little Glemham *Suffk* 55 TM3458
Little Gorsley *H & W* 47 SO6924
Little Gransden *Cambs* 52 TL2755
Little Green *Notts* 63 SK7243
Little Green *Somset* 22 ST7248
Little Grimsby *Lincs* 77 TF3291
Little Gringley *Notts* 75 SK7380
Little Habton *N York* 90 SE7477
Little Hadham *Herts* 39 TL4322
Little Hale *Lincs* 64 TF1441
Little Hallam *Derbys* 62 SK4640
Little Hallingbury *Essex* 39 TL5017
Little Hanford *Dorset* 11 ST8411
Little Harrowden *Nhants* 51 SP8771
Little Hartlip *Kent* 28 TQ8464
Little Haseley *Oxon* 37 SP6400
Little Hatfield *Humb* 85 TA1743
Little Hautbois *Norfk* 67 TG2521
Little Haven *Dyfed* 30 SM8512
Little Hay *Staffs* 61 SK1102
Little Haywood *Staffs* 73 SK0021
Little Heath *Staffs* 72 SJ8917
Little Heath *W Mids* 61 SP3482
Little Hereford *H & W* 46 SO5568
Little Hermitage *Kent* 28 TQ7170
Little Horkesley *Essex* 40 TL9532
Little Hormead *Herts* 39 TL4028
Little Horsted *E Susx* 16 TQ4718
Little Horton *W York* 82 SE1531
Little Horton *Wilts* 23 SU0462
Little Horwood *Bucks* 38 SP7930
Little Houghton *S York* 83 SE4205
Little Houghton *Nhants* 51 SP8059
Little Hucklow *Derbys* 74 SK1678
Little Hulton *Gt Man* 79 SD7203
Little Hungerford *Berks* 24 SU5173
Little Hutton *N York* 89 SE4576
Little Ingestre *Staffs* 72 SJ9824
Little Irchester *Nhants* 51 SP9066
Little Kelk *Humb* 91 TA0959
Little Keyford *Somset* 22 ST7746
Little Kimble *Bucks* 38 SP8207
Little Kineton *Warwks* 48 SP3350
Little Kingshill *Bucks* 26 SU8999
Little Knox *D & G* 100 NX8060
Little Langdale *Cumb* 86 NY3103
Little Langford *Wilts* 23 SU0436
Little Lashbrook *Devon* 18 SS4007
Little Laver *Essex* 39 TL5409
Little Leigh *Ches* 71 SJ6175
Little Leighs *Essex* 40 TL7117
Little Lever *Gt Man* 79 SD7507
Little Linford *Bucks* 38 SP8444
Little Linton *Cambs* 53 TL5547
Little Load *Somset* 21 ST4724
Little London *W York* 82 SE2039
Little London *Powys* 58 SO0488
Little London *Gloucs* 35 SO7018
Little London *Oxon* 37 SP6412
Little London *Hants* 23 SU3749
Little London *Hants* 24 SU6259
Little London *Lincs* 64 TF2321
Little London *Lincs* 77 TF3374
Little London *Lincs* 65 TF4323
Little London *Norfk* 65 TF5621
Little London *Cambs* 65 TL4196
Little London *Essex* 39 TL4729
Little London *Essex* 53 TL6835
Little London *E Susx* 16 TQ5620
Little Longstone *Derbys* 74 SK1871
Little Madeley *Staffs* 72 SJ7745
Little Malvern *H & W* 47 SO7640
Little Mancot *Clwyd* 71 SJ3266
Little Maplestead *Essex* 54 TL8234
Little Marcle *H & W* 47 SO6736
Little Marlow *Bucks* 26 SU8787
Little Massingham *Norfk* 65 TF7824
Little Melton *Norfk* 66 TG1607
Little Mill *Gwent* 34 SO3203
Little Milton *Oxon* 37 SP6100
Little Missenden *Bucks* 26 SU9299
Little Mongham *Kent* 29 TR3351
Little Moor *Somset* 21 ST3232
Little Musgrave *Cumb* 94 NY7612
Little Ness *Shrops* 59 SJ4019
Little Neston *Ches* 71 SJ2976
Little Newcastle *Dyfed* 30 SM9829
Little Newsham *Dur* 96 NZ1217
Little Norton *Staffs* 60 SK0207
Little Norton *Somset* 10 ST4715
Little Oakley *Nhants* 51 SP8985
Little Oakley *Essex* 41 TM2129
Little Odell *Beds* 51 SP9557
Little Offley *Herts* 38 TL1328
Little Onn *Staffs* 72 SJ8315
Little Ormside *Cumb* 94 NY7016
Little Orton *Cumb* 93 NY3555
Little Oxendon *Nhants* 50 SP7283
Little Packington *Warwks* 61 SP2184
Little Pannell *Wilts* 22 SU0053
Little Pattenden *Kent* 28 TQ7445
Little Paxton *Cambs* 52 TL1862
Little Petherick *Cnwll* 4 SW9172
Little Plumpton *Lancs* 80 SD3832
Little Plumstead *Norfk* 67 TG3112
Little Ponton *Lincs* 63 SK9232
Little Posbrook *Hants* 13 SU5304
Little Potheridge *Devon* 19 SS5214
Little Preston *W York* 83 SE3930
Little Preston *Nhants* 49 SP5854
Little Raveley *Cambs* 52 TL2579
Little Reedness *Humb* 84 SE8022
Little Ribston *N York* 83 SE3853
Little Rissington *Gloucs* 36 SP1819
Little Rollright *Oxon* 48 SP2930
Little Rowsley *Derbys* 74 SK2566
Little Ryburgh *Norfk* 66 TF9628
Little Ryle *Nthumb* 111 NU0111
Little Ryton *Shrops* 59 SJ4803
Little Salkeld *Cumb* 94 NY5636
Little Sampford *Essex* 40 TL6533
Little Sandhurst *Berks* 25 SU8262
Little Saredon *Staffs* 60 SJ9407
Little Saughall *Ches* 71 SJ3768
Little Saxham *Suffk* 54 TL8063
Little Scatwell *Highld* 139 NH3856
Little Sessay *N York* 89 SE4674
Little Shelford *Cambs* 53 TL4551
Little Silver *Devon* 9 SS8601
Little Silver *Devon* 9 SS9109
Little Singleton *Lancs* 80 SD3739
Little Skipwith *N York* 83 SE6538
Little Smeaton *N York* 83 SE5216
Little Snoring *Norfk* 66 TF9532
Little Sodbury *Avon* 35 ST7582
Little Sodbury End *Avon* 35 ST7483
Little Somborne *Hants* 23 SU3832
Little Somerford *Wilts* 35 ST9684
Little Soudley *Shrops* 72 SJ7128
Little Stainforth *N York* 88 SD8166
Little Stainton *Dur* 96 NZ3420
Little Stanney *Ches* 71 SJ4174
Little Staughton *Beds* 51 TL1062
Little Steeping *Lincs* 77 TF4362
Little Stoke *Staffs* 72 SJ9132
Little Stonham *Suffk* 54 TM1160
Little Stretton *Leics* 50 SK6600
Little Stretton *Shrops* 59 SO4491
Little Strickland *Cumb* 94 NY5619
Little Stukeley *Cambs* 52 TL2175
Little Sugnall *Staffs* 72 SJ8031
Little Sutton *Ches* 71 SJ3776
Little Sutton *Shrops* 59 SO5182
Little Sypland *D & G* 99 NX7253
Little Tew *Oxon* 48 SP3828
Little Tey *Essex* 40 TL8923
Little Thetford *Cambs* 53 TL5376
Little Thirkleby *N York* 89 SE4778
Little Thornage *Norfk* 66 TG0538
Little Thornton *Lancs* 80 SD3541
Little Thorpe *Dur* 96 NZ4242
Little Thurlow *Suffk* 53 TL6751
Little Thurlow Green *Suffk* 53 TL6851
Little Thurrock *Essex* 27 TQ6277
Little Torrington *Devon* 18 SS4916
Little Totham *Essex* 40 TL8811
Little Town *Cumb* 93 NY2319
Little Town *Lancs* 81 SD6635
Little Town *Ches* 79 SJ6494
Little Twycross *Leics* 62 SK3405
Little Wakering *Essex* 40 TQ9388
Little Walden *Essex* 39 TL5441
Little Waldingfield *Suffk* 54 TL9245
Little Walsingham *Norfk* 66 TF9337
Little Waltham *Essex* 40 TL7012
Little Warley *Essex* 40 TQ6090
Little Washbourne *Gloucs* 47 SO9833
Little Weighton *Humb* 84 SE9833
Little Weldon *Nhants* 51 SP9289
Little Welnetham *Suffk* 54 TL8859
Little Welton *Lincs* 77 TF3087
Little Wenham *Suffk* 54 TM0839
Little Wenlock *Shrops* 59 SJ6406
Little Weston *Somset* 21 ST6225
Little Whitefield *IOW* 13 SZ5889
Little Whittington *Nthumb* 102 NY9869
Little Wilbraham *Cambs* 53 TL5458
Little Witcombe *Gloucs* 35 SO9115
Little Witley *H & W* 47 SO7863
Little Wittenham *Oxon* 37 SU5693
Little Wolford *Warwks* 48 SP2635
Little Woodcote *Surrey* 27 TQ2861
Little Wratting *Suffk* 53 TL6847
Little Wymington *Beds* 51 SP9565
Little Wymondley *Herts* 39 TL2127
Little Wyrley *Staffs* 60 SK0105
Little Yeldham *Essex* 53 TL7839
Littlebeck *N York* 90 NZ8804
Littleborough *Gt Man* 81 SD9316
Littleborough *Notts* 75 SK8282
Littleborough *Devon* 19 SS8210
Littlebourne *Kent* 29 TR2057
Littlebredy *Dorset* 10 SY5889
Littlebury *Essex* 39 TL5139
Littlebury Green *Essex* 39 TL4838
Littlecott *Wilts* 23 SU1352
Littledean *Gloucs* 35 SO6713
Littledown *Hants* 23 SU3457
Littleham *Devon* 18 SS4323
Littleham *Devon* 9 SY0381
Littlehampton *W Susx* 14 TQ0201
Littleharle Tower *Nthumb* 103 NZ0183
Littlehempston *Devon* 7 SX8162
Littlehoughton *Nthumb* 111 NU2216
Littlemill *Highld* 140 NH9150
Littlemill *Gramp* 134 NO3295
Littlemoor *Derbys* 74 SK3663
Littlemore *Oxon* 37 SP5302
Littleover *Derbys* 62 SK3334
Littleport *Cambs* 53 TL5686
Littleport Bridge *Cambs* 53 TL5787
Littler *Ches* 71 SJ6366
Littlestone-on-Sea *Kent* 17 TR0824
Littlethorpe *N York* 89 SE3269
Littlethorpe *Leics* 50 SP5496
Littleton *D & G* 99 NX6355
Littleton *Ches* 71 SJ4466
Littleton *Somset* 21 ST4930
Littleton *Avon* 21 ST5563
Littleton *Dorset* 11 ST8904
Littleton *Hants* 24 SU4532
Littleton *Surrey* 25 SU9847
Littleton *Surrey* 26 TQ0668
Littleton Drew *Wilts* 35 ST8380
Littleton-on-Severn *Avon* 34 ST5989
Littletown *Dur* 96 NZ3343
Littletown *IOW* 13 SZ5390
Littlewick Green *Berks* 37 SU8379
Littlewindsor *Dorset* 10 ST4304
Littlewood *Staffs* 60 SJ9807
Littleworth *Staffs* 72 SJ9323
Littleworth *Staffs* 60 SK0111
Littleworth *H & W* 47 SO8850
Littleworth *H & W* 47 SO9962
Littleworth *Bucks* 38 SP8823
Littleworth *Oxon* 36 SU3197
Littleworth *W Susx* 15 TQ1920
Littleworth Common *Bucks* 26 SU9386
Littleworth End *Cambs* 52 TL2266
Littley Green *Essex* 40 TL6917
Litton *N York* 88 SD9074
Litton *Derbys* 74 SK1675
Litton *Somset* 21 ST5954
Litton Cheney *Dorset* 10 SY5490
Liverpool *Mersyd* 78 SJ3490
Liversedge *W York* 82 SE1923
Liverton *Cleve* 97 NZ7115
Liverton *Devon* 7 SX8075
Liverton Mines *Cleve* 97 NZ7117
Liverton Street *Kent* 28 TQ8750
Livesey Street *Kent* 28 TQ7054
Livingston *Loth* 117 NT0668
Livingston Village *Loth* 117 NT0366
Lixton *Devon* 7 SX6950
Lixwm *Clwyd* 70 SJ1671
Lizard *Cnwll* 2 SW7012
Llaingoch *Gwynd* 68 SH2382
Llaithddu *Powys* 58 SO0680
Llan-y-pwll *Clwyd* 71 SJ3752
Llanaber *Gwynd* 57 SH6018
Llanaelhaearn *Gwynd* 56 SH3844
Llanafan *Dyfed* 43 SN6872
Llanafan-fechan *Powys* 45 SN9750
Llanallgo *Gwynd* 68 SH5085
Llanarmon *Gwynd* 56 SH4239
Llanarmon Dyffryn Ceiriog *Clwyd* 58 SJ1532
Llanarmon-yn-Ial *Clwyd* 70 SJ1956
Llanarth *Dyfed* 42 SN4257
Llanarth *Gwent* 34 SO3710
Llanarthne *Dyfed* 32 SN5320
Llanasa *Clwyd* 70 SJ1081
Llanbabo *Gwynd* 68 SH3787
Llanbadarn Fawr *Dyfed* 43 SN6081
Llanbadarn Fynydd *Powys* 45 SO0977
Llanbadarn-y-garreg *Powys* 45 SO1148
Llanbadoc *Gwent* 34 ST3799
Llanbadrig *Gwynd* 68 SH3794
Llanbeder *Gwent* 34 ST3890
Llanbedr *Gwynd* 57 SH5826
Llanbedr *Powys* 45 SO1446
Llanbedr *Powys* 34 SO2320
Llanbedr-Dyffryn-Clwyd *Clwyd* 70 SJ1459
Llanbedr-y-cennin *Gwynd* 69 SH7669
Llanbedrgoch *Gwynd* 68 SH5180
Llanbedrog *Gwynd* 56 SH3231
Llanberis *Gwynd* 69 SH5760
Llanbethery *S Glam* 20 ST0369
Llanbister *Powys* 45 SO1173
Llanblethian *S Glam* 33 SS9873
Llanboidy *Dyfed* 31 SN2123
Llanbradach *M Glam* 33 ST1490
Llanbrynmair *Powys* 57 SH8902
Llancarfan *S Glam* 33 ST0470
Llancayo *Gwent* 34 SO3603
Llancillo *H & W* 46 SO3625
Llancloudy *H & W* 34 SO4921
Llancynfelyn *Dyfed* 43 SN6492
Llandaf *S Glam* 33 ST1577
Llandanwg *Gwynd* 57 SH5728
Llandawke *Dyfed* 31 SN2811
Llanddaniel Fab *Gwynd* 68 SH4970
Llanddarog *Dyfed* 32 SN5016
Llanddeiniol *Dyfed* 43 SN5571
Llanddeiniolen *Gwynd* 69 SH5465
Llandderfel *Gwynd* 58 SH9837
Llanddeusant *Gwynd* 68 SH3485
Llanddeusant *Dyfed* 44 SN7724
Llanddewi *W Glam* 32 SS4588
Llanddewi Brefi *Dyfed* 44 SN6655
Llanddewi Rhydderch *Gwent* 34 SO3512
Llanddewi Velfrey *Dyfed* 31 SN1415
Llanddewi Ystradenni *Powys* 45 SO1068
Llanddewi'r Cwm *Powys* 45 SO0348
Llanddoget *Gwynd* 69 SH8063
Llanddona *Gwynd* 69 SH5779
Llanddowror *Dyfed* 31 SN2514
Llanddrew *Powys* 45 SO0530
Llanddulas *Clwyd* 70 SH9178
Llanddyfnan *Gwynd* 68 SH5078
Llandecwyn *Gwynd* 57 SH6337
Llandefaelog Fach *Powys* 45 SO0332
Llandefaelogtrer-graig *Powys* 45 SO1229
Llandefalle *Powys* 45 SO1035
Llandegai *Gwynd* 69 SH5971
Llandegfan *Gwynd* 69 SH5674
Llandegla *Clwyd* 70 SJ2051
Llandegley *Powys* 45 SO1463
Llandegveth *Gwent* 34 ST3395
Llandegwning *Gwynd* 56 SH2629
Llandeilo *Dyfed* 32 SN6222
Llandeilo Graban *Powys* 45 SO0944
Llandeilo'r Fan *Powys* 45 SN8934
Llandeloy *Dyfed* 30 SM8626
Llandenny *Gwent* 34 SO4104
Llandevaud *Gwent* 34 ST4090
Llandevenny *Gwent* 34 ST4186
Llandinabo *H & W* 46 SO5128
Llandinam *Powys* 58 SO0288
Llandissilio *Dyfed* 31 SN1221
Llandogo *Gwent* 34 SO5203
Llandough *S Glam* 33 SS9972
Llandough *S Glam* 33 ST1673
Llandovery *Dyfed* 44 SN7634
Llandow *S Glam* 33 SS9473
Llandre *Dyfed* 43 SN6286
Llandre *Dyfed* 44 SN6741
Llandre Isaf *Dyfed* 31 SN1328
Llandrillo *Clwyd* 58 SJ0337
Llandrillo-yn-Rhos *Clwyd* 69 SH8380
Llandrindod Wells *Powys* 45 SO0561
Llandrinio *Powys* 58 SJ2817
Llandudno *Gwynd* 69 SH7882
Llandudno Junction *Gwynd* 69 SH7977
Llandudwen *Gwynd* 56 SH2736
Llandulas *Powys* 45 SN8841
Llandwrog *Gwynd* 68 SH4555
Llandybie *Dyfed* 32 SN6115
Llandyfaelog *Dyfed* 31 SN4111
Llandyfan *Dyfed* 32 SN6417
Llandyfriog *Dyfed* 31 SN3341
Llandyfrydog *Gwynd* 68 SH4485
Llandygwydd *Dyfed* 31 SN2443
Llandyrnog *Clwyd* 70 SJ1065
Llandyssil *Powys* 58 SO1995
Llandysul *Dyfed* 31 SN4140
Llanedeyrn *S Glam* 33 ST2181
Llanedi *Dyfed* 32 SN5806
Llanegryn *Gwynd* 57 SH6005
Llanegwad *Dyfed* 32 SN5221
Llaneilian *Gwynd* 68 SH4692
Llanelian-yn-Rhos *Clwyd* 69 SH8676
Llanelidan *Clwyd* 70 SJ1150
Llanelieu *Powys* 45 SO1834
Llanellen *Gwent* 34 SO3010
Llanelli *Dyfed* 32 SN5000
Llanelltyd *Gwynd* 57 SH7119
Llanelly *Gwent* 34 SO2314
Llanelwedd *Powys* 45 SO0451
Llanenddwyn *Gwynd* 57 SH5823
Llanengan *Gwynd* 56 SH2926
Llanerch *Gwynd* 57 SH8816
Llanerch *Powys* 59 SO3093
Llanerchymedd *Gwynd* 68 SH4184
Llanerfyl *Powys* 58 SJ0309
Llanfachraeth *Gwynd* 68 SH3182
Llanfachreth *Gwynd* 57 SH7522
Llanfaelog *Gwynd* 68 SH3373
Llanfaelrhys *Gwynd* 56 SH2026
Llanfaenor *Gwent* 34 SO4317
Llanfaes *Gwynd* 69 SH6077
Llanfaes *Powys* 45 SO0328
Llanfaethlu *Gwynd* 68 SH3186
Llanfair *Gwynd* 57 SH5728
Llanfair Caereinion *Powys* 58 SJ1006
Llanfair Clydogau *Dyfed* 44 SN6251
Llanfair Dyffryn Clwyd *Clwyd* 70 SJ1355
Llanfair Kilgeddin *Gwent* 34 SO3506
Llanfair P G *Gwynd* 68 SH5271
Llanfair Talhaearn *Clwyd* 70 SH9270
Llanfair Waterdine *Shrops* 45 SO2376
Llanfair-Nant-Gwyn *Dyfed* 31 SN1637
Llanfair-is-gaer *Gwynd* 68 SH5065
Llanfair-y-Cwmmwd *Gwynd* 68 SH4466
Llanfair-yn-Neubwll *Gwynd* 68 SH3076
Llanfairfechan *Gwynd* 69 SH6874
Llanfairynghornwy *Gwynd* 68 SH3290
Llanfallteg *Dyfed* 31 SN1520
Llanfallteg West *Dyfed* 31 SN1419
Llanfarian *Dyfed* 43 SN5877
Llanfechain *Powys* 58 SJ1920
Llanfechelli *Gwynd* 68 SH3791
Llanferres *Clwyd* 70 SJ1860
Llanfflewyn *Gwynd* 68 SH3588
Llanfihangel Tal-y-llyn *Powys* 45 SO1128
Llanfihangel Glyn Myfyr *Clwyd* 70 SH9849
Llanfihangel Nant Bran *Powys* 45 SN9434
Llanfihangel Rhydithon *Powys* 45 SO1566
Llanfihangel Rogiet *Gwent* 34 ST4587
Llanfihangel ar-Arth *Dyfed* 31 SN4540
Llanfihangel yn Nhowyn *Gwynd* 68 SH3277
Llanfihangel-nant-Melan *Powys* 45 SO1758
Llanfihangel-uwch-Gwili *Dyfed* 32 SN4922
Llanfihangel-y-Creuddyn *Dyfed* 43 SN6675
Llanfihangel-y-pennant *Gwynd* 57 SH5244
Llanfihangel-y-pennant *Gwynd* 57 SH6708
Llanfihangel-y-traethau *Gwynd* 57 SH5934
Llanfihangel-yng-Ngwynfa *Powys* 58 SJ0816
Llanfilo *Powys* 45 SO1132
Llanfoist *Gwent* 34 SO2813
Llanfor *Gwynd* 58 SH9336
Llanfrechfa *Gwent* 34 ST3293
Llanfrothen *Gwynd* 57 SH6241
Llanfrynach *Powys* 45 SO0725
Llanfwrog *Gwynd* 68 SH3084
Llanfwrog *Clwyd* 70 SJ1157
Llanfyllin *Powys* 58 SJ1419
Llanfynydd *Clwyd* 70 SJ2856
Llanfynydd *Dyfed* 44 SN5527
Llanfyrnach *Dyfed* 31 SN2231
Llangadfan *Powys* 58 SJ0110
Llangadog *Dyfed* 31 SN4207
Llangadog *Dyfed* 44 SN7028
Llangadwaladr *Gwynd* 68 SH3869
Llangadwaladr *Clwyd* 58 SJ1830
Llangaffo *Gwynd* 68 SH4468
Llangain *Dyfed* 31 SN3815
Llangammarch Wells *Powys* 45 SN9346
Llangan *S Glam* 33 SS9577
Llangarron *H & W* 34 SO5220
Llangasty-Talyllyn *Powys* 45 SO1326
Llangathen *Dyfed* 32 SN5822
Llangattock *Powys* 33 SO2117
Llangattock Lingoed *Gwent* 34 SO3620
Llangattock-Vibon-Avel *Gwent* 34 SO4515
Llangedwyn *Clwyd* 58 SJ1824
Llangefni *Gwynd* 68 SH4675
Llangeinor *M Glam* 33 SS9187
Llangeinwen *Gwynd* 68 SH4465
Llangeitho *Dyfed* 44 SN6259
Llangeler *Dyfed* 31 SN3739
Llangelynin *Gwynd* 57 SH5707
Llangendeirne *Dyfed* 32 SN4513
Llangennech *Dyfed* 32 SN5601
Llangennith *W Glam* 31 SS4291
Llangenny *Powys* 34 SO2417
Llangernyw *Clwyd* 69 SH8767
Llangian *Gwynd* 56 SH2928
Llangiwg *W Glam* 32 SN7205
Llangloffan *Dyfed* 30 SM9032
Llanglydwen *Dyfed* 31 SN1826
Llangoed *Gwynd* 69 SH6079
Llangoedmor *Dyfed* 42 SN2046

Lower Crossings *Derbys*	74	SK0480
Lower Cumberworth *W York*	82	SE2209
Lower Cwmtwrch *Powys*	32	SN7610
Lower Darwen *Lancs*	81	SD6825
Lower Dean *Beds*	51	TL0569
Lower Denby *W York*	82	SE2307
Lower Diabaig *Highld*	137	NG7960
Lower Dicker *E Susx*	16	TQ5511
Lower Dinchope *Shrops*	59	SO4584
Lower Down *Shrops*	59	SO3484
Lower Dunsforth *N York*	89	SE4464
Lower Egleton *H & W*	47	SO6245
Lower Elkstone *Staffs*	74	SK0658
Lower Ellastone *Staffs*	73	SK1142
Lower End *Bucks*	37	SP6809
Lower End *Nhants*	51	SP8861
Lower End *Bucks*	38	SP9238
Lower Everleigh *Wilts*	23	SU1854
Lower Exbury *Hants*	13	SZ4299
Lower Eythorne *Kent*	29	TR2849
Lower Failand *Avon*	34	ST5173
Lower Farringdon *Hants*	24	SU7035
Lower Feltham *Gt Lon*	26	TQ0971
Lower Fittleworth *W Susx*	14	TQ0118
Lower Frankton *Shrops*	59	SJ3732
Lower Freystrop *Dyfed*	30	SM9512
Lower Froyle *Hants*	24	SU7544
Lower Gabwell *Devon*	7	SX9169
Lower Gledfield *Highld*	146	NH5890
Lower Godney *Somset*	21	ST4742
Lower Gornal *W Mids*	60	SO9191
Lower Gravenhurst *Beds*	38	TL1035
Lower Green *Gt Man*	79	SJ7098
Lower Green *Staffs*	60	SJ9007
Lower Green *Nhants*	51	SP8159
Lower Green *Norfk*	66	TF9837
Lower Green *Herts*	39	TL1832
Lower Green *Herts*	39	TL4233
Lower Green *Essex*	39	TL4334
Lower Green *Suffk*	53	TL7465
Lower Green *Kent*	16	TQ5640
Lower Green *Kent*	16	TQ6341
Lower Hacheston *Suffk*	55	TM3156
Lower Halliford *Surrey*	26	TQ0866
Lower Halstock Leigh *Dorset*	10	ST5207
Lower Halstow *Kent*	28	TQ8567
Lower Hamworthy *Dorset*	11	SY9990
Lower Hardres *Kent*	29	TR1553
Lower Harpton *H & W*	46	SO2760
Lower Hartshay *Derbys*	74	SK3851
Lower Hartwell *Bucks*	38	SP7912
Lower Hatton *Staffs*	72	SJ8236
Lower Hawthwaite *Cumb*	86	SD2189
Lower Hergest *H & W*	46	SO2755
Lower Heyford *Oxon*	49	SP4824
Lower Heysham *Lancs*	87	SD4160
Lower Higham *Kent*	28	TQ7172
Lower Holbrook *Suffk*	54	TM1834
Lower Hordley *Shrops*	59	SJ3929
Lower Horncroft *W Susx*	14	TQ0017
Lower Howsell *H & W*	47	SO7848
Lower Irlam *Gt Man*	79	SJ7193
Lower Kilburn *Derbys*	62	SK3744
Lower Kilcott *Avon*	35	ST7889
Lower Killeyan *Strath*	104	NR2742
Lower Kingcombe *Dorset*	10	SY5599
Lower Kingswood *Surrey*	26	TQ2453
Lower Kinnerton *Ches*	71	SJ3462
Lower Langford *Avon*	21	ST4560
Lower Largo *Fife*	126	NO4102
Lower Leigh *Staffs*	73	SK0135
Lower Lemington *Gloucs*	48	SP2134
Lower Llanfadog *Powys*	45	SN9567
Lower Lovacott *Devon*	19	SS5227
Lower Loxhore *Devon*	19	SS6137
Lower Lydbrook *Gloucs*	34	SO5916
Lower Lye *H & W*	46	SO4066
Lower Machen *Gwent*	34	ST2288
Lower Maes-coed *H & W*	46	SO3430
Lower Mannington *Dorset*	12	SU0604
Lower Marston *Somset*	22	ST7644
Lower Meend *Gloucs*	34	SO5504
Lower Middleton Cheney *Nhants*	49	SP5041
Lower Milton *Somset*	21	ST5347
Lower Moor *W Mids*	47	SO9747
Lower Morton *Avon*	35	ST6491
Lower Nazeing *Essex*	39	TL3906
Lower Norton *Warwks*	48	SP2363
Lower Nyland *Dorset*	22	ST7521
Lower Penarth *S Glam*	20	ST1869
Lower Penn *Staffs*	60	SO8796
Lower Pennington *Hants*	12	SZ3193
Lower Penwortham *Lancs*	80	SD5327
Lower Peover *Ches*	79	SJ7474
Lower Place *Gt Man*	81	SD9011
Lower Pollicott *Bucks*	37	SP7013
Lower Pond Street *Essex*	39	TL4537
Lower Quinton *Warwks*	48	SP1847
Lower Rainham *Kent*	28	TQ8167
Lower Raydon *Suffk*	54	TM0338
Lower Roadwater *Somset*	20	ST0339
Lower Salter *Lancs*	87	SD6063
Lower Seagry *Wilts*	35	ST9580
Lower Sheering *Essex*	39	TL4914
Lower Shelton *Beds*	38	SP9942
Lower Shiplake *Oxon*	37	SU7679
Lower Shuckburgh *Warwks*	49	SP4862
Lower Shurlach *Ches*	79	SJ6772
Lower Slaughter *Gloucs*	36	SP1622
Lower Soothill *W York*	82	SE2523
Lower Soudley *Gloucs*	35	SO6609
Lower Standen *Kent*	29	TR2340
Lower Stanton St. Quintin *Wilts*	35	ST9180
Lower Stoke *Kent*	28	TQ8375
Lower Stone *Gloucs*	35	ST6794
Lower Stonnall *Staffs*	61	SK0803
Lower Stow Bedon *Norfk*	66	TL9694
Lower Street *Dorset*	11	SY8399
Lower Street *Norfk*	67	TG2635
Lower Street *Suffk*	53	TL7852
Lower Street *Suffk*	54	TM1052
Lower Street *E Susx*	16	TQ7012
Lower Stretton *Ches*	79	SJ6281
Lower Stroud *Dorset*	10	SY4598
Lower Sundon *Beds*	38	TL0526
Lower Swanwick *Hants*	13	SU4909
Lower Swell *Gloucs*	48	SP1725
Lower Tadmarton *Oxon*	48	SP4036
Lower Tale *Devon*	9	ST0601
Lower Team *Staffs*	73	SK0138
Lower Thurlton *Norfk*	67	TM4299
Lower Town *Dyfed*	30	SM9637
Lower Town *H & W*	47	SO6342
Lower Town *Cnwll*	2	SW6528
Lower Town *Devon*	7	SX7172
Lower Tregantle *Cnwll*	5	SX3953
Lower Treluswell *Cnwll*	3	SW7735
Lower Tysoe *Warwks*	48	SP3445
Lower Ufford *Suffk*	55	TM2952
Lower Upcott *Devon*	9	SX8880
Lower Upham *Hants*	13	SU5219
Lower Upnor *Kent*	28	TQ7571

Lower Vexford *Somset*	20	ST1135
Lower Walton *Ches*	78	SJ6086
Lower Waterston *Dorset*	11	SY7395
Lower Weare *Somset*	21	ST4053
Lower Welson *H & W*	46	SO2950
Lower Westmancote *H & W*	47	SO9337
Lower Whatcombe *Dorset*	11	ST8401
Lower Whatley *Somset*	22	ST7447
Lower Whitley *Ches*	71	SJ6179
Lower Wick *H & W*	47	SO8352
Lower Wick *Gloucs*	35	ST7096
Lower Wield *Hants*	24	SU6340
Lower Wigginton *Herts*	38	SP9409
Lower Willingdon *E Susx*	16	TQ5803
Lower Winchendon *Bucks*	37	SP7312
Lower Woodend *Bucks*	37	SU8187
Lower Woodford *Wilts*	23	SU1235
Lower Wraxhall *Dorset*	10	ST5700
Lower Wyche *H & W*	47	SO7743
Lower Wyke *W York*	82	SE1525
Lowerhouse *Lancs*	81	SD8032
Lowesby *Leics*	63	SK7207
Lowestoft *Suffk*	67	TM5493
Loweswater *Cumb*	92	NY1421
Lowfield Heath *W Susx*	15	TQ2739
Lowgill *Cumb*	87	SD6297
Lowgill *Lancs*	87	SD6564
Lowick *Nthumb*	111	NU0139
Lowick *Cumb*	86	SD2885
Lowick *Nhants*	51	SP9881
Lowick Bridge *Cumb*	86	SD2986
Lowick Green *Cumb*	86	SD2985
Lowlands *Dur*	96	NZ1325
Lowlands *Gwent*	34	ST2996
Lowsonford *Warwks*	48	SP1868
Lowther *Cumb*	94	NY5323
Lowther Castle *Cumb*	94	NY5223
Lowtherton *D & G*	101	NY2466
Lowthorpe *Humb*	91	TA0860
Lowton *Gt Man*	78	SJ6197
Lowton *Devon*	8	SS6604
Lowton *Somset*	20	ST1918
Lowton Common *Gt Man*	79	SJ6397
Lowton St. Mary's *Gt Man*	79	SJ6397
Loxbeare *Devon*	9	SS9116
Loxhill *Surrey*	25	TQ0038
Loxhore *Devon*	19	SS6138
Loxhore Cott *Devon*	19	SS6138
Loxley *Warwks*	48	SP2553
Loxley Green *Staffs*	73	SK0630
Loxter *H & W*	47	SO7140
Loxton *Avon*	21	ST3755
Loxwood *W Susx*	14	TQ0331
Lubcroy *Highld*	145	NC3501
Lubenham *Nhants*	50	SP7087
Lucas Green *Surrey*	25	SU9460
Lucasgate *Lincs*	77	TF4147
Luccombe *Somset*	20	SS9243
Luccombe Village *IOW*	13	SZ5879
Lucker *Nthumb*	111	NU1530
Luckett *Cnwll*	5	SX3873
Lucking Street *Essex*	54	TL8134
Luckington *Wilts*	35	ST8383
Lucklawhill *Fife*	127	NO4221
Lucknam *Wilts*	35	ST8272
Luckwell Bridge *Somset*	20	SS9038
Lucott *Somset*	19	SS8645
Lucton *H & W*	46	SO4364
Lucy Cross *N York*	89	NZ2112
Ludborough *Lincs*	77	TF2995
Ludbrook *Devon*	7	SX6654
Ludchurch *Dyfed*	31	SN1411
Luddenden *W York*	82	SE0426
Luddenden Foot *W York*	82	SE0325
Luddenham Court *Kent*	28	TQ9963
Luddesdown *Kent*	28	TQ6666
Luddington *Humb*	84	SE8316
Luddington *Warwks*	48	SP1652
Luddington in the Brook *Nhants*	51	TL1083
Ludford *Shrops*	46	SO5174
Ludford *Lincs*	76	TF1989
Ludgershall *Bucks*	37	SP6517
Ludgershall *Wilts*	23	SU2650
Ludgvan *Cnwll*	2	SW5033
Ludham *Norfk*	67	TG3818
Ludlow *Shrops*	46	SO5175
Ludney *Somset*	10	ST3812
Ludwell *Wilts*	22	ST9122
Ludworth *Dur*	96	NZ3641
Luffincott *Devon*	5	SX3394
Luffness *Loth*	118	NT4780
Lugar *Strath*	107	NS5921
Lugg Green *H & W*	46	SO4462
Luggate Burn *Loth*	118	NT5974
Luggiebank *Strath*	116	NS7672
Lugsdale *Ches*	78	SJ5285
Lugton *Strath*	115	NS4152
Lugwardine *H & W*	46	SO5540
Luib *Highld*	137	NG5627
Lulham *H & W*	46	SO4141
Lullington *Derbys*	61	SK2412
Lullington *Somset*	22	ST7851
Lullington *E Susx*	16	TQ5202
Lulsgate Bottom *Avon*	21	ST5165
Lulsley *H & W*	47	SO7455
Lulworth Camp *Dorset*	11	SY8381
Lumb *Lancs*	81	SD8324
Lumb *W York*	82	SE0221
Lumbutts *W York*	82	SD9523
Lumby *N York*	83	SE4830
Lumloch *Strath*	116	NS6370
Lumphanan *Gramp*	134	NJ5804
Lumphinnans *Fife*	117	NT1792
Lumsden *Gramp*	142	NJ4722
Lunan *Tays*	127	NO6851
Lunanhead *Tays*	127	NO4752
Luncarty *Tays*	125	NO0929
Lund *N York*	83	SE6532
Lund *Humb*	84	SE9647
Lundford Magna *Lincs*	76	TF1989
Lundie *Cent*	124	NN7304
Lundie *Tays*	126	NO2836
Lundin Links *Fife*	126	NO4002
Lundy Green *Norfk*	67	TM2392
Lunna *Shet*	155	HU4869
Lunsford *Kent*	28	TQ6959
Lunsford's Cross *E Susx*	17	TQ7210
Lunt *Mersyd*	78	SD3402
Luntley *H & W*	46	SO3955
Luppitt *Devon*	9	ST1606
Lupridge *Devon*	7	SX7163
Lupset *W York*	82	SE3119
Lupton *Cumb*	87	SD5581
Lurgashall *W Susx*	14	SU9326
Lurley *Devon*	9	SS9215
Lusby *Lincs*	77	TF3467
Luscombe *Devon*	7	SX7754
Luson *Devon*	6	SX6050
Luss *Strath*	115	NS3692
Lusta *Highld*	136	NG2656
Lustleigh *Devon*	8	SX7881
Luston *H & W*	46	SO4863

Luthermuir *Gramp*	135	NO6568
Luthrie *Fife*	126	NO3319
Lutley *W Mids*	60	SO9382
Luton *Devon*	9	ST0802
Luton *Devon*	9	SX9076
Luton *Beds*	38	TL0921
Luton *Kent*	28	TQ7766
Lutterworth *Leics*	50	SP5484
Lutton *Devon*	6	SX5959
Lutton *Dorset*	11	SY8980
Lutton *Lincs*	65	TF4325
Lutton *Nhants*	52	TL1187
Luxborough *Somset*	20	SS9738
Luxulyan *Cnwll*	4	SX0558
Luzley *Gt Man*	79	SD9600
Lybster *Highld*	151	ND2435
Lydbury North *Shrops*	59	SO3486
Lydcott *Devon*	19	SS6936
Lydd *Kent*	17	TR0420
Lydden *Kent*	29	TR2645
Lydden *Kent*	29	TR3567
Lyddington *Leics*	51	SP8797
Lyde Green *Hants*	24	SU7057
Lydeard St. Lawrence *Somset*	20	ST1332
Lydford *Devon*	5	SX5185
Lydford on Fosse *Somset*	21	ST5630
Lydgate *W York*	81	SD9225
Lydgate *W York*	82	SD9516
Lydham *Shrops*	59	SO3391
Lydiard Green *Wilts*	36	SU0885
Lydiard Millicent *Wilts*	36	SU0986
Lydiard Tregoze *Wilts*	36	SU1085
Lydiate *Mersyd*	78	SD3604
Lydiate Ash *H & W*	60	SO9775
Lydlinch *Dorset*	11	ST7413
Lydney *Gloucs*	35	SO6303
Lydstep *Dyfed*	31	SS0898
Lye *W Mids*	60	SO9284
Lye Cross *Avon*	21	ST4962
Lye Green *Warwks*	48	SP1965
Lye Green *Bucks*	38	SP9703
Lye Green *E Susx*	16	TQ5134
Lye Head *H & W*	60	SO7573
Lye's Green *Wilts*	22	ST8146
Lyford *Oxon*	36	SU3994
Lymbridge Green *Kent*	29	TR1244
Lyme *Border*	109	NT2041
Lyme Regis *Dorset*	10	SY3492
Lyminge *Kent*	29	TR1641
Lymington *Hants*	12	SZ3295
Lyminster *W Susx*	14	TQ0204
Lymm *Ches*	79	SJ6887
Lympne *Kent*	17	TR1135
Lympsham *Somset*	21	ST3354
Lympstone *Devon*	9	SX9984
Lynbridge *Devon*	19	SS7248
Lynch *Somset*	20	SS9047
Lynch Green *Norfk*	66	TG1505
Lynchat *Highld*	132	NH7801
Lyndhurst *Hants*	12	SU3008
Lyndon *Leics*	63	SK9004
Lyndon Green *W Mids*	61	SP1485
Lyne *Surrey*	26	TQ0166
Lyne Down *H & W*	47	SO6431
Lyne Hill *Staffs*	60	SJ9212
Lyne of Skene *Gramp*	135	NJ7610
Lyneal *Shrops*	59	SJ4433
Lynegar *Highld*	151	ND2257
Lyneham *Oxon*	36	SP2720
Lyneham *Wilts*	35	SU0278
Lyneham *Devon*	8	SX8579
Lyneholmford *Cumb*	101	NY5172
Lynemouth *Nthumb*	103	NZ2991
Lyness *Ork*	155	ND3094
Lyng *Somset*	21	ST3329
Lyng *Norfk*	66	TG0617
Lynhales *H & W*	46	SO3255
Lynmouth *Devon*	19	SS7249
Lynn *Shrops*	72	SJ7815
Lynn of Shenval *Gramp*	141	NJ2129
Lynsted *Kent*	28	TQ9460
Lynstone *Cnwll*	18	SS2005
Lynton *Devon*	19	SS7249
Lyon's Gate *Dorset*	11	ST6505
Lyonshall *H & W*	46	SO3355
Lytchett Matravers *Dorset*	11	SY9495
Lytchett Minster *Dorset*	11	SY9693
Lytham *Lancs*	80	SD3627
Lytham St. Anne's *Lancs*	80	SD3427
Lythbank *Shrops*	59	SJ4607
Lyth *Highld*	151	ND2762
Lythe *N York*	90	NZ8413
Lythmore *Highld*	150	ND0566

M

Mabe Burnthouse *Cnwll*	3	SW7634
Mabie *D & G*	100	NX9570
Mablethorpe *Lincs*	77	TF5085
Macclesfield *Ches*	79	SJ9173
Macclesfield Forest *Ches*	79	SJ9772
Macduff *Gramp*	142	NJ7064
Macharioch *Strath*	105	NR7309
Machen *M Glam*	33	ST2189
Machire *Strath*	112	NR2164
Machrie Farm *Strath*	105	NR9033
Machrihanish *Strath*	104	NR6320
Machrins *Strath*	112	NR3693
Machynlleth *Powys*	57	SH7400
Machynys *Dyfed*	32	SS5198
Mackworth *Derbys*	62	SK3137
Macmerry *Loth*	118	NT4372
Maddaford *Devon*	8	SX5494
Madderty *Tays*	125	NN9521
Maddington *Wilts*	23	SU0744
Maddiston *Cent*	116	NS9476
Madehurst *W Susx*	14	SU9810
Madeley *Shrops*	60	SJ6904
Madeley *Staffs*	72	SJ7744
Madeley Heath *Staffs*	72	SJ7845
Madford *Devon*	9	ST1411
Madingley *Cambs*	52	TL3960
Madley *H & W*	46	SO4238
Madresfield *H & W*	47	SO8047
Madron *Cnwll*	2	SW4531
Maen-y-groes *Dyfed*	42	SN3858
Maenaddwyn *Gwynd*	68	SH4684
Maenclochog *Dyfed*	31	SN0827
Maendy *S Glam*	33	ST0076
Maenporth *Cnwll*	3	SW7829
Maentwrog *Gwynd*	57	SH6640
Maer *Staffs*	72	SJ7938
Maerdy *Cnwll*	18	SS2008
Maerdy *M Glam*	33	SS9798

Maes-glas *Gwent*	34	ST2985
Maesbrook *Shrops*	59	SJ3021
Maesbury *Shrops*	59	SJ3026
Maesbury Marsh *Shrops*	59	SJ3125
Maesgwynne *Dyfed*	31	SN2024
Maeshafn *Clwyd*	70	SJ2061
Maesllyn *Dyfed*	42	SN3644
Maesmynis *Powys*	45	SO0146
Maesmynis *Powys*	45	SO0349
Maesteg *M Glam*	33	SS8590
Maesybont *Dyfed*	32	SN5616
Maesycwmmer *M Glam*	33	ST1594
Magdalen Laver *Essex*	39	TL5108
Maggieknockater *Gramp*	141	NJ3145
Maggots End *Essex*	39	TL4827
Magham Down *E Susx*	16	TQ6011
Maghull *Mersyd*	78	SD3703
Magor *Gwent*	34	ST4286
Maiden Bradley *Wilts*	22	ST8038
Maiden Head *Avon*	21	ST5666
Maiden Law *Dur*	96	NZ1749
Maiden Newton *Dorset*	10	SY5997
Maiden Rushett *Gt Lon*	26	TQ1761
Maiden Wells *Dyfed*	30	SR9799
Maidencombe *Devon*	7	SX9268
Maidenhay *Devon*	10	SY2795
Maidenhead *Berks*	38	SU8980
Maidens *Strath*	106	NS2107
Maidens Green *Berks*	25	SU8972
Maidenwell *Lincs*	77	TF3179
Maidford *Nhants*	49	SP6052
Maids Moreton *Bucks*	49	SP7035
Maidstone *Kent*	28	TQ7555
Maidwell *Nhants*	50	SP7476
Mains of Bainakettle *Gramp*	134	NO6274
Mains of Balhall *Tays*	134	NO5163
Mains of Cairnborrow *Gramp*	142	NJ4640
Mains of Dalvey *Highld*	141	NJ1132
Mains of Haulkerton *Gramp*	135	NO7172
Mains of Throsk *Cent*	116	NS8690
Mainsforth *Dur*	96	NZ3131
Mainsriddle *D & G*	92	NX9456
Mainstone *Shrops*	58	SO2787
Maisemore *Gloucs*	35	SO8121
Major's Green *H & W*	61	SP1077
Makeney *Derbys*	62	SK3544
Malborough *Devon*	7	SX7139
Malcoff *Derbys*	74	SK0782
Malden *Surrey*	26	TQ2166
Maldon *Essex*	40	TL8506
Malham *N York*	88	SD9063
Mallaig *Highld*	129	NM6796
Mallaigvaig *Highld*	129	NM6897
Malleny Mills *Loth*	117	NT1665
Mallows Green *Essex*	39	TL4726
Malltraeth *Gwynd*	68	SH4068
Mallwyd *Gwynd*	57	SH8612
Malmesbury *Wilts*	35	ST9387
Malmsmead *Somset*	19	SS7947
Malpas *Ches*	71	SJ4847
Malpas *Gwent*	34	ST3090
Malpas *Cnwll*	3	SW8442
Maltby *Cleve*	89	NZ4613
Maltby *S York*	75	SK5392
Maltby *Lincs*	77	TF3183
Maltby le Marsh *Lincs*	77	TF4681
Malting Green *Essex*	41	TL9720
Maltman's Hill *Kent*	28	TQ9043
Malton *N York*	90	SE7871
Malvern Link *H & W*	47	SO7947
Malvern Wells *H & W*	47	SO7742
Malzie *D & G*	99	NX3754
Mamble *H & W*	60	SO6871
Mamhilad *Gwent*	34	SO3003
Manaccan *Cnwll*	3	SW7624
Manafon *Powys*	58	SJ1102
Manaton *Devon*	8	SX7581
Mancetter *Warwks*	61	SP3296
Manchester *Gt Man*	79	SJ8497
Mancot *Clwyd*	71	SJ3167
Mandally *Highld*	131	NH2900
Manea *Cambs*	53	TL4789
Maney *W Mids*	61	SP1195
Manfield *N York*	89	NZ2113
Mangerton *Dorset*	10	SY4995
Mangotsfield *Avon*	35	ST6676
Mangrove Green *Herts*	38	TL1224
Manhay *Cnwll*	2	SW6930
Manish *W Isls*	154	NG1089
Mankinholes *W York*	82	SD9523
Manley *Ches*	71	SJ5071
Manmoel *Gwent*	33	SO1803
Mannel *Strath*	120	NL9840
Manning's Heath *W Susx*	15	TQ2028
Manningford Bohune *Wilts*	23	SU1357
Manningford Bruce *Wilts*	23	SU1358
Manningham *W York*	82	SE1435
Mannington *Dorset*	12	SU0605
Manningtree *Essex*	41	TM1031
Mannofield *Gramp*	135	NJ9104
Manor Park *Gt Lon*	27	TQ4285
Manorbier *Dyfed*	30	SS0697
Manorbier Newton *Dyfed*	30	SN0400
Manorhill *Border*	110	NT6632
Manorowen *Dyfed*	30	SM9336
Mansell Gamage *H & W*	46	SO3944
Mansell Lacy *H & W*	46	SO4245
Mansergh *Cumb*	87	SD6082
Mansfield *Strath*	107	NS6214
Mansfield *Notts*	75	SK5361
Mansfield Woodhouse *Notts*	75	SK5363
Mansriggs *Cumb*	86	SD2980
Manston *N York*	83	SE3634
Manston *Dorset*	11	ST8115
Manston *Kent*	29	TR3466
Manswood *Dorset*	11	ST9708
Manthorpe *Lincs*	63	SK9137
Manthorpe *Lincs*	64	TF0715
Manton *Humb*	84	SE9302
Manton *Notts*	75	SK6078
Manton *Leics*	63	SK8704
Manton *Wilts*	23	SU1768
Manuden *Essex*	39	TL4926
Manwood Green *Essex*	39	TL5412
Maolachy *Strath*	122	NM8913
Maperton *Somset*	22	ST6726
Maple Cross *Herts*	26	TQ0393
Maplebeck *Notts*	75	SK7060
Mapledurham *Oxon*	37	SU6776
Mapledurwell *Hants*	24	SU6851
Maplehurst *W Susx*	15	TQ1824
Maplescombe *Kent*	27	TQ5664
Mapleton *Derbys*	73	SK1647
Mapleton *Kent*	16	TQ4649
Mapperley *Derbys*	62	SK4342
Mapperley Park *Notts*	62	SK5844
Mapperton *Dorset*	10	SY5099
Mappleborough Green *Warwks*	48	SP0866
Mappleton *Humb*	85	TA2243
Mappowder *Dorset*	11	ST7306
Marazanvose *Cnwll*	3	SW7950

Marazion Middleton

Marazion *Cnwll* 2 SW5130
Marbury *Ches* 71 SJ5645
March *Strath* 108 NS9914
March *Cambs* 65 TL4196
Marcham *Oxon* 37 SU4596
Marchamley *Shrops* 59 SJ5929
Marchamley Wood *Shrops* 59 SJ5831
Marchington *Staffs* 73 SK1330
Marchington Woodlands *Staffs* 73 SK1128
Marchros *Gwynd* 56 SH3125
Marchwiel *Clwyd* 71 SJ3547
Marchwood *Hants* 12 SU3810
Marcross *S Glam* 20 SS9269
Marden *H & W* 46 SO5146
Marden *Wilts* 23 SU0857
Marden *Kent* 28 TQ7444
Marden Ash *Essex* 27 TL5502
Marden Beech *Kent* 28 TQ7442
Marden Thorn *Kent* 28 TQ7642
Mardens Hill *E Susx* 16 TQ5032
Mardleybury *Herts* 39 TL2618
Mardy *Gwent* 34 SO3015
Mare Green *Somset* 21 ST3326
Marefield *Leics* 63 SK7407
Mareham le Fen *Lincs* 77 TF2761
Mareham on the Hill *Lincs* 77 TF2867
Marehay *Derbys* 62 SK3947
Marehill *W Susx* 14 TQ0618
Maresfield *E Susx* 16 TQ4624
Marfleet *Humb* 85 TA1429
Marford *Clwyd* 71 SJ3556
Margam *W Glam* 32 SS7887
Margaret Marsh *Dorset* 22 ST8218
Margaretting *Essex* 40 TL6701
Margaretting Tye *Essex* 40 TL6800
Margate *Kent* 29 TR3571
Margnaheglish *Strath* 105 NS0332
Margrie *D & G* 99 NX5950
Margrove Park *Cleve* 97 NZ6515
Marham *Norfk* 65 TF7009
Marhamchurch *Cnwll* 18 SS2203
Marholm *Cambs* 64 TF1401
Marian-glas *Gwynd* 68 SH5084
Mariansleigh *Devon* 19 SS7422
Marine Town *Kent* 28 TQ9274
Marionburgh *Gramp* 135 NJ7006
Marishader *Highld* 136 NG4963
Maristow *Devon* 6 SX4764
Marjoriebanks *D & G* 100 NY0883
Mark *D & G* 98 NX1157
Mark *Somset* 21 ST3847
Mark Causeway *Somset* 21 ST3547
Mark Cross *E Susx* 16 TQ5010
Mark Cross *E Susx* 16 TQ5831
Mark's Corner *IOW* 13 SZ4692
Markbeech *Kent* 16 TQ4742
Markby *Lincs* 77 TF4878
Markeaton *Derbys* 62 SK3237
Market Bosworth *Leics* 62 SK4002
Market Deeping *Lincs* 64 TF1310
Market Drayton *Shrops* 72 SJ6734
Market Harborough *Leics* 50 SP7387
Market Lavington *Wilts* 22 SU0154
Market Overton *Leics* 63 SK8816
Market Rasen *Lincs* 76 TF1089
Market Stainton *Lincs* 76 TF2279
Market Street *Norfk* 67 TG2921
Market Weighton *Humb* 84 SE8741
Market Weston *Suffk* 54 TL9877
Markfield *Leics* 62 SK4809
Markham *Gwent* 33 SO1601
Markham Moor *Notts* 75 SK7173
Markinch *Fife* 126 NO2901
Markington *N York* 89 SE2865
Marks Tey *Essex* 40 TL9023
Marksbury *Avon* 22 ST6662
Markshall *Essex* 40 TL8425
Markwell *Cnwll* 5 SX3758
Markyate *Herts* 38 TL0616
Marl Bank *H & W* 47 SO7840
Marlborough *Wilts* 23 SU1868
Marlbrook *H & W* 46 SO5154
Marlbrook *H & W* 60 SO9774
Marlcliff *Warwks* 48 SP0950
Marldon *Devon* 7 SX8663
Marle Green *E Susx* 16 TQ5816
Marlesford *Suffk* 55 TM3258
Marley *Kent* 29 TR1850
Marley *Kent* 29 TR3353
Marley Green *Ches* 71 SJ5845
Marley Hill *T & W* 96 NZ2058
Marlingford *Norfk* 66 TG1309
Marloes *Dyfed* 30 SM7908
Marlow *H & W* 46 SO4076
Marlow *Bucks* 26 SU8486
Marlpit Hill *Kent* 16 TQ4347
Marlpits *E Susx* 16 TQ4528
Marlpits *E Susx* 16 TQ7013
Marlpool *Derbys* 62 SK4345
Marnhull *Dorset* 22 ST7818
Marnoch *Gramp* 142 NJ5950
Marple *Gt Man* 79 SJ9588
Marple Bridge *Gt Man* 79 SJ9688
Marr *S York* 83 SE5105
Marrick *N York* 88 SE0798
Marros *Dyfed* 31 SN2008
Marsden *T & W* 103 NZ3964
Marsden *W York* 82 SE0411
Marsden Height *Lancs* 81 SD8636
Marsett *N York* 88 SD9085
Marsh *W York* 82 SE0235
Marsh *Bucks* 38 SP8109
Marsh *Somset* 10 ST2510
Marsh Baldon *Oxon* 37 SU5699
Marsh Gibbon *Bucks* 37 SP6422
Marsh Green *Shrops* 59 SJ6014
Marsh Green *Staffs* 72 SJ8858
Marsh Green *Devon* 9 SY0493
Marsh Green *Kent* 16 TQ4344
Marsh Lane *Derbys* 74 SK4079
Marsh Lane *Gloucs* 34 SO5807
Marsh Street *Somset* 20 SS9944
Marsh The *Powys* 59 SO3197
Marshall's Heath *Herts* 39 TL1614
Marshalswick *Herts* 39 TL1608
Marsham *Norfk* 67 TG1923
Marshborough *Kent* 29 TR3057
Marshbrook *Shrops* 59 SO4489
Marshchapel *Lincs* 77 TF3599
Marshfield *Gwent* 34 ST2582
Marshfield *Avon* 35 ST7873
Marshgate *Cnwll* 4 SX1592
Marshland Green *Gt Man* 79 SJ6899
Marshside *Mersyd* 80 SD3619
Marshwood *Dorset* 10 SY3899
Marske *N York* 89 NZ1000
Marske-by-the-Sea *Cleve* 97 NZ6322
Marston *Ches* 79 SJ6775
Marston *Staffs* 60 SJ8313
Marston *Staffs* 72 SJ9227
Marston *Lincs* 63 SK8943
Marston *H & W* 46 SO3557
Marston *Warwks* 61 SP2094
Marston *Oxon* 37 SP5208
Marston *Wilts* 22 ST9656
Marston Green *W Mids* 61 SP1785
Marston Jabbet *Warwks* 61 SP3788
Marston Magna *Somset* 21 ST5922
Marston Meysey *Wilts* 36 SU1297
Marston Montgomery *Derbys* 73 SK1337
Marston Moretaine *Beds* 38 SP9941
Marston St. Lawrence *Nhants* 49 SP5341
Marston Stannet *H & W* 46 SO5655
Marston Trussell *Nhants* 50 SP6985
Marston on Dove *Derbys* 73 SK2329
Marstow *H & W* 34 SO5518
Marsworth *Bucks* 38 SP9114
Marten *Wilts* 23 SU2860
Marthall *Ches* 79 SJ7975
Martham *Norfk* 67 TG4518
Martin *Hants* 12 SU0619
Martin *Lincs* 76 TF1259
Martin *Lincs* 77 TF2466
Martin *Kent* 29 TR3447
Martin Dales *Lincs* 76 TF1762
Martin Drove End *Hants* 12 SU0520
Martin Hussingtree *H & W* 47 SO8860
Martindale *Cumb* 93 NY4319
Martinhoe *Devon* 19 SS6648
Martinscroft *Ches* 79 SJ6589
Martinstown *Dorset* 11 SY6489
Martlesham *Suffk* 55 TM2547
Martletwy *Dyfed* 30 SN0310
Martley *H & W* 47 SO7555
Martock *Somset* 21 ST4619
Marton *Cleve* 97 NZ5115
Marton *N York* 89 SE4162
Marton *N York* 90 SE7383
Marton *Shrops* 58 SJ2802
Marton *Ches* 71 SJ6267
Marton *Ches* 79 SJ8568
Marton *Lincs* 76 SK8381
Marton *Warwks* 48 SP4068
Marton *Humb* 85 TA1739
Marton-le-Moor *N York* 89 SE3770
Martyr Worthy *Hants* 24 SU5132
Martyr's Green *Surrey* 26 TQ0857
Marwick *Ork* 155 HY2324
Marwood *Devon* 19 SS5437
Mary Tavy *Devon* 5 SX5079
Marybank *Highld* 139 NH4853
Maryburgh *Highld* 139 NH5456
Maryculter *Gramp* 135 NO8599
Maryhill *Gramp* 143 NJ8245
Maryhill *Strath* 115 NS5669
Marykirk *Gramp* 135 NO6865
Maryland *Gwent* 34 SO5105
Marylebone *Gt Man* 78 SD5807
Marypark *Gramp* 141 NJ1938
Maryport *D & G* 98 NX1434
Maryport *Cumb* 92 NY0336
Marystow *Devon* 5 SX4382
Maryton *Tays* 127 NO6856
Marywell *Gramp* 134 NO5895
Marywell *Tays* 127 NO6544
Marywell *Gramp* 135 NO9399
Masham *N York* 89 SE2280
Mashbury *Essex* 40 TL6511
Mason *T & W* 103 NZ2073
Masongill *N York* 87 SD6675
Mastin Moor *Derbys* 75 SK4575
Matching *Essex* 39 TL5212
Matching Green *Essex* 39 TL5311
Matching Tye *Essex* 39 TL5111
Matfen *Nthumb* 103 NZ0371
Matfield *Kent* 28 TQ6541
Mathern *Gwent* 34 ST5290
Mathon *H & W* 47 SO7346
Mathry *Dyfed* 30 SM8832
Matlaske *Norfk* 66 TG1534
Matlock *Derbys* 74 SK3059
Matlock Bank *Derbys* 74 SK3060
Matlock Bath *Derbys* 74 SK2958
Matlock Dale *Derbys* 74 SK2959
Matson *Gloucs* 35 SO8515
Matterdale End *Cumb* 93 NY3923
Mattersey *Notts* 75 SK6889
Mattersey Thorpe *Notts* 75 SK6889
Mattingley *Hants* 24 SU7357
Mattishall *Norfk* 66 TG0511
Mattishall Burgh *Norfk* 66 TG0512
Mauchline *Strath* 107 NS4927
Maud *Gramp* 143 NJ9148
Maufant *Jersey* 152 JS0000
Maugersbury *Gloucs* 48 SP2025
Maughold *IOM* 153 SC4991
Mauld *Highld* 139 NH4038
Maulden *Beds* 38 TL0538
Maulds Meaburn *Cumb* 94 NY6216
Maunby *N York* 89 SE3586
Maund Bryan *H & W* 46 SO5650
Maundown *Somset* 20 ST0628
Mautby *Norfk* 67 TG4812
Mavesyn Ridware *Staffs* 73 SK0816
Mavis Enderby *Lincs* 77 TF3666
Maw Green *Ches* 72 SJ7057
Maw Green *W Mids* 60 SP0196
Mawbray *Cumb* 92 NY0846
Mawdesley *Lancs* 80 SD4914
Mawdlam *M Glam* 32 SS8081
Mawgan *Cnwll* 2 SW7025
Mawgan Cross *Cnwll* 2 SW7024
Mawgan Porth *Cnwll* 4 SW8567
Mawla *Cnwll* 2 SW7045
Mawnan *Cnwll* 3 SW7827
Mawnan Smith *Cnwll* 3 SW7728
Mawthorpe *Lincs* 77 TF4672
Maxey *Cambs* 64 TF1208
Maxstoke *Warwks* 61 SP2386
Maxted Street *Kent* 29 TR1244
Maxton *Border* 110 NT6130
Maxton *Kent* 29 TR3041
Maxwell Town *D & G* 100 NX9676
Maxwellheugh *Border* 110 NT7333
Maxworthy *Cnwll* 5 SX2593
May Bank *Staffs* 72 SJ8547
May's Green *Surrey* 26 TQ0957
Mayals *W Glam* 32 SS6089
Maybole *Strath* 106 NS2909
Maybury *Surrey* 26 TQ0159
Mayes Green *Surrey* 14 TQ1239
Mayfield *Loth* 118 NT3565
Mayfield *Staffs* 73 SK1446
Mayfield *E Susx* 16 TQ5826
Mayford *Surrey* 25 SU9956
Mayland *Essex* 40 TL9201
Maynard's Green *E Susx* 16 TQ5818
Maypole *Gwent* 34 SO4716
Maypole *W Mids* 61 SP0778
Maypole *Kent* 29 TR2064
Maypole Green *Suffk* 54 TL9159
Maypole Green *Suffk* 55 TM2767
Maypole Green *Norfk* 67 TM4195
Mead *Devon* 18 SS2217
Meadgate *Avon* 22 ST6758
Meadle *Bucks* 38 SP8005
Meadowtown *Shrops* 59 SJ3001
Meadwell *Devon* 5 SX4081
Meal Bank *Cumb* 87 SD5495
Mealrigg *Cumb* 92 NY1345
Mealsgate *Cumb* 93 NY2042
Meamskirk *Strath* 115 NS5455
Meanwood *W York* 82 SE2837
Mearbeck *N York* 88 SD8160
Meare *Somset* 21 ST4541
Meare Green *Somset* 20 ST2922
Mears Ashby *Nhants* 51 SP8366
Measham *Leics* 62 SK3311
Meathop *Cumb* 87 SD4380
Meaux *Humb* 85 TA0839
Meavy *Devon* 6 SX5467
Medbourne *Leics* 51 SP8093
Meddon *Devon* 18 SS2717
Medlam *Lincs* 77 TF3156
Medlar *Lancs* 80 SD4135
Medmenham *Berks* 37 SU8084
Medomsley *Dur* 95 NZ1154
Medstead *Hants* 24 SU6537
Meer Common *H & W* 46 SO3652
Meer End *W Mids* 61 SP2474
Meerbrook *Staffs* 72 SJ9860
Meesden *Herts* 39 TL4332
Meeson *Shrops* 72 SJ6421
Meeth *Devon* 19 SS5408
Meeting Green *Suffk* 53 TL7455
Meeting House Hill *Norfk* 67 TG3028
Meidrim *Dyfed* 31 SN2920
Meifod *Powys* 58 SJ1513
Meigle *Tays* 126 NO2844
Meikle Carco *D & G* 107 NS7813
Meikle Earnoch *Strath* 116 NS7053
Meikle Kilmory *Strath* 114 NS0560
Meikle Obney *Tays* 125 NO0337
Meikle Wartle *Gramp* 142 NJ7230
Meikleour *Tays* 126 NO1539
Meinciau *Dyfed* 32 SN4610
Meir *Staffs* 72 SJ9342
Meirheath *Staffs* 72 SJ9240
Melbourn *Cambs* 39 TL3844
Melbourne *Humb* 84 SE7543
Melbourne *Derbys* 62 SK3825
Melbury *Devon* 18 SS3719
Melbury Abbas *Dorset* 22 ST8820
Melbury Bubb *Dorset* 10 ST5906
Melbury Osmond *Dorset* 10 ST5707
Melbury Sampford *Dorset* 10 ST5705
Melchbourne *Beds* 51 TL0265
Melcombe Bingham *Dorset* 11 ST7602
Meldon *Nthumb* 103 NZ1183
Meldon *Devon* 8 SX5692
Meldreth *Cambs* 52 TL3746
Meldrum *Cent* 116 NS7299
Meledor *Cnwll* 3 SW9254
Melfort *Strath* 122 NM8313
Melgund Castle *Tays* 127 NO5455
Meliden *Clwyd* 70 SJ0680
Melin Court *W Glam* 33 SN8201
Melin-byrhedyn *Powys* 57 SN8198
Melin-y-coed *Gwynd* 69 SH8160
Melin-y-ddol *Powys* 58 SJ0807
Melin-y-wig *Clwyd* 70 SJ0448
Melinau *Dyfed* 31 SN1613
Melkinthorpe *Cumb* 94 NY5525
Melkridge *Nthumb* 102 NY7364
Melksham *Wilts* 22 ST9063
Mell Green *Berks* 37 SU4577
Mellangoose *Cnwll* 2 SW6826
Melldalloch *Strath* 114 NR9374
Mellguards *Cumb* 93 NY4445
Melling *Mersyd* 78 SD3800
Melling *Lancs* 87 SD5970
Melling Mount *Mersyd* 78 SD4001
Mellis *Suffk* 54 TM0974
Mellon Charles *Highld* 144 NG8491
Mellon Udrigle *Highld* 144 NG8996
Mellor *Lancs* 81 SD6530
Mellor *Gt Man* 79 SJ9888
Mellor Brook *Lancs* 81 SD6431
Mells *Somset* 22 ST7248
Mells *Suffk* 55 TM4076
Melmerby *Cumb* 94 NY6137
Melmerby *N York* 88 SE0785
Melmerby *N York* 89 SE3376
Melness *Highld* 149 NC5861
Melon Green *Suffk* 54 TL8456
Melplash *Dorset* 10 SY4898
Melrose *Border* 109 NT5434
Melsetter *Ork* 155 ND2689
Melsonby *N York* 89 NZ1908
Meltham *S York* 82 SE1010
Meltham Mills *W York* 82 SE1110
Melton *Humb* 84 SE9726
Melton *Suffk* 55 TM2850
Melton Constable *Norfk* 66 TG0432
Melton Mowbray *Leics* 63 SK7518
Melton Ross *Humb* 84 TA0610
Meltonby *Humb* 84 SE7952
Melvaig *Highld* 144 NG7486
Melverley *Shrops* 59 SJ3316
Melverley Green *Shrops* 59 SJ3317
Melvich *Highld* 150 NC8764
Membury *Devon* 10 ST2803
Memsie *Gramp* 143 NJ9762
Menabilly *Cnwll* 3 SX0951
Menagissey *Cnwll* 2 SW7146
Menai Bridge *Gwynd* 69 SH5571
Mendham *Suffk* 55 TM2782
Mendlesham *Suffk* 54 TM1065
Mendlesham Green *Suffk* 54 TM0963
Menheniot *Cnwll* 5 SX2863
Menithwood *H & W* 47 SO7069
Mennock *D & G* 108 NS8107
Menston *W York* 82 SE1643
Menstrie *Cent* 116 NS8597
Menthorpe *N York* 84 SE7034
Mentmore *Bucks* 38 SP9019
Meoble *Highld* 129 NM7987
Meole Brace *Shrops* 59 SJ4810
Meonstoke *Hants* 13 SU6119
Meopham *Kent* 27 TQ6466
Meopham Green *Kent* 27 TQ6465
Meopham Station *Kent* 27 TQ6467
Mepal *Cambs* 53 TL4481
Meppershall *Beds* 38 TL1336
Mere *Ches* 79 SJ7281
Mere *Wilts* 22 ST8132
Mere Brow *Lancs* 80 SD4218
Mere Green *H & W* 47 SO9562
Mere Green *W Mids* 61 SP1198
Mere Heath *Ches* 79 SJ6670
Mereclough *Lancs* 81 SD8730
Meresborough *Kent* 28 TQ8264
Mereworth *Kent* 28 TQ6553
Meriden *W Mids* 61 SP2482
Merkadale *Highld* 136 NG3931
Merlin's Bridge *Dyfed* 30 SM9414
Merrifield *Devon* 7 SX8147
Merrington *Shrops* 59 SJ4720
Merrion *Dyfed* 30 SR9397
Merriott *Somset* 10 ST4412
Merrivale *Devon* 6 SX5475
Merrow *Surrey* 26 TQ0250
Merry Field Hill *Dorset* 12 SU0201
Merry Hill *W Mids* 60 SO9286
Merry Hill *Herts* 26 TQ1394
Merry Lees *Leics* 62 SK4705
Merryhill *W Mids* 60 SO8897
Merrymeet *Cnwll* 5 SX2766
Mersham *Kent* 28 TR0540
Merstham *Surrey* 27 TQ2853
Merston *W Susx* 14 SU8902
Merstone *IOW* 13 SZ5285
Merther *Cnwll* 3 SW8644
Merthyr *Dyfed* 31 SN3520
Merthyr Cynog *Powys* 45 SN9837
Merthyr Dyfan *S Glam* 20 ST1168
Merthyr Mawr *M Glam* 33 SS8877
Merthyr Tydfil *M Glam* 33 SO0406
Merthyr Vale *M Glam* 33 ST0799
Merton *Oxon* 37 SP5717
Merton *Devon* 19 SS5212
Merton *Norfk* 66 TL9098
Merton *Gt Lon* 27 TQ2570
Meshaw *Devon* 19 SS7619
Messing *Essex* 40 TL8918
Messingham *Humb* 84 SE8904
Metfield *Suffk* 55 TM2980
Metherell *Cnwll* 5 SX4069
Metherin *Cnwll* 4 SX1174
Metheringham *Lincs* 76 TF0661
Methil *Fife* 118 NT3799
Methleigh *Cnwll* 2 SW6226
Methley *W York* 83 SE3926
Methley Junction *W York* 83 SE3925
Methlick *Gramp* 143 NJ8537
Methven *Tays* 125 NO0225
Methwold *Norfk* 65 TL7394
Methwold Hythe *Norfk* 65 TL7194
Mettingham *Suffk* 55 TM3689
Metton *Norfk* 67 TG2037
Mevagissey *Cnwll* 3 SX0144
Mexborough *S York* 75 SE4700
Mey *Highld* 151 ND2872
Meylltеyrn *Gwynd* 56 SH2332
Meysey Hampton *Gloucs* 36 SP1100
Miavaig *W Isls* 154 NB0834
Michaelchurch *H & W* 46 SO5225
Michaelchurch Escley *H & W* 46 SO3134
Michaelchurch-on-Arrow *Powys* 46 SO2450
Michaelston-le-Pit *S Glam* 33 ST1572
Michaelstone-y-Fedw *Gwent* 34 ST2484
Michaelstow *Cnwll* 4 SX0778
Michelcombe *Devon* 7 SX6969
Micheldever *Hants* 24 SU5139
Micheldever Station *Hants* 24 SU5143
Michelmersh *Hants* 23 SU3426
Mickfield *Suffk* 54 TM1361
Mickle Trafford *Ches* 71 SJ4469
Micklebring *S York* 75 SK5194
Mickleby *N York* 90 NZ8012
Micklefield *W York* 83 SE4432
Micklefield Green *Herts* 26 TQ0498
Mickleham *Surrey* 26 TQ1653
Mickleover *Derbys* 73 SK3033
Micklethwaite *Cumb* 93 NY2850
Micklethwaite *W York* 82 SE1041
Mickleton *Dur* 95 NY9623
Mickleton *Gloucs* 48 SP1643
Mickletown *W York* 83 SE4027
Mickley *N York* 89 SE2576
Mickley *Derbys* 74 SK3279
Mickley Green *Suffk* 54 TL8457
Mickley Square *Nthumb* 103 NZ0762
Mid Ardlaw *Gramp* 143 NJ9463
Mid Beltie *Gramp* 134 NJ6200
Mid Bockhampton *Hants* 12 SZ1796
Mid Calder *Loth* 117 NT0767
Mid Clyth *Highld* 151 ND2937
Mid Lavant *W Susx* 14 SU8508
Mid Mains *Highld* 139 NH4239
Mid Sannox *Strath* 105 NS0145
Mid Thorpe *Lincs* 77 TF2672
Mid Yell *Shet* 155 HU5190
Midbea *Ork* 155 HY4444
Middle Assendon *Oxon* 37 SU7385
Middle Aston *Oxon* 49 SP4726
Middle Chinnock *Somset* 10 ST4713
Middle Claydon *Bucks* 49 SP7225
Middle Duntisbourne *Gloucs* 35 SO9806
Middle Handley *Derbys* 74 SK4077
Middle Harling *Norfk* 54 TL9885
Middle Kames *Strath* 114 NR9189
Middle Littleton *H & W* 48 SP0847
Middle Madeley *Staffs* 72 SJ7745
Middle Maes-coed *H & W* 46 SO3333
Middle Mayfield *Staffs* 73 SK1444
Middle Mill *Dyfed* 30 SM8026
Middle Quarter *Kent* 28 TQ8938
Middle Rasen *Lincs* 76 TF0889
Middle Rocombe *Devon* 7 SX9069
Middle Salter *Lancs* 87 SD6062
Middle Stoford *Somset* 20 ST1821
Middle Stoke *Kent* 28 TQ8275
Middle Stoughton *Somset* 21 ST4249
Middle Street *Gloucs* 35 SO7704
Middle Street *Essex* 39 TL4005
Middle Taphouse *Cnwll* 4 SX1763
Middle Town *IOS* 2 SV8808
Middle Tysoe *Warwks* 48 SP3444
Middle Wallop *Hants* 23 SU2937
Middle Winterslow *Wilts* 23 SU2333
Middle Woodford *Wilts* 23 SU1136
Middle Yard *Gloucs* 35 SO8203
Middlebie *D & G* 101 NY2176
Middlebridge *Tays* 132 NN8866
Middlecliffe *S York* 83 SE4204
Middlecott *Devon* 8 SX7186
Middlegill *D & G* 108 NT0406
Middleham *N York* 89 SE1287
Middlehill *Wilts* 22 ST8168
Middlehill *Cnwll* 5 SX2869
Middlehope *Shrops* 59 SO4988
Middlemarsh *Dorset* 11 ST6707
Middlemore *Devon* 6 SX4973
Middlesbrough *Cleve* 97 NZ4919
Middlesceugh *Cumb* 93 NY4041
Middleshaw *Cumb* 87 SD5588
Middlesmoor *N York* 89 SE0973
Middlestone *Dur* 96 NZ2531
Middlestone Moor *Dur* 96 NZ2432
Middlestown *W York* 82 SE2617
Middlethird *Border* 110 NT6843
Middleton *Strath* 120 NL9443
Middleton *Tays* 126 NO1206
Middleton *Strath* 115 NS3952
Middleton *Loth* 118 NT3758
Middleton *Nthumb* 111 NU1035
Middleton *Cleve* 97 NZ5233

Middleton Mossbay

Middleton *Nthumb* **103** NZ0584
Middleton *Lancs* **87** SD4258
Middleton *Cumb* **87** SD6285
Middleton *Gt Man* **79** SD8705
Middleton *W York* **82** SE1249
Middleton *W York* **82** SE3028
Middleton *N York* **90** SE7885
Middleton *Shrops* **59** SJ3129
Middleton *Derbys* **74** SK1963
Middleton *Derbys* **73** SK2755
Middleton *H & W* **46** SO5469
Middleton *Shrops* **46** SO5477
Middleton *Warwks* **61** SP1798
Middleton *Nhants* **51** SP8489
Middleton *W Glam* **31** SS4287
Middleton *Hants* **24** SU4244
Middleton *Norfk* **65** TF6616
Middleton *Essex* **54** TL8639
Middleton *Suffk* **55** TM4267
Middleton Cheney *Nhants* **49** SP4941
Middleton Green *Staffs* **73** SJ9935
Middleton Hall *Nthumb* **111** NT9825
Middleton Moor *Suffk* **55** TM4167
Middleton One Row *Dur* **89** NZ3512
Middleton Priors *Shrops* **59** SO6290
Middleton Quernhow *N York* **89** SE3378
Middleton Scriven *Shrops* **60** SO6887
Middleton St. George *Dur* **89** NZ3412
Middleton Stoney *Oxon* **49** SP5323
Middleton Tyas *N York* **89** NZ2205
Middleton on the Hill *H & W* **46** SO5364
Middleton-in-Teesdale *Dur* **95** NY9425
Middleton-on-Leven *N York* **89** NZ4609
Middleton-on-Sea *W Susx* **14** SU9600
Middleton-on-the-Wolds *Humb* **84** SE9449
Middletown *Cumb* **86** NX9908
Middletown *Powys* **59** SJ3012
Middletown *Avon* **34** ST4571
Middlewich *Ches* **72** SJ7066
Middlewood *H & W* **46** SO2844
Middlewood *Cnwll* **5** SX2775
Middlewood Green *Suffk* **54** TM0961
Middleyard *Strath* **107** NS5132
Middlezoy *Somset* **21** ST3733
Middridge *Dur* **96** NZ2426
Midford *Avon* **22** ST7660
Midge Hall *Lancs* **80** SD5122
Midgeholme *Cumb* **94** NY6359
Midgham *Berks* **24** SU5567
Midgley *W York* **82** SE0226
Midgley *W York* **82** SE2714
Midhopestones *S York* **74** SK2399
Midhurst *W Susx* **14** SU8821
Midlem *Border* **109** NT5227
Midney *Somset* **21** ST4927
Midpark *Strath* **114** NS0259
Midsomer Norton *Avon* **22** ST6654
Midtown *Highld* **149** NC5861
Midtown Brae *Highld* **144** NG8284
Midville *Lincs* **77** TF3756
Midway *Ches* **79** SJ9182
Migvie *Gramp* **134** NJ4306
Milborne Port *Somset* **22** ST6718
Milborne St. Andrew *Dorset* **11** SY8097
Milborne Wick *Somset* **22** ST6620
Milbourne *Nthumb* **103** NZ1175
Milbourne *Wilts* **35** ST9587
Milburn *Cumb* **94** NY6529
Milbury Heath *Avon* **35** ST6790
Milby *N York* **89** SE4067
Milcombe *Oxon* **49** SP4134
Milden *Suffk* **54** TL9546
Mildenhall *Wilts* **36** SU2069
Mildenhall *Suffk* **53** TL7174
Mile Elm *Wilts* **35** ST9969
Mile End *Gloucs* **34** SO5811
Mile End *Essex* **41** TL9927
Mile End *Suffk* **55** TM3489
Mile Oak *Staffs* **61** SK1802
Mile Oak *E Susx* **15** TQ2407
Mile Oak *Kent* **28** TQ6743
Mile Town *Kent* **28** TQ9274
Milebrook *Powys* **46** SO3172
Milebush *Kent* **28** TQ7545
Mileham *Norfk* **66** TF9119
Miles Hope *H & W* **46** SO5764
Miles Platting *Gt Man* **79** SJ8599
Milesmark *Fife* **117** NT0688
Milfield *Nthumb* **110** NT9333
Milford *Staffs* **72** SJ9720
Milford *Derbys* **62** SK3545
Milford *Powys* **58** SO0991
Milford *Devon* **18** SS2322
Milford *Surrey* **25** SU9442
Milford Haven *Dyfed* **30** SM9005
Milford on Sea *Hants* **12** SZ2891
Milkwall *Gloucs* **34** SO5809
Mill Bank *W York* **82** SE0321
Mill Brow *Gt Man* **79** SJ9789
Mill Common *Norfk* **67** TG3201
Mill Common *Suffk* **55** TM4081
Mill Cross *Devon* **7** SX7361
Mill End *Bucks* **37** SU7885
Mill End *Herts* **39** TL3332
Mill Green *W Mids* **61** SK0701
Mill Green *Staffs* **73** SK0821
Mill Green *Lincs* **64** TF2223
Mill Green *Herts* **39** TL2410
Mill Green *Cambs* **53** TL6245
Mill Green *Essex* **40** TL6301
Mill Green *Suffk* **54** TL9542
Mill Green *Suffk* **54** TL9957
Mill Green *Suffk* **54** TM1360
Mill Green *Norfk* **54** TM1384
Mill Green *Suffk* **55** TM3161
Mill Hill *Gt Lon* **26** TQ2292
Mill Hill *E Susx* **16** TQ6205
Mill Meece *Staffs* **72** SJ8333
Mill Side *Cumb* **87** SD4484
Mill Street *Norfk* **66** TG0118
Mill Street *Suffk* **54** TM0672
Mill Street *Kent* **28** TQ6957
Mill of Drummond *Tays* **125** NN8315
Mill of Grange *Gramp* **141** NJ0460
Mill of Haldane *Strath* **115** NS3982
Mill of Uras *Gramp* **135** NO8680
Millais *Jersey* **152** JS0000
Milland *W Susx* **14** SU8328
Milland Marsh *W Susx* **14** SU8326
Millbeck *Cumb* **93** NY2526
Millbreck *Gramp* **143** NK0044
Millbrex *Gramp* **143** NJ8144
Millbridge *Surrey* **25** SU8442
Millbrook *Jersey* **152** JS0000
Millbrook *Gt Man* **79** SJ9799
Millbrook *Hants* **12** SU3813
Millbrook *Cnwll* **6** SX4252
Millbrook *Beds* **38** TL0138
Millbuie *Gramp* **135** NJ7909
Millburn *Strath* **107** NS4429
Millcombe *Devon* **7** SX8049
Millcorner *E Susx* **17** TQ8223
Millcraig *Highld* **146** NH6571
Milldale *Staffs* **73** SK1354
Millend *Gloucs* **34** SO5609
Millend *Gloucs* **35** ST7496
Miller's Dale *Derbys* **74** SK1473
Miller's Green *Essex* **40** TL5808
Millerhill *Loth* **118** NT3269
Millers Green *Derbys* **73** SK2852
Millerston *Strath* **116** NS6467
Millgate *Lancs* **81** SD8819
Millgreen *Shrops* **72** SJ6828
Millhalf *H & W* **46** SO2747
Millhayes *Devon* **9** ST2303
Millhead *Lancs* **87** SD4971
Millhouse *Strath* **114** NR9570
Millhouse *Cumb* **93** NY3637
Millhouse Green *S York* **82** SE2203
Millhousebridge *D & G* **100** NY1085
Millhouses *S York* **83** SE4204
Millhouses *S York* **74** SK3484
Millikenpark *Strath* **115** NS4162
Millin Cross *Dyfed* **30** SM9914
Millington *Humb* **84** SE8351
Millisle *D & G* **99** NX4547
Millness *Cumb* **87** SD5382
Millom *Cumb* **86** SD1780
Millook *Cnwll* **18** SX1899
Millpool *Cnwll* **2** SW5730
Millpool *Cnwll* **4** SX1170
Millport *Strath* **114** NS1755
Millthorpe *Derbys* **74** SK3167
Millthrop *Cumb* **87** SD6591
Milltimber *Gramp* **135** NJ8501
Milltown *Gramp* **133** NJ2609
Milltown *Gramp* **142** NJ4716
Milltown *D & G* **101** NY3375
Milltown *Derbys* **74** SK3561
Milltown *Devon* **19** SS5538
Milltown of Campfield *Gramp* **135** NJ6500
Milltown of Learney *Gramp* **134** NJ6303
Milnathort *Tays* **126** NO1204
Milngavie *Strath* **115** NS5574
Milnmark *D & G* **99** NX6582
Milnrow *Gt Man* **81** SD9212
Milnthorpe *Cumb* **87** SD4981
Milnthorpe *W York* **83** SE3317
Milovaig *Highld* **136** NG1549
Milson *Shrops* **47** SO6472
Milsted *Kent* **28** TQ9058
Milston *Wilts* **23** SU1645
Milthorpe *Nhants* **49** SP5946
Milthorpe *Lincs* **64** TF1130
Milton *Highld* **151** ND3451
Milton *Highld* **137** NG7043
Milton *Highld* **139** NH5749
Milton *Highld* **147** NH7674
Milton *Gramp* **142** NJ5163
Milton *Cent* **115** NN5001
Milton *Tays* **133** NO1357
Milton *Strath* **115** NS3569
Milton *Strath* **115** NS4274
Milton *D & G* **98** NX2154
Milton *D & G* **100** NX8470
Milton *Cumb* **101** NY5560
Milton *Staffs* **72** SJ9050
Milton *Derbys* **62** SK3126
Milton *Notts* **75** SK7173
Milton *Dyfed* **30** SN0403
Milton *Oxon* **49** SP4535
Milton *Avon* **21** ST3462
Milton *Gwent* **34** ST3688
Milton *Somset* **21** ST4621
Milton *Oxon* **37** SU4892
Milton *Cambs* **53** TL4762
Milton *Kent* **28** TQ6674
Milton Abbas *Dorset* **11** ST8002
Milton Abbot *Devon* **5** SX4079
Milton Bridge *Fife* **117** NT2562
Milton Bryan *Beds* **38** SP9730
Milton Clevedon *Somset* **22** ST6637
Milton Combe *Devon* **6** SX4866
Milton Common *Oxon* **37** SP6503
Milton Damerel *Devon* **18** SS3810
Milton End *Gloucs* **35** SO7110
Milton End *Gloucs* **36** SP1400
Milton Ernest *Beds* **51** TL0156
Milton Green *Ches* **71** SJ4658
Milton Hill *Oxon* **37** SU4790
Milton Keynes *Bucks* **38** SP8537
Milton Lilbourne *Wilts* **23** SU1960
Milton Malsor *Nhants* **49** SP7355
Milton Morenish *Tays* **124** NN6135
Milton Regis *Kent* **28** TQ9064
Milton Street *E Susx* **16** TQ5304
Milton of Auchinhove *Gramp* **134** NJ5503
Milton of Balgonie *Fife* **118** NO3200
Milton of Buchanan *Cent* **115** NS4490
Milton of Campsie *Strath* **116** NS6576
Milton of Cushnie *Gramp* **134** NJ5211
Milton of Tullich *Gramp* **134** NO3897
Milton on Stour *Dorset* **22** ST7928
Milton-under-Wychwood *Oxon* **36** SP2618
Milverton *Warwks* **48** SP3166
Milverton *Somset* **20** ST1225
Milwich *Staffs* **72** SJ9632
Milwr *Clwyd* **70** SJ1974
Minard *Strath* **114** NR9796
Minchington *Dorset* **11** ST9614
Minchinhampton *Gloucs* **35** SO8700
Mindrum *Nthumb* **110** NT8432
Mindrummill *Nthumb* **110** NT8433
Minehead *Somset* **20** SS9646
Minera *Clwyd* **70** SJ2751
Minety Lower Moor *Wilts* **35** SU0291
Minffordd *Gwynd* **57** SH5938
Mingarry Park *Highld* **129** NM6869
Miningsby *Lincs* **77** TF3264
Minions *Cnwll* **5** SX2671
Minishant *Strath* **106** NS3314
Minllyn *Gwynd* **57** SH8514
Minmore Hotel *Gramp* **141** NJ1929
Minnigaff *D & G* **99** NX4166
Minnis Bay *Kent* **29** TR2869
Minnonie *Gramp* **142** NJ7760
Minskip *N York* **89** SE3864
Minstead *Hants* **12** SU2811
Minsted *W Susx* **14** SU8520
Minster *Kent* **28** TQ9573
Minster *Kent* **29** TR3064
Minster Lovell *Oxon* **36** SP3111
Minsteracres *Nthumb* **95** NZ0156
Minsterley *Shrops* **59** SJ3705
Minsterworth *Gloucs* **35** SO7817
Minterne Magna *Dorset* **11** ST6504
Minterne Parva *Dorset* **11** ST6603
Minting *Lincs* **76** TF1873
Mintlaw *Gramp* **143** NJ9948
Minto *Border* **109** NT5620
Minton *Shrops* **59** SO4390
Minwear *Dyfed* **30** SN0413
Minworth *W Mids* **61** SP1691
Mirehouse *Cumb* **92** NX9715
Mirfield *W York* **82** SE2019
Miserden *Gloucs* **35** SO9308
Miskin *M Glam* **33** ST0480
Miskin *M Glam* **33** ST0498
Misson *Notts* **75** SK6895
Misterton *Notts* **75** SK7694
Misterton *Leics* **50** SP5583
Misterton *Somset* **10** ST4508
Mistley *Essex* **41** TM1231
Mistley Heath *Essex* **41** TM1230
Mitcham *Gt Lon* **27** TQ2768
Mitchel Troy *Gwent* **34** SO4910
Mitcheldean *Gloucs* **35** SO6618
Mitchell *Cnwll* **3** SW8554
Mitchellslacks *D & G* **100** NX9696
Mitford *Nthumb* **103** NZ1786
Mithian *Cnwll* **3** SW7450
Mitton *Staffs* **72** SJ8815
Mixbury *Oxon* **49** SP6033
Mixenden *W York* **82** SE0629
Mixon *Staffs* **74** SK0457
Moats Tye *Suffk* **54** TM0455
Mobberley *Ches* **79** SJ7879
Mobberley *Staffs* **73** SK0041
Moccas *H & W* **46** SO3543
Mochdre *Powys* **69** SH8278
Mochdre *Powys* **58** SO0788
Mochrum *D & G* **98** NX3446
Mockbeggar *Hants* **12** SU1609
Mockbeggar *Kent* **28** TQ7146
Mockerkin *Cumb* **92** NY0923
Modbury *Devon* **7** SX6651
Moddershall *Staffs* **72** SJ9236
Moelfre *Gwynd* **68** SH5186
Moelfre *Clwyd* **58** SJ1828
Moffat *D & G* **108** NT0805
Mogerhanger *Beds* **52** TL1449
Moira *Leics* **62** SK3115
Mol-chlach *Highld* **128** NG4513
Molash *Kent* **28** TR0251
Mold *Clwyd* **70** SJ2363
Moldgreen *W York* **82** SE1516
Molehill Green *Essex* **40** TL5624
Molehill Green *Essex* **40** TL7120
Molescroft *Humb* **84** TA0140
Molesden *Nthumb* **103** NZ1484
Molesworth *Cambs* **51** TL0775
Molland *Devon* **19** SS8028
Mollington *Ches* **71** SJ3870
Mollington *Oxon* **49** SP4447
Mollinsburn *Strath* **116** NS7171
Monachty *Dyfed* **44** SN5061
Monachylemore *Cent* **124** NN4719
Monday Boys *Kent* **28** TQ9045
Mondynes *Gramp* **135** NO7779
Monewden *Suffk* **55** TM2358
Moneydie *Tays* **125** NO0629
Moneygrow Green *Berks* **26** SU8977
Moniaive *D & G* **107** NX7890
Monifieth *Tays* **127** NO4932
Monikie *Tays* **127** NO4938
Monimail *Fife* **126** NO2914
Monington *Dyfed* **42** SN1344
Monk Bretton *S York* **83** SE3607
Monk Fryston *N York* **83** SE5029
Monk Hesleden *Dur* **97** NZ4537
Monk Sherborne *Hants* **24** SU6056
Monk Soham *Suffk* **55** TM2165
Monk Soham Green *Suffk* **55** TM2066
Monk Street *Essex* **40** TL6128
Monk's Gate *W Susx* **15** TQ2027
Monken Hadley *Gt Lon* **26** TQ2497
Monkhide *H & W* **46** SO6144
Monkhill *Cumb* **93** NY3458
Monkhopton *Shrops* **59** SO6293
Monkland *H & W* **46** SO4557
Monkleigh *Devon* **18** SS4520
Monknash *S Glam* **33** SS9170
Monkokehampton *Devon* **8** SS5805
Monks Eleigh *Suffk* **54** TL9647
Monks Heath *Ches* **79** SJ8474
Monks Kirby *Warwks* **50** SP4683
Monks Risborough *Bucks* **38** SP8104
Monkseaton *T & W* **103** NZ3472
Monksilver *Somset* **20** ST0737
Monkspath Street *W Mids* **61** SP1376
Monksthorpe *Lincs* **77** TF4465
Monkswood *Gwent* **34** SO3402
Monkton *Strath* **106** NS3527
Monkton *T & W* **103** NZ3363
Monkton *S Glam* **33** SS9270
Monkton *E Susx* **9** ST1803
Monkton *Kent* **29** TR2964
Monkton Combe *Avon* **22** ST7762
Monkton Deverill *Wilts* **22** ST8537
Monkton Farleigh *Wilts* **22** ST8065
Monkton Heathfield *Somset* **20** ST2526
Monkton Up Wimborne *Dorset* **11** SU0113
Monkton Wyld *Dorset* **10** SY3396
Monkwearmouth *T & W* **96** NZ3958
Monkwood *Hants* **24** SU6630
Monmore Green *W Mids* **60** SO9297
Monmouth *Gwent* **34** SO5012
Monnington on Wye *H & W* **46** SO3743
Monreith *D & G* **98** NX3541
Mont Saint *Guern* **152** GN0000
Montacute *Somset* **10** ST4916
Montcliffe *Gt Man* **81** SD6611
Montford *Shrops* **59** SJ4114
Montford Bridge *Shrops* **59** SJ4215
Montgarrie *Gramp* **142** NJ5717
Montgarswood *Strath* **107** NS5227
Montgomery *Powys* **58** SO2296
Montgreenan *Strath* **106** NS3343
Monton *Gt Man* **79** SJ7699
Montrave *Fife* **126** NO3806
Montrose *Tays* **127** NO7157
Monxton *Hants* **23** SU3144
Monyash *Derbys* **74** SK1566
Monymusk *Gramp* **142** NJ6815
Monzie *Tays* **125** NN8725
Moodiesburn *Strath* **116** NS6970
Moonzie *Fife* **126** NO3317
Moor Allerton *W York* **82** SE3038
Moor Crichel *Dorset* **11** ST9908
Moor End *Lancs* **80** SD3744
Moor End *W York* **82** SE0528
Moor End *N York* **83** SE6038
Moor End *Humb* **84** SE8137
Moor End *Beds* **38** SP9719
Moor End *Devon* **19** SS6609
Moor Green *Herts* **39** TL3226
Moor Head *W York* **82** SE1337
Moor Head *W York* **82** SE2329
Moor Monkton *N York* **83** SE5156
Moor Row *Cumb* **92** NY0014
Moor Row *Cumb* **93** NY2149
Moor Row *Dur* **96** NZ1515
Moor Side *Lancs* **80** SD4935
Moor Side *Lincs* **77** TF2557
Moor Street *W Mids* **60** SO9982
Moor Street *Kent* **28** TQ8265
Moorbath *Dorset* **10** SY4395
Moorby *Lincs* **77** TF2964
Moorcot *H & W* **46** SO3555
Moordown *Dorset* **12** SZ0994
Moore *Ches* **78** SJ5784
Moorend *Gloucs* **35** SO7303
Moorgreen *Hants* **13** SU4815
Moorhall *Derbys* **74** SK3074
Moorhampton *H & W* **46** SO3746
Moorhouse *Cumb* **93** NY2551
Moorhouse *Cumb* **93** NY3356
Moorhouse *W York* **83** SE4810
Moorhouse *Notts* **75** SK7566
Moorhouse Bank *Surrey* **27** TQ4353
Moorlinch *Somset* **21** ST3936
Moorgreen *Notts* **62** SK4847
Moorsholm *Cleve* **90** NZ6814
Moorside *Cumb* **86** NY0701
Moorside *Gt Man* **79** SD9407
Moorside *Dorset* **22** ST7919
Moorstock *Kent* **29** TR1038
Moorswater *Cnwll* **5** SX2364
Moorthorpe *W York* **83** SE4611
Moortown *W York* **82** SE2939
Moortown *Shrops* **59** SJ6118
Moortown *Hants* **12** SU1503
Moortown *Devon* **6** SX5274
Moortown *IOW* **13** SZ4283
Moortown *Lincs* **76** TF0798
Morangie *Highld* **147** NH7683
Morar *Highld* **129** NM6793
Morborne *Cambs* **64** TL1391
Morchard Bishop *Devon* **8** SS7707
Morcombelake *Dorset* **10** SY4094
Morcott *Leics* **51** SK9200
Morda *Shrops* **58** SJ2827
Morden *Dorset* **11** SY9195
Morden *Gt Lon* **27** TQ2666
Mordiford *H & W* **46** SO5737
Mordon *Dur* **96** NZ3226
More *Shrops* **59** SO3491
Morebath *Devon* **20** SS9525
Morebattle *Border* **110** NT7724
Morecambe *Lancs* **87** SD4364
Moredon *Wilts* **36** SU1487
Morefield *Highld* **145** NH1195
Morehall *Kent* **29** TR2136
Moreleigh *Devon* **7** SX7652
Morenish *Tays* **124** NN6035
Moresby *Cumb* **92** NX9921
Moresby Parks *Cumb* **92** NX9919
Morestead *Hants* **13** SU5025
Moreton *Mersyd* **78** SJ2689
Moreton *Staffs* **72** SJ7817
Moreton *Staffs* **73** SK1429
Moreton *H & W* **46** SO5064
Moreton *Oxon* **37** SP6904
Moreton *Dorset* **11** SY8089
Moreton *Essex* **39** TL5307
Moreton Corbet *Shrops* **59** SJ5623
Moreton Jeffries *H & W* **46** SO6048
Moreton Mill *Shrops* **59** SJ5723
Moreton Morrell *Warwks* **48** SP3155
Moreton Paddox *Warwks* **48** SP3154
Moreton Pinkney *Nhants* **49** SP5749
Moreton Say *Shrops* **59** SJ6334
Moreton Valence *Gloucs* **35** SO7809
Moreton on Lugg *H & W* **46** SO5045
Moreton-in-Marsh *Gloucs* **48** SP2032
Moretonhampstead *Devon* **8** SX7586
Morfa *Dyfed* **42** SN3053
Morfa Bychan *Gwynd* **57** SH5437
Morfa Glas *W Glam* **33** SN8606
Morfa Nefyn *Gwynd* **56** SH2840
Morgan's Vale *Wilts* **12** SU1920
Morganstown *S Glam* **33** ST1281
Morham *Loth* **118** NT5571
Moriah *Dyfed* **43** SN6279
Morland *Cumb* **94** NY6022
Morley *Dur* **96** NZ1227
Morley *W York* **82** SE2627
Morley *Ches* **79** SJ8282
Morley *Derbys* **62** SK3940
Morley Green *Ches* **79** SJ8281
Morley St. Botolph *Norfk* **66** TM0799
Mornick *Cnwll* **5** SX3272
Morningside *Strath* **116** NS8355
Morningside *Loth* **117** NT2470
Morningthorpe *Norfk* **67** TM2192
Morpeth *Nthumb* **103** NZ1986
Morphie *Gramp* **135** NO7164
Morrey *Staffs* **73** SK1218
Morridge Side *Staffs* **73** SK0254
Morridge Top *Staffs* **74** SK0365
Morriston *W Glam* **32** SS6697
Morston *Norfk* **66** TG0043
Mortehoe *Devon* **18** SS4545
Morthen *S York* **75** SK4788
Mortimer *Berks* **24** SU6564
Mortimer Common *Berks* **24** SU6565
Mortimer West End *Hants* **24** SU6363
Mortimer's Cross *H & W* **46** SO4263
Mortlake *Gt Lon* **26** TQ2075
Morton *Cumb* **93** NY3854
Morton *Cumb* **93** NY4539
Morton *Shrops* **59** SJ2924
Morton *Derbys* **74** SK4060
Morton *Notts* **75** SK7251
Morton *Lincs* **75** SK8091
Morton *IOW* **13** SZ6085
Morton *Lincs* **64** TF0923
Morton *Norfk* **66** TG1216
Morton Bagot *Warwks* **48** SP1164
Morton Hall *Lincs* **76** SK8863
Morton Tinmouth *Dur* **96** NZ1821
Morton-on-Swale *N York* **89** SE3291
Morvah *Cnwll* **2** SW4035
Morval *Cnwll* **5** SX2556
Morvich *Highld* **138** NG9621
Morville *Shrops* **60** SO6794
Morville Heath *Shrops* **60** SO6893
Morwenstow *Cnwll* **18** SS2015
Mosborough *S York* **74** SK4281
Moscow *Strath* **107** NS4840
Mose *Shrops* **60** SO7590
Mosedale *Cumb* **93** NY3532
Moseley *H & W* **47** SO8159
Moseley *W Mids* **60** SO9498
Moseley *W Mids* **61** SP0783
Moses Gate *Gt Man* **79** SD7306
Moss *Strath* **120** NL9544
Moss *S York* **83** SE5914
Moss *Clwyd* **71** SJ3053
Moss Bank *Mersyd* **78** SJ5197
Moss End *Ches* **79** SJ6778
Moss Side *Cumb* **93** NY1952
Moss Side *Lancs* **80** SD3730
Moss Side *Mersyd* **78** SD3802
Moss-side *Highld* **140** NH8555
Mossat *Gramp* **142** NJ4719
Mossbank *Shet* **155** HU4575
Mossbay *Cumb* **92** NX9927

Mossdale New Ridley

Mossdale D & G 99 NX6670
Mossend Strath 116 NS7460
Mossblown Strath 106 NS3925
Mossbrow Gt Man 79 SJ7089
Mossburnford Border 110 NT6616
Mossdale Strath 107 NS4904
Mosser Mains Cumb 92 NY1125
Mossgiel Strath 107 NS4828
Mossknowe D & G 101 NY2769
Mossley Gt Man 82 SD9701
Mossley Ches 72 SJ8861
Mossley Staffs 73 SK0417
Mosspaul Hotel Border 109 NY3999
Mosstodloch Gramp 141 NJ3259
Mossy Lea Lancs 80 SD5312
Mossyard D & G 99 NX5451
Mosterton Dorset 10 ST4505
Moston Gt Man 79 SD8701
Moston Shrops 59 SJ5626
Moston Green Ches 72 SJ7261
Mostyn Clwyd 70 SJ1580
Motcombe Dorset 22 ST8525
Mothecombe Devon 6 SX6047
Motherby Cumb 93 NY4228
Motherwell Strath 116 NS7457
Motspur Park Gt Lon 26 TQ2267
Mottingham Gt Lon 27 TQ4272
Mottisfont Hants 23 SU3226
Mottistone IOW 13 SZ4083
Mottram in Longdendale Gt Man 79 SJ9995
Mouilpied Guern 152 GN0000
Mouldsworth Ches 71 SJ5071
Moulin Tays 132 NN9459
Moulsecoomb E Susx 15 TQ3307
Moulsford Oxon 37 SU5883
Moulsoe Bucks 38 SP9141
Moultavie Highld 146 NH6371
Moulton N York 89 NZ2303
Moulton Ches 79 SJ6569
Moulton Nhants 50 SP7866
Moulton S Glam 33 ST0770
Moulton Lincs 64 TF3023
Moulton Suffk 53 TL6964
Moulton Chapel Lincs 64 TF2918
Moulton Seas End Lincs 64 TF3227
Moulton St. Mary Norfk 67 TG3907
Mount W York 82 SE0917
Mount Cnwll 3 SW7856
Mount Cnwll 4 SX1468
Mount Ambrose Cnwll 2 SW7043
Mount Bures Essex 40 TL9032
Mount Hawke Cnwll 2 SW7147
Mount Hermon Cnwll 2 SW6915
Mount Lothian Loth 117 NT2757
Mount Pleasant Dur 96 NZ2634
Mount Pleasant Ches 72 SJ8456
Mount Pleasant Derbys 74 SK3448
Mount Pleasant H & W 47 SP0064
Mount Pleasant Suffk 53 TL7347
Mount Pleasant Norfk 66 TL9994
Mount Pleasant E Susx 16 TQ4216
Mount Sorrel Wilts 23 SU0324
Mount Tabor W York 82 SE0527
Mountain W York 82 SE0930
Mountain Ash M Glam 33 ST0499
Mountain Cross Border 117 NT1547
Mountain Street Kent 29 TR0652
Mountblairy Gramp 142 NJ6854
Mountfield E Susx 17 TQ7320
Mountgerald House Highld 139 NH5661
Mountjoy Cnwll 4 SW8760
Mountnessing Essex 40 TQ6297
Mounton Gwent 34 ST5193
Mountsorrel Leics 62 SK5814
Mountstuart Strath 114 NS1159
Mousehill Surrey 25 SU9441
Mousehole Cnwll 2 SW4626
Mouswald D & G 100 NY0672
Mow Cop Ches 72 SJ8557
Mowhaugh Border 110 NT8120
Mowmacre Hill Leics 62 SK5807
Mowsley Leics 50 SP6489
Mowtie Gramp 135 NO8388
Moy Highld 140 NH7634
Moy Highld 131 NN4282
Moye Highld 138 NG8818
Moyles Court Hants 12 SU1608
Moylgrove Dyfed 42 SN1144
Muasdale Strath 105 NR6840
Much Birch H & W 46 SO5030
Much Cowarne H & W 46 SO6147
Much Dewchurch H & W 46 SO4831
Much Hadham Herts 39 TL4219
Much Hoole Lancs 80 SD4723
Much Hoole Town Lancs 80 SD4722
Much Marcle H & W 47 SO6532
Much Wenlock Shrops 59 SO6299
Muchalls Gramp 135 NO9092
Muchelney Somset 21 ST4224
Muchelney Ham Somset 21 ST4423
Muchlarnick Cnwll 5 SX2156
Mucking Essex 40 TQ6881
Muckingford Essex 40 TQ6779
Muckleford Dorset 10 SY6393
Mucklestone Staffs 72 SJ7237
Muckton Lincs 77 TF3781
Mucomir Highld 131 NN1884
Mud Row Kent 28 TR0072
Muddiford Devon 19 SS5638
Muddlebridge Devon 19 SS5232
Muddles Green E Susx 16 TQ5413
Mudeford Dorset 12 SZ1892
Mudford Somset 21 ST5719
Mudford Sock Somset 21 ST5519
Mudgley Somset 21 ST4545
Mugdock Cent 115 NS5577
Mugeary Highld 136 NG4439
Mugginton Derbys 73 SK2842
Muggintonlane End Derbys 73 SK2844
Muggleswick Dur 95 NZ0449
Muir of Fowlis Gramp 134 NJ5612
Muir of Miltonduff Gramp 141 NJ1859
Muir of Ord Highld 139 NH5250
Muir of Thorn Tays 125 NO0637
Muirden Gramp 142 NJ7054
Muirdrum Tays 127 NO5637
Muiresk Gramp 142 NJ6948
Muirhead Fife 126 NO2805
Muirhead Tays 126 NO3434
Muirhead Strath 116 NS6869
Muirhouselaw Border 110 NT6328
Muirhouses Cent 117 NT0180
Muirkirk Strath 107 NS6927
Muirmill Cent 116 NS7283
Muirshearlich Highld 131 NN1380
Muirtack Gramp 143 NJ9937
Muirton Mains Highld 139 NH4553
Muirton of Ardblair Tays 126 NO1643
Muirtown Tays 125 NN9211
Muker N York 88 SD9097
Mulbarton Norfk 67 TG1901
Mulben Gramp 141 NJ3550
Mulfra Cnwll 2 SW4534
Mulindry Strath 112 NR3659
Mullacott Cross Devon 19 SS5144
Mullion Cnwll 2 SW6719
Mumby Lincs 77 TF5174
Muncher's Green Herts 39 TL3126
Munderfield Row H & W 47 SO6451
Munderfield Stocks H & W 47 SO6550
Mundesley Norfk 67 TG3136
Mundford Norfk 66 TL8093
Mundham Norfk 67 TM3397
Mundon Hill Essex 40 TL8602
Mungrisdale Cumb 93 NY3630
Munlochy Highld 140 NH6453
Munnoch Strath 114 NS2548
Munsley H & W 47 SO6640
Munslow Shrops 59 SO5287
Munslow Aston Shrops 59 SO5186
Murchington Devon 8 SX6888
Murcot H & W 48 SP0640
Murcott Oxon 37 SP5815
Murcott Wilts 35 ST9591
Murkle Highld 151 ND1668
Murlaggan Highld 130 NN0192
Murrell Green Hants 24 SU7455
Murroes Tays 127 NO4635
Murrow Cambs 64 TF3707
Mursley Bucks 38 SP8128
Murthill Tays 134 NO4657
Murthly Tays 126 NO1038
Murton T & W 103 NZ3270
Murton Nthumb 111 NT9748
Murton Cumb 94 NY7221
Murton Dur 96 NZ3847
Murton N York 83 SE6452
Musbury Devon 10 SY2794
Muscoates N York 90 SE6879
Musselburgh Loth 118 NT3472
Muston Leics 63 SK8237
Muston N York 91 TA0979
Mustow Green H & W 60 SO8774
Muswell Hill Gt Lon 27 TQ2889
Mutehill D & G 99 NX6848
Mutford Suffk 55 TM4888
Muthill Tays 125 NN8717
Mutterton Devon 9 ST0205
Muxton Shrops 60 SJ7114
Mybster Highld 151 ND1652
Myddfai Dyfed 44 SN7730
Myddle Shrops 59 SJ4623
Mydroilyn Dyfed 42 SN4555
Mylor Cnwll 3 SW8135
Mylor Bridge Cnwll 3 SW8036
Mynachlog ddu Dyfed 31 SN1430
Mynydd-llan Clwyd 70 SJ1572
Myndtown Shrops 59 SO3989
Mynydd Buch Dyfed 43 SN7276
Mynydd Isa Clwyd 70 SJ2563
Mynydd-bach W Glam 32 SS6597
Mynydd-bach Gwent 34 ST4894
Mynyddgarreg Dyfed 31 SN4208
Mynytho Gwynd 56 SH3031
Myrebird Gramp 135 NO7398
Myredykes Border 102 NY5998
Mytchett Surrey 25 SU8855
Mytholm W York 82 SD9827
Mytholmroyd W York 82 SE0126
Mythop Lancs 80 SD3634
Myton-on-Swale N York 89 SE4366

N

Naast Highld 144 NG8283
Nab's Head Lancs 81 SD6229
Naburn N York 83 SE5945
Nackholt Kent 28 TR0543
Nackington Kent 29 TR1554
Nacton Suffk 55 TM2240
Nafferton Humb 91 TA0559
Nag's Head Gloucs 35 ST8898
Nailbridge Gloucs 35 SO6415
Nailsbourne Somset 20 ST2128
Nailsea Avon 34 ST4770
Nailstone Leics 62 SK4106
Nailsworth Gloucs 35 ST8499
Nairn Highld 140 NH8856
Nalderswood Surrey 15 TQ2445
Nancegollan Cnwll 2 SW6332
Nancledra Cnwll 2 SW4936
Nanhoron Gwynd 56 SH2731
Nannerch Clwyd 70 SJ1669
Nanpantan Leics 62 SK5017
Nanpean Cnwll 3 SW9556
Nanquidno Cnwll 2 SW3629
Nanstallon Cnwll 4 SX0367
Nant Gwynant Gwynd 69 SH6350
Nant Peris Gwynd 69 SH6058
Nant-ddu Powys 33 SO0014
Nant-glas Powys 45 SN9965
Nant-y-Bwch Gwent 33 SO1210
Nant-y-caws Dyfed 32 SN4518
Nant-y-derry Gwent 34 SO3306
Nant-y-gollen Shrops 58 SJ2428
Nant-y-moel M Glam 33 SS9392
Nant-y-pandy Gwynd 69 SH6973
Nanternis Dyfed 42 SN3756
Nantgaredig Dyfed 32 SN4921
Nantgarw M Glam 33 ST1285
Nantglyn Clwyd 70 SJ0061
Nantgwyn Powys 45 SN9776
Nantlle Gwynd 68 SH5153
Nantmawr Shrops 58 SJ2524
Nantmel Powys 45 SO0366
Nantmor Gwynd 57 SH6046
Nantwich Ches 72 SJ6552
Nantyffyllon M Glam 33 SS8492
Naphill Bucks 26 SU8496
Napleton H & W 47 SO8648
Nappa N York 81 SD8553
Napton on the Hill Warwks 49 SP4661
Narberth Dyfed 31 SN1015
Narborough Leics 50 SP5497
Narborough Norfk 65 TF7412
Narkurs Cnwll 5 SX3255
Nasareth Gwynd 68 SH4749
Naseby Nhants 50 SP6978
Nash H & W 46 SO3062
Nash Shrops 46 SO6071
Nash Bucks 38 SP7833
Nash Gwent 34 ST3483
Nash Gt Lon 27 TQ4063
Nash End H & W 60 SO7781
Nash Lee Bucks 38 SP8408
Nash Street Kent 27 TQ6469
Nash's Green Hants 24 SU6745
Nassington Nhants 51 TL0696
Nasty Herts 39 TL3524
Nateby Cumb 88 NY7706
Nateby Lancs 80 SD4644
Natland Cumb 87 SD5289
Naughton Suffk 54 TM0249
Naunton H & W 47 SO8645
Naunton H & W 47 SO8739
Naunton Gloucs 48 SP1123
Naunton Beauchamp H & W 47 SO9652
Navenby Lincs 76 SK9858
Navestock Essex 27 TQ5397
Navestock Side Essex 27 TQ5697
Navidale House Hotel Highld 147 ND0316
Navity Highld 140 NH7864
Nawton N York 90 SE6584
Nayland Suffk 54 TL9734
Nazeing Essex 39 TL4106
Nazeing Gate Essex 39 TL4105
Neacroft Hants 12 SZ1896
Neal's Green Warwks 61 SP3384
Nealhouse Cumb 93 NY3351
Neap Shet 155 HU5058
Near Cotton Staffs 73 SK0646
Near Sawry Cumb 87 SD3795
Neasden Gt Lon 26 TQ2185
Neasham Dur 89 NZ3210
Neath W Glam 32 SS7597
Neatham Hants 24 SU7440
Neatishead Norfk 67 TG3420
Nebo Gwynd 68 SH4850
Nebo Gwynd 69 SH8355
Nebo Dyfed 43 SN5465
Necton Norfk 66 TF8709
Nedd Highld 148 NC1331
Nedging Suffk 54 TL9948
Nedging Tye Suffk 54 TM0149
Needham Norfk 55 TM2281
Needham Market Suffk 54 TM0855
Needham Street Suffk 53 TL7265
Needingworth Cambs 52 TL3472
Neen Savage Shrops 60 SO6777
Neen Sollars Shrops 60 SO6672
Neenton Shrops 59 SO6387
Nefyn Gwynd 56 SH3040
Neilston Strath 115 NS4857
Nelson Lancs 81 SD8638
Nelson M Glam 33 ST1195
Nemphlar Strath 116 NS8544
Nempnett Thrubwell Avon 21 ST5260
Nenthall Cumb 94 NY7545
Nenthead Cumb 94 NY7743
Nenthorn Border 110 NT6837
Neopardy Devon 8 SX7999
Nep Town W Susx 15 TQ2115
Nercwys Clwyd 70 SJ2360
Nereabolls Strath 112 NR2255
Nerston Strath 116 NS6456
Nesbit Nthumb 111 NT9833
Nesfield N York 82 SE0949
Ness Ches 71 SJ3076
Nesscliffe Shrops 59 SJ3819
Neston Ches 71 SJ2977
Neston Wilts 22 ST8668
Netchwood Shrops 59 SO6291
Nether Alderley Ches 79 SJ8476
Nether Blainslie Border 109 NT5443
Nether Broughton Notts 63 SK6925
Nether Burrow Lancs 87 SD6174
Nether Cassock D & G 109 NT2303
Nether Cerne Dorset 11 SY6798
Nether Compton Dorset 10 ST5917
Nether Crimond Gramp 143 NJ8222
Nether Dallachy Gramp 141 NJ3563
Nether Exe Devon 9 SS9300
Nether Fingland Strath 108 NS9310
Nether Handley Derbys 74 SK4176
Nether Handwick Tays 126 NO3641
Nether Haugh S York 74 SK4196
Nether Headon Notts 75 SK7477
Nether Heage Derbys 74 SK3650
Nether Heyford Nhants 49 SP6658
Nether Howcleugh Strath 108 NT0312
Nether Kellet Lancs 87 SD5068
Nether Kinmundy Gramp 143 NK0543
Nether Moor Derbys 74 SK3866
Nether Newton Cumb 87 SD4082
Nether Padley Derbys 74 SK2478
Nether Poppleton N York 83 SE5654
Nether Row Cumb 93 NY3237
Nether Silton N York 89 SE4592
Nether Skyborry Shrops 46 SO2873
Nether Stowey Somset 20 ST1939
Nether Street Essex 40 TL5812
Nether Wallop Hants 23 SU3036
Nether Wasdale Cumb 86 NY1204
Nether Wellwood Strath 107 NS6526
Nether Welton Cumb 93 NY3545
Nether Westcote Oxon 36 SP2220
Nether Whitacre Warwks 61 SP2392
Nether Whitecleuch Strath 108 NS8319
Netheravon Wilts 23 SU1448
Netherbrae Gramp 143 NJ7959
Netherburn Strath 116 NS7947
Netherbury Dorset 10 SY4799
Netherby Cumb 101 NY3971
Netherby N York 83 SE3346
Nethercleuch D & G 100 NY1186
Nethercote Warwks 49 SP5164
Nethercott Devon 18 SS4839
Nethercott Devon 5 SX3596
Netherend Gloucs 34 SO5900
Netherfield Leics 62 SK5816
Netherfield Notts 62 SK6140
Netherfield E Susx 16 TQ7019
Netherfield Road E Susx 17 TQ7417
Nethergate Notts 75 SK7599
Nethergate Norfk 66 TG0529
Netherhampton Wilts 23 SU1029
Netherhay Dorset 10 ST4105
Netherland Green Staffs 73 SK1030
Netherlaw D & G 99 NX7444
Netherley Gramp 135 NO8493
Nethermill D & G 100 NY0487
Nethermuir Gramp 143 NJ9044
Netheroyd Hill W York 82 SE1419
Netherplace Strath 115 NS5255
Netherseal Derbys 61 SK2812
Netherstreet Wilts 22 ST9864
Netherthong W York 82 SE1309
Netherthorpe Derbys 75 SK4474
Netherton Tays 126 NO1452
Netherton Tays 134 NO5457
Netherton Cent 115 NS5579
Netherton Strath 116 NS7854
Netherton Nthumb 111 NT9807
Netherton Nthumb 103 NZ2381
Netherton W York 82 SE1213
Netherton W York 82 SE2816
Netherton H & W 46 SO5226
Netherton Shrops 60 SO7382
Netherton W Mids 60 SO9488
Netherton H & W 47 SO9941
Netherton Hants 23 SU3757
Netherton Oxon 36 SU4199
Netherton Devon 7 SX8971
Nethertown Highld 151 ND3578
Nethertown Cumb 86 NX9907
Nethertown Lancs 81 SD7236
Nethertown Staffs 73 SK1017
Netherwitton Nthumb 103 NZ0990
Nethy Bridge Highld 141 NJ0020
Netley Hants 13 SU4508
Netley Marsh Hants 12 SU3313
Nettacott Devon 9 SX8999
Nettlebed Oxon 37 SU6986
Nettlebridge Somset 21 ST6448
Nettlecombe Dorset 10 SY5195
Nettlecombe IOW 13 SZ5278
Nettleden Herts 38 TL0110
Nettleham Lincs 76 TF0075
Nettlestead Kent 28 TQ6852
Nettlestead Green Kent 28 TQ6850
Nettlestone IOW 13 SZ6290
Nettlesworth Dur 96 NZ2547
Nettleton Wilts 35 ST8278
Nettleton Lincs 76 TA1100
Nettleton Shrub Wilts 35 ST8277
Netton Wilts 23 SU1336
Netton Devon 6 SX5546
Neuadd Dyfed 32 SN7021
Neuadd Fawr Dyfed 44 SN7441
Neuadd-ddu Powys 45 SN9175
Nevendon Essex 40 TQ7390
Nevern Dyfed 31 SN0840
Nevill Holt Leics 51 SP8193
New Abbey D & G 100 NX9666
New Aberdour Gramp 143 NJ8863
New Addington Gt Lon 27 TQ3763
New Alresford Hants 24 SU5832
New Alyth Tays 126 NO2447
New Arram Humb 84 TA0344
New Ash Green Kent 27 TQ6065
New Balderton Notts 75 SK8152
New Barn Kent 27 TQ6169
New Barnet Gt Lon 27 TQ2695
New Barton Nhants 51 SP8564
New Bewick Nthumb 111 NU0620
New Bilton Warwks 50 SP4875
New Bolingbroke Lincs 77 TF3057
New Boultham Lincs 76 SK9670
New Bradwell Bucks 38 SP8341
New Brampton Derbys 74 SK3771
New Brancepeth Dur 96 NZ2241
New Bridge N York 90 SE8085
New Brighton Clwyd 70 SJ2565
New Brighton Mersyd 78 SJ3093
New Brinsley Notts 75 SK4550
New Brotton Cleve 97 NZ6920
New Broughton Clwyd 71 SJ3151
New Buckenham Norfk 54 TM0890
New Bury Gt Man 79 SD7304
New Byth Gramp 143 NJ8254
New Costessey Norfk 66 TG1810
New Cowper Cumb 92 NY1245
New Crofton W York 83 SE3817
New Cross Dyfed 43 SN6376
New Cross Somset 21 ST4119
New Cross Gt Lon 27 TQ3676
New Cumnock Strath 107 NS6213
New Cut E Susx 17 TQ8115
New Deer Gramp 143 NJ8847
New Delaval Nthumb 103 NZ2979
New Delph Gt Man 82 SD9907
New Denham Bucks 26 TQ0484
New Duston Nhants 49 SP7162
New Earswick N York 83 SE6155
New Eastwood Notts 62 SK4646
New Edlington S York 75 SK5398
New Elgin Gramp 141 NJ2261
New Ellerby Humb 85 TA1639
New Eltham Gt Lon 27 TQ4472
New End H & W 48 SP0560
New Farnley W York 82 SE2531
New Ferry Mersyd 78 SJ3385
New Fletton Cambs 64 TL1997
New Fryston W York 83 SE4526
New Galloway D & G 99 NX6377
New Gilston Fife 127 NO4208
New Grimsby IOS 2 SV8815
New Hartley Nthumb 103 NZ3076
New Haw Surrey 26 TQ0563
New Hedges Dyfed 31 SN1202
New Herrington T & W 96 NZ3352
New Hey Gt Man 82 SD9411
New Holkham Norfk 66 TF8839
New Holland Humb 85 TA0823
New Houghton Derbys 75 SK4965
New Houghton Norfk 66 TF7927
New Houses Gt Man 78 SD5502
New Houses N York 88 SD8073
New Hutton Cumb 87 SD5691
New Hythe Kent 28 TQ7159
New Inn Dyfed 44 SN4736
New Inn Gwent 34 ST3099
New Invention Shrops 46 SO2976
New Kelso Highld 138 NG9442
New Lakenham Norfk 67 TG2307
New Lambton Dur 96 NZ3051
New Lanark Strath 108 NS8842
New Lane Lancs 80 SD4212
New Lane End Ches 79 SJ6394
New Langholm D & G 101 NY3684
New Leake Lincs 77 TF4057
New Leeds Gramp 143 NJ9954
New Longton Lancs 80 SD5025
New Luce D & G 98 NX1764
New Malden Gt Lon 26 TQ2168
New Marston Oxon 37 SP5407
New Marton Shrops 59 SJ3334
New Mill Gramp 135 NO7883
New Mill W York 82 SE1609
New Mill Herts 38 SP9212
New Mill Cnwll 2 SW4534
New Mills Powys 58 SJ0901
New Mills Derbys 79 SK0085
New Mills Cnwll 3 SW8952
New Milton Hants 12 SZ2495
New Mistley Essex 41 TM1131
New Moat Dyfed 30 SN0625
New Ollerton Notts 75 SK6667
New Oscott W Mids 61 SP0994
New Oxted Surrey 27 TQ3952
New Pitsligo Gramp 143 NJ8855
New Polzeath Cnwll 4 SW9379
New Prestwick Strath 106 NS3424
New Quay Dyfed 42 SN3959
New Quay Essex 41 TM0223
New Rackheath Norfk 67 TG2812
New Radnor Powys 45 SO2161
New Rent Cumb 93 NY4536
New Ridley Nthumb 95 NZ0559

New Road Side North Luffenham

New Road Side *N York* 82 SD9743
New Romney *Kent* 17 TR0624
New Rossington *Notts* 75 SK6198
New Row *Lancs* 81 SD6438
New Row *Dyfed* 43 SN7273
New Scone *Tays* 126 NO1326
New Sharlston *W York* 83 SE3819
New Shoreston *Nthumb* 111 NU1932
New Silksworth *T & W* 96 NZ3853
New Skelton *Cleve* 97 NZ6618
New Somerby *Lincs* 63 SK9235
New Spilsby *Lincs* 77 TF4165
New Springs *Gt Man* 78 SD5906
New Stevenston *Strath* 116 NS7659
New Street *H & W* 46 SO3356
New Swannington *Leics* 62 SK4215
New Thundersley *Essex* 40 TQ7789
New Town *Loth* 118 NT4470
New Town *Nhants* 51 SP9677
New Town *Somset* 10 ST2712
New Town *Dorset* 22 ST8318
New Town *Dorset* 11 ST9515
New Town *Dorset* 11 ST9907
New Town *Dorset* 22 ST9918
New Town *Wilts* 36 SU2871
New Town *Beds* 52 TL1945
New Town *E Susx* 16 TQ4720
New Tredegar *M Glam* 33 SO1403
New Trows *Strath* 108 NS8038
New Tupton *Derbys* 74 SK3966
New Village *Humb* 84 SE8530
New Walsoken *Cambs* 65 TF4609
New Waltham *Humb* 85 TA2804
New Whittington *Derbys* 74 SK3975
New Wimpole *Cambs* 52 TL3549
New Winton *Loth* 118 NT4271
New Yatt *Oxon* 36 SP3713
New York *T & W* 103 NZ3270
New York *N York* 89 SE1963
New York *Lincs* 77 TF2455
New Zealand *Derbys* 62 SK3336
Newall *W York* 82 SE1946
Newark *D & G* 107 NS7808
Newark *Cambs* 64 TF2100
Newark-on-Trent *Notts* 75 SK7953
Newarthill *Strath* 116 NS7859
Newbarn *Kent* 29 TR1540
Newbattle *Loth* 118 NT3365
Newbie *D & G* 101 NY1764
Newbiggin *Cumb* 93 NY4729
Newbiggin *Cumb* 94 NY5549
Newbiggin *Cumb* 94 NY6228
Newbiggin *Dur* 95 NY9127
Newbiggin *Dur* 96 NZ1447
Newbiggin *Cumb* 86 SD0994
Newbiggin *Cumb* 86 SD2669
Newbiggin *N York* 88 SD9591
Newbiggin *N York* 88 SE0086
Newbiggin-by-the-Sea *Nthumb* 103 NZ3087
Newbiggin-on-Lune *Cumb* 87 NY7005
Newbigging *Tays* 126 NO2841
Newbigging *Tays* 127 NO4237
Newbigging *Strath* 117 NT0145
Newbold *Derbys* 74 SK3672
Newbold *Leics* 62 SK4019
Newbold Pacey *Warwks* 48 SP2957
Newbold Revel *Warwks* 50 SP4580
Newbold Verdon *Leics* 62 SK4403
Newbold on Avon *Warwks* 50 SP4877
Newbold on Stour *Warwks* 48 SP2446
Newborough *Gwynd* 68 SH4265
Newborough *Staffs* 73 SK1325
Newborough *Cambs* 64 TF2005
Newbottle *T & W* 96 NZ3351
Newbottle *Nhants* 49 SP5236
Newbourn *Suffk* 55 TM2743
Newbridge *Loth* 117 NT1272
Newbridge *D & G* 100 NX9479
Newbridge *Clwyd* 70 SJ2841
Newbridge *Dyfed* 30 SM9431
Newbridge *Dyfed* 44 SN5059
Newbridge *Oxon* 36 SP4001
Newbridge *Gwent* 33 ST2097
Newbridge *Hants* 12 SU2915
Newbridge *Cnwll* 2 SW4231
Newbridge *Cnwll* 3 SW7944
Newbridge *IOW* 13 SZ4187
Newbridge Green *H & W* 47 SO8439
Newbridge on Wye *Powys* 45 SO0158
Newbridge-on-Usk *Gwent* 34 ST3894
Newbrough *Nthumb* 102 NY8767
Newbuildings *Devon* 8 SS7903
Newburgh *Gramp* 143 NJ9659
Newburgh *Gramp* 143 NJ9925
Newburgh *Fife* 126 NO2318
Newburgh *Lancs* 78 SD4810
Newburgh Priory *N York* 90 SE5476
Newburn *T & W* 103 NZ1665
Newbury *Somset* 22 ST6949
Newbury *Wilts* 22 ST8241
Newbury *Berks* 24 SU4766
Newby *Cumb* 94 NY5921
Newby *N York* 90 NZ5012
Newby *N York* 88 SD7269
Newby *Lancs* 81 SD8146
Newby *N York* 91 TA0190
Newby Bridge *Cumb* 87 SD3686
Newby Cross *Cumb* 93 NY3653
Newby East *Cumb* 93 NY4758
Newby Head *Cumb* 94 NY5821
Newby West *Cumb* 93 NY3753
Newby Wiske *N York* 89 SE3687
Newcastle *Shrops* 58 SO2582
Newcastle *Gwent* 34 SO4417
Newcastle Emlyn *Dyfed* 31 SN3040
Newcastle upon Tyne *T & W* 103 NZ2464
Newcastle-under-Lyme *Staffs* 72 SJ8445
Newcastleton *D & G* 101 NY4887
Newchapel *Staffs* 72 SJ8654
Newchapel *Dyfed* 31 SN2239
Newchapel *Surrey* 15 TQ3641
Newchurch *Staffs* 73 SK1423
Newchurch *Gwent* 33 SO1710
Newchurch *Powys* 45 SO2150
Newchurch *H & W* 46 SO3550
Newchurch *Gwent* 34 ST4597
Newchurch *IOW* 13 SZ5685
Newchurch *Kent* 17 TR0531
Newchurch in Pendle *Lancs* 81 SD8239
Newcraighall *Loth* 118 NT3272
Newdigate *Surrey* 15 TQ1942
Newell Green *Berks* 25 SU8770
Newenden *Kent* 17 TQ8327
Newent *Gloucs* 47 SO7225
Newfield *Highld* 147 NH7877
Newfield *Dur* 96 NZ2033
Newfield *Dur* 96 NZ2452
Newfound *Hants* 24 SU5851
Newgale *Dyfed* 30 SM8522
Newgate *Norfk* 66 TG0443
Newgate *Cambs* 52 TL3990
Newgate Street *Herts* 39 TL3005
Newhall *Ches* 71 SJ6145
Newhall *Derbys* 73 SK2820
Newham *Nthumb* 111 NU1728
Newhaven *E Susx* 16 TQ4401
Newholm *N York* 90 NZ8610
Newhouse *Strath* 116 NS7961
Newick *E Susx* 15 TQ4121
Newingreen *Kent* 29 TR1236
Newington *Shrops* 59 SO4283
Newington *Oxon* 37 SU6096
Newington *Kent* 28 TQ8564
Newington *Kent* 29 TR1837
Newington Bagpath *Gloucs* 35 ST8194
Newland *Cumb* 86 SD3079
Newland *N York* 83 SE6824
Newland *Humb* 84 SE8029
Newland *Gloucs* 34 SO5509
Newland *H & W* 47 SO7948
Newland *Oxon* 36 SP3609
Newland *Somset* 19 SS8238
Newland *Humb* 84 TA0631
Newlandrig *Loth* 118 NT3762
Newlands *Cumb* 93 NY3439
Newlands *Border* 101 NY5094
Newlands *Nthumb* 95 NZ0855
Newlands of Dundurcas *Gramp* 141 NJ2951
Newlyn *Cnwll* 2 SW4628
Newmachar *Gramp* 143 NJ8919
Newmains *Strath* 116 NS8256
Newman's End *Essex* 39 TL5112
Newman's Green *Suffk* 54 TL8843
Newmarket *Cumb* 93 NY3438
Newmarket *Suffk* 53 TL6463
Newmill *Gramp* 142 NJ4352
Newmill *Border* 109 NT4510
Newmill of Inshewan *Tays* 134 NO4260
Newmillerdam *W York* 83 SE3215
Newmills *Fife* 117 NT0186
Newmills *Loth* 117 NT1667
Newmills *Gwent* 34 SO5107
Newmiln *Tays* 126 NO1230
Newmilns *Strath* 107 NS5337
Newnes *Shrops* 59 SJ3834
Newney Green *Essex* 40 TL6507
Newnham *H & W* 47 SO6469
Newnham *Gloucs* 35 SO6911
Newnham *Hants* 24 SU7053
Newnham *Herts* 39 TL2437
Newnham *Kent* 28 TQ9557
Newnham Paddox *Warwks* 50 SP4983
Newport *Highld* 151 ND1324
Newport *Humb* 84 SE8530
Newport *Shrops* 72 SJ7419
Newport *Dyfed* 30 SN0539
Newport *Devon* 19 SS5632
Newport *Gwent* 34 ST3188
Newport *Gloucs* 35 ST7097
Newport *Dorset* 11 SY8895
Newport *IOW* 13 SZ5089
Newport *Norfk* 67 TG5017
Newport *Essex* 39 TL5234
Newport Pagnell *Bucks* 38 SP8743
Newport-on-Tay *Fife* 127 NO4228
Newpound Common *W Susx* 14 TQ0627
Newquay *Cnwll* 4 SW8161
Newsam Green *W York* 83 SE3630
Newsbank *Ches* 72 SJ8366
Newseat *Gramp* 142 NJ7032
Newsham *N York* 89 NZ1010
Newsham *Nthumb* 103 NZ3080
Newsham *Lancs* 80 SD5136
Newsham *N York* 89 SE3784
Newsholme *Lancs* 81 SD8451
Newsholme *Humb* 84 SE7129
Newstead *Border* 109 NT5634
Newstead *Nthumb* 111 NU1527
Newstead *W York* 83 SE4014
Newstead *Notts* 75 SK5152
Newtack *Gramp* 142 NJ4446
Newthorpe *N York* 83 SE4632
Newtimber Place *W Susx* 15 TQ2613
Newton *Highld* 139 NH5850
Newton *Highld* 140 NH7448
Newton *Highld* 140 NH7866
Newton *Gramp* 141 NJ1663
Newton *Gramp* 141 NJ3362
Newton *Strath* 114 NS0498
Newton *Strath* 116 NS6760
Newton *Strath* 108 NS9331
Newton *Loth* 117 NT0977
Newton *Border* 110 NT6020
Newton *Nthumb* 110 NT9406
Newton *D & G* 100 NY1195
Newton *Nthumb* 103 NZ0364
Newton *Cumb* 86 SD2271
Newton *Lancs* 80 SD3436
Newton *Lancs* 80 SD4430
Newton *Lancs* 87 SD5974
Newton *Lancs* 81 SD6950
Newton *W York* 83 SE4527
Newton *N York* 90 SE8872
Newton *Ches* 71 SJ4167
Newton *Shrops* 59 SJ4234
Newton *Ches* 71 SJ5059
Newton *Staffs* 73 SK0325
Newton *Derbys* 75 SK4459
Newton *Notts* 63 SK6841
Newton *H & W* 46 SO3432
Newton *H & W* 46 SO3769
Newton *H & W* 46 SO5153
Newton *W Mids* 61 SP0393
Newton *Warwks* 50 SP5378
Newton *Nhants* 51 SP8883
Newton *W Glam* 32 SS6087
Newton *M Glam* 33 SS8377
Newton *Somset* 20 ST1038
Newton *Wilts* 23 SU2322
Newton *Lincs* 64 TF0436
Newton *Cambs* 65 TF4314
Newton *Norfk* 66 TF8315
Newton *Beds* 39 TL2344
Newton *Cambs* 53 TL4349
Newton *Suffk* 54 TL9240
Newton Abbot *Devon* 7 SX8571
Newton Arlosh *Cumb* 93 NY2055
Newton Aycliffe *Dur* 96 NZ2724
Newton Bewley *Cleve* 97 NZ4626
Newton Blossomville *Bucks* 38 SP9251
Newton Bromswold *Beds* 51 SP9966
Newton Burgoland *Leics* 62 SK3708
Newton Ferrers *Cnwll* 5 SX3466
Newton Ferrers *Devon* 6 SX5548
Newton Ferry *W Isls* 154 NF8978
Newton Flotman *Norfk* 67 TM2198
Newton Green *Gwent* 34 ST5191
Newton Harcourt *Leics* 50 SP6497
Newton Heath *Gt Man* 79 SD8700
Newton Hill *W York* 83 SE3222
Newton Kyme *N York* 83 SE4644
Newton Longville *Bucks* 38 SP8431
Newton Mearns *Strath* 115 NS5355
Newton Morrel *N York* 89 NZ2309
Newton Mountain *Dyfed* 30 SM9808
Newton Mulgrave *N York* 97 NZ7815
Newton Poppleford *Devon* 9 SY0889
Newton Purcell *Oxon* 49 SP6230
Newton Regis *Warwks* 61 SK2707
Newton Reigny *Cumb* 93 NY4731
Newton Row *Highld* 151 ND3449
Newton Solney *Derbys* 73 SK2825
Newton St. Cyres *Devon* 9 SX8898
Newton St. Faith *Norfk* 67 TG2217
Newton St. Loe *Avon* 22 ST7064
Newton St. Petrock *Devon* 18 SS4112
Newton Stacey *Hants* 24 SU4140
Newton Stewart *D & G* 99 NX4065
Newton Toney *Wilts* 23 SU2140
Newton Tracey *Devon* 19 SS5226
Newton Underwood *Nthumb* 103 NZ1486
Newton Valence *Hants* 24 SU7232
Newton by Toft *Lincs* 76 TF0487
Newton of Balcanquhal *Tays* 126 NO1610
Newton on Ouse *N York* 90 SE5159
Newton on Trent *Lincs* 76 SK8373
Newton on the Hill *Shrops* 59 SJ4823
Newton under Roseberry *Cleve* 90 NZ5713
Newton upon Derwent *Humb* 84 SE7149
Newton-le-Willows *N York* 89 SE2189
Newton-le-Willows *Mersyd* 78 SJ5995
Newton-on-the-Moor *Nthumb* 111 NU1705
Newtonairds *D & G* 100 NX8880
Newtongarry Croft *Gramp* 142 NJ5735
Newtongrange *Loth* 118 NT3364
Newtonhill *Gramp* 135 NO9193
Newtonloan *Loth* 118 NT3362
Newtonmill *Tays* 134 NO6064
Newtonmore *Highld* 132 NN7098
Newtown *Highld* 131 NH3504
Newtown *D & G* 107 NS7710
Newtown *Nthumb* 111 NT9631
Newtown *Nthumb* 103 NU0300
Newtown *Cumb* 92 NY1048
Newtown *Cumb* 101 NY5062
Newtown *Cumb* 94 NY5224
Newtown *Lancs* 80 SD5118
Newtown *Gt Man* 78 SD5604
Newtown *Shrops* 59 SJ4222
Newtown *Shrops* 59 SJ4731
Newtown *Ches* 71 SJ5375
Newtown *Ches* 72 SJ6247
Newtown *Ches* 72 SJ9060
Newtown *Staffs* 60 SJ9904
Newtown *Derbys* 79 SJ9984
Newtown *Powys* 58 SO1091
Newtown *Gwent* 33 SO1709
Newtown *H & W* 46 SO4757
Newtown *H & W* 46 SO5333
Newtown *H & W* 46 SO6145
Newtown *Gloucs* 35 SO6702
Newtown *H & W* 47 SO7037
Newtown *H & W* 47 SO8755
Newtown *H & W* 60 SO9478
Newtown *Devon* 19 SS7625
Newtown *M Glam* 33 ST0598
Newtown *Dorset* 10 ST4802
Newtown *Wilts* 22 ST9129
Newtown *Hants* 12 SU2710
Newtown *Wilts* 23 SU2963
Newtown *Hants* 24 SU4763
Newtown *Hants* 13 SU6013
Newtown *Cnwll* 2 SW5729
Newtown *Cnwll* 3 SW7423
Newtown *Cnwll* 3 SX1052
Newtown *Cnwll* 5 SX2978
Newtown *Dorset* 12 SZ0393
Newtown *IOW* 13 SZ4290
Newtown Linford *Leics* 62 SK5209
Newtown St. Boswells *Border* 110 NT5732
Newtown Unthank *Leics* 62 SK4904
Newtown of Beltrees *Strath* 115 NS3758
Newtyle *Tays* 126 NO2941
Newyears Green *Gt Lon* 26 TQ0788
Newyork *Strath* 122 NM9611
Nextend *H & W* 46 SO3357
Neyland *Dyfed* 30 SM9605
Niarbyl *IOM* 153 SC2177
Nibley *Gloucs* 35 SO6606
Nibley *Avon* 35 ST6982
Nibley Green *Gloucs* 35 ST7396
Nicholashayne *Devon* 9 ST1016
Nicholaston *W Glam* 32 SS5288
Nickies Hill *Cumb* 101 NY5367
Nidd *N York* 89 SE3060
Nigg *Highld* 147 NH8071
Nigg *Gramp* 135 NJ9402
Nightcott *Devon* 19 SS8925
Nine Elms *Wilts* 36 SU1085
Nine Wells *Dyfed* 30 SM7924
Ninebanks *Nthumb* 94 NY7853
Nineveh *H & W* 47 SO6265
Ninfield *E Susx* 16 TQ7012
Ningwood *IOW* 13 SZ3989
Nisbet *Border* 110 NT6725
Nisbet Hill *Border* 119 NT7950
Niton *IOW* 13 SZ5076
Nitshill *Strath* 115 NS5260
No Man's Heath *Ches* 71 SJ5148
No Man's Heath *Warwks* 61 SK2808
No Man's Land *Cnwll* 4 SW9470
No Man's Land *Cnwll* 5 SX2756
Noah's Ark *Kent* 27 TQ5557
Noak Bridge *Essex* 40 TQ6990
Noak Hill *Essex* 27 TQ5494
Noblethorpe *W York* 82 SE2805
Nobold *Shrops* 59 SJ4609
Nobottle *Nhants* 49 SP6763
Nocton *Lincs* 76 TF0564
Nogdam End *Norfk* 67 TG3900
Noke *Oxon* 37 SP5413
Nolton *Dyfed* 30 SM8618
Nolton Haven *Dyfed* 30 SM8618
Nomansland *Devon* 19 SS8313
Nomansland *Wilts* 12 SU2517
Noneley *Shrops* 59 SJ4828
Nonington *Kent* 29 TR2552
Nook *Cumb* 101 NY4679
Nook *Cumb* 87 SD5481
Norbiton Common *Gt Lon* 26 TQ2067
Norbreck *Lancs* 80 SD3140
Norbridge *H & W* 47 SO7144
Norbury *Ches* 71 SJ5547
Norbury *Staffs* 72 SJ7823
Norbury *Derbys* 73 SK1241
Norbury *Shrops* 59 SO3692
Norbury *Gt Lon* 27 TQ3069
Norbury Common *Ches* 71 SJ5548
Norbury Junction *Staffs* 72 SJ7923
Norchard *H & W* 47 SO8568
Norcott Brook *Ches* 78 SJ6080
Norcross *Lancs* 80 SD3341
Nordam *Humb* 84 SE8932
Nordelph *Norfk* 65 TF5501
Norden *Gt Man* 81 SD8614
Nordley *Shrops* 60 SO6996
Norham *Nthumb* 110 NT9047
Norland Town *W York* 82 SE0622
Norley *Ches* 71 SJ5772
Norleywood *Hants* 12 SZ3597
Norlington *E Susx* 16 TQ4413
Norman Cross *Cambs* 52 TL1690
Norman's Bay *E Susx* 16 TQ6805
Norman's Green *Devon* 9 ST0503
Normanby *Cleve* 97 NZ5418
Normanby *N York* 90 SE7381
Normanby *Humb* 84 SE8816
Normanby *Lincs* 76 SK9988
Normanby le Wold *Lincs* 76 TF1295
Normandy *Surrey* 25 SU9351
Normanton *W York* 83 SE3822
Normanton *Derbys* 62 SK3433
Normanton *Notts* 75 SK7054
Normanton *Leics* 63 SK8140
Normanton *Lincs* 63 SK9446
Normanton *Wilts* 23 SU1340
Normanton le Heath *Leics* 62 SK3712
Normanton on Soar *Notts* 62 SK5122
Normanton on Trent *Notts* 75 SK7868
Normanton on the Wolds *Notts* 62 SK6232
Normoss *Lancs* 80 SD3437
Norney *Surrey* 25 SU9444
Norrington Common *Wilts* 22 ST8864
Norris Green *Cnwll* 5 SX4169
Norristhorpe *W York* 82 SE2123
North Anston *S York* 75 SK5184
North Aston *Oxon* 49 SP4828
North Baddesley *Hants* 13 SU3920
North Ballachulish *Highld* 130 NN0560
North Barrow *Somset* 21 ST6129
North Barsham *Norfk* 66 TF9135
North Benfleet *Essex* 40 TQ7588
North Bersted *W Susx* 14 SU9201
North Berwick *Loth* 118 NT5485
North Biddick *T & W* 96 NZ3153
North Bitchburn *Dur* 96 NZ1732
North Boarhunt *Hants* 13 SU6010
North Bockhampton *Hants* 12 SZ1797
North Bovey *Devon* 8 SX7484
North Bradley *Wilts* 22 ST8555
North Brentor *Devon* 5 SX4881
North Brewham *Somset* 22 ST7236
North Bridge *Surrey* 14 SU9636
North Brook End *Cambs* 39 TL2944
North Buckland *Devon* 18 SS4840
North Burlingham *Norfk* 67 TG3609
North Cadbury *Somset* 21 ST6327
North Carlton *Notts* 75 SK5984
North Carlton *Lincs* 76 SK9477
North Cave *Humb* 84 SE8932
North Cerney *Gloucs* 35 SP0107
North Charford *Hants* 12 SU1919
North Charlton *Nthumb* 111 NU1622
North Cheam *Gt Lon* 26 TQ2365
North Cheriton *Somset* 22 ST6925
North Chideock *Dorset* 10 SY4294
North Cliffe *Humb* 84 SE8736
North Clifton *Notts* 75 SK8272
North Close *Dur* 96 NZ2532
North Cockerington *Lincs* 77 TF3790
North Collingham *Notts* 76 SK8362
North Common *E Susx* 15 TQ3921
North Connel *Strath* 122 NM9034
North Cornelly *M Glam* 33 SS8181
North Corner *Cnwll* 3 SW7818
North Corry *Highld* 122 NM8353
North Cotes *Lincs* 77 TA3400
North Country *Cnwll* 2 SW6943
North Cove *Suffk* 55 TM4689
North Cowton *N York* 89 NZ2803
North Crawley *Bucks* 38 SP9244
North Cray *Gt Lon* 27 TQ4872
North Creake *Norfk* 66 TF8538
North Curry *Somset* 21 ST3125
North Dalton *Humb* 84 SE9351
North Deighton *N York* 83 SE3951
North Duffield *N York* 83 SE6837
North Elham *Kent* 29 TR1844
North Elkington *Lincs* 77 TF2890
North Elmham *Norfk* 66 TF9820
North Elmsall *W York* 83 SE4712
North End *Cumb* 93 NY3259
North End *Mersyd* 78 SD3004
North End *Leics* 62 SK5715
North End *Nhants* 51 SP9668
North End *Avon* 21 ST4266
North End *Dorset* 22 ST8427
North End *Hants* 12 SU1016
North End *Hants* 24 SU5828
North End *Hants* 13 SU6502
North End *W Susx* 14 SU9703
North End *Humb* 85 TA1022
North End *Humb* 85 TA1941
North End *Humb* 85 TA2831
North End *Humb* 85 TA3101
North End *Lincs* 76 TF0499
North End *Lincs* 64 TF2341
North End *Lincs* 77 TF4289
North End *Essex* 40 TL6618
North End *Norfk* 66 TL9992
North End *W Susx* 14 TQ1109
North Erradale *Highld* 144 NG7480
North Evington *Leics* 62 SK6204
North Fambridge *Essex* 40 TQ8597
North Feorline *Strath* 105 NR9029
North Ferriby *Humb* 84 SE9826
North Frodingham *Humb* 85 TA1053
North Gorley *Hants* 12 SU1611
North Green *Norfk* 55 TM2288
North Green *Suffk* 55 TM3162
North Green *Suffk* 55 TM3966
North Grimston *N York* 90 SE8467
North Halling *Kent* 28 TQ7065
North Hayling *Hants* 13 SU7303
North Hazelrigg *Nthumb* 111 NU0533
North Heasley *Devon* 19 SS7333
North Heath *W Susx* 14 TQ0621
North Hele *Somset* 20 ST0323
North Hill *Cnwll* 5 SX2776
North Hillingdon *Gt Lon* 26 TQ0784
North Hinksey *Oxon* 37 SP4905
North Huish *Devon* 7 SX7156
North Hykeham *Lincs* 76 SK9465
North Kelsey *Humb* 84 TA0401
North Kessock *Highld* 140 NH6548
North Killingholme *Humb* 85 TA1417
North Kilvington *N York* 89 SE4285
North Kilworth *Leics* 50 SP6183
North Kingston *Hants* 12 SU1603
North Kyme *Lincs* 76 TF1552
North Lee *Bucks* 38 SP8308
North Lees *N York* 89 SE2973
North Leigh *Oxon* 36 SP3813
North Leigh *Kent* 29 TR1347
North with Habblesthorpe *Notts* 75 SK7882
North Littleton *H & W* 48 SP0847
North Lopham *Norfk* 54 TM0382
North Luffenham *Leics* 63 SK9303

North Marden Orford

North Marden W Susx 14 SU8016
North Marston Bucks 37 SP7722
North Middleton Loth 118 NT3559
North Middleton Nthumb 111 NT9924
North Milmain D & G 98 NX0852
North Molton Devon 19 SS7329
North Moreton Oxon 37 SU5689
North Mundham W Susx 14 SU8702
North Muskham Notts 75 SK7958
North Newbald Humb 84 SE9136
North Newington Oxon 49 SP4240
North Newnton Wilts 23 SU1257
North Newton Somset 20 ST3031
North Nibley Gloucs 35 ST7495
North Oakley Hants 24 SU5354
North Ockendon Gt Lon 27 TQ5985
North Ormsby Lincs 77 TF2893
North Otterington N York 89 SE3689
North Owersby Lincs 76 TF0594
North Perrott Somset 10 ST4709
North Petherton Somset 20 ST2833
North Petherwin Cnwll 5 SX2789
North Pickenham Norfk 66 TF8606
North Piddle H & W 47 SO9654
North Pool Devon 7 SX7741
North Poorton Dorset 10 SY5298
North Poulner Hants 12 SU1606
North Quarme Somset 20 SS9236
North Queensferry Fife 117 NT1380
North Radworthy Devon 19 SS7534
North Rauceby Lincs 76 TF0246
North Reston Lincs 77 TF3883
North Rigton N York 82 SE2749
North Ripley Hants 12 SZ1699
North Rode Ches 72 SJ8866
North Row Cumb 93 NY2232
North Runcton Norfk 65 TF6416
North Scale Cumb 86 SD1869
North Scarle Lincs 76 SK8466
North Seaton Nthumb 103 NZ2986
North Seaton Colliery Nthumb 103 NZ2985
North Shian Strath 122 NM9143
North Shields T & W 103 NZ3568
North Shoebury Essex 40 TQ9286
North Shore Lancs 80 SD3037
North Side Cumb 92 NX9929
North Side Cambs 64 TL2799
North Skelton Cleve 97 NZ6718
North Skirlaugh Humb 85 TA1439
North Somercotes Lincs 77 TF4296
North Stainley N York 89 SE2876
North Stainmore Cumb 95 NY8314
North Stifford Essex 40 TQ6080
North Stoke Avon 35 ST7069
North Stoke Oxon 37 SU6186
North Stoke W Susx 14 TQ0110
North Street Hants 12 SU1518
North Street Berks 24 SU6371
North Street Hants 24 SU6433
North Street Cambs 53 TL5868
North Street Kent 28 TQ8174
North Street Kent 28 TR0157
North Sunderland Nthumb 111 NU2131
North Tamerton Cnwll 5 SX3197
North Tawton Devon 8 SS6601
North Third Cent 116 NS7589
North Tidworth Wilts 23 SU2349
North Town Devon 19 SS5109
North Town Somset 21 ST5642
North Town Berks 26 SU8882
North Tuddenham Norfk 66 TG0314
North Walbottle T & W 103 NZ1767
North Walsham Norfk 67 TG2830
North Waltham Hants 24 SU5646
North Warnborough Hants 24 SU7351
North Weald Basset Essex 39 TL4904
North Wheatley Notts 75 SK7585
North Whilborough Devon 7 SX8766
North Wick Avon 21 ST5865
North Widcombe Somset 21 ST5758
North Willingham Lincs 76 TF1688
North Wingfield Derbys 74 SK4065
North Witham Lincs 63 SK9221
North Wootton Somset 21 ST5641
North Wootton Dorset 11 ST6514
North Wootton Norfk 65 TF6424
North Wraxall Wilts 35 ST8175
North Wroughton Wilts 36 SU1481
Northacre Norfk 66 TL9598
Northall Bucks 38 SP9520
Northall Green Norfk 66 TF9914
Northallerton N York 89 SE3694
Northam Devon 18 SS4529
Northam Hants 13 SU4312
Northampton H & W 47 SO8365
Northampton Nhants 49 SP7560
Northaw Herts 27 TL2702
Northay Somset 10 ST2811
Northborough Cambs 64 TF1507
Northbourne Kent 29 TR3352
Northbridge Street E Susx 17 TQ7324
Northbrook Oxon 37 SP4922
Northbrook Hants 24 SU5139
Northchapel W Susx 14 SU9529
Northchurch Herts 38 SP9708
Northcott Devon 9 ST0912
Northcott Devon 9 ST1209
Northcott Devon 5 SX3392
Northcourt Oxon 37 SU4998
Northdown Kent 29 TR3770
Northedge Derbys 74 SK3665
Northend Warwks 48 SP3952
Northend Bucks 37 SU7392
Northend Woods Bucks 26 SU9089
Northenden Gt Man 79 SJ8289
Northfield Gramp 135 NJ9008
Northfield W Mids 60 SP0279
Northfield Humb 84 TA0326
Northfields Lincs 64 TF0208
Northfleet Essex 27 TQ6374
Northiam E Susx 17 TQ8324
Northill Beds 52 TL1446
Northington Gloucs 35 SO7008
Northington Hants 24 SU5637
Northlands Lincs 77 TF3453
Northleach Gloucs 36 SP1114
Northleigh Devon 19 SS6034
Northleigh Devon 9 SY1995
Northlew Devon 19 SX5099
Northload Bridge Somset 21 ST4939
Northmooor Somset 20 SS9028
Northmoor Oxon 36 SP4202
Northmoor Green or Moorland Somset 21 ST3332
Northmuir Tays 126 NO3854
Northney Hants 13 SU7303
Northolt Gt Lon 26 TQ1384
Northop Clwyd 70 SJ2468
Northop Hall Clwyd 70 SJ2667
Northorpe W York 82 SE2221
Northorpe Lincs 76 SK8997
Northorpe Lincs 64 TF0917
Northorpe Lincs 64 TF2036
Northover Somset 21 ST4838
Northover Somset 21 ST5223
Northowram W York 82 SE1126
Northport Dorset 11 SY9288
Northrepps Norfk 67 TG2439
Northway W Glam 32 SS5889
Northway Somset 20 ST1329
Northwich Ches 79 SJ6673
Northwick H & W 47 SO8458
Northwick Somset 21 ST3548
Northwick Avon 34 ST5686
Northwold Norfk 65 TL7597
Northwood Shrops 59 SJ4633
Northwood Staffs 72 SJ8949
Northwood Derbys 74 SK2664
Northwood IOW 13 SZ4992
Northwood Gt Lon 26 TQ0990
Northwood End Beds 38 TL0941
Northwood Green Gloucs 35 SO7216
Norton Cleve 96 NZ4421
Norton S York 83 SE5415
Norton N York 90 SE7971
Norton Ches 78 SJ5581
Norton Shrops 59 SJ5609
Norton Shrops 60 SJ7200
Norton S York 74 SK3681
Norton Notts 75 SK5771
Norton Powys 46 SO3067
Norton Gwent 34 SO4420
Norton Shrops 59 SO4681
Norton Shrops 59 SO6382
Norton Gloucs 47 SO8524
Norton H & W 47 SO8751
Norton H & W 48 SP0447
Norton Nhants 49 SP5963
Norton W Glam 32 SS6188
Norton Avon 21 ST3463
Norton Wilts 35 ST8884
Norton W Susx 14 SU9206
Norton Cnwll 4 SX0869
Norton IOW 12 SZ3488
Norton Herts 39 TL2334
Norton Suffk 54 TL9565
Norton E Susx 16 TQ4701
Norton Bavant Wilts 22 ST9043
Norton Bridge Staffs 72 SJ8630
Norton Canes Staffs 60 SK0107
Norton Canon H & W 46 SO3847
Norton Corner Norfk 66 TG0928
Norton Disney Lincs 76 SK8859
Norton Ferris Wilts 22 ST7936
Norton Fitzwarren Somset 20 ST1925
Norton Green Staffs 60 SK0107
Norton Green IOW 12 SZ3488
Norton Hawkfield Avon 21 ST5964
Norton Heath Essex 40 TL6004
Norton Lindsey Warwks 48 SP2263
Norton Little Green Suffk 54 TL9766
Norton Malreward Avon 21 ST6064
Norton Mandeville Essex 40 TL5804
Norton St. Philip Somset 22 ST7755
Norton Subcourse Norfk 67 TM4198
Norton Wood H & W 46 SO3648
Norton in Hales Shrops 72 SJ7038
Norton in the Moors Staffs 72 SJ8951
Norton sub Hamdon Somset 10 ST4615
Norton-Juxta-Twycross Leics 61 SK3207
Norton-le-Clay N York 89 SE4071
Norwell Notts 75 SK7761
Norwell Woodhouse Notts 75 SK7362
Norwich Norfk 67 TG2308
Norwick Shet 155 HP6414
Norwood Cent 116 NS8793
Norwood S York 75 SK4681
Norwood Kent 17 TR0530
Norwood End Essex 40 TL5608
Norwood Green W York 82 SE1326
Norwood Green Gt Lon 26 TQ1378
Norwood Hill Surrey 15 TQ2343
Norwoodside Cambs 65 TL4197
Noseley Leics 50 SP7398
Noss Mayo Devon 6 SX5547
Nosterfield N York 89 SE2780
Nosterfield End Cambs 53 TL6344
Nostie Highld 138 NG8527
Notgrove Gloucs 36 SP1020
Nottage M Glam 33 SS8177
Notter Cnwll 5 SX3960
Nottingham Notts 62 SK5739
Nottington Dorset 11 SY6682
Notton W York 83 SE3413
Notton Wilts 35 ST9169
Nottswood Hill Gloucs 35 SO7018
Nounsley Essex 40 TL7910
Noutard's Green H & W 47 SO8066
Nox Shrops 59 SJ4110
Nuffield Oxon 37 SU6687
Nun Monkton N York 90 SE5057
Nuncargate Notts 75 SK5054
Nunclose Cumb 94 NY4945
Nuneaton Warwks 61 SP3691
Nuneham Courtenay Oxon 37 SU5599
Nunhead Gt Lon 27 TQ3475
Nunkeeling Humb 85 TA1449
Nunnerie Strath 108 NS9612
Nunney Somset 22 ST7345
Nunney Catch Somset 22 ST7344
Nunnington N York 90 SE6679
Nunnington H & W 46 SO5543
Nunnykirk Nthumb 103 NZ0793
Nuns Moor T & W 103 NZ2266
Nunsthorpe Humb 85 TA2607
Nunthorpe N York 83 SE6050
Nunthorpe Village Cleve 90 NZ5413
Nunton Wilts 23 SU1526
Nunwick Nthumb 102 NY8774
Nunwick N York 89 SE3274
Nup End Bucks 38 SP8619
Nupdown Avon 35 ST6395
Nupend Gloucs 35 SO7806
Nuptow Berks 25 SU8873
Nursling Hants 12 SU3716
Nursted Hants 13 SU7521
Nursteed Wilts 23 SU0260
Nurton Staffs 60 SO8399
Nutbourne W Susx 14 SU7705
Nutbourne W Susx 14 TQ0718
Nutfield Surrey 27 TQ3050
Nuthall Notts 62 SK5243
Nuthampstead Herts 39 TL4034
Nuthurst W Susx 15 TQ1925
Nutley Hants 24 SU6044
Nutley E Susx 16 TQ4427
Nuttal Lane Gt Man 81 SD7915
Nutwell S York 83 SE6304
Nybster Highld 151 ND3663
Nyetimber W Susx 14 SZ8998
Nyewood W Susx 14 SU8021
Nymet Rowland Devon 19 SS7108
Nymet Tracey Devon 8 SS7200
Nympsfield Gloucs 35 SO8000
Nynehead Somset 20 ST1422
Nythe Somset 21 ST4234
Nyton W Susx 14 SU9305

O

Oad Street Kent 28 TQ8762
Oadby Leics 50 SK6200
Oak Cross Devon 8 SX5399
Oak Tree Dur 89 NZ3613
Oakall Green H & W 47 SO8161
Oakamoor Staffs 73 SK0444
Oakbank Loth 117 NT0766
Oakdale Gwent 33 ST1898
Oake Somset 20 ST1525
Oaken Staffs 60 SJ8602
Oakenclough Lancs 80 SD5447
Oakengates Shrops 60 SJ7010
Oakenholt Clwyd 70 SJ2571
Oakenshaw Dur 96 NZ1937
Oakenshaw W York 82 SE1727
Oaker Side Derbys 74 SK2760
Oakerthorpe Derbys 74 SK3854
Oakford Dyfed 42 SN4558
Oakford Devon 20 SS9121
Oakfordbridge Devon 20 SS9122
Oakgrove Ches 79 SJ9169
Oakham Leics 63 SK8608
Oakhanger Ches 72 SJ7754
Oakhanger Hants 14 SU7635
Oakhill Somset 21 ST6347
Oakhurst Kent 27 TQ5550
Oakington Cambs 52 TL4164
Oaklands Powys 45 SO0450
Oakle Street Gloucs 35 SO7517
Oakley Bucks 37 SP6412
Oakley Oxon 37 SP7500
Oakley Hants 24 SU5650
Oakley Dorset 11 SZ0198
Oakley Beds 51 TL0153
Oakley Suffk 54 TM1677
Oakley Green Berks 26 SU9276
Oakley Park Powys 58 SN9886
Oakridge Gloucs 35 SO9103
Oaks Dur 96 NZ1525
Oaks Lancs 81 SD6733
Oaks Shrops 59 SJ4204
Oaks Green Derbys 73 SK1533
Oaksey Wilts 35 ST9993
Oakshaw Cumb 101 NY5176
Oakshott Hants 13 SU7427
Oakthorpe Leics 61 SK3212
Oakwood Nthumb 102 NY9465
Oakwoodhill Surrey 15 TQ1337
Oakworth W York 82 SE0338
Oare Somset 19 SS7947
Oare Wilts 23 SU1563
Oare Kent 28 TR0063
Oasby Lincs 63 TF0039
Oath Somset 21 ST3827
Oathlaw Tays 127 NO4756
Oatlands Park Surrey 26 TQ0865
Oban Strath 122 NM8629
Obley Shrops 46 SO3377
Obney Tays 125 NO0237
Oborne Dorset 11 ST6518
Obthorpe Lincs 64 TF0914
Occlestone Green Ches 72 SJ6962
Occold Suffk 54 TM1570
Ochiltree Strath 107 NS5021
Ockbrook Derbys 62 SK4235
Ocker Hill W Mids 60 SO9793
Ockeridge H & W 47 SO7762
Ockham Surrey 26 TQ0756
Ockle Highld 129 NM5570
Ockley Surrey 15 TQ1440
Ocle Pychard H & W 46 SO5945
Octon Humb 91 TA0369
Odcombe Somset 10 ST5015
Odd Down Avon 22 ST7462
Oddingley H & W 47 SO9159
Oddington Gloucs 48 SP2225
Oddington Oxon 37 SP5515
Odell Beds 51 SP9657
Odham Devon 18 SS4703
Odiham Hants 24 SU7451
Odsal W York 82 SE1529
Odsey Herts 39 TL2938
Odstock Wilts 23 SU1426
Odstone Leics 62 SK3907
Offchurch Warwks 48 SP3565
Offenham H & W 48 SP0546
Offerton T & W 96 NZ3455
Offham W Susx 14 TQ0208
Offham E Susx 15 TQ4012
Offham Kent 28 TQ6557
Offleymarsh Shrops 72 SJ7829
Offord Cluny Cambs 52 TL2267
Offord Darcy Cambs 52 TL2266
Offton Suffk 54 TM0649
Offwell Devon 9 SY1999
Ogbourne Maizey Wilts 36 SU1871
Ogbourne St. Andrew Wilts 36 SU1872
Ogbourne St. George Wilts 36 SU2074
Ogden W York 82 SE0730
Ogle Nthumb 103 NZ1378
Oglet Mersyd 78 SJ4481
Ogmore M Glam 33 SS8876
Ogmore Vale M Glam 33 SS9390
Ogmore-by-Sea M Glam 33 SS8675
Ogwen Bank Gwynd 69 SH6265
Okeford Fitzpaine Dorset 11 ST8010
Okehampton Devon 8 SX5995
Olchard Devon 9 SX8777
Old Nhants 50 SP7872
Old Aberdeen Gramp 135 NJ9407
Old Alresford Hants 24 SU5834
Old Auchenbrack D & G 107 NX7597
Old Basford Notts 62 SK5543
Old Basing Hants 24 SU6652
Old Bewick Nthumb 111 NU0621
Old Bolingbroke Lincs 77 TF3565
Old Bracknell Berks 25 SU8668
Old Bramhope W York 82 SE2343
Old Brampton Derbys 74 SK3371
Old Bridge of Urr D & G 100 NX7767
Old Buckenham Norfk 66 TM0691
Old Burghclere Hants 24 SU4657
Old Byland N York 90 SE5585
Old Cassop Dur 96 NZ3339
Old Castle M Glam 33 SS9079
Old Church Stoke Powys 58 SO2894
Old Clee Humb 85 TA2808
Old Cleeve Somset 20 ST0441
Old Colwyn Clwyd 69 SH8678
Old Dailly Strath 106 NX2299
Old Dalby Leics 63 SK6723
Old Dam Derbys 74 SK1179
Old Deer Gramp 143 NJ9747
Old Ditch Somset 21 ST5049
Old Edington S York 75 SK5397
Old Eldon Dur 96 NZ2427
Old Ellerby Humb 85 TA1637
Old Felixstowe Suffk 55 TM3135
Old Fletton Cambs 64 TL1997
Old Forge H & W 34 SO5518
Old Furnace H & W 46 SO4923
Old Glossop Derbys 74 SK0494
Old Goole Humb 84 SE7422
Old Grimsby IOS 2 SV8915
Old Hall Green Herts 39 TL3722
Old Hall Street Norfk 67 TG3033
Old Harlow Essex 39 TL4711
Old Heath Essex 41 TM0122
Old Hunstanton Norfk 65 TF6842
Old Hutton Cumb 87 SD5688
Old Kea Cnwll 3 SW8441
Old Kilpatrick Strath 115 NS4672
Old Knebworth Herts 39 TL2320
Old Lakenham Norfk 67 TG2205
Old Langho Lancs 81 SD7035
Old Leake Lincs 77 TF4050
Old Malton N York 90 SE7972
Old Micklefield W York 83 SE4433
Old Milton Hants 12 SZ2394
Old Milverton Warwks 48 SP2967
Old Newton Suffk 54 TM0562
Old Quarrington Dur 96 NZ3237
Old Radford Notts 62 SK5540
Old Radnor Powys 46 SO2558
Old Rattray Gramp 143 NK0857
Old Rayne Gramp 142 NJ6728
Old Romney Kent 17 TR0325
Old Scone Tays 126 NO1126
Old Shoreham W Susx 15 TQ2006
Old Shoremore Highld 148 NC2058
Old Soar Kent 27 TQ6254
Old Sodbury Avon 35 ST7581
Old Somerby Lincs 63 SK9633
Old Stratford Nhants 49 SP7741
Old Sunnford W Mids 60 SO9083
Old Tebay Cumb 87 NY6105
Old Thirsk N York 89 SE4382
Old Town Cumb 93 NY4743
Old Town Nthumb 102 NY8891
Old Town Cumb 87 SD5982
Old Town W York 82 SE0028
Old Town IOS 2 SV9110
Old Town E Susx 16 TV5999
Old Trafford Gt Man 79 SJ8196
Old Tupton Derbys 74 SK3865
Old Warden Beds 38 TL1343
Old Weston Cambs 51 TL0977
Old Wick Highld 151 ND3649
Old Windsor Berks 25 SU9874
Old Wives Lees Kent 29 TR0754
Old Woking Surrey 26 TQ0157
Old Wolverton Bucks 38 SP8041
Oldany Highld 148 NC0932
Oldberrow Warwks 48 SP1265
Oldbury Kent 27 TQ5956
Oldbury Shrops 60 SO7192
Oldbury W Mids 60 SO9888
Oldbury Warwks 61 SP3194
Oldbury Naite Avon 35 ST6293
Oldbury on the Hill Gloucs 35 ST8188
Oldbury-on-Severn Avon 34 ST6092
Oldcastle Gwent 46 SO3224
Oldcastle Heath Ches 71 SJ4745
Oldcotes Notts 75 SK5888
Oldfield W York 82 SE0037
Oldfield H & W 47 SO8464
Oldford Somset 22 ST7850
Oldhall Green Suffk 54 TL8956
Oldham Gt Man 79 SD9204
Oldhamstocks Loth 119 NT7470
Oldhurst Cambs 52 TL3077
Oldland Avon 35 ST6771
Oldmeldrum Gramp 143 NJ8127
Oldmill Cnwll 5 SX3673
Oldmixon Avon 21 ST3358
Oldridge Devon 8 SX8296
Oldstead N York 90 SE5379
Oldwall Cumb 101 NY4761
Oldwalls W Glam 32 SS4891
Oldways End Devon 19 SS8724
Oldwhat Gramp 143 NJ8651
Oldwoods Shrops 59 SJ4520
Olive Green Staffs 73 SK1118
Oliver Border 108 NT0924
Oliver's Battery Hants 13 SU4527
Ollaberry Shet 155 HU3680
Ollach Highld 137 NG5137
Ollerton Shrops 72 SJ6425
Ollerton Ches 79 SJ7776
Ollerton Notts 75 SK6567
Olmarch Dyfed 44 SN6255
Olmstead Green Cambs 53 TL6341
Olney Nhants 49 SP6643
Olney Bucks 38 SP8951
Olrig House Highld 151 ND1866
Olton W Mids 61 SP1382
Olveston Avon 34 ST6086
Ombersley H & W 47 SO8463
Ompton Notts 75 SK6865
Onchan IOM 153 SC3978
One House Suffk 54 TM0159
Onecote Staffs 73 SK0455
Onen Gwent 34 SO4314
Ongar Street H & W 46 SO3967
Onibury Shrops 46 SO4579
Onich Highld 130 NN0261
Onllwyn W Glam 33 SN8410
Onneley Staffs 72 SJ7542
Onslow Village Surrey 25 SU9849
Onston Ches 71 SJ5873
Openwoodgate Derbys 62 SK3647
Opinan Highld 137 NG7472
Orbliston Gramp 141 NJ3057
Orbost Highld 136 NG2543
Orby Lincs 77 TF4967
Orchard Portman Somset 20 ST2421
Orcheston Wilts 23 SU0545
Orcop H & W 46 SO4726
Orcop Hill H & W 46 SO4727
Ord Highld 129 NG6113
Ord Gramp 142 NJ6258
Ordhead Gramp 135 NJ6610
Ordie Gramp 134 NJ4501
Ordiequish Gramp 141 NJ3357
Ordley Nthumb 95 NY9459
Ordsall Notts 75 SK7079
Ore E Susx 17 TQ8311
Oreleton Common H & W 46 SO4768
Oreton Shrops 59 SO6580
Orford Ches 78 SJ6190

Orford Pen-y-lan

Orford *Suffk*	55	TM4250
Organford *Dorset*	11	SY9392
Orgreave *Staffs*	73	SK1415
Orlestone *Kent*	17	TR0034
Orleton *H & W*	46	SO4967
Orleton *H & W*	47	SO7067
Orlingbury *Nhants*	51	SP8572
Ormathwaite *Cumb*	93	NY2625
Ormesby *Cleve*	97	NZ5317
Ormesby St. Margaret *Norfk*	67	TG4914
Ormesby St. Michael *Norfk*	67	TG4714
Ormiscaig *Highld*	144	NG8590
Ormiston *Loth*	118	NT4169
Ormsaigmore *Highld*	121	NM4763
Ormsary *Strath*	113	NR7472
Ormskirk *Lancs*	78	SD4108
Ornsby Hill *Dur*	96	NZ1648
Oronsay *Strath*	112	NR3588
Orphir *Ork*	155	HY3404
Orpington *Gt Lon*	27	TQ4666
Orrell *Gt Man*	78	SD5303
Orrell *Mersyd*	78	SJ3496
Orrell Post *Gt Man*	78	SD5305
Orrisdale *IOM*	153	SC3292
Orroland *D & G*	92	NX7746
Orsett *Essex*	40	TQ6482
Orslow *Staffs*	72	SJ8015
Orston *Notts*	63	SK7740
Orthwaite *Cumb*	93	NY2534
Ortner *Lancs*	80	SD5354
Orton *Cumb*	87	NY6208
Orton *Staffs*	60	SO8795
Orton *Nhants*	51	SP8079
Orton Longueville *Cambs*	64	TL1796
Orton Rigg *Cumb*	93	NY3352
Orton Waterville *Cambs*	64	TL1595
Orton-on-the-Hill *Leics*	61	SK3003
Orwell *Cambs*	52	TL3650
Osbaldeston *Lancs*	81	SD6431
Osbaldeston Green *Lancs*	81	SD6432
Osbaldwick *N York*	83	SE6251
Osbaston *Shrops*	59	SJ3222
Osbaston *Leics*	62	SK4204
Osborne *IOW*	13	SZ5194
Osbournby *Lincs*	64	TF0638
Oscroft *Ches*	71	SJ5067
Osgathorpe *Leics*	62	SK4319
Osgodby *N York*	83	SE6433
Osgodby *N York*	91	TA0584
Osgodby *Lincs*	76	TF0792
Oskaig *Highld*	137	NG5438
Oskamull *Strath*	121	NM4540
Osmanthorpe *W York*	83	SE3333
Osmaston *Derbys*	73	SK1943
Osmington *Dorset*	11	SY7283
Osmington Mills *Dorset*	11	SY7381
Osmotherley *N York*	89	SE4596
Osney *Oxon*	37	SP4906
Ospringe *Kent*	28	TR0060
Ossett *W York*	82	SE2720
Ossington *Notts*	75	SK7564
Ostend *Essex*	40	TQ9397
Oswaldkirk *N York*	90	SE6278
Oswaldtwistle *Lancs*	81	SD7327
Oswestry *Shrops*	59	SJ2929
Otford *Kent*	27	TQ5359
Otham *Kent*	28	TQ7953
Otham Hole *Kent*	28	TQ8052
Othery *Somset*	21	ST3831
Otley *W York*	82	SE2045
Otley *Suffk*	55	TM2055
Otley Green *Suffk*	55	TM2156
Otter Ferry *Strath*	114	NR9384
Otterbourne *Hants*	13	SU4522
Otterburn *Nthumb*	102	NY8893
Otterburn *N York*	88	SD8857
Otterham *Cnwll*	4	SX1690
Otterham Quay *Kent*	28	TQ8366
Otterhampton *Somset*	20	ST2443
Ottershaw *Surrey*	26	TQ0263
Otterswick *Shet*	155	HU5285
Otterton *Devon*	9	SY0684
Otterwood *Hants*	13	SU4102
Ottery *Devon*	6	SX4475
Ottery St. Mary *Devon*	9	SY1095
Ottinge *Kent*	29	TR1642
Ottringham *Humb*	85	TA2624
Oughterby *Cumb*	93	NY2955
Oughtershaw *N York*	88	SD8780
Oughterside *Cumb*	92	NY1140
Oughtibridge *S York*	74	SK3093
Oughtrington *Ches*	79	SJ6987
Oulston *N York*	90	SE5474
Oulton *Cumb*	93	NY2450
Oulton *W York*	83	SE3628
Oulton *Staffs*	72	SJ7822
Oulton *Staffs*	72	SJ9035
Oulton *Norfk*	66	TG1328
Oulton *Suffk*	67	TM5294
Oulton Broad *Suffk*	67	TM5192
Oulton Street *Norfk*	66	TG1527
Oundle *Nhants*	51	TL0388
Ounsdale *Staffs*	60	SO8693
Ousby *Cumb*	94	NY6134
Ousden *Suffk*	53	TL7459
Ousefleet *Humb*	84	SE8323
Ouston *Nthumb*	103	NZ0770
Ouston *Dur*	96	NZ2554
Out Newton *Humb*	85	TA3821
Outchester *Nthumb*	111	NU1433
Outgate *Cumb*	87	SD3599
Outhgill *Cumb*	88	NY7801
Outhill *Warwks*	48	SP1066
Outlands *Staffs*	72	SJ7630
Outlane *W York*	82	SE0817
Outward Gate *Gt Man*	79	SD7805
Outwell *Norfk*	65	TF5103
Outwick *Hants*	12	SU1417
Outwood *W York*	83	SE3323
Outwood *Surrey*	15	TQ3145
Outwoods *Staffs*	72	SJ7817
Outwoods *Leics*	62	SK4018
Outwoods *Warwks*	61	SP2484
Ouzlewell Green *W York*	83	SE3326
Ovenden *W York*	82	SE0827
Over *Ches*	71	SJ6365
Over *Gloucs*	35	SO8119
Over *Avon*	34	ST5882
Over *Cambs*	52	TL3770
Over Burrows *Derbys*	73	SK2639
Over Compton *Dorset*	10	ST5816
Over End *Cambs*	51	TL0893
Over Green *Warwks*	61	SP1694
Over Haddon *Derbys*	74	SK2066
Over Kellet *Lancs*	87	SD5169
Over Kiddington *Oxon*	36	SP4021
Over Monnow *Gwent*	34	SO5012
Over Norton *Oxon*	48	SP3128
Over Silton *N York*	89	SE4493
Over Stenton *Fife*	117	NT2799
Over Stowey *Somset*	20	ST1838
Over Stratton *Somset*	10	ST4315
Over Tabley *Ches*	79	SJ7279
Over Wallop *Hants*	23	SU2838
Over Whitacre *Warwks*	61	SP2590
Over Woodhouse *Derbys*	75	SK4671
Over Worton *Oxon*	49	SP4329
Overbury *H & W*	47	SO9537
Overgreen *Derbys*	74	SK3273
Overleigh *Somset*	21	ST4835
Overley *Staffs*	73	SK1515
Overpool *Ches*	71	SJ3877
Overscaig Hotel *Highld*	149	NC4123
Overseal *Derbys*	73	SK2915
Oversland *Kent*	28	TR0557
Overstey Green *Warwks*	48	SP0957
Overstone *Nhants*	50	SP7966
Overstrand *Norfk*	67	TG2440
Overstreet *Wilts*	23	SU0637
Overthorpe *Nhants*	49	SP4840
Overton *Gramp*	143	NJ8714
Overton *Lancs*	87	SD4358
Overton *W York*	82	SE2516
Overton *N York*	83	SE5555
Overton *Clwyd*	71	SJ3741
Overton *Ches*	71	SJ5277
Overton *Shrops*	46	SO5072
Overton *W Glam*	32	SS4685
Overton *Hants*	24	SU5149
Overton Bridge *Clwyd*	71	SJ3542
Overton Green *Ches*	72	SJ8060
Overtown *Strath*	116	NS8053
Overtown *Lancs*	87	SD6275
Overtown *W York*	83	SE3516
Overtown *Wilts*	36	SU1579
Overy *Oxon*	37	SU5893
Overy Staithe *Norfk*	66	TF8444
Oving *Bucks*	37	SP7821
Oving *W Susx*	14	SU9004
Ovingdean *E Susx*	15	TQ3503
Ovingham *Nthumb*	103	NZ0863
Ovington *Nthumb*	103	NZ0663
Ovington *Dur*	89	NZ1314
Ovington *Hants*	24	SU5631
Ovington *Norfk*	66	TF9202
Ovington *Essex*	53	TL7642
Ower *Hants*	12	SU3215
Ower *Hants*	13	SU4702
Owermoigne *Dorset*	11	SY7685
Owl's Green *Suffk*	55	TM2869
Owlbury *Shrops*	59	SO3191
Owlerton *S York*	74	SK3389
Owlpen *Gloucs*	35	ST7998
Owlsmoor *Berks*	25	SU8462
Owlswick *Bucks*	37	SP7806
Owmby *Lincs*	85	TA0704
Owmby *Lincs*	76	TF0087
Owslebury *Hants*	13	SU5123
Owston *S York*	83	SE5511
Owston *Leics*	63	SK7707
Owston Ferry *Humb*	75	SE8000
Owstwick *Humb*	85	TA2732
Owthorne *Humb*	85	TA3328
Owthorpe *Notts*	63	SK6733
Oxborough *Norfk*	65	TF7401
Oxbridge *Dorset*	10	SY4797
Oxcombe *Lincs*	77	TF3177
Oxcroft *Derbys*	75	SK4873
Oxen End *Essex*	40	TL6629
Oxen Park *Cumb*	86	SD3187
Oxenholme *Cumb*	87	SD5290
Oxenhope *W York*	82	SE0335
Oxenpill *Somset*	21	ST4441
Oxenton *Gloucs*	47	SO9531
Oxenwood *Wilts*	23	SU3058
Oxford *Oxon*	37	SP5106
Oxhey *Herts*	26	TQ1295
Oxhill *Dur*	96	NZ1852
Oxhill *Warwks*	48	SP3146
Oxley *W Mids*	60	SJ9001
Oxley Green *Essex*	40	TL9014
Oxley's Green *E Susx*	16	TQ6921
Oxlode *Cambs*	53	TL4886
Oxnam *Border*	110	NT6918
Oxnead *Norfk*	67	TG2224
Oxshott *Surrey*	26	TQ1460
Oxshott Heath *Surrey*	26	TQ1361
Oxspring *S York*	82	SE2601
Oxted *Surrey*	27	TQ3852
Oxton *Border*	118	NT4953
Oxton *N York*	83	SE5043
Oxton *Notts*	75	SK6351
Oxwich *W Glam*	32	SS4986
Oxwich Green *W Glam*	32	SS4985
Oxwick *Norfk*	66	TF9125
Oykel Bridge *Highld*	145	NC3801
Oyne *Gramp*	142	NJ6725
Oystermouth *W Glam*	32	SS6187
Ozleworth *Gloucs*	35	ST7993

P

Packers hill *Dorset*	11	ST7110
Packington *Leics*	62	SK3614
Packmoor *Staffs*	72	SJ8654
Packmores *Warwks*	48	SP2866
Padanaram *Tays*	127	NO4251
Padbury *Bucks*	49	SP7230
Paddington *Ches*	79	SJ6389
Paddington *Gt Lon*	27	TQ2681
Paddlesworth *Kent*	28	TQ6862
Paddlesworth *Kent*	29	TR1939
Paddock Wood *Kent*	28	TQ6744
Paddolgreen *Shrops*	59	SJ5032
Padeswood *Clwyd*	70	SJ2762
Padfield *Derbys*	74	SK0296
Padgate *Ches*	79	SJ6389
Padhams Green *Essex*	40	TQ6497
Padiham *Lancs*	81	SD7933
Padside *N York*	89	SE1659
Padstow *Cnwll*	4	SW9175
Padworth *Berks*	24	SU6166
Page Bank *Dur*	96	NZ2335
Pagham *W Susx*	14	SZ8897
Paglesham *Essex*	40	TQ9293
Paignton *Devon*	7	SX8860
Pailton *Warwks*	50	SP4781
Paine's Cross *E Susx*	16	TQ6223
Painleyhill *Staffs*	73	SK0333
Painscastle *Powys*	45	SO1646
Painshawfield *Nthumb*	103	NZ0560
Painsthorpe *Humb*	90	SE8158
Painswick *Gloucs*	35	SO8609
Painter's Forstal *Kent*	28	TQ9958
Paisley *Strath*	115	NS4864
Pakefield *Suffk*	55	TM5390
Pakenham *Suffk*	54	TL9267
Pale *Gwynd*	58	SH9836
Pale Green *Essex*	53	TL6542
Palestine *Hants*	23	SU2640
Paley Street *Berks*	26	SU8776
Palfrey *W Mids*	60	SP0196
Palgrave *Suffk*	54	TM1178
Pallington *Dorset*	11	SY7891
Palmers Green *Gt Lon*	27	TQ3192
Palmersbridge *Cnwll*	5	SX1977
Palmerston *Strath*	107	NS5019
Palmerstown *S Glam*	20	ST1369
Palnackie *D & G*	92	NX8157
Palnure *D & G*	99	NX4563
Palterton *Derbys*	75	SK4768
Pamber End *Hants*	24	SU6158
Pamber Green *Hants*	24	SU6159
Pamber Heath *Hants*	24	SU6162
Pamington *Gloucs*	47	SO9433
Pamphill *Dorset*	11	ST9900
Pampisford *Cambs*	53	TL4948
Panborough *Somset*	21	ST4745
Panbride *Tays*	127	NO5635
Pancrasweek *Devon*	18	SS2905
Pancross *S Glam*	20	ST0469
Pandy *Gwynd*	57	SH6202
Pandy *Gwynd*	57	SH8729
Pandy *Powys*	58	SH9004
Pandy *Clwyd*	58	SJ1935
Pandy *Gwent*	34	SO3322
Pandy Tudur *Clwyd*	69	SH8564
Pandy'r Capel *Clwyd*	70	SJ0850
Panfield *Essex*	40	TL7325
Pangbourne *Berks*	37	SU6376
Pangdean *W Susx*	15	TQ2911
Panks Bridge *H & W*	47	SO6248
Pannal *N York*	82	SE3051
Pannal Ash *N York*	82	SE2953
Pannanich Wells Hotel *Gramp*	134	NO4097
Pant *Shrops*	58	SJ2722
Pant Mawr *Powys*	43	SN8482
Pant-Gwyn *Dyfed*	44	SN5925
Pant-glas *Gwynd*	68	SH4747
Pant-pastynog *Clwyd*	70	SJ0461
Pant-y-dwr *Powys*	45	SN9874
Pant-y-ffridd *Powys*	58	SJ1502
Pant-y-gog *M Glam*	33	SS9090
Pant-y-mwyn *Clwyd*	70	SJ1964
Pantasaph *Clwyd*	70	SJ1675
Pantersbridge *Cnwll*	4	SX1667
Pantglas *Powys*	43	SN7797
Panton *Lincs*	76	TF1778
Pantperthog *Gwynd*	57	SH7404
Pantyffynnon *Dyfed*	32	SN6210
Pantygasseg *Gwent*	34	ST2599
Pantymenyn *Dyfed*	31	SN1426
Panxworth *Norfk*	67	TG3513
Papcastle *Cumb*	92	NY1031
Papigoe *Highld*	151	ND3851
Papple *Loth*	118	NT5972
Papplewick *Notts*	75	SK5451
Papworth Everard *Cambs*	52	TL2862
Papworth St. Agnes *Cambs*	52	TL2664
Par *Cnwll*	3	SX0753
Paramour Street *Kent*	29	TR2961
Parbold *Lancs*	80	SD4911
Parbrook *Somset*	21	ST5736
Parbrook *W Susx*	14	TQ0825
Parc *Gwynd*	57	SH8834
Parc Seymour *Gwent*	34	ST4091
Parcllyn *Dyfed*	42	SN2451
Pardshaw *Cumb*	92	NY0924
Parham *Suffk*	55	TM3060
Park *Gramp*	135	NO7898
Park *D & G*	100	NX9091
Park *Nthumb*	102	NY6861
Park Bottom *Cnwll*	2	SW6642
Park Bridge *Gt Man*	79	SD9402
Park Corner *Oxon*	37	SU6988
Park Corner *Berks*	26	SU8582
Park Corner *E Susx*	16	TQ5336
Park End *Nthumb*	102	NY8675
Park End *Staffs*	72	SJ7851
Park End *Beds*	38	SP9952
Park Gate *W York*	82	SE1841
Park Gate *H & W*	60	SO9371
Park Gate *Hants*	13	SU5108
Park Green *Essex*	39	TL4628
Park Green *Suffk*	54	TM1364
Park Head *Cumb*	94	NY5841
Park Head *W York*	82	SE2007
Park Head *Derbys*	74	SK3654
Park Hill *Gloucs*	34	ST5799
Park Royal *Gt Lon*	26	TQ1982
Park Street *W Susx*	14	TQ1131
Parkend *Gloucs*	34	SO6108
Parkers Green *Kent*	16	TQ6148
Parkeston *Essex*	41	TM2332
Parkfield *Bucks*	37	SP8002
Parkfield *Cnwll*	5	SX3167
Parkgate *D & G*	100	NY0288
Parkgate *Cumb*	93	NY2146
Parkgate *Ches*	70	SJ2878
Parkgate *Ches*	79	SJ7873
Parkgate *Essex*	40	TL6829
Parkgate *Surrey*	15	TQ2043
Parkgate *Kent*	27	TQ5064
Parkgate *E Susx*	17	TQ7214
Parkgate *Kent*	17	TQ8534
Parkhall *Strath*	115	NS4871
Parkham *Devon*	18	SS3921
Parkham Ash *Devon*	18	SS3620
Parkhill *Notts*	75	SK6952
Parkhill House *Gramp*	143	NJ8914
Parkhouse *Gwent*	34	SO5003
Parkmill *W Glam*	32	SS5489
Parkside *Dur*	96	NZ4248
Parkside *Clwyd*	71	SJ3855
Parkeston Quay *Essex*	41	TM2332
Parkstone *Dorset*	12	SZ0391
Parley Green *Dorset*	12	SZ1097
Parlington *W York*	83	SE4235
Parmoor *Bucks*	37	SU7989
Parndon *Essex*	39	TL4308
Parr Bridge *Gt Man*	79	SD7001
Parracombe *Devon*	19	SS6745
Parrah Green *Ches*	72	SJ7145
Parrog *Dyfed*	30	SN0539
Parson Drove *Cambs*	64	TF3708
Parson's Cross *S York*	74	SK3492
Parson's Heath *Essex*	41	TM0226
Parson's Hill *Derbys*	73	SK2926
Parsonby *Cumb*	92	NY1438
Partick *Strath*	115	NS5467
Partington *Gt Man*	79	SJ7191
Partney *Lincs*	77	TF4068
Parton *D & G*	99	NX6970
Parton *Cumb*	92	NX9820
Partridge Green *W Susx*	15	TQ1919
Partrishaw *Powys*	34	SO2722
Parwich *Derbys*	73	SK1854
Paslow Wood Common *Essex*	27	TL5802
Passenham *Nhants*	38	SP7839
Passfield *Hants*	14	SU8234
Passingford Bridge *Essex*	27	TQ5097
Paston *Cambs*	64	TF1802
Paston *Norfk*	67	TG3234
Pasturefields *Staffs*	73	SJ9924
Patchacott *Devon*	5	SX4798
Patcham *E Susx*	15	TQ3008
Patchetts Green *Herts*	26	TQ1497
Patching *W Susx*	14	TQ0806
Patchole *Devon*	19	SS6142
Patchway *Avon*	34	ST6082
Pateley Bridge *N York*	89	SE1565
Paternoster Heath *Essex*	40	TL9115
Pateshall *H & W*	46	SO5262
Path of Condie *Tays*	125	NO0711
Pathe *Somset*	21	ST3730
Pathhead *Gramp*	135	NO7263
Pathhead *Strath*	107	NS6114
Pathhead *Fife*	117	NT2992
Pathhead *Loth*	118	NT3964
Pathlow *Warwks*	48	SP1758
Patmore Heath *Herts*	39	TL4425
Patna *Strath*	106	NS4110
Patney *Wilts*	23	SU0758
Patrick *IOM*	153	SC2482
Patrick Brompton *N York*	89	SE2190
Patricroft *Gt Man*	79	SJ7597
Patrington *Humb*	85	TA3122
Patrixbourne *Kent*	29	TR1855
Patterdale *Cumb*	93	NY3915
Pattingham *Staffs*	60	SO8299
Pattishall *Nhants*	49	SP6754
Pattiswick Green *Essex*	40	TL8124
Patton *Shrops*	59	SO5895
Paul *Cnwll*	2	SW4627
Paul's Dene *Wilts*	23	SU1432
Paulerspury *Bucks*	49	SP7145
Paull *Humb*	85	TA1626
Paulton *Avon*	21	ST6556
Paunton *H & W*	47	SO6650
Pauperhaugh *Nthumb*	103	NZ1099
Pave Lane *Shrops*	72	SJ7616
Pavenham *Beds*	51	SP9955
Pawlett *Somset*	20	ST2942
Pawston *Nthumb*	110	NT8532
Paxford *Gloucs*	48	SP1837
Paxton *Border*	119	NT9353
Payden Street *Kent*	28	TQ9254
Payhembury *Devon*	9	ST0901
Paythorne *Lancs*	81	SD8251
Paytoe *H & W*	46	SO4171
Peacehaven *E Susx*	15	TQ4101
Peak Dale *Derbys*	74	SK0976
Peak Forest *Derbys*	74	SK1179
Peak Hill *Lincs*	64	TF2615
Peakirk *Cambs*	64	TF1606
Pean *Kent*	29	TR1837
Peanmeanach *Highld*	129	NM7180
Pearsie *Tays*	134	NO3659
Pearson's Green *Kent*	28	TQ6943
Pease Pottage *W Susx*	15	TQ2633
Peasedown St. John *Avon*	22	ST7057
Peasehill *Derbys*	74	SK4049
Peaseland Green *Norfk*	66	TG0516
Peasemore *Berks*	37	SU4577
Peasenhall *Suffk*	55	TM3569
Peaslake *Surrey*	14	TQ0844
Peasley Cross *Mersyd*	78	SJ5294
Peasmarsh *Somset*	10	ST3312
Peasmarsh *Surrey*	25	SU9946
Peasmarsh *E Susx*	17	TQ8822
Peat Inn *Fife*	127	NO4509
Peathill *Gramp*	143	NJ9366
Peatling Magna *Leics*	50	SP5992
Peatling Parva *Leics*	50	SP5889
Peaton *Shrops*	59	SO5385
Pebmarsh *Essex*	40	TL8533
Pebworth *H & W*	48	SP1347
Pecket Well *W York*	82	SD9929
Peckforton *Ches*	71	SJ5356
Peckham *Gt Lon*	27	TQ3476
Peckleton *Leics*	62	SK4701
Pedair-ffordd *Powys*	58	SJ1124
Pedlinge *Kent*	17	TR1335
Pedmore *W Mids*	60	SO9182
Pedwell *Somset*	21	ST4236
Peebles *Border*	109	NT2540
Peel *IOM*	153	SC2483
Peel *Lancs*	80	SD3531
Peel Common *Hants*	13	SU5703
Peening Quarter *Kent*	17	TQ8828
Pegsdon *Beds*	38	TL1130
Pegswood *Nthumb*	103	NZ2287
Pegwell *Kent*	29	TR3664
Peinchorran *Highld*	137	NG5233
Peinlich *Highld*	136	NG4158
Pelaw *T & W*	96	NZ3061
Pelcomb *Dyfed*	30	SM9218
Pelcomb Bridge *Dyfed*	30	SM9317
Peldon *Essex*	41	TL9816
Pell Green *E Susx*	16	TQ6432
Pelsall *W Mids*	60	SK0203
Pelsall Wood *W Mids*	60	SK0204
Pelton *Dur*	96	NZ2553
Pelton Fell *Dur*	96	NZ2551
Pelutho *Cumb*	92	NY1249
Pelynt *Cnwll*	5	SX2055
Pemberton *Gt Man*	78	SD5503
Pemberton *Dyfed*	32	SN5300
Pembles Cross *Kent*	28	TQ8947
Pembrey *Dyfed*	31	SN4301
Pembridge *H & W*	46	SO3958
Pembroke *Dyfed*	30	SM9801
Pembroke Dock *Dyfed*	30	SM9603
Pembury *Kent*	16	TQ6240
Pen Rhiwfawr *W Glam*	32	SN7410
Pen-bont Rhydybeddau *Dyfed*	43	SN6783
Pen-ffordd *Dyfed*	31	SN0722
Pen-groes-oped *Gwent*	34	SO3106
Pen-llyn *Gwynd*	68	SH3582
Pen-lon *Gwynd*	68	SH4365
Pen-twyn *Gwent*	33	SO2000
Pen-twyn *Gwent*	34	SO2603
Pen-twyn *Gwent*	34	SO5209
Pen-y-Gwryd Hotel *Gwynd*	69	SH6655
Pen-y-bont *Clwyd*	58	SJ2123
Pen-y-bryn *Dyfed*	31	SN1742
Pen-y-bryn *M Glam*	33	SS8384
Pen-y-cae *Powys*	33	SN8413
Pen-y-cae-mawr *Gwent*	34	ST4195
Pen-y-cefn *Clwyd*	70	SJ1175
Pen-y-clawdd *Gwent*	34	SO4507
Pen-y-coedcae *M Glam*	33	ST0587
Pen-y-cwn *Dyfed*	30	SM8523
Pen-y-darren *M Glam*	33	SO0506
Pen-y-fai *M Glam*	33	SS8981
Pen-y-felin *Clwyd*	70	SJ1569
Pen-y-garn *Dyfed*	43	SN6285
Pen-y-genffordd *Powys*	45	SO1729
Pen-y-graig *Gwynd*	56	SH2033
Pen-y-lan *S Glam*	33	SS9976

Pen-y-pass Polglass

Pen-y-pass	*Gwynd*	**69**	SH6455
Pen-y-stryt	*Clwyd*	**70**	SJ1952
Pen-yr-Heol	*Gwent*	**34**	SO4311
Pen-yr-Heolgerrig	*M Glam*	**33**	SO0306
Penair	*Cnwll*	**3**	SW8445
Penallt	*Gwent*	**34**	SO5210
Penally	*Dyfed*	**31**	SS1199
Penalt	*H & W*	**46**	SO5629
Penare	*Cnwll*	**3**	SW9940
Penarth	*S Glam*	**33**	ST1871
Penbryn	*Dyfed*	**42**	SN2951
Pencader	*Dyfed*	**31**	SN4436
Pencaitland	*Loth*	**118**	NT4468
Pencalenick	*Cnwll*	**3**	SW8545
Pencarnisiog	*Gwynd*	**68**	SH3573
Pencarreg	*Dyfed*	**44**	SN5445
Pencarrow	*Cnwll*	**4**	SX1082
Pencelli	*Powys*	**45**	SO0925
Penclawdd	*W Glam*	**32**	SS5495
Pencoed	*M Glam*	**33**	SS9581
Pencombe	*H & W*	**46**	SO5952
Pencoyd	*H & W*	**46**	SO5126
Pencraig	*Powys*	**58**	SJ0426
Pencraig	*H & W*	**34**	SO5620
Pendeen	*Cnwll*	**2**	SW3834
Penderyn	*M Glam*	**33**	SN9408
Pendine	*Dyfed*	**31**	SN2208
Pendlebury	*Gt Man*	**79**	SD7802
Pendleton	*Lancs*	**81**	SD7539
Pendock	*H & W*	**47**	SO7832
Pendoggett	*Cnwll*	**4**	SX0279
Pendomer	*Somset*	**10**	ST5210
Pendoylan	*S Glam*	**33**	ST0576
Pendre	*M Glam*	**33**	SS9181
Penegoes	*Powys*	**57**	SH7600
Penelewey	*Cnwll*	**3**	SW8140
Pengam	*Gwent*	**33**	ST1597
Pengam	*S Glam*	**33**	ST2177
Penge	*Gt Lon*	**27**	TQ3570
Pengelly	*Cnwll*	**3**	SW8551
Pengelly	*Cnwll*	**4**	SX0783
Pengorffwysfa	*Gwynd*	**68**	SH4692
Pengover Green	*Cnwll*	**5**	SX2765
Pengrugla	*Cnwll*	**3**	SW9947
Pengwern	*Clwyd*	**70**	SJ0276
Penhale	*Cnwll*	**2**	SW6918
Penhale	*Cnwll*	**4**	SW9057
Penhale	*Cnwll*	**4**	SX0860
Penhale	*Cnwll*	**5**	SX4153
Penhallow	*Cnwll*	**3**	SW7651
Penhalurick	*Cnwll*	**2**	SW7038
Penhalvean	*Cnwll*	**2**	SW7038
Penhill	*Wilts*	**36**	SU1588
Penhow	*Gwent*	**34**	ST4290
Penhurst	*E Susx*	**16**	TQ6916
Peniarth	*Gwynd*	**57**	SH6105
Penifiler	*Highld*	**136**	NG4841
Peninver	*Strath*	**105**	NR7524
Penisar Waun	*Gwynd*	**69**	SH5563
Penistone	*S York*	**82**	SE2403
Penjerrick	*Cnwll*	**3**	SW7730
Penkelly	*Cnwll*	**4**	SX1854
Penketh	*Ches*	**78**	SJ5587
Penkill	*Strath*	**106**	NX2398
Penkridge	*Staffs*	**60**	SJ9213
Penlean	*Cnwll*	**5**	SX2098
Penley	*Clwyd*	**71**	SJ4040
Penllergaer	*W Glam*	**32**	SS6198
Penllyn	*S Glam*	**33**	SS9775
Penmachno	*Gwynd*	**69**	SH7950
Penmaen	*W Glam*	**32**	SS5288
Penmaen	*Gwent*	**33**	ST1897
Penmaenan	*Gwynd*	**69**	SH7175
Penmaenmawr	*Gwynd*	**69**	SH7276
Penmaenpool	*Gwynd*	**57**	SH6918
Penmark	*S Glam*	**20**	ST0568
Penmon	*Gwynd*	**69**	SH6280
Penmorfa	*Gwynd*	**57**	SH5540
Penmynydd	*Gwynd*	**68**	SH5074
Penn	*W Mids*	**60**	SO8895
Penn	*Bucks*	**26**	SU9193
Penn Street	*Bucks*	**26**	SU9295
Pennal	*Gwynd*	**57**	SH6900
Pennan	*Gramp*	**143**	NJ8465
Pennant	*Clwyd*	**58**	SJ0234
Pennant	*Powys*	**43**	SN8897
Pennant-Melangell	*Powys*	**58**	SJ0226
Pennard	*W Glam*	**32**	SS5688
Pennerley	*Shrops*	**59**	SO3599
Pennicott	*Devon*	**9**	SS8701
Pennington	*Cumb*	**86**	SD2677
Pennington	*Hants*	**12**	SZ3195
Pennington Green	*Gt Man*	**79**	SD6206
Pennorth	*Powys*	**45**	SO1125
Pennsylvania	*Avon*	**35**	ST7473
Penny Bridge	*Cumb*	**86**	SD3083
Penny Green	*Notts*	**75**	SK5475
Penny Hill	*Lincs*	**64**	TF3526
Pennycross	*Strath*	**121**	NM5025
Pennygate	*Norfk*	**67**	TG3423
Pennyghael	*Strath*	**121**	NM5125
Pennyglen	*Strath*	**106**	NS2710
Pennymoor	*Devon*	**19**	SS8611
Penparc	*Dyfed*	**42**	SN2047
Penparcau	*Dyfed*	**43**	SN5980
Penpedairheol	*Gwent*	**34**	SO3303
Penpedairheol	*M Glam*	**33**	ST1497
Penperlleni	*Gwent*	**34**	SO3204
Penpethy	*Cnwll*	**4**	SX0886
Penpillick	*Cnwll*	**3**	SX0856
Penpol	*Cnwll*	**3**	SW8139
Penpoll	*Cnwll*	**3**	SX1454
Penponds	*Cnwll*	**2**	SW6339
Penpont	*D & G*	**100**	NX8494
Penpont	*Powys*	**45**	SN9728
Penquit	*Devon*	**7**	SX6454
Penrest	*Cnwll*	**5**	SX3377
Penrherber	*Dyfed*	**31**	SN2938
Pen-rhiw	*Dyfed*	**31**	SN2440
Penrhiwceiber	*M Glam*	**33**	ST0597
Penrhiwllan	*Dyfed*	**31**	SN3641
Penrhiwpal	*Dyfed*	**42**	SN3445
Penrhos	*Gwynd*	**68**	SH2781
Penrhos	*Gwynd*	**56**	SH3433
Penrhos	*Powys*	**32**	SN8011
Penrhos	*Gwent*	**34**	SO4111
Penrhos garnedd	*Gwynd*	**69**	SH5670
Penrhyn Bay	*Gwynd*	**69**	SH8281
Penrhyn-side	*Gwynd*	**69**	SH8181
Penrhyncoch	*Dyfed*	**43**	SN6384
Penrhyndeudraeth	*Gwynd*	**57**	SH6139
Penrice	*W Glam*	**32**	SS4987
Penrioch	*Strath*	**105**	NR8744
Penrith	*Cumb*	**94**	NY5130
Penrose	*Cnwll*	**4**	SW8770
Penrose	*Cnwll*	**5**	SX2589
Penruddock	*Cumb*	**93**	NY4227
Penryn	*Cnwll*	**3**	SW7834
Pensarn	*Clwyd*	**70**	SH9578
Pensarn	*Dyfed*	**31**	SN4119
Pensax	*H & W*	**47**	SO7269
Pensby	*Mersyd*	**78**	SJ2782
Penselwood	*Somset*	**22**	ST7531
Pensford	*Avon*	**21**	ST6263
Pensham	*H & W*	**47**	SO9444
Penshaw	*T & W*	**96**	NZ3354
Penshurst	*Kent*	**16**	TQ5243
Penshurst Station	*Kent*	**16**	TQ5246
Pensilva	*Cnwll*	**5**	SX2970
Pensnett	*W Mids*	**60**	SO9189
Pensont	*Cnwll*	**4**	SX0874
Penstone	*Devon*	**8**	SS7700
Penstrowed	*Powys*	**58**	SO0691
Pentewan	*Cnwll*	**3**	SX0147
Pentir	*Gwynd*	**69**	SH5766
Pentire	*Cnwll*	**4**	SW7961
Pentlepoir	*Dyfed*	**31**	SN1105
Pentlow	*Essex*	**54**	TL8146
Pentlow Street	*Essex*	**54**	TL8245
Pentney	*Norfk*	**65**	TF7214
Penton Grafton	*Hants*	**23**	SU3247
Penton Mewsey	*Hants*	**23**	SU3247
Pentraeth	*Gwynd*	**68**	SH5278
Pentre	*Clwyd*	**70**	SJ0862
Pentre	*Clwyd*	**70**	SJ2840
Pentre	*Clwyd*	**71**	SJ3267
Pentre	*Shrops*	**59**	SJ3617
Pentre	*Powys*	**58**	SO0685
Pentre	*Powys*	**58**	SO1589
Pentre	*Gwent*	**34**	SO3106
Pentre	*M Glam*	**33**	SS9696
Pentre Bach	*Clwyd*	**70**	SJ2175
Pentre Berw	*Gwynd*	**68**	SH4772
Pentre Ffwrndan	*Clwyd*	**70**	SJ2572
Pentre Halkyn	*Clwyd*	**70**	SJ2072
Pentre Hodrey	*Shrops*	**46**	SO3277
Pentre Isaf	*Clwyd*	**70**	SH9871
Pentre Llanrhaeadr	*Clwyd*	**70**	SJ0863
Pentre Llifior	*Powys*	**58**	SO1598
Pentre Meyrick	*S Glam*	**33**	SS9675
Pentre bach	*Dyfed*	**44**	SN5547
Pentre ty gwyn	*Dyfed*	**44**	SN8135
Pentre'r Felin	*Gwynd*	**69**	SH8069
Pentre'r-felin	*Powys*	**45**	SN9230
Pentre-Gwenlais	*Dyfed*	**32**	SN6016
Pentre-Maw	*Powys*	**57**	SH8803
Pentre-bach	*Powys*	**45**	SN9132
Pentre-bont	*Gwynd*	**69**	SH7351
Pentre-cagel	*Dyfed*	**31**	SN3340
Pentre-celyn	*Powys*	**57**	SH8905
Pentre-celyn	*Clwyd*	**70**	SJ1453
Pentre-chwyth	*W Glam*	**32**	SS6794
Pentre-clawdd	*Shrops*	**59**	SJ2931
Pentre-cwrt	*Dyfed*	**31**	SN3838
Pentre-dwr	*W Glam*	**32**	SS6995
Pentre-llwyn-llwyd	*Powys*	**45**	SN9654
Pentre-llyn	*Dyfed*	**43**	SN6175
Pentre-llyn-cymmer	*Clwyd*	**70**	SH9752
Pentre-piod	*Gwent*	**34**	SO2601
Pentre-poeth	*Gwent*	**34**	ST2686
Pentre-tafarn-y-fedw	*Gwynd*	**69**	SH8162
Pentrebach	*M Glam*	**33**	SO0604
Pentrebeirdd	*Powys*	**58**	SJ1813
Pentredwr	*Clwyd*	**70**	SJ1946
Pentrefelin	*Gwynd*	**68**	SH4392
Pentrefelin	*Gwynd*	**57**	SH5239
Pentrefoelas	*Clwyd*	**69**	SH8751
Pentregalar	*Dyfed*	**31**	SN1831
Pentregat	*Dyfed*	**42**	SN3551
Pentrich	*Derbys*	**74**	SK3852
Pentridge Hill	*Dorset*	**12**	SU0317
Pentyrch	*M Glam*	**33**	ST1081
Penwithick	*Cnwll*	**3**	SX0256
Penwyllt	*Powys*	**33**	SN8515
Penybanc	*Dyfed*	**44**	SN6123
Penybont	*Powys*	**45**	SO1164
Pen-y-Bont-Fawr	*Powys*	**58**	SJ0824
Penycae	*Clwyd*	**70**	SJ2745
Penycaerau	*Gwynd*	**56**	SH1927
Penyffordd	*Clwyd*	**71**	SJ3061
Penygarnedd	*Powys*	**58**	SJ1023
Penygraig	*M Glam*	**33**	ST0090
Penygroes	*Gwynd*	**68**	SH4752
Penygroes	*Dyfed*	**32**	SN5813
Penysarn	*Gwynd*	**68**	SH4590
Penywaun	*M Glam*	**33**	SN9804
Penywern	*W Glam*	**32**	SN7609
Penzance	*Cnwll*	**2**	SW4730
Peopleton	*H & W*	**47**	SO9350
Peover Heath	*Ches*	**79**	SJ7973
Peper Harow	*Surrey*	**25**	SU9344
Peplow	*Shrops*	**59**	SJ6224
Pepper's Green	*Essex*	**40**	TL6110
Peppershill	*Oxon*	**37**	SP6709
Pepperstock	*Beds*	**38**	TL0817
Percie	*Gramp*	**134**	NO5992
Percyhorner	*Gramp*	**143**	NJ9665
Perelle	*Guern*	**152**	GN0000
Periton	*Somset*	**20**	SS9545
Perivale	*Gt Lon*	**26**	TQ1682
Perkin's Beach	*Shrops*	**59**	SJ3600
Perkins Village	*Devon*	**9**	SY0291
Perkinsville	*Dur*	**96**	NZ2553
Perlethorpe	*Notts*	**75**	SK6470
Perran Wharf	*Cnwll*	**3**	SW7738
Perranarworthal	*Cnwll*	**3**	SW7738
Perranporth	*Cnwll*	**3**	SW7554
Perranuthnoe	*Cnwll*	**2**	SW5329
Perranwell	*Cnwll*	**3**	SW7739
Perranwell	*Cnwll*	**3**	SW7752
Perranzabuloe	*Cnwll*	**3**	SW7752
Perrott's Brook	*Gloucs*	**35**	SP0106
Perry	*W Mids*	**61**	SP0792
Perry Barr	*W Mids*	**61**	SP0791
Perry Green	*Wilts*	**35**	ST9689
Perry Green	*Herts*	**39**	TL4317
Perry Green	*Essex*	**40**	TL8022
Perry Street	*Somset*	**10**	ST3305
Pershall	*Staffs*	**72**	SJ8129
Pershore	*H & W*	**47**	SO9446
Pertenhall	*Beds*	**51**	TL0865
Perth	*Tays*	**126**	NO1123
Perthy	*Shrops*	**59**	SJ3633
Pertwood	*Wilts*	**22**	ST8936
Pet Street	*Kent*	**29**	TR0846
Peter Tavy	*Devon*	**5**	SX5177
Peter's Green	*Herts*	**38**	TL1419
Peterborough	*Cambs*	**64**	TL1998
Peterchurch	*H & W*	**46**	SO3438
Peterculter	*Gramp*	**135**	NJ8300
Peterhead	*Gramp*	**143**	NK1246
Peterlee	*Dur*	**96**	NZ4241
Peters Marland	*Devon*	**18**	SS4713
Petersfield	*Hants*	**13**	SU7423
Petersham	*Gt Lon*	**26**	TQ1873
Peterstone Wentlooge	*Gwent*	**34**	ST2679
Peterstonsuper-Ely	*S Glam*	**33**	ST0876
Peterstow	*H & W*	**46**	SO5624
Petham	*Kent*	**29**	TR1251
Petherwin Gate	*Cnwll*	**5**	SX2889
Petrockstow	*Devon*	**19**	SS5109
Petsoe End	*Bucks*	**38**	SP8949
Pett	*E Susx*	**17**	TQ8714
Pett Bottom	*Kent*	**29**	TR1552
Pettaugh	*Suffk*	**54**	TM1659
Petterden	*Tays*	**127**	NO4240
Pettinain	*Strath*	**108**	NS9543
Pettistree	*Suffk*	**55**	TM3055
Petton	*Shrops*	**59**	SJ4326
Petton	*Devon*	**20**	ST0124
Petts Wood	*Gt Lon*	**27**	TQ4567
Pettycur	*Fife*	**117**	NT2686
Pettymuk	*Gramp*	**143**	NJ9023
Petworth	*W Susx*	**14**	SU9721
Pevensey	*E Susx*	**16**	TQ6405
Pevensey Bay	*E Susx*	**16**	TQ6504
Pewsey	*Wilts*	**23**	SU1660
Pheasant's Hill	*Bucks*	**37**	SU7887
Phepson	*H & W*	**47**	SO9459
Philadelphia	*T & W*	**96**	NZ3352
Philham	*Devon*	**18**	SS2522
Philiphaugh	*Border*	**109**	NT4327
Phillack	*Cnwll*	**2**	SW5638
Philleigh	*Cnwll*	**3**	SW8639
Philpot End	*Essex*	**40**	TL6118
Philpstoun	*Loth*	**117**	NT0577
Phocle Green	*H & W*	**47**	SO6326
Phoenix Green	*Hants*	**24**	SU7555
Phoines	*Highld*	**132**	NN7093
Pibsbury	*Somset*	**21**	ST4426
Pica	*Cumb*	**92**	NY0222
Piccotts End	*Herts*	**38**	TL0409
Pickering	*N York*	**90**	SE7984
Picket Piece	*Hants*	**23**	SU3947
Picket Post	*Hants*	**12**	SU1906
Pickford	*W Mids*	**61**	SP2881
Pickford Green	*W Mids*	**61**	SP2781
Pickhill	*N York*	**89**	SE3483
Picklescott	*Shrops*	**59**	SO4399
Pickmere	*Ches*	**79**	SJ6977
Pickney	*Somset*	**20**	ST1929
Pickstock	*Shrops*	**72**	SJ7223
Pickup Bank	*Lancs*	**81**	SD7122
Pickwell	*Leics*	**63**	SK7811
Pickwell	*Devon*	**18**	SS4540
Pickwick	*Wilts*	**35**	ST8670
Pickworth	*Leics*	**63**	SK9913
Pickworth	*Lincs*	**64**	TF0433
Pict's Cross	*H & W*	**46**	SO5526
Pictillum	*Gramp*	**142**	NJ7317
Picton	*N York*	**89**	NZ4107
Picton	*Clwyd*	**70**	SJ1182
Picton	*Ches*	**71**	SJ4371
Picton Ferry	*Dyfed*	**31**	SN2717
Piddinghoe	*E Susx*	**16**	TQ4303
Piddington	*Oxon*	**37**	SP6317
Piddington	*Nhants*	**51**	SP8054
Piddington	*Bucks*	**37**	SU8094
Piddlehinton	*Dorset*	**11**	SY7197
Piddletrenthide	*Dorset*	**11**	SY7099
Pidley	*Cambs*	**52**	TL3377
Pie Corner	*H & W*	**47**	SO6461
Piercebridge	*Dur*	**96**	NZ2115
Pierowall	*Ork*	**155**	HY4348
Piff's Elm	*Gloucs*	**47**	SO9026
Pig Oak	*Dorset*	**12**	SU0202
Pig Street	*H & W*	**46**	SO3647
Pigdon	*Nthumb*	**103**	NZ1588
Pigeon Green	*Warwks*	**48**	SP2260
Pikehall	*Derbys*	**74**	SK1959
Pilford	*Dorset*	**12**	SU0301
Pilgrims Hatch	*Essex*	**27**	TQ5895
Pilham	*Lincs*	**76**	SK8693
Pill	*Avon*	**34**	ST5275
Pillaton	*Staffs*	**60**	SJ9413
Pillaton	*Cnwll*	**5**	SX3664
Pillatonmill	*Cnwll*	**5**	SX3663
Pillerton Hersey	*Warwks*	**48**	SP2948
Pillerton Priors	*Warwks*	**48**	SP2947
Pilleth	*Powys*	**46**	SO2667
Pilley	*S York*	**74**	SE3300
Pilley	*Hants*	**12**	SZ3298
Pilley Bailey	*Hants*	**12**	SZ3398
Pillgwenlly	*Gwent*	**34**	ST3186
Pillhead	*Devon*	**18**	SS4726
Pilling	*Lancs*	**80**	SD4048
Pilling Lane	*Lancs*	**80**	SD3749
Pilning	*Avon*	**34**	ST5684
Pilot Inn	*Kent*	**17**	TR0818
Pilsbury	*Derbys*	**74**	SK1163
Pilsdon	*Dorset*	**10**	SY4199
Pilsgate	*Cambs*	**64**	TF0605
Pilsley	*Derbys*	**74**	SK2371
Pilsley	*Derbys*	**74**	SK4262
Pilson Green	*Norfk*	**67**	TG3713
Piltdown	*E Susx*	**16**	TQ4422
Pilton	*Leics*	**63**	SK9102
Pilton	*Somset*	**21**	ST5941
Pilton	*Nhants*	**51**	TL0284
Pilton Green	*W Glam*	**32**	SS4487
Pimlico	*Lancs*	**81**	SD7443
Pimlico	*Nhants*	**49**	SP6140
Pimperne	*Dorset*	**11**	ST9009
Pin Green	*Herts*	**39**	TL2525
Pinchbeck	*Lincs*	**64**	TF2425
Pinchbeck Bars	*Lincs*	**64**	TF1925
Pinchbeck West	*Lincs*	**64**	TF2024
Pincheon Green	*S York*	**83**	SE6517
Pinchinthorpe	*Cleve*	**90**	NZ5714
Pincock	*Lancs*	**80**	SD5417
Pindon End	*Bucks*	**38**	SP7847
Pineham	*Kent*	**29**	TR3145
Pinfold	*Lancs*	**80**	SD3811
Pinford End	*Suffk*	**54**	TL8459
Pinged	*Dyfed*	**31**	SN4203
Pingewood	*Berks*	**24**	SU6969
Pinhoe	*Devon*	**9**	SX9694
Pinkett's Booth	*W Mids*	**61**	SP2781
Pinkney	*Wilts*	**35**	ST8686
Pinley	*W Mids*	**61**	SP3577
Pinley Green	*Warwks*	**48**	SP2066
Pinmill	*Suffk*	**55**	TM2037
Pinminnoch	*Strath*	**106**	NX1993
Pinmore	*Strath*	**106**	NX2091
Pinner	*Gt Lon*	**26**	TQ1289
Pinner Green	*Gt Lon*	**26**	TQ1289
Pinsley Green	*Ches*	**71**	SJ5846
Pinvin	*H & W*	**47**	SO9549
Pinwherry	*Strath*	**98**	NX2086
Pinxton	*Derbys*	**75**	SK4554
Pipe Gate	*Shrops*	**72**	SJ7340
Pipe and Lyde	*H & W*	**46**	SO5043
Pipehill	*Staffs*	**61**	SK0907
Piperhill	*Highld*	**140**	NH8650
Pipers Pool	*Cnwll*	**5**	SX2584
Pipewell	*Nhants*	**51**	SP8485
Pippacott	*Devon*	**19**	SS5237
Pippin Street	*Lancs*	**81**	SD5924
Pipton	*Powys*	**45**	SO1637
Pirbright	*Surrey*	**25**	SU9455
Pirbright Camp	*Surrey*	**25**	SU9356
Pirnie	*Border*	**110**	NT6528
Pirton	*H & W*	**47**	SO8847
Pirton	*Herts*	**38**	TL1431
Pishill	*Oxon*	**37**	SU7389
Pistyll	*Gwynd*	**56**	SH3241
Pitagowan	*Tays*	**132**	NN8165
Pitblae	*Gramp*	**143**	NJ9864
Pitcairngreen	*Tays*	**125**	NO0627
Pitcalnie	*Highld*	**147**	NH8072
Pitcaple	*Gramp*	**142**	NJ7225
Pitcarity	*Tays*	**134**	NO3365
Pitch Green	*Bucks*	**37**	SP7703
Pitch Place	*Surrey*	**25**	SU8839
Pitch Place	*Surrey*	**25**	SU9852
Pitchcombe	*Gloucs*	**35**	SO8508
Pitchcott	*Bucks*	**37**	SP7720
Pitcher Row	*Lincs*	**64**	TF2933
Pitchford	*Shrops*	**59**	SJ5303
Pitchroy	*Gramp*	**141**	NJ1738
Pitcombe	*Somset*	**22**	ST6732
Pitcot	*M Glam*	**33**	SS8974
Pitcox	*Loth*	**118**	NT6475
Pitcur	*Tays*	**126**	NO2437
Pitfichie	*Gramp*	**142**	NJ6716
Pitfour Castle	*Tays*	**126**	NO1921
Pitglassie	*Gramp*	**142**	NJ6943
Pitgrudy	*Highld*	**147**	NH7991
Pitkennedy	*Tays*	**127**	NO5454
Pitlessie	*Fife*	**126**	NO3309
Pitlochry	*Tays*	**132**	NN9458
Pitmachie	*Gramp*	**142**	NJ6728
Pitmain	*Highld*	**132**	NH7400
Pitmedden	*Gramp*	**143**	NJ8827
Pitmuies	*Tays*	**127**	NO5649
Pitmunie	*Gramp*	**142**	NJ6614
Pitney	*Somset*	**21**	ST4528
Pitroddie	*Tays*	**126**	NO2125
Pitscottie	*Fife*	**126**	NO4112
Pitsea	*Essex*	**40**	TQ7488
Pitses	*Gt Man*	**79**	SD9403
Pitsford	*Nhants*	**50**	SP7567
Pitstone	*Bucks*	**38**	SP9415
Pitt	*Devon*	**9**	ST0316
Pitt	*Hants*	**24**	SU4528
Pitt Court	*Gloucs*	**35**	ST7496
Pitt's Wood	*Kent*	**16**	TQ6149
Pittarrow	*Gramp*	**135**	NO7274
Pittenweem	*Fife*	**127**	NO5502
Pitteuchar	*Fife*	**117**	NT2899
Pittington	*Dur*	**96**	NZ3244
Pittodrie	*Gramp*	**142**	NJ6924
Pitton	*Wilts*	**23**	SU2131
Pittulie	*Gramp*	**143**	NJ9567
Pity Me	*Dur*	**96**	NZ2645
Pityme	*Cnwll*	**4**	SW9576
Pivington	*Kent*	**28**	TQ9146
Pixey Green	*Suffk*	**55**	TM2475
Pixham	*Surrey*	**26**	TQ1750
Plain Street	*Cnwll*	**4**	SW9778
Plains	*Strath*	**116**	NS7966
Plaish	*Shrops*	**59**	SO5296
Plaistow	*Derbys*	**74**	SK3456
Plaistow	*H & W*	**47**	SO6939
Plaistow	*W Susx*	**14**	TQ0030
Plaistow	*Gt Lon*	**27**	TQ4082
Plaitford	*Hants*	**12**	SU2719
Plas Llanfair	*Gwynd*	**69**	SH5371
Plas Llysyn	*Powys*	**58**	SN9597
Plastow Green	*Hants*	**24**	SU5361
Platt	*Kent*	**27**	TQ6257
Platt Bridge	*Gt Man*	**78**	SD6002
Platt Lane	*Shrops*	**59**	SJ5136
Platts Heath	*Kent*	**28**	TQ8750
Plawsworth	*Dur*	**96**	NZ2647
Plaxtol	*Kent*	**27**	TQ6053
Play Hatch	*Oxon*	**37**	SU7376
Playden	*E Susx*	**17**	TQ9221
Playford	*Suffk*	**55**	TM2147
Playing Place	*Cnwll*	**3**	SW8141
Playley Green	*Gloucs*	**47**	SO7631
Plealey	*Shrops*	**59**	SJ4206
Plean	*Cent*	**116**	NS8386
Pleasance	*Fife*	**126**	NO2312
Pleasington	*Lancs*	**81**	SD6426
Pleasley	*Derbys*	**75**	SK5064
Pleck	*Dorset*	**11**	ST7010
Pledgdon Green	*Essex*	**40**	TL5626
Pledwick	*W York*	**83**	SE3316
Pleinheaume	*Guern*	**152**	GN0000
Plemont	*Jersey*	**152**	JS0000
Plemstall	*Ches*	**71**	SJ4570
Plenmeller	*Nthumb*	**102**	NY7163
Pleshey	*Essex*	**40**	TL6614
Plockton	*Highld*	**137**	NG8033
Ploughfield	*H & W*	**46**	SO3841
Plowden	*Shrops*	**59**	SO3887
Ploxgreen	*Shrops*	**59**	SJ3604
Pluckley	*Kent*	**28**	TQ9245
Pluckley Station	*Kent*	**28**	TQ9243
Pluckley Thorne	*Kent*	**28**	TQ9244
Plucks Gutter	*Kent*	**29**	TR2663
Plumbland	*Cumb*	**92**	NY1539
Plumgarths	*Cumb*	**87**	SD4994
Plumley	*Ches*	**79**	SJ7274
Plumpton	*Cumb*	**94**	NY4937
Plumpton	*E Susx*	**15**	TQ3613
Plumpton End	*Nhants*	**49**	SP7245
Plumpton Green	*E Susx*	**15**	TQ3616
Plumpton Head	*Cumb*	**94**	NY5035
Plumstead	*Norfk*	**66**	TG1334
Plumstead	*Gt Lon*	**27**	TQ4478
Plumstead Green	*Norfk*	**66**	TG1235
Plumtree	*Notts*	**62**	SK6132
Plumtree Green	*Kent*	**28**	TQ8245
Plungar	*Leics*	**63**	SK7634
Plurenden	*Kent*	**28**	TQ9337
Plush	*Dorset*	**11**	ST7102
Plusha	*Cnwll*	**5**	SX2580
Plushabridge	*Cnwll*	**5**	SX3072
Plwmp	*Dyfed*	**42**	SN3652
Plymouth	*Devon*	**6**	SX4754
Plympton	*Devon*	**6**	SX5456
Plymstock	*Devon*	**6**	SX5152
Plymtree	*Devon*	**9**	ST0502
Pockley	*N York*	**90**	SE6385
Pocklington	*Humb*	**84**	SE8048
Pode Hole	*Lincs*	**64**	TF2121
Podimore	*Somset*	**21**	ST5424
Podington	*Beds*	**51**	SP9462
Podmore	*Staffs*	**72**	SJ7835
Point Clear	*Essex*	**41**	TM1015
Pointon	*Lincs*	**64**	TF1131
Pokesdown	*Dorset*	**12**	SZ1292
Polapit Tamar	*Cnwll*	**5**	SX3389
Polbain	*Highld*	**144**	NB9910
Polbathic	*Cnwll*	**5**	SX3456
Polbeth	*Loth*	**117**	NT0264
Polbrock	*Cnwll*	**4**	SX0169
Polchar	*Highld*	**132**	NH8909
Pole Elm	*H & W*	**47**	SO8450
Pole Moor	*W York*	**82**	SE0615
Polebrook	*Nhants*	**51**	TL0686
Polegate	*E Susx*	**16**	TQ5804
Polelane Ends	*Ches*	**79**	SJ6479
Polesworth	*Warwks*	**61**	SK2602
Polgigga	*Cnwll*	**2**	SW3723
Polglass	*Highld*	**144**	NC0307

Q

Queensferry Ringwood

Queensferry *Clwyd* 71 SJ3168
Queenzieburn *Strath* 116 NS6977
Quendon *Essex* 39 TL5130
Queniborough *Leics* 63 SK6412
Quenington *Gloucs* 36 SP1404
Quernmore *Lancs* 87 SD5160
Quernmore Park Hall *Lancs* 87 SD5162
Queslett *W Mids* 61 SP0695
Quethiock *Cnwll* 5 SX3164
Quick's Green *Berks* 37 SU5876
Quidenham *Norfk* 54 TM0287
Quidhampton *Wilts* 23 SU1030
Quidhampton *Hants* 24 SU5150
Quina Brook *Shrops* 59 SJ5232
Quinberry End *Nhants* 49 SP6250
Quinish House *Strath* 121 NM4154
Quinton *W Mids* 60 SO9984
Quinton *Nhants* 49 SP7754
Quinton Green *Nhants* 50 SP7853
Quintrell Downs *Cnwll* 4 SW8460
Quither *Devon* 5 SX4481
Quixhall *Staffs* 73 SK1041
Quixwood *Border* 119 NT7863
Quoditch *Devon* 5 SX4097
Quorndon *Leics* 62 SK5616
Quothquan *Strath* 108 NS9939
Quoyburray *Ork* 155 HY5005
Quoyloo *Ork* 155 HY2420

R

RAF College (Cranwell) *Lincs* 76 TF0049
Rabbit's Cross *Kent* 28 TQ7847
Rableyheath *Herts* 39 TL2319
Raby *Cumb* 93 NY1951
Raby *Mersyd* 71 SJ3179
Rachan Mill *Border* 108 NT1134
Rachub *Gwynd* 69 SH6267
Rackenford *Devon* 19 SS8518
Rackham *W Susx* 14 TQ0413
Rackheath *Norfk* 67 TG2814
Rackwick *Ork* 155 ND2099
Radbourne *Derbys* 73 SK2836
Radcliffe *Nthumb* 103 NU2602
Radcliffe *Gt Man* 79 SD7806
Radcliffe on Trent *Notts* 63 SK6439
Radclive *Bucks* 49 SP6734
Radcot *Oxon* 36 SU2899
Raddington *Somset* 20 ST0225
Radernie *Fife* 127 NO4609
Radford Semele *Warwks* 48 SP3464
Radlet *Somset* 20 ST2038
Radlett *Herts* 26 TL1600
Radley *Devon* 19 SS7323
Radley *Oxon* 37 SU5398
Radley Green *Essex* 40 TL6205
Radmore Green *Ches* 71 SJ5955
Radnage *Bucks* 37 SU7897
Radstock *Avon* 22 ST6854
Radstone *Nhants* 49 SP5840
Radway *Warwks* 48 SP3648
Radway Green *Ches* 72 SJ7754
Radwell *Beds* 51 TL0057
Radwell *Herts* 39 TL2335
Radwinter *Essex* 53 TL6037
Radwinter End *Essex* 53 TL6139
Radyr *S Glam* 33 ST1280
Raecleugh *D & G* 108 NT0311
Rafford *Gramp* 141 NJ0556
Raftra *Cnwll* 2 SW3723
Ragdale *Leics* 63 SK6619
Ragdon *Shrops* 59 SO4591
Raginnis *Cnwll* 2 SW4625
Raglan *Gwent* 34 SO4107
Ragnall *Notts* 75 SK8073
Raigbeg *Highld* 140 NH8128
Rainbow Hill *H & W* 47 SO8555
Rainford *Gt Man* 78 SD4700
Rainham *Gt Lon* 27 TQ5282
Rainham *Kent* 28 TQ8165
Rainhill *Mersyd* 78 SJ4991
Rainhill Stoops *Mersyd* 78 SJ5090
Rainow *Ches* 79 SJ9475
Rainsough *Gt Man* 79 SD8002
Rainton *N York* 89 SE3675
Rainworth *Notts* 75 SK5858
Raisbeck *Cumb* 87 NY6407
Raise *Cumb* 94 NY7046
Raisthorpe *N York* 90 SE8561
Rait *Tays* 126 NO2226
Raithby *Lincs* 77 TF3084
Raithby *Lincs* 77 TF3766
Raithwaite *N York* 90 NZ8611
Rake *W Susx* 14 SU8027
Rakewood *Gt Man* 82 SD9414
Ralia *Highld* 132 NN7097
Ram *Dyfed* 44 SN5846
Ram Hill *Avon* 35 ST6779
Ram Lane *Kent* 28 TQ9646
Ramasaig *Highld* 136 NG1644
Rame *Cnwll* 3 SW7233
Rame *Cnwll* 6 SX4249
Rampisham *Dorset* 10 ST5602
Rampside *Cumb* 86 SD2366
Rampton *Notts* 75 SK8078
Rampton *Cambs* 53 TL4267
Ramridge End *Beds* 38 TL1023
Ramsbottom *Gt Man* 81 SD7916
Ramsbury *Wilts* 36 SU2771
Ramscraigs *Highld* 151 ND1427
Ramsdean *Hants* 13 SU7022
Ramsdell *Hants* 24 SU5857
Ramsden *H & W* 47 SO9246
Ramsden *Oxon* 36 SP3515
Ramsden Bellhouse *Essex* 40 TQ7194
Ramsden Heath *Essex* 40 TQ7095
Ramsey *IOM* 153 SC4594
Ramsey *Cambs* 52 TL2885
Ramsey *Essex* 41 TM2130
Ramsey Forty Foot *Cambs* 52 TL3087
Ramsey Heights *Cambs* 52 TL2484
Ramsey Island *Essex* 40 TL9405
Ramsey Mereside *Cambs* 52 TL2889
Ramsey St. Mary's *Cambs* 52 TL2587
Ramsgate *Kent* 29 TR3865
Ramsgill *N York* 89 SE1170
Ramshaw *Dur* 95 NY9547
Ramsholt *Suffk* 55 TM3141
Ramshope *Nthumb* 102 NT7304
Ramshorn *Staffs* 73 SK0845
Ramsley *Devon* 8 SX6593
Ramsnest Common *Surrey* 14 SU9432
Ranby *Notts* 75 SK6580
Ranby *Lincs* 76 TF2278
Rand *Lincs* 76 TF1078
Randwick *Gloucs* 35 SO8306
Ranfurly *Strath* 115 NS3865
Rangemore *Staffs* 73 SK1822
Rangeworthy *Avon* 35 ST6986
Rank's Green *Essex* 40 TL7418
Rankinston *Strath* 107 NS4513
Ranksborough *Leics* 63 SK8311
Rann *Lancs* 81 SD7124
Rannoch Station *Tays* 124 NN4257
Ranochan *Highld* 129 NM8282
Ranscombe *Somset* 20 SS9443
Ranskill *Notts* 75 SK6587
Ranton *Staffs* 72 SJ8524
Ranton Green *Staffs* 72 SJ8423
Ranworth *Norfk* 67 TG3514
Raploch *Cent* 116 NS7894
Rapness *Ork* 155 HY5141
Rapps *Somset* 10 ST3316
Rascarrel *D & G* 92 NX7948
Rashfield *Strath* 114 NS1483
Rashwood *H & W* 47 SO9165
Raskelf *N York* 90 SE4971
Rassau *Gwent* 33 SO1511
Rastrick *W York* 82 SE1421
Ratagan *Highld* 138 NG9119
Ratby *Leics* 62 SK5105
Ratcliffe Culey *Leics* 61 SP3299
Ratcliffe on Soar *Notts* 62 SK4928
Ratcliffe on the Wreake *Leics* 63 SK6314
Ratfyn *Wilts* 23 SU1642
Rathen *Gramp* 143 NJ9960
Rathillet *Fife* 126 NO3620
Rathmell *N York* 88 SD8059
Ratho *Loth* 117 NT1370
Rathven *Gramp* 142 NJ4465
Ratlake *Hants* 13 SU4123
Ratley *Warwks* 48 SP3847
Ratling *Kent* 29 TR2453
Ratlinghope *Shrops* 59 SO4096
Rattan Row *Norfk* 65 TF5114
Rattar *Highld* 151 ND2673
Ratten Row *Cumb* 93 NY3240
Ratten Row *Cumb* 93 NY3949
Ratten Row *Lancs* 80 SD4241
Rattery *Devon* 7 SX7461
Rattlesden *Suffk* 54 TL9758
Ratton Village *E Susx* 16 TQ5901
Rattray *Tays* 126 NO1845
Raughton *Cumb* 93 NY3947
Raughton Head *Cumb* 93 NY3745
Raunds *Nhants* 51 SP9972
Raven Meols *Mersyd* 78 SD2905
Ravenfield *S York* 75 SK4895
Ravenglass *Cumb* 86 SD0896
Ravenhills Green *H & W* 47 SO7454
Raveningham *Norfk* 67 TM3996
Ravenscar *N York* 91 NZ9801
Ravenscliffe *Staffs* 72 SJ8452
Ravensdale *IOM* 153 SC3592
Ravensden *Beds* 51 TL0754
Ravenshead *Notts* 75 SK5654
Ravensmoor *Ches* 71 SJ6150
Ravensthorpe *W York* 82 SE2220
Ravensthorpe *Nhants* 50 SP6670
Ravenstone *Leics* 62 SK4013
Ravenstone *Bucks* 38 SP8451
Ravenstonedale *Cumb* 88 NY7203
Ravenstruther *Strath* 116 NS9245
Ravensworth *N York* 89 NZ1308
Raw *N York* 91 NZ9305
Rawcliffe *N York* 83 SE5854
Rawcliffe *Humb* 83 SE6822
Rawcliffe Bridge *Humb* 83 SE6921
Rawdon *W York* 82 SE2139
Rawling Street *Kent* 28 TQ9059
Rawmarsh *S York* 75 SK4396
Rawnsley *Staffs* 60 SK0212
Rawreth *Essex* 40 TQ7893
Rawridge *Devon* 9 ST2006
Rawtenstall *Lancs* 81 SD8123
Raydon *Suffk* 54 TM0438
Raylees *Nthumb* 102 NY9291
Rayleigh *Essex* 40 TQ8090
Raymond Hill *Devon* 10 SY3296
Rayne *Essex* 40 TL7222
Raynes Park *Gt Lon* 26 TQ2368
Rea *Gloucs* 35 SO8016
Reach *Cambs* 53 TL5666
Read *Lancs* 81 SD7634
Reading *Berks* 24 SU7173
Reading Street *Kent* 17 TQ9230
Reading Street *Kent* 29 TR3869
Reagill *Cumb* 94 NY6017
Rearquhar *Highld* 146 NH7492
Rearsby *Leics* 63 SK6514
Rease Heath *Shrops* 72 SJ6454
Reaster *Highld* 151 ND2565
Reay *Highld* 150 NC9664
Reculver *Kent* 29 TR2269
Red Ball *Devon* 9 ST0917
Red Bull *Ches* 72 SJ8254
Red Cross *Cnwll* 18 SS2605
Red Cross *Cambs* 53 TL4754
Red Dial *Cumb* 93 NY2546
Red Hill *Warwks* 48 SP1356
Red Hill *Dorset* 12 SZ0995
Red Lumb *Gt Man* 81 SD8415
Red Rock *Gt Man* 78 SD5809
Red Roses *Dyfed* 31 SN2011
Red Row *T & W* 103 NZ2599
Red Street *Staffs* 72 SJ8251
Red Wharf Bay *Gwynd* 68 SH5281
Redberth *Dyfed* 31 SN0804
Redbourn *Herts* 38 TL1012
Redbourne *Lincs* 76 SK9799
Redbrook *Clwyd* 71 SJ5041
Redbrook *Gloucs* 34 SO5309
Redbrook Street *Kent* 28 TQ9336
Redburn *Highld* 140 NH9447
Redburn *Nthumb* 102 NY7764
Redcar *Cleve* 97 NZ6024
Redcastle *Highld* 139 NH5849
Redcastle *D & G* 100 NX8165
Redding *Cent* 116 NS9278
Reddingmuirhead *Cent* 116 NS9177
Reddish *Gt Man* 79 SJ8993
Redditch *H & W* 48 SP0467
Rede *Suffk* 54 TL8055
Redenhall *Norfk* 55 TM2684
Redenham *Hants* 23 SU3049
Redesmouth *Nthumb* 102 NY8682
Redford *Tays* 127 NO5644
Redford *Gramp* 135 NO7570
Redford *W Susx* 14 SU8626
Redfordgreen *Border* 109 NT3616
Redgate *M Glam* 33 ST0188
Redgorton *Tays* 125 NO0828
Redgrave *Suffk* 54 TM0477
Redhill *Gramp* 135 NJ7704
Redhill *Avon* 21 ST4962
Redhill *Herts* 39 TL3033
Redhill *Surrey* 27 TQ2750
Redisham *Suffk* 55 TM4084
Redland *Ork* 155 HY3724
Redland *Avon* 34 ST5775
Redlingfield *Suffk* 54 TM1870
Redlingfield Green *Suffk* 54 TM1871
Redlodge *Suffk* 53 TL6970
Redlynch *Somset* 22 ST7033
Redlynch *Wilts* 12 SU2021
Redmain *Cumb* 92 NY1333
Redmarley *H & W* 47 SO7666
Redmarley D'Abitot *Gloucs* 47 SO7531
Redmarshall *Cleve* 96 NZ3821
Redmile *Leics* 63 SK7935
Redmire *N York* 88 SE0491
Redmyre *Gramp* 135 NO7575
Rednal *Shrops* 59 SJ3628
Rednal *W Mids* 60 SP0076
Redpath *Border* 110 NT5835
Redruth *Cnwll* 2 SW6942
Redstocks *Wilts* 22 ST9362
Redstone *Tays* 126 NO1834
Redvales *Gt Man* 79 SD8008
Redwick *Gwent* 34 ST4184
Redwick *Avon* 34 ST5486
Redworth *Dur* 96 NZ2423
Reed *Herts* 39 TL3636
Reedham *Norfk* 67 TG4201
Reedness *Humb* 84 SE7923
Reeds Holme *Lancs* 81 SD8024
Reepham *Lincs* 76 TF0473
Reepham *Norfk* 66 TG1022
Reeth *N York* 88 SE0399
Reeves Green *W Mids* 61 SP2677
Reiff *Highld* 144 NB9614
Reigate *Surrey* 27 TQ2550
Reighton *N York* 91 TA1375
Reisque *Gramp* 143 NJ8819
Reiss *Highld* 151 ND3354
Rejerrah *Cnwll* 3 SW7956
Releath *Cnwll* 2 SW6532
Relubbus *Cnwll* 2 SW5631
Relugas *Gramp* 141 NH9948
Remenham *Berks* 37 SU7684
Remenham Hill *Berks* 37 SU7882
Remony *Tays* 124 NN7644
Rempstone *Notts* 62 SK5724
Rendcomb *Gloucs* 35 SP0209
Rendham *Suffk* 55 TM3464
Renfrew *Strath* 115 NS5067
Renhold *Beds* 38 TL0852
Renishaw *Derbys* 75 SK4577
Rennington *Nthumb* 111 NU2118
Renswick *Cumb* 94 NY5943
Renton *Strath* 115 NS3877
Repps *Norfk* 67 TG4217
Repton *Derbys* 73 SK3026
Resaurie *Highld* 140 NH7045
Rescassa *Cnwll* 3 SW9842
Rescorla *Cnwll* 3 SW9848
Resipole *Highld* 121 NM7264
Reskadinnick *Cnwll* 2 SW6341
Resolis *Highld* 140 NH6765
Resolven *W Glam* 33 SN8302
Rest and be Thankful *Strath* 123 NN2307
Reston *Border* 119 NT8862
Restronguet *Cnwll* 3 SW8136
Reswallie *Tays* 127 NO5051
Reterth *Cnwll* 4 SW9463
Retew *Cnwll* 4 SW9257
Retford *Notts* 75 SK7081
Retire *Cnwll* 4 SX0064
Rettendon *Essex* 40 TQ7698
Retyn *Cnwll* 4 SW8858
Revesby *Lincs* 77 TF2961
Rew *Devon* 7 SX7570
Rew Street *IOW* 13 SZ4794
Rewe *Devon* 9 SX9499
Rexon *Devon* 5 SX4188
Reydon *Suffk* 55 TM4977
Reymerston *Norfk* 66 TG0206
Reynalton *Dyfed* 31 SN0908
Reynoldston *W Glam* 32 SS4889
Rezare *Cnwll* 5 SX3677
Rhadyr *Gwent* 34 SO3602
Rhandirmwyn *Dyfed* 44 SN7843
Rhayader *Powys* 45 SN9768
Rheindown *Highld* 139 NH5147
Rhes-y-cae *Clwyd* 70 SJ1871
Rhewl *Clwyd* 70 SJ1060
Rhewl *Clwyd* 70 SJ1744
Rhewl Mostyn *Clwyd* 70 SJ1580
Rhewl-fawr *Clwyd* 70 SJ1381
Rhicarn *Highld* 148 NC0825
Rhiconich *Highld* 148 NC2552
Rhicullen *Highld* 146 NH6971
Rhigos *M Glam* 33 SN9205
Rhireavach *Highld* 144 NH0295
Rhives *Highld* 147 NC8200
Rhiwbina *S Glam* 33 ST1682
Rhiwbryfdir *Gwynd* 57 SH6946
Rhiwderyn *Gwent* 34 ST2687
Rhiwen *Gwynd* 69 SH5763
Rhiwinder *M Glam* 33 ST0287
Rhiwlas *Gwynd* 69 SH5765
Rhiwlas *Gwynd* 58 SH9237
Rhiwlas *Clwyd* 58 SJ1932
Rhiwsaeson *M Glam* 33 ST0682
Rhode *Somset* 20 ST2734
Rhoden Green *Kent* 28 TQ6845
Rhodes *Gt Man* 79 SD8505
Rhodes Minnis *Kent* 29 TR1542
Rhodesia *Notts* 75 SK5679
Rhodiad-y-brenin *Dyfed* 30 SM7627
Rhonehouse or Kelton Hill *D & G* 99 NX7459
Rhoose *S Glam* 20 ST0666
Rhos *Clwyd* 70 SJ1261
Rhos *Dyfed* 31 SN3835
Rhos *W Glam* 32 SN7302
Rhos *Powys* 45 SO1731
Rhos Haminiog *Dyfed* 43 SN5464
Rhos Lligwy *Gwynd* 68 SH4886
Rhos y-brithdir *Powys* 58 SJ1323
Rhos-fawr *Gwynd* 56 SH3838
Rhos-hill *Dyfed* 31 SN1940
Rhos-on-Sea *Clwyd* 69 SH8480
Rhos-y-garth *Dyfed* 43 SN6373
Rhos-y-gwaliau *Gwynd* 58 SH9434
Rhos-y-llan *Gwynd* 56 SH2337
Rhos-y-meirch *Powys* 46 SO2769
Rhoscefnhir *Gwynd* 68 SH5276
Rhoscolyn *Gwynd* 68 SH2267
Rhoscrowther *Dyfed* 30 SM9002
Rhosesmor *Clwyd* 70 SJ2168
Rhosgadfan *Gwynd* 68 SH5057
Rhosgoch *Gwynd* 68 SH4089
Rhosgoch *Powys* 45 SO1847
Rhoshirwaun *Gwynd* 56 SH2029
Rhoslan *Gwynd* 56 SH4840
Rhosllanerchrugog *Clwyd* 71 SJ2946
Rhosmaen *Dyfed* 44 SN6423
Rhosmeirch *Gwynd* 68 SH4677
Rhosneigr *Gwynd* 68 SH3173
Rhosnesni *Clwyd* 71 SJ3550
Rhosrobin *Clwyd* 71 SJ3252
Rhossili *W Glam* 31 SS4187
Rhostryfan *Gwynd* 68 SH4957
Rhostyllen *Clwyd* 71 SJ3148
Rhosybol *Gwynd* 68 SH4288
Rhosygadfa *Shrops* 59 SJ3234
Rhosymedre *Clwyd* 70 SJ2842
Rhu *Strath* 115 NS2684
Rhuallt *Clwyd* 70 SJ0775
Rhubodach *Strath* 114 NS0273
Rhuddall Heath *Ches* 71 SJ5562
Rhuddlan *Clwyd* 70 SJ0278
Rhulen *Powys* 45 SO1349
Rhunahaorine *Strath* 105 NR7048
Rhyd *Gwynd* 57 SH6341
Rhyd-Ddu *Gwynd* 69 SH5652
Rhyd-lydan *Clwyd* 69 SH8950
Rhyd-uchaf *Gwynd* 58 SH9037
Rhyd-y pennau *Dyfed* 43 SN6385
Rhyd-y-clafdy *Gwynd* 56 SH3234
Rhyd-y-foel *Clwyd* 70 SH9176
Rhyd-y-groes *Gwynd* 69 SH5867
Rhyd-y-meirch *Gwent* 34 SO3107
Rhyd-y-sarn *Gwynd* 57 SH6842
Rhyd-yr-onnen *Gwynd* 57 SH6102
Rhydargaeau *Dyfed* 31 SN4326
Rhydcymerau *Dyfed* 44 SN5738
Rhydd *H & W* 47 SO8345
Rhydding *W Glam* 32 SS7499
Rhyddlan *Dyfed* 44 SN4943
Rhydgaled *Clwyd* 70 SH9964
Rhydlanfair *Gwynd* 69 SH8252
Rhydlewis *Dyfed* 42 SN3447
Rhydlios *Gwynd* 56 SH1929
Rhydowen *Dyfed* 42 SN4445
Rhydrosser *Dyfed* 43 SN5667
Rhydspence *H & W* 46 SO2447
Rhydtalog *Clwyd* 70 SJ2354
Rhydycroesau *Shrops* 58 SJ2430
Rhydyfelin *Dyfed* 43 SN5979
Rhydyfelin *M Glam* 33 ST0988
Rhydyfro *W Glam* 32 SN7105
Rhydymain *Gwynd* 57 SH7821
Rhydymwyn *Clwyd* 70 SJ2066
Rhyl *Clwyd* 70 SJ0081
Rhymney *M Glam* 33 SO1107
Rhynd *Tays* 126 NO1520
Rhynie *Highld* 147 NH8479
Rhynie *Gramp* 142 NJ4927
Ribbesford *H & W* 60 SO7874
Ribbleton *Lancs* 81 SD5631
Ribby *Lancs* 80 SD4031
Ribchester *Lancs* 81 SD6535
Riber *Derbys* 74 SK3059
Riby *Lincs* 85 TA1807
Riccall *N York* 83 SE6237
Riccarton *Strath* 107 NS4236
Riccarton *Border* 101 NY5494
Richards Castle *H & W* 46 SO4969
Richings Park *Bucks* 26 TQ0278
Richmond *N York* 89 NZ1701
Richmond *S York* 74 SK4085
Richmond Fort *Guern* 152 GN0000
Richmond upon Thames *Gt Lon* 26 TQ1774
Richs Halford *Somset* 20 ST1434
Rickerscote *Staffs* 72 SJ9220
Rickford *Avon* 21 ST4859
Rickham *Devon* 7 SX7537
Rickinghall Inferior *Suffk* 54 TM0475
Rickinghall Superior *Suffk* 54 TM0375
Rickling *Essex* 39 TL4931
Rickling Green *Essex* 39 TL5129
Rickmansworth *Herts* 26 TQ0694
Riddell *Border* 109 NT5124
Riddings *Cumb* 101 NY4075
Riddings *Derbys* 74 SK4252
Riddlecombe *Devon* 19 SS6113
Riddlesden *W York* 82 SE0742
Ridge *Avon* 21 ST5556
Ridge *Wilts* 22 ST9531
Ridge *Dorset* 11 SY9386
Ridge *Herts* 26 TL2100
Ridge Green *Surrey* 15 TQ3048
Ridge Lane *Warwks* 61 SP2994
Ridge Row *Kent* 29 TR2042
Ridgebourne *Powys* 45 SO0560
Ridgehill *Avon* 21 ST5462
Ridgeway *Derbys* 74 SK3551
Ridgeway *Derbys* 74 SK4081
Ridgeway *H & W* 48 SP0461
Ridgeway Cross *H & W* 47 SO7147
Ridgewell *Essex* 53 TL7340
Ridgewood *E Susx* 16 TQ4719
Ridgmont *Beds* 38 SP9736
Riding Mill *Nthumb* 103 NZ0161
Ridley *Nthumb* 102 NY7963
Ridley *Kent* 27 TQ6164
Ridley Green *Ches* 71 SJ5554
Ridlington *Leics* 63 SK8402
Ridlington *Norfk* 67 TG3430
Ridlington Street *Norfk* 67 TG3430
Ridsdale *Nthumb* 102 NY9084
Rievaulx *N York* 90 SE5785
Rigg *D & G* 101 NY2966
Riggend *Strath* 116 NS7670
Righoul *Highld* 140 NH8851
Rigmadon Park *Cumb* 87 SD6184
Rigsby *Lincs* 77 TF4375
Rigside *Strath* 108 NS8735
Riley Green *Lancs* 81 SD6225
Rileyhill *Staffs* 61 SK1114
Rilla Mill *Cnwll* 5 SX2973
Rillaton *Cnwll* 5 SX2973
Rillington *N York* 90 SE8574
Rimington *Lancs* 81 SD8045
Rimpton *Somset* 21 ST6121
Rimswell *Humb* 85 TA3128
Rinaston *Dyfed* 30 SM9825
Rindleford *Shrops* 60 SO7395
Ring o'Bells *Lancs* 78 SD4510
Ring's End *Cambs* 65 TF3902
Ringford *D & G* 99 NX6957
Ringinglow *Derbys* 74 SK2883
Ringland *Norfk* 66 TG1313
Ringles Cross *E Susx* 16 TQ4722
Ringlestone *Kent* 28 TQ8755
Ringley *Gt Man* 79 SD7605
Ringmer *E Susx* 16 TQ4412
Ringmore *Devon* 7 SX6546
Ringmore *Devon* 7 SX9272
Ringorm *Gramp* 141 NJ2644
Ringsfield *Suffk* 55 TM4088
Ringsfield Corner *Suffk* 55 TM4087
Ringshall *Bucks* 38 SP9814
Ringshall *Suffk* 54 TM0452
Ringshall Stocks *Suffk* 54 TM0551
Ringstead *Nhants* 51 SP9875
Ringstead *Norfk* 65 TF7040
Ringwood *Hants* 12 SU1505

Ringwould Salfords

Ringwould *Kent* 29 TR3548
Rinsey *Cnwll* 2 SW5927
Ripe *E Susx* 16 TQ5110
Ripley *N York* 89 SE2860
Ripley *Derbys* 74 SK3950
Ripley *Hants* 12 SZ1698
Ripley *Surrey* 26 TQ0556
Riplingham *Humb* 84 SE9631
Riplington *Hants* 13 SU6623
Ripon *N York* 89 SE3171
Rippingale *Lincs* 64 TF0927
Ripple *H & W* 47 SO8737
Ripple *Kent* 29 TR3550
Ripponden *W York* 82 SE0319
Risabus *Strath* 104 NR3143
Risbury *H & W* 46 SO5455
Risby *Humb* 84 SE9114
Risby *Suffk* 54 TL8066
Risca *Gwent* 34 ST2391
Rise *Humb* 85 TA1542
Riseden *E Susx* 16 TQ6130
Risedown *Kent* 28 TQ7036
Risegate *Lincs* 64 TF2129
Riseholme *Lincs* 76 SK9775
Risehow *Cumb* 92 NY0234
Riseley *Berks* 24 SU7263
Riseley *Beds* 51 TL0462
Rishangles *Suffk* 54 TM1668
Rishton *Lancs* 81 SD7230
Rishworth *W York* 82 SE0318
Rising Bridge *Lancs* 81 SD7825
Risley *Cambs* 79 SJ6592
Risley *Derbys* 62 SK4535
Risplith *N York* 89 SE2468
Rivar *Wilts* 23 SU3161
Rivenhall End *Essex* 40 TL8316
River *W Susx* 14 SU9323
River *Kent* 29 TR2943
River Bank *Cambs* 53 TL5368
Riverford *Highld* 139 NH5454
Riverhead *Kent* 27 TQ5156
Rivers Corner *Dorset* 11 ST7712
Rivington *Lancs* 81 SD6214
Road Ashton *Wilts* 22 ST8856
Road Green *Norfk* 67 TM2693
Road Weedon *Nhants* 49 SP6359
Roade *Nhants* 49 SP7651
Roadhead *Cumb* 101 NY5174
Roadmeetings *Strath* 116 NS8649
Roadside *Highld* 151 ND1560
Roadside *Strath* 107 NS5717
Roadside of Catterline *Gramp* 135 NO8579
Roadside of Kinneff *Gramp* 135 NO8477
Roadwater *Somset* 20 ST0338
Roag *Highld* 136 NG2744
Roan of Craigoch *Strath* 106 NS2904
Roast Green *Essex* 39 TL4632
Roath *S Glam* 33 ST1977
Roberton *Strath* 108 NS9428
Roberton *Border* 109 NT4214
Robertsbridge *E Susx* 17 TQ7423
Roberttown *W York* 82 SE1922
Robeston Wathen *Dyfed* 31 SN0815
Robgill Tower *D & G* 101 NY2471
Robin Hill *Staffs* 72 SJ9057
Robin Hood *Lancs* 80 SD5211
Robin Hood *W York* 83 SE3227
Robin Hood's Bay *N York* 91 NZ9505
Robinhood End *Essex* 53 TL7036
Roborough *Devon* 19 SS5717
Roby *Mersyd* 78 SJ4390
Roby Mill *Lancs* 78 SD5107
Rocester *Staffs* 73 SK1039
Roch *Dyfed* 30 SM8821
Roch Gate *Dyfed* 30 SM8720
Rochdale *Gt Man* 81 SD8913
Roche *Cnwll* 4 SW9860
Rochester *Nthumb* 102 NY8298
Rochester *Kent* 28 TQ7468
Rochford *H & W* 47 SO6268
Rochford *Essex* 40 TQ8790
Rochville *Strath* 114 NS2390
Rock *Nthumb* 111 NU2020
Rock *H & W* 60 SO7371
Rock *W Glam* 32 SS7893
Rock *Cnwll* 4 SW9375
Rock *W Susx* 14 TQ1213
Rock Ferry *Mersyd* 78 SJ3386
Rock Hill *H & W* 47 SO9569
Rockbeare *Devon* 9 SY0194
Rockbourne *Hants* 12 SU1118
Rockcliffe *D & G* 92 NX8454
Rockcliffe *Cumb* 101 NY3561
Rockcliffe Cross *Cumb* 101 NY3463
Rockesta *Cnwll* 2 SW3722
Rockfield *Highld* 147 NH9282
Rockfield *Gwent* 34 SO4814
Rockford *Devon* 19 SS7547
Rockford *Hants* 12 SU1607
Rockgreen *Shrops* 46 SO5275
Rockhampton *Gloucs* 35 ST6593
Rockhead *Cnwll* 4 SX0784
Rockhill *Shrops* 46 SO2978
Rockingham *Nhants* 51 SP8691
Rockland All Saints *Norfk* 66 TL9996
Rockland St. Mary *Norfk* 67 TG3104
Rockland St. Peter *Norfk* 66 TL9897
Rockley *Notts* 75 SK7174
Rockley *Wilts* 36 SU1571
Rockliffe *Lancs* 81 SD8722
Rockwell End *Bucks* 37 SU7988
Rockwell Green *Somset* 20 ST1220
Rookwith *N York* 89 SE2086
Rodborough *Gloucs* 35 SO8404
Rodborough *Wilts* 36 SU1485
Rodbourne *Wilts* 35 ST9383
Rodd *H & W* 46 SO3262
Rodden *Dorset* 10 SY6184
Roddham *Nthumb* 111 NU0220
Roddymoor *Dur* 96 NZ1536
Rode *Somset* 22 ST8053
Rode Heath *Ches* 72 SJ8056
Rode Heath *Ches* 72 SJ8767
Rodel *W Isls* 154 NG0483
Roden *Shrops* 59 SJ5716
Rodhuish *Somset* 20 ST0139
Rodington *Shrops* 59 SJ5814
Rodington Heath *Shrops* 59 SJ5814
Rodley *W York* 82 SE2236
Rodley *Gloucs* 35 SO7411
Rodmarton *Gloucs* 35 ST9498
Rodmell *E Susx* 15 TQ4106
Rodmersham *Kent* 28 TQ9261
Rodmersham Green *Kent* 28 TQ9161
Rodney Stoke *Somset* 21 ST4849
Rodono Hotel *Border* 109 NT2321
Rodsley *Derbys* 73 SK2040
Rodway *Somset* 20 ST2540
Roe Cross *Gt Man* 79 SJ9896
Roe Green *Gt Man* 79 SD7501
Roe Green *Herts* 39 TL2107
Roe Green *Herts* 39 TL3133
Roecliffe *N York* 89 SE3765
Roehampton *Gt Lon* 26 TQ2273
Roewen *Gwynd* 69 SH7671
Roffey *W Susx* 15 TQ1932
Rogart *Highld* 146 NC7304
Rogate *W Susx* 14 SU8023
Roger Ground *Cumb* 87 SD3597
Rogerstone *Gwent* 34 ST2787
Rogiet *Gwent* 34 ST4587
Roke *Oxon* 37 SU6293
Roker *T & W* 96 NZ4058
Rollesby *Norfk* 67 TG4416
Rolleston *Staffs* 73 SK2327
Rolleston *Leics* 50 SK7300
Rolleston *Notts* 75 SK7452
Rolston *Humb* 85 TA2144
Rolstone *Avon* 21 ST3962
Rolvenden *Kent* 17 TQ8431
Rolvenden Layne *Kent* 17 TQ8530
Romaldkirk *Dur* 95 NY9922
Romanby *N York* 89 SE3693
Romanno Bridge *Border* 117 NT1647
Romansleigh *Devon* 19 SS7220
Romden Castle *Kent* 28 TQ8941
Romesdal *Highld* 136 NG4053
Romford *Dorset* 12 SU0709
Romford *Gt Lon* 27 TQ5188
Romiley *Gt Man* 79 SJ9490
Romney Street *Kent* 27 TQ5561
Romsey *Hants* 12 SU3521
Romsley *Shrops* 60 SO7883
Romsley *H & W* 60 SO9680
Ronachan *Strath* 113 NR7454
Rookhope *Dur* 95 NY9342
Rookley *IOW* 13 SZ5084
Rookley Green *IOW* 13 SZ5083
Rooks Bridge *Somset* 21 ST3652
Rooks Nest *Somset* 20 ST0933
Roos *Humb* 85 TA2830
Roosebeck *Cumb* 86 SD2567
Roothams Green *Beds* 51 TL0957
Ropley *Hants* 24 SU6431
Ropley Dean *Hants* 24 SU6232
Ropley Soke *Hants* 24 SU6533
Ropsley *Lincs* 63 SK9933
Rora *Gramp* 143 NK0650
Rorrington *Shrops* 59 SJ3000
Rosarie *Gramp* 141 NJ3850
Roscroggan *Cnwll* 2 SW6542
Rose *Cnwll* 3 SW7754
Rose Ash *Devon* 19 SS7921
Rose Green *W Susx* 14 SZ9099
Rose Green *Essex* 40 TL9028
Rose Green *Suffk* 54 TL9337
Rose Green *Suffk* 54 TL9744
Rose Hill *Lancs* 81 SD8231
Rose Hill *E Susx* 16 TQ4516
Rose Lands *E Susx* 16 TQ6200
Roseacre *Lancs* 80 SD4336
Rosebank *Strath* 116 NS8049
Rosebush *Dyfed* 31 SN0729
Rosecare *Cnwll* 4 SX1695
Rosecliston *Cnwll* 4 SW8159
Rosedale Abbey *N York* 90 SE7296
Roseden *Nthumb* 111 NU0321
Rosehall *Highld* 146 NC4701
Rosehearty *Gramp* 143 NJ9267
Rosehill *Shrops* 59 SJ4715
Roseisle *Gramp* 141 NJ1466
Rosemarket *Dyfed* 30 SM9508
Rosemarkie *Highld* 140 NH7357
Rosemary Lane *Devon* 9 ST1514
Rosemount *Tays* 126 NO1843
Rosenannon *Cnwll* 4 SW9566
Rosenithon *Cnwll* 3 SW8021
Roser's Cross *E Susx* 16 TQ5420
Rosevean *Cnwll* 4 SX0258
Rosevine *Cnwll* 3 SW8736
Rosewarne *Cnwll* 2 SW6036
Rosewell *Loth* 117 NT2862
Roseworth *Cleve* 96 NZ4221
Roseworthy *Cnwll* 2 SW6139
Rosgill *Cumb* 94 NY5316
Roshven *Highld* 129 NM7078
Roskhill *Highld* 136 NG2744
Roskorwell *Cnwll* 3 SW7923
Roskrow *Cnwll* 3 SW7635
Rosley *Cumb* 93 NY3245
Roslin *Loth* 117 NT2763
Rosliston *Derbys* 73 SK2416
Rosneath *Strath* 114 NS2583
Ross *Nthumb* 111 NU1337
Ross *D & G* 99 NX6444
Ross-on-Wye *H & W* 46 SO5923
Rossett *Clwyd* 71 SJ3657
Rossett Green *N York* 82 SE2952
Rossington *Notts* 75 SK6298
Rosskeen *Highld* 146 NH6869
Rossland *Strath* 115 NS4370
Roster *Highld* 151 ND2639
Rostherne *Ches* 79 SJ7483
Rosthwaite *Cumb* 93 NY2514
Roston *Derbys* 73 SK1340
Rosudgeon *Cnwll* 2 SW5529
Rosyth *Loth* 117 NT1082
Rothbury *Nthumb* 103 NU0501
Rotheirnorman *Gramp* 142 NJ7235
Rotherby *Leics* 63 SK6716
Rotherfield *E Susx* 16 TQ5529
Rotherfield Greys *Oxon* 37 SU7282
Rotherham *S York* 75 SK4392
Rothersthorpe *Nhants* 49 SP7156
Rotherwick *Hants* 24 SU7156
Rothes *Gramp* 141 NJ2749
Rothesay *Strath* 114 NS0864
Rothiebrisbane *Gramp* 142 NJ7437
Rothiemay *Gramp* 142 NJ5548
Rothley *Nthumb* 103 NZ0488
Rothley *Leics* 62 SK5812
Rothmaise *Gramp* 142 NJ6832
Rothwell *W York* 83 SE3428
Rothwell *Nhants* 51 SP8181
Rothwell *Lincs* 76 TF1499
Rothwell Haigh *W York* 83 SE3328
Rotsea *Humb* 84 TA0651
Rottal Lodge *Tays* 134 NO3769
Rottingdean *E Susx* 15 TQ3602
Rottington *Cumb* 92 NX9613
Roucan *D & G* 100 NY0277
Roud *IOW* 13 SZ5180
Rough Close *Staffs* 72 SJ9239
Rough Common *Kent* 29 TR1259
Rougham *Norfk* 66 TF8320
Rougham Green *Suffk* 54 TL9061
Roughlee *Lancs* 81 SD8440
Roughley *W Mids* 61 SP1399
Roughton *Shrops* 60 SO7594
Roughton *Lincs* 77 TF2464
Roughton *Norfk* 67 TG2136
Roughway *Kent* 27 TQ6153
Round Bush *Herts* 26 TQ1498
Round Street *Kent* 28 TQ6568
Roundbush *Essex* 40 TL8501
Roundbush Green *Essex* 40 TL5814
Roundham *Somset* 10 ST4209
Roundhay *W York* 83 SE3337
Rounds Green *W Mids* 60 SO9889
Roundstreet Common *W Susx* 14 TQ0528
Roundway *Wilts* 22 SU0163
Roundyhill *Tays* 126 NO3750
Rous Lench *H & W* 47 SP0153
Rousdon *Devon* 10 SY2991
Rousham *Oxon* 49 SP4724
Rout's Green *Bucks* 37 SU7898
Routenbeck *Cumb* 93 NY1930
Routenburn *Strath* 114 NS1961
Routh *Humb* 85 TA0942
Row *Cumb* 94 NY6234
Row *Cumb* 87 SD4589
Row *Cnwll* 4 SX0976
Row Ash *Hants* 13 SU5413
Row Green *Essex* 40 TL7420
Rowanburn *D & G* 101 NY4177
Rowardennan Hotel *Cent* 115 NS3698
Rowarth *Derbys* 79 SK0189
Rowberrow *Somset* 21 ST4558
Rowborough *IOW* 13 SZ4684
Rowde *Wilts* 22 ST9762
Rowden *Devon* 8 SX6499
Rowfield *Derbys* 73 SK1948
Rowfoot *Nthumb* 102 NY6860
Rowford *Somset* 20 ST2327
Rowhedge *Essex* 41 TM0221
Rowhook *W Susx* 14 TQ1234
Rowington *Warwks* 48 SP2069
Rowland *Derbys* 74 SK2172
Rowland's Castle *Hants* 13 SU7310
Rowland's Gill *T & W* 96 NZ1658
Rowledge *Surrey* 25 SU8243
Rowley *Dur* 95 NZ0848
Rowley *Humb* 84 SE9732
Rowley *Shrops* 59 SJ3006
Rowley Green *W Mids* 61 SP3483
Rowley Hill *W York* 82 SE1914
Rowley Regis *W Mids* 60 SO9787
Rowlstone *H & W* 46 SO3727
Rowly *Surrey* 14 TQ0440
Rowner *Hants* 13 SU5801
Rowney Green *H & W* 61 SP0471
Rownhams *Hants* 12 SU3817
Rows of Trees *Ches* 79 SJ8379
Rowsham *Bucks* 38 SP8417
Rowsley *Derbys* 74 SK2565
Rowstock *Oxon* 37 SU4789
Rowston *Lincs* 76 TF0856
Rowthorne *Derbys* 75 SK4764
Rowton *Shrops* 59 SJ3612
Rowton *Ches* 71 SJ4564
Rowton *Shrops* 59 SJ6119
Rowton *Shrops* 59 SO4180
Rowtown *Surrey* 26 TQ0363
Roxburgh *Border* 110 NT6930
Roxby *N York* 97 NZ7616
Roxby *Humb* 84 SE9116
Roxton *Beds* 52 TL1554
Roxwell *Essex* 40 TL6408
Roy Bridge *Highld* 131 NN2681
Royal Leamington Spa *Warwks* 48 SP3265
Royal Oak *Dur* 96 NZ2023
Royal Oak *Lancs* 78 SD4103
Royal Tunbridge Wells *Kent* 16 TQ5839
Royal's Green *Ches* 71 SJ6242
Roydhouse *W York* 82 SE2112
Roydon *Norfk* 65 TF7023
Roydon *Essex* 39 TL4010
Roydon *Norfk* 54 TM1080
Roydon Hamlet *Essex* 39 TL4107
Royston *S York* 83 SE3611
Royston *Herts* 39 TL3540
Royton *Gt Man* 79 SD9107
Rozel *Jersey* 152 JS0000
Ruabon *Clwyd* 71 SJ3043
Ruaig *Strath* 120 NM0747
Ruan High Lanes *Cnwll* 3 SW9039
Ruan Lanihorne *Cnwll* 3 SW8942
Ruan Major *Cnwll* 2 SW7016
Ruan Minor *Cnwll* 2 SW7115
Ruardean *Gloucs* 35 SO6217
Ruardean Hill *Gloucs* 35 SO6317
Ruardean Woodside *Gloucs* 35 SO6216
Rubery *H & W* 60 SO9977
Ruckcroft *Cumb* 94 NY5344
Ruckhall Common *H & W* 46 SO4539
Ruckinge *Kent* 17 TR0233
Ruckland *Lincs* 77 TF3378
Ruckley *Shrops* 59 SJ5300
Rudby *N York* 89 NZ4706
Rudchester *Nthumb* 103 NZ1167
Ruddington *Notts* 62 SK5732
Ruddle *Gloucs* 35 SO6811
Ruddlemoor *Cnwll* 3 SX0054
Rudford *Gloucs* 35 SO7721
Rudge *Somset* 22 ST8251
Rudgeway *Avon* 35 ST6386
Rudgwick *W Susx* 14 TQ0834
Rudhall *H & W* 47 SO6225
Rudheath *Ches* 79 SJ7471
Rudley Green *Essex* 40 TL8303
Rudry *M Glam* 33 ST2086
Rudston *Humb* 91 TA0967
Rudyard *Staffs* 72 SJ9557
Ruecastle *Border* 110 NT6120
Rufford *Lancs* 80 SD4615
Rufforth *N York* 83 SE5251
Rug *Clwyd* 70 SJ0543
Rugby *Warwks* 50 SP5075
Rugeley *Staffs* 73 SK0418
Ruggaton *Devon* 19 SS5545
Ruishton *Somset* 20 ST2625
Ruislip *Gt Lon* 26 TQ0987
Ruletown Head *Border* 110 NT6113
Rumbach *Gramp* 141 NJ3852
Rumbling Bridge *Tays* 117 NT0199
Rumburgh *Suffk* 55 TM3481
Rumby Hill *Dur* 96 NZ1634
Rumford *Cent* 116 NS9377
Rumford *Cnwll* 4 SW8970
Rumney *S Glam* 33 ST2178
Rumwell *Somset* 20 ST1923
Runcorn *Ches* 78 SJ5182
Runcton *W Susx* 14 SU8802
Runcton Holme *Norfk* 65 TF6109
Runfold *Surrey* 25 SU8647
Runhall *Norfk* 66 TG0507
Runham *Norfk* 67 TG4610
Runham *Norfk* 67 TG5108
Running Waters *Dur* 96 NZ3240
Runnington *Somset* 20 ST1221
Runsell Green *Essex* 40 TL7905
Runshaw Moor *Lancs* 80 SD5319
Runswick *N York* 97 NZ8016
Runtaleave *Tays* 133 NO2867
Runwell *Essex* 40 TQ7594
Ruscombe *Berks* 37 SU7976
Rush Green *Ches* 79 SJ6987
Rush Green *Herts* 39 TL2123
Rush Green *Herts* 39 TL3325
Rush Green *Essex* 41 TM1515
Rush Green *Gt Lon* 27 TQ5187
Rushall *W Mids* 60 SK0200
Rushall *H & W* 47 SO6435
Rushall *Wilts* 23 SU1255
Rushall *Norfk* 55 TM1982
Rushbrooke *Suffk* 54 TL8961
Rushbury *Shrops* 59 SO5191
Rushden *Nhants* 51 SP9566
Rushden *Herts* 39 TL3031
Rushenden *Kent* 28 TQ9071
Rusher's Cross *E Susx* 16 TQ6028
Rushett Common *Surrey* 14 TQ0242
Rushford *Devon* 5 SX4576
Rushford *Norfk* 54 TL9281
Rushlake Green *E Susx* 16 TQ6218
Rushmere *Suffk* 55 TM4986
Rushmere St. Andrew *Suffk* 55 TM1946
Rushmoor *Surrey* 25 SU8740
Rushock *H & W* 46 SO3058
Rushock *H & W* 60 SO8871
Rusholme *Gt Man* 79 SJ8594
Rushton *Ches* 71 SJ5863
Rushton *Shrops* 59 SJ6008
Rushton *Nhants* 51 SP8482
Rushton Spencer *Staffs* 72 SJ9362
Rushwick *H & W* 47 SO8254
Rushyford *Dur* 96 NZ2828
Ruskie *Cent* 116 NN6200
Ruskington *Lincs* 76 TF0851
Rusland *Cumb* 87 SD3488
Rusper *W Susx* 15 TQ2037
Ruspidge *Gloucs* 35 SO6611
Russ Hill *Surrey* 15 TQ2240
Russel's Green *Suffk* 55 TM2572
Russell Green *Essex* 40 TL7413
Russell's Green *E Susx* 16 TQ7011
Russell's Water *Oxon* 37 SU7089
Rusthall *Kent* 16 TQ5639
Rustington *W Susx* 14 TQ0402
Ruston *N York* 91 SE9583
Ruston Parva *Humb* 91 TA0661
Ruswarp *N York* 90 NZ8809
Ruthall *Shrops* 59 SO5990
Rutherford *Border* 110 NT6430
Rutherglen *Strath* 116 NS6161
Ruthernbridge *Cnwll* 4 SX0166
Ruthin *Clwyd* 70 SJ1258
Ruthrieston *Gramp* 135 NJ9204
Ruthven *Highld* 140 NH8132
Ruthven *Gramp* 142 NJ5046
Ruthven *Highld* 132 NN7699
Ruthven *Tays* 126 NO2848
Ruthven House *Tays* 126 NO3047
Ruthvoes *Cnwll* 4 SW9260
Ruthwaite *Cumb* 93 NY2336
Ruthwell *D & G* 100 NY0967
Ruxley Corner *Gt Lon* 27 TQ4770
Ruxton Green *H & W* 34 SO5419
Ruyton-XI-Towns *Shrops* 59 SJ3922
Ryal *Nthumb* 103 NZ0174
Ryall *H & W* 47 SO8640
Ryall *Dorset* 10 SY4095
Ryarsh *Kent* 28 TQ6660
Rycote *Oxon* 37 SP6705
Rydal *Cumb* 87 NY3606
Ryde *IOW* 13 SZ5992
Rye *E Susx* 17 TQ9220
Rye Cross *H & W* 47 SO7735
Rye Foreign *E Susx* 17 TQ8922
Rye Harbour *E Susx* 17 TQ9319
Rye Street *H & W* 47 SO7835
Ryebank *Shrops* 59 SJ5131
Ryeford *H & W* 35 SO6322
Ryeish Green *Nhants* 24 SU7267
Ryhall *Lincs* 64 TF0310
Ryhill *W York* 83 SE3814
Ryhope *T & W* 96 NZ4152
Rylah *Derbys* 75 SK4667
Ryland *Lincs* 76 TF0179
Rylands *Notts* 62 SK5335
Rylstone *N York* 88 SD9658
Ryme Intrinseca *Dorset* 10 ST5810
Ryther *N York* 83 SE5539
Ryton *T & W* 103 NZ1564
Ryton *N York* 90 SE7975
Ryton *Shrops* 60 SJ7602
Ryton *Warwks* 61 SP4086
Ryton Woodside *T & W* 96 NZ1462
Ryton-on-Dunsmore *Warwks* 61 SP3874

S

Sabden *Lancs* 81 SD7837
Sabine's Green *Essex* 27 TQ5496
Sacombe *Herts* 39 TL3319
Sacombe Green *Herts* 39 TL3419
Sacriston *T & W* 96 NZ2447
Sadberge *Dur* 96 NZ3416
Saddell *Strath* 105 NR7832
Saddington *Leics* 50 SP6691
Saddle Bow *Norfk* 65 TF6015
Saddlescombe *W Susx* 15 TQ2711
Sadgill *Cumb* 87 NY4805
Saffron Walden *Essex* 39 TL5438
Sageston *Dyfed* 30 SN0503
Saham Hills *Norfk* 66 TF9003
Saham Toney *Norfk* 66 TF8901
Saighton *Ches* 71 SJ4462
Saint Hill *Devon* 9 ST0908
Saint Hill *W Susx* 15 TQ3835
Saintbury *Gloucs* 48 SP1139
Salachail *Strath* 123 NN0551
Salcombe *Devon* 7 SX7439
Salcombe Regis *Devon* 9 SY1588
Salcott *Essex* 40 TL9413
Sale *Gt Man* 79 SJ7991
Sale Green *H & W* 47 SO9358
Saleby *Lincs* 77 TF4578
Salehurst *E Susx* 17 TQ7524
Salem *Gwynd* 69 SH5456
Salem *Dyfed* 44 SN6226
Salem *Dyfed* 43 SN6684
Salen *Strath* 121 NM5743
Salen *Highld* 121 NM6864
Salesbury *Lancs* 81 SD6832
Salford *Gt Man* 79 SJ8197
Salford *Oxon* 48 SP2828
Salford *Beds* 38 SP9339
Salford Priors *Warwks* 48 SP0751
Salfords *Surrey* 15 TQ2846

Salhouse Shaw Green

Salhouse *Norfk*	**67**	TG3114
Saline *Fife*	**117**	NT0292
Salisbury *Wilts*	**23**	SU1429
Salkeld Dykes *Cumb*	**94**	NY5437
Sall *Norfk*	**66**	TG1024
Sallachy *Highld*	**146**	NC5408
Salmonby *Lincs*	**77**	TF3273
Salmond's Muir *Tays*	**127**	NO5837
Salperton *Gloucs*	**36**	SP0720
Salph End *Beds*	**38**	TL0852
Salsburgh *Strath*	**116**	NS8262
Salt *Staffs*	**72**	SJ9527
Salt Cotes *Cumb*	**93**	NY1853
Salta *Cumb*	**92**	NY0845
Saltaire *W York*	**82**	SE1438
Saltash *Cnwll*	**6**	SX4258
Saltburn *Highld*	**146**	NH7270
Saltburn-by-the-Sea *Cleve*	**97**	NZ6621
Saltby *Leics*	**63**	SK8526
Saltcoats *Strath*	**106**	NS2441
Saltcoats *Cumb*	**86**	SD0797
Saltcoats *Lancs*	**80**	SD3728
Saltdean *E Susx*	**15**	TQ3802
Salterbeck *Cumb*	**92**	NX9926
Salterforth *Lancs*	**81**	SD8845
Salterswall *Ches*	**71**	SJ6266
Salterton *Wilts*	**23**	SU1236
Saltfleet *Lincs*	**77**	TF4593
Saltfleetby All Saints *Lincs*	**77**	TF4590
Saltfleetby St. Clements *Lincs*	**77**	TF4691
Saltfleetby St. Peter *Lincs*	**77**	TF4489
Saltford *Avon*	**22**	ST6867
Salthouse *Norfk*	**66**	TG0743
Saltley *W Mids*	**61**	SP1088
Saltmarsh *Gwent*	**34**	ST3482
Saltmarshe *Humb*	**84**	SE7824
Saltney *Ches*	**71**	SJ3865
Salton *N York*	**90**	SE7179
Saltrens *Devon*	**18**	SS4522
Saltwick *Nthumb*	**103**	NZ1780
Saltwood *Kent*	**29**	TR1535
Salvington *W Susx*	**14**	TQ1205
Salwarpe *H & W*	**47**	SO8762
Salwayash *Dorset*	**10**	SY4596
Sambourne *Warwks*	**48**	SP0662
Sambrook *Shrops*	**72**	SJ7124
Samlesbury *Lancs*	**81**	SD5930
Samlesbury Bottoms *Lancs*	**81**	SD6228
Sampford Arundel *Somset*	**20**	ST1118
Sampford Brett *Somset*	**20**	ST0741
Sampford Courtenay *Devon*	**8**	SS6301
Sampford Moor *Somset*	**20**	ST1118
Sampford Peverell *Devon*	**9**	ST0314
Sampford Spiney *Devon*	**6**	SX5372
Samson's Corner *Essex*	**41**	TM0818
Samsonlane *Ork*	**155**	HY6526
Samuelston *Loth*	**118**	NT4870
Sanaigmore *Strath*	**112**	NR2370
Sancreed *Cnwll*	**2**	SW4129
Sancton *Humb*	**84**	SE8939
Sand *Somset*	**21**	ST4346
Sand Cross *E Susx*	**16**	TQ5820
Sand Hills *W York*	**83**	SE3739
Sand Hole *Humb*	**84**	SE8137
Sand Hutton *N York*	**90**	SE6958
Sand Side *Cumb*	**86**	SD2282
Sandaig *Highld*	**129**	NG7102
Sandal Magna *W York*	**83**	SE3417
Sandale *Cumb*	**93**	NY2440
Sandavore *Highld*	**128**	NM4785
Sandbach *Ches*	**72**	SJ7560
Sandbank *Strath*	**114**	NS1680
Sandbanks *Dorset*	**12**	SZ0487
Sandend *Gramp*	**142**	NJ5566
Sanderstead *Gt Lon*	**27**	TQ3461
Sandford *Strath*	**107**	NS7143
Sandford *Cumb*	**94**	NY7316
Sandford *Shrops*	**59**	SJ3423
Sandford *Shrops*	**59**	SJ5833
Sandford *Devon*	**8**	SS8202
Sandford *Avon*	**21**	ST4259
Sandford *Hants*	**12**	SU1601
Sandford *Dorset*	**11**	SY9289
Sandford *IOW*	**13**	SZ5381
Sandford Orcas *Dorset*	**21**	ST6220
Sandford St. Martin *Oxon*	**49**	SP4226
Sandford-on-Thames *Oxon*	**37**	SP5301
Sandgate *Kent*	**29**	TR2035
Sandhaven *Gramp*	**143**	NJ9667
Sandhead *D & G*	**98**	NX0949
Sandhill *S York*	**75**	SK4496
Sandhills *Staffs*	**61**	SK0604
Sandhills *Oxon*	**37**	SP5507
Sandhills *Dorset*	**10**	ST5800
Sandhills *Dorset*	**11**	ST6810
Sandhills *Surrey*	**14**	SU9337
Sandhoe *Nthumb*	**102**	NY9666
Sandhole *Strath*	**114**	NS0098
Sandholme *Humb*	**84**	SE8230
Sandholme *Lincs*	**64**	TF3337
Sandhurst *Gloucs*	**47**	SO8223
Sandhurst *Berks*	**25**	SU8361
Sandhurst *Kent*	**17**	TQ8028
Sandhurst Cross *Kent*	**17**	TQ7827
Sandhutton *N York*	**89**	SE3881
Sandiacre *Derbys*	**62**	SK4736
Sandilands *Lincs*	**77**	TF5280
Sandiway *Ches*	**71**	SJ6070
Sandleheath *Hants*	**12**	SU1215
Sandley *Dorset*	**22**	ST7724
Sandling *Kent*	**28**	TQ7557
Sandlow Green *Ches*	**72**	SJ7865
Sandness *Shet*	**155**	HU1957
Sandon *Staffs*	**72**	SJ9429
Sandon *Herts*	**39**	TL3234
Sandon *Essex*	**40**	TL7404
Sandon Bank *Staffs*	**72**	SJ9428
Sandown *IOW*	**13**	SZ5984
Sandplace *Cnwll*	**5**	SX2557
Sandridge *Wilts*	**22**	ST9465
Sandridge *Herts*	**39**	TL1710
Sandringham *Norfk*	**65**	TF6928
Sands *Bucks*	**26**	SU8493
Sandsend *N York*	**90**	NZ8612
Sandside House *Highld*	**150**	NC9565
Sandtoft *Humb*	**84**	SE7408
Sandwich *Kent*	**29**	TR3358
Sandwick *Shet*	**155**	HU4323
Sandwick *Cumb*	**93**	NY4219
Sandwith *Cumb*	**92**	NX9614
Sandwith Newtown *Cumb*	**92**	NX9614
Sandy *Beds*	**52**	TL1649
Sandy Bank *Lincs*	**77**	TF2655
Sandy Cross *H & W*	**47**	SO6757
Sandy Haven *Dyfed*	**30**	SM8507
Sandy Lane *W York*	**82**	SE1135
Sandy Lane *Clwyd*	**71**	SJ4040
Sandy Lane *Wilts*	**22**	ST9668
Sandy Park *Devon*	**8**	SX7189
Sandycroft *Clwyd*	**71**	SJ3366
Sandyford *D & G*	**101**	NY2093
Sandygate *IOM*	**153**	SC3797
Sandygate *Devon*	**7**	SX8674
Sandyhills *D & G*	**92**	NX8855
Sandylands *Lancs*	**87**	SD4263
Sandylane *Staffs*	**72**	SJ7035
Sandylane *W Glam*	**32**	SS5589
Sandystones *Border*	**110**	NT5926
Sandyway *H & W*	**46**	SO4925
Sangobeg *Highld*	**149**	NC4266
Sangomore *Highld*	**149**	NC4067
Sankey Bridges *Ches*	**78**	SJ5887
Sankyn's Green *H & W*	**47**	SO7965
Sanna Bay *Highld*	**128**	NM4469
Santon *Cumb*	**86**	NY1001
Santon *IOM*	**153**	SC3171
Santon Bridge *Cumb*	**86**	NY1101
Santon Downham *Suffk*	**54**	TL8187
Sapcote *Leics*	**50**	SP4893
Sapey Common *H & W*	**47**	SO7064
Sapiston *Suffk*	**54**	TL9175
Sapley *Cambs*	**52**	TL2474
Sapperton *Derbys*	**73**	SK1834
Sapperton *Gloucs*	**35**	SO9403
Sapperton *Lincs*	**64**	TF0133
Saracen's Head *Lincs*	**64**	TF3427
Sarclet *Highld*	**151**	ND3443
Sarisbury *Hants*	**13**	SU5008
Sarn *Gwynd*	**56**	SH2432
Sarn *Powys*	**58**	SN9597
Sarn *Powys*	**58**	SO2090
Sarn *M Glam*	**33**	SS9083
Sarn-bach *Gwynd*	**56**	SH3026
Sarn-wen *Powys*	**58**	SJ2718
Sarnau *Gwynd*	**70**	SH9639
Sarnau *Powys*	**58**	SJ2315
Sarnau *Dyfed*	**42**	SN3150
Sarnau *Dyfed*	**31**	SN3318
Sarnau *Powys*	**45**	SO0232
Sarnesfield *H & W*	**46**	SO3750
Saron *Gwynd*	**69**	SH5365
Saron *Dyfed*	**31**	SN3737
Saron *Dyfed*	**32**	SN6012
Sarratt *Herts*	**26**	TQ0499
Sarre *Kent*	**29**	TR2565
Sarsden *Oxon*	**36**	SP2822
Sarson *Hants*	**23**	SU3044
Sartfield *IOM*	**153**	SC3599
Satley *Dur*	**95**	NZ1143
Satmar *Kent*	**29**	TR2539
Satron *N York*	**88**	SD9397
Satterleigh *Devon*	**19**	SS6622
Satterthwaite *Cumb*	**86**	SD3392
Satwell *Oxon*	**37**	SU7083
Sauchen *Gramp*	**135**	NJ7011
Saucher *Tays*	**126**	NO1933
Sauchieburn *Gramp*	**135**	NO6669
Saul *Gloucs*	**35**	SO7409
Saundby *Notts*	**75**	SK7888
Saundersfoot *Dyfed*	**31**	SN1304
Saunderton *Bucks*	**37**	SP7901
Saunton *Devon*	**18**	SS4637
Sausthorpe *Lincs*	**77**	TF3868
Saveock Water *Cnwll*	**3**	SW7645
Saverley Green *Staffs*	**72**	SJ9638
Savile Town *W York*	**82**	SE2420
Sawbridge *Warwks*	**50**	SP5065
Sawbridgeworth *Herts*	**39**	TL4814
Sawdon *N York*	**91**	SE9485
Sawley *Lancs*	**81**	SD7746
Sawley *N York*	**89**	SE2467
Sawley *Derbys*	**62**	SK4631
Sawston *Cambs*	**53**	TL4849
Sawtry *Cambs*	**52**	TL1683
Saxby *Leics*	**63**	SK8219
Saxby *W Susx*	**14**	SU9604
Saxby *Lincs*	**76**	TF0086
Saxby All Saints *Humb*	**84**	SE9816
Saxelbye *Leics*	**63**	SK6921
Saxham Street *Suffk*	**54**	TM0861
Saxilby *Lincs*	**76**	SK8975
Saxlingham *Norfk*	**66**	TG0239
Saxlingham Green *Norfk*	**67**	TM2396
Saxlingham Nethergate *Norfk*	**67**	TM2297
Saxlingham Thorpe *Norfk*	**67**	TM2197
Saxmundham *Suffk*	**55**	TM3863
Saxon Street *Cambs*	**53**	TL6759
Saxondale *Notts*	**63**	SK6839
Saxtead *Suffk*	**55**	TM2665
Saxtead Green *Suffk*	**55**	TM2564
Saxtead Little Green *Suffk*	**55**	TM2466
Saxthorpe *Norfk*	**66**	TG1130
Saxton *N York*	**83**	SE4736
Sayers Common *W Susx*	**15**	TQ2618
Scackleton *N York*	**90**	SE6472
Scaftworth *Notts*	**75**	SK6691
Scagglethorpe *N York*	**90**	SE8372
Scalasaig *Strath*	**112**	NR3993
Scalby *Humb*	**84**	SE8429
Scalby *N York*	**91**	TA0090
Scald End *Beds*	**51**	TL0457
Scaldwell *Nhants*	**50**	SP7672
Scale Houses *Cumb*	**94**	NY5845
Scaleby *Cumb*	**101**	NY4463
Scalebyhill *Cumb*	**101**	NY4463
Scales *Cumb*	**93**	NY3426
Scales *Cumb*	**86**	SD2772
Scales *Lancs*	**80**	SD4531
Scalesceugh *Cumb*	**93**	NY4449
Scalford *Leics*	**63**	SK7624
Scaling *N York*	**90**	NZ7413
Scaling Dam *N York*	**90**	NZ7412
Scalloway *Shet*	**155**	HU4039
Scamblesby *Lincs*	**77**	TF2778
Scammonden *W York*	**82**	SE0515
Scamodale *Highld*	**129**	NM8373
Scampston *N York*	**90**	SE8575
Scampton *Lincs*	**76**	SK9579
Scaniport *Highld*	**140**	NH6239
Scapegoat Hill *W York*	**82**	SE0916
Scarborough *N York*	**91**	TA0488
Scarcewater *Cnwll*	**3**	SW9154
Scarcliffe *Derbys*	**75**	SK4968
Scarcroft *W York*	**83**	SE3641
Scarcroft Hill *W York*	**83**	SE3741
Scarfskerry *Highld*	**151**	ND2674
Scargill *Dur*	**88**	NZ0510
Scarinish *Strath*	**120**	NM0444
Scarisbrick *Lancs*	**80**	SD3713
Scarness *Cumb*	**93**	NY2230
Scarning *Norfk*	**66**	TF9512
Scarrington *Notts*	**63**	SK7341
Scarth Hill *Lancs*	**78**	SD4206
Scarthingwell *N York*	**83**	SE4937
Scartho *Humb*	**85**	TA2606
Scawby *Humb*	**84**	SE9605
Scawsby *S York*	**83**	SE5305
Scawthorpe *S York*	**83**	SE5506
Scawton *N York*	**90**	SE5483
Scayne's Hill *W Susx*	**15**	TQ3623
Scethrog *Powys*	**45**	SO1025
Scholar Green *Staffs*	**72**	SJ8357
Scholes *Gt Man*	**78**	SD5905
Scholes *W York*	**82**	SE1507
Scholes *W York*	**82**	SE1625
Scholes *W York*	**83**	SE3736
Scholes *S York*	**74**	SK3895
Scholey Hill *W York*	**83**	SE3825
School Aycliffe *Dur*	**96**	NZ2523
School Green *W York*	**82**	SE1132
School Green *Ches*	**72**	SJ6464
School House *Dorset*	**10**	ST3602
Schoolgreen *Berks*	**24**	SU7367
Scissett *W York*	**82**	SE2410
Scleddau *Dyfed*	**30**	SM9434
Sco Ruston *Norfk*	**67**	TG2821
Scofton *Notts*	**75**	SK6280
Scole *Norfk*	**54**	TM1579
Sconser *Highld*	**137**	NG5132
Scoonie *Fife*	**126**	NO3801
Scopwick *Lincs*	**76**	TF0757
Scoraig *Highld*	**144**	NH0096
Scorborough *Humb*	**84**	TA0145
Scorrier *Cnwll*	**3**	SW7244
Scorriton *Devon*	**7**	SX7068
Scorton *N York*	**89**	NZ2500
Scorton *Lancs*	**80**	SD5048
Scot Hay *Staffs*	**72**	SJ7947
Scot Lane End *Gt Man*	**79**	SD6209
Scot's Gap *Nthumb*	**103**	NZ0386
Scotby *Cumb*	**93**	NY4455
Scotch Corner *N York*	**89**	NZ2105
Scotforth *Lancs*	**87**	SD4859
Scothern *Lincs*	**76**	TF0377
Scotland *W York*	**82**	SE2340
Scotland *Lincs*	**63**	TF0030
Scotland Gate *T & W*	**103**	NZ2584
Scotlandwell *Tays*	**126**	NO1801
Scotscalder Station *Highld*	**151**	ND0956
Scotscraig *Fife*	**127**	NO4428
Scotsdike *Cumb*	**101**	NY3872
Scotsmill *Gramp*	**142**	NJ5618
Scotstoun *Strath*	**115**	NS5267
Scotswood *T & W*	**103**	NZ2063
Scotter *Lincs*	**76**	SE8800
Scotterthorpe *Lincs*	**84**	SE8701
Scottlethorpe *Lincs*	**64**	TF0520
Scotton *N York*	**89**	SE1895
Scotton *N York*	**89**	SE3259
Scotton *Lincs*	**76**	SK8899
Scottow *Norfk*	**67**	TG2823
Scoughall *Loth*	**118**	NT6183
Scoulton *Norfk*	**66**	TF9800
Scounslow Green *Staffs*	**73**	SK0929
Scourie *Highld*	**148**	NC1544
Scouriemore *Highld*	**148**	NC1443
Scousburgh *Shet*	**155**	HU3717
Scouthead *Gt Man*	**79**	SD9605
Scrabster *Highld*	**151**	ND1070
Scraesburgh *Border*	**110**	NT6718
Scrafield *Lincs*	**77**	TF3068
Scrainwood *Nthumb*	**111**	NT9808
Scrane End *Lincs*	**64**	TF3841
Scraptoft *Leics*	**63**	SK6405
Scratby *Norfk*	**67**	TG5015
Scrayingham *N York*	**90**	SE7359
Scrays *E Susx*	**17**	TQ7619
Scredington *Lincs*	**64**	TF0940
Screel *D & G*	**92**	NX8053
Scremby *Lincs*	**77**	TF4467
Scremerston *Nthumb*	**111**	NU0148
Screveton *Notts*	**63**	SK7343
Scrivelby *Lincs*	**77**	TF2766
Scriven *N York*	**89**	SE3458
Scrooby *Notts*	**75**	SK6590
Scropton *Derbys*	**73**	SK1930
Scrub Hill *Lincs*	**76**	TF2355
Scruschloch *Tays*	**133**	NO2357
Scruton *N York*	**89**	SE2992
Scuggate *Cumb*	**101**	NY4474
Sculthorpe *Norfk*	**66**	TF8930
Scunthorpe *Humb*	**84**	SE8910
Scurlage *W Glam*	**32**	SS4687
Sea *Somset*	**10**	ST3412
Sea Palling *Norfk*	**67**	TG4226
Seaborough *Dorset*	**10**	ST4206
Seabridge *Staffs*	**72**	SJ8343
Seabrook *Kent*	**29**	TR1835
Seacombe *Mersyd*	**78**	SJ3290
Seacroft *W York*	**83**	SE3635
Seacroft *Lincs*	**77**	TF5661
Seafield *Highld*	**136**	NG4743
Seafield *Loth*	**117**	NT0066
Seaford *E Susx*	**16**	TV4899
Seaforth *Mersyd*	**78**	SJ3297
Seagrave *Leics*	**62**	SK6117
Seagry Heath *Wilts*	**35**	ST9581
Seaham *Dur*	**96**	NZ4149
Seahouses *Nthumb*	**111**	NU2231
Seal *Kent*	**27**	TQ5556
Seale *Surrey*	**25**	SU8947
Seamer *N York*	**90**	NZ4910
Seamer *N York*	**91**	TA0183
Seamill *Strath*	**114**	NS2047
Searby *Lincs*	**85**	TA0705
Seasalter *Kent*	**29**	TR0864
Seascale *Cumb*	**86**	NY0301
Seathwaite *Cumb*	**93**	NY2312
Seathwaite *Cumb*	**86**	SD2295
Seatle *Cumb*	**87**	SD3783
Seatoller *Cumb*	**93**	NY2413
Seaton *Cumb*	**92**	NY0130
Seaton *Nthumb*	**103**	NZ3276
Seaton *Dur*	**96**	NZ3949
Seaton *Leics*	**51**	SP9098
Seaton *Cnwll*	**5**	SX3054
Seaton *Devon*	**9**	SY2490
Seaton *Humb*	**85**	TA1646
Seaton *Kent*	**29**	TR2258
Seaton Burn *T & W*	**103**	NZ2373
Seaton Carew *Cleve*	**97**	NZ5229
Seaton Delaval *Nthumb*	**103**	NZ3075
Seaton Ross *Humb*	**84**	SE7840
Seaton Sluice *Nthumb*	**103**	NZ3376
Seatown *Dorset*	**10**	SY4291
Seave Green *N York*	**90**	NZ5500
Seaview *IOW*	**13**	SZ6291
Seaville *Cumb*	**92**	NY1553
Seavington St. Mary *Somset*	**10**	ST4014
Seavington St. Michael *Somset*	**10**	ST4015
Sebastopol *Gwent*	**34**	ST2998
Sebergham *Cumb*	**93**	NY3641
Seckington *Warwks*	**61**	SK2507
Sedbergh *Cumb*	**87**	SD6591
Sedbury *Gloucs*	**34**	ST5493
Sedbusk *N York*	**88**	SD8891
Sedgeberrow *H & W*	**48**	SP0238
Sedgebrook *Lincs*	**63**	SK8537
Sedgefield *Dur*	**96**	NZ3528
Sedgeford *Norfk*	**65**	TF7036
Sedgehill *Wilts*	**22**	ST8627
Sedgley *W Mids*	**60**	SO9193
Sedgley Park *Gt Man*	**79**	SD8202
Sedgwick *Cumb*	**87**	SD5186
Sedlescombe *E Susx*	**17**	TQ7818
Sedrup *Bucks*	**38**	SP8011
Seed *Kent*	**28**	TQ9456
Seend *Wilts*	**22**	ST9460
Seend Cleeve *Wilts*	**22**	ST9360
Seer Green *Bucks*	**26**	SU9692
Seething *Norfk*	**67**	TM3197
Sefton *Mersyd*	**78**	SD3501
Sefton Town *Mersyd*	**78**	SD3400
Seghill *Nthumb*	**103**	NZ2874
Seighford *Staffs*	**72**	SJ8825
Seion *Gwynd*	**69**	SH5466
Seisdon *Staffs*	**60**	SO8495
Selattyn *Shrops*	**58**	SJ2633
Selborne *Hants*	**24**	SU7433
Selby *N York*	**83**	SE6132
Selham *W Susx*	**14**	SU9320
Selhurst *Gt Lon*	**27**	TQ3267
Selkirk *Border*	**109**	NT4728
Sellack *H & W*	**46**	SO5627
Sellafirth *Shet*	**155**	HU5198
Sellan *Cnwll*	**2**	SW4230
Sellick's Green *Somset*	**20**	ST2119
Sellindge *Kent*	**29**	TR0938
Selling *Kent*	**28**	TR0456
Sells Green *Wilts*	**22**	ST9462
Selly Oak *W Mids*	**61**	SP0482
Selmeston *E Susx*	**16**	TQ5007
Selsdon *Gt Lon*	**27**	TQ3562
Selsey *W Susx*	**14**	SZ8593
Selsfield Common *Gwynd*	**15**	TQ3434
Selside *Cumb*	**87**	SD5399
Selside *N York*	**88**	SD7875
Selstead *Kent*	**29**	TR2144
Selston *Notts*	**75**	SK4553
Selworthy *Somset*	**20**	SS9246
Semer *Suffk*	**54**	TL9946
Semington *Wilts*	**22**	ST8960
Semley *Wilts*	**22**	ST8926
Send *Surrey*	**26**	TQ0155
Send Marsh *Surrey*	**26**	TQ0355
Senghenydd *M Glam*	**33**	ST1190
Sennen *Cnwll*	**2**	SW3525
Sennen Cove *Cnwll*	**2**	SW3526
Sennybridge *Powys*	**45**	SN9228
Serlby *Notts*	**75**	SK6389
Sessay *N York*	**89**	SE4575
Setchey *Norfk*	**65**	TF6313
Setley *Hants*	**12**	SU3000
Seton Mains *Loth*	**118**	NT4275
Settle *N York*	**88**	SD8163
Settlingstones *Nthumb*	**102**	NY8468
Settrington *N York*	**90**	SE8370
Seven Ash *Somset*	**20**	ST1533
Seven Kings *Gt Lon*	**27**	TQ4587
Seven Sisters *W Glam*	**33**	SN8208
Seven Springs *Gloucs*	**35**	SO9617
Seven Star Green *Essex*	**40**	TL9325
Seven Wells *Gloucs*	**48**	SP1134
Sevenhampton *Gloucs*	**36**	SP0321
Sevenhampton *Wilts*	**36**	SU2090
Sevenoaks *Kent*	**27**	TQ5255
Sevenoaks Weald *Kent*	**27**	TQ5250
Severn Beach *Avon*	**34**	ST5484
Severn Stoke *H & W*	**47**	SO8644
Sevicks End *Beds*	**51**	TL0954
Sevington *Kent*	**28**	TR0340
Sewards End *Essex*	**53**	TL5738
Sewardstonebury *Gt Lon*	**27**	TQ3995
Sewell *Beds*	**38**	SP9922
Sewerby *Humb*	**91**	TA1968
Seworgan *Cnwll*	**2**	SW7030
Sewstern *Leics*	**63**	SK8821
Sexhow *N York*	**89**	NZ4706
Sezincote *Gloucs*	**48**	SP1731
Shabbington *Bucks*	**37**	SP6606
Shacklecross *Derbys*	**62**	SK4234
Shackleford *Surrey*	**25**	SU9345
Shade *W York*	**81**	SD9323
Shader *W Isls*	**154**	NB3854
Shadforth *Dur*	**96**	NZ3440
Shadingfield *Suffk*	**55**	TM4384
Shadoxhurst *Kent*	**28**	TQ9737
Shadwell *W York*	**83**	SE3439
Shadwell *Norfk*	**54**	TL9383
Shaftenhoe End *Herts*	**39**	TL4037
Shaftesbury *Dorset*	**22**	ST8623
Shaftholme *S York*	**83**	SE5708
Shafton *S York*	**83**	SE3911
Shafton Two Gates *S York*	**83**	SE3910
Shalbourne *Wilts*	**23**	SU3163
Shalcombe *IOW*	**13**	SZ3985
Shalden *Hants*	**24**	SU6941
Shalden Green *Hants*	**24**	SU7043
Shaldon *Devon*	**7**	SX9372
Shalfleet *IOW*	**13**	SZ4189
Shalford *Essex*	**40**	TL7229
Shalford *Surrey*	**25**	TQ0047
Shalford Green *Essex*	**40**	TL7127
Shallowford *Staffs*	**72**	SJ8729
Shalmsford Street *Kent*	**29**	TR0954
Shalstone *Bucks*	**49**	SP6436
Shamley Green *Surrey*	**14**	TQ0343
Shandford *Tays*	**134**	NO4962
Shandon *Strath*	**114**	NS2586
Shandwick *Highld*	**147**	NH8575
Shangton *Leics*	**50**	SP7196
Shankhouse *Nthumb*	**103**	NZ2778
Shanklin *IOW*	**13**	SZ5881
Shap *Cumb*	**94**	NY5615
Shapwick *Somset*	**21**	ST4138
Shapwick *Dorset*	**11**	ST9301
Shard End *W Mids*	**61**	SP1588
Shardlow *Derbys*	**62**	SK4330
Shareshill *Staffs*	**60**	SJ9406
Sharlston *W York*	**83**	SE3918
Sharlston Common *W York*	**83**	SE3919
Sharman's Cross *W Mids*	**61**	SP1279
Sharnal Street *Kent*	**28**	TQ7974
Sharnbrook *Beds*	**51**	SP9959
Sharneyford *Lancs*	**81**	SD8824
Sharnford *Leics*	**50**	SP4891
Sharnhill Green *Dorset*	**11**	ST7105
Sharoe Green *Lancs*	**80**	SD5333
Sharow *N York*	**89**	SE3371
Sharp Green *Norfk*	**67**	TG3820
Sharpenhoe *Beds*	**38**	TL0630
Sharperton *Nthumb*	**102**	NT9503
Sharpness *Gloucs*	**35**	SO6702
Sharptor *Cnwll*	**5**	SX2573
Sharpway Gate *H & W*	**47**	SO9565
Sharrington *Norfk*	**66**	TG0337
Shatterford *H & W*	**60**	SO7981
Shatterling *Kent*	**29**	TR2658
Shaugh Prior *Devon*	**6**	SX5463
Shave Cross *Dorset*	**10**	SY4198
Shavington *Ches*	**72**	SJ6951
Shaw *Gt Man*	**79**	SD9308
Shaw *W York*	**82**	SE0235
Shaw *Wilts*	**22**	ST8965
Shaw *Wilts*	**36**	SU1185
Shaw *Berks*	**24**	SU4768
Shaw Common *Gloucs*	**47**	SO6826
Shaw Green *Lancs*	**80**	SD5218

Shaw Green Sloothby

Shaw Green N York 82 SE2652
Shaw Green Herts 39 TL3032
Shaw Hill Lancs 81 SD5720
Shaw Mills N York 89 SE2562
Shawbost W Isls 154 NB2646
Shawbury Shrops 59 SJ5521
Shawclough Gt Man 81 SD8914
Shawdon Hill Nthumb 111 NU0813
Shawell Leics 50 SP5480
Shawford Hants 13 SU4625
Shawforth Lancs 81 SD8920
Shawhead D & G 100 NX8675
Shear Cross Wilts 22 ST8642
Shearington D & G 100 NY0266
Shearsby Leics 50 SP6290
Shearston Somset 20 ST2830
Shebbear Devon 18 SS4409
Shebdon Staffs 72 SJ7625
Shebster Highld 150 ND0164
Shedfield Hants 13 SU5613
Sheen Derbys 74 SK1161
Sheep Hill Dur 96 NZ1757
Sheep-ridge W York 82 SE1519
Sheepbridge Derbys 74 SK3674
Sheepscar W York 82 SE3134
Sheepscombe Gloucs 35 SO8910
Sheepstor Devon 6 SX5667
Sheepwash Nthumb 103 NZ2585
Sheepwash Devon 18 SS4806
Sheepway Avon 34 ST4976
Sheepy Magna Leics 61 SK3201
Sheepy Parva Leics 62 SK3301
Sheering Essex 39 TL5014
Sheerness Kent 28 TQ9174
Sheerwater Surrey 26 TQ0461
Sheet Hants 13 SU7524
Sheffield S York 74 SK3587
Sheffield Cnwll 2 SW4526
Sheffield Bottom Berks 24 SU6469
Sheffield Green E Susx 15 TQ4125
Shefford Beds 38 TL1439
Shegra Highld 148 NC1860
Sheinton Shrops 59 SJ6003
Shelderton Shrops 46 SO4077
Sheldon Derbys 74 SK1768
Sheldon W Mids 61 SP1584
Sheldon Devon 9 ST1208
Sheldwich Kent 28 TR0156
Sheldwich Lees Kent 28 TR0156
Shelf W York 82 SE1228
Shelfanger Norfk 54 TM1083
Shelfield W Mids 61 SK0302
Shelfield Warwks 48 SP1263
Shelfield Green Warwks 48 SP1261
Shelford Notts 63 SK6642
Shelford Warwks 50 SP4288
Shellacres Border 110 NT8943
Shelley W York 82 SE2011
Shelley Essex 39 TL5505
Shelley Suffk 54 TM0238
Shelley Far Bank W York 82 SE2010
Shellingford Oxon 36 SU3193
Shellow Bowells Essex 40 TL6007
Shelsley Beauchamp H & W 47 SO7363
Shelsley Walsh H & W 47 SO7263
Shelton Shrops 59 SJ4613
Shelton Notts 63 SK7844
Shelton Beds 51 TL0368
Shelton Norfk 67 TM2291
Shelton Green Norfk 55 TM2390
Shelton Lock Derbys 62 SK3730
Shelton Under Harley Staffs 72 SJ8139
Shelve Shrops 59 SO3399
Shelwick H & W 46 SO5242
Shenfield Essex 40 TQ6095
Shenington Oxon 48 SP3742
Shenley Herts 26 TL1800
Shenley Brook End Bucks 38 SP8335
Shenley Church End Bucks 38 SP8336
Shenleybury Herts 26 TL1801
Shenmore H & W 46 SO3937
Shennanton D & G 98 NX3363
Shenstone Staffs 61 SK1004
Shenstone H & W 60 SO8673
Shenstone Woodend Staffs 61 SK1101
Shenton Leics 61 SK3800
Shepeau Stow Lincs 64 TF3012
Sheperdswell Kent 29 TR2647
Shephall Herts 39 TL2623
Shepherd's Bush Gt Lon 26 TQ2380
Shepherd's Green Oxon 37 SU7183
Shepherds Cnwll 3 SW8154
Shepherds Patch Gloucs 35 SO7304
Shepley W York 82 SE1909
Shepperdine Avon 35 ST6295
Shepperton Surrey 26 TQ0766
Shepperton Green Surrey 26 TQ0767
Shepreth Cambs 52 TL3947
Shepshed Leics 62 SK4819
Shepton Beauchamp Somset 10 ST4017
Shepton Mallet Somset 21 ST6143
Shepton Montague Somset 22 ST6831
Shepway Kent 28 TQ7753
Sheraton Dur 96 NZ4435
Sherborne Gloucs 36 SP1614
Sherborne Somset 21 ST5855
Sherborne Dorset 10 ST6316
Sherborne Causeway Dorset 22 ST8323
Sherborne St. John Hants 24 SU6255
Sherbourne Warwks 48 SP2661
Sherburn Dur 96 NZ3142
Sherburn N York 91 SE9576
Sherburn Hill Dur 96 NZ3342
Sherburn in Elmet N York 83 SE4933
Shere Surrey 14 TQ0747
Shereford Norfk 66 TF8829
Sherfield English Hants 23 SU2922
Sherfield on Loddon Hants 24 SU6858
Sherfin Lancs 81 SD7925
Sherford Devon 7 SX7844
Sherford Dorset 11 SY9193
Sheriff Hutton N York 90 SE6566
Sheriffhales Shrops 60 SJ7512
Sheringham Norfk 66 TG1543
Sherington Bucks 38 SP8846
Shermanbury W Susx 15 TQ2019
Shernborne Norfk 65 TF7132
Sherril Devon 7 SX6874
Sherrington Wilts 22 ST9639
Sherston Wilts 35 ST8586
Sherwood Notts 62 SK5643
Shettleston Strath 116 NS6464
Shevington Gt Man 78 SD5408
Shevington Moor Gt Man 78 SD5410
Shevington Vale Gt Man 78 SD5309
Sheviock Cnwll 5 SX3755
Shibden Head W York 82 SE0928
Shide IOW 13 SZ5088
Shidlaw Nthumb 110 NT8037
Shiel Bridge Highld 138 NG9318
Shieldaig Highld 137 NG8153
Shieldhill Cent 116 NS8976
Shieldhill House Hotel Strath 108 NT0040
Shieldhill D & G 100 NY0385
Shields Strath 116 NS7755
Shielhill Tays 134 NO4257
Shielhill Strath 114 NS2472
Shifford Oxon 36 SP3701
Shifnal Shrops 60 SJ7407
Shilbottle Nthumb 111 NU1908
Shildon Dur 96 NZ2226
Shillingford Devon 20 SS9824
Shillingford Oxon 37 SU5992
Shillingford Abbot Devon 9 SX9088
Shillingford St. George Devon 9 SX9087
Shillingstone Dorset 11 ST8211
Shillington Beds 38 TL1234
Shillmoor Nthumb 110 NT8807
Shilton Oxon 36 SP2608
Shilton Warwks 61 SP4084
Shilvinghampton Dorset 10 SY6284
Shimpling Suffk 54 TL8651
Shimpling Norfk 54 TM1583
Shimpling Street Suffk 54 TL8753
Shincliffe Dur 96 NZ2940
Shiney Row T & W 96 NZ3252
Shinfield Berks 24 SU7368
Shingay Cambs 52 TL3046
Shingle Street Suffk 55 TM3642
Shinnersbridge Devon 7 SX7862
Shinness Highld 146 NC5215
Shipbourne Kent 27 TQ5952
Shipbrookhill Ches 79 SJ6771
Shipdham Norfk 66 TF9507
Shipham Somset 21 ST4457
Shiphay Devon 7 SX8965
Shiplake Oxon 37 SU7678
Shiplake Row Oxon 37 SU7478
Shipley Nthumb 111 NU1416
Shipley W York 82 SE1537
Shipley Shrops 60 SO8095
Shipley W Susx 15 TQ1421
Shipley Bridge Surrey 15 TQ3040
Shipley Hatch Kent 28 TR0038
Shipmeadow Suffk 55 TM3790
Shippea Hill Halt Cambs 53 TL6484
Shippon Oxon 37 SU4898
Shipston on Stour Warwks 48 SP2540
Shipton N York 90 SE5558
Shipton Shrops 59 SO5692
Shipton Gloucs 36 SP0318
Shipton Bucks 49 SP7727
Shipton Bellinger Hants 23 SU2345
Shipton Gorge Dorset 10 SY4991
Shipton Green W Susx 14 SZ8099
Shipton Moyne Gloucs 35 ST8989
Shipton-on-Cherwell Oxon 37 SP4716
Shipton-under-Wychwood Oxon 36 SP2817
Shiptonthorpe Humb 84 SE8543
Shirburn Oxon 37 SU6995
Shirdley Hill Lancs 80 SD3612
Shire Cumb 94 NY6135
Shire Oak W Mids 61 SK0504
Shirebrook Notts 75 SK5267
Shiregreen S York 74 SK3691
Shirehampton Avon 34 ST5376
Shiremoor T & W 103 NZ3171
Shirenewton Gwent 34 ST4793
Shireoaks Notts 75 SK5580
Shirkoak Kent 17 TQ9435
Shirl Heath H & W 46 SO4359
Shirland Derbys 74 SK4058
Shirlett Shrops 59 SO6497
Shirley Derbys 73 SK2141
Shirley W Mids 61 SP1278
Shirley Hants 13 SU4014
Shirley Gt Lon 27 TQ3565
Shirrell Heath Hants 13 SU5714
Shirven Strath 113 NR8784
Shirwell Devon 19 SS6037
Shirwell Cross Devon 19 SS5936
Shittlehope Dur 95 NZ0039
Shobdon H & W 46 SO4062
Shobley Hants 12 SU1806
Shobrooke Devon 9 SS8601
Shoby Leics 63 SK6820
Shocklach Green Ches 71 SJ4349
Shoeburyness Essex 40 TQ9385
Sholden Kent 29 TR3552
Sholing Hants 13 SU4511
Shoose Cumb 92 NY0127
Shoot Hill Shrops 59 SJ4112
Shop Cnwll 18 SS2214
Shop Cnwll 4 SW8773
Shop Street Suffk 55 TM2268
Shopwyke W Susx 14 SU8805
Shore Gt Man 81 SD9216
Shoreditch Somset 20 ST2422
Shoreditch Gt Lon 27 TQ3382
Shoreham Kent 27 TQ5161
Shoreham-by-Sea W Susx 15 TQ2105
Shoreswood Nthumb 110 NT9446
Shorley Hants 13 SU5726
Shorncote Gloucs 35 SU0296
Shorne Kent 28 TQ6971
Shorne Ridgeway Kent 28 TQ6970
Short Heath W Mids 60 SJ9700
Short Heath W Mids 61 SP0992
Shorta Cross Cnwll 5 SX2857
Shortbridge E Susx 16 TQ4521
Shortfield Common Surrey 25 SU8442
Shortgate E Susx 16 TQ4915
Shortlanesend Cnwll 3 SW8047
Shorwell IOW 13 SZ4583
Shoscombe Avon 22 ST7156
Shotesham Norfk 67 TM2499
Shotgate Essex 40 TQ7592
Shotley Suffk 55 TM2335
Shotley Bridge Nthumb 95 NZ0953
Shotley Gate Suffk 41 TM2433
Shotley Street Suffk 55 TM2335
Shotleyfield Nthumb 95 NZ0553
Shottenden Kent 28 TR0454
Shottermill Surrey 14 SU8832
Shottery Warwks 48 SP1854
Shotteswell Warwks 49 SP4245
Shottisham Suffk 55 TM3244
Shottle Derbys 74 SK3149
Shottlegate Derbys 62 SK3147
Shotton Nthumb 110 NT8430
Shotton Nthumb 103 NZ2277
Shotton Dur 96 NZ3625
Shotton Dur 96 NZ4139
Shotton Clwyd 71 SJ3168
Shotwick Ches 71 SJ3371
Shougle Gramp 141 NJ2155
Shouldham Norfk 65 TF6709
Shouldham Thorpe Norfk 65 TF6607
Shoulton H & W 47 SO8159
Shover's Green E Susx 16 TQ6530
Shraleybrook Staffs 72 SJ7849
Shrawardine Shrops 59 SJ3915
Shrawley H & W 47 SO8065
Shreding Green Bucks 26 TQ0280
Shrewley Warwks 48 SP2167
Shrewsbury Shrops 59 SJ4912
Shrewton Wilts 23 SU0743
Shripney W Susx 14 SU9302
Shrivenham Oxon 36 SU2389
Shropham Norfk 66 TL9893
Shrub End Essex 41 TL9723
Shucknall H & W 46 SO5842
Shudy Camps Cambs 53 TL6244
Shurdington Gloucs 35 SO9218
Shurlock Row Berks 25 SU8374
Shurnock H & W 48 SP0360
Shurrery Highld 150 ND0458
Shurrery Lodge Highld 150 ND0456
Shurton Somset 20 ST2044
Shustoke Warwks 61 SP2290
Shut End W Mids 60 SO9089
Shut Heath Staffs 72 SJ8621
Shute Devon 9 SS8900
Shute Devon 10 SY2597
Shutford Oxon 48 SP3840
Shuthonger Gloucs 47 SO8935
Shutlanger Nhants 49 SP7249
Shutt Green Staffs 60 SJ8709
Shutterton Devon 9 SX9679
Shuttington Warwks 61 SK2505
Shuttlewood Derbys 75 SK4673
Shuttlewood Common Derbys 75 SK4773
Shuttleworth Lancs 81 SD8017
Sibbertoft Nhants 50 SP6882
Sibdon Carwood Shrops 59 SO4183
Sibford Ferris Oxon 48 SP3537
Sibford Gower Oxon 48 SP3537
Sible Hedingham Essex 53 TL7734
Sibley's Green Essex 40 TL6128
Siblyback Cnwll 5 SX2372
Sibsey Lincs 77 TF3550
Sibsey Fenside Lincs 77 TF3452
Sibson Leics 61 SK3500
Sibson Cambs 51 TL0997
Sibster Highld 151 ND3253
Sibthorpe Notts 75 SK7273
Sibthorpe Notts 63 SK7645
Sibton Suffk 55 TM3669
Sicklesmere Suffk 54 TL8760
Sicklinghall N York 83 SE3648
Sid Cop S York 83 SE3809
Sidbrook Somset 20 ST2527
Sidbury Shrops 60 SO6885
Sidbury Devon 9 SY1391
Sidcot Somset 21 ST4257
Sidcup Gt Lon 27 TQ4672
Siddick Cumb 92 NY0031
Siddington Ches 79 SJ8470
Siddington Gloucs 36 SU0399
Sidemoor H & W 60 SO9571
Sidestrand Norfk 67 TG2539
Sidford Devon 9 SY1390
Sidlesham W Susx 14 SZ8599
Sidlesham Common W Susx 14 SZ8599
Sidley E Susx 17 TQ7408
Sidmouth Devon 9 SY1287
Siefton Shrops 59 SO4883
Sigford Devon 7 SX7773
Sigglesthorne Humb 85 TA1545
Sigingstone S Glam 33 SS9771
Signet Oxon 36 SP2410
Silchester Hants 24 SU6261
Sileby Leics 62 SK6015
Silecroft Cumb 86 SD1381
Silfield Norfk 66 TM1299
Silian Dyfed 44 SN5751
Silk Willoughby Lincs 64 TF0542
Silkstead Hants 13 SU4424
Silkstone S York 82 SE2805
Silkstone Common S York 82 SE2904
Silksworth T & W 96 NZ3752
Silloth Cumb 92 NY1153
Silpho N York 91 SE9692
Silsden W York 82 SE0446
Silsoe Beds 38 TL0835
Silton Dorset 22 ST7829
Silver End Beds 38 TL1042
Silver End Essex 40 TL8119
Silver Street H & W 61 SP0776
Silver Street Somset 21 ST5432
Silver Street Kent 28 TQ8760
Silverburn Loth 117 NT2060
Silverdale Lancs 87 SD4674
Silverdale Staffs 72 SJ8146
Silverdale Green Lancs 87 SD4674
Silverford Gramp 142 NJ7763
Silvergate Norfk 66 TG1727
Silverlace Green Suffk 55 TM3160
Silverley's Green Suffk 55 TM2976
Silverstone Nhants 49 SP6743
Silverton Devon 9 SS9502
Silverwell Cnwll 3 SW7448
Silvington Shrops 47 SO6279
Simmondley Derbys 74 SK0293
Simonburn Nthumb 102 NY8773
Simons Burrow Devon 9 ST1416
Simonsbath Somset 19 SS7739
Simonstone Lancs 81 SD7734
Simonstone N York 88 SD8791
Simpson Bucks 38 SP8836
Simpson Cross Dyfed 30 SM8919
Sinclair's Hill Border 119 NT8150
Sinclairston Strath 107 NS4716
Sinderby N York 89 SE3482
Sinderhope Nthumb 95 NY8451
Sinderland Green Gt Man 79 SJ7389
Sindlesham Berks 25 SU7769
Single Street Gt Lon 27 TQ4359
Singleborough Bucks 49 SP7631
Singleton Lancs 80 SD3838
Singleton W Susx 14 SU8713
Singlewell Kent 28 TQ6570
Sinkhurst Green Kent 28 TQ8142
Sinnarhard Gramp 134 NJ4713
Sinnington N York 90 SE7485
Sinton H & W 47 SO8160
Sinton Green H & W 47 SO8160
Sipson Gt Lon 26 TQ0777
Sirhowy Gwent 33 SO1410
Sissinghurst Kent 28 TQ7937
Siston Avon 35 ST6875
Sitcott Devon 5 SX3691
Sithney Cnwll 2 SW6328
Sithney Common Cnwll 2 SW6428
Sithney Green Cnwll 2 SW6429
Sittingbourne Kent 28 TQ9063
Six Ashes Staffs 60 SO7988
Six Bells Gwent 34 SO2202
Six Mile Bottom Cambs 53 TL5756
Six Mile Cottages Kent 29 TR1344
Six Rues Jersey 152 JS0000
Sixhills Lincs 76 TF1787
Sixpenny Handley Dorset 11 ST9917
Sizewell Suffk 55 TM4762
Skaill Ork 155 HY5806
Skaith D & G 99 NX3766
Skares Strath 107 NS5317
Skateraw Loth 119 NT7375
Skeabost Highld 136 NG4148
Skeeby N York 89 NZ1902
Skeffington Leics 63 SK7402
Skeffling Humb 85 TA3719
Skegby Notts 75 SK4961
Skegby Notts 75 SK7869
Skegness Lincs 77 TF5663
Skelbo Highld 147 NH7895
Skelbo Street Highld 147 NH7994
Skelbrooke S York 83 SE5012
Skeldyke Lincs 64 TF3337
Skellingthorpe Lincs 76 SK9272
Skellorm Green Ches 79 SJ9281
Skellow S York 83 SE5310
Skelmanthorpe W York 82 SE2310
Skelmersdale Lancs 78 SD4606
Skelmorlie Strath 114 NS1967
Skelpick Highld 150 NC7256
Skelston D & G 100 NX8285
Skelton Cumb 93 NY4335
Skelton N York 89 NZ0900
Skelton Cleve 97 NZ6618
Skelton N York 89 SE3668
Skelton N York 83 SE5756
Skelton Humb 84 SE7625
Skelwith Bridge Cumb 87 NY3403
Skendleby Lincs 77 TF4369
Skene House Gramp 135 NJ7610
Skenfrith Gwent 34 SO4520
Skerne Humb 84 TA0455
Skerray Highld 149 NC6563
Skerricha Highld 148 NC2350
Skerton Lancs 87 SD4763
Sketchley Leics 50 SP4292
Sketty W Glam 32 SS6292
Skewen W Glam 32 SS7296
Skewsby N York 90 SE6270
Skeyton Norfk 67 TG2425
Skeyton Corner Norfk 67 TG2527
Skiall Highld 150 ND0267
Skidbrooke Lincs 77 TF4393
Skidbrooke North End Lincs 77 TF4395
Skidby Humb 84 TA0133
Skigersta W Isls 154 NB5461
Skilgate Somset 20 SS9827
Skillington Lincs 63 SK8925
Skinburness Cumb 92 NY1256
Skinflats Cent 116 NS9082
Skinidin Highld 136 NG2247
Skinners Green Berks 24 SU4465
Skinningrove Cleve 97 NZ7119
Skipness Strath 114 NR9057
Skipper's Bridge Cumb 101 NY3783
Skiprigg Cumb 93 NY3945
Skipsea Humb 85 TA1654
Skipsea Brough Humb 85 TA1454
Skipton N York 82 SD9851
Skipton-on-Swale N York 89 SE3679
Skipwith N York 83 SE6638
Skirling Border 108 NT0739
Skirmett Bucks 37 SU7790
Skirpenbeck Humb 84 SE7456
Skirwith Cumb 94 NY6132
Skirwith N York 87 SD7073
Skirza Highld 151 ND3868
Skitby Cumb 101 NY4465
Skittle Green Bucks 37 SP7703
Skulamus Highld 129 NG6622
Skullomie Highld 149 NC6161
Skyborry Green Shrops 46 SO2674
Skye Green Essex 40 TL8722
Skye of Curr Highld 141 NH9924
Skyreholme N York 88 SE0660
Slack W York 82 SD9728
Slack Derbys 74 SK3362
Slack Head Cumb 87 SD4978
Slack Side W York 82 SE1430
Slackadale Gramp 142 NJ7454
Slackcote Gt Man 82 SD9709
Slackholme End Lincs 77 TF5370
Slacks of Cairnbanno Gramp 143 NJ8445
Slad Gloucs 35 SO8707
Slade Devon 19 SS5046
Slade Somset 19 SS8327
Slade Devon 9 ST1108
Slade End Oxon 37 SU5990
Slade Green Kent 27 TQ5276
Slade Heath Staffs 60 SJ9106
Slade Hooton S York 75 SK5288
Sladen Derbys 74 SK0771
Slades Green H & W 47 SO8134
Sladesbridge Cnwll 4 SX0171
Slaggan Highld 144 NG8494
Slaggyford Nthumb 94 NY6752
Slagnaw D & G 99 NX7458
Slaid Hill W York 83 SE3240
Slaidburn Lancs 81 SD7152
Slaithwaite W York 82 SE0813
Slaley Nthumb 95 NY9657
Slaley Derbys 74 SK2757
Slamannan Cent 116 NS8572
Slapton Nhants 49 SP6446
Slapton Bucks 38 SP9320
Slapton Devon 7 SX8245
Slattocks Gt Man 79 SD8808
Slaugham W Susx 15 TQ2528
Slaughterford Wilts 35 ST8473
Slawston Leics 50 SP7894
Sleaford Hants 25 SU8038
Sleaford Lincs 64 TF0645
Sleagill Cumb 94 NY5919
Sleap Shrops 59 SJ4826
Sleapford Shrops 59 SJ6315
Sleasdairidh Highld 146 NH6496
Sledge Green H & W 47 SO8134
Sledmere Humb 91 SE9364
Sleight Dorset 11 SY9898
Sleightholme Dur 88 NY9510
Sleights N York 90 NZ8607
Slepe Dorset 11 SY9293
Slerra Devon 18 SS3124
Slickly Highld 151 ND2966
Sliddery Strath 105 NR9323
Sligachan Highld 136 NG4829
Sligrachan Strath 114 NS1791
Slimbridge Gloucs 35 SO7303
Slindon Staffs 72 SJ8232
Slindon W Susx 14 SU9608
Slinfold W Susx 14 TQ1131
Sling Gwynd 69 SH6066
Slingsby N York 90 SE6974
Slip End Beds 38 TL0718
Slip End Herts 39 TL2837
Slipton Nhants 51 SP9579
Slitting Mill Staffs 73 SK0217
Slockavullin Strath 113 NR8297
Slogarie D & G 99 NX6568
Sloley Norfk 67 TG2923
Sloncombe Devon 8 SX7386
Sloothby Lincs 77 TF4970

Slough St. Buryan

Slough *Berks* 26 SU9879
Slough Green *Somset* 20 ST2719
Slough Green *W Susx* 15 TQ2826
Slumbay *Highld* 138 NG8938
Slyfield Green *Surrey* 25 SU9952
Slyne *Lancs* 87 SD4765
Smailholm *Border* 110 NT6436
Small Dole *W Susx* 15 TQ2112
Small Heath *W Mids* 61 SP1085
Small Hythe *Kent* 17 TQ8930
Small Wood Hey *Lancs* 80 SD3948
Smallbridge *Gt Man* 81 SD9115
Smallbrook *Gloucs* 34 SO5900
Smallbrook *Devon* 9 SX8698
Smallburgh *Norfk* 67 TG3324
Smalldale *Derbys* 74 SK0977
Smalldale *Derbys* 74 SK1781
Smalley *Derbys* 62 SK4044
Smalley Common *Derbys* 62 SK4042
Smalley Green *Derbys* 62 SK4043
Smallfield *Surrey* 15 TQ3143
Smallridge *Devon* 10 ST3001
Smallthorne *Staffs* 72 SJ8850
Smallwood *Ches* 72 SJ8060
Smallworth *Norfk* 54 TM0080
Smannell *Hants* 23 SU3749
Smardale *Cumb* 88 NY7308
Smarden *Kent* 28 TQ8742
Smarden Bell *Kent* 28 TQ8742
Smart's Hill *Kent* 16 TQ5242
Smeafield *Nthumb* 111 NU0937
Smeale *IOM* 153 NX4102
Smearisary *Highld* 129 NM6476
Smeatharpe *Devon* 9 ST1910
Smeeth *Kent* 29 TR0739
Smeeton Westerby *Leics* 50 SP6892
Smelthouses *N York* 89 SE1964
Smerral *Highld* 151 ND1733
Smestow *Staffs* 60 SO8591
Smethwick *W Mids* 60 SP0287
Smethwick Green *Ches* 72 SJ8063
Smisby *Derbys* 62 SK3418
Smith End Green *H & W* 47 SO7752
Smith Green *Lancs* 80 SD4955
Smith's End *Herts* 39 TL4037
Smith's Green *Essex* 40 TL5721
Smith's Green *Essex* 53 TL6640
Smitheclose *IOW* 13 SZ5391
Smithfield *Cumb* 101 NY4465
Smithies *S York* 83 SE3508
Smithincott *Devon* 9 ST0611
Smithstown *Highld* 144 NG7977
Smithton *Highld* 140 NH7145
Smithy Green *Ches* 79 SJ7474
Smithy Green *Gt Man* 79 SJ8785
Smithy Houses *Derbys* 62 SK3846
Smockington *Leics* 50 SP4589
Smoo *Highld* 149 NC4167
Smythe's Green *Essex* 40 TL9218
Snade *D & G* 100 NX8485
Snaigow House *Tays* 125 NO0843
Snailbeach *Shrops* 59 SJ3702
Snailwell *Cambs* 53 TL6467
Snainton *N York* 91 SE9282
Snaith *Humb* 83 SE6422
Snape *N York* 89 SE2684
Snape *Suffk* 55 TM3959
Snape Green *Mersyd* 80 SD3813
Snape Street *Suffk* 55 TM3958
Snarestone *Leics* 62 SK3409
Snarford *Lincs* 76 TF0482
Snargate *Kent* 17 TQ9928
Snave *Kent* 17 TR0129
Sneachill *H & W* 47 SO9053
Snead *Powys* 59 SO3192
Sneath Common *Norfk* 54 TM1689
Sneaton *N York* 91 NZ8907
Sneatonthorpe *N York* 91 NZ9006
Snelland *Lincs* 76 TF0780
Snelston *Derbys* 73 SK1543
Snetterton *Norfk* 66 TL9991
Snettisham *Norfk* 65 TF6834
Snibston *Leics* 62 SK4114
Snig's End *Gloucs* 47 SO7828
Sniperhill *Kent* 28 TQ9163
Snitter *Nthumb* 103 NU0203
Snitterby *Lincs* 76 SK9894
Snitterfield *Warwks* 48 SP2159
Snitterton *Derbys* 74 SK2760
Snittlegarth *Cumb* 93 NY2138
Snitton *Shrops* 46 SO5575
Snoadhill *Kent* 28 TQ9442
Snodhill *H & W* 46 SO3240
Snodland *Kent* 28 TQ7061
Snoll Hatch *Kent* 28 TQ6648
Snow End *Herts* 39 TL4032
Snow Street *Norfk* 54 TM0981
Snowden Hill *S York* 74 SE2600
Snowshill *Gloucs* 48 SP0933
Soake *Hants* 13 SU6611
Soar *Powys* 45 SN9731
Soar *M Glam* 33 ST0983
Soberton *Hants* 13 SU6116
Soberton Heath *Hants* 13 SU6014
Sockbridge *Cumb* 94 NY4926
Sockburn *Nthumb* 89 NZ3406
Sodylt Bank *Shrops* 71 SJ3439
Soham *Cambs* 53 TL5973
Soham Cotes *Cambs* 53 TL5775
Solbury *Dyfed* 30 SM8912
Soldon *Devon* 18 SS3210
Soldon Cross *Devon* 18 SS3210
Soldridge *Hants* 24 SU6535
Sole Street *Kent* 28 TQ6567
Sole Street *Kent* 29 TR0949
Solihull *W Mids* 61 SP1679
Solitote *Highld* 136 NG4274
Sollas *W Isls* 154 NF8074
Sollers Dilwyn *H & W* 46 SO4255
Sollers Hope *H & W* 46 SO6132
Sollom *Lancs* 80 SD4518
Solva *Dyfed* 30 SM8024
Solwaybank *D & G* 101 NY3077
Somerby *Leics* 63 SK7710
Somerby *Lincs* 84 TA0606
Somercotes *Derbys* 74 SK4253
Somerford Keynes *Gloucs* 35 SU0195
Somerley *W Susx* 14 SZ8198
Somerleyton *Suffk* 67 TM4897
Somersal Herbert *Derbys* 73 SK1335
Somersby *Lincs* 77 TF3472
Somersham *Cambs* 52 TL3678
Somersham *Suffk* 54 TM0848
Somerton *Oxon* 49 SP4928
Somerton *Somset* 21 ST4928
Somerton *Suffk* 54 TL8153
Somerwood *Shrops* 59 SJ5614
Sompting *W Susx* 15 TQ1505
Sonning *Berks* 37 SU7575
Sonning Common *Oxon* 37 SU7180
Sonning Eye *Oxon* 37 SU7476
Sontley *Clwyd* 71 SJ3347
Sopley *Hants* 12 SZ1596
Sopworth *Wilts* 35 ST8286
Sorbie *D & G* 99 NX4346
Sorbietrees *Cumb* 101 NY4884
Sordale *Highld* 151 ND1462
Sorisdale *Strath* 120 NM2763
Sorn *Strath* 107 NS5526
Sortat *Highld* 151 ND2863
Sosgill *Cumb* 92 NY1024
Sotby *Lincs* 76 TF2078
Sots Hole *Lincs* 76 TF1264
Sotterly *Suffk* 55 TM4484
Sotwell *Oxon* 37 SU5890
Soughton *Clwyd* 70 SJ2466
Soulbury *Bucks* 38 SP8826
Soulby *Cumb* 93 NY4625
Soulby *Cumb* 88 NY7411
Souldern *Oxon* 49 SP5231
Souldrop *Beds* 51 SP9861
Sound Muir *Gramp* 141 NJ3652
Soundwell *Avon* 35 ST6575
Sourton *Devon* 8 SX5390
Soutergate *Cumb* 86 SD2281
South Acre *Norfk* 66 TF8114
South Alkham *Kent* 29 TR2441
South Allington *Devon* 7 SX7938
South Alloa *Cent* 116 NS8791
South Ambersham *W Susx* 14 SU9120
South Anston *S York* 75 SK5183
South Ascot *Berks* 25 SU9268
South Ashford *Kent* 28 TR0041
South Baddesley *Hants* 12 SZ3596
South Bank *Cleve* 97 NZ5320
South Bank *N York* 83 SE5950
South Barrow *Somset* 21 ST6028
South Beddington *Gt Lon* 27 TQ2863
South Beer *Cnwll* 5 SX3091
South Benfleet *Essex* 40 TQ7787
South Bersted *W Susx* 14 SU9300
South Bockhampton *Dorset* 12 SZ1795
South Bowood *Dorset* 10 SY4498
South Bramwith *S York* 83 SE6211
South Brent *Devon* 7 SX6960
South Brewham *Somset* 22 ST7236
South Broomhill *Nthumb* 103 NZ2499
South Burlingham *Norfk* 67 TG3807
South Cadbury *Somset* 21 ST6325
South Cairn *D & G* 98 NW9769
South Carlton *Notts* 75 SK5883
South Carlton *Lincs* 76 SK9476
South Cave *Humb* 84 SE9230
South Cerney *Gloucs* 36 SU0497
South Charlton *Nthumb* 111 NU1620
South Cheriton *Somset* 22 ST6924
South Church *Dur* 96 NZ2128
South Cleatlam *Dur* 96 NZ1218
South Cliffe *Humb* 84 SE8735
South Clifton *Notts* 75 SK8270
South Collingham *Notts* 75 SK8261
South Cornelly *M Glam* 33 SS8280
South Cove *Suffk* 55 TM4981
South Creake *Norfk* 66 TF8536
South Crosland *W York* 82 SE1112
South Croxton *Leics* 63 SK6810
South Dalton *Humb* 84 SE9645
South Duffield *N York* 83 SE6833
South Elkington *Lincs* 77 TF2988
South Elmsall *W York* 83 SE4711
South End *H & W* 47 SO7444
South End *Hants* 12 SU1015
South End *Humb* 85 TA1120
South End *Humb* 85 TA3918
South End *Norfk* 54 TL9990
South Erradale *Highld* 137 NG7471
South Fambridge *Essex* 40 TQ8694
South Fawley *Berks* 36 SU3880
South Feorline *Strath* 105 NR9028
South Ferriby *Humb* 84 SE9820
South Field *Humb* 84 TA0225
South Godstone *Surrey* 15 TQ3648
South Gorley *Hants* 12 SU1610
South Gosforth *T & W* 103 NZ2467
South Green *Kent* 28 TQ8560
South Hanningfield *Essex* 40 TQ7497
South Harting *W Susx* 14 SU7819
South Hayling *Hants* 13 SZ7299
South Hazelrigg *Nthumb* 111 NU0532
South Heath *Bucks* 26 SP9101
South Heighton *E Susx* 16 TQ4402
South Hetton *Cleve* 96 NZ3845
South Hiendley *W York* 83 SE3912
South Hill *Somset* 21 ST4726
South Hill *Cnwll* 5 SX3272
South Hinksey *Oxon* 37 SP5104
South Hole *Devon* 18 SS2220
South Holmwood *Surrey* 15 TQ1744
South Hornchurch *Gt Lon* 27 TQ5183
South Huish *Devon* 7 SX6941
South Hykeham *Lincs* 76 SK9364
South Hylton *T & W* 96 NZ3556
South Kelsey *Lincs* 76 TF0498
South Kessock *Highld* 140 NH6547
South Killingholme *Humb* 85 TA1416
South Kilvington *N York* 89 SE4284
South Kilworth *Nhants* 50 SP6081
South Kirkby *W York* 83 SE4410
South Knighton *Devon* 7 SX8172
South Kyme *Lincs* 76 TF1749
South Lambeth *Gt Lon* 27 TQ3077
South Lawn *Oxon* 36 SP2814
South Leigh *Oxon* 36 SP3909
South Leverton *Notts* 75 SK7881
South Littleton *H & W* 48 SP0746
South Lopham *Norfk* 54 TM0481
South Luffenham *Leics* 63 SK9301
South Mains *D & G* 107 NS7807
South Malling *E Susx* 16 TQ4210
South Marston *Wilts* 36 SU1987
South Merstham *Surrey* 27 TQ2952
South Middleton *Nthumb* 111 NT9923
South Milford *N York* 83 SE4931
South Milton *Devon* 7 SX7042
South Mimms *Herts* 26 TL2201
South Molton *Devon* 19 SS7125
South Moor *Dur* 96 NZ1951
South Moreton *Oxon* 37 SU5688
South Mundham *W Susx* 14 SU8700
South Muskham *Notts* 75 SK7957
South Newbald *Humb* 84 SE9035
South Newington *Oxon* 48 SP4033
South Newton *Wilts* 23 SU0834
South Normanton *Derbys* 75 SK4456
South Norwood *Gt Lon* 27 TQ3368
South Nutfield *Surrey* 15 TQ3049
South Ockendon *Essex* 27 TQ5983
South Ormsby *Lincs* 77 TF3675
South Ossett *W York* 82 SE2819
South Otterington *N York* 89 SE3787
South Owersby *Lincs* 76 TF0693
South Park *Surrey* 15 TQ2448
South Perrott *Dorset* 10 ST4706
South Petherton *Somset* 10 ST4316
South Petherwin *Cnwll* 5 SX3181
South Pickenham *Norfk* 66 TF8504
South Pill *Cnwll* 6 SX4259
South Pool *Devon* 7 SX7740
South Poorton *Dorset* 10 SY5297
South Quarme *Somset* 20 SS9236
South Queensferry *Loth* 117 NT1378
South Radworthy *Devon* 19 SS7432
South Rauceby *Lincs* 64 TF0245
South Raynham *Norfk* 66 TF8723
South Reddish *Gt Man* 79 SJ8891
South Reston *Lincs* 77 TF4083
South Runcton *Norfk* 65 TF6308
South Scarle *Notts* 76 SK8463
South Shian *Strath* 122 NM9042
South Shields *T & W* 103 NZ3666
South Shore *Lancs* 80 SD3033
South Skirlaugh *Humb* 85 TA1438
South Somercotes *Lincs* 77 TF4193
South Stainley *N York* 89 SE3063
South Stifford *Essex* 27 TQ5978
South Stoke *Avon* 22 ST7461
South Stoke *Oxon* 37 SU5983
South Stoke *W Susx* 14 TQ0209
South Stour *Kent* 28 TR0338
South Street *E Susx* 15 TQ3918
South Street *Kent* 27 TQ6363
South Street *Kent* 28 TR0557
South Street *Kent* 29 TR1265
South Tarbrax *Strath* 117 NT0353
South Tawton *Devon* 8 SX6594
South Thoresby *Lincs* 77 TF4076
South Tidworth *Hants* 23 SU2347
South Town *Hants* 24 SU6536
South Walsham *Norfk* 67 TG3613
South Warnborough *Hants* 24 SU7247
South Weald *Essex* 27 TQ5694
South Weston *Oxon* 37 SU7098
South Wheatley *Cnwll* 5 SX2492
South Widcombe *Somset* 21 ST5856
South Wigston *Leics* 50 SP5897
South Willesborough *Kent* 28 TR0240
South Willingham *Lincs* 76 TF1983
South Wingate *Dur* 96 NZ4134
South Wingfield *Derbys* 74 SK3755
South Witham *Lincs* 63 SK9219
South Wonston *Hants* 24 SU4636
South Woodham Ferrers *Essex* 40 TQ8097
South Wootton *Norfk* 65 TF6422
South Wraxall *Wilts* 22 ST8364
South Zeal *Devon* 8 SX6593
Southall *Gt Lon* 26 TQ1279
Southam *Gloucs* 47 SO9725
Southam *Warwks* 49 SP4161
Southampton *Hants* 13 SU4112
Southborough *Gt Lon* 27 TQ4267
Southborough *Kent* 16 TQ5842
Southbourne *W Susx* 14 SU7705
Southbourne *Dorset* 12 SZ1491
Southbrook *Dorset* 11 SY8494
Southburgh *Norfk* 66 TG0005
Southburn *Humb* 84 SE9854
Southchurch *Essex* 40 TQ9086
Southcott *Devon* 18 SS4416
Southcott *Wilts* 23 SU1659
Southcott *Cnwll* 5 SX1995
Southcott *Devon* 8 SX5495
Southcott *Devon* 8 SX7580
Southcourt *Bucks* 38 SP8112
Southease *E Susx* 16 TQ4205
Southend *Strath* 105 NR6908
Southend *Wilts* 36 SU1973
Southend-on-Sea *Essex* 40 TQ8885
Southernby *Cumb* 93 NY3639
Southernden *Kent* 28 TQ8645
Southerndown *M Glam* 33 SS8873
Southerness *D & G* 92 NX9754
Southery *Norfk* 65 TL6194
Southfield *Cent* 116 NS8472
Southfleet *Kent* 27 TQ6171
Southford *IOW* 13 SZ5179
Southgate *W Glam* 32 SS5587
Southgate *Norfk* 65 TF6833
Southgate *Norfk* 66 TF8635
Southgate *Norfk* 66 TG1324
Southgate *Gt Lon* 27 TQ2994
Southill *Beds* 39 TL1542
Southington *Hants* 24 SU5049
Southleigh *Devon* 9 SY2093
Southminster *Essex* 40 TQ9599
Southmoor *Oxon* 36 SU3998
Southmuir *Tays* 126 NO3852
Southoe *Cambs* 52 TL1864
Southolt *Suffk* 55 TM1968
Southorpe *Cambs* 64 TF0803
Southover *Dorset* 10 SY6294
Southover *E Susx* 16 TQ6525
Southowram *W York* 82 SE1123
Southport *Mersyd* 80 SD3317
Southrepps *Norfk* 67 TG2536
Southrey *Lincs* 76 TF1366
Southrop *Gloucs* 36 SP1903
Southrope *Hants* 24 SU6644
Southsea *Clwyd* 71 SJ3051
Southsea *Hants* 13 SZ6599
Southside *Dur* 95 NZ1026
Southtown *Somset* 10 ST3216
Southtown *Norfk* 67 TG5106
Southwaite *Cumb* 93 NY4445
Southwark *Gt Lon* 27 TQ3279
Southwater *W Susx* 15 TQ1526
Southwater Street *W Susx* 15 TQ1427
Southway *Somset* 21 ST5242
Southwell *Notts* 75 SK6953
Southwell *Dorset* 11 SY6870
Southwick *T & W* 96 NZ3758
Southwick *Somset* 21 ST3646
Southwick *Wilts* 22 ST8355
Southwick *Hants* 13 SU6208
Southwick *Nhants* 51 TL0292
Southwick *W Susx* 15 TQ2405
Southwold *Suffk* 55 TM5076
Southwood *Somset* 21 ST5533
Southwood *Norfk* 67 TG3905
Sowe Common *W Mids* 61 SP3782
Sower Carr *Lancs* 80 SD3743
Sowerby *W York* 82 SE0423
Sowerby *N York* 89 SE4380
Sowerby Bridge *W York* 82 SE0523
Sowerby Row *Cumb* 93 NY3940
Sowerhill *Somset* 19 SS8924
Sowhill *Gwent* 34 SO2700
Sowley Green *Suffk* 53 TL7050
Sowood *W York* 82 SE0818
Sowton *Devon* 6 SX5065
Sowton *Devon* 9 SX9792
Soyland Town *W York* 82 SE0320
Spa Common *Norfk* 67 TG2930
Spain's End *Essex* 53 TL6637
Spalding *Lincs* 64 TF2422
Spaldington *Humb* 84 SE7633
Spaldwick *Cambs* 52 TL1372
Spalford *Notts* 76 SK8369
Spanish Green *Hants* 24 SU6958
Sparham *Norfk* 66 TG0719
Sparhamill *Norfk* 66 TG0818
Spark Bridge *Cumb* 86 SD3084
Sparket *Cumb* 93 NY4325
Sparkford *Somset* 21 ST6025
Sparkhill *W Mids* 61 SP1083
Sparkwell *Devon* 6 SX5857
Sparrow Green *Norfk* 66 TF9414
Sparrowpit *Derbys* 74 SK0880
Sparrows Green *E Susx* 16 TQ6332
Sparsholt *Oxon* 36 SU3487
Sparsholt *Hants* 24 SU4331
Spartylea *Cumb* 95 NY8548
Spath *Staffs* 73 SK0835
Spaunton *N York* 90 SE7289
Spaxton *Somset* 20 ST2237
Spean Bridge *Highld* 131 NN2281
Spear Hill *W Susx* 15 TQ1317
Spearywell *Hants* 23 SU3127
Speen *Berks* 24 SU4567
Speen *Bucks* 26 SU8499
Speeton *N York* 91 TA1574
Speke *Mersyd* 78 SJ4383
Speldhurst *Kent* 16 TQ5541
Spellbrook *Herts* 39 TL4817
Spelmonden *Kent* 28 TQ7037
Spelsbury *Oxon* 36 SP3421
Spen *W York* 82 SE1925
Spen Green *Ches* 72 SJ8160
Spencers Wood *Berks* 24 SU7166
Spennithorne *N York* 89 SE1388
Spennymoor *Dur* 96 NZ2533
Spernall *Warwks* 48 SP0862
Spestos *Devon* 8 SX7298
Spetchley *H & W* 47 SO8953
Spettisbury *Dorset* 11 ST9102
Spexhall *Suffk* 55 TM3780
Spey Bay *Gramp* 141 NJ3565
Speybridge *Highld* 141 NJ0326
Speyview *Gramp* 141 NJ2541
Spilsby *Lincs* 77 TF4066
Spindlestone *Nthumb* 111 NU1533
Spinkhill *Derbys* 75 SK4578
Spinningdale *Highld* 146 NH6789
Spirthill *Wilts* 35 ST9976
Spital *Mersyd* 78 SJ3482
Spital *Berks* 26 SU9675
Spital Hill *Notts* 75 SK6193
Spital in the Street *Lincs* 76 SK9690
Spithurst *E Susx* 16 TQ4217
Spittal *Highld* 151 ND1654
Spittal *Loth* 118 NT4677
Spittal *Nthumb* 119 NU0051
Spittal *Humb* 84 SE7652
Spittal *Dyfed* 30 SM9723
Spittal of Glenmuick *Gramp* 134 NO3085
Spittal of Glenshee *Tays* 133 NO1070
Spittal-on-Rule *Border* 110 NT5819
Spittalfield *Tays* 126 NO1040
Spixworth *Norfk* 67 TG2415
Splatt *Devon* 8 SS6005
Splatt *Cnwll* 4 SW9476
Splatt *Cnwll* 5 SX2288
Splayne's Green *E Susx* 16 TQ4224
Splottlands *S Glam* 33 ST2077
Spodegreen *Ches* 79 SJ7385
Spofforth *N York* 83 SE3651
Spon Green *Clwyd* 70 SJ2863
Spondon *Derbys* 62 SK4036
Spooner Row *Norfk* 66 TM0997
Sporle *Norfk* 66 TF8411
Spott *Loth* 118 NT6775
Spottiswoode *Border* 110 NT6049
Spratton *Nhants* 50 SP7169
Spreakley *Surrey* 25 SU8341
Spreyton *Devon* 8 SX6996
Spriddlestone *Devon* 6 SX5351
Spridlington *Lincs* 76 TF0084
Spring Vale *S York* 82 SE2502
Springburn *Strath* 116 NS6068
Springfield *Fife* 126 NO3411
Springfield *D & G* 101 NY3268
Springfield *Essex* 40 TL7208
Springhill *Staffs* 60 SJ9704
Springhill *Staffs* 61 SK0705
Springholm *D & G* 100 NX8070
Springkell *D & G* 101 NY2575
Springside *Strath* 106 NS3738
Springthorpe *Lincs* 76 SK8789
Springwell *T & W* 96 NZ2858
Sproatley *Humb* 85 TA1934
Sproston Green *Ches* 72 SJ7366
Sprotbrough *S York* 83 SE5301
Sproughton *Suffk* 54 TM1244
Sprouston *Border* 110 NT7535
Sprowston *Norfk* 67 TG2512
Sproxton *N York* 90 SE6181
Sproxton *Leics* 63 SK8524
Sprytown *Devon* 5 SX4185
Spunhill *Shrops* 59 SJ4133
Spurstow *Ches* 71 SJ5657
Spyway *Dorset* 10 SY5293
Squirrel's Heath *Gt Lon* 27 TQ5389
St-y-Nyll *S Glam* 33 ST0977
St. Abbs *Border* 119 NT9167
St. Agnes *Loth* 118 NT6763
St. Agnes *Cnwll* 2 SW7150
St. Albans *Herts* 38 TL1407
St. Allen *Cnwll* 3 SW8250
St. Andrew *Guern* 152 GN0000
St. Andrew's Major *S Glam* 33 ST1371
St. Andrews *Fife* 127 NO5116
St. Andrews Well *Dorset* 10 SY4793
St. Ann's *D & G* 100 NY0793
St. Ann's Chapel *Cnwll* 5 SX4170
St. Ann's Chapel *Devon* 7 SX6647
St. Anne's *Lancs* 80 SD3228
St. Anthony *Cnwll* 3 SW7825
St. Anthony's Hill *E Susx* 16 TQ6201
St. Arvans *Gwent* 34 ST5296
St. Asaph *Clwyd* 70 SJ0374
St. Athan *S Glam* 20 ST0167
St. Aubin *Jersey* 152 JS0000
St. Austell *Cnwll* 3 SX0152
St. Bees *Cumb* 86 NX9711
St. Blazey *Cnwll* 3 SX0654
St. Blazey Gate *Cnwll* 3 SX0653
St. Boswells *Border* 110 NT5930
St. Brelade *Jersey* 152 JS0000
St. Brelades Bay *Jersey* 152 JS0000
St. Breock *Cnwll* 4 SW9771
St. Breward *Cnwll* 4 SX0977
St. Briavels *Gloucs* 34 SO5604
St. Bride's Major *M Glam* 33 SS8974
St. Brides *Dyfed* 30 SM8010
St. Brides Netherwent *Gwent* 34 ST4289
St. Brides Wentlooge *Gwent* 34 ST2982
St. Brides super-Ely *S Glam* 33 ST0977
St. Budeaux *Devon* 6 SX4558
St. Buryan *Cnwll* 2 SW4025

St.Cadoc Stockland

St. Cadoc Cnwll 4 SW8875
St. Catherine Avon 35 ST7769
St. Catherines Strath 123 NN1207
St. Chloe Gloucs 35 SO8401
St. Clears Dyfed 31 SN2816
St. Cleer Cnwll 5 SX2468
St. Clement Jersey 152 JS0000
St. Clement Cnwll 3 SW8543
St. Clether Cnwll 5 SX2084
St. Colmac Strath 114 NS0467
St. Columb Major Cnwll 4 SW9163
St. Columb Minor Cnwll 4 SW8362
St. Columb Road Cnwll 4 SW9159
St. Combs Gramp 143 NK0563
St. Cross South Elmham Suffk 55 TM2984
St. Cyrus Gramp 135 NO7464
St. David's Tays 125 NN9420
St. Davids Dyfed 30 SM7525
St. Day Cnwll 3 SW7242
St. Decumans Somset 20 ST0642
St. Dennis Cnwll 4 SW9557
St. Devereux H & W 46 SO4431
St. Dogmaels Dyfed 42 SN1645
St. Dogwells Dyfed 30 SM9727
St. Dominick Cnwll 5 SX4067
St. Donats S Glam 20 SS9368
St. Edith's Marsh Wilts 22 ST9764
St. Endellion Cnwll 4 SW9978
St. Enoder Cnwll 3 SW8956
St. Erme Cnwll 3 SW8449
St. Erney Cnwll 5 SX3559
St. Erth Cnwll 2 SW5535
St. Erth Praze Cnwll 2 SW5735
St. Ervan Cnwll 4 SW8970
St. Ewe Cnwll 3 SW9746
St. Fagans S Glam 33 ST1277
St. Fergus Gramp 143 NK0952
St. Fillans Tays 124 NN6924
St. Florence Dyfed 31 SN0801
St. Gennys Cnwll 4 SX1497
St. George Clwyd 70 SH9775
St. George's S Glam 33 ST1076
St. George's Hill Surrey 26 TQ0862
St. Georges Avon 21 ST3762
St. Germans Cnwll 5 SX3657
St Giles in the Wood Devon 19 SS5319
St. Giles-on-the-Heath Cnwll 5 SX3690
St. Harmon Powys 45 SN9872
St. Helen Auckland Dur 96 NZ1826
St. Helena Norfk 66 TG1816
St. Helens Cumb 92 NY0232
St. Helens IOW 13 SZ6289
St. Helens E Susx 17 TQ8212
St Helens Mersyd 78 SJ5195
St. Helier Jersey 152 JS0000
St. Helier Gt Lon 27 TQ2567
St. Hilary S Glam 33 ST0173
St. Hilary Cnwll 2 SW5431
St. Ibbs Herts 39 TL1926
St. Illtyd Gwent 34 SO2202
St. Ishmaels Dyfed 30 SM8307
St. Issey Cnwll 4 SW9271
St. Ive Cnwll 5 SX3167
St. Ives W York 82 SE0938
St. Ives Dorset 12 SU1204
St. Ives Cnwll 2 SW5140
St. Ives Cambs 52 TL3171
St. Jame's End Nhants 49 SP7460
St. James Norfk 67 TG2720
St. James South Elmham Suffk 55 TM3281
St. John Jersey 152 JS0000
St. John Cnwll 5 SX4053
St. John's IOM 153 SC2781
St. John's Chapel Dur 95 NY8837
St. John's Chapel Devon 19 SS5329
St. John's Fen End Norfk 65 TF5312
St. John's Highway Norfk 65 TF5214
St. John's Kirk Strath 108 NS9836
St. John's Town of Dalry D & G 99 NX6281
St. John's Wood Gt Lon 27 TQ2683
St. Johns Dur 95 NZ0633
St. Johns H & W 47 SO8454
St. Johns Surrey 25 SU9857
St. Johns Kent 27 TQ5356
St. Jude's IOM 153 SC3996
St. Just Cnwll 2 SW3731
St. Just Cnwll 3 SW8435
St. Just Lane Cnwll 3 SW8535
St. Katherines Gramp 142 NJ7834
St. Keverne Cnwll 3 SW7921
St. Kew Cnwll 4 SX0276
St. Kew Highway Cnwll 4 SX0375
St. Keyne Cnwll 5 SX2461
St. Laurence Kent 29 TR3665
St. Lawrence Jersey 152 JS0000
St. Lawrence Cnwll 4 SX0466
St. Lawrence IOW 13 SZ5376
St. Lawrence Essex 41 TL9604
St. Leonards Bucks 38 SP9007
St. Leonards Dorset 12 SU1103
St. Leonards E Susx 17 TQ8009
St. Leonards Street Kent 28 TQ6756
St. Levan Cnwll 2 SW3822
St. Lythans S Glam 33 ST1072
St. Mabyn Cnwll 4 SX0473
St. Margaret South Elmham Suffk 55 TM3183
St. Margaret's at Cliffe Kent 29 TR3544
St. Margarets H & W 46 SO3533
St. Margarets Herts 39 TL3811
St. Margarets Hope Ork 155 ND4493
St. Marks IOM 153 SC2974
St. Martin Guern 152 GN0000
St. Martin Jersey 152 JS0000
St. Martin Cnwll 5 SX2555
St. Martin's Tays 126 NO1530
St. Martin's Green Cnwll 3 SW7323
St. Martin's Moor Shrops 59 SJ3135
St. Martins Shrops 59 SJ3236
St. Mary Jersey 152 JS0000
St. Mary Bourne Hants 24 SU4250
St. Mary Church S Glam 33 ST0071
St. Mary Cray Gt Lon 27 TQ4768
St. Mary Hill S Glam 33 SS9678
St. Mary in the Marsh Kent 17 TR0627
St. Mary's Ork 155 HY4701
St. Mary's Bay Kent 17 TR0827
St. Mary's Grove Avon 21 ST4669
St. Mary's Hoo Kent 28 TQ8076
St. Marychurch Devon 7 SX9166
St. Marylebone Gt Lon 27 TQ2782
St. Maughans Gwent 34 SO4617
St. Maughans Green Gwent 34 SO4717
St. Mawes Cnwll 3 SW8433
St. Mawgan Cnwll 4 SW8765
St. Mellion Cnwll 5 SX3965
St. Mellons S Glam 34 ST2281
St. Merryn Cnwll 4 SW8874
St. Mewan Cnwll 3 SW9951
St. Michael Caerhays Cnwll 3 SW9642
St. Michael Church Somset 20 ST3030
St. Michael Penkevil Cnwll 3 SW8541
St. Michael South Elmham Suffk 55 TM3483
St. Michael's on Wyre Lancs 80 SD4641
St. Michaels H & W 46 SO5865
St. Michaels Kent 17 TQ8835
St. Minver Cnwll 4 SW9677
St. Monans Fife 127 NO5201
St. Neot Cnwll 4 SX1868
St. Neots Cambs 52 TL1860
St. Newlyn East Cnwll 3 SW8256
St. Nicholas Dyfed 30 SM9035
St. Nicholas S Glam 33 ST0974
St. Nicholas at Wade Kent 29 TR2666
St. Ninians Cent 116 NS7991
St. Olaves Norfk 67 TM4599
St. Osyth Essex 41 TM1215
St. Ouen Jersey 152 JS0000
St. Owens Cross H & W 46 SO5324
St. Paul's Walden Herts 39 TL1922
St. Pauls Cray Gt Lon 27 TQ4768
St. Peter Jersey 152 JS0000
St. Peter Port Guern 152 GN0000
St. Peter's Guern 152 GN0000
St. Peter's Kent 29 TR3868
St. Peter's Hill Cambs 52 TL2372
St. Petrox Dyfed 30 SR9797
St. Pinnock Cnwll 5 SX2063
St. Quivox Strath 106 NS3723
St. Ruan Cnwll 2 SW7115
St. Sampson Guern 152 GN0000
St. Saviour Guern 152 GN0000
St. Saviour Jersey 152 JS0000
St. Stephen Cnwll 3 SW9453
St. Stephens Cnwll 5 SX3285
St. Stephens Cnwll 5 SX4158
St. Stephen's Coombe Cnwll 3 SW9451
St. Teath Cnwll 4 SX0680
St. Tudy Cnwll 4 SX0676
St. Twynnells Dyfed 30 SR9597
St. Veep Cnwll 3 SX1455
St. Vigeans Tays 127 NO6443
St. Wenn Cnwll 4 SW9664
St. Weonards H & W 46 SO4924
Stableford Staffs 72 SJ8138
Stableford Shrops 60 SO7598
Stacey Bank Derbys 74 SK2890
Stackhouse N York 88 SD8165
Stackpole Dyfed 30 SR9896
Stacksford Norfk 54 TM0590
Stacksteads Lancs 81 SD8521
Stadbury Devon 7 SX6846
Staddiscombe Devon 6 SX5151
Staddlethorpe Humb 84 SE8328
Stadhampton Oxon 37 SU6098
Staffield Cumb 94 NY5442
Staffin Highld 136 NG4967
Stafford Staffs 72 SJ9223
Stag Green Cumb 86 SD1679
Stagsden Beds 38 SP9848
Stainburn Cumb 92 NY0129
Stainburn N York 82 SE2548
Stainby Lincs 63 SK9022
Staincross S York 83 SE3210
Staindrop Dur 96 NZ1220
Staines Surrey 26 TQ0371
Stainfield Lincs 64 TF0824
Stainfield Lincs 76 TF1172
Stainforth N York 88 SD8267
Stainforth S York 83 SE6411
Staining Lancs 80 SD3436
Stainland W York 82 SE0719
Stainsacre N York 91 NZ9108
Stainton Cumb 93 NY3857
Stainton Cumb 94 NY4828
Stainton Dur 95 NZ0718
Stainton Cleve 89 NZ4714
Stainton Cumb 87 SD5285
Stainton N York 89 SE1096
Stainton S York 75 SK5593
Stainton by Langworth Lincs 76 TF0677
Stainton le Vale Lincs 76 TF1794
Stainton with Adgarley Cumb 86 SD2472
Staintondale N York 91 SE9998
Stair Strath 107 NS4423
Stair Cumb 93 NY2321
Stair Haven D & G 98 NX2153
Stairfoot S York 83 SE3705
Staithes N York 97 NZ7818
Stake Pool Lancs 80 SD4147
Stakeford Nthumb 103 NZ2685
Stakes Hants 13 SU6808
Stalbridge Dorset 11 ST7317
Stalbridge Weston Dorset 11 ST7116
Stalham Norfk 67 TG3725
Stalham Green Norfk 67 TG3824
Stalisfield Green Kent 28 TQ9552
Stallen Dorset 10 ST6016
Stalling Busk N York 88 SD9186
Stallingborough Humb 85 TA1911
Stallington Staffs 72 SJ9439
Stalmine Lancs 80 SD3745
Stalmine Moss Side Lancs 80 SD3845
Stalybridge Gt Man 79 SJ9698
Stambourne Essex 53 TL7238
Stambourne Green Essex 53 TL6938
Stamford Nthumb 111 NU2219
Stamford Lincs 64 TF0307
Stamford Bridge Humb 84 SE7155
Stamford Bridge Ches 71 SJ4667
Stamford Hill Gt Lon 27 TQ3387
Stamfordham Nthumb 103 NZ0771
Stamton Lees Derbys 74 SK2562
Stanah Lancs 80 SD3542
Stanborough Herts 39 TL2211
Stanbridge Beds 38 SP9624
Stanbridge Dorset 11 SU0004
Stanbury W York 82 SE0137
Stand Strath 116 NS7668
Stand Gt Man 79 SD7905
Standburn Cent 116 NS9274
Standeford Staffs 60 SJ9107
Standen Kent 28 TQ8540
Standen Street Kent 17 TQ8030
Standerwick Somset 22 ST8150
Standford Hants 14 SU8134
Standingstone Cumb 92 NY0533
Standish Gt Man 78 SD5610
Standish Lower Ground Gt Man 78 SD5507
Standlake Oxon 36 SP3903
Standon Staffs 72 SJ8135
Standon Hants 13 SU4226
Standon Herts 39 TL3922
Standon Green End Herts 39 TL3620
Standwell Green Suffk 54 TM1369
Stane Strath 116 NS8859
Stanfield Norfk 66 TF9320
Stanford Shrops 59 SJ3313
Stanford Beds 39 TL1640
Stanford Kent 29 TR1238
Stanford Bishop H & W 47 SO6851
Stanford Bridge Shrops 72 SJ7024
Stanford Bridge H & W 47 SO7265
Stanford Dingley Berks 24 SU5771
Stanford Rivers Essex 27 TL5301
Stanford in the Vale Oxon 36 SU3493
Stanford le Hope Essex 40 TQ6882
Stanford on Avon Nhants 50 SP5978
Stanford on Soar Notts 62 SK5421
Stanford on Teme H & W 47 SO7065
Stanfree Derbys 75 SK4773
Stanghow Cleve 97 NZ6715
Stanground Cambs 64 TL2097
Stanhill Lancs 81 SD7227
Stanhoe Norfk 66 TF8036
Stanhope Border 108 NT1229
Stanhope Dur 95 NY9939
Stanhope Bretby Derbys 73 SK2921
Stanion Nhants 51 SP9186
Stanley Tays 126 NO1033
Stanley Dur 96 NZ1953
Stanley W York 83 SE3422
Stanley Staffs 72 SJ9352
Stanley Derbys 62 SK4140
Stanley Notts 75 SK4662
Stanley Shrops 60 SO7483
Stanley Common Derbys 62 SK4042
Stanley Crook Dur 96 NZ1637
Stanley Gate Lancs 78 SD4405
Stanley Moor Staffs 72 SJ9251
Stanley Pontlarge Gloucs 47 SP0030
Stanmer E Susx 15 TQ3309
Stanmore Hants 24 SU4628
Stanmore Berks 37 SU4778
Stanmore Gt Lon 26 TQ1692
Stannersburn Nthumb 102 NY7286
Stanningley W York 82 SE2234
Stannington Nthumb 103 NZ2179
Stannington S York 74 SK2987
Stansbatch H & W 46 SO3461
Stansfield Suffk 53 TL7852
Stanshope Staffs 73 SK1253
Stanstead Suffk 54 TL8449
Stanstead Abbots Herts 39 TL3811
Stanstead Street Suffk 54 TL8448
Stansted Kent 27 TQ6062
Stansted Mountfitchet Essex 39 TL5125
Stanton Nthumb 103 NZ1390
Stanton Staffs 73 SK1245
Stanton Derbys 73 SK2718
Stanton Gwent 34 SO3021
Stanton Gloucs 48 SP0634
Stanton Devon 7 SX7050
Stanton Suffk 54 TL9673
Stanton Butts Cambs 52 TL2372
Stanton Drew Avon 21 ST5963
Stanton Fitzwarren Wilts 36 SU1790
Stanton Harcourt Oxon 36 SP4105
Stanton Hill Notts 75 SK4760
Stanton Lacy Shrops 46 SO4978
Stanton Long Shrops 59 SO5791
Stanton Prior Avon 22 ST6762
Stanton St. Bernard Wilts 23 SU0961
Stanton St. John Oxon 37 SP5709
Stanton St. Quintin Wilts 35 ST9079
Stanton Street Suffk 54 TL9566
Stanton Wick Avon 21 ST6162
Stanton by Bridge Derbys 62 SK3726
Stanton by Dale Derbys 62 SK4637
Stanton in Peak Derbys 74 SK2364
Stanton on the Wolds Notts 63 SK6330
Stanton under Bardon Leics 62 SK4610
Stanton upon Hine Heath Shrops 59 SJ5624
Stantway Gloucs 35 SO7313
Stanwardine in the Field Shrops 59 SJ4124
Stanwardine in the Wood Shrops 59 SJ4227
Stanway Gloucs 48 SP0632
Stanway Essex 40 TL9424
Stanway Green Essex 40 TL9523
Stanway Green Suffk 55 TM2470
Stanwell Surrey 26 TQ0574
Stanwell Moor Surrey 26 TQ0474
Stanwick Nhants 51 SP9771
Stanwix Cumb 93 NY4057
Stape N York 90 SE7994
Stapehill Dorset 12 SU0500
Stapeley Ches 72 SJ6749
Stapenhill Staffs 73 SK2521
Staple Somset 20 ST1141
Staple Kent 29 TR2756
Staple Cross Devon 20 ST0320
Staple Cross E Susx 17 TQ7822
Staple Fitzpaine Somset 10 ST2618
Staple Hill H & W 60 SO9773
Staplefield W Susx 15 TQ2728
Stapleford Notts 62 SK4837
Stapleford Leics 63 SK8018
Stapleford Lincs 76 SK8857
Stapleford Wilts 23 SU0737
Stapleford Herts 39 TL3117
Stapleford Cambs 53 TL4751
Stapleford Abbotts Essex 27 TQ5194
Stapleford Tawney Essex 27 TQ5099
Staplegrove Somset 20 ST2126
Staplehay Somset 20 ST2121
Staplehurst Kent 28 TQ7843
Staplers IOW 13 SZ5189
Staplestreet Kent 29 TR0660
Staplet Cumb 101 NY5071
Stapleton N York 89 NZ2612
Stapleton Shrops 59 SJ4704
Stapleton H & W 46 SO3265
Stapleton Leics 50 SP4398
Stapleton Somset 21 ST4621
Stapley Somset 9 ST1913
Staploe Beds 52 TL1560
Staplow H & W 47 SO6941
Star Fife 126 NO3103
Star Dyfed 31 SN2434
Star Somset 21 ST4358
Starbeck N York 83 SE3255
Starbotton N York 88 SD9574
Starcross Devon 9 SX9781
Stareton Warwks 61 SP3371
Starkholmes Derbys 74 SK3058
Starklin H & W 60 SO8574
Starling Gt Man 79 SD7710
Starlings Green Essex 39 TL4631
Starr's Green E Susx 17 TQ7615
Starston Norfk 55 TM2384
Start Devon 7 SX8044
Startforth Dur 95 NZ0415
Startley Wilts 35 ST9482
Statenborough Kent 29 TR3155
Statham Ches 79 SJ6787
Stathe Somset 21 ST3728
Stathern Leics 63 SK7731
Station Town Dur 96 NZ4036
Staughton Green Cambs 52 TL1365
Staughton Highway Cambs 52 TL1364
Staunton Gloucs 34 SO5512
Staunton Gloucs 47 SO7829
Staunton Green H & W 46 SO3661
Staunton on Arrow H & W 46 SO3660
Staunton on Wye H & W 46 SO3644
Staveley Cumb 87 SD3786
Staveley Cumb 87 SD4698
Staveley N York 89 SE3662
Staveley Derbys 75 SK4374
Staverton Gloucs 47 SO8923
Staverton Nhants 49 SP5361
Staverton Wilts 22 ST8560
Staverton Devon 7 SX7964
Staverton Bridge Gloucs 35 SO8722
Stawell Somset 21 ST3738
Stawley Somset 20 ST0622
Staxigoe Highld 151 ND3852
Staxton N York 91 TA0179
Staylittle Dyfed 43 SN6489
Staylittle Powys 43 SN8891
Staynall Lancs 80 SD3643
Staythorpe Notts 75 SK7554
Stead W York 82 SE1446
Stean N York 89 SE0973
Steane Nhants 49 SP5538
Stearsby N York 90 SE6171
Steart Somset 20 ST2745
Stebbing Essex 40 TL6624
Stebbing Green Essex 40 TL6823
Stebbing Park Essex 40 TL6524
Stechford W Mids 61 SP1287
Stede Quarter Kent 28 TQ8738
Stedham W Susx 14 SU8622
Steel Nthumb 95 NY9458
Steel Cross E Susx 16 TQ5331
Steel Heath Shrops 59 SJ5436
Steele Road Border 101 NY5293
Steen's Bridge H & W 46 SO5357
Steep Hants 13 SU7425
Steep Lane W York 82 SE0223
Steephill IOW 13 SZ5477
Steeple Dorset 11 SY9080
Steeple Essex 41 TL9303
Steeple Ashton Wilts 22 ST9056
Steeple Aston Oxon 49 SP4725
Steeple Barton Oxon 49 SP4424
Steeple Bumpstead Essex 53 TL6841
Steeple Claydon Bucks 49 SP7026
Steeple Gidding Cambs 52 TL1381
Steeple Langford Wilts 23 SU0337
Steeple Morden Cambs 39 TL2842
Steeton W York 82 SE0344
Stein Highld 136 NG2656
Stella T & W 103 NZ1763
Stelling Minnis Kent 29 TR1447
Stembridge Somset 21 ST4220
Stenalees Cnwll 3 SX0156
Stenhouse D & G 100 NX8093
Stenhousemuir Cent 116 NS8783
Stenigot Lincs 77 TF2480
Stenscholl Highld 136 NG4767
Stenton Loth 118 NT6274
Stepaside Dyfed 31 SN1407
Stepney Gt Lon 27 TQ3681
Stepping Hill Gt Man 79 SJ9187
Steppingley Beds 38 TL0035
Stepps Strath 116 NS6568
Sternfield Suffk 55 TM3861
Sterridge Devon 19 SS5545
Stert Wilts 23 SU0259
Stetchworth Cambs 53 TL6459
Steven's Crouch E Susx 17 TQ7115
Stevenage Herts 39 TL2325
Stevenston Strath 106 NS2742
Steventon Oxon 37 SU4691
Steventon Hants 24 SU5447
Steventon End Essex 53 TL5942
Stevington Beds 51 SP9853
Stewartby Beds 38 TL0142
Stewarton Strath 105 NR6919
Stewarton Strath 115 NS4245
Stewkley Bucks 38 SP8526
Stewley Somset 10 ST3118
Stewton Lincs 77 TF3587
Steyne Cross IOW 13 SZ6487
Steyning W Susx 15 TQ1711
Steynton Dyfed 30 SM9107
Stibb Cnwll 18 SS2210
Stibb Cross Devon 18 SS4314
Stibb Green Wilts 23 SU2262
Stibbard Norfk 66 TF9828
Stibbington Cambs 51 TL0898
Stichill Border 110 NT7138
Sticker Cnwll 3 SW9750
Stickford Lincs 77 TF3560
Sticklepath Somset 20 ST0436
Sticklepath Devon 8 SX6494
Stickling Green Essex 39 TL4732
Stickney Lincs 77 TF3457
Stidd Lancs 81 SD6536
Stiff Green Kent 28 TQ8761
Stiffkey Norfk 66 TF9742
Stifford's Bridge H & W 47 SO7348
Stile Bridge Kent 28 TQ7547
Stileway Somset 21 ST4641
Stilligarry W Isls 154 NF7638
Stillingfleet N York 83 SE5940
Stillington Cleve 96 NZ3723
Stillington N York 90 SE5867
Stilton Cambs 52 TL1689
Stinchcombe Gloucs 35 ST7298
Stinsford Dorset 11 SY7091
Stirchley Shrops 60 SJ6907
Stirchley W Mids 61 SP0581
Stirling Gramp 143 NK1242
Stirling Cent 116 NS7993
Stirtloe Cambs 52 TL1966
Stirton N York 82 SD9752
Stisted Essex 40 TL8024
Stitchcombe Wilts 36 SU2369
Stithians Cnwll 3 SW7336
Stivichall W Mids 61 SP3376
Stixwould Lincs 76 TF1765
Stoak Ches 71 SJ4273
Stobo Border 109 NT1837
Stoborough Dorset 11 SY9286
Stoborough Green Dorset 11 SY9285
Stobs Castle Border 109 NT5008
Stobswood Nthumb 103 NZ2195
Stock Avon 21 ST4561
Stock Essex 40 TQ6998
Stock Green H & W 47 SO9859
Stock Wood H & W 47 SP0058
Stockbridge Hants 23 SU3535
Stockbriggs Strath 107 NS7936
Stockbury Kent 28 TQ8461
Stockcross Berks 24 SU4368
Stockdale Cnwll 3 SW7837
Stockdalewath Cumb 93 NY3845
Stocker's Hill Kent 28 TQ9650
Stockerston Leics 51 SP8397
Stocking H & W 47 SO6230
Stocking Green Bucks 38 SP8047
Stocking Pelham Herts 39 TL4529
Stockingford Warwks 61 SP3391
Stockland Devon 9 ST2404

Stockland Bristol Sutton le Marsh

Stockland Bristol Somset 20 ST2443
Stockland Green Kent 16 TQ5642
Stockleigh English Devon 8 SS8506
Stockleigh Pomeroy Devon 9 SS8703
Stockley Wilts 22 ST9967
Stockley Hill H & W 46 SO3738
Stocklinch Somset 10 ST3817
Stockmoor H & W 46 SO3954
Stockport Gt Man 79 SJ8990
Stocksbridge S York 74 SK2698
Stocksfield Nthumb 103 NZ0561
Stockstreet Essex 40 TL8222
Stockton Shrops 58 SJ2601
Stockton Shrops 72 SJ7716
Stockton H & W 46 SO5261
Stockton Shrops 60 SO7299
Stockton Warwks 49 SP4363
Stockton Wilts 22 ST9838
Stockton Norfk 67 TM3894
Stockton Brook Staffs 72 SJ9151
Stockton Heath Ches 78 SJ6185
Stockton on Teme H & W 47 SO7167
Stockton on the Forest N York 83 SE6556
Stockton-on-Tees Cleve 96 NZ4419
Stockwell Gloucs 35 SO9414
Stockwell End W Mids 60 SJ8900
Stockwell Heath Staffs 73 SK0521
Stockwood Dorset 10 ST5906
Stockwood Avon 21 ST6368
Stodday Lancs 87 SD4658
Stodmarsh Kent 29 TR2260
Stody Norfk 66 TG0535
Stoer Highld 148 NC0328
Stoford Somset 10 ST5613
Stoford Wilts 23 SU0835
Stogumber Somset 20 ST0937
Stogursey Somset 20 ST2042
Stoke W Mids 61 SP3778
Stoke Devon 18 SS2324
Stoke Hants 24 SU4051
Stoke Hants 13 SU7202
Stoke Kent 28 TQ8274
Stoke Abbott Dorset 10 ST4500
Stoke Albany Nhants 51 SP8088
Stoke Ash Suffk 54 TM1170
Stoke Bardolph Notts 63 SK6441
Stoke Bliss H & W 47 SO6563
Stoke Bruerne Nhants 49 SP7449
Stoke Canon Devon 9 SX9398
Stoke Charity Hants 24 SU4839
Stoke Climsland Cnwll 5 SX3674
Stoke Cross H & W 47 SO6250
Stoke D'Abernon Surrey 26 TQ1258
Stoke Doyle Nhants 51 TL0286
Stoke Dry Leics 51 SP8596
Stoke End Warwks 61 SP1797
Stoke Farthing Wilts 23 SU0525
Stoke Ferry Norfk 65 TF7000
Stoke Fleming Devon 7 SX8648
Stoke Gabriel Devon 7 SX8557
Stoke Gifford Avon 35 ST6279
Stoke Golding Leics 61 SP3997
Stoke Goldington Bucks 38 SP8348
Stoke Green Bucks 26 SU9882
Stoke Hammond Bucks 38 SP8829
Stoke Heath Shrops 72 SJ6529
Stoke Heath H & W 47 SO9468
Stoke Heath W Mids 61 SP3681
Stoke Holy Cross Norfk 67 TG2301
Stoke Lacy H & W 47 SO6249
Stoke Lyne Oxon 49 SP5628
Stoke Mandeville Bucks 38 SP8310
Stoke Newington Gt Lon 27 TQ3386
Stoke Orchard Gloucs 47 SO9128
Stoke Poges Bucks 26 SU9783
Stoke Pound H & W 47 SO9667
Stoke Prior H & W 46 SO5256
Stoke Prior H & W 47 SO9467
Stoke Rivers Devon 19 SS6335
Stoke Rochford Lincs 63 SK9127
Stoke Row Oxon 37 SU6884
Stoke St. Gregory Somset 21 ST3427
Stoke St. Mary Somset 20 ST2622
Stoke St. Michael Somset 22 ST6646
Stoke St. Milborough Shrops 59 SO5682
Stoke Talmage Oxon 37 SU6799
Stoke Trister Somset 22 ST7428
Stoke Wake Dorset 11 ST7606
Stoke Wharf H & W 47 SO9567
Stoke by Clare Suffk 53 TL7443
Stoke sub Hamdon Somset 10 ST4717
Stoke upon Tern Shrops 59 SJ6328
Stoke-by-Nayland Suffk 54 TL9836
Stoke-on-Trent Staffs 72 SJ8747
Stoke-upon-Trent Staffs 72 SJ8745
Stokeford Dorset 11 SY8687
Stokeham Notts 75 SK7876
Stokeinteignhead Devon 7 SX9170
Stokenchurch Bucks 37 SU7696
Stokenham Devon 7 SX8042
Stokesay Shrops 59 SO4381
Stokesby Norfk 67 TG4310
Stokesley N York 90 NZ5208
Stolford Somset 20 ST0332
Stolford Somset 20 ST2345
Ston Easton Somset 21 ST6253
Stondon Massey Essex 27 TL5800
Stone Staffs 72 SJ9034
Stone S York 75 SK5589
Stone H & W 60 SO8675
Stone Bucks 37 SP7812
Stone Somset 21 ST5834
Stone Gloucs 35 ST6895
Stone Kent 27 TQ5774
Stone Kent 17 TQ9427
Stone Allerton Somset 21 ST3951
Stone Bridge Corner Cambs 64 TF2700
Stone Chair W York 82 SE1227
Stone Cross E Susx 16 TQ5128
Stone Cross Kent 16 TQ5239
Stone Cross E Susx 16 TQ6104
Stone Cross E Susx 16 TQ6431
Stone Cross Kent 28 TR0236
Stone Cross Kent 29 TR3257
Stone Hill S York 83 SE6809
Stone House Cumb 88 SD7685
Stone Rows Leics 61 SK3214
Stone Street Suffk 54 TL9639
Stone Street Suffk 54 TM0143
Stone Street Suffk 55 TM3882
Stone Street Kent 27 TQ5754
Stone-edge-Batch Avon 34 ST4671
Stonea Cambs 65 TL4593
Stonebridge W Mids 61 SP2182
Stonebridge Avon 21 ST3859
Stonebridge Norfk 54 TL9290
Stonebroom Derbys 74 SK4059
Stonebury Herts 39 TL3828
Stonechrubie Highld 145 NC2419
Stonecross Green Suffk 54 TL8257
Stonecrouch Kent 16 TQ7033
Stoneferry Humb 85 TA1031
Stonefield Castle Hotel Strath 113 NR8671
Stonegarthside Cumb 101 NY4780
Stonegate N York 90 NZ7708
Stonegate E Susx 16 TQ6628
Stonegrave N York 90 SE6577
Stonehall H & W 47 SO8848
Stonehaugh Nthumb 102 NY7976
Stonehaven Gramp 135 NO8786
Stonehill Green Gt Lon 27 TQ5070
Stonehouse Strath 116 NS7546
Stonehouse D & G 100 NX8268
Stonehouse Nthumb 94 NY6958
Stonehouse Ches 71 SJ5070
Stonehouse Gloucs 35 SO8005
Stonehouse Devon 6 SX4654
Stoneleigh Warwks 61 SP3372
Stoneley Green Ches 71 SJ6151
Stonely Cambs 52 TL1167
Stoner Hill Hants 13 SU7225
Stones Green Essex 41 TM1626
Stonesby Leics 63 SK8224
Stonesfield Oxon 36 SP3917
Stonethwaite Cumb 93 NY2613
Stonetree Green Kent 29 TR0637
Stonewells Gramp 141 NJ2865
Stonewood Kent 27 TQ5972
Stoney Cross Hants 12 SU2611
Stoney Middleton Derbys 74 SK2375
Stoney Stanton Leics 50 SP4994
Stoney Stoke Somset 22 ST7032
Stoney Stratton Somset 21 ST6539
Stoney Stretton Shrops 59 SJ3809
Stoneybridge W Isls 154 NF7532
Stoneybridge H & W 60 SO9476
Stoneyburn Loth 117 NS9862
Stoneygate Leics 62 SK6002
Stoneyhills Essex 40 TQ9597
Stoneykirk D & G 98 NX0853
Stoneywood Gramp 135 NJ8811
Stoneywood Cent 116 NS7982
Stonham Aspal Suffk 54 TM1359
Stonnall Staffs 61 SK0603
Stonor Oxon 37 SU7388
Stonton Wyville Leics 50 SP7395
Stony Cross H & W 46 SO5466
Stony Cross H & W 47 SO7247
Stony Houghton Derbys 75 SK4966
Stony Stratford Bucks 38 SP7840
Stonyford Hants 12 SU3215
Stonywell Staffs 61 SK0712
Stoodleigh Devon 19 SS6532
Stoodleigh Devon 20 SS9218
Stopham W Susx 14 TQ0219
Stopsley Beds 38 TL1023
Stoptide Cnwll 4 SW9475
Storeton Mersyd 78 SJ3084
Storeyard Green H & W 47 SO7144
Stormy Corner Lancs 78 SD4707
Stornoway W Isls 154 NB4232
Storrington W Susx 14 TQ0814
Storth Cumb 87 SD4779
Storwood Humb 84 SE7144
Stotfold Beds 39 TL2136
Stottesdon Shrops 60 SO6782
Stoughton Leics 63 SK6402
Stoughton W Susx 14 SU8011
Stoughton Surrey 25 SU9851
Stoul Highld 129 NM7594
Stoulton H & W 47 SO9049
Stour Provost Dorset 22 ST7921
Stour Row Dorset 22 ST8221
Stourbridge W Mids 60 SO8983
Stourpaine Dorset 11 ST8609
Stourport-on-Severn H & W 60 SO8171
Stourton W York 83 SE3230
Stourton Staffs 60 SO8684
Stourton Warwks 48 SP2936
Stourton Wilts 22 ST7734
Stourton Caundle Dorset 11 ST7115
Stout Somset 21 ST4331
Stove Shet 155 HU4224
Stoven Suffk 55 TM4481
Stow Border 118 NT4544
Stow Lincs 76 SK8882
Stow Bardolph Norfk 65 TF6206
Stow Bedon Norfk 66 TL9596
Stow Longa Cambs 51 TL1070
Stow Maries Essex 40 TQ8399
Stow cum Quy Cambs 53 TL5260
Stow-on-the-Wold Gloucs 48 SP1925
Stowbridge Norfk 65 TF6007
Stowe Staffs 61 SK1210
Stowe Shrops 46 SO3173
Stowe Gloucs 34 SO5606
Stowe by Chartley Staffs 73 SK0026
Stowehill Nhants 49 SP6458
Stowell Somset 22 ST6822
Stowey Somset 21 ST5959
Stowford Devon 19 SS6541
Stowford Devon 5 SX4387
Stowford Devon 9 SY1189
Stowlangtoft Suffk 54 TL9568
Stowmarket Suffk 54 TM0458
Stowting Kent 29 TR1242
Stowting Common Kent 29 TR1243
Stowupland Suffk 54 TM0760
Straanruie Highld 141 NH9916
Strachan Gramp 135 NO6692
Strachur Strath 114 NN0901
Stradbroke Suffk 55 TM2373
Stradbrook Wilts 22 ST9152
Stradishall Suffk 53 TL7552
Stradsett Norfk 65 TF6605
Straight Soley Wilts 36 SU3172
Straiton Strath 106 NS3804
Straiton Loth 117 NT2766
Straloch Gramp 143 NJ8620
Straloch Tays 133 NO0463
Stramshall Staffs 73 SK0735
Strang IOM 153 SC3578
Strangford H & W 46 SO5827
Stranraer D & G 98 NX0560
Strata Florida Dyfed 43 SN7465
Stratfield Mortimer Berks 24 SU6664
Stratfield Saye Hants 24 SU6861
Stratfield Turgis Hants 24 SU6959
Stratford Beds 52 TL1748
Stratford Gt Lon 27 TQ3884
Stratford St. Andrew Suffk 55 TM3560
Stratford St. Mary Suffk 54 TM0434
Stratford Tony Wilts 23 SU0926
Stratford sub Castle Wilts 23 SU1332
Stratford-upon-Avon Warwks 48 SP2055
Strath Highld 151 ND2652
Strath Highld 144 NG7978
Strathan Highld 145 NC0821
Strathan Highld 149 NC5764
Strathan Highld 130 NM9791
Strathaven Strath 116 NS7044
Strathblane Cent 115 NS5679
Strathcarron Sta Highld 138 NG9442
Strathcoil Strath 122 NM6830
Strathdon Gramp 134 NJ3512
Strathkanaird Highld 145 NC1501
Strathkinness Fife 127 NO4516
Strathmashie House Tays 132 NN5891
Strathmiglo Fife 126 NO2109
Strathpeffer Highld 139 NH4858
Strathwhillan Strath 105 NS0235
Strathy Highld 150 NC8464
Strathy Inn Highld 150 NC8365
Strathyre Cent 124 NN5617
Stratton Gloucs 35 SP0103
Stratton Cnwll 18 SS2306
Stratton Dorset 11 SY6593
Stratton Audley Oxon 49 SP6025
Stratton St. Margaret Wilts 36 SU1786
Stratton St. Michael Norfk 67 TM2093
Stratton Strawless Norfk 67 TG2220
Stratton-on-the-Fosse Somset 22 ST6650
Stravithie Fife 127 NO5313
Stream Somset 20 ST0639
Streat E Susx 15 TQ3515
Streatham Gt Lon 27 TQ3071
Streatley Berks 37 SU5980
Streatley Beds 38 TL0728
Street N York 90 NZ7304
Street Lancs 80 SD5252
Street Somset 21 ST4836
Street Devon 9 SY1888
Street Ashton Warwks 50 SP4582
Street Dinas Shrops 71 SJ3338
Street End W Susx 14 SZ8599
Street End E Susx 16 TQ6023
Street End Kent 29 TR1453
Street Gate T & W 96 NZ2159
Street Houses Cleve 97 NZ7419
Street Houses N York 83 SE5245
Street Lane Derbys 74 SK3848
Street on the Fosse Somset 21 ST6239
Streethay Staffs 61 SK1410
Streetlam N York 89 SE3098
Streetly W Mids 61 SP0898
Strefford Shrops 59 SO4485
Strelitz Tays 126 NO1836
Strelley Notts 62 SK5141
Strensall N York 90 SE6360
Strensham H & W 47 SO9140
Stretcholt Somset 20 ST2943
Strete Devon 7 SX8446
Stretford Gt Man 79 SJ7994
Stretford H & W 46 SO4455
Stretford H & W 46 SO5257
Strethall Essex 39 TL4839
Stretham Cambs 53 TL5174
Strettington W Susx 14 SU8907
Stretton Ches 71 SJ4452
Stretton Ches 79 SJ6282
Stretton Staffs 60 SJ8811
Stretton Staffs 73 SK2526
Stretton Derbys 74 SK3961
Stretton Leics 63 SK9415
Stretton Grandison H & W 47 SO6344
Stretton Heath Shrops 59 SJ3610
Stretton Sugwas H & W 46 SO4642
Stretton Westwood Shrops 59 SO5998
Stretton en le Field Leics 61 SK3011
Stretton on Fosse Warwks 48 SP2238
Stretton under Fosse Warwks 50 SP4581
Stretton-on-Dunsmore Warwks 61 SP4072
Strichen Gramp 143 NJ9455
Strines Gt Man 79 SJ9786
Stringston Somset 20 ST1742
Strixton Nhants 51 SP9061
Stroat Gloucs 34 ST5797
Stromeferry Highld 138 NG8634
Stromness Ork 155 HY2508
Stronachlachar Cent 123 NN4010
Stronafian Strath 114 NS0281
Strone Highld 131 NN1481
Strone Strath 114 NS1980
Stronenaba Highld 131 NN2084
Stronmilchan Strath 123 NN1528
Strontian Highld 130 NM8161
Strood Kent 28 TQ7269
Strood Kent 17 TQ8532
Strood Green W Susx 14 TQ0224
Strood Green W Susx 15 TQ1332
Strood Green Surrey 15 TQ2048
Stroud Gloucs 35 SO8505
Stroud Hants 13 SU7223
Stroud Green Gloucs 35 SO8007
Stroud Green Essex 40 TQ8590
Stroude Surrey 25 TQ0068
Stroxton Lincs 63 SK9030
Struan Highld 136 NG3438
Struan Tays 132 NN8065
Strubby Lincs 77 TF4582
Strumpshaw Norfk 67 TG3407
Strutherhill Strath 116 NS7649
Struthers Fife 126 NO3709
Struy Highld 139 NH4040
Stryt-issa Clwyd 70 SJ2845
Stuartfield Gramp 143 NJ9745
Stubbers Green W Mids 61 SK0401
Stubbington Hants 13 SU5503
Stubbins Gt Man 81 SD7918
Stubbs Green Norfk 67 TM2598
Stubhampton Dorset 11 ST9113
Stubshaw Cross Gt Man 78 SJ5899
Stubton Lincs 76 SK8748
Stuchbury Nhants 49 SP5643
Stuckeridge Devon 20 SS9221
Stuckton Hants 12 SU1613
Stud Green Berks 26 SU8877
Studfold N York 88 SD8169
Studham Beds 38 TL0215
Studholme Cumb 93 NY2556
Studland Dorset 12 SZ0382
Studley Warwks 48 SP0764
Studley Wilts 35 ST9671
Studley Common H & W 48 SP0664
Studley Roger N York 89 SE2970
Studley Royal N York 89 SE2770
Stump Cross Cambs 39 TL5044
Stuntney Cambs 53 TL5578
Stunts Green E Susx 16 TQ6213
Sturbridge Staffs 72 SJ8330
Sturgate Lincs 76 SK8888
Sturmer Essex 53 TL6943
Sturminster Common Dorset 11 ST7812
Sturminster Marshall Dorset 11 ST9500
Sturminster Newton Dorset 11 ST7814
Sturry Kent 29 TR1760
Sturton Humb 84 SE9604
Sturton by Stow Lincs 76 SK8980
Sturton le Steeple Notts 75 SK7883
Stuston Suffk 54 TM1377
Stutton N York 83 SE4841
Stutton Suffk 54 TM1534
Styal Ches 79 SJ8383
Stynie Gramp 141 NJ3360
Styrrup Notts 75 SK6090
Succoth Strath 123 NN2905
Suckley H & W 47 SO7251
Suckley Green H & W 47 SO7253
Sudborough Nhants 51 SP9682
Sudbourne Suffk 55 TM4153
Sudbrook Lincs 63 SK9744
Sudbrook Gwent 34 ST5087
Sudbrooke Lincs 76 TF0376
Sudbury Derbys 73 SK1631
Sudbury Suffk 54 TL8741
Sudbury Gt Lon 26 TQ1685
Sudden Gt Man 81 SD8812
Suddie Highld 140 NH6554
Suddington H & W 47 SO8463
Sudgrove Gloucs 35 SO9308
Suffield N York 91 SE9890
Suffield Norfk 67 TG2232
Sugdon Shrops 59 SJ6015
Sugnall Staffs 72 SJ7931
Sugwas Pool H & W 46 SO4541
Suisnish Highld 129 NG5816
Sulby IOM 153 SC3894
Sulgrave Nhants 49 SP5544
Sulham Berks 24 SU6474
Sulhamstead Berks 24 SU6368
Sulhamstead Abbots Berks 24 SU6467
Sulhamstead Bannister Berks 24 SU6368
Sullington W Susx 14 TQ0913
Sullom Shet 155 HU3573
Sullom Voe Shet 155 HU4075
Sully S Glam 20 ST1568
Summer Heath Bucks 37 SU7490
Summer Hill Clwyd 71 SJ3153
Summerbridge N York 89 SE2062
Summercourt Cnwll 3 SW8856
Summerfield H & W 60 SO8473
Summerfield Norfk 65 TF7538
Summerhouse Dur 96 NZ2019
Summerlands Cumb 87 SD5386
Summerley Derbys 74 SK3778
Summersdale W Susx 14 SU8606
Summerseat Gt Man 81 SD7914
Summertown Oxon 37 SP5009
Summit Gt Man 79 SD9109
Summit Gt Man 82 SD9418
Sunbiggin Cumb 87 NY6608
Sunbury Surrey 26 TQ1168
Sundaywell D & G 100 NX8284
Sunderland Strath 112 NR2464
Sunderland Cumb 93 NY1735
Sunderland T & W 96 NZ3957
Sunderland Lancs 80 SD4255
Sunderland Bridge Dur 96 NZ2637
Sundhope Border 109 NT3325
Sundon Park Beds 38 TL0525
Sundridge Kent 27 TQ4855
Sunk Island Humb 85 TA2619
Sunningdale Surrey 25 SU9567
Sunninghill Surrey 25 SU9367
Sunningwell Oxon 37 SP4900
Sunniside Dur 96 NZ1438
Sunniside T & W 96 NZ2059
Sunny Bank Lancs 81 SD7720
Sunny Brow Dur 96 NZ1934
Sunnyhill Derbys 62 SK3432
Sunnyhurst Lancs 81 SD6722
Sunnylaw Cent 116 NS7998
Sunnymead Oxon 37 SP5009
Sunton Wilts 23 SU2454
Sunwick Border 119 NT9052
Surbiton Gt Lon 26 TQ1867
Surfleet Lincs 64 TF2528
Surfleet Seas End Lincs 64 TF2628
Surlingham Norfk 67 TG3106
Surrex Essex 40 TL8722
Sustead Norfk 66 TG1837
Susworth Lincs 84 SE8302
Sutcombe Devon 18 SS3411
Sutcombemill Devon 18 SS3411
Suton Norfk 66 TM0999
Sutterby Lincs 77 TF3872
Sutterton Lincs 64 TF2835
Sutton N York 83 SE4925
Sutton S York 83 SE5512
Sutton Shrops 59 SJ3527
Sutton Shrops 59 SJ5010
Sutton Mersyd 78 SJ5393
Sutton Shrops 72 SJ6631
Sutton Staffs 72 SJ7622
Sutton Notts 75 SK6784
Sutton Notts 63 SK7637
Sutton Dyfed 30 SM9115
Sutton Shrops 60 SO7386
Sutton Oxon 36 SP4106
Sutton Devon 8 SS7202
Sutton W Susx 14 SU9715
Sutton Devon 7 SX7042
Sutton Norfk 67 TG3823
Sutton Cambs 51 TL0998
Sutton Beds 52 TL2247
Sutton Cambs 53 TL4479
Sutton Suffk 55 TM3046
Sutton Gt Lon 27 TQ2564
Sutton Kent 29 TR3349
Sutton E Susx 16 TV4999
Sutton Bassett Nhants 50 SP7790
Sutton Benger Wilts 35 ST9478
Sutton Bingham Somset 10 ST5410
Sutton Bonington Notts 62 SK5024
Sutton Bridge Lincs 65 TF4721
Sutton Cheney Leics 50 SK4100
Sutton Coldfield W Mids 61 SP1295
Sutton Courtenay Oxon 37 SU5094
Sutton Crosses Lincs 65 TF4321
Sutton Grange N York 89 SE2873
Sutton Green Clwyd 71 SJ4048
Sutton Green Oxon 36 SP4107
Sutton Green Surrey 25 TQ0054
Sutton Howgrave N York 89 SE3179
Sutton Lane Ends Ches 79 SJ9270
Sutton Maddock Shrops 60 SJ7201
Sutton Mallet Somset 21 ST3736
Sutton Mandeville Wilts 22 ST9828
Sutton Manor Mersyd 78 SJ5190
Sutton Marsh H & W 46 SO5544
Sutton Montis Somset 21 ST6224
Sutton Poyntz Dorset 11 SY7083
Sutton Scansdale Derbys 75 SK4468
Sutton Scotney Hants 24 SU4639
Sutton St. Edmund Lincs 64 TF3613
Sutton St. James Lincs 65 TF3918
Sutton St. Nicholas H & W 46 SO5245
Sutton Street Kent 28 TQ8055
Sutton Valence Kent 28 TQ8149
Sutton Veny Wilts 22 ST9041
Sutton Waldron Dorset 11 ST8615
Sutton Weaver Ches 71 SJ5479
Sutton Wick Avon 21 ST5759
Sutton Wick Oxon 37 SU4894
Sutton at Hone Kent 27 TQ5569
Sutton in Ashfield Notts 75 SK4958
Sutton in the Elms Leics 50 SP5193
Sutton le Marsh Lincs 77 TF5280

T

Thornbury Totronald

Thornbury H & W 47 SO6259
Thornbury Devon 18 SS4008
Thornbury Avon 35 ST6390
Thornby Cumb 93 NY2851
Thornby Nhants 50 SP6775
Thorncliff Staffs 73 SK0158
Thorncombe Dorset 10 ST3703
Thorncombe Street Surrey 25 SU9941
Thorncott Green Beds 52 TL1547
Thorncross IOW 13 SZ4381
Thorndon Suffk 54 TM1469
Thorndon Cross Devon 8 SX5394
Thorne S York 83 SE6812
Thorne Somset 10 ST5217
Thorne St. Margaret Somset 20 ST1020
Thornecroft Devon 7 SX7767
Thornehillhead Devon 18 SS4116
Thorner W York 83 SE3740
Thornes W York 83 SE3219
Thornes Staffs 61 SK0703
Thorney Notts 76 SK8572
Thorney Somset 21 ST4223
Thorney Cambs 64 TF2804
Thorney Bucks 26 TQ0379
Thorney Hill Hants 12 SZ2099
Thorney Toll Cambs 64 TF3404
Thornfalcon Somset 20 ST2823
Thornford Dorset 10 ST6012
Thorngrafton Nthumb 102 NY7865
Thorngrove Somset 21 ST3632
Thorngumbald Humb 85 TA2026
Thornham Norfk 65 TF7343
Thornham Magna Suffk 54 TM1070
Thornham Parva Suffk 54 TM1072
Thornhaugh Cambs 64 TF0600
Thornhill Cent 116 NN6600
Thornhill D & G 100 NX8795
Thornhill W York 82 SE2518
Thornhill Derbys 74 SK1983
Thornhill M Glam 33 ST1584
Thornhill Hants 13 SU4612
Thornhill Lees W York 82 SE2419
Thornhills W York 82 SE1523
Thornholme Humb 91 TA1164
Thornicombe Dorset 11 ST8703
Thornington Nthumb 110 NT8833
Thornley Dur 95 NZ1137
Thornley Dur 96 NZ3639
Thornley Gate Cumb 95 NY8356
Thornliebank Strath 115 NS5559
Thorns Suffk 53 TL7455
Thorns Green Gt Man 79 SJ7884
Thornsett Derbys 79 SK0086
Thornthwaite Cumb 93 NY2225
Thornthwaite N York 89 SE1758
Thornton Tays 126 NO3946
Thornton Fife 117 NT2897
Thornton Nthumb 111 NT9547
Thornton Cleve 89 NZ4713
Thornton Mersyd 78 SD3301
Thornton Lancs 80 SD3342
Thornton W York 82 SE0932
Thornton Humb 84 SE7645
Thornton Leics 62 SK4607
Thornton Dyfed 30 SM9007
Thornton Bucks 49 SP7435
Thornton Lincs 77 TF2467
Thornton Curtis Humb 85 TA0817
Thornton Dale N York 90 SE8383
Thornton Green Ches 71 SJ4473
Thornton Heath Gt Lon 27 TQ3168
Thornton Hough Mersyd 78 SJ3080
Thornton Rust N York 88 SD9689
Thornton Steward N York 89 SE1787
Thornton Watlass N York 89 SE2385
Thornton in Lonsdale N York 87 SD6873
Thornton le Moor Lincs 76 TF0496
Thornton-in-Craven N York 81 SD9048
Thornton-le-Beans N York 89 SE3990
Thornton-le-Clay N York 90 SE6865
Thornton-le-Moor N York 89 SE3988
Thornton-le-Moors Ches 71 SJ4474
Thornton-le-Street N York 89 SE4186
Thorntonhall Strath 115 NS5955
Thorntonloch Loth 119 NT7574
Thornwood Common Essex 39 TL4604
Thornydykes Border 110 NT6148
Thornythwaite Cumb 93 NY3922
Thoroton Notts 63 SK7642
Thorp Arch W York 83 SE4345
Thorpe N York 88 SE0161
Thorpe Humb 84 SE9946
Thorpe Derbys 73 SK1550
Thorpe Notts 75 SK7649
Thorpe Lincs 77 TF4981
Thorpe Norfk 67 TM4398
Thorpe Surrey 26 TQ0168
Thorpe Abbotts Norfk 55 TM1979
Thorpe Acre Leics 62 SK5119
Thorpe Arnold Leics 63 SK7720
Thorpe Audlin W York 83 SE4715
Thorpe Bassett N York 90 SE8673
Thorpe Bay Essex 40 TQ9185
Thorpe Common S York 74 SK3895
Thorpe Constantine Staffs 61 SK2508
Thorpe End Norfk 67 TG2810
Thorpe Green Lancs 81 SD5923
Thorpe Green Suffk 54 TL9354
Thorpe Green Essex 41 TM1623
Thorpe Hesley S York 74 SK3796
Thorpe Langton Leics 50 SP7492
Thorpe Larches Dur 96 NZ3826
Thorpe Lea Surrey 26 TQ0170
Thorpe Malsor Nhants 51 SP8378
Thorpe Mandeville Nhants 49 SP5244
Thorpe Market Norfk 67 TG2436
Thorpe Morieux Suffk 54 TL9453
Thorpe Salvin S York 75 SK5281
Thorpe Satchville Leics 63 SK7311
Thorpe St. Andrew Norfk 67 TG2508
Thorpe St. Peter Lincs 77 TF4860
Thorpe Thewles Cleve 96 NZ3923
Thorpe Tilney Lincs 76 TF1257
Thorpe Underwood N York 89 SE4659
Thorpe Underwood Nhants 50 SP7981
Thorpe Waterville Nhants 51 TL0281
Thorpe Willoughby N York 83 SE5731
Thorpe by Water Leics 51 SP8996
Thorpe in Balne S York 83 SE5910
Thorpe in the Fallows Lincs 76 SK9180
Thorpe le Street Humb 84 SE8343
Thorpe on the Hill W York 82 SE3126
Thorpe on the Hill Lincs 76 SK9065
Thorpe-le-Soken Essex 41 TM1722
Thorpeness Suffk 55 TM4759
Thorpland Norfk 65 TF6108
Thorrington Essex 41 TM0919
Thorverton Devon 9 SS9202
Thrales End Beds 38 TL1116
Thrandeston Suffk 54 TM1176
Thrapston Nhants 51 SP9978
Threapland Cumb 92 NY1539
Threapland N York 88 SD9860
Threapwood Ches 71 SJ4344
Threapwood Staffs 73 SK0342
Threapwood Head Staffs 73 SK0342
Threave Strath 106 NS3306
Three Ashes H & W 34 SO5122
Three Bridges W Susx 15 TQ2837
Three Burrows Cnwll 3 SW7446
Three Chimneys Kent 28 TQ8238
Three Cocks Powys 45 SO1737
Three Crosses W Glam 32 SS5794
Three Cups Corner E Susx 16 TQ6320
Three Gates H & W 47 SO6862
Three Hammers Cnwll 5 SX2287
Three Holes Norfk 65 TF5000
Three Lane Ends Gt Man 79 SD8309
Three Leg Cross E Susx 16 TQ6831
Three Legged Cross Dorset 12 SU0805
Three Mile Cross Berks 24 SU7167
Three Mile Stone Cnwll 3 SW7745
Three Miletown Loth 117 NT0675
Three Oaks E Susx 17 TQ8314
Threehammer Common Norfk 67 TG3419
Threekingham Lincs 64 TF0836
Threepwood Border 109 NT5143
Threlkeld Cumb 93 NY3125
Threshfield N York 88 SD9863
Thrigby Norfk 67 TG4612
Thringarth Dur 95 NY9322
Thringstone Leics 62 SK4217
Thrintoft N York 89 SE3192
Thriplow Cambs 53 TL4346
Throapham S York 75 SK5387
Throckenhalt Lincs 64 TF3509
Throcking Herts 39 TL3330
Throckley T & W 103 NZ1566
Throckmorton H & W 47 SO9850
Throop Dorset 11 SY8292
Throop Dorset 12 SZ1195
Throphill Nthumb 103 NZ1285
Thropton Nthumb 103 NU0202
Througham Gloucs 35 SO9108
Throughgate D & G 100 NX8784
Throwleigh Devon 8 SX6690
Throwley Kent 28 TQ9955
Throwley Forstal Kent 28 TQ9854
Thrumpton Notts 62 SK5031
Thrumpton Notts 75 SK7080
Thrumster Highld 151 ND3345
Thrunscoe Humb 85 TA3107
Thrunton Nthumb 111 NU0810
Thrup Oxon 36 SU2999
Thrupp Gloucs 35 SO8603
Thrupp Oxon 37 SP4716
Thrushelton Devon 5 SX4487
Thrushesbush Essex 39 TL4909
Thrussington Leics 63 SK6515
Thruxton H & W 46 SO4334
Thruxton Hants 23 SU2945
Thrybergh S York 75 SK4695
Thulston Derbys 62 SK4031
Thundergarth D & G 101 NY1780
Thundersley Essex 40 TQ7988
Thurcaston Leics 62 SK5610
Thurcroft S York 75 SK4988
Thurdistoft Highld 151 ND2167
Thurdon Cnwll 18 SS2810
Thurgarton Notts 75 SK6949
Thurgarton Norfk 66 TG1834
Thurgoland S York 82 SE2901
Thurlaston Warwks 50 SP4670
Thurlaston Leics 50 SP5099
Thurlbear Somset 20 ST2621
Thurlby Lincs 76 SK9061
Thurlby Lincs 64 TF0916
Thurlby Lincs 77 TF4776
Thurleigh Beds 51 TL0558
Thurlestone Devon 7 SX6742
Thurlow Suffk 53 TL6750
Thurloxton Somset 20 ST2730
Thurlstone S York 82 SE2303
Thurlton Norfk 67 TM4198
Thurlwood Ches 72 SJ8057
Thurmaston Leics 62 SK6109
Thurnby Leics 63 SK6403
Thurne Norfk 67 TG4015
Thurnham Kent 28 TQ8057
Thurning Norfk 66 TG0729
Thurning Nhants 51 TL0882
Thurnscoe S York 83 SE4505
Thursby Cumb 93 NY3250
Thursden Lancs 81 SD9034
Thursford Norfk 66 TF9833
Thursley Surrey 25 SU9039
Thurso Highld 151 ND1168
Thurstaston Mersyd 78 SJ2484
Thurston Suffk 54 TL9265
Thurston Clough Gt Man 82 SD9707
Thurston Planch Suffk 54 TL9364
Thurstonfield Cumb 93 NY3156
Thurstonland W York 82 SE1610
Thurton Norfk 67 TG3200
Thurvaston Derbys 73 SK2437
Thuxton Norfk 66 TG0307
Thwaite N York 88 SD8998
Thwaite Suffk 54 TM1168
Thwaite Head Cumb 87 SD3490
Thwaite St. Mary Norfk 67 TM3395
Thwaites W York 82 SE0741
Thwaites Brow W York 82 SE0740
Thwing Humb 91 TA0470
Tibbermore Tays 125 NO0423
Tibbers D & G 100 NX8696
Tibberton Shrops 72 SJ6820
Tibberton Gloucs 35 SO7521
Tibberton H & W 47 SO9057
Tibbie Shiels Inn Border 109 NT2420
Tibenham Norfk 54 TM1389
Tibshelf Derbys 75 SK4461
Tibthorpe Humb 84 SE9555
Ticehurst E Susx 16 TQ6830
Tichborne Hants 24 SU5730
Tickencote Leics 63 SK9809
Tickenham Avon 34 ST4571
Tickford End Bucks 38 SP8843
Tickhill S York 75 SK5993
Ticklerton Shrops 59 SO4890
Ticknall Derbys 62 SK3523
Tickton Humb 84 TA0541
Tidbury Green W Mids 61 SP1075
Tidcombe Wilts 23 SU2858
Tiddington Warwks 48 SP2255
Tiddington Oxon 37 SP6404
Tidebrook E Susx 16 TQ6130
Tideford Cnwll 5 SX3559
Tideford Cross Cnwll 5 SX3461
Tidenham Gloucs 34 ST5595
Tideswell Derbys 74 SK1575
Tidmarsh Berks 24 SU6374
Tidmington Warwks 48 SP2538
Tidpit Hants 12 SU0718
Tiers Cross Dyfed 30 SM9010
Tiffield Nhants 49 SP7051
Tifty Gramp 142 NJ7740
Tigerton Tays 134 NO5364
Tigharry W Isls 154 NF7172
Tighnabruaich Strath 114 NR9873
Tigley Devon 7 SX7660
Tilbrook Cambs 51 TL0869
Tilbury Essex 27 TQ6476
Tilbury Green Essex 53 TL7441
Tile Cross W Mids 61 SP1687
Tile Hill W Mids 61 SP2777
Tilehouse Green W Mids 61 SP1776
Tilehurst Berks 24 SU6673
Tilford Surrey 25 SU8743
Tilgate W Susx 15 TQ2734
Tilgate Forest Row W Susx 15 TQ2632
Tilham Street Somset 21 ST5535
Tillers Green Gloucs 47 SO6932
Tillicoultry Cent 116 NS9197
Tillingham Essex 41 TL9904
Tillington H & W 46 SO4644
Tillington W Susx 14 SU9621
Tillington Common H & W 46 SO4545
Tilly Essex 40 TL5926
Tillybirloch Gramp 135 NJ6807
Tillycairn Gramp 134 NO4697
Tillyfourie Gramp 135 NJ6412
Tillygreig Gramp 143 NJ8822
Tillyrie Tays 126 NO1006
Tilmanstone Kent 29 TR3051
Tiln Notts 75 SK7084
Tilney All Saints Norfk 65 TF5618
Tilney High End Norfk 65 TF5617
Tilney St. Lawrence Norfk 65 TF5414
Tilshead Wilts 23 SU0347
Tilstock Shrops 59 SJ5437
Tilston Ches 71 SJ4650
Tilstone Bank Ches 71 SJ5659
Tilstone Fearnall Ches 71 SJ5660
Tilsworth Beds 38 SP9824
Tilton on the Hill Leics 63 SK7405
Tiltups End Gloucs 35 ST8497
Timberland Lincs 76 TF1258
Timbersbrook Ches 72 SJ8962
Timberscombe Somset 20 SS9542
Timble N York 82 SE1853
Timewell Devon 20 SS9625
Timpanheck D & G 101 NY3274
Timperley Gt Man 79 SJ7888
Timsbury Avon 22 ST6758
Timsbury Hants 23 SU3424
Timsgarry W Isls 154 NB0534
Timworth Suffk 54 TL8669
Timworth Green Suffk 54 TL8669
Tincleton Dorset 11 SY7692
Tindale Cumb 94 NY6159
Tindale Crescent Dur 96 NZ1927
Tingewick Bucks 49 SP6532
Tingley W York 82 SE2826
Tingrith Beds 38 TL0032
Tinhay Devon 5 SX3985
Tinker's Hill Hants 24 SU4047
Tinkersley Derbys 74 SK2664
Tinsley S York 74 SK4090
Tinsley Green W Susx 15 TQ2839
Tintagel Cnwll 4 SX0588
Tintern Parva Gwent 34 SO5200
Tintinhull Somset 21 ST4919
Tintwistle Derbys 79 SK0197
Tinwald D & G 100 NY0081
Tinwell Leics 63 TF0006
Tipp's End Norfk 65 TL5095
Tippacott Devon 19 SS7647
Tiptoe Hants 12 SZ2597
Tipton W Mids 60 SO9492
Tipton Green W Mids 60 SO9592
Tipton St. John Devon 9 SY0991
Tiptree Essex 40 TL8916
Tiptree Heath Essex 40 TL8815
Tir-y-fron Clwyd 70 SJ2859
Tirabad Powys 45 SN8741
Tiretigan Strath 113 NR7162
Tirley Gloucs 47 SO8328
Tiroran Strath 121 NM4827
Tirphil M Glam 33 SO1303
Tirril Cumb 94 NY5026
Tisbury Wilts 22 ST9429
Tisman's Common W Susx 14 TQ0632
Tissington Derbys 73 SK1752
Titchberry Devon 18 SS2427
Titchfield Hants 13 SU5405
Titchfield Common Hants 13 SU5206
Titchmarsh Nhants 51 TL0279
Titchwell Norfk 65 TF7643
Tithby Notts 63 SK6937
Titley H & W 46 SO3360
Titlington Nthumb 111 NU0915
Titmore Green Herts 39 TL2126
Titsey Surrey 27 TQ4054
Tittensor Staffs 72 SJ8738
Tittleshall Norfk 66 TF8921
Titton H & W 60 SO8370
Tiverton Ches 71 SJ5560
Tiverton Devon 9 SS9512
Tivetshall St. Margaret Norfk 54 TM1787
Tivetshall St. Mary Norfk 54 TM1686
Tivington Somset 20 SS9345
Tivy Dale S York 82 SE2707
Tixall Staffs 72 SJ9722
Tixover Leics 51 SK9700
Toab Shet 155 HU3811
Toadhole Derbys 74 SK3856
Toadmoor Derbys 74 SK3451
Tobermory Strath 121 NM5055
Toberonochy Strath 122 NM7408
Tocher Gramp 142 NJ6932
Tochieneal Gramp 142 NJ5165
Tockenham Wilts 36 SU0379
Tockenham Wick Wilts 36 SU0381
Tocketts Cleve 97 NZ6217
Tockington Avon 34 ST6086
Tockwith N York 83 SE4652
Todber Dorset 22 ST7919
Todburn Nthumb 103 NZ1295
Toddington Gloucs 48 SP0333
Toddington Beds 38 TL0128
Todds Green Herts 39 TL2226
Todenham Gloucs 48 SP2335
Todhills Tays 127 NO4239
Todhills Cumb 101 NY3762
Todhills Dur 96 NZ2133
Todmorden W York 81 SD9324
Todwick S York 75 SK4984
Toft Shet 155 HU4376
Toft Ches 79 SJ7576
Toft Warwks 50 SP4770
Toft Lincs 64 TF0717
Toft Cambs 52 TL3656
Toft Hill Dur 96 NZ1528
Toft Monks Norfk 67 TM4294
Toft next Newton Lincs 76 TF0388
Toftrees Norfk 66 TF8927
Tofts Highld 151 ND3668
Toftwood Norfk 66 TF9811
Togston Nthumb 103 NU2402
Tokavaig Highld 129 NG6011
Tokers Green Oxon 37 SU7077
Toldavas Cnwll 2 SW4226
Toldish Cnwll 4 SW9259
Toll Bar S York 83 SE5507
Tolland Somset 20 ST1032
Tollard Farnham Dorset 11 ST9515
Tollard Royal Wilts 11 ST9417
Tollbar End W Mids 61 SP3675
Toller Fratrum Dorset 10 SY5797
Toller Porcorum Dorset 10 SY5698
Toller Whelme Dorset 10 ST5101
Tollerton N York 90 SE5164
Tollerton Notts 62 SK6134
Tollesbury Essex 40 TL9510
Tolleshunt D'Arcy Essex 40 TL9211
Tolleshunt Knights Essex 40 TL9114
Tolleshunt Major Essex 40 TL9011
Tolpuddle Dorset 11 SY7994
Tolsta W Isls 154 NB5347
Tolvan Cnwll 2 SW7028
Tolver Cnwll 2 SW4832
Tolworth Gt Lon 26 TQ1966
Tomaknock Tays 125 NN8721
Tomatin Highld 140 NH8028
Tomchrasky Highld 131 NH2512
Tomdoun Highld 131 NH1500
Tomich Highld 146 NC6005
Tomich Highld 139 NH3027
Tomich Highld 139 NH5348
Tomich Highld 146 NH6971
Tomintoul Gramp 141 NJ1619
Tomintoul Gramp 133 NO1490
Tomlow Warwks 49 SP4563
Tomnacross Highld 139 NH5141
Tomnavoulin Gramp 141 NJ2126
Tompkin Staffs 72 SJ9451
Ton Gwent 34 SO3301
Ton Gwent 34 ST3695
Ton-teg M Glam 33 ST0986
Tonbridge Kent 16 TQ5846
Tondu M Glam 33 SS8984
Tonedale Somset 20 ST1321
Tong W York 82 SE2230
Tong Shrops 60 SJ7907
Tong Kent 28 TQ9556
Tong Green Kent 28 TQ9853
Tong Norton Shrops 60 SJ7908
Tong Street W York 82 SE1930
Tonge Leics 62 SK4223
Tongham Surrey 25 SU8848
Tongland D & G 99 NX6954
Tongue Highld 149 NC5957
Tongue End Lincs 64 TF1518
Tongwynlais S Glam 33 ST1382
Tonna W Glam 32 SS7798
Tonwell Herts 39 TL3316
Tonypandy M Glam 33 SS9991
Tonyrefail M Glam 33 ST0188
Toot Baldon Oxon 37 SP5600
Toot Hill Hants 12 SU3818
Toot Hill Essex 27 TL5102
Toothill Wilts 36 SU1183
Tooting Gt Lon 27 TQ2771
Tooting Bec Gt Lon 27 TQ2872
Top of Hebers Gt Man 79 SD8607
Top-y-rhos Clwyd 70 SJ2558
Topcliffe N York 89 SE3976
Topcroft Norfk 67 TM2693
Topcroft Street Norfk 67 TM2691
Topham S York 83 SE6217
Toppesfield Essex 53 TL7437
Toppings Gt Man 81 SD7213
Toprow Norfk 66 TM1698
Topsham Devon 9 SX9688
Torbeg Strath 105 NR8929
Torboll Highld 147 NH7599
Torbreck Highld 140 NH6441
Torbryan Devon 7 SX8266
Torcastle Highld 131 NN1378
Torcross Devon 7 SX8241
Tore Highld 140 NH6052
Torfrey Cnwll 3 SX1154
Torksey Lincs 76 SK8378
Tormarton Avon 35 ST7678
Tormitchell Strath 106 NX2394
Tormore Strath 105 NR8932
Tornagrain Highld 140 NH7650
Tornaveen Gramp 134 NJ6106
Torness Highld 139 NH5826
Torness Strath 121 NM6532
Tornewton Devon 7 SX8167
Toronto Nthumb 96 NZ1930
Torosay Castle Strath 122 NM7335
Torpenhow Cumb 93 NY2039
Torphichen Loth 117 NS9672
Torphins Gramp 134 NJ6202
Torpoint Cnwll 6 SX4355
Torquay Devon 7 SX9164
Torquhan Border 118 NT4448
Torr Devon 6 SX5851
Torran Highld 137 NG5949
Torrance Strath 116 NS6173
Torranyard Strath 115 NS3544
Torridon Highld 138 NG9055
Torridon House Highld 138 NG8657
Torrin Highld 129 NG5721
Torrisdale Highld 149 NC6761
Torrisdale Square Strath 105 NR7936
Torrish Highld 147 NC9718
Torrisholme Lancs 87 SD4563
Torrobull Highld 146 NC5904
Torry Gramp 135 NJ9405
Torryburn Fife 117 NT0286
Torrylin Strath 105 NR9521
Tortan H & W 60 SO8472
Torteval Guern 152 GN0000
Torthorwald D & G 100 NY0378
Tortington W Susx 14 TQ0004
Tortworth Avon 35 ST7093
Torvaig Highld 136 NG4944
Torver Cumb 86 SD2894
Torwood Cent 116 NS8385
Torwoodlee Border 109 NT4738
Torworth Notts 75 SK6586
Toscaig Highld 137 NG7138
Toseland Cambs 52 TL2462
Tosside Lancs 81 SD7656
Tostock Suffk 54 TL9563
Totaig Highld 136 NG2050
Tote Highld 136 NG4149
Tote Hill W Susx 14 SU8624
Tothill Lincs 77 TF4181
Totland IOW 12 SZ3287
Totley S York 74 SK3079
Totley Brook S York 74 SK3180
Totnes Devon 7 SX8060
Toton Notts 62 SK5034
Totronald Strath 120 NM1656

Totscore Twyford

Totscore *Highld* 136 NG3866
Tottenham *Gt Lon* 27 TQ3390
Tottenhill *Norfk* 65 TF6411
Totteridge *Gt Lon* 26 TQ2494
Totternhoe *Beds* 38 SP9821
Tottington *Gt Man* 81 SD7712
Tottleworth *Lancs* 81 SD7331
Totton *Hants* 12 SU3613
Touchen End *Berks* 26 SU8776
Toulston *N York* 83 SE4543
Toulton *Somset* 20 ST1931
Toulvaddie *Highld* 147 NH8880
Toux *Gramp* 142 NJ5459
Tovil *Kent* 28 TQ7554
Tow Law *Dur* 95 NZ1138
Towan *Cnwll* 4 SW8774
Towan *Cnwll* 3 SX0148
Toward *Strath* 114 NS1368
Toward Quay *Strath* 114 NS1167
Towcester *Nhants* 49 SP6948
Towednack *Cnwll* 2 SW4838
Towersey *Oxon* 37 SP7305
Towie *Gramp* 134 NJ4312
Town End *Cumb* 87 NY3406
Town End *Cumb* 94 NY6325
Town End *Cumb* 87 SD3687
Town End *Cumb* 87 SD4483
Town End *Lincs* 63 SK9943
Town End *Cambs* 65 TL4195
Town Green *Lancs* 78 SD4005
Town Green *Norfk* 67 TG3612
Town Head *Cumb* 87 NY4103
Town Head *N York* 88 SD8258
Town Head *N York* 82 SE1748
Town Kelloe *Dur* 96 NZ3536
Town Lane *Gt Man* 79 SJ6999
Town Littleworth *E Susx* 15 TQ4117
Town Moor *T & W* 103 NZ2465
Town Row *E Susx* 16 TQ5630
Town Street *Suffk* 53 TL7785
Town Yetholm *Border* 110 NT8128
Town of Lowdon *Mersyd* 78 SJ6196
Towngate *Cumb* 94 NY5246
Towngate *Lincs* 64 TF1310
Townhead *D & G* 100 NY0088
Townhead *Cumb* 92 NY0735
Townhead *Cumb* 94 NY6334
Townhead *S York* 82 SE1602
Townhead of Greenlaw *D & G* 99 NX7464
Townhill *Loth* 117 NT1089
Townlake *Devon* 5 SX4074
Towns End *Hants* 24 SU5659
Townsend *Somset* 10 ST3614
Townshend *Cnwll* 2 SW5932
Townwell *Avon* 35 ST7090
Towthorpe *N York* 90 SE6258
Towthorpe *Humb* 91 SE8962
Towton *N York* 83 SE4839
Towyn *Clwyd* 70 SH9779
Toxteth *Mersyd* 78 SJ3588
Toy's Hill *Kent* 27 TQ4651
Toynton All Saints *Lincs* 77 TF3963
Toynton Fen Side *Lincs* 77 TF3961
Toynton St. Peter *Lincs* 77 TF4063
Trabboch *Strath* 107 NS4421
Trabbochburn *Strath* 107 NS4621
Traboe *Cnwll* 3 SW7421
Tracebridge *Somset* 20 ST0621
Tradespark *Highld* 140 NH8656
Trafford Park *Gt Man* 79 SJ7896
Trallong *Powys* 45 SN9629
Tranent *Loth* 118 NT4072
Tranmere *Mersyd* 78 SJ3187
Trannack *Cnwll* 2 SW5633
Trantelbeg *Highld* 150 NC8952
Trantlemore *Highld* 150 NC8953
Tranwell *Nthumb* 103 NZ1883
Trap's Green *Warwks* 48 SP1069
Trap *Dyfed* 32 SN6518
Trapshill *Berks* 23 SU3763
Traquair *Border* 109 NT3334
Trash Green *Berks* 24 SU6569
Traveller's Rest *Devon* 19 SS6127
Trawden *Lancs* 81 SD9138
Trawscoed *Dyfed* 43 SN6672
Trawsfynydd *Gwynd* 57 SH7035
Tre Aubrey *S Glam* 33 ST0372
Tre'r-ddol *Dyfed* 43 SN6692
Tre-Gibbon *M Glam* 33 SN9905
Tre-Mostyn *Clwyd* 70 SJ1479
Tre-Vaughan *Dyfed* 31 SN3921
Tre-gagle *Gwent* 34 SO5207
Tre-groes *Dyfed* 42 SN4044
Tre-wyn *Gwent* 34 SO3222
Trealaw *M Glam* 33 ST0092
Treales *Lancs* 80 SD4332
Treamble *Cnwll* 3 SW7856
Trearddur Bay *Gwynd* 68 SH2579
Treaslane *Highld* 136 NG3953
Treator *Cnwll* 4 SW9075
Trebanos *W Glam* 32 SN7103
Trebartha *Cnwll* 5 SX2677
Trebarvah *Cnwll* 2 SW7130
Trebarwith *Cnwll* 4 SX0586
Trebeath *Cnwll* 5 SX2587
Trebehor *Cnwll* 2 SW3724
Trebelzue *Cnwll* 4 SW8464
Trebetherick *Cnwll* 4 SW9378
Trebudannon *Cnwll* 4 SW8961
Trebullett *Cnwll* 5 SX3278
Treburgett *Cnwll* 4 SX0579
Treburick *Cnwll* 4 SW8971
Treburley *Cnwll* 5 SX3577
Treburrick *Cnwll* 4 SW8670
Trebyan *Cnwll* 4 SX0763
Trecastle *Powys* 45 SN8829
Trecogo *Cnwll* 5 SX3080
Trecott *Devon* 8 SS6300
Trecwn *Dyfed* 30 SM9632
Trecynon *M Glam* 33 SN9903
Tredaule *Cnwll* 5 SX2381
Tredavoe *Cnwll* 2 SW4528
Tredegar *Gwent* 33 SO1408
Tredethy *Cnwll* 4 SX0672
Tredington *Gloucs* 47 SO9029
Tredington *Warwks* 48 SP2543
Tredinnick *Cnwll* 4 SW9270
Tredinnick *Cnwll* 4 SX0459
Tredinnick *Cnwll* 4 SX1666
Tredinnick *Cnwll* 5 SX2357
Tredinnick *Cnwll* 5 SX2957
Tredomen *Powys* 45 SO1231
Tredrissi *Dyfed* 31 SN0742
Tredrizzick *Cnwll* 4 SW9577
Tredunhock *Gwent* 34 ST3794
Tredustan *Powys* 45 SO1332
Treen *Cnwll* 2 SW3923
Treesmill *Cnwll* 3 SX0855
Treeton *S York* 75 SK4387
Trefacca *Powys* 45 SO1431
Trefasser *Dyfed* 30 SM8938
Trefdraeth *Gwynd* 68 SH4170
Trefeglwys *Powys* 58 SN9690
Trefenter *Dyfed* 43 SN6068
Treffgarne *Dyfed* 30 SM9523
Treffgarne Owen *Dyfed* 30 SM8625
Treffynnon *Dyfed* 30 SM8528
Trefil *Gwent* 33 SO1212
Trefilan *Dyfed* 44 SN5456
Treflach Wood *Shrops* 58 SJ2625
Trefnannau *Powys* 58 SJ2316
Trefnant *Clwyd* 70 SJ0570
Trefonen *Shrops* 58 SJ2526
Trefor *Gwynd* 68 SH3780
Treforda *Cnwll* 4 SX0988
Trefforest *M Glam* 33 ST0888
Trefrew *Cnwll* 4 SX1084
Trefriw *Gwynd* 69 SH7863
Tregadillett *Cnwll* 5 SX2983
Tregaian *Gwynd* 68 SH4580
Tregare *Gwent* 34 SO4110
Tregarne *Cnwll* 3 SW7823
Tregaron *Dyfed* 44 SN6759
Tregarth *Gwynd* 69 SH6067
Tregaswith *Cnwll* 4 SW8962
Tregatta *Cnwll* 4 SX0587
Tregawne *Cnwll* 4 SX0066
Tregear *Cnwll* 3 SW8650
Tregeare *Cnwll* 5 SX2486
Tregeiriog *Clwyd* 58 SJ1733
Tregele *Gwynd* 68 SH3592
Tregellist *Cnwll* 4 SX0177
Tregenna *Cnwll* 3 SW8743
Tregenna *Cnwll* 4 SX0973
Tregeseal *Cnwll* 2 SW3731
Tregew *Cnwll* 3 SW8034
Tregidden *Cnwll* 3 SW7523
Tregiddle *Cnwll* 2 SW6723
Tregidgeo *Cnwll* 3 SW9647
Tregiskey *Cnwll* 3 SX0146
Treglemais *Dyfed* 30 SM8229
Tregole *Cnwll* 5 SX1998
Tregolls *Cnwll* 3 SW7335
Tregonce *Cnwll* 4 SW9373
Tregonetha *Cnwll* 4 SW9563
Tregony *Cnwll* 3 SW9244
Tregoodwell *Cnwll* 4 SX1183
Tregoose *Cnwll* 2 SW6823
Tregoss *Cnwll* 4 SW9660
Tregowris *Cnwll* 3 SW7722
Tregoyd *Powys* 45 SO1937
Tregrehan Mills *Cnwll* 3 SX0453
Tregullon *Cnwll* 4 SX0664
Tregunna *Cnwll* 4 SW9673
Tregunnon *Cnwll* 5 SX2283
Tregurrian *Cnwll* 4 SW8565
Tregustick *Cnwll* 4 SW9866
Tregynon *Powys* 58 SO0998
Trehafod *M Glam* 33 ST0490
Trehan *Cnwll* 5 SX4058
Treharris *M Glam* 33 ST0996
Treharrock *Cnwll* 4 SX0178
Trehemborne *Cnwll* 4 SW8773
Treherbert *Dyfed* 44 SN5847
Treherbert *M Glam* 33 SS9498
Treheveras *Cnwll* 3 SW8046
Trehunist *Cnwll* 5 SX3263
Trekelland *Cnwll* 5 SX3480
Trekenner *Cnwll* 5 SX3478
Treknow *Cnwll* 4 SX0586
Trelan *Cnwll* 3 SW7418
Trelash *Cnwll* 4 SX1890
Trelassick *Cnwll* 3 SW8752
Trelawne *Cnwll* 5 SX2154
Trelawnyd *Clwyd* 70 SJ0979
Treleague *Cnwll* 3 SW7821
Treleaver *Cnwll* 3 SW7716
Trelech *Dyfed* 31 SN2830
Trelech a'r Betws *Dyfed* 31 SN3026
Treleddyd-fawr *Dyfed* 30 SM7528
Trelew *Cnwll* 3 SW8135
Trelewis *M Glam* 33 ST1096
Treligga *Cnwll* 4 SX0484
Trelights *Cnwll* 4 SW9979
Trelill *Cnwll* 4 SX0478
Trelinnoe *Cnwll* 5 SX3181
Trelion *Cnwll* 3 SW9252
Trelissick *Cnwll* 3 SW8339
Trelleck *Gwent* 34 SO5005
Trelleck Grange *Gwent* 34 SO4901
Trelogan *Clwyd* 70 SJ1180
Trelonk *Cnwll* 3 SW8941
Trelow *Cnwll* 4 SW9269
Trelowarren *Cnwll* 2 SW7124
Trelowia *Cnwll* 5 SX2956
Treluggan *Cnwll* 3 SW8838
Trelystan *Powys* 58 SJ2503
Tremadog *Gwynd* 57 SH5640
Tremail *Cnwll* 4 SX1686
Tremain *Dyfed* 42 SN2348
Tremaine *Cnwll* 5 SX2389
Tremar *Cnwll* 5 SX2568
Trematon *Cnwll* 5 SX3959
Trembraze *Cnwll* 5 SX2565
Tremeirchion *Clwyd* 70 SJ0873
Tremethick Cross *Cnwll* 2 SW4430
Tremollett *Cnwll* 5 SX2975
Tremore *Cnwll* 4 SX0164
Trenance *Cnwll* 3 SW8022
Trenance *Cnwll* 4 SW8568
Trenance *Cnwll* 4 SW9270
Trenarren *Cnwll* 3 SX0348
Trenault *Cnwll* 5 SX2683
Trench *Shrops* 60 SJ6912
Trench Green *Oxon* 37 SU6877
Trencreek *Cnwll* 4 SW8260
Trencreek *Cnwll* 4 SX1896
Trendeal *Cnwll* 3 SW8952
Trendrine *Cnwll* 2 SW4739
Treneague *Cnwll* 4 SW9871
Trenear *Cnwll* 2 SW6731
Treneglos *Cnwll* 5 SX2088
Trenerth *Cnwll* 2 SW6035
Trenewan *Cnwll* 4 SX1753
Trenewth *Cnwll* 4 SX0778
Trengothal *Cnwll* 2 SW3724
Trengune *Cnwll* 4 SX1893
Treninnick *Cnwll* 4 SW8160
Trenowah *Cnwll* 4 SW7959
Trenoweth *Cnwll* 3 SW7533
Trent *Dorset* 10 ST5918
Trent Port *Lincs* 76 SK8381
Trent Vale *Staffs* 72 SJ8643
Trentham *Staffs* 72 SJ8740
Trentishoe *Devon* 19 SS6448
Trentlock *Derbys* 62 SK4831
Treoes *S Glam* 33 SS9478
Treorchy *M Glam* 33 SS9597
Trequite *Cnwll* 4 SX0377
Trerhyngyll *S Glam* 33 ST0077
Trerulefoot *Cnwll* 5 SX3358
Tresahor *Cnwll* 3 SW7431
Tresaith *Dyfed* 42 SN2751
Tresawle *Cnwll* 3 SW8846
Trescott *Staffs* 60 SO8597
Trescowe *Cnwll* 2 SW5731
Tresean *Cnwll* 4 SW7858
Tresham *Avon* 35 ST7991
Tresillian *Cnwll* 3 SW8646
Tresinney *Cnwll* 4 SX1081
Treskinnick Cross *Cnwll* 5 SX2098
Treslea *Cnwll* 4 SX1368
Tresmeer *Cnwll* 5 SX2387
Tresparrett *Cnwll* 4 SX1491
Tressait *Tays* 132 NN8160
Tresta *Shet* 155 HU3650
Tresta *Shet* 155 HU6090
Treswell *Notts* 75 SK7879
Treswithian *Cnwll* 2 SW6241
Trethawle *Cnwll* 5 SX2662
Trethevey *Cnwll* 4 SX0789
Trethewey *Cnwll* 2 SW3823
Trethomas *M Glam* 33 ST1888
Trethosa *Cnwll* 3 SW9454
Trethurgy *Cnwll* 3 SX0355
Tretio *Dyfed* 30 SM7829
Tretire *H & W* 46 SO5123
Tretower *Powys* 33 SO1821
Treuddyn *Clwyd* 70 SJ2557
Trevadlock *Cnwll* 5 SX2679
Trevague *Cnwll* 5 SX2379
Trevalga *Cnwll* 4 SX0890
Trevalyn *Clwyd* 71 SJ3856
Trevanger *Cnwll* 4 SW9677
Trevanson *Cnwll* 4 SW9773
Trevarrack *Cnwll* 2 SW4731
Trevarren *Cnwll* 4 SW9160
Trevarrian *Cnwll* 4 SW8566
Trevarrick *Cnwll* 3 SW9843
Trevarth *Cnwll* 3 SW7240
Trevaughan *Dyfed* 31 SN2015
Treveal *Cnwll* 2 SW4740
Treveal *Cnwll* 4 SW7858
Treveale *Cnwll* 3 SW8751
Treveighan *Cnwll* 4 SX0779
Trevellas Downs *Cnwll* 3 SW7452
Trevelmond *Cnwll* 5 SX2063
Trevempor *Cnwll* 4 SW8159
Treveneague *Cnwll* 2 SW5432
Treveor *Cnwll* 3 SW9841
Treverbyn *Cnwll* 3 SW8849
Treverbyn *Cnwll* 4 SX0157
Treverva *Cnwll* 3 SW7531
Trevescan *Cnwll* 2 SW3524
Trevethin *Gwent* 34 SO2801
Trevia *Cnwll* 4 SX0983
Trevigro *Cnwll* 5 SX3369
Trevilla *Cnwll* 3 SW8239
Trevilledor *Cnwll* 4 SW8867
Trevilson *Cnwll* 3 SW8455
Trevine *Dyfed* 30 SM8432
Treviscoe *Cnwll* 3 SW9455
Treviskey *Cnwll* 3 SW9340
Trevissick *Cnwll* 3 SX0248
Trevithal *Cnwll* 2 SW4626
Trevithick *Cnwll* 4 SW8862
Trevithick *Cnwll* 3 SW9645
Trevivian *Cnwll* 4 SX1785
Trevoll *Cnwll* 4 SW8358
Trevone *Cnwll* 4 SW8975
Trevor *Gwynd* 56 SH3746
Trevor *Clwyd* 70 SJ2742
Trevorgans *Cnwll* 2 SW4025
Trevorrick *Cnwll* 4 SW8672
Trevorrick *Cnwll* 4 SW9273
Trevose *Cnwll* 4 SW8675
Trew *Cnwll* 2 SW6129
Trewalder *Cnwll* 4 SX0782
Trewalkin *Powys* 45 SO1531
Trewarlett *Cnwll* 5 SX3380
Trewarmett *Cnwll* 4 SX0686
Trewarthenick *Cnwll* 3 SW9044
Trewassa *Cnwll* 4 SX1486
Trewaves *Cnwll* 2 SW5926
Treween *Cnwll* 5 SX2182
Trewellard *Cnwll* 2 SW3733
Trewen *Cnwll* 5 SX0577
Trewennack *Cnwll* 2 SW6728
Trewent *Dyfed* 30 SS0197
Trewern *Powys* 58 SJ2811
Trewetha *Cnwll* 4 SX0080
Trewethern *Cnwll* 4 SX0076
Trewidland *Cnwll* 5 SX2559
Trewillis *Cnwll* 3 SW7717
Trewince *Cnwll* 3 SW8633
Trewint *Cnwll* 4 SX1072
Trewint *Cnwll* 5 SX2180
Trewint *Cnwll* 5 SX2963
Trewirgie *Cnwll* 3 SW8845
Trewithian *Cnwll* 3 SW8737
Trewoodloe *Cnwll* 5 SX3271
Trewoofe *Cnwll* 2 SW4425
Trewoon *Cnwll* 2 SW6819
Trewoon *Cnwll* 3 SW9952
Treworgan *Cnwll* 3 SW8349
Treworlas *Cnwll* 3 SW8938
Treworld *Cnwll* 4 SX1190
Treworthal *Cnwll* 3 SW8839
Treyarnon *Cnwll* 4 SW8673
Treyford *W Susx* 14 SU8218
Triangle *W York* 82 SE0422
Trickett's Cross *Dorset* 12 SU0800
Triermain *Cumb* 102 NY5966
Triffleton *Dyfed* 30 SM9724
Trillacott *Cnwll* 5 SX2689
Trimdon *Dur* 96 NZ3634
Trimdon Colliery *Dur* 96 NZ3735
Trimdon Grange *Dur* 96 NZ3635
Trimingham *Norfk* 67 TG2838
Trimley *Suffk* 55 TM2737
Trimley Heath *Suffk* 55 TM2738
Trimley Lower Street *Suffk* 55 TM2636
Trimpley *H & W* 60 SO7978
Trimsaran *Dyfed* 32 SN4504
Trimstone *Devon* 19 SS5043
Trinafour *Tays* 132 NN7264
Trinant *Gwent* 33 ST2099
Tring *Herts* 38 SP9211
Tring Wharf *Herts* 38 SP9212
Tringford *Herts* 38 SP9113
Trinity *Jersey* 152 JS0000
Trinity *Tays* 134 NO6061
Trinity Gask *Tays* 125 NN9718
Triscombe *Somset* 20 SS9237
Triscombe *Somset* 20 ST1535
Trislaig *Highld* 130 NN0874
Trispen *Cnwll* 3 SW8450
Tritlington *Nthumb* 103 NZ2092
Troan *Cnwll* 4 SW8957
Trochry *Tays* 125 NN9740
Troedrhiwfuwch *M Glam* 33 SO1204
Troedyraur *Dyfed* 42 SN3245
Troedyrhiw *M Glam* 33 SO0702
Trofarth *Clwyd* 69 SH8571
Trois Bois *Jersey* 152 JS0000
Troon *Strath* 106 NS3230
Troon *Cnwll* 2 SW6638
Troquhain *D & G* 99 NX6879
Trossachs Hotel *Cent* 124 NN5107
Troston *Suffk* 54 TL8972
Troswell *Cnwll* 5 SX2592
Trots Hill *H & W* 47 SO8855
Trottiscliffe *Kent* 27 TQ6460
Trotton *W Susx* 14 SU8322
Trough Gate *Lancs* 81 SD8821
Troughend *Nthumb* 102 NY8692
Troutbeck *Cumb* 93 NY3825
Troutbeck *Cumb* 87 NY4002
Troutbeck Bridge *Cumb* 87 NY4000
Troway *Derbys* 74 SK3879
Trowbridge *Wilts* 22 ST8558
Trowell *Notts* 62 SK4839
Trowle Common *Wilts* 22 ST8458
Trowse Newton *Norfk* 67 TG2406
Troy *W York* 82 SE2439
Trudoxhill *Somset* 22 ST7443
Trull *Somset* 20 ST2122
Trumfleet *S York* 83 SE6011
Trumpan *Highld* 136 NG2261
Trumpet *H & W* 47 SO6539
Trumpington *Cambs* 53 TL4454
Trumpsgreen *Surrey* 25 SU9967
Trunch *Norfk* 67 TG2834
Trunnah *Lancs* 80 SD3442
Truro *Cnwll* 3 SW8244
Truscott *Cnwll* 5 SX2985
Trusham *Devon* 8 SX8582
Trusley *Derbys* 73 SK2535
Trysull *Staffs* 60 SO8594
Tubney *Oxon* 36 SU4399
Tuckenhay *Devon* 7 SX8156
Tuckhill *Shrops* 60 SO7888
Tuckingmill *Wilts* 22 ST9329
Tuckingmill *Cnwll* 2 SW6540
Tuckton *Dorset* 12 SZ1492
Tucoyse *Cnwll* 3 SW9645
Tuddenham *Suffk* 53 TL7371
Tuddenham *Suffk* 55 TM1948
Tudeley *Kent* 16 TQ6245
Tudhoe *Dur* 96 NZ2535
Tudweiloig *Gwynd* 56 SH2436
Tuesley *Surrey* 25 SU9642
Tuffley *Gloucs* 35 SO8314
Tufton *Dyfed* 30 SN0428
Tufton *Hants* 24 SU4546
Tugby *Leics* 63 SK7601
Tugford *Shrops* 59 SO5587
Tughall *Nthumb* 111 NU2126
Tullibody *Cent* 116 NS8595
Tullich *Highld* 140 NH6328
Tullich *Highld* 147 NH8576
Tullich *Strath* 123 NN0815
Tulliemet *Tays* 125 NO0052
Tulloch *Gramp* 143 NJ8031
Tulloch *Cent* 124 NN5120
Tulloch Station *Highld* 131 NN3580
Tullochgorm *Strath* 114 NR9695
Tullybeagles Lodge *Tays* 125 NO0136
Tullynessie *Gramp* 142 NJ5519
Tumble *Dyfed* 32 SN5411
Tumbler's Green *Essex* 40 TL8025
Tumby *Lincs* 76 TF2359
Tumby Woodside *Lincs* 77 TF2757
Tummel Bridge *Tays* 132 NN7659
Tungate *Norfk* 67 TG2629
Tunstall *T & W* 96 NZ3953
Tunstall *Lancs* 87 SD6073
Tunstall *N York* 89 SE2196
Tunstall *Staffs* 72 SJ7727
Tunstall *Staffs* 72 SJ8651
Tunstall *Humb* 85 TA3031
Tunstall *Norfk* 67 TG4107
Tunstall *Suffk* 55 TM3655
Tunstall *Kent* 28 TQ8961
Tunstead *Derbys* 74 SK1074
Tunstead *Norfk* 67 TG3022
Tunstead Milton *Derbys* 79 SK0180
Tunworth *Hants* 24 SU6748
Tupsley *H & W* 46 SO5340
Tur Langton *Leics* 50 SP7194
Turgis Green *Hants* 24 SU6959
Turkdean *Gloucs* 36 SP1017
Turleigh *Wilts* 22 ST8060
Turleygreen *Shrops* 60 SO7685
Turn *Lancs* 81 SD8118
Turnastone *H & W* 46 SO3536
Turnberry *Strath* 106 NS2005
Turnchapel *Devon* 6 SX4953
Turnditch *Derbys* 73 SK2946
Turner Green *Lancs* 81 SD6030
Turner's Green *Warwks* 48 SP1969
Turner's Green *E Susx* 16 TQ6319
Turner's Hill *W Susx* 15 TQ3435
Turners Puddle *Dorset* 11 SY8393
Turnworth *Dorset* 11 ST8207
Turriff *Gramp* 142 NJ7250
Turton Bottoms *Gt Man* 81 SD7315
Turvey *Beds* 38 SP9452
Turville *Bucks* 37 SU7691
Turville Heath *Bucks* 37 SU7490
Turweston *Bucks* 49 SP6037
Tushielaw Inn *Border* 109 NT3017
Tushingham cum Grindley *Ches* 71 SJ5246
Tutbury *Staffs* 73 SK2128
Tutnall *H & W* 60 SO9970
Tutshill *Gloucs* 34 ST5494
Tuttington *Norfk* 67 TG2227
Tutwell *Cnwll* 5 SX3875
Tuxford *Notts* 75 SK7471
Twatt *Shet* 155 HU3253
Twatt *Ork* 155 HY2724
Twechar *Strath* 116 NS6975
Tweedmouth *Nthumb* 119 NT9952
Tweedsmuir *Border* 108 NT1024
Twelve Oaks *E Susx* 16 TQ6820
Twelveheads *Cnwll* 3 SW7542
Twemlow Green *Ches* 79 SJ7868
Twenty *Lincs* 64 TF1520
Twerton *Avon* 22 ST7264
Twickenham *Gt Lon* 26 TQ1673
Twigworth *Gloucs* 35 SO8422
Twineham *W Susx* 15 TQ2519
Twineham Green *W Susx* 15 TQ2520
Twinhoe *Avon* 22 ST7559
Twinstead *Essex* 54 TL8636
Twiss Green *Ches* 79 SJ6595
Twitchen *Shrops* 46 SO3779
Twitchen *Devon* 19 SS7930
Twitham *Kent* 29 TR2656
Two Bridges *Devon* 6 SX6174
Two Dales *Derbys* 74 SK2763
Two Gates *Staffs* 61 SK2101
Two Mile Oak Cross *Devon* 7 SX8468
Two Pots *Devon* 19 SS5344
Two Waters *Herts* 38 TL0505
Twycross *Leics* 62 SK3304
Twyford *Derbys* 62 SK3228
Twyford *Leics* 63 SK7210

Twyford Waen

Twyford *Lincs* 63 SK9323
Twyford *Bucks* 49 SP6626
Twyford *Hants* 13 SU4824
Twyford *Berks* 37 SU7976
Twyford *Norfk* 66 TG0123
Twyford Common *H & W* 46 SO5135
Twyn-carno *M Glam* 33 SO1108
Twyn-y-Sheriff *Gwent* 34 SO4005
Twyn-yr-Odyn *S Glam* 33 ST1173
Twynholm *D & G* 99 NX6654
Twyning *Gloucs* 47 SO8936
Twyning Green *Gloucs* 47 SO9036
Twynllanan *Dyfed* 44 SN7524
Twywell *Nhants* 51 SP9578
Ty'n-dwr *Clwyd* 70 SJ2341
Ty'n-y-coedcae *M Glam* 33 ST1988
Ty'n-y-groes *Gwynd* 69 SH7771
Ty-croes *Dyfed* 32 SN6010
Ty-nant *Gwynd* 58 SH9026
Ty-nant *Clwyd* 70 SH9944
Tyberton *H & W* 46 SO3839
Tyburn *W Mids* 61 SP1391
Tycrwyn *Powys* 58 SJ1018
Tydd Gote *Lincs* 65 TF4518
Tydd St. Giles *Cambs* 65 TF4216
Tydd St. Mary *Lincs* 65 TF4418
Tye *Hants* 13 SU7302
Tye Green *Essex* 39 TL5424
Tye Green *Essex* 53 TL5935
Tye Green *Essex* 40 TL7821
Tyersal *W York* 82 SE1932
Tyldesley *Gt Man* 79 SD6802
Tyler Hill *Kent* 29 TR1461
Tyler's Green *Essex* 39 TL5005
Tylers Green *Bucks* 26 SU9093
Tylers Green *Surrey* 27 TQ3552
Tylorstown *M Glam* 33 ST0095
Tylwch *Powys* 58 SN9780
Tyn-y-nant *M Glam* 33 ST0685
Tyndrum *Cent* 123 NN3230
Tyneham *Dorset* 11 SY8880
Tynemouth *T & W* 103 NZ3669
Tynewydd *M Glam* 33 SS9398
Tyninghame *Loth* 118 NT6179
Tynron *D & G* 100 NX8093
Tynygongl *Gwynd* 68 SH5082
Tynygraig *Dyfed* 43 SN6969
Tyringham *Bucks* 38 SP8547
Tyseley *W Mids* 61 SP1184
Tythegston *M Glam* 33 SS8578
Tytherington *Ches* 79 SJ9175
Tytherington *Avon* 35 ST6688
Tytherington *Somset* 22 ST7644
Tytherington *Wilts* 22 ST9141
Tytherleigh *Devon* 10 ST3103
Tywardreath *Cnwll* 3 SX0854
Tywardreath Highway *Cnwll* 3 SX0755
Tywyn *Gwynd* 69 SH7878

U

Ubbeston Green *Suffk* 55 TM3271
Ubley *Avon* 21 ST5258
Uckerby *N York* 89 NZ2402
Uckfield *E Susx* 16 TQ4721
Uckinghall *H & W* 47 SO8637
Uckington *Shrops* 59 SJ5709
Uckington *Gloucs* 47 SO9124
Uddingston *Strath* 116 NS6960
Uddington *Strath* 108 NS8633
Udimore *E Susx* 17 TQ8719
Udny Green *Gramp* 143 NJ8726
Uffcott *Wilts* 36 SU1277
Uffculme *Devon* 9 ST0612
Uffington *Shrops* 59 SJ5313
Uffington *Oxon* 36 SU3089
Ufford *Cambs* 64 TF0903
Ufford *Suffk* 55 TM2952
Ufton *Warwks* 48 SP3762
Ufton Nervet *Berks* 24 SU6367
Ugadale *Strath* 105 NR7828
Ugborough *Devon* 7 SX6755
Uggeshall *Suffk* 55 TM4480
Ugglebarnby *N York* 90 NZ8707
Ughill *Derbys* 74 SK2590
Ugley *Essex* 39 TL5228
Ugley Green *Essex* 39 TL5227
Ugthorpe *N York* 90 NZ7911
Uig *W Isls* 154 NB0533
Uig *Highld* 136 NG1952
Uig *Highld* 136 NG3963
Uig *Strath* 120 NM1654
Uigshader *Highld* 136 NG4346
Uisken *Strath* 121 NM3919
Ulbster *Highld* 151 ND3241
Ulcat Row *Cumb* 93 NY4022
Ulceby *Humb* 85 TA1014
Ulceby *Lincs* 77 TF4272
Ulceby Skitter *Humb* 85 TA1215
Ulcombe *Kent* 28 TQ8448
Uldale *Cumb* 93 NY2437
Uley *Gloucs* 35 ST7898
Ulgham *Nthumb* 103 NZ2392
Ullapool *Highld* 145 NH1294
Ullceby Cross *Lincs* 77 TF4173
Ullenhall *Warwks* 48 SP1267
Ullenwood *Gloucs* 35 SO9416
Ulleskelf *N York* 83 SE5239
Ullesthorpe *Leics* 50 SP5087
Ulley *S York* 75 SK4687
Ullingswick *H & W* 46 SO5949
Ullinish *Highld* 136 NG3237
Ullock *Cumb* 92 NY0724
Ulpha *Cumb* 86 SD1993
Ulpha *Cumb* 87 SD4581
Ulrome *Humb* 85 TA1656
Ulsta *Shet* 155 HU4680
Ulting Wick *Essex* 40 TL8009
Ulverley Green *W Mids* 61 SP1382
Ulverston *Cumb* 86 SD2878
Ulwell *Dorset* 12 SZ0280
Umachan *Highld* 137 NG6050
Umberleigh *Devon* 19 SS6023
Unapool *Highld* 148 NC2333
Under Burnmouth *D & G* 101 NY4783
Under River *Kent* 27 TQ5552
Underbarrow *Cumb* 87 SD4692
Undercliffe *W York* 82 SE1834
Underdale *Shrops* 59 SJ5013
Underley Hall *Cumb* 87 SD6179
Underling Green *Kent* 28 TQ7546
Underwood *Notts* 75 SK4750
Undley *Suffk* 53 TL6981
Undy *Gwent* 34 ST4386
Union Mills *IOM* 153 SC3577
Union Street *E Susx* 16 TQ7031
Unstone *Derbys* 74 SK3777
Unstone Green *Derbys* 74 SK3776
Unsworth *Gt Man* 79 SD8207
Unthank *Nthumb* 111 NT9848
Unthank *Cumb* 93 NY3948
Unthank *Cumb* 93 NY4536
Unthank *Cumb* 94 NY6040
Unthank *Derbys* 74 SK3075
Unthank End *Cumb* 93 NY4535
Up Cerne *Dorset* 11 ST6502
Up Exe *Devon* 9 SS9402
Up Holland *Lancs* 78 SD5205
Up Marden *W Susx* 14 SU7913
Up Mudford *Somset* 10 ST5718
Up Nately *Hants* 24 SU6951
Up Somborne *Hants* 23 SU3932
Up Sydling *Dorset* 10 ST6201
Upavon *Wilts* 23 SU1354
Upchurch *Kent* 28 TQ8467
Upcott *H & W* 46 SO3250
Upcott *Devon* 19 SS5838
Upcott *Devon* 19 SS7529
Upcott *Somset* 20 SS9025
Updown Hill *Surrey* 25 SU9363
Upend *Cambs* 53 TL7058
Upgate *Norfk* 66 TG1318
Upgate Street *Norfk* 66 TM0992
Upgate Street *Norfk* 67 TM2891
Uphall *Loth* 117 NT0671
Uphall *Dorset* 10 ST5502
Upham *Devon* 19 SS8808
Upham *Hants* 13 SU5320
Uphampton *H & W* 46 SO3963
Uphampton *H & W* 47 SO8364
Uphill *Avon* 21 ST3158
Uplawmoor *Strath* 115 NS4355
Upleadon *Gloucs* 47 SO7527
Upleatham *Cleve* 97 NZ6319
Uplees *Kent* 28 TR0064
Uploders *Dorset* 10 SY5093
Uplowman *Devon* 9 ST0115
Uplyme *Devon* 10 SY3293
Upminster *Gt Lon* 27 TQ5686
Upottery *Devon* 9 ST2007
Uppark *W Susx* 14 SU7717
Uppaton *Devon* 5 SX4380
Upper Affcot *Shrops* 59 SO4486
Upper Ardchronie *Highld* 146 NH6188
Upper Arley *H & W* 60 SO7680
Upper Arncott *Oxon* 37 SP6117
Upper Astrop *Nhants* 49 SP5137
Upper Basildon *Berks* 37 SU5976
Upper Batley *W York* 82 SE2325
Upper Beeding *W Susx* 15 TQ1910
Upper Benefield *Nhants* 51 SP9789
Upper Bentley *H & W* 47 SO9966
Upper Bighouse *Highld* 150 NC8856
Upper Birchwood *Derbys* 75 SK4355
Upper Boat *M Glam* 33 ST1086
Upper Boddington *Nhants* 49 SP4852
Upper Borth *Dyfed* 43 SN6088
Upper Brailes *Warwks* 48 SP3039
Upper Breakish *Highld* 129 NG6823
Upper Breinton *H & W* 46 SO4640
Upper Broadheath *H & W* 47 SO8056
Upper Broughton *Notts* 63 SK6826
Upper Bucklebury *Berks* 24 SU5468
Upper Burgate *Hants* 12 SU1516
Upper Bush *Kent* 28 TQ6966
Upper Cairn *D & G* 107 NS6912
Upper Caldecote *Beds* 52 TL1645
Upper Canada *Avon* 21 ST3658
Upper Canterton *Hants* 12 SU2612
Upper Catesby *Nhants* 49 SP5259
Upper Catshill *H & W* 60 SO9674
Upper Chapel *Powys* 45 SO0040
Upper Cheddon *Somset* 20 ST2328
Upper Chicksgrove *Wilts* 22 ST9529
Upper Chute *Wilts* 23 SU2953
Upper Clapton *Gt Lon* 27 TQ3487
Upper Clatford *Hants* 23 SU3543
Upper Clynnog *Gwynd* 56 SH4646
Upper Coberley *Gloucs* 35 SO9816
Upper Cokeham *W Susx* 15 TQ1605
Upper Cotton *Staffs* 73 SK0547
Upper Cound *Shrops* 59 SJ5505
Upper Cudworth *S York* 83 SE3909
Upper Cumberworth *W York* 82 SE2008
Upper Cwmtwrch *Powys* 32 SN7511
Upper Dallachy *Gramp* 141 NJ3662
Upper Deal *Kent* 29 TR3651
Upper Dean *Beds* 51 TL0467
Upper Denby *W York* 82 SE2207
Upper Denton *Cumb* 102 NY6165
Upper Dicker *E Susx* 16 TQ5509
Upper Dinchope *Shrops* 59 SO4583
Upper Dovercourt *Essex* 41 TM2330
Upper Drumbane *Cent* 124 NN6606
Upper Dunsforth *N York* 89 SE4463
Upper Eashing *Surrey* 25 SU9543
Upper Egleton *H & W* 47 SO6344
Upper Elkstone *Staffs* 74 SK0558
Upper Ellastone *Staffs* 73 SK1043
Upper Elmers End *Gt Lon* 27 TQ3667
Upper End *Derbys* 74 SK0875
Upper Enham *Hants* 23 SU3650
Upper Ethrie *Highld* 140 NH7662
Upper Farmcote *Shrops* 60 SO7791
Upper Farringdon *Hants* 24 SU7135
Upper Framilode *Gloucs* 35 SO7510
Upper Froyle *Hants* 24 SU7543
Upper Godney *Somset* 21 ST4842
Upper Gravenhurst *Beds* 38 TL1136
Upper Green *Gwent* 34 SO3818
Upper Green *Berks* 23 SU3763
Upper Green *Essex* 53 TL5935
Upper Green *Suffk* 53 TL7464
Upper Grove Common *H & W* 46 SO5526
Upper Hackney *Derbys* 74 SK2861
Upper Hale *Surrey* 25 SU8349
Upper Halliford *Surrey* 26 TQ0968
Upper Halling *Kent* 28 TQ6964
Upper Hambleton *Leics* 63 SK9007
Upper Harbledown *Kent* 29 TR1158
Upper Hardres Court *Kent* 29 TR1550
Upper Hardwick *H & W* 46 SO4057
Upper Hartfield *E Susx* 16 TQ4634
Upper Hartshay *Derbys* 74 SK3850
Upper Hatherley *Gloucs* 35 SO9220
Upper Hatton *Staffs* 72 SJ8237
Upper Haugh *S York* 74 SK4297
Upper Hayton *Shrops* 59 SO5181
Upper Heaton *W York* 82 SE1719
Upper Helmsley *N York* 83 SE6956
Upper Hergest *H & W* 46 SO2654
Upper Heyford *Oxon* 49 SP4925
Upper Heyford *Nhants* 49 SP6659
Upper Hill *H & W* 46 SO4753
Upper Hockenden *Kent* 27 TQ5069
Upper Hopton *W York* 82 SE1918
Upper Howsell *H & W* 47 SO7848
Upper Hulme *Staffs* 73 SK0160
Upper Ifold *Surrey* 14 TQ0033
Upper Inglesham *Wilts* 36 SU2096
Upper Keith *Loth* 118 NT4562
Upper Kilcott *Avon* 35 ST7988
Upper Killay *W Glam* 32 SS5892
Upper Kinchrackine *Strath* 123 NN1627
Upper Lambourn *Berks* 36 SU3080
Upper Landywood *Staffs* 60 SJ9805
Upper Langford *Avon* 21 ST4659
Upper Langwith *Derbys* 75 SK5169
Upper Largo *Fife* 127 NO4203
Upper Leigh *Staffs* 73 SK0136
Upper Ley *Gloucs* 35 SO7217
Upper Littleton *Avon* 21 ST5564
Upper Lochton *Gramp* 135 NO6997
Upper Longdon *Staffs* 61 SK0614
Upper Ludstone *Shrops* 60 SO8095
Upper Lybster *Highld* 151 ND2537
Upper Lydbrook *Gloucs* 34 SO6015
Upper Lyde *H & W* 46 SO4944
Upper Lye *H & W* 46 SO3965
Upper Maes-coed *H & W* 46 SO3334
Upper Midhope *Derbys* 74 SK2199
Upper Milton *H & W* 60 SO8172
Upper Minety *Wilts* 35 SU0091
Upper Moor *H & W* 47 SO9747
Upper Moor Side *W York* 82 SE2430
Upper Mulben *Gramp* 141 NJ3551
Upper Nesbet *Border* 110 NT6727
Upper Netchwood *Shrops* 59 SO6092
Upper Nobut *Staffs* 73 SK0335
Upper Norwood *W Susx* 14 SU9317
Upper Ollach *Highld* 137 NG5136
Upper Padley *Derbys* 74 SK2478
Upper Pennington *Hants* 12 SZ3095
Upper Pickwick *Wilts* 35 ST8571
Upper Pollicott *Bucks* 37 SP7013
Upper Pond Street *Essex* 39 TL4636
Upper Poppleton *N York* 83 SE5553
Upper Pulley *Shrops* 59 SJ4808
Upper Quinton *Warwks* 48 SP1846
Upper Ratley *Hants* 23 SU3223
Upper Rochford *H & W* 47 SO6367
Upper Ruscoe *D & G* 99 NX5661
Upper Sapey *H & W* 47 SO6863
Upper Seagry *Wilts* 35 ST9480
Upper Shelton *Beds* 38 SP9843
Upper Sheringham *Norfk* 66 TG1441
Upper Shuckburgh *Warwks* 49 SP5061
Upper Slaughter *Gloucs* 48 SP1523
Upper Soudley *Gloucs* 35 SO6510
Upper Spond *H & W* 46 SO3152
Upper Standen *Kent* 29 TR2139
Upper Staploe *Beds* 52 TL1459
Upper Stepford *D & G* 100 NX8681
Upper Stoke *Norfk* 67 TG2502
Upper Stondon *Beds* 38 TL1435
Upper Stowe *Nhants* 49 SP6456
Upper Street *Hants* 12 SU1518
Upper Street *Norfk* 67 TG3217
Upper Street *Norfk* 67 TG3616
Upper Street *Suffk* 53 TL7851
Upper Street *Suffk* 54 TM1050
Upper Street *Suffk* 54 TM1434
Upper Street *Norfk* 54 TM1779
Upper Sundon *Beds* 38 TL0428
Upper Swell *Gloucs* 48 SP1726
Upper Tankersley *S York* 74 SK3499
Upper Tasburgh *Norfk* 67 TM2095
Upper Tean *Staffs* 73 SK0139
Upper Threapwood *Ches* 71 SJ4345
Upper Town *Dur* 95 NZ0737
Upper Town *Derbys* 73 SK2351
Upper Town *Derbys* 74 SK2361
Upper Town *H & W* 46 SO5848
Upper Town *Avon* 21 ST5265
Upper Town *Suffk* 54 TL9267
Upper Tysoe *Warwks* 48 SP3343
Upper Ufford *Suffk* 55 TM2952
Upper Upham *Wilts* 36 SU2277
Upper Upnor *Kent* 28 TQ7570
Upper Victoria *Tays* 127 NO5336
Upper Vobster *Somset* 22 ST7049
Upper Wardington *Oxon* 49 SP4945
Upper Weald *Bucks* 38 SP8037
Upper Weedon *Nhants* 49 SP6258
Upper Wellingham *E Susx* 16 TQ4313
Upper Weston *Avon* 22 ST7267
Upper Weybread *Suffk* 55 TM2379
Upper Wick *H & W* 47 SO8252
Upper Wield *Hants* 24 SU6238
Upper Winchendon *Bucks* 37 SP7414
Upper Witton *W Mids* 61 SP0891
Upper Woodford *Wilts* 23 SU1237
Upper Wootton *Hants* 24 SU5754
Upper Wraxall *Wilts* 35 ST8074
Upper Wyche *H & W* 47 SO7643
Upperby *Cumb* 93 NY4153
Upperglen *Highld* 136 NG3151
Uppermill *Gt Man* 82 SD9905
Upperthong *W York* 82 SE1208
Upperthorpe *Derbys* 75 SK4580
Upperton *W Susx* 14 SU9522
Uppertown *Highld* 151 ND3576
Uppertown *Derbys* 74 SK3264
Upperup *Gloucs* 36 SU0496
Upperwood *Derbys* 73 SK2956
Uppincott *Devon* 9 SS9006
Uppingham *Leics* 51 SP8699
Uppington *Shrops* 59 SJ5909
Uppington *Dorset* 12 SU0206
Upsall *N York* 89 SE4586
Upsettlington *Border* 110 NT8846
Upshire *Essex* 27 TL4101
Upstreet *Kent* 29 TR2263
Upthorpe *Suffk* 54 TL9772
Upton *Cumb* 93 NY3139
Upton *W York* 83 SE4713
Upton *Mersyd* 78 SJ2788
Upton *Ches* 71 SJ4069
Upton *Ches* 78 SJ5087
Upton *Notts* 75 SK7354
Upton *Notts* 75 SK7476
Upton *Lincs* 76 SK8686
Upton *Dyfed* 30 SN0204
Upton *Warwks* 48 SP1257
Upton *Oxon* 36 SP2312
Upton *Leics* 61 SP3699
Upton *Nhants* 49 SP7159
Upton *Bucks* 37 SP7711
Upton *Cnwll* 18 SS2004
Upton *Somset* 20 SS9928
Upton *Devon* 9 ST0902
Upton *Somset* 21 ST4526
Upton *Hants* 23 SU3555
Upton *Hants* 12 SU3716
Upton *Oxon* 37 SU5187
Upton *Berks* 26 SU9779
Upton *Cnwll* 5 SX2772
Upton *Devon* 7 SX7043
Upton *Dorset* 11 SY7483
Upton *Dorset* 11 SY9893
Upton *Humb* 85 TA1454
Upton *Cambs* 64 TF1000
Upton *Norfk* 67 TG3912
Upton *Cambs* 52 TL1778
Upton Cheyney *Avon* 35 ST6970
Upton Cressett *Shrops* 59 SO6592
Upton Crews *H & W* 47 SO6527
Upton Cross *Cnwll* 5 SX2872
Upton End *Beds* 38 TL1234
Upton Grey *Hants* 24 SU6948
Upton Heath *Ches* 71 SJ4169
Upton Hellions *Devon* 8 SS8403
Upton Lovell *Wilts* 22 ST9440
Upton Magna *Shrops* 59 SJ5512
Upton Noble *Somset* 22 ST7139
Upton Pyne *Devon* 9 SX9198
Upton Scudamore *Wilts* 22 ST8647
Upton Snodsbury *H & W* 47 SO9454
Upton St. Leonards *Gloucs* 35 SO8615
Upton Towans *Cnwll* 2 SW5740
Upton Warren *H & W* 47 SO9267
Upton Wood *Kent* 29 TR2546
Upton upon Severn *H & W* 47 SO8540
Upwaltham *W Susx* 14 SU9413
Upware *Cambs* 53 TL5470
Upwell *Norfk* 65 TF4902
Upwey *Dorset* 11 SY6685
Upwick Green *Herts* 39 TL4524
Upwood *Cambs* 52 TL2582
Urchfont *Wilts* 23 SU0357
Urdimarsh *H & W* 46 SO5248
Ure Bank *N York* 89 SE3172
Urlay Nook *Cleve* 89 NZ4014
Urmston *Gt Man* 79 SJ7694
Urquhart *Gramp* 141 NJ2862
Urra *N York* 90 NZ5601
Urray *Highld* 139 NH5052
Ushaw Moor *Dur* 96 NZ2242
Usk *Gwent* 34 SO3700
Usselby *Lincs* 76 TF0993
Usworth *T & W* 96 NZ3057
Utley *W York* 82 SE0542
Uton *Devon* 8 SX8298
Utterby *Lincs* 77 TF3093
Uttoxeter *Staffs* 73 SK0933
Uwchmynydd *Gwynd* 56 SH1525
Uxbridge *Gt Lon* 26 TQ0584
Uyeasound *Shet* 155 HP5901
Uzmaston *Dyfed* 30 SM9714

V

Vale *Guern* 152 GN0000
Valley *Gwynd* 68 SH2979
Valley End *Surrey* 25 SU9564
Valley Truckle *Cnwll* 4 SX0982
Valtos *W Isls* 154 NB0936
Valtos *Highld* 137 NG5163
Van *M Glam* 33 ST1686
Vange *Essex* 40 TQ7186
Varteg *Gwent* 34 SO2606
Vatsetter *Shet* 155 HU5389
Vatten *Highld* 136 NG2843
Vaynor *M Glam* 33 SO0410
Velindre *Powys* 45 SO1836
Vellow *Somset* 20 ST0938
Velly *Devon* 18 SS2924
Venn *Devon* 7 SX8549
Venn Ottery *Devon* 9 SY0891
Venngreen *Devon* 18 SS3711
Vennington *Shrops* 59 SJ3309
Venny Tedburn *Devon* 8 SX8297
Venterdon *Cnwll* 5 SX3675
Ventnor *IOW* 13 SZ5677
Venton *Devon* 6 SX5956
Vernham Dean *Hants* 23 SU3356
Vernham Street *Hants* 23 SU3457
Vernolds Common *Shrops* 59 SO4780
Verwood *Dorset* 12 SU0809
Veryan *Cnwll* 3 SW9139
Veryan Green *Cnwll* 3 SW9140
Vickerstown *Cumb* 86 SD1868
Victoria *S York* 82 SE1705
Victoria *Gwent* 33 SO1707
Victoria *Cnwll* 4 SW9861
Vidlin *Shet* 155 HU4765
Viewfield *Gramp* 141 NJ2864
Viewpark *Strath* 116 NS7061
Vigo *Kent* 27 TQ6361
Ville la Bas *Jersey* 152 JS0000
Villiaze *Guern* 152 GN0000
Vine's Cross *E Susx* 16 TQ5917
Vinehall Street *E Susx* 17 TQ7520
Virginia Water *Surrey* 25 TQ0067
Virginstow *Devon* 5 SX3792
Virley *Essex* 40 TL9414
Vobster *Somset* 22 ST7048
Voe *Shet* 155 HU4062
Vowchurch *H & W* 46 SO3636
Vulcan Village *Ches* 78 SJ5894

W

Wackerfield *Dur* 96 NZ1522
Wacton *Norfk* 66 TM1791
Wadborough *H & W* 47 SO9047
Waddesdon *Bucks* 37 SP7416
Waddeton *Devon* 7 SX8756
Waddicar *Mersyd* 78 SJ3999
Waddingham *Lincs* 76 SK9896
Waddington *Lancs* 81 SD7343
Waddington *Lincs* 76 SK9764
Waddon *Dorset* 10 SY6285
Wadebridge *Cnwll* 4 SW9972
Wadeford *Somset* 10 ST3110
Wadenhoe *Nhants* 51 TL0183
Wadesmill *Herts* 39 TL3617
Wadhurst *E Susx* 16 TQ6431
Wadshelf *Derbys* 74 SK3170
Wadswick *Wilts* 22 ST8467
Wadworth *S York* 75 SK5696
Waen *Clwyd* 70 SH9962
Waen *Clwyd* 70 SJ1065
Waen *Powys* 58 SJ2319

Wheathill

Winterbourne Monkton

Wheathill *Somset* 21 ST5830
Wheatley *W York* 82 SE0726
Wheatley *Oxon* 37 SP5905
Wheatley *Hants* 25 SU7840
Wheatley Hill *Dur* 96 NZ3738
Wheatley Hills *S York* 83 SE5904
Wheatley Lane *Lancs* 81 SD8337
Wheaton Aston *Staffs* 60 SJ8512
Wheatsheaf *Clwyd* 71 SJ3253
Wheddon Cross *Somset* 20 SS9238
Wheel Inn *Cnwll* 2 SW6921
Wheelbarrow Town *Kent* 29 TR1445
Wheeler's Green *Oxon* 24 SU7672
Wheeler's Street *Kent* 28 TQ8444
Wheelerend Common *Bucks* 37 SU8093
Wheelerstreet *Surrey* 25 SU9440
Wheelock *Ches* 72 SJ7559
Wheelock Heath *Ches* 72 SJ7557
Wheelton *Lancs* 81 SD6021
Wheldale *W York* 83 SE4526
Wheldrake *N York* 83 SE6844
Whelpley Hill *Bucks* 38 SP9904
Whelpo *Cumb* 93 NY3139
Whelston *Clwyd* 70 SJ2076
Whempstead *Herts* 39 TL3221
Whenby *N York* 90 SE6369
Whepstead *Suffk* 54 TL8358
Wherstead *Suffk* 54 TM1540
Wherwell *Hants* 23 SU3841
Wheston *Derbys* 74 SK1376
Whetsted *Kent* 28 TQ6646
Whetstone *Leics* 50 SP5597
Whetstone *Gt Lon* 27 TQ2693
Wheyrigg *Cumb* 93 NY1948
Whicham *Cumb* 86 SD1382
Whichford *Warwks* 48 SP3134
Whickham *T & W* 96 NZ2061
Whiddon *Devon* 18 SX4799
Whiddon Down *Devon* 8 SX6992
Whight's Corner *Suffk* 54 TM1242
Whigstreet *Tays* 127 NO4844
Whiligh *E Susx* 16 TQ6431
Whilton *Nhants* 49 SP6364
Whim *Border* 117 NT2153
Whimble *Devon* 18 SS3503
Whimple *Devon* 9 SY0497
Whimpwell Green *Norfk* 67 TG3829
Whin Lane End *Lancs* 80 SD3941
Whinburgh *Norfk* 66 TG0009
Whinnie Liggate *D & G* 99 NX7252
Whinnow *Cumb* 93 NY3051
Whinny Hill *Cleve* 96 NZ3818
Whippingham *IOW* 13 SZ5193
Whipsnade *Beds* 38 TL0117
Whipton *Devon* 9 SX9493
Whisby *Lincs* 76 SK9067
Whissendine *Leics* 63 SK8214
Whissonsett *Norfk* 66 TF9123
Whistley Green *Berks* 25 SU7974
Whiston *Mersyd* 78 SJ4791
Whiston *Staffs* 60 SJ8914
Whiston *Staffs* 73 SK0347
Whiston *S York* 75 SK4489
Whiston *Nhants* 51 SP8460
Whiston Cross *Shrops* 60 SJ7903
Whiston Eaves *Staffs* 73 SK0446
Whiston Lane End *Mersyd* 78 SJ4690
Whitacre Fields *Warwks* 61 SP2592
Whitbeck *Cumb* 86 SD1184
Whitbourne *H & W* 47 SO7257
Whitburn *Loth* 116 NS9464
Whitburn *T & W* 96 NZ4062
Whitby *N York* 91 NZ8910
Whitby *Ches* 71 SJ3975
Whitbyheath *Ches* 71 SJ3974
Whitchurch *Shrops* 71 SJ5341
Whitchurch *Dyfed* 30 SM8025
Whitchurch *H & W* 34 SO5517
Whitchurch *Bucks* 38 SP8020
Whitchurch *S Glam* 33 ST1579
Whitchurch *Avon* 21 ST6167
Whitchurch *Hants* 24 SU4648
Whitchurch *Oxon* 37 SU6377
Whitchurch *Devon* 6 SX4972
Whitchurch Canonicorum *Dorset* 10 SY3995
Whitchurch Hill *Oxon* 37 SU6378
Whitcombe *Dorset* 11 SY7188
Whitcot *Shrops* 59 SO3791
Whitcott Keysett *Shrops* 58 SO2782
White Ball *Somset* 20 ST1019
White Chapel *Lancs* 81 SD5541
White Chapel *H & W* 48 SP0740
White Colne *Essex* 40 TL8729
White Coppice *Lancs* 81 SD6118
White Cross *Cnwll* 2 SW6821
White End *H & W* 47 SO7834
White Lackington *Dorset* 11 SY7198
White Ladies Aston *H & W* 47 SO9252
White Notley *Essex* 40 TL7818
White Ox Mead *Avon* 22 ST7258
White Pit *Lincs* 77 TF3777
White Roding *Essex* 40 TL5613
White Stake *Lancs* 80 SD5125
White Stone *H & W* 46 SO5642
White Waltham *Berks* 26 SU8577
White-le-Head *Dur* 96 NZ1654
Whiteacre *Kent* 29 TR1148
Whiteacre Heath *Warwks* 61 SP2292
Whiteash Green *Essex* 40 TL7930
Whitebirk *Lancs* 81 SD7028
Whitebridge *Highld* 139 NH4815
Whitebrook *Gwent* 34 SO5306
Whitecairns *Gramp* 143 NJ9218
Whitechapel *Gt Lon* 27 TQ3381
Whitechurch *Dyfed* 31 SN1536
Whitecliffe *Gloucs* 34 SO5609
Whitecraig *Loth* 118 NT3470
Whitecroft *Gloucs* 35 SO6206
Whitecrook *D & G* 98 NX1656
Whitecross *Cnwll* 2 SW5234
Whitecross *Cnwll* 4 SW9672
Whiteface *Highld* 146 NH7088
Whitefarland *Strath* 105 NR8642
Whitefield *Gt Man* 79 SD8006
Whitefield *Devon* 19 SS7035
Whitefield Lane End *Mersyd* 78 SJ4589
Whiteford *Gramp* 142 NJ7126
Whitegate *Ches* 71 SJ6269
Whitehall *Ork* 155 HY6528
Whitehall *Hants* 24 SU7452
Whitehall *W Susx* 15 TQ1321
Whitehaven *Cumb* 92 NX9718
Whitehill *Hants* 14 SU7934
Whitehill *Kent* 28 TR0059
Whitehills *Gramp* 142 NJ6565
Whitehouse *Gramp* 142 NJ6114
Whitehouse *Strath* 113 NR8161
Whitehouse Common *W Mids* 61 SP1397
Whitekirk *Loth* 118 NT5981
Whitelackington *Somset* 10 ST3815
Whiteley Bank *IOW* 13 SZ5581
Whiteley Green *Ches* 79 SJ9278
Whiteley Village *Surrey* 26 TQ0962
Whitemans Green *W Susx* 15 TQ3025
Whitemire *Gramp* 140 NH9854
Whitemoor *Staffs* 72 SJ8861
Whitemoor *Derbys* 62 SK3647
Whitemoor *Notts* 62 SK5441
Whitemoor *Cnwll* 4 SW9757
Whitenap *Hants* 12 SU3620
Whiteness *Shet* 155 HU3844
Whiteoak Green *Oxon* 36 SP3414
Whiteparish *Wilts* 23 SU2423
Whiterashes *Gramp* 143 NJ8523
Whiterow *Highld* 151 ND3648
Whiterow *Gramp* 141 NJ0257
Whiteshill *Gloucs* 35 SO8406
Whitesmith *E Susx* 16 TQ5213
Whitestaunton *Somset* 10 ST2810
Whitestone *Devon* 9 SX8694
Whitestone Cross *Devon* 9 SX8993
Whitestreet Green *Suffk* 54 TL9739
Whitewall Corner *N York* 90 SE7969
Whiteway *Avon* 22 ST7264
Whitewell *Lancs* 81 SD6646
Whitewell-on-the-Hill *N York* 90 SE7265
Whiteworks *Devon* 6 SX6171
Whitfield *Nthumb* 94 NY7758
Whitfield *Nhants* 49 SP6039
Whitfield *Avon* 35 ST6791
Whitfield *Kent* 29 TR3045
Whitfield Hall *Nthumb* 94 NY7756
Whitford *Clwyd* 70 SJ1478
Whitford *Devon* 10 SY2595
Whitgift *Humb* 84 SE8122
Whitgreave *Staffs* 72 SJ9028
Whithorn *D & G* 99 NX4440
Whiting Bay *Strath* 105 NS0425
Whitington *Norfk* 65 TL7199
Whitkirk *W York* 83 SE3633
Whitland *Dyfed* 31 SN1916
Whitlaw *Border* 109 NT5012
Whitletts *Strath* 106 NS3623
Whitley *N York* 83 SE5620
Whitley *S York* 74 SK3494
Whitley *Wilts* 22 ST8866
Whitley *Berks* 24 SU7270
Whitley Bay *T & W* 103 NZ3571
Whitley Chapel *Nthumb* 95 NY9257
Whitley Heath *Staffs* 72 SJ8126
Whitley Lower *W York* 82 SE2217
Whitley Row *Kent* 27 TQ4952
Whitlock's End *W Mids* 61 SP1076
Whitlow *S York* 74 SK3182
Whitminster *Gloucs* 35 SO7708
Whitmore *Staffs* 72 SJ8140
Whitmore *Dorset* 12 SU0609
Whitnage *Devon* 9 ST0215
Whitnash *Warwks* 48 SP3263
Whitney *H & W* 46 SO2747
Whitrigg *Cumb* 93 NY2038
Whitrigg *Cumb* 93 NY2257
Whitrigglees *Cumb* 93 NY2457
Whitsbury *Hants* 12 SU1219
Whitsford *Devon* 19 SS6633
Whitsome *Border* 119 NT8650
Whitson *Gwent* 34 ST3883
Whitstable *Kent* 29 TR1066
Whitstone *Cnwll* 5 SX2698
Whittingehame *Loth* 118 NT6073
Whittingham *Nthumb* 111 NU0611
Whittingslow *Shrops* 59 SO4388
Whittington *Lancs* 87 SD6075
Whittington *Shrops* 59 SJ3231
Whittington *Staffs* 61 SK1508
Whittington *Derbys* 74 SK3875
Whittington *Staffs* 60 SO8682
Whittington *H & W* 47 SO8753
Whittington *Gloucs* 35 SP0120
Whittington *Warwks* 61 SP2999
Whittle-le-Woods *Lancs* 81 SD5821
Whittlebury *Nhants* 49 SP6943
Whittlesey *Cambs* 64 TL2697
Whittlesford *Cambs* 53 TL4748
Whittlestone Head *Lancs* 81 SD7119
Whitton *Cleve* 96 NZ3822
Whitton *Humb* 84 SE9024
Whitton *Powys* 46 SO2767
Whitton *Shrops* 46 SO5772
Whitton *Suffk* 54 TM1447
Whittonditch *Wilts* 36 SU2872
Whittonstall *Nthumb* 95 NZ0757
Whitway *Hants* 24 SU4559
Whitwell *N York* 89 SE2899
Whitwell *Derbys* 75 SK5276
Whitwell *Leics* 63 SK9208
Whitwell *IOW* 13 SZ5277
Whitwell *Herts* 39 TL1820
Whitwell Street *Norfk* 66 TG1022
Whitwick *Leics* 62 SK4315
Whitwood *W York* 83 SE4024
Whitworth *Lancs* 81 SD8818
Whixall *Shrops* 59 SJ5134
Whixley *N York* 89 SE4458
Whorlton *Dur* 95 NZ1014
Whorlton *N York* 90 NZ4802
Whyle *H & W* 46 SO5561
Whyteleafe *Surrey* 27 TQ3358
Wibdon *Gloucs* 34 ST5797
Wibsey *W York* 82 SE1430
Wibtoft *Warwks* 50 SP4887
Wichenford *H & W* 47 SO7860
Wichling *Kent* 28 TQ9256
Wick *Highld* 151 ND3650
Wick *H & W* 47 SO9645
Wick *M Glam* 33 SS9271
Wick *Devon* 9 ST1704
Wick *Somset* 20 ST2144
Wick *Somset* 21 ST4026
Wick *Avon* 35 ST7072
Wick *Wilts* 12 SU1621
Wick *Dorset* 12 SZ1591
Wick *W Susx* 14 TQ0203
Wick End *Beds* 38 SP9850
Wick Rissington *Gloucs* 36 SP1821
Wick St. Lawrence *Avon* 21 ST3665
Wicken *Nhants* 49 SP7439
Wicken *Cambs* 53 TL5770
Wicken Bonhunt *Essex* 39 TL4933
Wickenby *Lincs* 76 TF0982
Wicker Street Green *Suffk* 54 TL9742
Wickersley *S York* 75 SK4791
Wickford *Essex* 40 TQ7493
Wickham *Berks* 36 SU3971
Wickham *Hants* 13 SU5711
Wickham Bishops *Essex* 40 TL8412
Wickham Green *Berks* 24 SU4072
Wickham Green *Suffk* 54 TM0969
Wickham Heath *Berks* 24 SU4169
Wickham Market *Suffk* 55 TM3055
Wickham Skeith *Suffk* 54 TM0969
Wickham St. Paul *Essex* 54 TL8336
Wickham Street *Suffk* 53 TL7654
Wickham Street *Suffk* 54 TM0869
Wickhambreaux *Kent* 29 TR2158
Wickhambrook *Suffk* 53 TL7554
Wickhamford *H & W* 48 SP0641
Wickhampton *Norfk* 67 TG4205
Wicklewood *Norfk* 66 TG0702
Wickmere *Norfk* 66 TG1733
Wickstreet *E Susx* 16 TQ5308
Wickwar *Avon* 35 ST7288
Widdington *Essex* 39 TL5331
Widdop *Lancs* 81 SD9233
Widdrington *T & W* 103 NZ2595
Widdrington Station *T & W* 103 NZ2494
Wide Open *T & W* 103 NZ2472
Widecombe in the Moor *Devon* 8 SX7176
Widegates *Cnwll* 5 SX2858
Widemouth Bay *Cnwll* 18 SS2002
Widford *Oxon* 36 SP2712
Widford *Herts* 39 TL4216
Widford *Essex* 40 TL6904
Widham *Wilts* 36 SU0988
Widmer End *Bucks* 26 SU8896
Widmerpool *Notts* 63 SK6327
Widmore *Gt Lon* 27 TQ4268
Widnes *Ches* 78 SJ5184
Wigan *Gt Man* 78 SD5805
Wigborough *Somset* 10 ST4415
Wiggaton *Devon* 9 SY1093
Wiggenhall St. Germans *Norfk* 65 TF5914
Wiggenhall St. Mary Magdalen *Norfk* 65 TF5911
Wiggenhall St. Mary the Virgin *Norfk* 65 TF5813
Wiggens Green *Essex* 53 TL6642
Wiggenstall *Staffs* 74 SK0960
Wiggington *Shrops* 59 SJ3335
Wigginton *N York* 90 SE6058
Wigginton *Staffs* 61 SK2006
Wigginton *Oxon* 48 SP3833
Wigginton *Herts* 38 SP9310
Wigglesworth *N York* 81 SD8156
Wiggold *Gloucs* 36 SP0404
Wiggonby *Cumb* 93 NY2952
Wiggonholt *W Susx* 14 TQ0616
Wighill *N York* 83 SE4746
Wighton *Norfk* 66 TF9439
Wigley *Hants* 12 SU3217
Wigmore *H & W* 46 SO4169
Wigmore *Kent* 28 TQ7964
Wigsley *Notts* 76 SK8570
Wigsthorpe *Nhants* 51 TL0482
Wigston *Leics* 50 SP6198
Wigston Fields *Leics* 50 SK6000
Wigston Parva *Leics* 50 SP4689
Wigthorpe *Notts* 75 SK5983
Wigtoft *Lincs* 64 TF2636
Wigton *Cumb* 93 NY2548
Wigtown *D & G* 99 NX4355
Wigtwizzle *S York* 74 SK2495
Wike *W York* 83 SE3342
Wilbarston *Nhants* 51 SP8188
Wilberfoss *Humb* 84 SE7350
Wilburton *Cambs* 53 TL4775
Wilby *Nhants* 51 SP8666
Wilby *Norfk* 54 TM0389
Wilby *Suffk* 55 TM2472
Wilcot *Wilts* 23 SU1360
Wilcrick *Gwent* 34 ST4088
Wilday Green *Derbys* 74 SK3274
Wildboarclough *Ches* 79 SJ9868
Wilden *H & W* 60 SO8272
Wilden *Beds* 51 TL0955
Wildhern *Hants* 23 SU3550
Wildhill *Herts* 39 TL2606
Wildmanbridge *Strath* 116 NS8253
Wildmoor *H & W* 60 SO9575
Wildsworth *Lincs* 75 SK8097
Wilford *Notts* 62 SK5637
Wilkesley *Ches* 71 SJ6241
Wilkhaven *Highld* 147 NH9486
Wilkieston *Fife* 117 NT1268
Wilkin's Green *Herts* 39 TL1907
Wilksby *Lincs* 77 TF2862
Willand *Devon* 9 ST0310
Willards Hill *E Susx* 17 TQ7124
Willaston *Ches* 71 SJ3377
Willaston *Ches* 72 SJ6852
Willcott *Shrops* 59 SJ3718
Willen *Bucks* 38 SP8741
Willenhall *W Mids* 60 SO9798
Willenhall *W Mids* 61 SP3676
Willerby *N York* 91 TA0079
Willerby *Humb* 84 TA0230
Willersey *Gloucs* 48 SP1039
Willersley *H & W* 46 SO3147
Willesborough *Kent* 28 TR0441
Willesborough Lees *Kent* 28 TR0342
Willesden *Gt Lon* 26 TQ2284
Willesleigh *Devon* 19 SS6033
Willesley *Wilts* 35 ST8588
Willett *Somset* 20 ST1033
Willey *Shrops* 60 SO6799
Willey *Warwks* 50 SP4984
Willey Green *Surrey* 25 SU9351
Williamscot *Oxon* 49 SP4845
Williamstown *M Glam* 33 ST0090
William *Herts* 39 TL2230
Willingdon *E Susx* 16 TQ5902
Willingham *Lincs* 76 SK8784
Willingham *Cambs* 52 TL4070
Willingham Green *Cambs* 53 TL6254
Willington *Dur* 96 NZ1935
Willington *Derbys* 73 SK2928
Willington *Warwks* 48 SP2639
Willington *Beds* 52 TL1150
Willington *Kent* 28 TQ7853
Willington Corner *Ches* 71 SJ5266
Willington Quay *T & W* 103 NZ3267
Willitoft *Humb* 84 SE7434
Williton *Somset* 20 ST0840
Willoughbridge *Staffs* 72 SJ7440
Willoughby *Warwks* 50 SP5167
Willoughby *Lincs* 64 TF0537
Willoughby *Lincs* 77 TF4771
Willoughby Hills *Lincs* 64 TF3545
Willoughby Waterleys *Leics* 50 SP5792
Willoughby-on-the-Wolds *Notts* 63 SK6325
Willoughton *Lincs* 76 SK9293
Willow Green *Ches* 71 SJ6076
Willows Green *Essex* 40 TL7219
Willsbridge *Avon* 35 ST6670
Willsworthy *Devon* 8 SX5381
Willtown *Somset* 21 ST3924
Wilmcote *Warwks* 48 SP1658
Wilmington *Avon* 22 ST6962
Wilmington *Devon* 9 SY2199
Wilmington *Kent* 27 TQ5372
Wilmington *E Susx* 16 TQ5404
Wilmslow *Ches* 79 SJ8481
Wilnecote *Staffs* 61 SK2200
Wilpshire *Lancs* 81 SD6832
Wilsden *W York* 82 SE0936
Wilsford *Wilts* 23 SU1057
Wilsford *Wilts* 23 SU1339
Wilsford *Lincs* 63 TF0042
Wilsham *Devon* 19 SS7548
Wilshaw *W York* 82 SE1109
Wilsill *N York* 89 SE1864
Wilsley Green *Kent* 28 TQ7736
Wilsley Pound *Kent* 28 TQ7837
Wilson *Leics* 62 SK4024
Wilson *H & W* 46 SO5523
Wilsontown *Strath* 116 NS9455
Wilstead *Beds* 38 TL0643
Wilsthorpe *Lincs* 64 TF0913
Wilstone *Herts* 38 SP9014
Wilstone Green *Herts* 38 SP9013
Wilton *Cumb* 86 NY0311
Wilton *Cleve* 97 NZ5819
Wilton *N York* 90 SE8582
Wilton *H & W* 46 SO5824
Wilton *Wilts* 23 SU0931
Wilton *Wilts* 23 SU2661
Wilton Dean *Border* 109 NT4914
Wimbish *Essex* 53 TL5936
Wimbish Green *Essex* 53 TL6035
Wimblebury *Staffs* 60 SK0111
Wimbledon *Gt Lon* 26 TQ2370
Wimblington *Cambs* 65 TL4192
Wimborne Minster *Dorset* 11 SZ0199
Wimborne St. Giles *Dorset* 12 SU0311
Wimbotsham *Norfk* 65 TF6205
Wimpstone *Warwks* 48 SP2148
Wincanton *Somset* 22 ST7128
Winceby *Lincs* 77 TF3268
Wincham *Ches* 79 SJ6775
Winchburgh *Loth* 117 NT0975
Winchcombe *Gloucs* 48 SP0228
Winchelsea *E Susx* 17 TQ9017
Winchelsea Beach *E Susx* 17 TQ9116
Winchester *Hants* 24 SU4829
Winchet Hill *Kent* 28 TQ7340
Winchfield *Hants* 24 SU7654
Winchmore Hill *Bucks* 26 SU9395
Winchmore Hill *Gt Lon* 27 TQ3194
Wincle *Ches* 72 SJ9566
Wincobank *S York* 74 SK3891
Winder *Cumb* 92 NY0417
Windermere *Cumb* 87 SD4098
Winderton *Warwks* 48 SP3240
Windhill *Highld* 139 NH5348
Windlehurst *Gt Man* 79 SJ9586
Windlesham *Surrey* 25 SU9364
Windmill *Derbys* 74 SK1677
Windmill *Cnwll* 4 SW8974
Windmill Hill *Somset* 10 ST3116
Windmill Hill *E Susx* 16 TQ6412
Windrush *Gloucs* 36 SP1913
Windsole *Gramp* 142 NJ5560
Windsor *Berks* 26 SU9576
Windsor Green *Suffk* 54 TL8954
Windsoredge *Gloucs* 35 SO8400
Windy Arbour *Warwks* 61 SP2971
Windy Hill *Clwyd* 71 SJ3054
Windygates *Fife* 118 NO3500
Windyharbour *Ches* 79 SJ8270
Wineham *W Susx* 15 TQ2320
Winestead *Humb* 85 TA2924
Winewall *Lancs* 81 SD9140
Winfarthing *Norfk* 54 TM1085
Winford *Avon* 21 ST5464
Winford *IOW* 13 SZ5584
Winforton *H & W* 46 SO2946
Winfrith Newburgh *Dorset* 11 SY8084
Wing *Leics* 63 SK8903
Wing *Bucks* 38 SP8822
Wingate *Dur* 96 NZ4036
Wingates *Nthumb* 103 NZ0995
Wingates *Gt Man* 79 SD6507
Wingerworth *Derbys* 74 SK3867
Wingfield *Wilts* 22 ST8256
Wingfield *Beds* 38 TL0026
Wingfield *Suffk* 55 TM2277
Wingfield Green *Suffk* 55 TM2177
Wingham *Kent* 29 TR2457
Wingham Well *Kent* 29 TR2356
Wingmore *Kent* 29 TR1946
Wingrave *Bucks* 38 SP8719
Winkburn *Notts* 75 SK7058
Winkfield *Berks* 25 SU9072
Winkfield Row *Berks* 25 SU8971
Winkfield Street *Berks* 25 SU8972
Winkhill *Staffs* 73 SK0651
Winkhurst Green *Kent* 16 TQ4949
Winkleigh *Devon* 19 SS6308
Winksley *N York* 89 SE2571
Winkton *Dorset* 12 SZ1696
Winlaton *T & W* 96 NZ1762
Winlaton Mill *T & W* 96 NZ1860
Winless *Highld* 151 ND3054
Winllan *Powys* 58 SJ2221
Winmarleigh *Lancs* 80 SD4647
Winnall *H & W* 47 SO8167
Winnall *Hants* 24 SU4829
Winnersh *Berks* 25 SU7870
Winnington *Ches* 79 SJ6474
Winscales *Cumb* 92 NY0226
Winscombe *Avon* 21 ST4257
Winsford *Ches* 72 SJ6566
Winsford *Somset* 20 SS9034
Winsh-wen *W Glam* 32 SS6896
Winsham *Devon* 19 SS5038
Winsham *Somset* 10 ST3706
Winshill *Staffs* 73 SK2623
Winskill *Cumb* 94 NY5834
Winslade *Hants* 24 SU6548
Winsley *Wilts* 22 ST7960
Winslow *Bucks* 49 SP7727
Winslow *Oxon* 36 SU2685
Winson *Gloucs* 36 SP0808
Winster *Cumb* 87 SD4193
Winster *Derbys* 74 SK2460
Winston *Dur* 96 NZ1416
Winston *Suffk* 54 TM1861
Winston Green *Suffk* 54 TM1761
Winstone *Gloucs* 35 SO9509
Winswell *Devon* 18 SS4913
Winterborne Came *Dorset* 11 SY7088
Winterborne Clenston *Dorset* 11 ST8303
Winterborne Herringston *Dorset* 11 SY6888
Winterborne Houghton *Dorset* 11 ST8204
Winterborne Kingston *Dorset* 11 SY8697
Winterborne Monkton *Dorset* 11 SY6787
Winterborne Stickland *Dorset* 11 ST8304
Winterborne Tomson *Dorset* 11 SY8897
Winterborne Whitechurch *Dorset* 11 ST8300
Winterborne Zelston *Dorset* 11 SY8997
Winterbourne *Avon* 35 ST6480
Winterbourne *Berks* 24 SU4572
Winterbourne Abbas *Dorset* 10 SY6190
Winterbourne Bassett *Wilts* 36 SU0974
Winterbourne Dauntsey *Wilts* 23 SU1734
Winterbourne Earls *Wilts* 23 SU1734
Winterbourne Gunner *Wilts* 23 SU1735
Winterbourne Monkton *Wilts* 36 SU0971

Winterbourne Steepleton Wye

Winterbourne Steepleton Dorset 10 SY6289
Winterbourne Stoke Wilts 23 SU0741
Winterbrook Oxon 37 SU6088
Winterburn N York 88 SD9358
Winteringham Humb 84 SE9221
Winterley Ches 72 SJ7457
Wintersett W York 83 SE3815
Winterslow Wilts 23 SU2332
Winterton Humb 84 SE9218
Winterton-on-Sea Norfk 67 TG4919
Winthorpe Notts 75 SK8156
Winthorpe Lincs 77 TF5665
Winton Cumb 88 NY7810
Winton N York 89 SE4196
Winton Dorset 12 SZ0893
Winton E Susx 16 TQ5103
Wintringham N York 90 SE8873
Winwick Ches 78 SJ6092
Winwick Nhants 50 SP6273
Winwick Cambs 51 TL1080
Wirksworth Derbys 73 SK2854
Wirswall Ches 71 SJ5444
Wisbech Cambs 65 TF4609
Wisbech St. Mary Cambs 65 TF4208
Wisborough Green W Susx 14 TQ0525
Wiseman's Bridge Dyfed 31 SN1406
Wiseton Notts 75 SK7189
Wishanger Gloucs 35 SO9109
Wishaw Strath 116 NS7955
Wishaw Warwks 61 SP1794
Wisley Surrey 26 TQ0659
Wispington Lincs 76 TF2071
Wissenden Kent 28 TQ9041
Wissett Suffk 55 TM3679
Wissington Suffk 40 TL9533
Wistanstow Shrops 59 SO4385
Wistanswick Shrops 72 SJ6629
Wistaston Ches 72 SJ6853
Wistaston Green Ches 72 SJ6854
Wisterfield Ches 79 SJ8371
Wiston Strath 108 NS9532
Wiston Dyfed 30 SN0218
Wiston W Susx 15 TQ1512
Wistow N York 83 SE5935
Wistow Cambs 52 TL2780
Wiswell Lancs 81 SD7437
Witby Mills Avon 22 ST6657
Witcham Cambs 53 TL4680
Witchampton Dorset 11 ST9806
Witchford Cambs 53 TL5078
Witcombe Somset 21 ST4721
Witham Essex 40 TL8214
Witham Friary Somset 22 ST7441
Witham on the Hill Lincs 64 TF0516
Withcall Lincs 77 TF2883
Witherenden E Susx 16 TQ6527
Witherenden Hill E Susx 16 TQ6426
Witheridge Devon 19 SS8014
Witherley Leics 61 SP3297
Withern Lincs 77 TF4282
Withernsea Humb 85 TA3427
Withernwick Humb 85 TA1940
Withersdale Street Suffk 55 TM2680
Withersfield Essex 53 TL6548
Witherslack Cumb 87 SD4384
Witherslack Hall Cumb 87 SD4385
Withiel Cnwll 4 SW9965
Withiel Florey Somset 20 SS9833
Withielgoose Cnwll 4 SX0065
Withington Shrops 59 SJ5713
Withington Ches 79 SJ8169
Withington Gt Man 79 SJ8492
Withington Staffs 73 SK0335
Withington H & W 46 SO5643
Withington Gloucs 35 SP0215
Withington Green Ches 79 SJ8071
Withleigh Devon 9 SS9012
Withnell Lancs 81 SD6322
Withybed Green H & W 60 SP0172
Withybrook Warwks 50 SP4383
Withycombe Somset 20 ST0141
Withyditch Avon 22 ST6959
Withyham E Susx 16 TQ4935
Withypool Devon 19 SS8435
Witley Surrey 25 SU9439
Witnesham Suffk 54 TM1751
Witney Oxon 36 SP3510
Wittering Cambs 64 TF0502
Wittersham Kent 17 TQ9027
Witton H & W 47 SO8962
Witton Norfk 67 TG3109
Witton Norfk 67 TG3331
Witton Gilbert Dur 96 NZ2345
Witton Green Norfk 67 TG4102
Witton Park Dur 96 NZ1730
Witton le Wear Dur 96 NZ1431
Wiveliscombe Somset 20 ST0827
Wivelrod Hants 24 SU6738
Wivelsfield E Susx 15 TQ3420
Wivelsfield Green E Susx 15 TQ3519
Wivelsfield Station W Susx 15 TQ3219
Wivenhoe Essex 41 TM0321
Wivenhoe Cross Essex 41 TM0423
Wiveton Norfk 66 TG0442
Wix Essex 41 TM1628
Wix Green Essex 41 TM1728
Wixford Warwks 48 SP0854
Wixhill Shrops 59 SJ5528
Wixoe Essex 53 TL7143
Woburn Beds 38 SP9433
Woburn Sands Bucks 38 SP9235
Wokefield Park Berks 24 SU6765
Woking Surrey 25 TQ0058
Wokingham Berks 25 SU8168
Wolborough Devon 7 SX8570
Wold Newton Humb 91 TA0473
Wold Newton Humb 77 TF2496
Woldingham Surrey 27 TQ3755
Wolf Hills Nthumb 94 NY7258
Wolf's Castle Dyfed 30 SM9526
Wolfclyde Strath 108 NT0236
Wolferlow H & W 47 SO6661
Wolferton Norfk 65 TF6528
Wolfhampcote Warwks 50 SP5265
Wolfhill Tays 126 NO1533
Wolfsdale Dyfed 30 SM9321
Wollaston Shrops 59 SJ3212
Wollaston Nhants 51 SP9062
Wollaton Notts 62 SK5239
Wollerton Shrops 59 SJ6130
Wollescote W Mids 60 SO9283
Wolseley Staffs 73 SK0220
Wolsingham Dur 95 NZ0737
Wolstanton Staffs 72 SJ8548
Wolstenholme Gt Man 81 SD8414
Wolston Warwks 50 SP4175
Wolsty Cumb 92 NY1050
Wolvercote Oxon 37 SP4910
Wolverhampton W Mids 60 SO9198
Wolverley Shrops 59 SJ4731
Wolverley H & W 60 SO8379
Wolverton Warwks 48 SP2062
Wolverton Bucks 38 SP8141
Wolverton Wilts 22 ST7831
Wolverton Hants 24 SU5558
Wolverton Kent 29 TR2642
Wolverton Common Hants 24 SU5659
Wolvesnewton Gwent 34 ST4599
Wolvey Warwks 50 SP4387
Wolvey Heath Warwks 50 SP4388
Wolviston Cleve 97 NZ4525
Wombleton N York 90 SE6683
Wombourne Staffs 60 SO8793
Wombwell S York 83 SE4002
Womenswold Kent 29 TR2250
Womersley N York 83 SE5319
Wonastow Gwent 34 SO4810
Wonersh Surrey 14 TQ0145
Wonford Devon 9 SX9491
Wonson Devon 8 SX6789
Wonston Hants 24 SU4739
Wooburn Bucks 26 SU9087
Wooburn Green Bucks 26 SU9188
Wooburn Moor Bucks 26 SU9189
Wood Bevington Warwks 48 SP0554
Wood Burcot Nhants 49 SP6946
Wood Dalling Norfk 66 TG0827
Wood Eaton Staffs 72 SJ8417
Wood End W Mids 60 SJ9400
Wood End Warwks 61 SP1171
Wood End Warwks 61 SP2498
Wood End Warwks 61 SP2987
Wood End Beds 38 TL0046
Wood End Beds 51 TL0866
Wood End Herts 39 TL3225
Wood End Cambs 52 TL3675
Wood End Gt Lon 26 TQ1385
Wood Enderby Lincs 77 TF2764
Wood Green Gt Lon 27 TQ3090
Wood Hayes W Mids 60 SJ9402
Wood Lane Shrops 59 SJ4132
Wood Lane Staffs 72 SJ8149
Wood Norton Norfk 66 TG0127
Wood Row W York 83 SE3827
Wood Street Surrey 25 SU9550
Wood Street Norfk 67 TG3722
Wood Top Lancs 81 SD5643
Wood Walton Cambs 52 TL2180
Wood's Corner E Susx 16 TQ6619
Wood's Green E Susx 16 TQ6333
Woodale N York 88 SE0279
Woodall S York 75 SK4880
Woodbastwick Norfk 67 TG3315
Woodbeck Notts 75 SK7777
Woodborough Notts 63 SK6347
Woodborough Wilts 23 SU1159
Woodbridge Dorset 22 ST8518
Woodbridge Suffk 55 TM2649
Woodbury Devon 9 SY0087
Woodbury Salterton Devon 9 SY0189
Woodchester Gloucs 35 SO8302
Woodchurch Mersyd 78 SJ2786
Woodchurch Kent 17 TQ9434
Woodcombe Somset 20 SS9546
Woodcote Shrops 72 SJ7615
Woodcote Oxon 37 SU6482
Woodcote Green H & W 60 SO9172
Woodcott Hants 24 SU4354
Woodcroft Gloucs 34 ST5495
Woodcutts Dorset 11 ST9717
Woodditton Cambs 53 TL6559
Woodeaton Oxon 37 SP5312
Woodend Highld 130 NM7861
Woodend Loth 116 NS9269
Woodend Staffs 73 SK1726
Woodend Nhants 49 SP6149
Woodend W Susx 14 SU8108
Woodend Green Essex 39 TL5528
Woodfalls Wilts 12 SU1920
Woodford Gt Man 79 SJ8882
Woodford Nhants 51 SP9676
Woodford Gloucs 35 ST6995
Woodford Devon 7 SX7950
Woodford Bridge Gt Lon 27 TQ4291
Woodford Green Bucks 49 SP6148
Woodford Halse Nhants 49 SP5452
Woodford Wells Gt Lon 27 TQ4093
Woodgate H & W 47 SO9666
Woodgate W Mids 60 SO9982
Woodgate Devon 9 ST1015
Woodgate W Susx 14 SU9304
Woodgate Norfk 66 TF8915
Woodgate Norfk 66 TG0215
Woodgreen Oxon 36 SP3610
Woodgreen Hants 12 SU1717
Woodhall N York 88 SD9790
Woodhall Hill W York 82 SE2035
Woodhall Spa Lincs 76 TF1963
Woodham Dur 96 NZ2826
Woodham Bucks 37 SP7018
Woodham Lincs 76 TF2267
Woodham Ferrers Essex 40 TQ7999
Woodham Mortimer Essex 40 TL8104
Woodham Walter Essex 40 TL8007
Woodhaven Fife 126 NO4126
Woodhead Gramp 142 NJ7838
Woodhill Somset 21 ST3527
Woodhorn Nthumb 103 NZ2988
Woodhorn Demesne Nthumb 103 NZ3088
Woodhouse W York 82 SE2935
Woodhouse W York 83 SE3821
Woodhouse S York 74 SK4284
Woodhouse Leics 62 SK5314
Woodhouse Eaves Leics 62 SK5214
Woodhouse Green Staffs 72 SJ9162
Woodhouse Mill S York 75 SK4385
Woodhouselee Fife 117 NT2364
Woodhouselees D & G 101 NY3975
Woodhouses Cumb 93 NY3252
Woodhouses Gt Man 79 SD9100
Woodhouses Staffs 61 SK0709
Woodhouses Staffs 73 SK1518
Woodhuish Devon 7 SX9152
Woodhurst Cambs 52 TL3176
Woodingdean E Susx 15 TQ3505
Woodkirk W York 82 SE2725
Woodland Gramp 143 NJ8723
Woodland Strath 106 NX1795
Woodland Dur 95 NZ0726
Woodland Devon 7 SX7968
Woodland Kent 29 TR1441
Woodland Head Devon 8 SX7796
Woodland Street Somset 21 ST5337
Woodland View S York 74 SK3188
Woodlands Gramp 135 NO7895
Woodlands N York 83 SE3254
Woodlands S York 83 SE5308
Woodlands Dorset 12 SU0509
Woodlands Hants 12 SU3211
Woodlands Kent 27 TQ5660
Woodlands Park Berks 26 SU8678
Woodlands St. Mary Berks 36 SU3375
Woodleigh Devon 7 SX7349
Woodlesford W York 83 SE3629
Woodley Gt Man 79 SJ9392
Woodley Berks 25 SU7773
Woodley Green Berks 26 SU8480
Woodmancote H & W 47 SO9142
Woodmancote Gloucs 47 SO9727
Woodmancote Gloucs 35 SP0008
Woodmancote Gloucs 35 ST7597
Woodmancote W Susx 14 SU7707
Woodmancote W Susx 15 TQ2314
Woodmancott Hants 24 SU5642
Woodmansey Humb 84 TA0538
Woodmansgreen W Susx 14 SU8627
Woodmansterne Surrey 27 TQ2759
Woodmarsh Wilts 22 ST8555
Woodmill Staffs 73 SK1320
Woodminton Wilts 22 SU0022
Woodnesborough Kent 29 TR3157
Woodnewton Nhants 51 TL0394
Woodnook Notts 75 SK4752
Woodplumpton Lancs 80 SD4934
Woodrising Norfk 66 TF9803
Woodrow H & W 60 SO8974
Woodseaves Shrops 72 SJ6831
Woodseaves Staffs 72 SJ7925
Woodsend Wilts 36 SU2176
Woodsetts S York 75 SK5483
Woodsford Dorset 11 SY7590
Woodside Tays 126 NO2037
Woodside Fife 127 NO4207
Woodside Cumb 92 NY0434
Woodside Berks 25 SU9371
Woodside Hants 12 SZ3294
Woodside Herts 39 TL2406
Woodside Essex 39 TL4704
Woodside Gt Lon 27 TQ3467
Woodside Green Kent 28 TQ9053
Woodstock Dyfed 30 SN0325
Woodstock Oxon 37 SP4416
Woodston Cambs 64 TL1897
Woodthorpe Derbys 75 SK4574
Woodthorpe Leics 62 SK5417
Woodthorpe Lincs 77 TF4380
Woodton Norfk 67 TM2994
Woodtown Devon 18 SS4123
Woodvale Mersyd 78 SD3010
Woodville Derbys 62 SK3118
Woodwall Green Staffs 72 SJ7831
Woody Bay Devon 19 SS6748
Woodyates Dorset 12 SU0219
Woofferton Shrops 46 SO5268
Wookey Somset 21 ST5145
Wookey Hole Somset 21 ST5347
Wool Dorset 11 SY8486
Woolacombe Devon 18 SS4643
Woolage Green Kent 29 TR2349
Woolaston Gloucs 34 ST5899
Woolaston Common Gloucs 34 SO5801
Woolavington Somset 21 ST3441
Woolbeding W Susx 14 SU8722
Woolcotts Somset 20 SS9631
Wooldale W York 82 SE1508
Wooler Nthumb 111 NT9927
Wooley Bridge Derbys 79 SK0194
Woolfardisworthy Devon 18 SS3321
Woolfardisworthy Devon 19 SS8208
Woolfold Gt Man 81 SD7811
Woolfords Strath 117 NT0056
Woolhampton Berks 24 SU5766
Woolhanger Devon 19 SS6945
Woolhope H & W 46 SO6135
Woolland Dorset 11 ST7707
Woollard Avon 21 ST6364
Woollensbrook Herts 39 TL3609
Woolley W York 83 SE3212
Woolley Derbys 74 SK3760
Woolley Cnwll 18 SS2516
Woolley Avon 22 ST7468
Woolley Cambs 52 TL1574
Woolmer Green Herts 39 TL2518
Woolmere Green H & W 47 SO9663
Woolmerston Somset 20 ST2833
Woolminstone Somset 10 ST4108
Woolpack Kent 28 TQ8537
Woolpit Suffk 54 TL9762
Woolpit Green Suffk 54 TL9761
Woolscott Warwks 50 SP5068
Woolsgrove Devon 8 SS7902
Woolsington T & W 103 NZ1870
Woolstaston Shrops 59 SO4598
Woolsthorpe Lincs 63 SK8333
Woolsthorpe Lincs 63 SK9224
Woolston Shrops 59 SJ3224
Woolston Ches 79 SJ6489
Woolston Shrops 59 SO4287
Woolston Somset 20 ST0939
Woolston Somset 21 ST6527
Woolston Hants 13 SU4310
Woolston Devon 7 SX7141
Woolston Devon 7 SX7150
Woolston Green Devon 7 SX7766
Woolstone Gloucs 47 SO9630
Woolstone Bucks 38 SP8738
Woolstone Oxon 36 SU2987
Woolton Mersyd 78 SJ4286
Woolton Hill Hants 24 SU4361
Woolverstone Suffk 54 TM1738
Woolverton Somset 22 ST7953
Woolwich Gt Lon 27 TQ4478
Woonton H & W 46 SO3552
Wooperton Nthumb 111 NU0420
Woore Shrops 72 SJ7342
Wooston Devon 8 SX7689
Wootten Breadmead Beds 38 TL0243
Wootten Green Suffk 55 TM2372
Wootton Shrops 59 SJ3327
Wootton Staffs 72 SJ8227
Wootton Staffs 73 SK1044
Wootton H & W 46 SO3252
Wootton Oxon 37 SP4419
Wootton Oxon 37 SP4701
Wootton Nhants 49 SP7656
Wootton Hants 12 SZ2498
Wootton IOW 13 SZ5392
Wootton Humb 85 TA0815
Wootton Beds 38 TL0044
Wootton Kent 29 TR2246
Wootton Bassett Wilts 36 SU0682
Wootton Bridge IOW 13 SZ5492
Wootton Common IOW 13 SZ5391
Wootton Courtenay Somset 20 SS9343
Wootton Fitzpaine Dorset 10 SY3695
Wootton Rivers Wilts 23 SU1962
Wootton St. Lawrence Hants 24 SU5953
Wootton Wawen Warwks 48 SP1563
Worbarrow Dorset 11 SY8779
Worcester H & W 47 SO8554
Worcester Park Gt Lon 26 TQ2165
Wordsley W Mids 60 SO8987
Worfield Shrops 60 SO7595
Worgret Dorset 11 SY9087
Workington Cumb 92 NY0028
Worksop Notts 75 SK5879
Worlaby Humb 84 TA0113
Worlaby Lincs 77 TF3476
World's End Berks 37 SU4877
Worlds End Bucks 38 SP8509
Worlds End Hants 13 SU6311
Worlds End W Susx 15 TQ3220
Worle Avon 21 ST3562
Worleston Ches 72 SJ6556
Worlingham Suffk 55 TM4489
Worlington Devon 19 SS7713
Worlington Suffk 53 TL6973
Worlingworth Suffk 55 TM2368
Wormald Green N York 89 SE3065
Wormbridge H & W 46 SO4230
Wormegay Norfk 65 TF6611
Wormelow Tump H & W 46 SO4930
Wormhill Derbys 74 SK1274
Wormhill H & W 46 SO4239
Wormingford Essex 40 TL9332
Worminghall Bucks 37 SP6308
Wormington Gloucs 48 SP0336
Worminster Somset 21 ST5743
Wormiston Border 117 NT2345
Wormit Tays 126 NO4026
Wormleighton Warwks 49 SP4553
Wormley Surrey 25 SU9438
Wormley Herts 39 TL3605
Wormley Hill S York 83 SE6616
Wormleybury Herts 39 TL3506
Wormshill Kent 28 TQ8857
Wormsley H & W 46 SO4247
Worplesdon Surrey 25 SU9753
Worrall S York 74 SK3092
Worsbrough S York 83 SE3602
Worsbrough Bridge S York 83 SE3503
Worsbrough Dale S York 83 SE3604
Worsley Gt Man 79 SD7500
Worsley Mesnes Gt Man 78 SD5703
Worstead Norfk 67 TG3025
Worsthorne Lancs 81 SD8732
Worston Lancs 81 SD7742
Worston Devon 6 SX5953
Worth Somset 21 ST5144
Worth W Susx 15 TQ3036
Worth Kent 29 TR3355
Worth Abbey Surrey 15 TQ3134
Worth Matravers Dorset 11 SY9777
Wortham Suffk 54 TM0877
Worthen Shrops 59 SJ3204
Worthenbury Clwyd 71 SJ4146
Worthing Norfk 66 TF9919
Worthing W Susx 15 TQ1403
Worthington Leics 62 SK4020
Worthybrook Gwent 34 SO4711
Worting Hants 24 SU5952
Wortley W York 82 SE2732
Wortley S York 74 SK3099
Worton N York 88 SD9589
Worton Wilts 22 ST9757
Wortwell Norfk 55 TM2784
Wotherton Shrops 58 SJ2800
Wothorpe Cambs 64 TF0205
Wotter Devon 6 SX5661
Wotton Surrey 14 TQ1247
Wotton Underwood Bucks 37 SP6815
Wotton-under-Edge Gloucs 35 ST7593
Woughton on the Green Bucks 38 SP8737
Wouldham Kent 28 TQ7164
Woundale Shrops 60 SO7793
Wrabness Essex 41 TM1731
Wrafton Devon 18 SS4935
Wragby W York 83 SE4116
Wragby Lincs 76 TF1378
Wramplingham Norfk 66 TG1106
Wrangaton Devon 7 SX6758
Wrangbrook W York 83 SE4913
Wrangle Lincs 77 TF4250
Wrangle Common Lincs 77 TF4253
Wrangle Lowgate Lincs 77 TF4451
Wrangway Somset 20 ST1218
Wrantage Somset 20 ST3022
Wrawby Humb 84 TA0108
Wraxall Avon 34 ST4971
Wraxall Somset 21 ST6036
Wray Lancs 87 SD6067
Wray Castle Cumb 87 NY3700
Wraysbury Berks 25 TQ0074
Wrayton Lancs 87 SD6172
Wrea Green Lancs 80 SD3931
Wreaks End Cumb 86 SD2286
Wreay Cumb 93 NY4348
Wreay Cumb 93 NY4423
Wrecclesham Surrey 25 SU8244
Wrekenton T & W 96 NZ2759
Wrelton N York 90 SE7686
Wrenbury Ches 71 SJ5947
Wrench Green N York 91 SE9689
Wreningham Norfk 66 TM1698
Wrentham Suffk 55 TM4982
Wrenthorpe W York 82 SE3122
Wrentnall Shrops 59 SJ4203
Wressle Humb 84 SE7131
Wressle Humb 84 SE9709
Wrestlingworth Beds 52 TL2547
Wretton Norfk 65 TF6900
Wrexham Clwyd 71 SJ3350
Wribbenhall H & W 60 SO7975
Wrickton Shrops 59 SO6486
Wright's Green Essex 39 TL5017
Wrightington Bar Lancs 80 SD5313
Wrinehill Staffs 72 SJ7547
Wrington Avon 21 ST4762
Wringworthy Cnwll 5 SX2658
Writhlington Somset 22 ST6954
Writtle Essex 40 TL6706
Wrockwardine Shrops 59 SJ6212
Wroot Humb 84 SE7103
Wrose W York 82 SE1636
Wrotham Kent 27 TQ6158
Wrotham Heath Kent 27 TQ6357
Wrottesley Staffs 60 SJ8200
Wroughton Wilts 36 SU1480
Wroxall Warwks 61 SP2271
Wroxall IOW 13 SZ5579
Wroxeter Shrops 59 SJ5608
Wroxham Norfk 67 TG3017
Wroxton Oxon 49 SP4141
Wyaston Derbys 73 SK1842
Wyberton Lincs 64 TF3240
Wyboston Beds 52 TL1656
Wybunbury Ches 72 SJ6949
Wych Dorset 10 SY4791
Wych Cross E Susx 15 TQ4131
Wychbold H & W 47 SO9266
Wychnor Staffs 73 SK1715
Wyck Hants 24 SU7539
Wycliffe Dur 95 NZ1114
Wycoller Lancs 81 SD9339
Wycomb Leics 63 SK7724
Wycombe Marsh Bucks 26 SU8892
Wyddial Herts 39 TL3731
Wye Kent 28 TR0546

Information on National Parks provided by the Countryside Commission for England & Wales.

Information on National Scenic Areas - Scotland provided by the Countryside Commission for Scotland.

Information on Forest Parks provided by the Forestry Commission.

Blue flag beaches are those designated by the European Blue Flag Campaign and sponsored by the Commission of the European Communities. The ones indicated in this atlas are the beaches which, in 1989, met certain environmental criteria.

The RSPB sites shown are a selection chosen by the Royal Society for the Protection of Birds.

Picnic sites are those inspected by the AA and are located on or near A and B roads.

Phone before you go

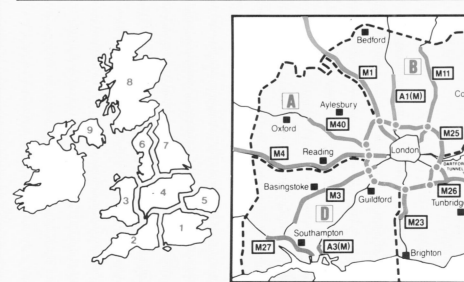